MEDIA EFFECTS

With contributions from some of the finest scholars in the discipline, *Media Effects* serves not only as a comprehensive reference volume for media effects study but also as an exceptional textbook for advanced courses in media effects. Covering the breadth of the media effects arena, this third edition provides updated material as well as new chapters focusing on effects of mobile media and other technologies. As this area of study continues to evolve, *Media Effects* will serve as a benchmark of theory and research for current and future generations of scholars.

This third edition includes:

- new ways of analyzing media effects.
- innovative perspectives from some of the finest scholars in the field.
- insightful advice as to how our theories can and should evolve to accommodate the rapidly changing media landscape.

New chapters discuss:

- framing
- psychophysiology
- civic participation
- sex-role stereotyping
- eating disorders and body image
- video and computer gaming
- the Internet
- mobile communication.

Jennings Bryant is CIS Distinguished Research Professor, holder of the Reagan Endowed Chair of Broadcasting, and Associate Dean for Graduate Studies and Research at the University of Alabama. He received the university's Blackmon-Moody Outstanding Professor Award for 2000 and was President of the International Communication Association in 2002–2003. In 2006 he received a Distinguished Scholar Award from the Broadcast Education Association and was elected a Fellow of the International Communication Association.

Mary Beth Oliver is a Professor in the department of Film/Video & Media Studies at Penn State University. She served as associate editor for the *Journal of Communication and Communication Theory* and is currently serving as co-editor of *Media Psychology*. She was the recipient of the Alumni Teaching Award at Virginia Tech and was awarded a Fulbright to conduct research in New Zealand in 2006.

COMMUNICATION SERIES
General Editors: Jennings Bryant and Dolf Zillmann

Selected titles in Communication Theory and Methodology subseries (Jennings Bryant, series advisor) include:

PLANNING STRATEGIC INTERACTION
Attaining Goals Through Communicative Action
Berger

AMERICAN COMMUNICATION RESEARCH
The Remembered History
Dennis and Wartella

CRAFTING SOCIETY
Ethnicity, Class, and Communication Theory
Ellis

MESSAGE PRODUCTION
Advances in Communication Theory
Greene

HUMAN COMMUNICATION THEORY AND RESEARCH
Concepts, Contexts, and Challenges, Second Edition
Heath and Bryant

HOLLYWOOD PLANET
Global Media and the Competitive Advantage of Narrative Transparency
Olsson

AMERICAN PRAGMATISM AND COMMUNICATION RESEARCH
Perry

ANALYZING MEDIA MESSAGES, Second Edition
Using Quantitative Content Analysis in Research
Riffe, Lacy, and Fico

AN INTEGRATED APPROACH TO COMMUNICATION THEORY AND RESEARCH, Second Edition
Salwen and Stacks

MEDIA EFFECTS

Advances in Theory and Research

Third Edition

Edited by

Jennings Bryant and Mary Beth Oliver

NEW YORK AND LONDON

First published 1994
by Lawrence Erlbaum Associates, Inc.
Second edition published 2002
by Lawrence Erlbaum Associates, Inc.
This edition published 2009
by Routledge
270 Madison Ave, New York, NY 10016

Simultaneously published in the UK
by Routledge
2 Park Square, Milton Park, Abingdon, Oxon 0X14 4RN

Routledge is an imprint of the Taylor & Francis Group, an informa business

Typeset in Goudy by
RefineCatch Limited, Bungay, Suffolk
Printed and bound in the United states of America on acid-free paper by
Edwards Brothers, Inc.

Library of Congress Cataloging-in-Publication Data
Media effects : advances in theory and research / Jennings Bryant, Mary Beth Oliver. – 3rd ed.
p. cm.
ISBN 978–0–8058–6449–6 – ISBN 978–1–4106–1877–1 1. Mass media–United States–Psychological aspects. 2. Mass media–Social aspects–United States. 3. Mass media–Political aspects–United States. 4. Mass media–United States–Influence. I. Bryant, Jennings. II. Oliver, Mary Beth.
HN90.M3M415 2008
302.23–dc22 2008012564

ISBN10: 0–8058–6449–0 (hbk)
ISBN10: 0–8058–6450–4 (pbk)
ISBN10: 0–4106–1877–3 (ebk)

ISBN13: 978–0–8058–6449–6 (hbk)
ISBN13: 978–0–8058–6450–2 (pbk)
ISBN13: 978–1–4106–1877–1 (ebk)

CONTENTS

TO DOLF ZILLMANN

On Your Shoulders
We Gratefully Stand

FIGURES

TABLES

PREFACE

When pundits discuss the major changes that characterize the latest phase of the information age, it is safe to say that few include "media effects" or the study thereof. They just might be wrong. In fact, if this third edition of *Media Effects: Advances in Theory and Research* is a valid indicator, they are. Over and over again, as the editors reviewed chapters by the contributors to this volume, our shared reaction was some variant of "My, how things have changed since the last edition." These changes include new ways of analyzing media effects, innovative perspectives, novel theories, fresh means of presenting results and conclusions, and insightful advice as to how our theories can and should evolve to accommodate the rapidly changing media landscape.

Change also is the order of the day in this edited volume via which we chronicle the state of the art in media effects. Most obvious might be a new co-editor: Dolf Zillmann, to whom we dedicate this volume, has retired, and Mary Beth Oliver now serves in his stead. She brings the perspectives of a new generation of media-effects scholars to this durable publishing project, which was born as *Perspectives on Media Effects* (1986) and matured through two intermediate editions (1994, 2002) that share the title of the present volume.

Only slightly less obvious is a change in publishers: Our previous publisher, Lawrence Erlbaum Associates, Inc. (LEA), was purchased by Informa's Taylor & Francis (T&F) in 2006. Now our publisher is Routledge, the imprint of Taylor & Francis that absorbed the lion's share of LEA's communication list. Fortunately, communication editor extraordinaire Linda Bathgate made the professional move from Mahwah, NJ (LEA) to New York City (T&F), so she remains a welcome beacon of stability among the myriad changes this volume represents.

As a tangible marker of Routledge's commitment to relevance in communication scholarship, when discussions about a new edition of *Media Effects* began, the publisher was most willing to undertake a systematic and extensive survey of adopters and potential adopters of the prior editions in order to guide our formative editorial decisions. The results of that in-depth survey have been invaluable in preparing the present volume. They were particularly useful as we made difficult content decisions—what we should keep, what needed major revision, what we should add, and what we should jettison. Should you be keeping score, we dropped three chapters and added eight. Among the additions are new chapters devoted to framing, psychophysiology, civic participation, sex-role stereotyping, eating disorders and body image, video and computer gaming, the Internet, and mobile communication.

From the editors' perspective, these macro-level changes were complemented beautifully by the microanalytic trenchwork of our contributors, who did the hard work. They masterfully documented the changes in epistemology, methodology, findings, and conclusions that characterize theory and research in their respective areas of specialization. As you read the chapters, we think you will be impressed by the quality and quantity of new developments in the study of media effects. This has become a very sophisticated, mature area of inquiry that retains considerable sizzle.

Permit us to provide you with a brief introductory overview of the content of this volume:

For all editions of *Media Effects*, our leadoff hitter has been Max McCombs, either writing alone or with able collaborators. In the current edition, Max McCombs and Amy Reynolds provide historical foundations, theoretical perspectives, and summaries of key empirical investigations of agenda setting and agenda building in their chapter titled "How the News Shapes Our Civic Agenda." Agenda setting has been and remains one of the most frequently studied approaches to media effects research (Bryant & Miron, 2004). Moreover, it is widely recognized not only within but also beyond the communication discipline.

New to this edition is "News Framing Theory and Research," contributed by David Tewksbury and Dietram A. Scheufele. They trace the sociological and psychological roots of framing theory, provide explanatory models of framing, carefully analyze its place in communication research, and provide a wealth of suggestions for future researchers who will undoubtedly continue to explore this important perspective. A "kissing cousin" of agenda setting, framing too has been among the most frequently researched approaches to media-effects inquiry, especially during recent years (Bryant & Miron, 2004).

Cultivation analysis is another theoretical approach that has enjoyed a wealth of research attention in the discipline (Bryant & Miron, 2004) and has consequently been a vital part of *Media Effects'* content since the beginning edition. Cultivation analysis lost its founding father, George Gerbner, in 2005. We join scholars throughout the communication discipline in mourning the passing of this intellectual giant. Fortunately for the well-being of this volume, three of his students, Michael Morgan, James Shanahan, and Nancy Signorielli, ably continue to advance the cultivation tradition in "Growing Up with Television: Cultivation Processes."

L. J. Shrum tackles a perennially popular topic of media effects in his chapter titled "Media Consumption and Perceptions of Social Reality: Effects and Underlying Processes." Noteworthy in this contribution is the innovative treatment of those governing psychological processes that explain and predict this category of media effects, including first-order and second-order cultivation effects. This chapter's overview of influences that develop *during* the process of viewing versus those that are manifest subsequent to viewing will undoubtedly serve as an important springboard for future scholarship interested in the role of media on viewers' values and beliefs.

Media priming is an often-cited but frequently misunderstood class of media-effects theories. However, reading "Media Priming: An Updated Synthesis" by David R. Roskos-Ewoldsen, Beverly Roskos-Ewoldsen, and Francesca Dillman Carpentier is a surefire antidote for any misunderstanding. Following the explication of various priming models, and following consideration of these models' applications with diverse media content (e.g., violence, political communication), the authors provide a cohesive rationale for the migration of priming into mental modeling.

Social cognitive theory is a vital and vibrant theory that has received extensive explication and application throughout the social sciences. In his extensively updated chapter titled "Social Cognitive Theory of Mass Communication," Albert Bandura reveals manifold ways by which the set of theories and propositions that compose social cognitive theory help explain and predict media effects.

Theories of persuasion have been an integral part of the media-effects tradition since its inception. In recent decades, the prevalent model of persuasion has been the elaboration likelihood model (ELM). Richard E. Petty, Pablo Briñol, and Joseph R. Priester masterfully present ELM and its applications to mass communication in their thoroughly updated and expanded chapter, "Mass Media Attitude Change: Implications of the Elaboration Likelihood Model of Persuasion."

Since its formal introduction in 1959, uses and gratifications has been one of the most widely utilized research perspectives in mass communication inquiry (Bryant & Miron, 2004). Since the publication of *Perspectives on Media Effects* in 1986, U-&-G's place has been eloquently represented in this collection by Alan M. Rubin, and we welcome his "Uses-and-Gratifications Perspective on Media Effects" in the current edition. Noteworthy in this chapter is the careful attention paid to linking media uses and effects.

One of the new contributions in this volume is Annie Lang, Robert F. Potter, and Paul Bolls' explanation of the place of psychophysiological research in mass communication inquiry. The increasingly prominent incursion of physiological measurement in a wide variety of communication scholarship is presented in their chapter titled "Where Psychophysiology Meets the Media: Taking the Effects Out of Mass Media Research."

Dhavan V. Shah, Hernando Rojas, and Jaeho Cho have provided another major new contribution to this edition with their chapter entitled "Media and Civic Participation: On Understanding and Misunderstanding Communication Effects." Their chapter goes a long way to correcting many of the mischaracterizations of media effects on civic life and recasts these questions and issues into a productive and important line of effects inquiry.

Systematic consideration of "Political Communication Effects" has been a major contribution of the last two editions of *Media Effects*. Douglas M. McLeod, Gerald M. Kosicki, and Jack M. McLeod continue with this important tradition with a major revamping and updating of their chapter from the previous edition. Readers will undoubtedly appreciate their intensive efforts to streamline and focus this massive body of scholarship, which has been so central to media-effects inquiry.

Another extremely popular perspective in media-effects inquiry, especially in the 21st century, has been the third-person effect, which has been tested in diverse investigations across a variety of communication genres. Richard M. Perloff provides historical background, detailed conceptualization, and a succinct summary of the research legacy of this vibrant tradition in "Mass Media, Social Perception, and the Third-Person Effect." We feel confident that readers not only will appreciate the expanded and updated literatures covered in this chapter but will also find Perloff's framework for interpreting these diverse findings particularly valuable.

The legacy of media-violence research is so rich and its theoretical lineage so convoluted that we had to call upon "a family of scholars" to write the chapter on "Media Violence." Glenn G. Sparks, Cheri W. Sparks, and Erin A. Sparks have gleaned these fertile fields and synthesized this massive tradition into a manageable and important compendium of knowledge.

One dimension of media violence that has emerged as its own relatively self-contained bailiwick is the topic of young people's fright reactions to media fare. Joanne Cantor is the grand master of this research domain and has integrated this ever-expanding research arena into a cohesive chapter that includes the topic's historical roots, essential conceptualization, research synthesis, and coping strategies, always keeping in mind important developmental and gender differences in "Fright Reactions to Mass Media."

As we turn the discussion from violence to sex, Richard Jackson Harris and Christopher P. Barlett explore issues such as where we learn about sex, what we learn about sex, and the ramifications of learning about sexuality and sexual behavior from diverse media sources. In "Effects of Sex in the Media," the nature of sexual content in the media is first explored systematically, and then both content and context effects are presented and discussed, concluding with the special case of sexual violence.

In prior editions of *Media Effects*, the treatment of media and stereotyping tended to focus most of its attention on racial stereotyping specifically. In this volume we expanded this focus to include both racial/ethnic stereotyping and sex-role stereotyping. As both of these research traditions have expanded and have taken on somewhat different characteristics and models, we commissioned independent chapters for these two traditions. Dana Mastro provides a valuable update to the contributions of prior editions in "Effects of Racial and Ethnic Stereotyping," and Stacy L. Smith and Amy D. Granados greatly expand our prior coverage of sexual stereotyping in a chapter that is new to this edition, "Content Patterns and Effects Surrounding Sex-Role Stereotyping on Television and Film." Both of these chapters not only do an exemplary job of overviewing the current state of media portrayals of stereotyping but also highlight the specific content and viewer characteristics that play important theoretical roles in how media may affect viewers' perceptions and beliefs about race and gender.

It would be difficult to overestimate the impact of marketing on the behavior of individual consumers, on society, and on cultural values. David W. Stewart and Paul A. Pavlou provide a detailed assessment of many of the "hot button" issues of marketing communications, especially in the world of rapidly evolving media, in "The Effects of Media on Marketing Communications."

Shalom M. Fisch provides an innovative and thorough look at the impact of media on education in his chapter titled "Educational Television and Interactive Media for Children: Effects on Academic Knowledge, Skills, and Attitudes." Included in this chapter are several new or enhanced models of learning via traditional and interactive media.

One area of media-effects inquiry that has undergone a substantial increase in sophistication during the past decade is that of planned communication campaigns. Accordingly, one of the chapters that received the most extensive and expansive updating is Ronald E. Rice and Charles K. Atkin's "Public Communication Campaigns: Theoretical Principles and Practical Applications."

Public attention to health-related media messages also has soared during the 21st century, especially with press coverage of "the obesity crisis" and "Generation Extra Large." Because Kim Walsh-Childers and Jane D. Brown have been contributing to this dialog for some time now, they are able to place the current concerns in a most valuable context, and they also highlight a number of other important health issues in "Effects of Media on Personal and Public Health."

Interestingly, the flip side of the obesity issue may be an equally critical social problem—the role of media in perpetuating the thin ideal and in precipitating or facilitating a wide variety of eating disorders. Michael P. Levine and Kristen Harrison consider these important issues in this newly added chapter, "Effects of Media on Eating Disorders and Body Image."

Many of the treatments of media effects in this volume are accompanied by some caveat to the effect that "not all effects are experienced by all people, at least not to the same extent." To some, these so-called "individual differences" that make some people more susceptible to media effects than others are some of the truly fascinating aspects of this area of investigation. Mary Beth Oliver and K. Maja Krakowiak tackle such issues head-on in "Individual Differences in Media Effects." In an era of specialized media, fragmented audiences, and user-generated media, this topic assumes ever-increasing importance.

Speaking of spiraling importance, the scientific study of entertainment seems to be claiming much more attention in the 21st century than it has in the past. Always equal to the task of examining "Entertainment and Enjoyment as Media Effects" are Peter Vorderer and Tilo Hartmann. Among the many useful approaches they bring to bear in examining this topic are evolutionary and environmental perspectives.

The final three chapters are new to this edition and are paeans to the diverse forms of media communication that permeate and characterize contemporary life. As you will see, each of these new media forms practically dictates new approaches to the study of media effects. Each also raises monumental new questions for the new generations of media scholars.

Kwan Min Lee, Wei Peng, and Namkee Park examine the "Effects of Computer/ Video Games and Beyond." Not only is digital gaming becoming more popular with each new generation of user and more sophisticated with each new generation of software and platform, but gaming is also routinely judged by users to be more entertaining than mainstream media fare. Add to this phenomenon the added dimensions of interactivity, agency, and competition that accompanies most gaming, and it becomes obvious that the potency of games to foster user engagement—and perhaps more robust media effects—warrants careful examination.

If we consider the single element that has changed post-industrial societies the most dramatically during the past couple of decades, it almost surely would be the Internet. The Net is now a major player in work, play, finances, relationships, and so much more. Carolyn A. Lin tackles this seemingly benign monster from an effects perspective in "Effects of the Internet."

Among all the social- and personal-level changes wrought by new media technologies, none may ultimately be more important than the effects of widespread adoption and use of mobile communications media. For most of the history of media communication, we have been tethered to networks. Suddenly, our networks permeate our lives, granting digital media heretofore-unimagined freedoms. Scott W. Campbell and Rich Ling explore the social consequences of such mobile communications, boldly suggesting ways that such technologies may cause us to rethink media effects.

We are greatly indebted to our wonderful contributors for teaching us so much about media effects in such an effortless manner. Accordingly, we enthusiastically remand their collective wisdom to the community of media-effects scholars.

Jennings Bryant
Mary Beth Oliver

Reference

Bryant, J., & Miron, D. (2004). Theory and research in mass communication. *Journal of Communication*, 54, 662–704.

1

HOW THE NEWS SHAPES OUR CIVIC AGENDA

Maxwell McCombs
University of Texas at Austin

Amy Reynolds
Indiana University at Bloomington

The war in Iraq dwarfed all other topics reported in the U.S. news media during the first three months of 2007. And public opinion polls during the same time showed that Americans thought the Iraq War was the most important issue as they began to think about electing a new president in 2008. Through their day-to-day selection and display of the news, journalists focus our attention and influence our perceptions of the most important issues facing the country, and in early 2007 the focus was on the Iraq war. This ability to influence the salience of topics on the public agenda has come to be called the agenda-setting role of the news media.

Establishing this salience among the public so that an issue becomes the focus of public attention, thought, and perhaps even action is the initial stage in the formation of public opinion. While many issues compete for public attention, only a few are successful in capturing public attention. The news media exert significant influence on our perceptions of what are the most salient issues of the day.

Because people use the media to help them sort through important political issues before they vote, scholars have spent nearly 70 years studying the effect of mass communication on voters. In the 1940 U.S. presidential election, Paul Lazarsfeld and his colleagues at Columbia University collaborated with pollster Elmo Roper to conduct seven rounds of interviews with voters in Erie County, Ohio (Lazarsfeld, Berelson, & Gaudet, 1944). Those surveys and many subsequent investigations in other settings over the next 20 years found little evidence of major mass communication effects on attitudes and opinions. Many scholars have argued that little evidence of effects was found because these early studies focused on the mass media's ability to persuade voters and change their attitudes. However, traditional journalism norms emphasize that the media are trying to inform, not persuade. These early studies did support that idea, demonstrating that people acquired information from the mass media, even if they didn't change their opinions. In an ironic turn of history for communication research, recent elaborations of agenda-setting theory discussed later in this chapter are investigating the relationship between the effects of agenda setting and public opinions and attitudes (Kim & McCombs, 2007).

But, as a result of the early election studies, a limited-effects model for mass communication emerged. Summarized in the law of minimal consequences (Klapper, 1960), this notion ran counter to the ideas that Walter Lippmann, the intellectual father of agenda setting, proposed back in the early 1920s. Lippmann's opening chapter in his 1922 classic, *Public Opinion*, which is titled "The World Outside and the Pictures in Our Heads," summarizes the agenda-setting idea even though he did not use that phrase. His thesis is that the news media, our windows to the vast world beyond our direct experience, determine our cognitive maps of that world. Public opinion, argued Lippmann, responds not to the environment, but to the pseudo-environment, the world constructed by the news media (Lippmann, 1922).

This scientific shift of perspective away from the law of minimal consequences took hold in the 1960s, and during the 1968 presidential election McCombs and Shaw (1972) launched a seminal study that would support Lippmann's notion that the information provided by the news media plays a key role in the construction of our pictures of reality. Their central hypothesis was that the mass media set the agenda of issues for a political campaign by influencing the salience of issues among voters. Those issues emphasized in the news come to be regarded over time as important by members of the public. McCombs and Shaw called this hypothesized influence agenda setting.

To test this hypothesis that the media agenda can set the public agenda, McCombs and Shaw conducted a survey among a sample of randomly selected undecided voters in Chapel Hill, North Carolina. These undecided voters were asked to name what they thought were the key issues of the day, regardless of what the candidates were saying. The issues named in the survey were ranked according to the percentage of voters naming each one to yield a description of the public agenda.

Concurrent with this survey of voters, the nine major news sources used by these voters—five local and national newspapers, two television networks, and two news magazines—were collected and content analyzed. The rank-order of issues on the media agenda was determined by the number of news stories devoted to each issue. The high degree of correspondence between these two agendas of political and social issues established a central link in what has become a substantial chain of evidence for an agenda-setting role of the press.

If this correlation between the voters' agenda and the total news agenda was the highest, it would be evidence of agenda setting. If the correlation with the voters' preferred party's agenda in the news coverage was higher, it would be evidence of selective perception. The concept of selective perception, which is often cited as an explanation for minimal media effects, locates central influence within the individual and stratifies media content according to its compatibility with an individual's existing attitudes and opinions. From this perspective, it is assumed that individuals minimize their exposure to non-supportive information and maximize their exposure to supportive information. The vast majority of the Chapel Hill evidence favored an agenda-setting effect.

ACCUMULATED EVIDENCE

Since the Chapel Hill study, researchers have conducted more than 425 empirical studies on the agenda-setting influence of the news media. This vast accumulated evidence comes from many different geographic and historical settings worldwide and covers numerous types of news media and a wide variety of public issues. The evidence also provides greater detail about the time-order and causal links between the media and public agendas.

Shaw and McCombs' (1977) follow-up to the Chapel Hill study examined a representative sample of all voters in Charlotte, North Carolina during the summer and fall of the 1972 presidential election and found that the salience of all seven issues on the public agenda was influenced by the pattern of news coverage in the *Charlotte Observer* and network television news. During the 1976 presidential election, voters in three very different settings—Lebanon, New Hampshire; Indianapolis, Indiana; and Evanston, Illinois—were interviewed nine times between February and December (Weaver, Graber, McCombs, & Eyal, 1981). Simultaneously, election coverage by the three national networks and local newspapers in the three cities was content analyzed. In all three communities the agenda-setting influence of both television and newspapers was greatest during the spring primaries.

Although election settings provide a strong natural laboratory in which to study agenda-setting effects, the evidence that supports the theory is not limited to elections. Winter and Eyal (1981) took a historical look at the civil rights issue between 1954 and 1976 using 27 Gallup polls. Comparison of the trends in public opinion with a content analysis of the *New York Times* yielded a correlation of +.71. Similar findings about the impact of news coverage on trends in public opinion come from an analysis of 11 different issues during a 41-month period in the 1980s (Eaton, 1989). In each of these analyses, the media agenda is based on a mix of television, newspapers, and news magazines, while the public agenda is based on 13 Gallup polls. All but one of the correlations (the issue of morality) were positive, although a pattern of considerable variability in the strength of the correlations was visible.

More recently, Holbrook and Hill (2005) explored the agenda-setting effect of entertainment media. They used data from two controlled lab experiments and the 1995 National Election Study Pilot Study to show that the viewing of crime dramas significantly increased concerns about crime and that those concerns affected viewers' opinions of the president. Gross and Aday (2003) compared the effects of watching local television news with direct experience measures of crime on fear of victimization and issue salience. They found that local news exposure did account for an agenda-setting effect. They did not, however, find that television viewing cultivated fear of becoming a victim of crime. Hester and Gibson (2003) combined data from four years of print and broadcast news about the economy in time series analyses with two indicators of consumer economic evaluations and three measures of real economic conditions. They concluded that the media's emphasis on negative economic news may have serious consequences for both economic performance and expectations.

Agenda-setting effects also have also been found outside of the U.S. In Pamplona, Spain during the spring of 1995, comparisons of six major concerns on the public agenda with local news coverage showed a high degree of correspondence (Canel, Llamas, & Rey, 1996). In Germany, a look at national public opinion patterns during 1986 through weekly comparisons of the public and media agendas showed that television news coverage had a significant impact on public concern about five issues, including the country's energy supply (Brosius & Kepplinger, 1990). Early in 1986 the energy supply issue had little salience on either the news agenda or the public agenda. But a rapid rise in May on the news agenda was followed within a week by a similar rise on the public agenda. When news coverage subsequently declined, so did the size of the constituency expressing concern about Germany's energy supply.

Again at the local level, agenda setting occurred in the October 1997 legislative elections in the Buenos Aires metropolitan area (Lennon, 1998). In September, the public agenda and the combined issue agenda of five major Buenos Aires newspapers only modestly agreed overall, but as election day approached in October, the correspondence between the agendas soared, an increase that suggests considerable learning from the news media in the closing weeks of the election campaign.

Using a cross-national comparative perspective that involved 14 European Union (EU) member states, Peter (2003) explored whether the amount of television coverage of the EU affected the extent to which EU citizens perceived European integration to be important. He found that the more EU stories people watched in countries in which the political elites disagreed about integration the more important they considered integration. But in countries in which elite opinion about integration was consensual this pattern did not repeat.

These real-world examples of agenda-setting effects are compelling but are not the best evidence for the core, causal proposition of agenda setting. The best evidence that the news media are the cause of these kinds of effects comes from controlled laboratory experiments, a setting where the theorized cause can be systematically manipulated, subjects are randomly assigned to various versions of the manipulation, and systematic comparisons are made among the outcomes. Evidence from laboratory experiments provides the final link in agenda setting's causal chain.

Changes in the salience of defense preparedness, pollution, arms control, civil rights, unemployment, and a number of other issues were produced in the laboratory among subjects who viewed TV news programs edited to emphasize a particular issue (Iyengar & Kinder, 1987). A variety of controls were used to show that changes in the salience of the manipulated issue were actually due to exposure to the news agenda. For example, in one experiment, control subjects viewed TV news programs that did not include the issue of defense preparedness. The change in salience of this issue was significantly higher for the test subjects who viewed stories on defense preparedness than for the subjects in the control group. There were no significant differences between the two groups from before to after viewing the newscasts for seven other issues. And a recent experiment documented the agenda-setting effects of an online newspaper. The salience of racism as a public issue was significantly higher among all three groups of subjects exposed to various versions of an online newspaper that discussed racism than among those subjects whose online newspaper did not contain a news report on racism (Wang, 2000).

These studies are far from all of the accumulated evidence that supports the theory of agenda setting. A meta-analysis of 90 empirical agenda-setting studies found a mean correlation of +.53, with most about six points above or below the mean (Wanta & Ghanem, 2000). There are, of course, a number of significant influences that shape individual attitudes and public opinion, including a person's personal experience as well as their exposure to the mass media. But the general proposition supported by this accumulation of evidence on agenda setting is that journalists do significantly influence their audience's picture of the world.

Many events and stories compete for journalists' attention. Because journalists have neither the capacity to gather all information nor the capacity to inform the audience about every single occurrence, they rely on a traditional set of professional norms to guide their daily sampling of the environment. The result is a limited view of the larger environment, something like the highly limited view of the outside world available through a small window.

Four portraits of public opinion—the major issues of the 1960s, the drug issue in the 1980s, crime in the 1990s, and the economy in the 2000s—tell us a great deal about the discretion of journalists and the discrepancies that are sometimes found in mass media portrayals of reality. In Funkhouser's (1973) study of public opinion trends during the 1960s, there was no correlation at all between the trends in news coverage of major issues and the reality of these issues. But there was a substantial correlation (+.78) between the patterns of news coverage and the public's perception of what were the most important issues. In the 1980s, there was an increasing trend in news coverage of drugs at a time when there was no change at all in the reality of the drug problem (Reese & Danielian, 1989). In the 1990s, there was an increase in the news coverage of crime at a time when there was a decreasing trend in the reality of crime (Ghanem, 1996). And, at the turn of the 21st century, Hester and Gibson (2003) noted that media coverage of the economy may have serious consequences for economic expectations and performance, particularly when the coverage is negative.

THE ACAPULCO TYPOLOGY

Explorations of agenda-setting effects have observed this mass communication phenomenon from a variety of perspectives. A four-part typology describing these perspectives is frequently referred to as the Acapulco typology because McCombs initially presented it in Acapulco, Mexico at the invitation of International Communication Association president Everett Rogers. The Acapulco typology contains two dichotomous dimensions. The first dimension distinguishes between two ways of looking at agendas. The focus of attention can be on the entire set of items that define the agenda, or the focus of attention can be narrowed to a single, particular item on the agenda. The second dimension distinguishes between two ways of measuring the salience of items on the agenda, either aggregate measures describing an entire population or measures that describe individual responses.

Perspective I includes the entire agenda and uses aggregate measures of the population to establish the salience of these items. The original Chapel Hill study took this perspective. For the media agenda, the salience of the issues was determined by the total percentage of news articles on each issue, while the public agenda was determined by the percentage of voters who thought the government should do something about each issue. This perspective is named "competition" because it examines an array of issues competing for positions on the agenda.

Perspective II is similar to the early agenda-setting studies with their focus on the entire agenda of items, but it shifts the focus to the agenda of each individual. When individuals are asked to rank-order a series of issues, there is little evidence of any correspondence at all between those individual rankings and the rank-order of those same issues in the news media. This perspective is labeled "automaton" because of its unflattering view of human behavior. An individual seldom reproduces to any significant degree the entire agenda of the media.

Perspective III narrows the focus to a single item on the agenda but like perspective I uses aggregate measures to establish salience. Commonly, the measures are the total number of news stories about the item and the percentage of the public citing an issue as the most important problem facing the country. This perspective is named "natural history" because the focus typically is on the degree of correspondence between the media agenda and the public agenda in the rise and fall of a single item over time. An example of this perspective is Winter and Eyal's (1981) study of the issue of civil rights over a 23-year period.

Perspective IV, like perspective II, focuses on the individual, but it narrows its observations to the salience of a single agenda item. This perspective, named "cognitive portrait," is illustrated by the experimental studies of agenda setting in which the salience of a single issue for an individual is measured before and after exposure to news programs where the amount of exposure to various issues is controlled.

The existence of these varied perspectives on the agenda-setting phenomenon, especially an abundance of evidence based on perspectives I and III, strengthens the degree of confidence about this media effect. Perspective I provides useful, comprehensive descriptions of the rich, ever-changing mix of mass media content and public opinion at particular points in time. This perspective strives to describe the world as it is. Perspective III provides useful descriptions of the natural history of a single issue but at the expense of the larger social context. Despite this, knowledge about the dynamics of a single issue over an extended time period is useful for understanding how the process of agenda setting works. Perspective IV also makes a valuable contribution to understanding the dynamics of agenda setting. From a scholarly viewpoint, evidence generated by perspectives III and IV is absolutely necessary for a detailed "how" and "why" explanation of agenda setting. But the ultimate goal of agenda-setting theory returns us to perspective I, which provides a comprehensive view of mass communication and public opinion in communities and nations.

ATTRIBUTE AGENDA SETTING

In most discussions of the agenda-setting role of the mass media, the unit of analysis on each agenda is an *object*, usually a public issue. But public issues are not the only objects that can be analyzed from the agenda-setting perspective. In party primaries, the objects of interest are the candidates vying for the nomination of their political party. Communication is a process that can be about any object or set of objects competing for attention. In all these instances, the term *object* is used in the same sense that social psychologists use the term *attitude object*.

Beyond the agenda of objects, there is another level of agenda setting. Each of the objects on an agenda has numerous attributes—characteristics and properties that describe the object. Just as objects vary in salience, so do their attributes. Both the selection of objects for attention and the selection of attributes for picturing those objects are powerful agenda-setting roles. An important part of the news agenda is the attributes that journalists and, subsequently, members of the public have in mind when they think about and talk about each object. These attributes have two dimensions, a cognitive component regarding information about substantive characteristics that describe the object and an affective component regarding the positive, negative, or neutral tone of these characteristics on the media agenda or the public agenda. The influence of attribute agendas in the news on the public's attribute agenda is the second level of agenda setting.

In an election setting, the theoretical distinction between the agenda of objects (the candidates) and the agendas of attributes (their images) is especially clear. Voters' images of the Democrat candidates during the 1976 presidential primaries illustrate this second level of agenda-setting effects. Eleven candidates were vying to be the Democrat challenger to incumbent Republican president Gerald Ford. Comparisons of New York voters' descriptions of these candidates with *Newsweek's* attribute agenda in its candidate sketches showed significant evidence of media influence (Becker & McCombs, 1978). Similar media effects on voters' images of political candidates have been found in such diverse cultural settings as the 1996 Spanish general election

(McCombs, Lopez-Escobar, & Llamas, 2000), the 1994 mayoral election in Taipei, Taiwan (King, 1997), and the 2002 Texas elections for governor and U.S. senator (Kim & McCombs, 2007).

Salience, which has been a central focus of agenda-setting theory, also can be examined at a second level. Public issues, like all other objects, have attributes. Different aspects of issues—their attributes—are emphasized to varying degrees in the news and in how people think and talk about issues. Again demonstrating the validity of agenda-setting theory across cultures, analysis of the 1993 Japanese general election found effects at both the first and second levels for the issue of political reform (Takeshita & Mikami, 1995). The more people used the news media, the greater the overall salience of the issue of political reform and, in particular, the greater the salience of system-related aspects of political reform, the aspect of the issue emphasized in the news.

Beyond election settings, in Minneapolis the correspondence between the local newspaper's reporting on the state of the economy and the salience of specific economic problems, causes, and proposed solutions among the public was a robust +.81 (Benton & Frazier, 1976). For an environmental issue in Indiana, the degree of correspondence was +.71 between the local newspaper's coverage of various aspects of this issue and the public's perspective on the development of a large lake (Cohen, 1975). In Japan, the correspondence between the coverage in two major dailies of the aspects of global environmental problems and Tokyo residents' concerns about these problems reached a peak of +.78 just prior to the United Nations' 1992 Rio de Janeiro environmental conference (Mikami, Takeshita, Nakada, & Kawabata, 1994).

Explication of attribute agenda setting also links the theory with the concept of framing. Both framing and attribute agenda setting call attention to the perspectives used by communicators and their audiences to picture topics in the daily news. However, because of the large number of definitions for framing, comparisons of the two approaches range from substantial overlap to total dissimilarity. Recent research has identified two types of frames, aspects and central themes, that do greatly resemble attribute agendas (McCombs, 2004).

An example of the aspects perspective, Ashley and Olson's (1998) catalog of the frames in news coverage of the women's movement ranges from feminists' appearance, used in more than a fourth of stories, to the seldom cited goals of the movement. Illustrating the convergence of the aspects framing perspective with attribute agenda setting, Miller, Andsager, and Riechert (1998) identified 28 frames describing four major candidates seeking the 1996 Republican presidential nomination. Although the study focused exclusively on identification of the frames in the campaign press releases and in news stories, subsequent analysis documented substantial attribute agenda-setting effects of the press releases on the news stories (McCombs, 2004).

In other framing research, the focus is on the dominant attribute defining the central theme of the news stories. Significant differences in the audience's responses were found in Nelson, Clawson, and Oxley's (1997) experiment comparing the effects of two contrasting themes, free speech versus public order, in news stories about a KKK rally and in McLeod and Detenber's (1999) experiment with news stories whose central theme varied in their level of support for civil protest. The idea that certain attributes of an object are *compelling arguments* for their salience (Ghanem, 1996) further links framing and agenda setting. Ghanem found that crime stories with low psychological distance—the crimes occurred locally or easily could happen to the audience member—drove the salience of crime as a public issue in Texas. Sheafer (2007) found that the negative valence of news stories was a compelling argument for the salience of the economy as the most important problem during five Israeli national elections.

Although Price and Tewksbury (1997) and Scheufele (2000) theorized a distinct difference between agenda setting and framing on the basis of the two aspects of knowledge activation (Higgins, 1996)—accessibility, which they linked to agenda setting, and applicability, linked to framing—these theories have found limited support. Focusing specifically on the accessibility of issue attributes, Kim, Scheufele, and Shanahan (2002) found that accessibility increased with greater newspaper use, but the resulting attribute agendas among the public bore no resemblance to the attribute agenda presented in the news and did not replicate attribute agenda-setting effects found over past decades. What emerged was a different version of media effects in which the *relative* amount of increased salience for the attributes among newspaper readers in comparison to persons unaware of the issue paralleled the media agenda. More recently, "Challenging the assumption that accessibility is responsible for shifts in importance judgments," Miller (2007) reported two experiments demonstrating that "the *content* of news stories is a primary determinant of agenda setting. Rather than solely relying on what is accessible in memory, people pay attention to the content of news stories . . ." (p. 689).

NEED FOR ORIENTATION

As already noted, the news media are not the only source of information or orientation to issues of public concern. Issues can be arrayed along a continuum ranging from obtrusive to unobtrusive. Obtrusive issues are those that we experience personally. For example, most people do not need the mass media to alert them to many aspects of the economy. Personal experience usually informs people about spending patterns during holidays or about the impact of rising gas prices. These are obtrusive issues. Some economic issues, however, are hard to understand personally. Typically, the mass media inform us about national trade deficits or balancing the national budget. These are unobtrusive issues, issues that we encounter only in the news and not in our daily lives. Some issues can be both obtrusive and unobtrusive, depending on individual circumstances. Unemployment is a good example. People who have never faced unemployment as a reality would see the issue as unobtrusive. But for workers who have been laid off or for anyone who has filed an unemployment claim, the issue is obtrusive. Their understanding of unemployment is first-hand.

Broad portraits of the agenda-setting role of the media reveal strong effects for unobtrusive issues and no effects for obtrusive issues (Weaver, Graber, McCombs, & Eyal, 1981; Zucker, 1978). More narrowly focused studies, which require knowing where an issue falls on the continuum for each individual, show similar results (Blood, 1981).

The concept of need for orientation provides a richer psychological explanation for variability in agenda-setting effects than simply classifying issues along the obtrusive/unobtrusive continuum. The concept of need for orientation is based on psychologist Edward Tolman's general theory of cognitive mapping. Tolman (1932, 1948) suggests that we form maps in our minds to help us navigate our external environment. His notion is similar to Lippmann's concept of the pseudoenvironment. The need for orientation concept suggests that there are individual differences in the need for orienting cues to an issue and in the need for background information about an issue.

Conceptually, an individual's need for orientation has been defined in terms of two lower order concepts, relevance and uncertainty, whose roles occur sequentially

(Weaver, 1977). Relevance is the initial defining condition. Most of us feel no discomfort or need for orientation to issues in a number of situations, especially in the realm of public affairs, because we don't see these issues as personally relevant. In the 2000 presidential election, most citizens showed little interest in the issue of U.S. and Russian relations, for example. People were much more concerned with Social Security and the growth of the American economy. In situations when the relevance of the issue to the individual is low, the need for orientation is low.

Among individuals who perceive a topic to be highly relevant, level of uncertainty must also be considered. This is the second and subsequent defining condition of need for orientation. If a person already possesses all the information he or she needs about an issue, uncertainty is low. Under conditions of high relevance and low uncertainty, the need for orientation is moderate. When relevance and uncertainty are high, however, need for orientation is high. This is often the situation during primary elections, when many unfamiliar candidates clutter the political landscape. As one might guess, the greater a person's need for orientation, the more likely he or she will attend to the mass media agenda, and the more likely he or she is to reflect the salience of the objects and attributes on the media agenda.

Need for orientation provides an explanation for the near-perfect match between the media agenda and the public agenda in the original Chapel Hill study. Although need for orientation was not initially provided as an explanation for that early study, it seems clear in retrospect that the original Chapel Hill findings regarding undecided voters were evidence of agenda-setting effects based exclusively on people with a high need for orientation.

On occasion, personal experience with an issue, rather than satisfying a need for orientation, triggers an increased need for more information and the validation that comes from the mass media (Noelle-Neumann, 1985). Sensitized to an issue, these individuals may become particularly adept at studying the media agenda.

Matthes (2006) noted that when taken together, agenda-setting studies that incorporate the need for orientation as a predictor of effects largely have been successful. But he notes that some studies with a focus on individual level analyses showed the strongest agenda-setting effects at moderate levels of need for orientation. For example, Schonbach and Weaver (1985) found that people with low interest and high uncertainty (a moderate need for orientation) showed the strongest agenda-setting effects. Matthes (2006) used these variable findings about the need for orientation to argue for a different theoretical and methodological approach. He suggested that three dimensions for need for orientation should be included in analyses—the need for orientation toward issues, the need for orientation toward facts, and the need for orientation toward journalistic evaluations. Although relevance and uncertainty could lead to need for orientation, the two lower order concepts do not allow for a direct measure of the need for orientation construct. This is why he argued for more direct indicators that express the motivation of respondents to turn to the news media. Matthes' scale continues to treat relevance and uncertainty as lower order constructs that allow a prediction for need for orientation. However, his need for orientation scale specifies three additional aspects. First is the need to orient to the issue itself; next is the need to orient to specific aspects or themes related to an issue (this dimension concerns the selection of background and factual information); and, finally, there is the need to orient to the journalist's evaluation, including the journalist's opinion and commentary about an issue.

Matthes (2007) tested his scale using a panel survey on the issue of unemployment combined with a content analysis of television and newspaper coverage of unemployment.

He found that the need for orientation did lead to increased issue salience and that a second level agenda-setting effect did occur. But need for orientation was not related to the perceived salience of issue attributes. He concluded that the need for orientation concept did explain the act of information seeking, but it did not influence the affective tone of the information that people sought.

CONSEQUENCES OF AGENDA-SETTING EFFECTS

The distinction between the first and second levels of agenda setting, object salience and attribute salience, also is related to consequences of agenda-setting effects for opinions about public figures or other elements in the news. There is a fundamental link between media attention to an object and the existence of opinions about it. During an election, for instance, the media focus their attention on the major candidates, which results in more people forming opinions about these candidates (Kiousis & McCombs, 2004). Other consequences for attitudes and opinions are *priming*, which is a consequence of first level agenda-setting effects, and *attribute priming*, a consequence of second level agenda-setting effects. The psychological basis of priming is the selective attention of the public. Rather than engaging in a comprehensive analysis based on their total store of information, citizens routinely draw upon those bits of information that are particularly salient at the time they make a judgment.

In their benchmark research on priming, Iyengar and Kinder (1987) noted, "By calling attention to some matters while ignoring others, television news [as well as other news media] influences the standards by which governments, presidents, policies, and candidates for public office are judged" (p. 63). Much of the research demonstrating priming has examined the impact of news coverage on presidential approval ratings, particularly news coverage that makes certain public issues salient among the public, issues that in turn become significant criteria for assessments of presidential performance.

Strong evidence of priming was found during the 1986 Iran-Contra scandal (Krosnick & Kinder, 1990). On November 25, 1986, the U.S. Attorney General announced that funds obtained by the U.S. government from the secret sale of weapons to Iran had been improperly diverted to the Contras, a group attempting to overthrow the Sandinista government in Nicaragua. The story received major news coverage. By coincidence, the National Election Study's post-1986 presidential survey was in the field at the time of these announcements, creating a natural before-and-after comparison of the elements of public opinion that influenced Americans' assessment of President Reagan. Public opinion about the importance of providing assistance to the Contras and about U.S. intervention in Central America substantially increased from before to after the Attorney General's announcement.

At the second level of agenda setting, the salience of attributes in the mass media is related to the opinions held by the audience. Focusing on the tone of the news about a wide variety of political and non-political attitude objects, research documenting significant links between the general affective tone of news coverage and public opinion includes German public opinion regarding Helmut Kohl across a decade (Kepplinger, Donsbach, Brosius, & Staab, 1989), voters' presidential candidate preferences during recent U.S. presidential campaigns (Shaw, 1999), and the negative tone of news stories and consumers' expectations about the economy (Blood & Phillips, 1997; Hester & Gibson, 2003). Kim and McCombs (2007) found that the affective tone of individual attributes was related to voters' opinions about the candidates for governor and U.S.

senator in the 2002 Texas elections. Moreover, the attributes most emphasized in news reports about these candidates were stronger predictors of opinions among heavy newspaper readers than among light newspaper readers. Combining both the first and second levels of agenda setting in an analysis of the 2000 U.S. presidential election, Son and Weaver (2006) found that the salience of both the candidates and their attributes predicted changes in the public opinion polls about voters' candidate preferences.

Attribute agenda setting in tandem with priming and attribute priming demonstrate that attention to the specific content of the news can provide a detailed understanding of the pictures in our heads and of our opinions grounded in those pictures. These effects of the news on our perspectives and opinions are not the result of any efforts at deliberate persuasion by the media but rather the inadvertent byproducts of the limited capacity of media agendas that must focus on a small number of topics and their attributes and, in turn, the limited amount of time and attention that the public devotes to public affairs.

WHO SETS THE MEDIA AGENDA?

As evidence accumulated about the agenda-setting influence of the mass media on the public, scholars in the early 1980s began to ask who set the media's agenda. In this new line of inquiry, researchers began to explore the various factors that shape the media agenda. Here the media agenda is the dependent variable whereas in traditional agenda-setting research the media agenda was the independent variable, the key causal factor in shaping the public agenda.

The metaphor of "peeling an onion" is useful for understanding the origins of the agenda of the mass media. The concentric layers of the onion represent the numerous influences that shape the media agenda, which is at the core of the onion. And the influence of an outer layer is, in turn, affected by layers closer to the core of the onion. A highly detailed elaboration of this metaphoric onion contains many layers, ranging from the prevailing social ideology to the beliefs and psychology of an individual journalist (Shoemaker & Reese, 1991).

At the surface of our theoretical onion are key external news sources. These include politicians, public officials, public relations practitioners, and any individual, like the president of the United States, who influences media content. For example, a study of Richard Nixon's State of the Union address in 1970 showed that the agenda of 15 issues in that address did influence the subsequent month's news coverage in the *New York Times*, the *Washington Post*, and two of the three national television networks (McCombs, Gilbert, & Eyal, 1982). No evidence was found in that study to suggest the media had an influence on the president. Examination of the *New York Times* and the *Washington Post* across a 20-year period found that nearly half of their news stories were based substantially on press releases and other direct information subsidies. About 17.5% of the total number of news stories was based, at least in part, on press releases and press conferences, and background briefings accounted for another 32% (Sigal, 1973).

Inside the onion are the interactions and influence of various mass media on each other, a phenomenon called intermedia agenda setting. To a considerable degree, these interactions reinforce and validate the social norms and traditions of journalism. Those values and practices are the layer of the onion surrounding the core that defines the ground rules for the ultimate shaping of the media agenda.

The *New York Times* frequently plays the role of intermedia agenda-setter because appearance on the front page of the *Times* can legitimize a topic as newsworthy. The contamination of Love Canal in upstate New York and the radon threat in Pennsylvania did not gain national prominence, despite intensive local media coverage, until these issues appeared on the *Times'* agenda (Mazur, 1987; Ploughman, 1984). The previous mention of the *Times'* coverage of the drug problem in the 1980s also demonstrates intermedia agenda setting. When the *New York Times* "discovered" the country's drug problem in late 1985, network news coverage and major newspaper coverage of the issue soon followed (Reese & Danielian, 1989).

In a laboratory experiment that examined the agenda-setting function of the Associated Press, researchers found a high degree of correspondence across topics between the proportion of news stories in a large wire file and the small sample selected by the subjects. The subjects were experienced newspaper and television wire editors (Whitney & Becker, 1982).

Recent intermedia agenda-setting studies have investigated the impact of web sites and other forms of new media on more traditional media content. Ku, Kaid, and Pfau (2003) found that web site campaigning during the 2000 presidential election had an impact on the agendas of the traditional news media much in the same way that a candidate's political advertising on television has historically influenced the media agenda. This supports the findings of studies like Boyle's (2001), which explored the impact that 116 political advertisements had on 818 newspaper and 101 network television news stories during the 1996 presidential election. Ku et al. (2003) also found that the candidate web sites' agendas were more likely to be associated with the public's agenda during the 2000 election.

In an extension of intermedia agenda setting to online news services, Lim (2006) found that some intermedia agenda setting did occur between the web sites of two major South Korean newspapers, the *Chosun Ilbo* and the *Joong Ang Ilbo*, and the web site of the South Korean wire service, the Yonhap News Agency. Lim found that while the wire service did not influence the issue agendas of the two newspapers, the leading online newspaper did influence the issue agendas of both the wire service and the other newspaper.

Finally, in an effort to explore the impact of blogs on the traditional media agenda, Schiffer's (2006) case study of the Downing Street Memo controversy in 2005 found that coverage of the controversy on the news pages of large papers and on television relied on Bush administration statements and official sources, while the op-ed pages of major newspapers showed coverage that was influenced by blog-based activism.

SUMMING UP

Many years ago, Harold Lasswell (1948) told us that mass communication had three broad social roles—surveillance of the larger environment, achieving consensus among segments of society, and transmission of the culture. Agenda setting is a significant part of the surveillance role because it contributes substantial portions of our pictures about the larger environment. And recent research on the consequences of both first-level and second-level agenda-setting effects outlines significant influence on attitudes and opinions.

The agenda-setting process also has implications for social consensus and transmission of the social culture. Evidence linking agenda setting and social consensus was found in Shaw and Martin's (1992) comparison of demographic groups in the North Carolina Poll. Although demographics typically are used to demonstrate differences among social groups, their analysis found increased similarities between demographic groups with increased levels of media use. The correlation between the issue agendas for men and women who infrequently read a daily newspaper was +.55. But for men and women who read a newspaper occasionally, the degree of correspondence rose to +.80. And, among men and women who read a newspaper regularly, the issue agendas were identical (+1.0). Similar patterns of increased consensus about the most important issues facing the country as a result of greater media exposure also were found in comparisons of young and old and black and white and was true for both newspaper and television use. These patterns of increased social consensus as a result of media exposure also have been found in Taiwan and Spain (Chiang, 1995; Lopez-Escobar, Llamas, & McCombs, 1998).

The transmission of culture is also linked to the agenda-setting process. Beyond the specifics of politics and election campaigns, the larger political culture is defined by a basic civic agenda of beliefs about politics and elections. Exploration of yet other cultural agendas is moving agenda-setting theory far beyond its traditional realm of public affairs. These new lines of cultural inquiry extend from the historical agenda defining a society's collective memory of the past to the contemporary agenda of attributes defining the ideal physical appearance of young women and men. The imprint of the mass media that begins with its basic agenda-setting influence on the focus of attention is found on many aspects of public opinion and behavior.

References

Ashley, L., & Olson, B. (1998). Constructing reality: Print media's framing of the women's movement, 1966 to 1986. *Journalism & Mass Communication Quarterly, 75*, 263–277.

Becker, L., & McCombs, M. E. (1978). The role of the press in determining voter reaction to presidential primaries. *Human Communication Research, 4*, 301–307.

Benton, M., & Frazier, P. J. (1976). The agenda-setting function of the mass media at three levels of information-holding. *Communication Research, 3*, 261–274.

Blood, D., & Phillips, P. (1997). Economic headline news on the agenda: New approaches to understanding causes and effects. In M. McCombs, D. Shaw, & D. Weaver (Eds.), *Communication and democracy: Exploring the intellectual frontiers in agenda-setting theory* (pp. 97–114). Mahwah, NJ: Erlbaum.

Blood, R. W. (1981). *Unobtrusive issues in the agenda-setting role of the press.* Unpublished doctoral dissertation, Syracuse University, Syracuse, NY.

Boyle, T. P. (2001). Intermedia agenda setting in the 1996 presidential election. *Journalism and Mass Communication Quarterly, 78*, 26–44.

Brosius, H. B., & Kepplinger, H. M. (1990). The agenda-setting function of television news: Static and dynamic views. *Communication Research, 17*, 183–211.

Canel, M. J., Llamas, J. P., & Rey, F. (1996). El primer nivel del efecto agenda setting en la informacion local: Los "problemas mas importantes" de la ciudad de Pamplona [The first level agenda setting effect on local information: The "most important problems" of the city of Pamplona]. *Communicacion y Sociedad, 9*, 17–38.

Chiang, C. (1995). *Bridging and closing the gap of our society: Social function of media agenda setting.* Unpublished master's thesis, University of Texas, Austin, TX.

Cohen, D. (1975). *A report on a non-election agenda-setting study.* Paper presented to the Association for Education in Journalism, Ottawa, Canada.

Eaton, H. Jr. (1989). Agenda setting with bi-weekly data on content of three national media. *Journalism Quarterly, 66*, 942–948.

Funkhouser, G. R. (1973). The issues of the sixties. *Public Opinion Quarterly, 37*, 62–75.

Ghanem, S. (1996). *Media coverage of crime and public opinion: An exploration of the second level of agenda setting*. Unpublished doctoral dissertation, University of Texas, Austin.

Gross, K., & Aday, S. (2003). The scary world in your living room and neighborhood: Using local broadcast news, neighborhood crime raters, and personal experience to test agenda-setting and cultivation. *Journal of Communication, 53*, 411–426.

Hester, J. B., & Gibson, R. (2003). The economy and second-level agenda-setting: A time series analysis of economic news and public opinion about the economy. *Journalism and Mass Communication Quarterly, 80*, 73–90.

Higgins, E. T. (1996). Knowledge activation: Accessibility, applicability, and salience. In E. T. Higgins & A. W. Kruglanski (Eds.), *Social psychology: Handbook of basic principles* (pp.133–168). New York: Guilford.

Holbrook, R. A., & Hill, T. G. (2005). Agenda-setting and priming in prime time television: Crime dramas as political cues. *Political Communication, 22*, 277–295.

Iyengar, S., & Kinder, D. R. (1987). *News that matters: Television and American opinion*. Chicago: University of Chicago Press.

Kepplinger, H. M., Donsbach, W., Brosius, H. B., & Staab, J. F. (1989). Media tone and public opinion: A longitudinal study of media coverage and public opinion on Chancellor Helmut Kohl. *International Journal of Public Opinion Research, 1*, 326–342.

Kim, K., & McCombs, M. (2007). News story descriptions and the public's opinions of political candidates. *Journalism and Mass Communication Quarterly, 84*, 299–314.

Kim, S.-H., Scheufele, D. A., & Shanahan, J. (2002). Think about it this way: Attribute agenda-setting function of the press and the public's evaluation of a local issue. *Journalism & Mass Communication Quarterly, 79*, 7–25.

King, P. (1997). The press, candidate images and voter perceptions. In M. E. McCombs, D. L. Shaw, and D. Weaver (Eds.), *Communication and democracy: Exploring the intellectual frontiers in agenda setting* (pp. 29–40). Mahwah, NJ: Erlbaum.

Kiousis, S., & McCombs, M. (2004). Agenda-setting effects and attitude strength: Political figures during the 1996 presidential election. *Communication Research, 31*, 36–57.

Klapper, J. (1960). *The effects of mass communication*. Glencoe, IL: Free Press.

Krosnick, J., & Kinder D. R. (1990). Altering the foundations of support for the president through priming. *American Political Science Review, 84*, 497–512.

Ku, G., Kaid, L. L., & Pfau, M. (2003). The impact of web site campaigning on traditional news media and public information processing. *Journalism and Mass Communication Quarterly, 80*, 528–547.

Lasswell, H. (1948). The structure and function of communication in society. In L. Bryson (Ed.), *The communication of ideas* (pp. 37–51). New York: Institute for Religious and Social Studies.

Lazarsfeld, P., Berelson, B., & Gaudet, H. (1944). *The people's choice*. New York: Columbia University Press.

Lennon, F. R. (1998). Argentina: 1997 elecciones. Los diarios nacionales y la campana electoral [The 1997 Argentina election. The national dailies and the electoral campaign]. Report by The Freedom Forum and Austral University.

Lim, J. (2006). A cross-lagged analysis of agenda setting among online news media. *Journalism and Mass Communication Quarterly, 83*, 298–312.

Lippmann, W. (1922). *Public opinion*. New York: Macmillan.

Lopez-Escobar, E., Llamas, J. P., & McCombs, M. E. (1998). Agenda setting and community consensus: First and second level effects. *International Journal of Public Opinion Research, 10*, 335–348.

Matthes, J. (2006). The need for orientation towards news media: revising and validating a classic concept. *International Journal of Public Opinion Research, 18*, 422–444.

Matthes, J. (2007). The need for orientation in agenda setting theory: testing its impact in a two-wave panel study. Presented to the International Communication Association, San Francisco, CA.

Mazur, A. (1987). Putting radon on the public risk agenda. *Science, Technology and Human Values, 12*, 86–93.

McCombs, M. E. (2004). *Setting the agenda: The mass media and public opinion*. Cambridge, England: Blackwell Polity Press.
McCombs, M. E., Gilbert, S., & Eyal, C. H. (1982). The State of the Union address and the press agenda: A replication. Presented to the International Communication Association, Boston, MA.
McCombs, M. E., Lopez-Escobar, E., & Llamas, J. P. (2000). Setting the agenda of attributes in the 1996 Spanish general election. *Journal of Communication, 50*, 77–92.
McCombs, M. E., & Shaw, D. L. (1972). The agenda-setting function of mass media. *Public Opinion Quarterly, 36*, 176–187.
McLeod, D., & Detenber, B. (1999). Framing effects of television news coverage of social protest. *Journal of Communication, 49*(3), 3–23.
Mikami, S., Takeshita, T., Nakada, M., & Kawabata, M. (1994). *The media coverage and public awareness of environmental issues in Japan*. Paper presented to the International Association for Mass Communication Research, Seoul, Korea.
Miller, J. M. (2007). Examining the mediators of agenda setting: A new experimental paradigm reveals the role of emotions. *Political Psychology, 28*, 689–717.
Miller, M. M., Andsager, J. L., & Riechert, B. P. (1998). Framing the candidates in presidential primaries: Issues and images in press releases and news coverage. *Journalism and Mass Communication Quarterly, 75*(2), 312–324.
Nelson, T. E., Clawson, R. A., & Oxley, Z. M. (1997). Media framing of a civil liberties conflict and its effect on tolerance. *American Political Science Review, 91*, 567–583.
Noelle-Neumann, E. (1985). The spiral of silence: A response. In K. Sanders, L. L. Kaid, & D. Nimmo (Eds.), *Political communication yearbook 1984* (pp. 66–94). Carbondale: Southern Illinois University Press.
Peter, J. (2003). Country characteristics as contingent conditions of agenda setting: The moderating influence of polarized elite opinion. *Communication Research, 30*, 683–712.
Ploughman, P. (1984). *The creation of newsworthy events: An analysis of newspaper coverage of the man-made disaster at Love Canal*. Unpublished doctoral dissertation, State University of New York at Buffalo, Buffalo.
Price, V., & Tewksbury, D. (1997). News values and public opinion: A theoretical account of media priming and framing. In G. A. Barnett and F. J. Boster (Eds.), *Progress in communication sciences: Advances in persuasion* (pp. 173–212). Greenwich, CT: Ablex.
Reese, S. D., & Danielian, L. (1989). Intermedia influence and the drug issue: Converging on cocaine. In P. Shoemaker (Ed.), *Communication campaigns about drugs* (pp. 29–46). Hillsdale, NJ: Erlbaum.
Scheufele, D. A. (2000). Agenda-setting, priming, and framing revisited: Another look at cognitive effects of political communication. *Mass Communication and Society, 3*, 297–316.
Schiffer, A. J. (2006). Blogswarms and press norms: News coverage of the Downing Street memo controversy. *Journalism and Mass Communication Quarterly*, 83, 494–510.
Schonbach, K., & Weaver, D. H. (1985). Finding the unexpected: Cognitive building in a political campaign. In S. Kraus & R. M. Perloff (Eds.), *Mass media and political thought: An information-processing approach* (pp. 157–176). Beverly Hills, CA: Sage.
Shaw, D. L., & Martin, S. (1992). The function of mass media agenda setting. *Journalism Quarterly*, 69, 902–920.
Shaw, D. L., & McCombs, M. E., Eds. (1977). *The emergence of American political issues*. St. Paul, MN: West.
Shaw, D. R. (1999). The impact of news media favorability and candidate events in presidential campaigns. *Political Communication, 16*, 183–202.
Sheafer, T. (2007). How to evaluate it: The role of story-evaluative tone in agenda setting and priming. *Journal of Communication, 57*, 21–39.
Shoemaker, P., & Reese, S. D. (1991). *Mediating the message: Theories of influences on mass media content*. New York: Longman.
Sigal, L. (1973). *Reporters and officials: The organization and politics of newsmaking*. Lexington, MA: D.C. Heath.

Son, Y. J., & Weaver, D. (2006). Another look at what moves public opinion: Media agenda setting and polls in the 2000 U.S. election. *International Journal of Public Opinion Research, 18*, 174–97.

Takeshita, T., & Mikami, S. (1995). How did mass media influence the voters' choice in the 1993 general election in Japan? *Keio Communication Review, 17*, 27–41.

Tolman, E. C. (1932). *Purposive behavior in animals and men*. New York: Appleton-Century-Crofts.

Tolman, E. C. (1948). Cognitive maps in rats and men. *Psychological Review, 55*, 189–208.

Wang, T. L. (2000). Agenda-setting online: An experiment testing the effects of hyperlinks in online newspapers. *Southwestern Mass Communication Journal, 15*(2), 59–70.

Wanta, W., & Ghanem, S. (2000). Effects of agenda-setting. In J. Bryant & R. Carveth (Eds.), *Meta-analyses of media effects*. Mahwah, NJ: Erlbaum.

Weaver, D. (1977). Political issues and voter need for orientation. In D. Shaw and M. McCombs (Eds.), *The emergence of American political issues* (pp. 107–119). St. Paul, MN: West.

Weaver, D., Graber, D. A., McCombs, M. E., & Eyal, C. H. (1981). *Media agenda-setting in a presidential election: Issues, images, and interest*. New York: Praeger.

Whitney, D. C., & Becker, L. (1982). "Keeping the gates" for gatekeepers: The effects of wire news. *Journalism Quarterly, 59*, 60–65.

Winter, J. P., & Eyal, C. H. (1981). Agenda-setting for the civil rights issue. *Public Opinion Quarterly, 45*, 376–383.

Zucker, H. G. (1978). The variable nature of news media influence. In B. D. Ruben (Ed.), *Communication yearbook 2* (pp. 225–240). New Brunswick, NJ: Transaction Books.

2

NEWS FRAMING THEORY AND RESEARCH

David Tewksbury
University of Illinois at Urbana-Champaign

Dietram A. Scheufele
University of Wisconsin-Madison

Artists know that the frame placed around a painting can affect how viewers interpret and react to the painting itself. As a result, some artists take great care in how they present their work, choosing a frame that they hope will help audiences see the image in just the right way. Journalists—often subconsciously—engage in essentially the same process when they decide how to describe the political world. They choose images and words that have the power to influence how audiences interpret and evaluate issues and policies. The simplicity of this analogy belies the complexity of the process and effects of framing in the news, however. Framing in the field of communication has been characterized by equal degrees of conceptual obliqueness and operational inconsistency (Scheufele & Tewksbury, 2007). Part of this vagueness at different levels stems from the fact that framing researchers have often approached the theory very inductively and examined framing as a phenomenon without careful explication of the theoretical premises and their operational implications.

This chapter provides an overview of framing research in three steps. In a first step we examine the theoretical foundations of framing in psychology, economics, sociology, and communication. Based on this theoretical framework, we then explicate the cognitive processes and mechanisms that explain framing effects. In this section, we also distinguish framing effects from other models of media effects. Finally, this chapter outlines agendas for future research in this area and discusses unresolved issues in framing research.

THEORETICAL FOUNDATIONS OF FRAMING

Framing theory has its roots in a number of disciplinary traditions, and different scholars have defined framing as a concept at different levels of analysis (Scheufele, 1999). In particular, the various approaches to framing can be distinguished along at least two distinct dimensions: *disciplinary origins* (psychological vs. sociological approaches) and *explanatory models* (applicability models vs. other effects models).

Disciplinary Origins

The disciplinary origins of framing are often traced back to more micro-level or psychological approaches and more macro-level or sociological approaches.

Sociological Roots

More macro-level or "sociological" approaches to framing, as Pan and Kosicki (1993) call them, draw heavily from assumptions outlined in attribution theory (Heider, 1959; Heider & Simmel, 1944) and frame analysis (Goffman, 1974). Heider's experimental work (1959) showed that human beings process complex information in their everyday lives by reducing social perception to judgments about causal attribution. A vast majority of subjects who were shown movies with abstract movements of geometrical shapes, for instance, interpreted these movements as actions of human beings with particular underlying motivations (Heider & Simmel, 1944). Based on these studies, Heider (1959) defined attribution as the perceived link between an observed behavior and a potential cause. Responsibility for observed actions can be attributed to personal factors or to societal or environmental factors. This distinction between societal and individual attributions of responsibility is mirrored in Iyengar's (1991) work on episodic and thematic political news framing and attributions of responsibility.

A separate but related intellectual tradition underlying sociological approaches to framing is Goffman's (1974) work on frames of reference. Rather than simple attributions of causality, individuals rely on broader interpretive schemas called "primary frameworks" (Goffman, 1974, p. 24). These primary frameworks are often described as relatively stable and socially shared category systems that human beings use to classify new information. In this sense, they are similar to the notion of "radical categories" and related constructs in cognitive linguistics (e.g., Lakoff, 1996).

The relevance of primary frameworks for communication research is two-fold. First, primary frameworks are socially constructed category systems that serve as important tools for information processing among citizens. Second, societal and media discourse is often tailored toward specific primary frameworks in order to influence audience interpretations. Or as Edelman (1993) put it: "The social world is . . . a kaleidoscope of potential realities, any of which can be readily evoked by altering the way in which observations are framed and categorized" (p. 232).

Psychological Roots

The psychological roots of framing are summarized in works on "frames of reference" (Sherif, 1967) and prospect theory (Kahneman, 2003; Kahneman & Tversky, 1979, 1984). In his experimental work, Sherif (1967) showed that all individual judgments and perceptions occur within certain frames of reference. Therefore, it is possible "to set up situations in which appraisal or evaluation of a social situation will be reflected in the perceptions and judgments of the individual" (Sherif, 1967, p. 382).

Kahneman and Tversky's Nobel Prize winning work (1979, 1984) expanded on this idea and claimed that all "perception is reference-dependent" (Kahneman, 2003, p. 459). The idea of reference dependency assumes that a given piece of information will be interpreted differently, depending on which interpretive schema an individual applies. More importantly, however, different interpretive schemas can be invoked by framing the same message in different ways (Scheufele, 2008). For example, "[a]n ambiguous stimulus that is perceived as a letter in a context of letters is seen as a number in a context of numbers" (Kahneman, 2003, p. 455). Kahneman's experimental work focused primarily on the impact of framing on economic and risk-related choices, but the implications for communication research are obvious.

Explanatory Models—Framing as an Applicability Process

Regardless of its theoretical underpinnings, framing research argues that news frames function to suggest how audiences can interpret an issue or event. In fact, news frames can exert a relatively substantial influence on citizens' beliefs, attitudes, and behaviors. Therefore, it is not surprising that they appear to be related to other consequential processes in news consumption and processing. There are three other processes and effects that bear at least passing resemblance to framing effects and, very likely, occur in parallel to framing. Distinguishing them from framing will help us understand how all of the processes operate.

Information Effects

News stories about political issues and events contain both information and frames. One question researchers have faced is how they distinguish between these two story elements and their effects. When Gamson and Modigliani (1987) discussed the framing process, they described packages that elites and media use to characterize an issue. These packages comprise arguments, information, symbols, metaphors, and images (Gamson & Modigliani, 1987). Presumably, packages can affect how people understand, interpret, and react to a problem or issue. At their core, issue packages have a frame, "a central organizing idea or story line that provides meaning to an unfolding strip of events" (1987, p. 143). Another element of a package is the information it provides about an issue. This may be detail about the people affected by a problem, its costs, implications, and so on. This information can affect audience members' beliefs about the issue and its treatment. A frame is what unifies information into a package that can influence audiences.

This description suggests that frames are the devices that build the associations between concepts; information in a news story can cement the link, but it relies on a frame to build the associations. If an issue and its frame are relatively novel to an audience reading an article, the presence of information (e.g., facts, figures, images) about the issue can serve to form the basis for the link the frame represents. However, if audiences already have the frame available to them, the mere presentation of a frame in a news story can exert an effect. Indeed, both a cultural approach to framing and common sense suggest that a frame effect is not due only to the associations that are explicitly introduced in some news effects. Rather, a very effective frame needs no supporting arguments to give it meaning within some text. Frame effects can rely upon culture-based meanings, norms, and values.

At their most powerful, frames invite people to think about an issue in particular ways. Simon and Jerit (2007) showed this efficiently in a recent experiment in which news articles about an abortion procedure used the word *fetus* or *baby* to describe the object of the procedure. There were no other differences between the articles. Not surprisingly—given American cultural norms regarding these words—audiences who read the "baby" article expressed significantly more support for regulating the procedure than did the other readers. Indeed, audiences who read a third version of the article, in which the words appeared with equal frequency, reported a level of support that matched that of the "baby" article readers (Simon & Jerit, 2007). Thus, it is possible in some situations for a single word to affect audience cognitions and attitudes, a conclusion that will certainly resonate with political scientists (e.g., Edelman, 1964).

In sum, information effects result from a process in which people acquire beliefs and impressions of an issue and its context. A framing effect occurs when a phrase, image, or statement suggests a particular meaning or interpretation of an issue. Frames link issues to particular beliefs that carry with them concepts for interpreting the origins, implications, and treatment of the issue. It is very likely that news stories frequently have both framing and information effects, but a story could presumably have one effect and not the other, as the Simon and Jerit (2007) study illustrates.

Persuasion Effects

On the surface, framing contains many elements that characterize basic persuasion processes (Hovland, Janis, & Kelly, 1953). Both concern the presentation of content that can influence attitudes in a predictable direction. What is more, framing research has examined the moderating effect of source credibility (Druckman, 2001), a standard concern in persuasion research. To be sure, framing effects research and a host of other experiment-based studies of message effects owe a basic debt to the persuasion studies of the World War II era. However, a number of elements distinguish these effects (see, for example, Nelson, Oxley, & Clawson, 1997).

The first is the basic process each seeks to describe. Framing theory encompasses the origin, evolution, presentation, and effects of frames, whereas persuasion theory is not typically concerned with the origin and evolution of messages. In addition, persuasion studies usually involve the presentation of intentionally persuasive content to audiences presumably aware of that intent. Frames in the news can take the form of journalists' descriptions of people and other political objects, their choice of elements of an event to include in the news, words used to name an issue, and more. The framing literature suggests that audiences of news frames are often not aware of the presence of frames and the influence they can wield (e.g., Tewksbury, Jones, Peske, Raymond, & Vig, 2000). As a result, the message processing that persuasion and frame audiences are undergoing is likely very different.

Of perhaps equal importance is the fact that persuasion and framing effect studies are typically concerned with different outcomes. The approaches share an interest in cognitive responses as dependent variables. However, cognitive responses that reveal audience issue interpretation is a primary effect of framing (e.g., Price, Tewksbury, & Powers, 1997), whereas persuasion research is typically concerned with responses as an indication of acceptance of persuasive messages. Much like information effects, persuasion effects are visible in what people know or believe about an issue (Nelson, Oxley, & Clawson, 1997). Framing effects are perhaps most visible in what people think is important about an issue or relevant to understanding it (e.g., Kinder & Sanders, 1990). Indeed, perhaps the most important distinction between the two processes lies in the fact that framing effects are not defined as attitude effects but as interpretation effects (e.g., Tewksbury et al., 2000). Although quite a few framing effects studies have examined attitudes toward an issue or its resolution as the effect of a frame, a growing body of studies focuses on interpretations of the issue as a primary focus of the effect (e.g., Brewer, 2002; Shah, Kwak, Schmierbach, & Zubric, 2004; Shen, 2004).

Agenda-Setting Effects

Framing effects may most clearly but superficially resemble agenda setting effects, a relationship that has garnered some attention (e.g., McCombs, 2004; Scheufele & Tewksbury, 2007). Agenda setting is the process by which audience exposure to news about an issue raises its *accessibility* (Price & Tewksbury, 1997). When people consider the issues that face a country, they may recall issues that have received attention in the news. Issues that have received the most attention may be perceived to be the most important, all else being equal (e.g., McCombs & Shaw, 1972). In work spanning the last decade, a number of studies have suggested that framing effects can be thought of as a second-step of agenda setting, after effects on perceived issue importance (McCombs, 2004). That is, the agenda setting model has been used to describe how news messages affect perceptions of both the importance of an issue and how the issue can be understood. As a result of this line of research, there is some disagreement about whether agenda setting and framing represent distinct processes. The resolution of this disagreement may be possible by looking at the basic psychological processes behind these effects.

Price and Tewksbury (1997) and Nelson, Clawson, and Oxley (1997) suggested that accessibility effects are distinct from framing processes in which the meaning, cause, implication, or treatment of an issue is characterized (i.e., framed). They claimed that the primary effect of a frame is to render specific information, images, or ideas *applicable* to an issue. The basis of a psychological difference between agenda setting and framing, therefore, lies in this accessibility/applicability distinction. Ironically, perhaps the best way to conceive of the difference between the two is to recognize that accessibility and applicability go hand-in-hand in everyday information processing.

Fundamental to basic models of priming effects in psychology research (e.g., Higgins, Rholes, & Jones, 1977) is the very explicit link between applicability and accessibility (Higgins, 1996). All else being equal, the greater the accessibility of a construct, the greater is the likelihood that it will be used to interpret some political issue. Likewise, the more applicable a construct is to an issue, the more likely it is to be used when thinking about the issue. Naturally, then, a construct that is both accessible and applicable is all that much more likely to be used (whether the relationship between these two processes is additive or interactive in this situation is unclear). In practice, priming effects in the laboratory are found for constructs that are both applicable and accessible. For example, Higgins et al. (1977) demonstrated that inapplicable constructs that were made accessible to subjects were not used in interpreting ambiguous information about a person. Thus, the ongoing conceptualization of framing as an applicability or accessibility effect is to some extent one of emphasis and nomenclature. Some part of the question boils down to how the field wants to name and classify framing effects.

Some studies have explicitly examined the question of whether framing effects result from accessibility or applicability processes. Nelson, Oxley, and Clawson (1997), for example, demonstrated that alternative news frames affected how audiences prioritized competing values relative to an issue and that this effect was independent of the accessibility of the values. These authors argued that frames work through building associations between concepts rather than by increasing their accessibility. Brewer, Graf, and Willnat (2003) similarly demonstrated that audiences exposed to news that suggested specific associations between foreign countries and other concepts relied on the associations in their perceptions and opinions regarding the countries. More importantly, Brewer et al. (2003) observed that information primes that merely raised the accessibility of potentially relevant concepts failed to prompt audiences to use those considerations in their judgments. Thus, there is some direct evidence bearing on the primacy of applicability in understanding framing effects.

There is quite a bit at stake in the discussion over names and interpretation. How the field classifies the framing process should influence how researchers conceptualize the conditions under which frames have their effect. A consideration of frames as creating primarily applicability effects emphasizes focusing scholarly attention on how links between concepts and interpretations are presented to audiences. That is, an applicability interpretation should encourage researchers to look at how news content builds the strengths of the connection of descriptors and considerations and an issue or policy. The more powerful the arguments for the links, the stronger the framing effects should be, ceteris paribus (Chong & Druckman, 2007). An accessibility emphasis, on the other hand, could suggest that researchers should look for repetitions of associations between concepts and issues as the prime cause of framing effects (e.g., Kim, Scheufele, & Shanahan, 2002). These two approaches suggest differences in both the characteristics of news that should be the cause of effects and the operation of studies designed to test framing effects.

In summary, perhaps the best way to consider the relationship between information, persuasion, agenda setting, and framing effects is to observe that all four effects can result from exposure to a news message. They are distinct processes and very likely operate in tandem, together determining the ultimate outcome of exposure to the news (Nelson, Oxley, & Clawson, 1997; Nelson & Oxley, 1999). The distinctions between them are worth recognizing and exploring, of course. Too often, research in one tradition ignores parallel traditions. We would know more about the impact of a message or class of messages if we were to examine multiple processes at the same time.

FRAMING IN COMMUNICATION RESEARCH

A much lamented phenomenon in communication research is the fact that framing remains an elusive concept without clear definitional boundaries (Entman, 1993; Scheufele, 1999; cf. D'Angelo, 2002). It is possible, however, to classify different approaches to framing research broadly into two groups: studies of framing as the dependent variable, and studies of framing as the independent variable. The former group usually deals with "frame building," i.e., the question of how frames get established in societal discourse and how different frames compete for adoption by societal elites and journalists. The latter group is mostly concerned with "frame setting," i.e., framing effects on audiences (Scheufele, 1999).

Frame Building

Frame building deals with the creation and social negotiation of frames in at least three related areas: journalistic norms, political actors, and cultural contexts. Work in this area is often based on sociological foundations of framing research (e.g., Gamson & Modigliani, 1987, 1989) and assumes that media frames might help set the terms of the debate among citizens as part of a "frame contest." In such a contest one interpretative package might gain influence because it resonates with popular culture or a series of events, fits with media routines or practices, and/or is heavily sponsored by elites (Scheufele & Nisbet, 2007).

Practices of News Production

Previous research on news production and selection suggests at least five aspects of news work that could potentially influence how journalists frame a given issue: larger societal norms and values, organizational pressures and constraints, external pressures from interest groups and other policy makers, professional routines, and ideological or political orientations of journalists (e.g., Shoemaker & Reese, 1996; Tuchman, 1978). Different studies have examined subsets of these five influences on frame building. Some have argued that the way news is framed in mass media is a result of social and professional routines of journalists (van Dijk, 1985), "driven by ideology and prejudice" (Edelman, 1993, p. 232), or shaped by an interaction of journalists' norms and practices and of the influence of interest groups (Gamson & Modigliani, 1987).

Political and Corporate Actors

The second potential influence on frame building comes from elites, including interest groups, government bureaucracies, and other political or corporate actors (Scheufele, 1999). All of these groups routinely engage in frame building efforts (e.g., Gamson & Modigliani, 1987; Miller, Andsager, & Riechert, 1998; Nisbet, Brossard, & Kroepsch, 2003; Nisbet & Huge, 2006). Empirical evidence on the link between elite communication and the way issues are framed in mass media, however, is inconsistent at best.

Edelman (1993), for instance, argued that "authorities and pressure groups categorize beliefs in a way that marshals support and opposition to their interests" (1993, p. 51). In fact, political campaigns are spending more and more resources on message testing and delivery in order to control how messages are framed in news media (e.g., Luntz, 2007). These efforts are consistent with Bennett's (1990) indexing hypothesis, which stated that "[m]ass media professionals . . . tend to 'index' the range of voices and viewpoints in both news and editorials according to the range of views expressed in mainstream government debate about a given topic" (p. 106). More recent analyses, however, suggest that media coverage of candidates in presidential primaries, for instance, is often different from the way candidates frame their issue stances in press releases, and that candidates are only moderately successful in getting their frames across in election coverage (Miller et al., 1998). Subsequent research, however, showed much stronger influences of the rhetoric put forth by various interest groups (Andsager, 2000) or policy players (Nisbet et al., 2003) on the ways journalists framed issues. These influences seem to be strongest for issues where journalists and various players in the policy arena can find shared narratives around which they can construct issue frames (e.g., Nisbet et al., 2003).

Cultural Contexts

As outlined earlier in this chapter, some of the earliest discussions of frames in communication settings (e.g., Goffman, 1974) assume that the meaning of a frame has implicit cultural roots. What a frame implies for the understanding of some event or issue is therefore not simply communicated in a news message. Rather, a frame makes reference to something resident in the surrounding culture, and the presence of the frame essentially invites audiences to apply the information and meanings within which the culture has imbued the frame. This context dependency of frames has been described as "cultural resonance" (Gamson & Modigliani, 1989) or "narrative fidelity" (Snow & Benford, 1988).

More recently, van Gorp (2007, p. 62) suggested that there is a "cultural stock of frames" available to a communicator and that this stock is both large and confining. On the one hand, there are many frames available in a culture, but on the other hand, building communication efforts around a concept without commonly shared cultural roots is unlikely to produce an effective frame. This culture-specific perspective suggests that the shared nature and cultural familiarity of most frames also means that they "often are unnoticed and implicit, their impact is by stealth" (van Gorp, 2007, p. 63). Journalists, by definition, are working within the culture of their society and will therefore rely unconsciously on commonly shared frames. As we outlined earlier, however, other players in the policy arena will likely make a very conscious effort to tailor their messages to the background culture in their attempts to create successful frames. The degree to which a frame resonates with the surrounding culture, Gamson and Modigliani (1989) argued, can also "facilitate the work of [frame] sponsors by tuning the ears of journalists to its symbolism. They add prominence . . . by amplifying the effects of sponsor activities and media practices" (p. 6).

Frame Setting

When media effects theorists conceptualize the potential outcome of the production and exhibition of news content, they typically consider both the macro-level and micro-level effects of that content. On the micro-level, theories of effects are used to predict and explain how individuals (potentially millions of them, to be sure) can be influenced by exposure to a message. Most theorizing about framing effects occurs on this level. As we argued earlier, frame setting can best be considered an applicability effect. The most widely cited description, penned by Entman (1993), stated, "To frame is to select some aspects of a perceived reality and make them more salient in a communicating text, in such a way as to promote a particular problem definition, causal interpretation, moral evaluation, and/or treatment recommendation for the item described" (p. 52). Entman suggested that a frame encourages audiences to make associative connections between an issue and particular considerations relevant to its definition, causes, implications, and treatment. The most effective frames are those that build all four of those associations, but, of course, not all frames are so powerful. In research, these four outcomes are rarely identified separately, and most attention is given to the definition and treatment linkages.

Following the focus of most of the research on framing and frame effects, our discussion of frame setting will examine the individual level cognitive and affective outcomes of frame exposure. Analyses of frame effects are rooted in a set of assumptions about how applicability processes operate, the individual-level locus of frame effects, and the nature of audience exposure to media messages. These assumptions will be discussed, with attention given to the implications of each for understanding frame effects.

Applicability Effects

The importance of building associations between concepts has been demonstrated in a number of studies that have examined how audiences receiving some news frame have come to interpret an issue. For example, Price and colleagues (Price, Tewksbury, & Powers, 1997) constructed different versions of a news story about a public policy issue. Exposure to story types featuring either conflict between policy makers, the consequences of policy change on citizens, or a human interest angle on the issue prompted audiences to describe the issue in open-ended comments in ways that reflected the frame they read. A number of other studies have demonstrated that how people think about an issue, including what they believe are the most important considerations that bear on it, can be influenced by exposure to a frame in the news (e.g., Brewer, 2002; Shen, 2004). Research in this area has focused on either the introduction of links between issues and their meanings or the reinforcement of those links. We consider each of these processes, in turn.

Most of the news framing research to date has examined issue-interpretation linkages. There are two primary ways framing processes operate. For one, both an issue and the considerations relevant to it can be introduced together in the body of a news account. This may occur for news about some emerging issue or a sudden event. For example, Tewksbury and colleagues (2000) introduced a local policy issue that had received only limited coverage and manipulated the considerations most relevant for understanding it. The issue—large, "factory style" hog farms—was presented as either an economic or environmental policy concern. Holding the news content constant but altering the headline and lead emphasis of news articles affected how news readers understood the issue. It stands to reason that news accounts addressing a novel issue should be particularly powerful for audiences. If news receivers lack a set of linkages between an issue and diverse or countervailing considerations (as we would expect with a novel issue), news framing should strongly determine how audiences understand the issue. Indeed, Tewksbury et al. (2000) observed that the different story versions exerted a substantial effect on audience interpretations immediately after exposure to an article, and the effect persisted when measured again three weeks later. Audience retention of associations between an issue and considerations after exposure to only one news article seems most likely to occur for an issue unfamiliar to audiences.

Frames may also create linkages between very familiar issues and existing beliefs, values, and attitudes (e.g., Brewer & Gross, 2005; de Vreese, 2004; Domke, McCoy, & Torres, 1999). In this case, the frame suggests to audiences that they think about an issue in some novel way. In one such instance, Nelson, Clawson, and Oxley (1997) tested the effects of news stories about a rally by the Ku Klux Klan. Different news stories linked the group alternately to considerations about free speech and public order, both very familiar concepts. People exposed to the free speech frame exhibited substantially more tolerance toward the Klan's speeches and rallies. Similarly, Terkildsen and Schnell (1997) reported that news accounts of women's rights issues framed in terms of economic equality versus political equality affected male news readers' endorsement of feminist values (the economic frame lowered support for feminist values).

Framing effects researchers have identified limits to the extent to which frames can directly build issue-interpretation links. Quite apart from rather obvious news-level factors such as the quality of the news presentation, the use of images, and factors that affect the likelihood of exposure to a story, there are audience-level factors that seem to influence how frames operate. For one, evidence suggests that the extent to which frames tap into existing beliefs and impressions will influence their effect (Rhee, 1997). For example, Shen (2004) reported that news frames appear most powerful when they activate existing constructs. Prior to exposure to news stories that depicted stem cell research and oil drilling in Alaska in economic or environmental terms, Shen (2004) measured the extent to which participants held schemas (structures of beliefs and attitudes) for economic and environmental considerations. The results showed that audiences will accept novel constructs made applicable to an issue, but they are significantly more likely to do so when they have existing schemas for those constructs. Similar findings have emerged in research that has looked at how frames tap into audiences' existing values (e.g., Domke, Shah, & Wackman, 1998; Shen & Edwards, 2005).

There is an important caveat to this process, of course. When a frame invites people to apply their existing schemas to an issue, the implication of that application depends, in part, on what is in that schema. As a general rule of thumb, the more the receivers know about politics, the more effective are frames (e.g., Druckman & Nelson, 2003). However, a frame producer (e.g., a journalist or an issue advocate) may not be able to predict whether audiences' existing knowledge or values will encourage the interpretation that they intend when they construct the frame (Brewer, 2002). For example, Clawson and Waltenburg (2003) reported that existing ideological beliefs can moderate the effects of news representations of an affirmative action court case. Similarly, Boyle et al. (2006) found that how people reacted to depictions of a political activist group was a partial function of how they felt about the group prior to reading a news account. Thus, it is not always possible to estimate the effects of a frame based purely on the linkages suggested in a news account.

Types of Effects

The applicability approach carries with it an assumption that the primary locus of interest to researchers and practitioners is the network of associations people have regarding issues. This hardly describes the range of research that has examined the effects of frames in the news, however. There are a number of other levels and types of effects that have received attention. Indeed, for many researchers, formation or changes to associative links between concepts is a mediating step on the way to some other effect. Attitude formation or change—the most commonly studied outcome of frame setting—is the most obvious next step. In an example of this research, Nelson and Oxley (1999) reported that frames in news accounts of an economic development issue affected perceptions of which considerations were most important; these perceptions were then linked to opinions about the issue itself. Similarly, Brewer (2002) demonstrated that exposure to frames can influence how people justify their attitude reports. Some researchers have taken the process a step further by looking at the potential influence of frames on receivers' behaviors (which, presumably, come as a result of attitude changes). For example, Valentino, Beckmann, and Buhr (2001) examined the effects of strategy and issue-based descriptions of political campaigns on citizens' intention to vote in an election. On a similar level, Boyle et al. (2006) examined the impact of framing of a political group on the audience members' willingness to take some action with respect to that group.

Some studies of framing effects focus on psychological processes other than applicability. One early discussion of framing effects examined the impact of news depictions of an issue on attributions of responsibility for problems (Iyengar, 1991; Iyengar & Kinder, 1987). Iyengar (1991) suggested that news about social problems can influence attributions of causal and treatment responsibility, an effect observed in both cognitive responses and evaluations of political leaders. Other research has looked at the effects of frames on receivers' evaluative processing style (Shah, Domke, & Wackman, 1996) and the complexity of audience members' thoughts about issues (Shah, Kwak, Schmierbach, & Zubric, 2004).

Framing effect research has opened a number of doors to thinking about the not-so-powerful but still consequential effects of the news media. However, the variety of dependent variables that have been studied may raise concerns about the validity of measurement. It is possible that researchers are using measures that are intended to tap different concepts but are all measuring a core phenomenon. For example, applicability effects are frequently studied by gathering and analyzing open-ended responses to questions about the news article (e.g., Price et al., 1997), the relevant issue (e.g., Shen, 2004), or attitudes about the issue (e.g., Brewer, 2002). One can look at these targets of audience thought as distinct, but it seems likely that they are strongly related to one another and might, in practice, all tap a basic set of considerations. A similar tale can be told for the relationship between attitudes toward an object (e.g., a policy proposal) and intentions to act toward it (expressing support for the policy). Attitude theory suggests that these are distinct phenomena (Fishbein & Ajzen, 1975), but researchers must take great care at the level of operationalization to ensure that they are measured accurately.

Nature of Exposure to Frames

How researchers talk about the frame setting process is substantially affected by how they assume audiences are exposed to frames. On an operational level, most studies of frame effects are set in contexts in which audiences are exposed to a news account about an issue. In these experiments, participants read print stories (and occasionally view televised stories; e.g., Nelson, Clawson, & Oxley, 1997) about an issue framed in a specific way. Immediately after this exposure, typically, participants report their interpretations, beliefs, and/or attitudes vis-à-vis the issue (this is not always the case, naturally; for a good counterexample, see Rhee, 1997). Most studies, therefore, are designed to measure the immediate effects of exposure to news stories. As such, these studies are not measuring long-term memory effects and, indeed, closely resemble studies of priming effects. A priming study may feature a manipulation of some construct and then measure whether audiences exposed to the construct use it to interpret a person, event, or issue (Roskos-Ewoldsen, Roskos-Ewoldsen, & Carpentier, 2002). Studies have demonstrated that framing effects are separate from such accessibility effects (e.g., Brewer et al., 2003; Nelson, Oxley, & Clawson, 1997), but their operational resemblance may be affecting how researchers understand the phenomena.

This issue is important for understanding framing effects because the knowledge activation model of Price and Tewksbury (1997) suggests that the framing effect is most clear in a longitudinal context. That is, applicability effects are most clear when the associations between issues and considerations are built at exposure but affect interpretations and judgments at a later point (Tewksbury et al., 2000). One may speculate, then, that applicability effects are most distinct from other news effects when they are perhaps most consequential, in interpersonal discussions, or even contexts that involve voting or responding to an opinion poll. These are impromptu situations in which people interpret issues and render judgments about them some time after exposure to news accounts. Of course, few framing models take into account what happens after the initial exposure. Researchers have noted that interpersonal discussion and other news content experienced after exposure to a news frame can mute its effects (Druckman & Nelson, 2003).

UNRESOLVED ISSUES

Research on framing during the last 30 years has tried to clarify the concept, its underlying mechanisms, and the contingencies under which framing works best. The sheer amount of research, however, has also raised new questions that have yet to be answered.

Types of Frames

The first question relates to the idea of specific sets of frames or interpretive schemas in various cultures (Scheufele & Nisbet, 2007). Previous research has conceptualized framing along very distinctive dimensions, examining the effects of these very specific frames on audience reactions. This includes sets of frames, such as gains vs. loss frames (Kahneman & Tversky, 1979), episodic vs. thematic frames (Iyengar, 1991), strategy vs. issue frames (Cappella & Jamieson, 1997), or human interest, conflict, and economic consequences frames (Price et al., 1997).

By taking this inductive approach, previous research has often identified unique sets of frames with each new study and paid significantly less attention to identifying what some scholars have called master frames (Snow & Benford, 1992) or more enduring cultural themes (Gamson & Modigliani, 1989), i.e., sets of frames that could potentially be applicable across issues. As a result, communication researchers continue to have an only limited understanding of the more generic sets of frames that can trigger certain underlying interpretive schemas among audiences and therefore lead to various behavioral or cognitive outcomes.

Researchers have begun to criticize this somewhat shortsighted tendency for frame reductionism (Scheufele, 2004) and have called for a more systematic effort to identify stable, consistent sets of schemas or frames (Scheufele & Nisbet, 2007). As Reese (2007) noted, "[h]ighlighting simple description of media frames is tempting, and a frequent approach given the easy availability of media texts, but this risks reifying them—locking them in place, as though they were not part of a larger conversation, serving particular interests, and undergoing changes over time" (p. 149).

Framing as a Multi-Level Problem: Internal Versus External Validity

The second issue that previous empirical research has left unanswered is the issue of framing as a multi-level problem. The different disciplinary traditions of the field outlined earlier also helped shape somewhat separate strands of research in the field of communication. They can be categorized, based on the types of manipulations each study is concerned with (see Figure 2.1).

Figure 2.1 classifies studies on framing effects in communication into four separate cells, based on the type of framing they examine empirically. Most research continues to approach frames in a very broad sense, i.e., using messages that confound pure framing effects with information effects. This makes a lot of sense, given that differences in framing in "real world" journalism usually go hand-in-hand with content differences. On the other hand, however, using these more externally valid messages also limits the ability of these studies to tap framing effects that are uncontaminated by information effects, and many of the behavioral and attitudinal outcomes measured by previous research are likely a function of both frame *and* content.

These studies are distinctively different from research that examines pure information or pure framing effects. An example for the former would be a study on media coverage of stem cell research that compares stories on the scientific processes behind stem cell research with stories about the religious and moral debates surrounding stem

		Informational Content Manipulation	
		Yes	**No**
Frame Manipulation	**Yes**	News stories in the "real world;" high external validity; limited internal validity due to frame/content confounds	"Pure" framing manipulation with informational content held constant; limited external validity; high internal validity
	No	"Pure" informational content manipulation without frames; limited external validity; high internal validity	No informational content or framing effects (e.g., agenda setting)

Figure 2.1 Internal and External Validity of Framing Research—Confounds of Frame and Content.

cell research. These stories present different facts and arguments about stem cell research and therefore have less to do with framing. An example of the latter would be Kahneman and Tversky's (1979) research on framing as purely presentational differences of the exact same information.

This distinction between uncontaminated framing and content effects is an important one for future framing research. Not only has the label "framing" been used to describe phenomena that are clearly not framing, but we have also yet to clearly delineate which effects in everyday news coverage of issues are due to informational content differences and which ones are a function of differences in the mode of presentation or other framing devices.

Over Time Versus Short-Term Effects—Method Versus Theory

Finally, media effects research often experiences something of a disjuncture between the hypothesized nature of some effect and the limitations of the methods chosen to study it. Framing effects are, almost exclusively, conceptualized as long-term in nature. To be sure, some researchers looking at survey or ballot wording are concerned about the very immediate effects of message framing. Most political communication researchers, however, are interested in the impact of exposure to messages on enduring beliefs and opinions about an issue. Thus, most studies are intended to examine long-term effects. Survey research is well poised to examine such effects, but the more common experiment-based studies are less well suited to the task.

The survey model offers researchers the opportunity to track ongoing news exposure and issue opinion development. In the news effects version of survey research, interviewers ask samples of people about their exposure to specific or even general classes of news content and then look for associations with issue interpretations and attitudes (e.g, Sotirovic, 2000). The question wording version of survey research is able to show that existing issue interpretations can be cued via questions that activate tightly organized sets of associations. Kinder and Sanders (1990), for example, asked survey respondents about their support for affirmative action policies. One version of their question encouraged people to apply an "undeserved advantage" (African-Americans receive unearned advantages) set of considerations about the policies, whereas a version suggested to a different group that they apply a "reverse discrimination" set (Affirmative Action policies discriminate against white Americans). These operations did not manipulate the meaning of the issue so much as tap into a set of considerations and feelings congruent with the frame the question mentioned. Thus, a survey approach to framing effects carries with it some ability to examine the long-term availability and influence of issue frames.

The experiment model provides researchers with more control over the nature of the news message and the terms of audience reception of it. However, most experiments are designed to examine short-term effects alone (e.g., Nelson, Clawson, & Oxley, 1997). Some experiments have examined the long-term effects of exposure to news frames, but they are the exception. For example, Tewksbury et al. (2000) found that exposure to a news article setting the frame for a relatively novel issue influenced perceptions of the gist of the issue three weeks after the exposure, whereas short-term influences on opinions about government regulation had disappeared at the time of the retest. This experiment was limited with its use of student subjects considering a relatively novel issue. More experienced and frequent news readers may hold pre-existing strong attitudes toward framed issues and be more likely to come across alternate framing of an issue in question, both factors that can reduce the influence of the frames (Chong & Druckman, 2007). At the same time, the knowledge activation approach suggests that frequent exposure to a relatively consonant framing of an issue should strengthen the applicability link between an issue and a frame while increasing the long-term accessibility of that link. Thus, future research designed to identify specific long-term applicability processes could help clarify the unique contributions of framing effects to political beliefs, opinion, and behaviors.

References

Andsager, J. L. (2000). How interest groups attempt to shape public opinion with competing news frames. *Journalism & Mass Communication Quarterly*, *77*, 577–592.

Bennett, W. L. (1990). Toward a theory of press-state relations in the United States. *Journal of Communication*, *40*(2), 103–125.

Boyle, M. P., Schmierbach, M., Armstrong, C. L., Cho, J., McCluskey, M., McLeod, D. M., & Shah, D. V. (2006). Expressive responses to news stories about extremist groups: A framing experiment. *Journal of Communication*, *56*, 271–288.

Brewer, P. R. (2002). Framing, value words, and citizens' explanations of their issue opinions. *Political Communication*, *19*, 303–316.

Brewer, P. R., Graf, J., & Willnat, L. (2003). Priming or framing: Media influences on attitudes toward foreign countries. *Gazette: The International Journal for Communication Studies*, *65*, 493–508.

Brewer, P. R., & Gross, K. (2005). Values, framing, and citizens' thoughts about policy issues: Effects on content and quantity. *Political Psychology*, *26*, 929–948.

Cappella, J. N., & Jamieson, K. H. (1997). *Spiral of cynicism: The press and the public good*. New York: Oxford University Press.

Chong, D., & Druckman, J. N. (2007). A theory of framing and opinion formation in competitive elite environments. *Journal of Communication*, *57*, 99–118.

Clawson, R. A., & Waltenburg, E. N. (2003). Support for a Supreme Court affirmative action decision: A story in black and white. *American Politics Research*, *31*, 251–279.

D'Angelo, P. (2002). News framing as a multiparadigmatic research program: A response to Entman. *Journal of Communication*, *52*, 870–888.

de Vreese, C. H. (2004). The effects of frames in political television news on issue interpretation and frame salience. *Journalism & Mass Communication Quarterly*, *81*, 36–52.

Domke, D., McCoy, K., & Torres, M. (1999). News media, racial perceptions, and political cognition. *Communication Research*, *26*, 570–607.

Domke, D., Shah, D. V., & Wackman, D. B. (1998). "Moral referendums": News media, and the process of candidate choice. *Political Communication*, *15*, 301–321.

Druckman, J. N. (2001). On the limits of framing effects: Who can frame? *The Journal of Politics*, *63*, 1041–1066.

Druckman, J. N., & Nelson, K. R. (2003). Framing and deliberation: How citizens' conversations limit elite influence. *American Journal of Political Science*, *47*, 729–745.

Edelman, M. (1964). *The symbolic uses of politics*. Urbana: University of Illinois Press.

Edelman, M. J. (1993). Contestable categories and public opinion. *Political Communication*, *10*, 231–242.

Entman, R. M. (1993). Framing: Towards clarification of a fractured paradigm. *Journal of Communication*, *43*, 51–58.

Fishbein, M., & Ajzen, I. (1975). *Belief, attitude, intention and behavior: An introduction to theory and research*. Reading: Addison-Wesley.

Gamson, W. A., & Modigliani, A. (1987). The changing culture of affirmative action. *Research in Political Sociology*, *3*, 137–177.

Gamson, W. A., & Modigliani, A. (1989). Media discourse and public opinion on nuclear power—A constructionist approach. *American Journal of Sociology*, *95*(1), 1–37.

Goffman, E. (1974). *Frame analysis: An essay on the organization of experience*. Cambridge, MA: Harvard University Press.

Heider, F. (1959). *The psychology of interpersonal relations* (2nd ed). New York: Wiley.

Heider, F., & Simmel, M. (1944). An experimental study of apparent behavior. *American Journal of Psychology*, *57*, 243–259.

Higgins, E.T. (1996). Knowledge activation: Accessibility, applicability, and salience. In E. T. Higgins & A.W. Kruglanski (Eds.), *Social psychology: Handbook of basic principles* (pp. 133–168). New York: Guilford Press.

Higgins, E. T., Rholes, W. S., & Jones, C. R. (1977). Category accessibility and impression formation. *Journal of Experimental Social Psychology*, *13*, 141–154.

Hovland, C. I., Janis, I. L., & Kelly, H. H. (1953). *Communication and persuasion: Psychological studies of opinion change*. New Haven, CT: Yale University Press.

Iyengar, S. (1991). *Is anyone responsible? How television frames political issues*. Chicago: University of Chicago Press.

Iyengar, S., & Kinder, D. R. (1987). *News that matters: Television and American opinion*. Chicago: University of Chicago Press.

Kahneman, D. (2003). Maps of bounded rationality: A perspective on intuitive judgment and choice. In T. Frängsmyr (Ed.), *Les Prix Nobel: The Nobel Prizes 2002* (pp. 449–489). Stockholm, Sweden: Nobel Foundation.

Kahneman, D., & Tversky, A. (1979). Prospect theory—Analysis of decision under risk. *Econometrica*, *47*(2), 263–291.

Kahneman, D., & Tversky, A. (1984). Choices, values, and frames. *American Psychologist*, *39*(4), 341–350.

Kim, S. H., Scheufele, D. A., & Shanahan, J. (2002). Think about it this way: Attribute agenda-setting function of the press and the public's evaluation of a local issue. *Journalism & Mass Communication Quarterly*, *79*, 7–25.

Kinder, D. R., & Sanders, L. M. (1990). Mimicking political debate with survey questions: The case of white opinion on affirmative action for blacks. *Social Cognition*, 8, 73–103.

Lakoff, G. (1996). *Moral politics: How liberals and conservatives think*. Chicago: University of Chicago Press.

Luntz, F. (2007). *Words that work: It's not what you say, it's what people hear*. New York: Hyperion.

McCombs, M. E. (2004). *Setting the agenda: The mass media and public opinion*. Malden, MA: Blackwell.

McCombs, M. E., & Shaw, D. (1972). The agenda setting function of the mass media. *Public Opinion Quarterly, 36*, 176–187.

Miller, M. M., Andsager, J. L., & Riechert, B. P. (1998). Framing the candidates in presidential primaries: Issues and images in press releases and news coverage. *Journalism and Mass Communication Quarterly, 75*, 312–324.

Nelson, T. E., Clawson, R. A., & Oxley, Z. M. (1997). Media framing of civil liberties conflict and its effects on tolerance. *American Political Science Review, 91*, 567–583.

Nelson, T. E., & Oxley, Z. M. (1999). Issue framing effects on belief importance and opinion. *The Journal of Politics, 61*, 1040–1067.

Nelson, T. E., Oxley, Z. M., & Clawson, R. A. (1997). Toward a psychology of framing effects. *Political Behavior, 19*, 221–246.

Nisbet, M. C., Brossard, D., & Kroepsch, A. (2003). Framing science—The stem cell controversy in an age of press/politics. *The Harvard International Journal of Press-Politics*, 8(2), 36–70.

Nisbet, M. C., & Huge, M. (2006). Attention cycles and frames in the plant biotechnology debate: Managing power and participation through the press/policy connection. *The Harvard International Journal of Press/Politics, 11*(2), 3–40.

Pan, Z., & Kosicki, G. M. (1993). Framing analysis: An approach to news discourse. *Political Communication, 10*, 59–79.

Price, V., & Tewksbury, D. (1997). News values and public opinion: A theoretical account of media priming and framing. In G. A. Barett & F. J. Boster (Eds.), *Progress in communication sciences: Advances in persuasion* (Vol. 13, pp. 173–212). Greenwich, CT: Ablex.

Price, V., Tewksbury, D., & Powers, E. (1997). Switching trains of thought: The impact of news frames on readers' cognitive responses. *Communication Research, 24*, 481–506.

Reese, S. D. (2007). The framing project: A bridging model for media research revisited. *Journal of Communication, 57*, 148–154.

Rhee, J. W. (1997). Strategy and issue frames in election campaign coverage: A social cognitive account of framing effects. *Journal of Communication, 47*, 26–48.

Roskos-Ewoldsen, D. R., Roskos-Ewoldsen, B., & Carpentier, F. R. (2002). Media priming: A synthesis. In J. Bryant and D. Zillmann (Eds.), *Media effects: Advances in theory and research* (pp. 97–120). Mahwah, NJ: Erlbaum.

Scheufele, B. T. (2004). Framing-effects approach: A theoretical and methodological critique. *Communications, 29*, 401–428.

Scheufele, D. A. (1999). Framing as a theory of media effects. *Journal of Communication*, 49(1), 103–122.

Scheufele, D. A. (2008). Framing theory. In W. Donsbach (Ed.), *The international encyclopedia of communication* (pp. 1862–1868). Malden, MA: Blackwell Publishing.

Scheufele, D. A., & Nisbet, M. C. (2007). Framing. In L. L. Kaid & C. Holz-Bacha (Eds.), *Encyclopedia of political communication* (pp. 254–257). Thousand Oaks, CA: Sage.

Scheufele, D. A., & Tewksbury, D. (2007). Framing, agenda-setting, and priming: The evolution of three media effects models. *Journal of Communication, 57*, 9–20.

Shah, D. V., Domke, D., & Wackman, D. B. (1996). "To thine own self be true": Values, framing, and voter decision-making strategies. *Communication Research, 23*, 509–560.

Shah, D. V., Kwak, N., Schmierbach, M., & Zubric, J. (2004). The interplay of news frames on cognitive complexity. *Human Communication Research, 30*, 102–120.

Shen, F. (2004). Effects of news frames and schemas on individuals' issue interpretations and attitudes. *Journalism & Mass Communication Quarterly, 81*, 400–416.

Shen, F., & Edwards, H. H. (2005). Economic individualism, humanitarianism, and welfare reform: A value-based account of framing effects. *Journal of Communication, 55*, 795–809.

Sherif, M. (1967). *Social interaction: Processes and products*. Chicago: Aldine.

Shoemaker, P. J., & Reese S. D. (1996). *Mediating the message* (2nd ed.). White Plains, NY: Longman.

Simon, A., & Jerit, J. (2007). Toward a theory relating political discourse, media, and public opinion. *Journal of Communication, 57,* 254–271.

Snow, D. A., & Benford, R. D. (1988). Ideology, frame resonance, and participant mobilization. In B. Klandermans, H. Kriesi, & S. Tarrow (Eds.), *International social movement research. Volume 1. From structure to action: Comparing social movement research across cultures* (pp. 197–217). Greenwich, CT: JAI Press.

Snow, D. A., & Benford, R. D. (1992). Master frames and cycles of protest. In A. D. Morris & C. McClurg Mueller (Eds.), *Frontiers in social movement theory* (pp. 133–155). New Haven, CT: Yale University Press.

Sotirovic, M. (2000). Effects of media use on audience framing and support for welfare. *Mass Communication & Society, 3,* 269–296.

Terkildsen, N., & Schnell, F. (1997). How media frames move public opinion: An analysis of the women's movement. *Political Research Quarterly, 50,* 879–900.

Tewksbury, D., Jones, J., Peske, M., Raymond, A., & Vig, W. (2000). The interaction of news and advocate frames: Manipulating audience perceptions of a local public policy issue. *Journalism & Mass Communication Quarterly, 77,* 804–829.

Tuchman, G. (1978). *Making news: A study in the construction of reality.* New York: The Free Press.

Valentino, N. A., Beckmann, M. N., & Buhr, T. A. (2001). A spiral of cynicism for some: The contingent effects of campaign news frames on participation and confidence in government. *Political Communication, 18,* 347–367.

van Dijk, T. A. (1985). Structures of news in the press. In T. A. van Dijk (Ed.), *Discourse and communication: New approaches to the analysis of mass media discourse and communication* (pp. 69–93). New York: de Gruyter.

van Gorp, B. (2007). The constructionist approach to framing: Bringing culture back in. *Journal of Communication, 57,* 60–78.

3

GROWING UP WITH TELEVISION

Cultivation Processes

Michael Morgan
University of Massachusetts Amherst

James Shanahan
Fairfield University

Nancy Signorielli
University of Delaware

Television is the source of the most broadly shared images and messages in history. It is the mainstream of the common symbolic environment into which our children are born and in which we all live out our lives. Even though new forms of media seem to sprout up weekly, television's mass ritual shows no signs of weakening as its consequences are increasingly felt around the globe.

In the 1960s, George Gerbner (1919–2005) developed a research project called Cultural Indicators, which was designed to provide a broad-based, integrated approach to studying television policies, programs, and impacts (Gerbner, 1969). He devised a theory of media effects he called *cultivation* to help us understand the consequences of growing up and living in a cultural environment dominated by television.

Cultivation analysis focuses on television's contributions to viewers' conceptions of social reality. Stated most simply, the central hypothesis guiding cultivation research is that those who spend more time watching television are more likely to perceive the real world in ways that reflect the most common and recurrent messages of the television world, compared to those who watch less television but are otherwise comparable in terms of important demographic characteristics. Over the years, literally hundreds of research studies have been based on (or critiqued) the theory and methods of cultivation. In this chapter, we summarize and illustrate the theory of the dynamics of the cultivation process, both in the United States and around the world (see also Shanahan & Morgan, 1999; Signorielli & Morgan, 1990).

CULTURAL INDICATORS

The Cultural Indicators paradigm entails a three-pronged research strategy (Gerbner, 1973). The first prong, called institutional process analysis, is designed to investigate the formation and systematization of policies directing the massive flow of media messages

(Gerbner, 1972). More directly relevant to this chapter are the other two pro message system analysis and cultivation analysis.

Message system analysis involves the systematic examination of week-long annual samples of network television drama, in order to reliably delineate selected features and trends in the world that television presents to its viewers. These analyses began in 1967 and have continued under various auspices until today. In recent years, cable programming and additional genres have been added into the analysis.

Gerbner developed the methodology of cultivation analysis in collaboration with Larry Gross (Gerbner & Gross, 1976). In cultivation analysis, we conduct surveys (or analyze data collected by others) that ask people questions about their attitudes and assumptions regarding various aspects of life and society. We then examine the responses to these questions among those with varying amounts of exposure to television. We want to determine whether those who spend more time watching television are more likely to perceive social reality in ways that reflect the potential lessons of the television world than are those who watch less television, other things held constant.

The concept of "cultivation" thus refers to the independent contribution television viewing makes to audience members' conceptions of social reality. Television viewing cultivates ways of seeing the world—those who spend more time "living" in the world of television are more likely to see the "real world" in terms of the images, values, portrayals, and ideologies that emerge through the lens of television. The "cultivation differential" is the margin of difference in conceptions of reality between lighter and heavier viewers in the same demographic subgroups. It represents the difference television viewing makes to some outlook or belief, in dynamic interaction with other factors and processes. Meta-analytic research has established the stability of the cultivation differential across different variables and populations, showing a remarkable consistency in the direction predicted by the theory over many dozens of studies (Shanahan & Morgan, 1999).

Although most early studies focused on the nature and functions of television violence, the Cultural Indicators project was broadly conceived from the outset. Even violence was approached primarily as a demonstration of power in the world of television, with serious implications for social control and for the confirmation and perpetuation of minority status (Gerbner, Gross, Signorielli, Morgan, & Jackson-Beeck, 1979; Morgan, 1983). As it developed, the project continued to take into account a wider range of topics, issues, and concerns. We (and many others) have investigated the extent to which television viewing contributes to audience conceptions and actions in areas such as gender, minority and age-role stereotypes, health, science, the family, educational achievement and aspirations, politics, religion, the environment, and numerous other topics, many of which have also been examined in a variety of cross-cultural comparative contexts.

TELEVISION IN SOCIETY

Television is a centralized system of storytelling. Its drama, commercials, news and other programs bring a relatively coherent system of images and messages into every home. Transcending historic barriers of literacy and mobility, television has become the primary common source of socialization and everyday information (usually cloaked in the form of entertainment) of otherwise heterogeneous populations. Television provides, perhaps for the first time since preindustrial religion, a daily ritual that elites share with many other publics. As with religion, the social function of television lies in the continual repetition of stories (myths, "facts," lessons, and so on) that serve to define the world and legitimize a particular social order.

Cultivation does not depend on whether or not viewers profess a belief in what they see on television or claim to be able to distinguish between factual and fictional presentations. Indeed, most of what we know, or think we know, is a mixture of all the stories and images we have absorbed. The labels of "factual," which may be highly selective, and "fictional," which may be highly realistic, are more questions of style than function.

Cultivation researchers approach television as a coherent *system* of messages produced for large and diverse populations and consumed in a relatively nonselective, almost ritualistic, way by most viewers. Despite obvious surface-level differences across genres and program types, deeper analysis often shows that surprisingly similar and complementary images of society, consistent ideologies, and stable accounts of the "facts" of life cut across many different types of programs. Exposure to the total pattern rather than to specific genres or programs is therefore what accounts for the historically distinct consequences of living with television: the cultivation of shared conceptions of reality among otherwise diverse publics.

In saying this, we do not deny the importance of specific programs, selective attention and perception, specifically targeted communications, individual and group differences, and attitude and behavior change. But compared to other media, television provides a relatively restricted set of choices for a virtually unrestricted variety of interests and publics. Even with the expansion of cable and satellite channels serving ever narrower *niche* audiences, most television programs are by commercial necessity designed to be watched by large and heterogeneous audiences. Moreover, amount of viewing follows the style of life of the viewer. The audience is always the group available at a certain time of the day, the week, and the season. Viewing decisions depend more on the clock than on the program. The number and variety of choices available to view when most viewers are available to watch is also limited by the fact that many programs designed for the same broad audience tend to be similar in their basic makeup and appeal (Signorielli, 1986).

In the typical U.S. home the television set is in use for over seven hours a day. The more people watch the less selective they can be (Sun, 1989). Researchers who attribute findings to news viewing or preference for action programs, and so forth, overlook the fact that most of those who watch more news or action programs watch more of all types of programs, and that many different types of programs share important features.

What is most likely to cultivate stable and common conceptions of reality is, therefore, the overall pattern of programming to which total communities are regularly exposed over long periods of time. That is the pattern of settings, casting, social typing, actions, and related outcomes that cuts across program types and viewing modes and defines the world of television. Viewers are born into that symbolic world and cannot avoid regular exposure to its recurrent patterns. This is not to claim that any individual program, type of program, or channel (e.g., family programs, talk shows, sports, cooking channels, news channels, violent films, and so on) might not have "effects" of some kind or another; rather, it is to emphasize that what we call "cultivation analysis" focuses on the consequences of long-term exposure to the entire *system* of messages, in the aggregate.

THE SHIFT FROM "EFFECTS" TO "CULTIVATION" RESEARCH

The bulk of scientific inquiry (and most public discourse) about television's social impact follows theoretical models and methodological procedures of marketing and persuasion research. Much time, energy, and money have been invested in efforts to use media to change people's attitudes and behaviors. Traditional effects research is based on evaluating specific informational, educational, political, or marketing efforts in terms of selective exposure and measurable before/after differences between those exposed to some message and others not exposed. Scholars steeped in those traditions find it difficult to accept the emphasis of cultivation analysis on total immersion rather than selective viewing.

Similarly, we are still imbued with the ideology of print culture and its ideals of freedom, diversity, and an active electorate. This ideal also assumes the production and selection of information and entertainment from the point of view of a variety of competing and conflicting interests. That is why many point to what they see as serious differences between cultivation theory and reception models of media texts (see McQuail, 2000). From the reception perspective, it seems logical to argue that other circumstances do intervene and can neutralize the cultivation process, that viewers do watch selectively, that program selections make a difference, and that how viewers construct meaning from texts is more important than how much they watch.

We do not dispute these contentions; the polysemy of mediated texts is well established. From the cultivation perspective, though, to say that audiences' interactions with media texts can produce enormous diversity and complexity does not negate that there can be important commonalities and consistencies across large bodies of media output. To explore those commonalities, as cultivation does, is not to deny that there are differences; similarly, the examination of differences need not (and, arguably, *can* not) deny the possibility of shared meanings in a culture.

Polysemy is not limitless, and preferred readings can have great power. Equally, concentrating on individual differences and immediate change misses the profound historical challenge television poses not only for research strategies but also for traditional theories of democratic government: the absorption of diverse conceptions and attitudes into a stable, common mainstream. Thus, although individual viewers certainly differ in their "reading" of any given program, cultivation does not ask people what they think *about television texts*. Rather, cultivation looks at what people absorb from their exposure to massive flows of messages over long periods of time. The process implies an *interaction* of the viewer with the message; neither the message nor the viewer is all-powerful.

Thus, cultivation does not see television's contribution to conceptions of social reality as a one-way, monolithic "push" process. The influences of a pervasive medium upon the composition and structure of the symbolic environment are subtle, complex, and intermingled with other influences. Moreover, the question of "which comes first" is misleading and irrelevant, as is the presumed dichotomy between an "active" or "passive" audience (see Shanahan & Morgan, 1999). People are born into a symbolic environment with television as its mainstream; viewing both shapes and is a stable part of lifestyles and outlooks. Many of those with certain social and psychological characteristics, dispositions, and world views, as well as those who have fewer alternatives, use television as their major vehicle of cultural participation. To the extent that television dominates their sources of entertainment and information, continued exposure to its messages is likely to reiterate, confirm, and nourish—that is, cultivate—its own values and perspectives (see Gerbner, 1990; Morgan & Signorielli, 1990).

The point is that cultivation is not conceived as a unidirectional but rather more like a gravitational process. The angle and direction of the "pull" depends on where groups of viewers and their styles of life are with reference to the line of gravity, the mainstream of the world of television. Each group may strain in a different direction, but all groups are affected by the same central current. Cultivation is thus a continual, dynamic, ongoing process of interaction among messages, audiences, and contexts.

METHODS OF CULTIVATION ANALYSIS

Cultivation analysis begins with message system analysis to identify the most recurrent, stable, and overarching patterns of television content. These are the consistent images, portrayals, and values that are embedded in the aggregate of messages (not necessarily in any particular program or genre) and that are virtually inescapable for regular (and especially for heavy) viewers.

There are many critical discrepancies between the world and the "world as portrayed on television." Findings from systematic analyses of television's message system are used to formulate questions about the potential "lessons" viewing may offer. Some questions are semi-projective, some use a forced-choice or forced-error format, and others simply measure beliefs, opinions, attitudes, or behaviors. (None ask respondents for their views about television itself or about any specific program or message.)

Using standard techniques of survey methodology, the questions are posed to samples (national probability, regional, convenience) of adults, adolescents, or children. Secondary analyses of large scale national surveys (for example, the General Social Surveys) have often been used when they include questions that relate to potential "lessons" of the television world and when viewing data are available for the respondents.

Television viewing is usually assessed by asking about the amount of time respondents watch television on an "average day." Multiple measures are used when available. Because these measures are assumed to provide relative, not absolute, indicators, the determination of what constitutes "light," "medium," and "heavy" viewing is made on a sample-by-sample basis. The relative differences in viewing levels are more important than the specific amount of viewing. The analysis of simple patterns across relatively light, medium, and heavy viewing groups (overall and in key subgroups) is useful to illuminate the general nature of the cultivation relationship, but it is normally followed up with more stringent multivariate analysis using continuous data.

The observable evidence of cultivation is likely to be modest in terms of absolute size. Even "light" viewers may be watching several hours a day and of course live in the same culture as heavy viewers. Therefore, the discovery of a consistent pattern of even small but pervasive differences between light and heavy viewers may be of far-reaching consequence. Extensive and systematic re-examination of hundreds of cultivation studies carried out over more than two decades (using the statistical techniques of meta-analysis; Shanahan & Morgan, 1999) has shown that cultivation relationships typically manifest a strength of about .09 using a common metric, the Pearson correlation coefficient.

This is not a statistically huge effect, but "small effects" often have significant repercussions. It takes but a few degrees shift in the average temperature to bring about an ice age or global warming. Recent Presidential elections have shown the havoc that can be wreaked by a minuscule percentage of votes. A range of 5% to 15% margins (typical of our "cultivation differentials") in a large and otherwise stable field often signals a landslide, a market takeover, or an epidemic, and it overwhelmingly tips the scale of any closely balanced choice, vote, or other decision. A single percentage point ratings difference is worth many millions of dollars in advertising revenue—as the media know only too well. Thus, a slight but pervasive shift in the cultivation of common perspectives may alter the cultural climate and upset the balance of social and political decision-making.

THE FINDINGS OF CULTIVATION ANALYSIS

Clear-cut divergences between symbolic reality and independently observable reality provide convenient tests of the extent to which television's versions of "the facts" are absorbed into what heavy viewers take for granted about the world. For example, consider how likely people on television are to encounter violence compared to the rest of us. Nearly four decades of message system analyses show that roughly half or more of television characters are involved each week in some kind of violent action. Although FBI statistics have clear limitations, they indicate that in any one year fewer than 1% of people in the U.S. are victims of criminal violence. We have found that heavy exposure to the world of television cultivates exaggerated perceptions of the number of people involved in violence in any given week (Gerbner et al., 1979, 1980; Shanahan & Morgan, 1999), as well as numerous other inaccurate beliefs about crime and law enforcement.

But cultivation analysis is not limited to cases when television "facts" vary from real-world (or even imaginary but different) statistics. The repetitive "lessons" we learn from television, beginning with infancy, can become the basis for a broader world view, making television a significant source of general values, ideologies, and perspectives as well as specific beliefs. Some of the most interesting and important issues for cultivation analysis involve the symbolic transformation of message system data into more general issues and assumptions, as opposed to the comparison of television and real world "facts" (see also Hawkins & Pingree, 1982).

One example of this is what we have called the "mean world" syndrome. Message data say little directly about either the selfishness or altruism of people, and there are certainly no real world statistics about the extent to which people can be trusted. Yet, we have found that long-term exposure to television tends to cultivate the image of a relatively mean and dangerous world. Compared to matching groups of lighter viewers, heavy viewers are more likely to say that most people "cannot be trusted," and most people are "just looking out for themselves" (Gerbner et al., 1980; Signorielli, 1990).

Other studies have dealt with assumptions about marriage and work. Signorielli (1993) found that television cultivates realistic views about marriage but contradictory views about work. Heavy viewing adolescents were more likely to want high status jobs and to earn a lot of money but also wanted to have their jobs be relatively easy with long vacations and time to do other things. Signorielli (1991) found that television viewing cultivates conceptions that reflect the ambivalent presentation of marriage on television. Adolescents who watched more television were more likely to say they wanted to get married, to stay married to the same person for life, and to have children.

Nevertheless, heavy viewers were more likely to believe that one sees so few good or happy marriages that one could question marriage as a way of life.

Many of television's families do not fit the "traditional nuclear" model, and single-parent families are over-represented. Morgan, Leggett, and Shanahan (1999) found that, beyond controls, heavy viewers were more likely than light viewers to approve of single-parenthood and out-of-wedlock childbirth. Nevertheless, the single parent on TV bears little resemblance to single-parent households in reality. On television, the single parent typically is a well-off male with full-time, live-in, domestic help. Heavy viewers may thus be more accepting of a highly fantasized and luxurious notion of single-parenthood.

Other studies have looked at the cultivation of attitudes toward science or the environment. For instance, Shanahan, Morgan, and Stenbjerre (1997) found that heavy viewers are less likely to be knowledgeable about the environment, less likely to be active on environmental issues, and more likely to be fearful about specific environmental problems or issues. A cultivated fearful withdrawal from science issues was adduced, echoing earlier work (Gerbner et al., 1981) on the cultivation of images of science (also see Shanahan & McComas, 1999, for more on TV and the environment).

Other extrapolations concern political views. We have argued that as television seeks large and heterogeneous audiences, its messages are designed to disturb as few as possible. Therefore they tend to "balance" opposing perspectives, and to steer a "middle course" along the supposedly non-ideological mainstream. We have found that heavy viewers are substantially more likely to label themselves as being "moderate" rather than either "liberal" or "conservative" (Gerbner et al., 1982, 1984). We have observed this finding in over two decades of General Social Survey data.

Implications of cultivation for foreign policy were reflected in a study of attitudes toward the war in the Persian Gulf (Morgan, Lewis, & Jhally, 1992). Heavy television viewers were more familiar with the military terminology used and more supportive of the war but less informed about issues and the Middle East in general. Overall amount of viewing was far more important than specific exposure to news.

COGNITIVE PROCESSES

The 1990s saw a great deal of progress in illuminating explanations for the cognitive mechanisms of cultivation: how does it "work"? A model offered by Hawkins and Pingree (1982) focused on how television contributes to conceptions "within the heads" of individuals by breaking down the process into two discrete steps, "learning" and "construction." Yet, no support for this model was found. Similarly, studies that attempted to shed light on black-box cognitive processes by highlighting the concept of the "perceived reality" produced few firm conclusions (Potter, 1986; Slater & Elliott, 1982).

Shapiro and Lang (1991) hypothesized that television can affect reality perceptions because people simply forget that what they see on TV is not real. Mares (1996) tested this hypothesis, and found that those who tended to confuse fiction programs for reality saw the world as a meaner, more violent place and also gave "TV answers" to questions about social class estimates. But Shrum (1997) presented evidence that people do not typically consider the source of their information when making social reality judgments.

Shrum's idea is that, because TV images are "heuristically" available to heavy viewers, they tend to use them more readily in making mental judgments, in a kind of cognitive shortcut. Shrum (1995, 1999) found that heavy viewers give faster responses to questions about social reality; a speedier response implies that an answer is more readily accessible, that the respondent does not have to dig very deeply to come up with an answer. Shrum's cognitive account is highly supportive of cultivation. It also suggests that television does not necessarily *change* attitudes, but that it makes them *stronger* (see also Shanahan & Morgan, 1999; Shrum, 2007).

MAINSTREAMING

Modern cultures consist of many diverse currents, but in the context of a dominant structure of beliefs, values, and practices. This dominant current is not simply the sum total of all the sub-currents. Rather, it is the most general, functional and stable mainstream, representing the broadest dimensions of shared meanings and assumptions. It is that which ultimately defines all the other cross-currents, including what Williams (1977) called "residual and emergent strains." Television's status as the primary storyteller in our society makes it the fundamental manifestation of the mainstream of our culture.

This mainstream can be thought of as a relative commonality of outlooks and values that heavy exposure to the television world tends to cultivate. The concept of "mainstreaming" means that heavy viewing may absorb or override differences in perspectives and behavior that ordinarily stem from other factors and influences. In other words, differences found in responses that usually are associated with the varied cultural, social, and political characteristics of different groups, are diminished in the responses of heavy viewers. For example, regional differences, political ideology, and socioeconomic differences are much less influential on the attitudes and beliefs of heavy viewers (Gerbner, Gross, Morgan, & Signorielli, 1980; Morgan, 1986).

The mean world syndrome also illustrates the mainstreaming implications of viewing. Signorielli (1990) found that heavy and light viewers who had not been to college were equally likely to score high on the mean world index: 53% of both the heavy and light viewers agreed with two or three of the items in the index. However, among those who had some college education, television viewing made a considerable difference: 28% of the light viewers compared to 43% of the heavy viewers in this subgroup had a high score on the mean world index. There is thus a 25-percentage point difference between the two subgroups of light viewers but only a 10-point spread between the two subgroups of heavy viewers. The heavy viewers of otherwise different groups are both in the "television mainstream."

Although, as we noted above, heavy viewers tend to call themselves "moderate," looking at the actual positions people take on political issues shows that the mainstream is not the "middle of the road." When we analyzed attitudes on racial segregation, homosexuality, abortion, minority rights, and other issues that traditionally divide liberals and conservatives, we found such divisions mostly among those who watch little television. Among heavy viewers, liberals and conservatives are much closer to each other. We have also noted (Gerbner et al., 1982) that while mainstreaming bends toward the right on political issues, it leans towards a populist stance on economic issues (with heavy viewers demanding more social services but lower taxes), reflecting the influence of a marketing orientation and setting up potential conflicts of demands and expectations.

As a process, mainstreaming represents the theoretical elaboration and empirical verification of television's cultivation of common perspectives. It represents a relative homogenization, an absorption of divergent views, and a convergence of disparate outlooks upon the overarching patterns of the television world. Traditional distinctions (which flourished, in part, through the relative diversity provided by print) become blurred as successive generations and groups are enculturated into television's version of the world. Through mainstreaming, television may have become the true "melting pot" of the American people—and increasingly of other countries around the globe.

INTERNATIONAL CULTIVATION ANALYSIS

Cultivation analysis is ideally suited to multinational and cross-cultural comparative study (Gerbner, 1977, 1989; Morgan, 1990). In fact, such study is the best test of system-wide similarities and differences across national boundaries, and of the actual significance of national cultural policies.

Every country's television system reflects the historical, political, social, economic, and cultural contexts within which it has developed (Gerbner, 1969). Although U.S. films and television are a significant presence on the screens of most countries, they combine with local and other productions to compose synthetic "worlds" that are culture specific. Other media systems may or may not project images and portrayals that are as stable, coherent, and homogeneous as those of U.S. media. As a result, cultivation (and mainstreaming) patterns tend to vary quite widely across different countries and cultures (see Gerbner, 1990; Morgan, 1990; Morgan & Shanahan, 1995; Tamborini & Choi, 1990).

In England, Wober (1978) found little support for cultivation in terms of images of violence, but there was little violence in British programs, and U.S. programs only made up about 15% of British screen time (see also Shanahan & Morgan, 1999). However, Piepe, Charlton, and Morey (1990) found evidence of political "homogenization" (mainstreaming) in Britain that was highly congruent with U.S. findings (Gerbner et al., 1982), as did Morgan and Shanahan (1995) in Argentina.

Pingree and Hawkins (1981) found that exposure to U.S. programs (especially crime and adventure) was significantly related to Australian students' scores on "mean world" and "violence in society" indices concerning Australia, but not the U.S. Viewing Australian programs was unrelated to these conceptions, but those who watched more U.S. programs were more likely to see Australia as dangerous and mean.

Cultivation analyses about conceptions of violence, sex roles, political orientations, "traditional" values, social stereotypes, and other topics have been conducted in numerous countries, including Sweden (Hedinsson & Windahl, 1984), Argentina (Morgan & Shanahan, 1995), the Philippines (Tan, Tan, & Tan, 1987), Taiwan and Mexico (Tan, Li, & Simpson, 1986), and Thailand (Tan & Suarchavarat, 1988), among others. These studies show the complex ways in which the viewing of local or imported programming can interact with distinct cultural contexts. For example, in Korea, Kang and Morgan (1988) found that exposure to U.S. television was associated with more "liberal" perspectives about gender-roles and family values among females, whereas in Japan, Saito (2007) found the opposite, with heavy viewing cultivating traditional views about gender especially among females.

Some international studies have explored the comparative aspects of cultivation analysis. Morgan and Shanahan (1992) analyzed adolescents in Taiwan and Argentina. In Argentina, where television is supported by commercials and features many U.S.

programs, heavy viewing cultivates traditional gender roles and authoritarianism. In Taiwan, where media are more state controlled, with fewer U.S. imports, and where overall viewing is much lighter, cultivation was much less apparent. Also, Morgan (1990) compared the cultivation of sex-role stereotypes in five different countries.

A study of U.S. and (what was then) Soviet television conducted in 1989 found that television played a different role in the two countries (Morgan, 1990). In the U.S., but not in the former USSR, television was associated with heightened anxieties about neighborhood safety, perhaps as a result of the much lower frequency of violence on Soviet television. In both countries, but especially in the former Soviet Union, the more people watched television the more likely they were to say that housework is primarily the responsibility of the woman. General satisfaction with life was consistently lower among heavy than among light television viewers in the United States, but not in the former USSR (where it was relatively low for everyone). In many ways, Soviet television actually presented more diversified fare than U.S. television. Perhaps due to this, television viewing seemed to have far greater mainstreaming consequences in the U.S. than in the former Soviet Union.

All this suggests that, in countries in which television's portrayals are less repetitive and homogeneous than in the U.S., the results of cultivation analysis also tend to be less predictable and consistent. The extent to which cultivation will occur in a given country depends on various structural factors, such as the number of channels available, overall amount of broadcasting time, and amount of time audiences spend viewing. But it seems especially to depend on the amount of diversity in the available content, which is not necessarily related to the number of channels. A few channels with a diverse and balanced program structure can foster (and, in fact, compel) more diversified viewing than many channels competing for the same audience.

RECENT FINDINGS

The number of studies looking at cultivation has continued to increase since the previous edition of this book, as have the number of new angles being explored. In this section, we briefly describe a few of the more noteworthy recent studies.

Crime

Although cultivation theory emphasizes overall exposure to television, many recent studies explore the contributions of specific genres. For example, Goidel, Freeman, and Procopio (2006) showed that attention to TV news in particular is associated with perceptions that juvenile crime is increasing. Watching reality crime shows is associated with the perception that overall crime is increasing. They found that TV news exposure is associated with exaggerated perceptions of the number of juveniles imprisoned for violent crimes. They also found that such exposure is related to the perception that imprisonment is more effective than rehabilitation. Finally, TV viewing was associated with the perception that sentencing is race neutral.

Holbrook and Hill (2005) found that viewing crime dramas was significantly related to concerns about crime. They argued that chronic accessibility of crime images drives perceptions, consistent with other research from cultivation, agenda-setting and priming literatures. Holbert, Shah, and Kwak (2004) examined relations between crime-related TV and views on capital punishment and gun ownership. Using a large marketing database, they found that viewing of TV news and police reality programming was associated with fear of crime. Viewing of police reality programs and crime drama is associated with support of capital punishment. Also, TV variables were associated with ownership of a gun.

Van den Bulck (2004) tested three competing models of relationships between exposure to fiction and fear of crime: the cultivation model, the withdrawal hypothesis (those afraid of crime will be afraid to leave the house) and the mood management hypothesis (frightened people watch more crime to help them manage their fear). His results from Belgium supported the cultivation hypothesis most strongly; TV viewing, but not direct experience of crime, was related to fear.

Busselle (2003) found that parents' viewing of crime-related TV predicted estimates of crime prevalence. This was in turn related to the frequency with which they gave crime warnings to their children. Then, such warnings were related to their children's memory of receiving such warnings. Finally, memory for such warnings was related to the children's own estimates of crime frequency.

Eschholz, Chiricos, and Gertz (2003) found that the perceived racial composition of neighborhood is a crucial dimension in structuring the TV/fear relationship, with television effects appearing primarily among individuals who perceive that they live in a neighborhood with high percentages of blacks.

Health and Mental Health

Gutschoven and Van den Bulck (2005) found that levels of television exposure among Flemish students was related to earlier onset of smoking initiation and also to more positive smoking attitudes. They speculate that both social learning from television role models and the cultivation of positive attitudes toward smoking are possible causal explanations.

Diefenbach and West (2007) continued the tradition of looking at TV's portrayal of mental health (see Signorielli, 1989) and found that mentally disordered individuals are still portrayed as violent and tending toward criminal behavior. Their accompanying survey found that heavy viewers were more likely to accept negative perceptions of those with mental illness.

Politics

Besley (2006) found that Europeans' TV use was associated with lower political participation. Following earlier mainstreaming analyses that found the strongest effects for self-identified liberals, Besley found the greatest decreases among those who identified with progressive values such as "self-transcendence" and "openness to change." Besley speculated that such effects may be due to TV's promotion of consumerism and a possible "annihilation" of the public sphere.

Sex Roles, Sexual Behaviors

Ward and Friedman (2006) found that exposure to sexual stereotypes in the lab affected respondents' acceptance of those stereotypes. Beyond the lab, their survey research indicated that regular media use is also associated with such beliefs as sex is desirable early in a relationship, that men are sex driven, and that women are sexual objects.

Zurbriggen and Morgan (2006) examined exposure to reality dating programs and attitudes toward sex and sexual behaviors. They found that such exposure was correlated with "adversarial" sexual beliefs, endorsement of a sexual double standard (that men should be more aggressive in sex roles), the belief that men are more driven by sex, that appearance is important in dating, and that dating is a game. They found few correlations with actual sexual behavior, however.

Harrison (2003) examined relations between TV exposure and female body ideals. She found that exposure to TV body image ideals was associated with approval of smaller waist, smaller hips, and a medium-sized bust, but only among females. Both males and females exposed to TV body image ideals were more likely to approve of surgical body alterations such as liposuction or breast surgery.

Contrary to earlier research that found relationships between TV exposure and negative conceptions of women, Holbert, Shah, and Kwak (2003) found that attention to "progressive dramas" and sitcoms was positively related to support for women's rights. Conversely, more conservative traditional drama use was negatively associated.

CULTIVATION IN THE 21ST CENTURY

The theory of cultivation was developed when "television" in the U.S. meant three national broadcast networks, plus a small handful of independent and public/educational stations. The three networks attracted well over 90% of the viewing audience, night after night. Fledgling cable systems mainly extended the reach of the networks, providing little competitive programming.

Those days of network dominance are long gone. Technological developments such as cable and satellite networks, VCRs, DVDs, DVRs, and the Internet have brought a significant erosion in audience share (and revenue) for the old "Big Three" broadcasting networks and have altered the marketing and distribution of programming. Yet, there is little evidence that proliferation of channels has led to any substantially greater diversity of content. Indeed, the mere availability of more channels does not fundamentally change the socio-economic dynamics that drive the production and distribution of programs. On the contrary, that dynamic is intensified by increased concentration of ownership and control and by the dissolution of the traditional barriers between and among networks, station owners, production studios, syndicators, MSOs, cable networks, and advertisers.

Viewers may feel a new sense of power and control derived from the ability to freeze a frame, review a scene, zip through commercials (or zap them entirely), interact with them, or call up a movie. The remarkable proliferation of DVDs and the increased choices offered via pay-per-view (PPV), On-Demand, and downloading also gives viewers an unprecedented range of *potential* choices. But again there is little evidence that any of this has changed viewing habits—or that the content that heavy television viewers consume most often presents world views and values fundamentally different from most network-type programs (Morgan, Shanahan, & Harris, 1990). Digital signal compression will soon flood viewers with even more channels, but with what programming? In fact, as channels proliferate, sources of original dramatic programming and perspectives decline, as channels continue to rely upon programs previously broadcast on network primetime programs to fill their programming needs. One reflection of the monopoly of market-orientation is the absence of poor (i.e. low-income) characters, and of diverse ideological (i.e., political, religious, etc.) orientations.

In particular, the Internet and digital downloading seem to threaten the stability of the traditional media landscape. But Nielsen//Netratings reports that average web usage amounts to just a fraction of the time most people spend watching television (Nielsen/Netratings, 2007). Figuring prominently among top sites are those with strong connections to dominant television networks, including Disney (owner of ABC), Time Warner, and News Corp. Clearly, the rise of the web—though of immense significance—still represents not only a relatively small amount of audience time, but also an ever greater role for dominant media corporations. Although the Internet may provide access to alternative channels of information, it can also deepen and sharpen the reach of dominant media corporations.

Despite revolutionary proclamations, only a tiny minority are using the Internet, cell phones, or iPods for viewing video or listening to audio programs as an alternative to dominant message providers. Even when new digital delivery systems threaten dominant interests, they are quickly swallowed up within the existing institutional structure. The much ballyhooed rise of user-generated video services such as YouTube have been absorbed by dominant players (Google) and are already being exploited for their benefits to advertisers. Despite widespread hopes (and fears) that the Internet will make possible a new information highway that will replace older media, there are no popular Internet or Web-based programs that yet threaten the network-cable alliance; on the contrary, networks and cable channels are working feverishly to drive their viewers to their websites, to allow them to obtain more personal information from viewers, and to create additional platforms for advertising. At most, the most popular online services gain audience share at any given time comparable to that of CNN or MTV, which is a rather small and specialized audience. As noted in a November 2000 study by Burke, Inc. viewers spend four hours a week watching television *while* on-line ("Individuals with Internet Access," 2000). The report noted that while "some have suggested that the Internet is killing TV," the results "show that Internet use not only coexists with TV viewing, it can encourage and enhance the viewing experience." Thus, cultivation theorists continue to proceed under the assumption that TV is "the dominant feature of Americans' free time" (Robinson & Godbey, 1997, p. 149).

Channels will continue to proliferate, by cable, satellite, and digital transmission. New developments such as digital video recorders will spread, allowing viewers to more easily indulge their own personal programming tastes (and, maybe, to ignore commercials, but with an increase of such strategies as product placement). Digital technologies for storing and manipulating personal video libraries will continue to emerge, as will options for direct, on-demand delivery of programs through set-top boxes, DVRs and high speed Internet connections. The broadcast network audience share will continue to shrivel (despite the occasional blockbuster series) and be divided among an ever increasing number of competing channels. Developments such as interactive TV that will allow advertisers to reach finely targeted groups, and even *individual* viewers, will be vigorously pursued.

Yet, all this is being accompanied by massive and unprecedented concentrations of ownership of media industries and program sources. Whether the most successful entertainment is delivered through television networks or in the form of video-on-demand through fiber-optic cable, satellites, or some other medium may make little difference if the messages don't change. Given that, there is little evidence to date that the dominant patterns of image cultivation will show any corresponding fragmentation. For most viewers, extended delivery systems signal even deeper penetration and integration of the dominant patterns of images and messages into everyday life. The empirical investigation of these developments, and their implications for cultivation analysis in general and for mainstreaming in particular, represents a major challenge for the new century.

References

Besley, J. (2006). The role of entertainment television and its interactions with individual values in explaining political participation. *Press/Politics, 11*(2), 41–63.

Busselle, R. (2003). Television exposure, parents' precautionary warnings and young adults' perceptions of crime. *Communication Research, 30*, 530–556.

Diefenbach, D., & West, M. (2007). Television and attitudes toward mental health issues: Cultivation analysis and third person effect. *Journal of Community Psychology, 35*, 181–195.

Eschholz, S., Chiricos T., & Gertz M. (2003). Television and fear of crime: Program types, audience traits, and the mediating effect of perceived neighborhood racial composition. *Social Problems, 50*, 395–415.

Gerbner, G. (1969). Toward "Cultural Indicators": The analysis of mass mediated message systems. *AV Communication Review, 17*, 137–148.

Gerbner, G. (1972). The structure and process of television program content regulation in the U.S. In G. A. Comstock & E. Rubinstein (Eds.), *Television and social behavior, Vol. 1: Content and control* (pp. 386–414). Washington, DC: U.S. Government Printing Office.

Gerbner, G. (1973). Cultural indicators: The third voice. In G. Gerbner, L. Gross, & W. H. Melody (Eds.), *Communications technology and social policy* (pp. 555–573). New York: Wiley.

Gerbner, G. (1977). Comparative cultural indicators. In G. Gerbner (Ed.), *Mass media policies in changing cultures* (pp. 199–205). New York: Wiley.

Gerbner, G. (1989). Cross-cultural communications research in the age of telecommunications. In The Christian Academy (Eds.), *Continuity and change in communications in post-industrial society* (Vol. 2, pp. 220–231). Seoul, Korea: Wooseok.

Gerbner, G. (1990). Epilogue: Advancing on the path of righteousness (maybe). In N. Signorielli & M. Morgan (Eds.), *Cultivation analysis: New directions in media effects research* (pp. 249–262). Newbury Park, CA: Sage.

Gerbner, G., & Gross, L. (1976). Living with television: The violence profile. *Journal of Communication, 26*(2), 173–199.

Gerbner, G., Gross, L., Morgan, M., & Signorielli, N. (1980). The "mainstreaming" of America: Violence profile no. 11. *Journal of Communication, 30*(3), 10–29.

Gerbner, G., Gross, L., Morgan, M., & Signorielli, N. (1981). Scientists on the TV screen. *Society*, May/June, 41–44.

Gerbner, G., Gross, L., Morgan, M., & Signorielli, N. (1982). Charting the mainstream: Television's contributions to political orientations. *Journal of Communication, 32*(2), 100–127.

Gerbner, G., Gross, L., Morgan, M., & Signorielli, N. (1984). Political correlates of television viewing. *Public Opinion Quarterly, 48*, 283–300.

Gerbner, G., Gross, L., Signorielli, N., Morgan, M., & Jackson-Beeck, M. (1979). The demonstration of power: Violence profile no. 10. *Journal of Communication, 29*(3), 177–196.

Goidel, R., Freeman, C., & Procopio, S. (2006). The impact of television on perceptions of juvenile crime. *Journal of Broadcasting and Electronic Media, 50*, 119–139.

Gutschoven, K., & Van den Bulck, J. (2005). Television viewing and age at smoking initiation: Does a relationship exist between higher levels of television viewing and earlier onset of smoking? *Nicotine and Tobacco Research, 7*, 381–385.

Harrison, K. (2003). Television viewers' ideal body proportions: The case of the curvaceously thin woman. *Sex Roles, 48*, 255–264.

Hawkins, R. P., & Pingree, S. (1982). Television's influence on social reality. In D. Pearl, L. Bouthilet, & J. Lazar (Eds.), *Television and behavior: Ten years of scientific progress and implications for the 80's, Vol. II, Technical reviews* (pp. 224–247). Rockville, MD: National Institute of Mental Health.

Hedinsson, E., & Windahl, S. (1984). Cultivation analysis: A Swedish illustration. In G. Melischek et al. (Eds.), *Cultural indicators: An international symposium* (pp. 389–406). Vienna: Verlag der Österreichischen Akademie der Wissenschaften.

Holbert, L., Shah, D., & Kwak, N. (2003). Political implications of prime-time drama and sitcom use: Genres of representation and opinions concerning women's rights. *Journal of Communication, 53*, 45–60.

Holbert, L., Shah, D., & Kwak, N. (2004). Fear, authority, and justice: Crime-related TV viewing and endorsements of capital punishment and gun ownership. *Journalism and Mass Communication Quarterly, 81*, 343–363.

Holbrook, R., & Hill, T. (2005). Agenda-setting and priming in prime time television: Crime dramas as political cues. *Political Communication, 22*, 277–295.

Individuals with internet access spend almost four hours per week watching TV while online. (2000, November 20). Retrieved November 21, 2000, from <http://biz.yahoo.com/bw/001120/oh_burke_n.html>.

Kang, J. G., & Morgan, M. (1988). Culture clash: US television programs in Korea. *Journalism Quarterly, 65*, 431–438.

Mares, M. (1996). The role of source confusions in television's cultivation of social reality judgments. *Human Communication Research, 23*, 278–297.

McQuail, D. (2000). *Mass communication theory*. Thousand Oaks, CA: Sage.

Morgan, M. (1982). Television and adolescents' sex-role stereotypes: A longitudinal study. *Journal of Personality and Social Psychology, 43*, 947–955.

Morgan, M. (1983). Symbolic victimization and real-world fear. *Human Communication Research, 9*, 146–157.

Morgan, M. (1986). Television and the erosion of regional diversity. *Journal of Broadcasting & Electronic Media, 30*, 123–139.

Morgan, M. (1990). International cultivation analysis. In N. Signorielli & M. Morgan (Eds.), *Cultivation analysis: New directions in media effects research* (pp. 225–248). Newbury Park, CA: Sage.

Morgan, M., Leggett, S., & Shanahan, J. (1999). Television and "family values": Was Dan Quayle right? *Mass Communication and Society, 2*, 47–63.

Morgan, M., Lewis, J., & Jhally, S. (1992). The media and the war: Public conceptions and misconceptions. In G. Gerbner, H. Mowlana, & H. Schiller (Eds.), *Global deception: The media's war in the Persian Gulf—An international perspective* (pp. 216–233). Boulder: Westview.

Morgan, M., & Shanahan, J. (1992). Comparative cultivation analysis: Television and adolescents in Argentina and Taiwan. In F. Korzenny & S. Ting-Toomey (Eds.), *Mass media effects across cultures: International and intercultural communication annual* (Vol. 16, pp. 173–197). Newbury Park, CA: Sage.

Morgan, M., & Shanahan, J. (1995). *Democracy tango: Television, adolescents, and authoritarian tensions in Argentina*. Cresskill, NJ: Hampton Press.

Morgan, M., Shanahan, J., & Harris, C. (1990). VCRs and the effects of television: New diversity or more of the same? In J. Dobrow (Ed.), *Social and cultural aspects of VCR use* (pp. 107–123). Hillsdale, NJ: Erlbaum.

Morgan, M., & Signorielli, N. (1990). Cultivation analysis: Conceptualization and methodology. In N. Signorielli & M. Morgan (Eds.), *Cultivation analysis: New directions in media effects research* (pp. 13–34). Newbury Park, CA: Sage.

Nielsen//Netratings. (2007). Internet audience metrics. Retrieved August 24, 2007, from <http://www.nielsen-netratings.com/resources.jsp?section=pr_netv&nav=1>.

Piepe, A., Charlton, P., & Morey, J. (1990). Politics and television viewing in England: Hegemony or pluralism? *Journal of Communication, 40*(1), 24–35.

Pingree, S., & Hawkins, R. P. (1981). U.S. programs on Australian television: The cultivation effect. *Journal of Communication, 31*(1), 97–105.

Potter, W. J. (1986). Perceived reality and the cultivation hypothesis. *Journal of Broadcasting & Electronic Media, 30*, 159–174.

Robinson, J., & Godbey, G. (1997). *Time for life: the surprising ways Americans use their time*. University Park: Pennsylvania State University Press.

Saito, S. (2007). Television and the cultivation of gender-role attitudes in Japan: Does television contribute to the maintenance of the status quo? *Journal of Communication, 57*, 511–531.

Shanahan, J., & McComas, K. (1999). *Nature stories*. Cresskill, NJ: Hampton Press.

Shanahan, J., & Morgan M. (1999). *Television and its viewers: Cultivation theory and research*. Cambridge: Cambridge University Press.

Shanahan, J., Morgan, M., & Stenbjerre, M. (1997). Green or brown? Television's cultivation of environmental concern. *Journal of Broadcasting & Electronic Media, 41*, 305–323.

Shapiro, M., & Lang, A. (1991). Making television reality: Unconscious processes in the construction of social reality. *Communication Research, 18*, 685–705.

Shrum, L. J. (1995). Assessing the social influence of television: A social cognition perspective on cultivation effects. *Communication Research, 22*, 402–429.

Shrum, L. J. (1997). The role of source confusion in cultivation effects may depend on processing strategy: A comment on Mares (1996). *Human Communication Research, 24*, 349–358.

Shrum, L. J. (1999). The relationship of television viewing with attitude strength and extremity: Implications for the cultivation effect. *Media Psychology, 1*, 3–25.

Shrum, L. J. (2007). The implications of survey method for measuring cultivation effects. *Human Communication Research, 33*, 64–80.

Signorielli, N. (1986). Selective television viewing: A limited possibility. *Journal of Communication, 36*, 64–75.

Signorielli, N. (1989). The stigma of mental illness on television. *Journal of Broadcasting and Electronic Media, 33*, 325–331.

Signorielli, N. (1990). Television's mean and dangerous world: A continuation of the cultural indicators perspective. In N. Signorielli & M. Morgan (Eds.), *Cultivation analysis: New directions in media effects research* (pp. 85–106). Newbury Park, CA: Sage.

Signorielli, N. (1991). Adolescents and ambivalence towards marriage: A cultivation analysis. *Youth & Society, 23*, 121–149.

Signorielli, N. (1993). Television and adolescents' perceptions about work. *Youth & Society, 24*, 314–341.

Signorielli, N., & Morgan, M. (Eds). (1990). *Cultivation analysis: New directions in media effects research*. Newbury Park, CA: Sage.

Slater, D., & Elliott, W. R. (1982). Television's influence on social reality. *Quarterly Journal of Speech, 68*, 69–79.

Sun, L. (1989). *Limits of selective viewing: An analysis of "diversity" in dramatic programming*. Unpublished M.A. thesis, The Annenberg School for Communication, University of Pennsylvania, Philadelphia.

Tamborini, R., & Choi, J. (1990). The role of cultural diversity in cultivation research. In N. Signorielli & M. Morgan (Eds.), *Cultivation analysis: New directions in media effects research* (pp. 157–180). Newbury Park, CA: Sage.

Tan, A. S., Li, S., & Simpson, C. (1986). American television and social stereotypes of Americans in Taiwan and Mexico. *Journalism Quarterly, 63*, 809–814.

Tan, A. S., & Suarchavarat, K. (1988). American TV and social stereotypes of Americans in Thailand. *Journalism Quarterly, 65*, 648–654.

Tan, A. S., Tan, G. K., & Tan, A. S. (1987). American TV in the Philippines: A test of cultural impact. *Journalism Quarterly, 64*, 65–72.

Van den Bulck, J. (2004). Research note: The relationship between television fiction and fear of crime. *European Journal of Communication, 19*, 239–248.

Ward, L., & Friedman, K. (2006). Using TV as a guide: Associations between television viewing and adolescents' sexual attitudes and behavior. *Journal of Research on Adolescence, 16*, 133–156.

Williams, R. (1977). *Marxism and literature*. Oxford: Oxford University Press.

Wober, J. M. (1978). Televised violence and paranoid perception: The view from Great Britain. *Public Opinion Quarterly, 42*, 315–321.

Zurbriggen, E., & Morgan, E. (2006). Who wants to marry a millionaire? Reality dating television programs, attitudes toward sex, and sexual behaviors. *Sex Roles, 54*, 1–17.

4

MEDIA CONSUMPTION AND PERCEPTIONS OF SOCIAL REALITY

Effects and Underlying Processes

L. J. Shrum
University of Texas at San Antonio

> Don't come to television for the truth. TV's a goddamned amusement park. We'll tell you the good guys always win. We'll tell you nobody ever gets cancer at Archie Bunker's house. We'll tell you any shit you want to hear.
>
> Paraphrasing Howard Beale, Paddy Chayefsky's character in *Network* (Chayefsky, 1976).

I opened this chapter in the second edition of Bryant and Zillmann's *Media Effects* series with the same quote. I retained it for this updated volume because it still rings true, despite some significant changes in the media landscape. Although in the movie it is unclear whether his words were those of a madman or a sage, few would be likely to question Howard Beale's claim that television presents a distorted view of reality. Certainly, one can argue that aspects of media content, format, and presentation have changed significantly in just the last few years, with a rise in so-called "reality programming," made popular by the initial success of programs such as *Survivor* and more recently by programs such as *American Idol*. Yet charges such as scripting of outcomes of competitions, selection of contestants based on audience appeal, and product placements have undermined the claim that these programs present the world as it really is.

But even if most people do not question the premise that typical television fare distorts reality, what they do question is if the distortion has any effect, and if so, why and how. These interrelated questions about the why and how of media effects lie at the heart of scholarly debates and critiques of media effects research. Over the past few decades, there have been two persistent criticisms. One is that the evidence accumulated to date has provided little indication of sizable media effects on viewers' thoughts, feelings, or actions, in spite of a generally held "myth of massive media impact" by many researchers (McGuire, 1986). The second criticism is that it has for the most part lacked any focus on explanatory mechanisms. That is, media effects research has been primarily concerned with relations between input variables (e.g., media information and its characteristics) and output variables (e.g., attitudes, beliefs, behavior), with little consideration of the cognitive processes that might mediate these relations (Hawkins & Pingree, 1990; Reeves, Chaffee, & Tims, 1982; see also Wyer, 1980).

Although the purpose of this chapter is to address the criticism of the lack of a cognitive process explanation for media effects, the two criticisms just noted are not independent. One of the useful features of process explanations is that models are developed that specify both moderating and mediating variables. McGuire (1986) notes in his review that even though research to date has shown remarkably small media effects, there are a number of possibilities that may ultimately allow for the "salvaging" of the massive effects notion. In particular, he notes that small main effects may be obscured by messages having different effects on different groups or as a function of different situations (moderators) and by focusing on direct effects at the expense of indirect ones (mediators). Thus, the development of cognitive process models for media effects has the potential to uncover new relations as well as make sense out of old ones.

The development of cognitive process models that can explain media effects has other advantages as well. For one, it has the potential to increase internal validity, or the extent to which we are confident that we are observing a true causal effect and not one that is spurious (Hawkins & Pingree, 1990), another common criticism of many media effects studies (see Hirsch, 1980; McGuire, 1986). A process model should provide clear links between the stimulus (e.g., media consumption) and the response (e.g., beliefs, behavior), and each link in the model should represent a testable proposition to be empirically verified. If these links stand on solid theoretical foundations and are empirically verified, then threats to internal validity such as spuriousness and reverse causality are rendered less plausible, as the threats would presumably have to occur at each stage. Another advantage is that process models may potentially address conflicting findings in previous research. A process model should provide boundary conditions for the effect; that is, a specification of the conditions under which the effect does *not* hold. To the extent that these boundary conditions are related to aspects of inconsistencies in previous research, disparate findings may be reconciled.

Given these advantages of a focus on process, my goals for this chapter are two-fold: 1) to discuss some of the general underlying principles in social cognition research that have particular implications for media effects, with reference to relevant media effects research that exemplify these principles; and 2) to discuss research to date that has focused on explicating the underlying processes of certain media effects such as cultivation (see chapter 3).

SOCIAL COGNITION AND MEDIA EFFECTS

Social cognition can best be described as an orientation toward the cognitive processes that occur in social situations (Reeves, Chaffee, & Tims, 1982). To be more specific, social cognition research attempts to open the "black box" that operates between a stimulus (e.g., information) and a response (e.g., a judgment) (Wyer, 1980) and has its focus on the cognitive processes that mediate the relations between social information and judgment (Wyer & Srull, 1989).

Social cognition research has had a profound effect not only on the field of social psychology, but on numerous other fields as well (e.g., marketing communications, see chapter 18; political communications, see chapter 11; cross-cultural psychology; organizational behavior). Given the maturity of the field, there are a number of models that have been developed to account for how people acquire, store, and use social information, the most complete of which is that provided by Wyer and Srull (1989; but see Wyer, 2004; Wyer & Radvansky, 1999, for revisions of this model).[1] Even though the various theories differ in important ways, they all share some basic underlying principles (Carlston & Smith, 1996; Wyer, 1980).

For the purposes of this discussion, there are two important and interrelated principles underlying social cognition research.[2] *Principle 1* (heuristic/sufficiency principle) concerns what information is retrieved in the course of constructing a judgment. This principle states that when people construct judgments, they typically do not search memory for all information that is relevant to the judgment, but instead retrieve only a small subset of the information available. Moreover, the criterion for what is retrieved is "sufficiency": That is, only the information that is sufficient to construct the judgment is retrieved, and the determinants of sufficiency are related to concepts such as motivation and ability to process information (Wyer & Srull, 1989; see also Chaiken, Liberman, & Eagly, 1989, for a similar perspective on attitude judgments).

Principle 2 (accessibility principle) concerns the role of the accessibility of information in the construction of judgments. In its simplest form, the principle states that the information that comes most readily to mind will be the information that comprises the small subset of available information that is retrieved, and in turn, is the information that is most likely to be used in constructing a judgment (Carlston & Smith, 1996; Higgins, 1996; Wyer, 1980).

Taken together, these two principles have important implications for explaining media effects. These implications revolve around the determinants and consequences of accessibility.

Determinants of Accessibility

There are a number of factors that may influence the ease with which something is recalled. Although a detailed discussion of these factors is beyond the scope of this chapter (for more extensive reviews, see Higgins, 1996; Higgins & King, 1981), certain ones have implications for media effects (Shrum, 1995). These factors are the frequency of construct activation, recency of construct activation, vividness of a construct, and relations with accessible constructs.

Frequency and Recency of Activation

Constructs that are frequently activated tend to be easily recalled (Higgins & King, 1981). This general finding has been shown both in studies of word recall and recognition (Paivio, 1971) as well as trait concepts (Wyer & Srull, 1980). Moreover, if activated frequently enough, particular constructs may become chronically accessible (for a review, see Higgins, 1996) such that they are spontaneously activated under many different situations. The same general relation holds for recency of activation: The more recently a construct has been activated, the easier it is to recall (Higgins, Rholes, & Jones, 1977; Wyer & Srull, 1980). However, research suggests that the effect of recency of activation on accessibility is relatively transitory, with frequency effects tending to dominate after a short period of time (Higgins, Bargh, & Lombardi, 1985; Wyer, 2004; Wyer & Radvansky, 1999).

This general relation of frequency and recency with accessibility has implications for potential media effects. For example, cultivation theory rests on the premise that the frequency of television viewing has effects on the beliefs of viewers. In terms of frequency of activation, heavier viewers should more frequently activate constructs portrayed on television than light viewers, particularly if those constructs tend to be portrayed more heavily on television than in real life. Moreover, heavy viewers have a higher probability of having viewed recently than light viewers; thus accessibility may be enhanced for heavy viewers through the recency of viewing.

Vividness

More vivid constructs are more easily activated from memory than less vivid ones (Higgins & King, 1981; Nisbett & Ross, 1980; Paivio, 1971). Like frequency and recency, vividness has particular applicability to media effects. It seems reasonable to think that television portrayals of particular actions or events may be more vivid than real world experiences, given the drama-enhancing goal of entertainment. Examples might include a fist-fight, an execution, family conflict, a natural disaster, military conflict, and so forth.

Vividness may also play a role in news reports. As Zillmann and colleagues have noted (for a review, see Zillmann, 2002), news reports often convey information in the form of case studies or extreme examples. Such a bias in favor of vivid examples over precise but pallid statistical information may make those examples relatively easy to remember.

Relations with Accessible Constructs

As the accessibility of a particular construct increases, so does the accessibility of a closely related construct. This concept is consistent with the associative network/spreading activation model of memory made popular in cognitive psychology as a means of explaining the interconnectedness of knowledge (Collins & Loftus, 1975). This model holds that constructs are stored in memory in the form of nodes, and links are formed between the nodes. When a particular node (stored construct) is activated, other constructs will also be activated to the extent that they are related to that node.

It seems likely that the relation between accessible constructs may have implications for media effects. One of the attributes of media portrayals, particularly on television programs and films, is the relatively consistent and formulaic way in which particular concepts (e.g., anger and aggression, particular classes of people, etc.) are portrayed. These portrayals may provide "scripts" (Schank & Abelson, 1977) or "situation models" (Wyer, 2004; see also chapter 5) for what represents a construct and how to react to it. Given the relations between accessible constructs, the activation of a particular construct (e.g., aggression, anger) may similarly activate scripts for behavior that are closely related to these constructs (e.g., crime, violence).

In summary, television consumption—whether it is the frequency, recency, or the content features of viewing—may serve to enhance the accessibility of particular constructs. This "media effect" is an example of the interrelatedness of the heuristic/sufficiency principle and the accessibility principle: Media consumption enhances accessibility, which influences the information that becomes a part of that small subset of available information.

Consequences of Accessibility

Simply demonstrating that media information may play a role in enhancing the accessibility of particular constructs is not sufficient to provide an explanation of media effects. It is also necessary to show that enhanced accessibility in turn produces effects that are consistent with the media effects literature.

The consequences of accessibility are directly related to principle 2: The information that is most accessible is most likely to be used to construct a judgment. Moreover, the way in which the most accessible information is used is a function of the type of judgment that is made.

Judgments about Persons

One of the more consistent findings in the social cognition literature is that when people make judgments about other persons, they tend to use the constructs that are most readily accessible from memory (accessibility principle). In the now-classic priming studies (e.g., Higgins et al., 1977; Srull & Wyer, 1979), when participants were required to form trait judgments based on the ambiguous behaviors of a target person, they tended to use the trait concepts that had been primed to interpret those ambiguous behaviors (for a review, see Higgins, 1996; see also chapter 5). The interpretations influenced participants' judgments about the target's behaviors (e.g., reckless, persistent) as well as judgments about how much they liked the target. These results have been replicated numerous times, even under conditions of subliminal presentation of the prime (Bargh & Pietromonaco, 1982).

Attitude and Belief Judgments

Evaluations of an object may be constructed from beliefs that are most accessible (Fishbein & Ajzen, 1975). In the Fishbein and Ajzen model, attitude construction is a function of particular beliefs and evaluations of those beliefs. It follows, then, that *which* beliefs are put into the attitude construction equation may be a function of which beliefs are most accessible at the moment. In a series of experiments, Wyer and colleagues (Henninger & Wyer, 1976; Wyer & Hartwick, 1984) examined the relation between accessible beliefs and evaluative judgments. In those experiments, which tested aspects of the *Socratic effect* (thinking about logically related beliefs makes those beliefs more consistent; McGuire, 1960), they showed that the accessibility of beliefs relating to premises increased the consistency between the beliefs in the premises and beliefs in the conclusions.

Judgments of Set-size and Probability

Set-size judgments pertain to judgments of the extent to which a particular category occurs within a larger, superordinate category (e.g., the percentage of women [subordinate category] in the U.S. population [superordinate category]; Manis, Shedler, Jonides, & Nelson, 1993). Probability judgments pertain to estimates of likelihood. A finding that has been documented consistently is the relation between the accessibility of a construct and judgments of set-size and probability (Sherman & Corty, 1984). In their seminal work on the *availability heuristic*, Tversky and Kahneman (1973) demonstrated that people tend to infer the frequency of a class or the probability of occurrence on the ease with which a relevant example can be recalled. For example, participants in one experiment estimated that words beginning with *k* occur more frequently in the English language than words having *k* as the third letter, even though the opposite is true. Presumably, words beginning with *k* are easier to recall because of how words tend to be organized in memory (by initial letters). Later work also identified a related heuristic, the *simulation heuristic*, in which people judge frequency and probability on the ease with which an example can be imagined (Kahneman & Tversky, 1982).

Media Effects and Accessibility Consequences

The three types of judgments just discussed and their relation to accessibility by no means exhausts the discussion of the types of judgments that have been shown to be influenced by the accessibility of information (Higgins & King, 1981). Rather, those judgments are singled out because of their relevance to the types of judgments that are often used in media effects studies.

Effects of News Reports on Issue and Person Perceptions

One domain in which information accessibility has been implicated is that of how information about particular issues presented in news reports affects judgments about those issues (e.g., attitudes, likelihood estimates). For example, research by Zillmann and colleagues has shown that information presented in the form of exemplars (e.g., case studies, vivid examples, etc.) tends to influence judgments to a greater degree than does more accurate but pallid base rate information. This general finding has been replicated for a variety of exemplar conditions, including manipulating the proportion of exemplars that are consistent with a story's focus, the degree of exaggeration of the exemplars, and the emotionality of the exemplars (for a review, see Zillmann, 2002). Other research has produced similar findings, with Iyengar (1990) reporting effects of the presence (vs. absence) of exemplars and Brosius and Bathelt (1994) finding an effect of number of exemplars on issue perceptions. Most of this research has conceptualized the results in terms of accessibility and the use of heuristics: The more vivid or frequent examples are easier to remember than less vivid or infrequent examples and thus tend to be used to construct judgments.

Iyengar and colleagues have also argued that media coverage can create an accessibility bias through its frequency of coverage of particular issues. In turn, this accessibility bias has been shown to influence a number of judgments, including issue salience, evaluations of politicians' performances, and voting behavior (Iyengar, 1990). Findings reported by Lichtenstein, Slovic, Fischhoff, Layman, and Combs (1978) have also been conceptualized in terms of accessibility and the application of the availability heuristic. They observed that roughly 80% of study participants estimated that death due to an accident is more likely to occur than death due to a stroke, even though strokes cause about 85% more deaths than accidents. Lichtenstein et al. suggest that examples of accidental deaths are easier to recall than examples of death by stroke, at least partially because the former tend to be reported more than the latter in the media.

Effects of Television Viewing on Social Perceptions

Another media effects domain in which accessibility has been used as an explanatory variable is in the relationship between television viewing and perceptions of social reality. This domain differs from news reports in that it considers all types of television viewing (e.g., fictional portrayals such as soap operas, action/adventure, dramas, situation comedies, etc.) rather than just news programs.

The results of a number of studies can be conceptualized in terms of the enhanced accessibility afforded by heavy television viewing and the subsequent application of judgmental heuristics, particularly when the dependent variables involve estimates of frequency of a class or likelihood of occurrence. For example, Bryant, Carveth, and Brown (1981) exposed participants, over a six-week period, to either heavy or light viewing of films depicting crime, and those in the heavy exposure condition saw crime portrayals that featured either just or unjust resolutions. They found that those in the heavy exposure conditions indicated a greater likelihood of being a victim of violence and more fear of victimization than those in the light exposure conditions, regardless of whether the resolutions were just or unjust. As with the other studies just discussed, these results are consistent with predictions made by the availability heuristic: The heavy viewing conditions made examples of crime more accessible than the light viewing conditions, and this accessibility, or ease of recall, influenced judgments of prevalence and likelihood of occurrence. Other studies have made this same connection between accessibility as a function of viewing and judgments (cf. Ogles & Hoffner, 1987; Tamborini, Zillmann, & Bryant, 1984).

The concepts of accessibility and the use of heuristics have also been used to explain the effects of sexual portrayals in the media (see chapter 15). Zillmann and Bryant (1982) found that participants who viewed portrayals of explicit sex scenes gave higher estimates of the prevalence of unusual sex practices among the general population, were less likely to object to public display of pornography, and recommended shorter jail sentences for a convicted rapist than did participants who viewed films that were not sexually explicit.

Effects of Media Portrayals on Aggression

Although the research just reviewed has focused predominantly on cognitive measures as dependent variables, the concept of accessibility has also been useful in explaining the effects of exposure to media violence on behavior. Berkowitz's *cognitive-neoassociationistic perspective* (1984; see also chapter 5) on the effects of violent media consumption posits that frequent viewing of violent media portrayals primes particular constructs (e.g., aggression, hostility) and thus makes these constructs more likely to be used in behavioral decisions as well as judgments about others. Note that this notion is very similar to the original trait priming studies that were discussed earlier: A particular trait concept is made accessible and thus is used disproportionately as a basis for subsequent judgments.

The relation between the activation of a construct such as aggression through media portrayals and the accessibility of aggression-related constructs has been demonstrated in several studies. For example, Bushman and Geen (1990) showed that viewing violent films elicited more aggressive thoughts than viewing nonviolent films. Berkowitz, Parker, and West (cited in Berkowitz, 1973) produced similar findings, showing that children who read a war comic book were more likely to select words with aggressive meanings than children who read a neutral comic book. Other studies have made the connection between activation (and presumed enhanced accessibility) of aggression constructs and subsequent judgments. Carver, Ganellen, Froming, and Chambers (1983) found that people who viewed a brief film portraying a hostile interaction between a business executive and his secretary perceived more hostility in an ambiguous target person than did people who viewed a non-hostile portrayal, and Berkowitz (1970) showed that similar effects of aggressive portrayals on judgments can be observed even when the aggressive behavior is in the form of comedy.

It is also worth noting that what is primed does not necessarily have to be directly related to an imminent judgment, but may only have to share similar features to a judgment situation. Recall that one of the antecedents of a construct's accessibility is its relation to other accessible constructs. This notion is useful in explaining possible media effects in which the type of aggressive action viewers observe in media content is only tangentially related to the type of aggressive action taken by viewers, a pattern of results that theories of learning, imitation, or "modeling" (Bandura, 1973; see chapter 6) have difficulty addressing (Berkowitz, 1984). In fact, as Berkowitz noted, the behavioral aggression measures that are used in studies are often quite different from the aggression observed in the media portrayals (whether they are experiments or field studies). For example, Phillips (1983) presented correlational data that showed that heavy media coverage of heavyweight championship boxing matches tended to be followed by an increase in homicides in the U.S. on certain days within a 10-day period following the fight (but see Freedman, 1984, for a criticism of this study). Similar aggression-related effects of viewing boxing matches have been reported in experimental studies as well (Turner & Berkowitz, 1972).

Indirect vs. Direct Investigations of Cognitive Processes

The research just presented is suggestive of the role of accessibility as a cognitive mediator of media effects. However, much of the evidence is still indirect in that many of the studies fall short of actually investigating the processes themselves, but rather offer process explanations for the obtained results. Exceptions to this generalization include Zillmann's work on excitation-transfer theory (Zillmann, 1983) and Berkowitz's cognitive-neoassociationistic perspective (Berkowitz, 1984).

In the following section, I discuss a series of studies that directly investigates such potential cognitive processes. The results of these studies are then used as the basis for the development of cognitive processing models that can account for a particular media effect, the cultivation effect. This model builds on the general principles discussed earlier (heuristic/sufficiency and accessibility) that underlie social cognition research.

PSYCHOLOGICAL PROCESSES UNDERLYING CULTIVATION EFFECTS

One area of media effects research that has generated considerable controversy is the research on the cultivation effect (see chapter 3). For the purposes of this discussion, a cultivation effect is defined as a positive relation between frequency of television viewing and social perceptions that are congruent with the world as it is portrayed on television, with the presumption that television viewing is the causal factor. Although considerable evidence has accumulated that supports the existence of at least a small-sized cultivation effect (Morgan & Shanahan, 1996), other researchers have challenged the validity of the effect. Some research suggests that the relationship between viewing and perceptions is not causal, but rather a spurious one resulting from third variable influences (e.g., direct experience, available time to view) on both television viewing and social perceptions (Doob & Macdonald, 1979; Hirsch, 1980; Hughes, 1980; Wober & Gunter, 1988). Other research suggests that the causal relation between viewing and social perceptions may be reversed; that is, aspects of the individual (including pre-existing social perceptions) may influence the amount and content of viewing (Zillmann, 1980).

As noted earlier, one of the advantages of developing a cognitive process model of media effects is that it has the potential to render implausible certain alternative explanations for the effect (e.g., spuriousness, reverse causality, etc.). Two caveats should be noted, however. First, rendering a particular alternative explanation implausible in a study merely means that the explanation cannot *completely* account for a particular pattern of results; it does not mean that the alternative explanation may not be operating simultaneously but independent of other effects. Second, the power of a process model is in the cumulative effect of a pattern of results, not a focus on a single study. Thus, even though alternative explanations may be possible for any one study, in the interest of parsimony, the alternative explanations should address the entire pattern of results to be an effective challenge.

In the following sections, I describe models that attempt to explain the underlying processes of cultivation effects. These models are grounded in the theories of social cognition that were described earlier. The models incorporate advances that have been made over the last few years and thus represent refinements of the model presented in the previous edition of *Media Effects* (Shrum, 2002). In fact, the models are now multiple ones that separately explain the processes underlying different types of cultivation effects, in particular what are generally referred to as effects on first-order (e.g., estimates of prevalence, probability) and second-order (attitudes, values, beliefs) judgments. Recent findings suggest that the processes by which television viewing influences judgments depend on the type of judgment that is made (Shrum, 2004, 2007a; Shrum, Burroughs, & Rindfleisch, 2004).

PROCESS MODEL FOR FIRST-ORDER CULTIVATION EFFECTS

The process model for first-order effects, which has been referred to as the heuristic processing model of cultivation effects (Shrum, 2002; Shrum, Wyer, & O'Guinn, 1998) and the accessibility model (Shrum, 2007a), starts with two general propositions that are based on the principles of heuristic/sufficiency and accessibility. The first general proposition is that television viewing enhances construct accessibility. As discussed earlier, aspects of television viewing may plausibly be related to the accessibility of constructs encountered in typical television fare. The second general proposition is that the social perceptions that serve as indicators of a cultivation effect are memory-based judgments that are constructed through heuristic processing. Specifically, rather than constructing judgments through an extensive search of memory for all available relevant information (systematic processing), only a subset of relevant information is retrieved, and specifically, the information retrieved is that which is most accessible from memory. A corollary of this second general proposition is that, at least for cases in which the judgments pertain to perceptions of frequency of a class (set-size) or likelihood of occurrence, judgments are constructed through the application of the availability heuristic; that is, the magnitude of the judgments is positively related to the ease with which an example can be brought to mind (Tversky & Kahneman, 1973).

Testable Propositions

These general propositions can themselves be used to generate testable propositions regarding the relation between television viewing and social perceptions and the cognitive mechanisms that may mediate this relation.

Proposition 1: Television Viewing Influences Accessibility

Proposition 1 is a necessary condition for testing whether the availability heuristic can explain cultivation effects. This proposition was initially tested by operationalizing accessibility as the speed with which judgments could be constructed. Shrum and O'Guinn (1993) had participants provide prevalence and likelihood estimates of constructs frequently portrayed on television (e.g., crime, prostitution, etc.) and measured the time it took participants to answer each question. If television information was more accessible for heavy viewers than for light viewers, heavy viewers should not only provide higher estimates than light viewers (a cultivation effect), but should also construct their judgments faster (an accessibility effect). The results of the study confirmed these hypotheses, even when controlling for individual baseline latencies, grade point average, and use of other media. These same general relations have been replicated using a variety of dependent variables, different operationalizations of television viewing, and multiple control variables (cf. O'Guinn & Shrum, 1997; Shrum, 1996; Shrum, O'Guinn, Semenik, & Faber, 1991).

Although the initial findings linking speed of constructing judgments to judgment magnitude were consistent with theory, speed of judgment is a relatively indirect way of measuring exemplar accessibility. Recent findings provide more direct evidence that television influences accessibility. Busselle and Shrum (2003) had participants recall examples of various constructs, some of which are portrayed frequently in television programs (trial, murder, highway accident), and rate the ease of that recall experience. Consistent with predictions, media examples were more frequently recalled for constructs that are portrayed often in television programs but infrequently experienced personally, whereas personal experiences were more frequently retrieved for events occurring often in real life, regardless of their frequency of occurrence in the media (highway accidents, dates). More important, rated ease of recall of the examples was positively related to frequency of television viewing, but only for the viewing of television programs in which the events were frequently portrayed (e.g., soap operas, dramas, news). Rated ease of recall was unrelated to viewing frequency for program categories in which the constructs were infrequently portrayed (e.g., comedies, sports) and for constructs in which personal experience (direct or indirect) was high (e.g., date, highway accident). These results not only bolster the proposition that television viewing increases accessibility, but also are consistent with research showing the direct experience with constructs enhances their accessibility. It is also consistent with research that shows that it is the subjective ease of recall (the *metacognitive* experience) that influences judgments, not frequency of recall per se (Schwarz, Bless, Strack, Klumpp, Rittenauer-Schatka, & Simons, 1991; Schwarz, Song, & Xu, in press).

Proposition 2: Accessibility Mediates the Cultivation Effect

Proposition 1 (viewing influences accessibility) is a necessary but not sufficient condition to implicate the availability heuristic as an explanation for cultivation effects. It is also necessary to demonstrate that accessibility mediates the relation between level of viewing and magnitude of judgments (Manis, Shedler, Jonides, & Nelson, 1993); that is, it is also necessary to demonstrate that the enhanced accessibility leads to higher estimates. Otherwise, it could be argued that television viewing impacts accessibility and the magnitude of the judgments independently.

Some indirect evidence of the mediating role of accessibility was provided by Shrum and O'Guinn (1993). When accessibility (speed of response) was controlled, the cultivation effect was for the most part reduced to nonsignificance. More direct evidence of mediation was provided by Shrum (1996). Path analyses were used to demonstrate that level of television viewing was related to accessibility (again, operationalized as response latencies), which in turn was related to the magnitude of the estimates. However, the path analyses also revealed that the mediation was only a partial one: Television viewing still had a direct effect on the magnitude of the estimates even when the influence of accessibility was controlled.

Busselle (2001) also provided evidence of the mediating role of accessibility by manipulating the conditions under which the prevalence estimates for particular constructs (e.g., a shooting) were constructed. Some participants provided their prevalence estimates before recalling an example of the construct (judgment-first condition), whereas other participants recalled an example before providing their estimates (recall-first condition). Level of television viewing was expected to make an example easier to recall in the judgment-first condition, whereas recalling an example before judgment was expected to make an example equally accessible for all participants, regardless of television viewing level. The results confirmed these expectations.

Proposition 3: Television Exemplars Are Not Discounted

An implicit assumption in the notion that the availability heuristic can explain cultivation effects is that the examples that are retrieved and used as a basis for judgment are considered applicable to the judgment. This is an important assumption because research has shown that accessibility effects typically obtain only when this condition is met (Higgins, 1996). Moreover, the judged applicability of the construct is a function of the overlap between its attended features and the features of the judgment.

In terms of the cultivation effect, the recalled construct would presumably be a television example. However, it is counterintuitive that people would perceive a television example (e.g., doctor, lawyer) as applicable to a judgment about its real-world prevalence. If they do not perceive the example as relevant, alternative information would be retrieved and used as a basis for judgment (Higgins, 1996; Higgins & Brendl, 1995; Shapiro & Lang, 1991).

One way in which a television example could be perceived as relevant to a real-world judgment is if people generally do not consider the source of the example they retrieve in the course of judgment construction. Note that perceived applicability is a function of the overlap between the *attended* features of the recalled construct and the features of the judgment. It may be that source characteristics of the retrieved construct are not salient features that are attended to, particularly when judgments are made with little effort. This may be a function of either lack of motivation to attend to source features (consistent with low involvement processing; Petty & Cacioppo, 1990) or lack of ability to recall source information (consistent with research on errors in source monitoring; Johnson, Hashtroudi, & Lindsay, 1993; Mares, 1996; Shrum, 1997). This process is also consistent with the weighing and balancing mechanism proposed by Shapiro and Lang (1991) to explain cultivation effects (for a review, see Shrum, 2007a).

To test proposition 3, Shrum, Wyer, and O'Guinn (1998) conducted two experiments in which source characteristics were primed prior to judgments. In the first experiment, the priming events consisted of a source-priming condition, in which participants provided information regarding their television viewing habits prior to providing prevalence and likelihood judgments of crime and occupations; and a relation-priming condition in which participants were told that the constructs they would be estimating appeared more often on television than in real life. In a third, no-priming condition, participants provided their estimates prior to providing television viewing information. Analyses revealed that when participants provided estimates under no-priming conditions, a cultivation effect was noted, but when they provided estimates under either source- or relation-priming conditions, the cultivation effect was eliminated. Follow-up analyses indicated that the estimates of light viewers did not differ as a function of priming conditions, but the priming conditions served to bring the estimates of heavy viewers more in line with those of light viewers. This pattern of results can be seen in Figure 4.1.

A second study replicated this pattern of results, and further suggested that the priming conditions induced a source-discounting process (heavy viewers discounted television information to a greater degree than light viewers) rather than an automatic adjustment process (heavy viewers adjusted their estimates downward because they were aware they were heavy viewers, but light viewers saw no need to adjust).

Proposition 4: Motivation to Process Information Moderates the Cultivation Effect

Proposition 4 is based on research showing that there are certain conditions under which heuristic processing (as opposed to systematic processing) is expected to occur (Sherman & Corty, 1984; see chapter 7). If so, then manipulating the types of processing in which people engage should have implications for whether a cultivation effect is obtained. To be specific, if people generally process heuristically in the course of constructing their judgments of prevalence or likelihood of occurrence, then inducing people to process heuristically should produce a cultivation effect that does not differ in magnitude from the cultivation effect obtained when people receive no such manipulation. But suppose people are induced to process systematically when constructing

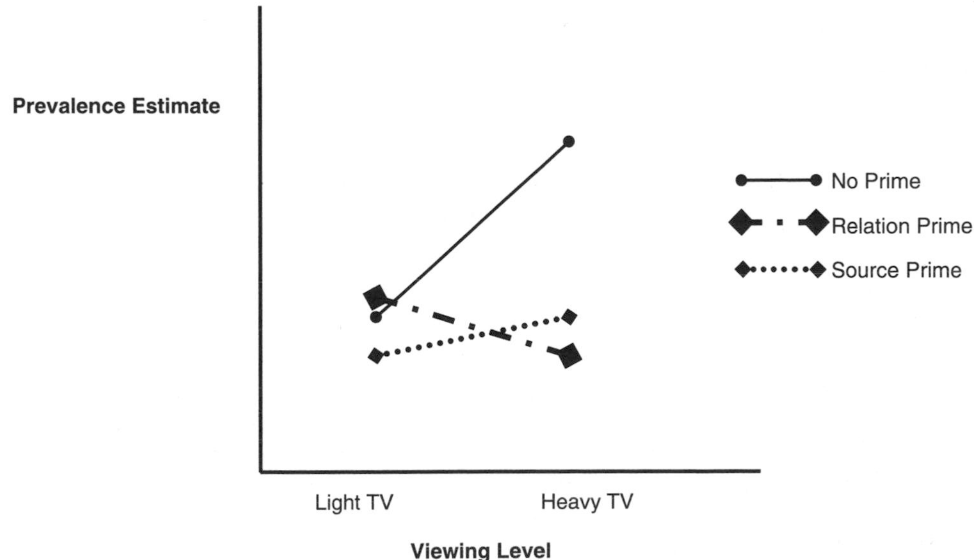

Figure 4.1 Prevalence Estimates as a Function of Priming Condition and Level of TV Viewing. Represents Pattern of Results across Dependent Variables (see Shrum, Wyer, & O'Guinn, 1998).

their judgments. Compared to heuristic processing, systematic processing is associated with the consideration of more information and greater scrutiny of the information that is considered. Systematic processing is used when it is important to determine the validity of information and has been shown to attenuate the effects of heuristics (Chaiken et al., 1989).

Under systematic conditions, it seems likely that the relation between level of viewing and social perceptions would be weakened or eliminated entirely. When people process systematically, they should be more likely to retrieve examples other than simply the first ones that come to mind, should be more likely to scrutinize the retrieved information, and thus should be more likely to ascertain and discount information from unreliable sources such as television programs, than when they process heuristically.

One condition that is related to whether heuristic or systematic processing strategies are adopted is the motivation to process information (Sherman & Corty, 1984). When motivation is high, systematic processing predominates; when motivation is low, heuristic processing predominates. Moreover, motivation is determined by a number of factors, including level of issue involvement (Petty & Cacioppo, 1990) and level of task involvement (Chaiken & Maheswaran, 1994).

To test proposition 4, Shrum (2001) manipulated the processing strategies that participants used to construct their estimates of the prevalence of crime, marital discord, affluence, and certain occupations. Some participants were induced to process systematically via an accuracy motivation/task importance manipulation (Chaiken & Maheswaran, 1994), others were induced to process heuristically by asking them to give the first answer that came to mind, and a third (control) group received no manipulation, but were simply instructed to provide their estimates. Television viewing was then measured after the judgments were made. The results were as expected. Both the control group and the heuristic group produced significant cultivation effects that did not differ from each other, whereas the systematic group showed no cultivation effect. Moreover, the pattern of results was very similar to those obtained by Shrum et al. (1998, Study 1): The estimates of light viewers did not differ as a function of condition, but the systematic condition affected only heavy viewers, bringing their estimates more in line with those of all light viewers, regardless of processing condition. This pattern of results can be seen in Figure 4.2.

Proposition 5: Ability to Process Information Moderates the Cultivation Effect

As with proposition 4, this proposition is based on the conditions that facilitate or inhibit the use of systematic or heuristic processing strategies. In addition to motivation to process information, the ability to process information is also associated with processing strategies (Chaiken et al., 1989; Petty & Cacioppo, 1986). One factor that relates to the ability to process information is time pressure (Moore, Hausknecht, & Thamodaran, 1986; Ratneshwar & Chaiken, 1991): the more time pressure, the greater the likelihood of adopting a heuristic processing strategy.

To test proposition 5, Shrum (2007b) used an experimental procedure that not only tested the proposition but also has implications for data collection methods. The experimental manipulation of time pressure was operationalized as either a mail survey (low time pressure) or a telephone survey (high time pressure) using a general population random sample. Pretests had indicated that the two data collection methods differed with respect to time pressure but did not differ in terms of respondents' self-reported

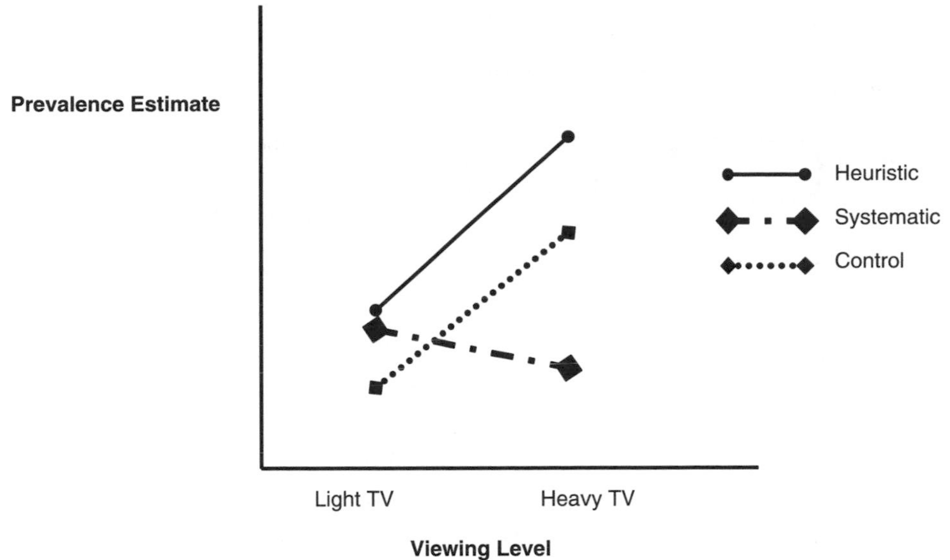

Figure 4.2 Prevalence Estimates as a Function of Processing Condition and Level of TV Viewing. Represents Pattern of Results across Dependent Variables (see Shrum, 2001).

level of involvement. The reasoning and predictions for the experiment were similar to Shrum (2001). If the cultivation effect is a function of heuristic processing, then larger effects should be noted under conditions that favor more heuristic processing (phone survey) than under conditions that favor less heuristic processing (mail survey). The results confirmed this speculation. Across five composite variables representing perceptions of societal crime, societal vice (e.g., prevalence of prostitution, drug abuse, etc.), marital discord, affluence, and the prevalence of particular occupations, the magnitude of the effects was significantly larger in the phone survey condition than in the mail survey condition for four of the five measures (as with Shrum, 2001, all but marital discord).

Other evidence also supports the notion that ability to process information has implications for the cultivation effect. Mares (1996) found that people who tend to make particular kinds of source confusions (mistaking fiction for fact) tend to exhibit a larger cultivation effect than those who do not tend to make such confusions. Thus, even in instances in which people may be motivated to process information (see Shrum, 1997), inability to properly process information (in this case, accurately ascertain source characteristics) may facilitate a cultivation effect.

Model Integration

The next step in model development is to integrate the testable propositions, and the implications of their supportive results, into a coherent conceptual framework. This conceptual framework, which is presented in the form of a flow chart in Figure 4.3, specifies a series of links, or steps, which lead from television viewing to the production of a cultivation effect. For the most part, each link (designated by an arrow) represents a testable proposition that has been empirically verified. As the figure indicates, there are in fact a number of ways in which media exposure will not have an effect on judgments (no cultivation effect), but only one way (path) in which a cultivation effect will be produced.

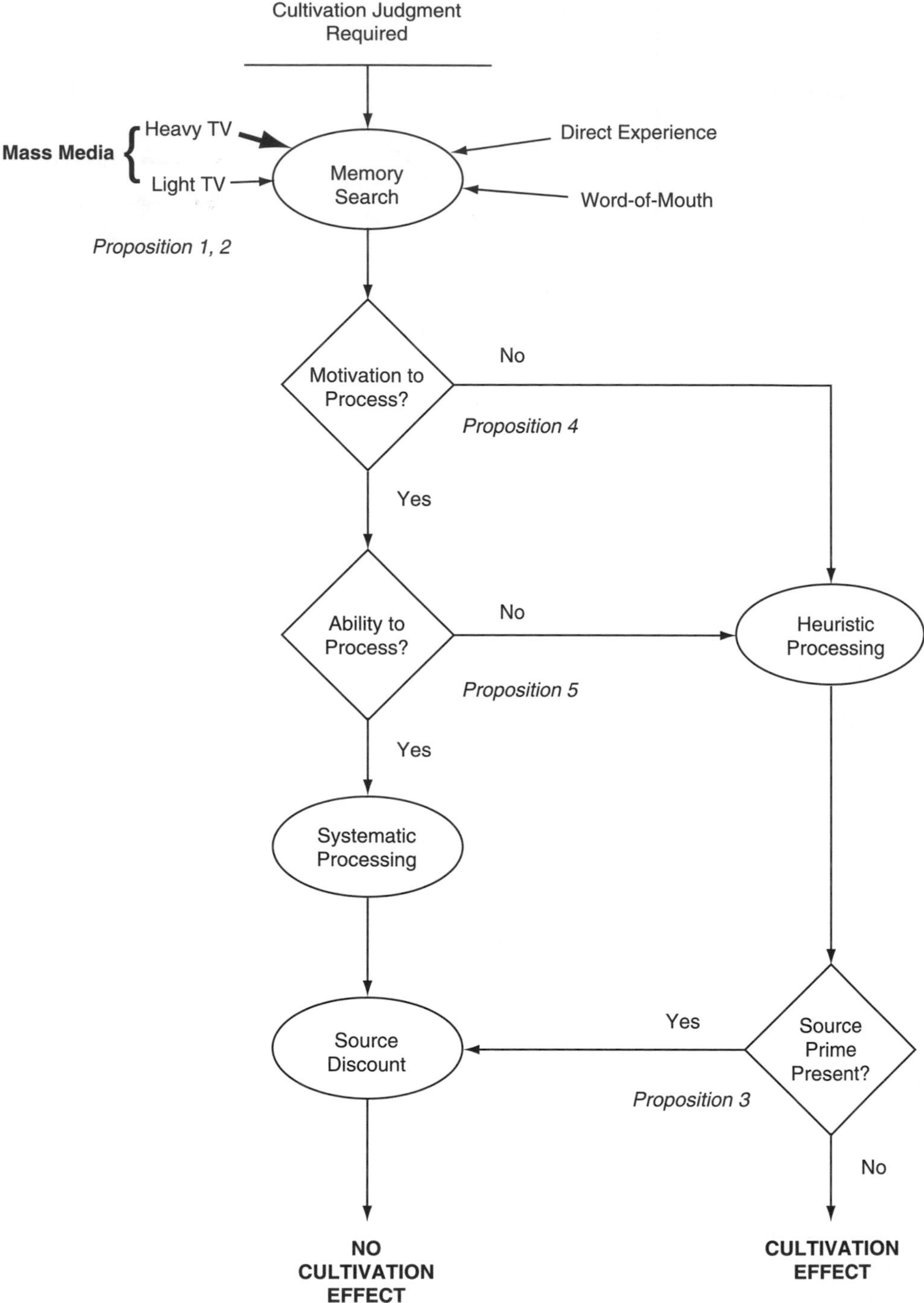

Figure 4.3 Flow Diagram of the Heuristic Processing Model of Television Effects. Circles Represent Mental Processes. The Thicker Arrow from Heavy TV to Memory Search Indicates a Greater Contribution to the Search Process.

In order to present as simple a model as possible, some misleading aspects arise that should be clarified. One of the misleading aspects of Figure 4.3 is that the links (Yes/No) and the outcomes (Effect/No Effect) are portrayed as dichotomous variables. In fact, it is more accurate to think of each as a continuum, and movement along the continuum has implications for the size of the outcome. For example, rather than interpreting the figure as "high motivation to process results in no cultivation effect," it may be better interpreted as "the higher the motivation to process, the smaller the cultivation effect."

Implausible Alternative Hypotheses

Although some, if not all, of the studies that have formed the basis of the model have potential alternative explanations, it is difficult for concepts such as spuriousness or reverse causality to account for the general pattern. For example, the initial studies that tested propositions 1 and 2 (accessibility) were strictly correlational and thus could be explained in terms of either spuriousness or reverse causality. However, these alternative explanations cannot account for the results of the experiments that tested propositions 3 through 5, particularly the pattern showing that both the experimental manipulations of source priming and of processing strategy produced nearly identical results, with the manipulations reducing estimates of heavy viewers to the equivalent of light viewers, but leaving the estimates of light viewers unaffected.

The consistency of results across the different types of dependent variables also argues against explanations other than a causal effect of television viewing. Consistent results tended to be found for judgments of occupational prevalence (doctors, lawyers, police officers), crime, and affluence (and to a lesser extent, marital discord). Although reverse causality or spuriousness explanations can be used (and often are) to explain the results for any one variable, it is difficult to account for the effects on all variables. Rather, the more parsimonious explanation is that the causal factor is the one that they most have in common: They are constructs over-represented in television portrayals relative to their real-world incidence.

Explaining Small Cultivation Effect Sizes

As mentioned earlier, one of the useful features of a process model for cultivation effects is that it has the potential to reconcile conflicting findings that have been reported. The myriad of paths toward little or no cultivation effect that are shown in Figure 4.3 has the potential to explain some of these conflicts.

Source-priming Explanations

The source-priming manipulation used by Shrum et al. (1998) had participants provide information on how much television they watch prior to providing their prevalence and likelihood estimates. This order of data collection was sufficient to eliminate the cultivation effect. As Morgan and Shanahan (1996) noted, a number of studies that have reported finding no evidence of a cultivation effect either measured television viewing prior to measuring social perceptions or introduced the study as one pertaining to television. Although Morgan and Shanahan's meta-analysis did not find support for such source-priming as a moderator, their results showed that the effect sizes for the non-source-primed studies tended to be slightly higher than the effect sizes for studies in which source was (inadvertently) primed. Thus, it seems possible that the inability to observe cultivation effects in previous studies may have been due to the inadvertent priming of source information.

Note also that it is not necessary to prime source through data collection. Priming simply refers to making a construct more accessible in memory. For some people, particular constructs may be chronically accessible (Higgins, 1996). So for whom might the construct of television, and its potential effects, be particularly accessible? One group may be communication majors, or for that matter, any student who might have had a course that deals with potential effects of television; in other words, people who may often comprise the subject pools that academics (and especially those in communication departments) use in their studies. Thus, it is plausible that null findings for cultivation effects in some studies may be due to the special characteristics of the sample.

Involvement Explanations

A number of factors may relate to level of involvement with constructing judgments. For example, level of involvement may differ as a function of sample composition. College students may be less intimidated than older adults or younger people by the university setting that may be used to collect data (Shrum, 1997). Alternatively, individual differences may exist that relate to involvement, such as interest in the topic (e.g., crime by those with direct experience with it) or general interest in solving problems (e.g., those high on need for cognition; Cacioppo & Petty, 1982). Involvement may also vary as a function of data collection method. Data that are collected through anonymous questionnaires may induce less accuracy motivation than data collected in, say, personal interviews (Shrum, 1997, 2001).

Time Pressure Explanations

Shrum (2007b) showed that simple differences in data collection methods, presumably related to differences in time pressure, can have a significant impact on the magnitude of cultivation effects. In that study, the difference was whether the data were collected via a phone or mail survey. Other situations can contribute to time pressure, whether real or imagined. Although not entirely independent of involvement, it has been my experience that a majority of the college students that comprise subject pools seem to be in quite a hurry to finish their task and leave. College students may be less interested in answering survey questions or in more of a hurry to complete the survey than older adults. If so, they would be more likely to use heuristics in their judgments, and thus should show a larger cultivation effect. There is actually some evidence that supports this possibility. Unreported data from Morgan and Shanahan's (1996) meta-analysis (reported in Shrum, 2007b) showed that college student samples produced markedly larger effect sizes than general population adult samples despite their lower incidence of television viewing.

Summary

The process model for first-order cultivation effects just discussed has provided robust findings that help explain the processes underlying the effect. This process explanation provides much needed support for the validity of the effect by explicating and testing the mediating processes. The model also specifies important boundary conditions or moderating effects. Cultivation effects tend to be strongest when motivation or ability to process information is low, and the effects tend to be reduced or eliminated when motivation or ability to process is high.

However, first-order effects are only a part of the picture. Although process research to date has tended to focus on first-order effects (perhaps because they have been shown to be more reliable; Hawkins & Pingree, 1982), second-order effects that look at television's influence on values, attitudes, and beliefs are arguably more important. As will be noted in the following section, first-order judgments are fairly uncommon and seldom spontaneous, usually coming only at the behest of one of life's researchers (Hastie & Park, 1986), whereas second-order judgments are typically spontaneous, everyday judgments that influence many aspects of our lives. In the next section, I provide a rough model of the processes underlying second-order cultivation effects and discuss evidence that supports this model.

PROCESS MODEL FOR SECOND-ORDER CULTIVATION EFFECTS

As just noted, second-order judgments differ from first-order judgments in some important ways, including how they are constructed (Shrum, 2004). First-order judgments tend to be memory-based judgments. Memory-based judgments are constructed by recalling information from memory and constructing the judgment in real time. In contrast, second-order cultivation judgments such as attitudes and values tend to be online judgments.[3] Online judgments are constructed by relying on information as it comes into memory storage from an outside source (e.g., an ad, a speech, etc.). As Hastie and Park (1986) noted, memory-based judgments are actually relatively rare, and often hard to produce, even in the lab. In contrast, online judgments are much more common and tend to be made spontaneously as information is received.

If indeed first-order and second-order judgments differ in how they are constructed, then it follows that the processes that underlie television effects on those judgments may also differ. In fact, as the next section illustrates, not only do the underlying processes differ, but in some cases appear to be exact opposites.

Cultivation as Online Persuasion

The premise of cultivation theory is that frequent viewing influences attitudes, values, and beliefs in the direction of the television message. Put this way, television viewing can be conceptualized as a persuasive communication. If so, and if in fact the attitudes, values, and beliefs are formed in an online fashion, there are a number of implications for the processes underlying the cultivation of second-order cultivation judgments. For one, it suggests that the influence of television on judgments occurs *during viewing*. Note that this differs from the influence of television on first-order judgments, in which the recall of television information influences judgments of frequency and probability at the time the judgment is requested. Second, if the cultivation is viewed as a persuasive communication, then it follows that factors that facilitate or inhibit persuasion would likewise facilitate or inhibit the cultivation effect. In particular, research on dual-process models of persuasion such as the ELM (see chapter 7) specify that motivation and ability to process information moderates the effects of persuasion: Persuasion is enhanced when motivation and ability to process information are high.[4] Given this, it follows that cultivation should be enhanced when motivation and ability are high during viewing.

Initial Tests

A few studies have provided initial support for this proposition. Shrum, Burroughs, and Rindfleisch (2005) conducted two studies that sought to determine whether motivation and ability to process information during viewing moderates the cultivation effect. The first study consisted of a randomly sampled general population survey of U.S. viewers that looked at the relation between frequency of television viewing and the personal value of materialism. Motivation to process information was operationalized as the extent to which viewers tend to elaborate during viewing (need for cognition; Cacioppo & Petty, 1982) and ability to process was operationalized as self-reported tendencies to pay attention to the program while viewing (Rubin, Perse, & Taylor, 1988). As expected, viewing frequency was positively related to level of materialism, but the effect was stronger for those who tend to elaborate more during viewing (high need for cognition) and for those who tend to pay attention more while viewing. A follow-up experiment confirmed the hypothesis that high need for cognition people who are heavy viewers tend to elaborate more, and also more positively, than low need for cognition heavy viewers. The heavy-viewing high need for cognition participants also reported being the most immersed into the program while they viewed. Note that these particular moderating effects for motivation and ability on second-order cultivation judgments are exactly the opposite of their moderating effects on first-order cultivation judgments. For the latter, high motivation and high ability to process information during recall *decreased* the cultivation effect (Shrum, 2001, 2007b).

The online nature of second-order cultivation judgments also has some implications for the accessibility of attitudes.[5] If in fact currently existing attitude and value structures get continuously accessed and updated during viewing, then the accessibility of those attitudes should be positively related to frequency of viewing. This proposition was confirmed in a study that measured television viewing and speed with which attitude judgments were made (Shrum, 1999). As expected, heavy viewers provided their attitude judgments faster than light viewers, and this effect held over-and-above the effects of attitude extremity.

CONCLUSION

When combined with the previous studies on memory-based processing and first-order cultivation judgments, the results of the most recent studies on online processing of second-order cultivation judgments make a convincing case that the processes underlying media effects such as cultivation depend on the type of judgment being made. This has important implications for reconciling various disparate findings in the media effects literature. To start, the articulation of boundary conditions for the cultivation effect can be extrapolated to certain conditions that may inhibit the cultivation effect, making it small and at times nonsignificant. The different "routes to cultivation," coupled with those boundary conditions, may also help explain why effects are often noted for one type of judgment but not the other (e.g., first-order effects may be more common and stronger than second-order effects; Hawkins & Pingree, 1982).

Specifying and documenting the underlying effects does more than simply contribute to the construct validity of the cultivation effect. The boundary conditions specified by the process models also imply ways in which unwanted effects of media consumption (e.g., increased materialism, less trust, inaccurate perceptions of society) may be mitigated. The models just articulated suggest that media literacy programs not only need to teach viewers to "read the media," but they also need to teach viewers to "read the judgment" by educating viewers as to the types of judgments that are often affected by television viewing and how to devise (different) strategies based on the different underlying processes.

Acknowledgement

Preparation of this chapter was supported in part by a Faculty Development Leave grant and a Faculty Research Award from the University of Texas at San Antonio and by a Faculty Summer Research Grant from the College of Business.

Notes

1 The comprehensive aspect of the Wyer and Srull (1989) model is that it specifies precise mechanisms for all stages in the information processing system (i.e., from input to output) and not necessarily that it is superior or more valid than other models. Most other models tend to focus on only selected aspects of the processing system (e.g., comprehension, storage, retrieval, response, etc.).

2 These two principles are discussed at more length by Carlston and Smith (1996) and Wyer (1980), who each use slightly different names for the principles. I have taken the liberty of renaming the principles to provide a better fit with the definitions and context of the discussions.

3 Of course, not all attitudes are formed in an online fashion. In certain instances, particularly when a current attitude is not very accessible or we are not confident in its validity, we may recompute our attitude from information we recall from memory (e.g., attitude toward a person, product, etc.). However, most of our attitudes, impressions, and perceptions are made spontaneously (and often automatically). As new information is encountered, new attitudes are formed or old ones are updated.

4 This is true only for strong (i.e., compelling) arguments. However, it is reasonable to think that heavy viewers find the story arguments compelling given that they watch frequently.

5 Note that this type of accessibility is different than the accessibility noted for first-order effects. Accessibility for first-order judgments refers to the accessibility of exemplars, which are used to construct memory-based judgments. Accessibility of attitudes or beliefs refers to the accessibility of a prior evaluative judgment.

References

Bandura, A. (1973). *Aggression: A social learning analysis.* Englewood Cliffs, NJ: Prentice Hall.

Bargh, J. A., & Pietromonaco, P. (1982). Automatic information processing and social perception: The influence of trait information presented outside of conscious awareness on impression formation. *Journal of Personality and Social Psychology, 43*, 437–449.

Berkowitz, L. (1970). Aggressive humors as a stimulus to aggressive responses. *Journal of Personality and Social Psychology, 16*, 710–717.

Berkowitz, L. (1973). Words and symbols as stimuli to aggressive responses. In J. Knutson (Ed.), *Control of aggression: Implications from basic research* (pp. 113–143). Chicago: Aldine-Atherton.

Berkowitz, L. (1984). Some effects of thoughts on anti- and prosocial influences of media events: A cognitive-neoassociation analysis. *Psychological Bulletin, 95*, 410–427.

Brosius, H., & Bathelt, A. (1994). The utility of examples in persuasive communication. *Communication Research, 21*, 48–78.

Bryant, J., Carveth, R. A., & Brown, D. (1981). Television viewing and anxiety: An experimental investigation. *Journal of Communication, 31*(1), 106–119.

Bushman, B., & Geen, R. (1990). Role of cognitive-emotional mediators and individual differences in the effects of media violence on aggression. *Journal of Personality and Social Psychology, 58*, 156–163.

Busselle, R. W. (2001). The role of exemplar accessibility in social reality judgments. *Media Psychology, 3*, 43–67.

Busselle, R. W., & Shrum, L. J. (2003). Media exposure and the accessibility of social information. *Media Psychology, 5*, 255–282.

Cacioppo, J. T., & Petty, R. E. (1982). The need for cognition. *Journal of Personality and Social Psychology, 42*, 116–131.

Carlston, D. E., & Smith, E. R. (1996). Principles of mental representation. In E. T. Higgins & A. W. Kruglanski (Eds.), *Social psychology: Handbook of basic principles* (pp. 184–210). New York: Guilford Press.

Carver, C., Ganellen, R., Froming, W., & Chambers, W. (1983). Modeling: An analysis in terms of category accessibility. *Journal of Experimental Social Psychology, 19*, 403–421.

Chaiken, S., Liberman, A., & Eagly, A. H. (1989). Heuristic and systematic processing within and beyond the persuasion context. In J. S. Uleman & J. A. Bargh (Eds.), *Unintended thought* (pp. 212–252). New York: Guilford Press.

Chaiken, S., & Maheswaran, D. (1994). Heuristic processing can bias systematic processing: Effects of source credibility, argument ambiguity, and task importance on attitude judgment. *Journal of Personality and Social Psychology, 66*, 460–473.

Chayefsky, P. (writer). (1976). *Network* [Film]. Metro-Goldwyn-Mayer, Inc.

Collins, A. M., & Loftus, E. F. (1975). A spreading-activation theory of semantic processing. *Psychological Review, 82*, 407–428.

Doob, A., & Macdonald, G. (1979). Television viewing and fear of victimization: Is the relationship causal? *Journal of Personality and Social Psychology, 37*, 170–179.

Fishbein, M., & Ajzen, I. (1975). *Belief, attitude, intention, and behavior: An introduction to theory and research*. Reading, MA: Addison-Wesley.

Freedman, J. L. (1984). Effect of television violence on aggressiveness. *Psychological Bulletin, 96*, 227–246.

Hastie, R., & Park, B. (1986). The relationship between memory and judgment depends on whether the judgment task is memory-based or on-line. *Psychological Review, 93*, 258–268.

Hawkins, R. P., & Pingree, S. (1982). Television's influence on constructions of social reality. In D. Pearl, L. Bouthilet, & J. Lazar (Eds.), *Television and behavior: Ten years of scientific progress and implications for the eighties* (Vol. 2, pp. 224–247). Washington, DC: Government Printing Office.

Hawkins, R. B., & Pingree, S. (1990). Divergent psychological processes in constructing social reality from mass media content. In N. Signorielli & M. Morgan (Eds.), *Cultivation analysis: New directions in media effects research* (pp. 33–50). Newbury Park, CA: Sage.

Henninger, M., & Wyer, R. S. (1976). The recognition and elimination of inconsistencies among syllogistically related beliefs: Some new light on the "Socratic effect." *Journal of Personality and Social Psychology, 34*, 680–693.

Higgins, E. T. (1996). Knowledge activation: Accessibility, applicability, and salience. In E. T. Higgins & A. W. Kruglanski (Eds.), *Social psychology: Handbook of basic principles* (pp. 133–168). New York: Guilford Press.

Higgins, E. T., Bargh, J. A., & Lombardi, W. (1985). The nature of priming effects on categorization. *Journal of Experimental Psychology: Learning, Memory, & Cognition, 11*, 59–69.

Higgins, E. T., & Brendl, C. M. (1995). Accessibility and applicability: Some "activation rules" influencing judgment. *Journal of Experimental Social Psychology, 31*, 218–243.

Higgins, E. T., & King, G. (1981). Accessibility of social constructs: Information processing consequences of individual and contextual variability. In N. Cantor & J. F. Kihlstrom (Eds.), *Personality, cognition and social interaction* (pp. 69–121). Hillsdale, NJ: Erlbaum.

Higgins, E. T., Rholes, W. S., & Jones, C. R. (1977). Category accessibility and impression formation. *Journal of Experimental Social Psychology*, *13*, 141–154.

Hirsch, P. (1980). The scary world of the nonviewer and other anomalies: A reanalysis of Gerbner et al.'s findings on cultivation analysis. *Communication Research*, *7*, 403–456.

Hughes, M. (1980). The fruits of cultivation analysis: A reexamination of some effects of television watching. *Public Opinion Quarterly*, *44*, 287–302.

Iyengar, S. (1990). The accessibility bias in politics: Television news and public opinion. *International Journal of Public Opinion Research*, *2*, 1–15.

Johnson, M. K., Hashtroudi, S., & Lindsay, D. S. (1993). Source monitoring. *Psychological Bulletin*, *114*, 3–28.

Kahneman, D., & Tversky, A. (1982). The simulation heuristic. In D. Kahneman, P. Slovic, & A. Tversky (Eds.), *Judgment under uncertainty: Heuristics and biases* (pp. 201–208). New York: Cambridge University Press.

Lichtenstein, S., Slovic, P., Fischhoff, G., Layman, M., & Combs, B. (1978). Judged frequency of lethal events. *Journal of Experimental Psychology: Human Learning and Memory*, *6*, 551–578.

Manis, M., Shedler, J., Jonides, J., & Nelson, T. E. (1993). Availability heuristic in judgments of set size and frequency of occurrence. *Journal of Personality and Social Psychology*, *65*, 448–457.

Mares, M. L. (1996). The role of source confusions in television's cultivation of social reality judgments. *Human Communication Research*, *23*, 278–297.

McGuire, W. J. (1960). Cognitive consistency and attitude change. *Journal of Abnormal and Social Psychology*, *60*, 345–353.

McGuire, W. J. (1986). The myth of massive media impact: Savagings and salvagings. In G. Comstock (Ed.), *Public communication and behavior* (Vol. 1, pp. 173–257). New York: Academic Press.

Moore, D. L., Hausknecht, D., & Thamodaran, K. (1986). Time compression, response opportunity, and persuasion. *Journal of Consumer Research*, *13*, 85–99.

Morgan, M., & Shanahan, J. (1996). Two decades of cultivation research: An appraisal and meta-analysis. In B. R. Burleson (Ed.), *Communication yearbook 20* (pp. 1–45). Newbury Park, CA: Sage.

Nisbett, R., & Ross, L. (1980). *Human inferences: Strategies and shortcomings of human judgment*. Englewood Cliffs, NJ: Prentice-Hall.

Ogles, R. M., & Hoffner, C. (1987). Film violence and perceptions of crime: The cultivation effect. In M. L. McLaughlin (Ed.), *Communication yearbook 10* (pp. 384–394). Newbury Park, CA: Sage.

O'Guinn, T. C., & Shrum, L. J. (1997). The role of television in the construction of consumer reality. *Journal of Consumer Research*, *23*, 278–294.

Paivio, A. (1971). *Imagery and verbal processes*. New York: Holt, Rinehart & Winston.

Petty, R. E., & Cacioppo, J. T. (1986). *Communication and persuasion: Central and peripheral routes to attitude change*. New York: Springer-Verlag.

Petty, R. E., & Cacioppo, J. T. (1990). Involvement and persuasion: Tradition versus integration. *Psychological Bulletin*, *107*, 367–374.

Phillips, D. (1983). The impact of mass media violence on U.S. homicides. *American Sociological Review*, *48*, 560–568.

Ratneshwar, S., & Chaiken, S. (1991). Comprehension's role in persuasion: The case of its moderating effect on the persuasive impact of source cues. *Journal of Consumer Research*, *18*, 52–62.

Reeves, B., Chaffee, S., & Tims, A. (1982). Social cognition and mass communication research. In M. E. Roloff & C. R. Berger (Eds.), *Social cognition and mass communication* (pp. 287–326). Newbury Park, CA: Sage.

Rubin, A. M., Perse, E. M., & Taylor, D. S. (1988). A methodological examination of cultivation. *Communication Research*, *15*, 107–134.

Schank, R., & Abelson, R. P. (1977). *Scripts, plans, goals, and understanding*. Hillsdale, NJ: Erlbaum.

Schwarz, N., Bless, H., Strack, F., Klumpp, G., Rittenauer-Schatka, H., & Simons, A. (1991). Ease of retrieval as information: Another look at the availability heuristic. *Journal of Personality and Social Psychology, 61*, 195–202.

Schwarz, N., Song, H., & Xu, J. (in press). When thinking is difficult: Metacognitive experiences as information. In M. Wänke (Ed.), *The social psychology of consumer behavior*. New York: Psychology Press.

Shapiro, M. A., & Lang, A. (1991). Making television reality: Unconscious processes in the construction of social reality. *Communication Research, 18*, 685–705.

Sherman, S. J., & Corty, E. (1984). Cognitive heuristics. In R. S. Wyer & T. K. Srull (Eds.), *Handbook of social cognition* (Vol. 1, pp. 189–286). Hillsdale, NJ: Erlbaum.

Shrum, L. J. (1995). Assessing the social influence of television: A social cognition perspective on cultivation effects. *Communication Research, 22*, 402–429.

Shrum, L. J. (1996). Psychological processes underlying cultivation effects: Further tests of construct accessibility. *Human Communication Research, 22*, 482–509.

Shrum, L. J. (1997). The role of source confusion in cultivation effects may depend on processing strategy: A comment on Mares (1996). *Human Communication Research, 24*, 349–358.

Shrum, L. J. (1999). The relationship of television viewing with attitude strength and extremity: Implications for the cultivation effect. *Media Psychology, 1*, 3–25.

Shrum, L. J. (2001). Processing strategy moderates the cultivation effect. *Human Communication Research, 27*, 94–120.

Shrum, L. J. (2002). Media consumption and perceptions of social reality: Effects and underlying processes. In J. Bryant & D. Zillmann (Eds.), *Media effects: Advances in theory and research* (2nd ed., pp. 69–95). Mahwah, NJ: Erlbaum.

Shrum, L. J. (2004). The cognitive processes underlying cultivation effects are a function of whether the judgments are on-line or memory-based. *Communications, 29*, 327–344.

Shrum, L. J. (2007a). Cultivation and social cognition. In D. R. Roskos-Ewoldsen & J. L. Monahan (Eds.), *Communication and social cognition: Theories and methods* (pp. 245–272). Mahwah, NJ: Erlbaum.

Shrum, L. J. (2007b). The implications of survey method for measuring cultivation effects. *Human Communication Research, 33*, 64–80.

Shrum, L. J., Burroughs, J. E., & Rindfleisch, A. (2004). A process model of consumer cultivation: The role of television is a function of the type of judgment. In L. J. Shrum (Ed.), *The psychology of entertainment media: Blurring the lines between entertainment and persuasion* (pp. 177–191). Mahwah, NJ: Erlbaum.

Shrum, L. J., Burroughs, J. E., & Rindfleisch, A. (2005). Television's cultivation of material values. *Journal of Consumer Research, 32*, 473–479.

Shrum, L. J., & O'Guinn, T. C. (1993). Processes and effects in the construction of social reality: Construct accessibility as an explanatory variable. *Communication Research, 20*, 436–471.

Shrum, L. J., O'Guinn, T. C., Semenik, R. J., & Faber, R. J. (1991). Processes and effects in the construction of normative consumer beliefs: The role of television. In R. H. Holman & M. R. Solomon (Eds.), *Advances in consumer research* (Vol. 18, pp. 755–763). Provo, UT: Association for Consumer Research.

Shrum, L. J., Wyer, R. S., & O'Guinn, T. C. (1998). The effects of television consumption on social perceptions: The use of priming procedures to investigate psychological processes. *Journal of Consumer Research, 24*, 447–458.

Srull, T. K., & Wyer, R. S. (1979). The role of category accessibility in the interpretation of information about persons: Some determinants and implications. *Journal of Personality and Social Psychology, 37*, 1660–1672.

Tamborini, R., Zillmann, D., & Bryant, J. (1984). Fear and victimization: Exposure to television and perceptions of crime and fear. In R. N. Bostrom (Ed.), *Communication yearbook 8* (pp. 492–518). Beverly Hills: Sage.

Turner, C., & Berkowitz, L. (1972). Identification with film aggressor (covert role taking) and reactions to film violence. *Journal of Personality and Social Psychology, 21*, 256–264.

Tversky, A., & Kahneman, D. (1973). Availability: A heuristic for judging frequency and probability. *Cognitive Psychology*, 5, 207–232.

Wober, M., & Gunter, B. (1988). *Television and social control*. Aldershot, England: Avebury.

Wyer, R. S. (1980). The acquisition and use of social knowledge: Basic postulates and representative research. *Personality and Social Psychology Bulletin*, 6, 558–573.

Wyer, R. S. (2004). *Social comprehension and judgment: The role of situation models, narratives, and implicit theories*. Mahwah, NJ: Erlbaum.

Wyer, R. S., & Hartwick, J. (1984). The recall and use of belief statements as bases for judgments: Some determinants and implications. *Journal of Experimental Social Psychology*, *20*, 65–85.

Wyer, R. S., & Radvansky, G. A. (1999). The comprehension and validation of social information. *Psychological Review*, *106*, 89–118.

Wyer, R. S., & Srull, T. K. (1980). The processing of social stimulus information: A conceptual integration. In R. Hastie, E. B. Ebbessen, T. M. Ostrom, R. S. Wyer, D. L. Hamilton, & D. E. Carlston (Eds.), *Person memory: The cognitive basis of social perception* (pp. 227–300). Hillsdale, NJ: Erlbaum.

Wyer, R. S., & Srull, T. K. (1989). *Memory and cognition in its social context*. Hillsdale, NJ: Erlbaum.

Zillmann, D. (1980). Anatomy of suspense. In P. H. Tannenbaum (Ed.), *The entertainment functions of television* (pp. 133–163). Hillsdale, NJ: Erlbaum.

Zillmann, D. (1983). Transfer of excitation in emotional behavior. In J. T. Cacioppo & R. E. Petty (Eds.), *Social psychophysiology: A sourcebook* (pp. 215–242). New York: Guilford.

Zillmann, D. (2002). Exemplification theory of media influence. In J. Bryant & D. Zillmann (Eds.), *Media effects: Advances in theory and research* (2nd ed., pp. 69–95). Mahwah, NJ: Erlbaum.

Zillmann, D., & Brosius, H. (2000). *Exemplification in communication: The influence of case reports on the perception of issues*. Mahwah, NJ: Erlbaum.

Zillmann, D., & Bryant, J. (1982). Pornography, sexual callousness, and the trivialization of rape. *Journal of Communication*, *32*(4), 10–21.

5

MEDIA PRIMING

An Updated Synthesis

David R. Roskos-Ewoldsen
University of Alabama

Beverly Roskos-Ewoldsen
University of Alabama

Francesca Dillman Carpentier
University of North Carolina

At a very general level, media priming refers to the short-term impact of exposure to the media on subsequent judgments or behaviors. Of course, what constitutes "short-term" varies depending on the research domain. In the last edition of this volume, we argued that the research on media priming had shifted its focus from whether media priming exists to testing of specific theories, and that this was a valuable trend because of the lack of clear theoretical models at that time (Roskos-Ewoldsen, Roskos-Ewoldsen, & Carpentier, 2002). While this shift in focus was accurate in our previous chapter, more recently research has tended to focus more on the different contexts in which priming occurs. So, for example, the research on priming violence and priming has shifted from a focus on TV and movies as a source of priming to a focus on video games as a source. Likewise, political priming has focused on how movies, TV series, and TV comedy can result in political priming effects. Finally, the impact of media priming of racial stereotypes has emerged as a major research focus in this area. So, the research on media priming has gone from a focus on whether media priming exists to how media priming works to how widespread a phenomenon media priming is. In this chapter we discuss three areas of research on media priming. Then we discuss theoretical models of priming. We conclude by continuing the argument we raised in the last edition, that traditional psychological explanations of priming (i.e., priming within network models of memory) has limited our progress towards understanding media priming. Instead, we suggest that a focus on how people comprehend media messages and the resulting mental representations provides a better explanation for media priming.

MEDIA PRIMING RESEARCH

Priming refers to the effect of some preceding stimulus or event on how we react, broadly defined, to some subsequent stimulus. As applied to the media, priming refers to the effects of the content of the media on people's later behavior or judgments related to the content that was processed. At one level, all media effects could be considered the result of media priming if one sticks with the definition that media priming refers to the effect of a previous exposure to the media on subsequent judgments or behavior. However, such a broad definition of priming serves no one's interests. Rather, it is important to understand that, with priming, the effect of the priming event is time bound. For example, in media priming focused on violence, studies often find that the priming effect fades quickly—often times within the time course of the experimental setting (Farrar & Krcmar, 2006; Josephson, 1987; Roskos-Ewoldsen, Klinger, & Roskos-Ewoldsen, 2007). For political priming, the effects are often argued to last for perhaps two months after media coverage of a politician has shifted. Further, it is important to understand that the ubiquitous nature of the media in our lives makes it a powerful tool for priming how we think and behave. Perhaps because of its nature, few media scholars have questioned whether media priming exists and, indeed, meta-analysis supports the existence of both political and violence media priming (Roskos-Ewoldsen et al., 2007), though the meta-analysis suggests they may be fundamentally different phenomena.

The meta-analysis of the media priming literature, using a loose definition of media, found only 63 published studies of media priming (Roskos-Ewoldsen et al., 2007). Representative studies from violence, political, and stereotype priming are described below to verify the existence of media priming.

Media Violence and Priming

Josephson (1987) investigated the priming effects of violent media on children's behavior. In this study, Josephson gathered measures of young boys' trait aggression from their teachers. The boys saw either a violent or a nonviolent television program, each of comparable excitement, likeability, and enjoyment value. The violent segment contained recurring images of walkie-talkies, whereas the nonviolent program contained no walkie-talkies. The walkie-talkies served as a cue for the violent television program, but not for the nonviolent program. Either before or after the television program, half the boys saw a 30-second nonviolent cartoon segment that had been edited to become increasingly static-ridden, eventually worsening to "snow." This cartoon segment was meant to frustrate the young viewers with its apparent technical malfunction.

After viewing their assigned programs, the boys were mock interviewed and then sent to the school gymnasium to play floor hockey. The boys then took turns playing hockey and were observed both on and off the court for signs of aggressive behavior, such as pushing other boys down, hitting other players with the hockey stick, or calling other boys abusive names. After three periods, each of three minutes of play, the boys were returned to the teachers.

Josephson (1987) found that violent television viewing primed boys who were high in trait aggressiveness to act more violently during initial sports activity (i.e., during the first period of play). This effect was heightened when violent programming was followed by frustration. However, this priming effect appeared to lessen with time, because violent programming and cues did not influence aggression in the later periods of play as strongly as in the initial period of play.

Recently, the research on media priming of violence has focused on video games. For example, Carnagey and Anderson (2005) tested the effects of reward and punishment in violent video games on participants' affect, cognitions, and behavior. In all three experiments, undergraduates were divided into three experimental conditions, each involving different versions of a competitive racing video game (Carmageddon 2). In one condition, killing pedestrians and racing opponents was punished, in the second condition killing pedestrians and racing opponents was rewarded, and in the last condition killing pedestrians and racing opponents was not possible. In the first experiment it was found that, even though more pedestrians were killed in the reward condition than the punishment condition, these two conditions generated similar levels of hostile affect and arousal. Interestingly, only ratings of frustration with the game and addiction to the game were predictors of aggressive affect. Across three studies, it was concluded that rewarding violence in video games can increase aggressive affect, the accessibility of aggressive cognitions, and aggressive behavior, and that these increases are not solely the result of the competitiveness in the games. Critical for a priming explanation of these findings, the results of the three experiments suggest that the priming of aggressive cognitions, not affect or arousal, is the primary method by which aggression is increased when playing violent video games. Other experimental research (e.g., Anderson & Murphy, 2003; Uhlmann & Swanson, 2004) supports the general conclusion that violent video games prime aggression, at least in the short term (see also Anderson, 2004; Anderson & Dill, 2000; Anderson & Murphy, 2003; cf. Bensley & Van Eenwyk, 2001; Williams & Skoric, 2005).

Consistent with this research, the meta-analysis by Roskos-Ewoldsen et al. (2007) found that depictions of violence or violence-related concepts (e.g., weapons) prime violence and aggression-related concepts in memory. The study of boys' aggression (Josephson, 1987) also suggested that priming may dissipate over time. Addressed next is the media priming literature regarding political news coverage.

Political News Coverage and Priming

Tests of political priming focus on the influence of media coverage of events on how people weight information when making judgments of politicians—typically the president. Historically, scholars in this area have focused on global judgments of presidential approval as the chief outcome variable. However, from a priming perspective, if the media have been predominately focused on domestic issues, then judgments of how well the president is doing specifically on domestic issues should weigh heavier in people's overall evaluations of the president, compared to the case where international news has been the predominant focus of the media. Importantly, political priming should focus on the kind of information people use to make judgments and how much that information is relied upon or weighted in making the judgment.

In a classic study, Krosnick and Kinder (1990) measured the priming effect of Iran-Contra media coverage on public evaluations of President Reagan's overall performance, using data from the 1986 National Election Study. In 1986, the Center for Political Studies at the University of Michigan conducted lengthy face-to-face interviews with adult respondents who were chosen randomly from the national population. Included in the interview of 1,086 citizens was a survey asking for evaluations of President Reagan, both overall and regarding his performance on foreign affairs, domestic policy, and other publicized issues. The interviews were conducted both before and after November 25, 1986, the date on which the Attorney General publicly confirmed the sale of arms to Iran and the subsequent distribution of the sale profits to the Contras.

The study focused on people's opinions regarding Reagan (i.e., overall performance, competence, and integrity) and his handling of foreign affairs (i.e., the Contras and

Central America, isolationism, and U.S. strength in foreign affairs) and domestic affairs (i.e., the national economy and aid to Blacks). Krosnick and Kinder (1990) compared responses obtained before and after the priming event—the Iran-Contra announcement—to see which foreign or domestic affairs issues contributed most to the respondents' overall performance evaluations of President Reagan. Before the priming event, domestic issues predicted overall evaluations of Reagan more than foreign affairs issues. After the priming event, the opposite was true; foreign affairs issues, especially those issues involving Central America, predicted the respondents' overall evaluations of Reagan more than domestic issues. This study shows that media coverage of political events can prime the information that people use when making judgments of presidential performance.

Recent research on political priming has focused on the boundaries of political priming. For example, research has recently demonstrated that movies (Holbert & Hansen, 2006), crime dramas (Holbrook & Hill, 2005), and late-night talk shows (Moy, Xenos, & Hess, 2005) can operate as political primes. Likewise, other studies have found that the media can prime evaluations of other politicians besides the president (Sheafer & Weimann, 2005; cf. McGraw & Ling, 2003). Further, simpler or familiar topics (such as general economic trends or issues of character) were more likely to prime evaluations of the president than more complex issues (such as domestic or international policies). However, there has been little or no evidence that the media prime the evaluations of different countries (Brewer, Graf, & Willnat, 2003).

In addition, there is a growing focus in research on political priming on the types of information that are primed by news coverage and what type of information people use when primed by the media (Kim & McCombs, 2007; Kim, Scheufele, & Shanahan, 2002). For example, political priming has generally been presented as a "hydraulic model" where the media prime people to use certain information at the expense of competing information. In a study of political priming in coverage of the first Gulf War, Kim (2005) found evidence that the types of information that are utilized are much more complex than the simple hydraulic model would suggest. Instead of a trade-off in the types of information that were used to make judgments of the president, Kim found that news coverage increased the variety of information that was used by people who pay careful attention to the media.

Media Priming and Stereotyping

The newest area of research on priming is media priming and stereotypes. A growing area of research concerns the potential for the media to prime various stereotypes, including both gender (Hansen & Hansen, 1988; Hansen & Krygowski, 1994) and racial stereotypes (Oliver, Ramasubramanian, & Kim, 2007; Power, Murphy, & Coover, 1996). This area of research has grown remarkably during the last six years with a focus on the impact of media primes on perceptions of both individuals in interpersonal settings and ambiguous individuals on the media, and on political judgments (Oliver et al., 2007).

Research involving perceptions of individuals in an interpersonal setting has used rock music videos as a prime. Exposure to rock music videos that portray stereotypical images of men and women resulted in more stereotypical impressions of a man and a woman interacting in a second videotape (Hansen & Hansen, 1988). In particular, participants perceived the woman as less dominant after exposure to these rock videos than after exposure to rock videos that included no stereotypical portrayals.

Also focusing on perceptions of individuals, Power et al. (1996) found that reading stereotypical information in a newsletter about either African Americans or women influenced judgments of later unrelated media events concerning the target group. For example, counter stereotypical depictions of women resulted in higher ratings in Anita Hill's credibility in the Clarence Thomas sexual harassment hearings, whereas stereotypical depictions lowered ratings of Hill's credibility (see also Brown Givens & Monahan, 2005; Monahan, Shtrulis, & Brown Givens, 2005) .

Regarding perceptions of ambiguous individuals, several studies found that the media prime rape myths, such as women enjoy being raped, which can influence later perceptions of the plaintiff and defendant in a rape trial (Intons-Peterson, B. Roskos-Ewoldsen, Thomas, Shirley, & Blut, 1989; Malamuth & Check, 1985). Specifically, men who ascribed to higher rape myths were less likely to believe that the man was guilty of the alleged rape, and if he were guilty, suggested less time in jail, compared to those who did not. An interesting area of research involves how representations of African Americans in the news influence people's attitudes toward various issues (Oliver et al., 2007). For example, Dixon (2006) found that participants had stronger support for the death penalty after viewing a newscast with African American suspects as compared to a newscast involving the same crimes but the race of the criminal was unspecified (see also Dixon, 2007). Likewise, Abraham and Appiah (2006) found that pictures of African Americans in newscasts about crime primed the racial stereotype of African Americans which resulted in more stereotypical judgments of African Americans regarding crime and educational policies (see also Richardson, 2005). Although these studies demonstrated that depictions of African Americans in the news could prime stereotypes which then influenced judgments of policy issues, Domke, McCoy, and Torres (1999) found that how a news story about a political issue (immigration) was framed (the story focused on the economic effects versus the ethics of immigration) could influence whether racial stereotypes of Hispanics were primed, despite the fact that Hispanics were not mentioned in the story. These activated stereotypes then influenced subsequent political judgments such as the effects of immigration on the economy (see also Domke, 2001).

In an intriguing extension of the stereotype priming literature to the health domain, several studies have shown that commercials can prime stereotypes. For example, Pechmann and Ratneshwar (1994) exposed adolescents to either anti-smoking advertisements that focused on how unattractive smoking was (e.g., smelly), cigarette advertisements, or control advertisements, all embedded within an age-appropriate magazine. After looking through the magazine, the adolescents read about a teenager who either smoked or did not smoke. Exposure to the anti-smoking advertisements resulted in more negative judgments of the teenager who smoked, compared with exposure to the other advertisements. Furthermore, the prime influenced judgments of the smoking teenager that were consistent with the participants' stereotypes of smokers (e.g., lacking common sense and immature) (see also Pechmann, Zhao, Goldberg, & Reibling, 2003).

As in the other domains, research in the stereotype domain indicates that the media can prime stereotypes and that these primed stereotypes influence how people are perceived. The research on media priming of stereotypes increases our confidence in the generality of the media as a prime because this research provides validation that the media can act as a prime in a unique research domain, and that a variety of media (e.g., advertisements, rock music videos, newsletters) can act as primes. Unfortunately, no research in this area has focused on behavioral manifestations of the media's priming of stereotypes, though the research by Pechmann and Ratneshwar (1994) suggests that these primed stereotypes influence adolescents' intention to smoke.

Conclusions

The research on media priming currently is disjointed. Clearly, the media act as a prime: a number of studies have demonstrated—and a meta-analysis has confirmed—that the media influence later judgments and behavior. In addition, the media operate as a prime in a number of different domains, through a number of different channels. In particular, the research on media priming demonstrates that the media can prime aggressive thoughts and feelings (Anderson, 1997; Anderson, Anderson, & Deuser, 1996; Bushman & Geen, 1990), aggressive behaviors (Bushman, 1995; Josephson, 1987), the information and criteria that we use in making judgments of the president (Iyengar & Kinder, 1987; Iyengar, Kinder, Peters, & Krosnick, 1984; Iyengar et al., 1982; Iyengar & Simon, 1993; Krosnick & Brannon, 1993; Krosnick & Kinder, 1990; Pan & Kosicki, 1997), and various stereotypes that influence how we make judgments of people from the stereotyped group (Hansen & Hansen, 1988; Hansen & Krygowski, 1994; Malamuth & Check, 1985; Pechmann, 2001; Power et al., 1996; Wyer et al., 1985).

Unfortunately, there has been little focus on understanding the cognitive mechanisms and processes underlying the media priming phenomenon. Further, the few explanations of the mechanisms by which the media acts as a prime vary from one domain to another. However, that may be necessary because the Roskos-Ewoldsen et al. (2007) meta-analysis suggests that violence priming and political priming may be different phenomena. Simply because both are called "priming" does not mean they are then the same phenomenon. In any case, there have been no attempts to integrate the research on media priming across the different areas. However, the models of media priming have a common reliance on the priming research from psychology. In the next section, we provide a brief background of the psychological research on priming and then discuss the current models of media priming within each domain.

MODELS OF PRIMING

Priming procedures were first used in cognitive psychology to explore the structure and representation of information within memory (e.g., Anderson, 1983). Network models of memory assumed that information is stored in memory in the form of nodes and that each node represents a concept. Furthermore, these nodes are connected to related nodes in memory by associative pathways. An additional assumption of network models of memory is that each node has an activation threshold. If a node's level of activation exceeds its threshold, then the node fires. When a node fires, it can influence the activation levels of other, associatively connected nodes. One consequence of spreading activation is that the related node now requires less additional activation for it to fire. The additional activation may accrue as a result of spreading activation from other related nodes, or it may result from environmental input. A typical behavioral outcome of spreading activation is that a judgment about or pronunciation of a word is faster when it is preceded by a related word than an unrelated word. A final assumption of network models of memory is that the activation level of a node will dissipate over time if no additional source of activation is present. Eventually, given no more activation, the activation level of the node returns to its resting state and is no longer considered to be activated. Using the procedure of priming a target word with a related or unrelated word was originally developed to test the assumptions of network models of memory, not as an explanation per se.

Research by both cognitive and social psychologists has demonstrated two important characteristics of priming. First, the extent of a prime's effect on a target behavior or thought is a dual function of the *intensity* and the *recency* of the prime (see the synapse model of priming, Higgins, Bargh, & Lombardi, 1985). The intensity of a prime refers to either the frequency of the prime (e.g., a single exposure vs. five exposures in quick succession) or the duration of the prime. Higher intensity primes produce larger priming effects, and these effects dissipate more slowly than lower intensity primes (see Higgins et al., 1985). Recency simply refers to the time lag between the prime and the target. Recent primes produce larger priming effects than temporally distant primes.

A second important characteristic of priming is that the effects of a prime fade with time. In lexical decision tasks (i.e., deciding whether the target is a word or a nonword), the effect of the prime usually fades within 700 milliseconds (Fazio, Sanbonmatsu, & Powell, 1986; Neely, 1977). In tasks that involve judgments or evaluations of a social stimulus, the effect of the prime also fades with time, though the effect appears to fade more slowly (Srull & Wyer, 1979, 1980). In these experiments, the priming effect can last up to 15 or 20 minutes, and possibly up to one hour (Srull & Wyer, 1979). Srull and Wyer (1979, 1980) found evidence of priming effects influencing judgments after 24 hours. However, we are aware of no replications of this latter effect. Most research on the influence of priming on subsequent judgments involves a maximum delay of 15 to 20 minutes. As mentioned previously, priming effects are consistent at these time delays.

Along these lines, it is important to differentiate priming effects, which temporarily increase the accessibility of a concept from memory, from chronic accessibility. Chronic accessibility refers to concepts that are always highly accessible from memory (see research by Bargh, Bond, Lombardi, & Tota, 1986; Fazio et al., 1986; Higgins, King, & Mavin, 1982). In the attitudinal domain, someone's attitude toward cockroaches is probably chronically accessible from memory. On the other hand, someone's attitude toward Tibetan food is probably not chronically accessible. Chronically accessible concepts can be primed so that they are temporarily even more accessible from memory (Bargh et al., 1986; Roskos-Ewoldsen et al., 2007). Nevertheless, without some form of reinforcement, even chronically accessible concepts eventually become less accessible across time (Grant & Logan, 1993).

Returning to the characteristics of priming, Roskos-Ewoldsen et al. (2007) investigated whether more intense primes produce larger priming effects, and whether the priming effect fades across time. First, none of the studies included in the meta-analysis directly tested the time course of priming effects. No study manipulated the time between the media violence prime and aggressive behavior to determine if aggressive behavior decreases at longer intervals from the media prime. Nevertheless, Roskos-Ewoldsen et al. (2007) found that, across all media priming studies, media priming effects appear to fade with time. However, the decrease in media priming effects was not statistically significant. Second, none of the studies directly tested the effect of prime intensity on later aggression. The meta-analysis provided mixed support for the supposition that media primes should become stronger when they are of greater intensity. For example, media primes that lasted 5 to 20 minutes in length had stronger effects than did media primes that were less than 5 minutes in length. On the other hand, media priming effects that resulted from media campaigns (e.g., coverage of the Gulf War), which were arguably of the longest duration (highest intensity), were significantly smaller than the priming effects from shorter duration (less intense) media primes. However, the lag between the priming event and the measure of the primes' effect was substantially longer in the campaign studies than in the other media priming studies, so there is a confound because of the lag between the priming event and the measurement of the prime's effect.

More recently, Carpentier, Roskos-Ewoldsen, and Roskos-Ewoldsen (2008) tested time course and prime intensity in the context of political priming. In this study, students read a historical sketch of President Ronald Reagan. Half of the participants were then asked to give impressions of Reagan immediately after reading the article, and half after approximately 30 minutes. Then participants completed the task involving ratings of President Reagan. The critical outcome involved how well students' evaluations of Reagan's economic policies predicted their overall evaluation of the former President. Evaluations of Reagan's economic policies were predictive of the overall evaluation, but generally the strength of the relation depended on the time course. The relation between judgments of Reagan's economic policy and his overall evaluation was weaker after a delay, particularly for participants who read the version that was favorable to Reagan, compared with the immediate judgments.

Reanalysis of priming effects for the 1991 Gulf War also suggest that there are short term effects of political priming that are distinct from the longer term effects, which supports the importance of considering the time course between the priming event and the judgment (Althaus & Kim, 2006; Kim, 2005).

Overall, several lines of research implicate the importance of the priming time course. The meta-analysis (Roskos-Ewoldsen et al., 2007) provided evidence that media priming of long and short duration may differ in terms of the mechanisms underlying priming. Likewise, Carpentier et al.'s (2008) findings and the reanalysis of the priming effects found for the Gulf War also suggest that models of media priming need to include time as a critical variable. Therefore, for models of media priming to be adequate, they need to incorporate time and should probably also include prime intensity. Of course, they must also be able to explain existing media priming results. For example, political priming effects last considerably longer than the typical priming effects found in psychological experiments (Iyengar & Simon, 1993; Krosnick & Brannon, 1993; Pan & Kosicki, 1997; Roskos-Ewoldsen et al., 2007). In the next section, we discuss the current models in each domain, with a focus on their ability to incorporate the two characteristics of media priming (time course and prime intensity) and to explain the media priming results.

Models of Media Violence Priming

One of the most prominent explanations of the consequences of media violence is Berkowitz's (1984, 1990, 1994, 1997) neo-associationistic model. Berkowitz's model draws heavily from network models of priming. The model hypothesizes that depictions of violence in the media activate hostility- and aggression-related concepts in memory. The activation of these concepts in memory increases the likelihood that a person will engage in aggressive behaviors and that others' behavior will be interpreted as aggressive or hostile. Without further activation, however, the activation levels of these hostile and aggressive concepts, and their associated likelihood of influencing aggressive behavior, fades with time.

Anderson (1997) proposed as an extension of Berkowitz's (1984) neo-associationistic model the general affective aggression model (or GAAM). This model incorporates affect and arousal into a network framework, and introduces a three-stage process by which situations influence aggressive behavior and affect. In the first stage, situational variables, such as pain, frustration, or depictions of violence, prime aggressive cognitions (e.g., hostile thoughts and memories) and affect (e.g., hostility, anger). These conditions result in increased arousal. In the second stage, the primed cognitions and affect, in conjunction with the increased arousal, influence *primary appraisal*. Primary appraisal involves the automatic interpretation of the situation (Fazio & Williams, 1986; Houston & Fazio, 1989) and of one's arousal in that situation (Fazio, Zanna, & Cooper, 1979; Schachter & Singer, 1962; Zanna & Cooper, 1974). The final stage of the model involves *secondary appraisals*, which are more effortful, controlled appraisals of the situation, and involve a more thoughtful consideration of various behavioral alternatives to the situation. This final stage can correct or override the primary appraisal (Gilbert, 1991; Gilbert, Tafarodi, & Malone, 1993).

Berkowitz's (1984, 1990, 1994, 1997) neo-associationistic model and Anderson's (1997) GAAM explain many of the findings of the research on priming and media violence. Both models predict that media violence will temporarily increase aggressive thoughts (Anderson et al., 1996; Bushman, 1998; Bushman & Geen, 1990), and aggressive behaviors (Bushman, 1995; Josephson, 1987). In addition, the affective aggression model predicts that hot temperatures, the presence of weapons, and competition will increase aggressive thoughts and affect (Anderson et al., 1995; Anderson et al., 1996; Anderson & Morrow, 1995). Finally, both models specifically predict that the effects of media priming will fade with time.

Models of Political Priming

Until recently, the theoretical mechanisms by which the media prime evaluations of the President have been largely unspecified. The first attempt used the availability heuristic to explain the effects of media coverage on political priming effects (Iyengar & Simon, 1993). According to this explanation, media coverage of an issue influences which exemplars are accessed from memory when people make judgments of the President. However, the availability explanation has not been well developed within the political priming domain and has not been subjected to any empirical tests within this domain.

Only one model of political priming has been developed sufficiently to explain the political priming results (Price & Tewksbury, 1997; Scheufele & Tewksbury, 2007). Similar to Berkowitz's (1984) neo-associationistic model, Price and Tewksbury's model of political priming is based on network models of memory and the role that the media play in increasing the accessibility of information from memory.[1] As discussed earlier, network models maintain that both chronic and temporary accessibility of constructs influences their likelihood of firing. In addition, Price and Tewksbury incorporate the *applicability* of information into their model of political priming. Applicability refers to deliberate judgments of the relevance of information to the current situation. Clearly, if primed information is not relevant, it will not be used when making political judgments. Within Price and Tewksbury's model, constructs that are activated by the media and judged as applicable to the current situation influence how the message is framed or interpreted. On the other hand, those constructs that are activated by the media and judged as not applicable to the current situation are not brought into working memory, but the activation of these constructs by the media means that they may act as a prime.

The research by Carpentier et al. (2008) is generally consistent with Price and Tewksbury's model of political priming. The one difficulty is the time frame of the priming effect. Carpentier et al. found that the effect of the prime was fading within 30 minutes after exposure. Likewise, Althaus and Kim (2006) also found short-term effects of the prime, which suggests that the short-term effects had dissipated within 24 hours of the media exposure. Although these time frames are consistent with Price and Tewksbury's model, they are difficult to reconcile with much of the political priming literature that looks at effects of exposure that last for several weeks. Price and Tewksbury's model can explain these long-term priming effects by resorting to assuming that continued media coverage makes the concepts chronically accessible. However, whether long-term coverage has this effect has not been demonstrated. In the next section, we will briefly present a model that we think incorporates Price and Tewksbury's model, but provides a clearer explanatory framework for the long-term effects of political priming.

As a final note, it is perhaps unfortunate that the cognitive/social priming research is cited as support in the political realm, because the phenomenon does not fit the characteristics of priming. It is more likely that the frequent and repeated stories on a particular issue (e.g., the Gulf War) increases the *chronic* accessibility of the information (Lau, 1989; Roskos-Ewoldsen, 1997; Roskos-Ewoldsen et al., 2007; Shrum, 1999; Shrum & O'Guinn, 1993). Rather than calling this phenomenon political priming, perhaps it would be better if we referred to it as political cultivation.

MENTAL MODELS: AN ALTERNATIVE FRAMEWORK FOR UNDERSTANDING MEDIA PRIMING

At one level, the theoretical development that has occurred in the area of media priming is impressive. There are currently two models that have been proposed to explain the cognitive processes that result in media priming: Anderson et al.'s (1995) affective aggression model and Price and Tewksbury's (1997) network model of political priming. Both of these models rely directly on network models of memory to explain media priming. Further, current research is beginning to test the assumptions of these models. For example, there has been extensive research on investigating the assumption that violent media prime violent constructs. Other research that directly tests the network models of political priming will surely follow.

Despite the commonalities across these network theories, their domains differ too much to afford a single theory of media priming. Further, neither model has been applied to stereotype priming. For example, GAAM's (Anderson et al., 1995) reliance on network models for explaining affective priming is problematic because recent research has seriously questioned the ability of network models to explain affective priming (Franks, Roskos-Ewoldsen, Bilbrey, & Roskos-Ewoldsen, 1999; Klinger, Burton, & Pitts, 2000). In addition, a unique feature of this model is that it incorporates secondary appraisals that can override the effect of the priming events on subsequent behavior. Clearly, this is a necessary addition to the model because it allows the model to explain how the priming of aggressive cognitions and affect does not always result in aggressive behavior. However, it is unclear how this component of the model would apply to political priming.

In our view, network models of media priming provide a starting point for understanding the effects of the media on subsequent judgments and behavior. However, we believe that network models need to be subsumed within a larger theoretical framework to explain adequately the phenomena that these models are attempting to explain. Below, we propose such a theoretical framework, one that focuses on comprehension processes and the resulting mental representations, to explain media priming effects.

Priming, as conceptualized by network models of memory, clearly occurs with the media. Commercials prime concepts, and this priming can influence the interpretation of other commercials or the show that the commercials were placed within (Yi, 1990a, 1990b). Likewise, watching a violent movie clip speeds the time it takes participants to pronounce aggression-related words, compared to participants who watched a violence-free movie clip (Anderson, 1997). Both of these findings are consistent with network models of priming. However, the phenomena of interest to media scholars studying priming (e.g., violent media influencing aggressive behavior, political coverage influencing what information is used to make judgments of the president, stereotyped portrayals of African Americans influencing judgments of other African Americans) cannot easily be explained by network-based theories of media priming. At a basic level, the priming effect that network models of memory address dissipates too quickly to explain many of the media priming effects. Of course, the time course issue can be addressed by assuming, as Price and Tewksbury (1997) do, that media portrayals increase the chronic accessibility of constructs and it is the chronic accessibility of the constructs that results in the media effects that are being studied (see also Arpan, Rhodes, & Roskos-Ewoldsen, 2007; Fazio & Roskos-Ewoldsen, 2005; Shrum, 1999; Shrum & O'Guinn, 1993). Although we believe that chronic accessibility is important (e.g., Arpan et al., 2007; Roskos-Ewoldsen, 1997; Roskos-Ewoldsen & Fazio, 1992a, 1992b, 1997), we propose that the phenomena of priming and of chronic accessibility should be incorporated into a larger theoretical frame that involves mental models of memory.

Consider political priming. Most people have little or no direct contact with the president of the United States and little or no direct contact with the events that the media are reporting on. The vast majority of Americans were not in the Middle East during the first Gulf War, which occurred during the first President Bush's term in office. Rather, people learned about these events from the media. Likewise, fortunately, most people do not have direct experience with murder, bombings, automatic weapons, and so forth. Again, information about these events is acquired via the media. At a very basic level, then, this information is acquired through the process of comprehending media stories. How the stories are comprehended influences the mental representations that are then stored in memory (Roskos-Ewoldsen, Davies, & Roskos-Ewoldsen, 2004). On the surface, comprehending a narrative, listening to a story teller, reading a book, having a conversation, or watching a movie appears to be a relatively simple matter. We see an image, hear or read words, and retrieve meanings from memory. However, each of these processes is complex and is only part of the mental work of comprehension. Many cognitive psychologists maintain that a basic component of the comprehension process involves the construction of a mental model (e.g. van Dijk & Kintsch, 1983; Zwann & Radvansky, 1998).

A mental model is a dynamic mental representation of a situation, event or object (van Dijk & Kintsch, 1983). We may use these mental models as a way to process, organize, and comprehend incoming information (Radvansky, Zwann, Federico, & Franklin, 1998; Zwann & Radvansky, 1998), make social judgments (Wyer & Radvansky, 1999), formulate predictions and inferences (Magliano, Dijkstra, & Zwann, 1996), or generate descriptions and explanations of how a system operates (Rickheit

& Sichelschmidt, 1999). A key notion of the mental model approach is that there is some correspondence between an external entity and our constructed mental representations of that entity (Johnson-Laird, 1983, 1989; Norman, 1983). An important element of mental models is the sense that they are "runable" (Williams, Hollan, & Stevens, 1983) in that elements of the model can be changed to see how other elements of the mental model or relationships between elements of the model would change.

One question that is often raised about mental models is how they differ from schemas. This is an important question because mental models and schemas are highly related. We and others have argued that mental models exist at many different levels (Roskos-Ewoldsen et al., 2002; Wyer & Radvansky, 1999; Zwann & Radvansky, 1998). However, we would argue that here there is a continuum of abstractness along which mental representations exist, from a situation model (least abstract) to a mental model to a schema (most abstract).

A situation model is a representation of a specific story or episode that has specific temporal and spatial constraints (Wyer, 2004). For example, a situation model of Rex Stout's (1948) story, *And Be a Villain*, takes place in 1949 in New York City and features the characters of Nero Wolfe, Archie Goodwin, Fritz, Madeline Fraser, and Deborah Koppel, among others. A mental model is a more abstract representation of a series of related stories. Like a situation model, a mental model has temporal and spatial constraints, but these constraints will typically be looser.

A mental model of a series of Rex Stout's Nero Wolfe stories would take place throughout the middle part of the 1900s and would be set primarily in and around New York City but include other parts of New York state, Washington, D.C., and so forth. Importantly, situation and mental models represent knowledge about some event or events. A schema is a more abstract representation that comprises knowledge of something (D'Andrade, 1995; Markman, 1999; Shore, 1996). For example, a schema for "mysteries" would include no temporal or spatial information. Rather, the schema would include information about what the important elements of a typical mystery are (e.g., a crime, an unknown perpetrator, someone trying to solve the crime, the possibility the crime will not be solved, etc.). Of course, astute readers will note that our example of a schema—the mystery schema—includes temporal information such as the crime has to occur before it is solved. However, although there may be temporal or spatial information about events within a schema, the schema itself is not contextualized within a specific time or place in the same way that a situation or mental model is situated.

Although there are a number of dimensions along which schemas, mental models, and situation models differ, three that we feel are critical are the degree of abstractness, with schemas being the most abstract and situation models the most concrete; the degree of contextualization, with schemas being the least contextualized and situation models the most contextualized; and the degree to which the structure is dynamic or mutable, with schemas being the least mutable and situation models the most mutable.

These characteristics of situation models and mental models are important enough to stress further. The first characteristic is that they are mutable. To return to the Nero Wolfe example, avid mystery readers could easily imagine substituting Sherlock Holmes in the place of Nero Wolfe and Watson in place of Archie (Nero Wolfe's sidekick) and envision what Holmes and Watson would do in the situation facing Wolfe and Archie. This flexibility is a critical component of situation and mental models. In other words, the components of a situation or mental model are interchangeable—much like building blocks can be used to construct various shapes (Wyer & Radvansky, 1999). This characteristic of models distinguishes them from other approaches to cognition, such as network models, or even schemas. Semantic networks, for instance, are static and rigid. Network models posit that knowledge is stored in nodes and, when stimulated, they activate closely related nodes. This results in the heightened accessibility of related exemplars. A mental model or situation model may be activated by similar processes, but once brought to mind these models interface with other knowledge structures in a much more dynamic way. The mutability of situation and mental models is critical for developing inferences about the possible outcomes of the model or for determining how the model operates, which involves "running" simulations using dynamic mental representations.

Thus, the second characteristic is that they are dynamic. That is, they are subject to user control and may be manipulated to generate inferences, test different scenarios, or draw conclusions about information that may or may not be contained in a text or situation. For example, movie viewers may use cinematic features—editing techniques, costumes, music, dialogue, etc.—as cues to make predictions about future events or to make inferences about previous events. When anomalous information is foregrounded by filmmakers, viewers attempt to find out why such information is presented. These predictions are generated through the manipulation of situation models that viewers create as they watch a film (Magliano et al., 1996).

Further, as people comprehend media stories, they construct situation models of the specific stories—models that are contextualized. In addition, they construct mental models of the larger events. The resulting mental models are then used to understand future stories as well as to generate inferences about future events and the relationships between various elements of the mental model as well as guide people's understanding of elements of the larger world that are related to the mental model (Wyer & Radvansky, 1999). Consider the first Gulf War. As people attended to news stories about the Gulf War, they built mental representations about the events in and surrounding the situation in the Gulf, including situation models of specific stories and a mental model of the larger situation. The mental model allowed people to develop a coherent understanding of the events and their relationships to the larger situation and to make predictions about future events (e.g., "A negotiated settlement is impossible because . . ."). Of course, an important element of mental models are the actors involved in the story (O'Brien & Albrecht, 1992; Zwann, Langston, & Graesser, 1995; Zwann & Radvansky, 1998), so President Bush would be an important component of the resulting mental model. Questions about President Bush would activate the mental model, which would then play a role in judgments about President Bush's performance.

A third characteristic of mental models is that they are situated in time. That is, they are contextualized. As time passes, specific mental models will be less applicable to a current situation, and this explains why mental models of an event are only utilized when making judgments for a while and then will fade. But, importantly, the time frame for the applicability of a mental model is much different than the time frame for priming the activation of a node within a network model of memory. That is, a mental model may be applied even after a few days or weeks.

At this point, there have been no direct tests of the mental models explanation of priming effects. However, the findings from several studies are consistent with the hypothesis that mental models are developed to represent media stories (Lee, Roskos-Ewoldsen, & Roskos-Ewoldsen, in press). For example, we have tested the mental models framework with framing effects (Kim, Roskos-Ewoldsen, & Roskos-Ewoldsen, 2007). In this study, participants who focused on the characteristic of a candidate and participants who focused on the issue being discussed by a candidate read a positively or negatively framed ad from a candidate sentence by sentence. After each sentence they rated all the concepts found in the ad in terms of how much the sentence made them think of each concept. From these ratings we created four landscapes of activation, one for characteristic-oriented participants who read a positively framed ad, one for characteristic-oriented participants who read a negatively framed ad, and the same for issue-oriented participants. These landscapes differed from each other, suggesting that these participants' mental models and thus their comprehension of the candidate's advertisement differed. The landscapes of activation were then used to predict recall of the concepts in the ads by another group of participants that was also divided into characteristic-oriented and issue-oriented participants. The results showed that landscapes created by characteristic-oriented participants predicted recall of the ads by characteristic-oriented readers. The same was true for issue-oriented participants: the landscapes created by issue-oriented participants predicted recall of the ads by issue-oriented participants. However, the relation between positively framed landscapes and positively framed ad recall, and between negatively framed landscapes and negatively framed ad recall, was much stronger than that for characteristic- and issue-oriented ads. These findings showed that differently framed political advertisements are comprehended differently, suggesting that it is the mental model that is created while reading the ad that produces the differential memory for positively and negatively framed advertisements. The mental models that occurred as a result of the comprehension process did an excellent job of predicting readers' memory for the political advertisements.

The mental models approach toward understanding political priming is also found in other literature. In particular, several studies have found that young children develop mental models of violence at a young age, with minimal exposure to violent programming (Krcmar & Curtis, 2003; Krcmar & Hight, 2007). Wyer and Radvansky (1999) hypothesize that the mental models that are developed when watching TV violence can translate into violent behavior.

In addition to research indicating that people develop mental models of media stories, recent research has also pointed to the complexity of the information that is used when making evaluations of the President. As Kim (2005) noted, network models of political priming assume a hydraulic model of information use when priming is operating. Specifically, the information that is primed will be used when making evaluations, whereas other domains of information are either ignored or weighted less. However, in addition to finding evidence of short-term priming effects, Kim (2005) demonstrated that priming actually increased the amount of information—both congruent and incongruent with the prime—that is used when making judgments.

Likewise, Althaus and Kim (2006) demonstrated that political priming operates from both short-term and long-term effects of the media coverage. Both of these studies suggest a more complex mental representation of information from media stories than is theorized by network models of memory. We concur that these studies clearly demonstrate that more complex representations result from media stories than is suggested by network models. We also believe that the traditional models of the judgmental processes accompanying media priming are too simple. In contrast, a mental models perspective can accommodate these findings easily through its three characteristics: mental models are mutable, dynamic, and contextualized. It is now time to test these characteristics in terms of their effects on thoughts, beliefs, attitudes, affect, and behavior.

CONCLUSION

Media priming is a well established phenomenon (Roskos-Ewoldsen et al., 2007). Recent research has explored the boundaries of media priming. For example, traditional political priming research had limited itself to exploring the effects of news coverage on the information that people use when judging the president. Recent research has explored both the effects of political priming on judgments of other entities besides the president (Sheafer & Weimann, 2005), as well as whether different types of media offerings, including political comedy shows or politically oriented documentaries, can prime presidential evaluations (Holbert & Hansen, 2006; Holbrook & Hill, 2005; Moy, Xenos, & Hess, 2005). Likewise, extensive research has been conducted looking at the potential of the media to prime gender and racial stereotypes (Brown Givens & Monahan, 2005; Dixon, 2006, 2007; Hansen & Hansen, 1988; Monahan et al., 2005; Oliver et al., 2007).

This new generation of research exploring the boundaries of media priming effects is important because it helps establish both the importance of the phenomenon and the external validity of this research domain. However, we agree with Scheufele and Tewksbury (2007) in that there has not been enough emphasis on the internal validity of the political priming effect. For example, are political priming, the priming potential of violent content, and racial/gender priming all the same phenomenon? The research on violent priming tends to involve very short time lags between the media prime and the measured effect of the prime. However, the work on political priming often includes delays of several weeks between the media prime and the measured effect of that prime (Roskos-Ewoldsen et al., 2007). These differences in the parameters of these two effects suggest that they are different phenomena. Further, although there has been an increased focus on research investigating the underlying theoretical mechanisms of political priming (e.g., Carpentier et al., 2007) more research is obviously needed in this area. We have come a long way in understanding the phenomenon of priming, yet we still have a long way to go.

Note

1 A study by Miller and Krosnick (2000), which rigorously tested the accessibility component of priming effects, found evidence that political priming was more likely to occur through deliberative processing. They argued that this deliberative processing runs counter to the predictions of network models because priming is typically conceived of as an automatic process. However, recent research on automaticity has demonstrated that automatic processing can lead to deliberative processing (Roskos-Ewoldsen, 1997; Roskos-Ewoldsen, Bichsel, & Hoffman, 2002; Roskos-Ewoldsen, Yu, & Rhodes, 2004).

References

Abraham, L., & Appiah, O. (2006). Framing news stories: The role of visual imagery in priming racial stereotypes. *Howard Journal of Communications*, *17*, 183–203.

Althaus, S. L., & Kim, Y. M. (2006). Priming effects in complex information environments: Reassessing the impact of news discourse on presidential approval. *Journal of Politics*, *68*, 960–976.

Anderson, C. A. (1997). Effects of violent movies and trait hostility on hostile feelings and aggressive thoughts. *Aggressive Behavior*, *23*, 161–178.

Anderson, C. A. (2004). An update on the effects of playing violent video games. *Journal of Adolescence*, *27*, 113–122.

Anderson, C. A., Anderson, K. B., & Deuser, W. E. (1996). Examining an affective aggression framework: Weapon and temperature effects on aggressive thoughts, affect, and attitudes. *Personality and Social Psychology Bulletin, 22*, 366–376.

Anderson, C. A., Deuser, W. E., & DeNeve, K. M. (1995). Hot temperatures, hostile affect, hostile cognition, and arousal: Tests of a general model of affective aggression. *Personality and Social Psychology Bulletin, 21*, 434–448.

Anderson, C. A., & Dill, K. E. (2000). Video games and aggressive thoughts, feelings, and behavior in the laboratory and in life. *Journal of Personality and Social Psychology, 78*, 772–790.

Anderson, C. A., & Morrow, M. (1995). Competitive aggression without interaction: Effects of competitive versus cooperative instructions on aggressive behavior in video games. *Personality and Social Psychology Bulletin, 21*, 1020–1030.

Anderson, C. A., & Murphy, C. R. (2003). Violent video games and aggressive behavior in young women. *Aggressive Behavior, 29*, 423–429.

Anderson, J. (1983). *The architecture of cognition.* Cambridge, MA: Harvard University Press.

Arpan, L., Rhodes, N., & Roskos-Ewoldsen, D. R. (2007). Accessibility, persuasion, and behavior. In D. R. Roskos-Ewoldsen & J. Monahan (Eds.), *Communication and social cognition: Theories and methods* (pp. 351–376). Mahwah, NJ: Erlbaum.

Bargh, J. A., Bond, R. N., Lombardi, W. J., & Tota, M. E. (1986). The additive nature of chronic and temporary sources of construct accessibility. *Journal of Personality and Social Psychology, 50*, 869–878.

Bensley, L. B., & Van Eenwyk, J. (2001). Video games and real-life aggression: Review of the literature. *Journal of Adolescent Health, 29*, 244–257.

Berkowitz, L. (1984). Some effects of thoughts on anti- and prosocial influences of media events: A cognitive-neoassociationistic analysis. *Psychological Bulletin, 95*, 410–427.

Berkowitz, L. (1990). On the formation and regulation of anger and aggression: A cognitive-neoassociationistic analysis. *American Psychologist, 45*, 494–503.

Berkowitz, L. (1994). Is something missing? Some observations prompted by the cognitive-neoassociationist view of anger and emotional aggression. In L. R. Huesmann (Ed.), *Aggressive behavior: Current perspectives* (pp. 35–57). New York: Plenum Press.

Berkowitz, L. (1997). Some thoughts extending Bargh's argument. In R. S. Wyer (Ed.), *The automaticity of everyday life: Advances in social cognition, volume 10* (pp. 83–92). Mahwah, NJ: Erlbaum.

Brewer, P. R., Graf, J., & Willnat, L. (2003). Priming or framing: Media influence on attitudes toward foreign countries. *Gazette: International Journal for Communication Studies, 65*, 493–508.

Brown Givens, S. M., & Monahan, J. L. (2005). Priming mammies, jezebels, and other controlling images: An examination of the influence of mediated stereotypes on perceptions of an African American woman. *Media Psychology, 7*, 87–106.

Bushman, B. J. (1995). Moderating role of trait aggressiveness in the effects of violent media on aggression. *Journal of Personality and Social Psychology, 69*, 950–960.

Bushman, B. J. (1998). Priming effects of media violence on the accessibility of aggressive constructs in memory. *Personality and Social Psychology Bulletin, 24*, 537–545.

Bushman, B. J., & Geen, R. G. (1990). Role of cognitive-emotional mediators and individual differences in the effects of media violence on aggression. *Journal of Personality and Social Psychology, 58*, 156–163.

Carnagey, N. L., & Anderson, C. A. (2005). The effects of reward and punishment in violent video games on aggressive affect, cognition, and behavior. *Psychological Science, 16*, 882–889.

Carpentier, F. D., Roskos-Ewoldsen, D. R., & Roskos-Ewoldsen, B. (2008). A test of the network models of political priming. *Media Psychology, 11*, 186–206.

D'Andrade, R. (1995). *The development of cognitive anthropology.* Cambridge: Cambridge University Press.

Dixon, T. L. (2006). Psychological reactions to crime news portrayals of Black criminals: Understanding the moderating roles of prior news viewing and stereotype endorsement. *Communication Monographs, 73*, 162–187.

Dixon, T. L. (2007). Black criminals and white officers: The effects of racially misrepresenting law breakers and law defenders on television news. *Media Psychology, 10*, 270–291.

Domke, D. (2001). Racial cues and political ideology: An examination of associative priming. *Communication Research, 28*, 772–801.

Domke, D., McCoy, K., & Torres, M. (1999). News media, racial perceptions, and political cognition. *Communication Research, 26*, 570–607.

Farrar, K., & Krcmar, M. (2006). Measuring state and trait aggression: A short, cautionary tale. *Media Psychology, 8*, 127–138.

Fazio, R. H., & Roskos-Ewoldsen, D. R. (2005). Acting as we feel: When and how attitudes guide behavior. In T. C. Brock and M. C. Green (Eds.), *The psychology of persuasion* (2nd ed.; pp. 41–62). New York: Allyn & Bacon.

Fazio, R. H., Sanbonmatsu, D. M., & Powell, M. C. (1986). On the automatic activation of attitudes. *Journal of Personality and Social Psychology, 50*, 229–238.

Fazio, R. H., & Williams, C. J. (1986). Attitude accessibility as a moderator of the attitude-perception and attitude behavior relations: An investigation of the 1984 presidential election. *Journal of Personality and Social Psychology, 51*, 505–514.

Fazio, R. H., Zanna, M. P., & Cooper, J. (1979). Dissonance and self-perception: An integrative view of each theory's proper domain of application. *Journal of Experimental Social Psychology, 13*, 464–479.

Franks, J. J., Roskos-Ewoldsen, D. R., Bilbrey, C. W., & Roskos-Ewoldsen, B. (1999). *Is attitude priming an artifact?* Unpublished data.

Gilbert, D. T. (1991). How mental systems believe. *American Psychologist, 46*, 107–119.

Gilbert, D. T., Tafarodi, R. W., & Malone, P. S. (1993). You can't not believe everything you read. *Journal of Personality and Social Psychology, 65*, 221–233.

Grant, S. C., & Logan, G. D. (1993). The loss of repetition priming and automaticity over time as a function of degree of initial learning. *Memory & Cognition, 21*, 611–618.

Hansen, C. H., & Hansen, R. D. (1988). How rock music videos can change what is seen when boy meets girl: Priming stereotypic appraisal of social interaction. *Sex Roles, 19*, 287–316.

Hansen, C. H., & Krygowski, W. (1994). Arousal-augmented priming effects: Rock music videos and sex object schemas. *Communication Research, 21*, 24–47.

Higgins, E. T., Bargh, J. A., & Lombardi, W. (1985). Nature of priming effects on categorization. *Journal of Experimental Psychology: Learning, Memory, & Cognition, 11*, 59–69.

Higgins, E. T., King, G. A., & Mavin, G. H. (1982). Individual construct accessibility and subjective impressions and recall. *Journal of Personality and Social Psychology, 43*, 35–47.

Holbert, R. L., & Hansen, G. J. (2006). Fahrenheit 9–11, need for closure and the priming of affective ambivalence. *Human Communication Research, 32*, 109–129.

Holbrook, R. A., & Hill, T. G. (2005). Agenda-setting and priming in prime time television: Crime dramas as political cues. *Political Communication, 22*, 277–295.

Houston, D. A., & Fazio, R. H. (1989). Biased processing as a function of attitude accessibility: Making objective judgments subjectively. *Social Cognition, 7*, 51–66.

Intons-Peterson, M. J., Roskos-Ewoldsen, B., Thomas, L., Shirley, M., & Blut, D. (1989). Will educational materials reduce negative effects of exposure to sexual violence? *Journal of Social and Clinical Psychology, 8*, 256–275.

Iyengar, S., & Kinder, D. R. (1987). *News that matters: Television and American opinion*. Chicago: The University of Chicago Press.

Iyengar, S., Kinder, D. R., Peters, M. D., & Krosnick, J. A. (1984). The evening news and presidential evaluations. *Journal of Personality and Social Psychology, 46*, 778–787.

Iyengar, S., Peters, M. D., & Kinder, D. R. (1982). Experimental demonstrations of the "not-so-minimal" consequences of television news programs. *American Political Science Review, 76*, 848–858.

Iyengar, S., & Simon, A. (1993). News coverage of the Gulf Crisis and public opinion: A study of agenda-setting, priming, and framing. *Communication Research, 20*, 365–383.

Johnson-Laird, P. N. (1983). *Mental models*. Cambridge, MA: Harvard University Press.

Johnson-Laird, P. N. (1989). Mental models. In M. I. Posner (Ed.), *Foundations of cognitive science* (pp. 469–499). Cambridge, MA: MIT Press.

Josephson, W. L. (1987). Television violence and children's aggression: Testing the priming, social script, and disinhibition predictions. *Journal of Personality and Social Psychology, 53*, 882–890.

Kim, K., & McCombs, M. (2007). New story descriptions and the public's opinions of political candidates. *Journalism & Mass Communication Quarterly, 84*, 299–314.

Kim, Y. M. (2005). Use and disuse of contextual primes in dynamic news environments. *Journal of Communication, 55*, 737–755.

Kim, K. S., Roskos-Ewoldsen, B., & Roskos-Ewoldsen, D. R. (2007). *Understanding the effects of message frames in political advertisements: A lesson from text comprehension*. Paper presented at the annual meeting of the International Communication Association, San Francisco, CA.

Kim, S., Scheufele, D. A., & Shanahan, J. (2002). Think about it this way: Attribute agenda-setting function of the press and the public's evaluation of a local issue. *Journalism & Mass Communication Quarterly, 79*, 7–25.

Klinger, M. R., Burton, P. C., & Pitts, S. (2000). Mechanisms of unconscious priming: I. Response competition, not spreading activation. *Journal of Experimental Psychology: Learning, Memory, and Cognition, 26*, 441–455.

Krcmar, M., & Curtis, S. (2003). Mental models: Understanding the impact of fantasy violence on children's moral reasoning. *Journal of Communication, 53*, 460–499.

Krcmar, M., & Hight, A. (2007). The development of aggressive mental models in young children. *Media Psychology, 10*, 250–269.

Krosnick, J. A., & Brannon, L. A. (1993). The impact of the Gulf War on the ingredients of presidential evaluations: multidimensional effects of political involvement. *American Political Science Review, 87*, 963–975.

Krosnick, J. A., & Kinder, D. R. (1990). Altering the foundations of support for the president through priming. *American Political Science Review, 84*, 497–512.

Lau, R. R. (1989). Construct accessibility and electoral choice. *Political Behavior, 11*, 5–32.

Lee, M., Roskos-Ewoldsen, B., & Roskos-Ewoldsen, D. R. (in press). Discourse processing during the comprehension of TV news stories. *Discourse Processes.*

Magliano, J. P., Dijkstra, K., & Zwann, R. A. (1996). Generating predictive inferences while viewing a movie. *Discourse Processes, 22*, 199–224.

Malamuth, N. M., & Check, J. V. P. (1985). The effects of aggressive pornography on beliefs in rape myths: Individual differences. *Journal of Research in Personality, 19*, 299–320.

Markman, A. B. (1999). *Knowledge Representation*. Mahwah, NJ: Erlbaum.

McGraw, K. M., & Ling, C. (2003). Media priming of president and group evaluations. *Political Communication, 20*, 23–40.

Miller, J. M., & Krosnick, J. A. (2000). News media impact on the ingredients of presidential evaluations: Politically knowledgeable citizens are guided by a trusted source. *American Journal of Political Science, 44*, 295–309.

Monahan, J. L., Shtrulis, I., & Brown Givens, S. (2005). Priming welfare queens and other stereotypes: The transference of media images into interpersonal contexts. *Communication Research Reports, 22*, 199–206.

Moy, P., Xenos, M. A., & Hess, V. K. (2005). Priming effects of late-night comedy. *International Journal of Public Opinion, 18*, 198–210.

Neely, J. H. (1977). Semantic priming and retrieval from lexical memory: Roles of inhibitionless spreading activation and limited-capacity attention. *Journal of Experimental Psychology: General, 106*, 225–254.

Norman, D. A. (1983). Some observations on mental models. In D. Gentner & A. L. Stevens (Eds.), *Mental models* (pp. 299–324). Mahwah, NJ: Erlbaum.

O'Brien, E. J., & Albrecht, J. E. (1992). Comprehension strategies in the development of a mental model. *Journal of Experimental Psychology: Learning, Memory, & Cognition, 18*, 777–784.

Oliver, M. B., Ramasubramanian, S., & Kim, J. (2007). Media and racism. In D. R. Roskos-Ewoldsen & J. Monahan (Eds.), *Communication and social cognition: Theories and methods* (pp. 273–292). Mahwah, NJ: Erlbaum.

Pan, Z., & Kosicki, G. M. (1997). Priming and media impact on the evaluations of the president's performance. *Communication Research, 24*, 3–30.

Pechmann, C. (2001). A comparison of health communication models: Risk learning versus stereotype priming. *Media Psychology, 3*, 189–210.

Pechmann, C., & Ratneshwar, S. (1994). The effects of anti-smoking and cigarette advertising on young adolescents' perceptions of peers who smoke. *Journal of Consumer Research, 21*, 236–251.

Pechmann, C., Zhao, G., Goldberg, M. E., & Reibling, E. T. (2003). What to convey in antismoking advertisements for adolescents? The use of protection motivation theory to identify effective message themes. *Journal of Marketing, 67*, 1–18.

Power, J. G., Murphy, S. T., & Coover, G. (1996). Priming prejudice: How stereotypes and counter-stereotypes influence attribution of responsibility and credibility among ingroups and out-groups. *Human Communication Research, 23*, 36–58.

Price, V., & Tewksbury, D. (1997). New values and public opinion: A theoretical account of media priming and framing. In G. A. Barnett & F. J. Boster (Eds.), *Progress in communication sciences: Advances in persuasion, Volume 13* (pp. 173–212). Greenwich, CT: Ablex Publishing.

Radvansky, G.A., Zwann, R. A., Federico, T., & Franklin, N. (1998). Retrieval from temporally organized situation models. *Journal of Experimental Psychology: Learning, Memory and Cognition, 24*, 1224–1237.

Richardson, J. D. (2005). Switching social identities: The influence of editorial framing on reader attitudes toward affirmative action and African Americans. *Communication Research, 32*, 503–528.

Rickheit, G., & Sichelschmidt, L. (1999). Mental models: some answers, some questions, some suggestions. In G. Rickheit and C. Habel (Eds.), *Mental models in discourse processing and reasoning* (pp. 9–40). New York: Elsevier.

Roskos-Ewoldsen, B., Davies, J., & Roskos-Ewoldsen, D. R. (2004). Implications of the mental models approach for cultivation theory. *Communications, 29*, 345–363.

Roskos-Ewoldsen, D. R. (1997). Attitude accessibility and persuasion: Review and a transactive model. In B. Burleson (Ed.), *Communication Yearbook 20* (pp. 185–225). Beverly Hills, CA: Sage.

Roskos-Ewoldsen, D. R., Bichsel, J., & Hoffman, K. (2002). The influence of accessibility of source likability on persuasion. *Journal of Experimental Social Psychology, 38*, 137–143.

Roskos-Ewoldsen, D. R., & Fazio, R. H. (1992a). The accessibility of source likability as a determinant of persuasion. *Personality and Social Psychology Bulletin, 18*, 19–25.

Roskos-Ewoldsen, D. R., & Fazio, R. H. (1992b). On the orienting value of attitudes: Attitude accessibility as a determinant of an object's attraction of visual attention. *Journal of Personality and Social Psychology, 63*, 198–211.

Roskos-Ewoldsen, D. R., & Fazio, R. H. (1997). The role of belief accessibility in attitude formation. *Southern Communication Journal, 62*, 107–116.

Roskos-Ewoldsen, D. R., Klinger, M., & Roskos-Ewoldsen, B. (2007). Media priming. In R. W. Preiss, B. M. Gayle, N. Burrell, M. Allen, & J. Bryant (Eds.), *Mass media theories and processes: Advances through meta-analysis* (pp. 53–80). Mahwah, NJ: Erlbaum.

Roskos-Ewoldsen, D. R., Roskos-Ewoldsen, B., & Carpentier, F. D. (2002). Media priming: A synthesis. In J. Bryant and D. Zillmann (Eds.), *Media Effects: Advances in theory and research* (2nd ed., pp. 97–120). Hillsdale, NJ: Erlbaum.

Roskos-Ewoldsen, D. R., Yu, H. J., & Rhodes, N. (2004). Fear appeal messages affect accessibility of attitudes toward the threat and adaptive behaviors. *Communication Monographs, 71*, 49–69.

Schachter, S., & Singer, S. (1962). Cognitive, social, and physiological determinants of the emotional state. *Psychological Review, 69*, 379–399.

Scheufele, D. A., & Tewksbury, D. (2007). Models of media effects. *Journal of Communication, 57*, 9–20.

Sheafer, T., & Weimann, G. (2005). Agenda-building, agenda-setting, priming, individual voting intentions, and the aggregate results: An analysis of four Israeli elections. *Journal of Communication, 55*, 347–365.

Shore, B. (1996). *Culture in Mind*. New York: Oxford University Press.

Shrum L. J., (1999). The relationship of television viewing with attitude strength and extremity: Implications for the cultivation effect. *Media Psychology, 1*, 3–25.

Shrum, L. J., & O'Guinn, T. C. (1993). Processes and effects in the construction of social reality. *Communication Research, 20*, 436–471.

Srull, T. K., & Wyer, R. S. (1979). The role of category accessibility in the interpretation of information about persons: Some determinants and implications. *Journal of Personality and Social Psychology, 37*, 1660–1672.

Srull, T. K., & Wyer, R. S. (1980). Category accessibility and social perception: Some implications for the study of person memory and interpersonal judgment. *Journal of Personality and Social Psychology, 38*, 841–856.

Stout, R. (1948). *And be a villain*. New York: Bantam Books.

Uhlmann, E., & Swanson, J. (2004). Exposure to violent video games increases automatic aggressiveness. *Journal of Adolescence, 27*, 41–52.

van Dijk, T. A., & Kintsch, W. (1983). *Strategies of discourse comprehension*. New York: Academic Press.

Williams, D., & Skoric, M. (2005). Internet fantasy violence: A test of aggression in an online game. *Communication Monographs, 72*, 217–233.

Williams, M. D., Hollan, J. D., & Stevens, A. L. (1983). Human reasoning about a simple physical system. In D. Gentner & A. L. Stevens (Eds.), *Mental models* (pp. 131–153). Hillsdale, NJ: Erlbaum.

Wyer, R. S., Jr., Bodenhausen, G. V., & Gorman, T. F. (1985). Cognitive mediators of reactions to rape. *Journal of Personality and Social Psychology, 48*, 324–338.

Wyer, R. S., Jr., & Radvansky, G. A. (1999). The comprehension and validation of social information. *Psychological Review, 106*, 89–118.

Wyer, R. S. (2004). *Social comprehension and judgment: The role of situation models, narratives, and implicit theories*. Mahwah, NJ: Erlbaum.

Yi, Y. (1990a). Cognitive and affective priming effects of the context for print advertisements. *Journal of Advertising, 19*, 40–48.

Yi, Y. (1990b). The effects of contextual priming in print advertisements. *Journal of Consumer Research, 17*, 215–222.

Zanna, M. P., & Cooper, J. (1974). Dissonance and the pill: An attribution approach to studying the arousal properties of dissonance. *Journal of Personality and Social Psychology, 29*, 703–709.

Zwann, R. A., Langston, M. C., & Graesser, A. C. (1995). The construction of situation models in narrative comprehension: An event-indexing model. *Psychological Science, 6*, 292–297.

Zwann, R. A., & Radvansky, G. A. (1998). Situation models in language comprehension and memory. *Psychological Bulletin, 123*, 162–185.

6

SOCIAL COGNITIVE THEORY OF MASS COMMUNICATION

Albert Bandura
Stanford University

Because of the influential role the mass media play in society, understanding the psychosocial mechanisms through which symbolic communication influences human thought, affect, and action is of considerable import. Social cognitive theory provides an agentic conceptual framework within which to examine the determinants and mechanisms of such effects. Human behavior has often been explained in terms of unidirectional causation. In these conceptions behavior is shaped and controlled either by environmental influences or by internal dispositions. Social cognitive theory explains psychosocial functioning in terms of triadic reciprocal causation (Bandura, 1986). In this transactional view of self and society, personal factors in the form of cognitive, affective, and biological events; behavioral patterns; and environmental events all operate as interacting determinants that influence each other bidirectionally (Figure 6.1).

Social cognitive theory is founded in an agentic perspective (Bandura, 1986; 2006c). People are self-developing, proactive, self-regulating, and self-reflecting, not just reactive organisms shaped and shepherded by environmental events or inner forces. Human self-development, adaptation, and change are embedded in social systems. Therefore, personal agency operates within a broad network of sociostructural influences. In these agentic transactions, people are producers of social systems, not just products of them. Personal agency and social structure operate as codeterminants in an integrated causal structure rather than as a disembodied duality.

Seen from the sociocognitive perspective, human nature is a vast potentiality that can be fashioned by direct and observational experience into a variety of forms within

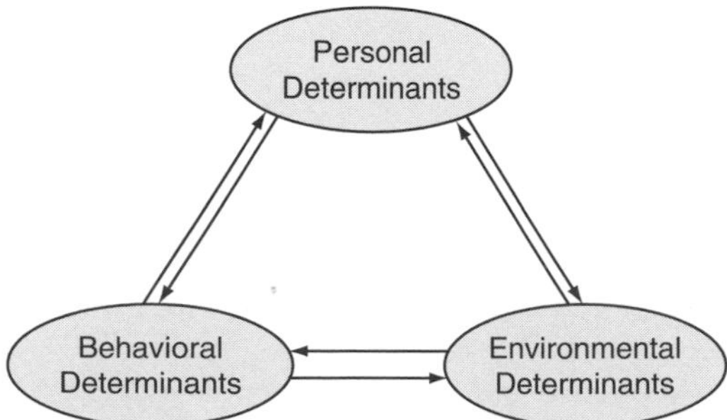

Figure 6.1 Schematization of Triadic Reciprocal Causation in the Causal Model of Social Cognitive Theory.

biological limits. To say that a major distinguishing mark of humans is their endowed plasticity is not to say that they have no nature or that they come structureless (Midgley, 1978). The plasticity, which is intrinsic to the nature of humans, depends upon neurophysiological mechanisms and structures that have evolved over time. These advanced neural systems are specialized for processing, retaining, and using coded information. They provide the capacity for the very capabilities that are distinctly human—generative symbolization, symbolic communication, forethought, evaluative self-regulation, and reflective self-consciousness (Bandura, 2008). These capabilities are addressed in the sections that follow.

SYMBOLIZING CAPABILITY

Social cognitive theory accords a central role to cognitive, vicarious, self-regulatory, and self-reflective processes. An extraordinary capacity for symbolization provides humans with a powerful tool for comprehending their environment and creating and regulating environmental events that touch virtually every aspect of their lives. Most external influences affect behavior through cognitive processes rather than directly. Cognitive factors partly determine which environmental events will be observed, what meaning will be conferred on them, whether they leave any lasting effects, what emotional impact and motivating power they will have, and how the information they convey will be organized for future use. It is with symbols that people process and transform transient experiences into cognitive models that serve as guides for judgment and action. Through symbols, people give meaning, form, and continuity to their experiences.

People gain understanding of causal relationships and expand their knowledge by operating symbolically on the wealth of information derived from personal and vicarious experiences. They construct possible solutions to problems and evaluate their likely outcomes, without having to go through a laborious trial-and-error process. Through the medium of symbols people can communicate with others at any distance in time and space. However, in keeping with the interactional perspective, social cognitive theory devotes much attention to the social origins of thought and the mechanisms through which social factors exert their influence on cognitive functioning. The other distinctive human capabilities are founded on this advanced capacity for symbolization.

SELF-REGULATORY CAPABILITY

People are not only knowers and performers, they are also self-reactors with a capacity for self-direction. Effective functioning requires the substitution of self-regulation for external sanctions and demands. The self-regulation of motivation, affect, and action operates partly through internal standards and evaluative reactions to one's own behavior (Bandura, 1991a). The anticipated self-satisfaction gained from fulfilling valued standards and discontent with substandard performances serve as incentive motivators for action. The motivational effects do not stem from the standards themselves, but from the evaluative self-investment in activities and positive and negative reactions to one's performances.

Most theories of self-regulation are founded on a negative feedback system in which people strive to reduce disparities between their perceived performance and an adopted standard. But self-regulation by negative discrepancy tells only half the story and not necessarily the more interesting half. In fact, people are proactive, aspiring organisms. Human self-regulation relies on *discrepancy production* as well as *discrepancy reduction*. People motivate and guide their actions through proactive control by setting themselves challenging goals and then mobilizing their resources, skills, and effort to fulfill them. After people attain the goal they have been pursuing, those with a strong sense of efficacy set higher goals for themselves. Adopting further challenges creates new motivating discrepancies to be mastered. Self-regulation of motivation and action thus involves a dual control process of disequilibrating discrepancy production (proactive control) followed by equilibrating discrepancy reduction (reactive control).

In areas of functioning involving achievement strivings and cultivation of competencies, the internal standards that are selected as a mark of adequacy are progressively altered as knowledge and skills are acquired and challenges are met. In many areas of social and moral behavior the internal standards that serve as the basis for regulating one's conduct have greater stability. People do not change from week to week what they regard as right or wrong or good or bad. After they adopt a standard of morality, their self-sanctions for actions that match or violate their personal standards serve as the regulatory influencers (Bandura, 1991b, 2004b). The exercise of moral agency has dual aspects—inhibitive and proactive. The inhibitive form is manifested in the power to refrain from behaving inhumanely. The proactive form of morality is expressed in the power to behave humanely.

The capability of forethought adds another dimension to the temporal extension of personal agency. Most human behavior is directed by forethought toward events and outcomes projected into the future. The future time perspective manifests itself in many different ways. People set goals for themselves, anticipate the likely consequences of their prospective actions, and otherwise plan courses of action that are likely to produce desired outcomes and to avoid undesired ones. Because future events have no actual existence they cannot be causes of current motivation and action. However, by being represented cognitively in the present, conceived futures can operate anticipatorily as motivators and regulators of current behavior. When projected over a long time course on matters of value, a forethoughtful perspective provides direction, coherence, and meaning to one's life.

SELF-REFLECTIVE CAPABILITY

The capability to reflect upon oneself and the adequacy of one's thoughts and actions is another distinctly human attribute that figures prominently in social cognitive theory. People are not only agents of action but self-examiners of their functioning. Effective cognitive functioning requires reliable ways of distinguishing between accurate and faulty thinking. In verifying thought by self-reflective means, people generate ideas, act on them or predict occurrences from them. They then judge from the results the adequacy of their thoughts, and change them accordingly. The validity and functional value of one's thoughts are evaluated by comparing how well thoughts match some indicant of reality. Four different modes of thought verification can be distinguished. They include enactive, vicarious, social, and logical forms.

Enactive verification relies on the adequacy of the fit between one's thoughts and the results of the actions they spawn. Good matches corroborate thoughts; mismatches tend to refute them. In *vicarious verification*, observing other people's transactions with the environment and the effects they produce provides a check on the correctness of one's own thinking. Vicarious thought verification is not simply a supplement to enactive experience. Symbolic modeling greatly expands the range of verification experiences that cannot otherwise be attained by personal action. When experiential verification is difficult or unfeasible, *social verification* is used, with people evaluating the soundness of their views by checking them against what others believe. In *logical verification* people can check for fallacies in their thinking by deducing from knowledge that is known what necessarily follows from it.

Such metacognitive activities usually foster veridical thought, but they can produce faulty thinking as well. Forceful actions arising from erroneous beliefs often create social environments that confirm the misbeliefs (Snyder, 1980). We are all acquainted with problem-prone individuals who, through offensive behavior, predictively breed negative social climates wherever they go. Verification of thought by comparison with distorted media versions of social reality can foster shared misconceptions of people, places, and things (Hawkins & Pingree, 1982). Social verification can foster bizarre views of reality if the shared beliefs of the reference group with which one affiliates are peculiar and the group is encapsulated from outside social ties and influences (Bandura, 1982; Hall, 1987). Deductive reasoning can lead one astray if the propositional knowledge on which it is based is faulty or biases intrude on logical reasoning processes (Falmagne, 1975).

Among the self-referent thought none is more central or pervasive than people's belief in their efficacy to exert control over their level of functioning and events that affect their lives. This core belief is the foundation of human agency (Bandura, 1997, 2008). Unless people believe that they can produce desired effects and forestall undesired ones by their actions, they have little incentive to act. Efficacy beliefs influence whether people think self-enhancingly or self-debilitatingly, optimistically or pessimistically; what courses of action they choose to pursue; the goals they set for themselves and their commitment to them; how much effort they put forth in given endeavors; the outcomes they expect their efforts to produce; how long they persevere in the face of obstacles; their resilience to adversity; how much stress and depression they experience in coping with taxing environmental demands; and the accomplishments they realize.

People do not live their lives in individual autonomy. They have to work together to secure what they cannot accomplish on their own. Social cognitive theory extends the conception of human agency to collective agency (Bandura, 1999a, 2000b). The more efficacious groups judge themselves to be, the higher their collective aspirations, the greater their motivational investment in their undertakings, the stronger their staying power in the face of impediments, the more robust their resilience to adversity, and the higher their performance accomplishments.

VICARIOUS CAPABILITY

Psychological theories have traditionally emphasized learning by the effects of one's actions. If knowledge and skills could be acquired only by response consequences human development would be greatly retarded, not to mention exceedingly tedious and hazardous. A culture could never transmit its language, mores, social practices, and requisite competencies if they had to be shaped tediously in each new member by response consequences without the benefit of models to exemplify the cultural patterns. Shortening the acquisition process is vital for survival as well as for self-development because natural endowment provides few inborn skills, hazards are ever present, and errors can be perilous. Moreover, the constraints of time, resources, and mobility impose severe limits on the places and activities that can be directly explored for the acquisition of new knowledge and competencies.

Humans have evolved an advanced capacity for observational learning that enables them to expand their knowledge and skills rapidly through information conveyed by the rich variety of models. Indeed, virtually all behavioral, cognitive, and affective learning from direct experience can be achieved vicariously by observing people's actions and its consequences for them (Bandura, 1986; Rosenthal & Zimmerman, 1978). Much social learning occurs either designedly or unintentionally from models in one's immediate environment. However, a vast amount of information about human values, styles of thinking, and behavior patterns is gained from the extensive modeling in the symbolic environment of the mass media.

A major significance of symbolic modeling lies in its tremendous reach and psychosocial impact. Unlike learning by doing, which requires altering the actions of each individual through repeated trial-and-error experiences, in observational learning a single model can transmit new ways of thinking and behaving simultaneously to countless people in widely dispersed locales. There is another aspect of symbolic modeling that amplifies its psychological and social impact. During the course of their daily lives, people have direct contact with only a small sector of the physical and social environment. They work in the same setting, travel the same routes, visit the same places, and see the same set of friends and associates. Consequently, their conceptions of social reality are greatly influenced by vicarious experiences—by what they see, hear, and read—without direct experiential correctives. To a large extent, people act on their images of reality. The more people's images of reality depend upon the media's symbolic environment, the greater is its social impact (Ball-Rokeach & DeFleur, 1976).

Most psychological theories were cast long before the advent of the extraordinary advances in the technology of communication. As a result, they give insufficient attention to the increasingly powerful role that the symbolic environment plays in present-day human lives. Whereas previously, modeling influences were largely confined to the behavior patterns exhibited in one's immediate environment, the accelerated growth of video delivery technologies has vastly expanded the range of models to which members of society are exposed day in and day out. By drawing on these modeled patterns of thought and behavior, observers can transcend the bounds of their immediate environment. New ideas, values, styles of behavior and social practices are now being rapidly diffused by symbolic modeling worldwide in ways that foster a globally distributed consciousness (Bandura, 1986, 2001). Because the symbolic environment occupies a major part of people's everyday lives, much of the social construction of reality and shaping of public consciousness occurs through electronic acculturation. At the societal level, the electronic modes of influence are transforming how social systems operate and serving as a major vehicle for sociopolitical change. The study of acculturation in the present electronic age must be broadened to include electronic acculturation.

MECHANISMS GOVERNING OBSERVATIONAL LEARNING

Because symbolic modeling is central to full understanding of the effects of mass communication, the modeling aspect of social cognitive theory is discussed in somewhat greater detail. Observational learning is governed by four subfunctions (Bandura, 1986) that are summarized in Figure 6.2.

Attentional processes determine what is selectively observed in the profusion of modeling influences and what information is extracted from ongoing modeled events. A number of factors influence the exploration and construal of what is modeled. Some of these determinants concern the cognitive skills, preconceptions and value preferences of the observers. Others are related to the salience, attractiveness, and functional value of the modeled activities themselves. Still other factors are the structural arrangements of human interactions and associational networks, which largely determine the types of models to which people have ready access.

People cannot be much influenced by observed events if they do not remember them. A second major subfunction governing observational learning concerns cognitive representational processes. Retention involves an active process of transforming and restructuring information conveyed by modeled events into rules and conceptions for memory representation. Retention is greatly aided by symbolic transformations of modeled information into memory codes and cognitive rehearsal of the coded information. Preconceptions and affective states exert biasing influences on these representational activities. Similarly, recall involves a process of reconstruction rather than simply retrieval of registered events.

In the third subfunction in modeling—the behavioral production process—symbolic conceptions are translated into appropriate courses of action (Carroll & Bandura, 1990). This is achieved through a conception-matching process in which conceptions guide the construction and execution of behavior patterns which are then compared against the conceptual model for adequateness. The behavior is modified on the basis of the comparative information to achieve close correspondence between conception and action. The mechanism for translating cognition into action involves both transformational and generative operations. Execution of a skill must be constantly varied to suit changing circumstances. Adaptive performance, therefore, requires a generative conception rather than a one-to-one mapping between cognitive representation and action. By applying an abstract specification of the activity, people can produce many variations on the skill.

Conceptions are rarely transformed into masterful performance on the first attempt. Monitored enactments serve as the vehicle for transforming knowledge into skilled action. Performances are perfected by corrective adjustments during behavior production. The more extensive the subskills that people possess, the easier it is to integrate them to produce new behavior patterns. When deficits exist, the subskills required for complex performances must first be developed by modeling and guided enactment.

The fourth subfunction in modeling concerns motivational processes. Social cognitive theory distinguishes between acquisition and performance because people do not perform everything they learn. Performance of observationally learned behavior is influenced by three major types of incentive motivators—direct, vicarious, and self-produced. People are more likely to exhibit modeled behavior if it results in valued outcomes than if it has unrewarding or punishing effects. The observed costs and benefits experienced by others influence the performance of modeled patterns in much the same way as do directly experienced consequences. People are motivated by the successes of others who are similar to themselves, but are discouraged from pursuing courses of behavior that they have seen often result in adverse consequences. Personal standards of conduct provide a further source of incentive motivation. The self-approving and self-censuring reactions people generate to their own behavior regulate which observationally learned

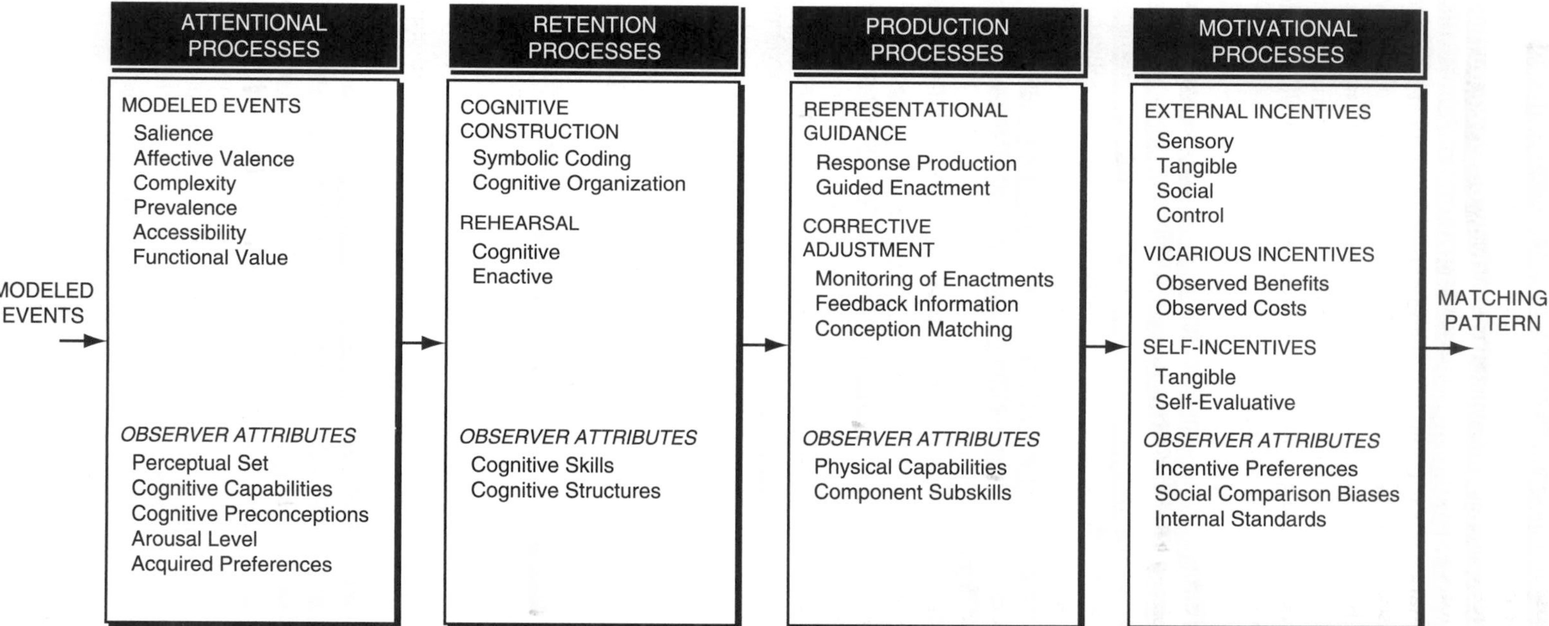

Figure 6.2 The Four Major Subfunctions Governing Observational Learning and the Influential Factors Operating within Each Subfunction.

activities they are most likely to pursue. They pursue activities they find self-satisfying and give them a sense of worth but reject those they personally disapprove.

The different sources of consequences may operate as complimentary or opposing influences on behavior (Bandura, 1986). Behavior patterns are most firmly established when social and self-sanctions are compatible. Under such conditions, socially approvable behavior is a source of self-pride and socially disapprovable behavior is self-censured. Behavior is especially susceptible to external influences in the absence of countervailing self-sanctions. People who are not much committed to personal standards adopt a pragmatic orientation, tailoring their behavior to fit whatever the situation seems to call for (Snyder & Campbell, 1982). They become adept at reading social situations and guiding their actions by expediency.

People commonly experience conflicts in which they are socially pressured to engage in behavior that violates their moral standards. When self-devaluative consequences outweigh the benefits for socially accommodating behavior, the social influences do not have much sway. However, the self-regulation of conduct operates through conditional application of moral standards. We shall see shortly that self-sanctions can be weakened or nullified by selective disengagement of internal control.

Another type of conflict between social and self sanctions arises when individuals are socially punished for behavior they highly value. Principled dissenters and nonconformists often find themselves in this predicament. Here, the relative strength of self-approval and social censure determine whether the behavior will be restrained or expressed. Should the threatened social consequences be severe, people hold in check self-praiseworthy acts in risky situations but perform them readily in relatively safe settings. There are individuals, however, whose sense of self-worth is so strongly invested in certain convictions that they will submit to prolonged maltreatment rather than accede to what they regard as unjust or immoral.

ABSTRACT MODELING

Modeling is not merely a process of behavioral mimicry, as commonly misconstrued. The proven skills and established customs of a culture may be adopted in essentially the same form as they are exemplified because of their high functional value. However, in most activities, subskills must be improvised to suit varying circumstances. Modeling influences convey rules for generative and innovative behavior as well. This higher-level learning is achieved through abstract modeling. Rule-based judgments and actions differ in specific content and other details but embody the same underlying rule. For example, a model may confront moral conflicts that differ widely in content but apply the same moral standard to them. In this higher form of abstract modeling, observers extract the rule governing the specific judgments or actions exhibited by others. Once they learn the rule, they can use it to judge or generate new instances of behavior that go beyond what they have seen or heard.

Much human learning is aimed at developing cognitive skills on how to gain and use knowledge for future use. Observational learning of thinking skills is greatly facilitated by having models verbalize their thoughts aloud as they engage in problem-solving activities (Bandura, 1986, 1997; Meichenbaum, 1984). The thoughts guiding their decisions and action strategies are thus made observable for adoption.

Acquiring generative rules from modeled information involves at least three processes: extracting the generic features from various social exemplars; integrating the extracted information into composite rules; and using the rules to produce new instances of behavior. Through abstract modeling, people acquire, among other things, standards for categorizing and judging events, linguistic rules of communication, thinking skills on how to gain and use knowledge, and personal standards for regulating one's motivation and conduct (Bandura, 1986; Rosenthal & Zimmerman, 1978). Evidence that generative rules of thought and conduct can be created through abstract modeling attests to the broad scope of observational learning.

Modeling also plays a prominent role in creativity. Few innovations are entirely new. Rather, creativeness usually involves synthesizing existing knowledge into new ways of thinking and doing things (Bandura, 1986; Bolton, 1993). There is variety in the profusion of social modeling. Innovators select useful elements from different exemplars, improve upon them, synthesize them into new forms, and tailor them to their particular pursuits. Models who exemplify novel perspectives to common problems also foster innovativeness in others, whereas modeled conventional styles of thinking and doing things diminish creativity (Harris & Evans, 1973). In these ways, selective modeling serves as the mother of innovation.

ACQUISITION AND MODIFICATION OF AFFECTIVE PROCLIVITIES

People are easily aroused by the emotional expressions of others. Vicarious arousal operates mainly through an intervening self-arousal process (Bandura, 1992). That is, seeing others react emotionally to instigating conditions activates emotion-arousing thoughts and imagery in observers. As people develop their capacity for cognitive self-arousal, they can generate emotional reactions to cues that are only suggestive of a model's emotional experiences (Wilson & Cantor, 1985). Conversely, they can neutralize or attenuate the emotional impact of modeled distress by thoughts that transform threatening situations into benign ones (Bandura, 1986; Cantor & Wilson, 1988; Dysinger & Ruckmick, 1993).

If the affective reactions of models only aroused observers fleetingly, it would be of some interest as far as momentary communication is concerned, but of limited psychological import. What gives significance to vicarious influence is that observers can acquire lasting attitudes, emotional reactions, and behavioral proclivities toward persons, places, or things that have been associated with modeled emotional experiences. They learn to fear the things that frightened models, to dislike what repulsed them, and to like what gratified them (Bandura, 1986; Duncker, 1938). Fears and intractable phobias are ameliorated by modeling influences that convey information about coping strategies for exercising control over the things that are feared. The stronger the instilled sense of coping self-efficacy, the bolder the behavior (Bandura, 1997; Williams, 1992). Values can similarly be developed and altered vicariously by repeated exposure to modeled preferences.

MOTIVATIONAL EFFECTS

The discussion thus far has centered on the acquisition of knowledge, cognitive skills, and new styles of behavior through observational learning. Social cognitive theory distinguishes among several modeling functions, each governed by different determinants and underlying mechanisms. In addition to cultivating new competencies, modeling influences have strong motivational effects. Vicarious motivators are rooted in outcome expectations formed from information conveyed by the rewarding and punishing outcomes of modeled courses of action. Seeing others gain desired outcomes by their actions can create outcome expectancies that function as positive incentives; observed punishing outcomes can create negative outcome expectancies that function as disincentives. These motivational effects are governed by observers' judgments of their ability to accomplish the modeled behavior, their perception of the modeled actions as producing favorable or adverse consequences, and their inferences that similar or unlike consequences would result if they, themselves, were to engage in similar activities.

Vicarious incentives take on added significance by their power to alter the valence and force of extrinsic incentives (Bandura, 1986). The value of a given outcome is largely determined by its relation to other outcomes rather than inheres in their natural qualities. The same outcome can function as a reward or punisher depending on social comparison between observed and personally experienced outcomes. For example, the same pay raise has negative valence for persons who have seen similar performances by others compensated more generously, but positive valence when others have been compensated less generously. Equitable rewards foster a sense of well-being; inequitable ones breed discontent and resentment.

Vicariously created motivators have been studied most extensively in terms of the inhibitory and disinhibitory effects of social justifications and outcomes accompanying modeled transgressive conduct (Anderson et al., 2003; Bandura, 1973; Berkowitz, 1984; Malamuth & Donnerstein, 1984; Zillmann & Bryant, 1984). In social cognitive theory, the latter effects are governed, in large part, by incentive motivators and the exercise of moral self-sanctions. Transgressive conduct is regulated by two major sources of sanctions—social sanctions and self-sanctions. Both control mechanisms operate anticipatorily. In motivators arising from social sanctions, people refrain from transgressing because they anticipate that such conduct will bring them social censure and other adverse consequences. In motivators rooted in self-sanctions, people refrain from behaving in ways that violate their moral standards because such conduct will bring self-condemnation. Media portrayals alter perceived social sanctions by the way in which the consequences of different styles of conduct are portrayed. For example, televised violence is often exemplified in ways that weaken restraints over aggressive conduct (Goranson, 1970; Halloran & Croll, 1972; Larsen, 1968). In televised representations of human discord, physical aggression is a preferred solution, is acceptable, is usually successful and socially sanctioned by superheroes triumphing over evil by violent means. Such portrayals legitimize, glamorize, and trivialize human violence.

Inhibitory and disinhibitory effects stemming from self-sanctions are mediated largely through self-regulatory mechanisms. After moral standards have been adopted, they serve as guides and deterrents to conduct by the self-approving and self-reprimanding consequences. However, moral standards do not function as perpetual internal regulators of conduct. Self-regulatory mechanisms do not operate unless they are activated, and there are many processes by which moral self-sanctions can be disengaged from inhumane conduct (Bandura, 1991b, 1999b). By selective activation and disengagement of self-sanctions, people can vary in their conduct with the same moral standards. Figure 6.3 shows the points in the self-regulatory process at which moral control can be disengaged from censurable conduct.

One set of disengagement practices operates at the behavior locus on the construal of the conduct itself by *moral justification*. People do not ordinarily engage in reprehensible

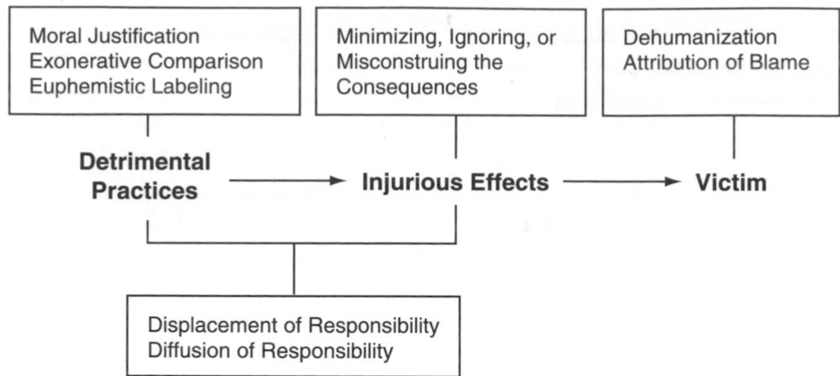

Figure 6.3 Mechanisms through Which Self-Sanctions are Selectively Activated and Disengaged from Detrimental Conduct at Critical Points in the Self-Regulatory Process.

conduct until they have justified to themselves the morality of their actions. What is culpable is made personally and socially acceptable by using worthy ends to sanctify harmful means. People then act on moral imperative. How behavior is viewed is also colored by what it is compared against. Self-deplored acts can be made benign or even honorable by contrasting them with more flagrant inhumanities. *Exonerative comparison* relies heavily on moral justification by utilitarian standards. Violence is made morally acceptable by claiming that one's harmful actions will prevent more human suffering than they cause. Activities can take on a very different appearance depending on what they are called. Sanitizing *euphemistic language* provides another convenient device for masking reprehensible activities or even conferring a respectable status upon them. Through convoluted verbiage, reprehensible conduct is made benign and those who engage in it are relieved of a sense of personal agency.

Sanctifying pernicious conduct through moral justifications, sanitizing language, and exonerating comparisons is the most effective set of psychological mechanisms for disengaging moral self-sanctions. Investing harmful conduct with high moral purpose not only eliminates self-censure but also engages self-approval in the service of destructive exploits.

Ball-Rokeach (1972) attaches special significance to evaluative reactions and social justifications presented in the media, particularly in conflicts of power. This is because relatively few viewers experience sufficient inducement to use the aggressive strategies they have seen, but the transmitted justifications and evaluations can help to mobilize public support for policy initiatives favoring either social control or social change. The justificatory changes can have widespread social and political ramifications.

The mass media, especially television, provide the best access to the public through their strong drawing power. For this reason, television is increasingly used as the principal vehicle of justification. Struggles to legitimize and gain support for one's values and causes and to discredit those of one's opponents are now waged more and more through the electronic media (Ball-Rokeach, 1972; Bandura, 2004a; Bassiouni, 1981). Because of its potential influence, the communication system itself is subject to constant pressures from different factions within society seeking to sway it to their ideology. Research on the role of the mass media in the social construction of reality carries important social implications.

Self-sanctions are activated most strongly when people acknowledge that they are contributors to harmful outcomes. Another set of disengagement practices operates, at the agency locus, by obscuring or minimizing the agentic role in the harm one causes. People will behave in ways they normally repudiate if a legitimate authority sanctions their conduct and accepts responsibility for its consequences (Milgram, 1974). Under conditions of *displacement of responsibility,* people view their actions as springing from the dictates of others rather than their being personally responsible for them. Because they are not the actual agent of their actions, they are spared self-prohibiting reactions. The deterrent power of self-sanctions is also weakened when personal agency is obscured by *diffusion of responsibility* for culpable conduct. Through division of labor, group decision making, and collective action, people can behave detrimentally without any one person feeling personally responsible (Kelman & Hamilton, 1989). Other ways of weakening moral conduct operate at the consequences locus by *minimizing, disregarding,* or *disputing the harmful effects* of one's activity. As long as the detrimental effects are out of sight and out of mind, there is little reason for self-censure to be activated.

The final set of disengagement practices operates at the victim locus. The strength of self-censure for detrimental conduct partly depends on how the perpetrators view the people toward whom the behavior is directed. To perceive another as human activates empathetic reactions through a sense of common humanity (Bandura, 1992). It is difficult to mistreat humanized persons without self-condemnation. Self-sanctions against cruel conduct can be disengaged or blunted by *dehumanization,* which divests people of human qualities or invests them with bestial qualities. While dehumanization weakens self-restraints against cruel conduct (Diener, 1977; Zimbardo, 2007), humanization fosters considerate, compassionate behavior (Bandura, Underwood, & Fromson, 1975).

Attribution of blame to one's antagonists is still another expedient that can serve self-exonerative purposes. Deleterious interactions usually involve a series of reciprocally escalative actions, in which the antagonists are rarely faultless. One can always select from the chain of events an instance of the adversary's defensive behavior and view it as the original instigation. Injurious conduct thus becomes a justifiable defensive reaction to belligerent provocations. Others can, therefore, be blamed for bringing suffering on themselves. Self-exoneration is similarly achievable by viewing one's detrimental conduct as forced by circumstances rather than as a personal decision. By blaming others or circumstances, not only are one's own actions excusable but one can even feel self-righteous in the process.

Because internalized controls can be selectively activated and disengaged, marked changes in moral conduct can be achieved without changing people's personality structures, moral principles, or self-evaluative systems. It is self-exonerative processes rather than character flaws that account for most inhumanities. The massive threats to human welfare stem mainly from deliberate acts of principle rather than from unrestrained acts of impulse.

Research in which the different disengagement factors are systematically varied in media portrayals of inhumanities attests to the disinhibitory power of mass media influences (Bandura, 1999b; Berkowitz & Green, 1967; Donnerstein, 1984; Meyer, 1972). Viewers' punitiveness is enhanced by exposure to media productions that morally justify injurious conduct, blame and dehumanize victims, displace or diffuse personal responsibility, and sanitize destructive consequences. Research on moral disengagement is clarifying how sanctioning social conditions fosters selective moral disengagement and the affective and psychosocial processes through which it regulates injurious conduct (Bandura, Barbaranelli, Caprara, & Pastorelli, 1996; Bandura et al., 1975).

This line of research has been extended to analysis of how the diverse mechanisms of moral disengagement operate in concert at the social systems level. These systems include injurious corporate practices (Bandura, 1999b; White, Bandura, & Bero, in press), application of the death penalty at the public policy, jury, and executioner levels (Bandura, 2007; Osofsky, Bandura, & Zimbardo, 2005), support of military force (McAlister, Bandura, & Owen, 2006) in terrorism and counterterrorism (Bandura, 2004a), and ecological sustainability (Bandura, 2007). With the advent of satellite transmission, battles are now fought in the airways to shape public perceptions and support for military campaigns.

The same disengagement mechanisms are enlisted heavily by the television industry in the production of programs that exploit human brutality for commercial purposes (Baldwin & Lewis, 1972; Bandura, 2004b). High moral purposes are assigned to the taking of human life, in the likeness of a national character building service. "The government wants kids to think that there are values worth fighting for, and that's basically what the leads on our show are doing." "If people who break the society's code resist the law, we have to use violence to suppress them. In doing so we are in the mainstream of American morality." Modeling violent solutions to problems allegedly builds character and affirms society's legal imperative.

Producers often excuse commercialization of violence by contrasting it with outrageous inhumanities, as though one form of human cruelty exonerates other forms. Why pick on television, the scapegoat disclaimer goes, when societies fight wars. "To examine violence where the end result is a dead body on television glosses over the point. This evades the culpability of a whole society which permits wars."

Another variant in the comparative exoneration is to sanctify brutalizing excesses on television by pointing to revered masterpieces containing some violent episodes. "There is violence in Oedipus and Hamlet, and it permeates the Bible." Gratuitous televised violence ain't Shakespeare. Here are some examples of television practices masquerading behind Hamlet's cloak. "I wish we could come up with a different device than running the man down with the car as we have done this now in three different shows. I like the idea of the sadism, but I hope we can come up with another approach for it." "Last week you killed three men; what are you going to do this week?" When the television programs are exported to other countries, much of the gratuitous violence is deleted. But we overdose our own children on it.

Producers of violent fare are quick to displace responsibility for violent events, to other sources. "Television and motion pictures are fall guys for a sick society." "Are kids from unstable environments triggered by television violence? Their not having parents is a more serious problem." Producers disclaim using gratuitous violence by attributing evident excesses to the characters they create. Ruthless individuals, or even peaceful folks, confronted with mortal jeopardy demand acts of violence. One of the more candid script writers discounted the asserted dramatic requirement for violence as analogous to saying, "I never put cotton in a wagon that's not prepared for cotton—but I never use anything but a cotton wagon."

Personal responsibility for gratuitous violence is also obscured by diffusing responsibilities for the product. Rewriters alter writers' scripts; directors fill in the details of the scenarios; and editors shape how the filmed events are depicted by what they select from the lengthy footage. Diffusion of the production process reduces a sense of personal responsibility for the final product.

Another way of escaping self-censure is to misrepresent, deny, or ignore harmful effects. Modeling violent solutions is purported to serve a public therapeutic function of draining viewers' aggressive drives. "Violence is a catharsis for kids." "Exposure to properly presented conflict which results in violence acts as a therapeutic release for anger and self-hatred." The claimed catharsis effect has long been discredited empirically. On the one hand the producers proclaim the therapeutic benefits of viewing violence, which are empirically refuted, but on the other hand they contend that the effects of televised violence can never be substantiated. "Nobody has been able to make a definitive statement about the effects of televised violence."

Viewers are divested of human sensitivities or invested with base qualities that justify serving them gory offerings. "Man's mind is connected to his stomach, his groin, and his fists. It doesn't float five feet above his body. Violence, therefore, cannot be eradicated." "Not as much action as some, but sufficient to keep the average bloodthirsty viewer fairly happy." The prevalence of violent content is attributed to the aggressive nature and desire of its viewers.

In fact, there is no relationship between the level of program violence and the Nielson index of program popularity (Diener & DeFour, 1978). Situational comedies and variety shows are the big draws. The answer to the prevalence of violent scenarios on TV lies in production costs and other structural factors, not in human craving for cruelty (Bandura, 1973; Brown, 1971).

Whenever a violent event occurs that stirs the public, the television networks run a predictable scenario. They assemble the cast of spokespersons for the major suspect sources of violence. The spokespersons promptly divert attention from their possible contributory influence by invoking and repudiating a single cause theory of violent conduct that no one really propounds. They portray themselves as convenient scapegoats and shift the blame to other contributors.

SOCIAL CONSTRUCTION OF REALITY

Televised representations of social realities reflect ideological bents in their portrayal of human nature, social relations, and the norms and structure of society (Adoni & Mane, 1984; Gerbner, 1972). Heavy exposure to this symbolic world may eventually make the televised images appear to be the authentic state of human affairs. Some disputes about the vicarious cultivation of beliefs have arisen over findings from correlational studies using global indices based on amount of television viewing (Gerbner, Gross, Morgan, & Signorielli, 1981; Hirsch, 1980). Televised influence is best defined in terms of the contents people watch rather than the sheer amount of television viewing. More particularized measures of exposure to the televised fare show that heavy television viewing shapes viewers' beliefs and conceptions of reality (Hawkins & Pingree, 1982). The relationship remains when other possible contributing factors are simultaneously controlled.

Vicarious cultivation of social conceptions is most clearly revealed in studies verifying the direction of causality by varying experimentally the nature and amount of exposure to media influences. Controlled laboratory studies provide converging evidence that television portrayals shape viewers' beliefs (Bryant, Carveth, & Brown, 1981; Flerx, Fidler, & Rogers, 1976; O'Bryant & Corder-Bolz, 1978). Portrayals in the print media similarly shape conceptions of social reality (Heath, 1984; Siegel, 1958). To see the world as the televised messages portray it is to harbor some misconceptions. Indeed, many of the shared misconceptions about occupational pursuits, ethnic groups, minorities, the elderly, social and sex roles, and other aspects of life are at least partly cultivated through symbolic modeling of stereotypes (Buerkel-Rothfuss & Mayes, 1981; Bussey & Bandura, 1999; McGhee & Frueh, 1980). Verification of personal conceptions against televised versions of social reality can thus foster some collective illusions.

SOCIAL PROMPTING FUNCTION

The actions of others can also serve as social prompts for previously learned behavior that observers can perform but have not done so because of insufficient inducements, rather than because of restraints. Social prompting effects are distinguished from observational learning and disinhibition because no new behavior has been acquired, and disinhibitory processes are not involved because the elicited behavior is socially acceptable and not encumbered by restraints.

The influence of models in activating, channeling, and supporting the behavior of others is abundantly documented in both laboratory and field studies (Bandura, 1986). By exemplification one can get people to behave altruistically, to volunteer their services, to delay or seek gratification, to show affection, to select certain foods and drinks, to choose certain kinds of apparel, to converse on particular topics, to be inquisitive or passive, to think creatively or conventionally, or to engage in other permissible courses of action. Thus, the types of models who predominate within a social milieu partly determine which human qualities, from among many alternatives, are selectively activated. The actions of models acquire the power to activate and channel behavior when they are good predictors for observers that positive results can be gained by similar conduct.

The fashion and taste industries rely heavily on the social prompting power of modeling. Because the potency of vicarious influences can be enhanced by showing modeled acts bringing rewards, vicarious outcomes figure prominently in advertising campaigns. Thus, drinking a certain brand of beer or using a particular shampoo wins the loving admiration of beautiful people, enhances job performance, masculinizes self-conception, actualizes individualism and authenticity, tranquilizes irritable nerves, invites social recognition and amicable reactions from total strangers, and arouses affectionate overtures from spouses.

The types of vicarious outcomes, model characteristics, and modeling formats that are selected vary depending on what happens to be in vogue at the time. Model characteristics are varied to boost the persuasiveness of commercial messages. Prestigeful models are often enlisted to capitalize on the high regard in which they are held. The best social sellers depend on what happens to be popular at the moment. Drawing on evidence that similarity to the model enhances modeling, some advertisements portray common folk achieving wonders with the wares being advertised. Because vicarious influence increases with multiplicity of modeling (Perry & Bussey, 1979), the beers, soft drinks, and snacks are being consumed with gusto in the advertised world by groups of wholesome, handsome, fun-loving models. Eroticism is another stimulant that never goes out of style. Therefore, erotic modeling does heavy duty in efforts to command attention and to make advertised products more attractive to potential buyers (Kanungo & Pang, 1973; Peterson & Kerin, 1979).

In sum, modeling influences serve diverse functions—as tutors, motivators, inhibitors, disinhibitors, moral engagers and disengagers, social prompters, emotion arousers, and shapers of values and public conceptions of reality. Although the different modeling functions can operate separately, in nature they often work in concert. Thus, for example, in the spread of new styles of aggression, models serve as both teachers and disinhibitors.

When novel conduct is punished, observers learn the conduct that was punished as well as the social sanctions. A novel example can both teach and prompt similar acts.

MATCHING METHODOLOGIES WITH SEPARABLE MEDIA EFFECTS

Each modeling effect requires a distinct methodology to advance understanding of the determinants and mechanisms through which it produces its effects. Research on the effects of televised violence is illustrative of the tailoring of methodology to separable effects. The conceptual and methodological issues, however, apply to the analysis of other media effects as well. Different lines of research identified four major effects of exposure to televised violence: it can teach novel aggressive styles of conduct; weaken restraints over the performance of preexisting styles of aggressive behavior; desensitize and habituate viewers to human cruelty; and shape public images of reality.

In observational *learning effects*, people acquire attitudes, values, emotional proclivities and new styles of thinking and behaving from the activities exemplified by models (Bandura, 1986). The widely cited Bobo doll laboratory experiments were designed to clarify the attentional, representational, translational, and motivational processes governing observational learning (Bandura, Ross, & Ross, 1963). The methodology for measuring learning effects requires simulated targets rather than live ones so that viewers will reveal all they have learned. To use human targets to assess the instructive function of televised influence would be as nonsensical as to require bombardiers to bomb San Francisco, New York, or some other inhabited area in testing whether they have acquired bombing skills. In short, tests for learning effects use simulated targets not live ones, a point that commentaries on the Bobo doll experiments often fail to recognize.

There is a difference between learning and performance. Tests of whether modeling influences alter the likelihood that individuals will act aggressively, however they learned it, requires human targets. In *performance effects*, social modeling operates on behavioral restraints through self-regulatory influence and incentive motivators rooted in outcome expectations. As previously noted, utility of aggressive behavior is influenced by three major types of incentive motivators: direct, vicarious, and self-produced (Bandura, 1986). Modeling can also contribute to impulsive aggression by heightening emotional arousal that can undermine self-restraint (Bandura, 1973; Berkovitz, 1984).

Repeated exposure to violence can desensitize and habituate people to human cruelty. They are no longer upset by it. The *desensitization effect* requires tests of the lack of emotional arousal to depicted violence as a function of the amount of exposure (Cline, Croft, & Courrier, 1973). Habituation to human brutality is tested by the level of aggression viewers will tolerate before they are willing to intervene (Thomas, Horton, Lippincott, & Drabman, 1977). The final modeling effect is the shaping of public consciousness. The mass media convey basic images about the social and political structure of societies, their ideological orientations, the conventional stereotyping of different groups, and the power relations among them. Examination of *the social construction of reality* requires methodologies that link the images conveyed by the mass media to peoples' conceptions of the world around them (Gerbner, Gross, Morgan, Shanahan, & Signorielli, 2001).

Verifying the effects of media violence requires diverse methodologies because no single method can provide a full explanation of human behavior. Rather it requires converging evidence from complementary methodologies. The four major research strategies include controlled laboratory experiments, correlational studies, controlled field studies, and naturalistic studies.

Controlled experimentation is well suited to verify the nature and direction of causation by systematically varying possible determinants and assessing the effects. Controlled experimentation has shed light on some of the determinants of aggressive behavior and the mechanisms through which they produce their effects (Anderson et al., 2003; Bandura, 1973). However, in the social sciences there are severe constraints on controlled experimentation. Its use is precluded for phenomena that are not producible in laboratory situations because they require a lengthy period of development, they are the product of complex constellations of influences from diverse social systems that are not manipulable or they are prohibited ethically. Experimental approaches are often mistakenly dismissed as "artificial." This, in fact, is their explanatory power. They address basic processes governing a given phenomenon and would lose their informative value if they mimiced surface similarities to the natural forms. Aerodynamic principles verified in wind tunnels got us airborne in gigantic airliners. Airplanes do not flap their wings like the flying creatures do in nature. The early inventors who tried to fly with flapping wings ended up in orthopedic wards.

Because there are limits to the variations one can produce experimentally, functional relations are examined in variations in natural concurrencies. Correlational studies establish whether violence viewing is related to aggressive conduct in everyday life (Anderson et al., 2003). But as the analytic mantra reminds us, correlation does not prove causation. Frequency of doctor visits correlates with patient deaths, but this does not mean the doctors are killing their patients. Correlations can arise through four different paths of influence: violence viewing fosters aggression; aggressive viewers are attracted to violent programs; the influence is bidirectional; or a third factor influences both aggression and violence viewing, creating a spurious causal relation. Multiple controls must be applied to rule out third-factor causation.

Controlled field studies help to clarify the directions of causation by systematically varying the level of exposure to media violence in the natural setting over a long period and assessing the level of interpersonal aggression as it occurs spontaneously in everyday transactions (Leyens, Camino, Parke, & Berkowitz, 1975). But this approach has certain limitations as well. One can never impose full control over naturally occurring events; social systems impose limits on the types of intervention they allow; it is difficult to maintain high fidelity of implementation over a lengthy period; experimental influences can spill over to control conditions; many important forms of aggression do not lend themselves to controlled manipulation; and ethical considerations place constraints on controlled field interventions.

The fourth method relies on informative naturalistic events (Philips, 1985). Some natural occurrences have characteristics that provide persuasive evidence of causality. They fit three criteria of a causative modeling relation. A highly novel style of behavior is modeled so there is no ambiguity about the source of their behavior. There is a temporal conjunction in which viewers exhibit the same style of behavior after the exposure. The behavioral watching occurs in the broadcast area.

Sometimes it is the fictional media that create an unintended natural experiment exemplifying social modeling (Bandura, 1978). The program called *Doomsday Flight* provides a notable example. In the plot line an extortionist threatens airline officials that an altitude sensitive bomb will be exploded on a transcontinental airliner as it descends below 5,000 ft. for the landing. In the end the pilot outwits the extortionist by selecting an airport located at an elevation above the critical altitude.

There was a substantial rise in extortion attempts using threats of altitude sensitive bombs. For two months following the telecasting of the program, there was an eight-fold increase in attempted extortions using the same scenario. Airlines were subjected to extortion threats a day or two after the program was shown as a rerun in different cities in the U.S. and abroad. Western Airlines paid $25,000 to an extortionist in Anchorage the day after the rerun was shown. A San Francisco rerun was followed by an extortion threat to United on a flight to Hawaii. The extortionist was apprehended as he picked up the money package dropped from a helicopter. Miami experienced an extortion attempt the day after the rerun. The day after the program was shown in Sydney, Australia, an extortionist informed Qantas officials that he had placed an altitude sensitive bomb on a flight in progress. He also directed the officials to a locker containing such a bomb to prove that he was not bluffing. Qantas paid $560,000 only to learn that the airliner contained no bomb. Following a showing of the "*Doomsday Flight*" on Montreal television, an extortionist used the bomb plot in an effort to extract a quarter of a million dollars from British Overseas Airways by warning that a barometric bomb was set to explode on a jet bound from Montreal to London when it descended below 5,000 ft. The hoaxer was unsuccessful because the airline officials, knowing the oft-repeated scenario, diverted the plane to Denver, which is at 5,339 ft. elevation. TWA bound for New York from Madrid was rerouted to the air force base in South Dakota, when a Madrid viewer called in the bomb hoax. A rerun in Paris produced the same extortion scenario.

An inventive hijacker, *D. B. Cooper*, devised an extortion technique in which he exchanged passengers for a parachute and a sizeable bundle of money. He then parachuted from the rear-door opening in a Boeing 207 which eliminates any danger of hitting the tail or stabilizers. Others were inspired by his successful feat. Within a few months there were 18 hijackers modeled on the parachute-extortion technique. It continued until a mechanical door lock was installed so that the rear exit could be opened only from the outside.

The preceding discussion demonstrates that social modeling has separable effects, each of which requires a distinct methodology to verify its determinants and governing mechanisms. Verification of the causative power of social modeling requires converging evidence from diverse analytic methodologies because no single method can do it alone. The common failure to distinguish among types of modeling effect linked to particular methodologies offering complementary evidence spawns a lot of misjudgments about media effects.

DUAL-LINK VERSUS MULTI-PATTERN FLOW OF INFLUENCE

It has been commonly assumed in theories of mass communication that modeling influences operate through a two-step diffusion process. Influential persons pick up new ideas from the media and pass them on to their followers through personal influence. Some communication researchers have claimed that the media can only reinforce preexisting styles of behavior but cannot create new ones (Klapper, 1960). Such a view is at variance with a vast body of evidence. Media influences create personal attributes as well as alter preexisting ones (Bandura, 1986; Williams, 1992).

The different modes of human influence are too diverse in nature to have a fixed path of influence or strengths. Most behavior is the product of multiple determinants operating in concert. Hence, the relative contribution of any given factor in a pattern of influences can change depending on the nature and strength of coexisting determinants. Even the same determinant operating within the same causal structure of factors can change in its causal contribution with further experience (Wood & Bandura, 1989). In the case of atypical behavior, it is usually produced by a unique constellation of determinants, such that if any one of them were absent the behavior would not have occurred. Depending on their quality and coexistence of other determinants, media influences may be subordinate to, equal to, or outweigh nonmedia influences. Given the dynamic nature of multifaceted causal structures, efforts to affix an average strength to a given mode of influence calls to mind the nonswimming analyst who drowned while trying to cross a river that averaged two feet in depth.

The view that the path of media influence is exclusively a filter-down process is disputed by a wealth of knowledge regarding modeling influences. Human judgment, values, and conduct can be altered directly by televised modeling without having to wait for an influential intermediary to adopt what has been shown and then to serve as the diffuser to others. Watt and van den Berg (1978) tested several alternative theories about how media communications relate to public attitudes and behavior. The explanatory contenders included the conceptions that media influence people directly; media influence opinion leaders who then affect others; media have no independent effects; media set the public agenda for discussions by designating what is important but do not otherwise influence the public; and finally, media simply reflect public attitudes and behavior rather than shape them. The direct-flow model from media to the public received the best empirical support. In this study, the behavior was highly publicized and could bring benefits without risks. When the activities being advocated require the investment of time and resources, and failures can be costly, people are inclined to seek verification of functional value from other sources as well before they act.

Chaffee (1982) reviewed substantial evidence that calls into question the prevailing view that interpersonal sources of information are necessarily more persuasive than media sources. People seek information that may be potentially useful to them from different sources. Neither informativeness, credibility, nor persuasiveness are uniquely tied to interpersonal sources or to media sources. How extensively different sources are used depends, in large part, on their accessibility and the likelihood that they will provide the kinds of information sought.

Modeling affects the adoption of new social practices and behavior patterns in several ways. It instructs people about new ways of thinking and behaving by informative demonstration or description. Learning about new things does not rely on a fixed hierarchy of sources. Efficacious modeling not only cultivates competencies but also enhances the sense of personal efficacy needed to transform knowledge and skills into successful courses of action (Bandura, 1997). The relative importance of interpersonal and media sources of information in initiating the adoption process varies for different activities and for the same activity at different stages in the adoption process (Pelz, 1983). As previously noted, models motivate as well as inform and enable. People are initially reluctant to adopt new practices that involve costs and risks until they see the advantages that have been gained by early adopters. Modeled benefits accelerate social diffusion by weakening the restraints of the more cautious potential adopters. As acceptance spreads, the new ways gain further social support. Models also display preferences and evaluative reactions, which can alter observers' values and standards. Changes in evaluative standards affect receptivity to the activities being modeled. Models not only exemplify and legitimate new practices, they also serve as advocates for them by directly encouraging others to adopt them.

In effecting large-scale changes, communications systems operate through two pathways (Figure 6.4). In the direct pathway, communications media promote changes by informing, enabling, motivating, and guiding participants. In the socially mediated pathway, media influences are used to link participants to social networks and community settings. These places provide continued personalized guidance, as well as natural incentives and social supports for desired changes (Bandura, 2006a). The major share of behavior changes is promoted within these social milieus.

The absence of individualized guidance limits the power of one-way mass communications. The revolutionary advances in interactive technologies provide the means to expand the reach and impact of communications media. On the input side, communications can now be personally tailored to factors that are causally related to the behavior of interest. Tailored communications are viewed as more relevant and credible, are better remembered and are more effective in influencing behavior than general messages (Kreuter, Strecher, & Glassman, 1999). On the behavioral guidance side, interactive technologies provide a convenient means of individualizing the type and level of behavioral guidance needed to bring desired changes to fruition (Bandura, 2004c). In the population-based approaches the communications are designed to inform, enable, motivate, and guide people to effect personal and social changes. In implementing the social linking function, communications media can connect people to interactive online self-management programs that provide intensive individualized guidance in their homes when they want it (Bandura, 2004c, 2006b; Taylor, Winzelberg, & Celio, 2001; Muñoz et al., 2007).

In short, there is no single pattern of social influence. The media can implant ideas either directly or through adopters. Analyses of the role of mass media in social diffusion must distinguish between their effect on learning modeled activities and on their adoptive use, and examine how media and interpersonal influences affect these separable processes. In some instances the media both teach new forms of behavior and create motivators for action by altering people's value preferences, efficacy beliefs, outcome expectations, and perception of opportunity structures. In other instances, the media teach but other adopters provide the incentive motivation to perform what has been learned observationally. In still other instances, the effect of the media may be entirely socially mediated. That is, people who have had no exposure to the media are influenced by adopters who have had the exposure and then, themselves, become the transmitters of the new ways. Within these different patterns of social influence, the media can serve as originating, as well as reinforcing, influences.

The hierarchical top-down model is characteristic mainly of the print media of yesteryear. In this electronic era, communication technologies and global interconnectedness provide people with ready direct access to information worldwide independently

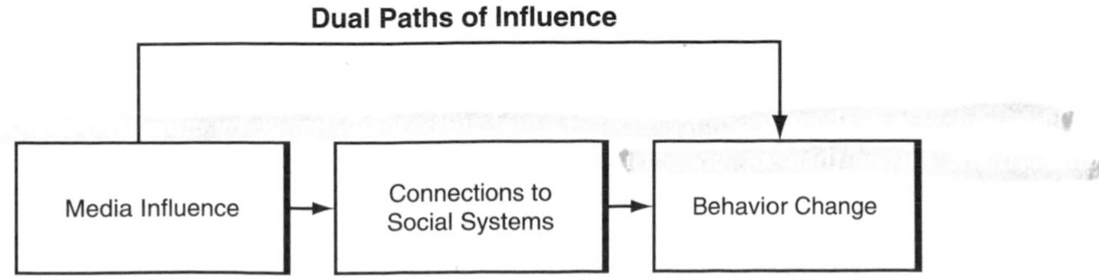

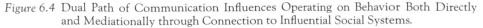

Figure 6.4 Dual Path of Communication Influences Operating on Behavior Both Directly and Mediationally through Connection to Influential Social Systems.

of time and place and unfettered by institutional and moneyed gatekeepers. The public is less dependent on a mediated filter-down system of persuasion and enlightenment. These vastly expanded opportunities for self-directedness underscore the growing primacy of agentic initiative in human adaptation and change in the electronic era (Bandura, 1997, 2002). Ready access to communication technologies will not necessarily enlist active participation unless people believe that they can achieve desired results by this means. Perceived personal and collective efficacy partly determines the extent to which people use this resource and the purposes to which they put it (Joo, Bong, & Choi, 2000; Newhagen, 1994a, b).

INTEGRATING SOCIAL COGNITIVE AND SOCIAL DIFFUSION THEORY

Much of the preceding discussion has centered on modeling at the individual level. As previously noted, a unique property of modeling is that it can transmit information of virtually limitless variety to vast numbers of people in diverse locales simultaneously through the medium of symbolic modeling. Extraordinary advances in technology of communication are transforming the nature, reach, speed and loci of human influence (Bandura, 2002). These technological developments have radically altered the social diffusion process. The video system feeding off telecommunications satellites has become the dominant vehicle for disseminating symbolic environments. Social practices are not only being widely diffused within societies, but ideas, values, and styles of behavior are being modeled worldwide. The electronic media are coming to play an increasingly influential role in transcultural change.

The most ambitious applications of social cognitive theory are aimed at abating some of the most pressing global problems (Bandura, 2006a; Singhal, Cody, Rogers, & Sabidó, 2004). These worldwide applications combine the functions of three models in ways that foster widespread changes. They combine a *theoretical model* that provides the guiding principles; a *translational and implementational model* that converts theory into innovative practice; and a *social diffusion* model that fosters adoption of changes through functional adaptations to diverse culture milieus.

Long-running serialized dramas serve as the principal vehicle for promoting personal and social changes. These productions bring life to people's everyday struggles and the effects of different social practices. The storylines speak ardently to people's fears, hopes, and aspirations for a better life. The dramatic productions are not just fanciful stories. They dramatize the realities of people's lives, the impediments with which they struggle and realistic solutions to them. The enabling dramas help viewers to see a better life and provide strategies and incentives that enable them to take the steps to achieve it. Hundreds of episodes allow viewers to form bonds to the models, who evolve in their thinking and behavior at a believable pace. Viewers are inspired and enabled by them to improve their lives.

This psychosocial approach fosters personal and social change by enlightenment and enablement rather than by coercion (Bandura, 1997). Global applications in Africa, Asia, and Latin America are helping to stabilize soaring population growth that is degrading the ecosystems that support life; raising the status of women in societies in which they are marginalized, disallowed aspirations and denied their liberty and dignity; curbing the spread of the AIDS epidemic; promoting national literacy; and fostering other changes that improve the quality of life.

Social cognitive theory analyzes social diffusion of new behavior patterns in terms of three constituent processes and the psychosocial factors that govern them (Bandura, 2006b). These include the acquisition of knowledge about innovative behaviors; the adoption of these behaviors in practice; and the social networks through which they spread and are supported. Diffusion of innovation follows a common pattern (Robertson, 1971; Rogers, 1995). New ideas and social practices are introduced by notable example. Initially, the rate of adoption is slow because new ways are unfamiliar, customs resist change, and results are uncertain. As early adopters convey more information about how to apply the new practices and their potential benefits, the innovation is adopted at an accelerating rate. After a period in which the new practices spread rapidly, the rate of diffusion slows down. The use of the innovation then either stabilizes or declines, depending upon its relative functional value.

MODELING DETERMINANTS OF DIFFUSION

Symbolic modeling usually functions as the principal conveyer of innovations to widely dispersed areas. This is especially true in the early stages of diffusion. Newspapers, magazines, radio, and television inform people about new practices and their likely risks or benefits. The Internet provides instant communicative access worldwide. Early adopters, therefore, come from among those who have had greater access to media sources of information about innovations. The psychosocial determinants and mechanisms of observational learning, which were reviewed earlier, govern the rate with which innovations are acquired.

Differences in the knowledge, skills and resources particular innovations require produce variations in rate of acquisition. Innovations that are difficult to understand and use receive more reluctant consideration than simpler ones (Tornatzky & Klein, 1982). When television models new practices on the screens in virtually every household, people in widely dispersed locales can learn them. However, not all innovations are promoted through the mass media. Some rely on informal personal channels. In such instances, physical proximity determines which innovations will be repeatedly observed and thoroughly learned.

It is one thing to acquire skills, it is another thing to use them effectively under difficult circumstances. The acquisition of personal resources includes not only knowledge and skills but also the self-belief in one's efficacy to use skills well. Modeling influences must, therefore, be designed to build self-efficacy as well as convey knowledge and rules of behavior. Perceived self-efficacy affects every phase of personal change (Bandura, 1997). It determines whether people even consider changing their behavior, whether they can enlist the motivation and perseverance needed to succeed should they choose to do so, and how well they maintain the changes they have achieved.

The influential role of people's beliefs in their efficacy in social diffusion is shown in their response to health communications aimed at fastening habits that promote health and reducing those that impair it. Meyerowitz and Chaiken (1987) examined four alternative mechanisms through which health communications could alter health habits—by transmission of factual information, fear arousal, change in risk perception, and enhancement of perceived self-efficacy. They found that health communications fostered adoption of preventive health practices by strengthening belief that one can exercise control. Beck and Lund (1981) have similarly shown that preventive health practices are better promoted by heightening self-efficacy than by elevating fear. Analyses of how community-wide media campaigns produce changes reveal that both the preexisting and created level of perceived self-efficacy play an influential role in the adoption and social diffusion of health practices (Maibach, Flora, & Nass, 1991; Slater, 1989). The stronger the preexisting perceived self-efficacy, and the more the media campaigns enhance people's beliefs in their self-regulative efficacy, the more likely they are to adopt the recommended practices. Health knowledge gets translated into healthful habits through the mediation of perceived self-efficacy (Rimal, 2000).

The findings reviewed above underscore the need to shift the emphasis from trying to scare people into healthy behavior to empowering them with the tools and self-beliefs for exercising personal control over their health habits. People must also experience sufficient success using what they have learned to become convinced of their efficacy and the functional value of what they have adopted. This is best achieved by combining modeling with guided mastery, in which newly acquired skills are first tried under conditions likely to produce good results, and then extended to more unpredictable and difficult circumstances (Bandura, 1986; 2000a).

Innovations require innovators. Turning visions into realities requires heavy investment of time, effort, and resources in ventures strewn with many hardships, unmerciful impediments, and uncertainties. A resilient sense of efficacy provides the necessary staying power in the tortuous pursuit of innovations. Indeed, perceived self-efficacy predicts entrepreneurship and which patent inventors are likely to start new business ventures (Chen, Greene, & Crick, 1998; Markman & Baron, 1999).

ADOPTION DETERMINANTS

As noted above, the acquisition of knowledge and skills regarding innovations is necessary, but not sufficient for their adoption in practice. A number of factors determine whether people will act on what they have learned. Environmental inducements serve as one set of regulators. Adoptive behavior is also highly susceptible to incentive influences, which may take the form of material, social, or self-evaluative outcomes. Some of the motivating incentives derive from the utility of the adoptive behavior. The greater the relative benefits provided by an innovation, the higher is the incentive to adopt it (Ostlund, 1974; Rogers & Shoemaker, 1971). However, benefits cannot be experienced until the new practices are tried. Promoters, therefore, strive to get people to adopt new practices by altering their preferences and beliefs about likely outcomes, mainly by enlisting vicarious incentives. Advocates of new technologies and ideologies create expectations that they offer better solutions than established ways do. Modeled benefits increase adoptive decisions. Modeling influences can, of course, impede as well as promote the diffusion process (Bandura, 1986). Modeling negative reactions to a particular innovation, as a result of having had disappointing experiences with it, dissuades others from trying it. Even modeled indifference to an innovation, in the absence of any personal experience with it, will dampen the interests of others.

Many innovations serve as a means of gaining social recognition and status. Indeed, status incentives are often the main motivators for adopting new styles and tastes. In many instances, the variant styles do not provide different natural benefits, or, if anything, the most innovative styles are the most costly. Status is thus gained at a price. People who strive to distinguish themselves from the common and the ordinary adopt new styles in clothing, grooming, recreational activities, artistic creations, and behavioral patterns, thereby achieving distinctive social standing. As the popularity of the new behavior grows, it loses its status-conferring value until eventually it, too, becomes commonplace. It is then discarded for a new form.

Adoptive behavior is also partly governed by self-evaluative reactions to one's own behavior. People adopt what they value, but resist innovations that violate their social and moral standards or that conflict with their self-conception. The more compatible an innovation is with prevailing social norms and value systems, the greater its adoptability (Rogers & Shoemaker, 1971). However, we saw earlier that self-evaluative sanctions do not operate in isolation from the pressures of social influence. People are often led to behave in otherwise personally devalued ways by strategies that circumvent negative self-reactions. This is done by changing appearances and meanings of new practices to make them look compatible with people's values.

The amenability of an innovation to brief trial is another relevant characteristic that can affect the ease of adoption. Innovations that can be tried on a limited basis are more readily adoptable than those that have to be tried on a large scale with substantial effort and costs. The more weight given to potential risks and the costs of getting rid of new practices should they fail to live up to expectations, the weaker is the incentive to innovate. And finally, people will not adopt innovations even though they are favorably disposed toward them if they lack the money, the skills, or the accessory resources that may be needed. The more resources innovations require, the lower is their adoptability.

Analysis of the determinants and mechanisms of social diffusion should not becloud the fact that not all innovations are useful, nor is resistance to them necessarily dysfunctional (Zaltman & Wallendorf, 1979). In the continuous flow of innovations, the number of faulty ones far exceeds those with truly beneficial possibilities. Both personal and societal well-being are well served by initial wariness to new practices promoted by unsubstantiated or exaggerated claims. The designations "venturesome" for early adopters and "laggards" for later adopters are fitting in the case of innovations that hold promise. However, when people are mesmerized by alluring appeals into trying innovations of questionable value, the more suitable designation is gullibility for early adopters and astuteness for resisters. Rogers (1983) has criticized the prevalent tendency to conceptualize the diffusion process from the perspective of the promoters. This tends to bias the search for explanations of nonadoptive behavior in negative attributes of nonadopters.

SOCIAL NETWORKS AND FLOW OF DIFFUSION

The third major factor that affects the diffusion process concerns social network structures. People are enmeshed in networks of relationships that include occupational colleagues, organizational members, kinships, and friendships, just to mention a few. They are linked not only directly by personal relationships. Because acquaintanceships overlap different network clusters, many people become linked to each other indirectly by interconnected ties. Social structures comprise clustered networks of people with various ties among them, as well as persons who provide connections to other clusters through joint membership or a liaison role. Clusters vary in their internal structure, ranging from loosely knit ones to those that are densely interconnected. Networks also differ in the number and pattern of structural linkages between clusters. They may have many common ties or function with a high degree of separateness. In addition to their degree of interconnectedness, people vary in the positions and status they occupy in particular social networks which can affect their impact on what spreads through their network. One is more apt to learn about new ideas and practices from brief contacts with casual acquaintances than from intensive contact in the same circle of close associates. This path of influence creates the seemingly paradoxical effect that innovations are extensively diffused to cohesive groups through weak social ties (Granovetter, 1983).

Information regarding new ideas and practices is often conveyed through multilinked relationships (Rogers & Kincaid, 1981). Traditionally, the communication process has been conceptualized as one of unidirectional persuasion flowing from a source to a recipient. Rogers emphasizes the mutuality of influence in interpersonal communication. Bidirectionality of influence is in keeping with the agentic perspective of social cognitive theory (Bandura, 2006c, in press). People share information, give meaning by mutual feedback to the information they exchange, gain understanding of each other's views, and influence each other. Specifying the channels of influence through which innovations are dispersed provides greater understanding of the diffusion process than simply plotting the rate of adoptions over time.

There is no single social network in a community that serves all purposes. Different innovations engage different networks. For example, birth control practices and agricultural innovations diffuse through quite different networks within the same community (Marshall, 1971). To complicate matters further, the social networks that come into play in initial phases of diffusion may differ from those that spread the innovation in subsequent phases (Coleman, Katz, & Menzel, 1966). Adoption rates are better predicted from the network that subserves a particular innovation than from a more general communication network. This is not to say that there is no generality to the diffusion function of network structures. If a particular social structure subserves varied activities, it can help to spread the adoption of innovations in each of those activities.

People with many social ties are more apt to adopt innovations than those who have few ties to others (Rogers & Kincaid, 1981). Adoption rates increase as more and more people in one's personal network adopt an innovation. The effects of social connectedness on adoptive behavior may be mediated through several processes. Multilinked relations can foster adoption of innovations because they convey more factual information, they mobilize stronger social influences, or it may be that people with close ties are more receptive to new ideas than those who are socially estranged. Moreover, in social transactions, people see their associates adopt innovations as well as talk about them. Multiple modeling alone can increase adoptive behavior (Bandura, 1986; Perry & Bussey, 1979).

If innovations are highly conspicuous, they can be adopted directly without requiring interaction among adopters. Television is widely used to forge large single-link structures, in which many people are linked directly to the media source, but they may have little or no direct relations with each other. For example, television evangelists attract loyal followers in widely dispersed locales who adopt the transmitted precepts as guides for how to behave in situations involving moral, social, and political issues. Although they share a common bond to the media source, most members of an electronic community may never see each other. Political power structures are similarly being transformed by the creation of new constituencies tied to a single media source, but with little interconnectedness. Mass marketing techniques, using computer identification and mass mailings, create special-interest constituencies that by-pass traditional political organizations in the exercise of political influence.

The evolving information technologies increasingly serve as a vehicle for building social networks. Online transactions transcend the barriers of time and space (Hiltz &

Turoff, 1978; Wellman, 1997). Through interactive electronic networking people link together in widely dispersed locals, exchange information, share new ideas, and transact any number of pursuits. Virtual networking provides a flexible means for creating diffusion structures to serve given purposes, expanding their membership, extending them geographically, and disbanding them when they have outlived their usefulness. With increasing interactivity through blogging and podpostings, Internet technology is interconnecting people globally in the virtual social networks of the cyberworld.

Although structural interconnectedness provides potential diffusion paths, psychosocial factors largely determine the fate of what diffuses through those paths. In other words, it is the transactions that occur within social relationships rather than the ties themselves that explain adoptive behavior. The course of diffusion is best understood by considering the interactions among psychosocial determinants of adoptive behavior, the properties of innovations that facilitate or impede adoption, and the network structures that provide the social pathways of influence. Sociostructural and psychological determinants of adoptive behavior should, therefore, be treated as complementary factors in an integrated comprehensive theory of social diffusion, rather than be cast as rival theories of diffusion.

References

Adoni, H., & Mane, S. (1984). Media and the social construction of reality: Toward an integration of theory and research. *Communication Research*, *11*, 323–340.

Anderson, C.A., Berkowitz, L., Donnerstein, E., Huesmann, L.R., Johnson, J.D., Linz, D., Malamuth, N.M., & Wartella. E (2003). The influence of media violence on youth. *Psychological Science in the Public Interest*, 4(3).

Baldwin, T. F., & Lewis, C. (1972). Violence in television: The industry looks at itself. In G. A. Comstock & E. A. Rubinstein (Eds.), *Television and social behavior: Vol. 1 Media content and control* (pp. 290–373). Washington, DC: U.S. Government Printing Office.

Ball-Rokeach, S., & DeFleur, M. (1976). A dependency model of mass media effects. *Communication Research*, *3*, 3–21.

Ball-Rokeach, S. J. (1972). The legitimation of violence. In J. F. Short, Jr. & M. E. Wolfgang (Eds.), *Collective violence* (pp. 100–111). Chicago: Aldine-Atherton.

Bandura, A. (1973). *Aggression: A social learning analysis*. Englewood Cliffs, NJ: Prentice-Hall.

Bandura, A. (1978, October). "Doomsday Flight" TV story leads to copies. *Stanford Observer*.

Bandura, A. (1982). The psychology of chance encounters and life paths. *American Psychologist*, *37*, 747–755.

Bandura, A. (1986). *Social foundations of thought and action: A social cognitive theory*. Englewood Cliffs, NJ: Prentice-Hall, Inc.

Bandura, A. (1991a). Self-regulation of motivation through anticipatory and self-regulatory mechanisms. In R. A. Dienstbier (Ed.), *Perspectives on motivation: Nebraska symposium on motivation* (Vol. 38, pp. 69–164). Lincoln: University of Nebraska Press.

Bandura, A. (1991b). Social cognitive theory of moral thought and action. In W. M. Kurtines & J. L. Gewirtz (Eds.), *Handbook of moral behavior and development* (Vol. A, pp. 45–103). Hillsdale, NJ: Erlbaum.

Bandura, A. (1992). Social cognitive theory and social referencing. In S. Feinman (Ed.), *Social referencing and the social construction of reality in infancy* (pp. 175–208). New York: Plenum Press.

Bandura, A. (1997). *Self-efficacy: The exercise of control*. New York: Freeman.

Bandura, A. (1999a). A social cognitive theory of personality. In L. Pervin & O. John (Eds.), *Handbook of personality* (2nd ed., pp. 154–196). New York: Guilford Publications.

Bandura, A. (1999b). Moral disengagement in the perpetration of inhumanities. *Personality and Social Psychology Review*, *3*, 193–209.

Bandura, A. (2000a). Self-regulation of motivation and action through perceived self-efficacy. In E. A. Locke (Ed.), *Handbook of principles of organization behavior* (pp. 120–136). Oxford, UK: Blackwell.

Bandura, A. (2000b). Exercise of human agency through collective efficacy. *Current Directions in Psychological Science*, 9, 75–78.

Bandura, A. (2002). Growing primacy of human agency in adaptation and change in the electronic era. *European Psychologist*, 7, 2–16.

Bandura, A. (2004a). The role of selective moral disengagement in terrorism and counterterrorism. In F. M. Mogahaddam & A. J. Marsella (Eds.), *Understanding terrorism: Psychological roots, consequences and interventions* (pp. 121–150). Washington, DC: American Psychological Association Press.

Bandura, A. (2004b). Selective exercise of moral agency. In T. A. Thorkildsen & H. J. Walberg (Eds.), *Nurturing morality* (pp. 37–57). Boston: Kluwer Academic.

Bandura, A. (2004c). Health promotion by social cognitive means. *Health Education & Behavior*, *31*, 143–164.

Bandura, A. (2006a). Going global with social cognitive theory: From prospect to paydirt. In S. I. Donaldson, D. E. Berger, & K. Pezdek (Eds.), *Applied psychology: New frontiers and rewarding careers* (pp. 53–79). Mahwah, NJ: Erlbaum.

Bandura, A. (2006b). On integrating social cognitive and social diffusion theories. In A. Singhal & J. Dearing (Eds.), *Communication of innovations: A journey with Ev Rogers* (pp. 111–135). Beverley Hills: Sage Publications.

Bandura, A. (2006c). Toward a psychology of human agency. *Perspectives on Psychological Science*, *1*, 164–180.

Bandura, A. (2007). Impeding ecological sustainability through selective moral disengagement. *The International Journal of Innovation and Sustainable Development*, 2, 8–35.

Bandura, A. (2008). The reconstrual of "free will" from the agentic perspective of social cognitive theory. In J. Baer, J. C. Kaufman, & R. F. Baumeister (Eds.), *Are we free? Psychology and free will* (pp. 86–127). Oxford: Oxford University Press.

Bandura, A. (in press). Moral disengagement in state executions. In B. L. Cutler (Ed.), *Encyclopedia of Psychology and Law*. Thousand Oaks, CA: Sage Publications.

Bandura, A., Barbaranelli, C., Caprara, G. V., & Pastorelli C. (1996). Mechanisms of moral disengagement in the exercise of moral agency. *Journal of Personality and Social Psychology*, *71*, 364–374.

Bandura, A., Ross, D., & Ross, S. A. (1963). Imitation of film-mediated aggressive models. *Journal of Abnormal and Social Psychology*, *66*, 3–11.

Bandura, A., Underwood, B., & Fromson, M. E. (1975). Disinhibition of aggression through diffusion of responsibility and dehumanization of victims. *Journal of Research in Personality*, 9, 253–269.

Bassiouni, M. C. (1981). Terrorism, law enforcement, and the mass media: Perspectives, problems, proposals. *The Journal of Criminal Law & Criminology*, *72*, 1–51.

Beck, K. H., & Lund, A. K. (1981). The effects of health threat seriousness and personal efficacy upon intentions and behavior. *Journal of Applied Social Psychology*, *11*, 401–405.

Berkowitz, L. (1984). Some effects of thoughts on anti- and prosocial influences of media events: A cognitive-neoassociation analysis. *Psychological Bulletin*, *95*, 410–427.

Berkowitz, L., & Green, R. G. (1967). Stimulus qualities of the target of aggression: A further study. *Journal of Personality and Social Psychology*, *5*, 364–368.

Bolton, M. K. (1993). Imitation versus innovation: Lessons to be learned from the Japanese. *Organizational Dynamics*, *21*(3), 30–45.

Brown, L. (1971). *Television: The business behind the box*. New York: Harcourt Brace Jovanovich.

Bryant, J., Carveth, R. A., & Brown, D. (1981). Television viewing and anxiety: An experimental examination. *Journal of Communication*, *31*, 106–119.

Buerkel-Rothfuss, N. L., & Mayes, S. (1981). Soap opera viewing: The cultivation effect. *Journal of Communication*, *31*, 108–115.

Bussey, K., & Bandura, A. (1999). Social cognitive theory of gender development and differentiation. *Psychological Review, 106*, 676–713.
Cantor, J., & Wilson, B. J. (1988). Helping children cope with frightening media presentations. *Current Psychological Research and Reviews, 7*, 58–75.
Carroll, W. R., & Bandura, A. (1990). Representational guidance of action production in observational learning: A causal analysis. *Journal of Motor Behavior, 22*, 85–97.
Chaffee, S. H. (1982). Mass media and interpersonal channels: Competitive, convergent, or complementary? In G. Gumpert & R. Cathart (Eds.), *Inter/Media: Interpersonal communication in a media world* (pp. 57–77). New York: Oxford University Press.
Chen, C. C., Greene, P. G., & Crick, A. (1998). Does entrepreneurial self-efficacy distinguish entrepreneurs from managers? *Journal of Business Venturing, 13*, 295–316.
Cline, V. B., Croft, R. G., & Courrier, S. (1973). Desensitization of children to television violence. *Journal of Personality and Social Psychology, 27*, 360–365.
Coleman, J. S., Katz, E., & Menzel, H. (1966). *Medical innovation: A diffusion study*. New York: Bobbs-Merrill.
Diener, E., (1977). Deindividuation: Causes and consequences. *Social Behavior and Personality, 5*, 143–156.
Diener, E., & DeFour, D. (1978). Does television violence enhance program popularity? *Journal of Personality and Social Psychology, 36*, 333–341.
Donnerstein, E. (1984). Pornography: Its effect on violence against women. In N. M. Malamuth & E. Donnerstein (Eds.), *Pornography and sexual aggression* (pp. 53–81). New York: Academic Press.
Duncker, K. (1938). Experimental modification of children's food preferences through social suggestion. *Journal of Abnormal Social Psychology, 33*, 489–507.
Dysinger, W. S., & Ruckmick, C. A. (1993). *The emotional responses of children to the motion-picture situation*. New York: Macmillan.
Falmagne, R. J. (1975). *Reasoning: Representation and process in children and adults*. Hillsdale, NJ: Erlbaum.
Flerx, V. C., Fidler, D. S., & Rogers, R. W. (1976). Sex role stereotypes: Developmental aspects and early intervention. *Child Development, 47*, 998–1007.
Gerbner, G. (1972). Communication and social environment. *Scientific American, 227*, 153–160.
Gerbner, G., Gross, L., Morgan, M., Shanahan, J., & Signorielli, N. (2001). Living with television: The dynamics of the cultivation process. In J. Bryant & D. Zillman (Eds.), *Perspectives on media effects, 2nd ed.* (pp. 43–67). Mahwah, NJ: Erlbaum.
Gerbner, G., Gross, L., Morgan, M., & Signorielli, N. (1981). A curious journey into the scary world of Paul Hirsch. *Communication Research, 8*, 39–72.
Gerbner, G., Gross, L., Signorielli, N., & Morgan, M. (1980). Television violence, victimization, and power. *American Behavioral Scientist, 23*, 705–716.
Goranson, R. E. (1970). Media violence and aggressive behavior. A review of experimental research. In L. Berkowitz (Ed.), *Advances in experimental social psychology* (Vol. 5, pp. 2–31). New York: Academic Press.
Granovetter, M. (1983). The strength of weak ties—A network theory revisited. In R. Collins (Ed.), *Sociological theory 1983* (pp. 201–233). San Francisco: Jossey-Bass.
Hall, J. R. (1987). *Gone from the promised land: Jonestown in American cultural history*. New Brunswick, NJ: Transaction Books.
Halloran, J. D., & Croll, P. (1972). Television programs in Great Britain: Content and control. In G. A. Comstock & E. A. Rubinstein (Eds.), *Television and social behavior: Vol. 1. Media content and control* (pp. 415–492). Washington, DC: U.S. Government Printing Office.
Harris, M. B., & Evans, R. C. (1973). Models and creativity. *Psychological Reports, 33*, 763–769.
Hawkins, R. P., & Pingree, S. (1982). Television's influence on social reality. In D. Pearl, L. Bouthilet, & J. Lazar (Eds.), *Television and behavior: Ten years of scientific progress and implications for the eighties* (Vol. II, pp. 224–247). Rockville, MD: National Institute of Mental Health.
Heath, L. (1984). Impact of newspaper crime reports on fear of crime: Multimethodological investigation. *Journal of Personality and Social Psychology, 47*, 263–276.

Hiltz, S. R., & Turoff, M. (1978). *The network nation: Human communication via computer*. Reading, MA: Addison-Wesley.

Hirsch, P. M. (1980). The "scary world of the nonviewer" and other anomalies: A reanalysis of Gerbner et al.'s findings on cultivation analysis. Part I. *Communication Research, 7*, 403–456.

Joo, Y. J., Bong, M., & Choi, H. J. (2000). Self-efficacy for self-regulated learning, academic self-efficacy, and Internet self-efficacy in web-based instruction. *Educational Technology Research & Development*, 48, 5–18.

Kanungo, R. N., & Pang, S. (1973). Effects of human models on perceived product quality. *Journal of Applied Psychology, 57*, 172–178.

Kelman, H. C., & Hamilton, V. L. (1989). *Crimes of obedience: Toward a social psychology of authority and responsibility*. New Haven, CT: Yale University Press.

Klapper, J. T. (1960). *The effects of mass communication*. New York: Free Press.

Kreuter, M. W., Strecher, V. J., & Glassman, B. (1999). One size does not fit all: The case for tailoring print materials. *Annals of Behavioral Medicine, 21*(4), 276–283.

Larsen, O. N. (Ed.). (1968). *Violence and the mass media*. New York: Harper & Row.

Leyens, J., Camino, L., Parke, R.D., & Berkowitz, L. (1975). The effects of movie violence on aggression in a field setting as a function of group dominance and cohesion. *Journal of Personality and Social Psychology, 32*, 346–360.

Maibach, E. W., Flora, J., & Nass, C. (1991). Changes in self-efficacy and health behavior in response to a minimal contact community health campaign. *Health Communication, 3*, 1–15.

Malamuth, N. M., & Donnerstein, E. (Eds.). (1984). *Pornography and sexual aggression*. New York: Academic Press.

Markham, G. D., & Baron, R. A. (1999, May). *Cognitive mechanisms: Potential differences between entrepreneurs and non-entrepreneurs*. Paper presented at the Babson College/Kauffman Foundation Entrepreneurship Conference.

Marshall, J. F. (1971). Topics and networks in intravillage communication. In S. Polgar (Ed.), *Culture and population: A collection of current studies* (pp. 160–166). Cambridge, MA: Schenkman Publishing Company.

McAlister, A. J., Bandura, A., & Owen, S. V. (2006). Mechanisms of moral disengagement in support of military force: The impact of Sept. 11. *Journal of Social and Clinical Psychology, 25*, 141–166.

McGhee, P. E., & Frueh, T. (1980). Television viewing and the learning of sex-role stereotypes. *Sex Roles*, 6, 179–188.

Meichenbaum, D. (1984). Teaching thinking: A cognitive-behavioral perspective. In R. Glaser, S. Chipman, & J. Segal (Eds.), *Thinking and learning skills (Vol. 2): Research and open questions* (pp. 407–426). Hillsdale, NJ: Erlbaum.

Meyer, T. P. (1972). Effects of viewing justified and unjustified real film violence on aggressive behavior. *Journal of Personality and Social Psychology, 23*, 21–29.

Meyerowitz, B. E., & Chaiken, S. (1987). The effect of message framing on breast self-examination attitudes, intentions, and behavior. *Journal of Personality and Social Psychology, 52*, 500–510.

Midgley, M. (1978). *Beast and man: The roots of human nature*. Ithaca, NY: Cornell University Press.

Milgram, S. (1974). *Obedience to authority: An experimental view*. New York: Harper & Row.

Muñoz, R. F., Lenert, L. L., Delucchi, K., Stoddard, J., Pérez, J. E., Penilla, C., & Pérez-Stable, E. J. (2006). Toward evidence-based Internet interventions: A Spanish/English web site for international smoking cessation trials. *Nicotine & Tobacco Research*, 8, 77–87.

Newhagen, J.E. (1994a) Self-efficacy and call-in political television show use. *Communication Research*, 21, 366–379.

Newhagen, J. E. (1994b). Media use and political efficacy: The suburbanization of race and class. *Journal of the American Society for Information Science*, 45, 386–394.

O'Bryant, S. L., & Corder-Bolz, C. R. (1978). The effects of television on children's stereotyping of women's work roles. *Journal of Vocational Behavior, 12*, 233–244.

Osofsky, M. J., Bandura, A., & Zimbardo, P. (2005). Role of moral disengagement in the execution process. *Law and Human Behavior, 29*, 371–393.

Ostlund, L. E. (1974). Perceived innovation attributes as predictors of innovativeness. *Journal of Consumer Research*, *1*, 23–29.

Pelz, D. C. (1983). Use of information channels in urban innovations. *Knowledge*, *5*, 3–25.

Perry, D. G., & Bussey, K. (1979). The social learning theory of sex differences: Imitation is alive and well. *Journal of Personality and Social Psychology*, *37*, 1699–1712.

Peterson, R. A., & Kerin, R. A. (1979). The female role in advertisements: Some experimental evidence. *Journal of Marketing*, *41*, 59–63.

Philips, D. P. (1985). Natural experiments on the effects of mass media violence on fatal aggression: Strengths and weaknesses of a new approach. In L. Berkowitz (Ed.), *Advances in experimental social psychology* (Vol. 19, pp. 207–250). New York: Academic.

Rimal, R. N. (2000). Closing the knowledge-behavior gap in health promotion: The mediating role of self-efficacy. *Health Communication*, *12*, 219–237.

Robertson, T. S. (1971). *Innovative behavior and communication*. New York: Holt, Rinehart & Winston.

Rogers, E. M. (1983). *Diffusion of Innovation (3rd Edition)*. New York: Free Press.

Rogers, E. M. (1987). Progress, problems and prospects for network research: Investigating relationships in the age of electronic communication technologies. *Social Networks*, *9*, 285–310.

Rogers, E. M. (1995). *Diffusion of innovations* (4th ed.). New York: Free Press.

Rogers, E. M., & Kincaid, D. L. (1981). *Communication networks: Toward a new paradigm for research*. New York: Free Press.

Rogers, E. M., & Shoemaker, F. (1971). *Communication of innovations: A cross-cultural approach* (2nd ed.). New York: Free Press.

Rosenthal, T. L., & Zimmerman, B. J. (1978). *Social learning and cognition*. New York: Academic Press.

Sabido, M. (1981). *Towards the social use of soap operas*. Mexico City, Mexico: Institute for Communication Research.

Siegel, A. E. (1958). The influence of violence in the mass media upon children's role expectation. *Child Development*, *29*, 35–56.

Singhal, A., Cody, M. J., Rogers, E. M., & Sabido, M. (2004, Eds.) *Entertainment-education and social change: History, research, and practice* (pp. 75–96). Mahwah, NJ: Erlbaum.

Singhal, A., & Rogers. E. M. (1999). *Entertainment-education: A communication strategy for social change*. Mahwah, NJ: Erlbaum.

Slater, M. D. (1989). Social influences and cognitive control as predictors of self-efficacy and eating behavior. *Cognitive Therapy and Research*, *13*, 231–245.

Snyder, M. (1980). Seek, and ye shall find: Testing hypotheses about other people. In E. T. Higgins, C. P. Herman, & M. P. Zanna (Eds.), *Social cognition: The Ontario Symposium on Personality and Social Psychology* (Vol. 1, pp. 105–130). Hillsdale, NJ: Erlbaum.

Snyder, M., & Campbell, B. H. (1982). Self-monitoring: The self in action. In J. Suls (Ed.), *Psychological perspectives on the self* (pp. 185–207). Hillsdale, NJ: Erlbaum.

Taylor, C. B., Winzelberg, A., & Celio, A. (2001). Use of interactive media to prevent eating disorders. In R. Striegel-Moor & L. Smolak (Eds.), *Eating disorders: New direction for research and practice* (pp. 255–270). Washington, DC: APA.

Thomas, M. H., Horton, R. W., Lippincott, E. C., & Drabman, R. S. (1977). Desensitization to portrayals of real-life aggression as function of exposure to television violence. *Journal of Personality and Social Psychology*, *35*, 450–458.

Tornatzky, L. G., & Klein, K. J. (1982). Innovation characteristics and innovation adoption-implementation: A meta-analysis of findings. *IEEE Transactions of Engineering and Management*, *EM-29*, 28–45.

Watt, J. G., Jr., & van den Berg, S. A. (1978). Time series analysis of alternative media effects theories. In R. D. Ruben (Ed.), *Communication Yearbook 2* (pp. 215–224). New Brunswick, NJ: Transaction Books.

Wellman, B. (1997). An electronic group is virtually a social network. In S. Kielser (Ed.), *Culture of the Internet* (pp. 179–205). Mahwah, NJ: Erlbaum.

White, J., Bandura, A., & Bero, L. (in press). Moral disengagement in the manipulation of research in the corporate world. *Journal of Business Ethics.*

Williams, S. L. (1992). Perceived self-efficacy and phobic disability. In R. Swarzer (Ed.), *Self-efficacy: Thought control of action* (pp. 149–176). Washington, D.C.: Hemisphere.

Wilson, B. J., & Cantor, J. (1985). Developmental differences in empathy with a television protagonist's fear. *Journal of Experimental Child Psychology, 39*, 284–299.

Wood, R. E., & Bandura, A. (1989). Social cognitive theory of organizational management. *Academy of Management Review, 14*, 361–384.

Zaltman, G., & Wallendorf, M. (1979). *Consumer behavior: Basic findings and management implications.* New York: Wiley.

Zillmann, D., & Bryant, J. (1984). Effects of massive exposure to pornography. In N. M. Malamuth & E. Donnerstein (Eds.), *Pornography and sexual aggression* (pp. 115–138). New York: Academic Press.

Zimbardo, P. G. (2007). *The Lucifer effect: Understanding how good people turn evil.* New York: Random House.

7

MASS MEDIA ATTITUDE CHANGE

Implications of the Elaboration Likelihood Model of Persuasion

Richard E. Petty
Ohio State University

Pablo Briñol
Universidad Autónoma de Madrid

Joseph R. Priester
University of Southern California

Undoubtedly, few social scientists today think that the mass media have the power to sway huge audiences to the extent once believed likely. Nevertheless, the technological advances of the last century—from the first primitive radio broadcasts to today's high speed mobile Internet devices—have made it possible for individual communicators to have access to unprecedented numbers of potential message recipients, and recipients to a constant barrage of messages. Millions of dollars are spent worldwide each year in attempts to change peoples' attitudes about political candidates, consumer products, health and safety practices, and charitable causes. In most of these instances, the ultimate goal is to influence people's behavior so that they will vote for certain politicians or referenda, purchase specific goods, engage in safer driving, eating, and sexual activities, and donate money to various religious, environmental, and educational organizations and institutions. To what extent are media persuasion attempts effective?

The success of media campaigns depends in part on: (a) whether the transmitted communications are effective in changing the attitudes of the recipients in the desired direction, and (b) whether these modified attitudes in turn influence people's behaviors. Our goal in this chapter is to present a brief overview of current psychological approaches to mass media influence, and to outline in more detail a general framework that can be used to understand the processes responsible for mass media attitude change. This framework is called the elaboration likelihood model of persuasion (ELM; see Petty & Cacioppo, 1981, 1986b; Petty & Wegener, 1999). Before addressing contemporary approaches, we provide a very brief historical overview of perspectives on mass media influence.

EARLY EXPLORATIONS OF MASS MEDIA PERSUASION

Direct Effects Model

The initial assumption about the effects of the mass media by social scientists in the 1920s and 1930s was that mass communication techniques were quite potent. For example, in an analysis of mass communication during World War I, Lasswell (1927) concluded that "propaganda is one of the most powerful instrumentalities in the modern world" (p. 220). During this period, there were several salient examples of seemingly effective mass communication effects. These included the panic following the 1929 stock market crash; the well-publicized mass hysteria following the radio broadcast of Orson Wells' *War of the Worlds* in 1938; and the rise in popularity of individuals such as Adolf Hitler in Germany, the right wing Catholic Priest, Father Coughlin, and Louisiana Senator Huey Long in the United States. The assumption of Lasswell and others was that transmission of information by mass communication produced direct effects on attitudes and behavior (e.g., Doob, 1935; Lippmann, 1922). In detailing the views about mass communication during this period, Sears and colleagues noted that it was assumed that "the audience was captive, attentive, and gullible . . . the citizenry sat glued to the radio, helpless victims" (Sears & Kosterman, 1994) and that "propaganda could be made almost irresistible" (Sears & Whitney, 1973, p. 2).

Many analysts of the period based their startling assessments of the power of the media on informal and anecdotal evidence rather than careful empirical research. For example, few attempts were made to measure the attitudes of message recipients prior to and following propaganda efforts. Thus, although it could be that the great propagandists of the time were changing the attitudes of their audience, it was also possible that the communicators were mostly attracting an audience that already agreed with them (called "selective exposure;" see Frey, 1986), or some combination of the two. Of course, not all analysts of the period were so optimistic about the prospects for the mass media to produce dramatic changes in opinion, but it was the dominant view (Wartella & Middlestadt, 1991).[1]

Although the Direct Effects Model has been replaced by more sophisticated theoretical perspectives, there do remain echoes of this model within both popular and academic writings. The news media, for example, have been represented in the popular literature as directly influencing and shaping political attitudes (e.g., Adams, 1993), the development of racism (e.g., Suber, 1997), and consumer preferences (e.g., Lohr, 1991). Traces of the Direct Effects Model can also be discerned in current theoretical perspectives. Zaller (1991), for instance, argues that information presentation is the key to public opinion formation and shift. Specifically, he provides some evidence that one can predict opinion change from the mere amount of information provided in the media for a particular stance. As we will see shortly, most current analyses of attitude change hold that it is not the amount or direction of the information per se that produces persuasion, but rather, people's idiosyncratic reactions to this information.

Indirect Effects Model

The Direct Effects Model was tempered considerably in the next two decades largely as a result of the subsequent empirical research conducted. For example, in analyzing survey information gathered by the National Opinion Research Center, Hyman and Sheatsley (1947) concluded that the effectiveness of mass communication campaigns could not be increased simply by increasing the number of messages. Rather, the specific psychological barriers to effective information dissemination must be considered and overcome (see also Cartwright, 1949). For example, they noted that people often distort incoming information to be consistent with prior attitudes, making change less likely. A similar conclusion was reached by Lazarsfeld, Berelson, and Gaudet (1948) in their influential study of the impact of the media in the 1940 Presidential campaign. A major result from this study was that the media appeared to reinforce people's already existing attitudes rather than producing new ones (see also Klapper, 1960; Lord, Ross, & Lepper, 1979). Some researchers argued that when public attitude change was produced, it was only indirectly attributable to the media. That is, the media were more effective in influencing various opinion leaders than the average person, and these opinion leaders were responsible for changes in the mass public (i.e., a "two-step" flow of communication; Katz & Lazarsfeld, 1955).

Studies conducted during World War II reinforced the "limited effects" view of the media. Most notably, the wartime studies by Carl Hovland and his colleagues showed that although various military training films had an impact on the knowledge of the soldier recipients, the films were relatively ineffective in producing mass changes in attitudes and behavior. Instead, the persuasive power of the films depended on a large number of moderating variables (Hovland, Lumsdaine, & Sheffield, 1949; see also Shils & Janowitz, 1948). When World War II ended, Hovland returned to Yale University, and the systematic examination of these moderating variables was begun in earnest.

CONTEMPORARY APPROACHES TO MASS MEDIA PERSUASION

The Attitude Construct

Contemporary social psychologists concerned with the study of media influence, like their predecessors (e.g., Peterson & Thurstone, 1933), have focused on the concept of "attitudes," or people's general predispositions to evaluate other people, objects, and issues favorably or unfavorably. People are aware of and can report most of their attitudes (explicit attitudes), but sometimes people come to have favorable or unfavorable automatic predispositions of which they might not be aware or deny (implicit attitudes). For example, people can harbor implicit prejudices (Devine, 1989) or other evaluative tendencies (Petty, Tormala, Briñol, & Jarvis, 2006) that they do not endorse (see also Greenwald & Banaji, 1995; Wilson, Lindsey, & Schooler, 2000).[2] The attitude construct achieved its preeminent position in research on social influence because of the assumption that a person's attitude—whether implicit or explicit—is an important mediating variable between exposure to new information, on the one hand, and behavioral change, on the other. For example, a television commercial might be based on the idea that giving people information about a candidate's issue-positions will lead to favorable attitudes toward the candidate and ultimately to contributing money to and voting for the candidate. Or, mere repeated exposure to a product name in a radio message might lead the listener to like the product name and therefore select it for purchase without much thought on the next shopping trip (Fazio, 1990).

Over the past 50 years, numerous theories of attitude change and models of knowledge-attitude-behavior relationships have been developed (see reviews by Eagly & Chaiken,

1993; Petty & Wegener, 1998a). Contemporary analyses of mass media persuasion have focused on the variables that determine when the media will be effective versus ineffective and what the underlying processes are by which the media induce change. Perhaps the most well known psychological framework for categorizing and understanding mass media persuasion effects was popularized by Hovland and his colleagues (e.g., Hovland, 1954; Hovland, Janis, & Kelley, 1953) and elaborated considerably by William McGuire (McGuire, 1985, 1989; see McGuire, 1996, for a review of the Hovland approach). After describing this early influential model, we turn to more contemporary approaches.

The Communication/Persuasion Matrix Model of Media Effects

One of the most basic assumptions of initial theories of attitude change (e.g., Strong, 1925), that is also evident in contemporary approaches (e.g., McGuire, 1985) was that effective influence required a sequence of steps (Petty & Cacioppo, 1984b). For example, Figure 7.1 presents McGuire's (1985, 1989) communication/persuasion matrix model of persuasion. This model outlines the inputs (or independent variables) to the persuasion process that media persuaders can control along with the outputs (or dependent variables) that can be measured to see if any influence attempt is successful.

Matrix Inputs

The inputs to the persuasion process in Figure 7.1 are based in part on Lasswell's (1964) classic question: Who says what to whom, when, and how? First, a communication typically has some *source*. The source can be expert or not, attractive or not, male or female, an individual or group, and so on. This source provides some information, the *message*, and this message can be emotional or logical, long or short, organized or not,

Outputs	SOURCE	MESSAGE	RECIPIENT	CHANNEL	CONTEXT
EXPOSURE					
ATTENTION					
INTEREST					
COMPREHENSION					
ACQUISITION					
YIELDING					
MEMORY					
RETRIEVAL					
DECISION					
ACTION					
REINFORCEMENT					
CONSOLIDATION					

Communication Inputs: (column headings)

Figure 7.1 The Communication/Persuasion Process as an Input/Output Matrix. The Figure Depicts the Primary Independent and Dependent Variables in Mass Media Persuasion Research (Adapted from McGuire, 1989).

directed at a specific or a general belief, and so forth. The message is presented to a particular *recipient* who can be high or low in intelligence, knowledge, experience, in a good or bad mood, and so on. The message is presented via some *channel* of communication. Different media allow different types of input such as audio only (e.g., radio), audio plus moving visual (television, Internet), print only, or print plus static visual (e.g., magazines, newspapers). Some media allow presentation of the message at the recipient's own pace (e.g., reading a magazine or browsing the Internet), whereas other media control the pace externally (e.g., radio and television). Finally, the message is presented to the recipient in some *context*. That is, the persuasion context can be one of group or individual exposure, noisy or quiet environment, and so forth.

Matrix Outputs

Each of the inputs to the persuasion process can have an impact on one or more of the outputs depicted in Figure 7.1. The communication/persuasion matrix model contends that in order for effective influence to occur, a person first needs to be *exposed* to some new information. Media are often selected by potential persuaders after an estimation of the number and type of people the message is likely to reach. Also, by deciding what to present, those who control the mass media help define the range of issues to which the public is exposed (e.g., Iyengar, Kinder, Peters, & Krosnick, 1984).

Secondly, the person must *attend* to the information presented. Just because a person is sitting in front of the television doesn't mean that he or she knows what is going on. For example, in order to gain and attract attention, TV commercials often present babies, puppies, or attractive men or women in proximity to the attitude object. Even if the person does notice the information, this doesn't mean that the person's *interest* will be engaged. The next two stages involve *comprehension* and *acquisition*, or the question of what part of the information presented the person actually understands and learns. It is only at step 6 that attitude change or *yielding* occurs. Once the person accepts the information in the message, the next step in the sequence involves *memory* or storage of the new information and the attitude that it supports. The next three steps detail the processes involved in translating the new attitude into a behavioral response. That is, at some subsequent behavioral opportunity, the person must *retrieve* the new attitude from memory, *decide* to act on it, and perform the appropriate *action*. Finally, the model notes that if the attitude-consistent behavior is not *reinforced*, the new attitude might be undermined. For example, if you act on your attitude and become embarrassed, that attitude will not persist. If the behavior is rewarding, however, the attitude-consistent behavior might lead to attitudinal *consolidation*, making the new attitude more likely to endure over time and guide future behavior.

Variants of this general information processing model were sometimes interpreted in theory and in practice as suggesting that a change early in the sequence (e.g., attention) would inevitably lead to a change later in the sequence (e.g., yielding). McGuire (1989) noted, however, that the likelihood that a message will evoke each of the steps in the sequence should be viewed as a conditional probability. Thus, even if the likelihood of achieving each of the first six steps in a mass media campaign was 60%, the maximum probability of achieving all six steps (exposure, attention, interest, comprehension, learning, and yielding) would be $.6^6$, or only 5%.

In addition, it is important to consider the fact that any one input variable can have different effects on the different output steps. For example, Hyman and Sheatsley (1947) noted that in the political domain, the knowledge and interest of a message recipient was positively related to exposure to political messages, but negatively related to attitude change. That is, high interest and knowledge tends to lead people to attend political rallies (exposure), but because people attend rallies of candidates they like, and because information is assimilated to existing opinions, attitude change (yielding) is low. In a cogent analysis of this point, McGuire (1968) noted that several variables might have opposite effects on the steps involving *reception* of information (e.g., exposure, attention, comprehension, acquisition, memory) versus yielding to it. For example, the intelligence of the message recipient is related positively to reception processes, but negatively related to yielding. The joint action of reception and yielding processes implies that people of moderate intelligence should be easier to persuade than people of low or high intelligence since this maximizes both reception and yielding (see also, Rholes & Wood, 1992).

Additional Issues for the Communication/Persuasion Matrix Model

Although McGuire's input/output matrix model serves as a very useful way to think about the steps involved in producing attitude and behavior change via the mass media or other means, it is important to appreciate a number of things that the model does not address. First, it is now clear that some of the steps in the postulated information processing sequence are completely independent of each other, rather than sequential. For example, although a person's ability to learn and recall new information (e.g., facts about a political candidate) was often thought to be an important causal determinant of attitude and behavior change (e.g., favoring and voting for a candidate), little empirical evidence has accumulated to support the view that message learning is a *necessary* step for persuasion (Greenwald, 1968; McGuire, 1985; Petty & Cacioppo, 1981). Rather, the existing evidence shows that message comprehension and learning can occur in the absence of attitude change, and that a person's attitudes can change without learning the specific information in the communication. That is, a person might be able to comprehend all of the intended information perfectly, but not be persuaded either because the information is counterargued, or seen as personally irrelevant. On the other hand, a person might get the information all wrong (scoring zero on a knowledge or recall test) but think about it in a manner that produces the intended change. That is, misunderstanding the message can sometimes produce more change than correct understanding.

This analysis helps to explain why previous research on mass media effects has sometimes found that message learning and changes in knowledge occur in the absence of attitude change and vice versa (Petty, Baker, & Gleicher, 1991). For example, after an extensive review of the mass media programs commonly used by government agencies to educate and to reduce social problems involving drugs and alcohol, Kinder, Pape, and Walfish (1980) concluded that although these programs were typically successful in increasing participants' knowledge about drugs, there was very little evidence that they were successful in changing attitudes and behavior.

Second, the model tells us little about the factors that produce yielding. Even though the initial steps in the information processing sequence are viewed as prerequisites to acceptance, McGuire did not mean to imply that people would invariably yield to all information they comprehended and learned. That is, the earlier steps were thought to be necessary but not sufficient for yielding. Rather, just as source and other variables determine the extent of attention, they also determine the extent of acceptance. As implied by the communication/persuasion matrix, current psychological research on influence focuses on how and why various features of a persuasion situation (i.e., aspects of the source, message, channel, recipient, and context) affect each of the steps in the communication sequence (e.g., how does the credibility of the source affect attention to the message?). The most research by far, however, focuses on the question of how variables affect the processes responsible for yielding to or resisting the communication.

Cognitive Response Approach

Cognitive response theory (Greenwald, 1968; Petty, Ostrom, & Brock, 1981) was developed explicitly to address two key issues unaddressed by the communication/persuasion matrix. That is, the cognitive response approach attempted to account for the low correlation between message learning and persuasion observed in many studies, and for the processes responsible for yielding. In contrast to the traditional view that acceptance of a message depended upon learning the message content, the cognitive response approach contends that the impact of variables on persuasion depends on the extent to which individuals articulate and rehearse their own individual thoughts to the information presented. The cognitive response perspective maintains that individuals are active participants in the persuasion process who attempt to relate message elements to their existing repertoires of information. The influence of cognitive responses —or one's own thoughts—on subsequent attitudes has been demonstrated in a variety of ways.

For example, in early research on "role playing," it was shown that asking people to self-generate arguments on an issue can lead to relatively enduring attitude change (e.g., Janis & King, 1954). When engaged in role playing (e.g., "generate a message to convince your friend to stop smoking"), people engage in a "biased scanning" of evidence on the issue and end up persuading themselves because the arguments they generate are seen as compelling (Greenwald & Albert, 1968). In related research, Tesser and his colleagues conducted a series of investigations of the effects of merely thinking about an attitude object. These studies have shown clearly that with mere thought, people's reactions and impressions to other people, objects, and issues can become more extreme, in either a positive or negative direction, depending on the valence of the initial thoughts generated (see Tesser, Martin, & Mendolia, 1995, for a review).

The cognitive response approach holds that even when external information is presented, people's own thoughts or cognitive responses to this information, rather than learning the information per se, determine the extent of influence. Most studies of cognitive responses to messages focus on the valence and the extent of thinking. Valence refers to the favorableness or unfavorableness of the thoughts with respect to the message, and extent of thinking refers to the number of thoughts generated. In general, the more favorable thoughts people have to the message, the more persuasion that occurs; and the more unfavorable thoughts people have to a message, the less influence (or even change in a direction opposite to the advocacy) that occurs (Greenwald, 1968; Petty, Ostrom, & Brock, 1981; Wright, 1973).

In addition to coding thoughts for valence and number, other categorization schemes have been used (e.g., coding for the origin of the thought, target, self-relevance, and so forth; see Cacioppo & Petty, 1981; Shavitt & Brock, 1986). One feature of thoughts that has proven to be useful is the confidence with which people hold their thoughts. That is, two people can have the same favorable thought about the message (e.g., "the proposed tax increase should help our schools"), but one person can have considerably more confidence in the validity of that thought than another person. According to *self-validation theory* (Petty, Briñol, & Tormala, 2002), the relationship between thoughts and attitudes should be greater when people have confidence rather than doubt in their thoughts. The self-validation approach says that many of the traditionally studied source, message, recipient, and channel variables can influence persuasion by influencing the extent to which people have confidence in the thoughts they have in response to a persuasive message (see Briñol & Petty, 2004, for a review). In a series of initial studies conducted to test the basic self-validation hypothesis, Petty et al. (2002) found that when the thoughts in response to a message were primarily favorable, increasing confidence in their validity increased persuasion, but increasing doubt about their validity decreased persuasion. When the thoughts to a message were mostly unfavorable, then increasing confidence reduced persuasion, but undermining confidence increased persuasion. These relationships held whether confidence in thoughts was measured or manipulated. Thus, research on cognitive responses suggest that generating favorable or unfavorable thoughts to a persuasive message is an important factor in producing attitude change, but it is not the only factor. Individuals also need to have confidence in the thoughts that they generate if these thoughts are to have an impact.

THE ELABORATION LIKELIHOOD MODEL OF PERSUASION

Although the cognitive response approach provided important insights into the persuasion process, it only focuses on those situations in which people are active processors of the information provided to them. The theory did not account very well for persuasion in situations where people were not actively thinking about the message content. To correct this deficit, the elaboration likelihood model of persuasion (ELM) was proposed. The ELM holds that persuasion can occur when thinking is high or low, but the processes and consequences of persuasion are different in each situation (Petty & Cacioppo, 1981, 1986a; Petty & Wegener, 1999). More specifically, the ELM holds that the processes that occur during the "yielding" stage of influence can be thought of as emphasizing one of two relatively distinct "routes to persuasion" (see Figure 7.2). The ELM focuses on yielding since this is the critical stage at which people accept or reject the message advocacy.

Central and Peripheral Routes to Persuasion

Central Route

The first, or *central route* to persuasion, involves effortful cognitive activity whereby the person draws upon prior experience and knowledge in order to carefully scrutinize all of the information relevant to determining the central merits of the position advocated (Petty, 1994; Petty & Cacioppo, 1986a). Consistent with the cognitive response approach to persuasion, the message recipient under the central route is actively generating favorable and/or unfavorable thoughts in response to the persuasive communication. The goal of this cognitive effort is to determine if the position advocated has any merit. Not every message received from the media is sufficiently interesting or important to think about, and not every situation provides the time and opportunity for careful reflection. When people are motivated and able to take the central route, they carefully appraise the extent to which the communication provides information that is fundamental or central to the perceived merits of the position advocated.

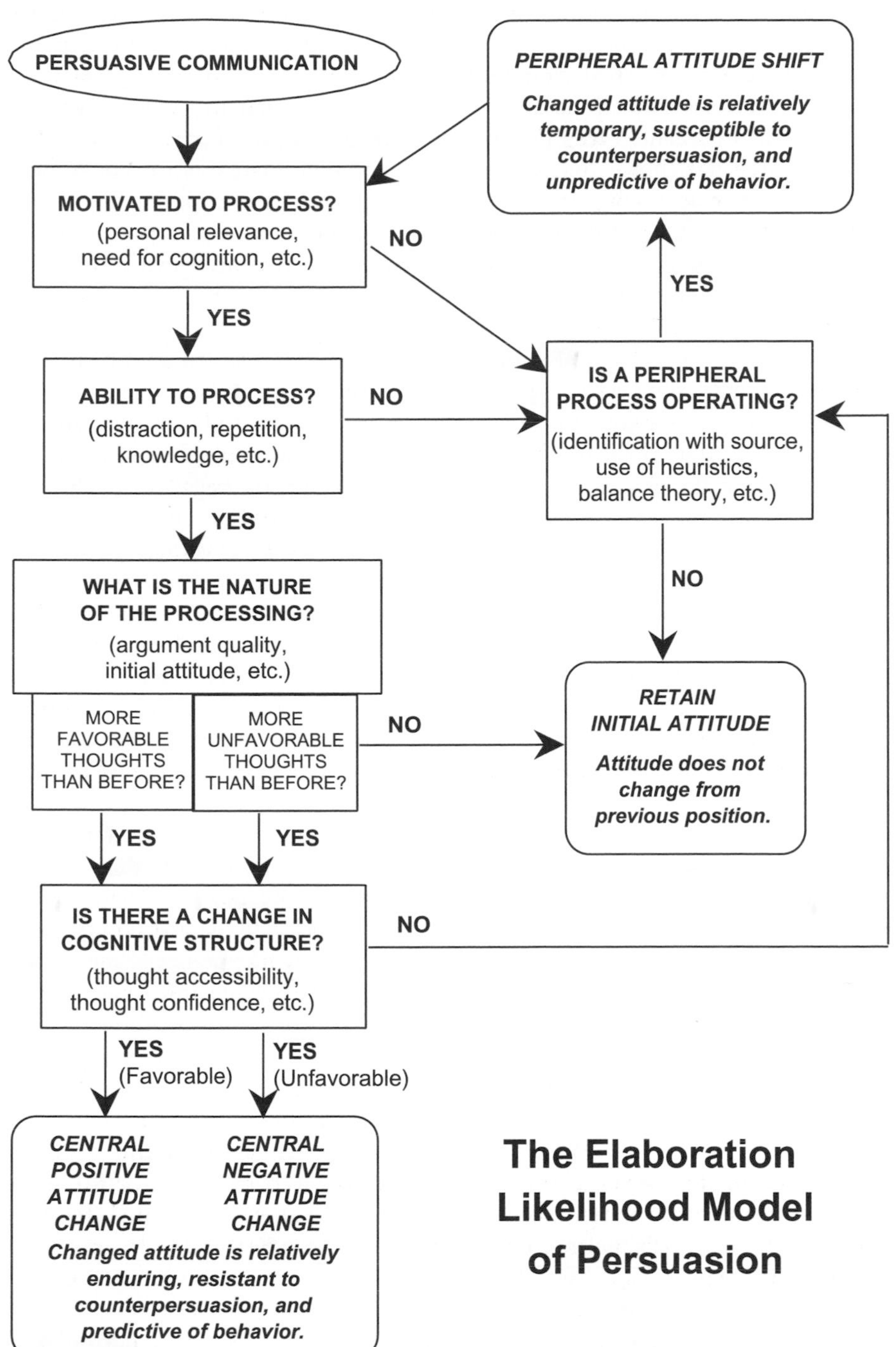

Figure 7.2 Schematic Depiction of the Elaboration Likelihood Model of Persuasion. The Figure Shows the Possible Endpoints after Exposure to a Persuasive Communication for People Following Central and Peripheral Routes to Attitude Change, and the Boxes Indicate the Roles that Variables can Play in the Persuasion Process (Adapted from Petty & Cacioppo, 1986a).

Of course, the particular kind of information that is perceived central to the merits of any particular issue can vary from person to person and from situation to situation. For example, when some people think about social issues (e.g., capital punishment), religious considerations and arguments are particularly persuasive, but for others, legalistic arguments carry the most weight (Cacioppo, Petty, & Sidera, 1982). Likewise, research has shown that when some people evaluate ads for consumer products, they are primarily concerned about how usage of the product will affect the image that they project; but for other people, this dimension is unimportant (DeBono & Packer, 1991; Snyder & DeBono, 1989). Dimensions that are most important will often receive the most scrutiny (Petty & Wegener, 1998b; Petty, Wheeler, & Bizer, 2000).

Research suggests that a key function of the media in the political domain is to make certain political and social issues more salient than others (see Iyengar & Kinder, 1987; McCombs & Reynolds, this volume). For example, a study of magazine stories showed that from the 1960s to the 1990s, stories about drug abuse and nutrition increased dramatically, stories about communism and desegregation declined, and stories on pollution remained about the same (Paisley, 1989). If people come to believe that certain issues are more important due to extensive media coverage, it is reasonable that these dimensions of judgment will become more central in evaluating the merits of political candidates. By giving a problem great coverage (e.g., whether it is global warming or a presidential sex scandal), newscasters render that problem highly accessible in the minds of recipients, making them more likely to think about that particular problem when they judge the "bottom line" on an attitude object (e.g., a presidential candidate; see Sherman, Mackie, & Driscoll, 1990). So, by setting the agenda of what is important to evaluate, the media can have important "indirect" effects on attitude change.[3]

In the central route, once people have thoughts about the message, the final step involves integrating the new thoughts into one's overall cognitive structure. Such integration is more likely to occur if one's thoughts are rehearsed and held with high confidence. It is important to note, however, that just because the attitude change process in the central route involves considerable cognitive work, does not mean that the attitude formed will be a rational or "accurate" one. The extensive information processing activity might be highly biased by factors such as one's prior attitude and knowledge, or one's current emotional state. The important point is that sometimes attitudes are changed by a rather thoughtful process in which people attend carefully to the issue-relevant information presented, examine this information in light of their relevant experiences and knowledge, and evaluate the information along the dimensions they perceive central to the merits of the issue. People engaged in this effortful cognitive activity have been characterized as engaging in "systematic" (Chaiken, Liberman, & Eagly, 1989), "mindful" (Palmerino, Langer, & McGillis, 1984), and "piecemeal" (Fiske & Pavelchak, 1986) processing (see Chaiken & Trope, 1999, for a discussion of various "dual route" models of social judgment).

Attitudes changed by the central route have been shown to have a number of distinguishing characteristics. Because these attitudes are well articulated and integrated into a person's cognitive structure, these attitudes have been found to be relatively easy to access from memory, held with high confidence, persistent over time, predictive of behavior, and resistant to change until they are challenged by cogent contrary information (Petty, Haugtvedt, & Smith, 1995; see Petty & Krosnick, 1995, for an extensive discussion of the determinants of attitude strength).

Peripheral Route

In stark contrast to the central route to persuasion, the ELM holds that attitude change does not always require effortful evaluation of the information presented by the mass media or other sources. Instead, when a person's motivation or ability to process the issue-relevant information is low, persuasion can occur by a *peripheral route* in which processes invoked by simple cues in the persuasion context influence attitudes. The peripheral route to persuasion recognizes that it is neither adaptive nor possible for people to exert considerable mental effort in thinking about all of the media communications to which they are exposed. In order to function in contemporary society, people must sometimes act as "lazy organisms" (McGuire, 1969) or "cognitive misers" (Taylor, 1981) and employ simpler means of evaluation (see also, Bem, 1972). For example, various features of a communication (e.g., pleasant scenery in a TV commercial) can elicit positive emotions (e.g., happiness) that become associated with the advocated position (as in classical conditioning, Staats & Staats, 1958). Or, the source of a message can trigger a relatively simple inference or heuristic such as "experts are correct" (Chaiken, 1987) that a person can use to judge the message. Similarly, the responses of other people who are exposed to the message can serve as a validity cue (e.g., "if so many agree, it must be true;" Axsom, Yates, & Chaiken, 1987). In the first half of the past century the Institute for Propaganda Analysis, in a report on propaganda techniques, listed a number of "tricks" that speakers of the time used to persuade their audiences that relied on peripheral cues (e.g., the "bandwagon" effect was giving the sense that most other people already supported the speaker; see Lee & Lee, 1939).

We do not mean to suggest that peripheral approaches are necessarily ineffective. In fact, they can be quite powerful in the short term. The problem is that over time, emotions dissipate, people's feelings about sources can change, and cues can become dissociated from the message. These factors would then undermine the basis of the attitude. Laboratory research has shown that attitude changes based on peripheral cues tend to be less accessible, enduring, and resistant to subsequent attacking messages than attitudes based on careful processing of message arguments (see Petty et al., 1995). In sum, attitudes changed via the central route tend to be based on active thought processes resulting in a well-integrated cognitive structure, but attitudes changed via the peripheral route are based on more passive acceptance or rejection of simple cues and have a less well-articulated foundation.[4]

The tendency for simple cue processes to dissipate over time along with the tendency for thought-based persuasion to persist can lead to interesting effects. For example, one such phenomenon is the often cited but infrequently found (Gillig & Greenwald, 1974) "sleeper effect" (Gruder, Cook, Hennigan, Flay, Alessis, & Halamaj, 1978; Hovland, Lumsdaine, & Sheffield, 1949; Peterson & Thurstone, 1970/1933). The sleeper effect  can occur when a persuasive message is followed by a discounting cue (e.g., you learn that some information was reported in the untrustworthy *National Enquirer* after exposure to it). The effect is that although the discounting cue suppresses attitude change initially, over time the message can increase in effectiveness—opposite to the typical decay pattern found. The ELM predicts that such an effect should be most likely to occur under conditions in which the initial message is very strong, processed carefully, and then discounted. If the message was processed carefully and a simple cue follows message processing then what should happen is the following: Over time the impact of the peripheral discounting cue should fade, and people's attitudes should be governed by their initial (and more memorable) favorable thoughts to the strong arguments (see Kumkale & Albarracin, 2004; Priester, Wegener, Petty, & Fabrigar, 1999).

Persuasion Processes in the Elaboration Likelihood Model

Variables Affecting the Amount of Thinking

Our discussion of the central and peripheral routes to persuasion has highlighted two basic processes of attitude change, but the depiction of the ELM in Figure 7.2 outlines more specific roles that variables can play in persuasion situations. First, some variables affect a person's general *motivation* to think about a message. Mendelsohn (1973) noted that placing potential media recipients "along a continuum ranging from those whose initial interest in a given subject area may be high to those who literally have no interest in what may be communicated becomes an essential step in developing effective public information campaigns" (p. 51). Several variables enhance interest in media messages. Perhaps the most important determinant of interest and motivation to process the message is the perceived personal relevance of the communication. In one study (Petty & Cacioppo, 1979b), for example, undergraduates were told that their own university (high personal relevance) or a distant university (low personal relevance) was considering implementing a policy requiring all seniors to pass an exam in their major as a prerequisite to graduation. The students then listened to a radio editorial that presented either strong or weak arguments in favor of the exam policy. As predicted by the ELM, when the speaker advocated that the exams should be instituted at the students' own campus, the quality of the arguments in the message had a greater impact on attitudes than when the speaker advocated that the exams should be instituted at a distant institution. That is, as the personal relevance of the message increased, strong arguments were more persuasive, but weak arguments were less persuasive than in the low relevance conditions (see top panel of Figure 7.3). In addition, an analysis of the thoughts that the students listed after the message suggested that the more extreme attitudes were accompanied by more extreme thoughts. When the arguments were strong, students exposed to the high relevance message produced more than twice as many favorable thoughts as low relevance students, and when the arguments were weak, high relevance students generated almost twice as many unfavorable thoughts as students exposed to the low relevance version.

In an interesting extension of this work, Burnkrant and Unnava (1989) have found that simply changing the pronouns in a message from the third person (e.g., "one" or "he and she") to the second person (i.e., "you") was sufficient to increase personal involvement and processing of the message arguments (see bottom panel of Figure 7.3). That is, when the messages contained the self-relevant pronouns, strong arguments were more persuasive and weak arguments were less persuasive than when third person pronouns were used. Yet another way to increase self-relevance is to frame a message to comport either with people's values or self-conceptions. For example, if a person is attuned to the image value of a product, framing the message as dealing with image can increase message processing (Petty & Wegener, 1998b; see Petty, Wheeler, & Bizer, 2000, for a review). Or, somewhat ironically, if people think of themselves as not liking to think, then by framing the message as being for people who don't like to think, thinking can be increased (Wheeler, Petty, & Bizer, 2005).

Although increasing the perceived personal relevance of a message is an important way to increase thinking (see Petty, Cacioppo, & Haugtvedt, 1992, for a review), it is hardly

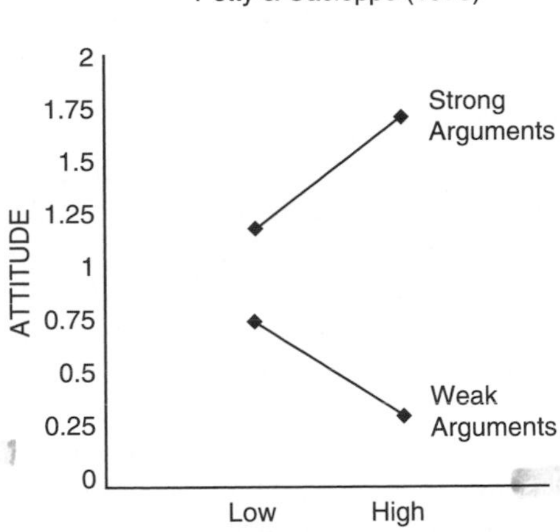

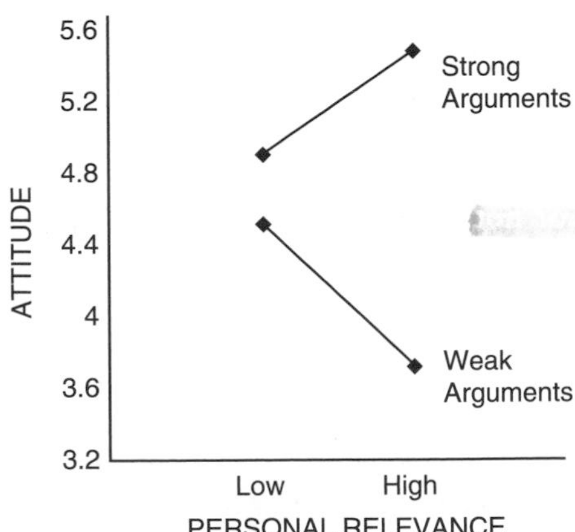

Figure 7.3 Self-Relevance Increases Message Processing. In Each Panel, as Self-Relevance (involvement) Increases, Argument Quality Becomes a More Important Determinant of the Attitudes Expressed after Exposure to a Persuasive Message. Data in the Top Panel are from an Experiment by Petty and Cacioppo (1979b). Data in the Bottom Panel are from an Experiment by Burnkrant and Unnava (1989). In Each Panel, Higher Numbers Indicate More Favorable Attitudes Toward the Position Taken in the Persuasive Message.

the only one. For example, the degree to which a source is perceived to be of questionable or low trustworthiness has also been found to increase the extent of elaboration (Priester & Petty, 1995). In this research, the extent to which a source could be trusted to convey accurate information was manipulated while keeping source expertise high. In one study, source trustworthiness was manipulated by either providing message recipients with background information that suggested that the speaker was honest and could be trusted or was dishonest and could not always be trusted to provide accurate information. In another study, trustworthiness was manipulated by having the source either advocate a self-serving position (relatively untrustworthy) or a position that violated the source's own self-interests (relatively trustworthy). Regardless of how source trustworthiness was manipulated, sources of questionable trustworthiness engendered greater elaboration than sources perceived to be trustworthy (see also Priester & Petty, 2003).

The increase in elaboration for untrustworthy sources occurs primarily for individuals who are not intrinsically motivated to think (i.e., low in need for cognition; Cacioppo & Petty, 1982), prompting them to elaborate when they would normally forgo such effortful processing. In contrast, individuals who intrinsically enjoy thinking (i.e., high need for cognition individuals) elaborated the messages equally regardless of source trustworthiness. Kaufman, Stasson, and Hart (1999) uncovered a similar pattern of results. Low need for cognition participants were more likely to elaborate the information presented by an untrustworthy (i.e., *National Enquirer*) than trustworthy (i.e., *Washington Post*) source.

Why does source trustworthiness influence thinking? The ELM postulates that individuals are motivated to hold correct attitudes. When a message source is perceived to be both expert and trustworthy (and hence likely to provide accurate information), individuals can be reasonably confident of the accuracy of their attitudes by merely accepting the position advocated. When the source is perceived to be an expert but of low trustworthiness, however, a message recipient cannot be assured of accuracy, and instead must scrutinize the information in order to be assured of an accurate attitude. As such, assuming the source has expertise (and is able to be accurate), perceived trustworthiness can influence the extent to which individuals engage in thinking. If a source has little knowledge (i.e., is low in expertise), there is little reason to process the message regardless of trustworthiness (Heesacker, Petty, & Cacioppo, 1983).

Another source characteristic that has been found to increase message elaboration is the degree to which a source is stigmatized or not. Specifically, research has provided evidence that when the source of a message is a member of a stigmatized group (e.g., gay or African American), message recipients are more likely to elaborate than when the source is a member of a non-stigmatized group (White & Harkins, 1994). Interestingly, this influence of source stigma is apparent only for people who reject prejudicial beliefs (e.g., are low in modern racism or homophobia; Petty, Fleming, & White, 1999). Individuals low in prejudice might be chronically concerned that stigmatized individuals are treated unfairly by others, or they might be concerned about their own implicit prejudices. As such, they pay particular attention to (i.e., elaborate) information presented by stigmatized sources in order to assure that the sources are treated fairly. The same appears to be the case when messages are about rather than by stigmatized individuals (Fleming, Petty, & White, 2005).

Other variables that have been found to increase elaboration include whether the key arguments are presented as questions or assertions, the number of message sources, and the expectedness of a position. For example, several studies have shown that when a person is not normally motivated to think about the message arguments, more thinking can be provoked by summarizing the major arguments as *questions* rather than as *assertions* (Howard, 1990; Petty, Cacioppo, & Heesacker, 1981; Swasy & Munch, 1985). Thus, if an argument in a radio commercial was followed by a question (Isn't this candidate the best one?) rather than by an assertion (This candidate is the best one), greater processing of the argument presented would result. Greater thinking about a message can also be induced by having the individual arguments presented by multiple sources rather than just one (Harkins & Petty, 1981; Moore & Reardon, 1987). The multiple source effect is attenuated if people suspect that the multiple sources are not providing independent analyses of the issue (Harkins & Petty, 1987; Wilder, 1990).

When some feature of the message is unexpected, processing can be increased. For example, if a newspaper headline implied that many people favored something that the message recipient disliked or that few people favored something the recipient liked, message scrutiny can be increased over cases in which the headline implied that few favored what the recipient disliked or many favored what the recipient liked (Baker & Petty, 1994). Of course, the enhanced thinking evoked by rhetorical questions, multiple sources, or surprising headlines will aid persuasion only if the arguments in the communication appear to be cogent when scrutinized. The enhanced thinking will be detrimental to persuasion if the arguments are found to be specious.

As outlined in Figure 7.2, having the necessary motivation to process a message is not sufficient for the central route to persuasion to occur. People must also have the ability to process a message. For example, a complex or long message might require more than one exposure for maximal processing, even if the recipient was highly motivated to think about it. The increased processing with multiple exposures should lead to more favorable thoughts and attitudes if the arguments are strong, but to more counterarguments and less favorable attitudes if the arguments are weak (Cacioppo & Petty, 1989). Of course, repetition is just one variable that has an impact on a person's ability to think about a message. For example, if a message is accompanied by distraction (Petty, Wells, & Brock, 1976) or if the speaker talks too fast (Smith & Shaffer, 1991), thinking about the message will be disrupted. When strong arguments are presented, disrupting thinking should diminish persuasion, but when weak arguments are presented, disrupting thinking should enhance persuasion by reducing counterarguing (see Petty & Brock, 1981). Different media channels have an impact on people's ability to think about the message. Specifically, people are generally better able to process messages in media that allow self-pacing (magazines, Internet) than those that are controlled externally (e.g., radio and television; Chaiken & Eagly, 1976; Wright, 1981).

A consideration of motivation and ability variables together suggests some interesting effects. For example, research shows clearly that moderate repetition of a message can be beneficial if arguments and cues are positive, but repeating the same message over and over eventually leads to boredom and reduced effectiveness. This "wearout" effect occurs regardless of whether the message is on a topic of high or low interest (Sawyer, 1981). Because of this, a number of investigators have suggested that introducing some variation into the repeated ads should forestall the inevitable tedium effect (see Pechman & Stewart, 1989). The ELM suggests that different kinds of message variation should be attempted in a media campaign depending on the recipient's overall motivation to think about the issue of the campaign. In a test of this hypothesis, Schumann, Petty, and Clemons (1990) found that for highly motivated message recipients (those expecting to make an imminent decision about the issue discussed in the communications), repeated presentations on the same topic could be made more effective if the messages varied the substantive arguments that they presented. Variation in peripheral cues made no difference. On the other hand, for recipients low in motivation, variation in simple cues across repeated exposures enhanced the effectiveness of the campaign, but variation in arguments did not.

Objective Versus Biased Thinking

In addition to influencing a person's general motivation or ability to think about a message, Figure 7.2 indicates that variables can also have an impact on persuasion by influencing the nature of the thoughts that come to mind. That is, some features of the persuasion situation increase the likelihood of favorable thoughts being elicited, but others increase the likelihood of unfavorable thoughts coming to mind. Although the subjective cogency of the arguments used in a message is a prime determinant of whether favorable or unfavorable thoughts are elicited when message thinking is high, other variables can also be influential in determining whether favorable or unfavorable thoughts predominate (Petty & Cacioppo, 1990). For example, instilling "reactance" in message recipients by telling them that they have no choice but to be persuaded on an important issue motivates counterarguing even when the arguments used are strong (Brehm, 1966; Petty & Cacioppo, 1979a). Thus, biased thinking often reduces the impact of message quality on persuasion (Petty & Cacioppo, 1986). Similarly, people who possess accessible attitudes bolstered by considerable attitude-congruent knowledge are better *able* to defend their attitudes than those who have inaccessible attitudes or attitudes with a minimal underlying foundation (Fazio & Williams, 1986; Wood, 1982).

Sometimes variables bias people's thinking and influence their responses to a persuasive message without any awareness of the effect. At other times, however, people can become aware of some potentially unwanted biasing influence on their thoughts and judgments. To the extent that people become aware of a possible bias and want to correct for it, they can take steps to debias their judgments. According to the flexible correction model (FCM) of debiasing (Petty & Wegener, 1993; Wegener & Petty, 1997), to the extent that people become aware of a potential contaminating factor and are motivated and able to correct for it, they consult their intuitive theory of the direction and magnitude of the bias, and adjust their judgment accordingly (see also, Wilson & Brekke, 1994). Because people are not always aware of a biasing factor, as we noted above, high elaboration attitude change is not necessarily bias free. Even attempts to correct for bias do not necessarily produce bias-free judgments because people can be unaware of the actual magnitude or direction of bias and therefore make an inaccurate correction.

If people overestimate a bias and attempt to correct for it, this can lead to an opposite bias. For example, in one study (Petty, Wegener, & White, 1998), students' attention was drawn to the possibly biasing impact of the attractiveness of the source or not. Under high thinking conditions, source attractiveness had no impact when attention was not drawn to it as a possibly biasing factor. However, when participants were told not to be biased by the attractiveness of the source, they actually showed more persuasion to the unattractive than the attractive source—a reverse bias brought on by their attempt to be unbiased.

Persuasive Impact of Arguments Versus Peripheral Cues

As we noted above, when people have the motivation and ability to think about an issue, they scrutinize the issue-relevant information presented, such as the arguments provided in the communication. An argument is any piece of information that says something about the merits of the position taken. Although we ordinarily think of arguments as features of the message content itself, source, recipient, and other factors can also serve as arguments or evidence. For example, if a spokesperson for a beauty product says that "if you use this product, you will look like me," the source's own physical appearance serves as relevant information for evaluating the effectiveness of the product (Petty & Cacioppo, 1984c). Or, a person might look to their own emotional state to provide evidence about the merits of something (e.g., "if I don't feel happy in your presence, I must not love you").

Just as source, recipient, and other factors can serve as persuasive arguments in the appropriate context, features of the persuasive message can serve as peripheral cues. A peripheral cue is a feature of the persuasion context that allows favorable or unfavorable attitude formation even in the absence of an effortful consideration of the true merits of the object or issue. Thus, just as source factors such as how expert or attractive the source is (Chaiken, 1980; Petty, Cacioppo, & Goldman, 1981; Petty, Cacioppo, & Schumann, 1983) can serve as a peripheral cue when motivation or ability to think are low, so too can the mere number of arguments in the message (Aaker & Maheswaran, 1997; Alba & Marmorstein, 1987; Petty & Cacioppo, 1984a) and the length of the arguments used (Wood, Kallgren, & Priesler, 1985; see Petty, Wheeler, & Bizer, 1999), since people can use the heuristic, "more is better."

Summary

The ELM holds that as the likelihood of elaboration is increased (as determined by factors such as the personal relevance of the message and the number of times it is repeated), the perceived quality of the issue-relevant information presented becomes a more important determinant of persuasion. Effortful evaluation of evidence can proceed in a relatively objective or a relatively biased fashion, however. As the elaboration likelihood is decreased, peripheral cues become more important in determining any attitude change that occurs. That is, when the elaboration likelihood is high, the central route to persuasion dominates, but when the elaboration likelihood is low, the peripheral route takes precedence (see Petty, 1994; Petty & Wegener, 1999, for additional discussion of the operation of central and peripheral processes along the elaboration likelihood continuum). Furthermore, as we articulate below, at different points along the elaboration likelihood continuum, any one variable (e.g., source attractiveness) can serve in different roles (e.g., being used as a peripheral cue when thinking is low, but being analyzed as evidence when thinking is high).

Multiple Roles for Variables in the Elaboration Likelihood Model

We have seen that one of the powerful features of the ELM is that it specifies a finite number of processes by which variables can affect persuasion. Now that we have explained all of these processes, it is important to note that another powerful feature of the ELM is that it holds that any one variable can have an impact on persuasion by affecting each of these processes in different situations. That is, the same feature of a persuasive message can, depending on the context, serve as an issue-relevant argument, or a peripheral cue, or affect the motivation or ability to think about the message, or bias the nature of the thoughts that come to mind, or affect structural properties of the thoughts such as how accessible they are, or how much confidence people have in them.

If any one variable can influence persuasion by several means, it becomes critical to identify the general conditions under which the variable acts in each of the different roles or the ELM becomes descriptive rather than predictive (cf. Stiff, 1986). The ELM holds that when the elaboration likelihood is high (such as when perceived personal relevance and knowledge are high, the message is easy to understand, no distractions are present, and so on), people typically know that they want to and are able to evaluate the merits of the arguments presented, and they do so. Variables in the persuasion setting are likely to have little direct impact on evaluations by serving as simple peripheral cues in these situations. Instead, when the elaboration likelihood is high, a variable (a) can serve as an argument if it is relevant to the merits of the issue, (b) can determine the nature of the ongoing information processing activity (e.g., it might bias the ongoing thinking), or (c) can influence structural properties of the thoughts that are generated (e.g., the confidence with which they are held).

On the other hand, when the elaboration likelihood is low (e.g., low personal relevance or knowledge, complex message, many distractions, and so on), people know that they do not want to or are not able to evaluate the merits of the arguments presented, or they do not even consider exerting effort to process the message. If any evaluation is formed under these conditions, it is likely to be the result of relatively simple associations or inferences based on salient cues in the situation. Under low thinking conditions, the cue effect of a variable is typically determined directly by its valence.

Finally, when the elaboration likelihood is moderate or unconstrained to be high or low (e.g., uncertain personal relevance, moderate knowledge, moderate complexity, and so on), people can be uncertain as to whether or not the message warrants or needs scrutiny and whether or not they are capable of providing this analysis. In these situations they will examine the persuasion context for indications (e.g., is the source trustworthy? is the message relevant?) of whether or not they are interested in or should process the message. A few examples should help to clarify the multiple roles that a variable can have in different situations. We organize our review by grouping variables into aspects of the persuasion source, message, and recipient.

Multiple Roles for Source Factors

Consider first the multiple processes by which source factors, such as expertise or attractiveness, can have an impact on persuasion (see Petty & Cacioppo, 1984c). In various studies, source factors have been found to influence persuasion by serving as peripheral cues when the likelihood of thinking was low. For example, when the personal relevance of a message was low, highly expert sources produced more persuasion than sources of low expertise regardless of the quality of the arguments they presented (Petty, Cacioppo, & Goldman, 1981; see also Chaiken, 1980). On the other hand, in several studies in which the personal relevance of the message was not specified and nothing else was done to make the likelihood of thinking especially high or low (i.e., moderate elaboration likelihood), the source factors of expertise and attractiveness affected how much thinking people did about the message (Heesacker et al., 1983; Moore, Hausknecht, & Thamodaran, 1986; Puckett, Petty, Cacioppo, & Fisher, 1983). That is, likable and expert sources led to more message processing such that persuasion was greater with the likable and expert than dislikable and not expert sources when the arguments were strong, but persuasion was reduced when the arguments were weak. The self-monitoring scale (see Snyder, 1987) has been used to distinguish people who tend to think more about what experts have to say (i.e., low self-monitors) from those who are more interested in what attractive sources have to say (i.e., high self-monitors; DeBono & Harnish, 1988).

When the likelihood of thinking is very high, source factors take on other roles. For example, if a source factor is relevant to the merits of a message, it can be used as a persuasive argument. Thus, as noted earlier, an attractive endorser might provide persuasive visual evidence for the effectiveness of a beauty product (Petty & Cacioppo, 1984c). In addition, Chaiken and Maheswaran (1994) demonstrated a biasing effect on information processing of source expertise. When recipients under high elaboration conditions received an ambiguous message (i.e., not clearly strong or weak), expertise biased the thoughts generated to the message. That is, people were more likely to interpret ambiguous information in a favorable way if it came from an expert than a non-expert. When the likelihood of thinking was low (i.e., the message was on an unimportant topic), expertise did not bias thinking but instead acted as a simple peripheral cue (see also Shavitt, Swan, Lowrey, & Wanke, 1994).

All of the effects for sources we have discussed already occurred when the source information was available prior to message receipt. One final role for sources has been obtained when the source information is revealed *after* message processing has already occurred. Specifically, in one study, when participants learned that the source was an expert after processing the message, confidence in the thoughts generated to the message was increased compared to learning that the source was of low credibility (Briñol, Petty, & Tormala, 2004). If a highly credible source can increase thought confidence compared to a low credibility source, this means that credibility can be associated with either more or less persuasion depending on the valence of the thoughts generated to the message. In a demonstration of this, Tormala, Briñol, and Petty (2006) presented recipients with either a strong or a weak persuasive message promoting *Confrin*, a new pain relief product, and then revealed information about the source (i.e., either from a federal agency that conducts research on medical products or from a class report written by a 14-year-old student). When the message was strong, the highly credible source led to more favorable attitudes than the source of low credibility because it instilled greater reliance on the positive thoughts generated. However, when the message was weak and participants generated mostly unfavorable thoughts, the effect of credibility was reversed. That is, the high credibility source produced less favorable attitudes than the low credibility source because participants exposed to the highly credible source had more confidence in their unfavorable thoughts to the weak message.

In sum, we have seen that source factors can take on multiple roles in persuasion settings. The role taken depends on how much thinking people are doing about the message and when the source information is revealed. When thinking is low, source factors serve as cues. This should be the case regardless of when the source information is uncovered. When thinking is unconstrained by other variables, source factors can affect the extent of thinking, but only if the source is revealed prior to thinking. When thinking is high, source factors can bias thinking if people are aware of the sources prior to their thinking, but can affect confidence in the thoughts already generated if revealed after thinking (Tormala, Briñol, & Petty, 2007). Finally, when thinking is high, source factors can be analyzed as arguments, if relevant to the advocacy, wherever they happen to appear in the persuasion context.

Multiple Roles for Message Factors

As we noted earlier, the mere number of arguments in a message can serve as a peripheral cue when people are either unmotivated or unable to think about the information. When motivation and ability are high, however, the informational items in a message are not simply counted as cues, but instead the information is processed for its cogency. When the number of items in a message serves as a cue (low elaboration conditions), adding weak reasons in support of a position enhances persuasion, but when the items in a message serve as arguments, adding weak reasons reduces persuasion (Aaker &

Maheswaran, 1997; Alba & Marmorstein, 1987; Friedrich, Fetherstonhaugh, Casey, & Gallagher, 1996; Petty & Cacioppo, 1984a).

One study examined multiple roles for message factors at three distinct levels of recipient elaboration. In this research, a regular advertisement for an unknown product was contrasted with an "upward comparison" ad that compared the new product to a well-established one (Pechmann & Estaban, 1993). Unlike a regular message that simply provides support for its position (e.g., You should vote for Candidate X because . . .), an upward comparison message suggests that the critical issue, product, or person is similar to one that is already seen as desirable (e.g., You should vote for Candidate X, who, like Person Y, favors tax cuts). In order to examine the multiple roles for this message variable, regular and upward comparison ads containing either strong or weak arguments were presented following instructions and procedures designed to elicit either a relatively low, moderate, or high motivation to think about the critical ad.

Effectiveness of the ads was assessed by asking recipients to rate their intentions to purchase the product advertised. When the low motivation instructions were used, the upward comparison ad produced more favorable intentions than the regular ad regardless of argument quality, but strong arguments did not produce more favorable intentions than weak ones. That is, under the low elaboration likelihood conditions, the comparison with the well known and liked product served as a simple peripheral cue, and argument processing was minimal. When the high motivation conditions were examined, the opposite resulted. That is, under the high elaboration instructions, the strong arguments produced more favorable intentions than the weak ones, but the upward comparison was completely ineffective as a cue for producing more favorable intentions. Finally, when the moderate motivation conditions were analyzed, the use of an upward comparison ad was found to motivate people to process the message arguments. Thus, when the upward comparison ad used strong arguments, it led to more persuasion than the direct ad, but when the upward comparison ad used weak arguments, it produced less persuasion than the regular ad.

There are many other message factors that can likewise serve in multiple roles in different situations (see Petty & Wegener, 1998a, for a review). To take one more example, consider the effects of matching, tailoring, or targeting the message to some characteristic of the message recipient (e.g., their personality, their gender or race, their group identity, etc.). Most theorists have predicted that matching should increase persuasion. However, as with any other variable, matching messages to individuals should influence persuasion by different processes depending on the likelihood of thinking. According to the ELM, depending on the process by which matching works, persuasion will not necessarily be increased (see Briñol & Petty, 2006; Petty, Barden, & Wheeler, 2002; Petty, Wheeler, & Bizer, 2000, for reviews).

Perhaps the individual variable that has been studied most with respect to matching a message type to a person characteristic is the personality trait of self-monitoring (Snyder, 1974). This individual difference makes a distinction between high self-monitors, who are oriented toward social approval, and low self-monitors, who are more motivated to be consistent with their internal beliefs and values. Much research on self-monitoring has shown that messages can be made more effective by matching the message to a person's self-monitoring status. For example, in one study Snyder and DeBono (1985) exposed high and low self-monitors to advertisements for a variety of products that contained arguments appealing either to the social adjustment function (i.e., describing the social image that consumers could gain from the use of the product) or to the value-expressive function (i.e., presenting content regarding the intrinsic quality or merit of the product). They found that high self-monitors were more influenced by ads with image content than ads with quality content. In contrast, the attitudes of low-self monitors were more vulnerable to messages that made appeals to values or quality (see also DeBono, 1987; Lavine & Snyder, 1996; Snyder & DeBono, 1989).

As noted, the ELM holds that there are several possible mechanisms by which matching can influence attitudes. For example, when thinking is set at a high level, then matching could bias the direction of thinking. Indeed, some research suggests that high self-monitors are more motivated to generate favorable thoughts to messages that make an appeal to image rather than an appeal to values (e.g., Lavine & Snyder, 1996). In contrast, when the circumstances constrain the likelihood of elaboration to be very low, a match of message to person is more likely to influence attitudes by serving as a simple cue (e.g., DeBono, 1987). That is, even when the content of the message is not processed, if a source simply asserted that the arguments are consistent with a person's values, a low self-monitor might be more inclined to agree than a high self-monitor by reasoning, "if it links to my values, it must be good." For high self-monitors, a link to image would enhance persuasion.

Furthermore, when thinking is not already constrained by other variables to be high or low, matching a message to a person could increase thinking about the message. This interpretation would be consistent with results obtained by Kreuter and colleagues (1999) in which participants generated more thoughts in response to messages designed to match the recipients (see also Brug et al., 1998; Skinner et al., 1994). Research that has manipulated the quality of the message arguments along with a matching manipulation has also provided evidence for the view that matching can affect the extent of thinking. For example, in one study, Petty and Wegener (1998b) matched or mismatched messages that were strong or weak to individuals who differed in their self-monitoring. In this research, high and low self-monitors read image (e.g., how good a product makes you look) or quality (e.g., how efficient a product is) appeals that contained either strong (e.g., beauty or efficacy that lasts) or weak arguments (e.g., momentary beauty or efficacy). The cogency of the arguments had a larger effect on attitudes when the message matched rather than mismatched the person's self-monitoring status indicating that matching increased attention to message quality (see also DeBono & Harnish, 1988; Updegraff, Sherman, Luyster, & Mann, 2007; Wheeler et al., 2005).

In sum, the accumulated research suggests that matching a message to some characteristic of the recipient can influence attitudes by serving as a peripheral cue when elaboration is low, by biasing thoughts when elaboration is high, and by enhancing the amount of information processing when elaboration is moderate. Matching message contents and/or frames with characteristics of people might influence attitude change by other mechanisms under other circumstances. For example, another possibility is that when a message is matched to the person, people might come to accept the message position simply because the message "feels right" (Cesario, Grant, & Higgins, 2004) or is easier to process (e.g., Lee & Aaker, 2004). These simple fluency experiences might impact attitudes directly under relatively low thinking conditions. Or, when thinking is high, processing fluency (Tormala et al., 2002) or having the message "feel right" (Cesario et al., 2004) could affect persuasion by influencing thought confidence. This enhanced confidence would increase persuasion if the thoughts generated are favorable, but reduce persuasion if the thoughts generated are unfavorable.

Multiple Roles for Recipient Factors

According to the ELM, recipient factors can serve in the same multiple roles as source and message factors. Consider the impact that a person's emotional state has on persuasion. The mass medium of television has special power to present messages (commercials) in contexts in which people's emotions vary (e.g., due to the television program they are watching). According to the ELM, when the likelihood of elaboration is relatively low, a person's internal feelings should impact attitudes by a peripheral process. Consistent with this view, a number of studies have shown that the non-thoughtful "classical conditioning" of affect to an attitude object occurs more easily when the likelihood of thinking is low (e.g., Cacioppo et al., 1992; Gorn, 1982; Priester, Cacioppo, & Petty, 1996). Also under low elaboration conditions, affective states have been postulated to influence attitudes by a simple inference process in which misattribution of the cause of the emotional state to the persuasive message or to the attitude object occurs (e.g., I must be happy because I like or agree with the message advocacy; see Petty & Cacioppo, 1983; Schwarz, 1990).

As the likelihood of elaboration increases, emotion takes on different roles (see also, Forgas, 1995). Specifically, when the elaboration likelihood is more moderate, emotions have been shown to have an impact on the extent of argument elaboration. According to the hedonic contingency theory (Wegener & Petty, 1994, 1996), happy people tend to pay attention to the hedonic rewards of situations and thus they are more likely than sad people to process a message that is thought to be hedonically rewarding if processed (see Wegener, Petty, & Smith, 1995). On the other hand, if the message will not be rewarding to think about (e.g., because it is on a counterattitudinal or a depressing topic), then sad individuals will engage in greater message processing than will happy people because sadness tends to put people in a problem solving mind set (Schwarz, Bless, & Bohner, 1991). Furthermore, since happiness is associated with more confidence than is sadness, when people feel happy (and confident) prior to receipt of a message, they might reason that they don't need to process the message because they are already confident in their views (Tiedens & Linton, 2001).

When the elaboration likelihood is high, the ELM holds that emotions can influence attitudes by influencing the nature of the thoughts that come to mind. Memory research has demonstrated that material of a positive valence is more accessible in memory when people are in a happy rather than a sad state, whereas negatively valenced material is more accessible when they are sad rather than happy (e.g., see Blaney, 1986; Bower, 1981; Isen, 1987). The increased accessibility of affect-congruent material in memory can lead to affect-congruent associations that further influence the evaluation of the target. In other words, when the elaboration likelihood is high, emotion can introduce a bias to the thoughts generated in response to the persuasive message. Thus, emotions can sometimes have a similar effect on attitudes under high and low elaboration conditions, but the process is different.

In one examination of the multiple roles for emotion under high and low thinking conditions, students watched a television commercial in the context of a program that induced either a happy or a neutral state (Petty, Schumann, Richman, & Strathman, 1993). The likelihood of thinking about the critical ad was varied by telling some of the students that they would be allowed to select a free gift at the end of the experiment from a variety of brands of the target product (high involvement), or that they would be allowed to select a free gift from another product category (low involvement). Following exposure to the television program containing the ads, the students reported on their emotions, rated their attitudes toward the target product, and listed the thoughts they had during the message. The results of this study revealed that the "happy" program led to more positive feelings and more positive evaluations of the product under both high and low elaboration conditions. Importantly, and consistent with the notion that the happiness from the TV program produces positive attitudes by different processes under high and low elaboration conditions, happiness was associated with more positive thoughts about the product when the elaboration likelihood was high, but not when it was low. Figure 7.4 presents the results from causal path analyses that simultaneously estimated the three paths between (a) manipulated emotion and attitude toward the product, (b) manipulated emotion and proportion of positive thoughts generated, and (c) proportion of positive thoughts and attitude toward the product. Under low involvement (low elaboration) conditions, emotion had a direct effect on attitudes, but did not influence thoughts (see top panel). In contrast, under high involvement (high elaboration) conditions, emotion had no direct effect on attitudes. Instead, increased happiness increased the production of positive thoughts, which in turn had an impact on attitudes (see bottom panel).

One way in which emotion biases thoughts is by affecting how likely people think the consequences mentioned in the message are to occur. Specifically, when in a happy state and thinking carefully, people believe that positive consequences mentioned in the communication are more likely, but negative consequences are less likely. The opposite occurs for sadness (e.g., Johnson & Tversky, 1983). Thus, positively framed arguments (e.g., if you stop smoking, you will live longer) are more effective when thoughtful people are in a happy rather than a sad state because people overestimate the likelihood of the positive consequence, but negatively framed arguments (if you don't stop smoking, you'll die sooner) are more effective in a sad than a happy state because thoughtful people overestimate the likelihood of the negative consequence (Wegener, Petty, & Klein, 1994). Research suggests that the effects of moods on perceived likelihoods are quite specific such that sad moods are especially effective in increasing the perceived likelihood of sad consequences and angering states are especially effective in increasing the perceived likelihood of angering consequences (DeSteno, Petty, Wegener, & Rucker,

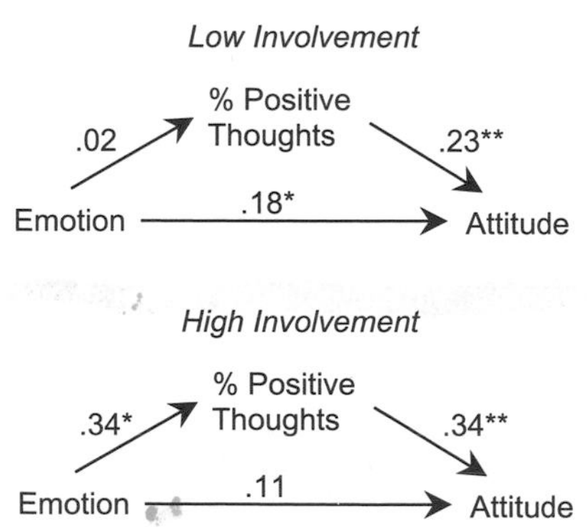

Figure 7.4 Direct and Indirect Effects of Positive Mood on Attitudes Under High and Low Involvement Conditions. Data in the Top Panel Show that when Involvement is Low and People are not Motivated to Process the Message, Mood has a Direct Effect on Attitudes. Data in the Bottom Panel Show that when Involvement is High and People are Motivated to Process the Message, the Effect of Mood on Attitudes is Mediated by the Generation of Positive Thoughts (Figure adapted from Petty, Schumann, Richman, & Strathman, 1993).

2000). Because of this, more specific types of matching of messages to emotional states have proven effective in situations in which people are being thoughtful. That is, presenting messages with sad consequences that might follow from some action are more effective than focusing on angering consequences when people are sad, but the opposite is true when people are angry (DeSteno, Petty, Rucker, Wegener, & Braverman, 2004).

In addition to biasing thoughts, recent research on the self-validation hypothesis has shown that under high elaboration conditions, emotions can also affect persuasion by influencing thought confidence when the emotions follow processing the message. This possibility follows directly from the finding mentioned earlier that emotional states can relate to confidence with happy people being more certain and confident than sad individuals (Tiedens & Linton, 2001). If emotion influences thought confidence, then people in a happy mood should be more reliant on their thoughts than people in a sad mood. In fact, Briñol, Petty, and Barden (2007) found that when placed in a happy versus a sad state following message processing, people were more reliant on their thoughts. This means that happy people were more persuaded than sad individuals when the thoughts generated to the message were primarily favorable, but happy people were less persuaded than sad people when thoughts generated were primarily unfavorable. Briñol et al. (2007) provided further support for the idea that self-validation effects are restricted to high elaboration conditions (i.e., need for cognition) and when confidence follows rather than precedes one's thinking.

Finally, it is important to note that the effects we have outlined for emotion under different elaboration conditions assume that the true source of the incidental emotions induced (e.g., from a TV show) are not obvious, and the emotions are not so salient that they are perceived as biasing. When people perceive a possible biasing impact from their emotions, they will often attempt to correct their judgments for the perceived contaminating impact of the emotional state (Schwarz & Clore, 1983). This can cause judgments to move in a direction opposite to people's intuitive theories of bias (Wegener & Petty, 1997, 2001). Thus, if people think that their happiness has produced a favorable impact on their judgments, and they overestimate this bias, the corrected judgment in a happy state can be more negative than the corrected judgment in a sad state (e.g., Berkowitz et al., 2000; Ottati & Isbell, 1996).

Consequences of Multiple Roles

Although we have only provided illustrative examples of particular source, message, and recipient variables, the accumulated research literature supports the ELM notion that variables can serve in different roles in different situations (see Petty & Wegener, 1998). That is, various source, message, and recipient variables have been shown to influence attitudes as: (a) a peripheral cue under low elaboration likelihood conditions, (b) a determinant of the extent of thinking about the message under moderate elaboration conditions, (c) a message argument when the variable was relevant to the attitude object and elaboration was high, and finally, depending on whether the variable was introduced before or after the message to (d) bias message processing, or (e) to influence confidence in one's message-relevant thoughts.

Because any one variable can produce persuasion in multiple ways, it is important to understand the process by which the variable has influenced a person's attitude. For example, our discussion of the two routes to persuasion suggests that if being happy has produced persuasion by serving as a simple cue under low elaboration conditions, the attitude induced will be less accessible, less persistent, less resistant, and less predictive of behavior than if being happy produced the same amount of persuasion but worked by increasing positive thoughts to the message arguments under high elaboration conditions. In empirical research on media campaigns in a variety of domains (see Rice & Atkin, 1989), many source, message, recipient, and contextual variables have been examined. Relatively little attention has been paid, however, to the processes by which these variables work. The ELM holds that the variables that determine persuasion can work by different processes in different situations, and that the process by which the variable induces change is critical for understanding the consequences of any attitude change that occurs (see Figure 7.2).

Directions for Future Research

Thus far we have reviewed evidence that has supported the primary ELM postulates about the processes responsible for attitude change. Before addressing the links between attitude change and behavior change, it is useful to consider where some future basic research on persuasion processes might be directed. Successful persuasion was said to occur when the recipients' attitudes were modified in the desired direction. After a long tradition of assessing the impact of persuasion treatments on attitudes with deliberative self reports (e.g., semantic differential scales such as rating one's attitude on a good-bad or favorable-unfavorable dimension), more recent work has begun to assess attitude change with measures that tap the more automatic evaluations associated with objects, issues and people. Thus, in the last decade, there has been a growing number of new measures of automatic attitudes available (e.g., evaluative priming; Fazio et al., 1995; implicit association test or IAT; Greenwald et al., 1998). These *implicit* measures aim to assess automatic evaluations without a person's knowledge of what is being assessed (see Petty, Fazio, & Briñol, 2008; and Wittenbrink & Schwarz, 2007, for reviews).

The very first assumptions about the nature of automatic evaluations suggested that such attitudes would be very difficult to change, in part because the underlying object-evaluation associations were assumed to be learned over a long period of time. For example, automatic evaluations reflecting prejudice have been viewed as resulting from passive, long-term exposure to negative portrayals in the media (Devine, 1989) and long-standing status differences between groups. However, recent research has demonstrated that automatic evaluations, like deliberative ones, can be affected by a variety of high and low thinking processes, including traditional elaborative forms of rhetorical persuasion (see Briñol, Petty, & McCaslin, 2008, for a review). For example, automatic evaluations have been shown to be affected by mere exposure and classical conditioning processes (e.g., Fazio & Olson, 2003), as well as by exposing people to advertisements, media campaigns, and other treatments involving verbal information (e.g., Briñol et al., 2008; Czyzewska & Ginsburg, 2007; Maio, Haddock, Watt, & Hewstone, 2008; Park, Felix, & Lee, 2007; see Gawronski & Bodenhausen, 2006, for a review).

Assessment of automatic evaluative reactions are potentially important to assess in addition to deliberative reactions for two reasons. First, the two kinds of measures do not always tap the same evaluation. Second, implicit measures are more likely to predict behavior in spontaneous situations (when people act without thinking), whereas deliberative measures are more likely to predict behavior in deliberative situations (e.g., Dovidio et al., 1997). Much attention has been paid recently to the discrepancies that can emerge between attitudes assessed with deliberative versus automatic measures (Gawronski & Bodenhausen, 2006; Petty & Briñol, 2008). The divergence between explicit and implicit measures opens a number of interesting possibilities for understanding attitude structure (Petty, Briñol, & DeMarree, 2007), and can also provide some potential insights for the study of mass media effects on persuasion. For example, recent research has demonstrated that when implicit and explicit evaluations are discrepant, people are more prone to process information regarding the attitude object than when the two evaluations are congruent (Briñol, Petty, & Wheeler, 2006; Petty et al., 2006).

Implicit measures can also reveal possibly hidden or previously unrecognized effects of media messages. For example, when people appear to have resisted persuasion on traditional deliberative measures, there might be some potentially important, yet previously hidden, persuasive effects on implicit measures. This is analogous to prior research showing that sometimes when a persuasive message seems to have failed, there have actually been changes in the underlying confidence with which the attitude is held—sometimes being increased, and sometimes decreased (e.g., Rucker & Petty, 2004; Rucker, Petty, & Briñol, 2008; Tormala & Petty, 2002; see Petty, Tormala, & Rucker, 2004, for a review). Thus, measures of the meta-cognitive properties associated with attitudes have proven informative in the absence of changes in the valence of the attitudes themselves (see Petty, Briñol, Tormala, & Wegener, 2007, for a review). It is plausible to imagine that under some circumstances, although participants were not influenced by persuasive messages on deliberative self-report measures (e.g., as a result of demand characteristics, evaluation apprehension, impression management, social desirability, and self-awareness limitations), there might still be some potentially hidden, persuasive effects on the automatic evaluative associations that exist with respect to the attitude object. If true, then researchers might sometimes be able to use automatic measures in the same way that researchers have used attitude confidence as a way of indicating that a message has had some (hidden) effect.

ATTITUDE-BEHAVIOR LINKS

As we noted earlier, the ELM provides a framework for understanding persuasion (yielding) processes and how variables have their effect on attitudes. Once a person's attitude has changed, however, behavior change requires that the person's new attitude rather than the old attitude or previous habits guide action. Considerable research has addressed the links between attitudes and behavior, and a number of situational and dispositional factors have been shown to enhance attitude-behavior consistency (see Ajzen 1988, for a comprehensive review).

Two general approaches to the process by which attitudes guide behavior have achieved widespread acceptance. One approach is exemplified by the theories of "reasoned action" (Fishbein & Ajzen, 1975) and "planned behavior" (Ajzen, 1991), which assume that "people consider the implications of their actions before they decide to engage or not engage in a given behavior" (Fishbein & Ajzen, 1975, p. 5). In this approach, people are hypothesized to form intentions to perform or not perform behaviors, and these intentions are based on the person's attitude toward the behavior as well as perceptions of the opinions of significant others (norms). This approach focuses on the relatively thoughtful processing involved in considering the personal costs and benefits of engaging in a behavior, and in one's perception of the ability to control the behavior. This approach has accumulated considerable empirical support (Sheppard, Hartwick, & Warshaw, 1988).

In contrast to the thoughtful processing highlighted by the theories of reasoned action and planned behavior, Fazio (1990, 1995) has proposed that much behavior is rather spontaneous and that attitudes can guide behavior by a relatively automatic process. That is, if the relevant attitude comes to mind, consistent behavior is likely to follow. Fazio argued that attitudes can guide behavior without any deliberate reflection or reasoning if (a) the attitude is activated spontaneously by the mere presence of the attitude object and (b) the attitude colors perception of the object so that, if the attitude is favorable (or unfavorable), the qualities of the object appear favorable (or unfavorable).

Importantly, Fazio (1990) further notes that motivational and ability factors are important in determining whether the reasoned action or the automatic activation process occurs. That is, just as the ELM holds that attitudes can be formed or changed by high or low thinking processes in different situations, Fazio's approach to attitude-behavior consistency (the MODE model) holds that attitudes can guide behavior by high or low thinking processes. For behavioral decisions that are high in perceived personal consequences, attitudes are likely to guide behavior by a deliberate reflection process, but when perceived consequences are low, spontaneous attitude activation should be more important as a determinant of behavior. Similarly, as the time allowed for a decision is reduced, the importance of spontaneous attitude activation processes should increase over more deliberative processes. When there is sufficient motivation and ability to think about one's behavior, a person can reflect upon the costs and benefits of the anticipated action.

Interestingly, depending upon what costs and benefits are salient at the moment, the deliberation process can lead to a behavior that is consistent or inconsistent with the underlying attitude. For example, the underlying attitude might be based on a combination of both emotional and cognitive (e.g., belief-based) factors (see Crites, Fabrigar, & Petty, 1994), but if reflection time is high, people might overweight cognitive over emotional considerations leading to later dissatisfaction with the decision (see Wilson, Dunn, Kraft, & Lisle, 1989). When motivation and ability to reflect are low, however, people's actions are determined by whichever attitudes are the most accessible.[5]

In some domains an accessible attitude is easily translated into behavior (e.g., I like candidate X, and so I will vote for this candidate). In other domains, however, translating new attitudes into new behaviors is rather complex even if the person has the desire to act on the attitude (e.g., I want to consume a low fat diet, but how do I do this?). Thus, for some media campaigns, attitude change, though an important first step, might still be insufficient to produce the desired behavioral responses even if appropriate attitudes were formed by the central route. People might also need to rehearse the attitude sufficiently so that it overcomes and replaces past attitudes (Petty, Gleicher, & Jarvis, 1993; Wilson et al., 2000), or people might need to become more confident in their new attitudes so that they will act on them (Rucker & Petty, 2006) or to acquire new skills and self-perceptions of efficacy that allow newly acquired attitudes and intentions to be translated into action. Bandura's (1977, 1986) social-cognitive theory provides a framework to understand the latter processes (see Bandura, this volume).

SUMMARY AND CONCLUSIONS

Although considerable research on mass media effects has shown that it is possible for media messages to change the knowledge or facts that people have about some object, issue, or person, we have argued that knowledge reception does not invariably result in attitude and behavior change. Our brief review of the ELM and the research supporting it has emphasized that information will be most successful in producing enduring changes in attitudes and behavior if people are motivated and able to process the information, and if this processing results in favorable thoughts and ideas that are integrated into the person's relatively enduring cognitive structure. Furthermore, once attitudes have changed, implementing changes in some behaviors might require overcoming past attitudes, developing confidence in new ones, and learning new skills and perceptions of self-efficacy.

Thus, current work on attitude and behavior change can help to account for some unsuccessful media campaigns in which knowledge acquisition failed to have attitudinal and/or behavioral consequences. First, the knowledge acquired could have been seen as irrelevant by the recipients, or might have led to unfavorable rather than favorable reactions. Second, even if favorable reactions were produced, people could have lacked confidence in those favorable thoughts, attenuating their reliance on them and reducing the likelihood of change. Third, even if appropriate attitude changes were induced, the changes might have been based on simple peripheral cues rather than on elaborative processing of the message. Thus, whatever changes were produced would be unlikely to persist over time and guide behavior. Fourth, even if attitude changes were produced by the central route, the people influenced could have lacked the necessary skills or self-confidence to translate their new attitudes into action, or the impact of attitudes on behavior might have been undermined by competing norms. Fifth, even when people appear to have resisted the influence of mass media on traditional measures of persuasion, there might have been some potentially important yet previously hidden persuasive effects on alternative measures. For example, a media campaign might have failed to get people to develop more negative attitudes toward smoking on traditional deliberative measures, but automatic measures of evaluation might reveal that people have become more negative, or meta-cognitive measures might reveal that people have lost some confidence in their prior positive evaluation paving the way for future attitude and behavior change.

Perhaps the three most important issues raised in our review are: (1) although some attitudes are based on an effortful reasoning process in which externally provided information is related to oneself and integrated into a coherent belief structure (central route), other attitudes are formed as a result of relatively simple cues in the persuasion environment (peripheral route); (2) any one variable (e.g., source expertise, mood) can be capable of inducing persuasion by either the central or the peripheral route in different situations by serving in one or more roles (i.e., affecting motivation or ability to think, biasing thinking, affecting thought confidence, serving as an argument, or a peripheral cue); and (3) although both central and peripheral route processes can lead to attitudes similar in their valence (how favorable or unfavorable they are), there are important consequences of the manner of attitude change such that more thoughtful attitude changes tend to be more consequential than less thoughtful ones.

If the goal of a mass media influence attempt is to produce long-lasting changes in attitudes with behavioral consequences, the central route to persuasion appears to be the preferred persuasion strategy. If the goal is immediate formation of a new attitude, even if it is relatively ephemeral (e.g., attitudes toward the charity sponsoring a telethon), the peripheral route could prove acceptable. Influence via the central route requires that the recipient of the new information have the motivation and ability to process it. As noted previously, one of the most important determinants of motivation to think about a message is the perceived personal relevance of that message. Most of the media messages people receive are probably not perceived as directly relevant and they have few immediate personal consequences. Thus, many of these messages will be ignored or processed primarily for peripheral cues. An important goal of any persuasion strategy aimed at enduring change will be to increase people's motivation to think about the messages by increasing the perceived personal relevance of the communications or employing other techniques to enhance processing (e.g., ending arguments with questions rather than statements; using multiple sources).

In conclusion, we note that research on mass media persuasion has come a long way from the early optimistic (and scary) notion that the mere presentation of information was sufficient to produce persuasion, and the subsequent pessimistic view that media influence attempts were typically ineffective. We now know that media influence, like other forms of influence, is a complex, though explicable process. We know that the extent and nature of a person's cognitive responses to external information can be more important than the information itself. We know that attitudes can be changed in different ways, such as central versus peripheral routes, and that some attitude changes are more accessible, stable, resistant, and predictive of behavior than others. We also know that even apparently simple variables such as how likable a source is or what emotion a person is experiencing can produce persuasion by very different processes in different situations.

Notes

1 In one of the relatively rare empirical efforts of the period, Peterson and Thurstone (1933) examined the power of movies such as D.W. Griffith's *Birth of a Nation*, controversial because of its depiction of Blacks, to modify the racial attitudes of adolescents. The conclusions of this research foreshadowed the modern period in that various moderators of effective influence were uncovered (e.g., greater influence for those with low knowledge rather than high issue-consistent knowledge; Wood, Rhodes, & Biek, 1995; see Wartella & Reeves, 1985).

2 The implicit/explicit distinction in attitudes is not new. For example, in their classic treatise, Hovland, Janis, and Kelley (1953) defined attitudes as "implicit responses" that were "sometimes unconscious" (p. 7). Attitudes were contrasted with "opinions" which were "verbal answers that one covertly expresses to (oneself)" (p. 8). Although in the 1950s, all that could be measured were explicit attitudes (opinions), more recently several implicit measures have been proposed to tap into one's automatic evaluative tendencies (e.g., Fazio et al., 1995; Greenwald et al., 1998).

3 Of course, much of the correlation between media coverage and ratings of issue-importance is due to the fact that the media cover issues people already think are important. Nevertheless, some research shows that the media coverage can precede public perceptions (e.g., MacKuen, 1981), and the mere accessibility of certain issues can cause people to give greater weight to them (Sherman et al., 1990).

4 For expository purposes we have emphasized the distinction between the central and the peripheral routes to persuasion. That is, we have focused on the prototypical processes at the end points of the elaboration likelihood continuum. In most persuasion situations (which fall somewhere along this continuum), some combination of central and peripheral processes are likely to have an impact on attitudes.

5 Because attitudes formed by the central route tend to be more accessible than attitudes formed by the peripheral route, peripheral cues in the behavioral environment are likely to have an impact on immediate actions only when the likelihood of reflection in the current situation is low and there are no accessible attitudes to guide behavior.

References

Aaker, J. L., & Maheswaran, D. (1997). The effect of cultural orientation on persuasion. *Journal of Consumer Research*, *24*(3), 315–328.

Adams, C. (1993, April 7). The power of the media. *Michigan Chronicle*, pp. A7.

Ajzen, I. (1988). *Attitudes, personality, and behavior*. Chicago: Dorsey Press.

Ajzen, I. (1991). The theory of planned behavior. *Organizational Behavior and Human Decision Processes, 50*, 179–210.

Alba, J. W., & Marmorstein, H. (1987). The effects of frequency knowledge on consumer decision making. *Journal of Consumer Research, 13*, 411–454.

Axsom, D., Yates, S., & Chaiken, S. (1987). Audience response as a heuristic cue in persuasion. *Journal of Personality and Social Psychology, 53*, 30–40.

Baker, S. M., & Petty, R. E. (1994). Majority and minority influence: Source advocacy as a determinant of message scrutiny. *Journal of Personality and Social Psychology, 67*, 5–19.

Bandura, A. (1977). *Social learning theory*. Englewood Cliffs, NJ: Prentice-Hall.

Bandura, A. (1986). *Social foundations of thought and action*. Englewood Cliffs, NJ: Prentice-Hall.

Bem, D. J. (1972). Self-perception theory. In L. Berkowitz (Ed.), *Advances in experimental social psychology* (Vol. 6, pp. 1–62). New York: Academic Press.

Berkowitz, L., Jaffee, S., Jo, E., & Troccoli, B. (2000). Some conditions affecting overcorrection of the judgment-distorting influence of one's feelings. In J. P. Forgas (Ed.), *Feeling and thinking: The role of affect in social cognition*. Cambridge, England: Cambridge University Press.

Blaney, P. H. (1986). Affect and memory: A review. *Psychological Bulletin, 99*, 229–246.

Bower, G. H. (1981). Mood and memory. *American Psychologist, 11*, 11–13.

Brehm, J. W. (1966). *A theory of psychological reactance*. New York: Academic Press.

Briñol, P., & Petty, R. E. (2004). Self-validation processes: The role of thought confidence in persuasion. In G. Haddock and G. Maio (Eds.), *Contemporary perspectives on the psychology of attitudes* (pp. 205–226). Philadelphia: Psychology Press.

Briñol, P., & Petty, R. E. (2005). Individual differences in persuasion. In D. Albarracin, B. T. Johnson, & M. P. Zanna (Eds.), *Handbook of attitudes and attitude change* (pp. 575–616). Hillsdale, NJ: Erlbaum.

Briñol, P., & Petty, R. E. (2006). Fundamental processes leading to attitude change: Implications for cancer prevention communications. *Journal of Communication, 56*, 81–104.

Briñol, P., Petty, R. E., & Barden, J. (2007). Happiness versus sadness as determinants of thought confidence in persuasion: A self-validation analysis. *Journal of Personality and Social Psychology, 93*, 711–727.

Briñol, P., Petty, R. E., & McCaslin, M. J. (2008). Automatic and deliberative attitude change from thoughtful and non-thoughtful processes. In R. E. Petty, R. H. Fazio, & P. Briñol (Eds.), *Attitudes: Insights from the new implicit measures* (pp. 285–326). New York: Psychology Press.

Briñol, P., Petty, R. E., & Tormala, Z. L. (2004). The self-validation of cognitive responses to advertisements. *Journal of Consumer Research, 30*, 559–573.

Briñol, P., Petty, R. E., & Wheeler, S. C. (2006). Discrepancies between explicit and implicit self-concepts: Consequences for information processing. *Journal of Personality and Social Psychology, 91*(1), 154–170.

Brug, J., Glanz, K., Van Assema, P., Kok, G., & Van Breukelen, G. J. P. (1998). The impact of computer-tailored feedback and iterative feedback on fat, fruit, and vegetable intake. *Health Education and Behavior*, 25, 517–531.

Burnkrant, R., & Unnava, R. (1989). Self-referencing: A strategy for increasing processing of message content. *Personality and Social Psychology Bulletin, 15*, 628–638.

Cacioppo, J. T., & Petty, R. E. (1981). Social psychological procedures for cognitive response assessment: The thought listing technique. In T. Merluzzi, C. Glass, and M. Genest (Eds.), *Cognitive assessment* (pp. 309–342). New York: Guilford.

Cacioppo, J. T., & Petty, R. E. (1982). The need for cognition. *Journal of Personality and Social Psychology, 42*, 116–131.

Cacioppo, J. T., & Petty, R. E. (1989). Effects of message repetition on argument processing, recall, and persuasion. *Basic and Applied Social Psychology, 10*, 3–12.

Cacioppo, J. T., Marshall-Goodell, B. S., Tassinary, L. G., & Petty, R. E. (1992). Rudimentary determinants of attitudes: Classical conditioning is more effective when prior knowledge

about the attitude stimulus is low than high. *Journal of Experimental Social Psychology, 28,* 207–233.

Cacioppo, J. T., Petty, R. E., & Sidera, J. (1982). The effects of a salient self-schema on the evaluation of proattitudinal editorials: Top-down versus bottom-up message processing. *Journal of Experimental Social Psychology, 18,* 324–338.

Cartwright, D. (1949). Some principles of mass persuasion. *Human Relations, 2,* 253–267.

Cesario, J., Grant, H., & Higgins, E. T. (2004). Regulatory fit and persuasion: Transfer from "feeling right." *Journal of Personality and Social Psychology, 86,* 388–404.

Chaiken, S. (1980). Heuristic versus systematic information processing and the use of source versus message cues in persuasion. *Journal of Personality and Social Psychology, 39,* 752–756.

Chaiken, S. (1987). The heuristic model of persuasion. In M. P. Zanna, J. Olson, & C. P. Herman (Eds.), *Social influence: The Ontario symposium* (Vol. 5, pp. 3–39). Hillsdale, NJ: Erlbaum.

Chaiken, S., & Eagly, A. H. (1976). Communication modality as a determinant of message persuasiveness and message comprehensibility. *Journal of Personality and Social Psychology, 34,* 605–614.

Chaiken, S., & Maheswaran, D. (1994). Heuristic processing can bias systematic processing: Effects of source credibility, argument ambiguity, and task importance on attitude judgment. *Journal of Personality and Social Psychology, 66,* 460–473.

Chaiken, S., Liberman, A., & Eagly, A. H. (1989). Heuristic and systematic processing within and beyond the persuasion context. In J. Uleman & J. Bargh (Eds.), *Unintended thought* (pp. 212–252). New York: Guilford Press.

Chaiken, S., & Trope, Y. (1999). *Dual-process theories in social psychology.* New York: Guilford Press.

Crites, S., Fabrigar, L., & Petty, R. E. (1994). Measuring the affective and cognitive properties of attitudes: Conceptual and methodological issues. *Personality and Social Psychology Bulletin, 20,* 619–634.

Czyzewska, M., & Ginsburg, H. J. (2007). Explicit and implicit effects of anti-marijuana and anti-tobacco TV advertisements. *Addictive Behaviors, 32,* 114–127.

DeBono, K. G. (1987). Investigating the social-adjustive and value-expressive functions of attitudes: Implications for persuasion processes. *Journal of Personality and Social Psychology, 52,* 279–287.

DeBono, K. G., & Harnish, R. J. (1988). Source expertise, source attractiveness, and processing or persuasive information: A functional approach. *Journal of Personality and Social Psychology, 55,* 541–546.

DeBono, K., & Packer, M. (1991). The effects of advertising appeal on perceptions of product quality. *Personality and Social Psychology Bulletin, 17,* 194–200.

DeSteno, D., Petty, R. E., Rucker, D. D., Wegener, D. T., & Braverman, J. (2004). Discrete emotions and persuasion: The role of emotion-induced expectancies. *Journal of Personality and Social Psychology, 86,* 43–56.

DeSteno, D., Petty, R. E., Wegener, D. T., & Rucker, D. D. (2000). Beyond valence in the perception of likelihood: The role of emotion specificity. *Journal of Personality and Social Psychology, 78,* 397–416.

Devine, P. G. (1989). Stereotypes and prejudice: Their automatic and controlled components. *Journal of Personality and Social Psychology, 56,* 5–18.

Doob, L. (1935). *Propaganda, its psychology and technique.* New York: Holt.

Dovidio, J. F., Kawakami, K., Johnson, C., Johnson, B., & Howard, A. (1997). On the nature of prejudice: Automatic and controlled processes. *Journal of Experimental Social Psychology, 33,* 510–540.

Eagly, A. H., & Chaiken, S. (1993). *The psychology of attitudes.* Fort Worth, TX: Harcourt, Brace, Jovanovich.

Fazio, R. H. (1990). Multiple processes by which attitudes guide behavior: The MODE model as an integrative framework. In M. Zanna (Ed.), *Advances in experimental social psychology* (Vol. 23, pp. 75–109). New York: Academic Press.

Fazio, R. H., Jackson, J. R., Dunton, B. C., & Williams, C. J. (1995). Variability in automatic activation as an unobtrusive measure of racial attitudes: A bona fide pipeline? *Journal of Personality and Social Psychology, 69*, 1013–1027.

Fazio, R. H., & Olson, M. A. (2003). Implicit measures in social cognition research: Their meaning and use. *Annual Review of Psychology, 54*, 297–327.

Fazio, R. H., & Williams, C. J. (1986). Attitude accessibility as a moderator of the attitude-perception and attitude-behavior relations: An investigation of the 1984 presidential election. *Journal of Personality and Social Psychology, 51*, 505–514.

Fishbein, M., & Ajzen, I. (1975). *Belief, attitude, intention, and behavior: An introduction to theory and research*. Reading, MA: Addison-Wesley.

Fiske, S. T., & Pavelchak, M. A. (1986). Category-based versus piecemeal-based affective responses: Developments in schema-triggered affect. In R. M. Sorrentino & E. T. Higgins (Eds.), *Handbook of motivation and cognition: Foundations of social behavior* (pp. 167–203). New York: Guilford Press.

Fleming, M. A., Petty, R. E., & White, P. H. (2005). Stigmatized targets and evaluation: Prejudice as a determinant of attribute scrutiny and polarization. *Personality and Social Psychology Bulletin, 31*, 496–507.

Forgas, P. (1995). Mood and judgment: The affect infusion model (AIM). *Psychological Bulletin, 117*, 39–66.

Frey, D. (1986). Recent research on selective exposure to information. In L. Berkowitz (Ed.), *Advances in experimental social psychology* (Vol. 19, pp. 41–80). San Diego, CA: Academic Press.

Friedrich, J., Fetherstonhaugh, D., Casey, S., & Gallagher, D. (1996). Argument integration and attitude change: Suppression effects in the integration of one-sided arguments that vary in persuasiveness. *Personality and Social Psychology Bulletin, 22*, 179–191.

Gawronski, B., & Bodenhausen, G. V. (2006). Associative and prepositional processes in evaluation: An integrative review of implicit and explicit attitude change. *Psychological Bulletin, 132*, 692–731.

Gillig, P. M., & Greenwald, A. G. (1974). Is it time to lay the sleeper effect to rest? *Journal of Personality and Social Psychology, 29*, 132–139.

Gorn, G. J. (1982). The effects of music in advertising on choice behavior: A classical conditioning approach. *Journal of Marketing, 46*, 94–101.

Greenwald, A. G. (1968). Cognitive learning, cognitive response to persuasion, and attitude change. In A. Greenwald, T. Brock, & T. Ostrom (Eds.), *Psychological foundations of attitudes*. New York: Academic Press.

Greenwald, A. G., & Albert, S. M. (1968). Observational learning: a technique for elucidating S-R mediation processes. *Journal of Experimental Psychology, 76*, 273–278.

Greenwald, A. G., & Banaji, M. R. (1995). Implicit social cognition: Attitudes, self-esteem, and stereotypes. *Psychological Review, 102*, 4–27.

Greenwald, A. G., McGhee, D. E., & Schwartz, J. L. K. (1998). Measuring individual differences in implicit cognition: The implicit association task. *Journal of Personality and Social Psychology, 74*, 1464–1480.

Gruder, C. L., Cook, T. D., Hennigan, K. M., Flay, B. R., Alessis, C., & Halamaj, J. (1978). Empirical tests of the absolute sleeper effect predicted from the discounting cue hypothesis. *Journal of Personality and Social Psychology, 36*, 1061–1074.

Harkins, S. G., & Petty, R. E. (1981). The effects of source magnification cognitive effort on attitudes: An information processing view. *Journal of Personality and Social Psychology, 40*, 401–413.

Harkins, S. G., & Petty, R. E. (1987). Information utility and the multiple source effect in persuasion. *Journal of Personality and Social Psychology, 52*, 260–268.

Haugtvedt, C., & Petty, R. E. (1992). Personality and persuasion: Need for cognition moderates the persistence and resistance of attitude changes. *Journal of Personality and Social Psychology, 63*, 308–319.

Heesacker, M., Petty, R. E., & Cacioppo, J. T. (1983). Field dependence and attitude change:

Source credibility can alter persuasion by affecting message-relevant thinking. *Journal of Personality, 51*, 653–666.

Hovland, C. I. (1954). Effects of the mass media of communication. In G. Lindzey (Ed.), *Handbook of social psychology* (Vol. 2, pp. 1062–1103). Cambridge, MA: Addison-Wesley Publishing Company.

Hovland, C. I. (1959). Reconciling conflicting results derived from experimental and survey studies of attitude change. *American Psychologist, 14*, 8–17.

Hovland, C. I., Janis, I., & Kelley, H. H. (1953). *Communication and persuasion.* New Haven, CT: Yale University Press.

Hovland, C. I., Lumsdaine, A., & Sheffield, F. (1949). *Experiments on mass communication.* Princeton, NJ: Princeton University Press.

Howard, D. J. (1990). Rhetorical question effects on message processing and persuasion: The role of information availability and the elicitation of judgment. *Journal of Experimental Social Psychology, 26*, 217–239.

Hyman, H., & Sheatsley, P. (1947). Some reasons why information campaigns fail. *Public Opinion Quarterly, 11*, 412–423.

Isen, A. (1987). Positive affect, cognitive processes, and social behavior. *Advances in experimental social psychology, 20*, 203–253.

Iyengar, S., & Kinder, D. R. (1987). *News that matters: Television and American opinion.* Chicago: University of Chicago Press.

Iyengar, S., Kinder, D. R., Peters, M. D., & Krosnick, J.A. (1984). The evening news and presidential evaluations. *Journal of Personality and Social Psychology, 46*, 778–787.

Janis, I. L., & King, B. T. (1954). The influence of role-playing on opinion change. *Journal of Abnormal and Social Psychology, 49*, 211–218.

Johnson, E., & Tversky, A. (1983). Affect, generalization, and the perception of risk. *Journal of Personality and Social Psychology, 45*, 20–31.

Katz, D., & Lazarsfeld, P. R. (1955). *Personal influence.* New York: Free Press.

Kaufman, D., Stasson, M., & Hart, J. (1999). Are the tabloids always wrong or is that just what we think? Need for cognition and perceptions of articles in print media. *Journal of Applied Social Psychology, 29*, 1984–1997.

Kinder, B. N., Pape, N. E., & Walfish, S. (1980). Drug and alcohol education programs: A review of outcome studies. *International Journal of the Addictions, 15*, 1035–1054.

Klapper, J. T. (1960). *The effects of mass communication.* New York: The Free Press.

Kreuter, M. W., Strecher, V. J., & Glassman, B. (1999). One size does not fit all: The case for tailoring print materials. *Annals of Behavioral Medicine, 21*, 276–283.

Kumkale, G. T., & Albarracin, D. (2004). The sleeper effect in persuasion: A meta-analytic review. *Psychological Bulletin, 130*, 143–172.

Lasswell, H. W. (1927). *Propaganda techniques in the World War.* New York: Peter Smith.

Lasswell, H. W. (1964). The structure and function of communication in society. In L. Bryson (Ed.), *Communication of ideas* (pp. 37–51). New York: Cooper Square Publishers.

Lavine, H., & Snyder, M. (1996). Cognitive processing and the functional matching effect in persuasion. The mediating role of subjective perceptions of message quality. *Journal of Experimental Social Psychology, 32*, 580–604.

Lazarsfeld, P., Berelson, B., & Gaudet, H. (1948). *The people's choice.* New York: Columbia University Press.

Lee, A.Y., & Aaker, J. L. (2004). Bringing the frame into focus: The influence of regulatory fit on processing fluency and persuasion. *Journal of Personality and Social Psychology, 86*, 205–218.

Lee, A., & Lee, E. B. (1939). *The fine art of propaganda: A study of Father Coughlin's speeches.* New York: Harcourt, Brace.

Lippmann, W. (1922). *Public opinion.* New York: Macmillan.

Lohr, S. (1991, February 18). Troubled banks and the role of the press. *New York Times*, pp. A33.

Lord, C. G., Ross, L., & Lepper, M. R. (1979). Biased assimilation and attitude polarization: The effects of prior theories on subsequently considered evidence. *Journal of Personality and Social Psychology, 37*, 2098–2109.

MacKuen, M. B. (1981). Social communication and the mass policy agenda. In M. B MacKuen & S. L. Coombs (Eds.), *More than news: Media power in public affairs* (pp. 19–144). Beverly Hills, CA: Sage.

Maheswaran, D., & Chaiken, S. (1991). Promoting systematic processing in low motivation settings: Effect of incongruent information on processing and judgment. *Journal of Personality and Social Psychology, 61*, 13–25.

Maio, G., Haddock, G., Watt, S. E., & Hewstone, M. (2008). Implicit measures in applied contexts: An illustrative examination of anti-racism advertising. In R. E. Petty, R. H. Fazio, & P. Briñol (Eds.), *Attitudes: Insights from the new implicit measures* (pp. 327–357). New York: Psychology Press.

McGuire, W. J. (1968). Personality and susceptibility to social influence. In E. F. Borgatta & W. W. Lambert (Eds.), *Handbook of personality theory and research* (pp. 1130–1187). Chicago: Rand McNally.

McGuire, W. J. (1969). The nature of attitudes and attitude change. In G. Lindzey & E. Aronson (Eds.), *Handbook of social psychology* (2nd ed., Vol. 3, pp. 136–314). Reading, MA: Addison-Wesley.

McGuire, W. J. (1985). Attitudes and attitude change. In G. Lindzey & E. Aronson (Eds.), *Handbook of social psychology* (3rd ed., Vol 2, pp. 233–346). New York: Random House.

McGuire, W. J. (1989). Theoretical foundations of campaigns. In R. E. Rice & C. K. Atkin (Eds.), *Public communication campaigns* (2nd ed., pp. 43–65). Newbury Park, CA: Sage.

McGuire, W. J. (1996). The Yale communication and attitude change program in the 1950s. In E. E. Dennis & E. Wartella (Eds.), *American communication research: The remembered history* (pp. 39–59). Mahwah, NJ: Erlbaum.

Mendelsohn, H. (1973). Some reasons why information campaigns can succeed. *Public Opinion Quarterly, 11*, 412–423.

Moore, D. L., & Reardon, R. (1987). Source magnification: The role of multiple sources in processing of advertising appeals. *Journal of Marketing Research, 24*, 412–417.

Moore, D. L., Hausknecht, D., & Thamodaran, K. (1986). Time pressure, response opportunity, and persuasion. *Journal of Consumer Research, 13*, 85–99.

Ottati, V. C., & Isbell, L. M. (1996). Effects of mood during exposure to target information on subsequently reported judgments: An on-line model of misattribution and correction. *Journal of Personality and Social Psychology, 71*, 39–53.

Paisley, W. (1989). Public communication campaigns: The American experience. In R. E. Rice & C. K. Atkin (Eds.), *Public communication campaigns* (2nd ed., pp. 15–41). Newbury Park, CA: Sage Publications.

Palmerino, M., Langer, E., & McGillis, D. (1984). Attitudes and attitude change: Mindlessness-mindfulness perspective. In J. R. Eiser (Ed.), *Attitudinal judgment* (pp. 179–195). New York: Springer-Verlag.

Park, J., Felix, K., & Lee, G. (2007). Implicit attitudes toward Arab-Muslims and the moderating effects of social information. *Basic and Applied Social Psychology, 29*, 35–35.

Pechman, C., & Stewart, D. W. (1989). Advertising repetition: A critical review of wearin and wearout. *Current Issues and Research in Advertising, 11*, 285–330.

Pechmann, C., & Estaban, G. (1993). Persuasion processes associated with direct comparative and noncomparative advertising and implications for advertising effectiveness. *Journal of Consumer Psychology, 2*, 403–432.

Peterson, R. E., & Thurstone, L. (1933). *Motion pictures and the social attitudes of children*. New York: Macmillan.

Petty, R. E. (1994). Two routes to persuasion: State of the art. In G. d'Ydewalle, P. Eelen, & P. Bertelson (Eds.), *International perspectives on psychological science* (Vol. 2, pp. 229–247). Hillsdale, NJ: Erlbaum.

Petty, R. E., Baker, S. M., & Gleicher, F. (1991). Attitudes and drug abuse prevention: Implications of the elaboration likelihood model of persuasion. In L. Donohew, H. E. Sypher, & W. J. Bukoski (Eds.), *Persuasive communication and drug abuse prevention* (pp. 71–90). Hillsdale, NJ: Erlbaum.

Petty, R.E., Barden, J., & Wheeler, S.C. (2002). The elaboration likelihood model of persuasion. In R. J. DiClemente, R. A. Crosby, & M. Kegler (Eds.), *Emerging theories in health promotion practice and research* (pp. 71–99). San Francisco: Jossey-Bass.

Petty, R. E., & Briñol, P. (2008). Implicit ambivalence: A meta-cognitive approach. In R. E. Petty, R. H. Fazio, & P. Briñol (Eds.), *Attitudes: Insights from the new implicit measures* (pp. 119–161). New York: Psychology Press.

Petty, R. E., Briñol, P., & DeMarree, K. G. (2007). The meta-cognitive model (MCM) of attitudes: Implications for attitude measurement, change, and strength. *Social Cognition, 25*, 609–642.

Petty, R. E., Briñol, P., & Tormala, Z. L. (2002). Thought confidence as a determinant of persuasion: The self-validation hypothesis. *Journal of Personality and Social Psychology, 82*, 722–741.

Petty, R. E., Briñol, P., Tormala, Z. L., & Wegener, D. T. (2007). The role of meta-cognition in social judgment. In E. T. Higgins & A. W. Kruglanski (Eds.), *Social psychology: A handbook of basic principles* (2nd ed., pp. 254–284). New York: Guilford Press.

Petty, R. E., & Brock, T. C. (1981). Thought disruption and persuasion: Assessing the validity of attitude change experiments. In R. Petty, T. Ostrom, & T. Brock (Eds.), *Cognitive responses in persuasion* (pp. 55–79). Hillsdale, NJ: Erlbaum.

Petty, R. E., & Cacioppo, J. T. (1979a). Effects of forewarning of persuasive intent on cognitive responses and persuasion. *Personality and Social Psychology Bulletin, 5*, 173–176.

Petty, R. E., & Cacioppo, J. T. (1979b). Issue-involvement can increase or decrease persuasion by enhancing message-relevant cognitive responses. *Journal of Personality and Social Psychology, 37*, 1915–1926.

Petty, R. E., & Cacioppo, J. T. (1981). *Attitudes and persuasion: Classic and contemporary approaches*. Dubuque: Wm. C. Brown.

Petty, R. E., & Cacioppo, J. T. (1983). Central and peripheral routes to persuasion: Application to advertising. In L. Percy & A. Woodside (Eds.), *Advertising and consumer psychology* (pp. 3–23). Lexington, MA: D. C. Heath.

Petty, R. E., & Cacioppo, J. T. (1984a). The effects of involvement on responses to argument quantity and quality: Central and peripheral routes to persuasion. *Journal of Personality and Social Psychology, 46*, 69–81.

Petty, R. E., & Cacioppo, J. T. (1984b). Motivational factors in consumer response to advertisements. In W. Beatty, R. Geen, & R. Arkin (Eds.), *Human motivation* (pp. 418–454). New York: Allyn & Bacon.

Petty, R. E., & Cacioppo, J. T. (1984c). Source factors and the elaboration likelihood model of persuasion. *Advances in Consumer Research, 11*, 668–672.

Petty, R. E., & Cacioppo, J. T. (1986a). *Communication and persuasion: Central and peripheral routes to attitude change*. New York: Springer/Verlag.

Petty, R. E., & Cacioppo, J. T. (1986b). The Elaboration Likelihood Model of persuasion. In L. Berkowitz (Ed.), *Advances in experimental social psychology* (Vol. 19, pp. 123–205). New York: Academic Press.

Petty, R. E., & Cacioppo, J. T. (1990). Involvement and persuasion: Tradition versus integration. *Psychological Bulletin, 107*, 367–374.

Petty, R. E., Cacioppo, J. T., & Goldman, R. (1981). Personal involvement as a determinant of argument-based persuasion. *Journal of Personality and Social Psychology, 41*, 847–855.

Petty, R. E., Cacioppo, J. T., & Haugtvedt, C. (1992). Involvement and persuasion: An appreciative look at the Sherifs' contribution to the study of self-relevance and attitude change. In D. Granberg & G. Sarup (Eds.), *Social judgment and intergroup relations: Essays in honor of Muzafer Sherif* (pp. 147–174). New York: Springer/Verlag.

Petty, R. E., Cacioppo, J. T., & Heesacker, M. (1981). The use of rhetorical questions in persuasion: A cognitive response analysis. *Journal of Personality and Social Psychology, 40*, 432–440.

Petty, R. E., Cacioppo, J. T., & Schumann, D. (1983). Central and peripheral routes to advertising effectiveness: The moderating role of involvement. *Journal of Consumer Research, 10*, 134–148.

Petty, R. E., Fazio, R. H., & Briñol, P. (Eds.). (2008). *Attitudes: Insights from the new implicit measures*. New York: Psychology Press.

Petty, R. E., Fleming, M. A., & White, P. (1999). Stigmatized sources and persuasion: Prejudice as a determinant of argument scrutiny. *Journal of Personality and Social Psychology, 76*, 19–34.

Petty, R. E., Gleicher, F. H., & Jarvis, B. (1993). Persuasion theory and AIDS prevention. In J. B. Pryor & G. Reeder (Eds.), *The social psychology of HIV infection* (pp. 155–182). Hillsdale, NJ: Erlbaum.

Petty, R. E., Haugtvedt, C., & Smith, S. M. (1995). Elaboration as a determinant of attitude strength: Creating attitudes that are persistent, restistant, and predictive of behaviour. In R. E. Petty & J. A. Krosnick (Eds.), *Attitude strength: Antecedents and consequences*, (pp. 93–130). Mahwah, NJ: Erlbaum.

Petty, R. E., & Krosnick, J. A. (Eds.). (1995). *Attitude strength: Antecedents and consequences*. Hillsdale, NJ: Erlbaum.

Petty, R. E., Ostrom, T. M., & Brock, T. C. (Eds.). (1981). *Cognitive responses in persuasion*. Hillsdale, NJ: Erlbaum.

Petty, R. E., Priester, J. R., & Wegener, D. T. (1994). Cognitive processes in attitude change. In R. S. Wyer & T. K. Srull (Eds.), *Handbook of social cognition* (2nd ed., Vol. 2, pp. 69–142). Hillsdale, NJ: Erlbaum.

Petty, R. E., Schumann, D., Richman, S., & Strathman, A. (1993). Positive mood and persuasion: Different roles for affect under high and low elaboration conditions. *Journal of Personality and Social Psychology, 64*, 5–20.

Petty, R. E., Tormala, Z. L., Briñol, P., & Jarvis, W. B. G. (2006). Implicit ambivalence from attitude change: An exploration of the PAST model. *Journal of Personality and Social Psychology, 90*, 21–41.

Petty, R. E., Tormala, Z. L., & Rucker, D. D. (2004). Resisting persuasion by counterarguing: An attitude strength perspective. In J. T. Jost, M. R. Banaji, & D. A. Prentice (Eds.), *Perspectivism in social psychology: The yin and yang of scientific progress* (pp. 37–51). Washington, D.C.: American Psychological Association.

Petty, R. E., & Wegener, D. T. (1993). Flexible correction processes in social judgment: Correcting for context induced contrast. *Journal of Experimental Social Psychology, 29*, 137–165.

Petty, R. E., & Wegener, D. T. (1998a). Attitude change: Multiple roles for persuasion variables. In D. Gilbert, S. Fiske, & G. Lindzey (Eds.), *The handbook of social psychology* (4th ed., Vol. 1, pp. 323–390). New York: McGraw-Hill.

Petty, R. E., & Wegener, D. T. (1998b). Matching versus mismatching attitude functions: Implications for scrutiny of persuasive messages. *Personality and Social Psychology Bulletin, 24*, 227–240.

Petty, R. E., & Wegener, D. T. (1999). The elaboration likelihood model: Current status and controversies. In S. Chaiken & Y. Trope (Eds.), *Dual process theories in social psychology* (pp. 41–72). New York: Guilford Press.

Petty, R. E., Wegener, D. T., & White, P. H. (1998). Flexible correction processes in social judgment: Implications for persuasion. *Social cognition, 16*, 93–113.

Petty, R. E., Wells, G. L., & Brock, T. C. (1976). Distraction can enhance or reduce yielding to propaganda. *Journal of Personality and Social Psychology, 34*, 874–884.

Petty, R. E., Wheeler, S. C., & Bizer, G. (1999). Is there one persuasion process or more? Lumping versus splitting in attitude change theories. *Psychological Inquiry, 10*, 156–153.

Petty, R. E., Wheeler, S. C., & Bizer, G. (2000). Matching effects in persuasion: An elaboration likelihood analysis. In G. Maio & J. Olson (Eds.), *Why we evaluate: Functions of attitudes* (pp. 133–162). Mahwah, NJ: Erlbaum.

Priester, J. R., Cacioppo, J. T., & Petty, R. E. (1996). The influence of motor processes on attitudes toward novel versus familiar semantic stimuli. *Personality and Social Psychology Bulletin, 22,* 442–447.

Priester, J. R., & Petty, R. E. (1995). Source attribution and persuasion: Perceived honesty as a determinant of message scrutiny. *Personality and Social Psychology Bulletin, 21,* 639–656.

Priester, J. R., & Petty, R. E. (2003). The influence of spokesperson trustworthiness on message elaboration, attitude strength, and advertising effectiveness. *Journal of Consumer Psychology, 13,* 408–421.

Priester, J. R., Wegener, D. T., Petty, R. E., & Fabrigar, L. F. (1999). Examining the psychological processes underlying the sleeper effect: The Elaboration Likelihood Model explanation. *Media psychology, 1,* 27–48.

Puckett, J., Petty, R. E., Cacioppo, J. T., & Fisher, D. (1983). The relative impact of age and attractiveness stereotypes on persuasion. *Journal of Gerontology, 38,* 340–343.

Rholes, N., & Wood, W. (1992). Self-esteem and intelligence affect influenceability: The mediating role of message reception. *Psychological Bulletin, 111,* 156–171.

Rice, R. E., & Atkin, C. K. (Eds.). (1989). *Public communication campaigns.* Newbury Park, CA: Sage.

Rucker, D. D., & Petty, R. E. (2004). When resistance is futile: Consequences of failed counterarguing on attitude certainty. *Journal of Personality and Social Psychology, 86,* 219–235.

Rucker, D. D., & Petty, R. E. (2006). Increasing the effectiveness of communications to consumers: Recommendations based on the elaboration likelihood and attitude certainty perspectives. *Journal of Public Policy and Marketing, 25,* 39–52.

Rucker, D. D., Petty, R. E., & Briñol, P. (2008). What's in a frame anyway? A meta-cognitive analysis of one versus two sided message framing. *Journal of Consumer Psychology, 18*(2), 137–149.

Sawyer, A. G. (1981). Repetition, cognitive responses and persuasion. In R. E. Petty, T. M. Ostrom, & T. C. Brock (Eds.), *Cognitive responses in persuasion* (pp. 237–261). Hillsdale, NJ: Erlbaum.

Schumann, D., Petty, R. E., & Clemons, S. (1990). Predicting the effectiveness of different strategies of advertising variation: A test of the repetition-variation hypothesis. *Journal of Consumer Research, 17,* 192–202.

Schwarz, N. (1990). Feelings as information: Informational and motivational functions of affective states. In E. T. Higgins & R. M. Sorrentino (Eds.), *Handbook of motivation and cognition: Foundations of social behavior* (Vol. 2, pp. 527–561). New York: Guilford.

Schwarz, N., Bless, H., & Bohner, G. (1991). Mood and persuasion: Affective states influence the processing of persuasive communications. In M. P. Zanna (Ed.), *Advances in experimental social psychology* (Vol. 24, pp. 161–201). San Diego: Academic Press.

Schwarz, N., & Clore, G. (1983). Mood, misattribution, and judgments of well-being: Informative and directive functions of affective states. *Journal of Personality and Social Psychology, 45,* 513–523.

Sears, D. O., & Kosterman, R. (1994). Mass media and political persuasion. In T. C. Brock & S. Shavitt (Eds.), *Persuasion: Psychological insights and perspectives* (pp. 251–278). Needham Heights, MA: Allyn & Bacon.

Sears, D. O., & Whitney, R. E. (1973). *Political persuasion.* Morristown, NJ: General Learning Press.

Shavitt, S., & Brock, T. C. (1986). Delayed recall of copytest responses: The temporal stability of listed thoughts. *Journal of Advertising, 19,* 6–17.

Shavitt, S., Swan, S., Lowrey, T. M., & Wanke, M. (1994). The interaction of endorser attractiveness and involvement in persuasion depends on the goal that guides message processing. *Journal of Consumer Psychology, 3,* 137–162.

Sheppard, B. H., Hartwick, J., & Warshaw, P. (1988). The theory of reasoned action: A meta-analysis of past research with recommendations for modifications and future research. *Journal of Consumer Research, 15*, 325–343.

Sherman, S. J., Mackie, D. M., & Driscoll, D. M. (1990). Priming and the differential use of dimensions in evaluation. *Personality and Social Psychology Bulletin, 16*, 405–418.

Shils, E. A., & Janowitz, M. (1948). Cohesion and disintegration in the Wehrmacht. *Public Opinion Quarterly, 12*, 300–306; 308–315.

Skinner, C. S., Strecher, V. J., & Hospers, H. (1994). Physicians; recommendations for mammography: Do tailored messages make a difference? *American Journal of Public Health, 84*, 43–49.

Smith, S. M., & Shaffer, D. R. (1991). Celebrity and cajolery: Rapid speech may promote or inhibit persuasion via its impact on message elaboration. *Personality and Social Psychology Bulletin, 17*, 663–669.

Snyder, M. (1974). Self-monitoring of expressive behavior. *Journal of Personality & Social Psychology, 30*, 526–537.

Snyder, M. (1987). *Public appearances, private realities: The psychology of self-monitoring*. New York: Freeman.

Snyder, M., & DeBono, K. G. (1985). Appeals to image and claims about quality: Understanding the psychology of advertising. *Journal of Personality and Social Psychology, 49*, 586–597.

Snyder, M., & DeBono, K. G. (1989). Understanding the functions of attitudes: Lessons from personality and social behavior. In A. Pratkanis, S. Breckler, & A. Greenwald (Eds.), *Attitude structure and function* (pp. 339–359). Hillsdale, NJ: Erlbaum.

Staats, A. W., & Staats, C. (1958). Attitudes established by classical conditioning. *Journal of Abnormal and Social Psychology, 67*, 159–167.

Stiff, J. B. (1986). Cognitive processing of persuasive message cues: A meta-analytic review of the effects of supporting information on attitudes. *Communication Monographs, 53*, 75–89.

Strong, E. K. (1925). *The psychology of selling and advertising*. New York: McGraw Hill.

Suber, B. (1997, December 3). Talk radio can fuel racism. *St Louis Post-Dispatch*, pp. B7.

Swasy, J. L., & Munch, J. M. (1985). Examining the target of receiver elaborations: Rhetorical question effects on source processing and persuasion. *Journal of Consumer Research, 11*, 877–886.

Taylor, S. E. (1981). The interface of cognitive and social psychology. In J. H. Harvey (Ed.), *Cognition, social behavior, and the environment* (pp. 189–211). Hillsdale, NJ: Erlbaum.

Tesser, A., Martin, L., & Mendolia, M. (1995). The impact of thought on attitude extremity and attitude-behavior consistency. In R. E. Petty & J. A. Krosnick (Eds.), *Attitude strength: Antecedents and consequences* (pp. 73–92). Mahwah, NJ: Erlbaum.

Tiedens, L. Z., & Linton, S. (2001). Judgment under emotional certainty and uncertainty: The effects of specific emotions on information processing. *Journal of Personality and Social Psychology, 81*, 973–988.

Tormala, Z. L., Briñol, P., & Petty, R. E. (2006). When credibility attacks: The reverse impact of source credibility on persuasion. *Journal of Experimental Social Psychology, 42*, 684–691.

Tormala, Z. L., Briñol, P., & Petty, R. E. (2007). Multiple roles for source credibility under high elaboration: It's all in the timing. *Social Cognition, 25*, 536–552.

Tormala, Z. L., & Petty, R. E. (2002). What doesn't kill me makes me stronger: The effects of resisting persuasion on attitude certainty. *Journal of Personality and Social Psychology, 83*, 1298–1313.

Tormala, Z. L., Petty, R. E., & Briñol, P. (2002). Ease of retrieval effects in persuasion: the roles of elaboration and thought-confidence. *Personality and Social Psychology Bulletin, 28*, 1700–1712.

Updegraff, J.A., Sherman, D. K., Luyster, F. S., & Mann, T. L. (2007). The effects of message quality and congruency on perceptions of tailored health communications. *Journal of Experimental Social Psychology, 43*, 249–257.

Wartella, E., & Middlestadt, S. (1991). Mass communication and persuasion: The evolution of direct effects, limited effects, information processing, and affect and arousal models. In L. Donohew, H. E. Sypher, & W. J. Bukoski (Eds.), *Persuasive communication and drug abuse prevention* (pp. 53–69). Hillsdale, NJ: Erlbaum.

Wartella, E., & Reeves, B. (1985). Historical trends in research on children and the media: 1900–1960. *Journal of Communications, 35*, 118–133.

Wegener, D. T., & Petty, R. E. (1994). Mood management across affective states: The hedonic contingency hypothesis. *Journal of Personality and Social Psychology, 66*, 1034–1048.

Wegener, D. T., & Petty, R. E. (1996). Effects of mood on persuasion processes: Enhancing, reducing, and biasing scrutiny of attitude-relevant information. In L. L. Martin, & A. Tesser (Eds.), *Striving and feeling: Interactions between goals and affect* (pp. 329–362). Mahwah, NJ: Erlbaum.

Wegener, D. T., & Petty, R. E. (1997). The flexible correction model: The role of naive theories of bias in bias correction. In M. P. Zanna (Ed.), *Advances in experimental social psychology* (Vol. 29, pp. 141–208). San Diego: Academic Press.

Wegener, D. T., & Petty, R. E. (2001). Understanding effects of mood through the elaboration likelihood and flexible correction models. In L. L. Martin & G. L. Clore (Eds.), *Theories of mood and cognition: A user's guidebook* (pp. 177–210). Mahwah, NJ: Erlbaum.

Wegener, D. T., Petty, R. E., & Klein, D. J. (1994). Effects of mood on high elaboration attitude change: The mediating role of likelihood judgments. *European Journal of Social Psychology, 23*, 25–44.

Wegener, D. T., Petty, R. E., & Smith, S. M. (1995). Positive mood can increase or decrease message scrutiny: The hedonic contingency view of mood and message processing. *Journal of Personality and Social Psychology, 69*, 5–15.

Wheeler, S. C., Petty, R. E., & Bizer, G. Y. (2005). Self-schema matching and attitude change: Situational and dispositional determinants of message elaboration. *Journal of Consumer Research, 31*, 787–797.

White, P. H., & Harkins, S. G. (1994). Race of source effects in the elaboration likelihood model. *Journal of Personality and Social Psychology, 67*, 790–807.

Wilder, D. A. (1990). Some determinants of the persuasive power of ingroups and outgroups: Organization of information and attribution of independence. *Journal of Personality and Social Psychology, 59*, 1202–1213.

Wilson, T. D., & Brekke, N. (1994). Mental contamination and mental correction: Unwanted influences on judgments and evaluations. *Psychological Bulletin, 116*, 117–142.

Wilson, T. D., Dunn, D. S., Kraft, D., & Lisle, D. (1989). Introspection, attitude change, and attitude-behavior consistency: The disruptive effects of explaining why we feel the way we do. In L. Berkowitz (Ed.), *Advances in experimental social psychology* (Vol. 22, pp. 287–343). San Diego, CA: Academic Press.

Wilson, T. D., Lindsey, S., & Schooler, T. Y. (2000). A model of dual attitudes. *Psychological Review, 107*, 101–126.

Wittenbrink, B., & Schwarz, N. (Eds.). (2007). *Implicit measures of attitudes*. New York: Guilford Press.

Wood, W. (1982). Retrieval of attitude relevant information from memory: Effects on susceptibility to persuasion and on intrinsic motivation. *Journal of Personality and Social Psychology, 42*, 798–810.

Wood, W., Kallgren, C., & Priesler, R. (1985). Access to attitude relevant information in memory as a determinant of persuasion. *Journal of Experimental Social Psychology, 21*, 73–85.

Wood, W., Rhodes, N., & Biek, M. (1995). Working knowledge and attitude strength: An information processing analysis. In R. E. Petty & J. A. Krosnick (Eds.), *Attitude strength: Antecedents and consequences* (pp. 283–313). Mahwah, NJ: Erlbaum.

Wright, P. L. (1973). The cognitive processes mediating acceptance of advertising. *Journal of Marketing Research, 10*, 53–62.

Wright, P. L. (1981). Cognitive responses to mass media advocacy. In R. E. Petty, T. M. Ostrom, & T. C. Brock (Eds.), *Cognitive responses in persuasion* (pp. 263–282). Hillsdale, NJ: Erlbaum.

Zaller, J. (1991). Information, values, and opinion. *American Political Science Review*, *85*, 1215–1237.

8

USES-AND-GRATIFICATIONS PERSPECTIVE ON MEDIA EFFECTS

Alan M. Rubin
Kent State University

Media effects researchers try to isolate elements of the communicator, channel, or message that explain the impact messages have on receivers. One view of this process emanates from a mechanistic perspective and assumes direct influence on message recipients. A mechanistic perspective sees audience members as passive and reactive, focuses on short-term, immediate, and measurable changes in thoughts, attitudes, or behaviors, and assumes direct influence on audiences.

Some have suggested other elements intervene between media messages and effects. Klapper (1960), for one, questioned the validity of mechanistic approaches. His phenomenistic approach proposed that several elements intercede between a message and a response so that, in most instances, media messages that are intended to persuade actually reinforce existing attitudes. These mediating factors include individual predispositions and selective perception processes, group norms, message dissemination via interpersonal channels, opinion leadership, and the free-enterprise nature of the media in some societies. Accordingly, we could argue (a) by themselves, media typically are not necessary or sufficient causes of audience effects, and (b) a medium or message is only a single influence in the social and psychological environment, although it is an important crucial one.

A PSYCHOLOGICAL PERSPECTIVE

According to uses and gratifications, a medium or message is a source of influence within the context of other possible influences. Media audiences are variably active communicators, rather than passive recipients of messages. The perspective underscores the role of social and psychological elements in mitigating mechanistic effects, and sees mediated communication as being socially and psychologically constrained. Rosengren (1974) wrote that uses and gratifications rests on a mediated view of communication influence, whereby individual differences constrain direct media effects. Therefore, to explain media effects, we must first understand the characteristics, motivation, selectivity, and involvement of individual communicators.

Uses and gratifications, then, is a psychological communication perspective. It shifts the focus of inquiry from a mechanistic perspective's interest in direct effects of media on receivers to assessing how people use the media: "that is, what purposes or functions the media serve for a body of active receivers" (Fisher, 1978, p. 159). The psychological perspective stresses individual use and choice. As such, researchers seek to explain media effects "in terms of the purposes, functions or uses (that is, uses and gratifications) as controlled by the choice patterns of receivers" (Fisher, 1978, p. 159).

In contrast to mechanistic views, writers have suggested functional and psychological views of media influence. In this chapter, I consider the roots of uses and gratifications, the objectives and functions of the paradigm, and the evolution of uses-and-gratifications research. Then, I address the links between media uses and effects, focusing on audience activity and media orientations, dependency and functional alternatives, and social and psychological circumstances. I also consider some directions, especially as linked to personal involvement, parasocial interaction, and newer media.

FUNCTIONAL APPROACHES TO MEDIA

Some early writings exemplify a functional approach. Lasswell (1948), for example, suggested that by performing certain activities—surveillance of the environment, correlation of different aspects of that environment, and transmission of social heritage—media content has common effects on those in a society. Lazarsfeld and Merton (1948) proposed that the media perform status-conferral and ethicizing functions and a narcotizing dysfunction. Wright (1960) added entertainment to Lasswell's three activities, and addressed the manifest and latent functions and dysfunctions of the media when performing surveillance, correlation, transmission, and entertainment activities.

Others suggested the media serve a myriad of functions for people and societies. For example, Horton and Wohl (1956) proposed that television provides viewers with a sense of parasocial relationship with media personalities. Pearlin (1959) argued that watching television allows viewers to escape from unpleasant life experiences. Mendelsohn (1963) noted that media entertainment reduces anxiety that is created by media news. Stephenson (1967) argued that television provides people the opportunity for play. And McCombs and Shaw (1972) hypothesized that media set the agenda in election campaigns.

Research focusing on audience motivation for using the media surrounded these functional studies. The belief that an object is best defined by its *use* guided such research. Klapper (1963) argued that mass communication research "too frequently and too long focused on determining whether some particular effect does or does not occur" (p. 517). He noted researchers had found few clear-cut answers to questions about the effects of the media. Consistent with Katz (1959), who suggested that a media message ordinarily could not influence a person who had no use for it, Klapper called for an expansion of uses-and-gratifications inquiry.

THE USES-AND-GRATIFICATIONS PARADIGM

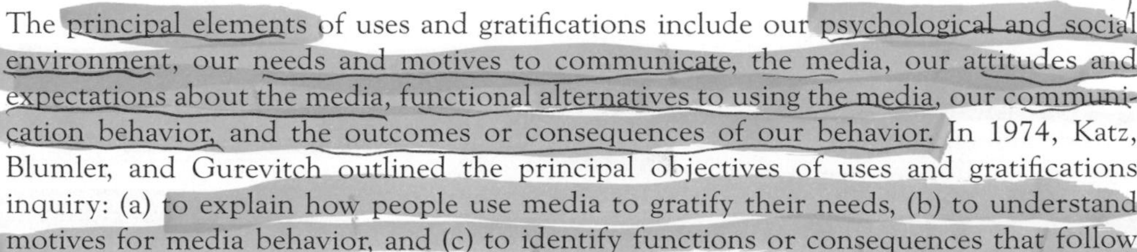

The principal elements of uses and gratifications include our psychological and social environment, our needs and motives to communicate, the media, our attitudes and expectations about the media, functional alternatives to using the media, our communication behavior, and the outcomes or consequences of our behavior. In 1974, Katz, Blumler, and Gurevitch outlined the principal objectives of uses and gratifications inquiry: (a) to explain how people use media to gratify their needs, (b) to understand motives for media behavior, and (c) to identify functions or consequences that follow from needs, motives, and behavior. Uses and gratifications focuses on: "(1) the social and psychological origins of (2) needs, which generate (3) expectations of (4) the mass media or other sources, which lead to (5) differential patterns of media exposure (or engagement in other activities), resulting in (6) need gratifications and (7) other consequences, perhaps mostly unintended ones" (Katz et al., 1974, p. 20).

A contemporary view of uses and gratifications is grounded in five assumptions (see, e.g., Palmgreen, 1984; Palmgreen, Wenner, & Rosengren, 1985; A. M. Rubin, 2002):

- Communication behavior, including the selection and use of the media, is goal-directed, purposive, and motivated. People are relatively active participants who choose media or media content. That functional behavior has consequences for people and societies.
- Audience members are variably active participants who initiate the selection and use of communication vehicles. Instead of being used by the media, people select and use media to satisfy felt needs or desires (Katz, Gurevitch, & Haas, 1973). Media use may respond to needs, but also satisfies wants or interests such as seeking information to solve a personal dilemma.
- Social and psychological factors guide, filter, or mediate behavior. Predispositions, the environment, and interpersonal interactions shape expectations about media and media content. Behavior responds to media and their messages, which are filtered through social and psychological circumstances such as personality, social categories and relationships, potential for interaction, and channel availability.
- The media compete with other forms of communication—or, functional alternatives—such as interpersonal interaction for selection, attention, and use to gratify our needs or wants. There are definite relationships between personal and mediated channels in this process. How well the media satisfy needs, motives, or desires varies based on individuals' social and psychological circumstances.
- People are typically more influential than the media in this process, but not always.  Individual initiative mediates the patterns and consequences of media use. Through this process, media may affect individual characteristics or social, political, cultural, or economic structures of society, and how people may come to rely on certain communication channels (Rosengren, 1974; A. M. Rubin & Windahl, 1986).

Katz and his colleagues (1974) listed two other early assumptions. First, methodologically, people can articulate their motives to communicate, so that self-reports can provide accurate data about media use. Second, value judgments about the cultural significance of media and their content should be suspended until we fully understand motives and gratifications. Self-reports are still typically used, but so are other qualitative and quantitative modes of inquiry. We also now have a clearer understanding of the role of motives and gratifications, so that inquiry does include questions of cultural significance. Some have advocated a shift in audience-based research toward examining cultural interaction of people and media (e.g., Massey, 1995).

The assumptions of uses and gratifications underscore the role of audience initiative and activity. Behavior is largely goal directed and purposive. People typically choose to participate and select media or messages from an array of communication alternatives in response to their expectations and desires.  These expectations and desires emanate from, and are constrained by, personal traits, social context, and interaction. A person has the capacity for subjective choice and interpretation and initiates such behavior as media or message selection. This initiative affects the outcomes of media use. Our degree of initiative or activity, though, has been seen as more variable than absolute over the past few decades (e.g., Blumler, 1979; Levy & Windahl, 1984, 1985; A. M. Rubin, 1993; A. M. Rubin & Perse, 1987a, 1987b).

THE EVOLUTION OF USES-AND-GRATIFICATIONS RESEARCH

Uses-and-gratifications research has focused on audience motivation and consumption. It has been guided by revised research questions shifting the focus to what people do with the media, instead of what the media do to people (Klapper, 1963). Research was descriptive and unsystematic in its early development, mostly identifying motives rather than explaining the processes or effects of media use. The early work was a precursor to research depicting typologies of media motives. For the most part, subsequent research became more systematic, and some investigators began to ask about the consequences of media use.

Media-Use Typologies

Early investigators of media gratifications sought to learn why people used certain media content. Lazarsfeld (1940), for example, considered the appeals of radio programs. Such studies preceded formal conceptualization of a uses-and-gratifications perspective. The early studies described audience motives rather than media effects. Examples include: (a) the competitive, educational, self-rating, and sporting appeals of a radio quiz program, *Professor Quiz*, for its listeners (Herzog, 1940); (b) the emotional-release, wishful-thinking, and advice-seeking gratifications listeners received from radio daytime serials (Herzog, 1944); and (c) the reasons why people read the newspaper—to interpret public affairs, as a daily tool for living, for social prestige, and to escape (Berelson, 1949). Such early descriptive research was largely abandoned in favor of studies of personal influence and media functions during the 1950s and 1960s.

In the early 1970s researchers sought to identify the motives of audience members for using the media, developing typologies of how people used the media to gratify social and psychological needs (Katz et al., 1973). Needs were related to social roles and psychological dispositions and often took the form of strengthening or weakening connections with self, family, or society. Katz et al., for example, developed a typology of the helpfulness of media in satisfying needs: strengthening understanding of self, friends, others, or society; strengthening the status of self or society; and strengthening contact with family, friends, society, or culture.

Lull (1980) addressed links between personal and mediated communication by observing the behavior of families when watching television. He developed a typology of the social uses of television. He suggested that television could be used *structurally*—as an environmental resource (e.g., for companionship) or as a behavioral regulator (e.g., punctuating time)—or *relationally*—to facilitate communication (e.g., an agenda for conversation), for affiliation or avoidance (e.g., conflict resolution), for social learning (e.g., behavioral modeling), or for competence or dominance (e.g., role reinforcement).

Researchers used such typologies to describe and explain media consumption. The typologies speak to connections between goals and outcomes, and suggest the complexities of media uses and effects. McQuail, Blumler, and Brown (1972), for example, categorized the types of gratifications people seek from viewing television content. They linked people's background and social circumstances with gratifications sought, and formulated a typology of media-person interactions. They observed that people are motivated to watch television for: diversion—to escape and for emotional release; personal relationships—for companionship and social utility; personal identity—for personal reference, reality exploration, and value reinforcement; and surveillance—to acquire news and information.

Rosengren and Windahl (1972) also considered the links between audience involvement, reality proximity, and media dependency. They noted that people might seek media as functional alternatives to personal interaction—as a supplement, complement, or substitute—for such reasons as compensation, change, escape, or vicarious experience. They suggested needs for interaction and identification can result in different degrees of media involvement: detachment, parasocial interaction, solitary identification, or capture. Rosengren and Windahl argued, by merging the traditions of media effects and media uses, it is possible "to ask what effect a given use made of the mass media, or a given gratification obtained from them, may have" (p. 176).

Criticisms

During this period, some criticized the early state of affairs and assumptions of uses and gratifications (e.g., Anderson & Meyer, 1975; Carey & Kreiling, 1974; Elliott, 1974; Swanson, 1977). The criticisms focused on (a) the compartmentalized nature of typologies, making it difficult to predict beyond those who were studied or to consider the implications of media use, (b) the lack of clarity of central constructs and how researchers attached different meanings to concepts such as motives and gratifications, (c) the treatment of the audience as being too active or rational in its behavior, and (d) the methodological reliance on self-report data.

Most criticisms have been addressed in the many studies of the past few decades. Researchers adapted and extended the use of consistent media-use measures across different contexts. Greenberg (1974), for example, developed motivation scales with British children and adolescents, and observed links among media behavior, television attitudes, aggressive attitudes, and viewing motives. A partial replication of that work in the U.S. identified six reasons why children and adolescents watched television: learning, habit/pass time, companionship, escape, arousal, and relaxation (A. M. Rubin, 1979). Habitual viewing related negatively to watching news and positively to television affinity and watching comedies. Viewing to learn related positively to perceived television realism. Arousal motivation was linked to watching action/adventure programs. Such results were similar to Greenberg's, presenting a consistent portrait across cultures.

This research also supported stability and consistency of responses via test-retest reliability of viewing-motive items and convergent validity of the motive scales with responses to open-ended queries of viewing reasons (A. M. Rubin, 1979). Participants were able to verbalize their reasons for using media. A similar technique in a later study supported convergent validity for a wider sample, ranging from children to older adults, and continued programmatic development and synthesis (A. M. Rubin, 1981a).

Besides supporting the consistency and accuracy of self-report motive scales, researchers also used experimental (e.g., Bryant & Zillmann, 1984), ethnographic (e.g., Lemish, 1985; Lull, 1980), and diary/narrative (e.g., Massey, 1995) methods. Investigators also sought to develop and extend conceptual, focused, and systematic lines of inquiry. They came to regard the audience as less than universally active and treated audience activity as a variable rather than an absolute (e.g., Blumler, 1979; Levy & Windahl, 1984, 1985; A. M. Rubin & Perse, 1987a, 1987b).

Contemporary Studies

Uses-and-gratifications research has demonstrated systematic progression during the past few decades. Research has helped explain media behavior and has furthered our understanding of media uses and effects. Researchers have provided a systematic analysis of media use by adapting similar motivation measures (e.g., Bantz, 1982; Eastman, 1979; Greenberg, 1974; Palmgreen & Rayburn, 1979; A. M. Rubin, 1979, 1981a, 1981b). Studies within and across research programs have included replication and secondary analysis. Several research directions are identified below. Some links to media effects research are drawn in the following sections:

- One direction has been the links among media-use motives and their associations with media attitudes and behaviors. This has led to the development of typologies of motives. Research suggests consistent patterns of media use such as meeting cognitive and affective needs, gratifying utilitarian and diversionary motivations, and fostering instrumental and ritualized orientations (e.g., Perse, 1986, 1990a; A. M. Rubin, 1983, 1984, 1985; A. M. Rubin & Bantz, 1989; A. M. Rubin & Rubin, 1982b). Lometti, Reeves, and Bybee (1977), for example, identified surveillance/entertainment, affective guidance, and behavioral guidance media-use gratification dimensions. Some focused on typologies and differences among types of consumers. Farquhar and Meeds (2007), for example, used Q-methodology to identify types of online fantasy sports users (e.g., casual, skilled, and isolationist thrill-seeking players). These types differed in their arousal and surveillance motives, whereby social interaction motives were only minimally important to these players.
- A second direction has been comparing motives across media and with newer media. This has produced analyses of newer media such as the Internet and comparative analyses of the appropriateness and effectiveness of channels—including evolving communication technologies such as the VCR, the Internet, and the World Wide Web—to meet people's needs and wants (e.g., Bantz, 1982; Cohen, Levy, & Golden, 1988; Dobos, 1992; Ferguson, 1992; Ferguson & Perse, 2000; Katz et al., 1973; Kaye & Johnson, 2002; Lichtenstein & Rosenfeld, 1983, 1984; Lin, 1999; Westmyer, DiCioccio, & Rubin, 1998). Elliott and Quattlebaum (1979), for example, reported various media serve similar needs, namely to maintain societal contact or to satisfy personal needs. Cowles (1989) found interactive media were felt to have more personal characteristics than noninteractive media. Perse and Courtright (1993) observed that interpersonal channels (i.e., conversation and telephone) had more social presence and better met personal needs, when compared with channels such as the computer. And Ko, Cho, and Roberts (2005) found that consumers with stronger information seeking motives engage in human-message interaction on a website, whereas those with stronger social interaction motives engage in human-to-human interaction.
- A third direction has been examining the different social and psychological circumstances of media use. Researchers have addressed how various factors influence media behavior (e.g., Adoni, 1979; Dimmick, McCain, & Bolton, 1979; Finn & Gorr, 1988; Hamilton & Rubin, 1992; Lull, 1980; Perse & Rubin, 1990; A. M. Rubin et al., 1985; A. M. Rubin & Rubin, 1982a, 1989; R. B. Rubin & Rubin, 1982;

Windahl, Hojerback, & Hedinsson, 1986). Researchers have examined the role of life position, lifestyle, personality, loneliness, isolation, need for cognition, religiosity, media deprivation, family-viewing environment, and the like.

- A fourth direction has been linking gratifications sought and obtained when using media or their content. This research has addressed how people's motives for using media are satisfied. Authors have proposed transactional, discrepancy, and expectancy-value models of media uses and gratifications (e.g., Babrow, 1989; Babrow & Swanson, 1988; Donohew, Palmgreen, & Rayburn, 1987; Galloway & Meek, 1981; Palmgreen & Rayburn, 1979, 1982, 1985; Palmgreen, Wenner, & Rayburn, 1980, 1981; Rayburn & Palmgreen, 1984; Wenner, 1982, 1986). For example, expectancy-value models predict gratification seeking from communication channels based on an expected outcome. They stress the consideration of expectancy and evaluative thresholds for behaviors, and comparisons of the congruence of expectation and outcome.
- A fifth direction has assessed how variations in background variables, motives, and exposure affect outcomes such as perceptions of relationship, cultivation, involvement, parasocial interaction, satisfaction, and political knowledge (e.g., Alexander, 1985; Carveth & Alexander, 1985; Garramone, 1984; Perse, 1990a; Perse & Rubin, 1988; A. M. Rubin, 1985; R. B. Rubin & McHugh, 1987). Others, for example, have observed that motivation for watching violent television content, personality characteristics such as locus of control, and experience with crime have been underemphasized in research and policy when considering viewer aggression (Haridakis, 2002; Haridakis & Rubin, 2003).
- A sixth direction includes theoretical developments in thinking and extensions that link uses and gratifications with other communication perspectives. For example, Slater's (2007) reinforcing spirals perspective is based on positive feedback loops in general systems theory, whereby attitudinal and behavioral outcomes of media use would feed back to influence people's selection of and attention to media content. In considering new measures of gratifications sought as outcome expectations, Peters, Rickes, Jockel, Criegern, and Deursen (2006) extended uses and gratifications in a social-cognitive framework of the model of media attendance (see LaRose & Eastin, 2004). And, in finding that habituated use of a public safety campaign predicted a third-person effect, Banning (2007) suggested uses and gratifications might be the root cause of third-person effects findings in other studies. Similarly, Haridakis and Rubin (2005) found locus of control and viewer motives to be important antecedents of third-person perceptual bias, suggesting an expansion of third-person effects research from perspectives such as uses and gratifications. Others have suggested models linking uses and gratifications and perspectives such as cultivation (Bilandzic & Rossler, 2004) or information processing (Eveland, 2004).
- A seventh direction has considered the method, reliability, and validity for measuring motivation (e.g., Babrow, 1988; Dobos & Dimmick, 1988; McDonald & Glynn, 1984).

MEDIA USES AND EFFECTS

Some have proposed a synthesis of uses-and-gratifications and media-effects research (e.g., Rosengren & Windahl, 1972; A. M. Rubin & Windahl, 1986; Windahl, 1981). The primary difference between the two traditions is that a media-effects researcher "most often looks at the mass communication process from the communicator's end," whereas a uses researcher begins with the audience member (Windahl, 1981, p. 176). Windahl argued that it is more beneficial to stress the similarities rather than the differences of the two traditions. One such similarity is that both uses and effects seek to explain the outcomes or consequences of communication such as attitude or perception formation (e.g., cultivation, third-person effects), behavioral changes (e.g., dependency), and societal effects (e.g., knowledge gaps). Uses and gratifications does so, however, recognizing the greater potential for audience initiative, choice, and activity.

Audience Activity and Media Orientations

Audience activity is the core concept in uses and gratifications. It refers to the utility, intentionality, selectivity, and involvement of the audience with the media (Blumler, 1979). Uses-and-gratifications researchers regard audience members to be variably—not universally—active; they are not equally active at all times. According to Windahl (1981), depicting the audience "as superational and very selective . . . invites criticism" (p. 176). A valid view of audience activeness lies on a continuum between being passive (and, perhaps, being more directly influenced by media or messages) and being active (and, perhaps, making more rational decisions in accepting or rejecting messages) (A. M. Rubin, 1993).

Levy and Windahl (1984) tested the proposition that audience activity is variable and identified three activity periods for Swedish television viewers: previewing, during viewing, and postviewing. Although they found preactivity or intention to watch to be weakly related to entertainment media use, it was strongly related to surveillance use. They argued that viewers actively seek news to gain information, but may not actively seek diversion. Lin (1993) noted that strongly motivated viewers engage in more activities and experience greater satisfaction when watching television as compared with weakly motivated viewers. She also found that the diversification of the home-media environment affects activity levels (Lin, 1994). Because they present more options, more diversified media households (e.g., greater cable, satellite, and computer opportunities) enable greater audience choice and selectivity.

Some researchers have approached motives as interrelated structures—or complex viewing orientations—rather than isolated entities (e.g., Abelman, 1987; Perse, 1986, 1990a; Perse & Rubin, 1988; A. M. Rubin, 1981b, 1983, 1984; A. M. Rubin & Perse, 1987a; A. M. Rubin & Rubin, 1982b). As such, Finn (1992) suggested proactive (mood management) and passive (social compensation) dimensions of media use. McDonald (1990) noted that two orientations—surveillance (i.e., needing to know about the community and world) and communication utility (i.e., using information in social interaction)—explained much of the variance in news-seeking behavior. Abelman and Atkin (1997) also supported interrelated patterns of television use by identifying three viewer archetypes: medium-, station-, and network-oriented viewers. Some of these approaches stem from work that suggested that media use could be described as primarily ritualized (diversionary) or instrumental (utilitarian) in nature (e.g., A. M. Rubin, 1984).

Ritualized and instrumental media orientations tell us about the amount and type of media use, and about one's media attitudes and expectations. These orientations reflect the complexity of audience activity. *Ritualized* use is using a medium more habitually to consume time and for diversion. It entails greater exposure to and affinity with the *medium*. Ritualized use suggests utility but an otherwise less active or less goal-directed state. *Instrumental* use is seeking certain message *content* for informational reasons.

It entails greater exposure to news and informational content and perceiving that content to be realistic. Instrumental use is active and purposive. It suggests utility, intention, selectivity, and involvement.

To a large extent, activity depends on the social context, potential for interaction, and attitude. Elements such as mobility and loneliness are important. Reduced mobility and greater loneliness, for example, result in ritualized media orientations and greater reliance on the media (Perse & Rubin, 1990; A. M. Rubin & Rubin, 1982a). Attitudinal dispositions such as affinity and perceived realism also are important. Attitudes affect our media expectations and how we perceive and interpret messages. They filter media and message selection and use. This is consistent with Swanson's (1979) notion of the importance of "the perceptual activity of interpreting or creating meaning for messages" (p. 42).

Potter (1986) and others have argued that such outcomes as cultivation are mediated by the differential perceptions people have about how realistic the media content is. For example, in one study we found watching action/adventure programs predicted a cultivation effect of feeling less safe, whereas watching television, in general, led to perceptions of greater safety (A. M. Rubin, Perse, & Taylor, 1988). Stronger cultivation effects were evident when media content was seen as being realistic. Perceived realism was also seen as a key element in explaining more variance in the enjoyment of reality-based versus fictional programming (Nabi, Stitt, Halford, & Finnerty, 2006).

Blumler (1979) argued that activity means imperviousness to influence. In other words, activity is a deterrent to media effects. This conclusion, though, is questionable. Activity plays an important intervening role in the effects process. Because activity denotes a more selective, attentive, and involved state of media use, it may actually be a catalyst to message effects. In two studies we found more active, instrumental television use led to cognitive (i.e., thinking about content), affective (i.e., parasocially interacting with media personalities), and behavioral (i.e., discussing content with others) involvement with news and soap opera programs (A. M. Rubin & Perse, 1987a, 1987b). Later, we observed that different activities could be catalysts or deterrents to media effects (Kim & Rubin, 1997). Activities—such as selectivity, attention, and involvement—facilitate such outcomes as parasocial interaction, cultivation, and communication satisfaction. Other activities—such as avoiding messages, being distracted, and being skeptical—inhibit these outcomes because they reduce message awareness and comprehension.

Therefore, it is reasonable to suggest that differences in audience activity—as evidenced in ritualized and instrumental orientations—have important implications for media effects. In other words, as Windahl (1981) argued, using a medium instrumentally or ritualistically leads to different outcomes. Instrumental orientations may produce stronger attitudinal and behavioral effects than ritualized orientations because instrumental orientations incorporate greater motivation to use and involvement with messages. Involvement suggests a state of readiness to select, interpret, and respond to messages.

Dependency and Functional Alternatives

According to McIlwraith, Jacobvitz, Kubey, and Alexander (1991), watching television can relax and distract viewers and decrease negative affect, and some viewers may excessively depend on television because they anticipate this effect. The notion of media

dependency is grounded in the availability and utilization of functional alternatives (Rosengren & Windahl, 1972). Dependency on a particular medium results from the motives we have to communicate, the strategies we use to obtain gratifications, and the restricted availability of functional alternatives. It mediates how we use the media and the potential impact of the media (e.g., Lindlof, 1986; Windahl et al., 1986).

On one hand, dependency results from an environment that restricts the availability of functional alternatives and produces a certain pattern of media use. Dotan and Cohen (1976), for example, found that fulfilling cognitive needs was most important and fulfilling escapist and affective needs was least important when using television, radio, and newspapers during and following the October, 1973, Middle East war. People turned to television and radio during a war-time crisis to fulfill most needs, especially surveillance needs. Recently, Diddi and LaRose (2006) suggested that strength of habit is the strongest predictor of news consumption.

Besides societal events and structure, individual life-position attributes—such as health, mobility, interaction, activity, life satisfaction, and economic security—also affect the availability and choice of communication alternatives, our motives to communicate, our strategies for seeking information and diversion, and dependency on a medium. In two studies of a life-position construct we called *contextual age*, for example, we found a negative link between one's degree of self-reliance and television dependency: the less healthy and less mobile depended more on television than did the healthier and more mobile (A. M. Rubin & Rubin, 1982a; R. B. Rubin & Rubin, 1982). Miller and Reese (1982) argued that "dependency on a medium appears to enhance the opportunity for that medium to have predicted effects" (p. 245). In their case, political effects (i.e., activity and efficacy) were more evident from exposure to a relied-upon medium.

We also proposed a model to highlight the links among media uses and effects. The *uses and dependency model* depicts links between one's needs and motives to communicate, strategies for seeking information, uses of media and functional alternatives, and media dependency (A. M. Rubin & Windahl, 1986). According to the model, needs and motives that produce narrow information-seeking strategies might lead to dependency on certain channels. In turn, dependency leads to other attitudinal or behavioral effects, and feeds back to alter other relationships in the society. Different outcomes would result from ritualized use of a medium and instrumental use of media content.

In one application of this model to development communication in Sierra Leone, Taylor (1992) found those who were dependent on radio for information about development used that medium instrumentally—they planned to acquire information and sought stimulating information from the radio. Those who were dependent on newspapers for information about development also used that medium instrumentally—they intentionally sought and selected stimulating information from the newspapers. As compared with the less dependent, Taylor observed that those who were more dependent on radio showed greater interest and participation in national development.

Social and Psychological Circumstances

The concept of media dependency highlights the interface of personal and mediated communication, including the importance of social and psychological circumstances—that is, individual differences—in media effects. Resourceful communicators have "a wider availability of alternative channels, a broader conception of the potential channels, and the capacity for using more diversified message- and interaction-seeking strategies"

(A. M. Rubin & Rubin, 1985, p. 39). They might, for example, use several available channels—including e-mail—to maintain their interpersonal relationships (Stafford, Kline, & Dimmick, 1999). Resourceful communicators are less likely to be dependent on any given person or communication channel. Effects should be more pronounced for those who come to depend on the messages of a particular medium such as talk radio or the Internet.

For example, telephoning a talk-radio host to express one's views is an accessible and nonthreatening alternative to interpersonal communication for those talk-radio listeners with restricted mobility, who are apprehensive about face-to-face interaction, and who feel others do not value what they have to say in interpersonal encounters (Armstrong & Rubin, 1989; also see Avery, Ellis, & Glover, 1978; Turow, 1974). Similarly, the Internet is a functional alternative to face-to-face communication for those who are anxious about interpersonal interaction and do not find such interaction to be rewarding (Papacharissi & Rubin, 2000; cf. Flaherty, Pearce, & Rubin, 1998). On the other hand, those who are extroverted and agreeable might prefer conversation with others instead of media (Finn, 1997). Such individual differences contribute to communication preferences and to the opportunity for certain sources to influence people.

Media uses and effects, then, depend on the potential for interaction and the context of interaction. This is heavily influenced by people's social and psychological circumstances, including lifestyle, life position, and personality (e.g., Finn & Gorr, 1988; A. M. Rubin & Rubin, 1982a). Life satisfaction, mobility, loneliness, and mood, to name a few factors, can determine media behavior. For example, crime victims who experience greater psychological distress and lower levels of felt social support use television to seek companionship, presumably to compensate for limited social interaction (Minnebo, 2005). Reduced life satisfaction and anxiety contribute to escapist television viewing (Conway & Rubin, 1991; A. M. Rubin, 1985), and restricted mobility and greater loneliness result in ritualized media behavior and reliance on television (Perse & Rubin, 1990; A. M. Rubin & Rubin, 1982a). Those who are heavily reliant on television—that is, self-reported television addicts—have been found to be neurotic, introverted, and easily bored, watching television to forget unpleasant thoughts, to regulate moods, and to fill time (McIlwraith, 1998). In addition, mood influences media choice so that boredom leads to selecting exciting content and stress to selecting relaxing content (Bryant & Zillmann, 1984).

Differences in personality, cognition, social affiliation, and motivation affect exposure, cultivation, satisfaction, parasocial interaction, identification, and content attention and elaboration (e.g., Carveth & Alexander, 1985; Perse, 1990b, 1992; R. B. Rubin & McHugh, 1987). Krcmar and Kean (2005) found that personality factors, including neuroticism, extroversion, openness, and agreeableness, are differentially related to watching or liking violent television content. Krcmar and Greene (1999) found that disinhibited adolescents tend to watch violent television programs, but sensation seekers who exhibit risky behavior are unlike those who watch violent content. Johnson (1995) noted that four motivations—gore, thrill, independent, and problem watching—affect adolescents' cognitive and affective responses to viewing graphic horror films. Harwood (1999) found that, by selecting programs that feature young characters, young adults increase age-group identification. Besides factors such as locus of control, gender differences also influence media exposure and mediate selection and impact. Haridakis (2006), for example, found motivation to be a more important predictor of viewer aggression for males than for females. Lucas and Sherry (2004) found that women are less motivated than men to play video games in social situations.

CONCLUSIONS AND DIRECTIONS

Uses and gratifications sees communication influence as being socially and psychologically constrained and affected by individual differences and choice. Variations in expectations, attitudes, activity, and involvement lead to different behaviors and outcomes. Personality, social context, motivation, and availability—based on culture and economic, political, and social structure—all affect the potential influence of media and their messages.

In 1974 Katz and his colleagues argued, "hardly any substantive or empirical effort has been devoted to connecting gratifications and effects" (p. 28). Five years later, Blumler (1979) echoed those sentiments: "We lack a well-formed perspective about which gratifications sought from which forms of content are likely to facilitate which effects" (p. 16). Although some precision has been lacking, this state of affairs has changed during the past three decades as investigators have sought to link social and psychological antecedents, motivation, attitudes, activity and involvement, behavior, and outcomes. More focused consideration of media orientations and audience activity has produced renewed interest in examining the place of motivation in explaining communication processes and outcomes. Yet, we still need increased specificity, especially as our attention continues to turn to newer media.

Blumler (1979) summarized cognitive, diversionary, and personal identity uses of the media. He proposed three hypotheses about media effects based on these uses: (a) cognitive motivation will facilitate information gain, (b) diversion or escape motivation will facilitate audience perceptions of the accuracy of social portrayals in entertainment media, and (c) personal identity motivation will promote reinforcement effects.

Such hypotheses have received some attention to date. For example, we have learned that cognitive or instrumental motivation leads to seeking information and to cognitive involvement (Perse, 1990a; A. M. Rubin, 1983, 1984; A. M. Rubin & Perse, 1987b; A. M. Rubin & Rubin, 1982b). Levy and Windahl (1984), for example, found that increased planning and intention to watch television was strongly related to surveillance use. Vincent and Basil (1997) found that increased surveillance needs resulted in greater use of all news media among a college-student sample. And researchers have observed links between cognitive or instrumental information-seeking motivation and information gain during a political campaign (McLeod & Becker, 1974), about political candidates (Atkin & Heald, 1976), and about candidates' stands on issues. They found that public affairs media use and interest lead to increased political knowledge (Pettey, 1988).

The second hypothesis about diversionary motivation and acceptance of role portrayals, though, must recognize the mediating role of attitudes and experiences in media effects. We have learned that attitudes and experience affect perceptions. Some studies support cultivation effects contingent on the perceived reality of content (Potter, 1986; A. M. Rubin et al., 1988), audience members' personal experiences with crime (Weaver & Wakshlag, 1986), and media utility and selectivity (Perse, 1986). There is much room for researchers to expand attention to links between attitudes, motivation, and involvement, on one hand, and perceptions of media content and role portrayals, on the other.

As to the third hypothesis, we have seen that media function as alternatives to personal interaction for the immobile, dissatisfied, and apprehensive (Armstrong & Rubin, 1989; Papacharissi & Rubin, 2000; Perse & Rubin, 1990; A. M. Rubin & Rubin, 1982a). In addition, social utility motivation might lead to a reduced sense of parasocial interaction with television personalities (A. M. Rubin & Perse, 1987a).

One fruitful path has been the study of personal involvement in the media uses and effects process. Involvement influences information acquisition and processing. It signifies attention, participation, cognitive processing, affect, and emotion. It also has led to the study of *parasocial interaction*, emphasizing the role of media personalities in real and perceived relationships with audience members. Parasocial interaction accentuates the relevance of interpersonal concepts such as attraction, similarity, homophily, impression management, and empathy to understanding the role and influence of media and newer technologies. Harrison (1997), for example, argued that interpersonal attraction to thin media characters promotes eating disorders in women college students. And O'Sullivan (2000) considered the role of mediated communication channels (e.g., telephone, answering machine, electronic mail) for managing impressions in relationships.

Over 50 years ago, Horton and Wohl (1956) proposed that television and radio personalities foster an illusionary parasocial relationship with viewers and listeners. Parasocial interaction is a sense of friendship with these media personae. It suggests an audience member's felt affective or emotional relationship with the media personality (Rosengren & Windahl, 1972; A. M. Rubin & Perse, 1987a), which may be experienced as "seeking guidance from a media persona, seeing media personalities as friends, imagining being part of a favorite program's social world, and desiring to meet media performers" (A. M. Rubin et al., 1985, pp. 156–157). Audience members often see particular media personalities in a manner parallel to their interpersonal friends—as natural, down-to-earth, attractive people holding similar attitudes and values. Media formats and techniques encourage and promote the development of parasocial relationships. As with other media, audience members must choose to participate or interact.

We have looked at parasocial interaction with television newscasters and soap-opera characters (A. M. Rubin & Perse, 1987a, 1987b), with talk-radio hosts (A. M. Rubin & Step, 2000), and with favorite television personalities (Conway & Rubin, 1991; R. B. Rubin & McHugh, 1987). We developed a measure to attempt to gauge the extent of the relationships (A. M. Rubin et al., 1985; A. M. Rubin & Perse, 1987a). Basically, involved viewers, not necessarily heavy viewers, appear to form parasocial relationships.

Parasocial interaction suggests involved and instrumental media use, that is, a more active orientation to media use (e.g., Kim & Rubin, 1997; Perse, 1990b; A. M. Rubin & Perse, 1987a). It has been linked to being socially and task-attracted to a favorite television personality (R. B. Rubin & McHugh, 1987), to reducing uncertainty in relationships (Perse & Rubin, 1989), and to attitude homophily with television personalities (Turner, 1993).

As affective and emotional involvement, parasocial interaction affects media attitudes, behaviors, and expectations, and should accentuate potential effects. For example, in an analysis of critical responses of British viewers, Livingstone (1988) suggested the personally involving nature of soap operas has important implications for media effects. Brown and Basil (1995) found that emotional involvement with a media celebrity mediates persuasive communication and increases personal concern about health messages and risky sexual behavior. Also, we found parasocially interacting with a public-affairs talk-radio host predicts planned and frequent listening, treating the host as an important source of information, and feeling the host influences how listeners feel about and act upon societal issues (A. M. Rubin & Step, 2000).

Windahl (1981) argued that a synthesis would help overcome limitations and criticisms of both media uses and media effects traditions. Such a synthesis recognizes that: media perceptions and expectations guide people's behavior; motivation is derived from needs, interests, and externally imposed constraints; there are functional alternatives to media consumption; there are important interpersonal dimensions to the media experience; and audience activity, involvement, and attitudes about media content play an important role in media effects.

Since the early days of media-use typologies, we have sought to address theoretical links among media uses and effects. We have learned more about audience members as variably active and involved communicators. We have seen the contributions of interpersonal communication for understanding media uses and effects. The media uses and effects process remains complex, requiring careful attention to antecedent, mediating, and consequent conditions. Single-variable explanations continue to have appeal to some researchers and policymakers. However, such explanations distract us from the conceptual complexity of media effects. As Ruggiero (2000) argued, uses and gratifications has been "a cutting-edge theoretical approach" in the early stages of new communication media. Uses and gratifications will continue to be especially valuable as we seek to understand the newer and continually evolving, interactive digital environment.

References

Abelman, R. (1987). Religious television uses and gratifications. *Journal of Broadcasting & Electronic Media, 31*, 293–307.

Abelman, R., & Atkin, D. (1997). What viewers watch when they watch TV: Affiliation change as case study. *Journal of Broadcasting & Electronic Media, 41*, 360–379.

Adoni, H. (1979). The functions of mass media in the political socialization of adolescents. *Communication Research, 6*, 84–106.

Alexander, A. (1985). Adolescents' soap opera viewing and relational perceptions. *Journal of Broadcasting & Electronic Media, 29*, 295–308.

Anderson, J. A., & Meyer, T. P. (1975). Functionalism and the mass media. *Journal of Broadcasting, 19*, 11–22.

Armstrong, C. B., & Rubin, A. M. (1989). Talk radio as interpersonal communication. *Journal of Communication, 39*(2), 84–94.

Atkin, C. K., & Heald, G. (1976). Effects of political advertising. *Public Opinion Quarterly, 40*, 216–228.

Avery, R. K., Ellis, D. G., & Glover, T. W. (1978). Patterns of communication on talk radio. *Journal of Broadcasting, 22*, 5–17.

Babrow, A. S. (1988). Theory and method in research on audience motives. *Journal of Broadcasting & Electronic Media, 32*, 471–487.

Babrow, A. S. (1989). An expectancy-value analysis of the student soap opera audience. *Communication Research, 16*, 155–178.

Babrow, A. S., & Swanson, D. L. (1988). Disentangling antecedents of audience exposure levels: Extending expectancy-value analyses of gratifications sought from television news. *Communication Monographs, 55*, 1–21.

Banning, S. A. (2007). Factors affecting the marketing of a public safety message: The third-person effect and uses and gratifications theory in public reaction to a crime reduction program. *Atlantic Journal of Communication, 15*(1), 1–18.

Bantz, C. R. (1982). Exploring uses and gratifications: A comparison of reported uses of television and reported uses of favorite program type. *Communication Research, 9*, 352–379.

Berelson, B. (1949). What "missing the newspaper" means. In P. F. Lazarsfeld & F. N. Stanton (Eds.), *Communications research 1948–1949* (pp. 111–129). New York: Harper.

Bilandzic, H., & Rossler, P. (2004). Life according to television: Implications of genre-specific cultivation effects. The gratification/cultivation model. *Communications: The European Journal of Communication Research, 29*, 295–326.

Blumler, J. G. (1979). The role of theory in uses and gratifications studies. *Communication Research, 6*, 9–36.

Brown, W. J., & Basil, M. D. (1995). Media celebrities and public health: Responses to "Magic" Johnson's HIV disclosure and its impact on AIDS risk and high-risk behaviors. *Health Communication, 7*, 345–370.

Bryant, J., & Zillmann, D. (1984). Using television to alleviate boredom and stress: Selective exposure as a function of induced excitational states. *Journal of Broadcasting, 28*, 1–20.

Carey, J. W., & Kreiling, A. L. (1974). Popular culture and uses and gratifications: Notes toward an accommodation. In J. G. Blumler & E. Katz (Eds.), *The uses of mass communications: Current perspectives on gratifications research* (pp. 225–248). Beverly Hills CA: Sage.

Carveth, R., & Alexander, A. (1985). Soap opera viewing motivations and the cultivation process. *Journal of Broadcasting & Electronic Media, 29*, 259–273.

Cohen, A. A., Levy, M. R., & Golden, K. (1988). Children's uses and gratifications of home VCRs: Evolution or revolution. *Communication Research, 15*, 772–780.

Conway, J. C., & Rubin, A. M. (1991). Psychological predictors of television viewing motivation. *Communication Research, 18*, 443–464.

Cowles, D. L. (1989). Consumer perceptions of interactive media. *Journal of Broadcasting & Electronic Media, 33*, 83–89.

Diddi, A., & LaRose, R. (2006). Getting hooked on news: Uses and gratifications and the formation of news habits among college students in an Internet environment. *Journal of Broadcasting & Electronic Media, 50*, 193–210.

Dimmick, J. W., McCain, T. A., & Bolton, W. T. (1979). Media use and the life span. *American Behavioral Scientist, 23*(1), 7–31.

Dobos, J. (1992). Gratification models of satisfaction and choice of communication channels in organizations. *Communication Research, 19*, 29–51.

Dobos, J., & Dimmick, J. (1988). Factor analysis and gratification constructs. *Journal of Broadcasting & Electronic Media, 32*, 335–350.

Donohew, L., Palmgreen, P., & Rayburn, J. D., II. (1987). Social and psychological origins of media use: A lifestyle analysis. *Journal of Broadcasting & Electronic Media, 31*, 255–278.

Dotan, J., & Cohen, A. A. (1976). Mass media use in the family during war and peace: Israel 1973–1974. *Communication Research, 3*, 393–402.

Eastman, S. T. (1979). Uses of television viewing and consumer life styles: A multivariate analysis. *Journal of Broadcasting, 23*, 491–500.

Elliott, P. (1974). Uses and gratifications research: A critique and a sociological alternative. In J. G. Blumler & E. Katz (Eds.), *The uses of mass communications: Current perspectives on gratifications research* (pp. 249–268). Beverly Hills CA: Sage.

Elliott, W. R., & Quattlebaum, C. P. (1979). Similarities in patterns of media use: A cluster analysis of media gratifications. *Western Journal of Speech Communication, 43*, 61–72.

Eveland, W. P. (2004). The effect of political discussion in producing informed citizens: The roles of information, motivation, and elaboration. *Political Communication, 21*, 177–193.

Farquhar, L. K., & Meeds, R. (2007). *Journal of Computer-Mediated Communication, 12*, 1208–1228.

Ferguson, D. A. (1992). Channel repertoire in the presence of remote control devices, VCRs, and cable television. *Journal of Broadcasting & Electronic Media, 36*, 83–91.

Ferguson, D. A., & Perse, E. M. (2000). The World Wide Web as a functional alternative to television. *Journal of Broadcasting & Electronic Media, 44*, 155–174.

Finn, S. (1992). Television addiction? An evaluation of four competing media-use models. *Journalism Quarterly, 69*, 422–435.

Finn, S. (1997). Origins of media exposure: Linking personality traits to TV, radio, print, and film use. *Communication Research, 24*, 507–529.

Finn, S., & Gorr, M. B. (1988). Social isolation and social support as correlates of television viewing motivations. *Communication Research, 15*, 135–158.

Fisher, B. A. (1978). *Perspectives on human communication*. New York: Macmillan.

Flaherty, L. M., Pearce, K. J., & Rubin, R. B. (1998). Internet and face-to-face communication: Not functional alternatives. *Communication Quarterly*, *46*, 250–268.

Galloway, J. J., & Meek, F. L. (1981). Audience uses and gratifications: An expectancy model. *Communication Research*, *8*, 435–449.

Garramone, G. M. (1983). Issue versus image orientation and effects of political advertising. *Communication Research*, *10*, 59–76.

Garramone, G. M. (1984). Audience motivation effect: More evidence. *Communication Research*, *11*, 79–96.

Greenberg, B. S. (1974). Gratifications of television viewing and their correlates for British children. In J. G. Blumler & E. Katz (Eds.), *The uses of mass communications: Current perspectives on gratifications research* (pp. 71–92). Beverly Hills: Sage.

Hamilton, N. F., & Rubin, A. M. (1992). The influence of religiosity on television use. *Journalism Quarterly*, *69*, 667–678.

Haridakis, P. M. (2002). Viewer characteristics, exposure to television violence, and aggression. *Media Psychology*, *4*, 323–352.

Haridakis, P. M. (2006). Men, women, and television violence: Predicting viewer aggression in male and female television viewers. *Communication Quarterly*, *54*, 227–255.

Haridakis, P. M., & Rubin, A. M. (2003). Motivation for watching television violence and viewer aggression. *Mass Communication & Society*, *6*(1), 29–56.

Haridakis, P. M., & Rubin, A. M. (2005). Third-person effects in the aftermath of terrorism. *Mass Communication & Society*, *8*(1), 39–59.

Harrison, K. (1997). Does interpersonal attraction to thin media personalities promote eating disorders? *Journal of Broadcasting & Electronic Media*, *41*, 478–500.

Harwood, J. (1999). Age identification, social identity gratifications, and television viewing. *Journal of Broadcasting & Electronic Media*, *43*, 123–136.

Herzog, H. (1940). Professor quiz: A gratification study. In P. F. Lazarsfeld (Ed.), *Radio and the printed page* (pp. 64–93). New York: Duell, Sloan & Pearce.

Herzog, H. (1944). What do we really know about daytime serial listeners? In P. F. Lazarsfeld & F. N. Stanton (Eds.), *Radio research 1942–1943* (pp. 3–33). New York: Duell, Sloan & Pearce.

Horton, D., & Wohl, R. R. (1956). Mass communication and para-social interaction. *Psychiatry*, *19*, 215–229.

Johnson, D. D. (1995). Adolescents' motivations for viewing graphic horror. *Human Communication Research*, *21*, 522–552.

Katz, E. (1959). Mass communication research and the study of popular culture. *Studies in Public Communication*, *2*, 1–6.

Katz, E., Blumler, J. G., & Gurevitch, M. (1974). Utilization of mass communication by the individual. In J. G. Blumler & E. Katz (Eds.), *The uses of mass communications: Current perspectives on gratifications research* (pp. 19–32). Beverly Hills CA: Sage.

Katz, E., Gurevitch, M., & Haas, H. (1973). On the use of the mass media for important things. *American Sociological Review*, *38*, 164–181.

Kaye, B. K., & Johnson, T. J. (2002). Online and in the know: Uses and gratifications of the web for political information. *Journal of Broadcasting & Electronic Media*, *46*(1), 54–72.

Kim, J., & Rubin, A. M. (1997). The variable influence of audience activity on media effects. *Communication Research*, *24*, 107–135.

Klapper, J. T. (1960). *The effects of mass communication*. New York: Free Press.

Klapper, J. T. (1963). Mass communication research: An old road resurveyed. *Public Opinion Quarterly*, *27*, 515–527.

Ko, H., Cho, C., & Roberts, M. S. (2005). Internet uses and gratifications. *Journal of Advertising*, *34*(2), 57–70.

Krcmar, M., & Greene, K. (1999). Predicting exposure to and uses of television violence. *Journal of Communication*, *49*(3), 24–45.

Krcmar, M., & Kean, L. G. (2005). Uses and gratifications of media violence: Personality correlates of viewing and liking violent genres. *Media Psychology*, *7*, 399–420.

LaRose, R., & Eastin, M. S. (2004). A social cognitive theory of Internet uses and gratifications: Toward a new model of media attendance. *Journal of Broadcasting & Electronic Media, 48,* 358–377.

Lasswell, H. D. (1948). The structure and function of communication in society. In L. Bryson (Ed.), *The communication of ideas* (pp. 37–51). New York: Harper.

Lazarsfeld, P. F. (1940). *Radio and the printed page.* New York: Duell, Sloan & Pearce.

Lazarsfeld, P. F., & Merton, R. K. (1948). Mass communication, popular taste and organized social action. In L. Bryson (Ed.), *The communication of ideas* (pp. 95–118). New York: Harper.

Lemish, D. (1985). Soap opera viewing in college: A naturalistic inquiry. *Journal of Broadcasting & Electronic Media, 29,* 275–293.

Levy, M. R., & Windahl, S. (1984). Audience activity and gratifications: A conceptual clarification and exploration. *Communication Research, 11,* 51–78.

Levy, M. R., & Windahl, S. (1985). The concept of audience activity. In K. E. Rosengren, L. A. Wenner, & P. Palmgreen (Eds.), *Media gratifications research: Current perspectives* (pp. 109–122). Beverly Hills CA: Sage.

Lichtenstein, A., & Rosenfeld, L. B. (1983). Uses and misuses of gratifications research: An explication of media functions. *Communication Research, 10,* 97–109.

Lichtenstein, A., & Rosenfeld, L. (1984). Normative expectations and individual decisions concerning media gratification choices. *Communication Research, 11,* 393–413.

Lin, C. A. (1993). Modeling the gratification-seeking process of television viewing. *Human Communication Research, 20,* 224–244.

Lin, C. A. (1994). Audience fragmentation in a competitive video marketplace. *Journal of Advertising Research, 34*(6), 30–38.

Lin, C. A. (1999). Online-service adoption likelihood. *Journal of Advertising Research, 39*(2), 79–89.

Lindlof, T. R. (1986). Social and structural constraints on media use in incarceration. *Journal of Broadcasting & Electronic Media, 30,* 341–355.

Livingstone, S. M. (1988). Why people watch soap operas: An analysis of the explanations of British viewers. *European Journal of Communication, 3,* 55–80.

Lometti, G., Reeves, B., & Bybee, C. R. (1977). Investigating the assumptions of uses and gratifications research. *Communication Research, 4,* 321–338.

Lucas, K., & Sherry, J. L. (2004). Sex-differences in video game play: A communication based explanation. *Communication Research, 31,* 499–523.

Lull, J. (1980). The social uses of television. *Human Communication Research, 6,* 197–209.

Massey, K. B. (1995). Analyzing the uses and gratifications concept of audience activity with a qualitative approach: Media encounters during the 1989 Loma Prieta earthquake disaster. *Journal of Broadcasting & Electronic Media, 39,* 328–349.

McCombs, M. E., & Shaw, D. L. (1972). The agenda-setting function of mass media. *Public Opinion Quarterly, 36,* 176–187.

McDonald, D. G. (1990). Media orientation and television news viewing. *Journalism and Mass Communication Quarterly, 67,* 11–20.

McDonald, D. G., & Glynn, C. J. (1984). The stability of media gratifications. *Journalism Quarterly, 61,* 542–549; 741.

McIlwraith, R. D. (1998). "I'm addicted to television": The personality, imagination, and TV watching patterns of self-identified TV addicts. *Journal of Broadcasting & Electronic Media, 42,* 371–386.

McIlwraith, R., Jacobvitz, R. S., Kubey, R., & Alexander, A. (1991). Television addiction: Theories and data behind the ubiquitous metaphor. *American Behavioral Scientist, 35*(2), 104–121.

McLeod, J. M., & Becker, L. B. (1974). Testing the validity of gratification measures through political effects analysis. In J. G. Blumler & E. Katz (Eds.), *The uses of mass communications: Current perspectives on gratifications research* (pp. 137–164). Beverly Hills CA: Sage.

McQuail, D., Blumler, J. G., & Brown, J. R. (1972). The television audience: A revised perspective. In D. McQuail (Ed.), *Sociology of mass communications* (pp. 135–165). Middlesex, England: Penguin.

Mendelsohn, H. (1963). Socio-psychological perspectives on the mass media and public anxiety. *Journalism Quarterly*, *40*, 511–516.

Miller, M. M., & Reese, S. D. (1982). Media dependency as interaction: Effects of exposure and reliance on political activity and efficacy. *Communication Research*, *9*, 227–248.

Minnebo, J. (2005). Psychological distress, perceived social support, and television viewing for reasons of companionship: A test of the compensation hypothesis in a population of crime victims. *Communications: The European Journal of Communication Research*, *30*, 233–250.

Nabi, R. L., Stitt, C. R., Halford, J., & Finnerty, K. L. (2006). Emotional and cognitive predictors of the enjoyment of reality-based and fictional television programming: An elaboration of the uses-and-gratifications perspective. *Media Psychology*, *8*, 421–447.

O'Sullivan, P. B. (2000). What you don't know won't hurt me: Impression management functions of communication channels in relationships. *Human Communication Research*, *26*, 403–431.

Palmgreen, P. (1984). Uses and gratifications: A theoretical perspective. *Communication Yearbook*, *8*, 20–55.

Palmgreen, P., & Rayburn, J. D., II. (1979). Uses and gratifications and exposure to public television: A discrepancy approach. *Communication Research*, *6*, 155–179.

Palmgreen, P., & Rayburn, J. D., II. (1982). Gratifications sought and media exposure: An expectancy value model. *Communication Research*, *9*, 561–580.

Palmgreen, P., & Rayburn, J. D., II. (1985). A comparison of gratification models of media satisfaction. *Communication Monographs*, *52*, 334–346.

Palmgreen, P., Wenner, L. A., & Rayburn, J. D., II. (1980). Relations between gratifications sought and obtained: A study of television news. *Communication Research*, *7*, 161–192.

Palmgreen, P., Wenner, L. A., & Rayburn, J. D., II. (1981). Gratification discrepancies and news program choice. *Communication Research*, *8*, 451–478.

Palmgreen, P., Wenner, L. A., & Rosengren, K. E. (1985). Uses and gratifications research: The past ten years. In K. E. Rosengren, L. A. Wenner, & P. Palmgreen (Eds.), *Media gratifications research: Current perspectives* (pp. 11–37). Beverly Hills CA: Sage.

Papacharissi, Z., & Rubin, A. M. (2000). Predictors of Internet use. *Journal of Broadcasting & Electronic Media*, *44*, 175–196.

Pearlin, L. I. (1959). Social and personal stress and escape television viewing. *Public Opinion Quarterly*, *23*, 255–259.

Perse, E. M. (1986). Soap opera viewing patterns of college students and cultivation. *Journal of Broadcasting & Electronic Media*, *30*, 175–193.

Perse, E. M. (1990a). Involvement with local television news: Cognitive and emotional dimensions. *Human Communication Research*, *16*, 556–581.

Perse, E. M. (1990b). Media involvement and local news effects. *Journal of Broadcasting & Electronic Media*, *34*, 17–36.

Perse, E. M. (1992). Predicting attention to local television news: Need for cognition and motives for viewing. *Communication Reports*, *5*, 40–49.

Perse, E. M., & Courtright, J. A. (1993). Normative images of communication media: Mass and interpersonal channels in the new media environment. *Human Communication Research*, *19*, 485–503.

Perse, E. M., & Rubin, A. M. (1988). Audience activity and satisfaction with favorite television soap opera. *Journalism Quarterly*, *65*, 368–375.

Perse, E. M., & Rubin, A. M. (1990). Chronic loneliness and television use. *Journal of Broadcasting & Electronic Media*, *34*, 37–53.

Perse, E. M., & Rubin, R. B. (1989). Attribution in social and parasocial relationships. *Communication Research*, *16*, 59–77.

Peters, O., Rickes, M., Jockel, S., Criegern, C., & Deursen, A. (2006). Explaining and analyzing audiences: A social cognitive approach to selectivity and media use. *Communications: The European Journal of Communication Research*, *31*, 279–308.

Pettey, G. R. (1988). The interaction of the individual's social environment, attention and interest, and public affairs media use on political knowledge holding. *Communication Research*, 15, 265–281.

Potter, W. J. (1986). Perceived reality and the cultivation hypothesis. *Journal of Broadcasting & Electronic Media*, *30*, 159–174.

Rayburn, J. D., II, & Palmgreen, P. (1984). Merging uses and gratifications and expectancy-value theory. *Communication Research*, *11*, 537–562.

Rosengren, K. E. (1974). Uses and gratifications: A paradigm outlined. In J. G. Blumler & E. Katz (Eds.), *The uses of mass communications: Current perspectives on gratifications research* (pp. 269–286). Beverly Hills: Sage.

Rosengren, K. E., & Windahl, S. (1972). Mass media consumption as a functional alternative. In D. McQuail (Ed.), *Sociology of mass communications* (pp. 166–194). Middlesex, England: Penguin.

Rubin, A. M. (1979). Television use by children and adolescents. *Human Communication Research*, 5, 109–120.

Rubin, A. M. (1981a). An examination of television viewing motivations. *Communication Research*, 8, 141–165.

Rubin, A. M. (1981b). A multivariate analysis of "*60 Minutes*" viewing motivations. *Journalism Quarterly*, 58, 529–534.

Rubin, A. M. (1983). Television uses and gratifications: The interactions of viewing patterns and motivations. *Journal of Broadcasting*, *27*, 37–51.

Rubin, A. M. (1984). Ritualized and instrumental television viewing. *Journal of Communication*, *34*(3), 67–77.

Rubin, A. M. (1985). Uses of daytime television soap opera by college students. *Journal of Broadcasting & Electronic Media*, *29*, 241–258.

Rubin, A. M. (1993). Audience activity and media use. *Communication Monographs*, *60*, 98–105.

Rubin, A. M. (2002). The uses-and-gratifications perspective of media effects. In J. Bryant & D. Zillmann (Eds.), *Media effects: Advances in theory and research* (2nd ed., pp. 525–548). Mahwah, NJ: Erlbaum.

Rubin, A. M., & Bantz, C. R. (1989). Uses and gratifications of videocassette recorders. In J. Salvaggio & J. Bryant (Eds.), *Media use in the information age: Emerging patterns of adoption and consumer use* (pp. 181–195). Hillsdale, NJ: Erlbaum.

Rubin, A. M., & Perse, E. M. (1987a). Audience activity and soap opera involvement: A uses and effects investigation. *Human Communication Research*, *14*, 246–268.

Rubin, A. M., & Perse, E. M. (1987b). Audience activity and television news gratifications. *Communication Research*, *14*, 58–84.

Rubin, A. M., Perse, E. M., & Powell, R. A. (1985). Loneliness, parasocial interaction, and local television news viewing. *Human Communication Research*, *12*, 155–180.

Rubin, A. M., Perse, E. M., & Taylor, D. S. (1988). A methodological examination of cultivation. *Communication Research*, *15*, 107–134.

Rubin, A. M., & Rubin, R. B. (1982a). Contextual age and television use. *Human Communication Research*, 8, 228–244.

Rubin, A. M., & Rubin, R. B. (1982b). Older persons' TV viewing patterns and motivations. *Communication Research*, *9*, 287–313.

Rubin, A. M., & Rubin, R. B. (1985). Interface of personal and mediated communication: A research agenda. *Critical Studies in Mass Communication*, *2*, 36–53.

Rubin, A. M., & Rubin, R. B. (1989). Social and psychological antecedents of VCR use. In M. R. Levy (Ed.), *The VCR age: Home video and mass communication* (pp. 92–111). Newbury Park, CA: Sage.

Rubin, A. M., & Step, M. M. (2000). Impact of motivation, attraction, and parasocial interaction on talk radio listening. *Journal of Broadcasting & Electronic Media*, *44*, 635–654.

Rubin, A. M., & Windahl, S. (1986). The uses and dependency model of mass communication. *Critical Studies in Mass Communication*, 3, 184–199.

Rubin, R. B., & McHugh, M. P. (1987). Development of parasocial interaction relationships. *Journal of Broadcasting & Electronic Media*, *31*, 279–292.

Rubin, R. B., & Rubin, A. M. (1982). Contextual age and television use: Reexamining a life-position indicator. *Communication Yearbook*, *6*, 583–604.

Ruggiero, T. E. (2000). Uses and gratifications theory in the 21st century. *Mass Communication & Society*, *3*(1), 3–37.

Slater, M. D. (2007). Reinforcing spirals: The mutual influence of media selectivity and media effects and their impact on individual behavior and social identity. *Communication Theory*, *17*, 281–303.

Stafford, L., Kline, S. L., & Dimmick, J. (1999). Home e-mail: Relational maintenance and gratification opportunities. *Journal of Broadcasting & Electronic Media*, *43*, 659–669.

Stephenson, W. (1967). *The play theory of mass communication*. Chicago: University of Chicago Press.

Swanson, D. L. (1977). The uses and misuses of uses and gratifications. *Human Communication Research*, *3*, 214–221.

Swanson, D. L. (1979). Political communication research and the uses and gratifications model: A critique. *Communication Research*, *6*, 37–53.

Swanson, D. L. (1987). Gratification seeking, media exposure, and audience interpretations: Some directions for research. *Journal of Broadcasting & Electronic Media*, *31*, 237–254.

Taylor, D. S. (1992). Application of the uses and dependency model of mass communication to development communication in the western area of Sierra Leone (Doctoral dissertation, Kent State University, 1991). *Dissertation Abstracts International*, *A52/12*, 4134.

Turner, J. R. (1993). Interpersonal and psychological predictors of parasocial interaction with different television performers. *Communication Quarterly*, *41*, 443–453.

Turow, J. (1974). Talk-show radio as interpersonal communication. *Journal of Broadcasting*, *18*, 171–179.

Vincent, R. C., & Basil, M. D. (1997). College students' news gratifications, media use and current events knowledge. *Journal of Broadcasting & Electronic Media*, *41*, 380–392.

Weaver, J., & Wakshlag, J. (1986). Perceived vulnerability to crime, criminal victimization experience, and television viewing. *Journal of Broadcasting & Electronic Media*, *30*, 141–158.

Wenner, L. A. (1982). Gratifications sought and obtained in program dependency: A study of network evening news programs and 60 Minutes. *Communication Research*, *9*, 539–560.

Wenner, L. A. (1986). Model specification and theoretical development in gratifications sought and obtained research: A comparison of discrepancy and transactional approaches. *Communication Monographs*, *53*, 160–179.

Westmyer, S. A., DiCioccio, R. L., & Rubin, R. B. (1998). Appropriateness and effectiveness of communication channels in competent interpersonal communication. *Journal of Communication*, *48*(3), 27–48.

Windahl, S. (1981). Uses and gratifications at the crossroads. *Mass Communication Review Yearbook*, *2*, 174–185.

Windahl, S., Hojerback, I., & Hedinsson, E. (1986). Adolescents without television: A study in media deprivation. *Journal of Broadcasting & Electronic Media*, *30*, 47–63.

Wright, C. R. (1960). Functional analysis and mass communication. *Public Opinion Quarterly*, *24*, 605–620.

9

WHERE PSYCHOPHYSIOLOGY MEETS THE MEDIA

Taking the Effects Out of Mass Media Research

Annie Lang
Indiana University

Robert F. Potter
Indiana University

Paul Bolls
University of Missouri

The use of physiological measures in the study of mass communication is not particularly new. Early research done in the 1960s and 1970s attempted to demonstrate that media have measurable effects on physiology (Cantor, Zillmann, & Einsiedel, 1978; Donnerstein & Barrett, 1978; Donnerstein & Hallam, 1978; Zillmann, 1971). Perhaps surprisingly, at least at the time, the findings of those studies did not demonstrate particularly robust or large effects, which led to the virtual disappearance of physiological measures from the communication discipline. This early work took place at a time when most mass communication researchers were looking for "effects" of the media. Physiological measures were being used primarily to demonstrate that the media had measurable effects on bodily functions, which in turn impacted how the messages were responded to. The physiological impact was part of the "effect" that was being searched for—a demonstrable change in physiology was expected in response to the media message. Sometimes, the sought-after change in physiology was thought to be an indicator of a change in state (e.g. arousal), but often simple change in physiology was the ultimate goal. The absence of reliable change in physiological systems in response to media, coupled with the economic and technical difficulties associated with collecting physiological data, virtually banished physiological measures from the toolbox of communication researchers for the next decade.

Not until the mid-1980s did physiological measures once again begin creeping into the published literature. This time, however, rather than making a brief appearance and then exiting the stage, the measures slowly and steadily increased their presence in the field. Today, in fact, not only are there one or two mass communication labs collecting physiological data and publishing results, but there are more than a dozen in this country and even more internationally (A. Lang, Bradley, Chung, & Lee, 2003). What changed?

Paradigm shift! Following the move of our colleagues in psychology from behaviorism to information processing (Lachman, Lachman, & Butterfield, 1979; Miller, 2003), mass communication researchers in the mid-1980s began shifting away from the study of media "effects" towards the study of media *processing* (Chaffee, 1980). Researchers who returned to the use of physiological measures in this decade did not view them as indicators of change in physiological states caused by the media but rather conceptualized them as indicators of cognitive and emotional events (Reeves, Thorson, & Schleuder, 1986). In other words, media researchers did not merely return to the use of physiological measures but instead embraced the discipline of psychophysiology.

As often happens at the intersection of disciplines, the blending of the new discipline and the old led to a new kind of thinking that has revolutionized the way some media researchers think about mass communication. In order to engage in psychophysiological research, that is to use physiological measures as indicators of thinking, rather than simply to use physiological measures, requires that one understand and accept the assumptions of psychophysiology. In many ways, the acceptance of these assumptions requires the rethinking of one's worldview, allowing for novel ways of exploring the same problems. Five primary assumptions of psychophysiology that impact the study of mass communication are discussed here (for a thorough discussion of the assumptions and conceptualization of psychophysiology, see Cacioppo, Tassinary, & Berntson, 2000a). The first and most central assumption of psychophysiology is the concept of the embodied mind. Psychophysiology has no place for Cartesian dualism. You cannot look for indicators of thought in heart rate or skin conductance or facial muscle activity if you believe that the soul or the mind is just riding around in the vehicle that is the body. Instead, psychophysiologists assume that thinking, feeling, meditation, awareness, and consciousness are side effects of the function of an organ called the brain, which is physiologically connected to every other organ and system in your body. It is an embodied brain. Thinking takes biological energy. It takes blood, oxygen, chemicals, enzymes, neurotransmitters, electricity, etc. A primary assumption of psychophysiology is that because thinking is an output of the body, you can see the effects of that embodied thinking in the systems that deliver these resources.

A second assumption is that the work of the brain and the body occur over time. Systems increase and decrease in an analog, not a digital, fashion. Therefore, thinking leads to changes that occur over the course of milliseconds or seconds, whose impacts on the biological and physiological systems grow and wane with the vagaries of thought.

Third, the body supports the body, not just the brain. Most of the variation in physiological systems is associated with living, not with thinking. Walking across a room has more effect on heart rate than thinking "Hmmm, that was interesting." However, both affect heart rate, and they do so simultaneously,

Fourth, this means that physiological measures are "monstrosities" (Cacioppo, Tassinary, & Berntson, 2000b, p. 20). That is to say, the value of a measure taken at any single moment in time is not related only with a single causal concept. Instead, at any one time, heart rate, or skin conductance, or EEG, or EMG is multiply determined by physical, biological, environmental, and systemic demands as well as by the thoughts and feelings going on in the brain. This means that in order to use psychophysiological measures to tease out the variation in a measure associated with or caused by the cognitive or emotional response elicited by a media message the researcher must have control over the context in which that message is encountered. Such control is necessary in order to control the multiple systems simultaneously determining variation in the physiological measure.

A fifth assumption of psychophysiology is that physiological systems are interactive and have both feedback and feed-forward mechanisms. This assumption results in the common question "*Which comes first, the thought or the physiological response?*" The assumption of the embodied brain leads naturally to a contemplation of whether the body's physiological fluctuations lead to the thought in the brain, support the thought, or are caused by the thought. In many contexts and with many kinds of thoughts psychophysiologists have done a great deal of empirical research to try to tease out the dynamic interactions between thinking and physiology. To summarize a large body of work, it is fair to conclude that an ongoing interaction exists between the physiological system and the cognitive system which feed back and feed forward to create the experiences we call consciousness, thought, and feeling. Research has shown that some physiological responses to mediated events occur extremely rapidly—within 17 to 75 ms of encountering the mediated stimulus. That means that these effects of media content happen a good 250 ms before the content that elicited the response has even been consciously perceived or identified. However, once it has been identified, the effects of this conscious thought immediately begin to feed down to the physiological systems and modify the ongoing response (Bradley, 2007; Bradley, Cuthbert, & P. Lang, 1990).

Accepting these five assumptions of psychophysiology required media researchers to reconceptualize what was meant by "media." It no longer makes sense to think of media as static categorical boxes (e.g. violence, news, radio, TV, porn). Instead media must be conceptualized as complex stimuli with multiple psychologically relevant variables continuously changing over time. The fluctuation of those variables will then initiate real-time interaction with the embodied brain, which means that media use is now an interaction over time between two complex dynamic systems (Reeves, 1989; Reeves & Thorson, 1986).

As mentioned previously, the return of parts of the communication field to physiological measures—and the subsequent union of those parts of the field with psychophysiology—was preceded by a more general shift away from an interest in static state changes, or effects, and towards the study of the *processing* of media and media messages. This turn was partially driven by the paradigm shift in psychology from behaviorism to information processing (Lachman, Lachman, & Butterfield, 1979). The parallel changes in both fields were driven by the notion that thinking takes time (Posner, 1978) and that what occurs during the time that thinking takes is the primary driver of what occurs after thought. In other words, the processes drive the eventual effects!

Researchers making this change in the 1980s began to advocate for and engage in the study of intra-, not just inter-, message effects (Thorson, Reeves, & Schleuder, 1986). That meant looking at how changes in the psychologically relevant variables that make up a media message influence the real-time processing of the mediated message. This led to a flurry of research examining the cognitive processing of media messages. Variables such as attention, encoding, storage, resource allocation, effort, and elaboration—which had previously been nonexistent or peripheral to the study of mass communication—became central; at least in the new sub-field of message processing. Growing interest in tracking over-time message processing and the dynamic changes in non-visible theoretical concepts like attention or resource allocation created a search for real-time indicators of these concepts. Hence, the turn to psychophysiology which contained measures shown to be good indicators of attention, cognitive effort, arousal, and emotional response. The very nature of physiological recording produces an over-time record of change in the system which can be time-locked to a media message presentation and thereby provide a window into how aspects of media messages reliably elicit change in a physiological system.

Indeed, some of the early studies using psychophysiological (rather than purely physiological) measures did take this somewhat inductive approach. For example, Reeves and his colleagues (Reeves et al., 1985; Reeves, A. Lang, Thorson, & Rothschild, 1989) measured EEG while participants viewed commercials. They then looked at the real-time record of alpha waves in the EEG and identified points of time at which the alpha waves disappeared from the spectrum, a phenomenon called alpha blocking. In the psychophysiological literature, alpha blocking had long been identified as an indicator of increased attention (Andreassi, 1995; Darrow, 1946; Stern, Ray, & Quigley, 2001). They then looked to see exactly what was happening at the moments in the message when alpha blocking occurred. What this research showed was that many structural and content aspects of television commercials elicited brief periods of alpha blocking indicative of increased attention.

This inductive approach was coupled with a deductive approach which tried to reconceptualize media and media messages in terms of variables which had psychological and emotional relevance rather than in terms defined by the media industries. Both existing psychological theory and the results of inductive studies like Reeves et al. (1985) led to several new ways of defining media messages. Examples of these variables, which can be tracked over time, include rate of structural change, rate of information change, level of movement, motion towards vs. motion away from the camera, emotional tone, arousing content, luminance, etc. In addition, media were rethought and talked about by scholars not as TV, print, or radio but as audio, visual, audiovisual, text, static visual, moving visual, etc.

These new variables and conceptualizations were useful because they were much more related to psychological and psychophysiological theories about cognition and emotion and they enabled media theorists to step out of the industry-defined boxes of genre and medium and create general theories of message processing that span the existing and yet-to-be-invented gamut of media contents and forms (Reeves, 1989; Reeves & Geiger, 1994). For example, to the extent that rate of change, or motion towards, or motion away, have impact on the embodied brain, they will exhibit these effects whether they occur in a commercial, a drama, or a news show, that is presented on the Web, on the TV screen, or in a movie theater. The ability to track change in these variables over time allows us to look within any message and analyze, theorize, and predict the real-time interaction between the message's structure, content, and the embodied cognitive processing system.

What has come out of this interdisciplinary approach to communication research? As is undoubtedly clear from the preceding section, the use of psychophysiology, as opposed to physiological measures, establishes an orientation which is focused on the psychological correlates of the physiological measures rather than on the measures themselves. For this reason, the following discussion is organized by the information or emotional processing variable of interest, presenting examples of media scholarship which use established physiological correlates to operationalize them.

ATTENTION

With the advent of message processing research came an intense interest in the concept of attention. A voluminous research exists in psychology attempting to conceptualize and explain what attention is and how it works. A detailed discussion of that body of research can be found in Pashler's (1998) book, *The Psychology of Attention*. We will not review the extensive literature on theories of attention here but we will borrow from it some basic concepts that have made their way into the study of mass communication and message processing. There are two broad areas of research on attention, selection and effort. Selective attention is related to short-term (often called phasic) actions and involves the choice of what aspects of the environment to focus on (Posner & Petersen, 1990). Effort, on the other hand, is a longer-term component of attention (often called tonic) and is related to how hard one is working at processing the stimulus that has been selected for attention (Posner & Petersen, 1990).

Current perspectives on attention conceptualize effort as the allocation of cognitive resources to encoding a stimulus (A. Lang, 2006a). Cognitive resources are a hypothetical construct that are theorized to be allocated, through automatic and controlled processes, to various tasks involved in processing stimuli. Automatic and controlled processing are two ends of a continuum. Processes which are more automatic tend to occur relatively involuntarily, require few resources, and cannot be stopped, while controlled processing requires conscious, effortful allocation of resources and can be consciously controlled (Schneider, Dumais, & Shiffrin, 1984; Shiffrin & Schneider, 1977).

One area of message processing research has been focused on linking elements of message structure and content to variations in attention as a function of both automatic and controlled processing. Psychophysiological measures prove to be invaluable in this area of research. Several psychophysiological measures can be used to track both the short and long-term shifts in automatic and controlled allocation of resources to processing mediated messages.

SELECTION AND SHORT-TERM RESPONSES

Research on children's television in the 1970s suggested that formal features of television messages automatically engaged the attention of children by eliciting an automatic mechanism called the orienting response (OR) (Anderson & Levin, 1976; Anderson & Lorch, 1983; Singer, 1980). The OR is a short-term, phasic response that is associated with a set of brief physiological changes. Theoretically, the OR is thought to be associated with the selection for additional processing of elements in the environment. These elements represent either a change in the environment (novelty) or something that is relevant to the observer (signal). In terms of processing, it has been suggested that once an orienting response is elicited this is associated with a brief increase in allocation of processing resources towards the stimulus which elicited the response (Graham, 1979; Ohman, 1979, 1997). This would mean that if structural elements or formal features of media elicited ORs then the occurrence of those features would result in intramessage fluctuation in attention. The ability to measure orienting responses would allow researchers to track that variation in attention.

Physiologically, ORs are associated with a brief increase in skin conductance (SC), a brief deceleration in heart rate (HR), a brief period of alpha blocking in the electroencephalogram (EEG), a brief increase in skin temperature, an increase in vasodilation in the brain, and a vasoconstriction in the periphery (Graham, 1979). The study referenced earlier by Reeves et al. (1985) was one of the first psychophysiological media studies done in the 1980s. By looking at points in time during the messages when alpha blocking occurred, these researchers hoped to identify elements of media messages which elicited orienting responses. While alpha blocking is correlated with the orienting response it also occurs for many other reasons. Therefore, while it is an indicator of an orienting response, it also often occurs when orienting does not. Psychophysiological research has demonstrated that the best solo indicator of an orienting response is the brief heart rate deceleration that accompanies it (Barry, 1990). This deceleration has a characteristic three to four beat deceleration followed by a return to baseline at the end of six to seven beats (Graham & Clifton, 1966). Subsequent research attempting to identify the aspects of mediated messages that elicit orienting responses has generally used phasic heart rate change as the operational definition of the OR. Table 9.1 provides selected (mostly recent) cites of research done over the last 20 years attempting to identify structural and content features of mediated messages which elicit orienting responses.

As can be seen, many aspects of different media elicit ORs. Interestingly, research has also identified some structural features which do not elicit orienting responses such as the onset of slow-motion video (Lee, 2006), the appearance of text or calm pictures on a computer screen (A. Lang, Borse, Wise, & David, 2002; Chung, 2007), and the sound of channel changing in radio messages (Potter, Lang, & Bolls, 1998). As new media come under the research microscope, each one can be examined to determine which aspects of its structure or content elicit orienting responses with the resultant brief increase in attention to the message.

Recent research has also begun to look at the effects of attention on selection of media content. The early research in this area was primarily done in contexts where the researcher had control over stimulus presentation. In the current media environment, media users have a great deal of control over content selection. This raises questions

Table 9.1 Recent Studies using Heart Rate to Indicate Orienting Responses

Medium	*Structure/Content feature*	*Study*
TV	Scene changes	A. Lang (1990); A. Lang, Geiger, Strickwerda, & Sumner (1993)
TV	On screen movement	Simons, Detenber, Roedema, & Reiss (1999)
TV	Onset of videographics	Thorson & A. Lang (1992)
TV	Color	Detenber, Simons, & Reiss (2000)
Radio	Voice changes	Potter (2000)
Still Images	Picture size	Codispoti & DeCesarei (2007)
Still Images	Emotional valence	Codispoti, Ferrari, & Bradley, M. (2006)
Still Images	Picture of risky products (i.e. alcohol)	A. Lang, Chung, Lee, & Zhao (2005)
Computer	Animation	A. Lang et al. (2002) Diao & Sundar (2004)
Computer	Textual warnings	A. Lang, Borse, Wise, & David (2002)
Computer	Pop-up windows	Diao & Sundar (2004)
Computer	Picture onset	Wise & Reeves (2007)

about how intentional selection affects orienting responses. Some research has been done examining this in both the computer and the television context. Work by Kevin Wise and his colleagues has examined how control influences orienting responses in a series of studies and has shown that having control over onset reduces or eliminates the OR even as it increases sympathetic activation (Lang, Borse, Wise, & David, 2002; Wise, Lee, Lang, Fox, & Grabe, 2008; Wise & Reeves, 2007). This means that when someone controls content, fewer resources are automatically allocated to messages by structural features. This reduction may or may not be negated by the additional allocation of controlled processing resources associated with controlling message onset through a mouse or a remote control. These findings suggest that the allocation of resources when acquiring content has a direct effect on the resources available for processing content once it has been acquired. Wise and Reeves (2007) refer to this as the relationship between "getting there" and "being there." While this work is still in its infancy, we can see that intent does seem to modulate automatic attention responses in ways which we need to understand better.

COGNITIVE EFFORT AND LONG-TERM RESPONSES

In addition to short-term fluctuations in attention related to structure and content, the long-term level of attention allocated to a message changes during media use. Physiological measures can help us here too. In general, the level of overall cognitive effort being exerted by a media user during message presentation can be tracked by the over-time deceleration and acceleration in the heart rate (A. Lang, 1994). Research has shown that in several media contexts (television viewing, radio listening, video game playing) deceleration in heart rate is a good indicator of overall cognitive effort even when the content of the messages is arousing (Bolls, Lang, & Potter, 2001; Lang, Bolls, Potter, & Kawahara, 1999; Schneider, Lang, Shin, & Bradley, 2004). However, tonic heart rate, as a measure of cognitive effort, has not yet been validated in the web surfing context.

Readers new to psychophysiology frequently find it odd that heart rate is used as a measure of attention and that *decreases* in heart rate are often indicative of *increases* in attention. This unexpected association is due to the fact that the speed with which the heart beats is dually determined by activation in both branches of the autonomic nervous system: the parasympathetic and the sympathetic nervous systems. Activation in the parasympathetic nervous system is associated with attention to external stimuli and with overall attention and vigilance. One of the results of parasympathetic activation is deceleration in the heart rate. One of the effects of activation in the sympathetic nervous system (often associated with arousal, which will be discussed later) is acceleration of the heart rate. When stimuli elicit both parasympathetic and sympathetic activation—something common with emotional and engrossing media messages—both signals are sent to the heart: speed up *and* slow down. Generally, one or the other will dominate depending on context. Because the associated arousal must be quite high to overcome the parasympathetic decelerations, most media research results in slower heart rate during higher levels of cognitive effort. Still, the dual-innervation of the heart means that for any given medium context, research needs to be done to determine the extent to which parasympathetic or sympathetic responses determine heart rate.

In addition, recent research has begun to look at heart rate variability (HRV) as another way to separate out the parasympathetic and sympathetic contributions to measures of heart rate (Koruth, Potter, Bolls, & Lang, 2007; Ravaja, 2004a, 2004b).

HRV measures are often based on spectral analyses of the regular variations in heart rate. For example, Ravaja (2004b) conducted a Fast-Fourier Transfer (FFT) on the milliseconds between heartbeats collected while subjects watched newscasts on a simulated handheld computer. Of specific interest was the frequency associated with breathing, known as the respiratory sinus arrhythmia or RSA, suppression of which has been shown to correlate with increased parasympathetic activation associated with sustained attention (Porges, 1991).

In addition to frequency-based analyses, HRV using time metrics can also help illuminate heart rate data (Allen, Chambers, & Towers, 2007). For example, Koruth et al. (2007) conducted a secondary analysis of cardiac data, previous analysis of which had found slower heart rates during negative radio messages compared to positive ones. HRV assessments showed that the cardiac sympathetic index (Toichi, Sugiura, Murai, & Sengoku, 1997) was significantly greater during positive messages. However, the parasympathetic indices showed no significant differences between messages of the two valences. The suggestion here is that what was previously interpreted as slower heart rate (or more attention) during negative messages was actually *faster* cardiac activity during positive messages due to sympathetic activation—or arousal.

A great deal of research has used heart rate as an indicator of overall cognitive effort during media use and Table 9.2 lists recent studies from that research. This research has demonstrated that among the content and structural variables which influence the long-term level of cognitive effort allocated to a message are emotion (both valence and arousal), structural pacing (which increases cognitive effort at medium levels but can decrease it at high levels), the inclusion of sensational packaging features, strong narrative structure, and variables related to content difficulty (which increases cognitive effort devoted to message processing at medium levels but can lead to decreases in effort at high levels).

It is worth noting here that because physiological activity is multiply determined, measures of that activity (e.g., heart rate) can be analyzed in different ways as indicators

Table 9.2 Recent Studies using Heart Rate as a Measure of Tonic Cognitive Effort

Medium	*Structure/Content feature*	*Study*
TV	Production pacing	A. Lang, Bolls, Potter, & Kawahara (1999); A. Lang, Zhou, Schwartz, Bolls, & Potter (2000)
TV	Emotional valence	A. Lang, Dhillon, & Dong (1995); A. Lang, Newhagen, & Reeves (1996)
TV	Screen size	Reeves, A. Lang, Kim, & Tatar (1999)
TV	Image motion	Ravaja (2004a)
TV	Sensational packaging	Grabe, Zhou, A. Lang, & Bolls (2000)
TV	News graphics	Fox et al. (2004)
Radio/Audio	Emotional valence	Bolls et al. (2001); Sammler, Grigutsch, Fritz, & Koelsch (2007)
Radio	Structural complexity	Potter & Choi (2006)
Radio	Imagery	Bolls (2002)
Still Images	Emotional valence	Sanchez-Navarro, Martinez-Selva, Roman, & Torrente (2006)
Computer	Computer audio (headphones vs. speakers)	Kallinen & Ravaja (2007)

of different cognitive processes. Thus, for example, we can look at the beat by beat short-term analysis of heart rate as an indicator of selective attention, we can look at the over-time long-term variation in heart rate as an indicator of cognitive effort, and we can look at the spectral analysis of heart rate as an indicator of relative activation in the parasympathetic and sympathetic nervous systems.

Although cardiac response is an easy and common operationalization of long-term attention, just as with the OR, other measures have been employed in media research. Both corrugator activation (firing of muscle groups associated with furrowing the brow) and skin conductance have at times been used as indicators of cognitive effort (Dawson, Schell, & Filion, 2000; Fox, Lang, Chung, Lee, Schwartz, & Potter, 2004). Again, empirical research needs to be done to completely understand the media contexts in which these measures are reliably indicating cognitive effort as opposed to some other cognitive or emotional affect. Research suggests that with visual media (such as television and video games) corrugator may indeed index cognitive effort (A. Lang & Schneider, 2001) but its reliability as an index of attention is likely strongly influenced by the emotional content of the messages being viewed. Similarly, one might tentatively conclude that skin conductance is an indicator of cognitive effort during relatively calm and unemotional television messages where the variations being assessed are not structural but are rather content-based. Thus, for example, skin conductance seems to indicate cognitive effort when comparing difficult and easy television content (both visual and verbal) if the messages are not emotional (Fox, et al., 2004).

Finally, EEG can also provide both phasic and tonic windows into attentional selectivity and cognitive effort. Both alpha blocking and activation of the beta frequency of the EEG can provide a real-time record of aspects of attentional processing. Activation in the beta frequency is often thought to be related to tonic cognitive effort. In addition, evoked-potential techniques (a probe technique used to assess attention levels) could potentially be used, like secondary task reaction times, to assess changes in resource allocation and attention. Only a few of today's media psychophysiologists have followed up on the early work by Reeves and colleagues and made the investment in time, money, and intellectual effort to engage in the necessary context-dependent empirical work to thoroughly understand the value of EEG in the media context. For example, Simons and colleagues (Simons, Detenber, Cuthbert, Schwartz, & Reiss, 2003) used EEG to demonstrate greater cognitive effort allocated to processing moving versus still images. EEG changes can also be observed at different cranial locations, as shown by Smith and Gevins (2004) who found posterior alpha blocking associated with structural changes in TV commercials while commercials high in self-reported attention were associated with attenuated alpha waves in the frontal brain regions. There is also some exploratory research being done by Geske (2007) and colleagues using EEG to examine differences in attention between reading printed text versus text on computer screens (Geske, 2007).

AROUSAL

The use of physiological measures as an indicator of arousal has a long history in media research. The vast majority of early research using physiological measures in communication was attempting to document changes in arousal (Bryant & Zillmann, 1984; Carruthers & Taggart, 1973; Levi, 1965; Zillmann, 1971, 1982). Since that early research, theoretical conceptualizations of arousal have shifted, necessitating a change in our understanding of what is being measured by the various physiological responses previously and currently thought to be associated with arousal. In the 1950s and 1960s most people subscribed to a unitary view of arousal (Duffy, 1951, 1962; Malmo, 1959). It was thought that arousal acted on all physiological systems simultaneously and that when it revved up everything revved up. Not surprisingly, most of the early research in communication tended to use this unitary conceptualization and argued that viewing arousing media (e.g. pornography, violence) would lead to increases in any and all physiological responses (Zillmann, 1978). A frequent specific prediction was that arousing media would increase heart rate (probably because HR is the easiest measure to collect). Unfortunately, many media scholars were frustrated because, as discussed previously, heart rate actually decelerated in an arousing media-viewing context because of the parasympathetic nervous system dominance in activation (Bryant & Zillmann, 1984).

Subsequent psychophysiological research demonstrated fairly early on that arousal did not have a uniform effect on all physiological systems. Instead, something called *directional fractionation* appeared to be the norm (Lacey, 1967; Libby, Lacey, & Lacey, 1973). This meant that in response to different kinds of arousing stimuli, physiological measures sometimes went up, sometimes went down, sometimes separate measures went up and down together, and sometimes some of them went up while others went down. Once again, context and content of the stimuli were the determining factors. The findings in strong support of directional fractionation of physiological systems led to a rethinking of arousal as a unitary force. In the 1980s a common conceptualization of arousal, one that made its way into the communication literature, was of a three-dimensional concept (Zillmann, 1982). Arousal comprised behavioral arousal, cognitive arousal, and physiological arousal. As the concept of arousal fractured, measurement of arousal became even more fractionated and psychophysiologists began to refer, not to overall levels of arousal, but more to the intensity of activation in individual physiological systems. Indeed, the most common current conceptualization of arousal, as a generic term, associates it quite narrowly with activation in the sympathetic nervous system. Probably because activation of the sympathetic nervous system is most commonly associated with preparation for fight or flight—likely the type of arousal people most commonly refer to when they use the term in a generic sense. From a measurement point of view, this narrow conceptualization allows for easy measurement because skin conductance is completely and solely enervated by the sympathetic nervous system. Therefore, increases in skin conductance (which are determined by increases and decreases in the level of sweat in the eccrine sweat glands on the palms or soles of the feet) provide a clear indication of variation in activation in the sympathetic nervous system.

However, the tripartite conceptualization of arousal as a construct, while useful for some areas of communication research, does not by itself solve the problem experienced when using physiological measures as the operational definition of arousal. While such a conceptual definition separates physiological arousal from cognitive or behavioral arousal, it does not tease apart the contributions of the different physiological systems to the experience of arousal. As mentioned previously, recent research using HRV may provide us with another indicator of sympathetic nervous system activation. Indeed, given that one is often interested in variations in sympathetic nervous system activation over fairly lengthy media-use periods, HRV may prove to be a better measure than skin conductance, which habituates quite quickly in the media viewing context while HRV effects do not.

Psychophysiological investigations of message processing have predicted increased arousal (primarily defined as sympathetic nervous system activation) in response to increases in message pacing, emotional content, message sensation value, screen size, presence of narrative, differences among media, and many other variables. Recent research in this area is listed in Table 9.3.

Table 9.3 Selected Studies using Skin Conductance as a Measure of Arousal

Medium	*Independent variable(s)*	*Study*
TV	Presence of Emotional Content in TV Ads	A. Lang (1990)
TV	Production Pacing & Content Arousal	A. Lang, Bolls, Potter, & Kawahara (1999); A. Lang, Zhou, Schwartz, Bolls, & Potter (2000); A. Lang, Chung, Lee, Schwartz, & Shin (2005)
TV	Picture Motion/Still Images	Detenber et al. (1998); Ravaja (2004a)
TV	Screen Size and Emotional Content	Reeves et al. (1999)
TV	Tabloid Production Effects	Grabe, Zhou, A. Lang, & Bolls (2000)
TV	Education Level	Grabe, A. Lang, Zhou, & Bolls (2000)
TV	Animation & Redundancy in News Graphics	Fox et al. (2004)
TV	Sensation Seeking Trait, Age, Production Pacing & Content Arousal	A. Lang et al. (2005)
TV	Message Sensation Value	Cappella et al. (2006)
TV	State Motivation Activation	Potter et al. (2006)
Film	Mood Induction & Regulation	Silvestrini & Gendolla (2007)
Computer/ Web	Speed of Web Page Loading	Sundar & Wagner (2002)
Computer/ Web	Animation in Web Ads	Sundar & Kalyanaraman (2004); Chung (2007)
Computer/ Web	Presence of Narrative in First-Person Shooter video game	Schneider et al. (2004)
Computer/ Web	Taboo nature of products in still images	A. Lang et al. (2005)
Computer/ Web	Player Performance in Video Games	Lin, Masaki, Wanhua, & Atsumi (2005)
Computer/ Web	Response to structural features in video games	Ravaja, Saari, Salminen, Laarni, & Kallinen (2006)
Computer/ Web	Technological Sophistication and Presence of Violence in Video Game	Ivory & Kalyanaraman (2007)
Computer/ Web	Valence & Arousal of Still Images, Trait Motivation Activation	A. Lang, Bradley, Sparks, & Lee (2007); A. Lang, Yegiyan, Bradley (2006)
Computer/ Web	User Control of Still Picture Onset	Wise & Reeves (2007)
Radio/Audio	Positive & Negative Ads	Bolls et al. (2001)
Radio/Audio	Production Pacing	Potter & Choi (2006)
Radio/Audio	Production Pacing, Content Arousal, Age	A. Lang, Schwartz, Lee, & Angelini (2007)
Radio/Audio	Tempo & Musical Genre	Dillman Carpentier & Potter (2007)

ANNIE LANG, ROBERT F. POTTER, AND PAUL BOLLS

EMOTION AND MOTIVATION

There is a long history of using psychophysiological measures to assess emotional responses. This is not surprising given that our personal experience of emotion and the language we use to talk about emotions are both very closely intertwined with the experience of physiological change. The authors of this chapter experienced stomach flip-flops and pounding hearts when they received the email from the book's editors reminding them that this chapter was due in two weeks; our palms were certainly sweating as we realized how much work remained to be done! Still, we didn't need to hook ourselves up with electrodes to know that fear and anxiety existed from the top of our brains right down through our physiological systems to the bottoms of our toes. A great deal of research in psychophysiology has explicated the physiological responses associated with emotion elicited by mediated messages. Over the last few years several media researchers have worked to translate this measurement paradigm into the media laboratory. It is difficult to separate theory and measurement when discussing this research; therefore we begin with a brief look at how emotion is conceptualized.

There are two primary approaches to studying emotion: the categorical and the dimensional. Researchers using a categorical conceptualization place their focus on specific emotions such as anger, sadness, disgust, etc. (Izard, 1972; Plutchik, 1980). The dimensional approach, on the other hand, focuses not on unique named emotions but on the dimensional building blocks of emotional states (Bradley, 2000). The primary dimensions of emotion have consistently been identified by a number of terms, all essentially synonymous for arousal/activation and valence/pleasure (Bradley, 1994; Mehrabian & Russell, 1974; Osgood, Suci, & Tannenbaum, 1957). Those conceptualizing emotion categorically have had little success identifying consistent, predictable patterns of physiological responses associated with specific emotions (Cacioppo, Berntson, Larsen, Poehlmann, & Ito, 2000). This is likely due to viewing emotion as discrete categories being somewhat more static and state-dependent than the dimensional approach which is more in harmony with most of the assumptions of psychophysiology including change over time, feedback, and multiple causality.

Most of the dimensional approaches conceptualize emotion as the result of activation in two underlying, perhaps independent, motivational systems; one supporting approach behavior (the appetitive motivational system) and one supporting avoidance behavior (the aversive motivational system) (Cacioppo & Berntson, 1994; Cacioppo, Gardner, & Berntson, 1997; A. Lang, 2006a, 2006b). Dimensional approaches recognize two primary contributors to emotion that are related to direction and intensity. The first dimension, *valence*, is related to the direction of motivational activation (approach, avoid). In other words, how positive or how negative the emotion is. The second dimension, called *arousal*, is related to the intensity of activation in the underlying motivational systems. In general, similar to the tripartite conceptualization of arousal itself, research on emotion acknowledges three primary sources of data for studying emotion: experiential, behavioral, and physiological (Bradley & P. J. Lang, 1999). The research explicating physiological responses associated with positive and negative emotions of varying intensity has included data from all three sources to validate the measures. A great deal of this research was done by psychophysiologists using still images as the emotional stimuli (P. J. Lang, Bradley, Fitzsimmons, Cuthbert, Scott, Moulder, et al., 1998; P. J. Lang, Greenwald, Bradley, & Hamm, 1993; Mallan & Lipp, 2007; Manber, Allen, Burton, & Kaszniak, 2000; Schupp, Junghofer, Weike, & Hamm, 2004). In their basic methodological paradigm participants viewed still images varying in terms of the positivity or negativity of the image and the intensity of the content. Positive images might range from a beautiful landscape (positive/calm) to a highly intense erotic sexual encounter (positive/arousing). The same continuum would exist for negative pictures (e.g. a cemetery being negative/calm to mutilated bodies being negative/arousing). Images were usually viewed for six seconds while multiple physiological measures were collected. Following each image, self-report ratings of emotional experience were collected. Based on this data, we know that in this media context (e.g. looking at still pictures for six seconds) skin conductance is an excellent measure of the arousal dimension of emotion and corrugator activation, zygomatic (smiling muscles) activation, startle magnitude, orbicularis oculi (eye-blinking muscles) activation, and heart rate all vary as a function of valence. Most of the valence measures also interact with arousing content so that the effects of valence are greater when the emotional stimulus is more arousing.

Research in mass communication has taken these findings and translated them into different media contexts. In particular, research has focused on validating the use of these indicators as measures of valence and arousal during television viewing (Bolls, Muehling, & Yoon, 2003; Detenber, Simons, & Bennet, 1998; A. Lang, Bolls, Potter, & Kawahara, 1999; Ravaja, 2004a; Potter, LaTour, Braun-LaTour, & Reichert, 2006; Ravaja, Saari, Kallinen, Jaarni, 2006), film viewing (Palomba, Sarlo, Angrilli, Mini, & Stegagno, 2000; Bruggemann & Barry, 2002; Dillmann Carpentier & Potter, 2007; Silvestrini & Gendolla, 2007) radio listening (Bolls, A. Lang, & Potter, 2001; A. Lang, Schwartz, Lee, & Angelini, 2007; Potter & Choi, 2006), and viewing images on the computer (A. Lang, Chung, Lee, & Zhao, 2005; Sundar & Wagner, 2002; Sundar & Kalyanaraman, 2004). In general most of these measures have translated quite well into these more dynamic and longer-lasting media contexts. Skin conductance remains a good measure of emotional arousal (aside from its tendency to habituate during extended periods of media use). Corrugator activation appears to be an excellent measure of both positive and negative emotional experience—increasing in activation during negative media messages and actually decreasing in activation compared to baseline during positive media messages (A. Lang, Bradley, Sparks, & Lee, 2007; A. Lang, Yegiyan, & Bradley, 2006; Potter et al., 2006). Zygomatic activation has been less successful as an indicator of positive emotional experience. While some studies measuring zygomatic activation during radio messages have shown the indicator to be valid (Bolls et al., 2001), the results are much less consistent and robust during television viewing and video game play. Instead, orbicularis oculi looks to be a better indicator of tonic or long-term positive emotional experience (A. Lang et al., 2007; A. Lang et al., 2006). Similarly, in the six-second image exposure paradigm, heart rate decelerates sharply and then returns to baseline for negative pictures, decelerates and then actually accelerates for positive pictures and is between those two responses when viewing neutral pictures (Bradley & P. J. Lang, 1999). Similar patterns are seen in cardiac response to emotional sounds, but only when they are highly arousing (Bradley & P. J. Lang, 2000). This pattern does not generally occur in the television and radio worlds, where we tend to see deceleration for both negative and positive messages (A. Lang, 1990; Potter et al., 1998). Still pictures presented on the Web may elicit the same pattern of heart rate change seen in the six second world, though more research is needed to confirm this finding (Chung, 2007; Diao & Sundar, 2004; Nadorff, Lee, Banerjee, A. Lang, 2007).

Recently probe measures like eyeblink startle have also been validated in the TV viewing environment (S. Bradley, 2007; Kaviani, Gray, Checkley, Veena, & Wilson, 1999; A. Lang et al., 2007). The eyeblink startle measure is an automatic attention response elicited by a fast rise time or sudden onset stimulus (P. Lang, Bradley, & Cuthbert, 1990; Stern et al., 2001). It is thought to be an indicator of aversive activation. When people are engaged in viewing emotional media messages the size of the startle response, measured by the amplitude of the associated eye blink, is modulated by the experienced emotion. When viewing negative media and feeling negative emotions, startle responses are larger than those elicited during neutral pictures. When viewing positive media and feeling positive emotions, startle responses are smaller than those elicited during neutral pictures (P. Lang et al., 1990). These patterns have been demonstrated during TV viewing with the caveat that startle probes need to be at least 75 ms away from any kind of orienting eliciting structural feature in the television message (Bradley, 2007).

Very recently psychophysiologists have begun to investigate the possibility that another probe measure, called the post-auricular response or PAR, might be an indicator of appetitive activation. PAR, like eyeblink startle, is elicited by a fast rise time stimulus and is measured by recording the activation in the small, somewhat vestigial muscles located behind the ears (O'Beirne & Patuzzi, 1999). Some recent research suggests that PAR demonstrates a reverse pattern of activation and inhibition to that seen with startle. Specifically, PAR appears to be facilitated during positive messages and perhaps inhibited during negative messages suggesting that it might be an indicator of appetitive activation (Benning, Patrick, & Lang, 2004; Hess, Sabourin, & Kleck, 2007). While more work needs to be done on the basic psychophysiology assessing the relationship between PAR and appetitive activation, a recent study using television stimuli did show facilitated PARs during positive media messages, with larger PARs during more arousing messages, and no facilitation of PAR during negative messages (Sparks, 2006).

Using these measures mass communication research has been able to begin to investigate many hypotheses about how the presence of emotional content in media messages influences the processing of the information contained in those messages and the attitudinal and behavioral responses that follow exposure. The accumulation of this research over time has led to an emerging perspective in this area called motivated cognition (A. Lang, 2006a, 2006b; A. Lang, Shin, & Lee, 2005). Following the development of emotional and cognitive research in psychology (M. Bradley, 1994; Cacioppo & Gardner, 1999; P. J. Lang, Bradley, & Cuthbert, 1997), this perspective no longer considers cognition and emotion to be separate or separable systems. Rather the information processing system is thought to be inseparably linked with the motivational systems in such a way that activation in the underlying appetitive and aversive systems modulates and fine-tunes the activities of the cognitive system in ways which better align cognitive function and behaviors to the goals associated with stimulus approach or avoidance respectively. Recent application of this perspective to studying mass communication is providing us with new tools that we can use to better answer old questions.

For example, a great deal of mass communication research has been concerned over the years with how the valence of messages (that is whether messages are positive or negative) influences memory for the messages, attention to the messages, and eventual behavioral and attitudinal responses to the messages. Research in this area has not provided a consistent answer. Some studies argue that negative messages are better (Christianson & Loftus, 1991; A. Lang, Newhagen, & Reeves, 1996; Shoemaker, 1996) while others showed that positive messages were better (A. Lang, 1990; A. Lang, Dhillon, & Dong, 1995; Ravaja, 2004a). Some show negative messages are better for one dependent variable while positive messages are better for another dependent variable (Bolls et al., 2001). Other studies have demonstrated that negative messages work for certain types of people but not for others (Grabe, A. Lang, Zhou, & Bolls, 2000). While each empirical study has added a piece of data to the puzzle, the motivated cognition perspective may allow us to develop theory which will help us fit those puzzle pieces together.

Within the motivated cognition perspective, the appetitive and aversive systems are thought to have different activation functions (Cacioppo & Gardner, 1999; A. Lang et al., 2005). This means that when confronted with a positive or a negative stimulus (say a chocolate cake or a pouncing tiger) the level of motivational activation elicited is determined by the intensity of the stimulus. The intensity of the chocolate cake or the pouncing tiger can be manipulated by distance. The chocolate cake held right under your nose where you can smell it, see it, and want nothing more than to taste it is a much more intense and arousing positive stimulus than a chocolate cake on the table 50 yards away. Similarly a pouncing tiger at the other end of a football field is much less arousing than a pouncing tiger 2 feet away! Research has shown that the two systems have different speeds of activation in response to increasingly arousing content. In a neutral environment (no chocolate cakes or pouncing tigers) the appetitive system appears to be more active than the aversive system (Cacioppo & Gardner, 1999; A. Lang, 2006a, 2006b). This makes sense, from an evolutionary perspective, since it encourages exploratory behavior, such as leaving the nest to search for mates and food. However, with increases in stimulus intensity, the aversive system activates much more quickly than the approach system (Miller, 1961, 1966; A. Lang et al., 2007). Once again, this makes evolutionary sense: slow approach to possible mates and food while gathering information about their suitability increases the likelihood of successfully obtaining your goals. On the other hand, swiftly avoiding negative stimuli may save your life.

What this means, in the mediated context, is that when messages are relatively calm, and contain little or no arousing content, positive messages will likely be attended to better than negative messages. On the other hand, with increasing arousing content, negative messages will activate the aversive system more quickly than positive messages. As a result, it is negative messages that receive more intense processing at a comparatively lower level of arousing content than positive messages. On the other hand, when negatively valenced messages are at very high levels of arousing content, it is likely that the aversive system will shift into flight mode, reducing message processing for negative messages whereas the appetitive system will continue to be in information-intake mode resulting in increased processing of highly arousing positive messages. Indeed, this reconceptualization of how emotional message processing predicts what we have seen in the data, that is great variation in whether positive or negative messages will be processed better as a function of context and arousal. Research using this motivated cognition paradigm also suggests that the resting levels of activation in the appetitive and aversive systems vary across individuals and across the life cycle (A. Lang et al., 2005; A. Lang et al., 2007) resulting in differences in how different people and groups of people process the same message. A great deal of work remains to be done to flesh out, test, and apply this perspective in mass communication research. However, it is an excellent example of how the use of psychophysiology has reconceptualized an old question—and may perhaps provide clues to the answer.

Dear reader, if you have read this far you may be wondering what this chapter is doing in a book on media effects. Perhaps the primary contribution that psychophysiological measures have made, and are making, to the study of mass communication is a relentless pressure on those who employ the measures to stop looking for static-state change ("effects") in response to media; to stop conceptualizing the study of media as looking for ways different aspects of the message influence post-message behavior without examining the real-time motivated cognition processing of the message that occurs during media use. Psychophysiological measures have made it possible for us to think about actually achieving the goal of explaining a good part of the complex interaction between a message and a viewer in such a way as to be able to predict how any given message might impact encoding, storage, emotional experience, and memory for the message. Psychophysiological theory and methods have provided tools which allow us to track the over-time interaction between message features and cognitive and emotional responses and, at the same time, to measure the impact of emotion on cognitive processing. Very recent research in this area is beginning to combine new tools of dynamic systems theory and cognitive modeling with the paradigms and tools of psychophysiology and apply them to an over-time conceptualization of media messages as continual variation in psychologically relevant variables. The result is actual prediction of motivated cognition in response to individual media messages. For example, in a recent dissertation, Wang (2007) created a dynamic cognitive model using second-by-second ratings of the emotional content in a 30-minute television viewing session to develop a dynamic time-series model which successfully predicted over 70% of the variance in individual physiological responses and channel changing behavior during viewing. Future research in this area is moving quickly into incorporating analyses that will allow for better understanding and prediction of the dynamic interplay between messages, physiology, and processing variables. In addition, researchers in this area must take the next step of going beyond the message processing time period and begin to theorize and investigate how the real-time experiences of messages influence post-media-use attitudes and behaviors.

References

Allen, J. J. B., Chambers, A. S., & Towers, D. N. (2007). The many metrics of cardiac chronotropy: A pragmatic primer and a brief comparison of metrics. *Biological Psychology, 74*, 243–262.

Anderson, D. R., & Levin, S.R. (1976). Young children's attention to "Sesame Street." *Child Development, 47*, 806–811.

Anderson, D. R., & Lorch, E. P. (1983). Looking at television: Action or reaction. In J. Bryant & D. R. Anderson (Eds.), *Children's understanding of television: Research on attention and comprehension* (pp. 1–34). New York: Academic Press.

Andreassi, J. L. (1995). *Psychophysiology: Human behavior & physiological response* (3rd ed.). Hillsdale, NJ: Erlbaum.

Barry, R. J., (1990). The orienting response: Stimulus factors and response measures. *Pavlovian Journal of Biological Science, 25*, 93–103.

Benning, S. D., Patrick, C. J., & Lang, A. R. (2004). Emotional modulation of the post-auricular reflex. *Psychophysiology, 41*, 426–432.

Bolls, P. D. (2002). I can hear you but can I see you? The use of visual cognition during exposure to high-imagery radio advertisements. *Communication Research, 29*, 537–563.

Bolls, P. D., Lang, A., & Potter, R. F. (2001). The effects of message valence and listener arousal on attention, memory, and facial muscular responses to radio advertisements. *Communication Research, 28*(5), 627–651.

Bolls, P. D., Muehling, D. D., & Yoon, K. (2003). The effects of television commercial pacing on viewers' attention and memory. *Journal of Marketing Communications, 9*, 17–28.

Bradley, M. M. (1994). Emotional memory: A dimensional analysis. In S. Van Goozen, N. E. Van de Poll, & J. A. Sergeant (Eds.), *Emotions: essays on emotion theory* (pp. 97–134). Hillsdale, NJ: Erlbaum.

Bradley, M. M. (2000). Emotion and Motivation. In J. T. Cacioppo, L. G. Tassinary, & G. G. Berntson (Eds.), *Handbook of Psychophysiology* (pp. 602–642). Cambridge, MA: Cambridge University Press.

Bradley, M. M., Cuthbert, B. N., & Lang, P. J. (1990). Pictures as prepulse: Attention and emotion in startle modification. *Psychophysiology, 30,* 541–545.

Bradley, M. M., & Lang, P. J. (1999). Measuring emotion: Behavior, feeling, and physiology. In R. D. Lane & L. Nadel (Eds.), *Cognitive neuroscience of emotion* (pp. 242–276). New York: Oxford University Press.

Bradley, M. M., & Lang, P. J. (2000). Affective reactions to acoustic stimuli. *Psychophysiology, 37,* 204–215.

Bradley, S. D. (2007). Examining the eyeblink startle reflex as a measure of emotion and motivation to television programming. *Communication Methods and Measures, 1,* 7–30.

Bruggemann, J. M., & Barry, R. J. (2002). Eysenck's P as a modulator of affective and electrodermal responses to violent and comic film. *Personality and Individual Differences, 32,* 1029–1048.

Bryant, J., & Zillmann, D. (1984). Using television to alleviate boredom and stress: Selective exposure as a function of induced excitational states. *Journal of Broadcasting, 28,* 1–20.

Cacioppo, J. T., & Berntson, G. G. (1994). Relationship between attitudes and evaluative space: A critical review, with emphasis on the separability of positive and negative substrates. *Psychological Bulletin, 115,* 401–423.

Cacioppo, J. T., Berntson, G. G., Larsen, J. T., Poehlmann, K. M., & Ito, T. A. (2000). The psychophysiology of emotion. In M. Lewis & J. M. Haviland-Jones (Eds.), *Handbook of emotion* (pp. 173–192). New York: Guilford Press.

Cacioppo, J. T., & Gardner, W. L. (1999). Emotion. *Annual Review of Psychology, 50,* 191–214.

Cacioppo, J. T., Gardner, W. L., & Berntson, G. G. (1997). Beyond bipolar conceptualizations and measures: The case of attitudes and evaluative space. *Personality & Social Psychology Review, 1,* 3–25.

Cacioppo, J. T., Tassinary, L. G., & Berntson, G. G. (2000a). *The handbook of psychophysiology.* New York, NY: Cambridge University Press.

Caccioppo, J. T., Tassinary, L. G., & Berntson, G. G. (2000b). Psychophysiological science. In J. T. Caccioppo, L. G. Tassinary, & G. G. Berntson (Eds.), *The handbook of psychophysiology* (pp. 3–26). New York, NY: Cambridge University Press

Cantor, J. R., Zillmann, D., & Einsiedel, E. F. (1978). Female responses to provocation after exposure to aggressive and erotic films. *Communication Research, 5,* 395–412.

Cappella, J. N., Fishbein, M., Kang, Y., Barrett, D. W., Zhao, X., Strasser, A., and Lerman, C. (2006, June). *Psycho-physiological responses to anti-marijuana PSAs: Validating the construct of message sensation value.* Paper presented at the annual meeting of the International Communication Association.

Carruthers, M., & Taggart, P. (1973). Vagotonicity of violence: Biochemical and cardiac responses to violent films and television programs. *British Medical Journal, 3,* 384–389.

Chaffee, S. H. (1980). Mass media effects: New research perspectives. In G. C. Wilhoit & H. de Bock (Eds.), *Mass Communication Review Yearbook* (Vol. 1, pp. 77–108). Beverly Hills, CA: Sage.

Christianson, S., & Loftus, E. (1991). Remembering emotional events: The fate of detailed information. *Cognition and Emotion, 5,* 81–108.

Chung, Y. (2007). *Processing web ads: The effects of animation and arousing content.* Youngstown, NY: Cambria Press.

Codispoti, M., & De Cesarei, A. (2007). Arousal and attention: Picture size and emotional reactions. *Psychophysiology, 44,* 680–686.

Codispoti, M., Ferrari, V., & Bradley, M.M. (2006). Repetitive picture processing: Autonomic and cortical correlates. *Brain Research, 1068,* 213–220.

Darrow, C. W. (1946). The electroencephalogram and psychophysiological regulation in the brain. *American Journal of Psychiatry, 102,* 791–798.

Dawson, M., Schell, A., & Filion, D. (2000). The electrodermal system. In J. Cacioppo, L. Tassinary, & G. Berntson (Eds.), *Handbook of Psychophysiology* (2nd ed.) (pp. 200–223). New York: Cambridge University Press.

Detenber, B. H., Simons, R. F., & Bennet, G. G. (1998). Roll 'em!: The effects of picture motion on emotional responses. *Journal of Broadcasting and Electronic Media, 42*, 113–127.

Detenber, B. H., Simons, R. F., & Reiss, J. E. (2000). The emotional significance of color in television presentations. *Media Psychology, 2*, 331–355.

Diao, F., & Sundar, S. S. (2004). Orienting response and memory for Web advertisements: Exploring effects of pop-up window and animation. *Communication Research, 31*, 537–567.

Dillman Carpentier, F., & Potter, R. F (2007). Effects of music on physiological arousal: Explorations into tempo & genre. *Media Psychology, 10*, 339–363.

Donnerstein, E., & Barrett, G. (1978). Effects of erotic stimuli on male aggression toward females. *Journal of Personality and Social Psychology, 36*, 180–188.

Donnerstein, E., & Hallam, J. (1978). Facilitating effects of erotica on aggression against women. *Journal of Personality and Social Psychology, 36*, 1270–1277.

Duffy, E. (1951). The concept of energy mobilization. *Psychological Review, 58*, 30–40.

Duffy, E. (1962). *Activation and behavior*. New York: Wiley.

Fox, J. R., Lang, A., Chung, Y., Lee, S., Schwartz, N., & Potter, D. (2004). Picture this: effects of graphics on the processing of television news. *Journal of Broadcasting & Electronic Media, 48*, 646–674.

Geske, J. (2007, May). *Differences in brain information processing between print and computer screens: Bottom-up and top-down attention factors*. Paper presented to the Information Systems Division of the International Communication Association, San Francisco, CA.

Grabe, M. E, Lang, A., Zhou, S., and Bolls, P. (2000). Cognitive access to negatively arousing news: An experimental investigation of the knowledge gap. *Communication Research, 27*, 3–26.

Grabe, M. E., Zhou, S., Lang, A., & Bolls, P. D. (2000). Packaging television news: The effects of tabloid on information processing and evaluative responses. *Journal of Broadcasting & Electronic Media, 44*, 581–598.

Graham, F. K. (1979). Distinguishing among orienting, defensive, and startle reflexes. In A. D. Kimmel, E. H. Van Olst, & J. F. Orlegeke (Eds.), *The orienting reflex in humans* (pp. 137–167). Hillsdale, NJ: Erlbaum.

Graham, F. K., & Clifton, R. K. (1966). Heart rate change as a component of the orienting response. *Psychological Bulletin, 65*, 305–320.

Hess, U., Sabourin, G., & Kleck, R. E. (2007). Postauricular and eyeblink startle responses to facial expressions. *Psychophysiology, 44*, 431–435.

Ivory, J. D., & Kalyanaraman, S. (2007). The effects of technological advancement and violent content in video games on players' feelings of presence, involvement, physiological arousal, and aggression. *Journal of Communication, 57*, 532–555.

Izard, C. E. (1972). *Patterns of emotions*. New York: Academic Press.

Kallinen, K., & Ravaja, N. (2007). Comparing speakers versus headphones in listening to news from a computer—individual differences and psychophysiological responses. *Computers in Human Behavior, 23*, 303–317.

Kaviani, H., Gray, J. A., Checkley, S. A., Veena, K., & Wilson, G. D. (1999). Modulation of the acoustic startle reflex by emotionally toned film-clips. *International Journal of Psychophysiology, 32*, 47–54.

Koruth, J., Potter, R.F., Bolls, P. D., & Lang, A. (2007). An examination of heart rate variability during positive and negative radio messages. *Psychophysiology, 43*, S60.

Lacey, J. I. (1967). Somatic response patterning and stress: Some revisions of activation theory. In M. H. Appley & R. Trumbull (Eds.), *Psychological stress: Issues in research* (pp. 14–38). New York: Appleton-Century-Crofts.

Lachman, R., Lachman, J. L., & Butterfield, E. C. (1979). *Cognitive psychology and information processing: An introduction*. Hillsdale: NJ: Erlbaum.

Lang, A. (1990). Involuntary attention and physiological arousal evoked by structural features and emotional content in TV commercials. *Communication Research, 17*, 275–299.

Lang, A. (1994). What can the heart tell us about thinking? In A. Lang (Ed.), *Measuring psychological responses to media messages* (pp. 99–111). Hillsdale, NJ: Erlbaum.

Lang, A. (2006a). Motivated cognition (LC4MP): The influence of appetitive and aversive activation on the processing of video games. In P. Messaris & L. Humphries (Eds.), *Digital Media: Transformation in Human Communication* (pp. 237–256). New York: Peter Lang Publishers.

Lang, A. (2006b). Using the limited capacity model of motivated mediated message processing to design effective cancer communication messages. *Journal of Communication, 56*, S57–S80.

Lang, A., Bolls, P. D., Potter, R. F., & Kawahara, K. (1999). The effects of production pace and arousing content on the information processing of television messages. *Journal of Broadcasting and Electronic Media, 43*, 451–475.

Lang, A., Borse, J., Wise, K., & David, P. (2002). Captured by the World Wide Web: Orienting to structural and content features of computer-presented information. *Communication Research, 29*, 215–245.

Lang, A., Bradley, S. D., Chung, Y., & Lee, S. (2003). Where the mind meets the message: Reflections on ten years of measuring psychological responses to media. *Journal of Broadcasting & Electronic Media, 47*, 650–655.

Lang, A., Bradley, S. D., Sparks Jr, J. V., & Lee, S. (2007). The Motivation Activation Measure (MAM): How well does MAM predict individual differences in physiological indicators of appetitive and aversive activation? *Communication Methods and Measures, 1*, 113–136.

Lang, A., Chung, Y., Lee, S., & Zhao, X. (2005). It's the product: Do risky products compel attention and elicit arousal in media users? *Health Communication, 17*, 283–300.

Lang, A., Chung, Y., Lee, S., Schwartz, N., & Shin, M. (2005). It's an arousing, fast-paced kind of world: The effects of age and sensation seeking on the information processing of substance-abuse PSAs. *Media Psychology, 7*(4), 421–454.

Lang, A., Dhillon, K., & Dong, Q. (1995). The effects of emotional arousal and valence on television viewers' cognitive capacity and memory. *Journal of Broadcasting & Electronic Media, 39*, 313–327.

Lang, A., Geiger, S., Strickwerda, M., & Sumner, J. (1993). The effects of related and unrelated cuts on viewers' memory for television: A limited capacity theory of television viewing. *Communication Research, 20*, 4–29.

Lang, A., Newhagen, J., & Reeves, B. (1996). Negative video as structure: Emotion, attention, capacity, and memory. *Journal of Broadcasting & Electronic Media, 40*, 460–477.

Lang, A. and Schneider, E. (2001). Physiological and emotional responses to first person shooter video games. *Psychophysiology, 38*, S60.

Lang, A., Schwartz, N., Lee, S., & Angelini, J. (2007). Processing radio PSAs: Production pacing, arousing content, and age. *Journal of Health Communication, 12*, 581–599.

Lang, A., Shin, M., & Lee, S. (2005). Sensation-seeking, motivation, and substance use: A dual system approach. *Media Psychology, 7*, 1–29.

Lang, A., Yegiyan, N., & Bradley, S. (2006). Effects of motivational activation on processing of health messages. *Psychophysiology, 41*(Supplement), S56.

Lang, A., Zhou, S., Schwartz, N., Bolls, P. D., & Potter, R. F. (2000). The effects of edits on arousal, attention, and memory for television messages: When an edit is an edit, can an edit be too much? *Journal of Broadcasting & Electronic Media, 44*(1), 94–109.

Lang, P. J., Bradley, M., & Cuthbert, M. (1990). Emotion, attention, and the startle reflex. *Psychological Review, 97*, 377–398.

Lang, P. J., Bradley, M., & Cuthbert, M. (1997). Motivated attention: Affect, activation and action. In P. Lang, R. Simons, & M. Balaban (Eds.), *Attention and orienting: Sensory and motivational processes* (pp. 97–136). Hillsdale, NJ: Erlbaum.

Lang, P. J., Bradley, M. M., Fitzsimmons, J. R., Cuthbert, B. N., Scott, J. D., Moulder, B., & Nangia, V. (1998). Emotional arousal and activation of the visual cortex: An fMRI analysis. *Psychophysiology, 35*, 199–210.

Lang, P. J., Greenwald, M., Bradley, M. M., & Hamm, A. O. (1993). Looking at pictures: Evaluative, facial, visceral, and behavioral responses. *Psychophysiology, 30*, 261–273.

Lee, S. (2006). *The impacts of slow motion on viewers' emotional, cognitive, and physiological processing*. Unpublished Masters Thesis. Indiana University, Bloomington.

Levi, L. (1965). The urinary output of adrenalin and noradrenalin during pleasant and unpleasant states: A preliminary report. *Psychosomatic Medicine, 27*, 80–85.

Libby, W. L., Lacey, B. C., & Lacey, J. I. (1973). Pupillary and cardiac activity during visual attention. *Psychophysiology, 10*, 270–294.

Lin, T., Masaki, O., Wanhua, H., & Atsumi, I. (2005). *Do physiological data relate to traditional usability indexes?* Paper presented at the Australasian Computer-Human Interaction Conference, Canberra, Australia.

Mallan, K. M., & Lipp, O. V. (2007). Does emotion modulate the blink reflex in human conditioning? Startle potentiation during pleasant and unpleasant cues in the picture-picture paradigm. *Psychophysiology, 44*, 737–748.

Malmo, R. B. (1959). Activation: A neuropsychological dimension. *Psychological Review, 66*, 367–386.

Manber, R., Allen, J. J. B., Burton, K., & Kaszniak, A. W. (2000). Valence-dependent modulation of psychophysiological measures: Is there consistency across repeated testing? *Psychophysiology, 37*, 683–692.

Mehrabian, A., & Russell, J. A. (1974). *An approach to environmental psychology*. Cambridge, MA: MIT Press.

Miller, G. A. (2003). The cognitive revolution: A historical perspective. *Trends in Cognitive Sciences, 7*, 141–144.

Miller, N. E. (1961). Some recent studies of conflict behavior and drugs. *American Psychologist, 16*, 12–24.

Miller, N. E. (1966). Some animal experiments pertinent to the problem of combining psychotherapy with drug therapy. *Comprehensive Psychiatry, 7*, 1–12.

Nadorff, G., Lee, S., Banerjee, M., & Lang, A. (2007). Children's physiological responses to animal and human emotional faces as a function of age. *Psychophysiology, 44*, S88.

O'Beirne, G. A., & Patuzzi, R. B. (1999). Basic properties of the sound-evoked post-auricular muscle response (PAMR). *Hearing Research, 138*, 115–132.

Ohman, A. (1979). The orientations response, attention, and learning: An information processing perspective. In H. D. Kimmel, E. H. V. Olst, & J. F. Orlebeke (Eds.), *The orienting reflex in humans* (pp. 443–472). Hillsdale, NJ: Erlbaum.

Ohman, A. (1997). As fast as the blink of an eye: Evolutionary preparedness for preattentive processing of threat. In P. J. Lang, R. F. Simons, & M. Balaban (Eds.), *Attention and orienting: Sensory and motivational processes* (pp. 165–184). Hillsdale, NJ: Erlbaum.

Osgood, C., Suci, G., & Tannenbaum, P. (1957). *The measurement of meaning*. Urbana: University of Illinois.

Palomba, D., Sarlo, M., Angrilli, A., Mini, A., & Stegagno, L. (2000). Cardiac responses associated with affective processing of unpleasant film stimuli. *International Journal of Psychophysiology, 36*, 45–57.

Pashler, H. (1998). *The psychology of attention*. Cambridge, MA: MIT Press.

Plutchik, R. (1980). A general psychoevolutionary theory of emotion. In R. Plutchik & H. Kellerman (Eds.), *Emotion: Theory, research and experience* (Vol. 1 (Theories of Emotion), pp. 3–31). New York: Academic Press.

Porges, S. W. (1991). Vagal Tone: An autonomic mediator of affect. In J. Garber & K. A. Dodge (Eds.), *The development of emotion regulation and dysregulation* (pp. 111–128). Cambridge, UK: Cambridge University Press.

Posner, M. I. (1978). *Chronometric explorations of mind*. Englewood Heights, NJ: Erlbaum.

Posner, M. I., & Petersen, S. E. (1990). The attention system of the human brain. *Annual Review of Neuroscience, 13*, 25–42.

Potter, R. F. (2000). The effects of voice changes on orienting and immediate cognitive overload in radio listeners. *Media Psychology*, *2*, 147–177.

Potter, R. F., & Choi, J. (2006). The effects of auditory structural complexity on attitudes, attention, arousal, and memory. *Media Psychology*, 8, 395–419.

Potter, R. F., Lang, A., & Bolls, P. D. (1998). Orienting to structural features in auditory media messages. *Psychophysiology*, *35*, S66.

Potter, R. F., LaTour, M. S., Braun-LaTour, K. A., & Reichert, T. (2006). The impact of program context on motivational system activation and subsequent effects on processing a fear appeal message. *Journal of Advertising*, *35*, 67–81.

Ravaja, N. (2004a). Effects of image motion on a small screen on emotion, attention, and memory: Moving-face versus static-face newscaster. *Journal of Broadcasting & Electronic Media*, *48*, 108–133.

Ravaja, N. (2004b). Contributions of psychophysiology to media research: Review and recommendations. *Media Psychology*, 6, 193–235.

Ravaja, N., Saari, T., Kallinen, K., & Jaarni, J. (2006). The role of mood in the processing of media messages from a small screen: Effects on subjective and physiological responses. *Media Psychology*, 8, 239–265.

Ravaja, N., Saari, T., Salminen, M., Laarni, J., & Kallinen, K. (2006). Phasic emotional reactions to video game events: A psychophysiological investigation. *Media Psychology*, 8, 343–367.

Reeves, B. (1989). Theories about news and theories about cognition: Arguments for a more radical separation. *American Behavioral Scientist*, *33*, 191–198.

Reeves, B., & Geiger, S. (1994). Designing experiments that assess psychological responses to media messages. In A. Lang (Ed.), *Measuring psychological responses to media messages* (pp. 165–180). Hillsdale: Erlbaum.

Reeves, B., Lang, A., Kim, E. Y., & Tatar, D. (1999). The effects of screen size and message content on attention and arousal. *Media Psychology*, *1*, 49–67.

Reeves, B., Lang, A., Thorson, E., & Rothschild, M. (1989). Emotional television scenes and hemispheric specialization. *Human Communication Research*, *15*, 493–508.

Reeves, B., & Thorson, E. (1986). Watching television: Experiments on the viewing process. *Communication Research*, *13*, 343–361.

Reeves, B., Thorson, E., Rothschild, M., McDonald, D., Hirsch, J., & Goldstein, R. (1985). Attention to television: Intrastimulus effects of movement and scene changes on alpha variation over time. *International Journal of Neuroscience*, *25*, 241–255.

Reeves, B., Thorson, E., & Schleuder, J. (1986). Attention to television: Psychological theories and chronometric measures. In J. Bryant & D. Zillmann (Eds.), *Perspectives on media effects* (pp. 251–279). Hillsdale, NJ: Erlbaum.

Sammler, D., Grigutsch, M., Fritz, T., & Koelsch, S. (2007). Music and emotion: Electrophysiological correlates of the processing of pleasant and unpleasant music. *Psychophysiology*, 44, 293–304.

Sanchez-Navarro, J., Martinez-Selva, J., Roman, F., & Torrente, G. (2006). The effect of content and physical properties of affective pictures on emotional responses. *The Spanish Journal of Psychology*, 9, 145–153.

Schneider, E. F., Lang, A., Shin, M., & Bradley, S. D. (2004). Death with a story. How story impacts emotional, motivational, and physiological responses to first-person shooter video games. *Human Communication Research*, *30*, 361–375.

Schneider, W., Dumais, S. T., & Shiffrin, R. M. (1984). Automatic and controlled processing and attention. In R. Parasuraman & D. R. Davies (Eds.), *Varieties of attention* (pp.1–25). Orlando, FL: Academic Press.

Schupp, H. T., Junghofer, M., Weike, A. I., & Hamm, A. O. (2004). The selective processing of briefly presented affective pictures: An ERP analysis. *Psychophysiology*, *41*, 441–449.

Shiffrin, R. M., & Schneider, W. (1977). Controlled and automatic human information processing: II. Perceptual learning, automatic attending and a general theory. *Psychological Review*, *84*, 127–189.

Shoemaker, P. J. (1996). Hardwired for news: Using biological and cultural evolution to explain the surveillance function. *Journal of Communication*, *46*, 32–47.

Silvestrini, N., & Gendolla, G. H. E. (2007). Mood effects on autonomic activity in mood regulation. *Psychophysiology*, *44*, 650–659.

Simons, R. F., Detenber, B., Roedema, T. M., & Reiss, J. E. (1999). Emotion processing in three systems: The medium and the message. *Psychophysiology*, *36*, 619–627.

Simons, R. F., Detenber, B. H., Cuthbert, B. N., Schwartz, D. D., & Reiss, J. E. (2003). Attention to television: Alpha power and its relationship to image motion and emotional content. *Media Psychology*, *5*, 283–301.

Singer, J. L. (1980). The power and limitations of television: A cognitive-affective analysis. In Tannenbaum (Ed.), *The entertainment functions of television*. NJ: Erlbaum.

Smith, M. E., & Gevins, A. (2004). Attention and brain activity while watching television: components of viewer engagement. *Media Psychology*, *6*, 285–305.

Sparks Jr., J. V. (2006). *The influence of sex and humor on motivated processing of mediated messages*. Unpublished doctoral dissertation, Indiana University, Bloomington, IN.

Stern, R. M., Ray, W. J., & Quigley, K. S. (2001). *Psychophysiological Recording* (2nd ed.). New York: Oxford University Press.

Sundar, S. S., & Kalyanaraman, S. (2004). Arousal, memory, and impression-formation effects of animation speed in Web advertising. *Journal of Advertising*, *33*, 7–17.

Sundar, S. S., & Wagner, C. B. (2002). The world wide wait: Exploring physiological and behavioral effects of download speed. *Media Psychology*, *4*, 173–206.

Thorson, E., & Lang, A. (1992). The effects of television videographics and lecture familiarity on adult cardiac orienting responses and memory. *Communication Research*, *19*, 346–369.

Thorson, E., Reeves, B., & Schleuder, J. (1986). Attention to local and global complexity in television messages. In M. L. McLaughlin (Ed.), *Communication Yearbook 10* (pp. 366–383). Beverly Hills, CA: Sage.

Toichi, M., Sugiura, T., Murai, T., & Sengoku, A. (1997). A new method of assessing cardiac autonomic function and its comparison with spectral analysis and coefficient of variation of R-R interval. *Journal of the Autonomic Nervous System*, *62*, 79–84.

Wang, Z. (2007). *Motivational processing and choice behavior during television viewing: An integrative dynamic approach*. Unpublished Doctoral Dissertation, Indiana University, Bloomington.

Wise, K., Lee, S., Lang, A., Fox, J.R., & Grabe, M.E. (2008). Responding to change on TV: How viewer-controlled changes in content differ from programmed changes in content. *Journal of Broadcasting & Electronic Media*, *52*(2), 182–199.

Wise, K., & Reeves, B. (2007). The effect of user control on the cognitive and emotional processing of pictures. *Media Psychology*, *9*, 549–566.

Zillmann, D. (1971). Excitation transfer in communication-mediated aggressive behavior. *Journal of Experimental Social Psychology*, *7*, 419–434.

Zillmann, D. (1978). Attribution and misattribution of excitatory reactions. In J. Harvey, W. J. Ickes, & R. F. Kidd (Eds.), *New directions in attribution research* (pp. 335–368). Englewood Cliffs: Erlbaum.

Zillmann, D. (1982). Television and arousal. In D. Pearl, L. Bouthilet, & J. Lazar (Eds.), *Television and behavior: Ten years of scientific progress and implications for the eighties* (Vol. 2, pp. 53–67). Washington DC: U.S. Department of Health and Human Services.

10

MEDIA AND CIVIC PARTICIPATION

On Understanding and Misunderstanding Communication Effects

Dhavan V. Shah
University of Wisconsin-Madison

Hernando Rojas
University of Wisconsin-Madison

Jaeho Cho
University of California, Davis

Inquiries into the health of civil society and engagement in public life have long rooted their accounts in citizens' personal traits and social standing (Almond & Verba, 1963; Habermas, 1979; Rosenstone & Hansen, 1993; Tocqueville, 1835/1840; Verba, Schlozman, & Brady, 1995). For many years, individuals' characteristics and connections were considered the keys to understanding differences in involvement in the public sphere, with age, gender, education, race, employment status, church attendance, residential stability, and general sociability the key factors explaining participation. More recently, scholars such as John Coleman (1990), Robert Putnam (1992), and Francis Fukuyama (1995) have theorized that these dispositional and situational factors may in fact be discrete indicators of latent constructs such as community integration, network membership, and a commitment to civic virtues and values (see Friedland, 2001; Friedland & Shah, 2005).

Much of the recent work on this topic has focused on explaining, implicitly or explicitly, the question of a four-decade decline in civic engagement and political participation that presumably threatens community life in America. Concern about the erosion of civil society, especially by communication scholars, is largely a response to Robert Putnam's (1995) "Bowling Alone" thesis, in which he contends that this loss of community solidarity, civic volunteerism, and political engagement is a result of the adverse effects of television viewing on *social capital*—i.e., "features of social life—networks, norms, and trust—that enable participants to act together more effectively to pursue shared objectives" (1995, p. 664). According to this view, time spent with television privatizes leisure time and therefore displaces other activities that build community. Further, as predicted by cultivation theory, the depiction of social reality on television is thought to cultivate a perception of the world as a "mean place," leading ultimately to social withdrawal (see Gerbner, Gross, Morgan, & Signorielli, 1980; cf. Hawkins & Pingree, 1981). The limited empirical support that exists for these links is based on crude hours-of-use measures, which are used to draw conclusions about complex multi-channel environments (Putnam, 2000; cf. Norris, 1996).

Nonetheless, these arguments have been extended to the Internet, with research relating time spent on-line to the erosion of psychological well-being, social trust, real-world ties, and community involvement (e.g., Kraut et al., 1998). Despite their failure to consider how these complex media forms are used, critics of television and the Internet have had considerable sway over the thinking of others examining the effect of electronic media on civic life (see Brehm & Rahn, 1997; Nie, 2001).

Over a decade of research on these issues has done much to correct these mischaracterizations of media effects on civic life. Many of these emergent insights echo the conclusions of the sizable body of theory and inquiry stretching back over the last 80 years that links mass communication—typically the local newspaper—to community engagement (see Dewey, 1927; Pan & McLeod, 1991; Park, 1940; Stamm, 1985; Tönnies, 1940). This new wave of research has not only found that electronic media use can have positive effects on civic engagement, it has helped create a number of new arenas of inquiry, each one clarifying how mass media and civic life intersect. In this chapter, we classify this rapidly developing scholarship within five domains of research, each one representing a new direction for communication effects research:

1. usage patterns, attending to disaggregated media effects on civic life;
2. generational differences, especially issues of media and civic socialization;
3. Internet dynamics, including individual, social, and institutional influences;
4. communication mediation, particularly channeling of campaign and news effects;
5. geographic/cross-national contexts, focusing on multi-level models.

The sizable body of research that falls within these domains has helped establish communication processes as central to understanding the health of civil society. It has found that mass media can be agents of engagement alongside personal characteristics and social connections. In fact, the most advanced efforts have integrated individual, situational, and contextual factors into broader models that consider the causes and consequences of media use as it relates to participation. Before we consider these advances, the claim of civic decline is first reviewed.

THE EROSION OF CIVIC LIFE

The thesis of an erosion in civic engagement and community health is intuitively appealing. The declaration of a decline resonates with older Americans, who often bemoan the loss of neighborliness and express concern about strains in the social fabric that binds citizens together. Available evidence suggests that by the end of the 20th century, face-to-face encounters with other community members had slid to a forty-year low. Measures of informal socializing indicate that people visit with friends, play cards, share meals, and go to bars at substantially lower levels than they did, on average, a generation ago. Americans seemingly are not as sociable as they once were.

At first glance, levels of volunteering and charitable contributions appear to buck this trend; however, cohort analyses suggest that older people bear a disproportionate amount of the service and financial burden. And although attendance at public events has remained high, it cannot match the sharp rise in privatized entertainment, particularly with the rise of home theatres and digital media. Political participation has also declined, with fewer than half of Americans voting in many recent national elections, and reduced numbers working for campaigns and running for political office (Rosenstone & Hansen, 1993). It seems, then, that between 1960 and 2000, Americans went from being a nation of participants to a nation of observers, with those under 30 years of age the most detached from public life (Putnam, 1995, 2000).

Research on *social capital* links these indicators of community health at the aggregate and individual level by conceiving of civic and political participation as a "by-product of activities engaged in for other purposes" (Coleman, 1990, p. 312). As Inglehart (1997) found, spending time with friends and participating in community life may strengthen social networks and reinforce norms of reciprocity, thereby sustaining democratic values. That is, individuals who are connected and confident about the return of their social investments feel a greater sense of belonging to their communities and take a more active role in politics (Rahn, Brehm, & Carlson, 1999), a "virtuous circle" of trust and participation that allows citizens to act together in the pursuit of joint objectives. Thus, social capital contributes indirectly to participation because individuals engaged in social and civic life are especially likely to take an interest in the political process.

Trying to determine the causes of the decline in civic and political engagement over the last 40 years has been one of the central concerns of recent scholarly inquiry. Many possible suspects have been named: increasing time pressure, economic conditions, residential mobility, suburbanization, the breakdown of the family, the disillusionment with authority, the growth of the welfare state, generational change, the women's liberation movement and civil rights revolution, and, most infamously, the rise of television (Putnam, 2000). Most of these suspects have been exonerated due to their failure to explain the totality of the downward trend, which, of course, ignores the possibility that each one of these factors may have played an incremental role in the erosion of community life, incrementally chipping away at community integration.

Instead, Putnam (1995) initially pointed to television as the culprit. Aggregate level evidence shows that the number of hours Americans spend with television on a daily basis has increased during the period in question, placing the decline of social capital in step with the rise of television. Putnam also used individual-level data to demonstrate that even when controlling for education, income, age, race, place of residence, work status, and gender, television viewing is strongly, negatively associated with both civic engagement and interpersonal trust. The same relationships are positive for newspaper reading. Putnam pointed to this contrast as support for his conclusion that television is to blame for the erosion of social capital.

This general thesis has faced criticism on a number of fronts. Some have argued that the decline in indicators of civic life is actually a change in the form rather than the amount of participation. Ladd (1996), for one, argued that although fraternal organizations like the Kiwanis, Optimists, and Lions have seen a decline in membership, others have grown to take their places, especially environmental and religious groups. The health club and the coffee shop have replaced the bowling alley and the corner bar. Likewise, Bennett (1998) and Skocpol (2003) argued that new forms of citizen activities such as consumer movements, lifestyle politics, and socially conscious consumption have been growing, replacing traditional forms of civic participation. Nonetheless, it does appear the rates of engagement in public life—organizational membership, civic participation, and political involvement—have not kept up with the increase in educational attainment over the past 50 years, which has risen sharply.

Yet this raises the question of whether it is appropriate to treat the early 1960s as a baseline simply because of the availability of data. This arbitrary starting point is perfect for framing a narrative of civic decline, even though prior eras have been characterized by downturns in civic activity (Schudson, 1998). Indeed, the introduction and rise of television, and its displacement of the newspaper as the dominant medium, may be indicative of a broader set of social changes that characterize the late 20th century, and may not be causally linked to the supposed decline. It could well be that both are the consequence of a period of unprecedented economic expansion and the culture of contentment that sprang up in the post-World War years, a period that hit its zenith in the early 1960s before the social upheavals of the late 1960s and beyond (Galbraith, 1992).

Even more troubling, this approach treats television—and, by extension, the Internet—as monolithic, reducible to the amount it is used, and capable only of direct effects. It pays little attention to the various ways a medium is consumed, the differential effects this may have, and the broader processes of which it is often a part. "Focusing on *hours of use* as opposed to *patterns of use*," this thesis directed attention to "*how much*" individuals use a medium as opposed to "*how* they use it" (Shah, Kwak, & Holbert, 2001, p. 142, emphasis in original). Although the volume of use may be important, a failure to understand it within its social context leads to misunderstandings.

USAGE PATTERNS AND DISAGGREGATED EFFECTS

This inattention to the complexity of media uses and media effects was the focus of a considerable amount of the political communication research that initially responded to the thesis of television as culprit. Whereas the rise of television may be partly responsible for the decline in social capital, the simplification of such a diverse medium to volume of use is problematic. This point was made explicit through Norris's (1996) analysis of the American Citizen Participation Study (see Verba et al., 1995). She finds that in addition to the role of age and education in equations predicting various forms of activism, viewing informational programming contributes positively to participation, whereas total television viewing contributes negatively. This is largely consistent with research by McLeod and colleagues (McLeod et al., 1996; McLeod, Scheufele, & Moy, 1999; Sotirovic & McLeod, 2001), which has demonstrated that local news viewing functions much like newspaper reading when related to civic participation at the community level.

Along these same lines, Lee, Cappella, and Southwell (2003) analyzed four data sets to explain the other half of the virtuous circle of engagement and trust. They found that age, education, and newspaper readership are consistent and strong associates of interpersonal trust, but that these social attitudes have no relationship with heavier or lighter consumption of television, rejecting Putnam's (and Gerbner's) hypothesis of "mean world" effects (see also Uslaner, 1998). Other studies have examined the time displacement argument and concluded that amount of television viewing does not produce the outcomes predicted by Putnam (Moy, Scheufele, & Holbert, 1999).

Thus, it appears that individuals use the news information they acquire via broadcast or print to reflect and deliberate about local issues. These scholars argue that media do more than educate; they help individuals organize their thoughts about their "imagined community" while also providing the basis for political discussion that can lead to civic action. We return to both of these points below when we consider the contextual effects of media and the idea of communication mediation. Despite their innovative nature, a number of these studies suffer from an important limitation: they only disaggregate one type of television use—news viewing—without considering the possibility that other television genres may have similar independent effects.

Shah's (1998) research addressed this issue while also examining the strength and direction of the relationships within the virtuous circle of participation and trust. He found that other types of television content also have the potential to provide information and foster reflection, the two presumed mechanisms to civic engagement. Analysis of DDB Life Style Study data revealed (a) that how individuals were using television (i.e., genre of viewing) was a more powerful predictor of trust and participation than volume of use (i.e., estimated hours of viewing) and (b) that some genres of use were positively related to civic participation and interpersonal trust (social dramas and situation comedies, respectively), whereas other forms were negatively related (e.g., science fiction viewing). These findings speak to the importance of disaggregating media use.

The positive relationship of drama and sitcom viewing with these outcomes is particularly relevant to the purposes of this chapter, because it suggests that entertainment programming may allow for complex and influential representations of the social and political "life-world." These programs are emotionally engaging, base their truth claims on experiential knowledge, and treat the audience as being physically present within the situation. Even finer-grained distinctions within television "genres of representation" have found that watching particular types of social dramas and crime programs shapes political attitudes toward topics ranging from women's rights to gun ownership (Holbert, Shah, & Kwak, 2003, 2004). As Shah (1998) notes:

> Television, it seems, is not the monolithic danger that some research on social capital might lead us to believe. Instead, the relationships between the use of television, civic engagement, and interpersonal trust must be viewed as more conditional—highly dependent on the type of programming one is considering and audience members' uses of it. How much television people watch appears to be less important than what they are watching. (p. 490)

This research, then, both reflects and complicates the distinctions suggested by theorizing on media uses and gratifications. Work in this area has tried to answer the question of why individuals choose to use particular types of media content and has discovered regular patterns of consumption that contrast *information and surveillance* motives for media use with the *entertainment and diversion* functions they serve (Blumler & Katz, 1974; McQuail, 1987; Rosengren, Palmgren, & Wenner, 1985). Recent scholarship by Prior (2005, 2007) on whether people have a preference for news or entertainment echoes this perspective. He argued that we have entered a "post-broadcast" environment in which media consumers have more and more control over their mode and type of use. In such a context, individuals inclined to avoid the news can do so with ease, whereas those who choose to follow current events can do so 24 hours a day. From this perspective, engagement in public life becomes more unequal and more polarized.

However, this conclusion may be too stark. As noted above, recent inquiries have concluded that the pro-civic effects of media use are not restricted to reading newspapers, watching news programs, and consuming public affairs content over the Internet. Indeed, Baum (2002) has written persuasively that soft news consumption, a category somewhere between news and entertainment, can have laudable effects on the citizenry, especially the politically inattentive (also Baum & Jamison, 2006). Content such as late night news satires such as *The Daily Show* and daytime talk shows such as *Oprah* allow viewers to gain knowledge about public affairs. Mobilizing information available in a wide range of media (e.g., rally information, relief donations) also facilitates civic involvement by making citizens aware of where and how to participate. Thus, the lines cannot be drawn so cleanly between news and entertainment when examining effects on civic life.

GENERATIONAL DIFFERENCES AND MEDIA SOCIALIZATION

The lack of clear distinctions between news and entertainment is particularly important to note when considering how patterns of media use vary across generational groups and the types of effects media have on socialization into public life. Generational differences and issues of political socialization have been central to the study of media and civic participation because the downward trend in core indicators of social capital appears to be both a cohort and life-cycle effect. That is, these changes appear to be based as much on differences between generational groups rooted in their formative experiences as they are on shifts that occur over the life-course. Said another way, the Baby Boomer parents of Generations X and Y are more participatory and trusting than their kids not only because they are older and more integrated into community life, but also because they were more participatory and trusting when they were young—a trait they carried with them as they aged. The same is true of the preceding "Civic Generation" relative to their Boomers progeny.

As a result, the gap in civic engagement and voting behavior between young and older adults has grown in recent years in most Western democracies, though there has been some recent reversal of this trend. Yet even when young people do vote, their action is not as likely to be accompanied by other public-spirited activities, at least those measured by conventional indicators. Youth are also less knowledgeable and politically attentive than their parents were at their age. There are substantial cohort differences in media use (Peiser, 2000), especially for newspapers and the Internet.

However, the differential influence of media on social capital production across generational groups may not simply reflect variation in levels in use; rather, age-cohort and life-cycle differences may be a function of media reliance—an affinity toward certain types of media as primary sources of gratification fulfillment (Ball-Rokeach, 1985; McLeod, Glynn, & McDonald, 1983). Directly relevant to this point, Shah, Kwak, and Holbert (2001), in their investigation of civic participation, found that Generation X was most influenced by the Internet, Boomers by television, and the Civic Generation by newspapers. This suggests that different age cohorts tend to rely on the medium that they were socialized into using for information and surveillance during adolescence. Each generation has a preferred medium that accounts for much of its reserves of social capital. This reasoning fits with recent theorizing about political socialization, which has argued for attention to generational differences and life-long learning models (Sears & Levy, 2003).

This shift in attention to young adulthood and even later life stages increases the import of media in models of civic socialization because parental and educational influence is comparatively reduced after adolescence. Of course, in some formulations, young adults, as heavy users of media, are thought to be most prone to the negative influences of television and the Internet. However, these assessments of adverse influence on participation have been called into question, as noted above. In their place, recent work has emerged that observes that news viewing, online news consumption, and other forms of media use have positive effects on youth engagement (Eveland, McLeod, & Horowitz, 1998; Jennings & Zeitner, 2003; Shah, McLeod, & Yoon, 2001).

Consequently, conventional models of political socialization have been altered over the last 40 years to account for changing communication patterns. Some of these new models take into account that television viewers often combine watching with other activities. Given that youth typically spend seven hours a day using media—comparable to the time they spend in school or sleeping—models must consider that they are often using two or more media simultaneously (Roberts, 2000). Further, media use does not occur in isolation; the socializing influences of mass media on youth are often complemented and reinforced by communication with parents and peers (Chaffee, McLeod, & Wackman, 1973). In particular, children who are encouraged to openly express their ideas—even those at odds with parents—tend to be more politically engaged, whereas children who are raised in contexts where conformity is emphasized are less engaged. Similarly, political discussion with family, friends, and others in one's social network has been found to help develop civic identity (Huckfeldt & Sprague, 1995).

To understand the effect of media use and political talk on adolescent socialization, we must consider both the *level* of activity and strength of *effect*. Adolescents' news consumption is small compared to their use of entertainment content, especially their use of newspapers. Yet newspaper reading has the strongest media effect on indicators of youth socialization, after demographic and other controls, in conveying knowledge, stimulating discussion, encouraging reflection, and shaping attitudes. Attentive television news viewing has a positive though weaker impact. That is, news consumption encourages youth socialization through these internal and external forms of deliberation (McLeod, 2000; Yoon, McLeod, & Shah, 2005). Recent analysis focused on adolescents finds high levels of use and positive linkages between public-spirited Internet use and civic engagement. Research on young adults examining online news use, political messaging over e-mail, and other Internet communication tools suggests even more optimistic outcomes for adolescents (Shah, Cho, Eveland, & Kwak, 2005).

For young adults, there are substantial differences in the relationship between media and civic socialization depending on life course. There are points of departure between the college-bound, trade-school students, and those who directly enter the workforce or armed services. For many, media take on a larger role as a means of connecting socially and maintaining contact through e-mail and social networking. Newspaper reading and television news viewing remains low for those under age 40 (McLeod, 2000). Internet use, writ large, displays an opposite pattern. Young adults are the heaviest users, with use declining across older groups (Yoon et al., 2005).

As with adolescents, newspaper reading is among the strongest positive predictors of civic engagement among young adults, despite its low levels of use (McLeod, 2000). The Internet, because of its very heavy use among younger adults, appears to provide a more potent opportunity for civic mobilization. For example, Shah, McLeod, and Yoon (2001) reported that Internet use for search and exchange of information was most strongly related to both trust in people and in civic participation among the youngest adult cohorts in their sample. Indeed, some recent studies suggest that young people are encountering news and building community through online channels such as customized homepages, blogs, and social networking sites (Boyd, 2008). Thus, use of

Internet by the most recent cohorts may partly offset the loss in conventional news consumption via newspapers and television.

INTERNET DYNAMICS AND DIGITAL TRANSFORMATION

Before the emergence of findings reporting beneficial effects of Internet use, some social critics claimed that Internet users become increasingly removed from meaningful social relationships and less likely to engage the community as they spend more and more time online (Stoll, 1995; Turkle, 1996). The initial field research—the little there was—provided some support for this pessimistic view; panel analyses linked frequent Internet use to withdrawal from social connections and increased feelings of malaise (Kraut et al., 1998). However, these conclusions were questioned because these preliminary studies provided participants with free Internet access and unconventional web devices and then assessed the social effects. This type of procedure likely biased results, since participants may have felt compelled to take advantage of the free services. In addition, many of the "users" studied did not come to the Internet on their own, and therefore were unlike those who adopted the Internet on their own.

Fortunately, other scholars responded to these assertions with theorizing and empirical assessments that countered these claims. Some heralded that these communication innovations were bringing about an information revolution that would transform the structure of society (Bimber, 2003; Castells, 2001; Rheingold, 2002). Others provided evidence that popular uses of the Internet—messaging and searching—were related to tighter social linkages and greater engagement (Shah, McLeod, & Yoon, 2001; Wellman, Quan-Haase, Witte, & Hampton, 2001).

Thus, the initial debate over the relationship between technological and social change was characterized in terms of utopian versus dystopian views of new communication technologies (see Graber, Bimber, Bennett, Davis, & Norris, 2004; Katz & Rice, 2002). The results of the first wave of research provided mixed results, in part because some studies employed access or time spent rather than specific uses, certain samples were not representative of the population, and causality and endogeneity problems were still being sorted out in this emerging field of inquiry (for a summary of this debate see Nie, 2001).

Since then, a new wave of studies has mostly refuted dystopian views of new communication technologies through distinct yet interrelated lines of inquiry. Probably the most robust line of inquiry is one that has extended the uses and gratifications approach to civic participation, showing that informational/news-seeking uses of new media are mostly related to increased engagement, whereas certain entertainment/diversion uses can be related to decreased participation (Shah, Kwak, & Holbert, 2001; Shah, McLeod, & Yoon, 2001). Related research has shown that online news use supplements, rather than displaces or replaces, traditional news consumption (Althaus & Tewksbury, 2000) and that consumption of a particular content area complements the consumption of other channels in that same area (Dutta-Bergman, 2006). It also links Internet use to volunteerism and public attendance (Shah, Schmierbach, Hawkins, Espino, & Donovan, 2002), civic engagement (Jennings & Zeitner, 2003), group membership, community involvement, and political activity (Kwak, Poor, & Skoric, 2006; Taveesin & Brown, 2006).

A related line of inquiry has focused on the effects of Internet adoption for whole communities. This work has explored the possibility that despite the positive effects of online information seeking and interpersonal messaging—making a world of information and a geographically dispersed groups of friends readily available—it could have a negative impact on spatially bounded communities that continue to be central for civic and political activity. Rather than drawing people away from local connections, assessments by Wellman and colleagues in Canadian communities have provided empirical support for the notion that the Internet has a modest yet positive effect on these spatial-based communities in terms of increased sociability, voluntary association membership, and increased political participation (Hampton & Wellman, 2003; Wellman et al., 2001; Wellmann, Quan-Haase, Boase, & Chen, 2003). Likewise, additional research has reported that individuals who participate in online communities are more likely to do so in spatial communities (Dutta-Bergman, 2006).

Emerging features, mostly based on network structures, provide new opportunities for researchers interested in new media and community building, particularly blogs, social networking sites, content sharing sites, and citizen journalism practices. Most prominent among these, blogs started in the mid 1990s, and gained traction during the turn of the millennium. These online journals typically feature a high level of interaction between the person in charge of the blog and those who participate in it and comment on it (Bausch, Haughey, & Hourihan, 2002). As such, blogs show signs of being virtual communities, including network connections in the form of links to other blogs, Web pages, and public forums (Bar-Ilan, 2005; Coleman, 2004; Drezner & Farrell, 2004; Johnson & Kaye, 2004; Singer, 2005; Thompson, 2003). This interactive quality, the reduced formality, and the ease of use have made blogs into breaking-news sites (Perlmutter, 2008; Thompson, 2003) that are increasingly central to communication and coordination by politicians (Kerbel & Bloom, 2005; Lawson-Borders & Kirk, 2005).

Studies have only begun to examine the general effects of blog use in the political realm (Eveland & Dylko, 2007). The most recent analyses indicate that political blog use functions similarly to news use, increasing engagement both online and offline (Gil de Zuniga, Puig-i-Abril, & Rojas, forthcoming; Rojas & Puig-i-Abril, 2007). This suggests a connection to citizen journalism, i.e., opening traditional news organizations to citizen participation in the news process or creating grass roots organizations based on citizen reporters' production of local content. Both of these possibilities should encourage civic engagement. This is also true of social networking sites, such as Facebook and MySpace, which seek to connect people by making their social networks visible, facilitating their preservation and growth. Ellison, Steinfield, and Lampe (2007) provided initial evidence that Facebook enhances the ability to stay connected with members of previous spatial communities and contributes to bridging social capital. It remains to be seen whether the capacity to maintain social bonds, particularly weak ties, will result in increased civic participation in traditional arenas, or whether it will recompose civic engagement along networked forms, in which attention and consumption practices become central mechanisms of engagement.

Computer mediated communications are not the only innovations impacting civic engagement. With the advent and ubiquity of mobile telephony and other portable devices that permit sustained social contact as well as access to information, research has begun to illustrate their potential for civic action. Initial research suggests that despite a reduced potential for surveillance uses of the Internet, mobile phones seem to contribute to maintaining larger social networks (Miyata, Boase, Wellmann, & Ikeda, 2006), though concerns have been raised about the potential for increased selectivity that might result in higher levels of homophily in social networks (Matsuda, 2006). In the coming years, this area of research promises to be vibrant, particularly with the convergence of increased content delivery capabilities to mobile phones as they merge with global positioning systems. In addition to existing lines of inquiry, research has also begun to explore new technologies as platforms for deliberation (Min, 2007; Pingree, 2007; Price & Cappella, 2002), the challenge of fostering civic engagement in virtual cities (Bers & Chau, 2006), and contextual differences in the effects of new technologies on civic engagement.

COMMUNICATION MEDIATION AND CHANNELED EFFECTS

As some of this work suggests, media effects on civic life, whether stemming from digital and conventional communication modalities, are often indirect. This insight grows out of work on the *communication mediation model*, which concludes that informational media use and political discussion largely channel the effects of background dispositions and orientations on citizen learning and participation (McLeod et al., 2001; Sotirovic & McLeod, 2001). A strength of this model is the integration of mass and interpersonal communication into processes that result in civic and political engagement, as previously demonstrated by Huckfeldt and Sprague (1995).

This mediational approach is an outgrowth of the introduction of the O-S-O-R framework into political communication from social psychology (Markus & Zajonc, 1985). Moving beyond the simple stimulus-response (S-R) perspectives of direct and universal effects, the O-S-O-R framework recognized that there are a host of contextual, cultural, and motivational factors that people bring with them to the reception experience that affect how they process the message. Just as important, new orientations form "between reception of the message and the response of the audience member" that mediate effects onto outcome behaviors (McLeod, Kosicki, & McLeod, 1994, pp. 146–147). This perspective provides the foundations for communication mediation.

Notably, the communication mediation model treats both news and talk as stimuli (S), focusing on how they jointly mediate the effects of demographic, dispositional, and structural factors on cognitive and behavioral outcomes. To further specify this process, Shah, Cho, Eveland, and Kwak (2005) advanced a *citizen communication mediation model*. This model theorizes and finds that media's influences are strong, but largely indirect, shaping participatory behaviors through effects on discussion about news.

This conclusion was reached through a series of panel analyses that tested distinct causal orderings of key variables in different types of change models. After testing nearly two-dozen structural models, this work finds that the same mediational process that channels the effects of conventional news use through face-to-face political conversation operates for information seeking and political expression via the Internet. This new model adds to research on the relationship between information and participation in two ways: (a) it situates communication among citizens as a critical mediator between information seeking via the mass media and democratic outcomes, adding another step in the causal chain; and (b) it asserts that online pathways to participation complement existing offline pathways, adding a new mediational route.

It is important to note that this *citizen communication mediation model* contends that there are similarities but also important differences between talking about politics face-to-face (i.e., political discussion) and expressing political views in online settings (i.e. political messaging) for engagement in public life. Face-to-face political talk largely occurs with family, friends, co-workers, and others within one's social network, and is thought to help citizens interpret media messages and construct meaning (Kim & Kim, 2008; Southwell & Yzer, 2007). Individuals who discuss politics are exposed to a wider range of perspectives, increasing their interest in politics, opinion quality, social tolerance, and participation (Gastil & Dillard, 1999; Mutz, 2002).

Political messaging may share some of these characteristics. However, it also permits the sharing of views with a much wider and dispersed array of people through "interactive messaging technologies such as e-mail, instant messaging, electronic bulletin boards, online chat, as well as feedback loops to news organizations and politicians" (Shah et al., 2005, p. 536). As such, the costs of mass expression and collective organizing are reduced, allowing individuals to "post, at minimal cost, messages and images that can be viewed instantly by global audiences" (Lupia & Sin, 2003, p. 316; cf. Hill & Hughes, 1998). Such messaging is also largely textual rather than verbal, and as such may produce stronger compositional effects associated with preparation for communication (Bargh & Schul, 1980; Lerner & Tetlock, 1999).

Recently, additional advances were made to this model under the rubric of the *campaign communication mediation model* (Shah et al., 2007). This model considers the effects of exposure to political advertising as a contextual factor in analyses including print, broadcast, and Internet news use, as well as interpersonal and online political expression. Given the highly targeted and structured nature of political ad placement in modern campaigns, the integration of ad exposure with the communication mediation model brought elite and citizen behavior together into a coherent framework, attending to campaign message placement and individual communication practices.

Increasingly, election campaigns have been characterized by adversarial politics, with negative ads and contrast ads comprising large portions of what voters encounter (Freedman & Goldstein, 1999). This has raised concerns about the impact of political advertising, especially "attack" ads, as it relates to civic engagement, campaign participation, and turnout (Pinkleton, Um, & Austin, 2002). Ansolabehere and Iyengar (1995) assert, based on survey and experimental evidence, that negative ads demobilize the electorate. They conclude that negativity suppresses turnout, in some cases by nearly 5%, and that it takes a broader toll on citizens' sense of efficacy, increasing cynicism and reducing their interest in the electoral process.

These assertions have been hotly disputed, especially claims of demobilization. For example, Finkel and Geer (1998) contended that even if attacks depress participation among some voters, the overall effect will be to increase interest in the election, strengthen ties to particular candidates, and stimulate political learning. Geer's (2006; also Martin, 2004) recent defense of campaign negativity extends this argument. Reviewing presidential campaigns from 1960 to 2004, he concluded that attack ads are more likely than positive ads to focus citizens' attention on the political issues defining the election, and in so doing, provide them with relevant political information to participate. This is consistent with Brader (2005), who finds that although positive ads may do a better job of motivating participation and activating partisan loyalties, negative ads stimulate vigilance and provide voters with persuasive information.

To examine these relationships, content-coded ad-buy data on the placement of campaign messages on a market-by-market and program-by-program basis were merged by Shah and his colleagues with a national panel data concerning patterns of traditional and digital media consumption and levels of civic and campaign participation. Exposure to campaign ads was estimated by developing an algorithm based on the market and program placement of specific ads *and* geo-coded survey respondents' viewing of the kinds of television content in which ads were placed. A series of structural equation models revealed that exposure to political advertising has direct effects on information seeking via mass media, especially newspaper and television news use, but also online news (see Shah et al., 2007). As the ratio of advertising exposure became more negative, however, information seeking via conventional news sources was reduced. Informational media use was consistently found to encourage citizen communication, which in turn spurred civic and political participation. These scholars (2007) concluded,

> Besides the direct effect of volume of campaign exposure on political participation, most campaign effects were mediated through other communication factors. Even the direct effects of newspaper use on civic and political participation did not diminish the general conclusion that media effects were largely indirect, channeled through political discussion and messaging. (p. 696)

Particularly noteworthy is the fact that Internet use not only functions as an information resource but also a communication forum, both of which have implications for civic engagement. This is consistent with previous work by Price and Cappella (2002). Equally important, the effects of advertising—a contextual level phenomenon—appear to work through individuals' communication practices: first their media consumption, and then offline and online forms of political expression. This brings campaign dynamics and individual behaviors together into a single model of communication effects on civic and political engagement.

These findings have led the scholars contributing to the communication mediation perspective to propose a revision to the longstanding O-S-O-R framework (Cho et al., 2008). In its place, they advocate an O-S-R-O-R model of communication processes and effects, adding reasoning (R) as a critical mediator of stimulus (S) effects. This additional step attempts to capture the critical role of mental elaboration and social deliberation as conduits of media effects on outcome orientations (O2) and responses (R2). Since the information utilized in this reflective process might be biased or inaccurate, reasoning here is not meant to refer to the rationality of the outcome, but the depth of processing. This is consistent with the cognitive mediation model (Eveland, 2001; Eveland, Shah, & Kwak, 2003), which focuses on how reflection mediates the effects of motivations and messages on knowledge.

Currently, the S-O portion of the model is a jumble of factors, including news consumption, thinking and talking about issues, and cognitions and attitudes that arise from this process. Mental elaboration and interpersonal discussion are particularly difficult to situate in this framework. They are not stimuli in the formal sense, since they have been found to be causally antecedent of exposure to mass media (Eveland et al., 2003; Shah et al., 2005). However, they are also not conventional outcome orientations in the sense of altered attitudes or developed cognitions. Instead, they are between stimuli and outcome orientations, indicative of efforts to form an understanding and reason through ideas. Notably, this model also takes into account the contextual, disposition, and demographic factors that help shape media consumption choices.

GEOGRAPHIC AND CROSS-NATIONAL CONTEXTS

Attention to the geographic context in which communication effects occur has defined the vanguard of research clarifying the links between media and civic participation.

Although it is well recognized that community properties influence civic engagement (Cho & McLeod, 2007; Haeberle, 1986; Huckfeldt, 1979; Oliver, 2000; Sampson, 1988), relatively little consideration is given to the intersection of local contexts and media use in studies of participation (cf. Kim & Ball-Rokeach, 2006; Paek, Yoon, & Shah, 2005). As a consequence, theorizing on contextual effects involving mass media—best illustrated by Pan and McLeod's "multi-level framework" (1991) and hinted by Anderson's notion of "imagined community" (1991)—has far outstripped the pace of empirical research. This is at least partly a function of the prevalence of individual-level data combined with the methodological and diagnostic complexities of multi-level analysis.

The first wave of formal efforts to understand the interplay of local media use with community norms (i.e., social stability and connectedness) was influenced by work that considered community properties as a force to moderate the connection between individuals' media use and civic engagement (see Kang & Kwak, 2003; Shah, McLeod, & Yoon, 2001). From this perspective, community solidarity and cohesion are thought to amplify media effects on civic participation. Cohesive communities create a pro-civic milieu with an excess of close ties and opportunities for political discussion. This makes it easier for residents to translate information into participation at the local level (Friedland & McLeod, 1999; Huckfeldt, Beck, Dalton, & Levine, 1995).

Media use is also thought to condition the influence of community characteristics on civic life. The media—particularly newspapers and local broadcast news—actively work to develop a local identity and symbolically reflect norms and features of the collective (Anderson, 1991; Kaniss, 1991). As a result, frequent news consumers are more likely to understand the symbolic properties and normative standards of the collective through the media (Stamm, 1985). The contextual influence of community properties on civic participation becomes greater as residents' informational media use increases and, accordingly, the awareness of community norms develops.

Research also indicates that individuals' media use functions as a mediator of the contextual influence of community properties on civic engagement. If one community is more socially connected and politically active than another, individuals within these communities feel certain pressures to keep track of community issues by attending to news media. That is, the norm of active citizenship increases the utility of being informed, and thus encourages residents to follow news coverage of community issues. Such informational media use, then, leads to engagement. Thus, certain features of community shape residents' media use patterns (Borgida et al., 2002; Olien, Donohue, & Tichenor, 1978; Sullivan, Borgida, Jackson, Riedel, & Oxendine, 2002), which in turn encourage engagement.

Analyses of these multi-level phenomena have been greatly advanced by developments in hierarchical linear modeling (HLM), which allows for more appropriate handling of multi-level data and, thus, more precise estimates of cross-level relationships (see Hayes, 2006; Raudenbush & Bryk, 2002). Utilizing this approach, Paek, Yoon, and Shah (2005) found that reading local news increases the likelihood of community participation both at the individual level and as a function of readership in communities with higher levels of social interaction. They also observed cross-level interactions between individual-level differences in community integration and contextual variation in print news readership, providing support for the idea that high levels of news readership at the community level create a local print culture that has pro-civic consequences for socially integrated non-readers. Of course, such analyses require contextual data, which can vary in how geographic boundaries are defined (e.g., state, city, zip code, or census track). Although aggregating individual scores of respondents within geographic units in survey data can give proxy measures of community properties (see Cho & McLeod, 2007; Shah, McLeod, & Yoon, 2001), this approach can be problematic if the number of individual cases used to create contextual measures is not adequately large.

A natural direction for future contextual analyses includes cross-national studies that consider how cultural, political, policy, and media environments shape communication effects on civic engagement. Research has already provided evidence that conventional and digital media use can (a) foster online and offline sociability in the European Union (Räsänen & Kouvo, 2007; Valkenburg & Peter, 2007) and Canada (Hampton & Wellman, 2003), (b) contribute to feelings of efficacy in Germany (Semetko & Valkenburg, 1998), (c) promote expressive political participation in Colombia (Puig-i-Abril & Rojas, 2007), Japan (Kobayashi, Ikeda, & Miyata, 2006), and the Netherlands (de Vreese, 2007), and (d) enhance civic and political participation across the globe (Chang, 2007; Kim & Han, 2005; Lee, 2007; Rojas, 2006; Vromen, 2007).

Media may also be critical to community life within Diasporic communities (Hiller & Franz, 2004). The use of new communication technologies to retain emotional, personal, cultural, and political ties among migrants to their areas of origin and how these ties will shape their civic engagement in their place of migration offer great potential for inquiry. For example, d'Haenens, Koeman, and Saeys (2007) suggested that youth ethnic minorities in the Netherlands and Flanders use new communication technologies to orient themselves to the country where they reside but also to their parents' country of origin. This echoes the view offered by Matei and Ball-Rokeach (2001) in their study of ethnic communities in Los Angeles: "strong anchoring to offline social and cultural groups links cyberspace to rather than separates it from people's local communities" (p. 560). Clearly, many others who study media and civic engagement now share their view.

CODA ON UNDERSTANDING MEDIA EFFECTS

Efforts to counter fundamental misunderstandings about the nature of media effects on civic life have required scholars (a) to examine usage patterns so that media effects could be disaggregated, (b) to consider generational differences in media use and their implications for youth and young adult socialization, (c) to explore the rapidly changing terrain of the Internet and its social implications, (d) to extend the communication mediation framework to incorporate digital media technologies and campaign message placement, and (e) to revisit multi-level models of communications effects. This unpacking of media effects on civic engagement has not only helped move us closer to a more nuanced and complete understanding of the linkages between communication and community life, it provides a template through which a range of questions regarding media effects beyond the issue of civic engagement might be tackled.

Indeed, many of these same approaches to untangling media effects have been outside the context of civic engagement and political participation, per se. They have been employed to understand the underpinnings of political consumerism and socially conscious consumption (Stolle, Hooghe, & Micheletti, 2005) as well as the issues of cultural capital (Holt, 1997). In this work, scholars have moved beyond monolithic treatment of media such as television and the Internet to consider patterns of use and effects (Keum, Devanathan, Deshpande, Nelson, & Shah, 2004). They have considered how older and younger adults differ not only in the media use, but how these modes of use help socialize and normalize certain forms of socially conscious consumption (de Vreese, 2007). The role of digital media has been examined alongside conventional media forms, with both related to use of various products and services to understand the social positioning of taste (Friedland et al., 2007). Studies have even applied the communication mediation framework to the question of lifestyle politics and political consumerism, yielding clear support for the model and new insights about the intersection of consumer and civic culture (Shah et al., 2007). Further, these studies have been conducted across different national and cultural contexts.

This body of research illustrates that the approaches used to correct misunderstanding about media and civic culture have great potential to be extended beyond that narrow scope into seemingly related and more distal domains of inquiry. Indeed, the subfields of political communication, health communication, and science communication would all benefit from a full and systematic application of these guiding frameworks to empirical analyses. Although these domains of research do not suffer from the types of mischaracterizations of media effects that motivated much of the early work on communication and social capital, it is clear that a more complex and comprehensive picture of media effects in relation to political judgment, health behaviors, and scientific attitudes would emerge if scholars were to disaggregate media effects, consider differences across the life cycle, and more fully incorporate digital media and interpersonal conversation into their models of influence. We are hopeful that this synthesis of the literature on media and civic life not only will advance research on communication and participation, but also will encourage scholars exploring media effects, more generally, to avoid some of the misunderstanding that has characterized this work.

References

Almond, G. A., & Verba, S. (1963). *The civic culture*. Princeton, NJ: Princeton University Press.

Althaus, S., & Tewksbury, D. (2000). Patterns of Internet and traditional news media use in a networked community. *Political Communication*, *17*, 21–45.

Anderson, B. (1991). *Imagined communities: Reflections on the origin and spread of nationalism*. New York: Verso.

Ansolabehere, S., & Iyengar, S. (1995). *Going negative: How political advertisements shrink and polarize the electorate*. New York: Free Press.

Ball-Rokeach, S. J. (1985). The origins of individual media-system dependency: A sociological framework. *Communication Research*, *4*, 485–510.

Bargh, J. A., & Schul, Y. (1980). On the cognitive benefits of teaching. *Journal of Educational Psychology*, *72*, 593–604.

Bar-Ilan, J. (2005). Information hub blogs. *Journal of Information Science*, *31*, 297–307.

Baum, M. A. (2002). Sex, lies and war: How soft news brings foreign policy to the inattentive public. *American Political Science Review*, *96*, 91–109.

Baum, M. A., & Jamison, A. (2006). The *Oprah* effect: How soft news helps inattentive citizens vote consistently. *Journal of Politics*, *68*, 946–959.

Bausch, P., Haughey, M., & Hourihan, M. (2002). *We blog: Publishing online with weblogs*. Indianapolis, IN: Wiley.

Bennett, W. L. (1998). The uncivic culture: Communication, identity, and the rise of lifestyle politics. *PS: Political Science and Politics*, *31*, 740–761.

Bers, M. U., & Chau, C. (2006). Fostering civic engagement by building a virtual city. *Journal of Computer-Mediated Communication*, *11*(3), article 4. Retrieved October 11, 2007 from http://jcmc.indiana.edu/vol11/issue3/bers.html

Bimber, B. (2003). *Information and American democracy: Technology in the evolution of political power*. Cambridge, MA: Cambridge University Press.

Blumler, J., & Katz, E. (Eds.) (1974). *The uses of mass communications: Current perspectives on gratifications research*. Beverly Hills, CA: Sage.

Borgida, E., Sullivan, J., Oxendine, A., Jackson, M., Riedel, E., & Gangl, A. (2002). Civic culture meets the digital divide: The role of community electronic networks. *Journal of Social Issues, 58*, 125–141.

Boyd, D. (2008). Why youth (heart) social network sites: The role of networked publics in teenage social life. In D. Buckingham (Ed.), *MacArthur Foundation series on digital learning—Youth, identity, and digital media volume* (pp. 119–142). Cambridge, MA: MIT Press.

Brader, T. (2005). Striking a responsive chord: How political ads motivate and persuade voters by appealing to emotions. *American Journal of Political Science, 49*, 388–405.

Brehm, J., & Rahn, W. M. (1997). Individual level evidence for the causes and consequences of social capital. *American Journal of Political Science, 41*, 999–1023.

Castells, M. (2001). *The Internet galaxy: Reflections on the Internet, business and society*. Oxford, UK: Oxford University Press.

Chaffee, S., McLeod, J. M., & Wackman, D. (1973). Family communication patterns and adolescent political participation. In J. Dennis (Ed.), *Socialization to politics: Selected readings* (pp. 349–364). New York: Wiley.

Chang, C. (2007). Politically mobilizing vs. demobilizing media: A mediation model. *Asian Journal of Communication, 17*, 362–380.

Cho, J., & McLeod, D. M. (2007). Structural antecedents to knowledge and participation: Extending the knowledge gap concept to participation. *Journal of Communication, 57*, 205–228.

Cho, J., Shah, D. V., McLeod, J. M., McLeod, D. M., Scholl, R. M., & Gotlieb, M. R. (2008). *Campaigns, reflection, and deliberation: Advancing an O-S-R-O-R model of communication effects*. Unpublished manuscript.

Coleman, J. (1990). *Foundations of social theory*. Cambridge, MA: Harvard University Press.

Coleman, S. (2004). *Political blogs: Craze or convention*. London: The Hansard Society.

de Vreese, C. H. (2007). Digital renaissance: Young consumer and citizen? *The ANNALS of the American Academy of Political and Social Science, 611*, 207–216.

Dewey, J. (1927). *The public and its problems*. New York: Henry Holt & Co.

d'Haenens, L., Koeman, J., & Saeys, F. (2007). Digital citizenship among ethnic minority youths in the Netherlands and Flanders. *New Media & Society, 9*, 278–299.

Drezner, D. W., & Farrell, H. (2004, September). *The power and politics of blogs*. Paper presented at the annual meeting of the American Political Science Association, Chicago, IL.

Dutta-Bergman, M. J. (2006). Community participation and Internet use after September 11: Complementarity in channel consumption. *Journal of Computer-Mediated Communication, 11*(2), article 4. Retrieved October 11, 2007 from http://jcmc.indiana.edu/vol11/issue2/dutta-bergman.html

Ellison, N. B., Steinfield, C., & Lampe, C. (2007). The benefits of Facebook "friends": Social capital and college students' use of online social network sites. *Journal of Computer-Mediated Communication, 12*(4), article 1. Retrieved October 11, 2007 from http://jcmc.indiana.edu/vol12/issue4/ellison.html

Eveland, W. P., Jr. (2001). The cognitive mediation model of learning from the news: Evidence from non-election, off-year election, and presidential election contexts. *Communication Research, 28*, 571–601.

Eveland, W. P., Jr., & Dylko, I. (2007). Reading political blogs during the 2004 election campaign: Correlates and political consequences. In M. Tremayne (Ed.), *Blogging, citizenship, and the future of media* (pp. 105–126). New York: Routledge.

Eveland, W. P., Jr., McLeod, J. M., & Horowitz, E. M. (1998). Communication and age in childhood political socialization: An interactive model of political development. *Journalism & Mass Communication Quarterly, 75*, 699–718.

Eveland, W. P., Jr., Shah, D. V., & Kwak, N. (2003). Assessing causality in the cognitive mediation model: A panel study of motivations, information processing and learning during campaign 2000. *Communication Research, 30*, 359–386.

Finkel, S. E., & Geer, J. G. (1998). A spot check: Casting doubt on the demobilizing effect of attack advertising. *American Journal of Political Science, 42*, 573–595.

Freedman, P., & Goldstein, K. (1999). Measuring media exposure and the effects of negative campaign ads. *American Journal of Political Science*, *43*, 1189–1208.

Friedland, L. W. (2001). Communication, community, and democracy: towards a theory of communicatively integrated community. *Communication Research*, *28*, 358–391.

Friedland, L. W., & McLeod, J. M. (1999). Community integration and mass media: A reconsideration. In D. Demers & K. Viswanath (Eds.), *Mass media, social control, and social change: A macrosocial perspective* (pp. 197–226). Ames, IA: Iowa State University Press.

Friedland, L. W., & Shah, D. V. (2005). Communication and community. In S. Dunwoody, L. Becker, G. Kosicki, & D. McLeod (Eds.), *The evolution of key mass communication concepts: Honoring Jack M. McLeod* (pp. 251–272). Cresskill, NJ: Hampton Press.

Friedland, L. W., Shah, D. V., Lee, N-J., Rademacher, M. A., Atkinson, L., & Hove, T. (2007). Capital, consumption, communication, and citizenship: The social positioning of taste and civic culture in the U.S. *The ANNALS of the American Academy of Political and Social Science*, *611*, 31–49.

Fukuyama, F. (1995). *Trust: The social virtues and the creation of prosperity*. New York: Free Press.

Galbraith, J. K. (1992). *The culture of contentment*. Boston: Houghton Mifflin Co.

Gastil, J., & Dillard, J. P. (1999). Increasing political sophistication through public deliberation. *Political Communication*, *16*, 3–23.

Geer, J. G. (2006). *In defense of negativity: Attack ads in presidential campaigns*. Chicago: University of Chicago Press.

Gerbner, G., Gross, L., Morgan, M., & Signorielli, N. (1980). The mainstreaming of America: Violence profile No. 11. *Journal of Communication*, *30*, 10–29.

Gil de Zuniga, H., Puig-i-Abril, E., & Rojas, H. (forthcoming). Blogs, traditional media online and political participation: An assessment of how the Internet is changing the political environment. *New Media & Society*.

Graber, D. A., Bimber, B., Bennett, W. L., Davis, R., & Norris, P. (2004). The Internet and politics: Emerging perspectives. In H. Nissenbaum & M. E. Price (Eds.), *Academy & the Internet* (pp. 90–119). New York: Peter Lang Publishing.

Habermas, J. (1979). *Communication and the evolution of society*. Boston: Beacon Press.

Haeberle, S. H. (1986). Good neighbors and good neighborhoods: Comparing demographic and environmental influences on neighborhood activism. *State and Local Government Review*, *18*, 109–116.

Hampton, K., & Wellman, B. (2003). Neighboring in Netville: How the Internet supports community and social capital in a wired suburb. *City & Community*, *2*, 277–311.

Hawkins, R. P., & Pingree, S. (1981). Uniform messages and habitual viewing: Unnecessary assumptions in social reality effects. *Human Communication Research*, *7*, 291–301.

Hayes, A. (2006). A primer on multilevel modeling. *Human Communication Research*, *32*, 385–410.

Hill, K. A., & Hughes, J. E. (1998). *Cyberpolitics: Citizen activism in the age of the Internet*. New York: Rowman & Littlefield.

Hiller, H., & Franz, T. M. (2004). New ties, old ties and lost ties: The use of the Internet in diaspora. *New Media & Society*, *6*, 731–752.

Holbert, R. L., Shah, D. V., & Kwak, N. (2003). Political implications of prime-time drama and sitcom use: Genres of representation and opinions concerning women's rights. *Journal of Communication*, *53*, 45–60.

Holbert, R. L., Shah, D. V., & Kwak, N. (2004). Fear, authority, and justice: TV news, police reality, and crime drama viewing influences on endorsements of capital punishment and gun ownership. *Journalism & Mass Communication Quarterly*, *81*, 343–363.

Holt, D. B. (1997). Poststructuralist lifestyle analysis: Conceptualizing the social patterning of consumption in postmodernity. *Journal of Consumer Research*, *23*, 326–350.

Huckfeldt, R. (1979). Political participation and the neighborhood social context. *American Journal of Political Science*, *23*, 579–592.

Huckfeldt, R., Beck, P. A., Dalton, R. J., & Levine, J. (1995). Political environments, cohesive social groups, and the communication of public opinion. *American Journal of Political Science*, *39*, 1025–1054.

Huckfeldt, R., & Sprague, J. (1995). *Citizens, politics, and social communication: Information and influence in an election campaign*. New York: Cambridge University Press.
Inglehart, R. (1997). *Modernization and postmodernization: Cultural, economic, and political change in 43 countries*. Princeton, NJ: Princeton University Press.
Jennings, M. K., & Zeitner, V. (2003). Internet use and civic engagement: A longitudinal analysis. *Public Opinion Quarterly, 67*, 311–334.
Johnson, T. J., & Kaye, B. (2004). Wag the blog: How reliance on traditional media and the Internet influence credibility perceptions of weblogs among blog users. *Journalism & Mass Communication Quarterly, 81*, 622–642.
Kang, N., & Kwak, N. (2003). A multilevel approach to civic participation: Individual length of residence, neighborhood residential stability, and their interactive effects with media use. *Communication Research, 30*, 80–106.
Kaniss, P. (1991). *Making local news*. Chicago: University of Chicago Press.
Katz, J. E., & Rice, R. E. (2002). *Social consequences of Internet use: Access, involvement, and interaction*. Cambridge, MA: MIT Press.
Kerbel, M. R., & Bloom, D. (2005). Blog for American and civic involvement. *Harvard International Journal of Press/Politics, 10*(4), 3–27.
Keum, H., Devanathan, N., Deshpande, S., Nelson, M. R., & Shah, D. V. (2004). The citizen-consumer: Media effects at the intersection of consumer and civic culture. *Political Communication, 21*, 369–391.
Kim, J., & Kim, E. J. (2008). Theorizing dialogic deliberation: Everyday political talk as communicative action and dialogue. *Communication Theory, 18*, 51–70.
Kim, S. H., & Han, M. (2005). Media use and participatory democracy in South Korea. *Mass Communication & Society, 8*, 133–153.
Kim, Y. C., & Ball-Rokeach, S. J. (2006). Community storytelling network, neighborhood context, and civic engagement: A multilevel approach. *Human Communication Research, 32*, 411–439.
Kobayashi, T., Ikeda, K., & Miyata, K. (2006). Social capital online: Collective use of the Internet and reciprocity as lubricants of democracy. *Information, Communication & Society, 9*, 582–611.
Kraut, R., Patterson, M., Lundmark, V., Kiesler, S., Mukopadhyay, T., & Scherlis, W. (1998). Internet paradox: A social technology that reduces social involvement and psychological well being? *American Psychologist, 53*, 1017–1031.
Kwak, N., Poor, N., & Skoric, M. M. (2006). Honey, I shrunk the world! The relation between Internet use and international engagement. *Mass Communication & Society, 9*, 189–213.
Ladd, E. C. (1996). The data just don't show erosion of America's "social capital." *Public Perspective, 7*, 5–21.
Lawson-Borders, G., & Kirk, R. (2005). Blogs in campaign communication. *American Behavioral Scientist, 49*, 548–559.
Lee, F. (2007). Talk radio listening, opinion expression and political discussion in a democratizing society. *Asian Journal of Communication, 17*, 78–96.
Lee, G. H., Cappella, J. N., & Southwell, B. (2003). The effects of news and entertainment on interpersonal trust: Political talk radio, newspapers, and television. *Mass Communication & Society, 6*, 413–434.
Lerner, J., & Tetlock, P. E. (1999). Accounting for the effects of accountability. *Psychological Bulletin, 125*, 255–275.
Lupia, A., & Sin, G. (2003). Which public goods are endangered? How evolving communication technologies affect the logic of collective action. *Public Choice, 117*, 315–331.
Markus, H., & Zajonc, R. B. (1985). The cognitive perspective in social psychology. In G. Lindzey & E. Aronson (Eds.), *The handbook of social psychology* (3rd ed.) (pp. 137–229). New York: Random House.
Martin, P. S. (2004). Inside the black box of negative campaign effects: Three reasons why negative campaigns mobilize. *Political Psychology, 25*, 545–562.
Matei, S., & Ball-Rokeach, S. J. (2001). Real and virtual social ties. *American Behavioral Scientist, 45*, 550–564.

Matsuda, M. (2006). Discourses of Keitai in Japan. In M. Ito, D. Okabe, & M. Matsuda (Eds.), *Personal, portable, pedestrian: Mobile phones in Japanese life* (pp. 19–40). Cambridge, MA: MIT Press.

McLeod, J. M. (2000). Media and civic socialization of youth. *Journal of Adolescent Health, 27*, 45–51.

McLeod, J. M., Daily, K., Guo, Z., Eveland, W. P. Jr., Bayer, J., Yang, S., & Wang, H. (1996). Community integration, local media use, and democratic processes. *Communication Research, 23*, 179–209.

McLeod, J. M., Glynn, C. J., & McDonald, D. G. (1983). Issues and images: The influence of media reliance in voting decisions. *Communication Research, 10*, 37–58.

McLeod, J. M., Kosicki, G. M., & McLeod, D. M. (1994). The expanding boundaries of political communication effects. In J. Bryant & D. Zillman (Eds.), *Media effects: Advances in theory and research* (pp. 123–162). Hillsdale, NJ: Erlbaum.

McLeod, J. M., Scheufele, D. A., & Moy, P. (1999). Community, communication, & participation: The role of mass media and interpersonal discussion in local political participation. *Political Communication, 16*, 315–336.

McLeod, J. M., Zubric, J., Keum, H., Deshpande, S., Cho, J., Stein, S., & Heather, M. (2001, August). *Reflecting and connecting: Testing a communication mediation model of civic participation.* Paper presented to the annual meeting of the Association for Education in Journalism and Mass Communication, Washington D.C.

McQuail, D. (1987). The functions of communication: A non-functionalist overview. In C. R. Berger & S. H. Chaffee (Eds.), *Handbook of communication science* (pp. 327–346). Beverly Hills, CA: Sage.

Min, S. (2007). Online vs. face-to-face deliberation: Effects on civic engagement. *Journal of Computer-Mediated Communication, 12*(4), article 11. Retrieved October 11, 2007 from http://jcmc.indiana.edu/vol12/issue4/min.html

Miyata, K., Boase, J., Wellman, B., & Ikeda, K. (2006). The mobile-izing Japanese: Connecting to the Internet by PC and Webphone. In M. Ito, D. Okabe, & M. Matsuda (Eds.), *Personal, portable, pedestrian: Mobile phones in Japanese life* (pp. 143–164). Cambridge, MA: MIT Press.

Moy, P., Scheufele, D. A., & Holbert, R. L. (1999). Television and social capital: Testing Putnam's time displacement hypothesis. *Mass Communication & Society, 2*, 27–45.

Mutz, D. (2002). Cross-cutting social networks: Testing democratic theory in practice. *American Political Science Review, 96*, 111–126.

Nie, N. H. (2001). Sociability, interpersonal relations and the Internet: Reconciling conflicting findings. *American Behavioral Scientist, 45*, 420–435.

Norris, P. (1996). Does television erode social capital? A reply to Putnam. *PS: Political Science & Politics, 293*, 474–480.

Olien, C. N., Donohue, G. A., & Tichenor, P. J. (1978). Community structure and media use. *Journalism Quarterly, 55*, 445–455.

Oliver, J. E. (2000). City size and civic involvement in metropolitan America. *American Political Science Review, 94*, 361–373.

Paek, H-J., Yoon, S-H., & Shah, D. V. (2005). Local news, social integration, and community participation: Hierarchical linear modeling of contextual and cross-level effects. *Journalism & Mass Communication Quarterly, 82*, 587–606.

Pan, Z., & McLeod, J. M. (1991). Multi-level analysis in mass communication research. *Communication Research, 18*, 140–173.

Park, R. E. (1940). News as a form of knowledge. *American Journal of Sociology, 45*, 669–686.

Peiser, W. (2000). Cohort replacement and the downward trend in newspaper readership. *Newspaper Research Journal, 21*(2), 11–22.

Perlmutter, D. D. (2008). *Blogwars: The new political battleground.* New York: Oxford University Press.

Pingree, R. (2007). Decision structure and the problem of scale in deliberation. *Communication Theory, 16*, 198–222.

Pinkleton, B. E., Um, N. H., & Austin, E. W. (2002). An exploration of the effects of negative political advertising on political decision making. *Journal of Advertising, 31*, 13–25.
Price, V., & Cappella, J. N. (2002). Online deliberation and its influence: The electronic dialogue project in campaign 2000. *IT & Society, 1*, 303–329.
Prior, M. (2005). News vs. entertainment: How increasing media choice widens the gap in political knowledge and turnout. *American Journal of Political Science, 49*, 577–592.
Prior, M. (2007). *Post-broadcast democracy: How media choice increases inequality in political involvement and polarizes elections.* New York: Cambridge University Press.
Puig-i-Abril, E., & Rojas, H. (2007). Internet use as an antecedent of expressive political participation among early Internet adopters in Colombia. *International Journal of Internet Science, 2*, 28–44.
Putnam, R. D. (Ed.). (1992). *Democracies in flux: The evolution of social capital in contemporary society.* Oxford: Oxford University Press.
Putnam, R. D. (1995). Bowling alone: America's declining social capital. *Journal of Democracy, 6*, 65–78.
Putnam, R. D. (2000). *Bowling alone: The collapse and revival of American community.* New York: Simon & Schuster.
Rahn, W. M., Brehm, J., & Carlson, N. (1999). National elections as institutions for generating social capital. In T. Skocpol & M. Fiorina (Eds.), *Civic engagement and American democracy* (pp. 111–160). Washington, DC: Brookings Institute.
Räsänen, P., & Kouvo, A. (2007). Linked or divided by the Web: Internet use and sociability in four European countries. *Information, Communication & Society, 10*, 219–241.
Raudenbush, S., & Bryk, A. S. (2002). *Hierarchical linear models: Applications and data analysis methods.* Newbury Park, CA: Sage.
Rheingold, H. (2002). *Smart mobs: The next social revolution.* Cambridge, MA: Basic Books.
Roberts, D. F. (2000). Media and youth: Access, exposure, and privatization. *Journal of Adolescent Health, 27*, 8–14.
Rojas, H. (2006). Comunicación, participación y democracia. *Universitas Humanistica, 62*, 109–142.
Rojas, H., & Puig-i-Abril, E. (2007, October). The Internet and civic engagement: How online news, political messaging and blog use matter for participation. Paper presented at the annual meeting of the Association for Internet Researchers, Vancouver, Canada.
Rosengren, K. E., Palmgren, P., & Wenner, L. (Eds.). (1985). *Media gratification research: Current perspectives.* Beverly Hills, CA: Sage.
Rosenstone, S. J., & Hansen, J. M. (1993). *Mobilization, participation and democracy in America.* New York: Macmillan.
Sampson, R. J. (1988). Local friendship ties and community attachment in mass society: A multi-level systemic model. *American Sociological Review, 53*, 766–779.
Schudson, M. (1998). *The good citizen.* New York: Martin Kessler Books.
Sears, D. O., & Levy, S. (2003). Childhood and adult development. In D. O. Sears, L. Huddy, & R. L. Jervis (Eds.), *Handbook of Political Psychology* (pp. 60–109). New York: Oxford University Press.
Semetko, H. A., & Valkenburg, P. M. (1998). The impact of attentiveness on political efficacy: Evidence from a three-year German panel study. *International Journal of Public Opinion Research, 10*, 195–210.
Shah, D. V. (1998). Civic engagement, interpersonal trust, and television use: An individual level assessment of social capital. *Political Psychology, 19*, 469–496.
Shah, D. V., Cho, J., Eveland, W. P., Jr., & Kwak, N. (2005). Information and expression in a digital age: Modeling Internet effects on civic participation. *Communication Research, 32*, 531–565.
Shah, D. V., Cho, J., Nah, S., Gotlieb, M. R., Hwang, H., Lee, N., Scholl, R. M., & McLeod, D. M. (2007). Campaign ads, online messaging, and participation: Extending the communication mediation model. *Journal of Communication, 57*, 676–703.
Shah, D. V., Kwak, N., & Holbert, R. L. (2001). Connecting and disconnecting with civic life:

Patterns of Internet use and the production of social capital. *Political Communication, 18*, 141–162.

Shah, D. V., McLeod, D. M., Kim, E., Lee, S-Y., Gotlieb, M. R., Ho, S., & Brevik, H. (2007). Political consumerism: How communication practices and consumption orientations drive "lifestyle politics." *The ANNALS of the American Academy of Political and Social Science, 611*, 217–235.

Shah, D. V., McLeod, J. M., & Yoon, S. H. (2001). Communication, context and community: An exploration of print, broadcast and Internet influences. *Communication Research, 28*, 464–506.

Shah, D. V., Schmierbach, M., Hawkins, J., Espino, R., & Donovan, J. (2002). Nonrecursive models of Internet use and community engagement: Questioning whether time spent online erodes social capital. *Journalism & Mass Communication Quarterly, 79*, 964–987.

Singer, J. B. (2005). The political j-blogger. "Normalizing" a new media form to fit old norms and practices. *Journalism: Theory, Practice, and Criticism, 6*, 173–198.

Skocpol, T. (2003). *Diminished democracy. From membership to management in American civic life.* Norman, OK: University of Oklahoma Press.

Sotirovic, M., & McLeod, J. M. (2001). Values, communication behavior, and political participation. *Political Communication, 18*, 273–300.

Southwell, B. G., & Yzer, M. C. (2007). The roles of interpersonal communication in mass media campaigns. *Communication Yearbook, 31*, 419–462.

Stamm, K. R. (1985). *Newspaper use and community ties: Toward a dynamic theory*. Norwood, NJ: Ablex.

Stoll, C. (1995). *Silicon snake oil*. New York: Doubleday.

Stolle, D., Hooghe, M., & Micheletti, M. (2005). Politics in the supermarket: Political consumerism as a form of political participation. *International Political Science Review, 26*, 245–269.

Sullivan, J., Borgida, E., Jackson, M., Riedel, E., & Oxendine, A. (2002). A tale of two towns: Assessing the role of political resources in a community electronic network. *Political Behavior, 24*, 55–84.

Taveesin, N. J., & Brown, W. J. (2006). The use of communication technology in Thailand's political process. *Asian Journal of Communication, 16*, 59–78.

Thompson, G. (2003). Weblogs, warblogs, the public sphere, and bubbles. *Transformations, 7*(September), 1–12.

Tocqueville, A. (1835). *Democracy in America*. Garden City, NY: Anchor Books.

Tönnies, F. (1940). *Fundamental concepts of sociology*. New York: American Book Company.

Turkle, S. (1996). Virtuality and its discontents: Searching for community in cyberspace. *American Prospect, 24*, 50–57.

Uslaner, E. (1998). Social capital, television, and the mean world: Trust, optimism and civic participation. *Political Psychology, 19*, 441–467.

Valkenburg, P. M., & Peter, J. (2007). Online communication and adolescent well-being: Testing the stimulation versus the displacement hypothesis. *Journal of Computer-Mediated Communication, 12*(4), article 2. Retrieved October 11, 2007 from http://jcmc.indiana.edu/vol12/issue4/valkenburg.html

Verba, S., Schlozman, K. L., & Brady, H. E. (1995). *Voice and equality: Civic volunteerism in American politics*. Cambridge, MA: Harvard University Press.

Vromen, A. (2007). Australian young people's participatory practices and Internet use. *Information, Communication & Society, 10*, 48–68.

Wellman, B., Quan-Haase, A., Boase, J., & Chen, W. (2003). The social affordances of the Internet for networked individualism. *Journal of Computer Mediated Communication*, 8(3), article 7. Retrieved October 11, 2007 from http://jcmc.indiana.edu/vol8/issue3/wellman.html

Wellman, B., Quan-Haase, A., Witte, J., & Hampton, K. (2001). Does the Internet increase, decrease or supplement social capital? *American Behavioral Scientist, 45*, 436–455.

Yoon, S. H., McLeod, J. M., & Shah, D. V. (2005). Communication and youth socialization. In L. Sherrod, C. Flanagan, & R. Kassimir (Eds.), *Youth activism: An international encyclopedia* (pp. 160–167). Westport, CT: Greenwood Publishing.

11

POLITICAL COMMUNICATION EFFECTS

Douglas M. McLeod
University of Wisconsin-Madison

Gerald M. Kosicki
The Ohio State University

Jack M. McLeod
University of Wisconsin-Madison

In this chapter, we survey various areas of political communication research ranging from micro-psychological effects to broader systemic effects. Relative to our chapter in Bryant and Zillmann's (2002) last volume on media effects (McLeod, Kosicki, & McLeod, 2002), this chapter is focused on specific types of political communication effects, omitting sections on the social and political contexts for effects, media content, and normative concerns about democratic functioning. We start by defining the boundaries of political communication research and then discuss: (1) individual-level effects, (2) conditional models of effects, and (3) systemic effects of political communication. We contextualize most of the major topics in political communication research, several of which are covered in greater detail in other chapters in this volume including agenda-setting, framing, and civic participation. Cites are provided as examples and are not exhaustive.

THE BOUNDARIES OF POLITICAL COMMUNICATION RESEARCH

Defining the boundaries of political communication has become a difficult task as the contributions from a variety of disciplines and research traditions—including political science, psychology, sociology, linguistics, rhetoric, and mass communication—have broadened the focus of research. Whereas the study of political communication once was confined to the relationship between print media use and voting choices, it has been expanded to other political aspects of communication as researchers have acknowledged that all facets of social behavior could be conceived of as political. For practical purposes, in this chapter, we have narrowed the boundaries of political communication to focus on the exchange of messages between political actors, the general public, and the news media.

Political communication effects are the consequences of political communication that can be attributed to either a personal or institutional source (e.g., a political leader, advertising, or news). Effects can be manifested at the micro level of individual behavior, the intermediary level of political groups, or at the macro level of the system itself. Defining effects more narrowly than our past chapter, this review emphasizes the most prominent forms of political communication effects on media audiences.

INDIVIDUAL-LEVEL POLITICAL COMMUNICATION EFFECTS

The political communication literature continues to be dominated by individual-level effects research. We distinguish four major classes of individual effects: (1) opinion formation and change, (2) cognitive, (3) perceptual, and (4) behavioral.

Opinion Formation and Change

A substantial body of research has investigated the media's impact on the formation, change, and stabilization of opinions on political issues and candidates. Research conceptualizing media effects as a form of persuasion has waxed and waned in terms of the extent to which it supports the notion of powerful media effects. In retrospect, it is clear that persuasion models fit better in the contexts of campaign effects studies (O'Keefe et al., 1996; Rice & Atkin, 2000) and political advertising (Shah et al., 2007) than they do in the less intentionally persuasive content of news (Ansolabehere & Iyengar, 1996). Examples of opinion change associated with media use are more frequently documented than are instances of its opposite, stabilization. However, debates and other forms of campaign information have been shown to affect voting intentions and increase the consistency of partisan attitudes (Hillygus & Jackman, 2003; Sears & Chaffee, 1979).

Cognitive Effects

The five examples of cognitive effects that we identify here have received considerable attention: agenda setting, priming, framing, knowledge gain, and cognitive complexity.

Agenda Setting

Agenda-setting research is based on two related propositions: (a) the media control the public agenda by selecting certain broad issue topics for prominent coverage, and (b) prominence subsequently determines which issues are judged as important (Cohen, 1963; McCombs, 2004; McCombs & Shaw, 1972). Agenda-setting has inspired a vast literature over the past four decades, providing substantial evidence supporting the proposition that public judgments of issue importance follow prominence on the media agenda. Early evidence took three distinct forms: time-series comparisons of the national news agenda with aggregated issue ratings from opinion polls (MacKuen, 1981; McCombs & Shaw, 1972); panel studies examining the sequencing of changes in the media agenda with corresponding changes in the issue saliences of individual respondents (McCombs, 1977; Tipton, Haney, & Basehart, 1975); and cross-sectional surveys comparing media agendas to audience salience judgments (McLeod, Becker, &

Byrnes, 1974). Experiments manipulating the agenda of televised newscasts (Iyengar & Kinder, 1987) not only strengthened the evidence, but also tied agenda-setting research to cognitive theories. Researchers have begun investigating "attribute agenda-setting," claiming that agenda-setting is a robust theoretical structure that encompasses not only issue salience, but the influence of specific attributes (Ghanem, 1997; McCombs, 2004). Agenda-setting effects on audiences should not be taken as indicative of powerful media as such effects are not necessarily powerful, consequential, and universal. The news media certainly serve at least as carriers of an agenda to the public and in some cases may have an independent influence on the agenda, but the literature is not always clear on the differences. Real-world events (such as wars and economic trends) and news sources are more likely to command the agenda than are fluctuations in media coverage (Iyengar & Kinder, 1987) and the effects of these forces are not often enough controlled.

Priming

First applied to media effects in the 1980s (Iyengar & Kinder, 1987; Krosnick & Kinder, 1990), priming occurs when a given message activates a mental concept, which for a period of time increases the probability that the concept, and thoughts and memories connected with it, will come to mind again (Berkowitz & Rogers, 1986). Priming experiments have examined the effects of television news in shaping the standards by which presidential performance is judged (Iyengar & Kinder, 1987). When primed by stories focusing on national defense, for example, respondents gave disproportionate weight to judgments of how well they thought the president had done on that issue in judging his overall performance. This held across six issues, for presidents from each party and for good news as well as for bad. Additional experiments showed priming influences may extend to vote choices and presidential evaluations (McGraw & Ling, 2003). Other research reveals that media coverage of the Gulf War and the economy primed evaluations of President George H.W. Bush (Pan & Kosicki, 1997).

Framing

As media effects, agenda-setting, priming, and framing have quite a bit in common. Several attempts have been made to locate them within a cognitive processing model and have helped to illuminate their similarities and key distinctions (Entman, 2007; Hwang et al., 2007; Price & Tewksbury, 1997; Scheufele & Tewksbury, 2007). Framing effects concern how the nature of news reports alters patterns of knowledge activation (Chong & Druckman, 2007; Pan & Kosicki, 2001; Price & Tewksbury, 1997). That is, framing suggests that news messages help determine what aspects of a problem the audiences focus on through both applicability and accessibility effects. Applicability involves effects of considerations activated at the time of message processing. Once activated, these ideas retain some potential for further use, making them likely to be drawn upon in making subsequent evaluations, a process called accessibility effects (Price, Tewksbury, & Powers, 1997). In other words, framing effects involve an interaction between message patterns and audience schema that guide the understanding of new information. News stories use standard forms such as the summary lead and the inverted pyramid style, but audience members assemble new information into a causal narrative or story that reflects their point of view (Kinder & Mebane, 1983).

Framing effects processes involve the use of cognitive shortcuts to satisfy whatever level of understanding a person considers "good enough" (Popkin, 1991). Typical information processing approaches can be categorized into three types of heuristic biases: categorization, selection, and integration of information about an issue or candidate. To analyze such biases, political communication research has borrowed heavily from cognitive psychology, using concepts such as availability (Krosnick, 1989), default values (Lau & Sears, 1986), schema (Graber, 1988), and causal attribution (Iyengar, 1991).

Just as differences in news frames can induce different interpretations of events and issues, audience understanding of a given news story may be characterized as polysemic—that is, a variety of different meanings and interpretations can be derived depending on an individual's predispositions and situational circumstances. Audience reactions to news stories are influenced by a variety of factors including news media "packages" (Gamson & Modigliani, 1989), a person's structural location, personal values (Shen & Edwards, 2005), political involvement (Valentino, Beckmann, & Buhr, 2001), political schema (Shen, 2004), knowledge (Zaller, 1992), and the norms of social groups. Audience interpretations may be consonant, oppositional or even independent of the news frame. As such, framing effects are not uniform. Most research in framing is taking place in laboratories, where it can be shown that framing has immediate effects, particularly when the message stimuli are perfectly balanced and equivalent (Sniderman & Theriault, 2004). More attention needs to be paid to framing effects with naturally occurring news and information in everyday life, which differs substantially from laboratory conditions (Kinder, 2007). Future research in framing effects must seek to further identify the factors that shape media frames as well as to more precisely isolate framing effects and the factors that moderate them.

Knowledge Gain

Learning from news media has long been a subject of political communication research. Special forms of political communication, debates, and conventions, along with standard news coverage, convey discernible if modest amounts of information to their audiences (Eveland et al., 2005; Jerit, Barabas, & Bolsen, 2006; McLeod, Bybee, & Durall, 1979; Neuman, 1986; Neuman, Just, & Crigler, 1992). Yet, despite the growth in access to media providing content about politics, citizens remain remarkably uninformed about public affairs as measured by population surveys. Despite a threefold increase in the proportion of Americans who have attended college, factual knowledge of politics has increased only marginally since the 1960s and has actually declined when education is controlled (Delli Carpini & Keeter, 1996). Yet, many voters feel the information they have is enough to make vote decisions by the time of the election (Dautrich & Hartley, 1999). In fact, there is some reason for optimism as Sotirovic and McLeod (2008) found that both media use and learning from media increased from past years during the 2004 campaign. Moreover, Popkin (1991) argued that although increments of learning from news are small, they may be sufficient for the purpose of separating candidates on the issues.

Many reasons have been offered for the relatively weak increments of political knowledge conveyed by news media. Most prominent is the charge that the "horse-race" coverage of political campaigns, focusing on who is winning and the political strategies employed by the campaigns rather than on issues, deters learning (Patterson, 1980). The selection of news stories for their entertainment and attention-getting value rather than for their political importance may block more complex issues from reaching the public. Television's shorter sound bites and presentation of "nuggetized factoids" devoid of historical and political context may lead to processing information episodically rather than reflectively and thematically. Though these charges emanate from critical observation of content alone, researchers have connected news content to learning (Delli Carpini & Keeter, 1996; Drew & Weaver, 2006; Ferejohn & Kuklinski, 1990; Sotirovic & McLeod, 2004).

Substantial research has examined questions about differential rates of knowledge acquisition across different social strata and groups, as articulated by Tichenor, Donohue, and Olien's (1970) "Knowledge Gap Hypothesis." For instance, research has fairly consistently identified difference in knowledge between high and low SES groups (Viswanath & Finnegan, 1996). The emergence of new information technologies and differences in the access and use patterns across SES groups (Roberts, 2000; Shah et al., 2000, November) has furthered concern about the "digital divide" and knowledge gaps (Jung et al., 2001; Loges & Jung, 2001). Studies have shown that knowledge gaps result from such factors as differences in cognitive complexity or processing abilities, disparities in media access and exposure, or differences in the perceived utility of being informed (McLeod & Perse, 1994; Ettema & Kline, 1977). For instance, higher levels of education facilitate knowledge acquisition; income provides greater access to information; social situations socialize people into different patterns of media use; and social circumstances reward different types of knowledge. Other research has shown that large-scale media events and intense media attention to issues can reduce knowledge gaps (Holbrook, 2002; McCann & Lawson, 2006; Viswanath et al., 2006), and that factors such as need for cognition, media choices, and interest moderate the size of the knowledge gap (Liu & Eveland, 2005). Work extending the knowledge gap research into the Internet age has focused on the "digital divide" highlighting access and use issues with new technology (Mossberger, Tolbert, & Stansbury, 2003; Shane, 2004).

Cognitive Complexity

Traditional measures of factual knowledge may be too limited to capture the full range of what audience members take away from political communication. To evaluate learning from the media, researchers have gone beyond the recognition or recall of specific factual knowledge to examine audience understanding more broadly. By using open-ended questions and recording of group discussion, researchers have assessed the structure and complexity of audience thinking (Shah et al., 2004; Sotirovic, 2001b). *Cognitive complexity* can be measured reliably by counting such features of open-ended responses as the number of arguments, time frames, causes and implications brought into the discussion (Sotirovic, 2001a). Cognitive complexity so measured is moderately correlated with factual knowledge from closed-ended questions, but the two criteria have distinct sets of structural and media use antecedents.

Perceptual Effects

Self-interest and Systemic Perceptions

Making connections between the individual-cognitive and social systems levels is a problem common to all areas of social science (Price, Ritchie, & Eulau, 1991). The problem is particularly acute for political communication, however. Most political action and power relationships operate at the societal or other systemic levels, whereas the bulk of empirical theory and research concentrates on the behavior of the individual citizen. Although we think of voting as a private act based on narrow self-interest, this highly individualized account may be illusory. Citizens may have difficulty recognizing their own self-interest, and their perception of it may not be entirely selfish in that such judgments include concern for the welfare of others (Popkin, 1991). Further, although the strength of the evidence is disputed (Kramer, 1983), voting decisions seem to be made less on the basis of perceived "pocketbook" self-interest than on "sociotropic" estimates of how well the country is doing economically (Fiorina, 1981; Kinder & Kiewiet, 1983). People clearly distinguish between their own economic situation and that of the nation. At levels between the nation and the individual lie a host of other entities and groups potentially consequential to individual voting and participation. The implications of sociotropic conceptions for media effects are quite clear. Given that systemic perceptions are based largely on media inputs, the news media have responsibilities for presenting an accurate and comprehensive picture of government operations. Many critics have expressed doubt as to how well the media play this role. Although the public is exposed to the moves of the president and prominent members of Congress, little emphasis is placed on how government actually works in terms of processes, compromises, and so on (Popkin, 1991).

Causal Attribution

Jones and Nisbett (1972) suggested that actors attribute causality or responsibility for their own behavior to situational factors, whereas observers attribute the actor's behavior to stable dispositions of the actor. Applied to political judgments, this can be seen in the tendency to ascribe weaknesses of public officials to their personal faults and in blaming the poor and the homeless for their condition. Iyengar (1989) showed that failure to link social problems with societal responsibility extends to poverty, racism, and crime. Media coverage may accentuate the attribution of personal causation. Television often portrays politics as conflict between individuals rather than as struggles between institutions and principles (Rubin, 1976; Weaver, 1972). Sotirovic (2003) found that television use, relative to newspaper reading, increased the tendency to make individual attributions for the causes of crime, which in turn were linked to support for the death penalty and opposition to welfare programs.

Iyengar (1991) provided experimental evidence that television influences attribution of responsibility for both the creation of problems (causal) and their resolution (treatment) by distinguishing between episodic framing (i.e., event-oriented news reports) and thematic framing (i.e., stories that focus on a more general issue context). Episodic stories, which made up nearly 80% of a sample of CBS news stories, decreased system-level responsibility relative to thematic stories. The consequences of episodic versus thematic framing have substantial implications for subsequent political behavior. Iyengar found that people who attribute the cause of a problem to systemic forces are more likely to bring that problem into their political judgments than are people citing dispositional causes.

Climate of Opinion

A crucial assumption in Noelle-Neumann's (1984) *Spiral of Silence* is that people make "quasi-statistical" judgments about which side is in the majority or gaining support on controversial issues. According to her theory, this diminishes opinion expression by the losing side, starting a spiral of silence, and ultimately changing opinions and political behaviors. Noelle-Neumann claimed that German television news affected electoral outcomes because the climate of opinion was portrayed as being unfavorable to the Christian Democratic party. More recent investigations of the spiral of silence have explored its fear of isolation mechanism in comparison to communication apprehension variables as antecedents to willingness to speak out (Ho & McLeod, 2008; Neuwirth, Frederick, & Mayo, 2007).

Other System Perceptions

Other systemic perceptions could be explored as outcomes of media effects. There is evidence that the horserace coverage of politics contributes to a "spiral of cynicism" that lowers interest in politics (Cappella & Jamieson, 1997). Moy and Pfau (2000) found that news coverage varies in cynicism across years and across political institutions. Use of network news, entertainment talk shows and political talk radio is associated with lower levels of confidence in institutions, while newspaper use is associated with positive evaluations. De Vreese (2005) tempers concern about media-induced cynicism, noting that it is correlated with political sophistication and is not antithetical to participation. Similarly, Valentino, Beckmann, and Buhr (2001) showed that negative effects of media-induced cynicism on participation and involvement are attenuated by sophistication and involvement.

Media portrayals are also linked to public attitudes toward racially charged attitudes such as views on welfare policy. Gilens (1999) demonstrated that news organizations have racialized discussions of poverty over decades and that these racialized discussions are systematically related to public support for welfare policies. Gilliam et al. (1996) have used creative experiments manipulating the race of perpetrators in local news coverage and found that the presence of racial cues activated stereotypic beliefs about African-Americans as antecedents of opinions about crime.

Behavioral Effects

Media effects on voting preferences have long dominated the political communication agenda. Voting decisions remain the ultimate criterion in much of the research reviewed here; however, recent work no longer looks for direct media effects and instead sees voting as a complex behavior influenced indirectly through the various cognitive influences. Another change is that interpersonal communication has become part of the participation process rather than simply an antecedent of voting.

Voter Turnout

Turnout was once thought to be a rather uninteresting phenomenon simply explained and highly stable, but it seems less predictable and more interesting in recent years. Turnout continues to be predicted by education, partisanship, age, church attendance, community involvement, and marital status (Strate, Parrish, Elder, & Ford, 1989; Wolfinger & Rosenstone, 1980), but abstention from voting continued to rise until the highly polarized and heavily advertised 2004 campaign produced a sharp increase in turnout particularly in battleground states.

In a panel study of the unusually high abstention rate in the 1970 British general election, media influences were found to be complex (Blumler & McLeod, 1974). Those most likely to abstain as a result of disenchantment with the televised image of the person's party leader, surprisingly, tended to be the more educated and better informed voters. Turnout studies in the United States suggest that exposure and attention to hard news in the print media are associated with turnout and with other forms of participation as well (Bybee, McLeod, Leutscher, & Garramone, 1981; McLeod & McDonald, 1985). Teixeira (1992) goes well beyond structural factors such as poverty and mobility to examine a range of motivational variables that are shown to affect turnout positively and negatively and suggests a number of campaign and media reforms designed to increase turnout. Negative campaigns and negative political advertising are forms of political communication that seem to stimulate voter turnout (Freedman & Goldstein, 1999; Jackson & Carsey, 2007; Kahn & Kenney, 1999; for arguments and evidence that negative advertising demobilizes and alienates voters see Ansolabehere, Iyengar, & Simon, 1999). Overton (2006) provides structural arguments for voter suppression based on examination of macro factors such as gerrymandering of voting districts, voter identification requirements and other so-called "anti-fraud" rules that make voting more difficult.

Interpersonal Communication

The Columbia voting studies treated interpersonal communication as an alternative to mass media influence, noting that on an average day, 10% more discussed the election than read or heard about it through the media (Lazarsfeld et al., 1948). Other observers have come to see this as a "synthetic competition" (Chaffee, 1982), arguing that media and interpersonal channels may have convergent, complementary, or other relationships as well. There is substantial evidence that both customary patterns of exposure and attention to newspaper public affairs content, and exposure to the media during the campaign, stimulate interpersonal discussion. Although not very efficient in conveying information about issues, the media do seem to stimulate interpersonal discussion and interest in the campaign (McLeod, Bybee, & Durall, 1979). Interpersonal discussion helps people decide how to vote and may stimulate turnout except where the others in the conversational network are of the opposite party. Even discussion with strangers may affect voting. Noelle-Neumann (1984) reported that willingness to express a particular side of an issue in conversations with strangers ultimately led to change in opinion toward that side.

Rising interest in deliberative democracy has led to increased attention to political talk of all kinds, including deliberation (Delli Carpini, Cook, & Jacobs, 2004). Although not without its critics (e.g. Sanders, 1997), deliberation is an increasing focus of many active research programs (e.g. Fishkin & Laslett, 2003; Gastil & Levine, 2005; Mutz, 2006 and Price & Cappella, 2002). It is also noteworthy that organizations such as AmericaSpeaks.org, National Issues Forum Institute, and Public Agenda, among others, have become quite active in recent years in promoting discussion forums around the country as well as online. The cumulative impact of these activities may be substantial in that they are reaching many thousands of people with their activities on an ongoing basis. People report a high level of satisfaction with these experiences, and often they are organized for the purpose of deciding local issues (e.g., Lukensmeyer, Goldman, & Brigham, 2005) at the invitation of local officials.

Media and Citizen Engagement

Discrepancies between the high normative standards of democratic theory and empirical evidence of low levels of citizen engagement have been noted repeatedly since the early Columbia voting studies (Berelson, Lazarsfeld, & McPhee, 1954). Narrow concern with falling voting turnout rates turned to near panic with the popular acceptance of Robert Putnam's (1995) "bowling alone" thesis and evidence for a 30-year decline in a wide range of other political and civic participation indicators. Twelve political and communal activities declined an average of 27% from 1973–74 to 1993–94, for example (Putnam, 2000, p. 45). Trust in other people, a key indicator in Putnam's concept of social capital, slipped from 55% to 35% from 1960 to 1999 (Putnam, 2000, p. 140). It appears many forms of participation have declined over the past 30 years, some forms are stable, and some may be increasing. One point of agreement is that participation rates have not kept up with the rising levels of education over recent decades. This same generalization holds for political knowledge as well (Delli Carpini & Keeter, 1996). Levels of knowledge have, overall, remained rather stable despite increased levels of educational attainment.

What is most striking is the failure of Putnam and others involved in the debate over declining civic engagement to deal with news media use in any meaningful way. Putnam's concern is confined to the alleged effects of time spent with television displacing participation. The evidence for displacement is weak and reverse causation is likely—those who stay home rather than going out to participate may well turn to television for diversion. More surprising is that researchers ignore decades of mass communication research showing positive effects of news media use (when adequately measured) on political knowledge and participation (e.g., Blumler & McLeod, 1974; Chaffee & Schleuder, 1986; McLeod & McDonald, 1985; McLeod et al., 1996a; Smith, 1986; Wattenberg, 1984). Declining patterns of regular newspaper reading, along with lower levels of availability of a local daily paper in many local areas, have not been investigated as sources of stagnation in civic life.

Civic Participation

The civic turn has markedly broadened the criteria for communication effects through the examination of local issues and nontraditional forms of participation (McLeod et al, 1996b; McLeod et al., 1999a) and interpersonal trust as a mediator (Shah, 1998; Shah, Kwak, & Holbert, 2001). It has redirected the study of participation toward the question of how civic engagement is stimulated conjointly by local media use, local issue discussion, and community ties (Kang & Kwak, 2003; McLeod et al., 1996b; McLeod et al., 1999a; Stamm, Emig, & Hesse, 1997). Recently, the knowledge gap concept has been extended to media effects on participation gaps (Cho & McLeod, 2007).

The ascendancy of the Internet as a central communication medium has inspired considerable research on its role as an antecedent to participation (Matei & Ball-Rokeach, 2003; Shah et al., 2002). For example, Shah et al. (2005) found that both online and traditional media use encourage political discussion and civic messaging, which in turn motivate civic participation. Xenos and Moy (2007) found that the effect of Internet use on participation was contingent on political interest.

Civic Socialization

Half a century of political behavior research has shown that citizen involvement increases with age. Research from the past decade indicates that a cohort phenomenon may be at work along with the maturational effect. For example, in the three presidential elections

(1988 to 1996), voter turnout in the 18–24 age group averaged 37%, 21% lower than among all citizens (Casper & Bass, 1998). This compares unfavorably with three previous elections (1972 to 1980) when the 18–24 years group averaged 44% turnout, 17% below that of all citizens. Recent cohorts have contributed most to the decline in other aspects of electoral participation (Miller & Shanks, 1996) and in civic engagement (Putnam, 2000). Also fueling concern are findings of cohort effects in the decline of newspaper reading in recent decades (Peiser, 2000). News use is a strong factor in stimulating youth participation (Chaffee, McLeod, & Wackman, 1973; Chaffee, Pan, & McLeod, 1995). The implication of the cohort effects findings is that the current pattern of low participation among the young is apt to translate into even lower rates of overall participation as they move through the life cycle. In recent elections, there is some cause for optimism as youth vote went up in 2004, but not in 2006. Early signs point to the fact that youth turnout is surging again during the 2008 campaign. However, it is too early to tell whether these signs of youth involvement represent any reversal of the general pattern of decline in participation.

Concern with declining youth participation has precipitated a reexamination of the political socialization research that was popular in the 1960s (Flanagan & Sherrod, 1998; Niemi, 1999). Political socialization work virtually disappeared after the 1970s, in large part because it was based on a flawed developmental transmission model. The developing adolescent was seen as a passive recipient in the learning process. As socialization has returned to the research agenda, researchers have proposed looking at the traditional models of socialization in new ways. For example, McDevitt and Chaffee (2002) inverted the top-down model of socialization to focus on the role that the developing adolescent serves as an impetus for change in the family dynamic relative to public affairs. The new civic socialization research conceives of youth as potential participants actively engaged in the world around them, often trying out roles in anticipation of adulthood. Civic knowledge, interpersonal trust, and efficacious attitudes remain as criteria for socialization effects, but so are news media use, issue discussion, thoughtful processing of information, listening and turn-taking in discussions, and working out compromises (McLeod, 2000).

Effects on Children

In the 1990s, concern with low levels of participation among the young led to the development of dozens of school-based intervention programs using media as sources of learning or media production by youth as a learning device (Sirianni & Friedland, 2001). The strong interest of adolescents in new media beyond television (e.g., computers and cell phones) provides the basis for such programs (Roberts, 2000). The low level of news media use among adolescents is partly compensated for by their use of new technologies. Young adults not only are more likely than older adults to use the Internet for information, but the strength of the effect of such use on civic engagement is also greater (Shah, McLeod, & Yoon, 2001). Though various media-based programs have been successful, the complex processes by which they achieve their goals are seldom evaluated. A Kids Voting USA project was successful in stimulating adolescent civic engagement by strategically combining the strengths of teachers, parents, and local media (Chaffee et al., 1995; McDevitt & Chaffee, 1998; McLeod, Eveland, & Horowitz, 1998). Local media provided publicity for the program and content for classroom assignments. The program also reduced knowledge and participation gaps by gender (McLeod et al., 1998a) and social class (McDevitt & Chaffee, 2000).

What lessons can be learned from the evaluation of these reform programs involving media? First, programs involving active and reflective learning have more lasting impact than do those confined to the passive learning of facts. Civics courses involving expressive activities were more effective in conveying knowledge (Niemi & Junn, 1998). Service learning in activities provides knowledge and skills lasting into adulthood (Youniss, McLellan, & Yates, 1997), particularly where the subject matter is tied to the field experience and where there is adequate reflection and evaluation (Niemi, Hepburn, & Chapman, 2000). Second, inducing change through media use is more likely to be effective when combined with the development of networks to discuss issues and support participation and sustain change. Media use patterns and networks developed around one issue are apt to carry over and provide the social capital for citizen action on other issues (Friedland, 2001). Finally, fundamental improvement in the quantity and quality of civic life requires not only change in individual citizens, but also the involvement of local associations and institutions in the community.

CONDITIONAL MODELS OF POLITICAL COMMUNICATION EFFECTS

Recent political communication effects research provides ample evidence that media impact is likely to be conditional rather than universal. Effects depend on orientations of audiences as well on exposure to media content stimuli. They take the form of O-S-O-R models (Markus & Zajonc, 1985). The first O represents the set of structural, cultural, cognitive, and motivational characteristics the audience brings to the reception situation that affect the impact of messages (S). They are often referred to as individual differences, although they are likely to be socially determined. They represent the person's *subjective* reactions to the *objective* conditions of the community and world in which he or she lives. These subjective orientations may alter effects either by directing the extent of use (dosage) of the messages or though interactions with message content magnifying or diminishing the strength (potency) of effect. In the former case, media use may *mediate* the effects of the orientations on some dependent variable. In the latter case, the orientation is said to act as a *moderator* of media effects (Baron & Kenny, 1986). The second O denotes various ways audiences may deal with media messages and indicates which is likely to happen between the reception of messages and the subsequent response (R) or outcome. Activity is the label given to various intervening orientations (Hawkins & Pingree, 1986). As is true for the first O, activities may be conceptualized at various levels ranging from a short-term physiological response to a complex set of interactions after the reception. New methodological work popularizing mediation and moderation is promoting interest in these approaches (Bucy & Tao, 2007; Holbert, 2005).

Prereception Orientations

Political Sophistication and Involvement

Educational and other status factors have produced large differences in how much citizens know and care about politics. Since the UN campaign study more than a half-century ago (Star & Hughes, 1950), evidence has consistently shown that those already informed are more likely to learn new information. Such sophistication also provides more complex schema for interpretation of ambiguous political campaign events (Graber, 1988). While enhancing learning, sophistication and involvement may moderate other campaign effects such as agenda setting (Iyengar & Kinder, 1987; McLeod et al., 1974; Weaver et al, 1981) and framing (Valentino, Beckmann, & Buhr, 2001).

Partisanship

Political partisanship serves as a heuristic device for political decision-making and as a key moderator of media effects through the selectivity processes of exposure, perception, and interpretation (Katz, 1987). Partisanship may minimize agenda-setting effects (Iyengar & Kinder, 1987; McLeod et al., 1974) and also priming effects when the primed news story is inconsistent with audience predispositions (Iyengar & Kinder, 1987). Partisanship led to different patterns of effects for exposure to late-night comedies (Young, 2004) and to different perceptions of media bias (Gunther & Schmitt, 2004; Vallone, Ross, & Lepper, 1985).

Worldviews and Values

Worldviews, personal beliefs or lay theories about how the world *is* (empirical) and normative theories of the world as it *ought* to be, can be powerful moderators of media effects (McLeod, Sotirovic, & Holbert, 1998b). Values that people hold as goals for their society and community have strong implications for media use and political participation (Inglehart, 1990). Holding strong *postmaterial* values (freedom to express ideas, helping each other, etc.) is strongly related to higher levels of public affairs media use and discussion of issues, and to reflection on how the content of news and discussion fits into their lives (McLeod et al., 1998b; Sotirovic & McLeod, 2001). Strong *material* values (order, control by defense and fighting crime, etc.) tend to have a dampening effect on citizen action through more soft entertainment media use and less frequent discussions that deter political engagement. Communication thus mediates the effects of worldviews and values on informed participation. Values may also act as moderators interacting with messages. Strength of values held by audience members interact with the value framing of content to affect decision-making outcomes (Shah, 2001).

News Media Orientations

"Common-sense" theories about the news media, both empirical and normative, affect learning from the news (Kosicki & McLeod, 1990). For example, people who see the news as having underlying patterns tend to learn more. Citizens who strongly value the normative roles of the media as a watchdog, a forum for ideas, and as a catalyst for participation, pay more attention to the news, and thus are indirectly more knowledgeable and participatory (McLeod et al., 1998b). In contrast, those more strongly advocating *consensual* functions were less knowledgeable and active due to their higher levels of attention to soft news and entertainment television.

Gratifications Sought from News

Research from the uses-and-gratifications approach has shown that motives for using media can be an important effects moderator. For example, strength of motivation acted as a moderator in enhancing information gain from party broadcasts (Blumler &

McQuail, 1969; McLeod & Becker, 1974). Gratifications sought may weaken as well as strengthen media effects. Readers with the strongest motivation to gain information failed to shift their salience ratings of issues in accordance with the agenda of the newspaper they read (McLeod et al., 1974). Studies of Internet use show that use motivations affect the nature of search behavior (Yang, 2004) and user satisfaction (Liang, Lai, & Ku, 2006), which ultimately shape exposure effects.

Reception Activity Orientations

Effects are also conditioned by orientations during exposure to news. These orientations can be measured physiologically below the level of the person's awareness (Reeves, Thorson, & Schleuder, 1986), or by using self-report measures that suffer the weaknesses of other self-report measures, but do reveal substantial variance between persons.

Attention

Attention is the conscious focusing of increased mental effort. As applied to news, it can be measured from closed-ended questions regarding various types of news content, and separately or combined across media. Attention is particularly important for television, where exposure takes place under very different levels of attention. In contrast, use of a newspaper or Internet information site demands more attention. Learning from news is enhanced at higher levels of attention (Chaffee & Choe, 1980; Chaffee & Schleuder, 1986), though effects vary according to type of news media used (de Vreese & Boomgaarden, 2006). Exposure and attention may have more than additive effects. Exposure to hard news interacted with attention to increase both knowledge about the economy and community participation (McLeod & McDonald, 1985).

Information-processing Strategies

Audience activity includes strategies people employ to cope with the "flood of information" (Graber, 1988). Surveys using a set of self-report items found three dimensions of audience news information-processing strategies (Kosicki & McLeod, 1990): *selective scanning; active processing*, going beyond the story to reinterpret it according to the person's needs; and *reflective integration*, replaying the story in the person's mind and using it as a topic of discussion. The extent of political learning, political interest, and participation were restricted by selective scanning and enhanced by reflective integration. Active processing had a little effect on learning, but does stimulate interest and participation. Processing research has focused on *reflection* or *elaboration* (Eveland, 2005), particularly as it mediates news effects on political knowledge (Fredin & Kosicki, 1989; Kosicki, Becker, & Fredin, 1994; McLeod, Scheufele, & Moy, 1999a; Sotirovic & McLeod, 2001), traditional participation (McLeod et al., 1999a; Sotirovic & McLeod, 2001), participation in public forums (McLeod et al., 1999b), and voting intentions (Hwang et al., 2007).

SYSTEMIC POLITICAL COMMUNICATION EFFECTS

Two very different processes are implied by systemic effects. The first are media effects on individuals that have consequences for societal and community systems. The second involves the influence of the collective features of institutions on individual behavior. The two are examples of micro-to-macro and macro-to-micro processes (McLeod, Pan, & Rucinski, 1995; Pan & McLeod, 1991).

Aggregated Individual Effects

Connecting micro individual-level effects and macro institutional-level consequences poses several difficult problems. First, systemic consequences are manifested through institutional policies, practices, and laws and other outcomes that transcend individual judgments. Second, systemic consequences are not reducible to the simple aggregation of individual-level effects. The distribution of effects, for example, can be of great theoretical significance, as in knowledge gap issues (Tichenor et al., 1970). Quite different concepts and theories are appropriate to various micro and macro levels (McLeod & Blumler, 1987). Finally, democratic practices involve collective forms of action such as social movements whose fate involves the connection of groups to information and power.

In lieu of formal attempts at cross-level theorizing, we can take current problems with the political system and work backward to possible ways in which the media might be responsible. The problems of the American political system are well documented. Despite substantial increases in educational attainment over several decades, there has been no corresponding increase in knowledge (Delli Carpini & Keeter, 1996) and a substantial decline in voter turnout and certain other indicators of participation have been noted with alarm (Putnam, 1995). Unfortunately, the search for causes of political system stagnation has been confined largely to the potential displacement effects of spending time with television.

Structural Effects

More substantial progress over the past decade has been made in research on macro-systemic to micro-individual effects. The structure of the person's discussion network influences participation (Huckfeldt & Sprague, 1995; McLeod et al., 1996a; Scheufele et al., 2006), though this relationship may be moderated by discussion frequency (Kwak et al., 2005). Beyond the effects of micro-social discussion networks, the contexts of the larger neighborhood and community may have consequences for individual media use and participation. The level of community stability, the contextual aggregation of residential stability (low likelihood and desire to move) across all individuals sampled in a community, was associated with higher levels of trust and participation after all individual level variables had been introduced (Shah, McLeod, & Yoon, 2001). Further, contextual community stability interacted with exchanging information on the Internet to bolster participation. Newspaper hard news reading interacted with two contextual variables, institutional confidence and connectedness, to bolster participation. Media impact depends on where we live collectively as well as how we live individually.

Evidence of political stratification depicts a political world sharply divided into a small group of sophisticated, involved citizens and a much larger group of uninterested and relatively uninformed citizens (Neuman, 1986). This stratified model of the political system may need qualification. Popkin (1991) has argued that increases in education have not deepened but nonetheless have broadened the number of issues seen as relevant to citizens' lives. It is likely that television news deserves some credit for this (Blumler & McLeod, 1974). Broadening may have led to an increase in the number of issue publics, that is, relatively small groups with intense interest in a particular issue, but with much less interest in most other issues. Issue specialization poses problems for political party mobilization and for coverage by news media increasingly constrained in resources.

Increasing attention to structural changes in the media environment are called for in light of the dramatic changes brought on by the disrupting technological effects of the Internet. Television content is increasingly delivered to consumers via DVD or through direct online downloading. Newspaper and magazine content is increasingly available online through the publication's own web sites, but also via a variety of content aggregators (e.g., Google News, Yahoo! News) enabled by search engine technology. It might be tempting from the standpoint of the user to say this makes no discernible difference in audience effects. But to the extent that aggregators are attracting advertising dollars for content they don't own, this is weakening the newsgathering operations of the large television networks, newspapers and magazines through loss of revenue. For example, revenue for Google Inc., a leading search engine and news aggregator founded in 1998, will likely exceed $16 billion in 2008. That is approximately the equivalent of the combined revenues of the four leading television networks in the United States.

While many individuals in the United States are accessing news online, the traditional mass media continue to serve large audiences (Ahlers, 2006). As the pace of innovation increases it is likely that traditional media will adapt by incorporating more of the characteristics of online environments. The implications of these trends for the future of media and democracy are discussed by Harrison & Falvey (2001). Sunstein (2006) discusses the collaborative possibilities of online environments, and Benkler (2006) focuses on the political economy of social production and the implications for the future of media and information availability and use in society.

SOME CONCLUDING REMARKS

Political communication effects research has continued to develop in ways that reflect: (a) the increased complexity of effects models; (b) augmented conceptions of media messages; and (c) an expanded emphasis on diverse types of effects. This development has included several promising trends. First, there has been some progress in connecting audience effects with other parts of the communication process: news sources, media organizations, and content. Second, investigation at the macro-social level of analysis has been revitalized to complement the already extensive research at the individual level. Coinciding with the resurgence of macrolevel concern, research making comparisons between communities, nations, and historical periods has also emerged (Bennett, 2000; Blumler, 1983; Blumler, McLeod, & Rosengren, 1992; Tichenor, Donohue, & Olien, 1980). A fourth trend is a renewed interest in language—not only the language of media content, but language as it relates to the production and interpretation of mediated information. Fifth, there has been an increase in the number of studies that combine methodologies and/or use multiple sources of data to provide more complete answers to research questions. Sixth, there has been a rebirth of interest in issues of civic socialization and community. Seventh, in assessing media effects, researchers are beginning to recognize the differences between the level of usage (dosage) and the strength of the effect (potency). Finally, researchers have developed more complex models of political communication processes. Each of the trends has been stimulated by the increasing complexity of the political environment and has facilitated the growth of knowledge in the field.

We have presented various ways in which the boundaries of political communication effects research have expanded in recent years. Movement has been "horizontal," connecting individual effects with other parts of the mass communication process as well as with their consequences for the political system. Broadening of effects also necessitates "vertical" linkages of individual behavior with political system institutions and interpersonal processes. Expansion is also seen in the diversity of media effects considered and in alternative conceptualizations of media messages. Political effects are now more likely to be seen as having varying impact contingent on characteristics of particular segments of the audience and as operating in an indirect and delayed fashion. Finally, we have shown how very different methodological strategies have informed the body of political communication knowledge.

In conclusion, we point out that the news media are by no means the sole cause nor even a major cause of current problems in the political system. Responsibility must be shared with other social institutions: the family, schools, political parties, and political leaders who have "joint custody" of democracy. However, this makes systematic study of the media's political effects no less necessary.

References

Ahlers, D. (2006). News consumption and the new electronic media. *Harvard International Journal of Press/Politics, 11*(1), 29–52.

Ansolabehere, S., & Iyengar, S. (1996). The craft of political advertising: A progress report. In D. C. Mutz, P. M. Sniderman, and R. A. Brody (Eds.), *Political persuasion and attitude change* (pp. 101–122). Ann Arbor: University of Michigan Press.

Ansolabehere, S., Iyengar, S., & Simon, A. (1999). Replicating experiments using aggregate and survey data: The case of negative advertising and turnout. *American Political Science Review, 93*, 901–909.

Baron, R. M., & Kenny, D. A. (1986). The moderator-mediator variable distinction in social psychological research: Conceptual, strategic, and statistical considerations. *Journal of Personality and Social Psychology, 51*, 1173–1182.

Benkler, Y. (2006). *The wealth of networks: How social production transforms markets and freedom.* New Haven: Yale University Press.

Bennett, W. L. (2000). Introduction: Communication and civic engagement in comparative perspective. *Political Communication, 17*, 307–312.

Berelson, B. R., Lazarsfeld, P. F., & McPhee, W. N. (1954). *Voting: A study of opinion formation in a presidential campaign*. Chicago: University of Chicago Press.

Berkowitz, L., & Rogers, K. H. (1986). A priming effect analysis of media influences. In J. Bryant & D. Zillmann (Eds.), *Perspectives on media effects* (pp. 57–81). Hillsdale, NJ: Erlbaum.

Blumler, J. G. (Ed.). (1983). *Communicating to voters: Television in the first European parliamentary election*. London: Sage.

Blumler, J. G., & McLeod, J. M. (1974). Communication and voter turnout in Britain. In T. Legatt (Ed.), *Sociological theory and social research* (pp. 265–312). London, Beverly Hills, CA: Sage.

Blumler, J. G., McLeod, J. M., & Rosengren, K. E. (1992). An introduction to comparative communication research. In J. G. Blumler, J. M. McLeod, & K. E. Rosengren (Eds.), *Comparatively speaking: Communication and culture across space and time* (pp. 3–18). Newbury Park, CA: Sage.

Blumler, J. G., & McQuail, D. (1969). *Television in politics: Its uses and influence*. Chicago: University of Chicago Press.

Bryant, J., & Zillmann, D. (Eds.). (2002). *Media effects: Advances in theory and research* (2nd ed.). Hillsdale, NJ: Erlbaum.

Bucy, E. P., & Tao, C. C. (2007). The Mediated Moderation Model of Interactivity. *Media Psychology, 9*, 647–672.

Bybee, C. R., McLeod, J. M., Leutscher, W., & Garramone, C. (1981). Mass communication and voter volatility. *Public Opinion Quarterly, 45*, 69–90.

Cappella, J. N., & Jamieson, K. H. (1997). *Spiral of cynicism: The press and the public good*. New York: Oxford University Press.

Casper, L. M., & Bass, L. E. (1998). Voting and registration in the election of November, 1996. *Current Population Reports, 20*, 20–504, Washington, DC: U.S. Bureau of the Census.

Chaffee, S. H., (1982). Mass media and interpersonal channels: Competitive, convergent or complementary? In G. Gumpert & R. Cathcart (Eds.), *Intermedia: Interpersonal communication in a media world* (pp. 57–77). New York: Oxford University Press.

Chaffee, S. H., & Choe, S. Y. (1980). Time of decision and media use during the Ford-Carter campaign. *Public Opinion Quarterly, 44*, 53–59.

Chaffee, S. H.. McLeod, J. M., & Wackman, D. B. (1973). Family communication patterns and adolescent political socialization. In J. Dennis (Ed.), *Socialization to politics* (pp. 349–363). New York: Wiley.

Chaffee, S. H., Pan, Z., & McLeod, J. M. (1995). Effects of kids voting in San Jose: A quasi-experimental evaluation. Final Report. Policy Study Center. Program in Media and Democracy, Annenberg School for Communication, University of Pennsylvania, 69 pages.

Chaffee, S. H., & Schleuder, J. (1986). Measurement and effects of attention to media news. *Human Communication Research, 13*, 76–107.

Cho, J., & McLeod, D. M. (2007). Structural antecedents to knowledge and participation: Extending the knowledge gap concept to participation. *Journal of Communication, 57*, 205–228.

Chong, D., & Druckman, J. N. (2007). Framing theory. *Annual Review of Political Science, 10*, 103–126.

Cohen, B. C. (1963). *The press and foreign policy*. Princeton, NJ: Princeton University Press.

Dautrich, K., & Hartley, T. H. (1999). How the news media fail American voters. New York: Columbia University Press.

Delli Carpini, M. X., Cook, F. L., & Jacobs, L. R. (2004). Public deliberation, discursive participation and citizen engagement: A review of the empirical literature. *Annual Review of Political Science* 7, 315–344.

Delli Carpini, M. X., & Keeter, S. (1996). *What Americans know about politics and why it matters*. New Haven: Yale University Press.

de Vreese, C. H. (2005). The spiral of cynicism reconsidered. *European Journal of Communication, 20*, 283–301.

de Vreese, C. H., & Boomgaarden, H. (2006). News, political knowledge and participation: The differential effects of news media exposure on political knowledge and participation. *Acta Politica, 41*, 317–341.

Drew, D., & Weaver, D. (2006). Voter learning in the 2004 presidential election: Did the media matter? *Journalism and Mass Communication Quarterly, 83*, 25–42.

Entman, R. M. (2007). Framing bias: Media in the distribution of power. *Journal of Communication, 57*, 163–173.

Ettema, J. S., & Kline, F. G. (1977). Deficits, differences, and ceilings: Contingent conditions for understanding the knowledge gap. *Communication Research, 4*, 179–202.

Eveland, W. P. (2005). Information processing strategies in mass communication research. In S. Dunwoody, L. B. Becker, D. M. McLeod, & G. M. Kosicki (Eds.), *The evolution of key mass communication concepts* (pp. 217–248). New York: Hampton Press.

Eveland, W. P., Hayes, A. F., Shah, D. V., & Kwak, N. (2005). Understanding the relationship between communication and political knowledge: A model comparison approach using panel data. *Political Communication, 22*, 423–446.

Ferejohn, J. A., & Kuklinski, J. H. (1990). *Information and democratic processes*. Urbana: University of Illinois Press.
Fiorina, M. P. (1981). *Retrospective voting in American national elections*. New Haven, CT: Yale University Press.
Fishkin, J. S., & Laslett, P. (Eds.) (2003). *Debating deliberative democracy*. Malden, MA: Blackwell.
Flanagan, C. A., & Sherrod, L. R. (1998). Youth political development: An introduction. *Journal of Social Issues, 54*, 447–456.
Fredin, E. S., & Kosicki, G. M. (1989). Cognitions and attitudes about community: Compensating for media images, *Journalism Quarterly, 66*, 571–578.
Freedman, P., & Goldstein, K. (1999). Measuring media exposure and the effects of negative campaign ads. *American Journal of Political Science, 43*, 1189–1208.
Friedland, L. A. (2001). Communication, community, and democracy: Toward a theory of the communicatively integrated community. *Communication Research, 28*, 358–391.
Gamson, W. A., & Modigliani, A. (1989). Media discourse and public opinion: A constructivist approach. *American Journal of Sociology, 95*, 1–37.
Gastil, J., & Levine, P. (Eds.). (2005). *The deliberative democracy handbook. Strategies for effective civic engagement in the 21st Century*. San Francisco: Jossey-Bass.
Ghanem, S. (1997). Filling in the tapestry: The second level of agenda setting. In M. E. McCombs, D. L. Shaw, & D. Weaver (Eds.), *Communication and democracy: Exploring the intellectual frontiers in agenda-setting theory* (pp. 3–14). Mahwah, NJ: Erlbaum.
Gilens, M. (1999). *Why Americans hate welfare*. Chicago: University of Chicago Press.
Gilliam, F. D., Iyengar, S., Simon, A., & Wright, O. (1996). Crime in black and white: The violent, scary world of local news. *Harvard International Journal of Press/Politics, 1*(1), 6–23.
Graber, D. (1988). *Processing the news: How people tame the information tide* (2nd ed.). New York: Longman.
Gunther, A. C., & Schmitt, K. (2004). Mapping boundaries of the hostile media effect. *The Journal of Communication, 54*, 55–75.
Harrison, T. M., & Falvey, L. (2001). Democracy and new communication technologies. *Communication Yearbook*, 25, 1–43.
Hawkins, R. P., & Pingree, S. (1986). Activity in the effects of television on children. In J. Bryant & D. Zillmann (Eds.), *Perspectives on media effects* (pp. 233–250). Hillsdale, NJ: Erlbaum.
Hillygus, D. S., & Jackman, S. (2003). Voter decision making in election 2000: Campaign effects, partisan activation, and the Clinton legacy. *American Journal of Political Science, 47*, 583–596.
Ho, S., & McLeod, D. M. (2008). Social-psychological influences on opinion expression in face-to-face and computer-mediated communication. *Communication Research, 35*(2), 190–207.
Holbert, R. L. (2005). Television news viewing, governmental scope, and postmaterialist spending: Assessing mediation by partisanship. *Journal of Broadcasting & Electronic Media, 49*, 416–434.
Holbrook, T. M. (2002). Presidential campaigns and the knowledge gap. *Political Communication, 19*, 437–454.
Huckfeldt, R., & Sprague, J. (1995). *Citizens, politics, and social communication*. Cambridge, UK: Cambridge University Press.
Hwang, H., Gotlieb, M. R., Nah, S., & McLeod, D. M. (2007). Applying a cognitive-processing model to presidential debate effects: Postdebate news analysis and primed reflection. *Journal of Communication, 57*, 40–59.
Inglehart, R. (1990). *Cultural shift in advanced industrial societies*. Princeton, NJ: Princeton University Press.
Iyengar, S. (1989). How citizens think about national issues. *American Journal of Political Science, 33*, 878–897.
Iyengar, S. (1991). *Is anyone responsible? How television frames political issues*. Chicago: University of Chicago Press.
Iyengar, S., & Kinder, D. R. (1987). *News that matters*. Chicago: University of Chicago Press.
Jackson, R. A., & Carsey, T. M. (2007). U.S. Senate campaigns, negative advertising, and voter mobilization in the 1998 midterm election. *Electoral Studies, 26*, 180–195.

Jerit, J., Barabas, J., & Bolsen, T. (2006). Citizens, knowledge, and the information environment. *American Journal of Political Science, 50*, 266–282.

Jones, E. E., & Nisbett, R. E. (1972). The actor and the observer: Divergent perceptions of the causes of behavior. In E. Jones, D. Kanouse, H. Kelley, R. Nisbett, S. Valins, & R. Kidd (Eds.), *New directions in attribution research* (pp. 79–94). Morristown, NJ: General Learning Press.

Jung, J. Y., Qiu, J. L., & Kim, Y. C. (2001). Internet connectedness and inequality. *Communication Research, 28*, 507–535.

Kahn, K. F., & Kenney, P. J. (1999). Do negative campaigns mobilize or suppress turnout?: Clarifying the relationship between negativity and participation. *American Political Science Review, 93*, 877–889.

Kang, N., & Kwak, N. (2003). A multilevel approach to civic participation: Individual length of residence, neighborhood residential stability, and their interactive effects with media use. *Communication Research, 30*, 80–106.

Katz, E. (1987). On conceptualizing media effects: Another look. In S. Oskamp (Ed.), *Applied Social Psychology Annual* (Vol. 8, pp. 32–42). Beverly Hills, CA: Sage.

Kinder, D. R. (2007). Curmudgeonly advice. *Journal of Communication, 57*, 155–162.

Kinder, D. R., & Kiewiet, D. R. (1983). Sociotropic politics: The American case. *British Journal of Political Science, 11*, 129–161.

Kinder, D. R., & Mebane, W. R., Jr. (1983). Politics and economics in everyday life. In K. Monroe (Ed.), *The political process and economic change* (pp. 141–180). New York: Agathon.

Kosicki, G. M., Becker, L. B., & Fredin, E. S. (1994). Buses and ballots: The role of media images in a local election, *Journalism Quarterly, 71*, 76–89.

Kosicki, G. M., & McLeod, J. M. (1990). Learning from political news: Effects of media images and information-processing strategies. In S. Kraus (Ed.), *Mass communication and political information processing* (pp. 69–83). Hillsdale, NJ: Erlbaum.

Kramer, G. H. (1983). The ecological fallacy revisited: Aggregate versus individual level findings on economics and elections and sociotropic voting. *American Political Science Review, 77*, 77–111.

Krosnick, J. A. (1989). Attitude importance and attitude accessibility, *Personality and Psychology Bulletin, 15*, 297–308.

Krosnick, J. A., & Kinder, D. R. (1990). Altering support for the president through priming: The Iran-Contra affair. *American Political Science Review, 84*, 497–512.

Kwak, N., Williams, A. E., Wang, X. R., & Lee, H. (2005). Talking politics and engaging in politics: An examination of the interactive relationships between structural features of political talk and discussion engagement. *Communication Research, 32*, 87–111.

Lau, R. R., & Sears, D. O. (1986). Social cognition and political cognition: The past, the present and the future. In R. Lau & D. Sears (Eds.), *Political cognition* (pp. 347–366). Hillsdale, NJ: Erlbaum.

Lazarsfeld, P. F., Berelson, B. R., & Gaudet, H. (1948). *The people's choice* (7th ed.). New York: Columbia University Press.

Liang, T. P., Lai, H. J., & Ku, Y. C. (2006). Personalized content recommendation and user satisfaction: Theoretical synthesis and empirical findings. *Journal of Management Information Systems, 23*, 45–70.

Liu, Y., & Eveland, W. P. (2005). Education, need for cognition, and campaign interest as moderators of news effects on political knowledge: An analysis of the knowledge gap. *Journalism & Mass Communication Quarterly, 82*, 910–929.

Loges, W. E., & Jung, J. Y. (2001). Exploring the digital divide: Internet connectedness and age. *Communication Research, 28*, 536–562.

Lukensmeyer, C. J., Goldman, J., & Brigham, S. (2005). A town meeting for the Twenty-First Century. In J. Gastil and P. Levine (Eds.), *Deliberative democracy handbook* (pp. 154–163). San Francisco: Jossey-Bass.

MacKuen, M. (1981). Social communication and the mass policy agenda. In M. MacKuen & S. Coombs (Eds.), *More than news: Media power in public affairs* (pp. 19–144). Beverly Hills, CA: Sage.

Markus, H., & Zajonc, R. B. (1985). The cognitive perspective in social psychology. In G. Lindzey & E. Aronson (Eds.), *The handbook of social psychology* (3rd ed., pp. 137–230). New York. Random House.

Matei, S., & Ball-Rokeach, S. (2003). The Internet in the communication infrastructure of urban residential communities: Macro- or mesolinkage? *Journal of Communication, 53*, 642–657.

McCann, J. A., & Lawson, C. (2006). Presidential campaigns and the knowledge gap in three transitional democracies. *Political Research Quarterly, 59*, 13–22.

McCombs, M. E. (1977). Newspapers versus television: Mass communication effects across time. In D. Shaw & M. McCombs (Eds.), *The emergence of American political issues: The agenda-setting function of the press* (pp. 89–105). St. Paul, MN: West Publishing.

McCombs, M. E. (2004). *Setting the agenda: The mass media and public opinion*. Malden, MA: Blackwell.

McCombs, M. E., & Shaw, D. L. (1972). The agenda-setting function of the mass media. *Public Opinion Quarterly, 36*, 176–187.

McDevitt, M., & Chaffee, S. H. (1998). Second chance political socialization: Trickle-up effects of children on parents. In T. Johnson, C. Hays, & S. Hays (Eds.), *Engaging the public: How government and the media can reinvigorate American democracy* (pp. 57–74). New York: Rowman & Littlefield.

McDevitt, M., & Chaffee, S. H. (2000). Closing gaps in political knowledge: Effects of a school intervention program via communication in the home. *Human Communication Research, 27*, 259–292.

McDevitt, M., & Chaffee, S. H. (2002). From top-down to trickle-up influence: Revisiting the assumptions about the family in political socialization. *Political Communication, 19*, 281–301.

McGraw, K. M., & Ling, C. (2003). Media priming of presidential and group evaluations. *Political Communication, 20*, 23–40.

McLeod, D. M., Kosicki, G. M., & McLeod, J. M. (2002). Resurveying the boundaries of political communication effects. In J. Bryant and D. Zillmann (Eds.), *Media effects: Advances in theory and research* (2nd ed.) (pp. 215–267). Hillsdale, NJ: Erlbaum.

McLeod, D. M., & Perse, E. M. (1994). Direct and indirect effects of socioeconomic status on public affairs knowledge. *Journalism Quarterly, 71*, 433–442.

McLeod, J. M. (2000). Media and civic socialization of youth. *Journal of Adolescent Health, 27S*, 45–51.

McLeod, J. M., & Becker, L. B. (1974). Testing the validity of gratification measures through political effects analysis. In J. G. Blumler & E. Katz (Eds.), *The uses of mass communication: Current perspectives on gratifications research* (pp. 137–164). Beverly Hills, CA: Sage.

McLeod, J. M., Becker, L. B., & Byrnes, J. E. (1974). Another look at the agenda-setting function of the press. *Communication Research, 1*, 131–165.

McLeod, J. M., & Blumler, J. G. (1987). The macrosocial level of communication science. In S. Chaffee & C. Berger (Eds.), *Handbook of communication science* (pp. 271–322). Beverly Hills, CA: Sage.

McLeod, J. M., Bybee, C. R., & Durall, J. A. (1979). The 1976 presidential debates and the equivalence of informed political participation. *Communication Research, 6*, 463–487.

McLeod, J. M., Daily, C., Guo, Z., Eveland, W. P., Bayer, J., Yang, S., & Wang, H. (1996a). Community integration, local media use, and democratic processes. *Communication Research, 23*, 179–209.

McLeod, J. M., Eveland, W. P., & Horowitz, E. M. (1998a). Going beyond adults and voter turnout: Evaluations of a socialization program involving schools, family and the media. In T. Johnson, C. Hays, & S. Hays (Eds.), *Engaging the public: How government and the media can reinvigorate American democracy* (pp. 195–205). New York: Rowman & Littlefield.

McLeod, J. M., Guo, S., Daily, C., Steele, C., Huang, H., Horowitz, E., & Chen, H. (1996b). The impact of traditional and non-traditional media forms in the 1992 presidential election. *Journalism and Mass Communication Quarterly, 73*, 401–416.

McLeod, J. M., & McDonald, D. G. (1985). Beyond simple exposure: Media orientations and their impact on political processes. *Communication Research*, *12*, 3–33.

McLeod, J. M., Pan, Z., & Rucinski, D. (1995). Levels of analysis in public opinion research. In T. Glasser & C. Salmon (Eds.), *Public opinion and the communication of consent* (pp. 55–85). Hillsdale, NJ: Erlbaum.

McLeod, J. M., Scheufele, D. A., & Moy, P. (1999a). Community, communication, and participation: The role of mass media and interpersonal discussion in local participation in a public forum. *Political Communication*, *16*, 315–336.

McLeod, J. M., Scheufele, D. A., Moy, P., Horowitz, E. M., Holbert, R. L., Zhang, W., Zubric, S., & Zubric, J. (1999b). Understanding deliberation: The effects of discussion networks on participation in a public forum. *Communication Research*, *26*, 743–774.

McLeod, J. M., Sotirovic, M., & Holbert, R. L. (1998b). Values as sociotropic judgments influencing communication patterns. *Communication Research*, *25*, 453–480.

Miller, W. E., & Shanks, J. (1996). *The New American Voter*. Cambridge, MA: Harvard University Press.

Mossberger, K., Tolbert, C. J., & Stansbury, M. (2003). *Virtual inequality: Beyond the digital divide*. Georgetown: Georgetown University Press.

Moy, P., & Pfau, M. W. (2000). *With malice towards all? The media and public confidence in democratic institutions*. Westport, CT: Greenwood Publishing Group Inc.

Mutz, D. C. (2006). *Hearing the other side: Deliberative versus participatory democracy*. New York: Cambridge University Press.

Neuman, W. R. (1986). *The paradox of mass politics: Knowledge and opinion in the American electorate*. Cambridge, MA: Harvard University Press.

Neuman, W. R., Just, M. R., & Crigler, A. N. (1992). *Common knowledge: News and the construction of political meaning*. Chicago: University of Chicago Press.

Neuwirth, K., Frederick, E., & Mayo, C. (2007). The spiral of silence and fear of isolation. *Journal of Communication*, *57*, 450–468.

Niemi, R. G. (1999). Editor's introduction. *Political Psychology*, *20*, 471–476.

Niemi, R. G., Hepburn, M. A., & Chapman, C. (2000). Community service by high school students: A cure for civic ills? *Political Behavior*, *22*, 45–69.

Niemi, R. G., & Junn, J. (1998). *Civic education: What makes students learn*. New Haven, CT: Yale University Press.

Noelle-Neumann, E. (1984). *The spiral of silence: Public opinion—our social skin*. Chicago: University of Chicago Press.

O'Keefe, G. J., Rosenbaum, D. P., Lavrakas, P. J., Reid, K., & Botta, R. A. (1996). *Taking a bite out of crime: The impact of the National Citizens' Crime Prevention Media Campaign*. Thousand Oaks, CA: Sage.

Overton, S. (2006). *Stealing democracy: The new politics of voter suppression*. New York: W. W. Norton.

Packard Foundation Report (2001). Reported in *The New York Times*, January 22, A11.

Pan, Z., & Kosicki, G. M. (1997). Priming and media impact on the evaluations of the president's performance. *Communication Research*, *24*, 3–30.

Pan, Z., & Kosicki, G. M. (2001). Framing as a strategic action in public deliberation. In S. D. Reese, O. H. Gandy. Jr., & A. E. Grant (Eds.), *Framing public life: Perspectives on media and our understanding of the social world* (pp. 35–65). Mahwah, NJ: Erlbaum.

Pan, Z., & McLeod, J. M. (1991). Multi-level analysis in mass communication research. *Communication Research*, *18*, 140–173.

Patterson, T. E. (1980). *The mass media election: How Americans choose their president*. New York: Praeger.

Peiser, W. (2000). Cohort replacement and the downward trend in newspaper readership. *Newspaper Research Journal*, *21*(2), 11–23.

Popkin, S. L. (1991). *The reasoning voter. Communication and persuasion in presidential campaigns*. Chicago: University of Chicago Press.

Price, V., & Cappella, J. N. (2002). Deliberation and its influence: The electronic dialogue project in campaign 2000. *IT and Society, 1*, 303–329.

Price, V., Ritchie, L. D., & Eulau, H. (1991). Micro-macro issues in communication research. *Communication Research, 18*, 133–273.

Price, V., & Tewksbury, D. (1997). News values and public opinion: A theoretical account of media priming and framing. In G. Barnett and F. J. Boster (Eds.), *Progress in communication sciences* (pp. 173–212). Greenwich, CT: Ablex.

Price, V., Tewksbury, D., & Powers, E. (1997). Switching trains of thought: The impact of news frames on reader's cognitive responses. *Communication Research, 24*, 481–506.

Putnam, R. D. (1995). Bowling alone: America's declining social capital. *Journal of Democracy, 6*(1), 65–78.

Putnam, R. D. (2000). *Bowling alone: the collapse and revival of American community*. New York: Simon & Schuster.

Reeves, B., Thorson, E., & Schleuder, J. (1986). Attention to television: Psychological theories and chronometric measures. In J. Bryant & D. Zillmann (Eds.), *Perspectives on media effects* (pp. 251–279). Hillsdale, NJ: Erlbaum.

Rice, R. E., & Atkin, C. K. (2000). *Public communication campaigns* (3rd ed.). Thousand Oaks, CA: Sage.

Roberts, D. F. (2000). Media and youth: Access, exposure and privatization. *Journal of Adolescent Health, 27S*, 8–14.

Rubin, R. (1976). *Party dynamics: The Democratic coalition and the politics of change*. New York: Oxford University Press.

Sanders, L. M. (1997). Against deliberation. *Political Theory*, 25, 347–376.

Scheufele, D. A., Hardy, B., Brossard, D., Waismel-Manor, I. S., & Nisbet, E.C. (2006). Democracy based on difference: Examining the links between structural heterogeneity, heterogeneity of discussion networks, and democratic citizenship. *Journal of Communication, 56*, 728–753.

Scheufele, D. A., & Tewksbury, D. (2007). Framing, agenda setting, and priming: The evolution of three media effects models. *Journal of Communication, 57*, 9–20.

Sears, D. O., & Chaffee, S. H. (1979). Uses and effects of the 1976 debates: An overview of empirical studies. In S. Kraus (Ed.), *The great debates, 1976: Ford vs. Carter* (pp. 223–261). Bloomington: Indiana University Press.

Shah, D. V. (1998). Civic engagement, interpersonal trust, and television use: An individual level assessment of social capital. *Political Psychology, 19*, 469–496.

Shah, D. V. (2001). The collision of convictions: Value framing and value judgments. In R. P. Hart & D. R. Shaw (Eds.), *Communication in U.S. elections* (pp. 55–74). Lanham, MD: Rowman & Littlefield.

Shah, D. V., Cho, J., Eveland, W. P., & Kwak, N. (2005). Information and expression in the digital age: Modeling Internet effects on civic participation. *Communication Research, 32*, 531–565.

Shah, D. V., Cho, J., Nah, S., Gotlieb, M. R., Hwang, H., Lee, N. J., Scholl, R. M., & McLeod, D. M. (2007). Campaign ads, online messaging, and participation: Extending the communication mediation model. *Journal of Communication, 57*, 676–703.

Shah, D. V., Kwak, N., & Holbert, R. L. (2001). "Connecting" and "disconnecting" with civic life: Patterns of Internet use and the production of social capital. *Political Communication, 18*, 141–162.

Shah, D. V., Kwak, N., & Schmierbach, M. (2000, November). Digital Media in America: Practices, Preferences and Policy Implications. Final report produced for the Digital Media Forum/Ford Foundation.

Shah, D. V., Kwak, N., Schmierbach, M., & Zubric, J. (2004). The interplay of news frames on cognitive complexity. *Human Communication Research, 30*, 102–120.

Shah, D. V., McLeod, J. M., & Yoon, S. H. (2001). Communication, context, and community: An exploration of print, broadcast, and Internet influences. *Communication Research, 28*, 464–506.

Shah, D. V., Schmierbach, M. G., Hawkins, J., Espino, R., & Donavan, J. (2002). Nonrecursive models of Internet use and community engagement questioning whether time spent online erodes social capital. *Journalism and Mass Communication Quarterly, 79*, 964–987.

Shane, P. (Ed.). (2004). *Democracy online: The prospects for political renewal through the Internet*. New York: Routledge.

Shen, F. (2004). Chronic accessibility and individual cognitions: Examining the effects of message frames in political advertisements. *Journal of Communication, 54*, 123–137.

Shen, F. Y., & Edwards, H. H. (2005). Economic individualism, humanitarianism, and welfare reform: A value-based account of framing effects. *Journal of Communication, 55*, 795–809.

Sirianni, C. J., & Friedland, L. A. (2001). *Civic innovation in America: Community, empowerment, public policy, and the movement for civic renewal*. Berkeley, CA: University of California Press.

Smith, H. H. III. (1986). Newspaper readership as a determinant of political knowledge and activity. *Newspaper Research Journal, 7*(2), 47–54.

Sniderman, P. M., & Theriault, S. M. (2004). The structure of political argument and the logic of issue framing. In W. Saris & P. M. Sniderman (Eds.), *Studies in public opinion* (pp. 133–165). Princeton NJ: Princeton University Press.

Sotirovic, M. (2001a). Affective and cognitive processes as mediators of media influence on crime policy preferences. *Mass Communication and Society, 3*, 269–296.

Sotirovic, M. (2001b). Effects of media use on complexity and extremity of attitudes toward the death penalty and prisoners' rehabilitation. *Media Psychology, 3*, 1–24.

Sotirovic, M. (2003). How individuals explain social problems: The influences of media use. *Journal of Communication, 33*, 122–137.

Sotirovic, M., & McLeod, J. M. (2001). Values, communication behavior, and political participation. *Political Communication, 18*, 273–300.

Sotirovic, M., & McLeod, J. M. (2004). Knowledge as understanding: The information processing approach to political learning. In L. Kaid (Ed.), *Handbook of Political Communication Research* (pp. 357–394). Mahwah, NJ: Erlbaum.

Sotirovic, M., & McLeod, J. M. (2008). U.S. election coverage. In J. Stromback & L. Kaid (Eds.). *Handbook of election coverage around the world*. Mahwah, NJ: Erlbaum.

Stamm, K. R., Emig, A. G., & Hesse, M. B. (1997). The contribution of local media to community involvement. *Journalism & Mass Communication Quarterly, 74*, 97–107.

Star, S. A., & Hughes, H. M. (1950). Report on an education campaign: The Cincinnati plan for the UN. *American Journal of Sociology, 55*, 389–400.

Strate, J. M., Parrish, C. J., Elder, C. D., & Ford, C., III. (1989). Life span and civic development and voting participation. *American Political Science Review, 83*, 443–464.

Sunstein, C. (2006). *Infotopia: How many minds produce knowledge*. New York: Oxford University Press.

Teixeira, R. A. (1992). *The disappearing American voter*. Washington, DC: Brookings.

Tichenor, P. J., Donohue, G. A., & Olien, C. N. (1980). *Community conflict and the press*. Beverly Hills, CA: Sage.

Tichenor, P. J., Donohue, G. A., & Olien, C. N. (1970). Mass media flow and differential growth of knowledge. *Public Opinion Quarterly, 34*, 159–170.

Tipton, L. P., Haney, R. D., & Basehart, J. R. (1975). Media agenda-setting in city and state election campaigns. *Journalism Quarterly, 52*, 15–22.

Valentino, N. A., Beckmann, M. N., & Buhr, T. A. (2001). A spiral of cynicism for some: the contingent effects of campaign news frames on participation and confidence in government. *Political Communication, 18*, 347–367.

Vallone, R. P., Ross, L., & Lepper, M. R. (1985). The hostile media phenomenon: Biased perception and perceptions of media bias in coverage of the "Beirut Massacre." *Journal of Personality and Social Psychology, 49*, 577–585.

Viswanath, K., Breen, N., Meissner, H., Moser, R. P., Hesse, B., Steele, W. R., & Rakowski, W. (2006). Cancer knowledge and disparities in the information age. *Journal of Health Communication, 11*(S1), 1–17.

Viswanath, K., & Finnegan, J. R. (1996). The Knowledge Gap Hypothesis: Twenty-five years later. In B. Burleson (Ed.), *Communication Yearbook 19* (pp. 187–227). Thousand Oaks, CA: Sage.

Wattenberg, M. P. (1984). *The decline of American political parties, 1952–1980*. Cambridge, MA: Harvard University Press.

Weaver, D. H., Graber, D. A., McCombs, M. E., & Eyal, C. H. (1981). *Media agenda-setting in a presidential election: Issues, images and interests*. New York: Praeger.

Weaver, P. (1972). Is television news biased? *Public Interest*, Winter, 57–74.

Wolfinger, R. E., & Rosenstone, S. J. (1980). *Who votes?* New Haven, CT: Yale University Press.

Xenos, M., & Moy, P. (2007). Direct and differential effects of the Internet on political and civic engagement. *Journal of Communication*, *57*, 704–718.

Yang, K. C. C. (2004). Effects of consumer motives on search behavior using Internet advertising. *Cyberpsychology & Behavior*, *7*, 430–442.

Young, D. G. (2004). Late-night comedy in election 2000: Its influence on candidate trait ratings and the moderating effects of political knowledge and partisanship. *Journal of Broadcasting and Electronic Media*, *48*, 1–22.

Youniss, J., McLellan, J. A., & Yates, M. (1997). What we know about engendering civic identity. *American Behavioral Scientist*, *40*, 620–631.

Zaller, J. R. (1992). *The nature and origin of mass opinion*. New York: Cambridge University Press.

12

MASS MEDIA, SOCIAL PERCEPTION, AND THE THIRD-PERSON EFFECT

Richard M. Perloff
Cleveland State University

What effect do the media have on you? Does news change your mind about issues? Do political commercials influence your beliefs? Does television violence make you more aggressive? Not really, you say. You make up your own mind, you form your own ideas about politics and products, and you're not much fazed by TV crime shows, though goodness knows, you've watched your share of them over the years. Okay—do me this favor, estimate the impact that news, commercials, and television violence have on other people. That is, guess how they influence other individuals who tune them in. Say what? You think that news, advertising, and TV violence have a strong effect on other people? That others buy into what they see in the newspaper, on television, and their computer screens?

Do we have a problem, Houston? Is there an inconsistency here?

According to the third-person effect hypothesis, there is. If you are right that other people are influenced by media, then it certainly stands to reason that you too should be affected. On the other hand, if you are correct that you're not affected and everyone else presumably claims the same lack of media influence, then you exaggerate the impact of media on others. "In either case," as James Tiedge and his colleagues (1991) noted, "most people appear to be willing to subscribe to the logical inconsistency inherent in maintaining that the mass media influence others considerably more than themselves" (Tiedge, Silverblatt, Havice, & Rosenfeld, 1991, p. 152).

Welcome to the domain of the third-person effect—a complex, labyrinth-like area in which perceptions become reality, reality is enshrouded by perceptions, and perceptions hinge on the very important factor of whether you are considering the media's impact on other people or yourself. As uses and gratifications did in the 1970s, the third-person effect hypothesis turns conventional media effects theorizing on its head. Instead of looking at media effects on beliefs, it examines beliefs about media effects. Rather than just assuming that media affect perceptions, it assumes that perceptions of media trigger behavioral effects. Indeed, it paradoxically posits that one of the strongest influences of media is the presumption that they have influences, stipulating that this presumption can itself engender a series of actions that would have been unthinkable in the absence of mediated communications.

A theoretical perspective of this kind is bound to generate interest, and the third-person effect has been nothing if not interesting to researchers. Ranked as the fifth most popular theory in 21st century mass communication research (Bryant & Miron, 2004), the third-person approach has generated hundreds of journal articles and convention papers, as well as an integrative volume (Andsager & White, 2007). What makes the effect all the more salient is that examples can be glimpsed easily in everyday life in contexts encompassing politics, celebrities, and advertising.

One recalls an intriguing CBS News poll, conducted when President Clinton was in the throes of the Monica Lewinsky scandal. The poll probed whether respondents believed that other people were more interested in news reports of President Clinton's sex life than they were. Only 7% of respondents indicated that they were fascinated by news stories on Clinton's sex life; 37% confessed they were mildly curious; and 50% claimed that they were not interested at all. Yet when asked to judge most people's interest in the stories, respondents reacted much differently. Twenty-five percent of the same sample said most people were fascinated, 49% claimed most people were mildly curious, and only 18% believed that most people harbored no interest at all (Berke, 1998).

An article on young children's fascination with celebrity gossip offers another view of self-other disparities. In speaking with a reporter, 11-year-old Arielle Urvater and her eight-year-old sister Jessie displayed an easy familiarity with the media antics of celebrity "bad girls" Lindsey Lohan, Paris Hilton, and Britney Spears. The girls knew all about the starlets' eating disorders, drinking problems, and misadventures. But did this translate into a belief that they were influenced by what they saw? "We're well educated," the 11-year-old explained. "We know that drugs aren't good and that smoking isn't good." On the other hand, she was quick to observe, girls her age cannot help but be affected by what they see in the media (Rosenbloom, 2007, p. 8).

A moment of introspection reveals how easy it is to uncover third-person perceptions in prosaic activities of everyday life. If you have ever thought twice about going to the mall to buy a highly advertised video game, out of fear that electronic stores would be packed with feverish customers influenced by glitzy ads promoting the product, you have fallen prey to the third-person perception. If you know someone who felt impelled to go on a diet because she assumed that everyone around her emulated thin models depicted in media advertisements, you can appreciate a third-person approach.

The third-person effect is a relatively new concept, as social science constructs go. It was invented in 1983 by sociologist W. Phillips Davison in a clever article that drew on intuition and public opinion theory. The third-person effect is an individual's perception that a message will exert a stronger impact on others than on the self. The "third-person" term derives from the expectation that a message will not have its greatest influence on "me" (the grammatical first person), or "you" (the second person), but on "them"—the third persons. Individuals may overestimate the impact media exert on others, underestimate effects on the self, or both.

Third-person biases probably operated throughout human history. People have long feared that new media—encompassing the written word in Plato's time, comic books in the 1950s, and violent video games in our own era—would have negative influences on others. However, these perceptions are of greater consequence today than in the pre-mass society era. When people's experiences of the world were limited by the contours of their communities and their life-space was restricted to the little towns in which they grew up, there was no possibility for opinions to spiral out and influence the world at large. Life is different today. Public opinion exerts a significant impact on social behavior and affects mass and elite decisions. Consequently, perceptions of public opinion can have direct and indirect "ripple" effects, particularly when these perceptions are widely reported in the mass media (Mutz, 1998). Indeed, the media have profoundly changed the calculus of perceived social influence. Albert C. Gunther and his colleagues have called attention to ways in which vivid portrayals, media formal features, and the wide-ranging reach of media invite attributions of strong effects. "Media direct attention outward, to the mass media audience and the undesirable influence that audience may experience," Gunther and Schmitt (2004, p. 69) observed. Contemporary mass media direct the gaze of individuals onto the audience, leading them to infer that the audience must be affected. This is itself a media effect.

Although the third-person effect is more hypothesis than full-blown theory, it has roots firmly planted in venerable communication concepts and respected research traditions. It is one of a family of concepts that bridges sociology and psychology and focuses on perceptions of social reality (Glynn, Ostman, & McDonald, 1995). A cross-disciplinary construct, it centers on public opinion, communication, and psychological processes. From a public opinion perspective, the third-person effect is subjectivist in its emphasis on perceived public opinion. As a communication concept, with roots in symbolic interactionism, it focuses on the intersection between self and other, the interaction between what I think and assume others think. By focusing not on just self or other, but their dynamic interaction seen through the prism of media effects, the third-person effect has strong foundations in communication.

At the same time, its emphasis on perception gives the third-person effect a strong psychological flavor. The third-person effect links up with the social psychology of risk, particularly the tendency to separate out judgments of risk for oneself and society at large (Tyler & Cook, 1984). The most direct linkage is with models of unrealistic optimism (Weinstein, 1980) and self-serving biases, notably people's self-serving tendency to assume that they are better than average and less susceptible to personal harm than everyone else.

The centerpiece of the third-person effect is perception and the implicit assumption that perceptions are not fixed at some final Archimedean point, but vary as a function of the gaze of the perceiver (toward others or self). Decidedly Western in its bifurcation of the subject (self) and the object (the world outside), the third-person effect hypothesis distinctively departs from other related public opinion concepts in its emphasis on the message or more precisely, the perceived effects of the message. What makes the effect all the more conceptually intriguing is the way individual-level perceptions of message influences play out on the larger social stage, interfacing with public and policy processes.

RESEARCH FINDINGS

The third-person effect (TPE) has been studied by asking participants to estimate communication effects on others and themselves. In many studies, individuals read or view a specific message and indicate their beliefs about the communication's impact on third persons and the self. In other investigations, participants estimate effects of a particular media genre on others and the self. Across different studies, contexts, and methodological procedures third-person effects emerge. Consider the following findings:

- A national sample of U.S. respondents estimated that the news media had a greater impact on others' opinions of the 1996 presidential candidates than on their own views (Salwen, 1998). More recently, research has found that individuals perceived others to be more influenced than themselves by news of the "millennium bug" in Y2K and environmental problems (Jensen & Hurley, 2005; Tewksbury, Moy, & Weis, 2004). In Israel, Tel Aviv residents believed that news of controversial development towns exerted a stronger influence on others than the self (Tsfati & Cohen, 2004). People maintain that opinion polls have little or no impact on themselves, while exerting a considerable influence on others (Pan, Abisaid, Paek, Sun, & Houden, 2006; Price & Stroud, 2006).

- Third-person perceptions also emerge in judgments about advertising. Individuals perceived that other people were more influenced than themselves by commercials for household products, liquor and beer, and cigarettes (Gunther & Thorson, 1992; Shah, Faber, & Youn, 1999). Even children exhibit third-person perceptions. Elementary and middle school students perceived that cigarette ads have a significantly greater impact on others than themselves (Henriksen & Flora, 1999).
- Extending the perceptual hypothesis to entertainment media, Gunther (1995) found that over 60% of U.S. adults believe that others are more negatively influenced by pornography than themselves. Similar findings emerge for antisocial rap music lyrics, television violence, and Internet pornography (Lee & Tamborini, 2005; McLeod, Eveland, & Nathanson, 1997; Salwen & Dupagne, 1999; Scharrer, 2002).
- Extrapolating the third-person effect from perceived media effects to perceptions of media uses, Peiser and Peter (2000) reported that German adults believe others are more likely than they are to gravitate to undesirable television viewing behaviors, such as escape and habit. By contrast, respondents perceived that they were more inclined to desirable TV viewing behaviors, like information seeking.

Even stronger support for the pervasiveness of the third-person effect is provided by a meta-analysis of 32 published and unpublished studies of the perceptual hypothesis. Using meta-analytic techniques to determine the strength of the perceptual effect, Paul, Salwen, and Dupagne (2000) found substantial support for the third-person perception. The effect size, or magnitude of difference between estimated media effects on self and others, was $r = .50$, considerably larger than that reported for the effect of TV violence on antisocial behavior ($r = .31$) and pornography on aggression ($r = .13$; cf. Paul et al., 2000). Sun, Pan, and Shen (2008), using a larger sample and more refined meta-analytic procedures, also reported a significant effect size for the third-person perception. Although the effect size they obtained ($r = .31$) was somewhat smaller than Paul et al.'s, Sun and her colleagues concluded the effect was robust and held up across different research conditions.

IS IT REAL OR ARTIFACT?

Third-person effects have emerged with such regularity that it is only natural for skeptics to wonder if the effects are real or in some sense artificial. Have researchers unwittingly encouraged respondents to make third-person perceptions by asking biased questions or framing the questions in such a way so as to lead respondents to exaggerate media effects on others?

Brosius and Engel (1996), hypothesizing that grammar is everything, argued that participants might be unwilling to acknowledge effects on self simply because the question "What impact does advertising have on you?" treats the respondent as the object of effects, an acknowledgment that people would rather not make. Reasoning that people might be more willing to acknowledge effects when the phrasing makes the respondent the active subject ("I let myself be influenced by advertising when I go shopping") than when it refers to the respondent in the typically passive fashion, Brosius and Engel varied the phrasing of questions, only to find that the third-person effect emerged regardless of how the question was worded.

If question wording does not attenuate the third-person effect, perhaps the order of questions does. Critics have speculated that the practice of asking self-other questions in a back-to-back format encourages individuals to contrast responses to a media-effects-on-others question with that of a media-effects-on-self query (Price & Tewksbury, 1996). The first question can serve as an anchor for the second, leading respondents to interpret the second in light of the orientation of the first. For example, answering the media-impact-on-others question first might lead respondents to estimate large effects on others and then to adjust the impact on self downward to preserve self-esteem. Such a contrast might not happen if respondents were asked to estimate effects on self first or if they were asked to make only a single estimate of media impact (either on themselves or others) rather than doing both.

A number of studies have examined whether the third-person effect disappears when question order is counterbalanced or experimentally manipulated. The answer that emerges from the overwhelming number of studies is: No, the effect persists, regardless of question order or format (e.g., Gunther, 1995; Price & Tewksbury, 1996; Salwen & Driscoll, 1997). Indeed, David, Liu, and Myser (2004), in a rigorous examination of methodological artifacts, found the third-person effect continued to emerge in a between-subjects design where one group of participants was asked to estimate perceived message impact on self and a different group was asked to judge perceived influence on others.

There remains a question about the frequency with which people attribute message effects to third persons in real life. Perhaps some people do not even think about third persons, let alone mass media effects, and the extent to which this occurs in everyday settings remains an interesting empirical question.

WHY THEE (AND THEM) MORE THAN ME?

At the heart of every political philosophy is an appraisal of human nature (Oreskes, 2000). The same is true of social scientific theories. What makes the TPE hypothesis intriguing is that explanatory mechanisms stake out different appraisals of human motivation and cognition (see Figure 12.1).

The prevailing interpretation is that the third-person effect is a subset of a universal human tendency to perceive the self in ways that make us look good or at least better than other people. Admitting that one has been influenced by media may be tantamount to acknowledging gullibility or that the self possesses socially undesirable traits. By assuming the self is invulnerable to communication effects while others are naively susceptible, individuals preserve a positive sense of self and reaffirm their belief that they are superior to others.

A second interpretation is that people are motivated by a need to control unpredictable life events. If we believed that every media program or stimulus had strong effects on us, we would be basket cases. By assuming that the self is not influenced by mass media, individuals can go about their days in a media-dominated world, using media, deriving gratifications, and sensibly integrating media into their lives.

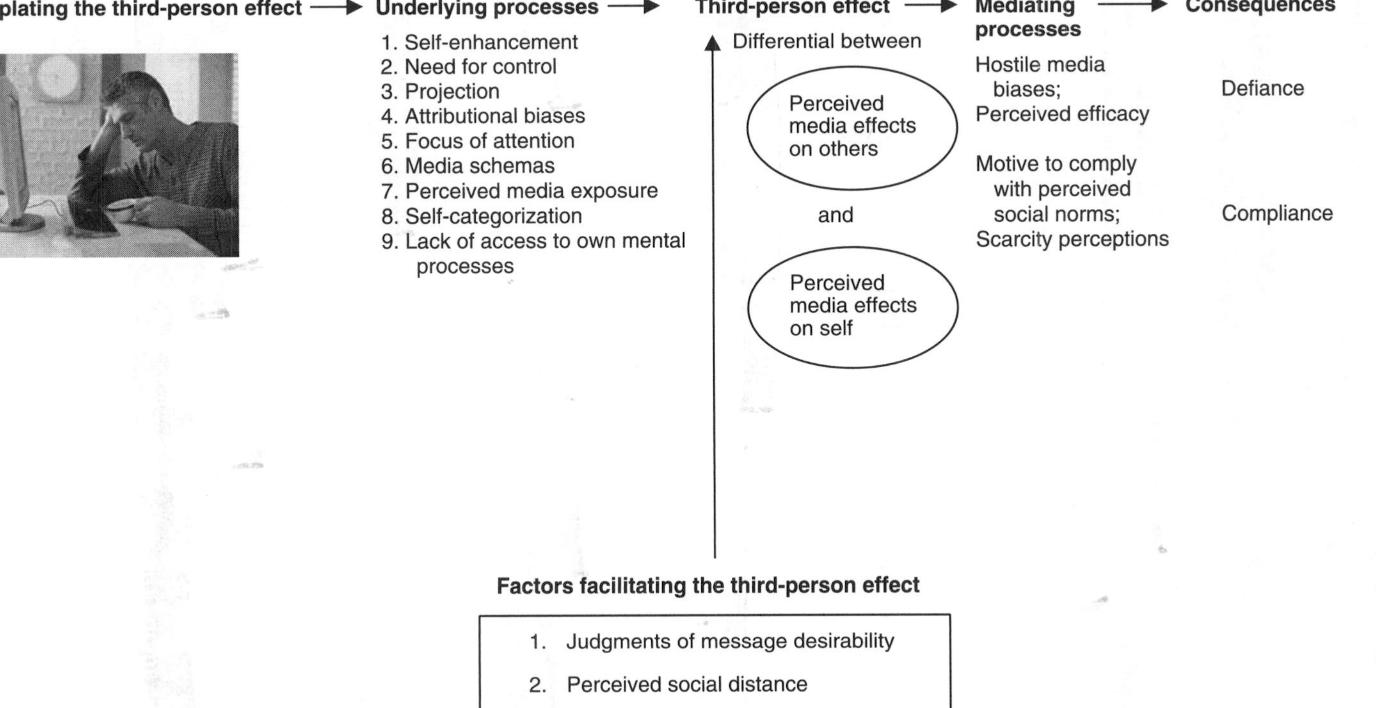
Contemplating the third-person effect
Underlying processes
1. Self-enhancement
2. Need for control
3. Projection
4. Attributional biases
5. Focus of attention
6. Media schemas
7. Perceived media exposure
8. Self-categorization
9. Lack of access to own mental processes
Third-person effect
Differential between
Perceived media effects on others
and
Perceived media effects on self
Mediating processes
Hostile media biases;
Perceived efficacy
Motive to comply with perceived social norms;
Scarcity perceptions
Consequences
Defiance
Compliance
Factors facilitating the third-person effect
1. Judgments of message desirability
2. Perceived social distance

Figure 12.1 The Third-Person Effect: Processes and Consequences.[1]

A third, related, explanation invokes projection, a psychodynamic process. According to this view, people are actually influenced by media, but cannot consciously acknowledge media influence. Admitting to media effects would threaten individuals' valued sense of self or reduce their perception of control over external events. As a result, people project media effects onto others, perhaps to defensively distance themselves from undesirable components of self that they would rather not acknowledge (Schimel, Greenberg, Pyszczynski, O'Mahen, & Arndt, 2000).

Other interpretations of the third-person effect emphasize cognitive, rather than motivational, mechanisms. An attributional approach assumes that people attribute their own actions to situational factors, but believe that others' behavior is governed by personality dispositions. Applying this to the third-person effect, Gunther (1991) suggested that when estimating media effects on themselves, people take into account the role played by external factors like persuasive intent. But when judging message effects on third persons, observers assume that others' dispositional shortcomings (e.g., gullibility) render them incapable of factoring in situational factors like persuasive intent. This logically leads observers to the conclusion that others will yield to messages that they see through (Lasorsa, 1992). More generally, people employ different criteria to determine perceived message effects on others than they use to judge perceived influences on the self (McLeod, Detenber, & Eveland, 2001).

A fifth and related interpretation calls attention to individuals' differential cognitive perspectives on themselves and others. More mentally attentive to their own dispositions than those of others, people notice that they have the wherewithal to see through harmful media content. Lacking this knowledge of others, they presume third persons are susceptible to media effects. When 11-year-old Arielle Urvater noted that she and her sister were "well educated" and therefore capable of recognizing the negative aspects of celebrity behavior, she evidenced this cognitive awareness.

A sixth view emphasizes media schemas. According to this view, people possess simple schemas of media effects—the time-honored hypodermic needle model, coupled with a "passive sheep" view of audience behavior. When asked to estimate media effects, respondents activate these beliefs and apply them to survey questions.

A seventh view also emphasizes lay theories of media effects, but with a focus on perceived media exposure. According to this account, observers assume that groups most susceptible to media fare are those with the greatest exposure to the content in question. Thus, third-person perceptions are rooted in observers' beliefs that audience members are exposed to media content, coupled with the assumption that with greater exposure comes stronger effects (Eveland, Nathanson, Detenber, & McLeod, 1999).

An eighth explanation emphasizes self-categorization, or how people view themselves in comparison with others (Reid & Hogg, 2005). Redressing an imbalance in the literature by focusing on group identification, this account stipulates that individuals try to determine the fit among themselves, a group of third persons, and the message. If, for example, observers perceive that a message is congruent with the values of a particular group, they assume that members of this group will naturally go along with the message. When the message is viewed as congenial with the "in-group"—one's own group, people on "my" side of the issue—an analogous process occurs. Individuals acknowledge that they will accept the message more readily than others. A reverse third-person effect or first-person effect ensues. On a broader level, this view calls attention to the ways that group membership can propel people to categorize others in particular ways and make assumptions about their susceptibility to media effects (e.g., Duck, Hogg, & Terry, 1995).

The ninth interpretation focuses on the flip side of the third-person issue—why individuals do not acknowledge media effects on themselves. It notes that people lack access to their own mental processes (Nisbett & Wilson, 1977) or do not have detailed episodic memory for previous behavior. Thus, if people employ audience prototypes to estimate media effects on others and engage in automatic thinking when it comes to their own media behavior, it is easy to understand why they might assume that others are more affected by mass communications than they are themselves.

There is considerable evidence consistent with a self-enhancement interpretation of the third-person effect (Andsager & White, 2007; see next section on message desirability). Even so, self-enhancement cannot account for all the findings. Other interpretations, such as perceived exposure, usefully explain some third-person effect findings. We lack air-tight, meta-analytic evidence to show that one view is more compelling than the others. A major reason is that the various interpretations overlap and simultaneously call on both cognitive and motivational processes. For example, individuals may categorize themselves in a particular way or compare themselves to hypothetical others for self-protective, as well as cognitive, reasons. Judgments that certain people are more susceptible to media effects may be based on reasonable inferences about who watches lots of television, biased assumptions that marginalized groups are more prone to watch TV (Scharrer, 2002), or on ego-enhancing presumptions that the self or in-group is too intelligent to waste time paying attention to particular media fare.

Efforts to tease out self-enhancement from cognitive processes are notoriously difficult (as is the related problem of discriminating overestimation of effects on others from underestimation of effects on the self; see Gunther, 1991 and Douglas & Sutton, 2004). Thus, until underlying processes are more carefully delineated or methodological techniques developed to permit more exact parceling out of mechanisms, it is prudent to adopt a pluralistic approach that recognizes that third-person effects are multiply determined.

WHAT CONDITIONS INFLUENCE THE STRENGTH OF THE TPE?

Early research on the third-person effect suggested that it was a universal phenomenon, one that emerged every time individuals were asked to estimate media effects on others and the self. With more research and inevitable dampening of panglossian perceptions has come the realization that, like most things in science, the effect is more likely to occur under particular conditions. What are the major factors that delimit third-person perceptions? The next section addresses this question.

Message Attributes

Self-enhancement theories tell us that people should be loath to admit that they are influenced by messages when such admission reflects negatively on the self. Third-person effects should be particularly pronounced when the message is perceived as undesirable—that is, when people infer that "this message may not be so good for me" or "it's not cool to admit you're influenced by this media program." In line with these predictions, research finds that people perceive content that is typically thought to be antisocial to have a larger impact on others than on themselves (e.g., television violence, pornography, antisocial rap). Indeed, violent and hateful messages have produced the strongest third-person perceptions in many studies (Andsager & White, 2007).

The flip side of these findings is more interesting. According to a self-enhancement view, if the third-person effect is driven by a desire to preserve self-esteem, people should be willing to acknowledge effects for communications that are regarded as socially desirable, healthy, or otherwise good for the self (Hoorens & Ruiter, 1996).

Research substantiates these predictions. People say they are more influenced than others by advertisements with positive emotional content, but not by neutral ads (Gunther & Thorson, 1992). They acknowledge greater personal influence for a persuasive message with strong, but not weak, arguments (White, 1997). When AIDS prevention ads are of high professional quality, students estimate they will be influenced more than others, but revert to a third-person effect for ads of low quality (Duck, Terry, & Hogg, 1995). Undergraduates perceive that others will be more influenced than themselves by cigarette ads but are quick to assume that they will be more affected by anti-tobacco and drunk-driving PSAs (Meirick, 2005; see also David, Liu, & Myser, 2004).

Thus, there is growing evidence of *first-person effects*. People will sometimes claim to be more influenced by messages than others. (The extent to which perceived self-influence equals authentic attitude change is another question.) First-person effects seem to emerge when agreement with the message reflects positively on the self, and to some degree when the message touches on topics that are congruent with the orientation of groups with which individuals identify.

In the past, these determinants of first- and third-person effects have been discussed under the umbrella of message characteristics. Increasingly, researchers believe that individuals' *social judgments* about the message determine the degree to which perceived message effects emerge.

Nature of the Others

Up to this point, I have implicitly treated the "third persons" in the third-person effect as a singular whole, making no effort to break the term down into smaller parts. But this oversimplifies matters. The nature of hypothetical audience members plays an important role in third-person perceptions. The magnitude of the third-person effect hinges on the particular others that observers have in mind when they estimate media effects. This is the heart of the *social distance corollary*, the notion that self-other disparities grow in magnitude with increases in perceived distance between self and comparison others.

There is empirical support for social distance predictions (e.g., Meirick, 2005; Tsfati & Cohen, 2004). After meta-analyzing the research, Andsager and White (2007) concluded that "Research consistently finds that others who are anchored to self as a point of reference are perceived to be less influenced by persuasive messages than are others who are not defined and, therefore, not anchored to any point of reference at all" (p. 92).

Even so, complications remain. Perceived social distance can encompass perceived similarity and predispositions of socially distant others (Meirick, 2005), size of the hypothetical audience (Tewskbury, 2002), and the extent to which the others are seen as members of a favorably-evaluated in-group or unfavorably-judged out-group (Duck, Hogg, & Terry, 1995; Meirick, 2004). What's more, the American public or public opinion is not only more removed from the self than "other university students"; it is also a more general, differentiated category. Complicating matters, as Tsfati and Cohen

(2004) pointed out, hypothetical others can be close to the self, but removed from the topic or distant from the self and close to the topic at hand. In their study, Israeli students assumed that news about Israeli settlements would have greater impact on other students, who were close to them but removed from the topic, than on Israeli settlers, who were remote from them, but close to the topic. Another complication lies in the fact that there may be cases in which specific others are viewed as more influenced than general, undefined others (Meirick, 2005; see also Neuwirth & Frederick, 2002). According to the *target corollary*, to the degree that a group is viewed as the target of a particular message, the perceived impact on group members will theoretically be greater (Meirick, 2005). (A complication is that one might predict under some conditions, such as ego-involvement, group members should be *less* influenced by messages; see Huge, Glynn, & Jeong, 2006. Thus, the theory underlying the target corollary needs to be explicated.) Andsager and White helpfully note that both corollaries draw on the social judgment theory notion of anchoring, with social distance focusing on the degree to which observers take the self as a point of reference and the target corollary focusing on the extent to which individuals take the message as a reference point. Even so, ambiguities in the meaning of social distance remain and lie behind different findings in the research literature (e.g., Andsager & White, 2007; Sun et al., 2008).

Summary

Synthesizing the literature, research indicates that third-person effects are most likely to occur when individuals: (a) perceive the message is undesirable or believe that message acceptance reflects negatively on the self; (b) view the hypothetical others as vulnerable to influence (Sun et al., 2008); (c) judge that the audience is composed of undefined others, who are not anchored to the self as a point of reference; and (d) perceive that the message is conveyed by mass media that reach a broad audience (Gunther & Schmitt, 2004). There is strong evidence for (a) (Sun, Pan, & Shen, 2008), solid support for (c) (though see Sun et al., 2008), and some evidence for (b) and (d).

Individual Differences

There is little evidence that demographic factors such as age, education, and gender reliably produce self-other disparities (Andsager & White, 2007; Paul, Salwen, & Dupagne, 2000). Thus, researchers have argued that psychological processes may be more crucial than exogenous factors like age or education in explaining third-person effects. Although a handful of individual difference factors (i.e., self-perceived knowledge; see Driscoll & Salwen, 1997) have been implicated as influencing third-person perceptions, the evidence for their impact is diminished by the paucity of theoretical underpinnings and empirical studies. One concept that has emerged with considerable regularity, stimulating theoretical and practical debate in the literature, is ego-involvement. When people are ego-involved in a topic covered by media, they perceive events passionately, stridently, and frequently through distorted perceptual lenses. People with strong attitudes and group identifications frequently charge that the media intentionally slant stories against their side, a phenomenon that falls under the rubric of hostile media bias (Vallone, Ross, & Lepper, 1985).

There is remarkable consistency in research on hostile media bias (Christen, Kannaovakun, & Gunther, 2002; Dalton, Beck, Huckfeldt, 1998; Giner-Sorolla & Chaiken, 1994; Gunther, Christen, Liebhart, & Chia, 2001; Perloff, 1989; Schmitt,

Gunther, & Liebhart, 2004). We can say with some confidence that if you pick an issue, locate partisans with extreme attitudes and ask them to view news coverage of the issue, you will find that activists on each side will tell you that the media is biased against their side and in favor of their opponents. But what are the implications of these beliefs for perceptions of media effects on third persons, or public opinion? This is where it gets even more interesting.

Research suggests that ego-involved partisans contrast their perceptions of media effects from those of third persons. Convinced that news media are biased against their side, partisans bring to bear simplistic lay theories of media exposure and impact, along with assumptions that the audience constitutes a political out-group (see Gunther & Christen, 2002; Perloff, 1989). Interestingly, you can also venture the opposite prediction. Partisans may also project their attitudes onto others, assuming that the public will naturally agree with what they have the foresight to recognize is the morally correct position. Consistent with this theorizing, there is evidence that people engage in projection (or biased assimilation, as it is sometimes called). A variety of studies show that partisans perceive that public opinion mirrors their own views on the issue (Christen et al., 2002; Gunther & Christen, 2002; Gunther et al., 2001).

Thus, ego-involvement produces two distorted—but opposing—perceptions: an egocentric belief that others see the world in precisely the same way as I do (biased assimilation), and the equally distorted conviction that news coverage will lead others to become more hostile to my side and more friendly toward my opponents (third-person-based contrast). Examples of this tendency are plentiful in real life. Consider two religious conservatives who perceive that presidential election coverage reflects a disturbing left-liberal bias. The first, an exemplar of the third-person effect, fears the news will "bully," sway or otherwise persuade gullible voters to support liberal Democratic candidates. The second, a proponent of biased assimilation, has faith in the basic goodness and decency of the American public. According to this view, voters will recognize the fundamental correctness of the conservative perspective, disregard news biases, and vote Republican.

It is, of course, possible that both views are correct, but under different conditions. Partisans are apt to resort to third-person, contrast-based judgments when the issue is historically and ethnically involving, like the Middle East, and news is vivid and graphic. Partisans may project their views onto others when they hold strong views, but the issue is not so central to self-identity, or when the information comes from a medium that does not have broad reach (Gunther & Schmitt, 2004). Or both third-person perceptions and biased assimilation may operate simultaneously, perhaps canceling each other to render a more accurate view of public opinion (Gunther & Christen, 2002) or alternatively exerting more random, unpredictable effects on public attitudes.

CONSEQUENCES OF THE THIRD-PERSON EFFECT

The field of social influence is filled with models that emphasize direct effects of messages on attitudes and behaviors. The path from message to attitude can be complex and multi-layered, to be sure, but most perspectives—for example, social cognitive theory, elaboration likelihood model, and framing—stipulate that effects can be understood by examining the processes by which the message (or source or persuasion situation) influences a receiver's own beliefs or attitudes about the issue at hand. The third-person effect is different. What made Davison's approach interesting was its suggestion that effects were indirect, paradoxical, and occurred through processes not intended by the communicator. Over the years, researchers have refined this notion, as exemplified in Gunther and Tsfati's research on the presumed influence hypothesis (Gunther, Perloff, & Tsfati, 2008; Gunther & Storey, 2003). Presumed influence focuses less on self-other disparities than on the attitudinal consequences of perceived effects on third persons.

Third-person perceptions exert two basic effects on opinions and behavior: defiance and compliance (see also Gunther, Perloff, & Tsfati, 2008 and Figure 12.1). The effects are polar opposites and work through different psychological processes. Defiance occurs when individuals presume that mediated messages have effects on third persons they find objectionable, and this presumption of effects motivates them to take some action, either active opposition or passive resistance. Theoretically, one would expect that the TPE should produce defiant responses to mediated messages by instigating hostile media biases, accessing selective perceptions of media content, including preexisting negative attitudes toward media (Giner-Sorolla & Chaiken, 1994; Schmitt, Gunther, & Liebhart, 2004), and triggering feelings of efficacy.

Attempts to censor media materials represent a prime example of defiance. Several years back, librarians expressed concern that the mention of the word "scrotum" on the first page of the Newberry award-winning *The Higher Power of Lucky* would have untoward effects on children's social development. They sought to ban or restrict the book, an apparent exemplar of consequences of the third-person effect.

Intrigued by the examples like these, researchers have explored the relationship between third-person perceptions and intent to censor controversial media. Research finds that the third-person effect predicts support for restricting pornography (Gunther, 1995), television violence (Hoffner et al., 1999; Rojas, Shah, & Faber, 1996; Salwen & Dupagne, 1999), as well as antisocial rap music (McLeod et al., 1997) and liquor and gambling advertising (Shah, Faber, & Youn, 1999). Few studies have employed behavioral measures, and the question of causality, always an issue in third-person effect research, remains open. Respondents may invoke perceptions of message effects to rationalize prior support for media censorship (Price & Stroud, 2006). Yet the more general hypothesis that individuals' expectations of media impact can induce them to consider action to thwart anticipated effects has received support (Tsfati & Cohen, 2005).

Compliance, the other consequence of third-person perceptions, works through a different set of psychological processes. In this case, presumptions of media effects on others influence perceptions of social reality. People assume that media content strongly influences others' opinions. Motivated to comply with the ("media-altered") views of hypothetical others (Ajzen & Fishbein, 2005), individuals change their own opinions so that they are congruent with perceived social norms. Another path from third-person perceptions to compliance involves scarcity perceptions. Exaggerated estimations of media impact on consumer behavior of third persons trigger a belief that an advertised product will be scarce and, therefore, more desirable (Brock, 1968; Cialdini, 2001). This may induce individuals to purchase the product.

Gunther and his colleagues explored consequences of presumed media effects in an intriguing study (Gunther, Bolt, Borzekowski, Liebhart, & Dillard, 2006). The researchers found that the more exposure sixth and seventh grade students had to smoking messages, the more they presumed their pre-adolescent peers also were exposed to the messages. Perceived peer exposure in turn predicted the belief that smoking was prevalent in their peer group. And in the perceptual coup de grace, believing peers smoked cigarettes pushed students to develop more favorable attitudes toward smoking themselves. It would seem that a desire to fit in with the perceived climate of opinion, a salient motive for pre-teens, pushed them to develop more favorable opinions about smoking cigarettes. The authors suggest that persuasion campaigns should try to counteract the tendency to overestimate prevalence of cigarette smoking, while at the same time promoting the perception that anti-smoking campaigns can influence attitudes toward smoking.

These findings are interesting and important in that they demonstrate that persuasion can occur indirectly, via perceived message effects on third persons. At the same time, questions emerge: Does presumed influence operate in situations in which conformist pressures are less salient? Are the different factors (e.g., perceived peer exposure, perceptions of smoking prevalence) conceptually independent? More generally from a persuasion perspective, perceptions of others' opinions has had a mixed record of influencing attitudes in one area where it has been tested, social norming. Convincing students that they overestimate how much peers drink has met with only partial success in reducing drinking (Polonec, Major, & Atwood, 2006). So there is much work to be done. But, given the difficulty of changing strongly held attitudes and the concomitant importance of using persuasion to advance public health, we need to take advantage of novel approaches that are beginning to develop a track record of empirical success. Gunther and others' research on presumed influence is intriguing, rife with implications for mass media and persuasion.

RESEARCH DIRECTIONS

An issue of pressing importance is to integrate the third-person effect with contemporary media technologies. There are interesting theoretical issues here. If perceived reach is an important determinant of third-person effects, then it becomes interesting to examine perceptions of message effects for Web sites whose reach may be perceived in qualitatively different ways than traditional mass media. If first-person effects are more likely when observers believe that message acceptance reflects positively on the self, can one, therefore, expect more first-person effects in the case of messages transmitted on popular sites like Facebook and MySpace? To the extent that third-person effects depend on judgments that the audience is composed of undefined others who are not anchored to the self as a point of reference, can we expect more first-person effects in the case of YouTube, MySpace, Facebook, and similar sites in which perceived similarity and personal reference points are the rule rather than the exception? At the same time, given the pervasiveness of third-person effects, should one not expect these effects to continue, varying in form to match the dominant media of the era? For example, if adolescent girls perceive that posted pictures of attractive young women are authentic (and not "photo-shopped"), might they not assume other Facebook users will be influenced by the photos? Might this instigate upward social comparisons that could have harmful effects on self-esteem?

Common to all these examples are convictions that mass media exert effects by triggering perceptions of media effects on others, media impacts are indirect and frequently unintended, and the underpinning of these effects is a paradoxical perceptual process that both transcends and uniquely fits the historical moment.

Note

1. I have adapted concepts advanced in Gunther, Perloff, and Tsfati (2008) to the consequences portion of the model. I am indebted to Al Gunther and Yariv Tsfati for their ideas on this topic.

References

Ajzen, I., & Fishbein, M. (2005). The influence of attitudes on behavior. In D. Albarracín, B. T. Johnson, & M. P. Zanna (Eds.), *The handbook of attitudes* (pp. 173–221). Mahwah, NJ: Erlbaum.

Andsager, J. L., & White, H. A. (2007). *Self versus others: Media, messages, and the third-person effect.* Mahwah, NJ: Erlbaum.

Berke, R. L. (1998, February 15). Clinton's O.K. in the polls, right? *The New York Times*, pp. 4–1, 4–5.

Brock, T. C. (1968). Implications of commodity theory for value change. In A. G. Greenwald, T. C. Brock, & T. M. Ostrom (Eds.), *Psychological foundations of attitudes* (pp. 243–275). New York: Academic Press.

Brosius, H. B., & Engel, D. (1996). The causes of third-person effects: Unrealistic optimism, impersonal impact, or generalized negative attitudes towards media influence? *International Journal of Public Opinion Research*, 8, 142–162.

Bryant, J., & Miron, D. (2004). Theory and research in mass communication. *Journal of Communication*, *54*, 662–704.

Christen, C. T., Kannaovakun. P., & Gunther, A. C. (2002). Hostile media perceptions: Partisan assessments of press and public during the 1997 United Parcel Service strike. *Political Communication*, *19*, 423–436.

Cialdini, R. B. (2001). *Influence: Science and practice* (4th ed.). Boston: Allyn & Bacon.

Dalton, R. J., Beck, P. A., & Huckfeldt, R. (1998). Partisan cues and the media: Information flows in the 1992 presidential election. *American Political Science Review*, *92*, 111–126.

David, P., Liu, K., & Myser, M. (2004). Methodological artifact or persistent bias?: Testing the robustness of the third-person and reverse third-person effects for alcohol messages. *Communication Research*, *31*, 206–233.

Davison, W. P. (1983). The third-person effect in communication. *Public Opinion Quarterly*, *47*, 1–15.

Douglas, K. M., & Sutton, R. M. (2004). Right about others, wrong about ourselves?: Actual and perceived self-other differences in resistance to persuasion. *British Journal of Social Psychology*, *43*, 585–603.

Driscoll, P. D., & Salwen, M. B. (1997). Self-perceived knowledge of the O. J. Simpson trial: Third-person perception and perceptions of guilt. *Journalism & Mass Communication Quarterly*, *74*, 541–556.

Duck, J. M., Hogg, M. A., & Terry, D. J. (1995). Me, us and them: Political identification and the third-person effect in the 1993 Australian federal election. *European Journal of Social Psychology*, *25*, 195–215.

Duck, J. M., Terry, D. J., & Hogg, M. A. (1995). The perceived influence of AIDS advertising: Third-person effects in the context of positive media content. *Basic and Applied Social Psychology*, *17*, 305–325.

Eveland, W. P., Jr., Nathanson, A. I., Detenber, B. H., & McLeod, D. M. (1999). Rethinking the social distance corollary: Perceived likelihood of exposure and the third-person perception. *Communication Research*, *26*, 275–302.

Giner-Sorolla, R., & Chaiken, S. (1994). The causes of hostile media judgments. *Journal of Experimental Social Psychology*, *30*, 165–180.

Glynn, C. J., Ostman, R. E., & McDonald, D. G. (1995). Opinions, perception, and social reality. In T. L. Glasser & C. T. Salmon (Eds.), *Public opinion and the communication of consent* (pp. 249–277). New York: Guilford.

Gunther, A. C. (1991). What we think others think: Cause and consequence in the third-person effect. *Communication Research, 18*, 355–372.

Gunther, A. C. (1995). Overrating the X-rating: The third-person perception and support for censorship of pornography. *Journal of Communication, 45(1)*, 27–38.

Gunther, A. C., Bolt, D., Borzekowski, D. L. G., Liebhart, J. L., & Dillard, J. P. (2006). Presumed influence on peer norms: How mass media indirectly affect adolescent smoking. *Journal of Communication, 56*, 52–68.

Gunther, A. C., & Christen, C. T. (2002). Projection or persuasive press?: Contrary effects of personal opinion and perceived news coverage on estimates of public opinion. *Journal of Communication, 52*, 177–195.

Gunther, A. C., Christen, C. T., Liebhart, J. L., & Chia, S. C.-Y. (2001). Congenial public, contrary press, and biased estimates of the climate of opinion. *Public Opinion Quarterly, 65*, 295–320.

Gunther, A. C., Perloff, R. M., & Tsfati, Y. (2008). Public opinion and the third-person effect. In W. Donsbach & M. Traugott (Eds.), *Handbook of public opinion* (pp. 184–191). Thousand Oaks, CA: Sage.

Gunther, A. C., & Schmitt, K. (2004). Mapping boundaries of the hostile media effect. *Journal of Communication, 54(1)*, 55–70.

Gunther, A. C., & Storey, J. D. (2003). The influence of presumed influence. *Journal of Communication, 53*, 199–215.

Gunther, A. C., & Thorson, E. (1992). Perceived persuasive effects of product commercials and public service announcements: Third-person effects in new domains. *Communication Research, 19*, 574–596.

Henriksen, L., & Flora, J. A. (1999). Third-person perception and children: Perceived impact of pro- and anti-smoking ads. *Communication Research, 26*, 643–665.

Hoffner, C., Buchanan, M., Anderson, J. D., Hubbs, L. A., Kamigaki, S. K., Kowalczyk, L., Pastorek, A., Plotkin, R. S., & Silberg, K. J. (1999). Support for censorship of television violence: The role of the third-person effect and news exposure. *Communication Research, 26*, 726–742.

Hoorens, V., & Ruiter, S. (1996). The optimal impact phenomenon: Beyond the third person effect. *European Journal of Social Psychology, 26*, 599–610.

Huge, M., Glynn, C. J., & Jeong, I. (2006). A relationship-based approach to understanding third-person perceptions. *Journalism & Mass Communication Quarterly, 83*, 530–546.

Jensen, J. D., & Hurley, R. J. (2005). Third-person effects and the environment: Social distance, social desirability, and presumed behavior. *Journal of Communication, 55*, 242–256.

Lasorsa, D. L. (1992). Policymakers and the third-person effect. In J. D. Kennamer (Ed.), *Public opinion, the press, and public policy* (pp. 163–175). Westport, CT: Praeger.

Lee, B., & Tamborini, R. (2005). Third-person effect and Internet pornography: The influence of collectivism and Internet self-efficacy. *Journal of Communication, 55*, 292–310.

McLeod, D. M., Detenber, B. H., & Eveland, W. P., Jr., (2001). Behind the third-person effect: Differentiating perceptual processes for self and others. *Journal of Communication, 51*, 678–695.

McLeod, D. M., Eveland, W. P., Jr., & Nathanson, A. I. (1997). Support for censorship of violent and misogynic rap lyrics: An analysis of the third-person effect. *Communication Research, 24*, 153–174.

Meirick, P. C. (2004). Topic-relevant reference groups and dimensions of distance: Political advertising and first- and third-person effects. *Communication Research, 31*, 234–255.

Meirick, P. C. (2005). Rethinking the target corollary: The effects of social distance, perceived exposure, and perceived predispositions on first-person and third-person perceptions. *Communication Research, 32*, 822–843.

Mutz, D. C. (1998). *Impersonal influence: How perceptions of mass collectives affect political attitudes.* New York: Cambridge University Press.

Neuwirth, K., & Frederick, E. (2002). Extending the framework of third-, first and second-person effects. *Mass Communication and Society, 5*, 113–140.

Nisbett, R. E., & Wilson, T. D. (1977). Telling more than we can know: Verbal reports on mental processes. *Psychological Review, 84*, 231–259.

Oreskes, M. (2000, June 4). Troubling the waters of nuclear deterrence. *New York Times*, Week in Review, p. 3.

Pan, Z., Abisaid, J. L., Paek, H-J., Sun, Y., & Houden, D. (2006). Exploring the perceptual gap in perceived effects of media reports of opinion polls. *International Journal of Public Opinion Research, 18*, 340–350.

Paul, B., Salwen, M. B., & Dupagne, M. (2000). The third-person effect: A meta-analysis of the perceptual hypothesis. *Mass Communication & Society, 3*, 57–85.

Peiser, W., & Peter, J. (2000). Third-person perception of television-viewing behavior. *Journal of Communication, 50*, 25–45.

Perloff, R. M. (1989). Ego-involvement and the third person effect of televised news coverage. *Communication Research, 16*, 236–262.

Polonec, L. D., Major, A. M., & Atwood, L. E. (2006). Evaluating the believability and effectiveness of the social norms message "Most Students Drink 0 to 4 Drinks When They Party." *Health Communication, 20*, 23–34.

Price, V., & Stroud, N. J. (2006). Public attitudes toward polls: Evidence from the 2000 U.S. presidential election. *International Journal of Public Opinion Research, 18*, 393–421.

Price, V., & Tewksbury, D. (1996). Measuring the third-person effect of news: The impact of question order, contrast and knowledge. *International Journal of Public Opinion Research, 8*, 120–141.

Reid, S. A., & Hogg, M. A. (2005). A self-categorization explanation for the third-person effect. *Human Communication Research, 31*, 129–161.

Rojas, H., Shah, D. V., & Faber, R. J. (1996). For the good of others: Censorship and the third-person effect. *International Journal of Public Opinion Research, 8*, 163–186.

Rosenbloom, S. (2007, May 27). Grade-school girls, grown-up gossip. *New York Times* (Sunday Styles), 1, 8–9.

Salwen, M. B. (1998). Perceptions of media influence and support for censorship: The third-person effect in the 1996 presidential election. *Communication Research, 25*, 259–285.

Salwen, M. B., & Driscoll, P. D. (1997). Consequences of third-person perception in support of press restrictions in the O. J. Simpson trial. *Journal of Communication, 47(2)*, 60–75.

Salwen, M. B., & Dupagne, M. (1999). The third-person effect: Perceptions of the media's influence and immoral consequences. *Communication Research, 26*, 523–549.

Scharrer, E. A. (2002). Third-person perception and television violence: The role of out-group stereotyping in perceptions of susceptibility to effects. *Communication Research, 29*, 681–704.

Schimel, J., Greenberg, J., Pyszczynski, T., O'Mahen, H., & Arndt, J. (2000). Running from the shadow: Psychological distancing from others to deny characteristics people fear in themselves. *Journal of Personality and Social Psychology, 78*, 446–462.

Schmitt, K. M., Gunther, A. C., & Liebhart, J. L. (2004). Why partisans see mass media as biased. *Communication Research, 31*, 623–641.

Shah, D. V., Faber, R. J., & Youn, S. (1999). Susceptibility and severity: Perceptual dimensions underlying the third-person effect. *Communication Research, 26*, 240–267.

Sun, Y., Pan, Z., & Shen, L. (2008). Understanding the third-person perception: Evidence from a meta-analysis. *Journal of Communication, 58(2)*, 280–300.

Tewksbury, D. (2002). The role of comparison group size in the third-person effect. *International Journal of Public Opinion Research, 14*, 247–263.

Tewksbury, D., Moy, P., & Weis, D. S. (2004). Preparations for Y2K: Revisiting the behavioral component of the third-person effect. *Journal of Communication, 54*, 138–155.

Tiedge, J. T., Silverblatt, A., Havice, M. J., & Rosenfeld, R. (1991). Discrepancy between perceived first-person and perceived third-person mass media effects. *Journalism Quarterly, 68*, 141–154.

Tsfati, Y., & Cohen, J. (2004). Object-subject distance and the third person perception. *Media Psychology, 6*, 335–361.

Tsfati, Y., & Cohen, J. (2005). The influence of presumed media influence on democratic legitimacy: The case of Gaza settlers. *Communication Research*, *32*, 794–821.

Tyler, T. R., & Cook, F. L. (1984). The mass media and judgments of risk: Distinguishing impact on personal and societal level judgments. *Journal of Personality and Social Psychology*, *47*, 693–708.

Vallone, R., Ross, L., & Lepper, M. (1985). The hostile media phenomenon: Biased perception and perceptions of media bias in coverage of the Beirut massacre. *Journal of Personality and Social Psychology*, *49*, 577–585.

White, H. A. (1997). Considering interacting factors in the third-person effect: Argument strength and social distance. *Journalism & Mass Communication Quarterly*, *74*, 557–564.

Weinstein, N. D. (1980). Unrealistic optimism about future life events. *Journal of Personality and Social Psychology*, *39*, 806–820.

13
MEDIA VIOLENCE

Glenn G. Sparks
Purdue University, West Lafayette, IN

Cheri W. Sparks
Indiana First Steps, Lafayette, IN

Erin A. Sparks
Florida State University, Tallahassee, FL

The history of research on media violence is frequently punctuated by new movies or TV programs that either push the envelope of violent content or attract attention because of their presumed "copy-cat" effects on some members of the audience. The fact that this trend continues unabated well into the new century may be disconcerting to some scholars who are concerned about the impact of media violence on society—but it probably reveals that the appetite for violent entertainment is relatively impervious to change. We opened the chapter in the previous edition of this volume by calling attention to the public controversy surrounding a violent movie made in Japan (*Battle Royale*). Japan's education minister, Nobutaka Machimura, called for theater owners to refrain from showing this movie because of its possible harmful effects on the nation's youth (Schaefer, 2000). As we seek here to update the scholarship on media violence, it is also worth noting some of the most recent media exemplars that have sparked controversy.

During the first few months of 2007, controversial billboards showed up in Los Angeles and ads on the roofs of taxi-cabs appeared in New York City. The ads were part of a campaign for the film, *Captivity*, and featured its star, Elisha Cuthbert, being tortured over a series of four storyboards. Each of the four storyboards respectively featured the labels, "abduction," "confinement," "torture," and "termination." While the public outrage and controversy that followed this ad campaign was, undoubtedly, exactly what the film promoters wanted to happen, they probably had not planned for the unprecedented action of the Motion Picture Association of America (MPAA). The MPAA placed a sanction on After Dark Films (a Lionsgate Films associate) that required prior approval for all of its future advertising purchases. The MPAA apparently believed that this ad campaign was simply not appropriate for general public viewing (Stewart, 2007). The film itself has also been featured in numerous articles and reviews, some of which maintain that its displays of gruesome violence have gone too far. One reviewer referred to the film as a "queasy and mostly nauseating piece of torture porn . . ." (*The Guardian*, 2007).

For scholars of media violence, the *Captivity* episode signals that, despite over half a century of academic scrutiny, the issues surrounding the controversy about the impact of media violence on consumers show no sign of diminishing. In fact, with the emerging of new media technologies that expand the venues of violent entertainment and research methodologies that permit scholars to probe events inside the brain during consumption of media violence, a number of important new themes are currently emerging in contemporary scholarship. Some of the questions that we take up in this chapter are familiar standbys. For example, perhaps the central question that has dominated the research in this area is, "To what extent does consumption of media violence lead directly to subsequent aggressive behavior?" Closely related to this question is the one that inquires after the theoretical mechanisms and processes that may operate in this domain. But in addition to these central questions, several new ones also deserve attention. For example, what effects other than ones associated with aggressive behavior seem noteworthy? What research methodologies appear to show new promise for the future study of media violence? What research themes emerge in the current scholarship that promise to shape the future research agenda? These are the main questions that we take up in this chapter. Prior to examining these questions, we turn first to a brief consideration of the history of the media violence controversy. Relative to other areas of media effects, the history of the concern about media violence is rather lengthy, and it is prudent not to ignore the highlights of that history.

A BRIEF HISTORY OF THE MEDIA VIOLENCE CONTROVERSY

For most scholars, the Payne Fund Studies mark the formal beginning of scientific inquiry into the study of media violence. The studies themselves were focused on a variety of different topics that reflected public concern about the impact of movies on children. An invitation issued by William Short, the Executive Director of the Motion Picture Research Council (a private educational group) resulted in private funding from a philanthropic foundation known as the Payne Fund. Two of the funded studies were particularly concerned with violence. In a study that signaled a long-term interest in the content of media messages, Dale (1935) conducted a content analysis of 1,500 movies that revealed a heavy emphasis upon crime. Blumer (1933), an early pioneer of the sample survey method, collected data from nearly 2,000 respondents that revealed that many people were conscious of the fact that they had directly imitated acts of violence that they had witnessed in violent movies. These studies helped to reinforce the concern about violent content in public entertainment—concerns that were exacerbated later in the 1950s when Wertham (1954) published an analysis of comic book content. Wertham claimed that a disproportionate amount of comic book content featured grotesque images of violence that contributed to juvenile delinquency on the part of young boys, many of whom tended to be heavy consumers of these images. Wertham's claims had more impact on the public and the self-censoring practices of the comic book industry than they did upon media scholars. Scientists were not inclined to accept claims that were based upon biased sample selection, imprecise coding techniques, and selected anecdotes based upon dramatic testimony from boys who were being treated for a wide range of psychological problems. It wasn't until television transformed the landscape of public media consumption during the 1950s that the issue of media violence gained sustained and serious traction in the research community.

The Rise of TV

By the beginning of the 1960s, 90% of American homes could receive TV signals. Almost immediately after TV began to pervade the American landscape, controversy about media violence was evident. Schramm, Lyle, and Parker (1961) discussed a number of examples of imitative violence that surfaced in news reports in the 1950s. The focus of their discussion was the notion that exposure to TV violence as a precursor to imitative acts that included violent crimes was a phenomenon to be treated quite seriously.

The U.S. government expressed early concern about the effects of televised violence in the 1950s—concern that continued through subsequent decades with major investigations and reports that focused on the link between exposure to media violence and aggressive behavior. Liebert, Sprafkin, and Davidson (1982) reviewed the early events surrounding the government's role in the media violence issue beginning with the role of Senator Estes Kefauver's 1954 Senate Subcommittee on Juvenile Delinquency (they questioned the need for violence on television). A steady stream of other reports followed, including the National Commission on the Causes and Prevention of Violence (1969), the U.S. Surgeon General's Scientific Advisory Committee (1972), which presented a collection of 23 different research projects, and the National Institute of Mental Health Report (1982), *Television and Behavior*. While these reports may have done more to fuel the controversy about the effects of media violence than to settle the issue, they certainly signaled the high priority that this topic would enjoy in the scholarly community for years to come.

Scholars have used numerous definitions of media violence to guide their research (see Potter, 2003, for a listing of at least eight different definitions). The pioneering content analytic work of George Gerbner gave rise to one definition that is still widely cited. Gerbner (1972) defined violence as, "the overt expression of physical force against others or self, or the compelling of action against one's will on pain of being hurt or killed" (p. 387). While this definition is limited to physical violence, it permitted Gerbner to arrive at very precise claims about the amount of violence on TV. He found that primetime TV contained about eight instances of violence per hour. He also estimated that about 80% of primetime programs contained some violence. By documenting the prevalence of violence on TV, Gerbner's research helped to set the stage for the central issue of concern: How did violence affect viewers? It should be noted that Gerbner himself was not so much interested in the effects of violent content on aggressive behavior. Instead, his theory of cultivation emphasized the cumulative effects of exposure to violence on beliefs that people held about the social world. Nevertheless, his content analyses were frequently cited as justification for the importance of raising the question about whether or not viewing violent content affected aggressive behavior.

DOES VIEWING MEDIA VIOLENCE CAUSE AGGRESSIVE BEHAVIOR?

Early research on the possible impact of media violence on aggressive behavior was marked by controversy and criticism. For example, in an early line of experimental research that is now regarded as among the hallmarks of the literature, Bandura, Ross, and Ross (1963a, 1963b) demonstrated that children were more likely to imitate the aggressive actions of a televised model when the model was rewarded instead of punished. But these studies were criticized for lacking construct validity. That is, the measure of aggression (hitting an inflatable doll) did not seem to be related to the construct of *human* aggression (see Liebert et al., 1982). The studies were also criticized for their reliance on programs that had little resemblance to programs that children were likely to view on television. These two criticisms were eventually addressed by Bandura and other researchers. Gradually, as more and more studies were designed, executed, and reported, the evidence accumulated in favor of the notion that exposure to media violence could definitely cause an increase in aggressive behavior.

The accumulating evidence has become so persuasive that on July 26, 2000, six professional health organizations issued a Joint Statement on the Impact of Entertainment Violence on Children. This statement signaled the strength and unity of an emerging consensus about the effects of media violence at the beginning of the new century. The statement was signed by the presidents and executive officers of the American Academy of Pediatrics, American Academy of Child and Adolescent Psychiatry, American Psychological Association, American Medical Association, American Academy of Family Physicians, and American Psychiatric Association. One portion of the statement referred to "well over 1,000 studies" that "point overwhelmingly to a causal connection between media violence and aggressive behavior in some children." It noted that "the conclusion of the public health community, based on over 30 years of research, is that viewing entertainment violence can lead to increases in aggressive attitudes, values and behavior, particularly in children" (Joint Statement, 2000, ¶4).

The consensus conclusion of the six professional health organizations is supported in many recent reviews of the voluminous literature on the topic—some prior to the Joint Statement (American Psychological Association, 1993; Center for Disease Control, 1991; Comstock & Scharrer, 1999; Gunter, 1994; Heath, Bresolin, & Rinaldi, 1989; Jason, Kennedy, & Brackshaw, 1999; Murray, 1998; National Academy of Science, 1993; Smith & Donnerstein, 1998; Wilson et al., 1997) and some afterwards (Anderson et al., 2003; Browne & Hamilton-Giachritsis, 2005; Cantor, 2003a; Strasburger & Wilson, 2003). The summary statement by Anderson et al. (2003) probably captures well the main consensus that currently exists among scholars about the effects of media violence:

> Research on violent television and films, video games, and music reveals unequivocal evidence that media violence increases the likelihood of aggressive and violent behavior in both immediate and long-term contexts. The effects appear larger for milder than for more severe forms of aggression, but the effects on severe forms of violence are also substantial (r = .13 to .32) when compared with effects of other violence risk factors or medical effects deemed important by the medical community (e.g., effect of aspirin on heart attacks). The research base is large; diverse in methods, samples, and media genres; and consistent in overall findings. The evidence is clearest with the most extensively researched domain, television and film violence. The growing body of video-game research yields essentially the same conclusions. (p. 81)

A Residue of Controversy

Although this recent conclusion and the Joint Statement seem absolutely unequivocal about the fact the exposure to media violence is causally related to aggressive behavior, it seems fair to say that a residue of controversy still exists surrounding this basic conclusion. This residue has several different contributing layers that are important to identify. First, the claim of a "causal" effect may be misunderstood as a claim of exclusive or singular causality and, consequently, may lead some to erroneously conclude that the consensus of the research community must be somehow flawed. In anticipation of this possibility, the Joint Statement (2000) contextualized more precisely the exact nature of the causal claim:

> We in no way mean to imply that entertainment violence is the sole, or even necessarily the most important factor contributing to youth aggression, antisocial attitudes, and violence. Family breakdown, peer influences, the availability of weapons, and numerous other factors may all contribute to these problems. (¶8)

However, clarification about the fact that media violence may be only one of many different causes of aggression introduces potential controversy about how to best interpret the statistical size of the causal effect. Distinct from the question of statistical *significance* (whether a particular finding is likely due to chance or not) is the issue of statistical *importance* that concerns the relative strength of the relationship to emerge from the research findings. On this point, the research community probably shares some blame for part of the confusion and controversy that exists. For example, in the above quotation from Anderson et al. (2003), the effects of media exposure on bringing about severe forms of violence are considered to be "substantial" with correlation coefficients ranging from .13 to .32. Perhaps, as the authors note, these effects are substantial when compared to other common effects that scientists take seriously (e.g., the effects of aspirin on heart attacks). This fact notwithstanding, a correlation of .13 indicates an effect that corresponds to less than 2% of the variance in aggressive behavior being accounted for by exposure to media violence. It seems at least possible to view such a small share of the variance as something less than a "substantial" effect, particularly if the comparative standard involves focusing on the proportion of the variance that is left unexplained (98% in this case). Too often, researchers have simply concluded that a causal effect exists without even addressing the possible vantage points from which the actual size of an effect can be gauged. To their credit, Anderson et al. (2003) compare the effect of media violence on aggression with another well-known phenomenon in order to provide some interpretive perspective.

Added to the controversy about the magnitude of the effect size (statistical *importance*) is the notion of *social* importance. Because media audiences sometimes number in the millions, even very small statistical effects can translate into important social problems. If just one person in several hundred thousand is influenced by a violent movie to commit a serious act of aggression, the social consequences of several million viewers watching that movie might be dramatic. Whereas this fact suggests that even tiny effect sizes ought to be taken quite seriously, another possible reaction is to conclude that given the huge size of the audience, such tiny effects seem nearly guaranteed, virtually unpreventable, and, consequently, not worth much attention.

These statistical issues that often arise in the discussion about media violence are hardly the only sources of potential confusion and controversy. For example, even if a clear causal connection between exposure to media violence and aggression can be demonstrated in a laboratory context, there is room for debate about the extent to which these effects are informative for drawing conclusions about the role of media violence in causing aggression in the world outside the lab. For example, Savage (2004) concluded that despite persistent claims to the contrary, the literature fails to establish a clear causal relationship between viewing violence and criminal behavior. Of course, there are real limitations to experimental evidence. It might be argued that many of the studies focus narrowly on college student participants and tend to use highly contrived measures of aggression that would never occur outside the laboratory context. Moreover, the effects demonstrated in these studies tend to be short-term effects that may diminish quickly. In response to some of these criticisms, Zillmann and Weaver (1999) have noted, "It seems that critics of media-violence research could only be satisfied with longitudinal experimental studies in which, within gender and a multitude of personality variables, random assignment is honored and exposure to violent fare is rigorously controlled—that is, with research that in a free society simply cannot be conducted" (p. 147). In addition, it would also seem that critics would demand that researchers be able to set up real-world opportunities for aggression in order to settle the controversy about the generalizability of laboratory findings to settings outside the lab. Of course, even if it were possible to do so, researchers would never want to set up such opportunities for ethical reasons.

Another persistent critic of the strong consensus that exists about the effects of media violence on aggression is Jonathan Freedman (Freedman, 1984, 1988, 2002). Although Freedman often raises legitimate criticisms of individual studies, his general critique is not held in high regard among most media effects scholars. This probably has to do with the fact that he doesn't seem to conduct his own empirical studies on the effects of media violence and he tends to dismiss the relevance of laboratory experiments and meta-analyses conducted by others. While scholars of media effects have certainly devoted space to refute Freedman's arguments (Cantor, 2003b; Huesmann & Taylor, 2003), we concur with Cantor when she stated that Freedman's ". . . reasoning flies in the face of decades of research on persuasion, imitation, and child development" and that ". . . between the tedium of the criticism of each research design, and the polemical nature of his arguments, I don't foresee it having much of an impact" (p. 468).

Controversy notwithstanding, the clear consensus of scholars who have devoted years to the objective study of the effects of media violence is that exposure is causally related to increased aggressive behavior. A number of excellent reviews of the empirical literature mentioned above lend credence to this consensus and another comprehensive rehash of these studies is beyond the purview of this chapter. However, we do highlight some of the major lines of evidence from different methodological approaches.

Types of Research Evidence

Experiments

Early laboratory experiments on the effects of media violence typically involved children as the participants and provided clear evidence for the facilitation of aggressive behavior after viewing violent media. For example, Liebert and Baron (1972) studied children from 5–9 years old by randomly assigning them to view a brief clip from either a violent program (*The Untouchables*) or a nonviolent sports program. Following exposure to one of these programs, the children were told that they could either "help" or "hurt" the progress of another child in an adjoining room who was trying to win a game. By pressing a "help" button the subjects were told that they could make it easier for the other child to turn a handle that was critical for success in the game. However, if they pressed the "hurt" button, they were told that the handle would become too hot to touch and, thus, would result in hurting the child's progress in the game. Those children who watched the violent film clip prior to being placed in this situation were more likely to press the "hurt" button and more likely to keep the button pressed for a long duration than were the children who watched the sports program.

Stein and Friedrich (1972) demonstrated that even cartoons featuring media violence could increase children's aggressive behavior. They conducted an experiment that randomly assigned children to view *Batman* and *Superman* cartoons (violent condition) or episodes of *Mister Rogers' Neighborhood* (prosocial condition). During the two weeks of observation following this manipulation, the children who viewed the violent cartoons were more likely to be aggressive in their interactions with other children than were the children who viewed the prosocial programming. Both of these early experiments, along with the ones by Bandura mentioned earlier, helped to attract attention to the potential problem of media violence as a facilitator of aggression.

Leonard Berkowitz and his associates conducted numerous experiments with older participants (mainly college students) that helped to expand the generalizability of the findings with children (Berkowitz & Alioto, 1973; Berkowitz & Geen, 1966, 1967; Berkowitz & LePage, 1967; Berkowitz & Powers, 1979; Berkowitz & Rawlings, 1963). The typical paradigm employed in these investigations was to expose subjects who were either provoked or unprovoked by an experimenter to either violent media or nonviolent media. Following exposure, Berkowitz discovered that provoked subjects behaved more aggressively to the experimenter after viewing violence than after viewing nonviolence.

A more recent experiment reported by Zillmann and Weaver (1999) exposed participants to either four consecutive days of gratuitous violence or nonviolence in the form of feature films. Like earlier experimental results, their findings showed that the participants who saw the violent films were more hostile in their behavior subsequent to exposure. Unlike prior experiments which tended to show that participants would only show hostility towards a person who had provoked them earlier, Zillmann and Weaver's participants showed such hostility regardless of whether they had been provoked earlier or not.

A significant extension to the traditional experimental studies on the effects of media violence is more recent research on exposure to violent video games. In general, the emerging evidence from this line of studies tends to be very consistent with the existing evidence on the effects of TV and movies (see Anderson, 2004). For example, Anderson and Dill (2000) found that participants in their study who played a violent video game had increases in both aggressive thoughts and behaviors. This general finding has been documented in other studies as well (Anderson et al., 2004; Bartholow & Anderson, 2002; Bushman & Anderson, 2002; Irwin & Gross, 1995).

In addition to laboratory experiments, there are a number of important field experiments that attempt to extend the basic causal link between media violence and aggression to more naturalistic settings. Berkowitz and his associates have conducted a number of studies in institutions for delinquent boys (Leyens, Camino, Parke, & Berkowitz, 1975; Parke, Berkowitz, Leyens, West, & Sebastian, 1977). These experiments assessed physical and verbal aggression in boys who had been assigned to watch media violence for several weeks and compared those levels of aggression with similar boys who did not watch violence. The findings of these studies converged with laboratory investigations; boys who watched media violence were more likely to engage in aggressive behavior. Along these same lines, the work of Williams (1986) is especially noteworthy in that she was able to study changes in aggression that occurred naturally over several years in a Canadian town that initially had no access to TV signals but, over the course of the natural experiment, gained TV access. The results of Williams' research converged with the findings of the laboratory studies: increases in exposure to media violence lead to increases in aggressive behavior. This type of evidence is especially rare because of the diminishing possibility of studying an environment that is free of media transmissions.

Another type of evidence on the impact of media violence comes from the natural experiment. The most notable results among studies of this type may be those reported by Phillips (1979, 1983, 1986) and Centerwall (1989). According to Centerwall, prior to television's emergence in the U.S., the national homicide rate was 3 per 100,000. By 1974, the homicide rate had doubled. Centerwall argued that this increase is directly linked to massive exposure to television throughout the culture. He noted that essentially the same kind of increase in homicide occurred in Canada. Moreover, he argued that despite its similarities on nearly any variable of interest, homicides did not increase in South Africa from 1945 to 1974 while a ban existed on TV. However, as soon as this ban was lifted, homicides began to increase there as well—more than doubling in less than 20 years just as it had in the United States and Canada. Centerwall concluded that the data he examined indicated that about half of all homicides in the United States are caused, in part, by exposure to TV. While Centerwall's claims are certainly intriguing, Savage (2004) argued that for a variety of reasons (including measurement procedures that are not replicable as well as the difficulties in making comparisons across countries), "Without further documentation, Centerwall's findings are merely suggestive and should not be weighed very heavily" (p. 108). She did acknowledge, however, that the U.S. did experience a dramatic increase in violent crime and homicide between the early 1960s and the mid-1970s that is in need of some explanation.

Phillips (1986) has also analyzed naturally occurring data and reached conclusions that are similar to Centerwall's. With respect to homicides, Phillips argued that after widely publicized heavy-weight prize fights, the homicide rate increased. Similarly, he notes that after news stories of widely publicized suicides, increases occurred in single-car fatalities and airplane crashes. Of course, unequivocal conclusions about causality are not possible based on the type of data presented by Centerwall and Phillips. It is also important to note that, like Centerwall's work, the studies by Phillips are not without criticism (see Wasserman, 1984), and some researchers have recently concluded that the alleged phenomenon of imitative suicides has yet to be firmly established (Hittner, 2005; Sullivan, 2007).

Surveys

In general, survey results that report on the relationship between exposure to media violence and aggressive behavior are less persuasive than laboratory experiments in documenting clear evidence in favor of the hypothesis that exposure causes aggression. Any statistically significant relationship between these two variables that emerges from survey research is invariably open to the possible interpretation that aggressive behavior could have preceded viewing or that some uncontrolled third variable that is empirically related to both media exposure and aggressive behavior could be at work. This tends to diminish the ultimate value of cross-sectional surveys in evaluating the causal hypothesis, even though several such studies report a relationship between aggression and exposure to media violence (see Anderson et al., 2003). The most pertinent survey evidence on the causal hypothesis is found in those surveys that employ a longitudinal design—thus eliminating the possibility that aggressive behavior preceded media exposure. But even in the most rigorous longitudinal designs that also attempt to control for a host of other possible contributing variables, it must be acknowledged that no list of control variables is ever complete.

The best longitudinal survey evidence on the question of media violence is probably found in the study reported by Huesmann, Moise-Titus, Podolski, and Eron (2003). This study collected data on several hundred children who were 6–9 years old in 1977–1978 and then again on those same individuals when they were 21–23 years old in 1992–1995. The authors concluded that early exposure to media violence is a significant predictor of later aggressive behavior for both males and females. This conclusion remained even after controlling for things like socio-economic status, parenting behaviors, and intellect. Another major longitudinal survey was reported by Milavsky, Kessler, Stipp, and Rubens (1982). While the findings of this study failed to converge with those of Huesmann et al. (2003), some scholars have pointed out that this study was funded and conducted by researchers who were with the NBC TV-network (Anderson et al., 2003). Moreover, there is some question about whether the most aggressive children in this study were actually dropped from the data analysis due to difficulties in getting reliable reports about media exposure.

Meta-analyses

Given the voluminous literature on media violence, it is a particularly attractive area for the application of meta-analysis, a statistical technique designed to gauge effect sizes over a large number of studies that employ different subject-populations as well as different independent and dependent variables. In general, the published meta-analyses tend to confirm a relationship between exposure to media violence and aggression (Christensen & Wood, 2007; Hearold, 1986; Paik & Comstock, 1994; Sherry, 2001; Wood, Wong, & Chachere, 1991). Christensen and Wood's (2007) recent analysis is particularly pertinent since it sought to update Wood et al.'s (1991) earlier analysis of aggression in a socially unconstrained environment. Consistent with the earlier findings, Christensen and Wood found that summarizing over the most recent investigations, exposure to media violence enhances viewer aggression. Their discussion of the size of this effect reflects some of the complicated issues discussed earlier. They stated that:

> We doubt that future investigations will find that exposure to violent media features prominently among the most important determinants of aggression in our society. Yet the impact of media violence on individual behavior is not trivial in comparison with the size of effects typically obtained with social-psychological predictors. (p. 161)

Theoretical Mechanisms for Understanding the Link Between Exposure and Aggression

An earlier version of this chapter (Sparks & Sparks, 2002) provided a brief outline of the major theoretical perspectives that scholars have brought to bear on the link between media violence and aggression. Essentially, these same mechanisms are also outlined in the comprehensive literature review by Anderson et al. (2003). We review briefly these four main mechanisms and add one new mechanism to the list that reflects recent research on the role of fundamental neurophysiological processes that may operate in the media context.

Social Learning

The theory of social learning was applied to media violence by Bandura (1965). This theory projected that media characters who serve as models for aggressive behavior may be attended to by viewers and, depending upon whether the behaviors are rewarded or punished, would either disinhibit or inhibit imitation of the behavior respectively. As discussed earlier, Bandura's program of studies offered considerable support for social learning processes. Bandura (2002; this volume) has updated his theoretical perspective in terms of social cognitive theory and demonstrates how the initial formulation has evolved over the years and currently stands as one of the major theoretical options for understanding the effects of media violence.

Priming

Initially, Berkowitz focused attention on media violence by emphasizing the "aggressive cues" contained in this type of content (Berkowitz & Geen, 1967; Berkowitz & LePage, 1967). He thought that these cues could combine psychologically with a viewer's emotional state of anger or frustration and trigger subsequent aggression. Jo and Berkowitz (1994) revised this formulation to focus on the fact that media violence could prime thoughts of aggressive behavior and, consequently, make actual aggressive behavior more likely. The priming hypothesis has received extensive support in the context of media violence (Anderson, 1983; Bushman & Geen, 1990). Perhaps most significantly, Zillmann and Weaver (1999) discussed how Bargh and his associates have extended the priming idea so that it can account not just for short-term effects of aggression after media exposure, but longer term effects as well (Bargh, 1984; Bargh, Lombardi, & Higgins, 1988). Summarizing the notion of priming, Jo and Berkowitz (1994) commented on one result by stating that "It is as if the thought of the particular action had, to some degree, activated the motor program linked to this action" (p. 48).

Arousal

In his theory of excitation transfer, Zillmann (1991) advanced the notion that the arousal-inducing properties of media violence were very important for understanding the intensity of emotional reactions that occur immediately after viewing. For example, if viewers became angry at some situation that developed following exposure to a highly arousing violent depiction, this arousal could subsequently transfer to the anger and intensify it—making aggressive behavior more likely. Similarly, the arousal could also intensify a positive emotion that might occur in response to some other stimuli confronted subsequent to viewing. The theory of excitation transfer is well documented in the study of media effects, and the arousing properties of media violence must be taken seriously given the evidence from studies by Zillmann and his colleagues.

Desensitization

One way that media violence might increase aggressive behavior is through emotional desensitization. According to this notion, with repeated exposure to media violence, a psychological saturation or emotional adjustment takes place such that initial levels of tension, anxiety, disgust, etc. diminish or weaken. These lower levels of negative emotion associated with exposure to media violence may reduce the urgency to respond to violence in real life. Some research with children supports this idea (Drabman & Thomas, 1976), and desensitization effects are commonly observed in studies that employ sexually violent stimulus materials (Dexter, Penrod, Linz, & Saunders, 1997; Krafka, Linz, Donnerstein, & Penrod, 1997). As people's sensitivities to violence become increasingly dull, violent behavior may increase, in part, because it is simply not recognized any longer as behavior that should be curtailed.

The most recent evidence in favor of emotional desensitization is reported by Carnagey, Anderson, and Bushman (2007) in the context of violent video games. College students were randomly assigned to play either a violent or non-violent video game for 20 minutes and then were asked to watch a 10-minute video that contained scenes of real-life violence. The participants who had played the violent video game showed significantly lower levels of heart-rate and galvanic skin response compared to participants who had played the non-violent game. While these results seem to support the notion that exposure to mediated violence can desensitize emotional reactions to real-life violence, it still points to the need to investigate behavioral responses and responses to violence that occur in one's natural environment instead of violence that is mediated by a screen.

Neurophysiological Activation

On the basis of recent studies with children, Murray et al. (2006) argued that when children watch TV violence, the neurophysiology of a "phylogenetically-old brain system" is recruited along with activation of limbic and neo-cortical systems that prepare the organism for motor plans associated with either fight or flight. These authors suggested that because of these fundamental brain processes that may be involved, responses to media violence may be essentially "preconscious" and have long-term implications that extend well beyond the viewing period. It may also be the case that these processes contribute to children's general lack of discrimination between real-life violence and fantasy violence. It should be noted that the involvement of neurophysiological mechanisms in the processing and effects of media violence is not incompatible with any of the other more traditional theoretical mechanisms discussed. To the extent that future research validates the involvement of these sorts of fundamental brain processes, our overall understanding of human responses to mediated violence stands to increase measurably.

FUTURE RESEARCH DIRECTIONS

With increasing clarification about the nature of the causal link between exposure to media violence and aggression, the future appears to hold a number of very promising avenues that will keep media violence at the forefront of media effects scholarship. Here, we identify five general lines of research that appear to hold great promise in continuing to enrich our understanding about media violence in the entertainment context. For each line of research, we provide some examples that in future years may appear in citation lists as examples of the early beginnings of areas that eventually grew into substantive literatures in their own right.

Individual Differences

One promising line of research is attempting to understand the individual difference variables that may be at work in either enhancing or diminishing the effects of exposure to violent content. For example, Grimes, Bergen, Nichols, Vernberg, and Fonagy (2004) discovered that children who had been diagnosed with Disruptive Behavior Disorders were more likely to show physiological reactivity to media violence. Sigurdsson, Gudjonsson, Bragason, Kristjansdottir, and Sigfusdottir (2006) focused on low empathy and attitudes that may predispose people to consume heavier diets of media violence. Other researchers have studied how anger and holding friendships with delinquents (Lee & Kim, 2004) or sensation seeking and alienation (Slater, Henry, Swaim, & Cardador, 2004) may also be linked to responses to media violence. Taken together, efforts such as these appear to be fruitful in making additional progress toward understanding populations who may be at considerably higher risk for suffering from the effects of exposure.

Enjoyment of Media Violence

In contrast to the traditional emphasis on how exposure to violence affects aggression, some scholars are turning attention to the study of the motivations associated with consumption of violent entertainment. Hoffner and Levine (2005) conducted a meta-analysis that focused on the enjoyment of mediated fright and violence. They discovered that enjoyment of violent material was greater for males, for viewers who were lower on measures of empathy, and for viewers who were high on sensation seeking. Sparks and Sparks (2000) attempted to untangle the various contributions to the enjoyment of mayhem and horror and concluded that there is very little data to conclusively establish the fact that programs containing media violence are generally preferred over versions of the same programs that contain no violence. One recent experiment reported by Sparks, Sherry, and Lubsen (2005) found that participants who watched a full-length movie that contained 15 minutes of violence enjoyed the film to the same extent as those who had been randomly assigned to watch the movie with the violence removed. An important line of future research may be designed to increase understanding about exactly what role violence plays in the enjoyment of this kind of entertainment.

Violent Video Games

The explosive growth of the video-gaming industry combined with the popularity of personal computing over the last two decades has produced a new line of research that appears to be burgeoning. This literature sometimes reflects the same issues that have been studied in the context of television and film such as desensitization (Bartholow, Bushman, & Sestir, 2006) or the enjoyment of violence (Jansz, 2005). The bulk of the literature still maintains the focus on the link between exposure and aggressive behavior (e.g., Anderson & Dill, 2000; Anderson, Gentile, & Buckley, 2007; Dill & Dill, 1998), but it might be expected that the future research will reflect theoretical innovations that are particular to the video-game context (e.g., the role of interactivity, personal control over violent scenarios, etc.).

Effects on Variables Other Than Aggressive Behavior

Clearly, the bulk of the literature on media violence has focused on aggressive behavior. While this preoccupation certainly seems justified given the serious implications of aggression, it has also tended to divert attention from other potentially serious and interesting effects. Of course, media cultivation effects on fear of victimization have been studied for several decades (Gerbner, Gross, Morgan, & Signorielli, 1994), but it may be that the focus on variables other than aggressive behavior will only fully mature in future years. For example, Smolej and Kivivuori (2006) recently studied the effects of crime news on fear of violence in Finland. Their results support the notion that reading about crime from headlines in the tabloids may lead to increased worry about becoming a victim of violence. Similarly, Fremont, Pataki, and Beresin (2005) expressed concern about increased news coverage of terrorist events and subsequent fears and anxieties that might form, particularly in children. Expanding the focus beyond some of the traditionally studied variables, Anastasio (2005) found that exposure to just eight minutes of justified violence in a media clip produced a tendency for experimental participants to devalue others. In the next decade, we anticipate a more sustained line of investigations that examine the impact of exposure to media violence on a host of outcomes other than direct aggressive behavior.

Advances in Brain Research

One of the most exciting new methodologies in the study of media effects involves the application of brain imaging through the use of a Magnetic Resonance Imaging scanner (MRI). In a recent special issue of the journal, *Media Psychology* (2006, Vol. 8, No. 1), two of the three research articles on the application of MRI technology reported results from studies on media violence. Murray et al. (2006) reported that based upon the observations on eight children who viewed televised violence or nonviolence, the MRI data revealed that viewing violence ". . . recruits a network of brain regions involved in the regulation of emotion, arousal and attention, episodic memory encoding and retrieval, and motor programming" (p. 26). The authors speculated that an understanding of the regions of the brain that are most active in processing may help to provide an increased understanding of the behavioral effects that are often observed in studies on media violence. In the second article of this special issue, Weber, Ritterfeld, and Mathiak (2006) reported results from 13 male participants who played a violent video game while being scanned with an MRI scanner. Their results suggested that exposure to virtual violence was associated with suppressed brain activity in the affective areas (anterior cingulate cortex and amygdala) of the brain. Although the application of MRI techniques does hold certain challenges (e.g., cost of the equipment, access to the equipment for research purposes, training in appropriate use of the equipment), we believe that the next decade in media effects research should yield some very promising insights as a result of more studies that provide a window in brain activity during processing of media stimuli.

Upon considering these five possible future directions for research on media violence, it seems evident that despite the continuing controversy that has marked this area of research over the years, there is no reason to think that the future decade of media effects research will not be heavily influenced by a continuing line of studies having to do with media violence and its various consequences.

References

American Psychological Association (1993). *Violence and youth: Psychology's response*. Washington, DC: American Psychological Association.

Anastasio, P. A. (2005). Does viewing "justified" violence lead to devaluing others? *Current Psychology, 23*, 259–266.

Anderson, C. A. (1983). Imagination and expectation: The effect of imagining behavioral scripts on personal intentions. *Journal of Personality and Social Psychology, 45*, 293–305.

Anderson, C. A. (2004). An update on the effects of playing violent video games. *Journal of Adolescence, 27*, 113–122.

Anderson, C. A., Berkowitz, L., Donnerstein, E., Huesmann, L. R., Johnson, J. D., Linz, D., et al. (2003). The influence of media violence on youth. *Psychological Science in the Public Interest, 4*, 81–110.

Anderson, C. A., Carnagey, N. L., Flanagan, M., Benjamin, A. J., Eubanks, J., & Valentine, J. C. (2004). Violent video games: Specific effects of violent content on aggressive thoughts and behavior. In M. Zanna (Ed.), *Advances in experimental social psychology* (Vol. 36, pp. 199–249). New York: Elsevier.

Anderson, C. A., & Dill, K. E. (2000). Video games and aggressive thoughts, feelings, and behavior in the laboratory and in life. *Journal of Personality and Social Psychology, 78*, 772–790.

Anderson, C. A., Gentile, D. A., & Buckley, K. E. (2007). *Violent video game effects on children and adolescents: Theory, research, and public policy*. New York: Oxford University Press.

Bandura, A. (1965). Influence of models' reinforcement contingencies on the acquisition of imitative responses. *Journal of Personality and Social Psychology, 1*, 589–595.

Bandura, A. (2002). Social cognitive theory of mass communication. In J. Bryant & D. Zillmann (Eds.), *Media effects: Advances in theory and research* (pp. 121–153). Mahwah, NJ: Erlbaum.

Bandura, A., Ross, D., & Ross, S. A. (1963a). Imitation of film-mediated aggressive models. *Journal of Abnormal and Social Psychology, 66*, 3–11.

Bandura, A., Ross, D., & Ross, S. A. (1963b). Vicarious reinforcement and imitative learning. *Journal of Abnormal and Social Psychology, 67*, 601–607.

Bargh, J. A. (1984). Automatic and conscious processing of social information. In R. S. Wyer & T. K. Srull (Eds.), *Handbook of social cognition* (Vol. 3, pp. 1–43). Hillsdale, NJ: Erlbaum.

Bargh, J. A., Lombardi, W. J., & Higgins, E. T. (1988). Automaticity of chronically accessible constructs in person x situation effects on person perception: It's just a matter of time. *Journal of Personality and Social Psychology, 55*, 599–605.

Bartholow, B. D., & Anderson, C. A. (2002). Effects of violent video games on aggressive behavior: Potential sex differences. *Journal of Experimental Social Psychology, 38*, 283–290.

Bartholow, B. D., Bushman, B. J., & Sestir, M. A. (2006). Chronic violent video game exposure and desensitization to violence: Behavioral and event-related brain potential data. *Journal of Experimental Social Psychology, 42*, 532–539.

Berkowitz, L., & Alioto, J. T. (1973).The meaning of an observed event as a determinant of its aggressive consequences. *Journal of Personality and Social Psychology, 28*, 206–217.

Berkowitz, L., & Geen, R. G. (1966). Film violence and the cue properties of available targets. *Journal of Personality and Social Psychology, 3*, 525–530.

Berkowitz, L., & Geen, R. G. (1967). Stimulus qualities of the target of aggression: A further study. *Journal of Personality and Social Psychology, 5*, 364–368.

Berkowitz, L., & LePage, A. (1967). Weapons as aggression-eliciting stimuli. *Journal of Personality and Social Psychology, 7*, 202–207.

Berkowitz, L., & Powers, P. C. (1979). Effects of timing and justification of witnessed aggression on the observers' punitiveness. *Journal of Research in Personality, 13*, 71–80.

Berkowitz, L., & Rawlings, E. (1963). Effects of film violence on inhibitions against subsequent aggression. *Journal of Abnormal and Social Psychology, 66*, 405–412.

Blumer, H. (1933). *Movies and conduct*. New York: The Macmillan Company.

Browne, K. D., & Hamilton-Giachritsis, C. (2005). The influence of violent media on children and adolescents: A public health approach. *Lancet, 365*, 702–710.

Bushman, B. J., & Anderson, C. A. (2002). Violent video games and hostile expectations: A test of the general aggression model. *Personality and Social Psychology Bulletin, 28*, 1679–1686.

Bushman, B. J., & Geen, R. G. (1990). Role of cognitive-emotional mediators and individual differences in the effects of media violence on aggression. *Journal of Personality and Social Psychology, 58*, 156–163.

Cantor, J. (2003a). Media violence effects and interventions: The roles of communication and emotion. In J. Bryant, D. Roskos-Ewoldson, & J. Cantor (Eds.), *Communication and emotion: Essays in honor of Dolf Zillmann* (pp. 197–219). Mahwah, NJ: Erlbaum.

Cantor, J. (2003b). [Review of the book *Media violence and its effect on aggression: Assessing the scientific evidence*.] *Journalism and Mass Communication Quarterly, 80*, 468–470.

Carnagey, N.L., Anderson, C.A., & Bushman, B.J. (2007). The effect of video game violence on desensitization to real-life violence. *Journal of Experimental Social Psychology, 43*, 489–496.

Center for Disease Control (1991). *Position papers from the third national injury conference: Setting the national agenda for injury control in the 1990s*. Washington, DC: Department of Health and Human Services.

Centerwall, B. S. (1989). Exposure to television as a cause of violence. In G. Comstock (Ed.), *Public communication and behavior* (Vol. 2, pp. 1–58). San Diego: Academic Press.

Christensen, P., & Wood, W. (2007). Effects of media violence on viewers' aggression in unconstrained social interaction. In R. W. Preiss, B. M. Gayle, N. Burrell, M. Allen, & J. Bryant (Eds.), *Mass media effects research: Advances through meta-analysis* (pp. 145–168). Mahwah, NJ: Erlbaum.

Comstock, G., & Scharrer, E. (1999). *Television: What's on, who's watching, and what it means*. San Diego: Academic Press.

Dale, E. (1935). *The content of motion pictures*. New York: The Macmillan Company.

Dexter, H. R., Penrod, S., Linz, D., & Saunders, D. (1997). Attributing responsibility to female victims after exposure to sexually violent films. *Journal of Applied Social Psychology, 27*, 2149–2171.

Dill, K. E., & Dill, J. C. (1998). Video game violence: A review of the empirical literature. *Aggression and Violent Behavior, 3*, 407–428.

Drabman, R. S., & Thomas, M. H. (1976). Does watching violence on television cause apathy? *Pediatrics, 57*, 329–331.

Freedman, J. L. (1984). Effect of television violence on aggressiveness. *Psychological Bulletin, 96*, 227–246.

Freedman, J. L. (1988). Television violence and aggression: What the evidence shows. In S. Oskamp (Ed.), *Television as a social issue. Applied social psychology annual* (Vol. 8, pp. 144–162). Newbury Park, CA: Sage.

Freedman, J. L. (2002). *Media violence and its effect on aggression: Assessing the scientific evidence*. Toronto: University of Toronto Press.

Fremont, W. P., Pataki, C., & Beresin, E. V. (2005). The impact of terrorism on children and adolescents: Terror in the skies, terror on television. *Child and Adolescent Psychiatric Clinics of North America, 14*, 429–451.

Gerbner, G. (1972). Violence in television drama: Trends and symbolic functions. In G. A. Comstock & E. A. Rubinstein (Eds.), *Television and social behavior (Vol. 1): Media content and control* (pp. 28–187). Washington, DC: United States Government Printing Office.

Gerbner, G., Gross, L., Morgan, M., & Signorielli, N. (1994). Growing up with television: The cultivation perspective. In J. Bryant & D. Zillmann (Eds.), *Media effects: Advances in theory and research* (pp. 17–41). Hillsdale, NJ: Erlbaum.

Grimes, T., Bergen, L., Nichols, K., Vernberg, E., & Fonagy, P. (2004). Is psychopathology the key to understanding why some children become aggressive when they are exposed to violent television programming? *Human Communication Research, 30*, 153–181.

Guardian, The (2007). Retrieved August 31, 2007, from (http://film.guardian.co.uk/News_Story/Critic_Review/Guardian_review/0,,2108250,00.html).

Gunter, B. (1994). The question of media violence. In J. Bryant & D. Zillmann (Eds.), *Media effects: Advances in theory and research* (pp. 163–211). Hillsdale, NJ: Erlbaum.

Hearold, S. (1986). A synthesis of 1,043 effects of television on social behavior. In G. Comstock (Ed.), *Public communication and behavior* (Vol. 1, pp. 65–133). New York: Academic Press.

Heath, L., Bresolin, L. B., & Rinaldi, R. C. (1989). Effects of media violence on children: A review of the literature. *Archives of General Psychiatry, 46*, 376–379.

Hittner, J. B. (2005). How robust is the Werther effect? A re-examination of the suggestion-imitation model of suicide. *Mortality, 10*, 193–200.

Hoffner, C. A., & Levine, K. J. (2005). Enjoyment of mediated fright and violence: A meta-analysis. *Media Psychology, 7*, 207–237.

Huesmann, L. R., Moise-Titus, J., Podolski, C. L., & Eron, L. D. (2003). Longitudinal relations between children's exposure to TV violence and their aggressive and violent behavior in young adulthood: 1977–1992. *Developmental Psychology, 39*, 201–221.

Huesmann, L. R., & Taylor, L. D. (2003). The case against the case against media violence. In D. A. Gentile (Ed.), *Media violence and children: A complete guide for parents and professionals* (pp. 107–130). Westport, CT: Praeger.

Irwin, A. R., & Gross, A. M. (1995). Cognitive tempo, violent video games, and aggressive behavior in young boys. *Journal of Family Violence, 10*, 337–350.

Jansz, J. (2005). The emotional appeal of violent video games for adolescent males. *Communication Theory, 15*, 219–241.

Jason, L. A., Kennedy, H. L., & Brackshaw, E. (1999). Television violence and children: Problems and solutions. In T. P. Gullotta & S. J. McElhaney (Eds.), *Violence in homes and communities: Prevention, intervention, and treatment. Issues in children's and families' lives* (Vol. 11, pp. 133–156). Thousand Oaks, CA: Sage.

Jo, E., & Berkowitz, L. (1994). A priming effect analysis of media influences: An update. In J. Bryant & D. Zillmann (Eds.), *Media effects: Advances in theory and research* (pp. 43–60). Hillsdale, NJ: Erlbaum.

Joint Statement. (2000). *Joint statement on the impact of entertainment violence on children*. Retrieved September 3, 2007, from http://www.aap.org/advocacy/releases/jstmtevc.htm.

Krafka, C., Linz, D., Donnerstein, E., & Penrod, S. (1997). Women's reactions to sexually aggressive mass media depictions. *Violence Against Women, 3*, 149–181.

Lee, E., & Kim, M. (2004). Exposure to media violence and bullying at school: Mediating influences of anger and contact with delinquent friends. *Psychological Reports, 95*, 659–672.

Leyens, J. P., Camino, L., Parke, R. D., & Berkowitz, L. (1975). Effects of movie violence on aggression in a field setting as a function of group dominance and cohesion. *Journal of Personality and Social Psychology, 32*, 346–360.

Liebert, R. M., & Baron, R. A. (1972). Short-term effects of televised aggression on children's aggressive behavior. In J. P. Murray, E. A. Rubinstein, & G. A. Comstock (Eds.), *Television and social behavior, Vol. II: Television and social learning* (pp. 181–201). Washington, DC: U.S. Government Printing Office.

Liebert, R., Sprafkin, J. N., & Davidson, E. S. (1982). *The early window: Effects of television on children and youth* (2nd ed.). New York: Pergamon Press.

Milavsky, J. R., Kessler, R. C., Stipp, H., & Rubens, W. S. (1982). *Television and aggression: A panel study*. New York: Academic Press.

Murray, J. P. (1998). Studying television violence: A research agenda for the 21st century. In J. K. Asamen & G. L. Berry (Eds.), *Research paradigms, television, and social behavior* (pp. 369–410). Thousand Oaks, CA: Sage.

Murray, J. P., Liotti, M., Ingmundson, P. T., Mayberg, H. S., Pu, Y., Zamarripa, F., et al. (2006). Children's brain activations while viewing televised violence revealed by fMRI. *Media Psychology, 8*, 25–37.

National Academy of Science. (1993). *Understanding and preventing violence*. Washington, DC: National Academy Press.

National Commission on the Causes and Prevention of Violence. (1969). *Commission statement on violence in television entertainment programs*. Washington, DC: U.S. Government Printing Office.

National Institute of Mental Health. (1982). *Television and behavior: Ten years of scientific progress and implications for the eighties. Vol. 1: Summary report* (DHHS Publication No. ADM 82–1195). Washington, DC: U.S. Government Printing Office.

Paik, H., & Comstock, G. (1994). The effects of television violence on antisocial behavior: A meta-analysis. *Communication Research, 21*, 516–546.

Parke, R. D., Berkowitz, L., Leyens, J. P., West, S. G., & Sebastian, R. J. (1977). Some effects of violent and non-violent movies on the behavior of juvenile delinquents. In L. Berkowitz (Ed.), *Advances in experimental social psychology* (Vol. 10, pp. 135–172). New York: Academic Press.

Phillips, D. P. (1979). Suicide, motor vehicle fatalities, and the mass media: Evidence toward a theory of suggestion. *American Journal of Sociology, 84*, 1150–1174.

Phillips, D. P. (1983). The impact of mass media violence on U.S. homicides. *American Sociological Review, 48*, 560–568.

Phillips, D. P. (1986). The found experiment: A new technique for assessing the impact of mass media violence on real-world aggressive behaviour. In G. Comstock (Ed.), *Public communication and behavior* (Vol. 1, pp. 259–307). Orlando, FL: Academic Press.

Potter, W. J. (2003). *The 11 myths of media violence*. Thousand Oaks, CA: Sage.

Savage, J. (2004). Does viewing violent media really cause criminal violence? A methodological review. *Aggression and Violent Behavior, 10*, 99–128.

Schaefer, G. (2000, December 17). Japan's teens ignore official's plea, line up to see violent film. *Journal and Courier*, p. A-9.

Schramm, W., Lyle, J., & Parker, E. (1961). *Television in the lives of our children*. Stanford, CA: Stanford University Press.

Sherry, J. L. (2001). The effects of violent video games on aggression: A meta-analysis. *Human Communication Research, 27*, 409–431.

Sigurdsson, J. F., Gudjonsson, G. H., Bragason, A. V., Kristjansdottir, E., & Sigfusdottir, I. D. (2006). The role of violent cognition in the relationship between personality and the involvement in violent films and computer games. *Personality and Individual Differences, 41*, 381–392.

Slater, M. D., Henry, K. L., Swaim, R. C., & Cardador, J. M. (2004). Vulnerable teens, vulnerable times: How sensation seeking, alienation, and victimization moderate the violent media content-aggressiveness relation. *Communication Research, 31*, 642–668.

Smith, S. L., & Donnerstein, E. (1998). Harmful effects of exposure to media violence: Learning of aggression, emotional desensitization, and fear. In R. G. Geen & E. Donnerstein (Eds.), *Human aggression: Theories, research, and implications for social policy* (pp. 167–202). San Diego: Academic Press.

Smolej, M., & Kivivuori, J. (2006). The relation between crime news and fear of violence. *Journal of Scandinavian Studies in Criminology and Crime Prevention, 7*, 211–227.

Sparks, G. G., Sherry, J., & Lubsen, G. (2005). The appeal of media violence in a full-length motion picture: An experimental investigation. *Communication Reports, 18*, 21–30.

Sparks, G. G., & Sparks, C. W. (2000). Violence, mayhem, and horror. In D. Zillmann & P. Vorderer (Eds.), *Media entertainment: The psychology of its appeal* (pp. 73–91). Mahwah, NJ: Erlbaum.

Sparks, G. G., & Sparks, C. W. (2002). Effects of media violence. In J. Bryant & D. Zillmann (Eds.), *Media effects: Advances in theory and research. LEA's communication series* (2nd ed., pp. 269–285). Mahwah, NJ: Erlbaum.

Stein, A. H., & Friedrich, L. K. (1972). Television content and young children's behavior. In J. P. Murray, E. A. Rubinstein, & G. A. Comstock (Eds.), *Television and social behavior, Vol. II: Television and social learning* (pp. 202–317). Washington, DC: U.S. Government Printing Office.

Stewart, R. (2007). "Captivity" controversy explodes to new level: MPAA slaps sanctions on, ratings process suspended. Retrieved July 23, 2007, from http://www.cinematical.com/2007/03/30/captivity-controversy-explodes-to-new-level-mpaa-slaps-sancti/

Strasburger, V. C., & Wilson, B. J. (2003). Television violence. In D. Gentile (Ed.), *Media violence and children: A complete guide for parents and professionals* (pp. 57–86). Westport, CT: Praeger.

Sullivan, G. (2007). Should suicide be reported in the media? A critique of research. In M. Mitchell (Ed.), *Remember me: Constructing immortality—beliefs on immortality, life and death* (pp. 149–158). New York: Routledge.

U.S. Surgeon General's Scientific Advisory Committee on Television and Social Behavior. (1972). *Television and growing up: The impact of televised violence* (DHEW Publication No. HSM 72–9086). Washington, DC: U.S Government Printing Office.

Wasserman, I. M. (1984). Imitation and suicide: A reexamination of the Werther effect. *American Sociological Review, 49*, 427–436.

Weber, R., Ritterfeld, U., & Mathiak, K. (2006). Does playing violent video games induce aggression? Empirical evidence of a functional magnetic resonance imaging study. *Media Psychology, 8*, 39–60.

Wertham, F. (1954). *Seduction of the innocent*. New York: Rinehart.

Williams, T. M. (1986). *The impact of television: A natural experiment in three communities*. New York: Academic Press.

Wilson, B. J., Kunkel, D., Linz, D., Potter, J., Donnerstein, E., Smith, S. L., Blumenthal, E., & Gray, T. (1997). Television violence and its context. In *National Television Violence Study, Vol. 1*. Thousand Oaks, CA: Sage (pp. 3–368).

Wood, W., Wong, F. Y., & Chachere, J. G. (1991). Effects of media violence on viewers' aggression in unconstrained social interaction. *Psychological Bulletin, 109*, 371–383.

Zillmann, D. (1991). Television viewing and physiological arousal. In J. Bryant & D. Zillmann (Eds.), *Responding to the screen: Reception and reaction processes* (pp. 103–133). Hillsdale, NJ: Erlbaum.

Zillmann, D., & Weaver, J. B. III. (1999). Effects of prolonged exposure to gratuitous media violence on provoked and unprovoked hostile behavior. *Journal of Applied Social Psychology, 29*, 145–165.

14

FRIGHT REACTIONS TO MASS MEDIA

Joanne Cantor
University of Wisconsin-Madison

The purpose of this chapter is to investigate fright reactions produced by mass media presentations. First, research findings related to the prevalence and intensity with which feelings of fear are experienced as a result of exposure to media drama are reviewed, and the neurophysiology of fear is invoked to explain the duration of lingering feelings of distress. Then the paradox that fright reactions to media fiction occur at all is discussed, and an explanation is based on principles of stimulus generalization. The theory is then refined to include other factors that are needed to account for observed effects in response to both dramatic and nonfictional presentations. Developmental differences in the media stimuli that frighten children and in the effectiveness of coping strategies are then discussed. Finally, gender differences are explored.

FEELINGS OF FRIGHT IN REACTION TO THE SCREEN

Anyone who has ever been to a horror film or thriller appreciates the fact that exposure to television shows, films, and other mass media presentations depicting danger, injury, bizarre images, and terror-stricken protagonists can induce intense fright responses in an audience. Most of us seem to remember at least one specific program or movie that terrified us when we were a child and that made us nervous, remained in our thoughts, and affected other aspects of our behavior for some time afterward. And this happened to us even after we were old enough to know that what we were witnessing was not actually happening and that the depicted dangers could not leave the screen and attack us directly. These reactions can also occur when we know that what is being portrayed never actually happened; at times we may have such reactions even when we understand that there is no chance that the depicted events could ever occur.

The predominant interest in this chapter is fright as an immediate emotional response that is typically of relatively short duration, but that may endure, on occasion, for several hours or days, or even longer. The focus here is on emotional reactions involving components of anxiety, distress, and increased physiological arousal, that are frequently engendered in viewers as a result of exposure to specific types of media productions.

Research interest in the phenomenon of fright reactions to mass media goes back as far as Herbert Blumer's (1933) studies of children's fright reactions to movies. Although sporadic attention was paid to the media as a source of children's fears in the succeeding several decades, research attention began to focus on this issue more prominently in the 1980s. One reason for this more recent focus on fright may have been the release of several blockbuster frightening films in the 1970s. As anecdotal reports of intense emotional responses to such popular films as *Jaws* and *The Exorcist* proliferated in the press, public attention became more focused on the phenomenon. Although many adults experience such reactions, the major share of public concern has been over children's responses. The furor over children's reactions to especially intense scenes in the 1984 movies *Indiana Jones and the Temple of Doom* and *Gremlins* prompted the Motion Picture Association of America to add "PG-13" to its rating system, in an attempt to caution parents that, for whatever reason, a film might be inappropriate for children under the age of 13 (Zoglin, 1984). In addition, the huge number of cable channels available means that most films produced for theatrical distribution, no matter how brutal or bizarre, eventually end up on television and thus become accessible to large numbers of children, often without their parents' knowledge. Finally, as television news became more graphically visual and sensational in the 1990s, observers began speculating about the effects of such images on children's psychological health.

Prevalence and Intensity of Media-Induced Fright Reactions

As early as the 1930s Blumer (1933) reported that 93% of the children he questioned said they had been frightened or horrified by a motion picture. More recently, about 75% of the respondents in two separate samples of preschool and elementary school children in Wisconsin said that they had been scared by something they had seen on television or in a movie (Wilson, Hoffner, & Cantor, 1987).

In other research, a survey of more than 2,000 third through eighth graders in Ohio public schools revealed that as the number of hours of television viewing per day increased, so did the prevalence of symptoms of psychological trauma, such as anxiety, depression, and posttraumatic stress (Singer, Slovak, Frierson, & York, 1998). Moreover, a survey of the parents of almost 500 public school children in kindergarten through fourth grade in Rhode Island revealed that the amount of television a child viewed (especially at bedtime) and having a television in his or her own bedroom were significantly related to sleep disturbances (Owens, Maxim, McGuinn, Nobile, Msall, & Alario, 1999). In addition, 9% of the parents reported that their child experienced TV-induced nightmares at least once a week. A more recent survey involving a representative sample of students in Belgium reported that approximately one-third of 13-year-old boys and girls said they experienced media-induced nightmares at least once a month (Van den Bulck, 2004). A study conducted in Finland indicates that the content and manner of children's viewing have important influences on the negative effects of television (Paavonen, Pennonen, Roine, Valkonen, & Lahikainen, 2006). In a randomized population-based survey of parents of 5- to 6-year-olds, the viewing of adult-targeted TV shows (movies, TV series, and news programs) and passive TV exposure (the amount of time the child was awake when the TV was on in the home) were strongly related to sleep disturbances, even when many demographic, psychiatric, and family influences were controlled statistically.

Although simple correlational studies cannot rule out the alternative explanation that anxious children or those with sleep problems seek out greater levels of television viewing, a recent longitudinal survey supports the interpretation that viewing precedes and promotes these problems. J. G. Johnson and colleagues (2004) conducted a prospective panel survey that measured children's television viewing and sleep problems at ages 14, 16, and 22 years. They reported that adolescents who watched more than three hours of television at age 14 were significantly more likely than lighter viewers to experience sleep problems at ages 16 and 22, even after controlling for previous sleep problems and other factors such as psychiatric disorders, and parental education, income, and neglect. In contrast, early sleep problems were not independently related to later television viewing. Moreover, respondents who reduced their amount of television viewing between the ages of 14 and 16 were significantly less likely to experience sleep disturbances at ages 16 and 22. These findings suggest that heavy viewing leads to difficulty falling asleep and to frequent nighttime awakenings, and that the correlation between viewing and sleep problems is not simply due to sleepless youth turning to television for relief. They also suggest that the effects of television viewing on sleep disturbances may be cumulative.

An experimental study suggests that witnessing scary media presentations may also lead children to avoid engaging in activities related to the events depicted (Cantor & Omdahl, 1991). In this study, kindergarten through sixth-grade children who were exposed to a dramatized depiction of a deadly house fire from *Little House on the Prairie* increased their self-reports of worry about similar events in their own lives. Moreover, they were also less interested in learning to build a fire in a fireplace than were children who were not shown the episode. Similarly, children who saw a scene involving a drowning expressed more concerns about water accidents and were less willing to learn canoeing than were children who had not watched that scene. Although the duration of such effects was not measured, the effects were undoubtedly short-lived, especially because debriefings were employed and safety guidelines were taught so that no child would experience long-term distress (Cantor & Omdahl, 1999).

There is an increasing body of evidence, in fact, that the fear induced by mass media exposure is often long-lasting, with sometimes intense and debilitating effects (Cantor, 1998). In a study designed to assess the severity of enduring fright reactions to mass media, B. R. Johnson (1980) asked a random sample of adults whether they had ever seen a motion picture that had disturbed them "a great deal." Forty percent replied in the affirmative, and the median length of the reported disturbance was three days. Respondents also reported on the type, intensity, and duration of symptoms such as nervousness, depression, fear of specific things, and recurring thoughts and images. Based on these reports, Johnson judged that 48% of these respondents (19% of the total sample) had experienced, for at least two days, a "significant stress reaction" as the result of watching a movie.

The most extreme reactions reported in the literature come from psychiatric case studies in which acute and disabling anxiety states enduring several days to several weeks or more (some necessitating hospitalization) are said to have been precipitated by the viewing of horror movies such as *The Exorcist*, *Invasion of the Body Snatchers*, and *Ghostwatch* (Buzzuto, 1975; Mathai, 1983; Simons & Silveira, 1994). Most of the patients in the cases reported had not had previously diagnosed psychiatric problems, but the viewing of the film was seen as occurring in conjunction with other stressors in the patients' lives.

Retrospective studies of adults' detailed memories of having been frightened by a television show or movie provide more evidence of the severity and duration of media-induced fear among "normal" individuals (Harrison & Cantor, 1999; Hoekstra, Harris, & Helmick, 1999). In these studies, involving samples of undergraduates from three universities, the presence of vivid memories of enduring media-induced fear was nearly universal. All of the participants in one study (Hoekstra et al., 1999) reported such an incident. In the other study (Harrison & Cantor, 1999), 90% of the participants reported an intense fear reaction to something in the media, in spite of the fact that the respondents could receive full extra credit for participating in the study if they simply said "no" (meaning "I never had such an experience") and thereby avoid writing a paper and filling out a three-page questionnaire.

Both studies revealed a variety of intense reactions, including generalized anxieties, specific fears, unwanted recurring thoughts, and disturbances in eating and sleeping. Moreover, Harrison and Cantor (1999) reported these fears to be long-lasting: One third of those who reported having been frightened said that the fear effects had lasted more than a year. Indeed, more than one-fourth of the respondents said that the emotional impact of the program or movie (viewed an average of six years earlier) was still with them at the time of reporting.

Recent analyses of adults' retrospective reports reveal that enduring, seemingly irrational effects on normal activities are common (Cantor, 2004a). For example, many people who saw *Jaws* as children still feel anxious swimming in lakes and pools as well as the ocean, even though they are consciously aware that sharks are not found in these locations. Such responses are consistent with LeDoux's (1996) two-system conceptualization of the neurophysiology of fear. According to LeDoux, unconscious traumatic memories are stored in the amygdala, which controls physiological reactions, such as increased heart rate, blood pressure, and muscle tension. These memories are highly resistant to change. In fact, LeDoux calls them "indelible." Conscious memories are stored in the hippocampus and involve appraisal processes, which are more malleable. This dual memory model may account for the fact that adults may understand that their media-induced fears are ungrounded but be unable to control their emotional distress.

A STIMULUS GENERALIZATION APPROACH TO MEDIA-INDUCED FEAR

As can be seen from the literature summarized here, there is a good deal of evidence regarding viewers' experiences of fear in response to mass media presentations. The next part of this chapter is devoted to speculations about why such fear reactions occur and the factors that promote or inhibit their occurrence.

Fear is generally conceived of as an emotional response of negative hedonic tone related to avoidance or escape, due to the perception of real or imagined threat (e.g., Izard, 1977). A classic fear-arousing situation is one in which the individual senses that he or she is in physical danger, such as upon encountering a poisonous snake on a walk through the woods. Fear can be conceived of as a response involving cognitions, motor behavior, and excitatory reactions that, except under extreme conditions, prepare the individual to flee from the danger.

Using this definition of fear, it is not difficult to explain the public terror that was produced by perhaps the most infamous frightening media drama on record—the 1938 radio broadcast of H. G. Wells' *War of the Worlds*. Many people who tuned in late thought they were listening to a live news bulletin informing them that Martians were taking over the United States (Cantril, 1940). Thus, if they believed what they heard, they justifiably felt that their own lives and indeed the future of their society were in great peril.

But in typical situations in which people are exposed to mass media drama, the audience understands that what is being depicted is not actually happening; in many cases, they know that it never did happen; and in some cases, they know that it never could happen. Objectively speaking, then, the viewer is not in any immediate danger. Why then, does the fright reaction occur? Although fright responses to media presentations are undoubtedly the result of the complex interaction of a variety of processes, a preliminary explanation for this phenomenon is based on the notion of stimulus generalization (see Pavlov, 1960). In conditioning terms, if a stimulus evokes either an unconditioned or conditioned emotional response, other stimuli that are similar to the eliciting stimulus will evoke similar, but less intense emotional responses. This principle implies that, because of similarities between the real and the mediated stimulus, a stimulus that would evoke a fright response if experienced first hand will evoke a similar, but less intense response when encountered via the mass media. In order to explore the implications of this explanation, it is instructive to identify major categories of stimuli and events that tend to induce fear in real-life situations and that are frequently depicted in frightening media productions, and, second, to delineate the factors that should promote or reduce the viewer's tendency to respond emotionally to the mediated stimulus.

Stimuli and Events that Generally Produce Fear

Based on a review of the literature on the sources of real-world fears and on the effects of frightening media, three categories of stimuli and events that tend to produce fear in real-life situations and that occur frequently in frightening presentations are proposed. They are (a) dangers and injuries, (b) distortions of natural forms, and (c) the experience of endangerment and fear by others. These categories are obviously not mutually exclusive: On the contrary, a frightening scene usually involves more than one of these categories.[1]

Dangers and Injuries

Stimuli that are perceived as dangerous should, by definition, evoke fear. The depiction of events that either cause or threaten to cause great harm is the stock-in-trade of the frightening film. Natural disasters such as tornadoes, volcanoes, plagues, and earthquakes; violent encounters on an interpersonal, global, or even intergalactic level; attacks by vicious animals; and large-scale industrial and nuclear accidents are typical events in frightening media fare. If any of these events were witnessed directly, the onlooker would be in danger, and fear would be the expected response. In addition, because danger is often present when injuries are witnessed, the perception of injuries should come to evoke fear as a conditioned response, even in the absence of the danger that produced the injuries. Through stimulus generalization, one might thus expect mediated depictions of danger, violence, and injury to produce fright reactions as well. Reports of fright produced by depictions of dangerous stimuli in media drama abound in the survey and experimental literature (e.g., Cantor, 1998; Harrison & Cantor, 1999).

Distortions of Natural Forms

In addition to dangerous stimuli and the outcomes of dangerous situations, a related set of stimuli that typically evoke fear might be referred to as deformities and distortions, or familiar organisms in unfamiliar and unnatural forms. Hebb (1946) observed fear responses to such "deviations from previously experienced patterns" in chimpanzees and argued that such responses are spontaneous, in that they do not require conditioning.

Organisms that have been mutilated as a result of injury could be considered to fall into this category as well as the previous category. In addition, distortions that are not the result of injury are often encountered in thrillers in the form of realistic characters like dwarves, hunchbacks, and mutants. Moreover, monsters abound in thrillers. Monsters are unreal creatures that are similar to natural beings in many ways, but deviant from them in other ways, such as through distortions in size, shape, skin color, or facial configuration. In scary movies, monstrous and distorted characters are typically, but not universally, depicted as evil and dangerous. Monsters, ghosts, vampires, mummies, and other supernatural beings are frequently cited as sources of children's fear in both surveys and anecdotal reports (e.g., Cantor, 1998; Cantor & Sparks, 1984).

The Experience of Endangerment and Fear by Others

Although in some cases, viewers seem to respond directly to depictions of fear-evoking stimuli such as dangers, injuries, and distortions, in most dramatic presentations these stimuli are shown to affect the emotional responses and outcomes of depicted characters. In many cases, the viewer can be said to respond indirectly to the stimuli through the experiences of the characters. One mechanism underlying such responses is empathy. Although there is controversy over the origins of empathic processes (see Berger, 1962; Feshbach, 1982; Hoffman, 1978), it is clear that under some circumstances, people experience fear as a direct response to the fear expressed by others. Many frightening films seem to stress characters' expressions of fear in response to dangers as much as the perceptual cues associated with the threat itself (see Wilson & Cantor, 1985).

Another indirect mechanism that may be proposed to account for emotional responses to the experiences of others derives from the fact that witnessing other people risk danger can produce the "vicarious" experience of fear, even when the persons at risk do not express fear. Zillmann and Cantor (1977) showed that people respond with dysphoria to the misfortunes of characters for whom they have affection, or for whom they at least do not feel antipathy. Therefore, fear may be seen as deriving from the anticipation of empathy with the distress responses of liked characters. Both survey and experimental findings indicate that the threat of harm to human or animal protagonists is a common source of media-induced fear (e.g., Cantor, 1998; Cantor & Omdahl, 1991).

Factors Affecting the Tendency to Respond Emotionally to Mediated Stimuli

Three factors have an impact on viewers' tendencies to respond emotionally to mediated fear-evoking stimuli. They are (a) the degree of similarity of the depicted stimuli to real-life fear-evokers, (b) viewers' motivations for media exposure, and (c) factors affecting emotionality, generally.

Similarity of Depicted Stimuli to Real-life Fear-evokers

The notion of stimulus generalization implies that the greater the similarity between a conditioned or unconditioned stimulus and the substitute stimulus, the stronger the generalization response will be. Perceptually speaking, realistic depictions of threatening events are more similar to events occurring in the real world than are animated or stylized depictions of the same events. Thus the stimulus generalization notion predicts more intense responses to live-action violence than to cartoon violence, or violence between puppets, for example. Experimental findings are consistent with this expectation (e.g., Gunter & Furnham, 1984).

The similarity of depicted stimuli to those stimuli that provoke fear in a particular individual should also enhance stimulus generalization. Experiments have shown that an individual's fears (for example, of spiders and of death) and prior experiences with stressful events (such as childbirth) intensify the emotional effects of related media presentations (e.g., Sapolsky & Zillmann, 1978; Weiss, Katkin, & Rubin, 1968).

The theory of stimulus generalization, while helpful, cannot account for all situations in which viewers respond with fear to media presentations. The theory also includes the notion of stimulus discrimination, which implies that as viewers come to recognize the different reinforcement contingencies associated with viewing a frightening stimulus on screen as opposed to being exposed to it in real life, their emotional reactions should diminish greatly. Because even adolescents and adults, who understand the mediated nature of frightening images, often experience intense media-induced fright reactions, it is necessary to invoke additional factors to explain their responses.

Motivations for Media Exposure

One set of factors that the stimulus generalization notion does not take into account are motivations for media exposure. In order to enhance the emotional impact of a drama, viewers may, for example, adopt the "willing suspension of disbelief," by cognitively minimizing the effect of knowledge that the events are mediated. In addition, mature viewers may enhance their emotional responses by generating their own emotion-evoking visual images or by cognitively elaborating on the implications of the portrayed events. Mature viewers who seek to avoid intense arousal may employ other appraisal processes to diminish fright reactions to media stimuli by using the "adult discount," for example (see Dysinger & Ruckmick, 1933), and concentrating on the fact that the stimuli are only mediated. Although such appraisal processes often operate, they are by no means universally effective. Moreover, such processes are especially limited in young children (Cantor & Wilson, 1984).

In addition to seeking entertainment, viewers may expose themselves to media for purposes of acquiring information. Because part of the emotional response to such stimuli might arise from viewers' anticipations of future consequences to themselves, depictions of real threats should evoke more fear than dramatic portrayals of events that could never happen. Moreover, depicted threatening agents that are considered to be proximate or imminent should evoke more fear than remote threats. Support for this notion comes from anecdotes regarding the especially intense reactions to *Jaws* by people who saw the movie while vacationing at the seashore. Similarly, in an experiment (Cantor & Hoffner, 1990), children who thought that the threatening agent depicted in a movie existed in their environment were more frightened by the movie than were children who did not believe that the threat could be found in their local area.

Factors Affecting Emotionality Generally

Because physiological arousal is an important component of fear, it is a critical element in viewers' reactions to frightening media. Experiments testing the role of excitation transfer (e.g., Zillmann, 1978) in responses to emotion-evoking films have demonstrated that excitatory residues from prior arousing experiences can combine with responses to unrelated, subsequently presented movie scenes and thereby intensify emotional reactions to the movie (e.g., Zillmann, Mody, & Cantor, 1974).

This reasoning leads to the expectation that factors within a frightening presentation that tend to produce arousal may combine with the depiction of fear-evoking stimuli to increase the viewer's arousal and thus the intensity of the fear experienced while viewing. Producers of frightening movies employ a variety of stylistic devices, including music and suspense, to intensify the audience's fright (see, e.g., Björkqvist & Lagerspetz, 1985; Cantor, Ziemke, & Sparks, 1984).

DEVELOPMENTAL DIFFERENCES AND MEDIA-INDUCED FEAR

Research has examined two major developmental issues in fright reactions to media: (a) the types of mass media stimuli and events that frighten children at different ages, and (b) the strategies for preventing or reducing unwanted fear reactions that are most effective for different-aged children. Experiments and surveys have been conducted to test expectations based on theories and findings in cognitive development. The experiments have tested rigorously controlled variations in program content and viewing conditions, using a combination of self-reports, physiological responses, the coding of facial expressions of emotion, and behavioral measures. For ethical reasons, only small excerpts from relatively mild stimuli are used in experiments. In contrast, the surveys have investigated the responses of children who were exposed to a particular media offering in their natural environment, without any researcher intervention. Although less tightly controlled, the surveys permit the study of responses to much more intensely frightening media fare.

Developmental Differences in the Media Stimuli That Produce Fright

One might expect that as children get older, they become less and less susceptible to all media-produced emotional disturbances. However, this is not the case. As children mature cognitively, some things become less likely to disturb them, whereas other things become potentially more upsetting. This generalization is consistent with developmental differences in children's fears in general. According to a variety of studies using diverse methodologies, children from approximately 3 to 8 years of age are frightened primarily by animals, the dark, supernatural beings, such as ghosts, monsters, and witches, and anything that looks strange or moves suddenly. The fears of 9- to 12-year-olds are more often related to personal injury and physical destruction and the injury and death of family members. Adolescents continue to fear personal injury and physical destruction, but school fears and social fears arise at this age, as do fears regarding political, economic, and global issues (see Cantor, Wilson, & Hoffner, 1986, for a review). The findings regarding the media stimuli that frighten children at different ages are consistent with observed changes in children's fears in general.

Perceptual Dependence

The first generalization about fright-provoking stimuli is that the relative importance of the immediately perceptible components of a fear-inducing media stimulus decreases as a child's age increases. Research on cognitive development indicates that, in general, very young children react to stimuli predominantly in terms of their perceptible characteristics and that with increasing maturity, they respond more and more to the conceptual aspects of stimuli (see Flavell, 1963; Melkman, Tversky, & Baratz, 1981). Research findings support the generalization that preschool children (approximately 3 to 5 years old) are more likely to be frightened by something that looks scary but is actually harmless than by something that looks attractive but is actually harmful; for older elementary school children (approximately 9 to 11 years), appearance carries much less weight, relative to the behavior or destructive potential of a character, animal, or object.

One set of data that supports this generalization comes from a survey conducted in 1981 (Cantor & Sparks, 1984), asking parents to name the programs and films that had frightened their children the most. In this survey, parents of preschool children most often mentioned offerings with grotesque-looking, unreal characters, such as the television series *The Incredible Hulk* and the feature film *The Wizard of Oz*; parents of older elementary school children more often mentioned programs or movies (like *The Amityville Horror*) that involved threats without a strong visual component and that required a good deal of imagination to comprehend. Sparks (1986) replicated this study, using children's self-reports rather than parents' observations, and obtained similar findings. Both surveys included controls for possible differences in exposure patterns in the different age groups.

A second investigation that supports this generalization was a laboratory study involving an episode of *The Incredible Hulk* (Sparks & Cantor, 1986). In the 1981 survey of parents, this program had spontaneously been mentioned by 40% of the parents of preschoolers as a show that had scared their child (Cantor & Sparks, 1984). The laboratory study concluded that preschool children's unexpectedly intense reactions to this program were partially due to their over-response to the visual image of the Hulk character. When participants were shown a shortened episode of the program and were asked how they had felt during different scenes, preschool children reported the most fear after the attractive, mild-mannered hero was transformed into the monstrous-looking Hulk. Older elementary school children, in contrast, reported the least fear at this time, because they understood that the Hulk was really the benevolent hero in another physical form, and that he was using his superhuman powers to rescue a character who was in danger.

Another study (Hoffner & Cantor, 1985), tested the effect of appearance more directly, by creating a story in four versions, so that a major character was either attractive and grandmotherly-looking or ugly and grotesque. The character's appearance was factorially varied with her behavior—she was depicted as behaving either kindly or cruelly. In judging how nice or mean the character was and in predicting what she would do in the subsequent scene, preschool children were more influenced than older children (6–7 and 9–10 years) by the character's looks and less influenced than older children by her kind or cruel behavior. As the age of the child increased, the character's looks became less important and her behavior carried increasing weight. A follow-up experiment revealed that all age groups engaged in physical appearance stereotyping in the absence of information about the character's behavior.

Harrison and Cantor's (1999) retrospective study of fright responses also provided evidence in support of the diminishing influence of appearance. When descriptions of the program or movie that had frightened respondents were categorized as whether they involved immediately perceptible stimuli (e.g., monstrous-looking characters, eerie noises), the percentage of respondents whose described scene fell into this category declined as the respondent's age at exposure increased.

Fantasy vs. Reality as Fear-inducers

A second generalization that emerges from research is that as children mature, they become more responsive to realistic, and less responsive to fantastic dangers depicted in the media. The data on trends in children's fears suggest that very young children are more likely than older children and adolescents to fear things that are not real, in the sense that their occurrence in the real world is impossible (e.g., monsters). The development of more "mature" fears seems to presuppose the acquisition of knowledge regarding the objective dangers posed by different situations. One important component of this knowledge includes an understanding of the distinction between reality and fantasy, a competence which develops only gradually throughout childhood (see Flavell, 1963; Morison & Gardner, 1978).

This generalization is supported by Cantor and Sparks' (1984) survey of parents. In general, the tendency to mention fantasy offerings as sources of fear—those depicting events that could not possibly occur in the real world—decreased as the child's age increased, and the tendency to mention fictional offerings, depicting events that could possibly occur, increased. Again, Sparks (1986) replicated these findings using children's self-reports. Further support for this generalization comes from a study of children's fright responses to television news (Cantor & Nathanson, 1996). A random survey of parents of children in kindergarten, second, fourth, and sixth grades showed that fear produced by fantasy programs decreased as the child's grade increased, while fear induced by news stories increased with age. Valkenburg, Cantor, and Peeters (2000), in a random survey of Dutch children, also found a decrease between the ages of 7 and 12 in fright responses to fantasy content.

Responses to Abstract Threats

The third generalization from research is that as children mature, they become frightened by media depictions involving increasingly abstract concepts. This generalization is clearly consistent with the general sources of children's fears, cited earlier. It is also consistent with theories of cognitive development (e.g., Flavell, 1963), which indicate that the ability to think abstractly emerges relatively late in cognitive development.

Data supporting this generalization come from a survey of children's responses to the television movie *The Day After*, which depicted the devastation of a Kansas community by a nuclear attack (Cantor et al., 1986). In a random telephone survey of parents conducted the night after the broadcast of this movie, children under 12 were reportedly much less disturbed by the film than were teenagers, and parents were the most disturbed. The very youngest children seem to have been the least frightened. The findings seem to be due to the fact that the emotional impact of the film comes from the contemplation of the potential annihilation of the earth as we know it—a concept that is beyond the grasp of the young child. The visual depictions of injury in the movie were quite mild compared to what most children have become used to seeing on television.

A study of children's reactions to television coverage of the war in the Persian Gulf also supports the generalization that, as they mature, children are increasingly responsive to abstract as opposed to concrete aspects of frightening media (Cantor, Mares, & Oliver, 1993). In a random survey of parents of children in public school in Madison,

Wisconsin, conducted shortly after the Gulf War, there were no significant differences between first, fourth, seventh, and eleventh graders in the prevalence or intensity of negative emotional reactions to television coverage of the war. However, children in different grades were upset by different aspects of the coverage. Parents of younger children, but not of adolescents, stressed the visual aspects of the coverage and the direct, concrete consequences of combat (e.g., the missiles exploding) in their descriptions of the elements that had disturbed their child the most. As the child's age increased, the more abstract, conceptual aspects of the coverage (e.g., the possibility of the conflict spreading) were cited by parents as the most disturbing.

Developmental Differences in the Effectiveness of Coping Strategies

Research in cognitive development has also been used to determine the best ways to help children cope with fear-producing stimuli or to reduce children's fear reactions once they occur (Cantor, 1998; Cantor & Wilson, 1988). Developmental differences in children's information-processing abilities yield differences in the effectiveness of strategies to prevent or reduce their media-induced fears. The findings of research on coping strategies can be summed up in the following generalization: Preschool children benefit more from "noncognitive" than from "cognitive" strategies; both cognitive and noncognitive strategies can be effective for older elementary school children, although this age group tends to prefer cognitive strategies.

Noncognitive Strategies

Noncognitive strategies generally do not involve the processing of verbal information and appear to be relatively automatic. The process of visual desensitization, or gradual exposure to threatening images in a nonthreatening context, is one such strategy that has been shown to be effective for both preschool and older elementary school children. In several experiments, prior exposure to a variety of stimuli—filmed footage of snakes (Wilson & Cantor, 1987), still photographs of worms (Weiss, Imrich, & Wilson, 1993), rubber replicas of spiders (Wilson, 1987), and live lizards (Wilson, 1989a)—reduced children's fear in response to movie scenes featuring similar creatures. Also, fear reactions to the Hulk character in *The Incredible Hulk* were reduced by viewing footage of Lou Ferrigno, the actor who plays the character, having his make-up applied so that he gradually took on the menacing appearance of the character (Cantor, Sparks, & Hoffner, 1988). None of these experiments revealed developmental differences in the effectiveness of desensitization techniques.

Other noncognitive strategies involve physical activities, such as clinging to an attachment object or having something to eat or drink. Although these techniques are available to viewers of all ages, younger children consider them to be more effective and report using them more often than older children do. In a study of children's perceptions of the effectiveness of strategies for coping with media-induced fright, preschool children's evaluations of "holding onto a blanket or a toy" and "getting something to eat or drink" were significantly more positive than those of older elementary school children (Wilson, et al., 1987). Harrison and Cantor's (1999) retrospective study also showed that the percentage of respondents who reported having used a "behavioral" (noncognitive) coping strategy to deal with media-induced fear declined as age at exposure to the frightening fare increased.

Another noncognitive strategy that has been shown to have more appeal and more effectiveness for younger than for older children is covering one's eyes during frightening portions of a presentation. In an experiment by Wilson (1989b), when covering the eyes was suggested as an option, younger children used this strategy more often than older children did. Moreover, the suggestion of this option reduced the fear of younger children, but actually increased the fear of older children. Wilson noted that the older children recognized the limited effectiveness of covering their eyes (while still being exposed to the audio features of the program) and may have reacted by feeling less in control, and therefore more vulnerable, when this strategy was offered to them.

Cognitive Strategies

In contrast to noncognitive strategies, cognitive strategies involve information that is used to cast the threat in a different light. These strategies involve relatively complex cognitive operations, and research consistently finds such strategies to be more effective for older than for younger children.

When dealing with fantasy depictions, the most typical cognitive strategy seems to be to provide an explanation focusing on the unreality of the situation. This strategy should be especially difficult for preschool children, who do not have a full grasp of the implications of the fantasy–reality distinction. In an experiment by Cantor and Wilson (1984), older elementary school children who were told to remember that what they were seeing in *The Wizard of Oz* was not real showed less fear than their classmates who received no instructions. The same instructions did not help preschoolers, however. A study by Wilson and Weiss (1991) also showed developmental differences in the effectiveness of reality-related strategies.

Children's beliefs about the effectiveness of focusing on the unreality of the stimulus have been shown to be consistent with these experimental findings. In Wilson et al.'s (1987) study of perceptions of fear-reducing techniques, preschool children's ranking of the effectiveness of "tell yourself it's not real" was significantly lower than that of older elementary school children.

For media depictions involving realistic threats, the most prevalent cognitive strategy seems to be to provide an explanation that minimizes the perceived severity of the depicted danger. This type of strategy is not only more effective with older children than with younger children, in certain situations it has been shown to have a fear-enhancing rather than anxiety-reducing effect with younger children. In an experiment involving the snake-pit scene from *Raiders of the Lost Ark* (Wilson & Cantor, 1987), children were either exposed or not exposed to reassuring information about snakes (e.g., the statement that most snakes are not poisonous). Although this information tended to reduce the fear of older elementary school children, kindergarten and first-grade children seem to have only partially understood the information, responding to the word "poisonous" more intensely than to the word "not." For them, negative emotional reactions were more prevalent if they had heard the supposedly reassuring information than if they had not heard it.

Data also indicate that older children use cognitive coping strategies more frequently than preschool children do. In the survey of reactions to *The Day After* (Cantor et al., 1986), parents' reports that their child had discussed the movie with them after viewing it increased with the age of the child. In a laboratory experiment involving exposure to a scary scene (Hoffner & Cantor, 1990), significantly more 9- to 11-year-olds than 5- to 7-year-olds reported spontaneously employing cognitive coping strategies (thinking about the expected happy outcome or thinking about the fact that what was happening was not real). Finally, Harrison and Cantor's (1999) retrospective study showed that the tendency to employ a cognitive strategy to cope with media-induced fear increased with the respondent's age at the time of the incident.

Studies have also shown that the effectiveness of cognitive strategies for young children can be improved by providing visual demonstrations of verbal explanations (Cantor et al., 1988), and by encouraging repeated rehearsal of simplified, reassuring information (Wilson, 1987). Recent research also suggests that young children enjoy talking with their caregivers when they are frightened, not so much to hear explanations of what they have seen, but to let them know how they are feeling and to solicit their comfort and support (Cantor, Byrne, Moyer-Gusé, & Riddle, 2007).

GENDER ISSUES AND MEDIA-INDUCED FRIGHT

Gender Differences in Media-Induced Fear

There is a common stereotype that girls are more easily frightened than boys (Birnbaum & Croll, 1984) and indeed that females in general are more emotional than males (e.g., Fabes & Martin, 1991; Grossman & Wood, 1993). Much research seems to support this contention, although the gender differences may be less strong than they appear at first glance, and the observed gender differences seem to be partially attributable to socialization pressures on girls to express their fears and on boys to inhibit them.

Peck (1999) conducted a meta-analysis of the studies of media-induced fear that were produced between 1987 and 1996. Her analysis, which included 59 studies that permitted a comparison between males and females, reported a moderate gender-difference effect size (.41), with females exhibiting more fear than males. Females' responses were more intense than those of males for all dependent measures. However, the effect sizes were largest for self-report and behavioral measures (those that are under the most conscious control) and smallest for heart rate and facial expressions. In addition, the effect size for gender differences increased with age.

Peck (1999) also conducted an experiment in which male and female college students were exposed to two scenes from the *Nightmare on Elm Street* series of movies, one featuring a male victim and the other featuring a female victim. She found that women's self-reports of fear were more intense than those of males, especially when the victim was female. However, when the victim was male, certain of the responses (pulse amplitude and hemispheric asymmetry) suggested that men were experiencing more intense physiological reactions than women.

Although more research is needed to explore the extent of gender differences in media-induced fear and the factors that contribute to them, these findings suggest that the size of the gender difference may be partially a function of social pressures to conform to gender-appropriate behavior.

Gender Differences in Coping Strategies

There is some evidence of gender differences in the coping strategies used to counteract media-induced fear, and these gender differences may also reflect gender-role socialization pressures. Hoffner (1995) found that adolescent girls reported using more noncognitive coping strategies than boys did, but that there were no gender differences in the use of cognitive strategies. Similarly Valkenburg et al. (2000) found that among 7- to 12-year-old Dutch children, girls reported resorting to social support, physical intervention and escape more often than boys did, but that there was no gender difference in the use of cognitive reassurance as a coping strategy.

Both of these findings are consistent with Hoffner's (1995) explanation that because boys are less willing than girls to show their emotions, they avoid noncognitive strategies, which are usually apparent to others. In contrast, the two genders employ cognitive strategies with equal frequency because these strategies are less readily observable.

SUMMARY AND CONCLUSIONS

In summary, research shows that children often experience anxiety and distress while watching mass media presentations and that these feelings, in varying intensities, often linger on after exposure. Recent surveys demonstrate that media-induced fears often interfere with children's sleep, and retrospective reports suggest that the negative effects of scary media can endure for years, even into adulthood.

Research on the relationship between cognitive development and emotional responses to television has been helpful in predicting the types of television programs and movies that are more or less likely to frighten children of different ages and in devising effective intervention and coping strategies for different age groups. In addition to providing empirical tests of the relationship between cognitive development and affective responses, these developmental findings can help parents and other care-givers make more sensible viewing choices for children (Cantor, 1998) and assist them in comforting children who have been frightened (see Cantor, 2004b).

Acknowledgment

Much of the research reported in this chapter was supported by Grant RO1 MH 35320 from the National Institute of Mental Health and by grants from the Graduate School of the University of Wisconsin.

Notes

1 These categories are also not considered exhaustive. Many theorists have proposed additional categories of stimuli that readily evoke fear, such as certain types of animals (especially snakes; see Jersild & Holmes, 1935; Yerkes & Yerkes, 1936) and loud noises, darkness, and stimuli related to loss of support (see Bowlby, 1973). These categories are not discussed separately here because it seems that in mass media productions, such stimuli tend to co-occur with danger or signal its imminence. For example, the snakes, bats, and spiders in horror films are usually depicted as poisonous as well as repulsive. Sudden loud noises, darkness, and the perception of rapid movement are often used to intensify the perceived dangerousness of situations.

References

Berger, S. M. (1962). Conditioning through vicarious instigation. *Psychological Review, 69*, 450–466.

Birnbaum, D. W., & Croll, W. L. (1984). The etiology of children's stereotypes about sex differences in emotionality. *Sex Roles, 10*, 677–691.

Björkqvist, K., & Lagerspetz, K. (1985). Children's experience of three types of cartoon at two age levels. *International Journal of Psychology, 20*, 77–93.

Blumer, H. (1933). *Movies and conduct*. New York: Macmillan.

Bowlby, J. (1973). *Separation: Anxiety and anger*. New York: Basic Books.

Buzzuto, J. C. (1975). Cinematic neurosis following *The Exorcist*. *Journal of Nervous and Mental Disease*, *161*, 43–48.

Cantor, J. (1998). *"Mommy, I'm scared": How TV and movies frighten children and what we can do to protect them*. San Diego, CA: Harvest/Harcourt.

Cantor, J. (2004a). "I'll never have a clown in my house": Why movie horror lives on. *Poetics Today: International Journal for Theory and Analysis of Literature and Communication*, *25*, 283–304.

Cantor, J. (2004b). *Teddy's TV troubles*. Madison, WI: Goblin Fern Press.

Cantor, J., Byrne, S., Moyer-Gusé, E., & Riddle, K. (2007, May). *Young children's descriptions of their media-induced fright reactions*. Paper presented at the Convention of the International Communication Association. San Francisco, CA.

Cantor, J., & Hoffner, C. (1990). Children's fear reactions to a televised film as a function of perceived immediacy of depicted threat. *Journal of Broadcasting & Electronic Media*, *34*, 421–442.

Cantor, J., Mares, M. L., & Oliver, M. B. (1993). Parents' and children's emotional reactions to televised coverage of the Gulf War. In B. Greenberg & W. Gantz (Eds.), *Desert Storm and the mass media* (pp. 325–340). Cresskill, NJ: Hampton Press.

Cantor, J., & Nathanson, A. (1996). Children's fright reactions to television news. *Journal of Communication*, *46*(4), 139–152.

Cantor, J., & Omdahl, B. (1991). Effects of fictional media depictions of realistic threats on children's emotional responses, expectations, worries, and liking for related activities. *Communication Monographs*, *58*, 384–401.

Cantor, J., & Omdahl, B. (1999). Children's acceptance of safety guidelines after exposure to televised dramas depicting accidents. *Western Journal of Communication*, *63*(1), 1–15.

Cantor, J., & Sparks, G. G. (1984). Children's fear responses to mass media: Testing some Piagetian predictions. *Journal of Communication*, *34*(2), 90–103.

Cantor, J., Sparks, G. G., & Hoffner, C. (1988). Calming children's television fears: Mr. Rogers vs. the Incredible Hulk. *Journal of Broadcasting & Electronic Media*, *32*, 271–188.

Cantor, J., & Wilson, B. J. (1984). Modifying fear responses to mass media in preschool and elementary school children. *Journal of Broadcasting*, *28*, 431–443.

Cantor, J., & Wilson, B. J. (1988). Helping children cope with frightening media presentations. *Current Psychology: Research & Reviews*, *7*, 58–75.

Cantor, J., Wilson, B. J., & Hoffner, C. (1986). Emotional responses to a televised nuclear holocaust film. *Communication Research*, *13*, 257–277.

Cantor, J., Ziemke, D., & Sparks, G. G. (1984). The effect of forewarning on emotional responses to a horror film. *Journal of Broadcasting*, *28*, 21–31.

Cantril, H. (1940). *The invasion from Mars: A study in the psychology of panic*. Princeton, NJ: Princeton University Press.

Dysinger, W. S., & Ruckmick, C. A. (1933). *The emotional responses of children to the motion picture situation*. New York: Macmillan.

Fabes, R. A., & Martin, C. L. (1991). Gender and age stereotypes of emotionality. *Personality and Social Psychology Bulletin*, *17*, 532–540.

Feshbach, N. D. (1982). Sex differences in empathy and social behavior in children. In N. Eisenberg (Ed.), *The development of prosocial behavior* (pp. 315–338). New York: Academic Press.

Flavell, J. (1963). *The developmental psychology of Jean Piaget*. New York: Van Nostrand.

Grossman, M., & Wood, W. (1993). Sex differences in the intensity of emotional experience: A social role interpretation. *Journal of Personality and Social Psychology*, *65*, 1010–1022.

Gunter, B., & Furnham, A. (1984). Perceptions of television violence: Effects of programme genre and type of violence on viewers' judgements of violent portrayals. *British Journal of Social Psychology*, *23*, 155–164.

Harrison, K., & Cantor, J. (1999). Tales from the screen: Enduring fright reactions to scary media. *Media Psychology*, *1*(2), 97–116.

Hebb, D. O. (1946). On the nature of fear. *Psychological Review*, *53*, 259–276.

Hoekstra, S. J., Harris, R. J., & Helmick, A. L. (1999). Autobiographical memories about the experience of seeing frightening movies in childhood. *Media Psychology, 1*(2), 117–140.

Hoffman, M. L. (1978). Toward a theory of empathic arousal and development. In M. Lewis & L. A. Rosenblum (Eds.), *The development of affect* (pp. 227–256). New York: Plenum.

Hoffner, C. (1995). Adolescents' coping with frightening mass media. *Communication Research, 22*, 325–346.

Hoffner, C., & Cantor, J. (1985). Developmental differences in responses to a television character's appearance and behavior. *Developmental Psychology, 21*, 1065–1074.

Hoffner, C., & Cantor, J. (1990). Forewarning of a threat and prior knowledge of outcome: Effects on children's emotional responses to a film sequence. *Human Communication Research, 16*, 323–354.

Izard, C. E. (1977). *Human emotions*. New York: Plenum Press.

Jersild, A. T., & Holmes, F. B. (1935). Methods of overcoming children's fears. *Journal of Psychology, 1*, 75–104.

Johnson, B. R. (1980). General occurrence of stressful reactions to commercial motion pictures and elements in films subjectively identified as stressors. *Psychological Reports, 47*, 775–786.

Johnson, J. G., Cohen, P., Kasen, S., First, M. B., & Brook, J. S. (2004). Association between television viewing and sleep problems during adolescence and early adulthood. *Archives of Pediatrics and Adolescent Medicine, 158*, 562–568.

LeDoux, J. (1996). *The emotional brain: The mysterious underpinnings of emotional life*. New York: Simon & Schuster.

Mathai, J. (1983). An acute anxiety state in an adolescent precipitated by viewing a horror movie. *Journal of Adolescence, 6*, 197–200.

Melkman, R., Tversky, B., & Baratz, D. (1981). Developmental trends in the use of perceptual and conceptual attributes in grouping, clustering and retrieval. *Journal of Experimental Child Psychology, 31*, 470–486.

Morison, P., & Gardner, H. (1978). Dragons and dinosaurs: The child's capacity to differentiate fantasy from reality. *Child Development, 49*, 642–648.

Owens, J., Maxim, R., McGuinn, M., Nobile, C., Msall, M., & Alario, A. (1999). Television-viewing habits and sleep disturbance in school children. *Pediatrics, 104*(3), e27.

Paavonen, E. J., Pennonen, M., Roine, M., Valkonen, S., & Lahikainen, A. R. (2006). TV exposure associated with sleep disturbances in 5- to 6-year-olds. *Journal of Sleep Research, 15*, 154–161.

Pavlov, I. P. (1960). *Conditioned reflexes* (G. V. Anrep, Trans.). London: Oxford University Press. (Original work published 1927)

Peck, E. Y. (1999). *Gender differences in film-induced fear as a function of type of emotion measure and stimulus content: A meta-analysis and a laboratory study*. Unpublished doctoral dissertation, University of Wisconsin-Madison.

Sapolsky, B. S., & Zillmann, D. (1978). Experience and empathy: Affective reactions to witnessing childbirth. *Journal of Social Psychology, 105*, 131–144.

Simons, D., & Silveira, W. R. (1994). Post-traumatic stress disorder in children after television programmes. *British Medical Journal, 308*, 389–390.

Singer, M. I., Slovak, K., Frierson, T., & York, P. (1998). Viewing preferences, symptoms of psychological trauma, and violent behaviors among children who watch television. *Journal of the American Academy of Child and Adolescent Psychiatry, 37*(10), 1041–1048.

Sparks, G. G. (1986). Developmental differences in children's reports of fear induced by the mass media. *Child Study Journal, 16*, 55–66.

Sparks, G. G., & Cantor, J. (1986). Developmental differences in fright responses to a television program depicting a character transformation. *Journal of Broadcasting and Electronic Media, 30*, 309–323.

Valkenburg, P. M., Cantor, J., & Peeters, A. L. (2000). Fright reactions to television: A child survey. *Communication Research, 27*, 82–99.

Van den Bulck, J. (2004). Media use and dreaming: The relationship among television viewing, computer game play, and nightmares or pleasant dreams. *Dreaming, 14*, 43–49.

Weiss, A. J., Imrich, D. J., & Wilson, B. J. (1993). Prior exposure to creatures from a horror film: Live versus photographic representations. *Human Communication Research, 20*, 41–66.

Weiss, B. W., Katkin, E. S., & Rubin, B. M. (1968). Relationship between a factor analytically derived measure of a specific fear and performance after related fear induction. *Journal of Abnormal Psychology, 73*, 461–463.

Wilson, B. J. (1987). Reducing children's emotional reactions to mass media through rehearsed explanation and exposure to a replica of a fear object. *Human Communication Research, 14*, 3–26.

Wilson, B. J. (1989a). Desensitizing children's emotional reactions to the mass media. *Communication Research, 16*, 723–745.

Wilson, B. J. (1989b). The effects of two control strategies on children's emotional reactions to a frightening movie scene. *Journal of Broadcasting & Electronic Media, 33*, 397–418.

Wilson, B. J., & Cantor, J. (1985). Developmental differences in empathy with a television protagonist's fear. *Journal of Experimental Child Psychology, 39*, 284–299.

Wilson, B. J., & Cantor, J. (1987). Reducing children's fear reactions to mass media: Effects of visual exposure and verbal explanation. In M. McLaughlin (Ed.), *Communication Yearbook 10* (pp. 553–573). Beverly Hills, CA: Sage.

Wilson, B. J., Hoffner, C., & Cantor, J. (1987). Children's perceptions of the effectiveness of techniques to reduce fear from mass media. *Journal of Applied Developmental Psychology, 8*, 39–52.

Wilson, B. J., & Weiss, A. J. (1991). The effects of two reality explanations on children's reactions to a frightening movie scene. *Communication Monographs, 58*, 307–326.

Yerkes, R. M., & Yerkes, A. W. (1936). Nature and conditions of avoidance (fear) response in chimpanzee. *Journal of Comparative Psychology, 21*, 53–66.

Zillmann, D. (1978). Attribution and misattribution of excitatory reactions. In J. H. Harvey, W. Ickes, & R. F. Kidd (Eds.), *New directions in attribution research* (Vol. 2, pp. 335–368). New York: Erlbaum.

Zillmann, D., & Cantor, J. (1977). Affective responses to the emotions of a protagonist. *Journal of Experimental Social Psychology, 13*, 155–165.

Zillmann, D., Mody, B., & Cantor, J. (1974). Empathetic perception of emotional displays in films as a function of hedonic and excitatory state prior to exposure. *Journal of Research in Personality, 8*, 335–349.

Zoglin, R. (1984, June 25). Gremlins in the rating system. *Time*, p. 78.

15

EFFECTS OF SEX IN THE MEDIA

Richard Jackson Harris
Kansas State University

Christopher P. Barlett
Iowa State University

Where do men and women, boys and girls, learn about sex? What is the impact of those influences? Throughout childhood, adolescence, and into adulthood people learn about sex from many sources, including parents, schools, friends, siblings, and media outlets such as movies, television, magazines, song lyrics, videos, and the Internet. For example, we may learn about French kissing from an older brother's stories, orgasms from a pornographic movie, oral sex from an erotic web site, and rape from a television movie.

Sexual themes in entertainment have been around as long as fiction itself. Many classics were often highly sexual in content, such as Aristophanes' *Lysistrata*, Chaucer's *Canterbury Tales*, or Shakespeare's *The Taming of the Shrew*, all of which are filled with overt sexuality and covert double entendres, some of which may be missed today due to the archaic language and the "classic" aura of these works. More broadly, sex has long been a part of popular culture. Roman gladiatorial contests sometime featured scantily clad women as combatants, and sex scandals, sexual entertainment, and young adults pushing the limits on acceptable dress and behavior have long diverted, and on occasion troubled, society.

According to a Time/CNN poll (Stodghill, 1998), 29% of U.S. teens identified television as their most important source of information about sex, up from 11% in 1986. Although the most-mentioned source (45%) was "friends," only 7% cited parents and 3% cited sex education. In one study, 90% of Toronto adolescent boys and 60% of the girls (mean age = 14) reported having seen at least one pornographic movie (Check & Maxwell, 1992, in Russell, 1998). Also, 29% of boys rated pornography as their *most significant source* of sex education, higher than schools, parents, books, peers or magazines (Check, 1995). Surveys of college men have shown that 35–55% report having consumed violent pornography in some form (Demare, Briere, & Lips, 1988; Garcia, 1986).

Throughout adolescence and early adulthood we continually learn about sex, and media are a major source of that information (Chia, 2006; Dorr & Kunkel, 1990; Sutton, Brown, Wilson, & Klein, 2002). Moreover, relative to other sources, media are becoming increasingly important (Check, 1995; Greenberg et al., 1993), especially women's magazines and television (Kallipolitis et al., 2004). The effects of this heavy consumption of sexually oriented media are the topic of this chapter. We begin by examining the nature of sex in the media, focusing on content analysis studies. The rest of the chapter presents a review of the research on how consuming sexually explicit media impacts sexual arousal, attitudes, and behavior.

THE NATURE OF SEX IN THE MEDIA

Types of Sexual Content

Sexually oriented media may encompass a wide variety of sources. Some materials in magazines, videos, films, and Internet web sites have labels like "erotic," "pornographic," "X-rated," or "sexually explicit." Pornography is big business, generating $13 billion just in the U.S. in 2006 (IT Facts, 2007). Although sex magazines have greatly declined in circulation since the mid-1990s, that drop has been more than compensated for by video sales and rentals, cable and pay-per-view TV, and especially the explosive growth of Internet pornography, producing over 20% of the total revenue in 2006.

Most scholars distinguish between *violent sexual* material, which portrays rape, bondage, torture, sadomasochism, hitting, spanking, hair pulling, and genital mutilation, and *nonviolent sexual* material. Further classifying the nonviolent sexual material is more difficult. Some nonviolent sexual material is entirely mutually consenting and affectionate (sometimes called *erotica*), depicting vaginal or oral intercourse in a loving, or at least non-coercive, fashion. On the other hand, some nonviolent sexual material is *sexually dehumanizing*, depicting *degradation, domination, subordination, or humiliation*. This nonviolent, but dehumanizing, material typically presents the woman with few human attributes besides body parts and sexual appetite. Although often verbally abused and degraded, she appears hysterically receptive and responsive to men's sexual demands. The man appears in the sexually dominant position, and the woman is far more likely than the man to be more exposed or nude.

Sex in media is not limited to explicit portrayals of intercourse or nudity, however, but may include any representation that portrays or implies sexual behavior, interest, or motivation. Sex also occurs in many other places besides explicitly sexual materials. Many news stories, including reports of sex crimes, sex scandals, celebrity starlet social gossip, or tragic excesses like the Abu Ghraib prison abuses, involve sexual content. Sex is rampant in advertising, particularly for products like perfume, cologne, and after-shave, but also for tires, automobiles, and kitchen sinks. For example, one automobile ad on network television featured two women discussing whether a man's choice of a car was related to the size of his penis ("I wonder what he's got under the hood"). See Reichert and Lambiase (2003) for a set of papers on sex in advertising.

Electronic Media

Since the advent of broadcast media in the 1920s, standards have usually been more conservative for radio and television than for print media, because it is easier to shield children from sexually oriented print media than from X-rated TV. With the advent of widespread cable and video technology, a sort of double standard has arisen, with greater acceptance of more sexual materials in video and premium cable channels than on network television. The logic appears to be that premium cable and rented movies are "invited" into the home, whereas network programming is there uninvited and accessible wherever a TV set is present. A greater problem is the easy availability of sexual materials on the Internet, which has virtually no effective restrictions (Ferguson

& Perse, 2000). Although there is much interest in legally restricting children's access to sexually explicit sites, there is considerable disagreement about what kinds of restrictions or blocking software would be both legal and effective, without blocking useful non-sexual sites like breast cancer information or art sites. According to a 2002 survey, it was reported that single males between the ages of 18 and 45 years visited pornographic websites more frequently than any other demographic group did (Buzzell, 2005).

Turning to television, the most-studied medium, content analyses have shown that, although the sex on network television is not usually explicit, sexual talk and innuendoes are rampant, most often occurring in a humorous context. One extensive content analysis study found that 68% of TV shows on network and cable in 1999–2000 contained sexual content, with 65% containing talk about sex and 27% presenting physical sexual behaviors (Kunkel, Biely, Eyal, Cope-Farrar, Donnerstein, & Fandrich, 2003). References to premarital and extra-marital sexual encounters outnumbered references to sex between spouses by at least 6:1 (Greenberg & Hofschire, 2000) and as high as 24:1 for unmarried versus married partners in soap operas or 32:1 in R-rated movies with teen characters (Greenberg et al., 1993)! The latter study also found that nudity occurred in all R-rated films in its sample, with female exceeding male nudity by a 4:1 margin. Sex in media is largely without consequences. One study showed only 14% of the discussions about sex on primetime TV contained any mention of risks or responsibilities of sex and only 3% of the portrayals of sexual behavior did (Cope-Farrar & Kunkel, 2002). For shows with "intercourse-related content," the percentage of shows mentioning any risk or responsibility of sex rose from 14 to 26%, but that is still low (Kunkel, Eyal, Donnerstein, Farrar, Biely, & Rideout, 2007).

In 2007, a longitudinal meta-analysis of 25 content analyses (from 1975 to 2004) on sexual content appearing on U.S. primetime network programming (NBC, ABC, CBS, and Fox) found a decrease in the frequency per hour for passionate kissing, touching and petting, and intercourse from the early 1990s to 2004. Interestingly, however, the amount of sex talk steadily increased from 1999 to 2004. This meta-analysis also found a significant positive correlation between the year and the amount of explicit sexual intercourse, although this type of content did not appear that often (0.025 occurrences per hour). Finally, results showed a recent increase in the frequency of unmarried intercourse and prostitution from 2000 to 2004 (Hetsroni, 2007).

Although content analyses of soap operas showed considerable sexual content in 1985, there was a 35% increase by 1994 (Greenberg & Busselle, 1996). Also in 1994, compared to 1985, there were more themes of (a) negative consequences of sex, (b) rejection of sexual advances, and (c) portrayals of rape. None of these three themes had been very common in the soaps of the 1970s and 1980s. Not surprisingly, R-rated movies and sex magazines had more explicit sex than appeared on television (Greenberg et al., 1993; Greenberg & Hofschire, 2000).

The major focus of this chapter is on sexually explicit materials, including, though not limited to, what is generally called "pornography" or "erotica," both violent and nonviolent. The term *pornography* is highly value laden, however, and as such is rather scientifically imprecise. Thus, we will most often refer to such materials as "sexually explicit" rather than "pornographic," although that term is so widely used it cannot be completed avoided. When we consider effects of sex in the media, however, we need to look more widely than only at what is typically considered "pornography."

EFFECTS OF CONSUMING SEXUAL MEDIA

Although many might wish it otherwise, sex, even very explicit sex, does sell. Sexually oriented print, video, broadcast, and Internet materials are highly profitable commercially, a condition which in itself ensures their continued presence. Aside from these economic effects, three major classes of effects of exposure have been identified, namely arousal, attitudinal changes, and behavioral effects. See Gunter (2002), Huston, Wartella, and Donnerstein (1998), Linz and Malamuth (1993), Malamuth (1993), Malamuth and Impett (2001), Mundorf, D'Alessio, Allen, and Emmers-Sommer (2007), Oddone-Paolucci, Genuis, and Violato (2000), and Pollard (1995) for more detailed reviews of various types of effects and media.

Research on effects of sex in the media has been guided by a variety of theoretical perspectives. Although these theories are not the focus of this chapter, the reader is referred to other chapters in this volume for thorough explications and reviews of these different perspectives: Morgan, Signorielli, and Shanahan (cultivation theory), Bandura (social cognitive theory), Petty, Briñol, and Priester (elaboration likelihood model), Roskos-Ewoldsen, Roskos-Ewoldsen and Carpentier (priming), and Rubin (uses and gratifications). Each of these perspectives has informed and guided certain areas of research on the effects of sexual media. These theoretical influences are alluded to below, although the focus of the rest of the chapter is on empirical findings on the effects of sexual media.

Arousal

One straightforward effect of consuming sexual media is sexual arousal, the heightened physiological state that energizes sexual behavior. Arousal is measured in either of two ways. The most common measures are self-ratings (e.g., "How aroused are you?" on a 7-point scale). It may also be measured more directly, albeit more obtrusively, through various physiological measures such as electronic sensors measuring penile tumescence, vaginal lubrication, or temperature (thermography).

By most measures, men are typically more aroused by sexual media than are women, especially in response to sexually violent or dehumanizing materials (Malamuth, 1996; Murnen & Stockton, 1997). Sexual violence may be particularly arousing to sex offenders and other violence-prone men and even to "normal" men if the victim is portrayed as being aroused by the assault. Sexually coercive men are more physiologically aroused by slides or verbal descriptions of coercive sex than are "normal" men, who may have developed the ability to inhibit a sexual response in the presence of coercive cues (Lohr, Adams, & Davis, 1997).

Sexual arousal in response to stimuli that would not normally be arousing may be learned through classical conditioning. For example, Rachman and Hodgson (1968) classically conditioned heterosexual men to be sexually aroused by women's boots by pairing the boots with nude female photos, thus providing a model of how sexual "turn-ons" can be learned. This process could account for the vast individual differences in the specific stimuli that arouse people sexually. Through different experiences, people have all been conditioned to respond to different stimuli through associations with those we love. Myers (2007) reported a friend who was turned on by the smell of onion breath, because his first girl friend loved to eat onions and he has associated that odor with kissing her, through the process of classical conditioning. Because of its connection with a particular person, someone may be aroused by a certain perfume or cologne, type of clothing, or specific behavior. Media provide many of the images and associations for such conditioning.

The degree of arousal need not be highly correlated with the degree of explicitness. Sometimes people are actually more aroused by a less sexually explicit story than a more explicit one. A scene which cuts suddenly from a bedroom one night to the next morning may sometimes be more arousing than a more explicit version with the intervening night uncut! Censoring a sex scene may make a film more arousing because viewers can fill in their own scripts. When people are allowed to use their own imaginations to construct the ending of a romantic scene, they are more likely to construct a reality that is more arousing to them personally than if they view someone else's idea of what is arousing. The individuality of sexual arousal is the concern that sex therapists have with certain sexual media from the Internet or adult video stores. It has been argued by Carnes (2001) that since the Internet has an unlimited number of websites that feature any sexual desire that the user wants, this leads to sexual arousal because the stimuli are "new." For instance, because of Internet sex websites, a viewer can see images of any desired fantasy, many of which typically do not occur in most people's sexual lives. These images are then "burned" into the brain and are fantasized about during sexual intercourse (Carnes, 2001).

Individual Differences in Viewers

Some early studies examined convicted rapists and found them to be aroused by both rape and consenting sex, whereas normal men were aroused only by the consenting sex (Abel, Barlow, Blanchard, & Guild, 1977; Quinsey, Chaplin, & Upfold, 1984), although subsequent studies did not find this consistent arousal effect in sex offenders (Baxter, Barbaree, & Marshall, 1986; Hall, 1989). Under some conditions, however, even "normal" college men were aroused by scenes of sexual violence. For example, men, though not women, were at least as aroused by a rape scene as by a consenting sex scene but only if the victim was portrayed as enjoying the rape and coming to orgasm (Malamuth & Check, 1983; Ohbuchi, Ikeda, & Takeuchi, 1994). The men were not aroused if the victim was shown to be terrorized. Using a similar design, Bushman, Bonacci, van Dijk, and Baumeister (2003) found that men scoring high in narcissism found a rape scene preceded by affection between the parties as more entertaining and more sexually arousing than low narcissists did. Yates, Barbaree, and Marshall (1984) showed that normal men were equally aroused by depictions of rape and consenting sex but only after they had been angered by a female confederate. Otherwise the consenting sex scene was more arousing. Finally, Bogaert (2001) found that the personality traits of dominance, Machiavellianism, psychoticism, and hypermasculinity were correlated with the likelihood of viewing erotica containing violence, child pornography, or women with insatiable sexual appetites but not with the likelihood of viewing erotica lacking in these themes.

The Gender Skew

Explicit sexual materials have traditionally been designed by men and for men. As such, they have a distinctly macho, hypermasculine orientation. Although magazines and videos show all varieties of heterosexual intercourse, they place little emphasis on associated foreplay, afterplay, cuddling, or general tenderness. Women are shown eagerly desiring and participating in intercourse, often with insatiable euphoria. There is little concern with the consequences of sex or the relational matrix within which most people experience it. Men are much more active seekers and users of sexual material than are women, with an estimated 71% of sex videos viewed by men by themselves (Gettleman, 1999). However, this cannot necessarily be assumed to be due to greater intrinsic male interest in sex; it may merely reflect the pornography industry's extreme slant to the hypermasculine fantasy. Indeed, a few studies have shown women to have more positive reactions to sexual videos written and directed by women and for women (Mosher & Maclan, 1994; Quackenbush, Strassberg & Turner, 1995; Senn & Desmarais, 2004), although men appear to be more likely to seek out sexual media and be aroused by it, even after controlling for content (Malamuth, 1996).

An evolutionary psychology explanation for sex differences in sexual behavior (Buss, 1995; Malamuth, 1996, 1999) would argue that men seek a greater number of sexual partners, while women are more interested in a longer-term commitment from a mate to help raise the offspring. These ideas are consistent with observed findings that men seek out and use sexual media more than women and are generally more aroused than women by them, especially media that visually represent many different potential partners. Women, however, are less aroused than men by typical pornography, preferring more contextually based sexual expressions like romance novels.

The Catharsis Legend

One often hears the argument that consuming sexually explicit material facilitates the expression of sexual urges and thus *decreases* arousal. This invokes the construct of *catharsis*, the emotional release that follows the expression of an impulse. This popular idea comes most directly from psychodynamic models of personality, notably Freud. Applied to sex, the catharsis argument predicts that consuming sexual media relieves sexual urges, with the magazine or video, perhaps in conjunction with masturbation, becoming a sort of imperfect substitute for the real behavior. Although a catharsis argument has been used to support loosening restrictions on pornography (Kutchinsky, 1973) and has been reported by sex offenders as a strategy for reducing impulses for committing an offense (Carter, Prentky, Knight, Vanderveer, & Boucher, 1987; Langevin, Lang, Wright, Handy, Frenzel, & Black, 1988), the research support for catharsis is weak to nonexistent (Bushman, Baumeister, & Stack, 1999). Viewing sexual material *increases*, not decreases, sexual arousal, and, after viewing, one is thus *more*, not *less*, motivated to engage in sexual behavior. Thus consuming pornography in order to reduce sexual arousal is likely to have the opposite effect. Nor will it reduce the propensity to rape, which is driven by a power motive, not a lack of sexual fulfillment (Prentky & Knight, 1991). See Scheele and DuBois (2006) for a recent conceptual examination of the history and current status of catharsis theory.

Attitudinal Effects

Sex and Values

Many concerns about sexually explicit media involve the attitudes and values they convey. Repeated exposure to media with a more-or-less consistent set of messages may cultivate a worldview that increasingly reflects the perspective of the media (Morgan, Shanahan, & Signorielli, this volume). For example, watching numerous sitcoms and movies where characters are routinely sexually active early in a relationship with little concern of consequences may cultivate acceptance of such a position in the viewer and thus weaken family-taught values against casual premarital sex. Increasing numbers of ads and movies with themes of coercion and sexual violence may desensitize readers to violence toward women. Such effects are especially likely to happen if the characters holding those values are respected characters with whom viewers identify. Sexual promiscuity by a prostitute is less likely to influence the values of a viewer than is similar behavior by a respected suburban mother.

One of the major social criticisms of pornography is that it is ideologically anti-women (Buchwald, Fletcher, & Roth, 1993; Russell, 1998), a concern especially leveled at violent and nonviolent dehumanizing pornography. It is usually women, not men, who are the playthings or victims of violence by the opposite sex. For example, one sex magazine showed a jackhammer in a woman's vagina as the opening photo to a story "How to Cure Frigidity," and another showed a photo spread of a gang rape turning into an orgy with the women appearing to be aroused by the assault. A sex video showed a woman's breast tied and squeezed for the entertainment of men who were watching.

Sexual Attitudes

A large body of research has shown effects on a variety of sexual attitudes and values after exposure to nonviolent sexually explicit materials. After seeing slides and movies of beautiful female nudes engaged in sexual activity, men rated their own partners as being less physically endowed, although they reported undiminished sexual satisfaction (Weaver, Masland, & Zillmann, 1984). Men even reported that they loved their own partners less after seeing sexually explicit videos of highly attractive models (Kenrick, Gutierres, & Goldberg, 1989). Men who saw a pornographic video responded more sexually to a subsequent female interviewer than did men seeing a control video, although this result was only found for men holding traditional gender-role attitudes (McKenzie-Mohr & Zanna, 1990). It is as if the voluptuous model has become the norm or "anchor" (Tversky & Kahneman, 1974) to which real people are compared.

Such effects are not limited to men. Relative to control groups, both men and women who watched weekly pornographic films later reported less satisfaction with the affection, physical appearance, sexual curiosity, and sexual performance of their real-life partners (Zillmann & Bryant, 1988a, 1988b). They also saw sex without emotional involvement as being relatively more important than did the control group, and they showed greater acceptance of premarital and extramarital sex and placed lesser value on marriage and monogamy. They also reported less desire to have children and greater acceptance of male dominance and female submission. Using the same methodology, Zillmann and Bryant (1982) found that participants who had watched sexually explicit films 1–3 weeks earlier consistently overestimated the frequency of oral sex, anal intercourse, sadomasochism, and bestiality in the general population, relative to perceptions of a control group seeing nonsexual films. Teens watching a heavy diet of daytime talk television with frank discussion of sexual topics later overestimated the frequency of such behaviors, relative to a low-viewing group (Greenberg & Smith, 2002). Heavy viewing of soap operas, primetime dramas and overall television predicts a lower sexual self-concept in young adult women (Aubrey, 2007). Such results reflect the cognitive heuristic of *availability*, whereby we judge the frequency of occurrence of various activities by the ease with which we can generate examples (Glassner, 1999; Tversky & Kahneman, 1973, 1974). Recent exposure to vivid media instances thus raises the estimation of the frequency of such occurrences in the real world.

The sexual material need not even be explicit or graphic to help shape attitudes. Bryant and Rockwell (1994) found that, compared to controls, adolescents who watched a heavy diet of highly sexual primetime programs were more lenient in their judgment about sexual impropriety and how much a victim had been wronged, although these effects were greatly attenuated by open family communication and active critical viewing. One may not even need the pictures. In one study all-verbal print descriptions of sex (e.g., the *Penthouse* Advisor column) were actually more conducive than photos to fantasizing about one's own partner (Dermer & Pyszczynski, 1978).

In a meta-analysis of studies examining the relationship of the exposure to sexual media to the acceptance of rape myths, Allen, Emmers, Gebhardt, and Giery (1995) concluded that experimental studies show a consistent positive effect between pornography exposure and rape myth acceptance, while correlational and field studies show only a very small positive or nonexistent effect. The relationship was consistently stronger when the pornography was violent than when it was nonviolent, although some experimental studies obtained effects with both types.

Alcohol consumption may enhance existing tendencies to either harshly judge or empathize with a female victim, although it generally decreased sensitivity to victim distress, especially so in "hypermasculine" men (Norris, George, Davis, Martell, & Leonesio, 1999). Alcohol can even affect women's judgments. Women reading an eroticized rape description while intoxicated were less likely than a sober control group to label coercive sex events as rape (Davis, Norris, George, Martell, & Heiman, 2006).

Pornography, especially videos, may be consumed for one or more of four different purposes (Gunter, 2002). *Sexual enhancement* creates the mood for sex or gives ideas about specific behaviors. *Diversion* offers an escape from boredom. *Sexual release* stimulates sexual fantasies. *Substitution* replaces a sexual partner. Men are more likely than women to report using pornography for sexual release and substitution. Those who used it for substitution were more likely to show acceptance of rape myths, although those who used it for sexual release were actually less likely to accept the rape myths (Gunter, 2002; Perse, 1994).

Slasher Films: Sex + Violence in Mainstream Movies

Although the studies discussed above used sexually explicit materials, attitudinal effects are by no means confined to clearly pornographic materials. Consider the highly successful horror-film series such as *I Know What You Did Last Summer, Halloween, Child's Play, Texas Chainsaw Massacre, Friday the Thirteenth, Scream, The Ring, Hostel,* and *Nightmare on Elm Street*, as well as many lesser known films of the last 40 years. Many are extremely violent with strong sexual overtones. Clover (1992, p. 21) defined a slasher film as a "generative story of a psychokiller who slashes to death a string of mostly female victims, one by one until he is subdued or killed, usually by the one girl who has survived." Although some, such as the *Scream* series and *Scary Movie*, are framed as "satires" of the slasher genre, it is not clear that the youthful audiences receive them very differently than the non-satirical films.

Although many slasher films have R ratings in the United States, others are released unrated or direct to video to avoid the "accompanied by parent" requirement of R-rated movies. Given that so many viewings of movies are in DVD format among youth (sometimes in "uncut" versions), the ratings are of limited use, however. Oliver (1993) found that punitive attitudes toward sexuality and traditional attitudes toward women's sexuality were associated with high school students' greater enjoyment of previews of slasher films. Although there has been some trend toward stronger, less victimized female characters in recent films such as *Urban Legend, I Know What You Did Last Summer*, and *Bride of Chucky*, the effects of such portrayals remains untested. Gender clearly remains a very salient aspect of these films and men and women respond somewhat differently to them. When young adults wrote descriptions of the most memorable slasher film they had seen and described their emotional reactions to the films, Nolan and Ryan (2000) found that men more often wrote of themes of fear of strangers, while women more often wrote of fear of horrors in the home and in intimate relationships.

Linz, Donnerstein, and Penrod (1984; see also Linz, Donnerstein, & Adams, 1989) examined the attitudinal effects of slasher films. After male college students were initially screened to exclude those with prior hostile tendencies or psychological problems, the remaining men in the experimental group watched one slasher film per day over one week. All of the films were very violent and showed multiple instances of women being killed in slow, lingering, painful deaths in situations associated with much erotic content (e.g., a woman masturbating in her bath is suddenly assaulted and killed by an intruder with a nail gun). Each day participants completed some personality measures and questionnaires evaluating that film.

Over the week, the men became generally less depressed, less annoyed, and less anxious in response to the films. The films themselves were rated as increasingly enjoyable, humorous, and socially meaningful, and progressively less violent, offensive, and degrading to women. Over the week's time, the violent episodes in general and rape episodes in particular were recalled as less frequent. Although these data provide clear evidence of desensitization in men, there is still the question of generalization to other situations.

To answer this question, Linz et al. arranged to have their participants later observe a rape trial at the law school and evaluate it in several ways. Compared to a control group, men who had seen the slasher films rated the rape victim as having been less physically and emotionally injured. These results are consistent with those of Zillmann and Bryant (1984), who found that massive exposure to sexually explicit media by jurors resulted in shorter recommended prison sentences for a rapist. Using Linz et al.'s methodology of rating movies followed by evaluation of an "unrelated" rape trial, Weisz and Earls (1995) showed men and women one of four films: man raping a man (*Deliverance*), man raping a woman (*Straw Dogs*), nonsexual male aggression toward both men and women (*Die Hard 2*), and nonaggressive action film (*Days of Thunder*). They found strong desensitizing effects of the two sexually violent films in men but not in women. Interestingly enough, it did not matter whether a man (*Deliverance*) or a woman (*Straw Dogs*) was the victim; both films desensitized men to the female rape trial victim, though neither effect appeared in women. Such findings show that attitudes inculcated by seeing slasher films do indeed transfer to new situations.

There have been some methodological (Weaver, 1991) and conceptual (Sapolsky & Molitor, 1996) criticisms of this research, and some effects have not been fully replicated in later work (Linz & Donnerstein, 1988). Some have questioned Donnerstein and Linz's conclusion of sharply different effects of viewing violent versus nonviolent sexual materials (Mundorf et al., 2007; Weaver, 1991).

Nor are violent sexual themes confined to horror, or even R-rated, movies. For example, the 1995 PG-rated James Bond movie *Goldeneye* featured a villain who seduces men to have sex with her and then crushes them to death. It also contains scenes of seduction with very violent mutual battering as a sort of foreplay. The major concern with such films is the juxtaposition of sex and violence. In countries like India and Japan, rape and other acts of violence against women are even more standard entertainment fare in action-adventure films.

Recently, Internet pornography has begun to be of interest to researchers (see Griffin-Shelley, 2003 for a review). Two early experimental studies (Barak & Fisher, 1997; Barak, Fisher, Belfry, & Lashambe, 1999) failed to find a consistent effect of amount of Internet sex exposure on any of several measures of misogynistic attitudes. Later work, however, has produced clearer effects. In an extensive correlational study investigating the effect of Internet pornography on adolescent male attitudes, a significant correlation was found between the amount of Internet pornography viewed and recreational sexual attitudes (which included items such as "It is OK to have sexual relationships with more than one partner"), but this effect was mediated by the realism of the pornography (Peter & Valkenburg, 2006). Thus, when the sexual actions on the Internet website looked as though they could happen in real life, teenage boys were more likely to have more liberal attitudes toward sex. Similarly, Lo & Wei (2005) found that exposure to Internet pornography was significantly correlated with attitudes toward extramarital sex and sexually permissive behavior (holding hands to sexual intercourse), such that, as the viewing amount increased, so did more accepting attitudes of infidelity, as well as the amount of self-reported sexual behavior by participants. A survey of college students found that viewing sexually explicit material on the Internet was significantly correlated with masturbating online, sending and receiving pornography online, and seeking new people online (Boies, 2002). The same study also sought the uses and gratifications for viewing pornography on the Internet, and responses indicated that men (more than women) use this form of media because they find it sexually arousing, to satisfy sexual needs, to fulfill sexual fantasies, and to satisfy curiosity about new sexual techniques (Boies, 2002).

Thus there is considerable evidence that exposure to erotica, in whatever medium, affects attitudes and values about sex and various sexual issues. We now turn to examining effects on behavior.

Behavioral Effects

Adolescent Socialization

Teenagers who watch a heavy diet of television with sexual content were twice as likely to engage in sexual intercourse over the following year as teens who were light viewers of sexual content, even after controlling for other possible factors (Collins, Elliott, Berry, Kanouse, Kunkel, & Hunter, 2004). Heavy TV viewing of sexual content was also associated with other non-coital sexual behaviors (heavy petting, deep kissing, etc.). These findings were the same regardless of whether the sexual content was explicitly shown in behavior or only discussed in dialogue.

On the other hand, sexual content in media can have positive effects of increasing knowledge and instigating information seeking. For example, after an *ER* episode with three minutes on emergency contraception, 51% of viewers reported talking with others about the issue, 23% sought information from another source, and 14% talked to their doctor about it (Kaiser Family Foundation, 2002). After an episode of *Friends* that portrayed a pregnancy resulting from condom failure, about two-thirds of viewers aged 12–17 reported learning that condoms could fail, and most remembered that six months later (Collins et al., 2003).

Teaching New Behaviors

Sometime media may actually teach new behaviors, potentially including some extremely violent and destructive ones. Although examples like men watching a movie depicting a gang rape on a pool table and soon afterward perpetrating a similar act are thankfully not commonplace, the juxtaposition of such events when they actually happen is compelling. Very violent and disturbing images are available on video and Internet, from extreme objectification like a naked woman on a hamburger bun smeared with condiments or women being tortured or even killed in a variety of ways (see Russell, 1998, for many gruesome examples). For obvious ethical reasons, there has been virtually no controlled scientific study of effects of viewing such extreme materials.

In a review of correlational research examining the role of pornography in the sexual development of sex offenders, including the possible role of pornography to incite sexual offenses, Bauserman (1996) concluded that such links have not been reliably demonstrated as general trends. However, sex offenders are a highly diverse group and there may be a subset that uses violent pornography in disturbing ways. Allen, D'Alessio, and Emmers-Sommer (2000) found that, although convicted sex offenders did not consume more pornography than did non-offender controls, they were more aroused by it and were more likely to commit some form of sexual act afterwards (masturbation, consensual, or coercive sex). Vega and Malamuth (2007) found that the amount of pornography consumption was a significant predictor of sexual aggression in men. Malamuth, Addison, and Koss (2000) came to a similar conclusion examining numerous meta-analyses and empirical studies, with the effect being strongest for violent pornography and those men at high risk for sexual aggression.

Cybersex, defined as communicating online and masturbating (Ferree, 2003), as well as viewing sexual images on the Internet while masturbating, has behavioral consequences for the user as well as the user's partner and family. Results from an online survey of those impacted by their significant other's frequent cybersex found that such behavior was a contributing factor in separation and divorce. Furthermore, the majority of couples abstained from having sexual intercourse, resulting from the partner's (usually female—97%) feelings of isolation and lower self-esteem from not feeling as pretty as the online women, and anger from being lied to (Schneider, 2000). If the user and partner had children, results showed that 14% of those children have seen pornographic images and/or the user masturbating, while 11% of children were adversely affected by the images and users' cybersex behavior (Schneider, 2003).

Disinhibition of Known Behaviors

Aside from teaching new behaviors, sexual media may also break down natural inhibitions of previously learned behaviors. For example, watching a video with oral sex or bondage may disinhibit the viewer's prior existing inhibitions against engaging in such behavior. Watching a rape scene where a woman appears to enjoy being assaulted may disinhibit the constraint against some men's secret urge to commit such a crime. Amount of violent pornography consumed significantly predicted self-rated likelihood to rape, although there was no effect of nonviolent pornography (Demare, Briere, & Lips, 1988). Check and Guloien (1989) found that men exposed to a steady diet of rape-myth sexual violence reported a higher likelihood of committing rape themselves, compared to a no-exposure control group, but the same result was found for a group exposed to nonviolent erotica.

Such effects appear to carry over to new settings. Donnerstein and Berkowitz (1981) showed men a sexually violent film where a woman is attacked, stripped, tied up, and raped. In one version of the film the woman was portrayed as enjoying the rape. Afterward, men who had seen that version administered more electric shocks to a female, though not to a male, confederate who had earlier angered them in an ostensibly unrelated study. In a similar vein, Zillmann and Bryant (1984) found that participants with repeated exposure to sexually explicit media recommended shorter prison sentences for a rapist than did a control group. Shope (2004) found that men who used pornography, especially if they also abused alcohol, were more likely to batter their partners.

Correlation of Sexual Media to Rape and Other Crimes

One of the main concerns about behavioral effects of viewing sexually explicit materials is their possible relationship with rape and other so-called sex crimes. Most Western nations have experienced since the 1960s a large increase both in the availability of sexually explicit media and in the rise in reported rapes. The relationship between the two, however, has been difficult to clarify. There have been many studies looking at correlations of rates of crimes like rape, sexual assault, exhibitionism, and child molestation, relative to sexual media consumption and changes in the availability of pornography in many different countries (see Bauserman, 1996, for a review). Results have sometimes shown an increase in availability of sexually explicit media associated with an increase in rape rates (e.g., Court, 1984; Jaffee & Straus, 1987), and other times a decrease or no difference in rates of rape and other crimes (e.g., Kutchinsky, 1973, 1991). This inconsistency in the literature may be in part due to sampling and procedural differences across studies and in part due to cultural and national differences in social attitudes toward rape, rates of reporting, and likelihood and severity of punishment.

One interesting example of cultural factors is seen in the case of Japan, which has a fairly high availability of sexually explicit materials, including sexual violence, but very low rape rates (Diamond & Uchiyama, 1999). Sexual themes in Japanese art and society go back centuries and continue to be common, without being associated with shame or guilt. Although Japan prohibits pictorial representations of adult genitalia, explicit sexual depictions are not restricted to "X-rated" magazines, books, and films, as in the United States. Why, then, is the incidence of reported rapes in Japan less than one tenth the rate in the U.S. and one-quarter the rate in Western Europe? Although rape in Japan may be more likely to be group instigated, perpetrated by juveniles, and greatly underreported by victims (Goldstein & Ibaraki, 1983), these factors are unlikely to entirely explain the difference (Abramson & Hayashi, 1984). Japanese society emphasizes order, obligation, cooperation, and virtue, and one who violates social norms is the object of shame. This probably discourages victims from reporting rape but also greatly discourages and stigmatizes those who perpetrate it.

Firmly establishing a causal relationship between the availability of sexually explicit materials and the incidence of crimes like rape is extremely difficult, due to the many other relevant factors, including the different varieties of sexual material, cultural differences, changes in social consciousness about reporting sexual assaults, and changing norms sanctioning such behavior. Although there may be positive correlations between specific measures like sex magazine circulation and reported rapes within a narrow geographical area (e.g., Court, 1984; Jaffee & Straus, 1987), a more general conclusion remains elusive, especially in the age of the Internet where material is available to users almost anywhere.

What About the Context?

Responses to sexual materials are not entirely due to the nature of the material itself. They also depend on a variety of intangible and hard-to-study contextual factors. For example, a documentary on rape or a tasteful drama on incest may be acceptable and noncontroversial, whereas a comedy with the same theme, even with far fewer sexually explicit depictions, may be highly offensive or even be considered pornographic. We react differently to a sexually explicit drawing by Picasso than we do to one in *Hustler* magazine. Because Shakespeare, Chaucer, *The Song of Solomon* in the Bible, and serious sex manuals are seen to have serious literary or didactic intentions, the sex therein is considered more acceptable and even healthy.

The context and expectations that are brought to the experience can greatly affect the experiencing of sex in the media. When watching an erotic film with one's parents, one's children, by oneself, in a group of close same-sex friends, or with one's spouse or significant other, reactions to it may differ greatly because of who else is there. Taking a first date to an unexpectedly explicit erotic movie may be a much less pleasant experience than seeing the same movie with a long-term companion. A photo of a nude woman being fed through a meat grinder might be unsurprising in *Hustler* but shocking if suddenly encountered in *Newsweek*.

One interesting contextual issue is how to respond to something of clear artistic worth but written at a time with different standards. For example, should Rhett Butler's forcing his attentions on Scarlett O'Hara in *Gone with the Wind* be seen as rape or as the noncontroversial romantic moment that it appeared to be in 1939? In many old Westerns of the 1940s and 1950s a man comes on sexually to a woman, she initially refuses, and finally she falls breathlessly into his arms. Ralph Kramden regularly threatened to punch his wife in the 1950s sitcom *The Honeymooners* (although he never did so), and Ricky Ricardo occasionally spanked his wife in *I Love Lucy*. Although such scenes were never sexually explicit, their effect on the modern viewer from a different world is unknown. Do these "safe" shows from an earlier "golden age" of television trivialize or even condone rape or spousal battering? There clearly are sexual messages there.

The relation and integration of sex to the overall plot is another important contextual factor. A sex scene, even a mild and nonexplicit one, may offend people if it appears to be added merely to spice up the story without having any connection to it. Something far more explicit may be accepted much better if it is seen as necessary and central to the plot. Sex scenes in a story about a prostitute may be much less gratuitous than similar scenes in a story about a female corporate executive. Few argued that the graphic pool table gang rape scene in *The Accused* was gratuitous in that story about the effects of rape on the victim.

The culture can provide important context. For example, some cultures do not consider female breasts to be particularly erotic or inappropriate for public display. Thus, most readers, at least over about age 14, do not consider topless women from some distant culture in *National Geographic* photos to be erotic, sexual, or pornographic. However, when *National Geographic* first began to publish such photographs in the early 20th century, it was a carefully reasoned, but risky, editorial decision (Lutz & Collins,

1993). Even within Western culture, standards have changed. In much of the 19th century, knees and calves were thought to be erotic, and the sight of a bare-kneed woman would be considered as scandalous as a topless woman would today. As societies go, North America overall is moderate in what is allowable sexual expression in dress, media, and behavior. Many Western European and Latin American cultures are far more permissive, while many Muslim and East Asian cultures are far more restrictive. Even today, the logic of conservative Islamic cultures insisting on a woman being largely covered stems from a belief that men seeing unclothed sections of women's bodies will be so sexually aroused that they will be unable to control themselves and thus may be driven to sexually assault the women. Thus the dress codes are seen as having the purpose of protecting women.

MITIGATING THE NEGATIVE EFFECTS OF SEXUAL MEDIA

Although not all questions have been answered, results from the research reviewed in this chapter are disturbing, especially given the widespread viewing of sexually violent films by children and young teens and their hugely increased availability through video and the Internet. Some studies have developed and evaluated extensive pre-exposure training and/or post-exposure debriefing procedures designed to lessen the desensitizing effects of sexual violence (Intons-Peterson, Roskos-Ewoldsen, Thomas, Shirley, & Blut, 1989; Linz, Fuson, & Donnerstein, 1990). These studies have typically shown mitigating effects on some measures and not on others. Linz et al. (1990) found that men were most strongly positively affected by the information that women are not responsible for sexual assaults perpetrated on them. Offering pertinent information about rape myths reduced desensitization and the inaccuracy of media portrayals *after* people had seen the sexually violent media. Participants were more impressed with such arguments after they had felt themselves excited and aroused by the film and had seen very specific examples to illustrate the point of the debriefing/mitigation information. In the context of having seen such a film, the specific points of the sensitization training had greater impact. Thus experimental participation may at least sometimes actually *decrease* rape myth acceptance.

Using a different approach, Wilson, Linz, Donnerstein, and Stipp (1992) measured the effect of seeing a prosocial TV movie about rape. Compared to a control group, people viewing the film generally showed more awareness and concern about rape. However, not all groups were so affected. Unlike women and young and middle-aged men, men over 50 had preexisting attitudes reinforced and actually blamed women more for rape *after* seeing the film. This suggests that attitudes and experiences of the target audience of interventions must be carefully considered.

In a recent meta-analysis, Mundorf et al. (2007) concluded that studies testing various methods of pre-warning and/or debriefing can completely undo the negative effects of sexual materials and often move attitudes to a less antisocial position than where they were before viewing the material.

Children and Sexual Media

All of the research discussed so far has tested adults or adolescents. For obvious ethical reasons, there is no research systematically showing young children sexually explicit material and measuring their reaction. However, children do see sexual media and are probably affected by them.

One study (Cantor, Mares, & Hyde, 2003) has used an ingenious methodology to study this problem without the unacceptable ethical situation of showing children sexual media. The study asked 196 college students to describe a memory for some sexual media content they had seen. Almost everyone (92%) did so, and 39% wrote about something they had seen at age 12 or younger. Most of these instances were R-rated movies playing in a home with older children or teens (but usually no adults) watching and the child as an incidental viewer. Memories of young children focused on salient physical aspects of the scene, such as nudity, kissing, and "sexual noises." This was in contrast to the over-age-13 memories, which focused more on dialogue, relationship, and themes like rape or same-gender sex. Overall, men's early memories were more positive than women's. Young children felt guilt and concern about what others would think of them. Older children responded more to the content (e.g., anger at rape scenes). Clearly there is need for parental mediation for children exposed to such content, and just as clearly they are often not receiving it.

CONCLUSION

What may we conclude from the research on the effects of sexual media? While there are documented negative effects of nonviolent (especially dehumanizing) pornography, particularly on attitudes toward women, the research is even more compelling in the case of sexual violence. Sexual violence arouses sex offenders, force-oriented men, and sometimes even "normal" young men if the woman is portrayed as being aroused by the assault. For reviews and meta-analyses of results from numerous experimental studies on the effects of viewing pornography, see Allen, D'Alessio, and Brezgel (1995); Davis and Bauserman (1993); Gunter (2002); Huston et al. (1998); Malamuth and Impett (2001); Mundorf et al. (2007); Oddone-Paolucci et al. (2000); and Pollard (1995).

Repeated exposure to sexual violence can lead to desensitization toward violence against women in general and greater acceptance of rape myths. However, the nature of the portrayal also matters. If the woman being assaulted is portrayed as being terrorized and brutalized, desensitizing effects on normal men are much less than if she is portrayed as being aroused and/or achieving orgasm through being attacked. There is nothing arousing or exciting about being raped in real life, and messages to the contrary do not help teenage boys understand the reality of how to relate to girls and women.

Finally, most of us believe that *other people* are more influenced by advertising (Gunther & Thorson, 1992) and news coverage (Gunther, 1991; Perloff, 1989) than we are; this is the *third-person effect* (Perloff, this volume). The same is true about the perceived effects of sexual media (Gunther, 1995); we believe it affects others more than it affects us. As society accepts increasingly explicit sexual materials, no one is immune from their reach. The influence is much more far-reaching that the adolescent boy's transient titillation from looking at a *Playboy* centerfold. What we learn about sexuality from the media forms a large part of what sexuality means to us.

Author Note

Thanks are expressed to Christopher Rodeheffer for comments on earlier drafts of this manuscript. Send correspondence to R.J. Harris, Department of Psychology, Kansas State University, Bluemont Hall 492, 1100 Mid-Campus Drive, Manhattan KS 66506-5302 USA, e-mail: rjharris@ksu.edu.

References

Abel, G. G., Barlow, D. H., Blanchard, E. B., & Guild, D. (1977). The components of rapists' sexual arousal. *Archives of General Psychiatry, 34*, 895–903.

Abramson, P. R., & Hayashi, H. (1984). Pornography in Japan: Cross-cultural and theoretical considerations. In N. M. Malamuth & E. Donnerstein (Eds.), *Pornography and sexual aggression* (pp. 173–183). Orlando: Academic Press.

Allen, M., D'Alessio, D., & Brezgel, K. (1995). A meta-analysis summarizing the effects of pornography II: Aggression after exposure. *Human Communication Research, 22*, 258–283.

Allen, M., D'Alessio, D., & Emmers-Sommer, T. M. (2000). Reactions of criminal sexual offenders to pornography: A meta-analytic summary. In M. Roloff (Ed.), *Communication Yearbook 22* (pp. 139–169). Thousand Oaks, CA: Sage.

Allen, M., Emmers, T., Gebhardt, L., & Giery, M. A. (1995). Exposure to pornography and acceptance of rape myths. *Journal of Communication, 45*(1), 5–26.

Aubrey, J. S. (2007). Does television exposure influence college-aged women's sexual self-concept? *Media Psychology, 10*, 157–181.

Barak, A., & Fisher, W. A. (1997). Effects of interactive computer erotica on men's attitudes and behavior toward women: An experimental study. *Computers in Human Behavior, 13*, 353–369.

Barak, A., Fisher, W. A., Belfry, S., & Lashambe, D. R. (1999). Sex, guys, and cyberspace: Effects of Internet pornography and individual differences on men's attitudes toward women. *Journal of Psychology and Human Sexuality, 11*, 63–91.

Bauserman, R. (1996). Sexual aggression and pornography: A review of correlational research. *Basic and Applied Social Psychology, 18*, 405–427.

Baxter, D. J., Barbaree, H. E., & Marshall, W. L. (1986). Sexual responses to consenting and forced sex in a large sample of rapists and nonrapists. *Behavior Research and Therapy, 24*, 513–520.

Bogaert, A. F. (2001). Personality, individual differences, and preferences for the sexual media. *Archives of Sexual Behavior, 30*, 29–53.

Boies, S. C. (2002). University students' uses of and reactions to online sexual information and entertainment: Links to online and offline sexual behaviour. *The Canadian Journal of Human Sexuality, 11*, 77–89.

Bryant, J., & Rockwell, S. C. (1994). Effects of massive exposure to sexually oriented prime time television programming on adolescents' moral judgment. In D. Zillmann, J. Bryant, and A. C. Huston (Eds.), *Media, children, and the family: Social scientific, psychodynamic, and clinical perspectives* (pp. 183–195). Hillsdale, NJ: Erlbaum.

Buchwald, E., Fletcher, P., & Roth, M. (Ed.). (1993). *Transforming a rape culture*. Minneapolis: Milkweed Eds.

Bushman, B. J., Baumeister, R. F., & Stack, A. D. (1999). Catharsis, aggression, and persuasive influences: Self-fulfilling or self-defeating prophecies? *Journal of Personality and Social Psychology, 76*, 367–376.

Bushman, B. J., Bonacci, A. M., van Dijk, M., & Baumeister, R. F. (2003). Narcissism, sexual refusal, and aggression: Testing a narcissistic reactance model of sexual coercion. *Journal of Personality and Social Psychology, 84*, 1027–1040.

Buss, D. M. (1995). Evolutionary psychology: A new paradigm for psychological science. *Psychological Inquiry, 6*, 1–30.

Buzzell, T. (2005). Demographic characteristics of persons using pornography in three technological contexts. *Sexuality and Culture*, *9*, 28–48.

Cantor, J., Mares, M.-L., & Hyde, J. S. (2003). Autobiographical memories of exposure to sexual media content. *Media Psychology*, *5*, 1–31.

Carnes, P. J. (2001). Cybersex, courtship, and escalating arousal: Factors in addictive sexual desire. *Sexual Addiction and Compulsivity*, *8*, 45–78.

Carter, D. L., Prentky, R. A., Knight, R. A., Vanderveer, P. L., & Boucher, R. J. (1987). Use of pornography in the criminal and developmental histories of sexual offenders. *Journal of Interpersonal Violence*, *2*, 196–211.

Check, J. V. P. (1995). Teenage training: The effects of pornography on adolescent males. In L. Lederer and R. Delgado (Eds.), *The price we pay: The case against racist speech, hate propaganda, and pornography* (pp. 89–91). New York: Hill and Wang.

Check, J. V. P., & Guloien, T. H. (1989). Reported proclivity for coercive sex following repeated exposure to sexually violent pornography, nonviolent pornography, and erotica. In D. Zillmann & J. Bryant (Eds.), *Pornography: Research advances and policy considerations* (pp. 159–184). Hillsdale, NJ: Erlbaum.

Chia, S. C. (2006). How peers mediate media influence on adolescents' sexual attitudes and sexual behavior. *Journal of Communication*, *56*, 585–606.

Clover, C. (1992). *Men, women, and chainsaws: Gender in the modern horror film*. Princeton, NJ: Princeton University Press.

Collins, R. L., Elliott, M. N., Berry, S. H., Kanouse, D. E., & Hunter, S. B. (2003). Entertainment television as a healthy sex educator: The impact of condom-efficiency information in an episode of *Friends*. *Pediatrics*, *112*, 1115–1121.

Collins, R. L., Elliott, M. N., Berry, S. H., Kanouse, D. E., Kunkel, D., & Hunter, S. B. (2004). Watching sex on television predicts adolescent initiation of sexual activity. *Pediatrics*, *114*, 280–289.

Cope-Farrar, K. M., & Kunkel, D. (2002). Sexual messages in teens' favorite prime-time television programs. In J. D. Brown, J. R. Steele, and K. Walsh-Childers (Eds.), *Sexual teens, sexual media* (pp. 59–78). Mahwah, NJ: Erlbaum.

Court, J. H. (1984). Sex and violence: A ripple effect. In N. M. Malamuth & E. Donnerstein (Eds.), *Pornography and sexual aggression* (pp. 143–172). Orlando: Academic Press.

Davis, C. M., & Bauserman, R. (1993). Exposure to sexually explicit materials: An attitude change perspective. In J. Bancroft (Ed.), *Annual Review of Sex Research* (Vol. 4, pp. 121–209). Mt. Vernon, IA: Society for the Scientific Study of Sex.

Davis, K. C., Norris, J., George, W. H., Martell, J., & Heiman, J. (2006). Rape-myth congruent beliefs in women resulting from exposure to violent pornography: Effects of alcohol and sexual arousal. *Journal of Interpersonal Violence*, *21*, 1208–1223.

Demare, D., Briere, J., & Lips, H. M. (1988). Violent pornography and self-reported likelihood of sexual aggression. *Journal of Research in Personality*, *22*, 140–153.

Dermer, M., & Pyszczynski, T. A. (1978). Effects of erotica upon men's loving and liking responses. *Journal of Personality and Social Psychology*, *36*, 1302–1309.

Diamond, M., & Uchiyama, A. (1999). Pornography, rape, and sex crimes in Japan. *International Journal of Law and Psychiatry*, *22*, 1–11.

Donnerstein, E., & Berkowitz, L. (1981). Victim reactions in aggressive erotic films as a factor in violence against women. *Journal of Personality and Social Psychology*, *41*, 710–724.

Dorr, A., & Kunkel, D. (1990). Children and the media environment: Change and constancy amid change. *Communication Research*, *17*, 5–25.

Ferguson, D. A., & Perse, E. M. (2000). The World Wide Web as a functional alternative to television. *Journal of Broadcasting & Electronic Media*, *44*, 155–174.

Ferree, M. C. (2003). Women and the web: Cybersex activity and implications. *Sexual and Relationship Therapy*, *18*, 385–393.

Garcia, L. T. (1986). Exposure to pornography and attitudes about women and rape: A correlational study. *Journal of Sex Research*, *22*, 378–385.

Gettleman, J. (1999, October 28). XXX=$$$, *Manhattan Mercury*, p. A6.

Glassner, B. (1999). *The culture of fear: Why Americans are afraid of the wrong things*. New York: Basic Books.

Goldstein, S., & Ibaraki, T. (1983). Japan: Aggression and aggression control in Japanese society. In A. Goldstein & M. Segall (Eds.), *Aggression in global perspective* (pp. 313–324). New York: Pergamon Press.

Greenberg, B. S., Brown, J. D., & Buerkel-Rothfuss, N. L. (Eds.). (1993). *Media, sex, and the adolescent*. Creskill, NJ: Hampton Press.

Greenberg, B. S., & Busselle, R. (1996). Soap operas and sexual activity: A decade later. *Journal of Communication*, *46*(4), 153–160.

Greenberg, B. S., & Hofschire, L. (2000). Sex on entertainment television. In D. Zillmann and P. Vorderer (Eds.), *Media entertainment: The psychology of its appeal* (pp. 93–111). Mahwah, NJ: Erlbaum.

Greenberg, B. S., & Smith, S. W. (2002). Daytime talk shows: Up close and in your face. In J. D. Brown, J. R. Steele, & K. Walsh-Childers (Eds.), *Sexual teens, sexual media* (pp. 79–93). Mahwah, NJ: Erlbaum.

Griffin-Shelley, E. (2003). The Internet and sexuality: A literature review—1983–2002. *Sexual and Relationship Therapy*, *18*, 354–370.

Gunter, B. (2002). *Media sex: What are the issues?* Mahwah, NJ: Erlbaum.

Gunther, A. C. (1991). What we think others think: Cause and consequence in the third-person effect. *Communication Research*, *18*, 355–372.

Gunther, A. C. (1995). Overrating the X-rating: The third-person perception and support for censorship of pornography. *Journal of Communication* *45*(1), 27–38.

Gunther, A. C., & Thorson, E. (1992). Perceived persuasive effects of product commercials and public-service announcements: Third-person effects in new domains. *Communication Research*, *19*, 574–596.

Hall, G. C. N. (1989). Self-reported hostility as a function of offense characteristics and response style in a sexual offender population. *Journal of Consulting and Clinical Psychology*, *57*, 306–308.

Harris, R. J. (1999). *A cognitive psychology of mass communication* (3rd ed.). Mahwah, NJ: Erlbaum.

Hetsroni, A. (2007). Three decades of sexual content on prime-time network programming: A longitudinal meta-analytic review. *Journal of Communication*, *57*, 318–348.

Huston, A. C., Wartella, E., & Donnerstein, E. (1998). *Measuring the effects of sexual content in the media: A report to the Kaiser Family Foundation*. Menlo Park, CA: The Henry J. Kaiser Family Foundation.

Intons-Peterson, M. J., Roskos-Ewoldsen, B., Thomas, L., Shirley, M., & Blut, D. (1989). Will educational materials reduce negative effects of exposure to sexual violence? *Journal of Social and Clinical Psychology*, *8*, 256–275.

IT Facts, (www.itfacts.biz/index.php?id=P7960). Retrieved July 5, 2007.

Jaffee, D., & Straus, M. A. (1987). Sexual climate and reported rape: A state-level analysis. *Archives of Sexual Behavior*, *16*, 107–123.

Kaiser Family Foundation. (2002). The impact of TV's health content: A case study of *ER* viewers. Menlo Park, CA: Kaiser Family Foundation.

Kallipolitis, G., Stefanidis, K., Loutradis, D., Siskos, K., Milingos, S., & Michalas, S. (2004). Knowledge, attitude, and behavior of female students concerning contraception in Athens, Greece. *Journal of Psychosomatic Obstetrics and Gynaecology*, *24*, 145–151.

Kenrick, D. T., Gutierres, S. E., & Goldberg, L. L. (1989). Influence of popular erotica on judgments of strangers and mates. *Journal of Experimental Social Psychology*, *25*, 159–167.

Kunkel, D., Biely, E., Eyal, K., Cope-Farrar, K. M., Donnerstein, E., & Fandrich, R. (2003). *Sex on TV 3: Content and context*. Menlo Park, CA: Henry J. Kaiser Family Foundation.

Kunkel, D., Eyal, K., Donnerstein, E., Farrar, K. M., Biely, E., & Rideout, V. (2007). Sexual socialization messages on entertainment television: Comparing content trends 1997–2003. *Media Psychology*, *9*, 595–622.

Kutchinsky, B. (1973). The effect of easy availability of pornography on the incidence of sex crimes: The Danish experience. *Journal of Social Issues*, *29*(3), 163–181.

Kutchinsky, B. (1991). Pornography and rape: Theory and practice? *International Journal of Law and Psychiatry*, *14*, 47–64.

Langevin, R., Lang, R. A., Wright, P., Handy, L., Frenzel, F. R., & Black, E. L. (1988). Pornography and sexual offenses. *Annals of Sex Research*, *1*, 335–362.

Linz, D., & Donnerstein, E. (1988). The methods and merits of pornography research. *Journal of Communication*, *38*(2), 180–184.

Linz, D., Donnerstein, E., & Adams, S. M. (1989). Physiological desensitization and judgments about female victims of violence. *Human Communication Research*, *15*, 509–522.

Linz, D., Donnerstein, E., & Penrod, S. (1984). The effects of multiple exposures to filmed violence against women. *Journal of Communication*, *34*(3), 130–147.

Linz, D., Fuson, I. A., & Donnerstein, E. (1990). Mitigating the negative effects of sexually violent mass communications through pre-exposure briefings. *Communication Research*, *17*, 641–674.

Linz, D., & Malamuth, N. (1993). *Pornography*. Newbury Park, CA: Sage.

Lo, V. H., & Wei, R. (2005). Exposure to Internet pornography and Taiwanese adolescents' sexual attitudes and behavior. *Journal of Broadcasting and Electronic Media*, *49*, 221–237.

Lohr, B. A., Adams, H. E., & Davis, J. M. (1997). Sexual arousal to erotic and aggressive stimuli in sexually coercive and noncoercive men. *Journal of Abnormal Psychology*, *106*, 230–242.

Lutz, C. A., & Collins, J. L. (1993). *Reading National Geographic*. Chicago: University of Chicago Press.

Malamuth, N. M. (1981). Rape fantasies as a function of exposure to violent sexual stimuli. *Archives of Sexual Behavior*, *10*, 33–47.

Malamuth, N. M. (1993). Pornography's impact on male adolescents. *Adolescent Medicine: State of the Art Reviews*, *4*, 563–576.

Malamuth, N. M. (1996). Sexually explicit media, gender differences, and evolutionary theory. *Journal of Communication*, 46(3), 8–31.

Malamuth, N. M. (1999). Pornography. *Encyclopedia of Violence, Peace, and Conflict*, *3*, 77–89.

Malamuth, N. M., Addison, T., & Koss, M. (2000). Pornography and sexual aggression: Are there reliable effects and can we understand them? *Annual Review of Sex Research*, *11*, 26–91.

Malamuth, N. M., & Check, J. V. P. (1980). Penile tumescence and perceptual responses to rape as a function of victim's perceived reactions. *Journal of Applied Social Psychology*, *10*, 528–547.

Malamuth, N. M., & Check, J. V. P. (1983). Sexual arousal to rape depictions: Individual differences. *Journal of Abnormal Psychology*, *92*, 55–67.

Malamuth, N. M., & Impett, E. A. (2001). Research on sex in the media: What do we know about effects on children and adolescents? In D. Singer & J. Singer (Eds.), *Handbook of Children and the Media* (pp. 269–278). Newbury Park, CA: Sage.

McKenzie-Mohr, D., & Zanna, M. P. (1990). Treating women as sexual objects: Look to the (gender schematic) male who has viewed pornography. *Personality and Social Psychology Bulletin*, *16*, 296–308.

Mosher, D. L., & Maclan, P. (1994). College men and women respond to X-rated videos intended for male or female audiences: Gender and sexual scripts. *The Journal of Sex Research*, *31*, 99–113.

Mundorf, N., D'Alessio, D., Allen, M., & Emmers-Sommer, T. M. (2007). Effects of sexually explicit media. In R. W. Preiss, B. M. Gayle, N. Burrell, M. Allen, and J. Bryant (Eds.), *Mass media effects research: Advances through meta-analysis* (pp. 181–198). Mahwah, NJ: Erlbaum.

Murnen, S. K., & Stockton, M. (1997). Gender and self-reported sexual arousal in response to sexual stimuli: A meta-analytic review. *Sex Roles*, *37*, 135–153.

Myers, D. G. (2007). *Psychology*. New York: Worth.

Nolan, J. M., & Ryan, G. W. (2000). Fear and loathing at the cineplex: Gender differences in descriptions and perceptions of slasher films. *Sex Roles*, *42*, 39–56.

Norris, J., George, W. H., Davis, K. C., Martell, J., & Leonesio, R. J. (1999). Alcohol and hypermasculinity as determinants of men's empathic responses to violent pornography. *Journal of Interpersonal Violence*, *14*, 683–700.

Oddone-Paolucci, E., Genuis, M., & Violato, C. (2000). A meta-analysis on the published research on the effects of pornography. In C. Violato, E. Oddone-Paolucci, & M. Genuis (Eds.), *The changing family and child development* (pp. 48–59). Aldershot, UK: Ashgate Publishing.

Ohbuchi, K., Ikeda, T., & Takeuchi, G. (1994). Effects of violent pornography upon viewer's rape myth beliefs: A study of Japanese males. *Psychology, Crime, & Law*, *1*, 71–81.

Oliver, M. B. (1993). Adolescents' enjoyment of graphic horror. *Communication Research*, *20*, 30–50.

Perloff, R. M. (1989). Ego-involvement and the third person effect of television news coverage. *Communication Research*, *16*, 236–262.

Perse, E. M. (1994). Uses of erotica and acceptance of rape myths. *Communication Research*, *21*, 488–515.

Peter, J., & Valkenburg, P. M. (2006). Adolescents' exposure to sexually explicit online material and recreational attitudes toward sex. *Journal of Communication*, *56*, 639–660.

Pollard, P. (1995). Pornography and sexual aggression. *Current Psychology: Developmental, Learning, Personality, Social*, *14*(3), 200–221.

Prentky, R. A., & Knight, R. A. (1991). Identifying critical dimensions for discriminating among rapists. *Journal of Consulting and Clinical Psychology*, *59*, 643–661.

Quackenbush, D. M., Strassberg, D. S., & Turner, C. W. (1995). Gender effects of romantic themes in erotica. *Archives of Sexual Behavior*, *24*, 21–35.

Quinsey, V. L., Chaplin, T. C., & Upfold, D. (1984). Sexual arousal to nonsexual violence and sadomasochistic themes among rapists and on sex offenders. *Journal of Consulting and Clinical Psychology*, *52*, 651–657.

Rachman, S., & Hodgson, R. J. (1968). Experimentally induced "sexual fetishism": Replication and development. *Psychological Record*, *18*, 25–27.

Reichert, T., & Lambiase, J. (Eds.). (2003). *Sex in advertising: Perspectives on the erotic appeal*. Mahwah, NJ: Erlbaum.

Russell, D. E. H. (1998). *Dangerous relationships: Pornography, misogyny, and rape*. Thousand Oaks, CA: Sage.

Sapolsky, B. S., & Molitor, F. (1996). Content trends in contemporary horror films. In J. B. Weaver and R. Tamborini (Eds.), *Horror films: Current research on audience preferences and reactions* (pp. 33–48). Mahwah, NJ: Erlbaum.

Scheele, B., & DuBois, F. (2006). Catharsis as a moral form of entertainment. In J. Bryant and P. Vorderer (Eds.), *Psychology of entertainment* (pp. 405–422). Mahwah, NJ: Erlbaum.

Schneider, J. P. (2000). Effects of cybersex addiction on the family: Results of a survey. *Sexual Addiction and Compulsivity*, *7*, 31–58.

Schneider, J. P. (2003). The impact of compulsive cybersex behaviours on the family. *Sexual and Relationship Therapy*, *18*, 329–354.

Senn, C. Y., & Desmarais, S. (2004). Impact of interaction with a partner or friend on the exposure effects of pornography and erotica. *Violence and Victims*, *19*, 645–658.

Shope, J. H. (2004). When words are not enough: The search for the effect of pornography on abused women. *Violence against Women*, *10*, 56–72.

Stodghill, R. (1998, June 15). Where'd you learn that? *Time*, 52–59.

Sutton, M. J., Brown, J. D., Wilson, K. M., & Klein, J. D. (2002). Shaking the tree of knowledge for forbidden fruit: Where adolescents learn about sexuality and contraception. In J. D. Brown, J. R. Steele, & K. Walsh-Childers (Eds.), *Sexual teens, sexual media* (pp. 25–55). Mahwah, NJ: Erlbaum.

Tversky, A., & Kahneman, D. (1973). Availability: A heuristic for judging frequency and probability. *Cognitive Psychology*, *5*, 207–232.

Tversky, A., & Kahneman, D. (1974). Judgment under uncertainty: Heuristics and biases. *Science*, *185*, 1124–1131.

Vega, V., & Malamuth, N. M. (2007). Predicting sexual aggression: The role of pornography in the context of general and specific risk factors. *Aggressive Behavior, 33*, 104–117.

Weaver, J. B. (1991). Responding to erotica: Perceptual processes and dispositional implications. In J. Bryant & D. Zillmann (Eds.), *Responding to the screen* (pp. 329–354). Hillsdale, NJ: Erlbaum.

Weaver, J. B., Masland, J. L., & Zillmann, D. (1984). Effects of erotica on young men's aesthetic perception of their female sexual partners. *Perceptual and Motor Skills, 58*, 929–930.

Weisz, M. G., & Earls, C. M. (1995). The effects of exposure to filmed sexual violence on attitudes toward rape. *Journal of Interpersonal Violence, 10*, 71–84.

Wilson, B. J., Linz, D., Donnerstein, E., & Stipp, H. (1992). The impact of social issue television programming on attitudes toward rape. *Human Communication Research, 19*, 179–208.

Yates, E., Barbaree, H. E., & Marshall, W. L. (1984). Anger and deviant sexual arousal. *Behavior Therapy, 15*, 287–294.

Zillmann, D., & Bryant, J. (1982). Pornography, sexual callousness, and the trivialization of rape. *Journal of Communication, 32*(4), 10–21.

Zillmann, D., & Bryant, J. (1984). Effects of massive exposure to pornography. In N. Malamuth and E. Donnerstein (Eds.), *Pornography and sexual aggression* (pp. 115–141). Orlando, FL: Academic Press.

Zillmann, D., & Bryant, J. (1988a). Pornography's impact on sexual satisfaction. *Journal of Applied Social Psychology, 18*, 438–453.

Zillmann, D., & Bryant, J. (1988b). Effects of prolonged consumption of pornography on family values. *Journal of Family Issues, 9*, 518–544.

16

EFFECTS OF RACIAL AND ETHNIC STEREOTYPING

Dana Mastro
University of Arizona

The effects of media exposure on the construction and maintenance of consumers' social perceptions, attitudes, beliefs, and actions have long been addressed by theoretical and empirical research in the domains of mass communication, social psychology, and cognitive psychology (Hardin & Higgins, 1996; Wyer & Radvansky, 1999). Accordingly, it should come as no surprise that media use has been determined to play a meaningful role in the development of racial/ethnic cognitions and intergroup behaviors. Indeed, research has consistently revealed modest but significant associations between viewing media portrayals of race/ethnicity and outcomes concerning evaluations of outgroup members' competence (Zuckerman, Singer, & Singer, 1980), socioeconomic status (Armstrong, Neuendorf, & Brentar, 1992), group status (Giles, Bourhis, & Taylor, 1977), social roles (Atkin, Greenberg, & McDermott, 1983), and judgments regarding a variety of race-based attributions and stereotypes (Dixon, 2006; Dixon & Maddox, 2005; Ford, 1997; Mastro, 2003; Mastro, Behm-Morawitz, & Ortiz, 2007; Mastro & Kopacz, 2006; Mastro, Tamborini, & Hullett, 2005; Oliver, Jackson, Moses, & Dangerfield, 2004).

Despite such evidence, racial/ethnic representation in the media and the implications of exposure to these messages remain intensely debated topics among consumers and producers alike; prompting a recurring stream of headlines in the popular press such as "White still a primary color" and "Same old Black and White" (Braxton, 2007, June 6; Stanley, 2006, March 22). In order to shed light on this issue, the present chapter synthesizes the extant research on the subject. In particular, quantitative examinations of (1) depictions of race/ethnicity in the media, (2) audience characteristics and media usage patterns, and (3) the effects of exposure will be addressed.

MEDIA DEPICTIONS OF RACE AND ETHNICITY

Theories of media effects (including those rooted in beliefs about active as well as passive audiences) collectively implicate the particular features of media content in outcomes associated with exposure. In other words, media effects depend (in part) on the specific images and messages depicted in the content. Accordingly, any discussion concerning effects must take into consideration the manner in which different racial/ethnic groups are characterized in the media. However, few universals can be offered with regard to contemporary media representations of race/ethnicity (see Greenberg,

Mastro, & Brand, 2002, for historical overview). In fact, research reveals that both the number and the nature of portrayals vary based on the race/ethnicity of the model. As such, a summary of current depictions of Latino Americans, Black Americans, Asian Americans, and Native Americans on television, in advertising, in the news, and in film (when available) is provided as these groups represent the four largest racial/ethnic minority groups in the U.S. population.

Black Americans

In terms of numeric representation on primetime TV, Black Americans and White Americans are the only racial/ethnic groups depicted at a rate exceeding their proportions of the U.S. population of approximately 12% and 69%, respectively (U.S. Census, 2000). Generally speaking, African Americans constitute between 14–17% of the primetime population and Whites comprise between 73–80% of the characters appearing on primetime television (Children Now, 2001; Children Now, 2004; Mastro & Behm-Morawitz, 2005; Mastro & Greenberg, 2000). Although images of White Americans can be seen relatively evenly distributed across the TV genres, Black Americans are nearly exclusively seen in sitcoms or crime dramas (Mastro & Behm-Morawitz, 2005; Mastro & Greenberg, 2000; Matabane & Merritt, 1996; Stroman, Merritt, & Matabane, 1989–1990). When in dramas, Black Americans are featured in mixed-race casts (Children Now, 2004) whereas on sitcoms they appear in a cast that is predominately Black American. The importance of these clusterings is two-fold. First, genre conventions and constraints inevitably result in differing race-based presentations. Accordingly, differential effects are likely to be associated with exposure to the different content features normative for various genres (Armstrong, Neuendorf, & Brentar, 1992). Second, this tendency leaves open the possibility that depending on TV viewing preferences, a viewer may be exposed to one-sided images of Blacks, or simply not see them at all. Given that intergroup contact in the media conveys messages to consumers regarding race-based norms and the value attached to diversity in society (Harwood & Roy, 2005), the extent to which Black Americans, or any group, is isolated/integrated into the general media landscape should not be ignored. As Entman (1994) argued, images of race/ethnicity on television not only have the potential to provide (mis)information about *who* racial/ethnic minorities are, but additionally offer evidence to corroborate (mis)perceptions regarding *why* they should be viewed in a certain way.

In terms of the manner in which Black Americans are depicted on television, the typical Black character on primetime is a middle-class male in his thirties. He is likely to be a law enforcer or professional, discussing work-related topics (Children Now, 2001; Children Now, 2004; Mastro & Behm-Morawitz, 2005; Mastro & Greenberg, 2000). This character enjoys moderate levels of both job and social authority (Mastro & Behm-Morawitz, 2005) and is among the least aggressive figures on TV (Mastro & Greenberg, 2000). However, Black Americans on primetime are also characterized by more provocative and less professional dress than their White counterparts (Mastro & Greenberg, 2000).

Much the same can be said for images in film. Again, the preponderance of lead characters are White Americans (80%) followed by Black Americans (19%) (Escholtz, Bufkin, & Long, 2002). Although their rate of appearance exceeds their proportion of the real-world population, Black Americans are not seen across a variety of film genres. Instead, they are most frequently featured in films primarily starring Black American characters. On average, these characters are younger than their White counterparts and are more likely to be employed in positions with lower levels of occupational prestige than Whites.

The images offered by advertising are not altogether different. Here again, the vast majority of characters are White Americans (86%), with Black Americans representing about 11% of the actors featured in commercials (Coltrane & Messineo, 2000). Most often, Black characters are found in ads for food/beverages (Taylor & Stern, 1997) and financial services (Mastro & Stern, 2003). In addition, Licata and Biswas (1993) note an inverse relationship between product value and interface with Black Americans in advertisements such that as interactions with Black Americans increase product values decrease.

News coverage depicting Black Americans presents an altogether more unfavorable picture, both on an absolute and comparative basis (Entman, 1992). Although Blacks and Whites appear with relatively equal frequency in news stories unrelated to crime, Black Americans are seen at nearly twice the rate as Whites when the topic is crime (Romer, Jamieson, & DeCoteau, 1998). In such news stories, Black Americans are more likely to be depicted as crime perpetrators (Dixon & Linz, 2000a), appearing nameless and restrained, and with a disheveled and threatening appearance (Entman, 1990, 1992, 1994). In addition, findings from Dixon and Linz (2002) reveal that prejudicial information (e.g., providing information on prior arrests) is more frequently reported when the defendant is a Black American as opposed to White.

Black Americans' rate of representation as criminals in the news is not only discrepant when compared with depictions of Whites, but is additionally inconsistent with real-world arrest reports (Dixon & Linz, 2000a). When contrasted with real-world crime statistics, African American adults are overrepresented as perpetrators on TV news whereas Whites are presented either at a rate equivalent to (Dixon & Linz, 2000b) or below (Dixon & Linz, 2000a) that in the real world. The same is true of images of Black youth in the news. Results from Dixon and Azocar (2006) indicate that Black American youth are seen as perpetrators on TV news more frequently than Whites. In fact, 39% of all juvenile perpetrators depicted in the news are Black (18% in Department of Justice statistics) whereas 24% are White (22% in Department of Justice statistics).

Alongside their overrepresentation as criminals on TV news, when compared with Whites, African Americans also are underrepresented as victims—but at a rate in proportion with real-world crime reports (Dixon & Linz, 2000b). In addition, Black Americans are seen as police officers on the news (3%) (Dixon, Azocar, & Casas, 2003) and in reality-based police shows (9.3%) (Oliver, 1994) at a rate substantially below their proportion of the U.S. police population.

Latino Americans

Although Latinos are the largest racial/ethnic minority group in the U.S., at approximately 13% of the population (U.S. Census, 2000), they comprise only between 2% and 6.5% of the primetime television population (Children Now, 2001; Children Now, 2004; Mastro & Behm-Morawitz, 2005; Mastro & Greenberg, 2000) and a mere 1% of lead characters in top grossing, U.S. motion pictures (Eschholz, Bufkin, & Long, 2002). Like Black Americans, Latino images on primetime television are primarily confined to sitcoms and crime dramas. The typical Latino character is a family member, engaged in conversation about crime (Mastro & Behm-Morawitz, 2005; Mastro & Greenberg, 2000). Compared with their on-air counterparts Latinos are younger, lower in job authority, lazier, less articulate, less intelligent, more seductively dressed (Mastro & Behm-Morawitz, 2005), and four times more likely to be characterized as a domestic worker (Children Now, 2004). In addition, alongside Black Americans, Latinos are deemed the most hot-tempered characters on primetime TV.

Consistent with their negligible representation in the movies, in commercial advertising few images of Latinos are likely to be found. Here again, only 1% of characters depicted are Latino (Coltrane & Messineo, 2000; Mastro & Stern, 2003). When present, they are primarily in background roles and in group settings (Taylor & Stern, 1997). Moreover, Latinos in commercial advertising are significantly more likely than other racial/ethnic groups to be presented in a sexualized manner, engaging in sexual glances, displaying alluring behavior, and adorning provocative attire (Mastro & Stern, 2003).

When it comes to television news, Latinos (like Blacks) are depicted as crime perpetrators more frequently than Whites (Dixon & Linz, 2000a). However, their rate of representation falls below real-world arrest reports (Dixon & Linz, 2000b). The same pattern emerges for depictions of Latino youth on the news. Although Latino youth appear as perpetrators more frequently than Whites, this proportion is below Department of Justice Statistics (Dixon & Azocar, 2006). Alternatively, when it comes to representation as victims on TV news, Latinos also are seen at a rate below both their White, on-air counterparts and below real-world crime reports (Dixon & Linz, 2000b).

The content of crime-related news stories also varies depending on the race/ethnicity of the perpetrator. Consistent with their findings regarding Black Americans, Dixon and Linz's (2002) results indicate that reporting prejudicial information (such as an existing arrest record) is more likely to be associated with Latino defendants than with Whites, particularly in cases involving White victims.

Asian Americans

In terms of numeric representation, Asian Americans constitute between 1% and 3% of the characters on primetime TV (Children Now, 2001; Children Now, 2004; Mastro & Behm-Morawitz, 2005; Mastro & Greenberg, 2000), compared with 4% of the U.S. population (U.S. Census, 2000). When they are seen on TV, Asian Americans are found primarily in minor and non-recurring roles (Children Now, 2001; Children Now, 2004). Despite the scarcity of these images, Asian American characters are often in high-status (37%), professional positions (Children Now, 2004). As a result of their infrequent presence, however, little more is known about the manner in which they are depicted on primetime.

When it comes to images in commercial advertising, Asian Americans make up 2% of the characters depicted (Coltrane & Messineo, 2000; Mastro & Stern, 2003). They are most commonly portrayed in conservative attire in the workplace and are characterized by their passive nature (Mastro & Stern, 2003). Asian American images can be found most frequently in technology ads (Mastro & Stern, 2003).

Native Americans

Native Americans represent between 0 and 0.4% of the characters appearing on primetime television (Children Now, 2001; Children Now, 2004; Mastro & Behm-Morawitz, 2005; Mastro & Greenberg, 2000), and make up slightly less than 1% of the U.S. population (U.S. Census, 2000). Their occasional roles are typically based in an historical context (Merskin, 1998). Similarly, .02% of newspaper articles and .002% of films depict Native Americans (Fryberg, 2003). When they appear in these media outlets, they are seen as spiritual, as warriors, and as a social problem.

Television Newsmakers

Although not a content feature, per se, Harwood and Roy (2005) maintained that media control and ownership are inherently tied to issues associated with the quantity and quality of race-based media offerings. They argued, "control over media production and dissemination is a crucial dimension of group vitality . . . [in] that media ownership and control can function as a means to support the subordination of disadvantaged groups" (p. 191). Notably, not only are numeric disparities evident in the racial/ethnic breakdown of both on-air television newsmakers (Gant & Dimmick, 2000) and those working off-air (Papper, 2005), but the overall proportion of the racial/ethnic minority TV news workforce (21%) as well as the percentage of minority TV news directors (12.5%) has dropped slightly from previous years (Papper, 2005). Although the proportion of Black Americans in the broadcast news workforce has remained relatively stable in recent years (at 10%), the percentages of Asian Americans (2%), Latinos (9%), and Native Americans (0.3%) all are down. Among news directors, 6% are Latino, 3.5% are Black Americans, 1.3% are Asian American, and 1.0% are Native American. In terms of TV news general managers, the vast majority are White (93%).

When it comes to on-air appearances, Whites account for 77% of newsmakers and Black Americans 22%—with Asian Americans and Latino Americans combined at 1% (Gant & Dimmick, 2000). Moreover, White newsmakers appear as experts/professionals significantly more than Black American newsmakers.

AUDIENCE CHARACTERISTICS

Of course content features alone address only a portion of the relationship between exposure and effects. Theory and empirical research alike demonstrate that the amount of consumption and the particular characteristics of the audience members each play a role in determining effects.

Usage Patterns

Research in the domains of social cognitive theory (see Chapter 6 in this volume), cultivation theory (see Chapter 3), and priming (see Chapter 5), among others, have long established that media effects are, in large part, a reflection of what and how much viewers consume. Accordingly, effects are likely to vary based on media preferences and patterns. Although this has implications for all audience members, it suggests that certain audience features may result in increased vulnerability to media messages. Thus, identifying what is known about race-related media consumption patterns is critical.

Black Americans

Despite the increasing variety of new media offerings, television remains the dominant media choice for consumers, and audience analyses reveal Black Americans to be among the heaviest consumers in the U.S. (Nielsen, 1998, 2007). According to Nielsen Media Research, in the typical Black American home the television is on for 20 hours per week more than in the average White American household. On a daily basis, this amounts to a 3 hour per day disparity in time spent watching TV; a pattern which has consistently emerged in studies of viewing rates (Brown, Campbell, & Fischer, 1986; Greenberg & Linsangan, 1993). Moreover, as Brown, Campbell, and Fischer (1986) noted, this tendency is not isolated to adult viewers. Indeed, their findings indicate that Black teens are exposed to up to 7 more hours of television viewing per week than White teens. Botta's (2000) investigation of the influence of television consumption on adolescent girls' self-concept yielded parallel outcomes. Her findings demonstrate that compared with their White counterparts, Black adolescent girls watch substantially higher levels of television.

In terms of content preferences and uses for media, differences based on race additionally have been documented. Across ages and genders, Black Americans report a preference for programs featuring Black characters and Black casts (Eastman & Liss, 1980; Nielsen, 1998; Poindexter & Stroman, 1981). Use of television in the average Black American household is primarily for entertainment and educational purposes (Becker, Kosicki, & Jones, 1992; Poindexter & Stroman, 1981); however, research additionally suggests that program choices (including both selection and avoidance) may be used to support racial identity needs (Abrams & Giles, 2007). Black audiences (and children in particular) also report greater belief in the veracity of television messages (Poindexter & Stroman, 1981) and reveal higher levels of identification with Black characters (Greenberg & Atkin, 1982) particularly when highly identified with their race/ethnicity (Whittler, 1991).

Latino Americans

Among Latino viewers, both adult and adolescent television consumption rates have increased on a yearly basis (Nielsen, 2007), making this group second to Blacks in amount of TV viewing. In terms of preferences and uses for media, audience analyses have yielded mixed findings. Some research has noted a preference for Latino-associated content (Greenberg et al., 1983) and Latino characters (Eastman & Liss, 1980) whereas other findings have suggested that preferences for Latino-based programming are only marginal. Of course, given the small number of Latino characters depicted on mainstream U.S. programming, selectivity may not be an option. Not surprisingly, Nielsen (1997) ratings reveal that many of the most popular programs in Latino households (e.g., telenovellas) come from the Spanish-language networks such as Univision and Telemundo. In fact, since the addition of Spanish language programming into the Nielsen rankings, Univision has emerged as the fifth most watched TV network in the U.S. (*LA Times*, Feb 17, 2006); reaching 98% of all Latino TV households (Univision, 2005). Additional evidence in support of a preference for Spanish language content can be derived from research on the persuasive appeal of Spanish language television commercials. This research has demonstrated that advertisements for the same brands are found to be significantly more persuasive in Spanish than in English among both bilingual and Spanish-dominant Latinos in the U.S. (Roslow & Nicholls, 1996).

Variations in preferences may also reflect the diversity of gratifications sought from Latino consumers with differing levels of acculturation. Among Latinas with low levels of acculturation, television is likely to be used to learn about social norms in the U.S. and to improve English-speaking skills (Johnson, 1996). Stilling's (1997) data yielded parallel results, revealing use of English-language television among Latinos to increase levels of acculturation. Alternatively, for those seeking to maintain racial/ethnic identity, ethnic media content is preferred (Jeffres, 2000; Ríos & Gaines, 1999).

Inconsistencies also have been found in studies investigating Latinos' perceptions about the quality of television content. Formative research by Greenberg et al. (1983) indicates that Latino youth believe in the authenticity and decency of Latino television models. Alternatively, in their research examining adult TV viewers Faber, O'Guinn, & Meyer (1987) revealed Latinos to be greatly dissatisfied with both the number and quality of Latino TV characterizations. Notably, their findings additionally showed that Whites who were heavy TV consumers were more likely to report that the quality of images of Latinos was fair, whereas Latinos who were heavy television viewers noted quite the opposite.

Asian Americans and Native Americans

Little is known about the media choices, patterns, and preferences of Asian American and Native American consumers. What can be said about Native American media use and beliefs about representations of Native Americans in the media is derived from survey research by Merskin (1998), who sampled 190 self-identified Native American college students from a university in the Northwest U.S. Her findings indicated that although the majority of students own television sets (82%), viewing rates peak at 1 to 2 hours per day. Additionally, the majority of students who participated (69%) reported dissatisfaction with the programming available for adults, most often declaring that TV portrayals of Native Americans were both negative and inaccurate.

Audience Attributes

Alongside the usage patterns documented above, a variety of individual difference variables have also been found to impact on outcomes associated with racial/ethnic stereotyping and race-based evaluations. Such features are not only likely to influence effects of media exposure but also the interpretation of media messages themselves. In particular, viewers' own racial (ingroup) identification, adherence to stereotypes (e.g., racial attitudes), and real-world interracial contact each serve as moderators of race-based media effects.

Racial Identification

Research identifying the influential role of ingroup (racial) identification on race-based effects is rooted in the literature on social identity theory and self-categorization theory which suggests that manifestations of racial/ethnic bias are likely to vary as a result of the importance of one's own racial/ethnic identification to their own self-concept (Reid, Giles, & Harwood, 2005). From this perspective, as ingroup identification increases so too does the motivation to protect the status and interests of that group (Verkuyten & Brug, 2004). Accordingly, it is the degree of group salience that determines responses to intergroup contexts (Espinoza & Garza, 1985), including mediated, intergroup contexts (Mastro, 2003), such that individuals who are highly ingroup identified perceive greater disparities between ingroup and relevant outgroup members and judge outgroup members accordingly (Oakes, Haslam, & Turner, 1994). Thus for media consumers high in racial/ingroup identification, exposure to stereotypical characterizations of outgroup races/ethnicities is particularly likely to provoke more unfavorable/stereotypical judgments of those outgroup members and more advantageous evaluations of ingroup members (Mastro, 2003). Of course the availability of images privileging one's ingroup varies greatly depending on the race/ethnicity of the consumer. Consequently, the primary messages offered by the media may, for some, facilitate intergroup comparisons in favor of self. For others, these same images offer a threat to self, requiring more thoughtful selection of media content and necessitating strategic efforts to manage self-concept.

Racial Attitudes

Not surprisingly, existing racial attitudes also have been found to impact the effects of media exposure to racial/ethnic stereotypes. However, research in this domain has met with somewhat inconsistent results. To some extent, findings have revealed that a variety of stereotype endorsement measures and racial attitude measures moderate the relationship between exposure to media stereotypes and subsequent stereotypical judgments (Dixon, 2006; Gilliam et al., 1996; Peffley, Shields, & Williams, 1996). Among these studies, data suggest that for those high in racial antipathy, more punitive responses are triggered as a result of exposure to racial/ethnic stereotypes in the media. Still, others have been unable to replicate this relationship in seemingly parallel designs (Oliver et al., 2004; Oliver & Fonash, 2002), raising questions about the exact nature of this association.

Interracial Contact

Of course our own personal experiences also are known to moderate the effects of exposure to media messages (Hawkins & Pingree, 1990). Accordingly, racial/ethnic stereotypes in the media have been found to produce the greatest effect on consumers when real-world experiences are consistent with the messages offered by the media and/or when audience members have minimal/no real-world contact to pull from in forming their judgments (Fujioka, 1999; Tan, Fujioka, & Lucht, 1997; Mastro, Behm-Morawitz, & Ortiz, 2007). From a more prosocial perspective, it could be said that positive contact experiences in the real-world minimize the effect of exposure to unfavorable racial/ethnic stereotypes in the media.

EFFECTS OF MEDIA ON RACIAL/ ETHNIC STEREOTYPING

Given the discrepancies in portrayals of different racial/ethnic groups in the media and the varying usage patterns associated with different races/ethnicities, it should come as no surprise that a variety of race-based effects have been linked with exposure. Indeed, these studies indicate that when it comes to effects of media exposure on majority as well as minority group members, the quality of content is critical. Although this may appear to be an oversimplification of a complex relationship, in essence it reflects the core findings in this area.

Priming Stereotypes in Majority Group Members

The bulk of the quantitative research examining the influence of racial/ethnic stereotypes in the media on consumers has utilized a priming framework. Priming in this context refers to the process through which information that has been recently activated by media consumption is used to guide judgments regarding target outgroup members. In the main, results from such investigations have demonstrated that even a single exposure to racial/ethnic stereotypes in the media can, at least in the short term, influence real-world evaluations of minorities (Dixon, 2006, 2007; Givens & Monahan, 2005), provoke stereotypic responses (Gilliam & Iyengar, 2000; Mendelberg, 1997), and guide intergroup outcomes (Fryberg, 2003; Mastro, 2003).

A handful of experimental studies have provided evidence for these assertions. Johnson, Adams, Hall, and Ashburn (1997) examined the role of exposure to race and violent crime on attributions about Blacks. Their results demonstrated that alongside prompting stereotype-consistent responses, priming racialized depictions of crime additionally resulted in differential attributions for the behavior such that dispositional explanations are provided for Black perpetrators (particularly those implicated in violent crimes) whereas situational explanations are offered for White defendants. Consistent with these findings, Peffley, Shields, and Williams' (1996) investigation of the influence of race primes in crime news coverage on subsequent judgments revealed a significant association between the race of the depicted suspect and stereotypic evaluations. Similarly, data from Abraham and Appiah's (2006) examination of the role of implicit racial cues in news stories revealed that exposure to even subtle depictions of race/ethnicity can generate stereotypic responses in White consumers. The authors argued that this result demonstrates that the effect of media primes is more pronounced when the depicted trait is stereotypically associated with the target (Banaji, Hardin, & Rothman, 1993).

More blatantly prejudicial outcomes emerge in studies by Dixon and Maddox (2005) and Oliver et al. (2004). Their findings indicate that Black criminality is stereotypically and erroneously linked to overtly physical attributes such as skin tone and Afrocentric features. In particular, findings from Oliver et al. (2004) establish a link between exposure to crime news stories and misperceptions regarding the Afrocentric qualities of the Black individual depicted in the article; with these attributes identified as more pronounced when exposed to a violent crime story (compared with a non-stereotype story and a non-crime stereotype story). Further, Dixon and Maddox's (2005) results reveal that exposure to dark-skinned Black perpetrators (compared with Whites) generated increased concern and sympathy for the victim.

Alongside priming specific constructs, exposure is likely to activate semantically related cognitive constructs that can serve to bias a broader array of social judgments. Valentino's (1999) research demonstrated that certain issues (e.g., crime, welfare) have become race-coded topics and, as such, media coverage prompts stereotype-based responses regarding both the activated construct and associated constructs. Findings from Ford (1997) yielded parallel results revealing that priming a particular construct in memory not only affects judgments along that particular trait, but also activates broader schema for the target; influencing a variety of stereotypical traits beyond that which was primed.

Notably, the outlook is not all bad. Results from Bodenhausen et al. (1995) as well as Power, Murphy, and Coover (1996) each have shown that exposure to positive, counter-stereotypes in the media promotes more favorable race-based judgments. In particular,

Bodenhausen et al. (1995) examined the influence of exposure to Black media exemplars (i.e. Oprah Winfrey, Michael Jordan) on Whites' racial attitudes. Their results indicated that activating positive media exemplars generates more sympathetic responses towards discrimination as a social problem and more favorable attitudes about outgroup members as a whole. Power, Murphy, and Coover (1996) investigated the effects of exposure to negative stereotypes and counter-stereotypes of Blacks in the news on White consumers' evaluations of Blacks. Although somewhat mixed, their results show that exposure to negatively stereotypic representations of Blacks generates more negative judgments of Blacks in unrelated news events whereas exposure to positive counter-stereotypes results in more favorable evaluations (compared with a control condition).

But priming alone provides only a portion of the picture. Researchers have begun to appreciate the importance of including measures of both immediate and long term exposure in tests of media effects. Indeed, findings from Gorham (2006) clearly demonstrated that both short term and over-time exposure to stereotypic depictions of Blacks in the media influence subsequent stereotype-based responses. In this case, these outcomes manifest in variations in language abstractness, used to reflect subtle (and unconscious) discriminatory responses. Dixon and Azocar (2007) further advance this notion by specifying the underlying mechanisms involved in this process. Consistent with findings outside the domain of stereotyping (Price & Tewksbury, 1997; Shrum, 2002), they argued that whereas recently activated constructs will be more accessible for use in processing and interpreting information, as the rate of exposure increases, the cognitive associations between the attribute and the attitude object will additionally strengthen (Dixon & Azocar, 2007). Accordingly, based on content analytic results looking at depictions of Blacks in the news, heavy consumption should lead to increased exposure to Blacks as criminals which in turn strengthens this cognitive association. Over time and repeated exposure this construct becomes chronically accessible in the minds of consumers when rendering judgments about Blacks. Consequently, when exposed to images of Black criminality in the news, the priming effect should be stronger among heavy viewers; ultimately influencing race-based evaluations. However, only inconsistent support was yielded from Dixon and Azocar's (2007) experimental test of these relationships. Nonetheless, their results suggest that increased exposure (*à la* cultivation) indeed contributes to the construction of race-based cognitions.

Cultivating Stereotypes in Majority Group Members

According to cultivation theory, television consumption provides audiences with a consistent set of messages that, over time and persistent exposure, influence consumers' real-world social perceptions such that the more a viewer watches, the more their views reflect those presented by TV, regardless of the veracity of the messages (Gerbner et al., 2002). Consequently, cultivation theory does not direct attention to the effects of exposure to any single message; rather, it is concerned with consumption of the system of messages presented by television—for example racial/ethnic stereotypes.

Initial survey research into the cultivation of racial/ethnic stereotypes revealed a significant relationship between exposure to television content and real-world racial perceptions (Armstrong, Neuendorf, & Brentar, 1992). Specifically, in their survey of White college students, Armstrong, Neuendorf, and Brentar (1992) found that increased exposure to TV news was associated with negative judgments regarding Blacks' socio-economic status (consistent with content analytic results for the genre). The reverse was found for exposure to entertainment programming. Here, heavy exposure resulted in more favorable estimates of Black socioeconomic status relative to Whites (again consistent with genre-specific depictions). Similar results were yielded in Busselle and Crandall's (2002) survey of White college students. As exposure to TV news increased, so too did the belief that differences in the socioeconomic status of Blacks versus Whites were a result of lack of motivation on the part of Blacks, rather than lack of opportunity. Alternatively, increasing exposure to sitcoms was associated with higher estimates of Blacks' educational attainment (with no such effect emerging regarding Whites' level of education). Finally, as exposure to dramatic programming increased, perceptions regarding disparities in the educational attainment of Whites versus Blacks also increased.

In order to provide additional clarity regarding the mechanisms involved in learning stereotypes from the media, Mastro, Behm-Morawitz, and Ortiz (2007) incorporated mental models assumptions into the cultivation framework to examine the association between media use, perceptions about media content, and real-world stereotyping of Latinos. In this context, mental models can be considered cognitive devices that allow viewers to incorporate subjective and objective components of mediated information into malleable versions of knowledge, or mental representations, for use in interpreting incoming messages (Johnson-Laird, 1983; Radvansky & Zacks, 1997). Accordingly, both the features of media massages and the manner in which viewers interpret and store these messages each come into play when determining exposure-based effects. The findings from their survey yielded support for this cultivation-based mental models approach, revealing that amount of consumption and perceptions regarding the content impact on stereotyping. In other words, how much people watch and what they perceive they are seeing in the content each contribute to forming stereotypes. In particular, their results indicate that the relationship between viewers' perceptions of television portrayals of Latinos and real-world evaluations of Latinos is stronger for heavier viewers. Notably, their findings additionally offer some support for the assertion that positive real-world contact can mitigate the impact of exposure.

Stereotypes and Political Reasoning among Majority Group Members

Assumptions from priming, cultivation, and models of policy reasoning each contribute to our understanding of the effects of exposure to media depictions of race/ethnicity on policy reasoning and political decision making. Although not rooted in one particular theory, the findings from this research provide valuable insights into the influence of exposure to media depictions of race/ethnicity on consumers' voting intentions. Here, research links racialized depictions of crime in the news with Whites' decision-making about policy issues (Mendelberg, 1997; Valentino, 1999). To illustrate, audience members exposed to news stories about a furloughed African American convict were more likely than those who were not exposed to be resistant to government efforts to reduce racial inequality (Mendelberg, 1997). Similar results are yielded in investigations of political candidates. Valentino's (1999) research examining the influence of racialized crime news stories on evaluations of presidential candidates reveals that less support was offered for Democratic (vs Republican) candidates when voters were exposed to minority perpetrators in crime news stories. Valentino contents that these news stories activated existing cognitions that Democrats are sympathetic to minorities and weak on crime, resulting in unfavorable evaluations of their candidates.

Studies addressing overall media consumption offer comparable results to those yielded in priming-based research. Both Tan, Fujioka, and Tan (2000) and Mastro and Kopacz (2006) found that exposure to unfavorable media portrayals of racial/ethnic minorities led Whites to make more stereotypic evaluations of real-life minorities. These stereotypic evaluations, then, were negatively related to support for race-related policies such as affirmative action. In both studies, media exposure was the initial causal variable in a model of policy reasoning revealing that consumption of racial/ethnic stereotypes in the media can indeed sway real-world perceptions, ultimately predicting political decision making.

Media and Intergroup Outcomes Associated with Majority Group Members

Effects studies rooted in social identity theory also have begun to emerge which investigate the extent to which exposure to media portrayals of race can serve identity-based needs. From this perspective, viewing media depictions of race/ethnicity would be expected to provoke group-based comparisons in order to maintain and enhance self-concept (Harwood & Roy, 2005). Findings in this area have revealed that exposure to stereotypical portrayals of outgroup races on television can initiate race-based social comparisons which may be utilized to advantage the ingroup and bolster self-esteem (Mastro, 2003). Moreover, these media-generated intergroup comparisons favoring the ingroup are more pronounced among those high in racial ingroup identification.

When these social identity based notions are merged with assumptions from aversive racism, a more complete picture is provided with regard to the diverse intergroup outcomes that can be anticipated from exposure to particular features of media content. Specifically, although exposure to negative, stereotypic images of outgroup races/ethnicities can prompt intergroup comparisons favoring the ingroup, ambiguous or affiliative depictions appear to generate responses consistent with assumptions derived from aversive racism (Coover, 2001; Mastro, Behm-Morawitz, & Kopacz, 2008). According to this framework, in an effort to maintain an egalitarian self-image, viewers will avoid discriminatory responses to media when behaviors could be attributed to race-based motives (Gaertner & Dovidio, 1986). Indeed, when exposed to media images that present harmonious interracial contact, attempts to overcompensate for the appearance of racism have been found to emerge (Coover, 2001). This finding parallels self-categorization based research which demonstrates that viewing highly assimilated images of race/ethnicity results in more favorable evaluations of racial/ethnic outgroup members, among White viewers (Mastro, Tamborini, & Hullett, 2005). This is not to suggest, however, that prejudicial responses are on the decline. Instead, experimental research has demonstrated that race-based discriminatory reactions remain likely to surface if an opportunity to privilege the ingroup arises which would allow for continued maintenance of a non-racist self-image, such as an anonymous media viewing context or an ambiguous media message (Mastro et al., 2008).

The Influence of Media Exposure on Minority Group Members

What little is known about the effects of exposure to stereotypical media content on racial/ethnic minorities themselves, is somewhat mixed. Although it has been theorized that consuming negative images of one's ingroup could have a negative influence on self-concept and self-esteem, few empirical studies have explored this relationship. In one notable exception, Fryberg (2003) experimentally investigated the effects of exposure to stereotypical depictions of Native Americans on Native American consumers. Her results indicated that consumption of unfavorable representations of one's ingroup has a negative effect on self-esteem and ingroup efficacy. Similarly, results from Rivadeneyra, Ward, and Gordon's (2007) survey of Latino high school students found that different dimensions of self-esteem were impacted negatively as a result of exposure to a variety of media genres. Global self-esteem, however, was unrelated to television viewing in their study. On the other hand, Subervi-Velez and Necochea (1990) found no relationship between television exposure and self-concept (for either English and Spanish-language TV) among Latino, elementary school children.

CONCLUDING THOUGHTS

Taken together, what do these findings tell us? From the perspective of shared reality theory (Hardin & Higgins, 1996), the features of media content (alongside the attributes of audience members and the subsequent effects of exposure) work together to create a common version of the reality of race/ethnicity in society. According to this approach, reality itself is based on social verification, as collective legitimization (rather than individual experience) is the force that moves the subjective into the objective (Hardin & Higgins, 1996). If we acknowledge the conceivability of such claims, then the significance of media representations of race/ethnicity and their subsequent effects on consumers can not be over-emphasized as no channel for the creation of mutually shared reality has broader influence. This is particularly relevant to stereotypes as they "exist in part *because* they are based in social consensus" (Hardin & Higgins, 1996, p. 61). Given this, the implications of the current body of evidence on media and race may seem inauspicious—at least at first glance. However, this perspective offers cause for optimism. In particular, it implies that mass media can serve as a powerful mechanism for re-shaping and re-defining social reality to redress current inequities. All that remains is for racial/ethnic stereotyping in the media to be perceived with the same critical importance as issues such as violence and sex in the media.

References

Abraham, L., & Appiah, O. (2006). Framing news stories: The role of visual imagery in priming racial stereotypes. *The Howard Journal of Communications*, *17*, 183–203.

Abrams, J., & Giles, H. (2007). Ethnic identity gratifications selection and avoidance by African Americans: A group vitality and social identity perspective. *Media Psychology*, 9, 115–134.

Armstrong, G., Neuendorf, K., & Brentar, J. (1992). TV entertainment, news, and racial perceptions of college students. *Journal of Communication*, *42*, 153–176.

Atkin, C., Greenberg, B., & McDermott, S. (1983). Television and race role socialization. *Journalism Quarterly*, *60*, 407–414.

Banaji, M., Hardin, C., & Rothman, A. (1993). Implicit stereotyping in person judgment. *Journal of Personality and Social Psychology*, *65*, 272–281.

Becker, L., Kosicki, G., & Jones, F. (1992). Racial differences in evaluations of the mass media. *Journalism Quarterly*, *69*, 124–134.

Bodenhausen, G., Schwarz, N., Bless, H., & Wanke, M. (1995). Effects of atypical exemplars on racial beliefs: Enlightened racism or generalized appraisals? *Journal of Experimental Social Psychology*, *31*, 48–63.

Botta, R. (2000). The mirror of television: A comparison of Black and White adolescents' body image. *Journal of Communication*, *50*, 144–159.

Braxton, G. (2007, June 6). White still a primary color; Black, Latino and Asian groups feel multicultural momentum at the major networks has been lost. *Los Angeles Times*, p. 1, Part E.
Brown, J., Campbell, K., & Fischer, L. (1986). American adolescents and music videos—Why do they watch? *Gazette*, *37*, 19–32.
Busselle, R., & Crandall, H. (2002). Television viewing and perceptions about race differences in socioeconomic success. *Journal of Broadcasting & Electronic Media*, *46*, 256–282.
Children Now. (2001). *Fall colors, 2000–2001: Prime time diversity report*. Oakland, CA: Children Now.
Children Now. (2004). *Fall colors, 2003–2004: Prime time diversity report*. Oakland, CA: Children Now.
Coltrane, S., & Messineo, M. (2000). The perpetuation of subtle prejudice: Race and gender imagery in 1990s television advertising. *Sex Roles*, *42*, 363–389.
Coover, G. (2001). Television and social identity: Race representation as "White" accommodation. *Journal of Broadcasting and Electronic Media*, *45*, 413–431.
Dixon, T. (2006). Psychological reactions to crime news portrayals of black criminals: Understanding the moderating roles of prior news viewing and stereotype endorsement. *Communication Monographs*, *73*, 162–187.
Dixon, T. (2007). Black criminals and White officers: The effects of racially misrepresenting law breakers and law defenders on television news. *Media Psychology*, *10*, 270–291.
Dixon, T., & Azocar, C. (2006). The representation of juvenile offenders by race on Los Angeles area television news. *The Howard Journal of Communications*, *17*, 143–161.
Dixon, T., & Azocar, C. (2007). Priming crime and activating Blackness: Understanding the psychological impact of the overrepresentation of Blacks as lawbreakers on television news. *Journal of Communication*, *57*, 229–253.
Dixon, T., Azocar, C., & Casas, M. (2003). The portrayal of race and crime on television network news. *Journal of Broadcasting & Electronic Media*, *47*, 498–523.
Dixon, T., & Linz, D. (2000a). Overrepresentation and underrepresentation of African Americans and Latinos as lawbreakers on television news. *Journal of Communication*, *50*, 131–154.
Dixon, T., & Linz, D. (2000b). Race and the misrepresentation of victimization on local television news. *Communication Research*, *27*, 547–573.
Dixon, T., & Linz, D. (2002). Television news, prejudicial pretrial publicity, and the depiction of race. *Journal of Broadcasting & Electronic Media*, *46*, 112–136.
Dixon, T., & Maddox, K. (2005). Skin tone, crime news, and social reality judgments: Priming the stereotype of the dark and dangerous Black criminal. *Journal of Applied Social Psychology*, *35*, 1555–1570.
Eastman, H., & Liss, M. (1980). Ethnicity and children's preferences. *Journalism Quarterly*, *57*, 277–280.
Entman, R. (1990). Modern racism and the images of Blacks in local television news. *Critical Studies in Mass Communication*, *7*, 332–345.
Entman, R. (1992). Blacks in the news: Television, modern racism and cultural change. *Journalism Quarterly*, *69*, 341–361.
Entman, R. (1994). Representation and reality in the portrayal of Blacks on network television news. *Journalism Quarterly*, *71*, 509–520.
Eschholz, S., Bufkin, J., & Long, J. (2002). Symbolic reality bites: Women and racial/ethnic minorities in modern film. *Sociological Spectrum*, *22*, 299–334.
Espinoza, J., & Garza, R. (1985). Social group salience and interethnic cooperation. *Journal of Experimental Social Psychology*, *21*, 380–392.
Faber, R., O'Guinn, T., & Meyer, T. (1987). Televised portrayals of Hispanics. *International Journal of Intercultural Relations*, *11*, 155–169.
Ford, T. (1997). Effects of stereotypical television portrayals of African-Americans on person perception. *Social Psychology Quarterly*, *60*, 266–278.
Fryberg, S. (2003). Really? You don't look like an American Indian: Social representations and social group identities. *Dissertation Abstracts International*.

Fujioka, Y. (1999). Television portrayals and African-American stereotypes: Examination of television effects when direct contact is lacking. *Journalism & Mass Communication Quarterly, 76*, 52–75.

Gaertner, S. L., & Dovidio, J. F. (1986). The aversive form of racism. In J. Dovidio & S. Gaertner (Eds.), *Prejudice, discrimination, and racism* (pp. 61–89). New York: Academic Press.

Gant, C., & Dimmick, J. (2000). African Americans in television news: From description to explanation. *Howard Journal of Communications, 11*, 189–205.

Gerbner, G., Gross, L., Morgan, M., Signorielli, N., & Shanahan, J. (2002). Growing up with television: Cultivation processes. In J. Bryant & D. Zillmann (Eds.), *Media effects: Advances in theory and research* (pp. 43–68). Hillsdale, NJ: Erlbaum.

Giles, H., Bourhis, R., & Taylor, D. (1977). Towards a theory of language in ethnic group relations. In H. Giles (Ed.), *Language, ethnicity, and intergroup relations* (pp. 307–348). London: Academic Press.

Gilliam, F., & Iyengar, S. (2000). Prime suspects: The influence of local television news on the viewing public. *American Journal of Political Science, 44*, 560–573.

Gilliam, F., Iyengar, S., Simon, A., & Wright, O. (1996). Crime in Black and White: The violent scary world of local news. *Harvard International Journal of Press/Politics, 1*, 6–23.

Givens, S., & Monahan, J. (2005). Priming mammies, jezebels, and other controlling images: An examination of the influence of mediated stereotypes on perceptions of an African American woman. *Media Psychology, 7*, 87–106.

Gorham, B. (2006). News media's relationship with stereotyping: The linguistic intergroup bias in response to crime news. *Journal of Communication, 56*, 289–308.

Greenberg. B. S., & Atkin, C. (1982). Learning about minorities from television: A research agenda. In G. Berry & C. Mitchell-Kernan (Eds.), *Television and the socialization of the minority child* (pp. 215–243). New York: Academic Press.

Greenberg, B. S., Heeter, C., Graef, D., Doctor, K., Burgoon, J., & Korzenny, F. (1983). Mass communication and Mexican Americans. In B. Greenberg, M. Burgoon, J. Burgoon, & F. Korzenny (Eds.), *Mexican Americans and the mass media* (pp. 305–323). Norwood, NJ: Ablex.

Greenberg, B., & Linsangan, R. (1993). Gender differences in adolescents' media use, exposure to sexual content, parental mediation and self-perceptions. In B. S. Greenberg, J. Brown, & N. Boerkel-Rothfoss (Eds.), *Media, sex and the adolescents* (pp. 134–144). Cresskill, NJ: Hamilton Press.

Greenberg, B., Mastro, D., & Brand, J. (2002). Minorities and the mass media: Television into the 21st century. In J. Bryant & D. Zillmann (Eds.), *Media effects: Advances in theory and research* (pp. 333–351). Hillsdale: NJ: Erlbaum.

Hardin, C. D., & Higgins, E. T. (1996). Shared reality: How social verification makes the subjective objective. In R. M. Sorrentino & E. T. Higgins (Eds.), *Handbook of motivation and cognition: Volume 3* (pp. 28–84). New York, NY: Guilford Press.

Harwood, J., & Roy, A. (2005). Social identity theory and mass communication research. In J. Harwood & H. Giles (Eds.), *Intergroup Communication* (pp. 189–211). New York: Peter Lang.

Hawkins, R., & Pingree, S. (1990). Divergent psychological processes in constructing social reality from mass media content. In N. Signorielli & M. Morgan (Eds.), *Cultivation analysis: New directions in media effects research* (pp. 35–50). Newbury Park, CA: Sage.

Jeffres, L. W. (2000). Ethnicity and ethnic media use: A panel study. *Communication Research, 27*, 496–535.

Johnson, J. D., Adams, M. S., Hall, W., & Ashburn, L. (1997). Race, media, and violence: Differential racial effects of exposure to violent news stories. *Basic and Applied Social Psychology, 19*, 81–90.

Johnson, M. (1996). Latinas and television in the United States: Relationships among genre identification, acculturation, and acculturation stress. *The Howard Journal of Communications, 7*, 289–313.

Johnson-Laird, P. N. (1983). *Mental models: Towards a cognitive science of language, inference, and consciousness*. Cambridge, MA: Harvard University Press.

LA Times. (February 17, 2006). *Television en fuego*. Retrieved February 17, 2006, from: http://www.latimes.com/news/printedition/opinion/la-ed-spanish17feb17,1,4061267.story?ctrack=1&cset=true

Licata, J., & Biswas, A. (1993). Representation, roles, and occupational status of Black models in television advertisements. *Journalism Quarterly, 70*, 868–882.

Mastro, D. (2003). A social identity approach to understanding the impact of television messages. *Communication Monographs, 70*, 98–113.

Mastro, D., & Behm-Morawitz, E. (2005). Latino representation on primetime television. *Journalism & Mass Communication Quarterly, 82*, 110–130.

Mastro, D., Behm-Morawitz, E., & Kopacz, M. (2008). Exposure to television portrayals of latinos: The implications of aversive racism and social identity theory. *Human Communication Research 34*, 1–33.

Mastro, D., Behm-Morawitz, E., & Ortiz, M. (2007). The cultivation of social perceptions of Latinos: A mental models approach. *Media Psychology, 9*, 1–19.

Mastro, D., & Greenberg, B. (2000). The portrayal of racial minorities on prime time television. *Journal of Broadcasting & Electronic Media, 44*, 690–703.

Mastro, D., & Kopacz, M. (2006). Media representations of race, prototypicality, and policy reasoning: An application of self-categorization theory. *Journal of Broadcasting & Electronic Media, 50*, 305–322.

Mastro, D., & Stern, S. (2003). Representations of race in television commercials: A content analysis of primetime advertising. *Journal of Broadcasting & Electronic Media, 47*, 638–647.

Mastro, D., Tamborini, R., & Hullett, C. (2005). Linking media to prototype activation and subsequent celebrity attraction: An application of self-categorization theory. *Communication Research, 32*, 323–348.

Matabane, P., & Merritt, B. (1996). African Americans on television: Twenty-five years after Kerner. *The Howard Journal of Communications, 7*, 329–337.

Mendelberg, T. (1997). Executing Hortons. Racial crime in the 1988 presidential campaign. *Public Opinion Quarterly, 61*, 134–157.

Merskin, D. (1998). Sending up signals: A survey of Native American media use and representation in the mass media. *The Howard Journal of Communications, 9*, 333–345.

Nielsen Media Research. (1998). *1998 Report on Television*. New York: Author.

Nielsen Media Research. (2007). Retrieved on July 3, 2007, from http://www.nielsenmedia.com/nc/portal/site/Public/menuitem.55dc65b4a7d5adff3f65936147a062a0/?vgnextoid=4156527aacccd010VgnVCM100000ac0a260aRCRD

Oakes, P. J., Haslam, S. A., & Turner, J. C. (1994). *Stereotyping and social reality*. Oxford: Blackwell.

Oliver, M. B. (1994). Portrayals of crime, race, and aggression in reality-based police shows: A content analysis. *Journal of Broadcasting & Electronic Media, 38*, 179–192.

Oliver, M. B., & Fonash, D. (2002). Race and crime in the news: Whites' identification and misidentification of violent and nonviolent criminal suspects. *Media Psychology, 4*, 137–156.

Oliver, M. B., Jackson II, R., Moses, N., & Dangerfield, C. (2004). The face of crime: Viewers' memory of race-related facial features of individuals pictured in the news. *Journal of Communication, 54*, 88–104.

Papper, B. (2005). Running in place: Minorities and women in television see little change, while minorities fare worse in radio. *Communicator, July/August*, 26–32.

Peffley, M., Shields, T., & Williams, B. (1996). The intersection of race and crime in television news stories: An experimental study. *Political Communication, 13*, 309–327.

Poindexter, P. M., & Stroman, C. (1981). Blacks and television: A review of the research literature. *Journal of Broadcasting, 25*, 103–122.

Power, J., Murphy, S., & Coover, G. (1996). Priming prejudice: How stereotypes and counter-stereotypes influence attribution of responsibility and credibility among ingroups and outgroups. *Human Communication Research, 23*, 36–58.

Price, V., & Tewksbury D. (1997). News values and public opinion: A theoretical account of media priming and framing. In G. Barnett & F. Boster (Eds.), *Progress in the communication sciences* (pp. 173–212). New York, NY: Ablex.

Radvansky, G. A., & Zacks, R. T. (1997). The retrieval of situation-specific information. In M. Conway (Ed.), *Cognitive models of memory* (pp. 173–213). Cambridge, MA: MIT Press.

Reid, S., Giles, H., & Harwood, J. (2005). A self-categorization perspective on communication and intergroup relations. In J. Harwood & H. Giles (Eds.), *Intergroup Communication* (pp. 241–263). New York: Peter Lang.

Ríos, D., & Gaines, S. (1999). Latino media use for cultural maintenance. *Journalism & Mass Communication Quarterly*, *75*, 746–761.

Rivadeneyra, R., Ward, L. M., & Gordon, M. (2007). Distorted reflections: Media exposure and Latino adolescents' conception of self. *Media Psychology*, *9*, 261–290.

Romer, D., Jamieson, K., & DeCoteau, N. (1998). The treatment of persons of color in local television news: Ethnic blame discourse or realistic group conflict. *Communication Research*, *25*, 286–305.

Roslow, P., & Nicholls, A. F. (1996). Targeting the Hispanic market: Comparative persuasion of TV commercials in Spanish and English. *Journal of Advertising Research*, *30*, 66–77.

Shrum, L. J. (2002). Media consumption and perceptions of social reality: Effects and underlying processes. In J. Bryant & D. Zillmann (Eds.), *Media effects: Advances in theory and research* (2nd ed.). Mahwah, NJ: Erlbaum.

Stanley, A. (2006, March 22). Same old Black and White in two series' take on race. *The New York Times*, p. 5, section E.

Stilling, E. (1997). The electronic melting pot hypothesis: The cultivation of acculturation among Hispanics through television viewing. *The Howard Journal of Communication*, 8, 77–100.

Stroman, C., Merritt, B., & Matabane, P. (1989–1990). Twenty years after Kerner: The portrayals of African Americans on prime-time television. *The Howard Journal of Communications*, *2*, 44–56.

Subervi-Velez, F., & Necochea, J. (1990). Television viewing and self-concept among Hispanic American children—A pilot study. *The Howard Journal of Communications*, *2*, 315–329.

Tan, A., Fujioka, Y., & Lucht, N. (1997). Native American stereotypes, TV portrayals, and personal contact. *Journalism & Mass Communication Quarterly*, *74*, 265–284.

Tan, A., Fujioka, Y., & Tan, G. (2000). Television use, stereotypes of African Americans and opinions on affirmative action: An effective model of policy reasoning. *Communication Monographs*, *67*, 362–371.

Taylor, C., & Stern, B. (1997). Asian-Americans: Television advertising and the "Model Minority" stereotype. *Journal of Advertising*, *26*, 47–60.

Univision Communications. (2005). Univision. Retrieved September 26, 2005, from http://www.univision.net/corp/en/index.jsp

U.S. Census. (2000). Retrieved July 2, 2007, from http://www.census.gov/population/pop-profile/2000/chap02.pdf.

Valentino, N. A. (1999). Crime news and the priming of racial attitudes during evaluations of the president. *Public Opinion Quarterly*, *63*, 293–320.

Verkuyten, M., & Brug, P. (2004). Multiculturalism and group status: The role of ethnic identification, group essentialism and protestant ethic. *European Journal of Social Psychology*, *34*, 647–661.

Whittler, T. (1991). The effects of actors' race in commercial advertising: Review and extension. *Journal of Advertising*, *20*, 54–60.

Wyer, R. S., & Radvansky, G. A. (1999). The comprehension and validation of social information. *Psychological Review*, *106*, 89–118.

Zuckerman, D., Singer, C., Singer, J. (1980). Children's television viewing, racial and sex role attitudes. *Journal of Applied Social Psychology*, *10*, 281–294.

17

CONTENT PATTERNS AND EFFECTS SURROUNDING SEX-ROLE STEREOTYPING ON TELEVISION AND FILM

Stacy L. Smith
University of California, Santa Barbara

Amy D. Granados
University of California, Santa Barbara

Among activists, parents, and educators, renewed interest has emerged regarding the negative impact of sex-role stereotyping in the media (See Invisible Women, 2007; Jane, 2005). As one caregiver stated, "Though it's been more than 30 years since feminists first drew attention to the stereotyped gender messages delivered by mainstream television, movies, and books, men and women are still often portrayed in very traditional roles" (Mithers, 2001, ¶18). Another writer pointed out that television programs "still show mom with the babies and kids. Most domicile publications still show women vacuuming, cleaning and cooking" (Cohen, 2006, ¶23).

These quotes raise two interesting questions: (1) how are males and females presented in today's dynamic media environment, and (2) what impact do such portrayals have on the consuming audience? The purpose of this chapter is to answer these questions. To this end, the manuscript is divided into three major sections.

In the first section, we examine content patterns surrounding the portrayal of sex-roles in film and television. Documenting how males and females are featured in media content is the first step towards understanding the impact exposure may be having on viewers. The second section focuses on theoretical mechanisms (e.g., social cognitive theory, gender schema theory) that have been used to explain and predict the effects of exposure to media content on sex-role socialization. This section also overviews intervening variables that may moderate or mediate the media exposure-stereotyping link. The third section tackles effects, focusing heavily on studies involving youth as participants. We organized our review rather narrowly, by concentrating on a few areas within the stereotyping arena that have received a considerable amount of empirical attention (i.e., sex-typing, occupations, romantic relationships, physical appearance concerns).

CONTENT PATTERNS

Innumerable content studies have been conducted on sex-role stereotyping in the media. Because of this, we limited our review in two ways. First, we focus on studies examining sex roles in fictional screen media (i.e., film, TV, commercials). This was done in an attempt to document trends in content popular among younger audiences. Second, we only review those studies published during or after 1990. This decision seemed prudent given the dynamic and changing nature of the entertainment industry.

Film

Several studies have been conducted on sex roles in movies. A few claims can be made from this body of work. First, gender equity is non existent in film (Bazzini, McIntosh, Smith, Cook, & Harris, 1997; Lauzen & Dozier, 2005). Smith,[1] Granados, Choueiti, and Pieper (2007) examined over 15,000 single, speaking characters across 400 top-grossing (Nielsen EDI©) G, PG, PG-13, and R-rated films theatrically released in North America between 1990 and 2006. The results showed that 73% of all characters were male and 27% were female. Significant but trivial variation occurred by rating (G=2.5 to 1 ratio; PG=2.6 to 1; PG-13=2.8 to 1; R=2.9 to 1), but not by date of film release. This later finding suggests that a lack of gender parity has existed in popular films for at least 16 years.

Gender also affects how characters are portrayed (Bazzini et al., 1997; Lauzen & Dozier, 2005; Markson & Taylor, 2000). Table 17.1 illustrates some of the patterns we have found in our own work. Females have a tendency to be shown more traditionally (i.e., caregiver, relational partner) as well as younger than their male counterparts. The age-related finding is consistent with the results from other studies (Bazzini et al., 1997), suggesting that appearance is a more discriminating screen feature for females than males. Indeed, our results show that many females in film function as eye candy (see Table 17.1). Females are more likely than males to be shown scantily clad, top heavy, and with little room for a womb or other internal organs.

Perhaps the most surprising finding is that hypersexuality varies with rating. G-rated films are the worst offenders when it comes to sexualizing females, which is consistent with Herbozo, Tantleff-Dunn, Gokee-Larose, and Thompson's (2004) research. In explanation, female characters in general audience movies are more likely than those in PG, PG-13, or R-rated ones to be young and/or possess unrealistically small waists ($G_{females}$=34.6%, $PG_{females}$=20.7%, PG-$13_{females}$=22.8%, $R_{females}$=23.7%, respectively), unusually large chests ($G_{females}$ =20.6%, $PG_{females}$=13.9%, PG-$13_{females}$=14.3%, $R_{females}$=13.8%), and unattainable hourglass figures ($G_{females}$=16.3%, $PG_{females}$=6.3%, PG-$13_{females}$=11.1%, $R_{females}$=10.3%). Sexually revealing clothing varied, but this was due to PG females showing less alluring attire than PG-13 or R females ($G_{females}$=20.3%, $PG_{females}$=15.6%, PG-$13_{females}$=24.5%, $R_{females}$=23.5%). Clearly, our findings suggest that general audience gals[2] are prey, on the prowl, or both.

To see if this was the case, we conducted a qualitative analysis of 10 popular G-rated films featuring a lead female teen (Smith, Pieper, Granados, & Choueiti, 2005). We were interested in the frequency of "prototypical" characters found in these films as well as common themes contained therein. The findings revealed a lack of originality in storytelling on the part of the creative community (see Table 17.2). Most of the young, hypersexualized protagonists are depicted as "good virgins," fighting against an older, power hungry overlord or hag. The good virgin often has an

Table 17.1 Demographic and Hypersexuality Variables by Gender within Media

	Films	
Variables	*Males*	*Females*
Demographics		
% 21 years or under	11.%$_a$ (n=1,301)	17.9%$_b$ (n=735)
% 21 to 64 years	81.8%$_b$ (n=8,974)	75.6%$_a$ (n=3,103)
% 65 years or older	6.4% (n=698)	6.5% (n=265)
% that are parents	40.4%$_a$ (n=590)	52.2%$_b$ (n=515)
% that are in a committed relationship	47.4%$_a$ (n=733)	59.9%$_b$ (n=632)
Hypersexuality		
% wearing sexually revealing clothing	3.9%$_a$ (n=390)	21.3%$_b$ (n=814)
% with small waist	8.0%$_a$ (n=716)	24.7%$_b$ (n=848)
% with large chest	14.8% (n=1,428)	15.2% (n=556)
% with unrealistic ideal	3.4%$_a$ (n=321)	10.6%$_b$ (n=382)
Variables	*Children's shows*	
Demographics		
% that are a child	47.7%$_a$ (n=4,362)	58.7%$_b$ (n=3,200)
% that are an adult	52.3%$_b$ (n=4,775)	41.3%$_a$ (n=2,256)
% that are parents	61.9%$_a$ (n=672)	71.9%$_b$ (n=683)
% that are in a committed relationship	57.8%$_a$ (n=559)	67.9%$_b$ (n=523)
Hypersexuality		
% wearing sexually revealing clothing	5.4%$_a$ (n=325)	20.7%$_b$ (n=826)
% shown partially naked	8.4%$_a$ (n=503)	18.8%$_b$ (n=739)
% with small waist	14.4%$_a$ (n=850)	25.6%$_b$ (n=994)
% with large chest	11.7% (n=701)	8.4% (n=332)
% with unrealistic ideal	8.8%$_a$ (n=527)	13.9%$_b$ (n=550)

Note: The film sample included 400 top-grossing theatrically released fictional movies in North American between January 1990 and September 2006. The television sample included a composite week of 1,034 (534 hours) randomly selected children's shows. A total of 67 shows (34 hours) were depicted on network channels, 95 on public broadcast (53.5 hours), and 872 on cable (446.5 hours) outlets. All chi-square analyses are per measure and different row subscripts denote significance at $p < .05$ level. Cells contain column percentages and within cell sample size. The measures reported above only pertain to single speaking characters. Reliability coeffecients for all of the measures are well above .70, using the Potter and Levine-Donnerstein (1999) formula.

unrealistic peer group, comprising strange male friends or animals from a variety of species. Love is a common plot device, with Eros often striking at first sight (see also Tanner, Haddock, Zimmerman, & Lund, 2003). The consummation of love typically happens *after* the good virgin has an extreme makeover, however. The heroine will sometimes fall for the bad boy or even her captor, with the later case glamorizing an instance of Stockholm Syndrome (e.g., *Beauty and the Beast*) in an allegedly benign children's film.

In sum, the gender composition of film is imbalanced at best. The range of roles for females is restricted to the young, domestic, or sexual. Some of these trends are problematic in general audience films, potentially cultivating unrealistic beliefs and norms about romance and appearance (see Levine & Harrison, this volume) in the most vulnerable of viewers—young children.

Table 17.2 Character Prototypes in G-Rated Films Featuring Young Female Protagonists

Label	*Definition*
The Good Virgin	Young and innocent protagonist desiring more than her mundane life. Sexually attractive (e.g., Ariel, Belle, Anastasia).
The Queen Hag	Chief antagonist that desires to bring the good virgin to ruin. Queen Hag is often repulsive (e.g., Ursula, Stepmother).
Wicked Overlord	Attempts to seek or maintain power, which may be threatened by the good virgin (e.g., Rasputin).
Prince Charming	The handsome love interest (e.g., Eric, Phillip) of the good virgin. Their love may be the problem of the plot.
Bad Boy	A handsome suitor that may be a threat to the good virgin's reputation (e.g. Beast, John Smith, Nicholas).
Mother Figure	She is older and provides wisdom, support, and magical powers to aid the good virgin (e.g., G-mother Willow).
Father Figure	May be bumbling (e.g., Maurice) or overprotective/dominating (i.e., King Triton) father.
Male Friends	The good virgin usually has a group of strange male friends (e.g., Dwarfs). They also may be animals or artifacts.
Theme	*Definition*
Desire for More	Protagonist states or sings about a desire for more. The more may be romance, adventure, or simply a change of scenery.
Love at 1st Sight	Characters barely know the object of their affection. Often, they are willing to take large risks to secure a relationship.
Unrealistic Peers	The protagonist is usually befriended by groups of animals or creatures who are almost always male.
Extreme Makeover	Protagonists' physical appearance are altered from slight to drastic.
Feminine Sacrifice	Females surrender their talents and desires or risk life/limb for unfounded causes in light of the possible consequences.

Note: Ten films were assessed qualitatively (Smith et al., 2005): *Snow White and the Seven Dwarfs, The Wizard of Oz, The Little Mermaid, Beauty and the Beast, Pocahontas, Mulan, Anastasia, The Princess Diaries, The Princess. Diaries II*, and *Cinderella*.

Television

Historically, most content analyses of sex roles on television have focused on specific day parts or program genres. Two of the most popular programming outlets are primetime and children's shows, which we will review below. We also cover research on sex-roles in commercials, given the large number of studies examining the effects of such content on viewers.

Prime Time

Sex-roles in primetime are very similar to those depicted in motion picture content. Females are underrepresented, comprising anywhere between 34% to 40% of the speaking cast (Glascock, 2001; Lauzen & Dozier, 1999a, 2002, 2004; Lauzen, Dozier, & Cleveland, 2006; Signorielli & Bacue, 1999; Signorielli & Kahlenberg, 2001). Across

20 years, Gerbner (1997) found that 31.5% of all characters were female. His data also suggest that the percentage has increased over time. In terms of demography, primetime females are younger than primetime males (Gerbner, 1997; Glascock, 2001; Lauzen & Dozier, 1999a; Signorielli & Bacue, 1999) and more likely to be married and/or parents (Gerbner, 1997; Glascock, 2001).

Occupationally, a character's sex affects primetime employment. Males are more likely than females to have a determinable job (Glascock, 2001; Signorielli & Bacue, 1999) and to be shown working (Signorielli & Kahlenberg, 2001). Lauzen and Dozier (2004) found that males are more likely than females to hold positions of occupational leadership, power, and to be depicted with discernible goals. Signorielli and Kahlenberg (2001) found that women are just as likely as men to be shown in professional and white collar occupations. Their findings also show that professional jobs are overrepresented on TV when compared to U.S. labor statistics, potentially heightening the appeal of such prestigious occupations.

Scholars have also begun to look at the nature of workplace environments. Grauerholz and King (1997) examined the presence of sexual harassment across three networks. A full 84% of the shows featured at least one offensive incident, with an average of 3.4 depicted per program. The perpetrators are overwhelmingly male (73.9%), with the recipient most likely a female in a peer or subordinate role. Roughly a third of the acts involved sexist comments. Nearly 13% of the acts concerned inappropriate body language (i.e., leering, standing close), and 11.7% of the acts pertained to physical advances or sexual propositioning.

Other research has focused on more general patterns of language use. Zhao and Gantz (2003) examined how gender affects character interruptions. Of the 435 interruptions coded, 56% were initiated by males and 43% by females. In terms of strategy use, males (81%) were more likely to interrupt disruptively than were females (68%). As such, males were also less likely than females to be shown interrupting cooperatively (19% vs. 32%, respectively). Yet other studies have found that females are more likely than males to be verbally hostile or negative (Glascock, 2001) and competitive in scripted shows written by men (Lauzen, Dozier, & Cleveland, 2006).

Sex differences in behaviors also have been assessed. Glascock (2001) examined a variety of role-related actions across 67 hours of content. Consistent with research in the violence arena (Gerbner, 1997), he found that males were more likely than females to be depicted as physically aggressive and threatening—but not in comedic series. Females were more likely than males to be affectionate, make negative comments, use hostile remarks, and show concern in situation comedies.

Children's Shows

Television content made for children seems to be the most balanced fictional story-telling fare. Examining sex roles in 1,034 children's shows across 11 broadcast and cable outlets, Smith, Granados, Choueiti, Pieper, and Lee (2006) found that 63.2% of characters were male (n=9,716) and 36.8% were female (n=5,655). This translates into a ratio of 1.72 males to every one female, which is more equitable than what has been found in earlier research (Calvert, Stolkin, & Lee, 1997; Jones, Abelli, & Abelli, 1994; Stevens-Aubrey & Harrison, 2004; Thompson & Zerbinos, 1995). The ratio varied by rating and style of presentation, however. Shows rated TVG (55.3%, males) were more balanced than those rated TVY (64.5%, males) or TVY7 (64.8%, males). Live action programs (55.3%, males) depicted a more egalitarian snapshot of the sexes than did animated programs (65%, males).

The nature of characters in children's content has also been explored. Gender affects demography and hypersexuality of characters in ways that mirror primetime and film content (see Table 17.1). In terms of work, about a third (31.7%) of the main and supporting characters in the Smith et al. (2006) study were depicted with a job. Studies show that the presence of an occupation varies with gender (Smith et al., 2006; Thompson & Zerbinos, 1995), with males more likely than females to be shown gainfully employed. Smith et al. (2006) found gender differences across occupations, with males more likely to hold blue collar jobs and females more likely to hold professional ones. Assessing 15 episodes of *Sesame Street*, Jones et al. (1994) found that males and females were shown in stereotypical occupations ten times as often as non-stereotypical ones.

Scholars have also looked at gender differences in characters' personality traits and social behaviors in children's programs, yet many of the studies use different samples (i.e., animation, educational fare, favorite shows) and a variety of measures making cross study comparisons difficult. Despite this, a general pattern reveals that females are more likely to be depicted as nurturing, affectionate and/or compassionate, whereas males are more likely to be physically aggressive, braggarts, dominant, and/or leaders (Barner, 1999; Leaper, Breed, Hoffman, & Perlman, 2002; Smith et al., 2006; Stevens-Aubrey & Harrison, 2004; Thompson & Zerbinos, 1995).

Overall, the creators of television and film are sending similar gender-related messages to viewing audiences. However, children's shows seem to be the most egalitarian. Yet even kids' content hypersexualizes females, creating a potentially hostile developmental environment for young viewers.

Commercials

Approximately 45% to 49.5% of all characters in commercials are female (Coltrane & Messineo, 2000; Ganahl, Prinsen, & Netzley, 2003). A few studies have found a nearly equal distribution of men and women in primetime (Craig, 1992) and children's programming (Larson, 2001). Bartsch, Burnett, Diller, and Rankin-Williams (2000) observed that a majority of characters in primetime ads are female (59%), and Craig (1992) noted a similar trend for daytime TV. Clearly, advertisers may pitch gender parity during popular programming knowing full well that half of the buying audience is female.

Though balanced, the sexes are still portrayed stereotypically in commercial content. Females across the life span, save young adults, are more likely to be shown at home, not working (Stern & Mastro, 2004), and promoting household products (Bartsch et al., 2000; Ganahl et al., 2003). Domestic chores are also performed more often by women than men (Kaufman, 1999; Scharrer, Kim, Lin & Liu, 2006). Similar to fictional content, women are more likely than men to be depicted as parents or relational partners (Craig, 1992).

Males are more likely than females to be portrayed as professionals (Craig, 1992). They are often shown working as their primary behavior, particularly if they are younger than 35. Not surprisingly, males are routinely portrayed in job-related or outdoor settings (Craig, 1992; Stern & Mastro, 2004). Men also can be found promoting non-domestic products (Bartsch et al., 2000; Stern & Mastro, 2004) such as auto supplies, electronics, or appliances (Ganahl et al., 2003). About half of the men engaging in housework are disparaged with humor about their chore performance (Scharrer et al., 2006), thus potentially reinforcing sex-typed norms that only certain domestic activities are appropriate for men.

Traditional gender roles are further reinforced by the sexualization of female characters in commercials. Women are more likely than men to be younger (Ganahl et al., 2003, Stern & Mastro, 2004), more attractive, and suggestively dressed. A quarter of young adult women, in comparison to 2% of men, are shown engaging in alluring behavior in commercials. Though equitable in terms of ratio, the way in which males and females in commercial content are portrayed is very similar to primetime and children's shows.

Taken together, most of the media landscape lacks gender balance. Males saturate fictional story telling in film and television, though commercial content depicts a more impartial world view. The nature of the portrayal varies greatly between the sexes. Whether four or forty, the consumer of media content is exposed to roughly the same one-dimensional storyline regarding the importance, appearance, occupational aspiration, personality, and life experiences of on screen females in the 21st century.

THEORETICAL MECHANISMS

A few theories can be used to explain and/or predict the impact of seeing traditional and hypersexualized media portrayals on sex-role stereotyping of viewers. Most research has focused on the child audience, out of concern that viewing media content may have negative effects on sex-role socialization. As such, two of the most frequently used mechanisms are social cognitive and gender schema theory, which we now turn to review.

Social Cognitive Theory

According to Bandura (1986), children acquire sex-typed behavior through direct experience or observational learning. Such learning takes place via exposure to live or mediated models. Observational learning is guided by four specific sub-processes. The first is attention. Attributes of the modeled event can sway viewers' attention, with physical attractiveness being one potent feature. Many of the females in general audience fare should be eye-catching characters, due to their hypersexualized appearance. As an indicator of their appeal, sales for Disney© "princess" products in 2003 reached $1.3 billion (Strauss, 2004), epitomizing the economic success and pull these attractive characters have on females of all ages.

Attractiveness can also be associated with demographic markers such as sex, race, or social class. Based on notions of perceived similarity, same-sex characters should be highly attractive role models for young viewers' sex-role socialization. Studies show that individuals are more likely to identify with, have positive affect for, and select same-sex characters as their favorites (Hoffner & Buchanan, 2005; Jose & Brewer, 1984), though some research demonstrates that these effects are stronger for boys than girls (Hoffner, 1996; Reeves & Miller, 1978). These differences have been explained (Hoffner, 1996) by (1) the imbalanced nature of sex-roles on television or (2) the fact that it is more tolerable for females to engage in masculine actions than it is for males to engage in feminine ones.

Does research reveal that viewers actually attend to same-sex characters more than opposite-sex ones? Studies conducted in the laboratory and more natural environments show that children do not pay reliably more attention to same-sex characters (Alwitt et al., 1980; Schmitt, Anderson, & Collins, 1999; Slaby & Frey, 1975). Bandura (1986) has argued that only examining the impact of gender similarity between characters and viewers on learning is sometimes not enough.

In explanation, he (1986, p. 95) states, "when the modeled behavior is highly sex-typed, the sex-appropriateness of the behavior generally exerts greater influence on which observed activities children choose to perform than does the sex of the model." Indeed, Sprafkin and Liebert (1978) found that 1st and 2nd graders were more likely to attend to programming showing same-sex characters engaging in sex-typed activities. Following this logic, the sex of the media model *and* the degree to which s/he engages in stereotypic actions are important message features that may independently and interactively affect viewers' attentional properties.

The second process is retention. Viewers have to encode characters' actions for sex-role learning to take place. Retention can be facilitated by cognitive rehearsal of the coded information (Huesmann, 1988). Repeated exposure to stereotypic mass media fare may function as a form of cognitive rehearsal, thereby strengthening sex-typed scripts in memory. Two meta-analyses show that heavy viewing is positively associated with sex-role stereotyping in children and adults (Herrett-Skjellum & Allen, 1995; Oppliger, 2007).

The third process is production. Reproducing an act involves translating symbolic conceptions into courses of action. As such, production is affected by coordination skills and the ability to enact the modeled event. The final sub-process is motivation. Motivation is influenced by the social sanctions delivered to media models. Studies show that children are more likely to imitate violent characters that are rewarded or not punished (Bandura, 1965; Bandura, Ross, & Ross, 1963). Thus, youngsters are more likely to learn "appropriate" sex-typed behaviors by watching response consequences delivered to media characters when they act in traditional or nontraditional ways.

Together, social cognitive theory purports that imitation of a media event is heightened when all four conditions are met. A portrayal that is optimal for learning gender stereotypical attitudes and behaviors involves a child seeing a same-sex media model engaging in sex-typed behavior that is rewarded or not punished by other characters.

Gender Schema Theory

Another mechanism that can be evoked to explain the effects of media content on sex-role socialization is gender schema theory. A schema is defined as "a cognitive structure that represents knowledge about a concept or type of stimulus, including its attributes and the relations among those attributes" (Fiske & Taylor, 1991, p. 98). Children have schemas for all sorts of concepts, even gender. Such schemas steer individuals' cognitive processing of real world and mediated information about males and females.

According to this perspective, an individual's understanding of sex stereotypes may be particularly strong because gender is salient from a very early age (Huston, 1983). Children form schemas for males and females, though the template for one's own gender is more elaborate. Girls tend to score lower on measures of sex typing than do boys (see Huston, 1983), and thus may be more accepting of counter stereotypical actions. Females presumably have more flexible gender schemas because they are at less risk of social condemnation for masculine behavior than are boys who engage in conventionally feminine behavior (Calvert, 1999).

As schemas form, information is judged as appropriate for one's gender and subsequently as fitting for oneself or not (Huston, 1983). After formation, children seek out content that confirms the mental template. As Martin and Halverson (1981) stated, "By observing same-sex models, children learn about what members of the in-group do, thereby learning what things are sex-appropriate . . . By observing opposite-sex models, children learn about what members of the in-group do not do, thereby learning what things are sex-inappropriate" (p. 1129).

Young viewers need to look no further than their TV sets for a steady stream of schema-consistent depictions. Viewing traditional portrayals may contribute to the development of gender stereotypic schemas in young children. Older viewers may activate or strengthen existing schemas with exposure, thereby reinforcing stereotypic thoughts and attitudes about masculinity and femininity.

When viewers are exposed to highly counter stereotypic information, gender schema theory predicts that such content may be distorted or ignored (Calvert, 1999). Studies support this theorizing (Cordua, McGraw, & Drabman, 1979; Drabman et al., 1981). Across three investigations, Drabman et al. (1981) showed preschool and elementary school-aged children a short clip of a child at the pediatrician's office interacting with a female doctor and male nurse. Immediately after, children were asked to indicate the names or identify photos of the medical professionals in the video. Results showed that many preschool and elementary school aged children selected male names for the physician and female names for the nurse. A follow-up experiment demonstrated similar findings (Cordua et al., 1979), noting also that the male nurse was inaccurately relabeled significantly more often than the female physician. One other interesting effect was observed: correct labeling was more likely to occur when participants' mothers were employed or they had had prior real-world experience with male nurses.

Individuals for which gender is a salient schema may be affected most by viewing stereotypical content. List, Collins, and Westby (1983) found that sex-typed children are better able than their less sex-typed counterparts to recall information consistent with their own sex. Results also showed that androgynous children were just as likely to retain gender relevant as irrelevant information.

Summing up, this perspective suggests that gender is an important organizing tool in children's processing of media content. Schemas will not only affect children's encoding of and responses to mass media fare, but their mental muscles can also be changed in the process of viewing. From a gender schema approach or social cognitive theory, the effects of exposure to sex-role portrayals on children's information processing may be influenced by intervening variables, which is the focus of the next section.

Intervening Variables

Theoretically, a few characteristics of the viewer and his/her viewing environment should mediate and/or moderate the impact of sex-role portrayals in the media. The first is the nature of the message. Males and females can be shown on screen in a multitude of ways. A growing body of experimental, survey, and field research (Davidson, Yasuna, & Tower, 1979; Davies et al., 2002; Flerx et al., 1976; Geis et al., 1984; Johnston & Ettema, 1982; Wroblewski & Huston, 1987) demonstrates that when characters are shown in *counter stereotypic roles* the likelihood of a sex-typing effect decreases. Given that schemas are often resistant to inconsistent information (see Cordua et al., 1979; Drabman et al., 1981), the effects may be dependent on repeated exposures and the extent to which the mediated action of males and females deviates from highly sex-typed norms.

The second is the age of the viewer or his/her level of cognitive development. A few skills have implications for children's sex-role learning from media. One pertains to achieving gender constancy. According to Kohlberg (1966), a child's cognitive organization of gender will change during the early childhood years (cf. Huston, 1983, p. 397).

First, a child will learn to identify or correctly label him/herself as a boy or girl. This typically occurs around age 3 (see Huston, 1983; Calvert, 1999). Somewhere between pre- and early elementary school, most children will understand that their gender is constant and invariant across time and situations (Slaby & Frey, 1975). After this developmental milestone, children will strive to act in ways that are "appropriate" for their sex and may avoid those actions that are "inappropriate" (Cobb, Stevens-Long, & Goldstein, 1982; Ruble, Balaban, & Cooper, 1981).

This process may have implications for media effects. According to this perspective, we might expect to see increases in patterns of attention to, learning from, and imitation of, same-sex characters *after* children achieve gender constancy. Some research on attention (Luecke-Aleksa, Anderson, Collins, & Schmitt, 1995; Slaby & Frey, 1975) supports this theorizing, especially with boys. Yet Bussey and Bandura (1984) found that independent of level of gender constancy, 2- to 5-year olds were more likely to imitate same-, as opposed to, opposite-sex models engaging in gender neutral behaviors.

A child's ability to process conceptual content should also affect their responses to media portrayals of sex-role stereotyping (e.g., Hoffner & Cantor, 1985). Categorization studies (Melkman & Deutsch, 1977; Melkman, Tversky, & Baratz, 1981; Sigel, 1953) show that young children are more likely than their older counterparts to classify and sort objects based on perceptual characteristics. Near the middle of elementary school, older children begin grouping items based on conceptual attributes.

The shift from perceptual to conceptual processing may developmentally moderate the types of sex-role related features children attend to and learn from on screen. Younger children may be more likely to focus on visual aspects of characters' gender, such as their physical appearance (i.e., clothing, figure) and overt activities and behaviors (i.e., chores, toys). Older children may be more likely than younger children to attend to abstract qualities such as characters' personality traits (i.e., assertive, competent, leadership) and verbally communicated information (i.e., dating scripts, sexist comments) pertaining to sex roles.

The sex of a viewer may also influence his/her selection of and/or preference for different types of media content (Oliver, 2000). Social cognitive theory suggests that children learn sex-typed media selections by observing the choices of role models (e.g., siblings, peers, parents) in their natural environment. Gender schema theory may imply that children seek out programming consistent with conceptualizations of their own sex. Indeed, studies show that there are gender differences in types of media fare that males and females report appreciating (Hoffner & Levine, 2007). Interviewing parents of k, 2nd, 4th, and 6th graders, Cantor and Nathanson (1997) found that boys were reportedly more interested than girls in action cartoons (e.g., *Ninja Turtles*) and live action shows (e.g., *Power Rangers*)—two types of program genres with violence. Using books, Collins-Standley, Gan, Yu, and Zillmann (1996) found that 2- to 4- year old girls' interest for romantic tales *increases* across these ages, whereas their interest for violent tales *decreases*. The opposite pattern emerged for boys, but the age-related trends were not as clear cut. Without doubt, gender-linked media preferences begin early in life. Indeed, at least one study found that labeling media content for "boys" or "girls" *decreases* children's enjoyment of opposite-sex categorized films (Oliver & Green, 2001).

Parents also play a role in the effects of sex-role stereotyping on children. Caregivers' media choices and commentary about shows may teach youngsters norms and beliefs about what is acceptable for males and females to watch. Research has revealed that mediation can affect children's responses to violent content and advertising (Buijzen & Valkenburg, 2005; Nathanson & Yang, 2003). Can the effects of sex-role stereotyping in the media be reduced? In an attempt to answer this question, Nathanson, Wilson, McGee, and Sebastian (2002) recently assessed the impact of mediation on children's gender stereotyping. Children were shown a series of clips featuring stereotypically female attitudes (i.e., expressive negativity toward camping) or behaviors (e.g., facial treatment). During viewing, the children received either a counter-stereotypical mediation strategy (i.e., "The show is wrong. Lots of girls like camping"), neutral information (i.e., benign commentary), or no information (control). Among k–2nd graders, the results revealed that mediation significantly increased children's acceptance of females participating in conventionally masculine behaviors. These findings tentatively suggest that parents offering very simple statements expressing contradictory attitudes and beliefs than those depicted in programs may be able to alter younger children's sex-role schemas. More research on the types of strategies that are effective is needed, however.

EFFECTS OF SEX-ROLE STEREOTYPING

As noted earlier, the film and television landscape is littered with traditional and hypersexualized portrayals of the sexes, particularly females. In this section, we examine the impact these depictions may be having on children and adults.

Sex Typing

Television may contribute to the sex typing of viewers' personalities and behaviors. Sex typing has been conceptualized in a variety of ways, usually focusing on psychological characteristics (i.e., affectionate/compassionate vs. ambitious/aggressive) or social behaviors associated with societal roles for males and females. Though there are exceptions (Perloff, 1977), correlational research shows that heavy viewers hold more sex-typed personality characteristics than do light viewers (Frueh & McGhee, 1975; McGhee & Frueh, 1980; Volgy & Schwarz, 1980)—which is consistent with a schematic processing perspective. Ross et al. (1982) found evidence of this relationship among college students, but only with heavy viewers of traditional television content (e.g., Bem scale).

Experiments also have revealed that the way in which characters (traditional roles vs. non-traditional roles) are shown can affect sex typing (Geis et al., 1984; Jennings-Walstedt, Geis, & Brown, 1980). Davidson, Yasuna, and Tower (1979) found that female kindergartners exposed to a reversed stereotyped cartoon (i.e., girls shown building, being athletic) had significantly lower scores on a sex-typing scale after viewing than did those exposed to neutral (i.e., teens solving a mystery) or highly stereotyped (i.e., girls shown jealous, lacking interest in outdoors) cartoons. Similar message effects have been obtained with adult female participants (Jennings-Walstedt et al., 1980), elementary schoolers (Flerx et al., 1976) and adolescents (Johnston & Ettema, 1982). The results from these experiments reveal that nontraditional roles can reduce stereotyping in viewers.

Another aspect of sex typing involves the gender "appropriateness" of different activities. Some studies have found no relationship between television exposure and sex-typed attitudes (Repetti, 1984). Signorielli and Lears (1992) found that television viewing was a significant and positive predictor of boys' attitudes towards chores, despite controls. Kimball (1986) found that two years after the introduction of television into a Canadian town, boys' sex-typed attitudes towards a variety of activities (e.g., sports, housework) increased. Longitudinally, Morgan (1987) found that adolescents'

exposure to television at time 1 was a significant and positive predictor of their sex-typed attitudes towards division of labor at time 2 (6 months later), controlling for initial attitudes, behaviors, and SES. The results also showed that early sex-typed attitudes predicted later viewing, but only among adolescent boys. Morgan and Rothschild (1983) found that adolescents' television exposure and chore-related attitudes are positively related over time, particularly among those with access to cable and few social connections.

A final group of studies has measured attributes of sex-role stereotyping of women using items across different categories. Researchers have combined measures that tap personality characteristics (i.e., men are more driven/successful), social behaviors (e.g., swearing is worse for a girl than a boy), occupations (e.g., should mothers, fathers, or both have a full time job) and roles (e.g., women should take care of running their home and leave running the country up to men). These combined measures have been labeled as indicators of "sexism" (Gross & Jeffries-Fox, 1978; Morgan, 1982).

Most of the studies show that exposure can positively affect sexism indices (Ward & Rivadeneyra, 1999), save one (Signorielli, 1989). Gross and Jeffries-Fox (1978) found that television viewing correlates with sexist attitudes, but primarily among boys. Morgan (1982) found that early television viewing was a significant and positive predictor of 6th through 10th grade girls' sexism scores two years later, even after controlling for demographics and Time 1 sexism scores.

Quite clearly, sex-role stereotyping can be affected by exposure to media content. A meta-analysis (Herrett-Skjellum & Allen, 1995) showed that television exposure is positively correlated with attitudes (r = .08) and behaviors (r =. 11), though the magnitude of these correlations is weak.

Occupations

Much of the sex-role stereotyping research has looked at occupational outcomes. Some researchers have assessed the role of television in cultivating career aspirations. The survey evidence here is conflicting, with one study demonstrating a difference between heavy and moderate viewers (Beuf, 1974) and another revealing no relationship (Meyer, 1980). Interviewing 10- to 13-year olds, Wroblewski and Huston (1987) found that girls with a television diet filled with traditional content but lacking nontraditional content "were more likely to consider feminine television occupations than those with other viewing patterns" (p. 294).

Experimental evidence is consistent with these latter findings (Geis et al., 1984; O'Bryant & Corder-Bolz, 1978). Using college students as participants, Davies et al. (2002) found that females exposed to stereotypic commercials express significantly less interest in jobs requiring mathematical skill than did those females exposed to neutral commercials. When aspirations involving verbal skills were assessed, the pattern reversed. The authors reasoned that traditional content in commercials primed a stereotype threat, which *increased* evaluation apprehension pertaining to a traditionally masculine domain (e.g., math) and thus *decreased* females' vocational interests.

Attitudes towards occupations can also be affected by television exposure. Studies have assessed the gender appropriateness of different jobs. Research reveals that exposure is not correlated with attitudes about employment (Meyer, 1980; Repetti, 1984; Wroblewski & Huston, 1987). However, Kimball (1986) found evidence of an effect using a naturalistic design. Two years after television was introduced into a Canadian town, boys' attitudes towards occupations were significantly more sex-typed.

No effect was observed for girls. Experiments and field studies show (Atkin & Miller, 1975; Flerx et al., 1976; Johnston & Ettema, 1982; Pingree, 1978) that viewing women in *nontraditional* occupations across media can *increase* the acceptability of females' working in nonconventional careers.

Television viewing may also affect individuals' estimations of real-world jobs, which is consistent with research on the availability heuristic (see Shrum, this volume). The evidence here is by no means universal, with two studies finding no relationship between television viewing and children's occupational estimations (Miller & Reeves, 1976; Wroblewski & Huston, 1987). Using adult participants (Buerkel-Rothfuss & Mayes, 1981; Carveth & Alexander, 1985; Potter & Chang, 1990), studies show that exposure is associated with occupational estimations (i.e., number of women at home or in professional contexts), but the nature of the relationship varies by media genre exposure (i.e., soaps, action shows).

Together, the research presented above suggests that television impacts all three occupational outcomes. Traditional roles for males and females may teach or reinforce viewers' sex-typed occupational schemas. Indeed, a meta-analysis (Herrett-Skjellum & Allen, 1995) reveals that the effect size between television viewing and occupational stereotyping is small and positive ($r = .22$).

Romantic Relationships

Many of the elements surrounding romantic relationships in television and film are unsettling. G-rated films are a staple in many children's media diets. As such, younger children are repeatedly exposed to stories about females falling in love at first sight (Smith et al., 2006; Tanner et al., 2003), often engaging in little or no dialogue with the handsome suitor. These types of portrayals may have negative implications when characters are then shown riding off into the sunset or getting married. As Segrin and Nabi (2002) argued, "the presentation of marriage in children's media (e.g., Disney movies, fairy tales) cultivates a 'happily ever after' schema" (p. 260). Sure enough, at least one study has shown that young viewers may develop relational expectancies or romance schemas from exposure to media portrayals (Bachen & Illouz, 1996).

What impact does exposure to love stories have on viewers? Some research has revealed that individuals may develop idealized beliefs about romance through exposure to television (Haferkamp, 1999; Shapiro & Kroeger, 1991), such that relationships will involve mind reading or sexual perfectionism. Signorielli (1991) found that TV viewing is associated with more cynical views of marriage, despite controls. Other studies have found that levels of reality-dating show exposure correlate with adversarial attitudes (i.e., sexual double standard, men as sex driven, dating is a game, women are sex objects) and beliefs about romantic relationships (Ferris, Smith, Greenberg, & Smith, 2007; Zurbriggen & Morgan, 2006). Clearly, the research suggests that media exposure may be contributing to distorted perceptions, attitudes, and beliefs about mature, romantic relationships. More research is needed, which tests causal linkages and longitudinal trends over time.

Physical Appearance

As noted above, unrealistic and sexualized female bodies often appear in television and film content approved for general audiences (Smith et al., 2006, 2007). Yet the impact of these types of depictions on developing youth is relatively unknown. Most of the research in this area has focused on adolescents and young adults. Studies show that

media exposure to thin ideals can affect females' desire for a smaller body, eating disorder symptoms, and drive for thinness (see Levine & Harrison, this volume; also Harrison, 1997; Harrison, 2003; Hargreaves & Tiggemann, 2002; Stice, Schupak-Neuberg, Shaw, & Stein, 1994). In fact, the results from a recent meta-analysis of 25 studies reveal that women experience significantly more body dissatisfaction ($d = -.31$) after viewing images of thin ideals than after viewing images of average size or overweight media figures or neutral depictions (Groesz, Levine, & Murnen, 2001).

Even younger children may be susceptible to the effects of exposure to thin media models. Evidence suggests that girls start developing a "desire to be thin" somewhere between the ages of 6 and 7 (Ambrosi-Randic, 2000; Dohnt & Tiggemann, 2004, 2006; Williamson & Delin, 2001). And, more recent research shows that children in this age bracket can be affected by the thin ideal perpetuated in the media. Surveying 5- to 8-year olds, Dohnt and Tiggemann (2006) found that exposure to women's appearance magazines was a significant and positive predictor of girls' self reports of dieting awareness (but not body dissatisfaction) even after controlling for body mass index, peer influences, and other media. It must be noted that viewing children's TV content (e.g., *ABC Play, Play School*) was a significant and negative predictor of the girls' dieting concerns. Experimentally, Dittmar, Halliwell, and Ive (2006) found that 5- to 7-year-old girls shown images of Barbie© experienced significant *decreases* in body satisfaction and self esteem immediately after viewing than did those same-aged girls shown images of Emme© (a heavier doll) or neutral depictions. More research is necessary in this area given that many young viewers spend their formative years as enthusiastic fans of exaggerated and unrealistic media figures.

Taken as a whole, sex-role stereotyping on television or in film can contribute to a series of outcomes. Such portrayals can skew perceptions, attitudes, and beliefs about males and females' personality characteristics, social behaviors, and occupations. There is also some preliminary evidence to cautiously suggest that media exposure may be cultivating distorted schemas for romance and unattainable ideals for beauty and thinness.

CONCLUSION

The aim of this chapter was to overview what is known about content patterns and effects of sex-role stereotyping on television and film. Despite the Civil Rights Movement in the 1950/60s and the rise of second wave Feminism in the 1970s, on-screen gender equality still does not exist. Across media, women are still featured in a traditional and sexualized way that supports patriarchy and hegemonic forces that reinforce limiting gender roles.

What can be done to change these content patterns? Within the entertainment industry, one factor that seems to foster gender parity is having a female in a position of creative influence. Lauzen and Dozier's (1999b) program of research revealed that the presence of a female writer or producer increases the number of on-screen females as well as the nature of how women are portrayed. Until more females saturate the industry and create a sea change, the efforts to reduce sex-role stereotypes are left in the hands of parents, teachers, and advocacy groups.

The research on sex-role stereotyping reveals that media content can play a role in children's gender socialization. With viewing, children may develop distorted attitudes, beliefs, and perceptions of males and females. Perhaps where our knowledge is lacking the most pertains to the effects of hypersexualized females found across television and films. With repeated viewing of these "lusty ladies," girls may develop distorted schemas about what it means to be female in today's society. Such portrayals can also impact boys, however. Young males may form unrealistic expectancies about how females should dress or act. Perhaps with heavy viewing, young males may acquire beliefs that females are to be valued for how they look as opposed to who they are. Clearly, a great deal of research is needed to ascertain the short- and long-term effects of exposure to these types of portrayals on children's sex-role socialization.

In conclusion, the media's portrayal of males and females is distorted at best. Although we do not know the full impact of exposure to these skewed depictions, we do know that viewing stereotypes may have serious consequences for children's information processing of and schema development for gender.

Notes

1. All of our content analytic work was funded generously by *See Jane*, a program under an umbrella non profit started by actor Geena Davis to reduce gender imbalance in media aimed at children 0 to 11 years of age.
2. Many of the differences found in G-rated films may be a function of presentational style. To explore this, we separated general audience females into two categories: those presented in live action and those featured in animated action. Then, we reran the analyses. The results showed pronounced differences between animated and live action females on all of the body variables: small waist ($45.2\%_{\text{animated}}$ vs. $22.4\%_{\text{live}}$), large chest ($27.7\%_{\text{animated}}$ vs. $12.5\%_{\text{live}}$), and unrealistic hourglass ($24.6\%_{\text{animated}}$ vs. $6.6\%_{\text{live}}$). These analyses suggest that style of presentation can account for a lot, but not all, of the waif-like figures found in general audience films.

References

Alwitt, L. F., Anderson, D. R., Lorch, D. R., & Levin, S. R. (1980). Preschool children's visual attention to attributes of television. *Human Communication Research*, *7*, 52–67.

Ambrosi-Randic, N. (2000). Perception of current and ideal body size in preschool age children. *Perceptual & Motor Skills*, *90*, 885–889.

Atkin, C., & Miller, M. (April, 1975). *The effects of television advertising on children: Experimental evidence*. Paper presented to the Mass Communication Division at the annual meeting of the International Communication Association, Chicago, IL.

Bachen, C. M., & Illouz, E. (1996). Imagining romance: Young people's cultural models of romance and love. *Critical Studies in Mass Communication*, *13*, 279–308.

Bandura, A. (1965). Influence of models' reinforcement contingencies on the acquisition of imitative responses. *Journal of Personality and Social Psychology*, *1*, 589–595.

Bandura, A. (1986). *Social foundations of thought and action: A social cognitive theory*. Englewood Cliffs, NJ: Prentice Hall.

Bandura, A., Ross, D., & Ross, S.A. (1963). Vicarious reinforcement and imitative learning. *Journal of Abnormal and Social Psychology*, *67*, 601–607.

Barner, M. R. (1999). Sex-role stereotyping in FCC-mandated children's educational television. *Journal of Broadcasting Electronic & Media*, *43*, 551–564.

Bartsch, R. A., Burnett, T., Diller, T. R., & Rankin-Williams, E. (2000). Gender representation in television commercials: Updating the update. *Sex Roles*, *43*, 735–743.

Bazzini, D. G., McIntosh, W. D., Smith, S. M., Cook, S., & Harris, C. (1997). The aging woman in popular film: Underrepresented, unattractive, unfriendly, and unintelligent. *Sex Roles*, *36*, 531–543.

Beuf, A. (1974). Doctor, lawyer, household drudge. *Journal of Communication*, *24*(2), 142–145.

Buerkel-Rothfuss, N. L., & Mayes, S. (1981). Soap opera viewing: The cultivation effect. *Journal of Communication*, *31*(3), 108–115.

Buijzen, M. & Valkenburg, P. (2005). Parental mediation of undesired advertising effects. *Journal of Broadcasting and Electronic Media*, *49*, 153–165.

Bussey, K., & Bandura, A. (1984). Influence of gender constancy and social power on sex-linked modeling. *Journal of Personality & Social Psychology*, *47*, 1292–1302.

Calvert, S. (1999). *Children's journeys through the information age*. Boston, MA: McGraw Hill.

Calvert, S., Stolkin, A., & Lee, J. (April, 1997). *Gender and ethnic portrayals in Saturday morning television programs*. Paper presented at the biennial meeting of the Society for Research in Child Development, Washington D.C.

Cantor, J., & Nathanson, A. (1997). Predictors of children's interest in violent television programs. *Journal of Broadcasting & Electronic Media*, *41*, 155–168.

Carveth, R., & Alexander, A. (1985). Soap opera viewing motivations and the cultivation process. *Journal of Broadcasting & Electronic Media*, *29*, 259–273.

Children Now. (2001). *Fair play? Violence gender and race in video games*. Oakland, CA: Children Now.

Cobb, N. J., Stevens-Long, J., & Goldstein, S. (1982). The influence of televised models on toy preference in children. *Sex Roles*, *8*, 1075–1080.

Cohen, E. (2006, June 18). Daddy's home: And as a stay-at-home father, he's been there all day. *Press & Sun-Bulletin*, p. Lifestyle.

Collins-Standley, T., Gan, S., Yu, H. J., & Zillmann, D. (1996). Choice of romantic, violent, and scary film fairy-tale books by preschool girls and boys. *Child Study Journal*, *26*, 279–302.

Coltrane, S., & Messineo, M. (2000). The perpetuation of subtle prejudice: Race and gender imagery in 1990s television advertising. *Sex Roles*, *42*, 363–389.

Cordua, G. D., McGraw, K. O., & Drabman, R. S. (1979). Doctor or nurse: Children's perception of sex typed occupations. *Child Development*, *50*, 590–593.

Craig, R. S. (1992). The effect of television day part on gender portrayals in television commercials: A content analysis. *Sex Roles*, *26*, 197–211.

Davidson, E. S., Yasuna, A., & Tower, A. (1979). The effects of television cartoons on sex-role stereotyping in young girls. *Child Development*, *50*, 597–600.

Davies, P. G., Spencer, S. J., Quinn, D. M., & Gerhardstein, R. (2002). Consuming images: How television commercials that elicit stereotype threat can restrain women academically and professionally. *Personality & Social Psychology Bulletin*, *28*, 1615–1628.

Dittmar, H., Halliwell, E., & Ive, S. (2006). Does Barbie make girls want to be thin? The effect of experimental exposure to images of dolls on the body image of 5- to 8-year-old girls. *Developmental Psychology*, *42*, 283–292.

Dohnt, H. K., & Tiggemann, M. (2004). Development of perceived body size and dieting awareness in young girls. *Perceptual & Motor Skills*, *99*, 790–792.

Dohnt, H. K., & Tiggemann, M. (2006). Body image concerns in young girls: The role of peers and media prior to adolescence. *Journal of Youth & Adolescence*, *35*, 141–151.

Drabman, R. S., Robertson, S. J., Patterson, J. N., Jarvie, G. J., Hammer, D., and Cordua, G. (1981). Children's perception of media-portrayed sex roles. *Sex Roles*, *7*, 379–389.

Ferris, A., Smith, S., Greenberg, B. S., & Smith, S. L. (2007). The content of reality dating shows and viewer perceptions of dating. *Journal of Communication*, *57*, 490–510.

Fiske, S. T., & Taylor, S. E. (1991). *Social cognition*. New York: McGraw Hill.

Flerx, V. C., Fidler, D. S., & Rogers, R. W. (1976). Sex role stereotypes: Developmental aspects and early intervention. *Child Development*, *47*, 998–1007.

Frueh, T., & McGhee, P. E. (1975). Traditional sex role development and amount of time spent watching television. *Developmental Psychology*, *11*, 109.

Ganahl, D. J., Prinsen, T. J., & Netzley, S. B. (2003). A content analysis of prime time commercials: A contextual framework of gender representation. *Sex Roles*, *49*, 545–551.

Geis, F. L., Brown, V., Jennings-Walstedt, J., & Porter, N. (1984). TV commercials as achievement scripts for women. *Sex Roles*, *10*, 513–525.

Gerbner, G. (1997). Gender and age in prime-time television. In S. Kirschner & D. A. Kirschner

(Eds.), *Perspectives on psychology and the media* (pp. 69–94). Washington, DC: American Psychological Society.

Gerbner, G., Gross, L., Morgan, M., Signorielli, N., & Shanahan, J. (2002). Growing up with television: Cultivation processes. In J. Bryant & D. Zillmann (Eds.), *Media effects: Advances in theory and research* (2nd ed., pp. 43–67). Mahwah, NJ: Erlbaum.

Glascock, J. (2001). Gender roles on prime-time network television: Demographics and behaviors. *Journal of Broadcasting & Electronic Media, 45*, 656–669.

Grauerholz, E., & King, A. (1997). Prime time sexual harassment. *Violence Against Women, 3*, 129–148.

Groesz, L. M., Levine, M. P., & Murnen, S. K. (2001). The effect of experimental presentation of thin media images on body satisfaction: A meta-analytic review. *International Journal of Eating Disorders, 31*, 1–16.

Gross, L., & Jeffries-Fox, S. (1978). What do you want to be when you grow up little girl? In G. Tuchman, A. K. Daniels, & J. Benet (Eds.), *Hearth & home: Images of women in the mass media* (pp. 240–265). New York: Oxford University Press.

Haferkamp, C. J. (1999). Beliefs about relationships in relation to television viewing, soap opera viewing, and self-monitoring. *Current Psychology, 18*, 193–204.

Hargreaves, D., & Tiggemann, M. (2002). The effect of television commercials on mood and body dissatisfaction: The role of appearance-schema activation. *Journal of Social & Clinical Psychology, 21*, 287–308.

Harrison, K. (1997). Does interpersonal attraction to thin media personalities promote eating disorders? *Journal of Broadcasting & Electronic Media, 41*, 478–500.

Harrison, K. (2003). Television viewers' ideal body proportions: The case of the curvaceously thin woman. *Sex Roles, 48*, 255–263.

Herbozo, S., Tantleff-Dunn, S., Gokee-Larose, J., & Thompson, J. K. (2004). Beauty and thinness messages in children's media: A content analysis. *Eating Disorders, 12*, 21–34.

Herrett-Skjellum, J., & Allen, M. (1995). Television programming and sex stereotyping: A meta-analysis. In B. R. Burleson (Ed.), *Communication yearbook 19* (pp. 157–185). Thousand Oaks, CA: Sage.

Hoffner, C. (1996). Children's wishful identification and parasocial interaction with favorite television characters. *Journal of Broadcasting & Electronic Media, 40*, 389–402.

Hoffner, C., & Buchanan, M. (2005). Young adults' wishful identification with television characters: The role of perceived similarity and character attributes. *Media Psychology, 7*, 325–351.

Hoffner, C., & Cantor, J. (1985). Developmental differences in responses to television characters' appearance and behavior. *Developmental Psychology, 21*, 1065–1074.

Hoffner, C., & Levine, K. (2007). Enjoyment of mediated horror and violence: A meta-analysis. In R. W. Preiss, B. M. Gayle, N. Burrell, M. Allen, & J. Bryant (Eds.), *Mass media effects research: Advances through meta-analysis* (pp. 199–214). Mahwah, NJ: Erlbaum.

Huesmann, L. R. (1988). An information processing model for the development of aggression. *Aggressive Behavior, 14*, 13–24.

Huston, A. C. (1983). Sex typing. In E. M. Hetherington (Ed.), P. H. Mussen (Series Ed.), *Handbook of child psychology: Vol. 4. Socialization, personality, and social development* (pp. 387–467). New York: Wiley.

Invisible Women. (2007). Invisible women productions. Retrieved November 15, 2007 from http://www.invisiblewomen.com/

Jennings-Walstedt, J., Geis, F. L., & Brown, V. (1980). Influence of television commercials on women's self-confidence and independent judgment. *Journal of Personality & Social Psychology, 38*, 203–210.

Johnston, J., & Ettema, J. S. (1982). *Positive images: Breaking stereotypes with children's television*. Beverly Hills, CA: Sage.

Jones, R. W., Abelli, D. M., & Abelli, R. B. (August, 1994). *Ratio of female:male characters and stereotyping in educational programming*. Paper presented at the annual meeting of the American Psychological Association, Los Angeles, CA.

Jose, P. E., & Brewer, W. F. (1984). Development of story liking: Character identification, suspense, and outcome resolution. *Developmental Psychology, 20*, 911–924.

Kaufman, G. (1999). The portrayal of men's family roles in television commercials. *Sex Roles, 41*, 439–458.

Kimball, M. M. (1986). Television and sex-role attitudes. In T. M. Williams (Ed.), *The impact of television* (pp. 265–298). London: Academic Press.

Kohlberg, L. A. (1966). A cognitive developmental analysis of children's sex role concepts and attitudes. In E. E. Maccoby (Ed.), *The development of sex differences* (pp. 82–173). Stanford, CA: Stanford University Press.

Larson, M. (2001). Interactions, activities, and gender in children's television commercials: A content analysis. *Journal of Broadcasting & Electronic Media, 45*, 41–56.

Lauzen, M. M., & Dozier, D. M. (1999a). Making a difference in prime time: Women on screen and behind the scenes in the 1995–96 season. *Journal of Broadcasting & Electronic Media, 43*, 1–19.

Lauzen, M. M., & Dozier, D. M. (1999b). The role of women on screen and behind the scenes in the television and film industries: Review and a program of research. *Journal of Communication Inquiry, 23*, 355–373.

Lauzen, M. M., & Dozier, D. M. (2002). You look mahvelous: An examination of gender and appearance comments in the 1999–2000 prime-time season. *Sex Roles, 46*, 429–437.

Lauzen, M. M., & Dozier, D. M. (2004). Evening the score in prime time: The relationship between behind the scenes women and on-screen portrayals in the 2002–2003 season. *Journal of Broadcasting & Electronic Media, 48*, 484–500.

Lauzen, M. M., & Dozier, D. M. (2005). Maintaining the double standard: Portrayals of age and gender in popular films. *Sex Roles, 52*, 437–446.

Lauzen, M. M., Dozier, D. M., & Cleveland, E. (2006). Genre matters: An examination of women working behind the scenes and on-screen portrayals in reality and scripted prime-time programming. *Sex Roles, 55*, 445–455.

Leaper, C., Breed, L., Hoffman, L., & Perlman, C. A. (2002). Variations in the gender-stereotyped content of children's television cartoons across genres. *Journal of Applied Social Psychology, 32*, 1653–1662.

List, J. A., Collins, W. A., & Westby, S. D. (1983). Comprehension and inferences from traditional and nontraditional sex-role portrayals on television. *Child Development, 54*, 1579–1587.

Luecke-Aleksa, D., Anderson, D. R., Collins, P. A., & Schmitt, K. L. (1995). Gender constancy and television viewing. *Developmental Psychology, 31*, 773–780.

Markson, E. W., & Taylor, C. A. (2000). The mirror has two faces. *Ageing & Society, 20*, 137–160.

Martin, C. L., & Halverson, C. F., Jr. (1981). A schematic processing model of sex typing and stereotyping in children. *Child Development, 52*, 1119–1134.

McGhee, P. E., & Frueh, T. (1980). Television viewing and the learning of sex-role stereotypes. *Sex Roles, 6*, 179–188.

Melkman, R., & Deutsch, C. (1977). Memory functioning as related to developmental changes in bases of organization. *Journal of Experimental Child Psychology, 23*, 84–97.

Melkman, R., Tversky, B., & Baratz, D. (1981). Developmental trends in the use of perceptual and conceptual attributes in grouping, clustering, and retrieval. *Journal of Experimental Child Psychology, 31*, 470–486.

Meyer, B. (1980). The development of girls' sex-role attitudes. *Child Development, 51*, 508–514.

Miller, M. M., & Reeves, B. (1976). Dramatic TV content and children's sex-role stereotypes. *Journal of Broadcasting, 20*, 35–50.

Mithers, C. L. (2001). Sugar & spice. *Parenting, 15(7)*, 90–92, 95–96.

Morgan, M. (1982). Television and adolescents' sex role stereotypes: A longitudinal study. *Journal of Personality & Social Psychology, 43*, 947–955.

Morgan, M. (1987). Television, sex-role attitudes, and sex-role behavior. *Journal of Early Adolescence, 7*, 269–282.

Morgan, M., & Rothschild, N. (1983). Impact of the new television technology: Cable TV, peers, and sex-role cultivation in the electronic environment. *Youth & Society, 15*, 33–50.

Nathanson, A. I., Wilson, B. J., McGee, J., & Sebastian, M. (2002). Counteracting the effects of female stereotypes on television via active mediation. *Journal of Communication, 52*, 922–937.

Nathanson, A. I., & Yang, M. S. (2003). The effects of mediation content and form on children's responses to violent television. *Human Communication Research, 29*(1), 111–134.

O'Bryant, S. L., & Corder-Bolz, C. R. (1978). The effects of television on children's stereotyping of women's work roles. *Journal of Vocational Behavior, 12*, 233–244.

Oliver, M. B. (2000). The respondent gender gap. In D. Zillmann & P. Vorderer (Eds.), *Media entertainment: The psychology of its appeal* (pp. 215–234). Mahwah, NJ: Erlbaum.

Oliver, M. B., & Green, S. (2001). Development of gender differences in children's responses to animated entertainment. *Sex Roles, 45*, 67–88.

Oppliger, P. A. (2007). Effects of gender stereotyping on socialization. In R. W. Preiss, B. M. Gayle, N. Burrell, M. Allen, & J. Bryant (Eds.), *Mass media effects research: Advances through meta-analysis* (pp. 199–214). Mahwah, NJ: Erlbaum.

Perloff, R. M. (1977). Some antecedents of children's sex-role stereotypes. *Psychological Reports, 40*, 463–466.

Pingree, S. (1978). The effects of nonsexist television commercials and perceptions of reality on children's attitudes about women. *Psychology of Women Quarterly, 2*, 262–277.

Potter, W. J., & Chang, I. C. (1990). Television exposure measures and the cultivation hypothesis. *Journal of Broadcasting & Electronic Media, 34*, 313–333.

Potter, W. J., & Levine-Donnerstein, D. (1999). Rethinking validity and reliability in content analysis. *Journal of Applied Communication Research, 27*, 258–284.

Reeves, B., & Miller, M. M. (1978). A multidimensional measure of children's identification with television characters. *Journal of Broadcasting, 22*, 71–86.

Repetti, R. L. (1984). Determinants of children's sex stereotyping: Parental sex-role traits and television viewing. *Personality & Social Psychology Bulletin, 10*, 457–468.

Ross, L., Anderson, D. R., & Wisocki, P. A. (1982). Television viewing and adult sex-role attitudes. *Sex Roles, 8*, 589–592.

Ruble, D. N., Balaban, T., & Cooper, J. (1981). Gender constancy and the effects of sex-typed televised toy commercials. *Child Development, 52*, 667–673.

Scharrer, E., Kim, D. D., Lin, K., & Liu, Z. (2006). Working hard or hardly working? Gender, humor, and the performance of domestic chores in television commercials. *Mass Communication and Society, 9*, 215–238.

Schmitt, K. L., Anderson, D. R., & Collins, P. A. (1999). Form and content: Looking at visual features of television. *Developmental Psychology, 35*, 1156–1167.

See Jane. (2005). Retrieved November 7, 2005, from http://www.seejane.org.

Segrin, C., & Nabi, R. L. (2002). Does television viewing cultivate unrealistic expectations about marriage? *Journal of Communication, 52*, 247–263.

Shapiro, J., & Kroeger, L. (1991). Is life just a romantic novel? The relationship between attitudes about intimate relationships and the popular media. *American Journal of Family Therapy, 19*, 226–236.

Sigel, I. E. (1953). Developmental trends in the abstraction ability of children. *Child Development, 24*, 131–144.

Signorielli, N. (1989). Television and conceptions about sex roles: Maintaining conventionality and the status quo. *Sex Roles, 21*, 341–360.

Signorielli, N. (1991). Adolescents and ambivalence toward marriage: A cultivation analysis. *Youth Society, 23*, 121–149.

Signorielli, N., & Bacue, A. (1999). Recognition and respect: A content analysis of prime-time television characters across three decades. *Sex Roles, 40*, 527–544.

Signorielli, N., & Kahlenberg, S. (2001). Television's world of work in the nineties. *Journal of Broadcasting & Electronic Media, 45*, 4–22.

Signorielli, N., & Lears, M. (1992). Children, television, and conceptions about chores: Attitudes and behaviors. *Sex Roles, 27*, 157–170.

Slaby, R. G., & Frey, K. S. (1975). Development of gender constancy and selective attention to same-sex models. *Child Development*, 46, 849–856.

Smith, S. L., Granados, A. D., Choueiti, M., & Pieper, K. (2007). *Gender prevalence and hypersexuality in top grossing, theatrically released G, PG, PG-13, and R-rated films.* Unpublished data.

Smith, S. L., Granados, A. D., Choueiti, M., Pieper, M. & Lee, E. (2006). Equity or eye-candy? Exploring the Nature of Sex-Roles in Children's Television Programming. Final report prepared for the See Jane Program at Dads and Daughters, Duluth, MN.

Smith, S. L., Pieper, K., Granados, A. D., & Choueiti, M. (2005). *General audience or G-porn: Assessing gender-related portrayals in top-grossing G-rated films.* Manuscript prepared for Dads and Daughters, Duluth, MN.

Sprafkin, J. N., & Liebert, R. M. (1978). Sex typing and children's preferences. In G. Tuchman, A. K. Daniels, & J. Benet (Eds.), *Hearth & home: Images of women in the mass media* (pp. 228–239). New York: Oxford University Press.

Stern, S. & Mastro, D. E. (2004). Gender portrayals across the life span: A content analysis look at broadcast commercials. *Mass Communication & Society*, 7, 215–236.

Stevens-Aubrey, M. J., & Harrison, K. (2004). The gender-role content of children's favorite television programs and its links to their gender-related perceptions. *Media Psychology*, 6, 111–146.

Stice, E., Schupak-Neuberg, E., Shaw, H. E., & Stein, R. I. (1994). Relation of media exposure to eating disorder symptomatology: An examination of mediating mechanisms. *Journal of Abnormal Psychology*, *103*, 836–840.

Strauss, G. (2004). Princesses rule the hearts of little girls. *USA Today*. Retrieved November 11, 2005, from http://www.usatoday.com/life/lifestyle/2004-03-02-princess_x.htm

Tanner, L. R., Haddock, S. A., Zimmerman, T. S., & Lund, L. K. (2003). Images of couples and families in Disney feature-length animated films. *The American Journal of Family Therapy*, *31*, 355–373.

Thompson, T. L., & Zerbinos, E. (1995). Gender roles in animated cartoons: Has the picture changed in 20 years? *Sex Roles*, *32*, 651–673.

Volgy, T. J., & Schwarz, J. E. (1980). TV entertainment programming and sociopolitical attitudes. *Journalism Quarterly*, *57*, 150–155.

Ward, L. M., & Rivadeneyra, R. (1999). Contributions of entertainment television to adolescents' sexual attitudes and expectations: The role of viewing amount versus viewer involvement. *Journal of Sex Research*, 36, 237–249.

Williamson, S., & Delin, C. (2001). Young children's figural selections: Accuracy of reporting and body size dissatisfaction. *International Journal of Eating Disorders*, *29*, 80–84.

Wroblewski, R., & Huston, A. C. (1987). Televised occupational stereotypes and their effects on early adolescents: Are they changing? *Journal of Early Adolescence*, *7*, 283–297.

Zhao, X., & Gantz, W. (2003). Disruptive and cooperative interruptions in prime-time television fiction: The role of gender, status, and topic. *Journal of Communication*, *53*, 347–362.

Zurbriggen, E. L., & Morgan, E. M. (2006). Who wants to marry a millionaire? Reality dating television programs, attitudes toward sex, and sexual behaviors. *Sex Roles*, *54*, 1–17.

18

THE EFFECTS OF MEDIA ON MARKETING COMMUNICATIONS

David W. Stewart and Paul A. Pavlou
University of California, Riverside

In this chapter, we examine research and theory related to the characteristics of media, how these characteristics influence responses to marketing communications, and the processes by which this influence occurs. More specifically, we examine the unique and interactive effects of particular media types and vehicles, and how marketing communication affects individual consumers and markets. In earlier reviews of this area (Stewart, Pavlou, and Ward, 2002; Stewart & Ward, 1994), we examined relatively traditional effects of media in the context of marketing communications. We briefly introduced the then nascent new interactive media and considered the potential changes these new interactive media suggested in both the characteristics of media and the influence of such media on advertising practice. We suggested that the continuing rapid evolution of media presented new opportunities for research, but that such research would require a change of focus from the stimulus—media characteristics—to the individual or the purposes and functions served by various media for individual consumers. Much that we suggested about the evolution of media has come to pass with the continuing development of the Internet, interactive television, and mobile communication, and also the rise of social networks, user-generated content, and branded entertainment. Nevertheless, traditional media, such as broadcast and cable television, continue to account for a larger share of expenditures than any other advertising media by a large margin. In the present chapter, we will examine the roles of traditional and newer media in marketing communications and the increasing integration of media.

Characteristics of particular media certainly influence managerial decisions about marketing communications: what particular media types and/or vehicles to use, how expenditures should be allocated among different media, and the specific mix and schedule of media. These media characteristics are ultimately linked, directly or indirectly, to how individuals use and respond to various media, however. Thus, in this chapter, we will focus more on how individuals interact with and respond to marketing communications, rather than with the effects of specific media characteristics on managerial decisions about marketing communications. Our focus will also be on the more general topic of marketing communications rather than the narrower domain of advertising. The increasing interactivity of various media, ranging from the World Wide Web to mobile devices and digital assistants (PDAs), started to blur the boundaries among various types of marketing communications. Advertising, personal selling, service before and after a sale, distribution, and even the product itself have all become difficult to clearly differentiate. User-generated content has also become an important element in marketing communications, further blurring the domain of marketing communications.

DEFINING MEDIA FOR MARKETING COMMUNICATIONS

At the most general level, a *medium* refers to any transmission vehicle or device through which communication may occur. In the context of marketing communication, the term *advertising* has traditionally been applied to mass communication media, to distinguish advertising from personal selling, which occurs through the medium of interpersonal communication, and from sales promotion activities which can occur through various media. Advertising media have traditionally been characterized as *measured* media, to refer to the availability of quantitative information to assess the number of viewers or readers potentially exposed to advertising messages. However, unmeasured media have become a far more common form of marketing communication. In addition, advertising has traditionally been conceptualized as one-way communication from an advertiser to a recipient with the advertiser in control of both the content of the message and the selection of the medium used to deliver the message. Personal selling and direct response marketing have more typically been characterized as interactive.

Both the practice of marketing management—the organizational domain in which advertising decisions are generally made—and the technological environment have made traditional conceptions of advertising media open to discussion. Several scholars have argued that the increasing availability of information, and the sophistication of the technology for obtaining, processing, and analyzing this information, are blurring the boundaries of several elements of the marketing mix (Glazer, 1989; Ray, 1985). There have also been calls for changes in the organization of both the marketing function and the firm itself to accommodate this blurring of the traditional functional lines within marketing and between marketing and other functional disciplines within and external to the firm (Glazer, 1989; Webster, 1989). Organizations are increasingly aware that there are more opportunities for controlled communications with consumers and other corporate stakeholders advertising alone, and that many marketing communication decisions must be coordinated and rationalized within the context of the organization's objectives. For example, the choice of retail outlets represents a kind of communications medium decision. Whether a good is sold through Tiffany's or through discount merchandisers is an issue that is conceptually similar to whether an advertisement has the same impact in *The New Yorker* as it does in *Tennis* magazine. Similarly, a salesperson is a communications medium in the same sense as an ad in a weekly newsmagazine, although the characteristics of the medium are quite different.

In addition to the trend toward an expanded view of organizational communications media, trends and developments have extended the traditional definition of advertising and marketing communications media beyond the mass media. For example, sponsorships and place-based communication have become an important means for reaching consumers with marketing messages. The logos of well-known brands covered the bicycle and athletic wear of Lance Armstrong as he won the Tour de France. Such sponsorships, along with cable television, computer-based information services, facsimile machines, mobile telephones, and Web-enabled PDAs now allow marketers to reach much more concentrated and focused audiences than with traditional mass media. Many of these communication technologies have also made it increasingly easier for the consumer to respond to the marketer's communications and even initiate communication with the marketer.

Consumers have accepted the Internet as a communication medium with marketers; hence, a new type of marketing communication, interactive advertising, has emerged mainly as a result of traditional advertising embracing interactive technologies. Consistent with the view that the boundaries of the marketing mix are indeed blurring, interactive advertising shares some characteristics with personal selling, direct response marketing, and even distribution channels. Expenditures for online advertising, only a single form of interactive communication, reached $15 billion in the year 2005 and are expected to exceed $26 billion by 2010, as reported by Forrester (http://www.forrester.com/ER/Press/Release/0,1769,1003,00.html). Although this will still be only about 10% of all advertising expenditures, there is reason to believe that this figure will dramatically increase as both consumers and marketers recognize the benefits of interactive advertising that largely occurs online.

The communication objectives associated with the use of nontraditional media tend to be similar to those for traditional mass media. For example, sponsorship of an athlete, such as Lance Armstrong, may influence attitude formation and change because an advertiser is associated with the athlete or a particular sporting event. At the very least, marketers hope for very high levels of brand name exposure, as event audiences and audiences that may witness the event on television are repeatedly exposed to the sponsor's brand name via messages during the event, billboards at the event, or attachment of the brand name to the object of the event (such as a sports clothing company's logo appearing on players' uniforms). On the other hand, interactive media greatly expand the potential objectives for marketing communication. For example, in contrast to traditional advertising, an interactive medium not only provides information, it can take the order and, in cases where products and services can be digitized, even deliver the product. As we noted above, we believe that much of what is known about the influence of more traditional media on response to marketing communication is generalizable to the new media under appropriate circumstances, although the new media will alter traditional uses of mass media by both the consumer and the marketer. Thus, we will consider the extant body of empirical and theoretical literature regarding more traditional media before turning to a discussion of the new media.

The Nature of Media Effects on Marketing Communications

It is probably safe to say that the early advertisers were less concerned with media choices and effects than they were with simply initiating communication. Mass communications historians tell us that the earliest models of communication effects posited that communications were very powerful, the early "bullet" or "hypodermic needle" models of mass communication (Katz & Lazarsfeld, 1955, p. 16) that gave rise to the earliest conception of communication effects (who says what to whom through what medium with what effects). Very quickly, marketers learned that advertising and other types of marketing communications are not so powerful. Virtually all advertising textbooks recall John Wanamaker's lament, after witnessing the failure of advertising to stimulate sales in his department store chain: "I know that half of my advertising budget is wasted; the trouble is, I don't know which half." The problem, of course, is that the effects of marketing communications are due to a myriad of factors, some related to the characteristics of the communication itself (and, therefore, under the control of the marketer) and some to relatively uncontrollable factors, such as consumer characteristics, marketing communications of competitors, and so forth. Further complicating the problem is the fact that the effects of marketing communications are not necessarily direct. That is, it is exceedingly difficult to separate the effects of media from message variables effects, both in the day-to-day practice of communications management and in empirical research on media effects. Communications and consumer characteristics also interact: it is difficult to partial out the unique effects of communication from the prior attitudes and experiences of consumers who see or hear it.

Managerial Approaches to Understanding Media Effects: Media Planning Models

With the advent of commercial television, and printing technologies to make narrow, segment-specific magazines possible, advertisers came to believe that individual media have unique capabilities and effects. Marketing communications managers evolved rules of thumb to account for these effects, e.g., print media are better to explain complex products, television is better because it can show product demonstrations, etc. There was an evolving idea that there are "qualitative" media factors, but generally these were—and are today—relegated to the subjective judgment of media influences. Similarly, the advent of interactive technologies, such as mobile telephones and the Internet, has given rise to efforts to individualize communications or, at the very least, customize marketing communications for very small but especially relevant audiences for the marketer's messages.

Early rules of thumb about media effects evolved into attempts to explicitly model these effects. This evolution was stimulated at least as much by the availability of large databases on the media habits of individuals, by computer technology, and by communication or psychological theory. Generally, media models contain information concerning readership, viewership, listenership, Web browsing among households, and data about household purchasing behavior, among other things. Armed with such information, a marketing planner can quickly identify the characteristics of heavy users of a brand or product category, and determine the media habits of such users. Models employing such demographic and behavioral analysis merely offer insight into which media particular consumers use, and by implication, which media are most likely to reach the marketer's intended audience.

The Advertising Response Function

At the heart of most media planning models is an *advertising response function*. This is the hypothesized relationship between the cumulative number of exposures of an individual (or aggregate of individuals) to communication for a product (within the same medium or across different media), and some dependent variable, such as purchase probability, product knowledge, etc. The specific form of this response function has been the subject of considerable debate. In general however, one of two functions is thought to apply (Stewart 1989): (a) a gentle S-curve indicating that advertising requires a few exposures to have any impact (hence a threshold for any effect at all), a few more exposures to reach its maximum impact, and then a declining marginal impact; and (b) a simple ogive function that also consists of a rapidly rising level of effectiveness with each additional exposure, followed by diminishing marginal impact of each subsequent exposure, but no threshold. Both functions have been documented extensively in the literature, which suggests that the specific form of the function may be contingent on other factors. Consistent with this contingency perspective is the suggestion by Burke and Srull (1988) that the threshold portion of the model is observed under conditions of competitive advertising. Their reasoning is consistent with a long tradition of research on interference effects in the learning literature. Simply put, Burke and Srull argued that the threshold effect represents the minimal advertising for a product to overcome the interference created by the advertising for competitive products. Thus, the threshold is likely to be most prominent in heavily advertised product categories and may disappear altogether when competitive advertising is relatively modest. This suggests that at least one dimension of the broader media context, the density of competing messages, may influence the very shape of the advertising response function.

Media Impact

Finally, most media planning models include a capability for the media planner to specify *impact* factors. These are subjective weights that the planner can assign to certain factors, such as media types and vehicles, and types of consumers that will influence the model to select particular media types and/or vehicles that reach specified audience segments. There is a general consensus among advertisers and media planners that media do differentially impact the effectiveness of communications embedded within them (Stewart, Pavlou, & Ward, 2002; Stewart & Ward, 1994). General recognition that there exist qualitative differences among media that may influence response to advertising has not brought with it substantial skill in identifying and accommodating to these differences, however. Not only is there some debate about how to characterize different media across various dimensions, rather little is actually known about how people interact with different media. Media planners have tried to capture these effects through the use of subjective judgments. Unfortunately, subjective media judgments have not proven very reliable, even in simple cases (Haley, 1985).

This discussion of computer-based models actually used by media planners provides an overview of how advertisers estimate the nature of media effects, and the knowledge advertisers use in accounting for variance in media effects. Variants of such models have been employed in making decisions about almost all media used in marketing communications, including such traditional media as television and magazines, nontraditional media such as event sponsorship, and newer forms of advertising such as banner ads on the Internet. Despite years of experience with such models, there is little empirical evidence to indicate with much precision the unique effects of media types and vehicles. Again, this is largely the result of media vehicle effects interacting with a variety of other effects and the difficulty of isolating unique media effects from the total "gestalt" of message characteristics, repetition effects, consumer characteristics and the like, on consumer responses. The models do require subjective judgments about *receivers* of advertising messages in different media. For example, media vehicle weights demand that the media planner weight characteristics of individuals who attend to particular media vehicles. However, these characteristics are normally only understood in terms of demographic characteristics, or in some cases, *psychographic* characteristics that attempt to characterize individuals in terms of attitudes, opinions, beliefs, and lifestyle habits. In contrast, academic research has focused on individual characteristics that may be correlated with demographics, but are oriented more toward processes by which individuals interact with communication media. We now turn to these research streams.

THEORETICAL AND EMPIRICAL APPROACHES TO UNDERSTANDING MEDIA EFFECTS

Marshall McLuhan is well known for his "Medium is the Message" statement, implying that a medium communicates an image or generates effects independent of any single message it contains (McLuhan & Fiore, 1967). In fact, as the preceding discussion makes clear, media effects can only be understood in the context of consumer characteristics that influence the effectiveness of marketing communications in particular media. While there are many such consumer characteristics, five factors have received considerable attention in empirical research and theory development:

1. Attitudes toward the medium;
2. Uses of the medium;
3. Involvement while using the medium;
4. Mood states affecting media usage; and
5. Interactivity of the medium.

In addition to these five factors, media effects are also conditional on media scheduling decisions, which result in differences in repetition of the same message, and the frequency of exposure to marketing communication in the medium.

Attitudes Toward Media

The attitude of a consumer toward a specific medium can radically alter how that medium affects the consumer and any marketing communications it carries. In an early landmark study, the Politz Research Organization compared the vehicle effects of *McCall's* with that of *Look* and *Life* magazines (Politz Research, Inc., 1962). Matched samples of readers were shown the same sets of advertisements, controlling for copy effects, but were told that they appeared in one magazine or the other. There were no differences in brand awareness and knowledge of brand claims, but there were significant differences in brand quality rating and in brand preference. For example, the gain attributed to one advertised brand as the "very highest quality" was 3.8% when the advertisement was said to run in *McCall's* magazine, but only 1.0% when the ad was said to run in the other two magazines.

In a similar vein, Aaker and Brown (1972) examined the interaction of media vehicle types ("prestige" versus "expert" magazines) and copy appeals ("image" advertisements versus "reason-why" advertisements). The dependent variables were consumers' expected price, quality, and reliability. The results showed strong interaction effects among respondents who had not used the advertised products previously. Image advertisements performed better in prestige magazines than did reason-why advertisements. However, reason-why advertisements did not perform better in expert magazines than in prestige magazines in terms of the dependent variables. These studies provide some empirical basis for the notion that individual attitudes toward media vehicles condition their responses to marketing communications in those vehicles.

The Role of Relationship and Trust

One particularly important attitude toward a medium is related to its perceived credibility or trustworthiness (Shimp, 1990). Particularly for media that are interactive, the perceived trustworthiness of the medium is likely to play an especially important role in determining its influence on consumers. There is also considerable consistency with the conclusion that marketers' relationships with consumers play an important role in how consumers respond to marketing communications (Fontenot & Vlosky, 1998; Hoffman & Novak, 1996). Perhaps the most important element of a successful marketer-consumer relationship is the notion of trust. Research has shown that trust reduces transaction costs (Ganesan, 1994), lowers transaction risk (Pavlou, 2003; Pavlou & Gefen, 2004) and transaction uncertainty (Pavlou, Liang, & Xue, 2007), improves attitudes, and increases future transaction intentions (Pavlou & Fygenson, 2006), and brings more favorable pricing terms (Ba & Pavlou, 2002; Pavlou & Ba, 2000; Pavlou & Dimoka, 2006). Moreover, Keen (2000) posited that the very foundation of electronic commerce rests on trust. While consumers may decide to interact with a marketer in a variety of contexts, any transaction will be largely determined by trust.

Although trust has long been recognized as an extremely important element of every interaction (Dwyer, Schurr, & Oh, 1987), traditional advertising media provide the marketer with limited ability to raise the level of consumers' trust since one-way communication is unlikely to build trust (Mayer, Davis, & Schoorman, 1995). However, reciprocal interaction, communication, and cooperation facilitate trust building and commitment (Anderson & Narus, 1990; Anderson & Weitz, 1989). Hoffman, Novak, and Peralta (1999) noted that consumers do not trust most Internet marketers enough to engage in *relationship exchanges* involving money and personal information.

Trust is a subjective evaluation of another entity's characteristics based on limited information (Beccera & Gupta, 1999). In the context of marketing, limited information about products' attributes and the intent of the marketer to provide a fair transaction can give rise to the need for consumers either to trust the marketer based on the marketer's reputation (Pavlou, 2003), rely on third parties for additional information (Ba & Pavlou, 2002; Pavlou & Dimoka, 2006), or take other actions to reduce risk, such as institutional third parties (Pavlou & Gefen, 2004).

Consumers' trust toward a marketer can be defined broadly as the subjective probability with which consumers believe that the marketer will perform a particular interaction in a manner consistent with their expectations. While it is generally agreed that trust has an economic value (Hill, 1990) and can be a source of competitive advantage (Barney & Hansen, 1994), traditional advertising has not necessarily been focused on building trust, despite the fact that trust has an important influence on the behavior of consumers (Schurr & Ozanne, 1985). On the other hand, interactive media have the potential to promote consumers' trust towards the advertiser and product through reciprocal information exchange, customer support and technical assistance, reciprocal communication, operational linkages, and other specific adaptations by the marketer to the needs of the consumer (Forrest & Mizerski, 1996).

It is certainly clear that audiences have different perceptions of and attitudes toward different media. Knowing that consumers of various media perceive them differently and have different attitudes toward them still does not tell us how people interact with a given medium or how this interaction influences response. Chook (1983) made just this point when he stated that "the attitudinal approach is simple and relatively inexpensive, but at the same time is one that raises a number of critical questions. For one thing, measures of media interest, confidence, and enjoyment have no proven bearing on the performance of advertising. For another, such measures are too generalized for application to specific types of advertising" (p. 250).

Uses of Mass Media

In a broader sense, media effects may be considered in the context of the stream of research examining uses and gratifications that individuals obtain from using mass media. This paradigm holds that social and psychological needs generate expectations of the mass media, which lead to differential patterns of exposure, need gratification, and other outcomes (Atkin, 1985; Katz, Blumler, & Gurevitch, 1974; Rubin, 1986). While this research approach has been criticized on many grounds (see O'Guinn & Faber, 1991), the notion that people have uses for and obtain gratifications from exposure to marketing communications in different media is appealing. There is also some empirical support for the notion. For example, research has found that *social utility* motives influence the viewing of commercials on television. O'Guinn and Faber suggest that uses and gratification approaches may be most usefully applied to media such as special interest magazine readership.

Evidence for different uses and gratifications from mass media is seen in studies of differential loyalty among consumers of media types and vehicles. In addition, there are selective patterns of exposure or preferential attitudinal dispositions toward certain kinds of media and vehicles within media that are not constant across all viewers (Gunter, 1985). How people think and feel about various vehicles or the extent to which the audience flows toward or across certain programs varies between demographic divisions of the population. More significant, however, are Gunter's findings that indicate differences in viewing patterns or attitudinal preferences for programs associated with enduring psychological characteristics of viewers.

The Role of Selective Exposure

There is also strong evidence that people selectively attend to information based on its relevance to them at a given point in time (Broadbent, 1977; Greenwald & Leavitt, 1984; Krugman, 1988; Pechmann & Stewart, 1988; Tolley & Bogart, 1994). Research is rather clear on the point that characteristics of consumers directly influence media effects. For example, in her review of consumer processing of advertising, Thorson (1990) identifies such individual difference factors as motivation (involvement), ability, prior learning, and emotion, among others, that influence how, and even whether, consumers process advertising messages. The theoretical foundation for these effects is *selective exposure*, the proposition that consumers tend to see and hear communications that are favorable, congenial, or consistent with their predispositions and interests (Zillmann & Bryant, 1994).

For our purposes, the key issue is whether these findings are in some way related to the effectiveness of marketing communications in different media. It may be that the effects of commercial messages will differ substantially depending on how a particular consumer uses a given medium. For example, readers of certain publications and viewers of certain programs indicate that advertising content is an important reason for selecting a given medium, and in some cases is the sole reason for using a particular medium. On the other hand, it is likely that some commercial messages will not even gain an individual's attention, if they are inconsistent with the individual purpose in using a mass medium, i.e., they may spoil the mood, distract from the flow, etc. Evidence on these hypotheses stems from research on the concept of *involvement*, which we address below.

Involvement

The concept of involvement has become a key construct in a number of theories of attitude formation and change (see Chaiken, 1980; Chaiken, Liberman, & Eagly, 1989; Greenwald & Leavitt, 1984; Petty & Cacioppo, 1986). Involvement has generally been conceptualized in terms of how consumers interact with a given medium or message. Messages and media are conceived of as more or less involving for a particular consumer, and such involvement is posited to influence the amount and type of information processing in which a consumer engages. Involvement has also been one of the more frequently researched and controversial constructs within the disciplines of social psychology, advertising, and communication (see Zaichowsky, 1985). One problem with an examination of the research on the effects of involvement is the lack of a generally accepted definition for the construct. Researchers have used the term to mean a number of distinctly different things. For example, Schwerin (1958) defined involving programs as "tense" programs. Kennedy (1971) defined involvement as interest in the program storyline, while Soldow and Principe (1981) interpreted involvement as suspense. Thorson, Reeves, Schleuder, Lang, and Rothschild (1985) used liking for a television program and an assessment of cortical arousal as measures of involvement.

Related to these differences in the operationalization of the involvement construct is the issue of where to measure involvement. Marketing researchers have defined involvement in terms of the medium (or specific vehicle), in terms of the message, and in terms of the product that is the focus of the message. It is likely that the general inconsistency of research findings regarding involvement is due to differences in the way involvement has been defined and operationalized across studies (see Singh and Hitchon, 1989, for a review of this literature). With these caveats in mind, research in this area has yielded important findings on media effects.

In early work on the subject, Krugman (1965, 1966) posited the concept of involvement to counter the prevalent model of mass communications effects in the late 1950s and early 1960s, the so-called *transactional model*. In contrast to the earlier "bullet" or "hypodermic needle" models that posited strong communications effects, the essential notion of the transactional model is that mass media effects are quite limited. Individual characteristics, attitudes, experiences, predispositions, etc., all mediate mass media effects. As some have put it, the conceptual shift was to change the focus from "what media do to people," to "what people do to mass media." Contemporary versions of the transactional model are still popular among attitude researchers today under the general rubric of cognitive response theory.

Cognitive response theory posits that the receivers of communications actively process information as it is received by generating thoughts (Greenwald, 1968). Cognitive response theory, of which there are a number of variations, suggests that people are not so much persuaded by communication as they persuade themselves through their own idiosyncratic thoughts in response to communications. The best known cognitive response theory in advertising research is the elaboration likelihood model (ELM) associated with Petty and Cacioppo (1986). ELM posits a number of specific characteristics of receivers of communication that influence the likelihood of cognitive response (hence the name, elaboration likelihood). The two characteristics that have received the most attention from researchers are the ability of the receiver to use the information and the involvement of the receiver.

Krugman (1965, 1966) suggested that early transaction models were flawed because mass media effects are most often viewed as attitude changes regarding important issues—the focus of most empirical research in the area. Krugman argued that people are much less involved with content of marketing communications, especially in what he called "low involvement" media, such as television. Cognitive response theory has not, by any means, ignored low involvement situations. It suggests that there are differences between high involvement and low involvement situations. The underlying cognitive response mechanism is the same in both situations, however. What is hypothesized to differ is the content of the thoughts elicited by the communication. More involving situations elicit more thoughts directly related to the message, while less involving situations elicit more thoughts related to such non-message cues as source expertise, liking for the source, and so forth. In both high and low involvement circumstances the message recipient is viewed as an active information processor. What changes as a function of involvement is the nature of the information attended and processed.

Several studies have specifically examined the effect of various kinds of involvement on responses to marketing communication. Lloyd and Clancy (1989) and Audits and Surveys (1986) reported large-scale studies that demonstrate that more highly involving media (i.e., print) are better vehicles for delivering product messages. This is true regardless of whether the measure of effectiveness of communication is recall, persuasion, or message credibility. Buchholz and Smith (1991) investigated the effect of the interaction of involvement and type of medium on a variety of measures. For these authors, involvement is a situational variable, which they induced by instructions that directed respondents either to pay careful attention to an advertisement or to pay attention to material surrounding the advertisement of interest. Their research demonstrated that in high involvement situations, message recipients were equally likely to process and remember advertising messages embedded in radio and television commercials. Under high involvement situations, message recipients tended to generate more thoughts, and especially personally relevant thoughts, about the commercial message. In low involvement situations, television, with its dual channel input (audio and visual), was the superior medium. Cognitive responses and the number of personally relevant connections were substantially reduced in the low involvement situation. Television was nonetheless superior to radio in low involvement circumstances.

In sum, the involvement notion is an important one for this chapter's topic because it has formed the basis for research that attempts to directly compare media effects. In general, findings show that media differ in the extent to which they invite different kinds of attentiveness and information processing of advertising. Additionally, despite the ambiguity of the construct, research has directly examined the complex interactions between effects of the medium itself, viewer characteristics, products, and perhaps the situation in which the communication occurs.

Mood

The term *mood* denotes specific subjective feeling states at the time of exposure to a marketing communication. A rather substantial body of research makes it quite clear that mood influences an array of psychological processes: attention, information processing, decision making, memory, and attitude formation. Srull (1990), Isen (1989), and Gardner (1985) provide reviews of much of this work and its implications for advertising and consumer behavior. Conceptually related to *uses and gratifications* research discussed earlier, the concept of mood and the related construct of arousal, focus on affective, rather than cognitive factors that link individuals to media. The essential idea is that people use media to maintain or change feeling states (moods) or excitatory states (arousal). Self-report data suggest that people use television to both increase and decrease arousal (Condry, 1989), and physiological studies have shown that television viewing can alter blood pressure, heart rate, and other physiological states that presumably reflect arousal states (Klebber, 1985).

There is certainly evidence that moods induced by television programs interact with commercials embedded within these programs to produce differential responses among viewers. For example, Kennedy (1971) found viewers of suspense programs had poorer recall of a brand name in an embedded commercial than viewers of a comedy. However, attitudes toward the advertised brand were more positive among viewers of the suspense program than among viewers of a comedy. Similar results for recall are reported by Soldow and Principe (1981). Goldberg and Gorn (1987) found that compared to commercials viewed in the context of a sad program, commercials viewed in the context of a happy television program resulted in happier moods during viewing of both the program and commercials, more positive cognitive responses about the commercials, and higher evaluations of commercial effectiveness. They also found that the mood induced by the program had a greater effect on commercials with a greater emotional appeal than commercials with more informational appeals. They did not examine whether there was an interaction between the emotional tone of the commercials and the programs in which they were embedded.

The potential interaction of the emotional tone of commercials and programs was investigated by Kamins, Marks, and Skinner (1991). They found that a "sad" commercial embedded within a "sad" program was rated by viewers as more likeable and produced higher ratings of purchase intention than a humorous commercial embedded within a "sad" program. Conversely, a humorous commercial embedded within a humorous program performed better than a humorous commercial embedded within a "sad" program. The authors interpreted these results in terms of consistency theory, which suggests that viewers seek to maintain a mood throughout a program. Since commercials represent interruptions, Kamins et al. suggested that commercials that are more consistent in emotional tone with the program will perform better than those that are inconsistent in tone.

In an earlier study, Krugman (1983) also examined the relationship between responses to advertising and the programming context. While he did not explicitly address the question of mood, his hypotheses reflect processes that would seem to be conceptually related to the construct of mood: he tested the conventional wisdom that "commercials are particularly objectionable when they interrupt interesting programs." Thus, some reasoned, "the more interesting the program, the less effective the commercial" (Soldow & Principe, 1981). Krugman first distinguished between viewer opinion, and impact on viewers, as separate phenomena. Then, he examined the impact of advertising in 56 television programs that were determined to vary in interest level. He found a pattern that is just the reverse of the conventional wisdom: commercials interrupting interesting programs are more effective. This is consistent with Krugman's earlier hypothesis that involvement with advertising tends to be consistent with interest in the editorial environment. While this study does not make comparisons with other media, and the notion of interest relates as much to message variables as it may relate to media effects, the finding is indicative of the importance of the media viewing context as a mediator of advertising effects.

Finally, a major field experiment (Yuspeh, 1977) examined the programming context as a determinant of responses to television advertising. This time, the programming context was manipulated by having viewers watch either situation comedies or action programs. Yuspeh did not offer explanatory concepts to suggest what it is about the different programming types that might account for different effects, but the implicit idea seems to be that linkage between programming stimuli and advertising responses is attributable to variations in mood, or excitatory states experienced while watching. Individuals were asked to watch particular programs (experimentally manipulated so that half watched three action programs and half watched three situation comedies). Commercials for six products were embedded in the programs, and effects were measured with multiple indicators, such as brand recall, attitudes and buying intention, and commercial element playback. Interestingly, there were only slight differences between the two types of programming contexts on commercial effectiveness. However, there were significant differences among specific episodes with each program type, across products and performance measures. It appears that different episodes of the same program may have different effects on the performance of commercials appearing in those programs. It is likely that such an effect is the outcome of a complex set of interactions between program type, advertising message, and viewer characteristics, especially programming-induced moods.

None of the studies that explore the relationship between programming context and advertising response clarify whether the effects of prior moods differ from programming-induced moods. Nor is it clear whether the types of mood effects that occur in a television context occur in other media, although it is certain that other media are capable of creating or changing moods (Gardner, 1985; Isen, 1989).

Interactivity

Within the last few years, a new form of marketing communication has emerged. This new form is predominantly electronic, but it has many of the characteristics of other forms of communication: (a) it can be interactive, but without the human touch of personal selling; (b) it provides the opportunity for direct response from and to the consumer; (c) it allows mass communication among consumers without the marketer's intervention; and (d) it shares some of the characteristics of print and broadcast advertising, at least with respect to the more traditional advertising that appears on it (banner ads, e-announcements). Cutler (1990) defined the new media as media that provide the capability to instantaneously advertise, execute a sale, and collect payment. With the advent of the Internet and other technologies (interactive web technologies, streaming media, wireless devices, interactive TV, etc.), these new media go well beyond these basic capabilities to allow a more comprehensive interaction between consumers and marketers and among consumers (Anderson, 1996). Therefore, perhaps the most interesting and novel attribute of the new media is their capability for *interactivity*, which is becoming increasingly more pronounced with the infusion of more advanced communication media.

Using interactive media, consumers can collect and provide information by searching and navigating through commercial Web sites, interact with marketers through interactive Web-based software and mobile telephones, post and customize their preferences, communicate with other consumers and product and service providers, and conduct transactions anytime from anywhere. Similarly, marketers can use information obtained from consumers to customize their messages, segment their audiences, facilitate consumer search for selected types of information and products, and collect information about consumers' preferences to improve future products and services. Moreover, marketers can potentially provide consumers with a more enjoyable and informative experience by offering such services as personalized information, live messaging and entertainment, and quick customer service and technical support through e-mail, "smart" Web sites, live operators, streaming media, and video conferencing. Thus, interactive media provide new capabilities (Burke, 1997) that are not found in more traditional media.

The notion of interactivity has tended to be associated primarily with the Internet, but this is a limiting conceptualization in an era that is providing increasing opportunities for interactivity through a variety of different media ranging from interactive television to mobile devices that use WAP-enabled mobile sites (Balasubramanian, Peterson, & Jarvenpaa, 2002). Moreover, the concept of interactivity will strongly influence the conceptualization and practice of relationship marketing (Thirkwell, 1997) and change the way marketers think about communication. Leckenby and Li (2000) defined interactive advertising as the presentation and promotion of products, services, and ideas by an identified sponsor through mediated means, involving mutual interaction between consumers and marketers.

The use of interactive media also draws attention to the theoretical differences between traditional conceptualizations on advertising and its applications to today's marketplace. Traditional approaches to advertising practice and research have implicitly assumed that advertising is something the marketer does *to* the consumer. In contrast, interactive advertising makes it clear that what advertising does to the consumer is only one limited dimension of advertising, highlighting the need to understand what consumers do to advertising (Cross & Smith, 1995), and how interactive media affect this two-way interaction (Stewart & Pavlou, 2002). The reasons consumers seek, self-select, process, use and respond to information are critical for understanding interactive marketing communication. Moreover, communication among multiple consumers over interactive media (e.g. portals, chat rooms, blogs, online product reviews) has the potential to alter the way consumers respond to marketers' communications (Dellarocas, 2003). Interactive media of various types not only open new opportunities for communication with and among consumers (Spalter, 1996), but they also create opportunities for creating new measures of consumer response to such communications, as well as to product offerings and other marketing initiatives. Interactive media highlight the importance of the consumer in marketing communication (Pavlou & Stewart, 2000, Stewart & Pavlou, 2002).

Benefits of Interactive Media

Interactive media will soon achieve the reach of television, the selectivity of direct marketing, and the richness of personalized interaction rivaled only by an expert salesperson (Braunstein & Levine, 2000). Interactive media combine the dynamic delivery of broadcast media to send targeted streaming ad messages to consumers, while attracting new audiences that may not respond to traditional non-interactive media. Moreover, interactive media can offer communications that provide consumers with the ability to complete a transaction instantaneously (McKenna, 1997), while simultaneously monitoring results, analyzing consumer preferences, and adjusting the message and promotions to increase performance. This allows advertisers to target advertisements to consumers with different content type based on past online behavior, geographical location, and demographic information.

Keeney (1999) has suggested a variety of ways in which the Internet might create value for consumers. These include minimizing errors in transactions, lowering costs of products and services, designing optimal products or product bundles, minimizing shopping time, and increasing the enjoyment of shopping, among others. These outcomes are undoubtedly valuable to consumers; nevertheless, the effects of interactive advertising go well beyond cost and convenience benefits to include satisfaction, customization, participation and involvement, mutual confidence and trust, and better product understanding and purchasing decision quality (Pavlou & Fygenson, 2006).

By using interactive media, marketers can create profiles of consumers by either direct self-reporting or by tracking behavior. Consumers can also generate their own profile preferences, provided they see a benefit from doing this. For example, Mypoints.com (www.mypoints.com) promises to send personalized messages to consumers for products and services they care about if they reveal their preferences. In this sense, consumers receive value by learning about goods they are interested in. Apart from self-reporting, data mining is a powerful approach that allows marketers to learn about consumer preferences by tracking patterns of behavior, such as clickstream and purchase history data. For example, *cookies* are widely used software programs that keep track of consumers' Web behavior. Therefore, depending on the "expertise" of the system, Web tracking helps marketers learn more about their consumers and improve and target their messages and product offerings. Interactive advertising can also act as a *product simulator*, providing a substitute for physical on-site selling. As bandwidth limitations become less restrictive, marketers can advertise their products by employing virtual showrooms where consumers can view products in interactive 360-degree views with zooming capabilities (Jiang & Benbasat, 2005, 2007a, 2007b). Furthermore, *live consultation* can also be employed by the power of interactive media that can help marketers respond to consumer inquiries in a manner similar to live consultation without employing human salespeople. In sum, interactive advertising offers a variety of benefits to both consumers and marketers, enabling a better and more fruitful interaction among consumers and marketers (Wikstrom, 1996).

While interactive media may never achieve the human touch of personal interaction and might not translate the tone and body language of an expert salesperson, they can still offer an opportunity for a form of personal selling, one-to-one marketing (Burke, 1997). Since the interactive media can provide customized solutions to mass markets, they may enable marketing communication to enter areas where the "high touch" of a human salesperson is required. Indeed, Stewart, Frazier, and Martin (1996) argued that the Internet is merging traditional advertising and personal selling into a new integrated form of marketing communication. According to Lovelock (1996), interactive media can establish a channel of communication among consumers and marketers and give rise to better relationships. Customized and personalized media also have the potential to improve customer service after the sale (Berry 1987, 1995; Peterson, Balasubramanian, & Bronnenberg, 1997).

The concept of *build-to-order* products is a possible consequence of employing interactive media. For example, Helper and MacDuffie (2000) proposed a hypothetical scenario where consumers can actively participate in a form of personal selling through interactive media to order custom-configured automobiles. In addition, *automatic replenishment* is a form of one-to-one marketing where the consumer is automatically notified about reordering new products. Automatic replenishment can be considered another form of personal selling that adds value to the consumer experience, brings back existing customers, delivers new sales, and enhances customer relationships. Interactivity is a key element for the success of automatic replenishment since this form of advertising needs a customer-marketer relationship.

Despite such enormous possibilities arising from the use of interactive media in advertising, e-mail communication is still the most common form of personal selling within today's interactive media. For example, Coolsavings.com (www.coolsavings.com) sends personalized e-mails to targeted consumers asking them to visit a site and purchase certain discounted products. The ability to reach individual users immediately and reliably without significant costs makes e-mail communication more efficient than the traditional letter, telephone, or even broadcast medium. Consumers are also more likely to respond to e-mail offers that are personalized to their interests than to the mass media.

Interactive media can replace personal selling when the marketer knows enough about the consumer to provide knowledgeable and personalized ad messages. While marketers could ideally use any information to benefit the consumer in terms of tailoring a message based on the consumers' preferences, collecting personal information could practically result in an invasion of the consumers' privacy (Culnan & Armstrong, 1999; Malhotra, Kim, & Agarwal, 2004). Online profiling is the practice of collecting information, often secretly, about consumers' Web surfing habits and other personal purchasing preferences (Smith, Milberg, & Burke, 1996).

One of the unique dimensions of the Internet is anonymity; hence, consumers are rightfully concerned about the privacy of their personal information gathered by marketers during their Web surfing. Whereas Web tracking can have an enormous potential for marketers, concerns over loss of the consumer's privacy may hinder the marketers' efforts to understand consumers better (Malhotra et al., 2004). Similar to traditional forms of personal selling, interactive advertising can achieve a legitimate one-to-one communication when consumers are intentionally seeking such interaction.

Word-of-Mouth Communication in Interactive Media

Word-of-mouth (WOM) communication has long been regarded as the most credible, unbiased, and effective form of marketing communication (Cafferky, 1996; Hoyer & Macinnis, 2001; Kiely, 1993; Rosen, 2000). WOM communication is defined as all informal exchange of information among consumers about the characteristics, usage, and ownership of products and services. Many Internet portals allow consumers to actively communicate through e-mail group discussions, message boards, and chat rooms without marketer intervention, providing a viable form of mass WOM communication (Chevalier & Mayzlin, 2006). Whereas consumers have always had the ability to spread information to other consumers (word-of-mouth), this "pass-it-on" phenomenon has become a prominent use of the new interactive media (Buttle, 1998). The term *viral marketing* describes the fact that consumers spread a marketer's message to other consumers with little or no effort by the marketer. For example, Web sites offering virtual greeting cards (e.g., www.bluemountain.com) spread information about the availability of such cards when consumers send them to each other.

A new venue for a third-party-driven form of interactive communication has emerged in interactive media. Independent portals such as Yahoo.com (www.yahoo.com) host virtual communities, message boards, and chat rooms, and e-mail group discussions, which offer convenient ways to connect consumers who share the same interests and ideas. For example, eGroups.com (www.egroups.com) is an e-mail group service that allows consumers to easily create and join e-mail groups. This provides a form of dynamic WOM communication among millions of consumers. While WOM communication is usually not marketer-driven, advertisers can monitor and perhaps influence what information is communicated among consumers (Chen & Xie, 2005).

Online WOM communication in the form of *online product reviews* has become a major informational source since online product reviews can reach far beyond traditional settings and reach a virtually infinite number of consumers. Indeed, the marketing literature suggests that consumers do pay attention to online product reviews and act upon them to make purchasing decisions (Chatterjee, 2001; Chevalier & Mayzlin,

2006). Therefore, firms like Amazon.com and Circuitcity.com encourage their consumers to read and write product reviews, while other firms, such as Epinions.com and BizRate.com specialize in collecting, synthesizing, and disseminating online product reviews. Pew Internet's August 2006 survey reported that 28% of Internet users rate their product purchases, while Pew Internet's March 2005 survey showed that 78% of Internet users read product reviews before purchasing a product. Accordingly, many studies (e.g., Chevalier & Mayzlin, 2006; Godes & Mayzlin, 2004; Liu, 2006) used online product reviews to predict product sales. For example, Chevalier and Mayzlin examined the effect of online product reviews on book sales on Amazon's and Barnes and Noble's Web sites, showing that an improvement in a book's mean of online product reviews enhances book sales. Most studies show that online product reviews have a significant effect on product sales (e.g., Chevalier & Goolsbee, 2003; Clemons, Gao, & Hitt, 2006). However, other studies (e.g., Liu, 2006) show that it is the *volume* of product reviews that significantly influences sales, while the *valence* does not show any significant effects. In sum, the nature and impact of online product reviews as an instance of WOM communication is still an open research question.

Not only does monitoring WOM communication in public venues not violate consumer privacy, it can also provide valuable information about what information consumers find most important. Rather than copiously tracking consumer preferences, marketers can use publicly available information to understand how consumers form their preferences. Moreover, marketers can influence WOM communication by "seeding" sites (Rosen, 2000). In sum, consumer-to-consumer communication over interactive media can provide a form of a dynamic WOM communication that can complement marketer-driven communications.

A dynamic component of online WOM communication that rapidly increases in importance and can complement marketer-driven communications are *blogs*. Blogs are the fastest growing online medium for communication, and they represent the latest method of personal expression. While there were only 5 million blogs worldwide in 2004, this figure increased to 50 million by 2005 (Wright, 2006). According to Blogpulse (www.blogpulse.com), in a typical day there are over 70,000 newly created blogs and more than 700,000 individual blog posts. Fortune magazine (2005) argues that blogs are so important that companies cannot afford to ignore them (http://money.cnn.com/magazines/fortune/fortune_archive/2005/01/10/8230982/index.htm). Interestingly, many mainstream TV news reports quote news stories from blogs. While blogs started as a means for personal publishing and low-scale communication, they have recently become marketing tools. For example, Microsoft, General Motors, and Disney Studios have adopted blogs for disseminating information, building relationships, and managing knowledge (Wright, 2006). Over 1,000 Microsoft developers and product managers communicate directly with customers daily via blogs to understand how customers respond to the company's products and services (Wright, 2006). General Motors (GM) has introduced FastLane Blog (http://fastlane.gmBlogs.com/) to distribute company news, offer product information, and create an online community where GM customers can participate. Disney has over 130 technicians working around the clock to guard the smooth operation of two Disney blogs (Disney Channel & Toon Disney). These examples suggest that blogs are replacing traditional means of communication among consumers and between consumers and companies, and they have implications for consumer-marketer communications.

The availability of interactive media on a large scale is a very recent phenomenon. Thus, the full implications of these media in the context of marketing communications remain to be identified and explored. Nevertheless, interactivity fundamentally changes the nature of marketing communication. The traditional paradigm in marketing practice and research implicitly has assumed that communication is something the marketer does to the consumer. As we have pointed out, this is a very limited view. The traditional paradigm for research on marketing communication has served the profession well, but it is incomplete in an increasingly interactive context (Pavlou & Stewart, 2000). The future of interactive communication highlights the need for a new paradigm that focuses on what consumers do to marketing communication and how they respond to it. The focus of this new paradigm must also be the consumers' active participation in marketing communication, not merely their responses to it (Roehm & Haugtvedt, 1999).

This new paradigm requires that the focus of research on the influence and effects of marketing communications will need to shift from a focus on outcomes to a focus on both process and outcome. The role of the consumer in selecting opportunities for communication, in choosing when and how to interact (if at all), and the goals and purposes of consumers involved in the interaction will be especially important dimensions of marketing communications that will require new measures and new conceptualizations of how communication works. It is also likely that as the marketing mix becomes increasingly integrated and the same vehicles assume multiple functions (communication, distribution, etc.), it will become increasingly difficult to conduct relevant research on marketing communications without consideration of the larger context of the full marketing mix. In addition, the consumers' use of other information sources, especially the consumers' interaction with other consumers, will be important for understanding how and why consumers respond as they do to marketing communications.

Media Context as a Mediator of the Influence of Marketing Communications

In the broadest sense, the five consumer characteristics discussed to this point form a complex context for media exposure. That is, attitudes toward media types and vehicles, uses and gratifications from media, involvement, mood states motivating and characterizing media use, and interactivity, all form the context that influences consumers' decisions about whether or not to attend to particular media and consumers' cognitive and affective states while attending to media. However, a few studies focus more on media stimuli themselves than on consumer characteristics that determine communication effects in different media. We refer to these studies as focusing on the *media context*. Studies in this area seek to explain relatively immediate outcomes of exposure to advertising, such as cognitive responses, attention behavior, and physiological responses, in terms of exposure to different media types. Other studies examine longer-term responses to advertising as a function of frequency and timing of exposure, and these will be reviewed in the next section.

Krugman's (1965) involvement construct, discussed earlier, suggests that the inherent characteristics of media, in addition to consumer characteristics and product characteristics, interact in order to determine one's *involvement* with media. Terms such as *hot* (broadcast media) or *cool* (print media), however, do not tell us much about particular media characteristics that may be functionally related to different effects on individuals. A primary concern is whether the media context affects consumer responses to marketing communications, and if so, what the nature of these responses would be. Research that addresses these questions falls into several types: studies of cognitive response, observational studies, studies employing physiological measures, studies of *priming*, and research on the mediating effects of various situational or environmental factors.

Cognitive Response

A classic study by Wright (1973) examined the interaction of media and receiver involvement on a range of cognitive responses. Drawing heavily on previous research in psychology, Wright argued that individuals may experience an array of responses when exposed to marketing communications, and the nature and intensity of these responses is directly related to the degree of involvement. These cognitive responses include counterarguments, source derogation, support arguments, and, in other research, *connections*—a construct very similar to Krugman's (1965) discussion of *bridging* that may occur as individuals relate what they see in advertising to some aspect of their personal lives.

Wright (1973) was interested in the mediating role these cognitive response variables might play in determining consumer responses to marketing communications in different media, under different involvement conditions. Receiver involvement was manipulated by telling some subjects they would have to make a short-term decision after viewing advertising for a new soybean-based product (high involvement). Other subjects were not told of the impending decision (low involvement). Messages were transmitted either by audio means, similar to radio advertising, or by print means, similar to newspaper or magazine advertising. Wright found significantly more total cognitive responses, less source derogation, and more support arguments for a print version of an advertisement than for a radio version. Although acceptance of the ad message was not affected by the medium, buying intention was higher for the print condition than for the radio condition. In addition to the immediately measured cognitive response activity, delayed responses were elicited two days later; among the more highly involved subjects, supportive responses to the radio ad increased, but not for the print ad. Initially, the rapid transmission rate of broadcast media, compared to the more audience-controlled input of print, probably inhibits both the amount and variability of response activity. Over time, relatively more opportunity exists for increases in cognitive responses to broadcast media; the responses may in turn be related to different amounts of persistence of attitude change and behavior.

Observational Studies

Other studies also directly examine consumer responses while viewing marketing communications in different media contexts. While Wright (1973) examined self-reports of cognitive responses while viewing marketing communications in different media, some researchers have examined actual behaviors while attending to media. For example, Ward, Levinson, and Wackman (1972) and Bryant and Anderson (1983), among others, examined actual behavior while watching television. Tolley (1991) used a unique lamp-like device to unobtrusively track the eye movements of readers of newspapers. Rothschild and others (Rothschild & Hyun, 1990; Rothschild, Hyun, Reeves, Thorson, & Goldstein, 1988) have measured physiological responses among individuals exposed to television commercials. Unfortunately, most of these behavioral studies do not compare responses across media, unlike Wright's study that compared responses to print and audio advertising.

In the Ward et al. (1972) research, mothers observed one of their children watching television, and coded attention behavior. Results show a great deal of activity while watching television generally, ranging from not attending to the television set at all, to full attention. During strings of commercials, the children's attention initially increased when commercials interrupted programming, but decreased steadily over the "pod" of commercials. Interestingly, there was some tendency for attention to increase later in commercial pods, apparently because children anticipated the return of programming. Bryant and Anderson's (1983) work has sought to identify those attributes of television programs that attract the attention of children. Attention was operationalized as visual selection, that is, the time the children's eyes were directed toward the television screen. Program characteristics most likely to draw attention to the television screen included movement, high levels of physical activity, and auditory changes in the program. Such findings have not been lost on the creators of children's advertising. Most of such advertising routinely includes those elements that draw attention. Simply focusing on a television screen does not however assure that information is processed by the viewer.

Tolley (1991) found that readers of newspapers scan pages to decide whether and to what they will attend. Most individual newspaper pages received virtually no attention. Debriefings with readers suggested that they were using the quick scan as a means for identifying those items, editorial matter, ads, etc., that were personally relevant. Such findings are consistent with research that suggests that there exists a pre-attentional process that acts to filter irrelevant information and helps the individual determine those environmental elements for which information processing is worth the effort (Broadbent, 1977; Greenwald & Leavitt, 1984). Tolley also observed that individuals appear to have consistent but idiosyncratic styles of reading.

Physiological Measures

Rothschild et al. (1988) examined physiological (EEG: electroencephalographic) responses of individuals watching television commercials and examined the relationship between EEG responses and memory for components of TV commercials (Rothschild and Hyun, 1990). They found significant EEG activity during commercial exposure, and some differences in hypothesized directions for greater dominance by one brain hemisphere or the other. The latter is the topic of *hemispheric lateralization*, referring to specialization of the right and left sides of the brain in information processing (Hellige, 1990). Some advance the idea that the right side of the brain is better at processing stimuli, such as pictures and music, while the left side of the brain is better at processing words and numbers.

Priming

Another stream of research on the effects of media context has examined the degree to which media *prime* attention to specific elements of advertising and other types of marketing communications (Herr, 1989; Higgins & King, 1981; Wyer & Srull, 1981; Yi, 1990a, 1990b). Research in contexts other than advertising (Berkowitz & Rogers, 1986) suggests the presence of such an effect. The notion of priming suggests that the media context may predispose an individual to pay more attention to some elements of a communication message than others and may influence the interpretation that a viewer gives a complex or ambiguous stimulus. For example, the presence of an older model in an advertisement could be interpreted in terms of maturity, experience, conservatism, sophistication, steadfastness, or any of a number of other more or less positive attributes. Depending on the product, some of these interpretations would be more desirable to the marketer than others. For a perfume, associations of experience and sophistication might be appropriate, while conservatism and steadfastness would be less appropriate (though they might be appropriate for a different product, such as a bank). The media context might serve to prime one or more of these interpretations. For example, if the advertising were embedded in a program about a sensuous older woman, the associations elicited by an older female model in an ad might well include sophistication and experience. On the other hand, if the program in which the advertising was embedded dealt with the struggle of an older woman to adjust to a near-fatal illness, rather different associations might be elicited.

Several empirical studies demonstrate that such priming does occur. Further, this priming may occur for both cognitive and affective responses. For example, Yi (1990a) showed that a media context that emphasized one particular interpretation of an automobile attribute (size) resulted in greater salience for the primed interpretation. Similar effects have also been identified in other studies (Herr, 1989; Yi, 1990b) and are consistent with Wyer and Srull's (1981) model of cognitive accessibility and with recent research on framing effects (Bettman & Sujan, 1987). Yi (1990a) also demonstrated *affective priming*, a type of mood effect in which a mood is induced by the media context, in contrast to a mood that the individual brings to the medium. Yi found that the more positive the tone of the editorial matter, the more effective the ad (as measured by attitude toward the brand and purchase intention). He further demonstrated that this effect appeared to be mediated by more positive attitudes toward the ad.

Research on priming has generally assumed that priming is unidirectional, that is, the effect is induced by media context on response to a message. This is probably not an unreasonable assumption under most circumstances given the embeddedness of commercials within the more dominant media environment. It may be possible to have an opposite effect, however, with a commercial (say, prior to the beginning of a television program) serving to prime response to the medium. Another related question is the degree to which advertisements in the same medium or the same "pod" of commercials, or page in a magazine, might prime response to other advertisements. The role of priming in an interactive media context also poses an array of interesting questions. For example, the context in which a banner ad occurs on a Web site may influence both the propensity to respond to the ad as well as the nature of the response that follows.

EFFECTS OF MEDIA SCHEDULING

Evidence suggests that there are different effects of marketing communication in different media, depending on *media scheduling*, that is, how often individuals are exposed to advertising in a given time frame (frequency and repetition effects). Pechmann and Stewart (1988), after reviewing the substantial literature on advertising wearout, suggested that three *quality* exposures to a communication are probably sufficient for a message to have its effect, but noted that it may take many exposure opportunities to produce the effect of three quality exposures. This is because potential message recipients may elect not to attend to a message even when it is present or may see or hear only a portion of the total message. It is also likely that marketing communications for competing products, as well as marketing communications in general, may interfere with the processing of a commercial message at any given point in time.

Several studies tend to support the view that there are rapidly diminishing returns to repeated exposures. Blair (1987/1988) and Blair and Rabuck (1998) reported tests of television commercials that demonstrate that increased spending on advertising (with a concomitant increase in the average number of exposures and gross rating points) in a market increased sales in those cases where the commercial scored well on a measure of persuasion. Spending differences seemed to make no difference when persuasion was low. In other words, if an ad was not persuasive to begin with, even an infinite number of exposures was insufficient to produce a response. More relevant to the current discussion is the finding that the persuasive effect of advertising took place quickly and this effect was in direct proportion to the number of gross rating points purchased for the commercial. Further, once commercials had reached their targeted consumers, there was no further effect of additional exposures. Once consumers were exposed to the advertising and had been persuaded or not, that was the end of the matter. Consumers did not become more persuaded with additional exposures.

While Blair's (1987/1988) studies examined television advertising, a study carried out in the early 1980s by Time, Inc., in collaboration with Joseph E. Seagram & Sons, Inc., examined repetition and frequency effects of print advertising. While this study was restricted to one product category (liquor) and only two magazines (*Time* and *Sports Illustrated*), the study was well-controlled and extended over a 48-week period. The results of this study found that measures of brand awareness, brand attitude, and willingness to buy increased sharply after the very first opportunity to see the advertising. All measures tended to level off, then remain constant in the latter weeks of the campaign for brands that had a high level of awareness at the beginning of the campaign. However, for brands that began with a low level of initial awareness, all measures tended to show a steady increase over the 48 weeks of the campaign. The influence of greater advertising frequency was greater for low-awareness brands than for high-awareness brands. These results are consistent with a learning view of marketing communication (Pechmann & Stewart, 1988). Thus, it is useful to compare processes of learning and forgetting marketing communication with basic research in memory processes.

Learning and Memory Effects

Most studies of media scheduling on advertising effects examine recall and other variables (especially attitude change) as a function of the frequency of exposure and/or repetition of advertising stimuli. This is quite similar to the methods of research on the psychology of learning. One of the pioneers of learning research, Ebbinghaus (1902), identified three basic memory processes:

(1) *A negatively accelerating forgetting curve*. After 20 minutes, Ebbinghaus observed that subjects forgot one third of what was learned; after six days, about one fourth; and a full month later, about one fifth.

(2) *Serial position effects*. Items at the beginning or end of a series were most easily learned; items in the middle were learned most slowly and forgotten most rapidly.

(3) *Over-learning*. Over-learning or repetition beyond the point of repetition made very long conscious memory possible (for example: "Things go better with______").

The processes of learning and forgetting marketing communications and marketing-related stimuli are considerably more complex than learning simple stimuli in the laboratory, of course. Consumer characteristics, such as prior experiences, shape these processes, as well as such communications factors as message characteristics and media effects. Nevertheless, much of the laboratory research on verbal learning and forgetting appears to generalize well to a marketing communications context.

Unlike the laboratory setting, the marketing communications context provides less control over the frequency of repetition. Media in which marketing communications appear are often defined by their frequency of appearance, e.g. nightly news, monthly magazine, daily newspaper, regularly updated Web pages. These characteristics of media limit the advertiser's flexibility for scheduling repetitions. Further, as noted earlier in this chapter, an exposure opportunity (the placement of a communication in a particular medium) is not the same as an actual exposure. It is likely that there are many more exposure opportunities than actual exposures to any particular marketing communication. This fact, coupled with the temporal characteristics of various media, create problems for the marketer that are not present in the laboratory. Thus, a considerable body of research has addressed the issue of scheduling.

Advertising Scheduling

Strong (1974, 1977) examined the scheduling and repetition effects of print advertising and found that greater advertising recognition occurred when consumers were exposed to weekly intervals of magazine advertising than to monthly or daily intervals. Another classic study used direct mail advertising. Zielske (1959) found that repetition was very effective in increasing advertising recall, both when repetitions occurred over a relatively short period of time, and when repetitions occurred in a pulsed fashion, over one year. Shortly after the thirteenth exposure, 63% of the people who had been mailed ads weekly recalled some of the content, as did 48% of those receiving monthly ads. After the monthly ads stopped, that group showed decay of recall, similar to the negatively accelerating forgetting curve observed by Ebbinghaus (1902). In a later study, Zielske and Henry (1980) demonstrated similar effects for television advertising. Ray and Sawyer (1971) found that the percentages of subjects recalling an ad increased from 27 to 74% as the number of repetitions increased from one to six. Although recognition and recall increased as the number of repetitions increased, there were diminishing returns: additional repetitions resulted in decreasing magnitudes of gains in recall and recognition. Similar results have been found by a number of other researchers (see Pechmann & Stewart, 1988, for a review of this research).

There may be circumstances in which repetitions have a negative effect on recall and recognition. When consumers have negative attitudes toward a product, increased repetitions may result in more negative attitudes. Negative effects may also result from very high levels of repetition, regardless of consumer attitudes due to irritation (Pechmann & Stewart, 1988). As in many other areas of communication research, most studies of media scheduling effects do not compare effects across various media, and they do not isolate media effects from interactions. Few longitudinal studies have been conducted that would provide a basis for definitive statements about repetition and frequency effects of advertising in different media. In addition, scheduling and repetition factors cannot be separated from message variables. Particularly compelling or particularly dreary messages may accelerate or hamper the kinds of results found in studies reviewed here. Greenberg (1988) for example suggested that "critical images" in television programming may have profound effects, in contrast to the view that television effects occur slowly and incrementally. He calls these strong effects the *drench* hypothesis:

> The drench hypothesis, in its current, primitive form, asserts that critical images may contribute more to impression-formation and image-building than does the sheer frequency of television and behaviors that are viewed. The hypothesis provides an alternative to the no-effects hypothesis and to the view that the slow accretion of impressions cumulate across an indefinite time period. Finally, it also suggests that striking new images can make a difference—that a single character or collection of characters may cause substantial changes in beliefs, perceptions, or expectations about a group or a role, particularly among young viewers. (pp. 100–101).

Finally, the advent of interactive media creates new and interesting issues with respect to media scheduling. Much of the work on media scheduling to date revolves around the question of how best to reach consumers who may not be actively seeking information, at least at the time of message exposure. Increasingly, consumers are becoming active users of interactive media in the quest for information, products, and services. The rapid growth of interactive media and specific vehicles within these media, e.g., Web sites, confront the consumer with the need for assistance in finding the information they need. Thus, there is increasing reliance on such tools as search engines, portals, and virtual communities to locate sites and sources of additional information. Assuring prominence for an organization, product, or service within these tools has become the latest challenge in scheduling media.

In addition, consumers are increasingly integrating different media, making the use of some media complementary rather than substitutes for other media. For example, consumers have already begun to provide evidence that they have integrated the Internet experience into their broader media use. Almost half of all personal computers are in the same room as the television set, and simultaneous viewing of television and access to the Internet are common (Cox, 1998). Web site addresses are now common in television and print advertising. Traditional media now routinely encourage consumers to seek out additional information on Web sites or via telephone. These traditional media are not simply offering advertising that is extended to another media environment. Entertainment programs on broadcast media and editorial content in print media may refer consumers to additional information about the program or editorial content. However, the site of this additional information may include marketing communications that were not present in the original broadcast or print medium. In addition, outdoor advertising or voice yellow pages may refer users of mobile telephones to Web sites or telephone numbers that provide information or opportunities for product or service purchase. As consumers integrate their own use of various media, it will become more difficult to separate passive media from interactive media. Such integration will also raise interesting issues with respect to the scheduling of marketing communications in complementary media.

MEDIA-RELATED OUTCOMES OF EXPOSURE TO MARKETING COMMUNICATIONS

To this point, we have related results from a number of studies, focusing more on independent variables than on dependent variables. Our focus has been on the independent and joint effects of marketing communications in various media types and vehicles on a variety of outcomes. Selection of dependent variables in many of these studies has been driven by the interests of marketing, consumer, and advertising researchers. Therefore, dependent variables usually pertain to effects having to do with consumption, such as *hierarchy of communication* effects (McGuire, 1969) thought to lead up to purchase behavior, cognitive processes mediating advertising effects, and learning outcomes (effects on long- and short-term memory). These variables include various recognition and recall measures, measures of product knowledge, interest and attitude, and purchase intention and brand choice (see Stewart, Furse, & Kozak, 1983; Stewart et al., 1985, for a review of the use of these measures for assessing the effectiveness of advertising).

In addition, traditional measures of the effects and effectiveness of marketing communication have tended to focus on the response of a relatively passive consumer responding to an action by a marketer. Although there has been recognition of a reciprocal relationship between marketer-driven communications and actions and consumer responses, this reciprocity has generally been safely ignored because it has occurred over very long time periods. The advent of interactive media has changed all of this and produced a need to reconsider how the effects and effectiveness of marketing communications are measured.

Measuring the Effectiveness of Marketing Communications

The rise of interactive media poses new and difficult challenges related to the measurement of the success of marketing communication. Traditional measures of advertising effectiveness, such as recall, attitude change, and brand choice, while still useful, are only a subset of the potential measures of the effectiveness of marketing communications employing interactive media (Pavlou & Stewart, 2000). These traditional measures focus on the influence of communication on the consumer, offering limited insight into what the consumer does to and with advertising. This perspective views marketing communication as a causal independent variable and the consumer's response as the dependent variable. The typical research paradigm involves a forced exposure to some marketing message followed by some measure of consumer response. Assuming that consumers interact with marketing messages, the simple relationship between the independent and the dependent variables becomes obsolete. Therefore, in the interactive media environment this relationship becomes reciprocal and contingent on a host of other factors. When consumers actively decide to interact, their actions become powerful determinants of response to marketing communication.

Whereas advertising in the interactive media can take many forms, the most common method has been the *display banner ad* that occupies a small portion on a computer monitor and through clicking on it redirects the consumer to the marketer's own Web site. Whereas many studies have examined where ad banners should be located to increase clickthrough (see a summary at webreference.com 2000), a universal measure of effectiveness for this popular advertising form has not yet been established. Clickthrough is only one of many proposed measures of the effectiveness of interactive communications. Another proposed measure of online advertising is the *eyeball* method, or the number of unique visits to a given Web site. An additional measure of the quality of online relationships is the metric of *stickiness*, or the length of time viewers remain attached to a marketer's Web site. In general, these metrics, like the measures of traditional media that preceded them, measure the quantity of viewing, not the quality. Therefore, none of these measures has been widely adopted.

Fundamental to any discussion of interactive marketing communications is the question of how different it is from marketing communications using more traditional media. Although interactive media have been touted as more powerful, responsive, and customizable than traditional media (Hoffman & Novak, 1996; Port, 1999), the empirical evidence suggests that consumers respond to interactive advertising in the same ways they respond to advertising in more traditional media, at least with respect to traditional measures of advertising effectiveness. For example, Drèze and Hussherr (1999) found response to advertising on the Internet to be similar to response to advertising in other media, except that advertising on the Internet appeared to be easier to ignore. Similarly, Lynch and Ariely (2000) found that consumers are less price sensitive when providers on the Internet offer different rather than identical products, a finding that directly parallels findings in more traditional retail settings.

Despite the potential importance of interactive media in the future, very few studies have examined the interactivity of marketers, consumers, and ad messages (Oh, Cho, & Leckenby, 1999). Rodgers and Thorson (2000) have proposed a new model for conceptualizing the ways in which users perceive and process online advertising, but little empirical research exists to inform such a model. Interactive media place the consumer at the center of the study of marketing communication because effectiveness of marketing communications in such media hinges not only on how the marketer's message influences the consumer, but also on how the consumer shapes and responds to the message. Therefore, research on interactive media will need to focus on the consumer and the marketer in order to maximize the reciprocal gains of interaction and collaboration (Pavlou & Stewart, 2000). This will give rise to the need for measures of the effectiveness of marketing communication that go beyond traditional measures. These new measures will focus on process as well as outcome and are likely to include measures of effectiveness that have previously been regarded as mediating variables.

Involvement

As reviewed earlier, consumer involvement refers to a subjective psychological state of the consumer and defines the importance and personal relevance that consumers attach to an advertisement. While involvement has long been considered an important variable mediating the influence of communication, it has been poorly defined and operationalized, as noted above. It has long been possible to obtain self-reports of consumers' involvement, but interactive media have the potential to provide a direct measure of consumers' involvement through examination of the frequency and type of interaction with the marketer. Interactive media can involve the consumer in the communication process in a significant way. Indeed, enhanced consumer involvement can be an important benefit arising from the use of interactive media. For example, many commercial Web sites focus on involving consumers in the communication process by allowing them to actively search and collect information. The amount of time spent on a particular interactive medium, as well as the frequency of return to the medium, may be particularly useful measures of consumer involvement.

Comprehension

Comprehension refers to the recall of the message intended by the marketer in response to a product category and brand cue (Stewart & Furse, 1986; Stewart & Koslow, 1989). For marketing communication to be effective, both the marketer and the consumer must mutually agree that the consumer has understood the message (Clark & Brennan, 1991; Clark & Wilkes-Gibbs, 1986). Given the anonymous and ambiguous nature of much of the marketing communication on the Internet and interactive shopping (Alba et al., 1997), consumers may have difficulty comprehending the messages of marketers and may not fully understand the true characteristics of a product. Thus, comprehension is a vital part of interactive marketing communication, as it is with communication involving more traditional media. Interactive media have the potential advantage of providing a means for obtaining measures of comprehension on a real-time basis.

Feedback

Feedback from the consumer to the marketer plays an important role in marketing, and business more generally, since the consumer should understand what the marketer intends, and the marketer should in turn adjust the message so that it is clearly understood. To the extent that marketing communication fails to elicit feedback of some type, it is by definition not interactive regardless of the marketer's intent and the medium used. Feedback of some type is an objective of most marketing communication, since sales and customer satisfaction are almost always an ultimate objective. Both sales and customer satisfaction have always been measures of business success. Interactive media have the potential to provide such measures of success (feedback) instantaneously.

Besides feedback from the consumer to the marketer, feedback mechanisms, such as those on eBay (www.ebay.com), facilitate exchange of feedback about product and seller quality among consumers. The importance of feedback among consumers has been widely touted (Dellarocas, 2003). Notably, Ba and Pavlou (2002) showed the effect of positive and negative feedback ratings on a seller's prices by building trust in a seller, while Pavlou and Dimoka (2006) showed the effect of feedback text comments (feedback in the form of text) on price premiums by enhancing a customer's trust (credibility and benevolence) in sellers.

Persuasion

Persuasion implies an attempt to move, affect, or determine a purchasing decision (Schwerin & Newell, 1981). Interactive marketing communication may be a far more powerful persuasive tool than communication using traditional advertising media since it provides opportunities to personalize information presentation, promote trust, identify objections and points in need of further clarification, and modify the offering itself, much as is the case of personal selling. Therefore, interactive media should further enhance the ability of the marketer to persuade. Indeed, Zigurs, Poole, and DeSanctis (1988) have proposed that the pattern of persuasive behavior should be different depending on the degree to which communication is interactive. For example, resistance to the adoption of new products and services is an especially significant obstacle faced by marketers. Interactive communication may well have the effect of decreasing resistance to new products (Lucas, 1974) by reducing the communication of irrelevant or unimportant features of the product and by improving the consumers' understanding of the product (Robey & Farrow, 1982; Stewart, 1986). On the other hand, interactive media are likely to make much more obvious those consumers who are impervious to the persuasive efforts of marketers. This may prove to be a benefit to both consumers and marketers. Consumers may be spared from unwanted communications, and marketers may find their communication efforts more effective when focused on consumers who regard the marketer's message as relevant to their needs.

Quality of Purchasing Decisions

Consumer satisfaction, loyalty, and trust are likely to be by-products of the quality of the consumer's decision. Lam (1997) has demonstrated that the quality of decisions is better for complex tasks when interactive communication is involved. As noted earlier, interaction with consumers can provide significant information about the nature of consumers' preferences with respect to products and product features. Such information can provide marketers with the opportunity to modify and improve future products and make better decisions regarding product features that consumers find most useful. Moreover, interactive media can promote marketers' learning about consumers' characteristics and preferences, which should in turn improve customer support, technical assistance, and future promotions. Therefore, an important effect of interactive communication should be better quality of decisions for future marketing communications and products by the marketer even as it also improves the quality of decisions by consumers. This is a very important and distinctive characteristic of interactive communication. In addition, the satisfaction of consumers with the *experience* of communication and the subsequent purchase decision (or decision not to purchase) will also be especially important measures of the effectiveness of marketing communication.

Decision Efficiency

Prior research suggests that effective communication reduces the time required to make decisions (Short, Williams, & Christie, 1976). Dennis, George, Jessup, Nunamaker, and Vogel (1988) concluded that an important outcome of interactive technologies is reduction in the time required to make a decision. As noted earlier, interactive media have the potential to combine the processes of advertising, transacting the sale, and collecting payment (Cutler, 1990). Since all of these actions can be performed nearly simultaneously via interactive media, the total time and effort required to communicate a message and sell a product should be substantially reduced. Stated somewhat differently, measures of efficiency are likely to be more important and more useful in the context of interactive media than more traditional media.

EMERGING ISSUES IN THE USE OF INTERACTIVE MEDIA

The emergence of interactive media and its adoption as a means for marketing communications highlight a variety of issues related to the characteristics and use of these media that are rather different from the issues associated with the use of traditional media for marketing communications. Insofar as traditional media continue to play an important role in marketing communications, and they will, issues related to media context and media scheduling will continue to be relevant to marketers. These issues are also important in the use of interactive media, but by definition, interactive media provide consumers with much more control over both the media context and the schedule with which they are exposed (or not exposed) to marketing communications. On the other hand, there are issues that are relevant to all media used for marketing communications that are especially salient in the context of interactive media.

The Necessity of Content Management

While interactive media can bring a wealth of information, most of this information may be irrelevant and meaningless to consumers (Wurman 2000). Tillman (1995) has observed that "within the morass of networked data are both valuable nuggets and an incredible amount of junk." Given consumers' limited capacity to process information and the enormous amount of information available through the new media, content management will be of fundamental importance. According to Simon (1957), a wealth of information creates a poverty of attention. There is already a realization that interactive media, such as the Internet and mobile communication, have had the effect of increasing consumers' search costs (Stewart & Zhao, 2000). Web sites are growing faster than they can be cataloged and a variety of techniques and economic incentives now operate to increase the likelihood that a site will be cataloged and occupy a coveted position near the beginning of a list of sites identified by a search engine or a portal.

Content management will play an especially important role in interactive marketing communications. Marketers will need to assure that consumers can readily identify sources of information, as well as focus on what customers want and need to learn (assuming these things may be delivered at a profit), rather than provide an abundance of unnecessary information. Relevant and clear content can accelerate consumers' decision making process and facilitate transactions. While relevance and clarity have always been important elements of traditional advertising, these elements become essential in interactive advertising. Two content management tools, dynamic content and data mining combined with collaborative filtering, already play an important role in increasing the efficacy of interactive media in marketing communications.

Dynamic Content

Dynamic content involves changing information over time and in response to interaction with the consumer. The availability of relevant new information and new offerings serves to attract consumers and increase involvement with an interactive medium. Personalization engines and document management solutions will play an especially important role in dynamic content management. In addition, combinations of media will play an ever more important role in marketing communications. Thus, e-mail or voice mail may be used to inform consumers of new information and offerings that are available in some other medium (e.g., Web site, physical store location).

Information portals are electronic intermediaries that allow marketers to send their advertising messages and consumers to either respond to them or communicate among themselves. For example, Google.com (www.google.com) is a popular Internet information portal that draws many marketers and consumers. Information portals can be separated into *vertical* ones that focus on specific information, or *horizontal* portals that deal with a variety of issues. While messages through horizontal portals have the ability to reach the masses, vertical portals reach a targeted audience, which can integrate community building. According to Meckler (2000), the future of content management favors vertical focus and original content as consumers seek greater customization and personalization.

Data Mining and Collaborative Filtering

Interactivity provides opportunities for gathering enormous amounts of information about the behavior of consumers. Although the collection and use of such data raise a variety of issues related to consumer privacy (Culnan & Armstrong, 1999), these data also provide opportunities for marketers to provide more personalized information and more customized assortments of products and services (Malhotra et al., 2004). Data mining tools provide a means for identifying patterns in the behavior of individual consumers and across groups of consumers that are far more specific than even the most sophisticated segmentation approaches in use today. The results obtained from data mining exercises may be combined with collaborative filtering to improve content management. Collaborative filtering is essentially a *recommendation engine* that provides consumers with suggestions about products and services that consumers with similar preferences have purchased. For example, Amazon.com (www.amazon.com) uses collaborative filtering to offer consumers information about what customers who had bought a particular book had also bought in addition.

Recommendation agents, such as MyProductAdvisor.com (www.myproductadvisor.com) and DiscoverYourRide.com (www.discoveryourride.com), have become important means for online consumer-marketer communications (Ansari, Essegaier, & Kohli, 2000), and they have been successfully implemented by many Web sites, such as Amazon.com and Yahoo! Recommendation agents are Internet-based software tools that provide product advice based on the consumers' profiles, preferences, needs, and past purchasing behavior (Wang & Benbasat, 2005). Recommendation agents facilitate consumers' decision making by narrowing down the consideration set with products that better fit the consumers' preferences and reducing their information overload (Maes, 1994). Recommendation agents have become very popular and are prevalent in multiple Web sites (Häubl & Trifts, 2000), as they have been shown to improve the quality of purchase decisions (Hostler, Yoon, & Guimaraes, 2005). To demonstrate the importance of recommendation agents, eBay paid $620 million to acquire Shopping.com (www.shopping.com), a Web site that specializes in recommendation agents (*The Economist*, June 4, 2005).

Mobile Commerce: Anytime, Anyplace

The advent of mobile telephones and small wireless digital assistants provides new opportunities for marketing communication and new opportunities for consumers to obtain information when and where they need it (Balasubramanian et al., 2002). Mobile commerce not only facilitates commerce by enabling transactions that would otherwise not be feasible, but also generates new opportunities for shaping the traditional nature of consumer-marketer relationships, such as real-time personalization of the transaction based on the consumer's location (Ngai & Gunasekaran, 2007). For example, these new devices offer the ability to access information on demand, like a list of French restaurants in an unfamiliar city. In fact, personalization has been touted as one of the greatest advantages of mobile commerce (Xu, 2003). For marketers, mobile devices provide an opportunity to communicate with consumers wherever consumers might be. A real estate agent might provide information about a specific house for a potential home buyer, or an automobile manufacturer might provide information about the make of an automobile that the consumer sees in a dealership or parking lot. The ability for anywhere-anytime transactions has been termed *ubiquitous commerce* (Watson, Pitt, Berthon, & Zinkhan, 2002). Such communications will tend to be more under the control of the consumer, but not always. Using permission marketing, a marketer might provide a consumer with the opportunity to identify types of information or types of products about which the consumer wishes to receive information (Scharl, Dickinger, &

Murphy, 2005). The consumer would then receive a telephone call, e-mail, or voice mail message when such information or products are available.

The emerging literature on mobile commerce has studied this new phenomenon under different perspectives. For example, Venkatesh and Ramesh (2006) viewed mobile commerce adoption as a system usability problem, using Microsoft's usability guidelines as the antecedents of using mobile devices for commerce. Hung, Ku, and Chang (2003) used the technology acceptance model (Davis, 1989) as the theory basis, thus focusing on the usefulness and user-friendliness of mobile devices. Pavlou, Lie, and Dimoka (2007) used the theory of planned behavior as the underlying theory, while they modeled mobile commerce adoption as a set of three behaviors of using mobile devices for getting and giving information and purchasing product and services.

Mobile commerce places new demands on marketers in terms of responsiveness. Consumers will want to obtain information when they need it, not at the convenience of the marketer. Indeed, the immediate availability of information may be the difference between a customer making a purchase or not. Pavlou et al. (2007) showed that delay in downloading data in a mobile device is an important impediment to getting information and purchasing. Screen size is another major limitation of mobile commerce (Jones et al., 1999), since consumers have a difficult time getting information on small, low-resolution screens (Buchanan et al., 2001). Therefore, content organization, layout, links, intuitive organization and navigation links, and a well-structured hierarchy of links enable users to navigate easily around the mobile site and get relevant information (Karkkainen & Laarni, 2002). Rather than focusing on the scheduling of media in particular vehicles or time slots, as is the case with traditional media scheduling in advertising, the marketer will need to assure that information is available whenever and wherever the customer needs it. For example, Tsang, Ho, and Liang (2004) showed that useful information helps build positive attitudes toward mobile sites.

Branded Entertainment: Blurring the Medium and the Message

During the past five years there has been an enormous growth in what is variously called *branded entertainment* or *brand integration*. Brand entertainment involves the combination, or integration, of an audio-visual program (TV, radio, computer or interactive game, podcast, etc.) and a brand. Branded entertainment provides an opportunity for brands to promote their name and image to a target audience by creating positive links between the brand and the program in the viewers. Spending on branded entertainment was estimated at almost $53 billion in 2007 and is expected to be nearly double this amount by 2011 (Mahmud, 2007).

Branded entertainment is not new. Indeed, in some ways this use of media for advertising is coming full cycle. Early in the history of both radio and television, many programs were sponsored by and identified with a specific sponsor. Early soap operas on radio and television are examples. Although such programs never fully disappeared, the practice diminished over time until the late 1990s, as advertisers shifted to the use of short, freestanding commercials. The increasing clutter of such freestanding commercials led advertisers to explore other ways to communicate with consumers in a way that did not seem so intrusive or commercial. The increase in branded entertainment is in part a response to the fragmentation of media and the increasing cost of traditional broadcast commercials, especially on a cost-per-exposure basis. The traditional 15- or 30-second commercial has become less efficient in reaching consumers who now have hundreds of channels from which to choose and new ways to manage and spend time with media, including Internet streaming, interactive games, and digital video recording devices. Advertisers have returned to branded entertainment in an attempt to increase exposure to their advertising, obtain greater efficiencies in advertising and create stronger associations between their brands and the media content.

The branded entertainment that is now emerging is different from earlier sponsorships of programs. It is also more than just simply product advertising or incidental product placement within a piece of entertainment. Rather, contemporary branded entertainment seeks to integrate a brand and its attributes with a piece of entertainment. For example, *City Hunters*, a Latin American animated television series, was coproduced by Unilever and features its AXE brand of body sprays for men. The program revolves around the adventures of a Dr. Lynch and Axel (a not so subtle association with AXE). In the series Dr. Lynch is a mentor to Axel and tries to develop Axel's skills in seduction. There is also an interactive Internet link associated with the program (http://www.cityhunters.tv/ar). Other examples include Bud TV, sponsored by Anheuser-Busch; the "Hottest Mom in America," sponsored by Medicis Pharmaceutical; and *Extreme Makeover: Home Edition*, sponsored by Sears. Branded entertainment has also emerged on the Internet and in computer games. For example, Burger King has developed a series of computer games in which Burger King products play a central role. Brands populate "Second Life," and even the online version of "The Sims" provides an opportunity to buy a kiosk and sell McDonalds' products.

Unlike traditional product placement, in which the product is just a background element or prop, in branded entertainment the brand is an integral part of plot or media experience. One advantage of branded entertainment is that it makes it nearly impossible for the viewer to avoid exposure to the brand if he or she is attending to the content of the media. Another potential advantage is that the exposure to the brand message may be more engaging, and therefore more persuasive than traditional advertising exposures.

To date there has been little published academic research that has focused on the effectiveness of branded entertainment. This will no doubt change. Some proprietary research does suggest that branded entertainment can increase awareness and positive brand associations. Awareness and positive brand associations have not been shown to be universally related to measures of persuasion or sales, however.

Engagement

Over the past five years the advertising industry has been obsessed with finding a replacement for the traditional measure of advertising frequency, that is, the number of times a consumer is exposed to an advertising message. Engagement has been defined as "turning on a prospect to a brand idea enhanced by the surrounding context" (Advertising Research Foundation, 2007). Although it has become the focus of intense industry attention, including a joint task force of the Association of National Advertisers, the American Association of Advertising Agencies, and the Advertising Research Foundation, the idea behind engagement is not new. In many ways, engagement is just the latest incarnation of the well-studied constructs of relevance, involvement, and persuasion. Recent focus on the concept of engagement has failed to produce an operational definition of the construct or a standard measure of engagement.

THE FUTURE OF RESEARCH ON MEDIA INFLUENCE IN MARKETING COMMUNICATIONS

The media landscape is undergoing profound changes that are creating a need to rethink how marketing communications are managed. These changes are also giving rise to the need for a new and different paradigm for theory and research on the role of media in marketing communications. The very rapid increase in the media options available to consumers and the greater selectivity exercised by individual consumers with respect to these options means, on the one hand, that it will be more difficult to reach target audiences through traditional mass media. On the other hand, the increase in the number of media vehicles available to consumers and consumers' selectivity in using these vehicles may also provide more opportunities to reach precisely defined audiences with the optimal message for the medium and the media use occasion. Realizing this possibility requires several things: (a) a better understanding of how and when people use and interact with various media, (b) a better understanding of how the mode of interaction with various media influences the processing of commercial messages, and (c) a better understanding of how to create commercial messages and distribution strategies that are appropriate in the context of specific media uses. Note that what is needed is not a better understanding of *media*, but rather a better understanding of how people interact with various forms of media and embedded commercial messages. Indeed, the increasing use of interactive media by marketers and consumers makes it critical to place the consumer at the center of any theory of marketing communications.

The linking pins between channels of communication and marketing outcomes are the factors that influence the individual's self-selection process and the dimensions of interaction with media. The goals and purposes of the users of media are primary determinants of media effects when users have options. Unfortunately, this is an area that still has received rather little attention from researchers (Becker & Schoenbach, 1989; Pavlou & Stewart, 2000; Stewart, Pavlou, & Ward, 2002; Stewart & Ward, 1992). We do not believe that this is the result of lack of theory to guide such research. Rather, it appears to be a result of the fact that, until recently, there have been relatively few genuinely different media options available. In such situations the behavior of individuals is restricted and largely dwarfed by such differences in media as they exist.

There are numerous candidate theories for guiding future research on the use of media and subsequent effects on advertising response. Control theory (Powers, 1973, 1978), with its origins in human factors research and its emphasis on purpose as the link between stimulus inputs and behavioral outcomes, may be particularly appropriate given its emphasis on how people get things done. Bandura's (1986) notion of self-efficacy and Ajzen and Madden's (1986) work on goal-directed behavior are also potential candidates. In any case, theoretical approaches to future studies of media effects should surely focus on individual characteristics that determine media usage patterns, factors that influence interactivity, and dependent measures that reflect the diversity of outcomes that may arise when consumers are in control of their information environment.

References

Aaker, D. A., & Brown, P. K. (1972). Evaluating vehicle source effects. *Journal of Advertising Research*, *12*, 11–16.

Advertising Research Foundation. (2007). Engagement. Retrieved Sept. 12, 2007. http://www.thearf.org/research/engagement.html.

Ajzen, I., & Madden, J. T. (1986). Prediction of goal-directed: attitudes, intentions and perceived behavioral. *Journal of Experimental Social Psychology, 22*, 453–474.

Alba, J., Lynch, J., Weitz, B., Janiszewski, C., Lutz, R., Sawyer, A., & Wood, S. (1997). Interactive home shopping: consumer, retailer, and manufacturer incentives to participate in electronic marketplaces. *Journal of Marketing, 61*(July), 38–53.

Anderson, C. (1996). Computer as audience, mediated interactive messages. In E. Forrest & R. Mizerski (Eds.), *Interactive Marketing: The Future Present* (pp. 149–162). IL: American Marketing Association, NTC Business Books.

Anderson, E., & Narus, J. A. (1990). A model of distributor firm and manufacturer firm working partnership. *Journal of Marketing, 54*, 42–58.

Anderson, E., & Weitz, B. (1989). Determinants of continuity in conventional industrial channel dyads. *Marketing Science*, 8(4), 310–323.

Ansari, A., Essegaier, S., & Kohli, R. (2000). Internet recommendation systems. *Journal of Marketing Research, 37*(3), 363–375.

Atkin, C. K. (1985). Informational utility and selective exposure to entertainment media. In D. Zillman & J. Bryant (Eds.), *Selective Exposure to Communication* (pp. 63–92). Hillsdale, NJ: Erlbaum.

Audits and Surveys, Inc. (1986). *A Study of Media Involvement*. New York: Audits and Surveys.

Ba, S., & Pavlou, P. A. (2002). Evidence of the effect of trust building technology in electronic markets: price premium and buyer behavior. *MIS Quarterly, 26*(3), 243–268.

Balasubramanian, S., Peterson, R. A., & Jarvenpaa, S. L. (2002). Exploring the implications of m-commerce for markets and marketing. *Journal of the Academy of Marketing Science, 30*(4), 348–361.

Bandura, A. (1986). *Social foundations of thought and action: A social cognitive theory*. Englewood Cliffs, NJ: Prentice Hall.

Barney, J. B., & Hansen, M. H. (1994). Trustworthiness as a source of competitive advantage [Special issue]. *Strategic Management Journal, 15*, 175–190.

Becerra, M., & Gupta, A. K. (1999). Trust within the organization: integrating the trust literature with agency theory and transaction cost economics. *Public Administration Quarterly, 23*(2), 177–203.

Becker, L. B., & Schoenbach, K. (1989). When media content diversifies: anticipating audience behaviors. In L. B. Becker & K. Schoenbach (Eds.), *Audience Response to Media Diversification, Coping with Plenty* (pp. 1–28). Hillsdale, NJ: Erlbaum.

Berkowitz, L. & Rogers, K. H. (1986). A priming effect analysis of media influences. In J. Bryant & D. Zillman (Eds.), *Perspectives on Media Effects*, (pp. 57–81). Hillsdale, NJ: Erlbaum.

Berry, L. L. (1987). Big ideas in services marketing. *Journal of Services Marketing, 1*, 5–9.

Berry, L. L. (1995). Relationship marketing of services—growing interest, emerging perspectives. *Journal of the Academy of Marketing Science, 24*(4), 236–245.

Bettman, J. R., & Sujan, M. (1987). Effects of framing on evaluation of comparable and non-comparable alternatives by expert and novice consumers. *Journal of Consumer Research, 14*(September), 141–154.

Blair, M. H. (1987/88). An empirical investigation of advertising wearin and wearout. *Journal of Advertising Research, 27*, 45–50.

Blair, M. H., & Rabuck, M. J. (1998). Advertising wearin and wearout: ten years later—more empirical evidence and successful practice. *Journal of Advertising Research, 38*(October), 7–18.

Braunstein, M., & Levine, E. H. (2000). *Deep branding on the Internet*. Roseville, CA: Prima Venture.

Broadbent, D. (1977). The hidden pre-attentive processes. *American Psychologist, 32*(2), 109–118.

Bryant, J., & Anderson, D. (1983). *Children's understanding of television: research on attention and comprehension*. New York: Academic Press.

Buchanan, G., Ferrant, S., Jones, M., Thimbelby, H., Marsden, G., & Pazzani, M. (2001). Improving mobile Internet usability. *Proceedings of the 10th ACM WWW Conference, New York*, 673–680.

Buchholz, L. M., & Smith, R. E. (1991). The role of consumer involvement in determining cognitive response to broadcast advertising. *Journal of Advertising, 20*, 4–17.

Burke, R. R. (1997). Do you see what I see? The future of virtual shopping. *Journal of the Academy of Marketing Science, 25*(4), 352–360.

Burke, R. R., & Srull, T. K. (1988). Competitive interference and consumer memory for advertising. *Journal of Consumer Research, 15*(June), 55–68.

Buttle, F. A. (1998). Word-of-mouth: understanding and managing referral marketing. *Journal of Strategic Marketing, 6*, 241–254.

Cafferky, M. (1996). *Let your customers do the talking*. Chicago, IL: Upstart Publishing Company.

Chaiken, S. (1980). Heuristic versus systematic information processing and the use of source versus message cues in persuasion. *Journal of Personality and Social Psychology, 29*(5), 751–766.

Chaiken, S., Liberman, A., & Eagly, A. H. (1989). Heuristic and systematic information processing within and beyond the persuasion context. In J. S. Uleman & J. A. Bargh (Eds.), *Unintended thought: Limits of awareness, intention and control* (pp. 212–252). New York: Guilford.

Chatterjee, P. (2001). Online reviews: do consumers use them? *Advances in Consumer Research, 28*(1), 129–133.

Chen, Y., & Xie, J. (2005). Third-party product review and firm marketing strategy. *Marketing Science, 24*(2), 218–240.

Chevalier, J., & Goolsbee, A. (2003). Measuring prices and price competition online: Amazon and Barnes and Noble. *Quantitative Marketing and Economics, 1*(2), 203–222.

Chevalier, J., & Mayzlin, D. (2006). The effect of word of mouth on sales: online book reviews. *Journal of Marketing Research, 43*(3), 345–354.

Chook, P. H. (1983). ARF model for evaluating media, making the promise a reality. *Advertising Research Foundation Transcript Proceedings of the Intermedia Comparisons Workshop*. New York: Advertising Research Foundation.

Clark, H. H., & Brennan, S. E. (1991). Grounding in communication. In L. B. Resnick, J. M. Levine, & S. D. Teasley (Eds.), *Perspectives on Socially Shared Cognition* (pp. 127–149). Washington, DC: American Psychological Association.

Clark, H. H., & Wilkes-Gibbs, D. (1986). Referring as a collaborative process. *Cognition, 22*, 1–39.

Clemons, E. K., Gao, G., & Hitt, L. M. (2006). When online reviews meet hyper differentiation: a study of craft beer industry. *Journal of Management Information Systems, 23*(2), 149–171.

Condry, J. (1989). *The Psychology of Television*. Hillsdale, NJ: Erlbaum.

Cox, B. (1998, November 17). Report: TV, PC get equal time. *Advertising Report Archives, InternetNews.com*.

Cross, R., & Smith, J. (1995). Internet marketing that works for customers (part 1). *Direct Marketing, 58*(4), 22–23.

Culnan, M., & Armstrong, P. (1999). Information privacy concerns, procedural fairness, and impersonal trust: an empirical investigation. *Organization Science, 10*(1), 104–115.

Cutler, B. (1990). The fifth medium. *American Demographics, June*, 24–29.

Davis, F. D. (1989). Perceived usefulness, perceived ease of use and user acceptance of information technology. *MIS Quarterly, 13*(3), 319–340.

Dellarocas, C. (2003). The digitization of word-of-mouth: promise and challenges of online reputation mechanisms. *Management Science, 49*(10), 1407–1424.

Dennis, A. R., George, J. F., Jessup, L. M., Nunamaker, J. F. Jr., & Vogel, D. R. (1988). Information technology to support electronic meetings. *MIS Quarterly, 12*(December), 591–624.

Drèze, X., & Hussherr, F.-X. (1999). *Internet advertising: is anybody watching?* Working Paper, Department of Marketing, Marshall School of Business, University of Southern California.

Dwyer, F. R., Schurr, P. H., & Oh, S. (1987). Developing buyer-seller relationships. *Journal of Marketing, 52*, 21–34.

Ebbinghaus, H. (1902). *Grundzuge der Psychologie* (p. 123). Leipzig: Viet.

Economist; 6/4/2005; Vol. 375, Issue 8429.

Fontenot, R. J., & Vlosky, R. P. (1998). Exploratory study of internet buyer-seller relationships.

Proceedings of the 1998 American Marketing Association Winter Educators Conference, Chicago: American Marketing Association, 169–170.

Forrest, E., & Mizerski, R. (1996). Interactive marketing: the future present. *American Marketing Association*. IL: NTC Business Books.

Ganesan, S. (1994). Determinants of long-term orientation in buyer-seller relationships. *Journal of Marketing*, *58*, 1–19.

Gardner, M. P. (1985). Mood states and consumer behavior: a critical review. *Journal of Consumer Research*, *12*(December), 281–300.

Glazer, R. (1989). Marketing and the changing information environment: implications for strategy, structure, and the marketing mix. Report No. 89–108. Cambridge, MA: Marketing Science Institute.

Godes, D., & Mayzlin, D. (2004). Using online conversations to study word of mouth communication, *Marketing Science*, *23*(4), 545–560.

Goldberg, M. E., & Gorn, G. J. (1987). Happy and sad tv programs: how they affect reactions to commercials. *Journal of Consumer Research*, *14*(December), 387–403.

Greenberg, B. S. (1988). Some uncommon television images and the drench hypothesis. In S. Oskamp (Ed.), *Television as a social issue* (pp. 88–102). Newbury Park, CA: Sage.

Greenwald, A. C., (1968). Cognitive learning, cognitive response to persuasion, and attitude change. In A. G. Greenwald, T. C. Brock, & T. Ostrom (Eds.), *Psychological Foundations of Attitudes* (pp. 147–170). New York: Academic Press.

Greenwald, A. C., & Leavitt, C. (1984). Audience involvement in advertising: four levels. *Journal of Consumer Research*, *11*(June), 581–592.

Gunter, B. (1985). Determinants of television viewing preferences. In D. Zillmann & J. Bryant (Eds.), *Selective Exposure to Communication* (pp. 93–112). Hillsdale, NJ: Erlbaum.

Haley, R. I. (1985). *Developing effective communications strategy*. New York: Wiley.

Häubl, G., & Trifts, V. (2000). Consumer Decision Making in Online Shopping Environments: The Effects of Interactive Decision Aids. *Marketing Science*, *19*, 4–21.

Hellige, J. B. (1990). Hemispheric asymmetry. *Annual Review of Psychology*, *41*, 55–80.

Helper, S., & MacDuffie, J. P. (2000). E-volving the auto industry: e-commerce effects on consumer and supplier relationships. In *E-Business and the Changing Terms of Competition: A View From Within the Sectors*, Working Paper, Stanford University.

Herr, P. M. (1989). Priming price: prior knowledge and context effects. *Journal of Consumer Research*, *16*(June), 67–75.

Higgins, E. T., & King, G. (1981). Accessibility of social constructs: information processing consequences of individual and contextual variability. In N. Cantor & J. Kihlstrom (Eds.), *Personality, Cognition, and Social Interaction* (pp. 69–122). Hillsdale, NJ: Erlbaum.

Hill, C. W. L. (1990). Cooperation, opportunism, and the invisible hand: implications for transaction cost theory. *Academy of Management Review*, *15*, 500–513.

Hoffman, D. L., & Novak, T. P. (1996). Marketing in computer-mediated environments: conceptual foundations. *Journal of Marketing*, *60*(July), 50–68.

Hoffman, D. L., Novak, T. P., & Peralta, M. (1999). Building consumer trust online. *Communications of the ACM*, *42*(4), 80–85.

Hostler, R. E., Yoon, V. Y., & Guimaraes, T. (2005). Assessing the impact of Internet agent on end users' performance. *Decision Support Systems*, *41*(1), 313–323.

Hoyer, W. D., & Macinnis, D. J. (2001). *Consumer Behavior*. Boston, MA: Houghton Mifflin.

Hung, S.-Y., Ku, C.-Y., & Chang, C.-M. (2003). Critical factors of WAP services adoption: an empirical study. *Electronic Commerce Research and Applications*, *2*(1), 42–60.

Isen, A. M. (1989). Some ways in which affect influences cognitive processes: implications for advertising and consumer behavior. In P. Cafferata & A. Tybout (Eds.), *Cognitive and Affective Responses to Advertising* (pp. 91–118). Lexington, MA: Lexington Books.

Jiang, Z., & Benbasat, I. (2005). Virtual product experience: effects of visual and functional control of products on perceived diagnosticity and flow in electronic shopping. *Journal of Management Information Systems*, *21*(3), 111–148.

Jiang, Z. J., & Benbasat, I. (2007). The effects of presentation formats and task complexity on online consumers' product understanding. *MIS Quarterly, 31*; 475–500.

Jiang, Z. H., & Benbasat, I. (2007). Investigating the influence of the functional mechanisms of online product presentations. *Information Systems Research, 18*, 454–470.

Jones, M., Marsden, G., Mohd-Nasir, N., Boone, K., & Buchanan, G. (1999). Improving Web interaction in small screen displays. *Proceedings of the 8th WWW Conference, Toronto, Canada*, 51–59.

Kamins, M. A., Marks, L. J., & Skinner, D. (1991). Television commercial evaluation in the context of program induced mood: congruency versus consistency effects. *Journal of Advertising, 20*(2), 1–14.

Karkkainen, L., & Laarni, J. (2002, October 19–23). Designing for small display screens. *Proceedings of the 2nd Nordic Conference on Human-Computer Interaction*, 227–230.

Katz, E., Blumler, J. G., & Gurevitch, M. (1974). Utilization of mass communication by the individual. In J. Blumler & E. Katz (Eds.), *The Uses of Mass Communication* (pp. 19–32). Beverly Hills, CA: Sage.

Katz, E., & Lazarsfeld, P. F. (1955). *Personal influence: the part played by people in the flow of mass communications*. New York, NY: Free Press.

Keen, P. G. W. (2000). Ensuring e-trust. *Computerworld, 34*(11), 13, 46.

Keeney, R. L. (1999). The value of Internet commerce to the customer. *Management Science, 45*(April), 533–542.

Kennedy, J. R. (1971). How program environment affects tv commercials. *Journal of Advertising Research, 11*, 33–38.

Kiely, M. (1993). Word-of-mouth marketing. *Marketing, September*, 6.

Klebber, J. M. (1985). Physiological measures of research: a review of brain activity, electrodermal response, pupil dilation, and voice analysis methods and studies. In J. H. Leigh & C. Martin, Jr. (Eds.), *Current Issues and Research in Advertising* (pp. 53–76). Ann Arbor: University of Michigan.

Krugman, H. E. (1965). The impact of television advertising: learning without involvement. *Public Opinion Quarterly, 29*, 349–356.

Krugman, H. E. (1966). The measurement of advertising involvement. *Public Opinion Quarterly, 30*, 583–596.

Krugman, H. E. (1983). Television program interest and commercial interruption: are commercials on interesting programs less effective? *Journal of Advertising Research, 23*(February/March), 21–23.

Krugman, H. E. (1988). Point of view: limits of attention to advertising. *Journal of Advertising Research, 28*(October/November), 47–50.

Lam, S. S. K. (1997). The effects of group decision support systems and task structures on group communication and decision quality. *Journal of Management Information Systems, 13*(4), 193–215.

Lazarsfeld, P. F., Berelson, B. R., & Gaudet, H. (Eds.). (1948). *The People's Choice*. New York: Columbia University Press.

Leckenby, J. D., & Li, H. (2000). From the editors: Why we need the Journal of Interactive Advertising. *Journal of Interactive Advertising, 1, 1 (Fall)*. Retrieved Aug. 31, 2007. Online: http://jiad.org/vol1/no1/editors/index.html

Liu, Y. (2006). Word-of-mouth for movies: its dynamics and impact on box office revenue. *Journal of Marketing, 70*(3), 74–89.

Lloyd, D. W., & Clancy, K. J. (1989). The effects of television program involvement on advertising response: implications for media planning. *Transcript Proceedings of the First Annual Advertising Research Foundation Media Research Workshop*. New York: Advertising Research Foundation.

Lovelock, C. H. (1996). *Services marketing* (3rd ed.). NJ: Prentice Hall.

Lucas, H. C., Jr. (1974). Systems quality, user reactions, and the use of information systems. *Management Informatics, 3*(4), 207–212.

Lynch, J. G., & Ariely, D. (2000). Wine online: search costs and competition on price, quality, and distribution. *Marketing Science*, *19*(1), 83–103.

Maes, P. (1994). Agents that reduce work and information overload. *Communications of the ACM*, *37*(7), 31–40.

Mahmud, S. (2007). Brand content, mobile to grow. *Adweek*, August 8, retrieved Aug. 31, 2007 from http://www.adweek.com/aw/national/article_display.jsp?vnu_content_id=1003622588.

Malhotra, N., Kim, S. K., & Agarwal, J. (2004). Internet users' information privacy concerns (IUIPC): the construct, the scale, and a causal model. *Information Systems Research 15*(4), 336–355.

Mayer, R. C., Davis, J. H., & Schoorman, F. D. (1995). An integrative model of organizational trust. *Academy of Management Review*, *20*(3), 709–734.

McGuire, W. J. (1969). The nature of attitudes and attitude change. In G. Lindzey & E. Aronson (Eds.), *The Handbook of Social Psychology* (Vol. 3, pp. 136–314). New York: Random House.

McKenna, R. (1997, July–August). Real-time marketing. *Harvard Business Review*, 87–98.

McLuhan, M., & Fiore, Q. (1967). *The Medium is the Message*. New York: Bantam Books.

Meckler, A. (2000, September 26). I want my N-TV. *Business 2.0*, 124–126.

Ngai, E. W. T., & Gunasekaran, A. (2007). A review for mobile commerce research and applications. *Decision Support Systems*, *43*, 3–15.

O'Guinn, T. C., & Faber, R. J. (1991). Mass communication and consumer behavior. In T. S. Robertson & H. Kassarjian (Eds.), *Handbook of Consumer Behavior* (pp. 349–400). Englewood Cliffs, NJ: Prentice-Hall.

Oh, K. W., Cho, C. H., & Leckenby, J. D. (1999). A comparative analysis of Korean and U.S. Web advertising. *Proceedings of the 1999 Conference of the American Academy of Advertising*, 73–86.

Pavlou, P. A. (2003). Consumer acceptance of electronic commerce: integrating trust and risk with the technology acceptance model. *International Journal of Electronic Commerce*, *7*(3), 69–103.

Pavlou, P. A., & Ba, S. (2000). Does online reputation matter? An empirical investigation of reputation and trust in online auction markets. *Proceedings of the 6th Americas Conference in Information Systems, Long Beach, CA*.

Pavlou, P. A. and Dimoka, A. (2006), The nature and role of feedback text comments in online marketplaces: Implications for trust building, price premiums, and seller differentiation. *Information Systems Research*, *17*(4), 391–412.

Pavlou, P. A., & Fygenson, M. (2006). Understanding and predicting electronic commerce adoption: an extension of the theory of planned behavior. *MIS Quarterly*, *30*(1), 115–143.

Pavlou, P. A., & Gefen, D. (2004). Building effective online marketplaces with institution-based trust. *Information Systems Research*, *15*, 27–53.

Pavlou, P. A., Liang, H., & Xue, Y. (2007). Understanding and mitigating uncertainty in online environments: an agency theory perspective. *MIS Quarterly*, *31*(1), 105–136.

Pavlou, P. A., Lie, T., & Dimoka, A. (2007, November 3–4). An integrative model of mobile commerce adoption. *Proceedings of the Conference on Information Systems and Technology (CIST/INFORMS)*, Seattle, WA.

Pechmann, C., & Stewart, D. W. (1988). A critical review of wearin and wearout. *Current Issues and Research in Advertising*, 285–330.

Peterson, R., Balasubramanian, S., & Bronnenberg, B. J. (1997). Exploring the implications of the Internet for consumer marketing. *Journal of the Academy of Marketing Science*, *25*(4), 329–346.

Petty, R. E., & Cacioppo, J. T. (1986). *Communication and Persuasion: Central and Peripheral Routes to Attitude Change*. New York: Springer-Verlag.

Politz Research, Inc. (1962, November). *A Measurement of Advertising Effectiveness: The Influence of Audience Selectivity and Editorial Environment*.

Port, O. (1999, October 4). Customers move into the driver's seat. *Business Week*, 103–106.

Powers, W. T. (1973, January 26). Feedback: beyond behaviorism. *Science*, *179*, 351–356.

Powers, W. T. (1978). Quantitative analysis of purposive systems: some spadework at the foundations of scientific psychology. *Psychological Review*, *85*, 417–435.

Ray, M. L. (1985). An even more powerful consumer? In R. Buzzell (Ed.), *Marketing in an Electronic Age* (pp. 238–241). Cambridge, MA: Harvard University Press.

Ray, M. L., & Sawyer, A. G. (1971, February). Repetition in media models: a laboratory technique. *Journal of Marketing Research, 8*, 20–29.

Robey, D., & Farrow, D. L. (1982). User involvement in information system development: a conflict model and empirical test. *Management Science, 28*, 73–85.

Rodgers, S., & Thorson, E. (2000). The interactive advertising model: how users perceive and process online ads. *Journal of Interactive Advertising, 1*. Retrieved Sept. 1, 2007. Online: http://jiad.org/vol1/no1/pavlou/index.html

Roehm, H. A., & Haugtvedt, C. P. (1999). Understanding interactivity of cyberspace advertising. In D. W. Schumann & E. Thorson (Eds.), *Advertising and the World Wide Web* (pp. 27–39). Mahwah, NJ: Erlbaum.

Rosen, E. (2000). *The Anatomy of Buzz: How to Create Word of Mouth Marketing*. New York: Doubleday.

Rothschild, M. L., & Hyun, Y. J. (1990, March). Predicting memory for components of tv commercials from EEG. *Journal of Consumer Research, 16*, 472–479.

Rothschild, M. L., Hyun, Y. J., Reeves, B., Thorson, E., & Goldstein, R. (1988, September). Hemispherically lateralized EEG as a response to television commercials. *Journal of Consumer Research, 15*, 185–198.

Rubin, A. M. (1986). Uses, gratification, and media effects research. In J. Bryant & D. Zillman (Eds.), *Perspectives on Media Effects* (pp. 281–302). Hillsdale, PA: Erlbaum.

Scharl, A., Dickinger, A., & Murphy, J. (2005). Diffusion and success factors of mobile marketing. *Electronic Commerce Research and Applications, 4*, 159–173.

Schurr, P. H., & Ozanne, J. L. (1985). Influences on exchange processes: buyers' preconceptions of a seller's trustworthiness and bargaining toughness. *Journal of Consumer Research, 11*(4), 939–953.

Schwerin, H. (1958). Do today's programs provide the wrong commercial climate? *Television Magazine, 15*(8), 45–47, 90–91.

Schwerin, H., & Newell, H. H. (1981). *Persuasion in Marketing*. New York: Wiley.

Shimp, T. A. (1990). *Promotion Management and Marketing Communications* (2nd ed.). Hinsdale, IL: Drydn Press.

Short, J., Williams, E., & Christie, B. (1976). *The Social Psychology of Telecommunications*. New York: John Wiley.

Simon, H. (1957). *Organizations*. New York: McGraw Hill.

Singh, S. N., & Hitchon, J. C. (1989). The intensifying effects of exciting television programs on the reception of subsequent commercials. *Psychology and Marketing*, 6(Spring), 1–31.

Smith, H. J., Milberg, S., & Burke, S. (1996). Information privacy: measuring individuals' concerns about organizational practices. *MIS Quarterly, 20*(2), 167–196.

Soldow, G. F., & Principe, V. (1981). Response to commercials as a function of program context. *Journal of Advertising Research, 21*(2), 59–65.

Spalter, M. (1996). Maintaining a customer focus in an interactive age, the seven i's to success. In E. Forrest & R. Mizerski (Eds.), *Interactive Marketing: The Future Present* (pp. 163–188). Chicago, IL: American Marketing Association, NTC Business Books.

Srull, T. K. (1990). Individual responses to advertising: mood and its effects from an information processing perspective. In S. J. Agres, J. A. Edell, & T. M. Dubitsky (Eds.), *Emotion in advertising, theoretical and practical explorations* (pp. 19–34). New York: Quorum Books.

Stewart, D. W. (1986, April/May). The moderating role of recall, comprehension, and brand differentiation on the persuasiveness of television advertising. *Journal of Advertising Research, 25*, 43–47.

Stewart, D. W. (1989, June/July). Measures, methods, and models of advertising response. *Journal of Advertising Research, 29*, 54–60.

Stewart, D. W., Frazier, G., & Martin, I. (1996). Integrated channel management: merging the communication and distribution functions of the firm. In E. Thorson & J. Moore

(Eds.), *Integrated communication: Synergy of persuasive voices* (pp. 185–216). Hillsdale, NJ: Erlbaum.

Stewart, D. W., & Furse, D. H. (1986). *Effective Television Advertising: A Study of 1000 Commercials*. Lexington, MA: Lexington Books.

Stewart, D. W., Furse, D. H., & Kozak, R. (1983). A descriptive analysis of commercial copy-testing services. In C. Martin & J. Leigh (Eds.), *Current Issues and Research in Advertising, 6*, 1–44.

Stewart, D. W., & Koslow, S. (1989). Executional factors and advertising effectiveness: a replication. *Journal of Advertising, 18*(3), 21–32.

Stewart, D. W., & Pavlou, P. A. (2002). From consumer response to active consumer: Measuring the effectiveness of interactive media. *Journal of the Academy of Marketing Science, 30*(4), 376–396. Online: http://jam.sagepub.com/cgi/content/abstract/30/4/376.

Stewart, D. W., Pavlou, P. A., & Ward, S. (2002). Media influences on marketing communications. In J. Bryant & D. Zillmann (Eds.), *Media Effects: Advances in Theory and Research* (Rev. ed.) (pp. 353–396). Hillsdale, NJ: Erlbaum.

Stewart, D. W., Pechmann, C., Ratneshwar, S., Stroud, J., & Bryant, B. (1985). Methodological and theoretical foundations of advertising copy testing: a review. *Current Issues and Research in Advertising, 2*, 1–74.

Stewart, D. W., & Ward, S. (1994). Media effects on advertising. In J. Bryant & D. Zillman (Eds.), *Media Effects: Advances in Theory and Research* (pp. 315–364). Hillsdale, NJ: Erlbaum.

Stewart, D. W., & Zhao, Q. (2000). Internet marketing, business models, and public policy. *Journal of Public Policy and Marketing, 19*, 287–296.

Strong, E. C. (1974, November). The use of field experimental observations in estimating recall. *Journal of Marketing Research, 11*, 369–378.

Strong, E. C. (1977, December). The spacing and timing of advertising. *Journal of Advertising Research, 16*, 25–31.

Thirkwell, P. C. (1997). Caught by the Web: implications of Internet technologies for the evolving relationship marketing paradigm. *Proceedings of the Third American Marketing Association Special Conference, New and Evolving Paradigms, Dublin, Ireland*, 334–348.

Thorson, E. (1990). Consumer processing of advertising. In J. H. Leigh & C. Martin, Jr. (Eds.), *Current Issues and Research in Advertising* (Vol. 12) (pp. 197–230). Ann Arbor: University of Michigan.

Thorson, E., Reeves, B., Schleuder, J., Lang, A., & Rothschild, M. L. (1985). Effect of program context on the processing of television commercials. *Proceedings of the American Academy of Advertising*, R58–63.

Tillman, H. (1995, September 6). Evaluating the quality of information on the Internet or finding a needle in a haystack (a presentation delivered at the John F. Kennedy School of Government, Harvard University, Cambridge, Massachusetts).

Time, Inc. (1981). *A study of the effectiveness of advertising frequency in magazines: the relationship between magazine advertising frequency and brand awareness, advertising recall, favorable brand rating, willingness to buy, and product use and purchase*. New York: Research Department, Magazine Group, Time Inc.

Tolley, B. S., & Bogart, L. (1994) *Attention, Altitude and Affect in Response to Advertising* (pp. 69–78). Hillsdale, NJ: Erlbaum.

Tsang, M. M., Ho, S. C., & Liang, T. P. (2004). Consumer attitudes toward mobile advertising: an empirical study. *International Journal of Electronic Commerce*, 8(3), 65–78.

Venkatesh, V., & Ramesh, V. (2006). Web and wireless site usability: understanding differences and modeling use. *MIS Quarterly, 30*(1), 181–206.

Wang, W., & Benbasat, I. (2005). Trust in and adoption of online recommendation agents. *Journal of the Association for Information Systems*, 6(3), 72–101.

Ward, S., Levinson, D., & Wackman, D. (1972). Children's attention to television advertising. In G. A. Comstock & J. P. Murray (Eds.), *Television and Social Behavior: Vol. 4, Television in Day-to-Day Life* (pp. 491–515). Rockville, MD: National Institute of Mental Health.

Watson, R. T., Pitt, L. F., Berthon, P., and Zinkhan, G. M. (2002). U-commerce: expanding the universe of marketing. *Journal of the Academy of Marketing Science*, *30*(4), 333–347.

Webster, F. E., Jr. (1989). It's 1990—do you know where your marketing is? *MSI White Paper*. Cambridge, MA: Marketing Science Institute.

Wikstrom, S. (1996). An integrated model of buyer-seller relationships. *Journal of the Academy of Marketing Science*, *23*(4), 335–345.

Wright, J. (2006). *Blog Marketing*. McGraw-Hill.

Wright, P. L. (1973). The cognitive processes mediating acceptance of advertising. *Journal of Marketing Research*, *10*, 53–62.

Wurman, R. S. (2000, November 28). Redesign the data pump. *Business 2.0*, 210–220.

Wyer, R. S., & Srull, T. K. (1981). Category accessibility: some theoretical and empirical issues concerning the processing of social stimulus information. In E. T. Higgins, C. P. Herman, & M. P. Zanna (Eds.), *Social cognition: The Ontario Symposium* (pp. 161–197). Hillsdale, NJ: Erlbaum.

Xu, Y. (2003). Mobile data communications in China. *Communications of the* ACM, *46*(12), 81–85.

Yi, Y. (1990a). Cognitive and affective priming effects of the context for print advertisements. *Journal of Advertising*, *19*(2), 40–48.

Yi, Y. (1990b, September). The effects of contextual priming in print advertisements. *Journal of Consumer Research*, *17*, 215–222.

Yuspeh, S. (1977, November). On-air: are we testing the message or the medium? Paper delivered to J. Walter Thompson Research Conference, New York.

Zaichowsky, J. (1985). Measuring the involvement construct. *Journal of Consumer Research*, *12*, 341–352.

Zielske, H. A. (1959). The remembering and forgetting of advertising. *Journal of Marketing*, 239–243.

Zielske, H. A., & Henry, W. (1980, April). Remembering and forgetting television ads. *Journal of Advertising Research*, *20*, 7–13.

Zigurs, I., Poole, M. S., & DeSanctis, G. L. (1988, December). A study of influence in computer-mediated group decision making. *MIS Quarterly*, *12*, 625–644.

Zillmann, D., & Bryant, J. (1994). Entertainment as media effect. In J. Bryant & D. Zillmann (Eds.), *Media Effects: Advances in Theory and Research* (pp. 437–462). Hillsdale, NJ: Erlbaum.

19

EDUCATIONAL TELEVISION AND INTERACTIVE MEDIA FOR CHILDREN

Effects on Academic Knowledge, Skills, and Attitudes

Shalom M. Fisch
Sesame Workshop

All too often, discussions of the effects of electronic media on children focus solely on the negative. Some critics have argued—with little, if any, basis in empirical data—that exposure to television can lead to outcomes such as reduced attention spans, lack of interest in school, or children's becoming passive "zombie viewers" (e.g., Healy, 1990; Postman, 1985; Winn, 1977). Discussions regarding interactive media often have been more ambivalent; for example, efforts to bring computers and Internet access into classrooms reflect perceptions of interactive media as an educational necessity (e.g., Roberts, 2000), but others have focused on negative consequences such as the potential for widespread "video game addiction" (e.g., Bruner & Bruner, 2006). While many negative claims have been either attenuated or completely refuted by research, other negative effects of media have found more support in the literature, such as the modeling of aggressive behavior (e.g., Weber, Ritterfield, & Kostygina, 2006; Wilson et al., 1997) or persuasive effects of advertising (e.g., John, 1999; Kunkel, 2001).

However, even those negative effects that are supported by data do not present the entire picture. Often, far less attention has been paid to the positive effects that can result from use of educational media such as educational television programs or video games. Yet, if we believe that children can learn negative lessons from media, then it stands to reason that they can learn positive lessons, too. The same medium that conveys product information through a television commercial can also convey science concepts in an educational television program. And the same medium that can influence children to act more aggressively via violent games should also be able to motivate them to engage in educational activities.

This chapter reviews research on the impact of educational media on children's knowledge, skills, and attitudes in academic areas such as literacy, science, and mathematics. The first section reviews key findings regarding television, the second focuses on interactive media, and the third discusses theoretical mechanisms that have been proposed to explain effects. Due to space limitations, the focus will be on efforts designed for children rather than adults (e.g., Greenberg & Gantz, 1976; Lowe, 2005;

Singhal & Rogers, 1999; Winsten, 1994) and primarily on unaided use by children, rather than use accompanied by adult-led follow-up discussions or activities (e.g., Block, Guth, & Austin, 1993; Cognition and Technology Group at Vanderbilt, 1997; Lampert, 1985; Sanders & Sonnad, 1980).

EDUCATIONAL TELEVISION

Academic effects of educational television have been investigated in several subject areas, each of which is discussed in turn below. First, research on the impact of preschool educational programming on young children's school readiness is reviewed. Next, effects of school-age programming in four areas—literacy, mathematics and problem solving, science and technology, and civics and social studies—are explored.

School Readiness

Numerous educational television series have been created to promote school readiness among preschool children. Of course, the term "school readiness" encompasses not only academic skills, but also interpersonal skills and attitudes, such as self-confidence and cooperation with peers (Zero to Three/National Center for Clinical Infant Programs, 1992). This chapter reviews research on the impact of preschool television programs in the academic domain. Readers interested in the impact of prosocial programs on children's interpersonal skills are directed to a recent review by Mares and Woodard (2001).

Because of its particular prominence in this literature, the section will begin by reviewing several landmark studies on the impact of *Sesame Street*. (More detail on these studies may be found in Fisch & Truglio, 2001.) Next, research on the impact of other preschool series will be reviewed.

Sesame Street

The earliest indications of the educational power of *Sesame Street* emerged in a pair of experimental/control, pretest/posttest studies conducted by the Educational Testing Service (ETS) after the first and second seasons of production (Ball & Bogatz, 1970; Bogatz & Ball, 1971). Each study found that among 3- to 5-year-olds, heavier viewers of *Sesame Street* showed significantly greater pretest-posttest gains on an assortment of academic skills related to the alphabet, numbers, body parts, shapes, relational terms, and sorting and classification. The areas that showed the greatest effects were the ones that had been emphasized the most in *Sesame Street* (e.g., letters). These effects held across age, sex, geographic location, socioeconomic status (SES) (with low-SES children showing greater gains than middle-SES children), native language (English or Spanish), and whether the children watched at home or in school. Indeed, even when Cook and his colleagues (1975) conducted a re-analysis of these data that controlled for other, potentially contributing factors such as mothers' discussing *Sesame Street* with their child, the above effects were reduced but many remained statistically significant.

These effects have found parallels in summative evaluations of several international co-productions of *Sesame Street* outside the United States. Significant differences in cognitive skills (often focused on literacy and mathematics) have been found between viewers and nonviewers of *Plaza Sésamo* in Mexico (Diaz-Guerrero & Holtzman, 1974; UNICEF, 1996), *Susam Sokagi* in Turkey (Sahin, 1990), *Rua Sésamo* in Portugal

(Brederode-Santos, 1993), and *Ulitsa Sezam* in Russia (*Ulitsa Sezam* Department of Research and Content, 1998). Only one Mexican study failed to replicate this pattern of differences (Diaz-Guerrero, Reyes-Lagunes, Witzke, & Holtzman, 1976), but it turned that the control group had, in fact, been exposed to *Plaza Sésamo* as well. (See Cole, Richman, & McCann Brown, 2001, for a more detailed review of this research.)

Sesame Street has been found to hold long-term benefits for viewers as well. One component of the Bogatz and Ball (1971) study was a follow-up on a subset of the children who had participated in their earlier study (Ball & Bogatz, 1970). Teachers rated their students on several dimensions of school readiness (e.g., verbal readiness, quantitative readiness, attitude toward school, relationship with peers) without knowing their prior viewership of *Sesame Street*. Results indicated that those children who had been frequent *Sesame Street* viewers were rated as better prepared for school than their non- or low-viewing classmates.

More than 25 years later, the immediate and long-term effects of *Sesame Street* were confirmed by other data. A three-year longitudinal study of low-SES preschoolers found that after controlling statistically for background variables such as parents' level of education, native language, and preschool attendance, preschool viewing of educational programs—and *Sesame Street* in particular—predicted time spent in reading and educational activities, letter-word knowledge, math skills, vocabulary size, and school readiness on age-appropriate standardized achievement tests. Also, as in the earlier Bogatz and Ball (1971) study, teachers more often rated *Sesame Street* viewers as well-adjusted to school (Wright & Huston, 1995; Wright, Huston, Scantlin, & Kotler, 2001). A second study was a correlational analysis of data representing approximately 10,000 children from the U.S. Department of Education's National Household Education Survey in 1993. Although the data were correlational (and, thus, can suggest but not prove causality), results indicated that preschoolers who viewed *Sesame Street* were more likely to be able to recognize letters of the alphabet and tell connected stories when pretending to read; these effects were strongest among children from low-income families, and held true even after the effects of other contributing factors (e.g., parental reading, preschool attendance, parental education) were removed statistically. In addition, first and second graders who had viewed *Sesame Street* as preschoolers were more likely to be reading storybooks on their own and less likely to require remedial reading instruction (Zill, 2001; Zill, Davies, & Daly, 1994).

Finally, the longest-term impact of *Sesame Street* was found in a "recontact" study that examined high school students who either had or had not watched educational television as preschoolers; the bulk of this viewing had consisted of watching *Sesame Street*. Results showed that high school students who had watched more educational television—and *Sesame Street* in particular—as preschoolers had significantly higher grades in English, Mathematics, and Science. They also used books more often, showed higher academic self-esteem, and placed a higher value on academic performance. These differences held true even after the students' early language skills and family background variables were factored out (Anderson, Huston, Wright, & Collins, 1998; Huston, Anderson, Wright, Linebarger, & Schmitt, 2001).

Other Preschool Series

Research on other preschool series has explored several different approaches to school readiness, exploring impact on children's knowledge, their willingness to pursue challenges, and their problem-solving skills.

A series of studies by Jerome and Dorothy Singer and their colleagues assessed the impact of *Barney & Friends* (a series featuring a purple dinosaur, which makes extensive use of songs set to familiar children's tunes) on preschoolers' knowledge (see Singer & Singer, 1998 for a review). Research with a largely white, middle-SES sample of 3- and 4-year-old children found that unaided viewing of 10 episodes resulted in viewers' performing significantly better than nonviewers in counting skills, identifying colors, vocabulary, and knowledge of neighborhood, although not in identifying shapes or labeling emotions (Singer & Singer, 1994). However, a replication that included a greater representation of children from low-SES and minority families found that, for this population, viewing 10 episodes of the series without teacher follow-up produced only a small advantage over nonviewers (although effects were greater when *Barney & Friends* was combined with teacher-driven lessons; Singer & Singer, 1995). Additional studies found no significant effects for 5½-year-old kindergartners, which was attributed to ceiling effects, but suggested that prosocial effects could exist for children as young as 2 years old (Singer & Singer, 1998; Singer, Singer, Miller, & Sells, 1994).

Another approach toward school readiness is embodied by *Dragon Tales*, an animated series in which a pair of Latino siblings help a group of friendly dragons in the magical world of Dragon Land. Targeted at children aged 2 to 6, *Dragon Tales* was designed to stimulate preschoolers' motivation to pursue age-appropriate physical, cognitive, social, and emotional challenges. In an experimental, pretest-posttest study, ratings from researchers, teachers, and parents indicated that *Dragon Tales* had a significant positive impact on the frequency with which children chose challenging tasks, initiated or organized play with others, and asked others to play. More direct evidence from children emerged from task-based interviews in which viewers were more likely to describe their block building in terms of a coherent goal, and free play tasks in which viewers were more likely to spontaneously make things (Rust, 2001).

A third approach to school readiness lies in building problem-solving skills, as in several of the series produced for Nickelodeon's "Nick Jr." programming block. One set of studies examined the combined effects of *Allegra's Window* (a live-action series featuring a little girl puppet named Allegra) and *Gullah Gullah Island* (a live-action series about a black family set on a tropical island) as preschool children either viewed or did not view the pair of series for two years. Caregiver ratings indicated that caregivers perceived viewers as showing significantly greater increases than nonviewers on scales of flexible thinking (e.g., seeing things from multiple points of view, showing curiosity) and problem solving (e.g., trying different approaches to solve problems, concentrating well on activities, not giving up). The largest gains appeared within the first month of viewing and were sustained over the entire two-year viewing period (Bryant et al., 1997). Data collected directly from children revealed that viewers produced significantly more correct answers in three sets of hands-on problem-solving tasks (e.g., simplified versions of the classic Tower of Hanoi problem) than nonviewers. They also solved four of the six Tower of Hanoi problems in fewer moves than nonviewers, but no significant difference was found for response time in a Go-NoGo task (akin to signal detection) in which children distinguished between shapes and/or colors (Mulliken & Bryant, 1999).

Subsequently, parallel research assessed the impact of *Blue's Clues* (a participatory series about an animated dog named Blue and her human friend Steve, who asks viewers directly for assistance in solving games and puzzles) on preschool children's knowledge and cognitive development during a two-year viewing period (Anderson, Bryant, Wilder, Santomero, Williams, & Crawley, 2000; Bryant et al., 1999). On the most basic level, when presented with the same puzzles shown in individual episodes of *Blue's Clues* (incorporating skills such as matching, sequencing, and relational concepts, among others), viewers gave significantly more correct answers than nonviewers, suggesting recall of the material seen on television. More broadly, subscales from the Kaufman Assessment Battery for Children (K-ABC) and the Kaufman Brief Intelligence Test (K-BIT) revealed that viewers performed significantly better than nonviewers in solving nonhumorous riddles (e.g., "What is small, has two wings, and can fly?"), Gestalt closure of incomplete inkblot drawings, and a matrices task that tapped nonverbal problem-solving; these effects were sustained throughout the two-year viewing period. No effect was found for children's expressive vocabulary or self-esteem.

One unique feature of *Blue's Clues* is the degree to which it solicits viewer participation, with the aim of engaging viewers actively in its educational content. Based on observations of children during viewing (Crawley, Anderson, Wilder, Williams, & Santomero, 1999), though, Anderson and his colleagues have hypothesized that (at least among preschoolers), viewer participation does not so much contribute to learning as reflect mastery *after* learning has occurred. As a result, they found participation to increase with repeated viewing of the same episode, as more children, presumably, learned the answers.

Language Development

Each of the preceding studies assessed the educational impact of one or more series within the specific domain of their stated educational goals. More broadly, one area of impact that has been examined across several different preschool television series is language development (see Naigles & Mayeux, 2001 for a review). A series of content analyses by Rice and her colleagues compared the spoken language used in television series such as *Sesame Street*, *Mister Rogers' Neighborhood*, and *The Electric Company* to the language parents use in child-directed speech for young children (Rice, 1984; Rice & Haight, 1986). In contrast to situation comedies such as *Gilligan's Island*, the researchers found that the language in the educational television series contained many of the same features that are believed to promote language development in child-directed speech: short length of utterance, repetition, language tied to immediate, concrete referents, and so on. Thus, the potential existed for such television series to contribute to language development.

However, subsequent research supported this hypothesis with regard to some aspects of language development but not others. Although not every study has found effects on children's vocabulary acquisition (e.g., Bryant et al., 1999), many studies have shown educational programs to contribute to lexical development. That is, preschool children can acquire new words from television (e.g., Rice, Huston, Truglio, & Wright, 1990; Rice & Woodsmall, 1988; Singer & Singer, 1994; cf. Naigles & Mayeux, 2001). However, the few studies that have examined the role of television in grammatical development (i.e., the acquisition of syntax) provide little evidence for a significant effect of television in this area (e.g., Singer & Singer, 1981). Naigles and Mayeux (2001) hypothesize that grammatical development may require a socially based construction of meaning that the one-way communication of television does not provide.

Significant effects on vocabulary acquisition have been found in second-language learning as well. For example, Linebarger (2001) assessed the impact of *Dora the Explorer* (a participatory problem-solving series about a Latina girl, whose dialogue frequently includes Spanish words and phrases) on knowledge of Spanish words among English- and Spanish-speaking children. Among Spanish-speaking children, pretest-posttest gains were associated more strongly with children's general language development than their exposure to the series, but small but significant gains were observed among English-speaking children. English-speaking children who were 4 years old at the beginning of the study gained one Spanish word per 14 episodes viewed; 3-year-olds gained one word per 58 episodes viewed.

Finally, it is worth noting that, under some conditions, educational television programs may also have unintended negative effects on language development. Naigles et al. (1995) found that, after watching 10 episodes of *Barney & Friends*, children demonstrated *decreased* understanding of the difference between the mental state verbs *know* (which reflects certainty) and *think* and *guess* (which are less certain). A subsequent examination of the 10 *Barney & Friends* episodes explained why: they included numerous uses of *know* or *think* in situations of certainty. Just as exposure to novel words in appropriate televised contexts can have positive effects on young children's vocabulary, it seemed that consistent misuses of words could have negative effects as well.

Television for Very Young Children?

Traditionally, educational television for preschoolers has been produced for an audience of 3- to 5-year-old children. As a result, the vast majority of the preceding research was conducted with this age group. More recently, though, television and videos aimed at even younger children have become big business, as is evident from examples such as *Teletubbies, Baby Einstein*, and *Baby First TV*, an entire 24-hour TV channel targeted at the youngest viewers. However, the lack of research with younger children has left open the question of whether effects might be found among children below the age of 3. Do such programs hold educational benefits for very young children? Or are toddlers not yet cognitively ready to comprehend and learn from educational television programs? Certainly, the latter point of view would be consistent with the American Academy of Pediatrics' (1997, 2001) recommendation that television be avoided completely for children under 2 years of age.[1]

Some insight into comprehension of television among very young children can be gained from several studies that have assessed the degree to which children below the age of 3 are able to imitate simple actions or acquire rudimentary bits of knowledge from television. Meltzoff (1988) found that, after watching a videotape of an experimenter pulling apart and reassembling a dumbbell-like toy, even 14- and 24-month-old children could imitate the actions they had seen. In fact, the level of imitation was consistent with that found in another study using live models (Meltzoff, 1985). By contrast, other studies have suggested that toddlers' imitation from video increases with age and depends on the complexity of the behavior being imitated. McCall, Parke, and Kavanaugh (1977) found that, among 18-, 24-, and 36-month-olds, only 36-month-olds imitated a sequence of actions as frequently when it was presented on video as when it was demonstrated live. Barr and Hayne (1999) manipulated the complexity of the behavior being modeled; they found that, one day after watching an adult model a simple behavior (either live or on videotape), 15- and 18-month-olds produced similar levels of imitation from the live and videotaped presentations, but 12-month-olds did not. By contrast, when the model demonstrated a longer sequence of behaviors, only the 18-month-olds showed as much imitation from the videotape as from the live model.

Using a different methodology, several studies have presented 2- to 3-year-olds with either video or live demonstrations of an adult hiding a toy in a neighboring room. After viewing, the children were brought into the room to attempt to find the toy

(Schmitt & Anderson, 2002; Troseth, 2003; Troseth & DeLoache, 1998). Results indicated that 24- and 30-month-olds were less accurate in finding the toy if they watched the video than if they watched the equivalent scene live; 36-month-olds were equally accurate in both conditions, but faster after the live presentation.

Taken together, the preceding studies suggest that, below the age of 2 or 3 years, children can acquire simple behaviors or information from television, but they are less able to learn from a televised portrayal than from a live demonstration. One reason may lie in the social nature of live presentations and interaction between the model and viewer, as Troseth, Saylor, and Archer (2006) found that video was just as powerful as live presentations if they used a live (rather than pre-taped) video that allowed the on-screen adult to interact directly with the viewers.

Naturally, the videos used in these studies are far simpler than anything that would be seen on broadcast television. To my knowledge, only one study to date has attempted to gauge the impact of commercial "baby videos" on the cognitive abilities of young children. A survey of parents found a significant negative correlation between the language development of 8- to 16-month-olds and the amount of time that the children reportedly spent watching baby videos; one hour of viewing per day was associated with a 17-point deficit in language scores. No such effect was found for 17- to 24-month-olds, or for other genres of video, such as educational television and DVDs, entertainment television, or adult television (Zimmerman, Christakis, & Meltzoff, 2007).

It is interesting to consider the point that, because no effect was found for other genres of video, this finding does not seem to be a result of watching television *per se*; rather, the effect may relate to some aspect of the format of baby videos themselves. We might speculate that, because baby videos often employ little language, and other research has shown that the presence of background television can reduce parent-child interaction (Schmidt, Pempek, Kirkorian, Lund, & Anderson, in press), it is possible that such videos could displace some of the language-rich interaction that might otherwise occur. However, it is important to note that Zimmerman et al.'s data are correlational, so they cannot establish a causal link between baby videos and language development. Indeed, an equally possible explanation is that children with less developed language might be more likely to watch videos that require relatively little language proficiency from viewers.

Without additional research, it is difficult to draw definitive conclusions about the potential positive or negative effects of educational television among toddlers. It appears that very young children can acquire some knowledge from television; for example, in the first trial in the Schmitt and Anderson (2002) study, 60% of the 2-year-olds found the object after seeing it hidden on television. Still, it also seems that children below the age of 3 are better able to learn from live experiences than from television. Clearly, future research will be needed to expand our understanding of these issues. Until then, it is probably safest to say that, if educational television is to be used among children under 3, it should be used judiciously, and as a supplement to other enriching activities that children can experience hands-on.

Literacy

Many of the effects of preschool programming on 3- to 5-year-olds' school readiness have concerned literacy. These range from fairly immediate effects on letter recognition to long-term effects on subsequent reading performance.

Among school-age television series, too, many have been claimed as "literacy shows," but the term has been used quite broadly. Often, producers or broadcasters have labeled television series as serving literacy simply because their characters have been taken from books, regardless of whether the series is designed to model reading or writing skills. For example, *The New Adventures of Winnie the Pooh* was labeled as a literacy series, even though its storylines actually focused on socioemotional issues and were not adapted from books.

In fact, such claims are not completely without merit. Anecdotal evidence suggests that the existence of television series based on books can stimulate greatly increased sales of the books on which they are based, a point to which I shall return in discussing effects on motivation below. Nevertheless, this review focuses more narrowly on television series that explicitly attempt to promote reading and/or writing among children.

Basic Reading Skills

The first substantive research in this area was a pair of summative studies on *The Electric Company*, a magazine-format series in which each episode comprised a combination of comedy sketches, songs, and animations (e.g., the adventures of "Letterman," a super hero who solved problems by changing letters in words). *The Electric Company* targeted poor readers in the second grade, and, in keeping with leading educational practice of the time, much of its focus lay in demonstrating the correspondence between letters (or combinations of letters) and their associated sounds.

Ball and Bogatz (1973) assessed the impact of the first season of *The Electric Company* in an experimental/control, pretest-posttest study with more than 8,000 children in grades 1 through 4. Approximately one-half of the children were shown *The Electric Company* in school for six months, while the remaining children were not. Pretests and posttests included a paper-and-pencil battery of assessments that addressed all of *The Electric Company*'s 19 goal areas (e.g., the ability to read consonant blends, digraphs, sight words, and final E, among others); a subset of more than 1,000 children were also tested orally in one-on-one sessions with researchers.

The data showed significant gains among viewers of *The Electric Company* in almost all of the 19 goal areas, including a broad range of phonics-based skills, as well as their ability to read for meaning. These gains were greatest for first and second graders, presumably because they had shown the lowest initial performance in the pretest. (Recall also that *The Electric Company*'s target audience was poor readers in the second grade.) The effects held across sex, ethnicity, and native language (English or Spanish), and were confirmed by similar, though less pronounced, effects in a subsequent study on the impact of the second season of *The Electric Company* (Ball, Bogatz, Karazow, & Rubin, 1974).

Parallel effects were found more than 25 years later for another PBS early literacy series, *Between the Lions*. Like *The Electric Company, Between the Lions* is a humorous magazine-format series whose goals include promoting concepts of print, phonemic awareness, and letter-sound correspondences (plus other topics, such as whole language elements) among early readers. Linebarger (2000) presented 17 half-hour episodes to children in kindergarten and first grade over a period of three to four weeks. Using an experimental/control, pretest/posttest design, viewers' and nonviewers' reading performance was assessed on several levels: specific program content (e.g., ability to read words that had been shown in the program), three particular emergent literacy skills (i.e., letter naming, phonemic segmentation fluency, nonsense word fluency), and more generalized early reading ability as measured via a standardized test (including knowledge of the alphabet and its functions, and print conventions such as reading left to right). At the posttest, after controlling statistically for a variety of background variables, kindergarten viewers performed significantly better than nonviewers on three out of five measures of specific program content, all three measures of emergent literacy skill, and the test of early reading ability. However, apart from one significant effect in phonemic segmentation fluency, there were no significant differences among first graders. This appeared to be due largely to ceiling effects; first graders already possessed the bulk of the skills modeled in *Between the Lions*.

Reading Comprehension

Impact has been assessed on a somewhat broader level with regard to *Reading Rainbow* (Leitner, 1991). Aimed at 5- to 8-year-olds, each episode of *Reading Rainbow* presents a specific children's book that is read on-air as the camera shows illustrations taken from the book; other segments in the episode deal with related topics in a variety of formats (e.g., songs, documentaries, interviews with children). In this study, fourth graders read a book about cacti in the desert after one of three treatments: (1) watching a 30-minute episode of *Reading Rainbow* that featured the book along with other segments about the desert and animals that live there, (2) a hands-on opportunity to touch and examine a potted cactus, or (3) a verbal pre-reading discussion in which groups of children were asked to imagine the kinds of things that might be in a book about the desert. Among the results of the study, children who viewed the relevant *Reading Rainbow* episode showed significantly greater comprehension than those who engaged in pre-reading discussions; no difference emerged between the pre-reading discussion and hands-on conditions. Leitner explained the data in terms of modality effects. However, her alternate explanation—that the effect was due to previewing the book through *Reading Rainbow*—seems at least as likely, since only the children in the *Reading Rainbow* condition heard the book read (via television) before they read it themselves. Thus, the crucial factor may not have been television *per se*, but, rather, an additional exposure to the book. Yet, while this may pose a confound for the research, it holds less serious implications in the real world. Indeed, this is much of the idea behind *Reading Rainbow*: to expose children to books with the intent of inspiring them to read these books subsequently on their own.

Motivation to Read and Write

As noted earlier, anecdotal evidence suggests that popular television series based on books can stimulate greatly increased sales of the books that inspired them, whether the television series are intended as educational (e.g., *Arthur*) or not (e.g., *Goosebumps*). More systematic research on *Reading Rainbow* has reported increases of 150% to 900% in the sales of books featured in the series, and a survey of librarians found that 82% reported children asking for books they had seen on *Reading Rainbow* (Wood & Duke, 1997). However, it is not clear in these cases whether the television programs stimulated increased amounts of reading (i.e., reading that would not have occurred otherwise), or whether the television-related books merely displaced reading of other books by children who would have been reading anyway.

More direct assessments of impact on motivation to read and write were conducted in research on *Between the Lions* and *Ghostwriter*. Data on the motivational effects of *Between the Lions* have been mixed, with significant effects on parent and teacher ratings in some areas but not others. Among kindergartners, parents and teachers reported no difference in several measures (e.g., children's looking at books or magazines alone, how often they asked people to read to them), but parents reported viewers' going to libraries or bookstores more and writing significantly more than nonviewers. The only significant effects for first graders were in parents' ratings of how often children read books alone and teachers' reports of writing during free time (Linebarger, 2000).

Providing compelling opportunities to read and write was an explicit goal of *Ghostwriter*, a television series and multiple-media initiative for children aged 7 to 10. *Ghostwriter* featured a team of children who used literacy to solve mysteries with the aid of Ghostwriter, an invisible ghost who could communicate only via reading and writing. To date, there have been no experimental/control studies of the impact of *Ghostwriter*. However, findings from several pieces of research speak to the issue of providing children with compelling opportunities to engage in reading and writing.

On the most basic level, several studies have found that viewers typically chose to read the print that was shown on-screen in *Ghostwriter* (e.g., in the form of messages to and from *Ghostwriter* or characters' recording information in their "casebooks"); one survey found that 83% of respondents said they read along, and an additional 8% "sometimes" did so (Nielsen New Media Services, 1993). Another study found that approximately 25% of the girls who viewed *Ghostwriter* kept casebooks of their own, and about 20% of the children said they regularly wrote in code (KRC Research & Consulting, 1994).

Perhaps the clearest evidence of *Ghostwriter*'s impact on children's pursuit of literacy activities lay in the large numbers of children who wrote letters to *Ghostwriter* and participated in mail-in contests that required them to engage in complex activities such as writing songs or creating their own original super-heroes. Such activities were almost completely self-motivated on the part of children, and some reported that it was the first time they had written a letter. Children's participation required substantial effort—not only in writing the letters themselves, but also in learning how to address an envelope, obtaining the necessary postage, using zip codes, and so on. Despite all of these potential obstacles, more than 450,000 children wrote letters to *Ghostwriter* during its first two seasons (Children's Television Workshop, 1994)—direct evidence of *Ghostwriter*'s ability to motivate children to engage in reading and writing.

Long-term Impact

As discussed in the section on school readiness above, longitudinal studies of *Sesame Street* have found preschool viewing to carry long-term effects on children's literacy in first and second grade (Wright et al., 2001; Zill, 2001) and as late as high school (Anderson et al, 1998; Huston et al., 2001). Very little longitudinal research has assessed the long-term impact of school-age television programs on literacy, but summative research on the second season of *The Electric Company* suggests that such series can also hold long-term benefits (Ball et al., 1974). Participants in the study included a subsample of children who had participated in Ball and Bogatz's (1973) study of the first season of the series. Data from the pretest (i.e., before children saw any additional episodes of *The Electric Company*) indicated that the effect of viewers' initial exposure sustained itself, even though *The Electric Company* had not been broadcast during the several-month interval between studies. Interestingly, however, posttest data showed that the effect of viewing two seasons was not considerably greater than the effect of viewing one. Thus, the major impact of *The Electric Company* appeared to come from children's initial six-month exposure to the series, and this impact was sufficiently enduring to sustain itself several months after viewing.

Mathematics and Problem Solving

The impact of school-age mathematics programs has been assessed on three types of outcome variables: knowledge of mathematics, mathematical problem-solving ability, and attitudes toward mathematics. Each is discussed below.

Knowledge of Mathematics

Effects on knowledge of mathematics have been found across studies and for two different school-age television series. Harvey, Quiroga, Crane, and Bottoms (1976) evaluated the impact of eight episodes of *Infinity Factory*, a magazine-format mathematics series for 8- to 11-year-old children, that had a particular focus on African-American and Latino children. The study found that viewers showed significant gains in mathematics performance at posttest, although white children showed greater gains than minority viewers.

Knowledge of mathematics was also the focus of an early summative study of *Square One TV*. Aimed at 8- to 12-year-olds, *Square One TV* employed a magazine format that included comedy sketches, game shows with real children, music videos, animation, and an ongoing mathematical detective serial, "Mathnet." The goals of the series were to promote positive attitudes toward mathematics, to promote the use and application of problem-solving processes, and to present sound mathematical content in an interesting, accessible, and meaningful manner. Peel, Rockwell, Esty, and Gonzer (1987) assessed children's comprehension of 10 mathematical problem-solving segments from the first season of *Square One TV*. Although limited by the absence of a pretest or nonviewing control group (because the study was intended to measure comprehension rather than learning), the study is notable for measuring comprehension on three different levels: *recall* of the problem and solution in each segment, *understanding* of the mathematics that underlay the segment, and *extension* of the mathematics content to new, related problems. As one might expect, comprehension at all levels varied somewhat across the segments tested, but a general trend emerged: The highest performance was found in recall, followed by understanding, which was followed in turn by extension. By drawing these distinctions explicitly, the study raises an important issue that must be considered in evaluating the effectiveness of educational television—namely, that researchers may find different results depending upon the way they have defined "comprehension." I will return to this point in the "Theoretical Mechanisms" section below.

Effects on Problem Solving

In keeping with an emerging reform movement in mathematics education that recommended embedding mathematics content in a context of problem solving (e.g., National Council of Teachers of Mathematics, 1989), *Square One TV* placed a heavy emphasis on mathematical problem solving. Hall, Esty, and Fisch (1990a; Hall et al., 1990b) assessed its impact in this area.

In this study, fifth graders in two elementary schools in Corpus Christi, TX (where *Square One TV* had not been broadcast) were shown 30 episodes of *Square One TV*, while children in two other schools were not. A subsample of viewers and nonviewers were individually matched for sex, SES, ethnicity, and performance on a standardized mathematics test. At pretest and posttest, these children attempted several hands-on, nonroutine mathematical problem-solving activities (e.g., figuring out what was wrong with a mathematical game and fixing it), with interviewers and coders blind as to whether children were viewers or nonviewers. Results indicated that, from pretest to posttest, viewers showed significant gains in the number and variety of problem-solving heuristics they used to solve problems (e.g., looking for patterns, working backward), and they used significantly more than nonviewers at posttest. At the same time, viewers' solutions to two of the three problems became significantly more complete and sophisticated, while nonviewers showed no significant change. (Viewers showed no change on the third problem because of ceiling effects.) Thus, exposure to *Square One TV* affected both the ways in which children approached problems and the solutions they reached—effects that occurred regardless of the children's sex, ethnicity, SES, or performance on standardized mathematics tests.

Similar results were found in a summative study of *Cyberchase*, an animated, humorous adventure series in which a group of resourceful kids use mathematics to thwart the schemes of the villainous Hacker. In this study, impact was evaluated on three levels: direct learning (i.e., children's ability to replicate the characters' solutions to on-screen problems), near transfer (solving problems similar to those seen in the series), and far transfer (solving problems that bore little surface similarity to the on-screen problems, although they employed similar mathematics). Significant effects were found on all three levels. However, consistent with research on classroom learning (e.g., Detterman & Sternberg, 1993), the strongest and most consistent effects were found for direct learning, followed by near transfer, and fewer significant effects were found for far transfer. As in the *Square One TV* study, the significant effects that emerged in the far transfer tasks reflected both children's use of problem-solving heuristics and their solutions to one of the problems (Fisch, 2003, 2005).

Attitudes toward Mathematics

The same study of *Square One TV* also assessed the series' effects on children's attitudes toward mathematics (Hall et al., 1990b). In contrast to previous studies in mathematics education, which had assessed attitudes via fairly limited pencil-and-paper scales, attitudes in this study were assessed via in-depth interviews, which were then coded by blind coders. Pretest-posttest comparisons showed significant effects in several domains: Viewers showed a broader conception of "math" (i.e., beyond basic arithmetic) than nonviewers, a greater desire than nonviewers to pursue challenging mathematical tasks, and significantly greater gains than nonviewers in the number of times they spontaneously talked about enjoying mathematics and problem solving throughout the interview (i.e., without being asked directly about enjoyment). Again, there was no consistent effect of sex, ethnicity, or SES. Only one domain, children's conceptions of the usefulness of mathematics, produced no significant effect.

Science and Technology

Television has a long tradition of broadcasting educational science series, from the debut of *Mr. Wizard* in 1951 through more recent efforts, such as *Beakman's World*, *Science Court*, and *Magic Schoolbus*. This section examines the impact of a few science-based series on children's knowledge of science, exploration and experimentation, and attitudes toward the subject. It is interesting to note that these series span several very different genres—presenter-based demonstrations, magazine-format documentary, and

Saturday morning cartoon—but all have produced consistent patterns of significant effects.

Knowledge of Science

Numerous educational television series have been found to produce significant gains in children's knowledge of specific science content. Perhaps the greatest number of studies has concerned *3-2-1 Contact*, a daily magazine-format series targeting 8- to 12-year-olds. *3-2-1 Contact* relied heavily on live-action, mini-documentary segments with teenage hosts, but also included animations, songs, and a dramatized mystery serial called "The Bloodhound Gang." Each week of shows was built around a specific theme (e.g., electricity, outer space), with many of that week's segments corresponding to some aspect of that theme.

Research on the impact of *3-2-1 Contact* is somewhat limited by the methods used; almost all of the existing studies relied largely on paper-and-pencil (typically multiple-choice) quizzes to assess comprehension. Despite this limitation, however, a consistent pattern of effects has been observed with regard to comprehension. Studies have varied in the number of episodes presented to children (from 10 to more than 40). At all levels of exposure, these studies found that viewing *3-2-1 Contact* resulted in positive effects on children's comprehension of the science topics presented (Cambre & Fernie, 1985; Johnston, 1980; Johnston & Luker, 1983; Wagner, 1985). The effects were often strongest among girls, one of the populations that has often been found to demonstrate lower levels of science achievement (e.g., Levin, Sabar, & Libman, 1991).

Other studies have found parallel effects among school-age children for other science-based television series, such as *Bill Nye the Science Guy* (Rockman Et Al., 1996), *Cro* (Fay, Teasley, Cheng, Bachman, & Schnakenberg, 1995a; Goodman, Rylander, & Ross, 1993; cf. Fay et al., 1995b; Fisch et al., 1995), and *Fetch* (Peterman, 2006) in the United States, the Australian series *Australia Naturally* (Noble & Creighton, 1981), and an assortment of individual episodes of *Owl TV*, *Know How*, *Tomorrow's World*, *Body Matters*, and *Erasmus Microman* in the United Kingdom (Clifford, Gunter, & McAleer, 1995).

Of course, comprehension of science content is dependent on the effectiveness of its presentation, as illustrated by research on *Cro*. *Cro* was a Saturday-morning animated series about a Cro-Magnon boy, designed to promote knowledge of and interest in science and technology among 6- to 11-year-old children. Summative research on the first season of *Cro* found that viewers demonstrated a significantly greater understanding of the technological principles presented in some episodes than nonviewers did. However, no differences were found in extension of these principles to new problems, and even on the level of understanding, differences were not significant for every episode tested (Goodman et al., 1993). Several factors distinguished between episodes that produced significant effects and those that did not: they focused on concrete devices rather than abstract principles, they embedded content in a context of problem solving in which characters continually refined solutions to make them more effective, and their educational content was central, rather than tangential, to the narrative plotline. The hypothesis was confirmed when these characteristics were subsequently built into all of the *Cro* episodes produced in Season II, and significant differences between viewers and nonviewers were found for all of the episodes tested (Fay et al., 1995a).

Exploration and Experimentation

Beyond comprehension of science concepts shown, Rockman Et Al. (1996) assessed the impact of exposure to *Bill Nye the Science Guy* on children's hands-on science experimentation. Targeting children aged 8 to 10, each episode of *Bill Nye the Science Guy* featured real-life comedian/scientist Bill Nye conducting experiments and demonstrating scientific concepts (often with surprising effects) in a variety of settings. In this study, a series of hands-on science tasks (e.g., classifying animals, figuring out interesting ways in which tops might be used in *Bill Nye the Science Guy*) were presented to viewers and nonviewers before an extended viewing period in which viewers watched at least 12 episodes of the series in school or at home; the same problems were presented to a second group of viewers and nonviewers after the viewing period. Viewers' process of exploration showed significant improvement in the posttest (e.g., they made more observations and comparisons), as did the sophistication with which they classified animals (e.g., using categories such as "mammals" instead of number of legs). Although limited somewhat by the lack of within-subject controls, then, the data suggested that exposure to *Bill Nye the Science Guy* enhanced both the processes children used and the sophistication of their solutions—a finding consistent with mathematical problem solving data on *Square One TV* (Hall et al., 1990a, 1990b).

It is worth noting that these effects with school-age children have found parallels in some research with preschoolers as well. Beck and Murack (2004) found that when 38 3- to 5-year-old children were given the opportunity to engage in the same sorts of science explorations that some of them had seen in the preschool animated series *Peep and the Big Wide World*, viewers were significantly more likely than nonviewers to initiate predictions and observations, identify problems, use problem-solving strategies, and solve the problems.

Attitudes toward Science

Apart from conveying knowledge and modeling process, the goals of *3-2-1 Contact*, *Bill Nye the Science Guy*, and *Cro* also included stimulating positive attitudes toward science and/or technology. As in the research on knowledge described above, research on the impact of *3-2-1 Contact* on children's attitudes toward science is somewhat limited by its reliance on pencil-and-paper measures. Nevertheless, significant effects on children's interest in science and images of scientists have been found across these studies, although they have been moderate in size and less consistent than effects on knowledge (Cambre & Fernie, 1985; Johnston, 1980; Johnston & Luker, 1983; Wagner, 1985). It is not clear whether *3-2-1 Contact* had less impact in this area, or whether the more moderate effects were due to the relatively limited measures used.

A wider array of measures was used to measure the impact of *Cro* on interest in science and technology, including pencil-and-paper measures, in-depth interviews, and behavioral observations of children as they chose to engage in technology-related vs. -unrelated activities (Fay et al., 1995a, 1995b). Under an experimental/control, pretest/posttest design, children who viewed eight episodes of *Cro* were compared to nonviewers, who watched eight episodes of another animated educational series that did not concern science (*Where on Earth Is Carmen Sandiego?*). Results pointed to a variety of significant effects concerning interest: *Cro* viewers showed significantly greater pretest-posttest gains than nonviewers in their interest in doing technology activities related to episodes of *Cro* (e.g., making a catapult), exhibited greater interest in learning more about the technology content of particular episodes, and were significantly more likely to engage in hands-on activities connected to two episodes when given a choice among these activities and other, non-technology activities (although parallel effects were not found for other episodes tested). However, gains were not significant for interest in technology activities that were not presented in *Cro*, perhaps because the children did not possess a mental construct of "technology" that was sufficiently broad to encompass all of these types of activities.

Rockman Et Al. (2003) found significant pretest-posttest gains in children's perceptions of the importance of experimental methods after viewing *Dragonfly TV*. However, Rockman Et Al.'s (1996) evaluation of *Bill Nye the Science Guy* found little change in viewers' attitudes toward science as reflected in pencil-and-paper measures; this was attributed to ceiling effects, as children scored highly even in the pretest. Some positive effects appeared in parents' reports: 61% believed their children's interest in science increased after watching *Bill Nye the Science Guy*, almost all believed their interest in participating in science activities increased, and 35% reported that their children talked with them about the content of specific episodes. Naturally, however, these data must be interpreted with caution since they reflect parent perceptions rather than direct assessments of children.

Civics and Social Studies

Research in this domain has focused primarily on two areas: children's recall of current events content from television news, and the impact of televised *Schoolhouse Rock* songs on children's understanding of American history or the workings of government.

News and Current Events

Although Comstock and Paik (1991) observed that children get most of their news information from television, as opposed to newspapers, radio, or discussions with others, most research on television news has focused on adults rather than children. This is understandable, as the primary audience for news programming is typically adults, although Atkin and Gantz (1978) found that even elementary school children showed moderate increases in knowledge of political affairs and current events after watching adult news programs.

Issues concerning children's learning from television news take on greater significance when we consider news programs produced specifically for children. A series of studies in the Netherlands compared fourth and sixth graders' recall of news stories presented in one such program, *Jeugdjournaal* (*Children's News*), with print and audio versions of the same stories (Walma van der Molen & van der Voort, 1997, 1998, 2000). These studies consistently found immediate recall of news stories to be greater when presented on television than in any other form. However, the effect was greatest when the information in the televised visuals was redundant with (rather than complementary to) information in the audio track. This led the researchers to explain the advantages of the televised versions using Paivio's (1971) dual-coding hypothesis, which posits a greater likelihood of recall when the same material is presented in two modalities (audio and visual) than when it is presented in only one.

Perhaps the most prominent—and certainly the most controversial—example of American news programming for children is *Channel One*, a 10-minute news program (plus two minutes of commercials) that is broadcast, not to homes, but directly to middle and high schools. In exchange for delivering the program to students on at least 90% of school days, schools receive a satellite dish, two VCRs, and televisions in each classroom from Whittle Communications, the producer of *Channel One*. Several studies have measured learning from *Channel One* via forced-choice, paper-and-pencil assessments. Although one study found no effect (Knupfer & Hayes, 1994), most have found exposure to *Channel One* to result in viewers' knowing more about the news topics covered in the broadcasts than nonviewers (Greenberg & Brand, 1993; Johnston & Brzezinski, 1994). However, even when effects were found, they were not always equal across viewers; some were not significant for children with grade-point averages of "C" or "D," or were stronger for students who were motivated or whose teachers discussed the news on a regular basis (Johnston & Brzezinski, 1994). Although some question how often teachers actually hold discussions to follow up on *Channel One* broadcasts (see Bachen, 1998, for a review), the latter finding raises a question as to the degree to which effects are attributable to the program *per se* or to the discussions it might stimulate.

Nevertheless, greater controversy has been provoked by data showing that viewers learn, not only from the news portion of the program, but also from its commercials. Children have been found to evaluate products more highly and express greater intent to buy products (although they were not significantly more likely to have bought them) if they had seen the products advertised on *Channel One* (Brand & Greenberg, 1994; Greenberg & Brand, 1993). The effectiveness of such in-school advertising, coupled with the increasing presence of advertising and commercial initiatives in schools, has led to debate over the propriety of such efforts (e.g., Richards, Wartella, Morton, & Thompson, 1998; Wartella & Jennings, 2001).

American History and Government

In the 1970s, a series of 3-minute educational interstitials, *Schoolhouse Rock*, aired between children's programs on ABC. Each animated interstitial presented a song about a topic in English, mathematics, science, or American history. At the time, no research was conducted to assess the educational effectiveness of *Schoolhouse Rock*. However, when *Schoolhouse Rock* was rebroadcast in the 1990s, a series of studies by Calvert and her colleagues (Calvert, 1995; Calvert & Pfordresher, 1994; Calvert, Rigaud, & Mazella, 1991; Calvert & Tart, 1993) tested children's and adults' comprehension of two *Schoolhouse Rock* interstitials: "I'm Just a Bill" (the steps through which a bill becomes a law) and "The Shot Heard Round the World" (the Revolutionary War). A third interstitial, "The Preamble" (verbatim text of the Preamble to the Constitution), was tested only with adults. Data from these studies suggested that the interstitials were less effective than alternate versions in which the audio track was spoken rather than sung. Repeated exposure to the original, musical versions improved verbatim recall, but was less effective than prose in promoting deeper comprehension of the educational content.

The researchers attributed this to modality effects (i.e., songs are better suited to verbatim recall) and/or a better match between the prose presentation and verbal recall measures. Yet, when others have found poor comprehension for individual songs in educational television programs, they have generally pointed to factors that were more specific to the particular songs involved; for example, Palmer attributed poor comprehension of one *Sesame Street* song to the rhyme scheme's emphasizing the wrong words and drawing attention away from the educational content (Palmer & Fisch, 2001). While one might hesitate, then, to conclude that songs never lend themselves to deep processing of content, it is clear that these three *Schoolhouse Rock* interstitials succeeded only on the level of verbatim recall.

Interest in News

Interest in and motivation to seek out news was assessed only in research on *Channel One*. Self-report data showed students and teachers reporting examples of having sought out information or contributing to dinnertime conversation because of *Channel One* (Ehman, 1995). However, quantitative comparisons of viewers and nonviewers found no significant difference in students' reports of talking about news stories outside class or using other media to learn about news stories (Johnston & Brzezinski, 1992; Johnston, Brzezinski, & Anderman, 1994). The latter findings, coupled with the issues that always surround self-report data, leave open the question of whether *Channel One* truly increased children's interest in seeking out news. To paraphrase Johnston et al. (1994): To the degree that *Channel One* held benefits for its viewers, it may have satisfied, rather than stimulated, their need to know.

INTERACTIVE MEDIA

In virtually all of the preceding research on educational television, children's learning consists of acquiring concepts, skills, or attitudes that are modeled on the screen. Some learning from interactive media (which we might term "learning *from* interactive media") operates similarly, as in cases where children play an educational computer game about world history and gain a greater understanding of the causes of World War II (McDivitt, 2006) or learn how to manage their asthma or diabetes by playing video games about these topics (Lieberman, 1999, 2001). However, other types of learning (which we might term "learning *with* interactive media") operate differently and do not arise from presentations of specific educational concepts *per se*. Rather, in this case, interactive media provide tools that can facilitate a child's own creativity or learning in a broad array of subject areas. For example, at various times, Druin and her colleagues have developed an authoring tool that allows children to create presentations on any topic, and a digital library that provides access to online e-books about assorted subjects (e.g., Druin et al., 1999; Druin, Weeks, Massey, & Bederson, 2007). We will consider both types of learning below.

Indeed, the distinction between learning from and with interactive media represents only one aspect of the sheer diversity of interactive media. For example, a broad range of diverse media are included under the category of "interactive media," running the gamut from electronic stuffed toys to video games to cell phone applications to computer-based software applications for classroom use. Moreover, even within a given interactive medium, digital technology continues to evolve with meteoric speed, so that (for instance) the term "computer game" could refer either to today's massively multiplayer online games or to the simple educational games that were designed to be played on 64K home computers in the 1980s. Third, the design of some interactive media products for children has been grounded firmly in educational or developmental principles (e.g., Strommen & Alexander, 1999), whereas others have been guided by little more than the gut instincts of their designers. However, despite these challenges, many commonalities do exist across different forms of interactive media, allowing broad conclusions to be drawn—and to be applied to other forms of interactive media in the future.

The educational value of some forms of interactive media seems almost self-evident. For example, word processing software certainly has the potential to facilitate children's writing, just as a pencil and paper might. Emergent online platforms such as blogs (i.e. online diaries) and video sites such as YouTube offer new opportunities to stimulate literacy and disseminate the products of children's creativity, although I am not yet aware of any empirical research to gauge the educational impact of engaging in such activities.

Some scholars have argued that, by their very nature, computer games provide a compelling context for children's learning (e.g., Gee, 2003; Jenkins, 2002; Papert, 1998). Interactive games can motivate children to learn via features such as appealing activities or the inherent game-like challenge to achieve goals. Moreover, they can continually challenge children by adjusting their level of difficulty to match children's level of knowledge and/or skill, thus engaging children in what Papert has referred to as educationally rich "hard fun." Games can stimulate spatial perception, dexterity, and eye-hand coordination. They can provide opportunities for situated learning of substantive content, practicing problem-solving skills, and self-monitoring of one's own performance and understanding. (For expanded discussions of these sorts of issues, see, e.g., Gee, 2003; Lieberman, 2006.) As in the case of television, of course, the content of the game is of key importance—there is a vast difference between a social studies game such as *Making History* and a violent entertainment game such as *Mortal Kombat*—but the very format of a challenging game can engage children in ways that have the potential to promote learning.

Empirical Studies

Beyond the conceptual arguments discussed above, several studies have evaluated the impact of children's use of educational interactive media. To date, only some of these studies have employed tightly controlled experimental designs, and interactive media have not yet been the subject of the sorts of years-long longitudinal research conducted for television series such as *Sesame Street*. Nevertheless, the existing studies provide evidence of immediate educational benefits in various subject areas.

Literacy

Research has shown that interactive media can support several aspects of children's learning to read (e.g., Reinking, 2005). On one level, a series of studies by Olson, Wise, and their colleagues demonstrated that interactive media can support children's decoding—that is, their ability to identify written words and the correspondence between written letters and their sounds. These studies determined that synthetic speech could support emergent readers' recognition of targeted words as well as spoken language (Olson, Foltz, & Wise, 1986), that computer-based audio feedback accelerated children's progress beyond that of a control group (Wise et al., 1989), and that children who came to the software with an existing level of phonemic awareness benefited more than children who did not (Olson & Wise, 1992). Similarly, McKenna, Reinking, and Bradley (2003) had kindergarteners and first graders read online versions of popular children's books, in which children could click on a word to hear phonics analogies (e.g., comparing *fix* to *six*). They found that children who already had some awareness of the correspondence between sounds and symbols showed an increase in their reading of sight words, whereas children who had not yet reached that stage did not show a meaningful change.

Interactive media also have been found to support children's vocabulary knowledge. For example, Miller and Gildea (1987) showed fifth graders segments from the film *Raiders of the Lost Ark*, and then presented written computer-based text descriptions of the movie scenes; children could click on words to see definitions, sample usage, or video illustrating the words' meaning. They found that children who used this software recognized more meanings of the targeted words and used them more appropriately. Along similar lines, children who engaged in a set of interactive and offline activities centered on the film *Young Sherlock Holmes* spontaneously used targeted vocabulary more than a control group did, and also exhibited better story comprehension and use of historical information to draw inferences (Kinzer & Risko, 1988).

Apart from supplying support for basic reading skills, interactive media can also provide texts for children to read and tools to locate those texts. Druin et al. (2007) reported case studies of children from four countries as they used an online library of nearly 2,000 children's books in 39 languages. Because this was not an experimental study and only a relatively small number of children participated, the data must be interpreted with caution. Nevertheless, the researchers found that the children using the digital library continued to value physical books and libraries, but also increased the variety of books they read online, showed interest in exploring different cultures, and became more motivated to read (although they were inclined to read shorter books online than offline).

Interactive media can stimulate children's writing as well. Jenkins (2006) reported a case study of a 13-year-old who, inspired by her love of the *Harry Potter* books, decided to promote literacy by founding an online "school newspaper" for the fictional Hogwarts school. Within one year, the online newspaper had grown to a staff of 102 children from around the world. The site provided a vehicle for children to submit and evaluate each other's fictional "news articles" and fan fiction stories about the characters of *Harry Potter*. These were rich literacy experiences for both the children who wrote the submissions and those who read and commented on them, with some submissions as long as 50,000 words.

Taken together, then, the preceding research studies and case studies suggest that interactive media have the potential to make multifaceted contributions to children's literacy, by supporting decoding skills and vocabulary acquisition, providing access to a wide variety of reading material, and providing opportunities for children to create their own written material and share it with others.

Mathematics

As in the case of literacy, interactive media have been found to promote positive outcomes for mathematics education among adult and child learners alike. (For a review that includes outcomes for adult learners, see Atkinson, 2005.) For example, one study compared elementary school children's performance in solving addition and subtraction number sentences (i.e., equations) with or without the support of animated graphics. In one version of the software, the number sentences were presented alone; in another, they were accompanied by animations of a bunny that moved along a number line. The researchers found that, in difficult problems, children who saw the animations demonstrated significantly greater pretest-posttest gains than the other children did.

Still, it is noteworthy that no such difference was found for the easier items, and that a second experiment by the same researchers found that the animations were of greater benefit to children of high spatial ability than to children with low spatial ability

(Moreno & Mayer, 1999). Thus, parallel to literacy research that found greater impact for early readers who were stronger in phonemic awareness (Olson & Wise, 1992), Moreno and Mayer's study illustrates the point that the impact of a given piece of interactive media may not be the same for all users under all circumstances. Even if the interactive activity is sufficiently well designed to produce significant outcomes, these outcomes may be moderated by features of both the educational content (e.g., difficulty) and the pre-existing skills and knowledge that the user brings to the screen.

Science

Building upon the preceding point, research on science-based interactive media suggests that observed outcomes can also depend on the match between the on-screen material and the outcome measures. In a study conducted in Turkey, eighth-grade science students learned about physical and chemical changes via either standard lectures or software that allowed them to simultaneously view presentations at the macroscopic level (videos of experiments), symbolic level (chemical equations), and molecular level (molecular drawings and simple animations). Posttest results indicated that, if the subsequent test items employed molecular representations (similar to those used in the software), children who used the software performed better than other children. In addition, they also displayed more particulate representations and greater conceptual accuracy (Ardac & Akaygun, 2004).

Similarly, Kozma (2000) presented older students with chemistry software that portrayed an experiment involving gas-phase equilibrium. As the phenomenon progressed, it was presented in three ways, via three windows; one window presented video, a second showed nanoscale animation, and a third plotted data on a graph. Each student saw one of the three windows (or all three). Kozma found that students who saw the animation performed best on subsequent test items that concerned the dynamic nature of gas-phase equilibrium, whereas those who saw the graph performed best on items regarding relative pressure. Thus, it seems likely that each aspect of the process lent itself best to one form of representation or another, so the most relevant representation carried the greatest educational strength. It is interesting to note that students who saw all three windows did not outperform the other groups, perhaps because the three continual streams of information were more than students could process and comprehend simultaneously.

Therefore, as these studies of science, literacy, and mathematics indicate, there is no one "best" way to design educational software (or, indeed, any form of educational media). The effectiveness of a piece of educational media depends on the match between characteristics of the user, the media product, and the content that is conveyed. I will return to this point in the section on "Theoretical Mechanisms" below.

Social Studies

Most (although not all) research within the realm of social studies has consisted of case studies that cannot definitively establish causality. However, the existing research has suggested impact on several aspects of children's understanding of history and current events, with several different age groups.

In the early grades, one challenge for history education is that young children often have difficulty conceptualizing the scope of time that separates events in "the past"; in their minds, there is little difference between ten, one hundred, and even one thousand years ago. In an attempt to overcome this misconception, Masterman and Rogers (2002) developed a computer-based activity in which children traveled along a road map timeline; along the way, they found text, photos, video, and audio clips about events in British history. The children used this material to work on several sequencing tasks, such as unscrambling diary pages and spotting anachronisms. Despite young children's prevalent misconceptions about time, these activities seemed to facilitate reasoning about time among five pairs of 6- and 7-year-olds. Supported by the software, the pairs of children sequenced events correctly and engaged in lively debate over anachronisms.

Among high school students, history teacher David McDivitt (2006) conducted a semi-experimental study regarding 110 students' understanding of European history prior to World War II. Some classes received standard classroom sessions, while other classes learned through classroom discussions that centered on playing the video game *Making History*, in which players take leadership of a country between 1938 and 1945. The data were not analyzed through formal inferential statistics, so we cannot be certain that differences between the classes are significant beyond chance. Nevertheless, they suggest some considerable differences between the groups; for example, 90% of those who played the game (vs. 55% of non-players) could explain the meaning of the Munich conference of 1938, and 67% could explain the reasons for the start of World War II (vs. 35% of non-players).

Finally, like the case studies of *Harry Potter* fan fiction reported by Jenkins (2006), interactive media can also stimulate children's writing about current events. A Canadian Broadcasting Company Web site called Outburst was designed to provide opportunities for 8- to 12-year-olds to submit written opinions about news stories and current events. In fact, many children took advantage of the opportunity. Antle (2004) reported that, in the space of a single month, 250 children submitted opinions through the site. A content analysis of 36 of these submissions suggested that the site provided a vehicle for children's emotional and personal expression, as well as their empathy or exploration of the impact of the event on the people involved.

THEORETICAL MECHANISMS

Having established *that* children learn from educational media, the next question one might ask is *how* they learn. That is, what cognitive mechanisms are responsible for children's processing of and learning from such media? This section reviews four such theoretical approaches. The first typically has been applied to learning from interactive multimedia, whereas the others describe aspects of children's processing of educational television. Yet, although each theory was posited initially with regard to a particular medium, all have the potential to apply to other electronic media as well. Together, they span processing of educational media from the micro level of encoding and processing, through comprehension, transfer of learning, and ultimately, the long-term benefits of educational media.

Multimedia: The Cognitive Theory of Multimedia Learning

The cognitive theory of multimedia learning (CTML; e.g., Mayer, 2001, 2003; Moreno, 2006) is intended to describe the processing by which users encode and learn from multimedia. The CTML has its roots in three assumptions that grow out of the research literature in cognitive psychology: that humans take in visual and auditory information through two separate information-processing channels, that each channel has a limited capacity for processing information at any given time, and that active learning entails carrying out a coordinated set of cognitive processes during learning. Since multimedia presentations typically present information via more than one modality (e.g., visual images and auditory narration, or on-screen text and animated images), the model tracks the processing of elements of information through the visual and auditory channels as they make their way through the three classic cognitive structures of cognition and memory: sensory memory (responsible for the initial encoding of external stimuli), working memory (in which active processing of information occurs), and long-term memory (where information is stored beyond a matter of moments). The CTML posits that, when a user engages with an instructional message via multimedia, bits of visual and auditory information are encoded and processed separately, to yield a pictorial mental model of the visual information and a verbal mental model of the auditory information. These two models are then integrated into a single representation in which corresponding elements of the pictorial and verbal models are mapped onto each other (see Figure 19.1).

Under this model, an effective piece of educational software must be clear and well-organized, with little extraneous information. If the software includes too much extraneous material (e.g., unnecessary animation, text, graphics, or music), or requires users to engage in too much extraneous cognitive processing, then the demands will exceed the limited capacity of working memory, and the material will not be well learned (or, perhaps, even well understood).

Comprehension of Educational Content: The Capacity Model

Although initially developed in the context of educational television rather than interactive multimedia, the *capacity model* (Fisch, 2000, 2004) shares several features with Mayer's CTML—particularly its roots in cognitive psychology and the limited capacity of working memory. Several studies have demonstrated that, as in the case of other complex stimuli, viewers' comprehension of television involves processing that draws on the limited capacity of working memory (Armstrong & Greenberg, 1990; Beentjes & van der Voort, 1993; Lang, Geiger, Strickwerda, & Sumner, 1993; Lorch & Castle, 1997; Meadowcroft & Reeves, 1989; Thorson, Reeves, & Schleuder, 1985).

Like the CTML, the capacity model argues that the limited capacity of working memory poses challenges for viewers of educational television programs. However, whereas the CTML focuses on challenges stemming from the need to process both visual and auditory information (as well as information that is either intrinsic or extrinsic to the lesson being taught), the capacity model focuses on challenges that stem from the fact that educational television programs typically present narrative content and educational content simultaneously. For example, consider the example of a program about a boy who wants to join a band (narrative content) and, in the process, learns how different musical instruments create sound through vibration (educational content). The capacity model proposes that comprehension of educational content depends, not only on the cognitive demands of processing the educational content itself, but also on the demands presented by the narrative in which it is embedded. In addition, the model argues that comprehension is affected by *distance*, that is, the degree to which the educational content is integral or tangential to the narrative (see Figure 19.2). To best understand the notion of distance, imagine a television mystery in which the hero suddenly stops to give a lesson on mathematical rate-time-distance problems.

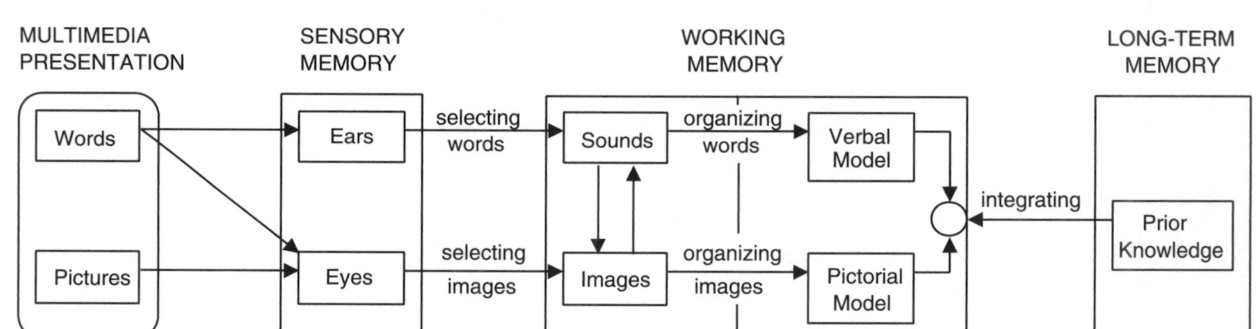

Figure 19.1 Cognitive Theory of Multimedia Learning (after Mayer, 2003).

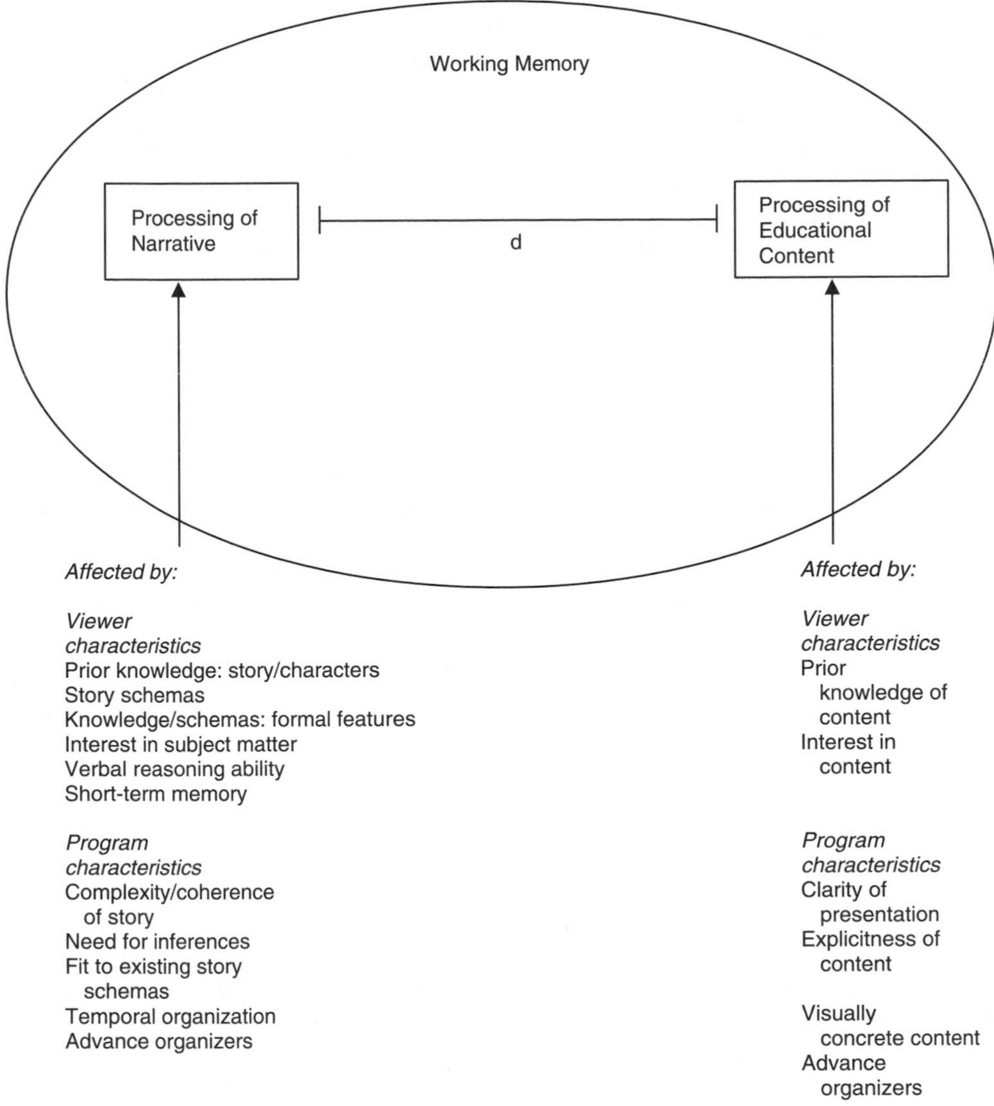

Figure 19.2 Theoretical Construct Described by the Capacity Model, with Factors that Determine the Resource Demands for Comprehending Narrative and Educational Content (after Fisch, 2004).

If the mathematical content is not directly relevant to the mystery, it would be tangential to the narrative and distance would be large. Conversely, if the hero uses the rate-time-distance concept to prove that only one suspect was near enough to commit the crime (i.e., if it provides the key clue to solve the mystery), then the mathematical content is integral to the narrative and distance would be small.

According to the capacity model, if distance is large, the mental resources needed for comprehension are generally devoted primarily to the narrative; less resources are available for processing the educational content. However, if the educational content is integral to the narrative, then the two complement, rather than compete with, each other; the same processing that permits comprehension of the narrative simultaneously contributes to comprehension of the educational content. Thus, comprehension of educational content typically would be stronger under any of the following conditions: (1) when the processing demands of the narrative are relatively small (e.g., because few inferences are needed to understand the story or the viewer's language skills are sufficiently sophisticated to follow the narrative easily; see Figure 19.2 and Fisch, 2004, for a full list of contributing factors), (2) when the processing demands of the educational content are small (e.g., because it is presented clearly or the viewer has some knowledge of the subject already), or (3) when distance is small. The model is consistent with a large body of existing literature on children's comprehension of television, but at the time of this writing, it has yet to be tested for predictive validity in new research.

Transfer of Learning

Comprehension—and even learning—of the educational content in a television program does not guarantee that viewers also will be able to apply the material successfully in new problems or situations. Recall, for example, Goodman et al.'s (1993) finding significant differences between *Cro* viewers' and nonviewers' understanding of the science content presented, but not in extension to new problems. Actually, this phenomenon is not exclusive to educational television; some researchers have noted that it is relatively rare to find transfer of learning for even classroom learning (e.g., Detterman & Sternberg, 1993). Yet, some studies have found evidence of transfer from educational television, such as significant effects on children's experimentation and problem solving in contexts different than those shown in the television programs (e.g., Hall et al., 1990a, 1990b; Mulliken & Bryant, 1999; Rockman Et Al., 1996).

Why, then, has educational television been successful in producing transfer of learning in some studies but not in others? Speaking in terms of education more generally, Bransford, Brown, and Cocking (1999) have argued that successful transfer requires several key elements, including: a rich understanding of the subject matter that has been presented, a representation of the knowledge that is abstracted beyond its original context, and a match between the representation of the knowledge and the new situation in which it might be applied. Yet, applying these principles to educational television would almost seem to produce a contradiction under the capacity model discussed above (Fisch, 2000): According to the capacity model, one of the chief ways to enrich comprehension of educational content (as is required for transfer) is to maintain a small distance between narrative and educational content. However, content that is overly tied to a narrative context may not be represented abstractly enough to transfer to new problems in different contexts (e.g., Cognition and Technology Group at Vanderbilt, 1997).

As I have proposed elsewhere (Fisch, 2004), the optimal solution may lie in maintaining a small distance between narrative and educational content, but also presenting the same educational content several times in several different narrative contexts (a principle demonstrated outside the realm of television by researchers such as Gick & Holyoak, 1983). Thus, for example, Goodman et al. (1993) found significant effects on understanding but not transfer for *Cro*, in which each discrete science concept was presented in only one episode and one narrative context. However, Hall et al. (1990a, 1990b) found significant transfer of the problem-solving heuristics modeled in *Square One TV*, where the same heuristic (e.g., considering probability) was embedded in several different contexts (e.g., a game show in which contestants used probability to play strategically, a music video about choosing the right key to escape a haunted house). These multiple treatments of the same underlying content may have contributed toward a more abstract representation of the mathematical concepts involved and also may have encouraged a sense of these concepts as applicable in a broader variety of situations, thus encouraging transfer.

Long-term Effects: The Early Learning Model

The above conceptions of comprehension and transfer are useful in considering the relatively immediate effects of educational television, but they are not sufficient to explain longer-term effects, particularly if the eventual outcomes bear little resemblance to the educational content that was presented on television. For example, when preschool viewing of *Sesame Street* was found to predict grade-point averages in high school (Anderson et al., 1998; Huston et al., 2001), it was unlikely that students were applying the material they had learned from *Sesame Street* directly to their high school classes.

To explain such effects, Huston et al. proposed the *early learning model*. Under this model, three facets of early development are proposed as pathways by which long-term effects can result: (1) learning pre-academic skills, particularly related to language and literacy, (2) developing motivation and interest, and (3) acquiring behavioral patterns of attentiveness, concentration, nonaggressiveness, and absence of restlessness or distractibility. (Note that the latter point runs directly counter to claims by Healy [1990] and others that *Sesame Street* reduces children's attention spans.) These factors contribute to early success in school, which then plays a significant role in determining children's long-term academic trajectories; children who demonstrate good skills early on are likely to be placed in higher ability groups, to be perceived as more competent by teachers, to receive more attention, to feel successful, and to be motivated to do well (Entwistle, Alexander, & Olson, 1997). In addition, these early successes may also affect the types of activities in which children choose to engage; for example, good readers may choose to read more on their own. Each of these outcomes can then result in further success over time. In this way, the model posits a cascading effect in which early exposure to educational television (or, by extension, any educational media) leads to early academic success, which in turn, contributes to a long-term trajectory of success that can endure for years.

CONCLUSION

Perhaps the broadest conclusion to be drawn from this review is that educational media work. Thoughtfully crafted educational media can hold many significant benefits for children of various ages. Moreover, the benefits of such media can last for years.

This is not to say, of course, that all media are beneficial for children, any more than it would be reasonable to claim that all media are bad for them. Indeed, Wright et al.'s (2001) three-year longitudinal study of the impact of *Sesame Street* found not only that exposure to *Sesame Street* was associated with positive effects on literacy and school readiness, but also that preschool viewing of commercial entertainment cartoons sometimes had significant negative effects on the same outcome measures. Clearly, the critical factor is not the medium itself, but the content it carries.

Along with the content of media, we must also consider the context in which they are viewed and in which their effects are observed. For example, numerous studies have shown that children's learning from educational television can be increased through activities and follow-up discussion with parents or teachers (e.g., Reiser, Tessmer, & Phelps, 1984; Reiser, Williamson, & Suzuki, 1988; Salomon, 1977; Singer & Singer, 1995). Indeed, Huston et al.'s (2001) early learning model highlights the point that offline experiences play an important role, not only while using media, but also at the time when effects subsequently appear. Educational advantages provided by exposure to educational media can combine with other factors, such as positive feedback from teachers or engagement in other informal education activities, to result in effects that are stronger and more enduring than the effects of simple exposure to media.

To that end, we might also consider the potential synergy that might arise from joint use of several different forms of educational media themselves. Today, it is common for an educational media project to encompass multiple media, such as an educational television series with an accompanying Web site. For example, in contrast to its beginnings in 1969, today's *Sesame Street* includes not only a television series, but also books, *Sesame Street Magazine*, the www.sesamestreet.com Web site, traditional and electronic toys, hands-on activities for outreach settings, broadcasts to cell phones, and so on. Often, multiple media are employed with the assumption that they will yield greater educational benefits than would result from any one medium alone, perhaps because the different treatments of similar educational content reinforce each other or because they provide multiple points of entry for users with diverse learning styles. At the time of this writing, this assumption has not yet been tested empirically, but my colleagues and I have recently embarked on a program of naturalistic and experimental research to investigate this issue.

Clearly, given the complex interactions at work among all of the relevant variables, there is a long way to go before the effects of educational media will be understood completely. However, even in striving toward a distant goal of understanding effects, we must not lose sight of a more immediate point: Effective educational media products already exist. The greatest value of research in this area does not lie in theoretical models, but in the concrete benefits that such media have already been shown to hold for our children.

Note

1. Note that the AAP intentionally issued a very conservative recommendation because virtually no research with this age group was available at the time.

References

American Academy of Pediatrics. (1997). *Media Matters: A national media education campaign*. Elk Grove Village, IL: Author.

American Academy of Pediatrics. (2001). Children, adolescents, and television. *Pediatrics, 107*, 423–426.

Anderson, D. R., Bryant, J., Wilder, A., Santomero, A., Williams, M., & Crawley, A. M. (2000). Researching *Blue's Clues*: Viewing behavior and impact. *Media Psychology, 2*, 179–194.

Anderson, D. N., Huston, A. C., Wright, J. C., & Collins, P. A. (1998). *Sesame Street* and educational television for children. In R. G. Noll & M. E. Price (Eds.), *A communications cornucopia: Markle Foundation essays on information policy* (pp. 279–296). Washington, DC: Brookings Institution Press.

Antle, A. (2004). Supporting children's online emotional expression and exploration in online environments. In A. Druin, J. P. Hourcade, & S. Kollett (Eds.), *Interaction Design and Children conference proceedings: Building a community* (pp. 97–104). New York: Association for Computing Machinery.

Ardac, D., & Akaygun, S. (2004). Effectiveness of multimedia-based instruction that emphasizes molecular representations on students' understanding of chemical change. *Journal of Research in Science Teaching, 41*(4), 317–337.

Armstrong, G. B., & Greenberg, B. S. (1990). Background television as an inhibitor of cognitive processing. *Human Communication Research, 16*, 355–386.

Atkin, C. K., & Gantz, W. (1978). Television news and the child audience. *Public Opinion Quarterly, 42*, 183–198.

Atkinson, R. K. (2005). Multimedia learning of mathematics. In R. E. Mayer (Ed.), *The Cambridge handbook of multimedia learning* (pp. 393–409). New York: Cambridge University Press.

Bachen, C. M. (1998). *Channel One* and the education of American youths. *Annals of the American Academy of Political and Social Science, 557*, 132–146.

Ball, S., & Bogatz, G. A. (1970). *The first year of Sesame Street: An evaluation*. Princeton, NJ: Educational Testing Service.

Ball, S., & Bogatz, G. A. (1973). *Reading with television: An evaluation of The Electric Company*. Princeton, NJ: Educational Testing Service.

Ball, S., Bogatz, G. A., Karazow, K. M., & Rubin, D. B. (1974). *Reading with television: A follow-up evaluation of The Electric Company*. Princeton, NJ: Educational Testing Service.

Barr, R., & Hayne, H. (1999). Developmental changes in imitation from television during infancy. *Child Development, 70*, 1067–1081.

Beck, J., & Murack, J. (2004). *Peep and the Big Wide World, Season One Evaluation: Television Series Final Report*. Cambridge, MA: Goodman Research Group.

Beentjes, J. W. J., & van der Voort, T. H. A. (1993). Television viewing versus reading: Mental effort, retention, and inferential learning. *Communication Education, 42*, 191–205.

Block, C., Guth, G. J. A., & Austin, S. (1993). *Galaxy Classroom project evaluation: Language arts, grades 3–5, final report*. San Francisco: Far West Laboratory for Educational Research and Development.

Bogatz, G. A., & Ball, S. (1971). *The second year of Sesame Street*: A continuing evaluation. Princeton, NJ: Educational Testing Service.

Brand, J. E., & Greenberg, B. S. (1994). Commercials in the classroom: The impact of *Channel One* advertising. *Journal of Advertising Research, 34*, 18–27.

Bransford, J. D., Brown, A. L., & Cocking, R. R. (Eds.) (1999). *How people learn: Brain, mind, experience, and school*. Washington, DC: National Academy Press.

Brederode-Santos, M. E. (1993). *Learning with television: The secret of Rua Sésamo*. [English translation of Portuguese, Brederode-Santos, M. E. (1991). *Com a Televiso o Segredo da Rua Sésamo*. Lisbon: TV Guia Editora.] Unpublished research report.

Bruner, O., & Bruner, K. (2006). *Playstation nation: Protect your child from video game addiction*. Nashville, TN: Center Street.

Bryant, J., McCollum, J., Ralstin, L., Raney, A., McGavin, L., Miron, D., Maxwell, M., Venugopalan, G., Thopson, S., DeWitt, D., & Lewis, K. (1997). *Effects of two years' viewing of Allegra's Window and Gullah Gullah Island*. Tuscaloosa, AL: Institute for Communication Research, University of Alabama.

Bryant, J., Mulliken, L., Maxwell, M., Mundorf, N., Mundorf, J., Wilson, B., Smith, S., McCollum, J., & Owens, J. W. (1999). *Effects of two years' viewing of Blue's Clues*. Tuscaloosa: Institute for Communication Research, University of Alabama.

Calvert, S. L. (1995). *Impact of televised songs on children's and young adults' memory of verbally-presented content*. Unpublished manuscript, Department of Psychology, Georgetown University, Washington, DC.

Calvert, S. L., & Pfordresher, P. Q. (1994, August). Impact of a televised song on students' memory of information. Poster presented at the annual meeting of the American Psychological Association, Los Angeles, CA.

Calvert, S. L., Rigaud, E., & Mazella, J. (1991). Presentational features for students' recall of televised educational content. Poster presented at the biennial meeting of the Society for Research in Child Development, Seattle, WA.

Calvert, S. L., & Tart, M. (1993). Song versus verbal forms for very-long-term, long-term, and short-term verbatim recall. *Journal of Applied Developmental Psychology, 14*, 245–260.

Cambre, M. A., & Fernie, D. (1985). *Formative evaluation of Season IV, 3-2-1 Contact*: Assessing the appeal of four weeks of educational television programs and their influence on children's science comprehension and science interest. New York: Children's Television Workshop.

Children's Television Workshop. (1994). *Learning from Ghostwriter: Strategies and outcomes.* New York: Author.

Clifford, B. R., Gunter, B., & McAleer, J. (1995). *Television and children: Program evaluation, comprehension, and impact*. Hillsdale, NJ: Erlbaum.

Cognition and Technology Group at Vanderbilt. (1997). *The Jasper Project: Lessons in curriculum, instruction, assessment, and professional development*. Mahwah, NJ: Erlbaum.

Cole, C. F., Richman, B. A., & McCann Brown, S. K. (2001). The world of *Sesame Street* research. In S. M. Fisch & R. T. Truglio (Eds.), *"G" is for "growing": Thirty years of research on children and Sesame Street* (pp. 147–179). Mahwah, NJ: Erlbaum.

Comstock, G., & Paik, H. (1991). *Television and the American child*. New York: Academic Press.

Cook, T. D., Appleton, H., Conner, R. F., Shaffer, A., Tamkin, G., & Weber, S. (1975). *Sesame Street revisited*. New York: Russell Sage Foundation.

Crawley, A. M., Anderson, D. R., Wilder, A., Williams, M., & Santomero, A. (1999). Effects of repeated exposures to a single episode of the television program *Blue's Clues* on the viewing behaviors and comprehension of preschool children. *Journal of Educational Psychology, 91*, 630–637.

Detterman, D. K., & Sternberg, R. J. (Eds.) (1993). *Transfer on trial: Intelligence, cognition, and instruction*. Norwood, NJ: Ablex.

Diaz-Guerrero, R., & Holtzman, W. H. (1974). Learning by televised *Plaza Sésamo* in Mexico. *Journal of Educational Psychology, 66*(5), 632–643.

Diaz-Guerrero, R., Reyes-Lagunes, I., Witzke, D. B., & Holtzman, W. H. (1976). *Plaza Sésamo* in Mexico: An evaluation. *Journal of Communication, 26*, 145–154.

Druin, A., Bederson, B., Boltman, A., Miura, A., Knotts-Callahan, D., & Platt, M. (1999). Children as our technology design partners. In A. Druin (Ed.), *The design of children's technology* (pp. 51–72). San Francisco: Morgan Kaufman.

Druin, A., Weeks, A., Massey, S., & Bederson, B. B. (2007). Children's interests and concerns when using the International Children's Digital Library: A four country case study. Paper presented at the Joint Conference on Digital Libraries, Vancouver, Canada.

Ehman, L. (1995, April). A case study of *Channel One* in the instruction and curriculum of a middle school. Paper presented at the annual meeting of the American Education Research Association, San Francisco, CA.

Entwistle, D. R., Alexander, K. L., & Olson, L. S. (1997). *Children, schools, and inequality*. Boulder, CO: Westview Press.

Fay, A. L., Teasley, S. D., Cheng, B. H., Bachman, K. M., & Schnakenberg, J. H. (1995a). *Children's interest in and their understanding of science and technology: A study of the effects of Cro*. Pittsburgh, PA: University of Pittsburgh and New York: Children's Television Workshop.

Fay, A. L., Yotive, W. M., Fisch, S. M., Teasley, S. D., McCann, S. K., Garner, M. S., Ozaeta, M., Chen, L., & Lambert, M. H. (1995b, August). The impact of *Cro* on children's interest in and understanding of technology. In Fisch, S. M. (Chair; 1995, August) *Science on Saturday morning: The Children's Television Act and the role of Cro*. Symposium presented at the annual meeting of the American Psychological Association, New York, NY.

Fisch, S. M. (2000). A capacity model of children's comprehension of educational content on television. *Media Psychology, 2*(1), 63–91.

Fisch, S. M. (2003). *The impact of Cyberchase on children's mathematical problem solving: Cyberchase season 2 summative study*. Teaneck, NJ: MediaKidz Research & Consulting.

Fisch, S. M. (2004). *Children's learning from educational television: Sesame Street and beyond*. Mahwah, NJ: Erlbaum.

Fisch, S. M. (2005, April). Transfer of learning from educational television: Near and far transfer from *Cyberchase*. Poster session presented at the biennial meeting of the Society for Research in Child Development, Atlanta, GA.

Fisch, S. M., Goodman, I. F., McCann, S. K., Rylander, K., & Ross, S. (1995, April). The impact of informal science education: *Cro* and children's understanding of technology. Poster presented at the 61st annual meeting of the Society for Research in Child Development, Indianapolis, IN.

Fisch, S. M., Kirkorian, H., & Anderson, D. R. (2005). Transfer of learning in informal education: The case of television. In J. P. Mestre (Ed.), *Transfer of learning from a modern multidisciplinary perspective* (pp. 371–393). Greenwich, CT: Information Age Publishing.

Fisch, S. M., & Truglio, R. T. (Eds.). (2001). *"G" is for "growing": Thirty years of research on children and Sesame Street* (pp. 115–130). Mahwah, NJ: Erlbaum.

Gee, J. P. (2003). *What video games have to teach us about learning and literacy*. New York: Palgrave-MacMillan.

Gick, M. L., & Holyoak, K. J. (1983). Schema induction and analogical transfer. *Cognitive Psychology, 15*, 1–38.

Goodman, I. F., Rylander, K., & Ross, S. (1993). *Cro Season I summative evaluation*. Cambridge, MA: Sierra Research Associates.

Greenberg, B. S., & Brand, J. E. (1993). Television news and advertising in school: The "Channel One" controversy. *Journal of Communication, 43*, 143–151.

Greenberg, B. S., & Gantz, W. (1976). Public television and taboo topics: The impact of *VD Blues*. *Public Telecommunications Review, 4*(1), 56–59.

Hall, E. R., Esty, E. T., & Fisch, S. M. (1990a). Television and children's problem-solving behavior: A synopsis of an evaluation of the effects of *Square One TV*. *Journal of Mathematical Behavior, 9*, 161–174.

Hall, E. R., Fisch, S. M., Esty, E. T., Debold, E., Miller, B. A., Bennett, D. T., & Solan, S. V. (1990b). *Children's Problem-Solving Behavior and their Attitudes toward Mathematics: A Study of the Effects of Square One TV* (Vols. 1–5). New York: Children's Television Workshop.

Harvey, F. A., Quiroga, B., Crane, V., & Bottoms, C. L. (1976). *Evaluation of eight Infinity Factory programs*. Newton, MA: Education Development Center.

Healy, J. M. (1990). *Endangered minds: Why our children don't think*. New York: Simon & Schuster.

Huston, A. C., Anderson, D. R., Wright, J. C., Linebarger, D. L., & Schmitt, K. L. (2001). *Sesame Street* viewers as adolescents: The recontact study. In S. M. Fische & R. T. Truglio (Eds.), *"G" is for "growing": Thirty years of research on children and Sesame Street* (pp. 131–144). Mahwah, NJ: Erlbaum.

Jenkins, H. (2002, 29 March). Game theory: How should we teach kids Newtonian physics? Simple. Play computer games. *Technology Review*. Retrieved September 11, 2007 from http://www.techreview.com/articles/02/03/wo_jenkins032902.asp.

Jenkins, H. (2006). *Convergence culture: Where old and new media collide*. New York: NYU Press.

John, D. R. (1999). Consumer socialization of children: A retrospective look at 25 years of research. *Journal of Consumer Research, 26*, 183–213.

Johnston, J. (1980). *An exploratory study of the effects of viewing the first season of 3-2-1 Contact*. New York: Children's Television Workshop.

Johnston, J., & Brzezinski, E. (1992). *Taking the measure of Channel One: The first year*. Ann Arbor: Institute for Social Research, University of Michigan.

Johnston, J., & Brzezinski, E. (1994). *Executive summary, Channel One: A three year perspective*. Ann Arbor: Institute for Social Research, University of Michigan.

Johnston, J., Brzezinski, E., & Anderman, E. M. (1994). *Taking the measure of Channel One: A three year perspective*. Ann Arbor: Institute for Social Research, University of Michigan.

Johnston, J., & Luker, R. (1983). *The "Eriksson Study": An exploratory study of viewing two weeks of the second season of 3-2-1 Contact*. New York: Children's Television Workshop.

Kinzer, C. K., & Risko, V. J. (1988). Macrocontexts to facilitate learning. Paper presented at the 33rd annual conference of the International Reading Association, Toronto, Ontario.

Knupfer, N., & Hayes, P. (1994). The effects of the *Channel One* broadcast on students' knowledge of current events. In A. DeVaney (Ed.), *Watching Channel One: The convergence of students, technology, and private business* (pp. 42–60). Albany: State University of New York Press.

Kozma, R. B. (2000). The use of multiple representations and the social construction of understanding in chemistry. In M. Jacobson & R. Kozma (Eds.), *Innovations in science and mathematics education: Advanced designs for technologies of learning* (pp. 11–46). Mahwah, NJ: Erlbaum.

KRC Research & Consulting. (1994). *An evaluative assessment of the Ghostwriter project*. New York: Author.

Kunkel, D. (2001). Children and television advertising. In D. G. Singer & J. L. Singer (Eds.), *Handbook of children and the media* (pp. 375–393). Thousand Oaks, CA: Sage.

Lampert, M. (1985). Mathematics learning in context: *The Voyage of the Mimi*. *Journal of Mathematical Behavior*, *4*, 157–167.

Lang, A., Geiger, S., Strickwerda, M., & Sumner, J. (1993). The effects of related and unrelated cuts on television viewers' attention, processing capacity, and memory. *Communication Research*, *20*, 4–29.

Leitner, R. K. (1991). *Comparing the effects on reading comprehension of educational video, direct experience, and print*. Unpublished doctoral thesis, University of San Francisco, CA.

Levin, T., Sabar, N., & Libman, Z. (1991). Achievements and attitudinal patterns of boys and girls in science. *Journal of Research in Science Teaching*, *28*, 315–328.

Lieberman, D. (1999). The researcher's role in the design of children's media and technology. In A. Druin (Ed.), *The design of children's technology* (pp. 73–97). San Francisco: Morgan Kaufman.

Lieberman, D. A. (2001). Management of chronic pediatric diseases with interactive health games: Theory and research findings. *Journal of Ambulatory Care Management*, *24*(1), 26–38.

Lieberman, D. A. (2006). What can we learn from playing interactive games? In P. Vorderer & J. Bryant (Eds.), *Playing video games: Motives, responses, and consequences* (pp. 379–398). Mahwah, NJ: Erlbaum.

Linebarger, D. L. (2000). *Summative evaluation of Between the Lions: A final report to WGBH Educational Foundation*. Kansas City, KS: Juniper Gardens Children's Project, University of Kansas.

Linebarger, D. L. (2001). *Summative evaluation of Dora the Explorer, Part 1: Learning outcomes*. Kansas City, KS: Media & Technology Projects, ABCD Ventures, Inc.

Lorch, E. P., & Castle, V. J. (1997). Preschool children's attention to television: Visual attention and probe response times. *Journal of Experimental Child Psychology*, *66*, 111–127.

Lowe, R. K. (2005). Multimedia learning of meteorology. In R. E. Mayer (Ed.), *The Cambridge handbook of multimedia learning* (pp. 429–446). New York: Cambridge University Press.

Mares, M. L., & Woodard, E. H. (2001). Prosocial effects on children's social interactions. In D. G. Singer & J. L. Singer (Eds.), *Handbook of children and the media* (pp. 183–205). Thousand Oaks, CA: Sage.

Masterman, E., & Rogers, Y. (2002). A framework for designing interactive multimedia to scaffold young children's understanding of historical chronology. *Instructional Science*, *30*, 221–241.

Mayer, R. E. (2001). *Multimedia learning* (pp. 31–48). New York: Cambridge University Press.

Mayer, R. E. (2003). *Learning and instruction*. Upper Saddle River, NJ: Merrill Prentice Hall.

Mayer, R. E. (2005). Cognitive theory of multimedia learning. In R. E. Mayer (Ed.), *The Cambridge handbook of multimedia learning* (pp. 31–48). New York: Cambridge University Press.

McCall, R. B., Parke, R. D., & Kavanaugh, R. D. (1977). Imitation of live and televised models by children one to three years of age. *Monographs of the Society for Research in Child Development*, *42*, 5.

McDivitt, D. (2006). Do gamers score better in school? *Serious Game Source*. Retrieved September 11, 2007 from: http:// seriousgamesource.com/features/feature_051606.php.

McKenna, M. C., Reinking, D., & Bradley, B. A. (2003). The effects of electronic trade books on the decoding growth of beginning readers. In R. M. Joshi, C. K. Leong, & B. L. J. Kaczmarek

(Eds.), *Literacy acquisition: The role of phonology, morphology, and orthography* (pp. 193–202). Amsterdam: IOS Press.

Meadowcroft, J. M., & Reeves, B. (1989). Influence of story schema development on children's attention to television. *Communication Research, 16*, 352–374.

Meltzoff, A. N. (1985). Immediate and deferred imitation in fourteen- and twenty-four month-old infants. *Child Development, 56*, 62–72.

Meltzoff, A. N. (1988). Imitation of televised models by infants. *Child Development, 59*, 1221–1229.

Miller, G. A., & Gildea, P. M. (1987). How children learn words. *Scientific American, 257*(3), 94–99.

Moreno, R. (2006). Learning in high-tech and multimedia environments. *Current Directions in Psychological Science, 15*, 63–67.

Moreno, R., & Mayer, R. E. (1999). Multimedia-supported metaphors for meaning making in mathematics. *Cognition and Instruction, 17*, 215–248.

Mulliken, L., & Bryant, J. A. (1999, May). Effects of curriculum-based television programming on behavioral assessments of flexible thinking and structured and unstructured prosocial play behaviors. Poster presented at the 49th annual conference of the International Communication Association, San Francisco, CA.

Naigles, L. R., & Mayeux, L. (2001). Television as incidental language teacher. In D. G. Singer & J. L. Singer (Eds.), *Handbook of children and the media* (pp. 135–152). Thousand Oaks, CA: Sage.

Naigles, L., Singer, D., Singer, J., Jean-Louis, B., Sells, D., & Rosen, C. (1995). Watching "Barney" affects preschoolers' use of mental state verbs. Paper presented at the annual meeting of the American Psychological Association, New York, NY.

National Council of Teachers of Mathematics (1989). *Curriculum and evaluation standards for school mathematics*. Reston, VA: Author.

Nielsen New Media Services. (1993). *Ghostwriter study, wave II: May, 1993*. Dunedin, FL: Author.

Noble, G., & Creighton, V. M. (1981). *Australia Naturally—Children's reactions*. Armidale, Australia: Author.

Olson, R. K., Foltz, G., & Wise, B. W. (1986). Reading instruction and remediation using voice synthesis in computer interaction. *Proceeding of the Human Factors Society, 2*, 1336–1339.

Olson, R. K., & Wise, B. W. (1992). Reading on the computer with orthographic and speech feedback: An overview of the Colorado Remedial Reading Project. *Reading and Writing: An Interdisciplinary Journal, 4*, 107–144.

Paivio, A. (1971). *Imagery and verbal processes*. New York: Holt.

Palmer, E. L., & Fisch, S. M. (2001). The beginnings of *Sesame Street* research. In S. M. Fische & R. T. Truglio (Eds.), *"G" is for "growing": Thirty years of research on children and Sesame Street* (pp. 3–23). Malwah, NJ: Erlbaum.

Papert, S. (1998, June). Does easy do it?: Children, games, and learning. *Game Developer*, 88.

Peel, T., Rockwell, A., Esty, E., & Gonzer, K. (1987). *Square One Television: The comprehension and problem solving study*. New York: Children's Television Workshop.

Peterman, K. (2006). *Summative Evaluation of FETCH Season I: Executive Summary*. Cambridge, MA: Goodman Research Group.

Postman, N. (1985). *Amusing ourselves to death*. New York: Penguin.

Reinking, D. (2005). Multimedia learning of reading. In R. E. Mayer (Ed.), *The Cambridge handbook of multimedia learning* (pp. 355–374). New York: Cambridge University Press.

Reiser, R. A., Tessmer, M. A., & Phelps, P. C. (1984). Adult-child interaction in children's learning from *Sesame Street*. *Educational Communication and Technology Journal, 32*, 217–223.

Reiser, R. A., Williamson, N., & Suzuki, K. (1988). Using *Sesame Street* to facilitate children's recognition of letters and numbers. *Educational Communication and Technology Journal, 36*, 15–21.

Rice, M. L. (1984). The words of children's television. *Journal of Broadcasting, 28*, 445–461.

Rice, M. L., & Haight, P. L. (1986). "Motherese" of Mr. Rogers: A description of the dialogue of educational television programs. *Journal of Speech and Hearing Disorders, 51*, 282–287.

Rice, M. L., Huston, A. C., Truglio, R., & Wright, J. C. (1990). Words from *Sesame Street*: Learning vocabulary while viewing. *Developmental Psychology*, *26*, 421–428.

Rice, M. L., & Woodsmall, L. (1988). Lessons from television: Children's word learning when viewing. *Child Development*, *59*, 420–429.

Richards, J. I., Wartella, E. A., Morton, C. & Thompson, L. (1998). The growing commercialization of schools: Issues and practices. *Annals of the American Academy of Political and Social Science*, *557*, 148–163.

Roberts, L. (2000). Federal programs to increase children's access to educational technology. *The Future of Children*, *10*(2), 181–185.

Rockman Et Al. (1996). *Evaluation of Bill Nye the Science Guy: Television series and outreach*. San Francisco, CA: Author.

Rockman Et Al. (2003). *DragonflyTV Evaluation Report*. San Francisco, CA: Author.

Rust, L. W. (2001). *Summative evaluation of Dragon Tales: Final report*. Briarcliff Manor, NY: Langbourne Rust Research, Inc.

Sahin, N. (1990, September). Preliminary report on the summative evaluation of the Turkish coproduction of Sesame Street. Paper presented at the International Conference on Adaptations of *Sesame Street*, Amsterdam, The Netherlands.

Salomon, G. (1977). Effects of encouraging Israeli mothers to co-observe *Sesame Street* with their five-year-olds. *Child Development*, *48*, 1146–1151.

Sanders, J. R., & Sonnad, S. R. (1980). *Research on the introduction, use, and impact of Thinkabout: Executive summary*. Bloomington, IN: Agency for Instructional Television.

Schmidt, M. E., Pempek, T. A., Kirkorian, H. L., Lund, A. F. & Anderson, D. R. (in press). The effects of background television on the toy play behavior of very young children. *Child Development*.

Schmitt, K., & Anderson, D. R. (2002). Television and reality: Toddlers' use of information from video to guide behavior. *Media Psychology*, *4*, 51–76.

Singer, D. G., Singer, J. L., Miller, R. H., & Sells, D. J. (1994). *Barney and Friends as education and entertainment: Phase 2, kindergarten sample—Can children learn through kindergarten exposure to Barney and Friends?* New Haven, CT: Yale University Family Television Research and Consultation Center.

Singer, J. L., & Singer, D. G. (1981). *Television, imagination, and aggression: A study of preschoolers*. Hillsdale, NJ: Erlbaum.

Singer, J. L., & Singer, D. G. (1994). *Barney and Friends as education and entertainment: Phase 2—Can children learn through preschool exposure to Barney and Friends?* New Haven, CT: Yale Univerity Family Television Research and Consultation Center.

Singer, J. L., & Singer, D. G. (1995). *Barney and Friends as education and entertainment: Phase 3—A national study: Can children learn through preschool exposure to Barney and Friends?* New Haven, CT: Yale Univerity Family Television Research and Consultation Center.

Singer, J. L., & Singer, D. G. (1998). *Barney & Friends* as entertainment and education: Evaluating the quality and effectiveness of a television series for preschool children. In J. K. Asamen & G. L. Berry (Eds.), *Research paradigms, television, and social behavior* (pp. 305–367). Thousand Oaks, CA: Sage.

Singhal, A., & Rogers, E. M. (1999). *Entertainment-education: A communication strategy for social change*. Mahwah, NJ: Erlbaum.

Strommen, E. F., & Alexander, K. J. (1999, April). Learning from computers with interactive toy characters as learning companions. Poster session presented at the biennial meeting of the Society for Research in Child Development, Albuquerque, NM.

Thorson, E., Reeves, B., & Schleuder, J. (1985). Message complexity and attention to television. *Communication Research*, *12*, 427–454.

Troseth, G. L. (2003). Getting a clear picture: Young children's understanding of a televised image. *Developmental Science*, *6*, 247–253.

Troseth, G. L., & DeLoache, J. (1998). The medium can obscure the message: Understanding the relation between video and reality. *Child Development*, *69*, 950–965.

Troseth, G. L., Saylor, M. M., & Archer, A. H. (2006). Young children's use of video as a source of socially relevant information. *Child Development, 77*, 786–799.

Ulitsa Sezam Department of Research and Content. (1998, November). Preliminary report of summative findings. Report presented to the Children's Television Workshop, New York, NY.

UNICEF. (1996). Executive summary: Summary assessment of *Plaza Sésamo* IV—Mexico. [English translation of Spanish.] Unpublished research report. Mexico City, Mexico: Author.

Wagner, S. (1985). *Comprehensive evaluation of the fourth season of 3-2-1 Contact*. New York: Children's Television Workshop.

Walma van der Molen, J., & van der Voort, T. (1997). Children's recall of television and print news: A media comparison study. *Journal of Educational Psychology, 89*, 82–91.

Walma van der Molen, J., & van der Voort, T. (1998). Children's recall of the news: TV news stories compared with three print versions. *Educational Technology Research and Development, 46*, 39–52.

Walma van der Molen, J., & van der Voort, T. (2000). The impact of television, print, and audio on children's recall of the news: A study of three alternative explanations for the dual-coding hypothesis. *Human Communications Research, 26*, 3–26.

Wartella, E., & Jennings, N. (2001). Hazards and possibilities of commercial TV in the schools. In D. G. Singer & J. L. Singer (Eds.), *Handbook of children and the media* (pp. 557–570). Thousand Oaks, CA: Sage.

Weber, R., Ritterfield, U., & Kostygina, A. (2006). Aggression and violence as effects of playing violent video games? In Vorderer, P., & Bryant, J. (Eds.), *Playing video games: Motives, responses, and consequences* (pp. 347–362). Mahwah, NJ: Erlbaum.

Wilson, B. J., Kunkel, D., Linz, D., Potter, J., Donnerstein, E., Smith, S. L., Blumenthal, E., & Gray, T. (1997). *National television violence study* (Vol. 1). Thousand Oaks, CA: Sage.

Winn, M. (1977). *The Plug-in drug*. New York: Penguin.

Winsten, J. A. (1994). Promoting designated drivers: The Harvard Alcohol Project. *American Journal of Preventive Medicine, 10*(3), 11–14.

Wise, B. W., Olson, R. K., Anstett, M., Andrews, L., Terjak, M., Schnider, V., & Kostuch, J. (1989). Implementing a long-term computerized remedial reading program with synthetic speech feedback: Hardware, software, and real-world issues. *Behavior Research Methods, Instruments, and Computers, 21*, 173–180.

Wood, J. M., & Duke, N. K. (1997). Inside "Reading Rainbow": A spectrum of strategies for promoting literacy. *Language Arts, 74*, 95–106.

Wright, J. C., & Huston, A. C. (1995). *Effects of educational TV viewing of lower income preschoolers on academic skills, school readiness, and school adjustment one to three years later: A report to the Children's Television Workshop*. Lawrence: Center for Research on the Influences of Television on Children, The University of Kansas.

Wright, J. C., Huston, A. C., Scantlin, R., & Kotler, J. (2001). The Early Window project: *Sesame Street* prepares children for school. In S. M. Fisch & R. T. Truglio (Eds.), *"G" is for "growing": Thirty years of research on children and Sesame Street* (pp. 97–114). Mahwah, NJ: Erlbaum.

Zero to Three/National Center for Clinical Infant Programs. (1992). *Heart Start: The emotional foundations of school readiness*. Arlington, VA: Author.

Zill, N. (2001). Does *Sesame Street* enhance school readiness?: Evidence from a national survey of children. In S. M. Fisch & R. T. Truglio (Eds.), *"G" is for "growing": Thirty years of research on children and Sesame Street* (pp. 115–130). Mahwah, NJ: Erlbaum.

Zill, N., Davies, E., & Daly, M. (1994). *Viewing of Sesame Street* by preschool children and its relationship to school readiness: Report prepared for the Children's Television Workshop. Rockville, MD: Westat, Inc.

Zimmerman, F. J., Christakis, D. A., & Meltzoff, A. N. (2007). Associations between media viewing and language development in children under age 2 years. *Journal of Pediatrics, 151*, 364–368.

20

PUBLIC COMMUNICATION CAMPAIGNS

Theoretical Principles and Practical Applications

Ronald E. Rice
University of California at Santa Barbara

Charles K. Atkin
Michigan State University

Public communication campaigns can be broadly defined as (1) purposive attempts (2) to inform, persuade, or motivate behavior changes (3) in a relatively well-defined and large audience, (4) generally for noncommercial benefits to the individuals and/or society at large, (5) typically within a given time period, (6) by means of organized communication activities involving mass media, and (7) often complemented by interpersonal support (adapted and expanded from Rogers & Storey, 1987). The use of digital media in campaigns extends the traditional definition a bit. The International Society for Research on Internet Interventions (www.isrii.org) defined "Internet interventions [as] treatments, typically behaviorally based, that are operationalized and transformed for delivery via the Internet. Usually, they are highly structured; self-guided or partly self-guided; based on effective face-to-face interventions; personalized to the user; interactive; enhanced by graphics, animations, audio, and video; and tailored to provide follow-up and feedback," but do not include sites that just provide information (Ritterband, Andersson, Christensen, Carlbring & Cuijpers, 2006).

Paisley (2001) distinguished public service campaigns (in which goals are generally supported by a broad array of stakeholders) from advocacy campaigns (in which goals are controversial and challenged by significant stakeholders). Over time, some topics may shift from one type to another, such as gender equality or smoking. Paisley (1998, 2001) mentioned several other conceptual distinctions: (1) *Objectives or methods* (emphasizing campaigns as strategies of social control to achieve objectives, or campaigns as a genre of communication with associated methods, communication channels, and kinds of results), (2) *Strategies of change* (whether the campaign emphasizes education or providing information about how to change behaviors or attitudes, enforcement or negative consequences for not complying with accepted or desired behavior, or engineering or designing social systems to prevent unwanted behaviors or consequences), (3) *Individual or collective* benefits (whether campaigns emphasize individual or social changes and outcomes), (4) *First-party* and *second-party* entitlement (whether campaign sources pay the direct consequences and have a primary stake in the issue or whether they are not directly affected and represent other stakeholders who may not be able to present their case), and (5) *Types of stakeholders* (whether the primary campaign sponsors and actors are associations, government agencies, foundations, trade unions, corporations, mass media, and social scientists, as they all differentially affect the public agenda, funding sources, campaign design, access to media, objectives and audiences).

Extensive advances in research and practice related to campaign theorizing, design, implementation, evaluation, and critique have been introduced since our initial summary chapter (Rice & Atkin, 1994), and an increasing number of campaigns have attained success in the past 15 years. Nevertheless, some current campaigns still fall far below expectations, certain theoretical aspects of campaigns are still only partially understood, and a variety of unexpected or uncontrollable factors may undermine the direction, implementation, and outcomes of campaigns. Only when we understand underlying general principles of communication, persuasion and social change, and the relationships among the components of a campaign, can we properly design and evaluate campaign efforts. This is especially true precisely for the reasons that social science is often criticized by practitioners: Reality is too complex to identify what really causes what, and what is and is not effective, especially when perceptions are based solely on experience gained in a few campaigns.

The following sections summarize general campaign components according to a framework derived from both Atkin (2001) and McGuire (2001), with increased attention to implications of online/digital media for campaigns. Additional sources for campaign summaries and reviews are available in Table 20.1; the appendix of Rice and Atkin (2001); Backer, Rogers, and Sopory (1992), who suggested 27 generalizations about successful health communication campaigns (pp. 30–32); and Salmon and Atkin (2003).

UNDERSTAND THE HISTORICAL AND POLITICAL CONTEXT

A rich history of American communication campaigns existed before the era of federal government and social science involvement (Paisley, 2001). Early examples include the pamphleteers and individual reformers in the 18th century such as Cotton Mather and public inoculations, Benjamin Franklin and abolitionism, Thomas Paine and independence, and Dorethea Dix and treatment of the mentally ill. The 19th century saw the rise of associations using legislative testimony, mass communication, confrontation, and local organizing (Bracht, 2001) to promote slavery abolition, women's suffrage, temperance unions, and wilderness preservation. In the early 20th century, muckrakers harnessed the powerful reach of inexpensive newspapers to address issues such as child labor and adulterated food products. As the century progressed, the federal government played an increasingly central role with regulations concerning commerce, food and drugs, and the environment, as well as programs providing social services after the New Deal. By mid-century, campaigners were applying social science to the development and evaluation of campaigns; initial perspectives held that mass media campaigns had no direct effect, that audiences were largely uninterested or applied selective exposure and perception, and that most effects operated indirectly through opinion leaders, while more recent theories suggest that well-conceived campaigns can achieve moderate success by using appropriate mixes of social change, media advocacy, community participation, audience targeting, message design, channel usage, and time frames.

Table 20.1 Recent Campaign Resource Books

An increasing number of monographs, textbooks, and readers have been published on the subject of campaign communication, primarily by scholars in the areas of mass communication, social psychology, and public health. This section briefly identifies the basic content of key books published since 2000:

- Crano and Burgoon (2002) organized a series of theoretical perspectives and research studies focusing on the role of the media in drug abuse prevention
- Cox (2006) focused on the role of media and public forums (scientists, lobbyists, corporations, advocacy groups, etc.) in shaping perceptions of the environment and actions relating to the environment
- Edgar, Noar, and Freimuth (2007) analyzed public and private communication about HIV/AIDS in the US and other countries
- Hornik (2002) presented 16 major studies using various methods to investigate health communication programs in many nations
- Klingermann and Roemmele (2002) packaged an array of chapters about public information campaigns in European countries, with an emphasis on practical applications
- Kotler et al. (2002) discussed social marketing approaches to health promotion
- Lederman and Stewart (2005) examined campaign strategies in the context of alcohol prevention programs
- Moser and Dilling (2007) presented various perspectives on effective communication, public outreach and education influencing policy, collective action and behavior change related to climate change
- Perloff (2003) described persuasion theories and applications relevant to campaign message design
- Rice and Atkin (2001) assembled more than two dozen perspectives on public communication campaigns (this chapter summarizes the main points of many of these)
- Rice and Katz (2001) and Murero and Rice (2006) brought together a wide range of researchers who analyzed changes in health care, information seeking, and support associated with Internet technologies
- Singhal et al. (2004) traced the history and reviewed international cases of the expanding practice of entertainment-education to promote health
- Stiff and Mongeau (2003) provided an overview of theoretical models pertinent to persuasive strategies in communication campaigns
- Thompson, Dorsey, Miller, and Parrott (2003) presented a comprehensive handbook featuring coverage of health campaigns
- Thorogood and Coombes (2004) provided a tutorial on methods (qualitative and quantitative) for implementing and evaluating health promotion interventions
- Tones and Green (2004) offered an international perspective on the complexities of health promotion strategies
- Valente (2002) comprehensively explained the frameworks, theories, research designs, and analytical methods used to evaluate health promotion programs
- Wilbur (2006) provided a tutorial on social marketing and then applies the principles to water-related environmental contexts
- Witte, Meyer, and Martell (2001) presented a detailed blueprint for constructing effective health messages
- The U.S. Department of Health and Human Services (2003) developed an elaborate manual presenting useful guidance on the design of health programs

Also crucial to the success of campaigns is the ability to become an important and enduring part of the public agenda, and to obtain first-party entitlement for significant stakeholders (Paisley, 2001). Some topics rise and fall over time, such as energy conservation, global warming, busing, endangered species, cancer, HIV/AIDS, drugs, drunk driving, tobacco, starvation due to famine, abortion, or civil rights. It seems that some periods are more "ideological," at which time issues are debated in the public agenda more extensively. One challenge in campaigns is to understand and try to shape these agenda items, and to cut through the very cluttered set of public agenda items that compete for people's attention and understanding. Paisley (1998) concluded that campaigns must advise, inform, advocate, and reinforce rather than simply exhorting, because only the individual can grasp the various aspects of their social context.

REVIEW THE REALITIES, AND UNDERSTAND THE SOCIOCULTURAL SITUATION

In undertaking campaigns, it is advisable to first review the realities (choose a significant problem offering a cost-effective solution, and then identify available resources and determine the optimum apportionment), the sociocultural situation, and the campaign ethics.

This includes identifying the focal behaviors of high-priority audiences, their media usage patterns, social factors and institutional constraints, and what constitutes meaningful and acceptable change. It also involves identifying whether the campaign objectives are essentially creating awareness, instructing/educating, or persuading. Among the "strategies of change" mentioned by Paisley (1998), campaigns traditionally rely on the educational component rather than the enforcement or engineering aspects. The current trend broadens the scope to include a greater emphasis on environmental change to complement media influence at the individual level.

Part of this understanding is the philosophical foundation of the campaign. For example, the perspectives of Sense-Making, community and two-way symmetric public relations campaigns have reconceptualized audience members (including publics, communities and institutions) as peers and collaborators in the mutual and interactive development and implementation of a change effort (Bracht, 2001; Dervin & Frenette, 2001; Dozier, Grunig, & Grunig, 2001). These approaches differ from traditional campaigns by giving greater emphasis to audiences' social and cultural contexts, by replacing experts' goals with audience-derived goals, and by using audience networks as ways to generate, frame, and share messages (Dervin & Frenette, 2001).

All communication campaigns and their components involve a wide array of ethical issues, from underlying assumptions (such as individual or social causes) to actual intervention choices, although they are usually implicit and embedded within campaign decision-making processes (Guttman, 2003). Identifying and resolving these ethical issues have both moral grounds (attempting to change people) as well as practical benefits (such as increased trust and respect). Guttman reviews aspects of different perspectives on ethics, such as means/ends, do good/avoid harm, justice, connectedness, truth, completeness, correctness, sincerity, comprehensibility, and inclusion. Specific concerns relating to health communication interventions include: who chooses and who has the mandate to select and impose the campaign's goals; the extent to which audience segmentation creates inequities and unequal utilities; the implications and unintended consequences of targeting one vs. another segment; using persuasion strategies that involve exaggeration, omission, fear and emotional appeals; the extent to which tailoring to cultural meanings is a form of co-optation, appropriation, or reinforcement of stereotyping or associated negative behaviors; the representation of blame, shame, culpability and responsibility in messages; unintended consequences such as harm, stigma, labeling, knowledge and social gaps; altering the role of health itself in the public agenda; and obligations the health campaigns have to individuals, the community, organizations, stakeholders, the profession, and society (Guttman, 2003).

UNDERSTAND THE AUDIENCE

One approach to improved understanding of the audience is segmentation—identifying subaudiences. Segmentation may involve demographics, media usage patterns, lifestyle, psychographics, ZIP code, uses and gratifications, predispositions toward the topic, and channel accessibility. This enables allocation of campaign efforts to the audience groups that are most in need of change and most receptive to the campaign, and to design messages appropriate to the audience preferences, media usage, and abilities.

Campaign designers typically emphasize three basic types of audiences. *Focal segments* are audiences grouped by levels of risk or illness, readiness, income and education, and other factors such as sensation-seeking. *Interpersonal influencers* are opinion leaders, media advocates, peer and role models, who can mediate the campaign (positively or negatively!) and help set the public agenda. *Societal policymakers* affect the legal, political and resource infrastructure, such as through regulations on media messages, environmental conditions, or safety standards, and social action such as community-based campaigns, federal allocations (such as the gasoline or tobacco tax), and insurance and health care programs. Atkin (2001) argued that campaigns may want to develop a *product line* or continuum of intended outcomes, so that audiences with different levels of receptivity or resistance can find their comfortable location in the campaign mix.

One way of understanding the audience is the Sense-Making methodology, which aims to "ensure as far as possible that dialogue is encouraged in every aspect of communication campaign research, design, and implementation" (Dervin & Frenette, 2001, p. 72). The method helps participants communicate about their attempts to move through discontinuities (gaps in meaning across time, people and space) in their life experiences by means of making sense, internally and externally, in the context of the intersection of past, present and future. Cognitions, attitudes, beliefs, emotions, and narratives serve as bridges—or obstacles—across these gaps. The primary interviewing approach is called the micro-moment time-line, whereby participants are asked to describe a situation and how they experienced it through time, identifying both how they saw themselves as stopped or moving at a particular moment on the timeline, and how various utilities helped them move through time and space.

The concept of *two-way symmetrical campaigns* derived from public relations theory (Dozier, Grunig, & Grunig, 2001, p. 239) emphasizes negotiating with an activist public, using conflict resolution in dealing with publics, helping management understand the opinions of particular publics, and determining how publics react to the organization. In particular, Dozier et al. highlighted the significance of *invisible clients*, those organizations that employ public relations activities to influence audiences without being explicitly identified as associated with the message. Examples include the tobacco industry, political ideologies (see Proctor, 2001), the milk industry (through its "Got Milk?" campaigns—see Butler, 2001), and environmental lobbyists (Cox, 2006).

APPLY APPROPRIATE THEORY

After assessing the factors described above, the campaign strategist should identify appropriate theoretical approaches. While campaigns are typically viewed as merely applied communication research, the most effective campaigns carefully review and apply relevant theories; further, campaign results can be used to extend and improve theories about media effects and social change. Atkin (2001) advocated using informed diversification of campaign approaches and channels rather than a single strategy. Salmon and Atkin (2003) briefly reviewed the frameworks and research on persuasive message strategies, including diverse incentive appeals (negative, positive, multiple), the use of evidence (one-sided vs. two-sided), and the addition of instruction (knowledge gain, skills acquisition, resistance to peer influence, media literacy, inoculation) and awareness (recognition, activation, compliance, information-seeking, sensitize) messages.

Theories most commonly invoked to guide successful campaigns include the following:

Social learning (Bandura, 1977b; Flora, 2001): Individuals are likely to exhibit behavior similar to that of role models who are credible, who explicitly model intended behaviors, and who receive appropriate negative or positive reinforcements.

Social comparison (Festinger, 1954; Flora, 2001): People compare the salience and outcomes of others' behavior, which, along with social norms, attitudes, and intentions, influence one's subsequent behavior.

Reasoned action (Ajzen & Fishbein, 1980): A combination of one's personal attitudes, perceived norms of influential others, and motivation to comply provides a parsimonious model of predictors of intended behavior. This model is derived from *expectancy-value* theory, which postulates that one's beliefs about how likely a given behavior leads to certain consequences, multiplied by one's evaluation of those consequences, are likely to predict attitudes and behavior.

Self-efficacy (Bandura, 1977a): The extent to which one feels one has control over one's actions, or can in fact accomplish a task, affects the extent to which one engages in changing one's own attitudes and behaviors. Thus an intermediary goal of a campaign would be to improve the self-efficacy of the at-risk group, such as those attempting to stop smoking or adolescents attempting to learn and practice behaviors that reduce their risk of AIDS.

The extended parallel process model (EPPM) (Stephenson & Witte, 2001): Fear appeals, through arousal, perceived susceptibility and vulnerability, awareness of likelihood of a hazard, framing of messages in terms of potential gains or losses, and perceived threat, can be effective in changing risky attitudes and behaviors. However, two, parallel, responses to fear may occur: a cognitive process involving ways to control or avert a danger, which may take advantage of the health message using a fear appeal, and an emotional process that attempts to control the fear, often by denial or coping, which will generally reject the message due to the fear appeal. (The third possible response is to ignore the message if it is deemed irrelevant or insignificant to the respondent.) The EPPM argues that perceived threat influences the strength of a danger or fear control response, while perceived efficacy influences whether danger or fear control responses are elicited. So a fear appeal must successfully convey both that the threat is salient and significant, and that the audience member can do something about it, and probably by emphasizing efficacy before threat.

Diffusion and influence through social networks (Piotrow & Kincaid, 2001; Rice, 1993; Rogers, 1981): Ideas, norms, and practices are diffused through—or rejected by—interpersonal networks because of the strong influence that evaluations and behavior of others—especially opinion leaders—have on network members. For example, students' estimates of their peers' drinking behaviors are typically significantly higher than the peers' actual behaviors; these inaccurate social projections encourage students to engage in excessive drinking until campaigns such as the RU Sure? Project (Lederman et al., 2001) provide accurate evidence from the individuals' own peer networks. Thus, perceived network influence is an important goal as well as a mechanism of campaigns taking social network theory seriously.

Integrative theory of behavior change (Cappella, Fishbein, Hornik, Ahern, & Sayeed, 2001): This model integrates three major theories: Health Belief Model, social cognitive theory, and the theory of reasoned action. Outcome behaviors are influenced by skills, environmental constraints, and intentions. Intentions are influenced by attitudes, norms, and self-efficacy. Attitudes are influenced by behavioral beliefs and their evaluative aspects. Norms are influenced by normative beliefs and motivations to comply (such as with network members or opinion leaders or enforcement threats). Self-efficacy is influenced by efficacy beliefs. All the beliefs are influenced by a variety of external variables (situational, institutional and infrastructural), demographics, attitudes, personality traits, and other individual differences (such as gender, race and culture). Different implications follow for the proximate influences (environmental, intention, and skills and attitudes), the intermediate influences (attitudes, norms, self-efficacy), the underlying beliefs (behavioral, normative and control), and background influences (past behavior, demographics and culture, attitudes toward the target behavior, personality and emotions, other individual differences, and exposure to the intervention or media messages) (Fishbein & Cappella, 2006). Identifying what audience segments hold what beliefs, or what social groupings are more influenced by social norms, helps campaign implementers focus their efforts.

The transtheoretical (or stages of change) model (Buller et al., 2001; Prochaska, DiClemente, & Norcross, 1992; Prochaska & Velicer, 1997): This model identifies subaudiences on the basis of their stage in the process of behavior change with respect to a specific health behavior: precontemplation, contemplation, preparation, action, or maintenance. Progression along these stages is influenced by a variety of processes: consciousness raising, dramatic relief, self-reevaluation, environmental reevaluation, self-liberation, helping relationships, counterconditioning, contingency management, stimulus, control, and social liberation. Thus, based on the audience's stage, a campaign should emphasize different processes, behaviors and messages. This is an ideal challenge for interactive web sites, as users can first assess their own stage, and then be provided material and activities appropriate for that stage and the associated processes.

The *health communication-behavior change model*, the basis of the Stanford Three-Community Campaign to reduce cardiovascular disease through integrated community-side projects, outlines three major project components: communication inputs (media, face-to-face, and community programs), communication functions for the receiver (attention, information, incentives, models, training, cues to action, support, self-management) and behavior objectives for the receiver (awareness, knowledge, motivation, skills, action, practice self-management skills, social network members) (Flora, 2001).

APPLY THE COMMUNICATION/PERSUASION MATRIX TO MESSAGE DESIGN

It is important to understand the role of and interaction among communication input variables and output variables. Communication *input variables* include source, message, channel, audience, and outcomes. Campaign *output variables* include the 13 possibly sequential persuasion steps of exposure, attention, liking, comprehension, generating related cognitions, acquiring skills, attitude change, storing, retrieving, decision to act in accord with retrieved position, action, cognitive integration of behavior, and encouraging others to behave similarly (McGuire, 2001). This model extends the traditional *instrumental learning* approach (Hovland, Janis, & Kelley, 1953). Several variants to the straightforward communication/persuasion matrix (McGuire, 2001) include the *elaboration likelihood model* (Petty & Cacioppo, 1986), *self-persuasion* (McGuire, 1960), and *alternate causal chains* (Bem, 1970).

Typical source (or messenger) variables include credibility, attractiveness and power. However, their effect may co-vary with other factors, such as attractiveness with formality of dress, and credibility with sameness of gender or ethnicity between source and audience.

Interesting message variables include credibility, attractiveness, relevance, understandability, argument structure, evidence, one-sided vs. two-sided content, types of arguments, types of appeals, and style (humor, clarity). At the most elemental level, effective appeals generally associate some valued (positive/negative) incentive with a sufficient probability that the promised/threatened outcome will occur. Typical incentives relate to health, time/effort, economics, ideology, aspirations, social acceptance and status. For example, well-designed fear appeals can increase the smoker's perceived likelihood of social rejection even though they may not bring the distant likelihood of lung cancer to salient levels. Atkin (2001) asserted that probability is more effective than valence when both cannot be achieved, and that multiple appeals are a more efficient as well as effective strategy. Presentation of evidence is more important for forming beliefs when the source lacks complete credibility or when the audience is highly involved. Other message variables include stylistic, modality, and production factors, which should be appropriately matched to the nature of the argument, audience, and desired outcomes.

Channel variables differ across various media in terms of reach, specialization, informativeness, interactivity, modalities, cognitive effort, effect on agenda setting, accessibility, homogeneity of audience, efficiency of production and dissemination, and context in which the audience uses the medium (Atkin, 2001; McGuire, 2001). Salmon and Atkin (2003) compared 25 channels across six major media features relevant to campaign design and effectiveness (access, reach, ability to reach specific target, depth [detailed and complex content], credibility, and agenda-setting). Other relevant features include intrusiveness, safeness, participation, sensory modalities, personalization, decodability, efficiency (both in production and dissemination). Audience variables include risk, cognitive development, education, and susceptibility to social influence (affected by anxiety, peer norms and behaviors, self-efficacy, compensatory mechanisms such as threat-avoiding coping habits). Central outcomes include beliefs, attitudes, behavior, persistence of outcome, and resistance to persuasion. McGuire (2001) discussed how each of these may be moderated by, or interact with, other factors.

Potentially valuable output variables to consider include audience choices and social settings of media use, differential paths to persuasion, varied sequencing of these 13 steps for different people or settings, the role played by liking, comprehension and recall in affecting behavioral outcomes, and whether the goal is to promote positive behaviors and attitudes or reduce or prevent negative ones. This latter issue, for example, raises questions of whether fear appeals, counter-arguing, or social benefits from alternative behaviors are most appropriate.

Atkin (2001) pointed out that depending on the nature of the campaign goal and type of message—awareness, instruction or persuasion—different input and output variables would be emphasized. For example, messages intended to create awareness need to stimulate and facilitate audience members to seek additional information, or sensitize or prime them to note particular kinds of messages. Some messages are designed to instruct or educate, such as procedures to use to resist peer pressure to engage in unhealthy behaviors, or to inoculate audiences against misleading advertisements. Finally, persuasion messages create or change attitudes through the promise, or association, of positive or negative incentives, located in the present or the future, in one's person or one's social interactions. Crucial to successful persuasion messages is activating or creating the salience and likelihood of positive outcomes. The communication inputs and the output response steps—creating what is typically called the communication/persuasion matrix—interact to mediate the persuasive response, so all the stages must work together to identify the appropriate campaign components and timing.

CONDUCT FORMATIVE EVALUATION

Formative Evaluation Stages

An important part of this campaign planning and design is *formative evaluation*, which provides data and perspectives to improve messages during the course of creation (Atkin & Freimuth, 2001; Flora, 2001), and helps avoid unintended outcomes such as boomerang effects or shifting unhealthy behaviors to other domains. A general goal of formative evaluation is to understand what McGuire called the "sociocultural situation," encompassing situational circumstances (e.g., economic, cultural, political, psychological, etc.) that instigate and maintain the undesirable target behavior or that sustain the desired target behavior. This understanding is obtained through *preproduction research*. Atkin and Freimuth identified four stages in preproduction research:

1 *Identify the target audiences:* Who is at risk, who is accessible through communication channels, who can influence others at risk, and who is most and least persuasible? The Stanford project also involved community stakeholders such as health agencies, commercial organizations (restaurants and work places), and community leaders, so its formative evaluation included an *organizational needs analysis* (Flora, 2001).
2 *Specify the target behavior:* Insofar as most global behaviors consist of component behaviors that are influenced by contextual factors, campaign messages should focus on specific effective component behaviors. For example, formative evaluation of weight-loss messages in the Stanford Community Studies found that whereas women were aware of their weight problems and motivated to change, men greatly underestimated their weight problem, were not generally motivated to change, and had low self-efficacy about their ability to lose weight (Flora, 2001).
3 *Elaborate intermediate responses:* The hierarchy-of-effects model suggests a long causal chain between exposure and integrated behavior. Formative evaluation can identify how these steps are linked and what intermediate steps are most amenable to campaign efforts. Some of the intermediate responses include knowledge and lexicon, beliefs and images, attitudes and values, salience priorities, and efficacy and skills. For example, Cialdini (2001) argued that campaigns must avoid unintentionally providing persuasive models of undesirable but popular norms while explicitly concentrating on desirable but unpopular prescriptive norms.
4 *Ascertain channel use:* Using any kind of media without knowing which media the target audience uses, at what times, for how long or how many times, and in what combination is an ineffective use of campaign resources. Formative evaluation can identify media exposure and attitudes toward the different media, either via custom surveys or utilization of marketing and advertising databases.

Next, *pretesting research* is performed to refine the messages. Evaluators help develop key concepts by asking test audiences to suggest and amplify more appropriate message ideas or more relevant message sources (e.g., should the source be a doctor or a celebrity?). Words, phrases, or descriptions used by target audiences in their discussions about the campaign topic can also be incorporated into message content. Rough, preliminary versions of messages can be tested for the following attributes: attention, comprehensibility, strong and weak points, relevance, or controversial aspects. Several methods are useful in pretesting messages, including focus group interviews, in-depth interviews, central-location intercept interviews, self-administered questionnaires, theater testing, day-after recall, media gatekeeper review, and physiological response analysis.

Challenges to Formative Evaluation of Online/Digital Media Campaigns

With web-based interventions, formative evaluation and audience assessment stages need to identify whether the requirements of the site match users' computer/online literacy (concerning, reading, computer use, information searching, understanding health information, ability to contextualize the information). One approach is to provide something like the eHeals literacy scale, based in social cognitive and self-efficacy theories (Norman & Skinner, 2006), and tailor the interface to literacy levels.

Another challenge in designing online campaign components is to decide on and implement an appropriate information architecture. Danaher, McKay, and Seeley (2005) identified four main types: free-form/matrix (provides a range of possibly interrelated hyperlinks for users to choose and "forage"), directive tunnel (step-by-step guidance through a structured sequence of pages), hierarchical (top-down, guiding the user to specific content), and hybrid (using elements of the other designs, possibly at different stages of the intervention or different user responses). Each has varying implications for usability, perceived complexity, retracing one's path, mentally modeling the layered content, involvement, tailoring, and behavior change goals, as illustrated through analysis of several tobacco cessation sites. Given the range of content, software, and hardware components of online campaigns, system and research design and formative evaluation should involve interdisciplinary participants (designers, researchers) as well as users, which also means support for interdisciplinary projects by funding and implementation agencies, and the consideration of similarities across and overlaps between iterative/cyclic user-centered systems design and health services research paradigms (Pagliari, 2007). Formative evaluation of online campaigns often encounters many challenges, such as coordination of teams, understanding of differing terminologies and methods and forms of evidence, balancing design innovation with robust development, and the usual tensions between academic studies and applied projects.

One implication of taking advantage of web sites through interactivity and multimedia content is that the user's computer and connection bandwidth may be insufficient for interactivity and multi-media, or more fundamentally, the required server's bandwidth may not be sufficient for a given total of concurrent users. Danaher et al. (2005) developed a bandwidth usage index (assessing how well a site can be used within dial-up or broadband conditions), and applied it to three intervention web sites under a number of conditions, including comparing a video-rich version, an audio-rich version, and a web-enabled CD which contained the media-rich content. Even with a variety of bandwidth-reducing techniques (such as scaling, compression, streaming, preloading, etc.), only the web-enabled CD-ROM was suitable for dial-up use. As an example, even though from half to two-thirds of participants in two cancer program patient education web sites felt the sites were more useful than any other source on the topic, they still experienced problems with video and audio clips (Cumbo et al., 2002).

ACCESSING THE MEDIA

Campaigns must make their messages available through a variety of communication media that are appropriate for the target audience. The message must also communicate specific information, understandings, and behaviors that are actually accessible, feasible, and culturally acceptable (Rice & Atkin, 1989, p. 10). We have seen that the communication/persuasion matrix, along with formative evaluation, can be used to design or identify persuasive and informational attributes of source, message, and channel.

Social Marketing

A *social marketing* perspective also emphasizes the need to understand the competition, particularly alternative messages and behaviors. Social marketing is similar to communication campaigns, especially its emphasis on behavioral and not just awareness change, and altering the social structure so as to facilitate the intended behavioral changes, except for its reliance on commercial marketing concepts and its orientation toward the consumer (Alcalay & Bell, 2000). These include consumer product orientation, audience segmentation, channel analysis, strategy for the highest probability goals, and process tracking. The more familiar emphases of social marketing include product (may be an action or material), price (financial and social costs), place (distribution, access, and socially acceptable), promotion (developing attitudes and intentions leading to the behaviors), and positioning (maximize benefits and minimize cost, relative to other activities and materials, including re-positioning a familiar concept). Social marketing and product marketing have consequential differences, however, including: focusing on behavioral and social systems change (not merely preference or attitude), expected changes in a large percentage of the relevant audience, salient and central attitudes and values, only a probability of causal outcomes or gratifications, long-term or preventative outcomes, a more neutral informational tone, dependency on trust based on credibility of the source and benefits to the consumer, and limited budget including in-kind services and volunteerism. Any mass media message competes with hundreds of other messages. Any concept competes with dozens of related mental concepts. So, there is a need to identify the "competitive advantage" of the particular campaign objective. For example, exercising as a means of preventing heart disease can also be advertised as a social activity.

Approaches to Media Dissemination: Placement, Data, Services

Alcalay and Taplin (1989) highlighted the importance and utility of *public relations* ("news about an issue, service, client, or product," p. 116) and *public affairs* ("lobbying and working on regulatory or legislative issues with administrators and legislators," p. 122). Because it has "third party" credibility, public relations can be very useful in not only increasing public awareness of a campaign, but also in deterring opposition to an otherwise controversial issue, such as family planning. Public affairs is important not only in shaping legislation that may advance campaign objectives, but also in gaining support for resources and spokespeople. Editorials, press releases, and hard news coverage may be powerful media modes, when managed properly.

Commercial *broadcast rating services* such as Nielsen can help identify the most effective and efficient channels. Similar data are available for newspapers, magazines, billboards, mailing lists, and even bus posters. By providing figures to calculate the percentage of the target audience exposed to the program or channel at specific time periods, as well as the extent to which audiences change across time periods or are consistent, campaign implementers can determine the *reach* (number of different individuals in the audience) or *frequency* (number of times any individual may be exposed). Different campaign objectives would be achieved through increased reach or increased frequency. For example, increasing awareness about a common issue by the public at large could be achieved more cost effectively through using a specific time/channel combination to maximize reach. However, achieving and maintaining learning or attitude change in a specific at-risk audience would require increased frequency, which may involve a different time/channel mix. A jazz or classical music station, for example, may have high frequency but low reach.

The global reach of some television programs provides new opportunities for taking advantage of minimal marginal costs after initial production, and of reaching youth audiences. For example, MTV aired a global media campaign, "Staying Alive," in 2002 to promote HIV prevention among 16- to 25-year-olds (Geary et al., 2007) and made all the materials copyright free to non-MTV broadcasters. At least some portions of the campaign were available to nearly 800 million households in 166 countries, with example exposure rates among 16- to 25-year-olds of 12% in Kathmandu to 82% in Dakar.

The Advertising Council provides in-kind creative and agency services to support approximately 36 public communication campaigns a year in the United States. Further, in-place commercial distribution channels can be used to support delivery of campaign messages and materials. For example, the annual Muscular Dystrophy campaign enlists the cooperation of 7–11 convenience stores to provide immediate delivery channels across the United States. To overcome limitations in free access to the media, certain campaigns have sought government or corporate funding for paid message placement. The Office of National Drug Control Policy began requiring networks and stations to match the time that ONDCP buys with donated time for other groups communicating about substance abuse prevention (Browning, 2002). Nationally, this approach has been most prevalent for drug, tobacco, and drunk driving prevention campaigns; a healthy media budget can significantly increase audience exposure to messages combating unhealthy behavior.

It is common practice to request local and sometimes national media to place *public service announcements* (PSAs). The practice of broadcasting PSAs was in large part an outgrowth of Federal Communication Commission requirements that stations using the broadcasting frequencies served the public interest and necessity. With the proliferation of media outlets and the deregulation of the media, opportunities to broadcast PSAs continue to decline. It can be argued that PSAs are typically of limited value anyway, because they cannot be scheduled for times when the specific target audience is most likely to be watching or listening, or in known amounts of exposure. Nevertheless, PSAs can be still be placed in specialized outlets such as local radio stations or community newspapers that are likely to reach a target audience, such as teenagers or retired people.

PSAs appear online, too (Browning, 2002). Examples range from the Benton Foundation/Ad Council "Connect for Kids" campaign that received nearly 1 million site visits per month, to a cancer research foundation that ran over 15 million online ads in two months but received only nine new donors. Exposure can be substantial: Doubleclick provided around 200 million PSA impressions per month in 2001, and America Online provided about $25 million worth of online PSAs, supporting between 10 to 15 campaigns per month, though in a rather random fashion, filling unsold ad space. The Coalition for Organ Donation reported 109,000 visitors to its site, with around 6,000 coming from banner ads on a wide variety of websites. Keeping up with the changing media scene, The Interactive Advertising Bureau began in 1998 committing 5% of its online advertising for PSAs, while the Ad Council reported it received close to $400 million in donated online ad space in 2001. YouTube enables charity organizations to benefit from massive exposure. The channel (http://uk.youtube.com/user/DontYouForgetAboutMe) was launched in the UK in 2007, with the goal of bringing the plight of missing children to a wider and younger audience.

However, as the online PSAs are distributed through intermediaries, campaign sponsors have little control over or knowledge about how those other websites choose to place their banner ad, or what is the nature of the site's users. Indeed, often the target audience is among those least likely to have access to or have the knowledge and expertise to use the Internet. Extreme limitations exist in a message that must be delivered in a quickly observed 1 inch by 3 inch banner ad, which also have very low click-through rates (estimated at 0.5% in 2000). Internet ads—as well as traditional TV commercials—are also being blocked or skipped over with computer software and digital TV recorders. And many people are increasingly concerned about privacy, monitoring, and data-mining issues associated with computer/Internet use, and increasingly so with digital TV recording and even mobile phone use. Further, there is no associated "public service" mandate to motivate web sites to host online PSAs.

Education-Entertainment Approaches

Some campaigns have engaged in cooperative efforts with the entertainment industry to produce attractive music videos and PSAs, to insert themes in popular TV programs, or to create prosocial television series (Singhal, Cody, Rogers, & Sabido, 2004). Examples include the PBS Freestyle programs seeking to diversify gender occupation roles (LaRose, 1989), designated driver portrayals inserted in primetime entertainment programs (Winsten & DeJong, 2001), and the South African TV series *Soul City* to promote healthy practices (Singhal & Rogers, 2001). This form of campaign consciously mixes theories of *social modeling* (providing role models for behavior and attitudes), *parasocial interaction* (getting the audience personally involved in the characters and content), and *expectancy value* (combining perceived social norms with beliefs about the source's normative expectations) with commercial entertainment values, media personalities, and wide-scale distribution. Celebrities often provide credible and influential sources, especially for certain at-risk populations who distrust, or are not otherwise exposed to, traditional authority figures. This campaign approach also generates revenues through successful programming that allows sustainability, improvement, and expansion over time.

However, Singhal and Rogers (2001) noted a variety of ethical issues in such campaigns, including (1) how well the social change goals match the moral and values guidelines of the campaign, (2) who establishes just exactly what is or is not "prosocial,"

(3) the extent to which all audience segments receive the positive and helpful messages equally or eventually, (4) whether the entertaining message is somehow indirect or even subliminal rather than an explicit communication campaign, (5) how sociocultural equality—inclusion of all relevant voices—can be achieved through entertainment-education, and (6) how to avoid unintended negative effects.

Media Advocacy

A complementary approach to campaign implementation is *media advocacy* (Piotrow & Kincaid, 2001; Wallack & Dorfman, 2001). In line with the critique that most campaigns emphasize individual blame and personal responsibility, this approach emphasizes the wide range of social forces that influence public health, particularly the salient and consequential policy issues that are ignored by most communication campaigns. This approach has been notably successful using the media to initiate societal level reforms relating to alcohol and tobacco issues.

While the media are key vehicles for communication campaigns, certain types of media content can also produce a wide variety of contradictions for public communication campaigns (Wallack, 1989). A wide variety of unhealthy behaviors and antisocial attitudes are shown in both programs and commercials on television. Stereotypes of gender roles, race relations, age-specific behaviors, behavior by medical personnel, sexual relations, and treatments of physical and mental problems are all developed and reinforced through media portrayals that overwhelm attempts by other messages to reduce such stereotypes. In the media, health and social problems are also portrayed as individually caused and individually solved, avoiding discussion of the social and economic causes.

Instead, successful campaigns must be linked to broader community action (see Bracht, 2001; Dervin & Frennette, 2001; Dozier, Grunig, & Grunig, 2001; Flora, 2001). As the systems model proposed by Rice and Foote (2001) indicated, many broad and pervasive pre-state conditions can overwhelm or prevent any campaign intentions or messages. Thus, populations, policy, and public agendas should be the primary targets of health campaigns—the salient audiences are the stakeholders and potential participants in any social change process.

This requires a media advocacy approach—"the strategic use of mass media in combination with community organizing to advance healthy public policies" (Wallack & Dorfman, 2001, p. 393). It explicitly attempts to associate social problems with social structures and inequities, change public policy rather than individual behavior, reach opinion leaders and policymakers, work with groups to increase involvement in the communication process, and reduce the power gap instead of simply providing more information. The four primary activities involved in media advocacy include (1) develop an overall strategy that involves formulating policy options, identifying the stakeholders that have power to create relevant change and apply pressure to foster change, and developing messages for these stakeholders; (2) set the agenda, including gaining access to the news media through stories, news events, and editorials; (3) shape the debate, including framing the public health problems as policy issues salient to significant audiences, emphasizing social accountability, and providing evidence for the broader claims; and (4) advance the policy, including maintaining interest, pressure and coverage over time.

ACCESSING ONLINE AND DIGITAL MEDIA

Increasing Use of Online and Digital Media for Communication Campaigns

The Internet is becoming a major source for online health information, discussion, therapy, access to physicians, and, more recently, campaigns and interventions (Rice, 2006; see also The International Society for Research on Internet Interventions, http://www.isrii.org). The Internet may be particularly relevant for college students and young adults, as they search (equally by men and women) for online health information more than other groups, although emphasizing certain kinds of health topics, such as diet and nutrition (Hanauer et al., 2004). However, shortcomings of online health information include inconsistent quality, difficulties in finding and using the information, access problems for population segments, and harm from inaccurate or misleading information (Benigeri & Pluye, 2003; Rice & Katz, 2001).

The interactive CHESS system, designed for adolescents, was one of the first computer-based campaigns (Hawkins et al., 1987). It provided confidential, nonjudgmental health information, behavioral change strategies, and sources of referral across five adolescent health areas: alcohol and other drugs, human sexuality, smoking prevention and cessation, stress management and diet and exercise. More recently, the number of Medline citations to "web-based therapies" rose 12-fold from 1996 to 2003 (569 citations overall), leading Wantland et al. (2004) to prepare the first meta-analysis comparing behavioral change outcomes of web-based vs. non-web-based interventions. Twenty-two articles, involving nearly 12,000 participants, reported effect sizes from –.01 to .75. Outcomes involved exercise time, nutritional status knowledge, asthma treatment knowledge, healthcare participation, reduced decline in health, perception of body shape, and maintenance of weight loss. Other reviews of online/digital media interventions are provided by Griffiths et al. (2006), Neuhauser and Kreps (2003), Rice and Katz (2001), and Walther et al. (2005). Table 20.2 provides some examples of such campaigns.

Researchers are examining the potential roles of new communication media, such as electronic mail, voice response systems, interactive video, DVD and CD-ROM, and computer games, in reaching particular at-risk populations and in influencing learning, attitudes, and behaviors (Buller et al., 2001; Lieberman, 2001; Piotrow & Kincaid, 2001; Rice, 1984; Rice & Katz, 2001). Lieberman (2001, p. 377) recommended that campaign designers take advantage of the interactive, multi-media, networked, personalized, and portable aspects of these new media. This allows computer-mediated campaigns to apply young people's media and genres, use characters that appeal to that age group, support information seeking, incorporate challenges and goals, use learning-by-doing, create functional learning environments, facilitate social interaction, allow user anonymity when appropriate, and involve young people in product design and testing.

Email is a straightforward campaign medium. Interpersonal components of campaigns might be extended through the use of email, such as in the Digital Heroes Campaign (DHC), in which online mentors were matched with 242 youths for two years to foster better youth development (Rhodes et al., 2006). One workplace health campaign sent emails daily for one year providing health tips suggesting physical activity, increased fruit and vegetable intake, and relevant web sites including self-monitoring and comparison tools (Franklin et al., 2006).

Even the Internet will not be the only, or in some cases the best, form of convergence across digital communication/information technologies. Different technologies can be

Table 20.2 Examples of Online and Digital Media Campaigns

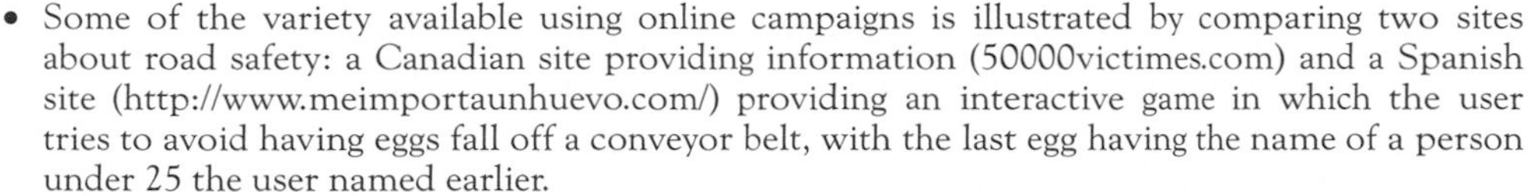

- Some of the variety available using online campaigns is illustrated by comparing two sites about road safety: a Canadian site providing information (50000victimes.com) and a Spanish site (http://www.meimportaunhuevo.com/) providing an interactive game in which the user tries to avoid having eggs fall off a conveyor belt, with the last egg having the name of a person under 25 the user named earlier.
- "Check Your Drinking" is a component of the online Alcohol Help Center, which compares participants' self-reported drinking to others in similar demographics (Cunningham et al., 2006). Users in one small trial reported greater usefulness and accuracy (for problem drinkers compared to moderate drinkers), and decreased drinking three months later. Two potentials of such sites is the ability to be used by groups who might not otherwise seek help from clinics and agency services, and to improve the screening questions over time.
- A Canadian campaign (http://www.protectyourhead.com/) (with associated print ads) to raise awareness around the risks of brain injuries seeks to convince people to wear a helmet every time they perform potentially risky activities, such as biking, skating, but also working in a construction site. The website features a 3D brain that simulates what everyday social situations may be like after suffering brain injury. Users can take a series of tests by answering questions or playing little games that show how one's capabilities may result if the head is not protected.
- A Spanish campaign draws attention on the importance of donating blood on a regular basis (http://www.5segons.com/watch.php?id=2&v=K9hsIu6jPIg).
- An alcohol education CD-ROM featuring video, text, music, graphics, and animation was most effective at reducing estimates of peer alcohol consumption among students compared to a lecture about alcohol education and to a control group (Reis, Riley, & Baer, 2000).
- An intriguing, if somewhat disgusting, viral campaign (http://www.pourquoitutousses.be/site/index.asp) launched in Belgium by OgilvyInteractive for Pfizer and the World No Tobacco Day allows visitors to send "personalized" smoker's coughs to their friends, adjusted by volume, duration, and dryness of the cough.
- CDC's 2006 Seasonal Influenza Campaign used new media to enhance promotion of influenza vaccination uptake among traditional and new audiences, including: specialized podcast episodes, wide distribution of a customized graphical bug, a webinar for blog writers, virtual vaccinations for younger audiences, and messaging via online social networks (Edgerton et al., 2007).
- From Australia, an edutainment "Battle for the Bronchs" site (http://www.battleforthebronchs.com.au/) is an interactive comic book combining live action video set in an illustrated city inside a pair of lungs, aimed at young people who may suffer from asthma but tend to ignore the warning signs and avoid traditional health management messages.
- In France a new site was launched to spread the word about the risk of sexual encounters, and explain to teenagers (but not only to them) what can put them at risk of contracting AIDS. The site, called www.touteslesrencontressontpossibles.com (all possible encounters) was developed using a style that is serious but engagingly amusing at the same time. The site uses graphics and drawings to picture typical summer situations and send out straightforward messages to teens. Users can select an avatar and follow the path unveiled after the choice.
- In the UK, MTV launched an educational advergame (http://www.staying-alive.org/me/game/index.html) to guide teens through life's sensitive issues. The edugame was produced with the support of the Youth Peer Education Network and it represents a good example of online communication to teens.
- The ElectroCity (http://electrocity.co.nz/) site was designed to allow users to become involved with virtual town planning in order to better understand the generation, costs, and effects of energy. It also provides prizes and encourages users to forward the link to others.

Note: The non-referenced examples are from www.adverblog.com.

combined to take advantage of their specific features. For example, one trial assessed the effect on perceived control, intention to exercise, and moderate physical activity of a completely automated Internet and mobile phone system (compared to a no-support control group) (Hurling et al., 2007). The participants entered their perceived barriers and received tailored solutions, a dialogue therapy module to help shape beliefs about exercise, a schedule for planning exercise sessions, mobile phone and/or email reminders, a message board for use by all participants, feedback on their activity, and a wristband accelerometer (which captured and reported activity data in real-time, via a wireless connection to the mobile phone). Adults who participated in an intervention featuring an automated, computer-controlled telephone system offering educational feedback, advice and behavioral counseling showed improvements in their nutrition behavior and overall diet (Delichatsios et al., 2001).

As a greater percent of the US (and more so in most countries) has adopted mobile phones than the Internet, and as income is less a factor in the mobile phone digital divide than in the Internet digital divide (Rice & Katz, 2003), and because they are, well, mobile, personal, and increasingly multi-media, mobile phones may be more effective media for tailored, wide-reaching, interactive and continuing health interventions (Tufano & Karras, 2005). Computers and personal digital assistants (PDAs) are limited in developing countries because of their expense and requirement for additional equipment, such as relatively complex network connections. Cell phones, which are ubiquitous and cheaper than most computers and PDAs, offer a simple complement or alternative. Curioso (2006) described an application of a telehealth program using cell phones and the Internet to collect, transmit and monitor data in real-time from female sex workers (FSW) who were part of a 20-city randomized trial in Peru to reduce sexually transmitted diseases (STDs). Electronic short message service (SMS) may be used to provide health promotional messages, though apparently more successfully for younger and higher social class users (Trappey & Woodside, 2005).

RSS feeds are already being used in campaigns such as the Johns Hopkins Bloomberg School of Public Health's Center for Communication Programs to distribute up-to-date changes and new entries about health information. Blogs allow users with similar health information needs and concerns to share their views and experiences. Podcasts are another, audio-based, means of providing relevant information to target audiences at their convenience, while wikis support collaboration among project members (Haylock & Rabi, 2007). The Kaiser Family Foundation's Program for the Study of Entertainment Media and Health is especially interested in how health-related and other non-profit and government agencies can use new digital media such as social networking, user-generated content, and gaming to enhance their communications strategies (http://www.kff.org/about/entmediastudies.cfm).

Lieberman (2006) reviewed nine kinds of learning associated with videogame use. Four of those are directly relevant to campaigns: knowledge, skills and behaviors, self-regulation and therapy, and attitudes and values. Concerning knowledge, interactive games require the processing of new information and feedback in order to solve a problem. Interactive health games for those with chronic health conditions (such as diabetes or asthma) or in need of health knowledge (such as children's vegetable and fruit consumption) can improve self-care skills and behaviors, leading to improved health outcomes. Dealing with physical or mental treatment and problems may be improved through interactive games as well, by means of increased self-regulation, emotion management, social interaction, distraction from pain, and tolerance of phobias. Self-efficacy can be improved through success in vicarious experiences. Role-playing and modeling through videogames may both allow more direct experience with modeled and rewarded behaviors, although most commercial popular games include negative and aggressive roles and behaviors. Three-dimensional massively multiplayer online role-playing games (MMORPGs) are another opportunity for promoting health and behavior change, allowing users to simulate behaviors and their consequences, in interaction with other users (by means of online avatars) (Annang, Muilenburg, & Strasser, 2007).

Characteristics of Online and Digital Media for Campaigns

Central to an understanding of the role of new media in campaigns are the concepts of *interactivity, narrowcasting*, and *tailoring*.

McMillan (2002) explicated two primary dimensions of *interactivity*—direction of communication and level of receiver control over the communication process. Based upon the two dimensions, the four kinds of relationships between the user and the source include *monologue, feedback, responsive dialogue*, and *mutual discourse*. These four cells can be associated with specific design features, such as surveys, games, purchasing products or services, email, hyperlinks, chat rooms, etc. Understanding the concept, and application, of interactivity has significant implications for both the underlying philosophy of an Internet-based campaign as well as the design features and evaluation criteria—for example, concerning the directionality and symmetry of the relations between the source and the audience. However, the majority of health-related websites use some, but not many, interactive components, and those are more frequent in .com vs. .gov or .org. sites (McMillan, 2002; Rice, Peterson, & Christine, 2001; Stout, Villegas, & Kim, 2001).

In order to avoid by now familiar problems associated with online health information (noted above), Rimal and Adkins (2003) suggested applying social marketing principles to *narrowcasting via segmentation* and targeting Internet users. The goal is to find the best mix among the least number of media channels and messages to be effective, and the audience segment most homogeneous (based on theory) about the particular risk. The characteristics of the various targeted media must be matched with the campaign goals, and the messages must be tailored to match the theoretically relevant audience characteristics. This is how the Internet and other digital media are especially relevant, as some of their characteristics are much better matched to some campaign goals, audience segments, and especially message tailoring. Interactive/individualized feedback is more effective at increasing motivation to make more healthy food choices than is general nutrition information, likely because of the increased attention and cognitive processing from the user, and less redundant content (Brug, Oenema, & Campbell, 2003). As an example of narrowcasting and the value of anonymity and peer communication, in an online survey of more than 4,600 people, most people indicated that they would visit a STD/HIV prevention website to get information, but that they would not open an email or chat about the information within the website (Bull, McFarlane, & King, 2001). However, those most at risk were more likely to do so, implying a useful alternative to physical STD prevention settings and complement to STD information in clinic settings.

The CDC-sponsored Guide to Community Preventive Services (2005) has stressed the importance of *tailoring* to individual and/or targeted population characteristics (Tufano & Karras, 2005). "Tailoring is a process of designing messages to reflect individual's needs, interests, abilities and motivations, which are derived from an individual assessment (Kreuter, Farrell, Olevitch, & Brennan, 2000). Based on the screening data, the program chooses the most suitable responses, which are then integrated into an advice and displayed to the respondent" (Brunsting & van den Putte, 2006, pp. 314–315; see also Ryan & Lauver, 2002). Aspects of tailoring that seem particularly responsible for positive results is providing feedback, self-monitoring, and even the process of entering one's own data, in some cases fostered by regular prompts. Tailored communication is generally more effective than generic messages in promoting health behavior change (Neuhauser & Kreps, 2003).

Rimal and Adkins (2003) reviewed studies showing the positive outcomes (exposure, attention, use, recall, credibility, behavior change) of campaigns using tailored messages in general, and online- or digital media-based tailored messages in particular. These positive outcomes seem to be due largely to increased relevance, perceived risk, and self-efficacy, all enhanced through feedback. Computers (online, disk-based, mobile, etc.) in particular support tailoring and feedback through interactivity ("complexity of choice, effort exerted by users, responsiveness, monitoring of information use, ease of adding information, and facilitation of interpersonal communication," p. 506 [Heeter, 1989], and "multimodality, telepresence, networkability, temporal flexibility, sensory vividness, and anonymity," p. 507 [Rimal & Flora, 1997]).

Computer-based interactivity, narrowcasting and tailoring are good matches with the transtheoretical (stages of change) model (Prochaska & Velicer, 1997) as the system can ask questions that identify the user's stage of change (and thus potential motivators such as intention, attitude, self-efficacy, subjective norms, etc.), and then provide appropriate information and activities. For example, a study to identify the demographic factors influencing 10,000 self-registered heavy drinkers' exposure, use, attrition, completion, and self-reported impact (on dependency, harms, and mental health) of a 6-week web-based intervention (Down Your Drink) (Linke et al., 2007) was based explicitly on the transtheoretical model. There were six stages, with a different module each week, involving motivational enhancement, cognitive behavioral therapy, relapse prevention, drinking diary, consumption calculator, quizzes, behavioral analysis of drinking situations, email or SMS that send reminders and tips, and a nonmoderated listserve. Although attrition was high (83.5% did not finish all six weeks; most of these left after the first week; and those were more likely at risk of alcohol dependency and of harm from alcohol use), outcomes were all improved for those who did. The authors note that while attrition is high, the marginal cost for any completion is very low; consider that this intervention provided significant results on all outcome measures for over 1,500 heavy drinkers. Brunsting and van den Putte (2006) analyzed the effectiveness of a Dutch computer-tailored intervention that targeted excessive alcohol users who are not inclined to seek treatment, and which also was based on the transtheoretical model. The site attracted over 100,000 users in the first two weeks, and 10,000 per month thereafter. Such tailored drink tests can also be integrated with other forms of support, such as, after receiving the tailored advice, calling a help-desk or sending questions about the advice by e-mail. Etter (2005) analyzed use and smoking quitting rates of nearly 12,000 users of two sites at time 1 and over 4,200 users at time 2. Only former smokers, and smokers in the contemplation stage of change, increased their abstinence rates after using the original version of a tailored program (Stop-tabac.ch) that was shorter and provided more information on nicotine dependence and nicotine replacement therapy, and less on health risks and coping strategies, compared to a more comprehensive and interactive version of the tailored program. An innovative use of "tailoring" is to provide an interactive website for patients to gain tailored feedback about their condition and then be provided related questions to ask their physicians (Hartmann et al., 2007). Other examples explicitly applying this model include the Consider This web-based smoking cessation and prevention program for children (Buller et al., 2001) and children's interactive CD-ROMs and videogames (Lieberman, 2001).

Other relevant characteristics include ". . . presence, homophily, social distance [including stigma management], anonymity/privacy, and interaction management [including both degree of participation and forms of expression]" (Walther et al., 2005). Walther et al. explored the theoretical foundations for why each of these attributes should facilitate such outcomes, through mediating processes of learning, social influence (including patient compliance) and coping.

ENGAGE THE COMMUNITY

A related means of integrating media and interpersonal communication is to conduct and involve campaign activities at and by the community level (Bracht, 2001). Dearing (2001, p. 305) observed that "social change occurs because of complementary and reinforcing information circulating through social and organized systems that constitute a community . . . [by means of] multiple positively related interventions at multiple levels of impact with a given geographic area." Note that while we list community engagement late in the list of campaign components a truly community-based campaign would engage stakeholders right from the start. Indeed, many funding agencies now require community involvement as part of the design and implementation protocol. One of the central motivations for community-based campaigns is to empower communities, their voluntary associations and their members through local initiation and activities. This "social ecology-based" approach is fundamentally different from the typical "social planning" approach in which external change agencies provide expertise and solutions for individuals (or "clients") within a community but with some form of community sponsorship (Dearing, 2003). Dearing reviewed the elements of successful community organizing, emphasizing the necessary but difficult balance between external and community-based resources, expertise, and agendas. Sustainability and institutionalization of the initiative's objectives should be a central focus for health communication practitioners.

Bracht (2001) described five key stages in organizing community campaigns: (1) Conduct a community analysis, including identifying the community's assets and history; defining the community according to geographic, population, and political jurisdiction; collecting data with community participation; and assessing community capacity and readiness for change; (2) Design and initiate the campaign, including developing an organizational structure for collaboration, increasing community participation and membership in the organization, and developing an initial intervention plan; (3) Implement the campaign, including clarifying the roles and responsibilities of all partners, providing orientation and training to citizens and volunteers, refining the intervention plan to accommodate local contexts, and generate broad citizen participation; (4) Consolidate program maintenance, including maintaining high levels of volunteer effort, and continuing to integrate intervention activities into community networks; and (5) Disseminate results and foster sustainability of the community campaign, including reassessing campaign activities and outcomes, refining the sustainability plan, and updating the community analysis.

Community-level approaches were emphasized in the Stanford heart disease prevention programs (Flora, 2001). Three models of community mobilization were applied as appropriate: (1) *consensus development*, or participation by diverse community members, (2) *social action*, or mobilizing the community to create new social structures and engage in the political process, and (3) *social planning*, or using expert data to propose and plan system-wide change. Campaign messages, resources, and activities were developed and implemented through media, training instructors, workplace contests and workshops, schools, restaurants and grocery stores, health professionals, and contests or lotteries.

New media may be especially useful for community campaigns. In 2001, a Canadian urban community used an interactive web site (with messages about health risks and about city council events) and email as the primary components (in addition to public posters and billboards, and media coverage) of a campaign to advocate revising a smoking bylaw (to better protect children under 18 from second-hand smoke) in a conservative province resistant to government regulation. An Internet survey and focus group found that over two-thirds contacted the city council during the campaign (about a third had ever contacted the council before the campaign), and half indicated they were more likely to become involved in civic issues, partially due to increased capacity for political involvement (Grierson et al., 2006). This led to a final revision of the smoking bylaws, though not as complete as had been desired. Involvement in the web site influenced 76.4% to discuss the bylaw with others, and 63.8% to forward the site link to friends. Evaluation of the campaign emphasized the importance of "community capacity building," which includes individual and collective assets from community residents to improve quality of life, especially when some issue inspires or threatens their well-being, and which requires reliable access to decision-making processes and to the knowledge and skills necessary to create community change. Citizen participation (diverse members, collective action, and defining as well as implementing change) and social trust are two major indicators of community capacity building (Grierson et al., 2006).

Online or CD-ROM resources are becoming available for community campaign development and implementation. Finnegan et al. (2001) describe the use of the World Wide Web to make available to communities intervention technology addressing the problem of patient delay in seeking care for heart attack symptoms, based on their experiences with an 18-month 20-community treatment/control field experiment involving the effectiveness of fostering rapid response to heart attacks. They discuss the 10 steps they used in implementing the site, similar to stages in social marketing: (1) Preliminary questions, data gathering, (2) Define scope and mission, (3) Detailed outline of web site sections, (4) Visual representation of site organization, (5) Site layout, page design decisions, and user interface, (6) Collection of materials, (7) Technical training, (8) Technical development (implementation) of the design, (9) Development and implementation of a maintenance plan, and (10) Development and implementation of an evaluation plan. The site provided detailed information on how to develop community-based interventions, including case material from each of the field experiment treatment communities. CD-ROMs for health communication campaign planning and evaluation are available from the Centers for Disease Control (CDCynergy) and the Johns Hopkins School of Public Health's Center for Communication Program (SCOPE--Strategic Communication Planning & Evaluation). Other community-oriented campaign resources include The Benton Foundation (2007), The Communications Network (2007), Smart Chart 2.0 (2007), and The SPIN Project (2007) (all specifically oriented toward nonprofit organizations).

Lieberman (2006) advocated integrating community campaigns with online community games, which involve considerable social interaction, knowledge sharing, collaboration, and collective benefits, with both diverse as well as very targeted participants. Associated with the popular games are fan sites and discussion groups, which increase identification, knowledge, and social contacts. Mobile services and devices are also becoming part of virtual communities for health interventions (Leimeister & Krcmar, 2006), as they allow real anytime-anyplace access to the community platform.

CONDUCT SUMMATIVE EVALUATION

"Evaluation is the systematic application of research procedures to understand the conceptualization, design, implementation, and utility of interventions" (Valente, 2001, p. 106). Valente proposed that a comprehensive evaluation framework includes (1) assessing needs, (2) conducting formative research to design messages, (3) designing treatments, comparisons, instruments, and monitoring methods, (4) process research, (5) summative research, and (6) sharing results with stakeholders and other researchers. Developing an evaluation plan as an initial part of the campaign forces implementers and researchers to explicitly state the desired outcomes of the campaign, and how it will be implemented to obtain those goals. The actual financial and time costs of evaluation are real, but are extremely valuable investments, both for the current campaign stakeholders as well as for stakeholders of subsequent campaigns.

Valente (2001, 2002) summarized classical study designs that help reduce threats to validity due to selectivity, testing, history and maturation, and sensitization. Levels and timing of interventions and outcomes influence whether cross-sectional, cohort, panel, time-series or event-history designs are most appropriate, and whether interventions occur at the individual, group or community. Other factors to consider are the roles of self-selection, treatment diffusion across communities, and communication and influence through interpersonal and mediated networks.

Proper summative evaluation can distinguish between *theory failure*, the extent to which underlying causal chains are rejected by the evaluation results, and *process or program failure*, the extent to which the implementation of the campaign was inadequate or incorrect, thus allocating blame, credit, and lessons for future campaigns accordingly (Valente, 2002). Note that theory drives the design of messages and interventions, and thus the basis for evaluation, as theory is required to specify the causal processes and temporal sequence of inputs and outcomes. *Summative evaluation* consists of identifying and measuring answers to questions about six campaign aspects: (1) the *audience* (e.g., size, characteristics), (2) *implementation* of the planned campaign components (e.g., dissemination of messages and/or services), (3) *effectiveness* (e.g., influence on attitudes, behaviors, and health conditions), (4) *impacts* on larger aggregations (e.g., families or government agencies), (5) *cost* (e.g., total expenditures, and cost-effectiveness), and (6) *causal processes* (e.g., isolating the reasons why effects occurred or not) (Flay & Cook, 1989).

A Systems Perspective

Rice and Foote (2001) suggested a *systems-theoretical* approach to planning campaign evaluation, with particular application to health communication campaigns in developing countries. The basic assumption underlying this systems approach is that campaign inputs intended to alter prior states are mediated by a set of system constraints and enter into a process whereby some inputs are converted into outputs, thus evolving into a new post-state and altering system constraints. Campaign evaluation planning must match the timing and nature of inputs (such as media channels, messages, and material resources) and measurements with relevant phases of the system. The approach includes these stages: (1) specifying the goals and underlying assumptions of the project, (2) specifying the model at the project level, (3) specifying prior states, system phases, and system constraints, (4) specifying immediate as well as long-term intended post states, and guarding against unintended outcomes (boomerang effects), such as normalizing the unhealthy behavior, psychological reactance, and generating anxiety through fear appeals to those with low self-efficacy (Atkin, 2001), (5) specifying the model at the individual and the social (e.g., community network) levels, (6) choosing among research approaches appropriate to the system, and (7) assessing implications for design.

As a part of a process evaluation, Rice and Foote distinguished between *planned*, *real*, and *engaged* inputs. Informed campaign evaluations should measure and analyze these kinds of inputs separately. For example, Snyder's (2001) meta-analysis of 48 U.S. health campaigns found that an average of only 40% of people in intervention communities reported being exposed to their particular campaign. The Stanford Five-Community Study collected extensive data on message objectives, content, reach, and exposure, so it could explicitly evaluate the quantity of programming, broadcasting and interpersonal delivery, and engagement of a broad range of communication interventions. Similarly comprehensive programs of systems planning and integrated campaigns have been applied to complex problems such as rat control in grain-producing countries and community-wide issues such as adolescent drinking (Adhikarya, 2001; Bracht, 2001).

Challenges to Evaluating Online/Digital Media Campaigns

While online/digital media campaign components provide many benefits and opportunities (see below), they also present many new challenges. These include the increasing inability to identify and to reach known subpopulations, the shift from the broadcast mode of traditional mass media to the increased personalization of new media, the individual user's creation of and even interaction with specific sequences and forms of content, the use of multiple media forms to learn more about a particular topic, and the significance of peer-to-peer communication (Livingstone, 2004). These challenges create several methodological problems, including trying to observe actual behavior, and determining the meaning of these individually created multi-media experiences (with sites and content that themselves change or even disappear without any archival record).

Other challenges include how recruitment methods, and patient characteristics, are related to participation rates, engagement, and continued participation (Glasgow et al., 2007). Getting people to use web-based interventions, even when randomly assigned into that condition, is difficult (Verheijden et al., 2007). There is considerable variation in how to assess "exposure" to the intervention. Using the example of ChewFree.com, a randomized control trial of a smokeless tobacco cessation program on the web, Danaher et al. (2006) identified and defined measures such as email prompts (related to the intended "quit date" tailored to the quitting method, support messages, and messages encouraging those who were not using the site regularly), sessions/visits (number, duration, pattern, usage atrophy rate), and viewing (number, page types, postings). Online interventions run the risk of not only selective enrollment, but also selective retention (that is, use over multiple times, or through the length of the intervention). Verheijden et al.'s (2007) analysis of the use of a tailored online lifestyle/physical speculated that the minimization of stigmatization about bodyweight through individual, anonymous Internet sites may help account for the greater ongoing use by the specific target obese audience; but they also note that other target categories (those higher in physical activity and in vegetable consumption) were less likely to continue using the site. Another challenge to the use of interactive and tailored sites is determining the reliability and validity of the measures, because of different psychometric properties (for example, different groups of respondents answer only different small subsets of the entire set of questions, questions may be grouped on the basis of commonly understood symptoms rather than an underlying concept, sufficient sample size for each subset of answered items may be difficult to determine) (Ruland, Bakken, & Røislien, 2007). Dynamic, hyperlinked web sites are not amenable to all traditional evaluation methods, and few standard criteria yet exist for evaluating health-related web sites. Schneider et al. (2001) developed a multi-method evaluation of the US federal Medicare site (online survey of Internet users, online survey of visitors to the site, an expert review, focus groups, and a focus group with visually impaired Internet users). They recommend using the above methods as well as usability testing, interviews with web site managers, interviews with stakeholders, online focus groups, asynchronous forums, web usage/log analysis, analysis of emails from users, and backward compatibility assessments (to see how users with older browsers or systems would experience the site).

Assessing Effectiveness and Effects

Regarding the degree of effects, a meta-analysis of 48 mediated health campaigns (Snyder, 2001) showed 7% to 10% more overall behavior change by people in intervention communities than in control communities, representing a correlation of .09. Promoting new behaviors seems more effective than stopping old behaviors or preventing new behaviors (12% compared to 5% and 4%), and enforcement strategies and provision of new information both noticeably increased outcomes (17% and 14% change).

However, assessing campaign effectiveness is not easily achieved, even with sophisticated summative evaluation designs. This is because "effects" are not the same as "effectiveness", and what constitutes "effectiveness" itself is controversial and often ambiguous (Salmon & Atkin, 2003; Salmon & Murray-Johnson, 2001). At least six measures of "effectiveness" may be considered:

1. *Definitional effectiveness* is somewhat political: it is the extent to which various stakeholders attain success in having a social phenomenon defined as a social problem. As noted above, Paisley (2001) considered this problem in terms of getting the problem on the public agenda—just how important *is* this health problem, anyway?—and defining campaign interests as first-party or second-party advocacy. For example, Butler (2001) showed how the "Got Milk?" campaign was fraught with issues of industry sponsorship and lack of evaluation in spite of federal regulations and counter-indicative research.

2. *Ideological effectiveness* concerns whether the problem is defined as primarily individual or social; that is, should alcohol abuse be seen, and treated as, primarily an issue of individual responsibility (as in the "designated driver" television campaign—see Winsten & DeJong, 2001), or should it be considered as embedded in extensive advertising and entertainment portrayals of drinking?

3. *Political effectiveness* is the extent to which a campaign creates visibility or symbolic value for some stakeholder, regardless of other outcome measures.

4. *Contextual effectiveness* assesses the extent to which the intervention achieved its goals within a particular context. For example, education, enforcement or engineering approaches are differently appropriate for different problems (Paisley, 2001), so it would

be unfair to evaluate (and probably unwise to implement) an attitude-change campaign if engineering approaches are the most suitable (such as reducing automobile exhaust).

5. *Cost-effectiveness* concerns the tradeoffs between different inputs and outputs, over time. For example, prevention campaigns may in fact save much more money over time than treatment campaigns, but the outcomes are harder to measure and occur over lengthier time spans. Further, treating some problems (such as those with low prevalence, or those that generate widespread fear) may generate increased costs in other areas, thus lowering health effectiveness overall.

6. Finally, *programmatic effectiveness* is probably the most familiar approach, whereby campaign performance is assessed relative to its stated goals and objectives.

Salmon and Murray-Johnson (2001) showed that campaigns should be assessed on two dimensions: whether or not effects were obtained, and whether or not the campaign was effective. The resulting four conditions lead to very different overall evaluations. For example, public service announcements for local health agencies may be quite effective in attaining high and measurable exposure while failing to achieve an effect in measurably increasing referrals or visits or reduced illness.

Unintended Effects

Campaign evaluations rarely consider potential unintended harmful consequences (such as decreasing pressure to provide interpersonal support, increased isolation, reducing the visibility of the problem and thus reinforcing the stigma, etc.), or of associated costs not specifically part of the intervention (such as costs to local health services or patients' social networks) (Griffiths et al., 2006). Discussion among participants in an online campaign intervention (such as through a chat or discussion feature) is one possible unintended effect, as it may generate a boomerang effect (due to increased discussion about the topic, earlier counter-arguing, greater portrayal of consensus or majority attitudes, possibly by more dominant or deviant members) or increased adherence to initial beliefs (David, Cappella, & Fishbein, 2006). Cho and Salmon (2007) developed a typology of unintended effects that provides a conceptual framework for such possibilities. Their model first identifies five dimensions where unintended campaign effects may occur—time (short or long term), level (individual or societal), audience (targeted or other), content (related to specific content or indirectly related to the use of the medium), and valence (desirable or undesirable). Across these five dimensions, 11 types of unintended effects may differentially occur (for example, all 11 may be associated with undesirable valence, but only three are associated with short-term): obfuscation, dissonance, boomerang, epidemic of apprehension, desensitization, culpability, opportunity cost, social reproduction, social norming, enabling, and system activation (pp. 299–301).

CONSIDER ONGOING CHALLENGES

A variety of theoretical and practical challenges and tensions continue to exist in the design, implementation, and evaluation of public communication campaigns. Many important social problems involve *collective benefits* (such as reduced litter), yet most campaigns have succeeded only when they promote *individual benefits*. How can campaigns increase the salience of collective benefits, the focus of many campaigns in China (see Liu, 2001), or the foundation of environmental campaigns (Cox, 2006)? What is the proper mix of *education* and *entertainment*? Will or should new "infotainment" campaigns be embedded in the commercial media mainstream (Singhal et al., 2004; Singhal & Rogers, 2002)? How can campaigns, which generally use the media channels, overcome the *simultaneous pervasive negative influence of the mass media* on campaign issues such as drinking, violence and environmental damage (Moser & Dilling, 2007; Wallack & Dorfman, 2001)? Few theories or campaign designs explicitly distinguish *short-term* from *long-term* effects and objectives. What should be the relative emphasis on each, and how can campaigns achieve longer term outcomes (McGuire, 2001; Valente, 2002)? What is the proper mix of *interpersonal, mass media* and *new interactive media* communication for specific campaign goals (Cappella et al., 2001; Murero & Rice, 2006; Rice & Katz, 2001)? How can campaigns successfully promote a *prevention* approach in order to avoid the more expensive *treatment* approach typically favored by organizations, government agencies, and the electorate (Dervin & Frennette, 2001; Rice, 2001; Wallack & Dorfman, 2001)? What are the relative influences of *individual differences* versus *social structure* on the problems targeted by communication campaigns (Piotrow & Kincaid, 2001; Rice & Foote, 2001)? How can campaigns *communicate effectively with young people*, who have fundamentally different evaluations of risk and future consequences, who are using radically different interactive and personal media, and who are deeply embedded in both face-to-face and, increasingly, online and wireless peer networks (Kim, Kim, Park, & Rice, 2007; Piotrow & Kincaid, 2001)? Finally, how can campaigns resolve the wide-ranging *ethical implications* of the many choices required throughout the process (Guttman, 2003)?

References

Adhikarya, R. (2001). The strategic extension campaigns on rat control in Bangladesh. In R. E. Rice & C. K. Atkin (Eds.), *Public communication campaigns* (3rd ed., pp. 283–285). Thousand Oaks, CA: Sage.

Ajzen, I., & Fishbein, M. (1980). *Understanding attitudes and predicting social behavior*. Englewood Cliffs, NJ: Prentice-Hall.

Alcalay, R., & Bell, R. A. (2000). What is social marketing? From *Promoting nutrition and physical activity through social marketing: Current practices and recommendations*. Center for Advanced Studies in Nutrition and Social Marketing, Davis, CA: University of California. Retrieved March, 2008 from http://socialmarketing-nutrition.ucdavis.edu

Alcalay, R., & Taplin, S. (1989). Community health campaigns: From theory to action. In R. E. Rice & C. Atkin (Eds.), *Public communication campaigns* (2nd ed., pp. 105–130). Newbury Park, CA: Sage.

Annang, L., Muilenburg, J., & Strasser, S. (2007). Three-dimensional online virtual worlds: An opportunity to expand the horizons of health promotion. Paper presented at *135th American Public Health Association conference*, Nov 2007, Washington, D.C.

Atkin, C. K. (2001). Theory and principles of media health campaigns. In R. E. Rice & C. K. Atkin (Eds.), *Public communication campaigns* (3rd ed., pp. 49–68). Thousand Oaks, CA: Sage.

Atkin, C. K., & Freimuth, V. (2001). Formative evaluation research in campaign design. In R. E. Rice & C. K. Atkin (Eds.), *Public communication campaigns* (3rd ed., pp. 125–145). Thousand Oaks, CA: Sage.

Backer, T., Rogers, E. M., & Sopory, P. (1992). *Designing health communication campaigns: What works?* Newbury Park, CA: Sage.

Bandura, A. (1977a). Self-efficacy: Toward a unifying theory of behavioral change. *Psychological Review, 84*(2), 191–215.

Bandura, A. (1977b). *Social learning theory*. Englewood Cliffs, NJ: Prentice-Hall.

Bem, D. (1970). *Beliefs, attitudes and human affairs.* Belmont, CA: Brooks/Cole.

Benigeri, M., & Pluye, P. (2003). Shortcomings of health information on the Internet. *Health Promotion International, 18*(4), 381–386.

Benton Foundation. (2007). Retrieved March, 2008 from http://www.benton.org/publibrary/toolkits/community.html.

Bracht, N. (2001). Community partnership strategies in health campaigns. In R. E. Rice & C. K. Atkin (Eds.), *Public communication campaigns* (3rd ed., pp. 323–342). Thousand Oaks, CA: Sage.

Browning, G. (2002). PSAs in a new media age. In V. Rideout, & T. Hoff (Eds.), Shouting to be heard: PSAs in a new media age. Kaiser Family Foundation report. Retrieved March, 2008 from http://www.kff.org/entmedia/loader.cfm?url=/commonspot/security/getfile.cfm& PageID=13937

Brug, J., Oenema, A., & Campbell, M. (2003). Past, present, and future of computer tailored nutrition education. *American Journal of Clinical Nutrition, 77*(4), 1028S–1034S.

Brunsting, S., & van den Putte, B. (2006). Web-based computer-tailored feedback on alcohol use: Motivating excessive drinkers to consider their behavior. In M. Murero & R. E. Rice (Eds.), *The Internet and health care: Theory, research and practice* (pp. 313–333). Mahwah, NJ: Erlbaum.

Bull, S. S., McFarlane, M., & King, D. (2001). Barriers to STD/HIV prevention on the Internet. *Health Education Research, 16*(6), 661–670.

Buller, D., Woodall, W. G., Hall, J., Borland, R., Ax, B., Brown, M., & Hines, J. M. (2001). A web-based smoking cessation and prevention program for children aged 12–15. In R. E. Rice & C. K. Atkin (Eds.), *Public communication campaigns* (3rd ed., pp. 357–372). Thousand Oaks, CA: Sage.

Butler, M. (2001). America's sacred cow. In R. E. Rice & C. K. Atkin (Eds.), *Public communication campaigns* (3rd ed., pp. 309–314). Thousand Oaks, CA: Sage.

Cappella, J., Fishbein, M., Hornik, R., Ahern, R. K., & Sayeed, S. (2001). Using theory to select messages in anti-drug media campaigns: Reasoned action and media priming. In R. E. Rice & C. K. Atkin (Eds.), *Public communication campaigns* (3rd ed., pp. 214–230). Thousand Oaks, CA: Sage.

Cho, H., & Salmon, C. T. (2007). Unintended effects of health communication campaigns. *Journal of Communication, 57*(2), 293–317.

Cialdini, R. (2001). Littering: When every litter bit hurts. In R. E. Rice & C. K. Atkin (Eds.), *Public communication campaigns* (3rd ed., pp. 280–282). Thousand Oaks, CA: Sage.

The Communications Network. (2007). Retrieved March, 2008 from www.comnetwork.org.

Cox, R. (2006). *Environmental communication and the public sphere.* Thousand Oaks, CA: Sage.

Crano, W., & Burgoon, M. (Eds.). (2002). *Mass media and drug prevention: Classic and contemporary theories and research.* Mahwah, NJ: Erlbaum.

Cumbo, A., Agre, P., Dougherty, J., Callery, M., Tetzlaff, L., Pirone, J., & Tallia, R. (2002). Online cancer patient education: Evaluating usability and content. *Cancer practice, 10*(3), 155–161.

Cunningham, J. A., Humphreys, K., Kypri, K., & van Mierlo, T. (2006). Formative evaluation and three-month follow-up of an online personalized assessment feedback intervention for problem drinkers. *Journal of Medical Internet Research,* 8(2):e5. Retrieved March, 2008 from <http://www.jmir.org/2006/2/e5/>

Curioso, W. (2006). New technologies and public health in developing countries: The cell PREVEN Project. In M. Murero & R. E. Rice (Eds.), *The Internet and health care: Theory, research and practice* (pp. 375–393). Mahwah, NJ: Erlbaum.

Danaher, B. G., Boles, S. M., Akers, L., Gordon, J. S., & Severson, H. H. (2006). Defining participant exposure measures in web-based health behavior change programs. *Journal of Medical Internet Research,* 8(3):e15. Retrieved March, 2008 from <http://www.jmir.org/2006/3/e15/>

Danaher, B. G., Jazdzewski, S. A., McKay, H. G., & Hudson, C. R. (2005). Bandwidth constraints to using video and other rich media in behavior change websites. *Journal of Medical Internet Research,* 7(4):e49. Retrieved March, 2008 from <http://www.jmir.org/2005/4/e49/>

Danaher, B. G., McKay, H. G., & Seeley, J. R. (2005). The information architecture of behavior change websites. *Journal of Medical Internet Research,* 7(2):e12. Retrieved March, 2008 from <http://www.jmir.org/2005/2/e12/>

David, C., Cappella, J., & Fishbein, M. (2006). The social diffusion of influence among adolescents: Group interaction in a chat room environment about antidrug advertisements. *Communication Theory*, *16*(1), 118–140.

Dearing, J. W. (2001). The cumulative community response to AIDS in San Francisco. In R. E. Rice & C. K. Atkin (Eds.), *Public communication campaigns* (3rd ed., pp. 305–308). Thousand Oaks, CA: Sage.

Dearing, J. W. (2003). The state of the art and the state of the science of community organizing. In T. L. Thompson, A. M. Dorsey, K. I. Miller, & R. Parrott (Eds.), *Handbook of health communication* (pp. 207–220). Mahwah, NJ: Erlbaum.

Delichatsios, H. K., Friedman, R. H., Glanz, K., Tennstedt, S., Smigelski, C., Pinto, B. M., Kelley, H., & Gillman, M. W. (2001). Randomized trial of a "talking computer" to improve adults' eating habits. *American Journal of Health Promotion*, *15*(4), 215–224.

Dervin, B., & Frenette, M. (2001). Applying sense-making methodology: Communicating communicatively with audiences as listeners, learners, teachers, confidantes. In R. E. Rice & C. K. Atkin (Eds.), *Public communication campaigns* (3rd ed., pp. 69–87). Thousand Oaks, CA: Sage.

Dozier, D., Grunig, L., & Grunig, J. (2001). Public relations as communication campaign. In R. E. Rice & C. K. Atkin (Eds.), *Public communication campaigns* (3rd ed., pp. 231–248). Thousand Oaks, CA: Sage.

Edgar, T., Noar, S., & Freimuth, V. (2007). *Communication perspectives on HIV/AIDS for the 21st century*. Mahwah, NJ: Erlbaum.

Edgerton, E., Nall, J., Burnett, A., & Maze, T. (2007). Health campaigns and new media: Seasonal flu. Paper presented at *135th American Public Health Association conference*, Nov 2007, Washington, D.C.

Etter, J. (2005). Comparing the efficacy of two internet-based, computer-tailored smoking cessation programs: A randomized trial. *Journal of Medical Internet Research*, 7(1):e2. Retrieved March, 2008 from <http://www. jmir.org/2005/1/e2/>

Festinger, L. (1954). A theory of social comparison processes. *Human Relations*, *7*, 117–140.

Finnegan, J. Jr., Alexander, D., Rightmyer, J., Estabrook, B., Gloeb, B., Voss, M., Leviton, L., & Luepker, R. (2001). Using the web to assist communities in public health campaign planning: A case study of the REACT project. In R. E. Rice & J. E. Katz (Eds.) (2001). *The Internet and health communication: Expectations and experiences* (pp. 147–166). Thousand Oaks, CA: Sage.

Fishbein, M., & Cappella, J. N. (2006). The role of theory in developing effective health communications. *Journal of Communication*, *56*(Supplement), S1–S17.

Flay, B., & Cook, T. (1989). Three models for summative evaluation of prevention campaigns with a mass media component. In R. E. Rice & C. Atkin (Eds.), *Public communication campaigns* (2nd ed., pp. 175–196). Newbury Park, CA: Sage.

Flora, J. (2001). The Stanford community studies: Campaigns to reduce cardiovascular disease. In R. E. Rice & C. K. Atkin (Eds.), *Public communication campaigns* (3rd ed., pp. 193–213). Thousand Oaks, CA: Sage.

Franklin, P. D., Rosenbaum, P. F., Carey, M. P., & Roizen, M. F. (2006). Using sequential email messages to promote health behaviors: Evidence of feasibility and reach in a worksite sample. *Journal of Medical Internet Research*, 8(1):e3. Retrieved March, 2008 from http://www.jmir.org/2006/1/e3/

Geary, C., Burke, H. M, Castelnau, L., Neupane, S., Sall, Y. B., & Wong, E. (2007). Exposure to MTV's global HIV prevention campaign in Kathmandu, Nepal; Sao Paulo, Brazil; and Dakar, Senegal. *AIDS Education and Prevention*, *19*(1), 36–50.

Glasgow, R. E., Nelson, C. C., Kearney, K. A., Reid, R., Ritzwoller, D. P., Strecher, V. J., Couper, M. P., Green, B., & Wildenhaus, K. (2007). Reach, engagement, and retention in an internet-based weight loss program in a multi-site randomized controlled trial. *Journal of Medical Internet Research*, 9(2):e11. Retrieved March, 2008 from <http://www.jmir.org/2007/2/e11/>

Grierson, T., Van Dijk, M. W., Dozois, E., & Mascher, J. (2006). Using the Internet to build community capacity for healthy public policy. *Health Promotion Practice*, *7*(1), 13–22.

Griffiths, F., Lindenmeyer, A., Powell, J., Lowe, P., & Thorogood, M. (2006). Why are health care interventions delivered over the internet? A systematic review of the published literature. *Journal of Medical Internet Research*, 8(2):e10. Retrieved March, 2008 from http://www.jmir.org/2006/2/e10/

Guide to Community Preventive Services. http://www.thecommunityguide.org/pa/pa-int-indiv-behav-change.pdf [accessed 2008 Mar 21]

Guttman, N. (2003). Ethics in health communication interventions. In T. L. Thompson, A. M. Dorsey, K. I. Miller, & R. Parrott (Eds.), *Handbook of health communication* (pp. 651–679). Mahwah, NJ: Erlbaum.

Hanauer, D., Dibble, E., Fortin, J., & Col, N. F. (2004). Internet use among community college students: Implications in designing healthcare interventions. *Journal of American College Health*, *52*(5), 197–202.

Hartmann, C. W., Sciamanna, C. N., Blanch, D. C., Mui, S., Lawless, H., Manocchia, M., Rosen, R. K., & Pietropaoli, A. (2007). A website to improve asthma care by suggesting patient questions for physicians: Qualitative analysis of user experiences. *Journal of Medical Internet Research*, 9(1):e3. Retrieved March, 2008 from http://www.jmir.org/2007/1/e3/

Hawkins, R., Gustafson, D. H., Chewning, B., Bosworth, K., & Day, P. (1987). Reaching hard-to-reach populations: Interactive computer programs as public information campaigns for adolescents. *Journal of Communication*, *37*(2), 8–28.

Haylock, C. & Rabi, M. (2007). Wikis, RSS, Blogs, Podcasts: How Web 2.0 technologies can enhance public health Web sites. Paper presented at *135th American Public Health Association conference*, Nov 2007, Washington, D.C.

Heeter, C. (1989). Implications of new interactive technologies for conceptualizing communication. In J. L. Salvaggio & J. Bryant (Eds.), *Media use in the information age: Emerging patterns of adoption and consumer use* (pp. 217–235). Hillsdale, NJ: Erlbaum.

Hornik, R. (2002). *Public health communication: Evidence for behavior change*. Mahwah, NJ: Erlbaum.

Hovland, C., Janis, I., & Kelley, H. (1953). *Communication and persuasion*. New Haven, CT: Yale University Press.

Hurling, R., Catt, M., De Boni, M., Fairley, B. W., Hurst, T., Murray, P., Richardson, A., & Sodhi, J. S. (2007). Using internet and mobile phone technology to deliver an automated physical activity program: Randomized controlled trial. *Journal of Medical Internet Research*, 9(2):e7. Retrieved March, 2008 from http://www.jmir.org/2007/2/e7/

Kim, H., Kim, G. J., Park, H. W., & Rice, R. E. (2007). Configurations of relationships in different media: FtF, Email, Instant Messenger, Mobile Phone, and SMS. *Journal of Computer-Mediated Communication*, *12*(4). Retrieved March, 2008 from htttp://jcmc.indiana.edu/vol12/issue4/kim.html and http://www.blackwell-synergy.com/doi/full/10.1111/j.1083–6101.2007.00369.x

Klingermann, H., & Roemmele, A. (Eds.). (2002). *Public information campaigns and opinion research: A handbook for the student and practitioner*. London: Sage.

Kotler, P., Roberto N., & Lee, N. (2002). *Social marketing: Improving the quality of life*. Thousand Oaks, CA: Sage.

Kreuter, M., Farrell, D., Olevitch, L., & Brennan, L. (2000). *Tailoring health messages: Customizing communication with computer technology*. Mahwah, NJ: Erlbaum.

LaRose, R. (1989). Freestyle, revisited. In R. E. Rice & C. Atkin (Eds.), *Public communication campaigns* (2nd ed., pp. 206–209). Newbury Park, CA: Sage.

Lederman, L. C., & Stewart, L. P. (2005). *Changing the culture of college drinking: A socially situated health communication campaign*. Cresskill, NJ: Hampton Press.

Lederman, L. C., Stewart, L., Barr, S., Powell, R., Laitman, L., & Goodhart, F. W. (2001). RU sure? Using communication theory to reduce dangerous drinking on a college campus. In R. E. Rice & C. K. Atkin (Eds.), *Public communication campaigns* (3rd ed., pp. 295–299). Thousand Oaks, CA: Sage.

Leimeister, J. M., & Krcmar, H. (2006). Designing and implementing virtual patient support communities: A German case study. In M. Murero & R. E. Rice (Eds.), *The Internet and health care: Theory, research and practice* (pp. 255–276). Mahwah, NJ: Erlbaum.

Lieberman, D. A. (2001). Using interactive media in communication campaigns for children and adolescents. In R. E. Rice & C. K. Atkin (Eds.), *Public communication campaigns* (3rd ed., pp. 373–388). Thousand Oaks, CA: Sage.

Lieberman, D. A. (2006). What can we learn from playing interactive games? In P. Vorderer & J. Bryant (Eds.), *Playing video games: Motives, responses, and consequences* (pp. 379–397). Mahwah, NJ: Erlbaum.

Linke, S., Murray, E., Butler, C., & Wallace, P. (2007). Internet-based interactive health intervention for the promotion of sensible drinking: Patterns of use and potential impact on members of the general public. *Journal of Medical Internet Research*, 9(2):e10. Retrieved March, 2008 from <http://www.jmir.org/2007/2/e10/>

Liu, A. P. (2001). Mass campaigns in the People's Republic of China during the Mao era. In R. E. Rice & C. K. Atkin (Eds.), *Public communication campaigns* (3rd ed., pp. 286–289). Thousand Oaks, CA: Sage.

Livingstone, S. (2004). The challenge of changing audiences: Or, what is the audience researcher to do in the age of the Internet? *European Journal of Communication, 19*(1), 75–86.

McGuire, W. J. (1960). A syllogistic analysis of cognitive relationships. In M. J. Rosenberg & C. I. Hovland (Eds.), *Attitude organization and change* (pp. 65–111). New Haven, CT: Yale University Press.

McGuire, W. (2001). Input and output variables currently promising for constructing persuasive communications. In R. E. Rice & C. K. Atkin (Eds.), *Public communication campaigns* (3rd ed., pp. 22–48). Thousand Oaks, CA: Sage.

McMillan, S. (2002). A four-part model of cyber-interactivity: Some cyber-places are more interactive than others. *New Media & Society*, 4(2), 271–291.

Moser, S. & Dilling, L. (Eds.) (2007). *Creating a climate for change: Communicating climate change and facilitating social change*. New York: Cambridge University Press.

Murero, M. & Rice, R. E. (Eds.) (2006). *The Internet and health care: Theory, research and practice*. Mahwah, NJ: Erlbaum.

Neuhauser, L., & Kreps, G. L. (2003). Rethinking communication in the e-Health era. *Journal of Health Psychology*, 8(1), 7–22.

Norman, C. D., & Skinner, H. A. (2006). eHEALS: The eHealth literacy scale. *Journal of Medical Internet Research*, 8(4):e27. Retrieved March, 2008 from <http://www.jmir.org/2006/4/e27/>

Pagliari, C. (2007). Design and evaluation in ehealth: Challenges and implications for an interdisciplinary field. *Journal of Medical Internet Research*, 9(2):e15. Retrieved March, 2008 from <http://www.jmir.org/2007/2/e15/>

Paisley, W. (1998). Scientific literacy and the competition for public attention and understanding. *Science Communication, 20*, 70–80.

Paisley, W. (2001). Public communication campaigns: The American experience. In R. E. Rice & C. K. Atkin (Eds.), *Public communication campaigns* (3rd ed., pp. 3–21). Thousand Oaks, CA: Sage.

Perloff, R. (2003). *The dynamics of persuasion: Communication and attitudes in the 21st century*. Mahwah NJ: Erlbaum.

Petty, R., & Cacioppo, J. (1986). *Communication and persuasion: Central and peripheral routes to attitude change*. New York: Springer-Verlag.

Piotrow, P., & Kincaid, L. (2001). Strategic communication for international health programs. In R. E. Rice & C. K. Atkin (Eds.), *Public communication campaigns* (3rd ed., pp. 249–266). Thousand Oaks, CA: Sage.

Prochaska, J. O., DiClemente, C. C., & Norcross, J. C. (1992). In search of how people change: Applications to addictive behaviors. *American Psychologist, 47*, 1102–1114.

Prochaska, J. O., & Velicer, W. F. (1997). The Transtheoretical Model of health behavior change. *American Journal of Health Promotion, 12*, 38–48.

Proctor, R. (2001). The Nazi anti-tobacco campaign. In R. E. Rice & C. K. Atkin (Eds.), *Public communication campaigns* (3rd ed., pp. 315–319). Thousand Oaks, CA: Sage.

Reis, J., Riley, W., & Baer, J. (2000). Interactive multimedia preventive alcohol education: An evaluation of effectiveness with college students. *Journal of Educational Computing Research, 23*(1), 41–65.

Rhodes, J. E., Spencer, R., Saito, R., & Sipe, C. L. (2006). Online mentoring: The promise and challenges of an emerging approach to youth development. *Journal of Primary Prevention, 27*(5), 497–513.

Rice, R. E. (1993). Using network concepts to clarify sources and mechanisms of social influence. In W. Richards, Jr. & G. Barnett (Eds.), *Progress in communication sciences, vol. 12: Advances in communication network analysis* (pp. 43–52). Norwood, NJ: Ablex.

Rice, R. E. (2001). Smokey Bear. In R. E. Rice & C. K. Atkin (Eds.), *Public communication campaigns* (3rd ed., pp. 276–279). Thousand Oaks, CA: Sage.

Rice, R. E. (2006). Influences, usage, and outcomes of Internet health information searching: Multivariate results from the Pew surveys. *International Journal of Medical Informatics, 75*(1), 8–28.

Rice, R. E., and Associates (1984). *The new media: Communication, research and technology*. Newbury Park, CA: Sage.

Rice, R. E., & Atkin, C. (Eds.). (1989). *Public communication campaigns* (2nd ed.). Newbury Park, CA: Sage.

Rice, R. E., & Atkin, C. (1994). Principles of successful communication campaigns: A summary from recent research. In J. Bryant & D. Zillmann (Eds.), *Media effects: Advances in theory and research* (pp. 365–387). Mahwak, NJ: Erlbaum.

Rice, R. E., & Foote, D. (2001). A systems-based evaluation planning model for health communication campaigns in developing countries. In R. E. Rice & C. K. Atkin (Eds.), *Public communication campaigns* (3rd ed., pp. 146–167). Thousand Oaks, CA: Sage.

Rice, R. E., & Katz, J. E. (Eds.) (2001). *The Internet and health communication*. Thousand Oaks, CA: Sage.

Rice, R. E., & Katz, J. E. (2003). Comparing internet and mobile phone usage: Digital divides of usage, adoption, and dropouts. *Telecommunications Policy, 27*(8/9), 597–623.

Rice, R. E., Peterson, M., & Christine, R. (2001). A comparative features analysis of publicly accessible commercial and government health database web sites. In R. E. Rice & J. E. Katz (Eds.), *The Internet and health communication: Expectations and experiences* (pp. 213–231). Thousand Oaks, CA: Sage.

Rimal, R. N., & Adkins, A. D. (2003). Using computers to narrowcast health messages: The role of audience segmentation, targeting, and tailoring in health promotion. In T. L. Thompson, A. M. Dorsey, K. I. Miller, & R. Parrott (Eds.), *Handbook of health communication* (pp. 497–513). Mahwah, NJ: Erlbaum.

Rimal, R. N., & Flora, J. A. (1997). Interactive technology attributes in health promotion: Practical and theoretical issues. In R. Street & T. Manning (Eds.), *Using interactive computing in health promotion* (pp. 19–38). Mahwah, NJ: Erlbaum.

Ritterband, L. M., Andersson, G., Christensen, H. M., Carlbring, P., & Cuijpers, P. (2006). Directions for the International Society for Research on Internet Interventions. *Journal of Medical Internet Research*, 8(3):e23. Retrieved March, 2008 from <http://www.jmir.org/2006/3/e23/>

Rogers, E. M. (1981). *Communication networks: A new paradigm for research*. New York: Free Press.

Rogers, E. M., & Storey, D. (1987). Communication campaigns. In C. Berger & S. Chaffee (Eds.), *Handbook of communication science* (pp. 817–846). Newbury Park, CA: Sage.

Ruland, C. M., Bakken, S., & Røislien, J. (2007). Reliability and validity issues related to interactive tailored patient assessments: A case study. *Journal of Medical Internet Research*, 9(3):e22. Retrieved March, 2008 from http://www.jmir.org/2007/3/e22/

Ryan, P., & Lauver, D. R. (2002). The efficacy of tailored interventions. *Journal of Nursing Scholarship, 34*(4), 331–337.

Salmon, C., & Atkin, C. (2003). Using media campaigns for health promotion. In T. L. Thompson, A. M. Dorsey, K. I. Miller, & R. Parrott (Eds.), *Handbook of health communication* (pp. 449–472). Mahwah, NJ: Erlbaum.

Salmon, C., & Murray-Johnson, L. (2001). Communication campaign effectiveness: Some critical distinctions. In R. E. Rice & C. K. Atkin (Eds.), *Public communication campaigns* (3rd ed., pp. 168–180). Thousand Oaks, CA: Sage.

Schneider, S., Frechtling, J., Edgar, T., Crawley, B., & Goldstein, E. (2001). Evaluating a federal health-related web site: A multi-method perspective on *Medicare.Gov.* In R. E. Rice & J. E. Katz (Eds.), *The Internet and health communication: Expectations and experiences* (pp. 167–187). Thousand Oaks, CA: Sage.

Singhal, A., & Rogers, E. M. (2001). The entertainment-education strategy in communication campaigns. In R. E. Rice & C. K. Atkin (Eds.), *Public communication campaigns* (3rd ed., pp. 343–356). Thousand Oaks, CA: Sage.

Singhal, A., & Rogers, E. M. (2002). A theoretical agenda for entertainment-education. *Communication Theory, 12*(2), 117–135.

Singhal, A., Cody, M., Rogers, E., & Sabido, M. (2004). *Entertainment-education and social change: History, research, and practice*. Mahwah, NJ: Erlbaum.

Smart Chart 2.0. (2007). Retrieved March, 2008 from www.smartchart.org.

Snyder, L. (2001). How effective are mediated health campaigns? In R. E. Rice & C. K. Atkin (Eds.), *Public communication campaigns* (3rd ed., pp. 181–190). Thousand Oaks, CA: Sage.

SPIN Project. (2007). Retrieved March, 2008 from www.spinproject.org.

Stephenson, M., & Witte, K. (2001). Creating fear in a risky world: Generating effective health risk messages. In R. E. Rice & C. K. Atkin (Eds.), *Public communication campaigns* (3rd ed., pp. 88–102). Thousand Oaks, CA: Sage.

Stiff, J. B., & Mongeau, P. (2003). *Persuasive communication*. New York: Guilford Press.

Stout, P. A., Villegas, J., & Kim, H. (2001). Enhancing learning through use of interactive tools on health-related websites. *Health Education Research, 16*(6), 721–733.

Thompson, T., Dorsey, A., Miller, K., & Parrott, R. (Eds.) (2003). *Handbook of health communication*. Mahwah, NJ: Erlbaum.

Thorogood, M., & Coombes, Y. (Eds.) (2004). *Evaluating health promotion: Practice and methods* (2nd ed.). New York: Oxford University Press.

Tones, K., & Green, G. (2004). *Health promotion: Planning and strategies*. London: Sage.

Trappey, R. J., & Woodside, A. G. (2005). Consumer responses to interactive advertising campaigns coupling short-message-service direct marketing and TV commercials. *Journal of Advertising Research, 45*(4), 382–401.

Tufano, J. T., & Karras, B. T. (2005). Mobile eHealth interventions for obesity: A timely opportunity to leverage convergence trends. *Journal of Medical Internet Research,* 7(5):e58. Retrieved March, 2008 from <http://www.jmir.org/2005/4/e1/>

U.S. Department of Health and Human Services (2003). *Making health communication programs work*. Bethesda, MD: Office of Cancer Communications, National Cancer Institute.

Valente, T. (2001). Evaluating communication campaigns. In R. E. Rice & C. K. Atkin (Eds.), *Public communication campaigns* (3rd ed., pp. 105–124). Thousand Oaks, CA: Sage.

Valente, T. (2002). *Evaluating health promotion programs*. New York: Oxford University Press.

Verheijden, M. W., Jans, M. P., Hildebrandt, V. H., & Hopman-Rock, M. (2007). Rates and determinants of repeated participation in a web-based behavior change program for healthy body weight and healthy lifestyle. *Journal of Medical Internet Research,* 9(1):e1. Retrieved March, 2008 from <http://www.jmir.org/2007/1/e1/>

Wallack, L. (1989). Mass media and health promotion: A critical perspective. In R. E. Rice & C. Atkin (Eds.), *Public communication campaigns* (2nd ed., pp. 353–368). Newbury Park, CA: Sage.

Wallack, L., & Dorfman, L. (2001). Putting policy into health communication: The role of media advocacy. In R. E. Rice & C. K. Atkin (Eds.), *Public communication campaigns* (3rd ed., pp. 389–401). Thousand Oaks, CA: Sage.

Walther, J. B., Pingree, S., Hawkins, R. P., & Buller, D. B. (2005). Attributes of interactive online health information systems. *Journal of Medical Internet Research,* 7(3):e33. Retrieved March, 2008 from <http://www.jmir.org/2005/3/e33/>

Wantland, D. J., Portillo, C. J., Holzemer, W. L., Slaughter, R., & McGhee, E. M. (2004). The effectiveness of web-based vs. non-web-based interventions: A meta-analysis of behavioral change outcomes. *Journal of Medical Internet Research,* 6(4):e40 http://www.jmir.org/2004/4/e40/

Wilbur, J. (2006). *Getting your feet wet with social marketing: A social marketing guide for watershed programs*. Salt Lake City, UT: Utah Department of Agriculture and Food. Retrieved March, 2008 from http://www.ag.utah.gov/conservation/GettingYourFeetWet1.pdf

Winsten, J., & DeJong, W. (2001). The designated driver campaign. In R. E. Rice & C. K. Atkin (Eds.), *Public communication campaigns* (3rd ed., pp. 290–294). Thousand Oaks, CA: Sage.

Witte, K., Meyer, G., & Martell, D. (2001). *Effective health risk messages*. Thousand Oaks, CA: Sage.

21

EFFECTS OF MEDIA ON PERSONAL AND PUBLIC HEALTH

Kim Walsh-Childers
University of Florida

Jane D. Brown
University of North Carolina-Chapel Hill

Health-related messages are in every kind of media one might use in a typical day. The breakfast cereal is advertised as "heart-healthy," the margarine and toast "trans-fat free." The morning newspaper contains stories about the latest medical research, presidential candidates' health care reform proposals, and the nationwide obesity epidemic. The songs on the radio include explicit, even degrading sexual lyrics. Magazines offer weight loss advice, images of physical ideals and advertising for alcohol, cigarettes, and numerous health-related products. In Fall 2007, the evening TV lineup included ABC's "Fat March," a reality show featuring 12 obese individuals attempting to walk 575 miles in 10 weeks; "Nip/Tuck," an FX Networks drama about plastic surgeons; and Fox's "House, M.D.," about an antisocial medical genius who always succeeds in pinpointing his patients' mysterious illnesses. And almost anything about health can be found on the Internet—medical advice, support groups, health blogs, and even the opportunity to purchase prescription or non-prescription drugs.

Interest in the effects of such content has increased over the past 20 years as it has become clearer that the media do shape individuals' health-related beliefs and behaviors. Studies typically have focused on the negative effects of advertising (e.g., for cigarettes, alcohol) and entertainment (e.g., unprotected sex) on individuals. In chapter 20 in this volume, Atkin and Rice examined how the intentional use of media, such as in public health media campaigns, can result in positive health attitudes and behaviors.

In this chapter we have organized the research on the health effects of the mass media along three dimensions: (1) level of influence (personal/public), (2) intention of the message producer regarding effects (intended/unintended), and (3) outcome (positive/negative). At the *personal level*, the mass media may provide information and models that stimulate changes—either positive or negative—in health-related attitudes and behaviors. At the *public level*, the mass media may influence both policy-makers' and the public's opinions about health issues; when policy makers respond by enacting new regulations or laws, these media influences contribute to changing the context in which people make choices about their health. The effects of the media may be *intended* by the message producer, as is the case when health educators develop public information campaigns, or may be *unintended*, as is the case when viewers adopt unhealthy behaviors that are portrayed only for entertainment value on television programs. The outcome may be either *positive* or *negative* from a public health point of view. A typology of the kinds of effects generated by these three dimensions and some examples are presented in Table 21.1.[1]

PERSONAL-LEVEL EFFECTS

Commercial Product Advertising

Advertising is ubiquitous in all forms of the media in the United States and increasingly in other countries. Some of the most frequently advertised products, such as cigarettes and alcohol, have severe negative personal health effects.

Tobacco

Tobacco use, including cigarette and cigar smoking and the use of smokeless tobacco, continues to be the leading preventable cause of death in the United States and increasingly around the world. The World Health Organization (2007a) estimated that tobacco is responsible for one in 10 deaths in the world every year. Recognition of the harmful effects of smoking has led many countries to restrict tobacco advertising. More than 140 nations, including the United States, have signed a treaty agreeing to limit tobacco advertising, as well as protect nonsmokers from second-hand smoke (WHO, 2007b). In the United States, cigarette advertising was banned on television and radio in 1971, but flourished in other kinds of media, especially newspapers, magazines, billboards and in event promotion such as the Winston Cup stock car races. In the 1990s, as care for those with smoking-related illnesses claimed more of states' budgets and as evidence grew that the tobacco companies had been deceptive in promoting a deadly product, an

Table 21.1 Examples of the Potential Effects of the Mass Media on Personal and Public Health

	Personal-level health effects
Intended	**Positive** Entertainment-education: People have more positive beliefs about organ donation after *Grey's Anatomy* episode about organ transplantation **Negative** Marketing unhealthy products: Cigarette & alcohol ads directed at young people increases smoking & drinking
Unintended	**Positive** Risk awareness: News about a young singer's breast cancer diagnosis increases mammography screenings **Negative** Activity displaced by "screen time": More media use, less physical activity, greater body weight
	Public-level health effects
Intended	**Positive** Media advocacy campaigns: Increased media coverage raises community involvement in tobacco control efforts, leads to ban on smoking in public places **Negative** Advertising leverage: Cigarette industry's advertising clout reduces editorial content re: cancer risk, increases framing of smoking bans as imposition on personal freedom
Unintended	**Positive** Agenda-setting/framing: Positive news coverage of obesity epidemic leads to more federal funding for research **Negative** Budget priorities: Media coverage increases funding for war on drugs at expense of other health and social issues

agreement between the state Attorneys General and the tobacco companies further restricted the tobacco product promotions (Master Settlement Agreement, 1998). Despite these restrictions, the tobacco industry spent more than $15.2 billion in 2003 to promote their products in the United States, the world's second-largest cigarette market (Federal Trade Commission, 2005).

Effects of Tobacco Marketing

Restrictions on tobacco marketing have been based to a large extent on research that has shown that all but about 10% of smokers begin during adolescence (U.S. Dept. of Health and Human Services, 1994) and that the younger people begin smoking, the more likely they are to become strongly addicted to nicotine (CDC, 1994). It is also clear that even young children are influenced by the allure of cigarette smoking aggressively promulgated by the tobacco industry. Studies have shown, for example, that one-third of 3-year-olds could make the association between the cartoon character Old Joe the Camel and a pack of cigarettes. In the three years after Old Joe was introduced, preference for Camel cigarettes increased from 0.5% to 32% among adolescent smokers (DiFranza et al., 1991). Studies in both the United States and England consistently have shown that the most popular brands among young people are the most heavily advertised (Pierce et al., 1991; Substance Abuse and Mental Health Services Administration, 2005; Vickers, 1992). Smoking initiation among young women increased abruptly when campaigns targeting women, such as the Virginia Slims' "You've come a long way, baby," were introduced (Pierce, Lee, & Gilpin, 1994).

Cross-sectional and longitudinal studies have shown that receptivity and exposure to cigarette advertising in magazines, on the radio, and increasingly on the Internet, as well as ownership of promotional materials (e.g., caps, lighters with cigarette brand logos), is related to increased tobacco use among young people (e.g., Biener & Siegel, 2000). Studies have found that awareness of and involvement with tobacco promotions even exceeds the influence of family members and peers who smoke (e.g., Pierce, Distefan, Jackson, et al., 2002). Experimental studies suggest that advertising promotions increase the perception among young people that smoking is normative, glamorous and risk-free (Pechmann & Ratneshwar, 1994).

Point-of-Purchase Marketing

As restrictions on tobacco advertising have tightened, tobacco companies in the United States have shifted their marketing strategies to spend more money on point-of-purchase marketing than all other forms of promotion (newspaper, magazine, billboard, and transit advertising) combined (Rabin, 2007). Much of this promotion is in convenience stores that young people visit frequently. Tobacco ads are more numerous and in children's line of sight (near candy and below three feet) in stores located near schools (Woodruff, Agro, Wildey, & Conway, 1995) and in neighborhoods with a higher proportion of residents younger than 18 (Pucci, Joseph, & Siegel, 1998). Studies have found, on average, 14 to 27 tobacco ads inside the stores and 3.6 to 7.5 ads outside (Feighery, Ribisl, Achabal, & Tyebjee, 1999). Experimental research suggests that in-store promotions affect adolescents' perceptions of the availability, use, and popularity of cigarettes, all factors that contribute to the likelihood that an adolescent will begin smoking (Henriksen & Flora, 2001).

The Internet as Tobacco Marketing Tool

In the future, research on tobacco marketing effects probably will focus on alternative marketing strategies such as in-store and Internet promotion as the tobacco industry looks for ways to recruit new users and keep current smokers. A few studies of the currently unregulated Internet suggest that it may be an important new venue for tobacco promotion. The number of Internet cigarette vendors appears to have increased substantially since 2000, especially as states have increased excise taxes on cigarette sales (Ribisl, Kim, & Williams, 2007). As Ribisl et al. warned in the Institute of Medicine's (2007) blueprint for ending the tobacco problem in the United States: "the Internet has the potential to be a more potent medium than static print advertising in magazines because of its ability to individually tailor marketing strategies and to engage in these activities relatively unnoticed in the vast World Wide Web" (p. 291). In 2004, more than one-third of U.S. middle school and high school students reported having seen advertisements for tobacco products on the Internet (CDC, 2005). It remains to be seen if such marketing tactics have an effect on youths' smoking and if proposed efforts to reduce the ease of obtaining tobacco products from Web vendors are effective (Bonnie et al., 2007).

Alcohol

Misuse of alcohol exacts a psychological, physical, and financial toll on individuals and families. Alcohol use is linked to family violence toward spouses and children, sexual assault, and homicide (Fals-Stewart, 2003; Grant, 2000). Increasing focus has turned to the problems of alcohol consumption among young people, as recent research suggests that earlier initiation has dramatic short- and long-term health consequences (Grube, 2004). In the United States each year, about 5,000 people younger than 21 die from alcohol-related injuries involving under-age drinking, including motor vehicle crashes, homicides and suicides (Stahre, Brewer, Naimi, & Miller, 2004).

Alcohol is used more frequently by more young people than any other drug, including cigarettes and marijuana; a majority of U.S. high school seniors say they currently drink alcohol, and more than one-quarter report binge drinking (five or more drinks consumed on one occasion) (Johnston et al., 2004). Despite prevailing misconceptions that European traditions of training children to drink at home prevent later problems with alcohol, binge drinking among adolescents is an even bigger problem in France, Germany, and Denmark than in the United States (Kantrowitz & Underwood, 2007).

Although parents and peers have a large impact on adolescents' decisions to drink, alcohol advertising and marketing also affect youths' expectations and attitudes about drinking. In the late 1990s, the U.S. Federal Trade Commission acknowledged the probable effects of alcohol marketing on underage drinking and encouraged the alcohol industry to adhere more closely to their own rules limiting marketing to people younger than 21 (Federal Trade Commission, 1999). Youth are more likely than adults to see alcohol marketing messages (Center on Alcohol Marketing and Youth, 2006). The distilled spirits industry lifted its self-imposed ban on television advertising in 1996; CAMY estimated that between 2001 and 2005, youths' exposure to TV alcohol ads increased by 41%, primarily due to the rise in distilled spirits advertising.

The alcohol industry has moved into other forms of media especially attractive to young people as well, including Internet websites that offer games, brand-logoed gifts and clothes, and sponsorships of sporting events and concerts featuring popular musicians (Jernigan & O'Hara, 2004). Using "viral marketing" techniques, Anheuser-Busch encouraged users to send e-mail and mobile phone text messages to friends using the "Whassup?" phrase featured in its television ads (Cooke et al., 2002).

In alcohol ads, drinking is portrayed as normative and fun, with no negative consequences (Grube, 1993) and often includes images of physical and outdoor activities such as swimming, boating, and skiing that would be risky if engaged in while consuming alcohol, and animals such as the Budweiser lizards, ferrets and Clydesdale horses, that are especially appealing to children and adolescents (Collins, Ellickson, McCaffrey, & Hambarsoomians, 2007; Zwarun & Farrar, 2005).

Effects of Alcohol Advertising

Recent rigorous prospective studies suggest that increased exposure to alcohol advertising increases the likelihood of earlier initiation of drinking, especially among early adolescents (Ellickson, Collins, Hambarsoomians, & McCaffrey, 2005; Snyder, Milici, Slater, Sun, & Strizhakova, 2006; Stacey, Zogg, Unger, & Dent, 2004). One study of the effects of exposure to six sources of advertising (television beer advertisements, alcohol ads in magazines, in-store beer displays and concessions, radio-listening time, and ownership of beer promotional items) found that exposure at grade 6 (about 11 years old) was strongly predictive of 7th-grade intentions to drink and drinking (Collins, Ellickson, MCaffrey, & Hambarsoomians, 2007).

Recently, increased attention has been paid to the concept of "alcohol expectancies"—the idea that models of drinking as socially and physically rewarding can affect young people's own expectations about the positive benefits of drinking. Typically, children's earliest alcohol expectancies are negative (e.g., having three or four drinks would make me feel sick), but by 10 or 11 years old, expectancies become more positive (e.g., alcohol would make me feel happy, have a lot of fun). The stronger and more positive the alcohol expectancies, the more likely an individual is to begin drinking early in adolescence, and to develop problem drinking patterns (Dunn & Goldman, 1998).

Austin and colleagues' Message Interpretation Process (MIP) model helps explain how exposure to alcohol advertising may lead to underage drinking by influencing alcohol expectancies (Austin & Knaus, 2000). They have found that identification with and perceived desirability of the models in alcohol ads is a strong predictor of positive alcohol expectancies and alcohol use for adolescents; however, parental guidance decreases alcohol use directly and indirectly by decreasing the child's positive affect toward alcohol advertising (Austin, Chen, & Grube, 2006). More research like this that examines message processing, advertising's role in generating expectations about alcohol use, and individual use contexts will move us closer to understanding the sometimes subtle and indirect effects of alcohol advertising.

Prescription Drug Advertising

Direct-to-consumer (DTC) advertising of prescription drugs has been the subject of fierce controversy in the United States since 1997, when the Food and Drug Administration first began allowing consumer-targeted ads to include both the product name and the condition it is meant to treat without listing all possible risks. Growth in advertising expenditures has been dramatic, with total dollars spent growing 330% from 1996 to 2005. DTC ads are now common in both magazines (Curry, Jarosch, & Pacholok, 2005) and on television (Brownfield et al., 2004). Frosch et al. (2007, p. 6) estimated that "American television viewers see as many as 16 hours of prescription drug advertisements (ads) each year."

Content analyses of both magazine (Curry, Jarosch, & Pacholok, 2005) and DTC ads on television (Frosch et al., 2007) generally have not supported manufacturers' claims that such advertising helps educate consumers. Frosch et al. (2007) examined DTC drug ads presented on the four major networks (ABC, NBC, CBS and Fox). None of the ads mentioned behavior changes that could substitute for drugs in managing conditions such as high cholesterol, hypertension or insomnia, although 19% of the ads mentioned behavior changes along with drug use. Nearly one in five of the ads (18%), however, suggested that behavior change alone—without use of a drug—would *not* be sufficient to manage the condition.

Effects of DTC Advertising of Prescription Drugs

Research has produced evidence of some positive and some negative effects of DTC advertising on behavior (Datti & Carter, 2006; DeLorme et al., 2006; Spence et al., 2005). Sumpradit, Fors, and McCormick (2002) found, for instance, that respondents generally felt that DTC advertising makes these drugs seem "harmless" and helps them make decisions about taking the drugs, although 70% of those who had talked with their doctors about an advertised drug said their primary purpose was to gather more information, not to request a prescription. Another survey of U.S. adults revealed that DTC ads prompted 6% of respondents to ask their physician about preventive care (Murray et al., 2004). Among those who had discussed an advertised drug with their doctor, 14% had disclosed a health concern, and 12% were told that they either had or were at risk for the condition mentioned in the ad. About 30% of respondents who discussed a drug ad with their doctor were prescribed the advertised drug and were told the drug likely would help them; 11.5% received the advertised drug despite the physician doubting it would help.

Food and Nutrition

Dramatic increases in obesity and obesity-related chronic diseases have occurred worldwide, and children have grown heavier in most countries in the world since the 1990s (James et al., 2001; Wang et al., 2002). In the United States about one in three children and teens are either overweight or at risk of becoming overweight (Ogden et al., 2002), increasing their risk for cardiovascular disease and other chronic diseases such as diabetes (e.g., Cook et al., 2003; Pinhas-Hamiel et al., 1996). Although a large body of research suggests that increased exposure to food advertising contributes to childhood obesity, at present, we know little about how other kinds of program and advertising content affect knowledge, attitudes, and diet quality, or the underlying mechanisms that may lead to obesity, such as overeating or snacking while viewing television and/or less physical activity (Committee on Food Marketing, 2006).

Food Advertising

The effects of food advertising have received extensive scholarly attention. In the United States and increasingly around the world, children and adolescents are now the "target of intense and specialized food marketing and advertising efforts" (Story & French, 2004, p. 1). In the United States and Great Britain, children view an average of more than 20 commercials per hour. Half are for food products, and about 90% of the advertised foods are high in fat, sugar, and/or salt (e.g., Lewis & Hill, 1998). Even brief exposure to televised food commercials has been shown to affect preschool children's food preferences (Borzekowski & Robinson, 2001). TV viewing is related to children's requests for their parents to buy foods advertised on TV, as well as with higher overall caloric intakes (Story & French, 2004; Taras & Gage, 1995). The Institute of Medicine's recent analysis of more than 120 studies of food marketing to youth concluded that there is compelling evidence linking TV food advertising to childhood obesity increases (Committee on Food Marketing, 2006).

Entertainment Media (TV, Movies, Music)

Entertainment media also have significant unintended and typically negative effects on health-related knowledge, attitudes, and behaviors. We begin with the health subject of the previous section, food and nutrition.

Obesity and Overweight

Time Spent Using Sedentary Media

Media effects studies have tended to focus on the effects of content, but some studies have found associations between the sheer amount of time a child watches television and the child's weight (Saelens et al., 2002). Some have even shown a dose-response relationship between hours of usual TV viewing and the child's weight or Body Mass Index (Berkey et al., 2000; Dennison et al., 2002). Time spent watching TV may lower energy expenditure, given that the metabolic rate for watching television is the same or lower (when reclining) than the rate for resting (Montoye et al., 1996). Surprisingly, studies to date have not shown strong support for the corollary hypothesis that more time spent using sedentary media results in less time spent in more strenuous physical activity (Robinson, 1999, 2000).

Eating Snack Foods

Another possible mechanism is that media use provides a context for eating snack foods high in fat and/or sugar (Coon et al., 2001). A marked increase in snacking behavior has been observed concurrent with the U.S. obesity epidemic (Jahns, Siega-Riz, & Popkin, 2001). Snacking appears to be related to TV viewing patterns (Coon et al., 2001; Matheson et al., 2004). Francis et al. (2003) found what we might call the "couch potato chip" effect; TV viewing was associated with both higher intakes of energy-dense snacks and higher BMI in young U.S. girls.

Diet/Activity Knowledge

Some surveys have suggested that television is a primary source of nutrition information —with negative effects (Brook & Tepper, 1997; Nowak & Speare, 1996). In one longitudinal study of American elementary school children, TV viewing frequency predicted declines in nutritional knowledge and reasoning, especially for foods marketed as weight-loss aids (e.g., "fat free") (Harrison, 2005). Obviously, more research is needed to parse out the apparently multiple pathways between media use and obesity.

Substance Use and Abuse

Portrayals of Alcohol, Tobacco, and Other Drugs

The frequency and kind of portrayals of alcohol, tobacco, and illicit drugs differ within and across entertainment media. The Roberts and Christenson (2000) analysis of portrayals across three popular kinds of media (movies, television, and music) still stands as the most comprehensive (see Table 21.2). More recent smaller-scale studies paint similar portraits of pervasive smoking and alcohol use in movies, frequent alcohol use on primetime television, with illicit drug use rare in most media except rap/hip-hop music (e.g., Gruber et al., 2005; Thompson & Yokota, 2001).

MOVIES

Alcohol and tobacco are depicted in almost all movies (Everett, Schnuth, & Tribble, 1998; Roberts & Christenson, 2000), in part due to paid product placements for alcohol (Jernigan & O'Hara, 2004). Although the tobacco industry agreed to ban paid product placement in movies in 1990, at least one study found that cigarette brands appeared as frequently after the ban as they had before (Sargent et al., 2001). Even G-rated animated movies and 75% of Disney's animated classics include alcohol, cigarettes or both—think of the beer keg in *Snow White and the Seven Dwarfs* and Cruella De Vil chain-smoking cigarettes in *101 Dalmations* (Thompson & Yokota, 2001; Ryan & Hoerrner, 2004). Actors in movies now smoke almost as often as they did in the 1950s (Glantz, Kacirk, & McCulloch, 2004).

In nearly all movie portrayals, smoking conveys physical attractiveness and social status (Everett, Schnuth, & Tribble, 1998) and is often associated with other risky activities, including sexual, violent, or dangerous behavior. Thus, tobacco may be used as a kind of character cue for "bad" women and "tough" men (Sargent et al., 2000), which may be attractive characteristics, especially for adolescent viewers. However, an analysis of 50 G-rated, animated feature films released between 1937 and 1997 found that "good" characters were shown using tobacco and alcohol as frequently as "bad" characters (Goldstein, Sobel, & Newman, 1999). No consequences of drinking were depicted in more than half of the 200 most popular movie rentals in 1996 and 1997. Characters' statements about drinking were far more likely to be positive than negative (Roberts, Henriksen, & Christenson, 1999).

Table 21.2 Frequency of Depiction and Consequences to Users of Alcohol, Tobacco, and Illicit Drugs in Movies, Entertainment TV, and Popular Songs

% referring or depicting substance/% depicting consequences to user			
	Movies	*TV*	*Popular songs*
Alcohol	93% / 43%	75% / 23%	17% / 9%
Tobacco	89% / 13%	22% / 1%	3% / —
Illicit drugs	22% / 48%	20% / 67%	18% / 19%

Note: Proportions are based on 200 most popular movie rentals and 1,000 most popular songs from 1996 and 1997 (Roberts, Hendricksen, & Christenson, 1999), as well as four consecutive episodes of the 42 top-rated primetime series of the 1998–1999 season (Christenson, Henriksen, & Roberts, 2000), as summarized in Roberts and Christenson (2000). There were so few references to tobacco in the songs analyzed that the frequencies of consequences were not calculated.

Illicit drugs are rarely portrayed in mainstream movies. Illicit drug users are more likely to be shown to suffer negative consequences than alcohol or cigarette users. Addiction is rarely shown, and addicts usually are portrayed as evil rather than ill (Roberts & Christenson, 2000).

TELEVISION

Portrayals of smoking on television also have risen in recent years. About 20% of episodes of popular, non-educational primetime television programs depict tobacco use (Roberts & Christenson, 2000), and pro-smoking portrayals outnumber anti-smoking portrayals by a ratio of 10 to one (Dozier, Lauzen, Day, et al., 2005). References to alcohol use—visual and/or verbal—occur several times during an average hour of primetime television. An analysis of the top-20 teen and top-20 adult shows from Fall 1998–1999 found that more than three-fourths of the episodes included references to alcohol (Christenson, Henriksen, & Roberts, 2000). Alcohol was the drink of choice only on the adult-oriented shows, but even in teen shows one or more major characters were shown drinking, on average, 1.6 minutes per hour (Christenson et al., 2000). Adult drinkers on television tend to be regular and attractive characters, whereas young drinkers typically are portrayed less positively (Mathios, Avery, Bisogni, & Shanahan, 1998).

MUSIC AND MUSIC VIDEOS

Little systematic research has been done on substance use in music or music videos. It is clear, though, that portrayals differ dramatically by musical genre. About 10% of country music songs mentioned alcohol use. Most characterized drinking as problematic in some way, yet the same songs often presented alcohol use as normal and functional, a typical way of escaping problems, getting over a lost love, etc. (Roberts & Christenson, 2000).

Analyses of music videos have found that rap/hip-hop and rock music videos are the most likely to portray alcohol use and illicit drug use (Durant et al., 1997; Gruber et al., 2005). In one study across all music genres, no consequences were mentioned in 91% of the lyrics that included references to drinking (Roberts, Henriksen, & Christenson, 1999). Young adults were shown smoking in about 75% of music videos in the late 1990s (Durant et al., 1997).

Entertainment Content Effects on Alcohol, Tobacco, and Illicit Drug Use

Social cognitive theory predicts that behaviors that are shown frequently and without negative consequence are more likely imitated, and that behaviors of attractive characters are more likely modeled by observers (Bandura, 1986; Chapter 6, this volume). Robinson, Chen, and Killen (1998), for example, found that for every extra hour per day spent watching music videos, adolescents (13–14 years old) were 31% more likely to begin drinking alcohol during the next 18 months; an extra hour of regular television viewing increased their chances of drinking by nearly 10%. A longitudinal study of 10- to 14-year olds found that those with higher exposure to movie alcohol use were more likely than those who saw fewer alcohol-depicting movies to have started drinking one to two years later (Sargent, Wills, Stoolmiller, et al., 2006).

Studies have found that adolescent smokers were more likely than non-smokers to name actors who smoked either on- or off-screen as their favorite stars (Distefan,

Gilpin, Sargent, & Pierce, 1999). Three longitudinal studies have found associations between movie exposure and smoking initiation prospectively (Dalton, Sargent, Beach et al., 2003; Jackson, Brown, & L'Engle, 2007; Sargent, Beach, Adachi-Mejia, et al., 2005). Given the evidence so far, it appears reasonable to conclude that the unrealistic picture of tobacco and alcohol use presented in the movies and on television is contributing to the continued high levels of smoking and alcohol use among young people and may be undermining the extensive anti-smoking and underage drinking media campaigns underway across the country (see Chapter 20, this volume).

Few studies have tied portrayals of illicit drug use in any of the media directly to beliefs, attitudes or behaviors. Some have suggested, though, that aggregate patterns indicate media effects. Illicit drug use among adolescents declined significantly from the early 1980s through the early 1990s, but began to increase in the late 1990s, just as there seemed to be a comeback of marijuana in Hollywood movies such as *There's Something About Mary* (Strasburger & Wilson, 2002). More research is needed on how the frequency of positive or negative portrayals contributes to attitudes toward illicit drug use.

Sexuality

Because Chapter 15 in this volume focuses primarily on sexually explicit content and pornography, we'll limit our discussion to mainstream entertainment content. In these media in the United States, sexual talk and displays are frequent and increasingly explicit, but rarely include the three Cs of healthy sexual behavior: Commitment, Contraceptives and Consequences (for reviews, see Escobar-Chaves et al., 2005; Kunkel et al., 2007). Although more than half of the couples who engage in sexual intercourse on television are in an established relationship, one in 10 are couples who have met only recently; more than one-quarter do not maintain a relationship after having sex (Kunkel et al., 1999). Only about one in 17 of the sexual scenes on television includes any message about the risks or responsibilities of sexual activity (Kunkel et al., 2007). Sexually transmitted diseases other than HIV/AIDS are almost never discussed, and unintended pregnancies are rarely shown. Abortion is a taboo topic, too controversial for commercial television and magazines (Walsh-Childers, Gotthoffer, & Lepre, 2002).

In the past decade, three large-scale longitudinal survey studies have shown that increased exposure to sexual content on television (Ashby, Arcari, & Edmonson, 2006; Collins et al., 2004) as well as in music, movies and magazines (Brown et al., 2006) predicts earlier transition to sexual intercourse among U.S. adolescents. Across the four kinds of media analyzed in the Brown et al. study, less than 1% of the sexual content contained any kind of sexual health information (defined as any mention or depiction of puberty, masturbation, contraception, unplanned pregnancy, or abortion) (Hust, Brown, & L'Engle, 2008).

The Internet and Health

An impressive body of research already has suggested important individual-level health effects of the Internet. Among Internet users—71% of all American adults in 2007 (Demographics of Internet Users, 2006)—seeking health information has become one of the most common online activities (Greenberg, D'Andrea, & Lorence, 2003). By 2006, 80% of U.S. Internet users—113 million adults—had searched online for health information at least once, with higher use among women, college graduates, more experienced Internet users, people younger than 65 and those with high-speed Internet access (Fox, 2006) and among individuals with chronic illnesses, the uninsured and those who have to travel longer distances for health care (Bundorf et al., 2006).

Respondents to the 2006 Pew survey generally gave online health information positive marks, with 56% saying online health information increased their confidence in doctor–patient conversations. However, 25% were overwhelmed by the amount of information, 22% were frustrated by inability to find information they sought, 18% found the information confusing, and 10% rated the information as frightening (Fox, 2006).

Health information-seeking on the Internet appears to have important outcomes, with more than half (53%) reporting that information found in their most recent online health information search affected how they care for themselves or for someone else; 42% classified the effect as minor, but 11% said the impact was "major" (Fox, 2006). Most respondents to an earlier Pew study used online information to supplement health professionals' advice, but about 18% reported using online information to diagnose or decide how to treat a medical condition without consulting their doctor (Fox & Rainie, 2002). In one study examining Internet use among newly diagnosed cancer patients, Bass et al. (2006) found patients who sought health information online were more likely to prepare lists of questions to ask their doctor and to actually ask questions during doctor visits. However, the study also showed *less* compliance with doctors' treatment recommendations among online health information users.

Numerous studies have raised doubts about the quality of health websites. In fact, low information quality was the characteristic most often mentioned in more than 160 articles evaluating online health information (Powell et al., 2005). Similarly, Eysenbach et al.'s (2002) review of 79 articles evaluating website quality showed that most expressed concerns about lack of completeness, inaccuracy and the difficulty of finding high-quality sites.

Thus far, relatively little research has examined in any depth exactly how consumers search for and process Internet health information. One exception was a study of English women's use of the Internet for information about hormone replacement therapy. The researchers found that women evaluated websites based on three key influences: information credibility, relevance and accessibility, and social identity, meaning the extent to which women felt they were like the women who produced or were featured in the websites. The study participants rejected several "medically credible sites . . . because they lacked sufficient social identification markers" (Sillence et al., 2007, p. 8).

Other researchers have found that although consumers *say* the source of website information plays a key role in their evaluations of its trustworthiness, in actual practice they often do not check either the author or website information or the site's owner/sponsor, nor do they read disclosure or disclaimer statements (Eysenbach & Köhler, 2002). The researchers found that after finding information quickly, only 21% of the German consumers participating could remember either the name of the website or the sponsoring organization where they had found specific information; only 23% could identify the type of website (.gov, .com, etc.). Fewer than 25% of consumers regularly follow recommended procedures for assessing online health information quality, such as checking the date and source of information (Fox, 2006).

News Coverage of Health

About 40% of American adults report following health news closely, with the greatest amount of attention going to stories about public health issues, followed by health policy stories and stories about specific diseases (Brodie et al., 2003). In our typology of kinds of effects, we would consider the outcomes of exposure to health stories in the news as unintended individual-level effects, given that most news organizations would not acknowledge themselves as providing health education.

Effects on Individual Health Knowledge and Behavior

Several studies have revealed behavioral effects of exposure to health news, especially stories about celebrities' health problems. For instance, news coverage of former First Lady Nancy Reagan's decision to undergo a mastectomy influenced the behavior of other women diagnosed with breast cancer (Nattinger et al., 1998), and coverage of popular Australian singer Kylie Minogue's breast cancer diagnosis dramatically increased the number of mammography appointments made by Australian women, especially those who had not previously had a mammogram (Chapman et al., 2005).

Even without celebrities, however, news coverage can have unintended effects on individual health behaviors, some of them positive, some potentially negative. Researchers have found that news coverage had significant effects on both smoking cessation rates (Pierce & Gilpin, 2001) and adolescents' attitudes about and use of marijuana (Stryker, 2003). Other researchers have found effects of news coverage on use of iodized salt (Li et al., 2007), prostate cancer screening (Rai et al., 2007) and use of hormone replacement therapy (Haas et al., 2007). Research on "suicide contagion" has shown that news stories about suicide can have dramatic negative effects by encouraging "copycat" suicides (Stack, 2005); news outlets can reduce these effects by stressing negative definitions of suicide (Stack, 2005), not publishing details about how the individual died and including information about assistance available to those contemplating suicide (Stack, 2002).

POLICY-LEVEL EFFECTS

News and Health Policy

In addition to affecting individual health behaviors, news coverage can have important, usually unintended,[2] impacts on public health policy. Agenda-setting theory suggests that news media can help set the health policy agenda for citizens and policymakers by focusing attention on certain issues or diseases and ignoring others. The framing of health issues (e.g., focusing on individual behavior, rather than environmental factors, as the primary causes of poor health) also can affect the types of policy solutions the public and policymakers consider (Dorfman & Wallack, 2007). News influences on policy can be negative if media pressure spurs legislators to approve policies that have not been carefully considered or evaluated (Reese & Danielian, 1989). For instance, Shoemaker, Wanta, and Leggett (1989) argued that the media's intense coverage of the drug problem during Summer 1986 likely influenced the U.S. Congress's rapid—and, some argued, ill-considered—passage of a $1.7 billion antidrug legislation package. Similarly, Benelli (2003) argued that overwhelmingly positive Italian news coverage of a controversial and unproven cancer treatment drove Italian government officials to authorize expenditures of more than 50 billion Italian lira[3] to test the effectiveness of the treatment.

Case studies have suggested that news coverage is most likely to influence public health policy development when health experts agree on the solutions, when the change can occur at the local or state policy level, and when private citizen groups and/or public officials are working toward policy changes supported by the news content (Walsh-Childers, 1994a, 1994b). Research on news media influence on public policy has been relatively limited, however, and much remains to be studied in this area.

Intended Public-Level Effects

A growing number of public health advocates have begun to incorporate media advocacy—the strategic use of mass media, especially news media, for advancing social or public policy initiatives (Pertschuk, 1988)—into public health campaigns. Some researchers have found evidence that media advocacy can indeed promote positive health outcomes. Treno and Holder (1997) found that media advocacy played a key role in community mobilization in a project aimed at reducing alcohol-related injuries. Harwood et al. (2005), however, found increased press coverage of proposed legislation to reduce underage drinking in Louisiana decreased the bill's likelihood of passage. They suggested that "press inattention has possible benefits for policy advocacy in at least two ways—to prevent mobilization of opponents and to permit stakeholders the opportunity to compromise during negotiations on bill content and wording" (Harwood et al., 2005, p. 255). Niederdeppe, Farrelly, and Wenter (2007) found that media advocacy activities by the Florida Tobacco Control Program contributed to passage of county ordinances regulating the placement of tobacco products to restrict children and adolescents' access, but the ordinances did not reduce youth smoking rates. The researchers cautioned that increased news coverage of youth smoking issues may have undermined efforts to support more comprehensive tobacco-control programs.

CONCLUSIONS

Since the first edition of this book was published in 1994, we have seen a dramatic increase in research on media effects on health. Some of this research has been supported by federal agencies and states that have begun to realize that significant shifts in cultural norms are necessary if individuals are to be expected to behave in healthy ways and that mass media have significant potential to influence those cultural norms. For example, initial funds from a few states' settlements with the tobacco companies generated excellent new research on the effects of cigarette advertising on youth that ultimately affected the content of the Master Settlement Agreement and increased restrictions on tobacco product promotion. More recently, tobacco settlement funds have been used to support media advocacy efforts to encourage communities to enact tobacco control measures.

Another trend obvious here is that the research on the media's impact on health is becoming increasingly sophisticated and theoretically based, moving toward more complicated longitudinal designs that put media exposure into the context of individuals' lives. Austin's research on how alcohol advertising affects children's beliefs about alcohol and subsequent drinking is a good example of theory-based research that helps explain as well as describe the process of media effects (Austin, Pinkleton, & Fujioka, 2000). Similar theoretically driven research is needed to understand the effects of both news coverage (unintentional) and media advocacy efforts (intentional) on public policies that alter the health environment. The health impact of the Internet, which had only begun to be studied when the second edition of this book was published in 2002, now has been the subject of hundreds of studies. We will need more theory-based research if we are to harness the Internet's potential to produce health benefits and limit its negative effects at both individual and public health levels.

Much of the early research on the media's impact on health focused on media impacts on children and young people, largely because of the perception that media effects would be greatest among these apparently more vulnerable groups. The growth in research on the Internet, on news effects, and on prescription drug advertising, however, reflects growing recognition that individuals do not "outgrow" vulnerability to media's effects, whether positive or negative.

Studying the media's health effects on children and adolescents remains a crucial endeavor, and one that—we hope—will continue to develop in sophistication. It is important to improve our ability to predict when, how and in which young people effects are most likely to occur with an eye toward what types of interventions may be most useful in forestalling negative effects and promoting positive outcomes. It is also clear, however, that as the Baby Boom generation ages, we will need more research that examines the media's health effects on adults, especially older adults. In 2002, U.S. Comptroller General David Walker, testifying before the U.S. Senate's Special Committee on Aging, predicted that as the Baby Boom generation becomes elderly, spending on Medicare, Medicaid, and Social Security "will nearly double as a share of the economy by 2035" (Walker, 2002, p. 1). At the least, then, economic concerns should motivate research leading to reducing the negative health effects of mass media and improving our use of the media's power to improve the health environment and individual health outcomes. We look forward to seeing what research in the next decade and beyond will reveal about media impacts on health and how we can increase the ratio of positive to negative effects.

Notes

1. In this chapter we define health broadly, adopting the World Health Organization's definition: "Health is a state of complete physical, mental, and social well-being and not merely the absence of disease or infirmity." We do not consider the media's effects on violence or on body image and eating disorders, two of the most intensively studied health-related topics, or public health campaigns because those topics are covered elsewhere in this volume (Chapters 13, 20, 22).
2. In the United States, journalists rarely acknowledge writing about health issues with the intent of spurring policy change. This may be less true outside the United States. Interviews with Irish health journalists, for instance, revealed that many see themselves as "advocates" for health care consumers, particularly those among the less powerful segments of society (Walsh-Childers, 2006). Similar results were produced in a survey of Swedish health journalists (Finer, Tomson, & Björkman, 1997).
3. Italy now uses the euro, so it's difficult to determine the dollar value of 50 billion lira in 2000, when the case occurred. However, based on a 2007 exchange rate, this would amount to $36.71 million.

References

Ashby, S. L., Arcari, C. M., & Edmonson, M. B. (2006). Television viewing and risk of sexual initiation by young adolescents. *Archives of Pediatric Adolescent Medicine*, *160*(4), 375–380.

Austin, E. W., Chen, M.-J., & Grube, J. W. (2006). How does alcohol advertising influence underage drinking? The role of desirability, identification and skepticism. *Journal of Adolescent Health, 38*(4), 376–384.

Austin, E. W., & Knaus, C. (2000). Predicting the potential for risky behavior among those "too young" to drink, as the result of appealing advertising. *Journal of Health Communication, 5*(1), 13–27.

Austin, E. W., Pinkleton, B., & Fujioka, Y. (2000). The role of interpretation processes and parental discussion in the media's effects on adolescents' use of alcohol. *Pediatrics, 105*(2), 343–349.

Bandura, A. (1986). *Social foundations of thought and action: A social cognitive theory*. Englewood Cliffs, NJ: Prentice-Hall.

Bass, S. B., Ruzek, S. B., Gordon, T. F., Fleisher, L., McKeown, N., & Moore, D. (2006). Relationship of Internet health information use with patient behavior and self-efficacy: Experiences of newly diagnosed cancer patients who contact the National Cancer Institute's Cancer Information Service. *Journal of Health Communication, 11*(2), 219–236.

Benelli, E. (2003). The role of the media in steering public opinion on healthcare issues. *Health Policy, 63*(2), 179–186.

Berkey, C. S., Rockett, H. R., Field, A. E., Gillman, M. W., Frazier, A. L., Camargo, C. A. Jr., & Colditz, G. A. (2000). Activity, dietary intake, and weight changes in a longitudinal study of preadolescent and adolescent boys and girls. *Pediatrics, 105*(4), 446–452.

Biener, L., & Siegel, M. (2000). Tobacco marketing and adolescent smoking: More support for a causal inference. *American Journal of Public Health, 90*(3), 407–411.

Bonnie, R. J., Stratton, K., & Wallace, R. B. (Eds.). (2007). *Ending the tobacco problem: A blueprint for the nation*. Washington, DC: Board on Population Health and Public Health Practice, Institute of Medicine of the National Academies.

Borzekowski, D. L., & Robinson, T. N. (2001). The 30-second effect: An experiment revealing the impact of television commercials on food preferences of preschoolers. *Journal of the American Diabetic Association, 101*(1), 42–46.

Brodie, M., Hamel, E. C., Altman, D. E., Blendon, R. J., & Benson, J. M. (2003). Health news and the American public, 1996–2002. *Journal of Health Politics, Policy and Law, 28*(5), 927–950.

Brook, U., & Tepper, I. (1997). High school students' attitudes and knowledge of food consumption and body image: Implications for school based education. *Patient Education and Counseling, 30*(3), 283–288.

Brown, J. D., L'Engle, K. L., Pardun, C. J., Guo, G., Kenneavy, K., & Jackson, C. (2006). Sexy media matter: Exposure to sexual content in music, movies, television, and magazines predicts black and white adolescents' sexual behavior. *Pediatrics, 117*(4), 1018–1027.

Brownfield, E. D., Bernhardt, J. M., Phan, J. L., Williams, M. V., & Parker, R. M. (2004). Direct-to-consumer drug advertisements on network television: An exploration of quantity, frequency, and placement. *Journal of Health Communication, 9*(6), 491–497.

Bundorf, M. K., Wagner, T. H., Singer, S. J., & Baker, L. C. (2006). Who searches the internet for health information? *Health Services Research, 41*(3), 819–836.

CDC. (1994). *Preventing tobacco use among young people: A report of the Surgeon General*. Atlanta, GA: U.S. Department of Health and Human Services.

CDC. (2005, April 1). Tobacco use, access, and exposure to tobacco in media among middle and high school students—United States, 2004. *Morbidity & Mortality Weekly Report, 54*(12), 297–301.

Center on Alcohol Marketing and Youth. (2006). *Still growing after all these years: Youth exposure to alcohol advertising on television, 2001–2005*. Washington, DC: Center on Alcohol Marketing and Youth.

Chapman, S., McLeod, K., Wakefield, M., & Holding, S. (2005). Impact of news of celebrity illness on breast cancer screening: Kylie Minogue's breast cancer diagnosis. *The Medical Journal of Australia, 183*(5), 247–250.

Christenson, P. G., Henriksen, L., and Roberts, D. F. (2000). *Substance Use in Popular Prime Time Television*. Washington, DC: Office of National Drug Control Policy.

Collins, R. L., Ellickson, P. L., McCaffrey, D., & Hambarsoomians, K. (2007). Early adolescent exposure to alcohol advertising and its relationship to underage drinking. *Journal of Adolescent Health*, *40*(6), 527–534.

Collins, R. L., Elliott, M. N., Berry, S. H., Kanourse, D., Kunkel, D., & Hunter, S. B. (2004). Watching sex on television predicts adolescent initiation of sexual behavior. *Pediatrics*, *114*(3), e280–e289.

Committee on Food Marketing and the Diets of Children and Youth. (2006). *Food marketing to children and youth: Threat or opportunity?* Washington, DC: National Academy Press.

Cook, S., Weitzman, M., Auinger, P., Nguyen, M., & Dietz, W. H. (2003). Prevalence of a metabolic syndrome phenotype in adolescents. *Archives of Pediatrics and Adolescent Medicine*, *157*(8), 821–827.

Cooke, E., Hastings, G., & Anderson, S. (2002). *Desk research to examine the influence of marketing and advertising by the alcohol industry on young people's alcohol consumption: Research prepared for the World Health Organization*. Glasgow: Centre for Social Marketing at the University of Strathclyde.

Coon, K. A., Goldberg, J., Rogers, B. L., & Tucker, K. (2001). Relationships between use of television during meals and children's food consumption patterns. *Pediatrics*, *107*(1), e7.

Curry, T. J., Jarosch, F., & Pacholok, S. (2005). Are direct to consumer advertisements of prescription drugs educations? Comparing 1992 to 2002. *Journal of Drug Education*, *35*(3), 217–232.

Dalton, M. A., Sargent, J. D., Beach, M. L., Titus-Ernstoff L., Gibson J. J., Ahrens M. B., et al. (2003). Effect of viewing smoking in movies on adolescent smoking initiation: A cohort study. *The Lancet*, *362*(3280), 281–285.

Datti, B., & Carter, M. W. (2006). The effect of direct-to-consumer advertising on prescription drug use by older adults. *Drugs and Aging*, *23*, 71–81.

DeLorme, D. E., Huh, J., & Reid, L. N. (2006). Age differences in how consumers behave following exposure to DTC advertising. *Health Communication*, *20*(3), 255–265.

Demographics of Internet Users (2006). Washington, DC: Pew Internet and American Life Project. Retrieved October 12, 2007, from http://www.pewinternet.org/trends/User_Demo_4.26.06.htm

Dennison, B. A., Erb, T. A., & Jenkins, P. L. (2002). Television viewing and television in bedroom associated with overweight risk among low-income preschool children. *Pediatrics*, *109*(6), 1028–1035.

DiFranza, J. R., Richards, J. W., Paulman, P. M., Wolf-Gillespie, N., Fletcher, C., Jaffe, R. D., & Murray, D. (1991). RJR Nabisco's cartoon camel promotes Camel cigarettes to children. *Journal of the American Medical Association*, *266*(22), 3149–3153.

Distefan, J. M., Gilpin, E. A., Sargent, J. D., & Pierce, J. P. (1999). Do movie stars encourage adolescents to start smoking? Evidence from California. *Preventive Medicine*, *28*(1), 1–11.

Dorfman, L., & Wallack, L. (2007). Moving nutrition upstream: The case for reframing obesity. *Journal of Nutrition Education and Behavior*, *39*(2), S45–S50.

Dozier, D. M., Lauzen, M. M., Day, C. A., Payne, S. M., & Tafoya, M. R. (2005). Leaders and elites: Portrayals of smoking in popular films. *Tobacco Control*, *14*(1), 7–9.

Dunn, M. E., & Goldman, M. S. (1998). Age and drinking-related differences in the memory organization of alcohol expectancies in 3rd-, 6th-, 9th-, and 12th-grade children. *Journal of Consulting and Clinical Psychology*, *66*(3), 579–585.

Durant, R. H., Rome, E. S., Rich, M., Allred, E., Emans, S. J., & Woods, E. R. (1997). Tobacco and alcohol use behaviors portrayed in music videos: A content analysis. *American Journal of Public Health*, *87*(7), 1131–1135.

Ellickson, P. L., Collins, R. L., Hambarsoomians, K., & McCaffrey, D. R. (2005). Does alcohol advertising promote adolescent drinking? Results from a longitudinal assessment. *Addiction*, *100*(2), 235–246.

Escobar-Chaves, S. L., Tortolero, S., Markham, C. M., Low, B. J., Eitel, P., & Thickstun, P. (2005). Impact of the media on adolescent sexual attitudes and behaviors. *Pediatrics*, *116*, 303–326.

Everett, S. A., Schnuth, R. L., & Tribble, J. L. (1998). Tobacco and alcohol use in top-grossing American films. *Journal of Community Health, 23*(4), 317–324.

Eysenbach, G., & Köhler, C. (2002). How do consumers search for and appraise health information on the world wide web? Qualitative study using focus groups, usability tests, and in-depth interviews. *British Medical Journal, 324*(7337), 573–577.

Eysenbach, G., Powell, J., Kuss, O., & Sa, E. R. (2002). Empirical studies assessing the quality of health information for consumers on the World Wide Web: A systematic review. *Journal of the American Medical Association, 287*(20), 2691–2700.

Fals-Stewart, W. (2003). The occurrence of partner physical aggression on days of alcohol consumption: A longitudinal diary study. *Journal of Consulting and Clinical Psychology, 71*, 41–52.

Federal Trade Commission. (2005). *Cigarette report for 2003*. Washington, DC: Federal Trade Commission.

Federal Trade Commission. (1999). *Self-regulation in the alcohol industry: A review of industry efforts to avoid promoting alcohol to underage consumers*. Washington, DC: Federal Trade Commission.

Feighery, E. C., Ribisl, K. M., Achabal, D. D., & Tyebjee, T. (1999). Retail trade incentives: How tobacco industry practices compare with those of other industries. *American Journal of Public Health, 89*(10), 1564–1566.

Finer, D., Tomson, G., & Björkman, N. M. (1997). Ally, advocate, analyst, agenda-setter? Positions and perceptions of Swedish medical journalists. *Patient Education and Counseling, 30*(1), 71–81.

Fox, S. (2006). Online Health Search 2006. Washington, DC: Pew Internet and American Life Project. Retrieved Oct. 12, 2006, from http://www.pewinternet.org/pdfs/PIP_Online_Health_2006.pdf.

Fox, S., & Rainie, L. (2002). Vital decisions: How Internet users decide what information to trust when they or their loved ones are sick. Washington, DC: Pew Internet & American Life Project. Retrieved September 16, 2006, from http://www.pewinternet.org/pdfs/PIP_Vital_Decisions_May2002.pdf.

Francis, L. A., Lee, Y. & Birch, L. (2003). Parental weight status and girls' television viewing, snacking and body mass indexes. *Obesity Research, 11*, 143–151.

Frosch, D. L., Krueger, P. M., Hornik, R. C., Cronholm, P. F., & Barg, F. K. (2007). Creating demand for prescription drugs: A content analysis of television direct-to-consumer advertising. *Annals of Family Medicine, 5*, 6–13.

Glantz, S., Kacirk, K. W., & McCulloch, C. (2004). Back to the future: Smoking in movies in 2002 compared with 1950 levels. *American Journal of Public Health, 94*(2), 261–263.

Goldstein, A. O., Sobel, R. A., & Newman, G. R. (1999). Tobacco and alcohol use in G-rated children's animated films. *Journal of the American Medical Association, 281*(12), 1131–1136.

Grant, B. F. (2000). Estimates of US children exposed to alcohol abuse and dependence in the family. *American Journal of Public Health, 90*, 112–115.

Greenberg, L., D'Andrea, G., & Lorence, D. (2003). Setting the public agenda for online health search: A white paper and action agenda. Washington, DC: Utilization Review Accreditation Commission Inc (URAC). Retrieved September 16, 2006, from http://www.urac.org/documents/URAC_CWW_Health_%20Search_White_Paper1203.pdf?arch=%22%22Setting%20the%20Public%20Agenda%20for%20Online%20Health%20Search%22%22.

Grube, J. W. (1993). Alcohol portrayals and alcohol advertising on television. *Alcohol Health & Research World, 17*(1), 61–66.

Grube, J. W. (2004). Alcohol in the media: Drinking portrayals, alcohol advertising, and alcohol consumption among youth. In R. J. Bonnie & M. E. O'Connell (Eds.), *Reducing underage drinking: A collective responsibility* (pp. 597–622). Washington, DC: The National Academy of Sciences.

Gruber, E. L., Thau, H. M., Hill, D. L., Fisher, D. A., & Grube, J. W. (2005). Alcohol, tobacco and illicit substances in music videos: A content analysis of prevalence and genre. *Journal of Adolescent Health, 37*, 81–83.

Haas, J. S., Miglioretti, D. L., Geller, B., Buist, D. S., Nelson, D. E., Kerlikowske, K., Carney, P. A.,

Dash, S., Breslau, E. S., & Ballard-Barbash, R. (2007). Average household exposure to newspaper coverage about the harmful effects of hormone therapy and population-based declines in hormone therapy use. *Journal of General Internal Medicine*, *22*(1), 68–73.

Harrison, K. (2005). Is "fat free" good for me? A panel study of television viewing and children's nutritional knowledge and reasoning. *Health Communication*, *17*(2), 117–132.

Harwood, E. M., Witson, J. C., Fan, D. P., & Wagenaar, A. C. (2005). Media advocacy and underage drinking policies: A study of Louisiana news media from 1994 through 2003. *Health Promotion Practice*, *6*(3), 246–257.

Henriksen, L., & Flora, J. A. (2001). *Effects of adolescents' exposure to retail tobacco advertising*. Paper presented at the annual conference of the International Communication Association, Washington, DC.

Hust, S., Brown, J. D., & L'Engle, K. L. (2008). Boys will be boys and girls better be prepared: An analysis of the rare sexual health messages in young adolescents' media. *Mass Communication and Society*, *11*, 3–23.

Jackson, C., Brown, J. D., & L'Engle, K. L. (2007). R-rated movies, bedroom televisions, and initiation of smoking by white and black adolescents. *Archives of Pediatric and Adolescent Medicine*, *161*(3), 260–268.

Jahns, L., Siega-Riz, A. M., & Popkin, B. M. (2001). The increasing prevalence of snacking among U.S. children and adolescents from 1977–1996. *Journal of Pediatrics*, *138*(4), 493–498.

James, P. T., Leach, R., Kalamara, E., & Shayeghi, M. (2001). The worldwide obesity epidemic. *Obesity Research*, *9*(S4), 228S–233S.

Jernigan, D., & O'Hara, J. (2004). Alcohol advertising and promotion. *Reducing underage drinking: A collective responsibilityy* (pp. 625–652). Washington, DC: The National Academy of Sciences.

Johnston, L. D., O'Malley, P. M., Bachman, J. G., & Schulenberg, J. E. (2004). *Monitoring the future, national survey results on drug use, 1975–2004. Vol. 1: Secondary school students*. NIH Publication No. 05–5727. Bethesda, MD: National Institute on Drug Abuse.

Kantrowitz, B., & Underwood, A. (2007, June 25). The teen drinking dilemma. *Newsweek*, 36–37.

Kunkel, D., Cope, K., Farinola, W., Biely, E., Rollin, E., & Donnerstein, E. (1999). *Sex on TV: A biennial report to the Kaiser Family Foundation*. Menlo Park, CA: The Henry J. Kaiser Family Foundation.

Kunkel, D., Eyal, K., Donnerstein, E., Farrar, K. M., Biely, E., & Rideout, V. (2007). Sexual socialization messages on entertainment television: Comparing content trends 1997–2002. *Media Psychology*, *9*(3), 595–622.

Lewis, M. K., & Hill, A. J. (1998). Food advertising on British children's television: A content analysis and experimental study with nine year olds. *International Journal of Obesity*, *22*(3), 206–214.

Li, M., Chapman, S., Agho, K., & Eastman, C. J. (July 16, 2007). Can even minimal news coverage influence consumer health-related behavior? A case study of iodized salt sales, Australia. *Health Education Research*, Retrieved July 16, 2007 from http://tobacco.health.usyd.edu.au/site/supersite/contact/pdfs/HERiodine.pdf, 6 pages.

Master Settlement Agreement. (1998). National Association of Attorneys General. Retrieved December 12, 2000, from http://www.naag.org/tobaccopublic/library.cfm.

Matheson, D. M., Killen, J. D., Wang, Y., Varady, A. & Robinson, T. N. (2004). Children's food consumption during television viewing. *American Journal of Clinical Nutrition*, *79*(6), 1088–1094.

Mathios, A., Avery, R., Bisogni, C., & Shanahan, J. (1998). Alcohol portrayal on prime-time television: Manifest and latent messages. *Journal of Studies on Alcohol*, *59*(3), 305–310.

Montoye, H. J., Kemper, H. C. G., Saris, W. H. M, & Washburn, R. A. (1996). *Measuring physical activity and energy expenditure*. Champaign, IL: Human Kinetics.

Murray, E., Lo, B., Pollack, L., Donelan, K., & Lee, K. (2004). Direct-to-consumer advertising: Public perceptions of its effects on health behaviors, health care, and the doctor-patient relationship. *Journal of the American Board of Family Practice*, *17*, 6–18.

Nattinger, A. B., Hoffmann, R. G., Howell-Pelz, A., & Goodwin, J. S. (1998). Effect of Nancy Reagan's mastectomy on choice of surgery for breast cancer by U.S. women. *Journal of the American Medical Association, 279*(10), 762–767.

Niederdeppe, J., Farrelly, M. C., & Wenter, D. (2007). Media advocacy, tobacco control policy change and teen smoking in Florida. *Tobacco Control, 16*, 47–52.

Nowak, M., & Speare, R. (1996). Gender differences in food related concerns, beliefs and behaviours of North Queensland adolescents. *Journal of Paediatrics and Child Health, 32*(5), 424–427.

Ogden, C. L., Flegal, K. M., Carroll, M. D., & Johnson, C. L. (2002). Prevalence and trends of overweight among US children and adolescents, 1999–2000. *Journal of the American Medical Association, 288*(14), 1728–1732.

Pechmann, C., & Ratneshwar, S. (1994). The effects of antismoking and cigarette advertising on young adolescents' perceptions of peers who smoke. *Journal of Consumer Research, 21*(2), 236–251.

Pertschuk, M. (1988). *Smoking Control: Media Advocacy Guidelines*. Washington, DC: Advocacy Institute for the National Cancer Institute, National Institutes of Health.

Pierce, J. P., Distefan, J. M., Jackson, C., White, M. M., & Gilpin, E. A. (2002). Does tobacco marketing undermine the influence of recommended parenting in discouraging adolescents from smoking? *American Journal of Preventive Medicine, 23*(2), 73–81.

Pierce, J. P., & Gilpin, E. A. (2001). News media coverage of smoking and health is associated with changes in population rates of smoking cessation but not initiation. *Tobacco Control, 10*(2), 145–153.

Pierce, J. P., Gilpin, E. A., Burns, D. M., Whalen, E., Rosbrook, B., Shopland, D., & Johnson, M. (1991). Does tobacco advertising target young people to start smoking? *Journal of the American Medical Association, 266*(22), 3154–3158.

Pierce, J. P., Lee, L., & Gilpin, E. A. (1994). Smoking initiation by adolescent girls, 1944 through 1988: An association with targeted advertising. *Journal of the American Medical Association, 271*(8), 608–611.

Pinhas-Hamiel, O., Dolan, L. M., Daniels, S. R., Standiford, D., Khoury, P. R., & Zeitler, P. (1996). Increased incidence of non-insulin-dependent diabetes mellitus among adolescents. *Journal of Pediatrics, 128*(5), 608–615.

Powell, J. A., Low, P., Griffiths, F. E., & Thorogood, J. (2005). A critical analysis of the literature on the Internet and consumer health information. *Journal of Telemedicine and Telecare, 11*(Supplement 1), 41–43.

Pucci, L. G., Joseph, H. M., Jr., & Siegel, M. (1998). Outdoor tobacco advertising in six Boston neighborhoods: Evaluating youth exposure. *American Journal of Preventive Medicine, 15*(2), 155–159.

Rabin, R. L. (2007). Controlling the retail sales environment: Access, advertising, and promotional activities. In R. J. Bonnie, K. Stratton, & R. B. Wallace (Eds.), *Ending the tobacco problem: A blueprint for the nation* (pp. 641–652). Washington, DC: Board on Population Health and Public Health Practice, Institute of Medicine of the National Academies.

Rai, T., Clements, A., Bukach, C., Shine, B., Austoker, J., & Watson, E. (2007). What influences men's decision to have a prostate-specific antigen test? A qualitative study. *Family Practice, 24*(4), 365–371.

Reese, S. D., & Danielian, L. H. (1989). Intermedia influence and the drug issue: Converging on cocaine. In P. J. Shoemaker (Ed.), *Communication campaigns about drugs: Government, media and the public* (pp. 29–45). Hillsdale, NJ: Erlbaum.

Ribisl, K. M., Kim, A. E., & Williams, R. S. (2007). Sales and marketing of cigarettes on the Internet: Emerging threats to tobacco control and promising policy solutions. In R. J. Bonnie, K. Stratton, & R. B. Wallace (Eds.), *Ending the tobacco problem: A blueprint for the nation* (pp. 653–678). Washington, DC: Board on Population Health and Public Health Practice, Institute of Medicine of the National Academies.

Roberts, D. F., & Christenson, P. G. (2000). *"Here's Looking at You, Kid": Alcohol, drugs and tobacco in entertainment media*. Washington, DC: Kaiser Family Foundation.

Roberts, D. F., Henriksen, L., & Christenson, P. G. (1999). *Substance use in popular movies and music*. Washington, DC: Office of National Drug Control Policy.

Robinson, T. N. (1999). Reducing children's television viewing to prevent obesity: A randomized, quasi-experimental trial. *Journal of the American Medical Association*, *282*(16), 1561–1517.

Robinson, T. N. (2000). Can a school-based intervention to reduce television use decrease adiposity in children in grades 3 and 4? *Western Journal of Medicine*, *173*(1), 40.

Robinson, T. N., Chen, H. L., & Killen, J. D. (1998). Television and music video exposure and risk of adolescent alcohol use. *Pediatrics*, *102*(5), E54.

Ryan, E. L., & Hoerrner, K. L. (2004). Let your conscience be your guide: Smoking and drinking in Disney's animated classics. *Mass Communication & Society*, *7*(3), 261–278.

Saelens, B. E., Sallids, J. F., Nader, P. R., Broyles, S. L., Berry, C. C., & Taras, H. L. (2002). Home environmental influences on children's television watching from early to middle childhood. *Journal of Developmental and Behavioral Pediatrics*, *23*(3), 127–132.

Sargent, J. D., Dalton, M., Beach, M. L., Bernhardt, A., Heatherton, T. F., & Stevens, M. (2000). Effect of cigarette promotions on smoking intake among adolescents. *Preventive Medicine*, *30*(4), 320–327.

Sargent, J. D., Tickle, J. J., Beach, M. L., Dalton, M. A., Ahrens, M. B., & Heatherton, T. F. (2001). Brand appearances in contemporary cinema films and contribution to global marketing of cigarettes. *Lancet*, *357*(9249), 29–32.

Sargent, J. D., Beach, M. L., Adachi-Mejia, A. M., Gibson, J. J., Titus-Ernstoff, L. T., Carusi, C. P., et al. (2005). Exposure to movie smoking: Its relation to smoking initiation among US adolescents. *Pediatrics*, *116*, 1183–1191.

Sargent, J. D., Wills, T. A., Stoolmiller, M., Gibson, J., & Gibbons, F. X. (2006). Alcohol use in motion pictures and its relation with early-onset teen drinking. *Journal of Studies on Alcohol*, *67*(1), 54–65.

Shoemaker, P. J., Wanta, W., & Leggett, D. (1989). Drug coverage and public opinion, 1972–1986. In P. J. Shoemaker (Ed.), *Communication campaigns about drugs: Government, media and the public* (pp. 67–80). Hillsdale, NJ: Erlbaum.

Sillence, E., Briggs, P., Harris, P. R., & Fishwick, L. (2007). How do patients evaluate and make use of online health information? *Social Science & Medicine*, *64*(9), 1853–1862.

Snyder, L. B., Milici, F. F., Slater, M., Sun, H., & Strizhakova, Y. (2006). Effects of alcohol advertising exposure on drinking among youth. *Archives of Pediatrics and Adolescent Medicine*, *160*, 18–24.

Spence, J. M., Teleki, S. S., Cheetham, T. C., Schweitzer, S. O., & Millares, M. (2005). Direct-to-consumer advertising of COX-2 inhibitors: Effect on appropriateness of prescribing. *Medical Care Research and Review*, *62*(5), 544–559.

Stack, S. (2002). Media coverage as a risk factor in suicide. *Injury Prevention*, 8(Suppl IV), 30–32.

Stack, S. (2005). Suicide in the media: A quantitative review of studies based on non-fictional stories. *Suicide & Life-Threatening Behavior*, *35*(2), 121–133.

Stacey, A. W., Zogg, J. B., Unger, J. B., & Dent, C. W. (2004). Exposure to televised alcohol ads and subsequent adolescent alcohol use. *American Journal of Health Behavior*, *28*(6), 498–509.

Stahre, M., Brewer, R., Naimi, T., & Miller, J. (2004). Alcohol-attributable deaths and years of potential life lost—United States, 2001. *Morbidity and Mortality Weekly Report*, *53*(37), 866–870.

Story, M., & French, S. (2004). Food advertising and marketing directed at children and adolescents in the US. *International Journal of Behavioral Nutrition and Physical Activity*, *1*(1), 3.

Strasburger, V. C., & Wilson, B. (2002). *Children, adolescents, and the media*. Thousand Oaks, CA: Sage Publications.

Stryker, J. E. (2003). Media and marijuana: A longitudinal analysis of news media effects on adolescents' marijuana use and related outcomes, 1977–1999. *Journal of Health Communication*, 8(4), 305–328.

Substance Abuse and Mental Health Services Administration. (2005). *The National Survey on Drug Use and Health: 2004 detailed tables, tobacco brands*. Rockville, MD: Substance Abuse and Mental Health Services Administration, Office of Applied Studies.

Sumpradit, N., Fors, S. W., & McCormick, L. (2002). Consumers' attitudes and behavior toward prescription drug advertising. *American Journal of Health Behavior*, *26*, 68–75.

Taras, H. L., & Gage, M. (1995). Advertised foods on children's television. *Archives of Pediatrics and Adolescent Medicine*, *149*(6), 649–652.

Thompson, K. M., & Yokota, F. (2001). Depiction of alcohol, tobacco, and other substances in G-rated animated films. *Pediatrics*, *107*(6), 1369–1374.

Treno, A. J., & Holder, H. D. (1997). Community mobilization: Evaluation of an environmental approach to local action. *Addiction*, *92*(Supplement 2), S173–S187.

U.S. Dept. of Health and Human Services. (1994). *Preventing tobacco use among young people: Report of the Surgeon General*. Washington, DC: U.S. Government Printing Office.

Vickers, A. (1992). Why cigarette advertising should be banned. *British Medical Journal*, *304*(6836), 1195–1196.

Walker, D. M. (2002). *Long term care: Aging Baby Boom generation will increase demand and burden on federal and state budgets*. Testimony before the Special Committee on Aging, U.S. Senate. Washington, DC: General Accounting Office.

Walsh-Childers, K. (1994a). Newspaper influence on health policy development: A case study investigation. *Newspaper Research Journal*, *15*(3), 89–104.

Walsh-Childers, K. (1994b). "A Death in the Family": A case study of newspaper influence on health policy development. *Journalism Quarterly*, *71*(4), 820–829.

Walsh-Childers, K. (2006). Trolleys and other health service targets: Irish journalists' perceptions of their influence on health policy development. Paper presented at the annual conference of the Association for Education in Journalism and Mass Communication, San Francisco, CA, August 2006.

Walsh-Childers, K., Gotthoffer, A., & Lepre, C. R. (2002). From "just the facts" to "downright salacious": Teens' and women's magazines' coverage of sex and sexual health. In J. D. Brown, J. R. Steele, & K. Walsh-Childers (Eds.), *Sexual teens, sexual media* (pp. 153–171). Mahwah, NJ: Erlbaum.

Wallack, L., & Dorfman, L. (1992). Television news, hegemony and health. *American Journal of Public Health*, *82*(1), 125–126.

Wang, Y., Monteiro, C., & Popkin, B. M. (2002). Trends of overweight and underweight in children and adolescents in the United States, Brazil, China, and Russia. *American Journal of Clinical Nutrition*, *75*(6), 971–977.

Woodruff, S., Agro, A., Wildey, M., & Conway, T. (1995). Point-of-purchase tobacco advertising: Prevalence, correlates, and brief intervention. *Health Values*, *19*(5), 56–62.

World Health Organization. (2007a). Tobacco causes 1 in 10 deaths worldwide. Retrieved October 20, 2007, from http://www.who.int/mediacentre/factsheets/fs310/en/index2.html

World Health Organization. (2007b). WHO Tobacco Treaty. Retrieved October 20, 2007, from http://www.who.int/mediacentre/news/notes/2007/np26/en/index.html

Zwarun, L., & Farrar, K. M. (2005). Doing what they say, saying what they mean: Self-regulatory compliance and depictions of drinking in alcohol commercials in televised sports. *Mass Communication and Society*, *8*(4), 347–371.

22

EFFECTS OF MEDIA ON EATING DISORDERS AND BODY IMAGE

Michael P. Levine
Kenyon College

Kristen Harrison
University of Illinois at Urbana-Champaign

INTRODUCTION AND OVERVIEW

The third edition of this volume marks the first time a chapter has been devoted to media effects on body image and disordered eating. In the past 10 years there has been an explosion of advanced theory and research concerning sociocultural factors in general and mass media in particular (see, e.g., Cash & Prusinky, 2002; Thompson, Heinberg, Altabe, & Tantleff-Dunn, 1999). Few media effects research areas have grown so rapidly in such a short time. Every day millions of people of all ages, including many as young as 2 years old, are engaged with a wide variety of media that extol the virtues of an extremely lean body. As we will demonstrate, it is neither possible nor defensible to interpret this fact as a public health issue of marginal importance, relevant only to a handful of privileged White American teenage girls.

Further, it is invalid to deny a potential link between media use and disordered eating simply because research has established a link between media use and obesity (see Chapter 21 of this volume). Longitudinal research has shown that excessive dieting and other unhealthful weight control behaviors in childhood and adolescence increase the risk of overeating and obesity years later, even for youngsters who were thin when they started dieting (Neumark-Sztainer, Wall, Guo, Story, Haines, & Eisenberg, 2006; Stice, Cameron, Killen, Hayward, & Taylor, 1999). Therefore, research demonstrating media effects on body dissatisfaction and excessive dieting goes hand-in-hand with research on obesity. Both literatures investigate the role of media use in encouraging and reinforcing health risks such as negative body image, imbalanced consumption, and counter-productive efforts at weight and shape management.

The present chapter extends our recent attempts (Groesz, Levine, & Murnen, 2002; Harrison & Hefner, 2006; Levine & Harrison, 2004; Levine & Smolak, 2006; Murnen, Levine, Groesz, & Smith, 2007) to introduce media effects researchers and students to the significant theoretical, methodological, and empirical issues framing the following proposition: Mass media exposure is a key factor in the development of body image disturbance and disordered eating among youth and adolescents.

Definitions, Prevalence, and Consequences

Definitions

Eating disorders such as anorexia nervosa (AN), bulimia nervosa (BN), and variants (Eating Disorders Not Otherwise Specified, or EDNOS) are serious and frequently chronic conditions (American Psychiatric Association, 2000). These disorders are the extremes of a "disordered eating behavior" (DEB) spectrum that encompasses varying combinations and degrees of negative body image, binge eating, and unhealthy forms of weight and shape management such as restrictive dieting, self-induced vomiting after eating, and abuse of laxatives, diuretics, diet pills, and exercise (Levine & Smolak, 2006).

One's "image" of one's "body" (hair, face, shape, weight, degree of visible fat and muscle, posture, etc.) represents a complex synthesis of visual memory, emotions, assumptions about gender and attractiveness, and kinesthetic sense of comfort or awkwardness (Cash & Pruzinsky, 2002). Body image also incorporates feelings of trust or mistrust in one's own needs, emotions, and desires, along with a sense of efficacy or helplessness in regard to the body's connections to (or disconnections from) the self, other people, and the physical world (Piran, 2001). In most research on media effects, the construct of body image is represented by measures of body dissatisfaction. Perceptual-emotional conclusions (e.g., "I look too fat [and/or puny] to myself and others" and "I am ashamed of this") result from, and feed a schema that integrates an idealization of slenderness, leanness, and/or muscularity, an irrational fear of fat, and a belief in weight and shape as central determinants of one's identity as a female or male.

Prevalence

In the United States, Canada, and the United Kingdom, the prevalence of BN and AN among girls and young women in ages 10 through 25 is roughly 2% and 0.2–0.5%, respectively. A reasonable, conservative estimate of the prevalence of DEB that produces *significant* physical, psychological, and social problems, but does not meet the full criteria of AN or BN, is 6% to 8% (Bisaga & Walsh, 2005; Levine & Smolak, 2006). Thus, the DEB spectrum probably affects between 8% and 10% of adolescent girls and young women. Males suffer from DEB, too, but, with the exception of binge-eating disorder (experienced by three females for every two males), 8:1 is a conservative estimate of the ratio of females to males for the more severe syndromes. A significant minority of adolescent males suffers from obsessive anxieties about becoming more muscular and less fat (Pope, Phillips, & Olivardia, 2000).

In contrast to DEB, the prevalence of "*unhealthy* negative body image" (U-NBI) that causes problematic levels of emotional distress, interpersonal problems, and risky behaviors among girls and women ages 10 through 30 is unknown. A safe but noteworthy estimate is 15–20% (Cash, 2002; L. Smolak, personal communication, October 3, 2007). The prevalence of U-NBI among boys and men ages 10 through 30 is also unknown, but it is at least 10% (see Levine & Smolak, 2006). U-NBI and DEB appear among youth of all social classes, ethnicities, and geographic locations (Cash & Pruzinsky, 2002; Levine & Smolak, 2006; Pope et al., 2000).

Consequences

The DEB spectrum has serious, sometimes debilitating, emotional and physical effects. DEB is typically accompanied by, or may lead to and worsen, one or more of the following: depression, social anxiety, obsessions and compulsions, emotional instability, and substance abuse. The medical consequences include renal, reproductive, cardiovascular, digestive, and dental problems (Rome & Ammerman, 2003; Thompson, 2004). These physical and psychological consequences make it extremely difficult for people with eating disorders or DEB to establish healthy relationships with others and to function effectively and consistently at school or at work (Thompson, 2004). The availability of effective multidimensional therapies means that even full-blown AN, BN, and EDNOS are not necessarily life-long problems. Nevertheless, all types of eating disorders can become debilitating, chronic, and isolating. There is less certainty about the long-term outcomes of BN, but approximately 5–10% of adolescents and adults suffering from AN die prematurely of starvation-induced organ failures, suicide, or non-specific causes (Nielsen et al., 1998).

U-NBI is itself an important public health issue (Elliot & Goldberg, 2008; Harrison & Hefner, 2006; Levine & Smolak, 2006). Body dissatisfaction in adolescent girls and young women is not a harmless, phasic indulgence; rather, it is a prospective risk factor for cigarette smoking, binge-eating, low levels of physical activity, unhealthy weight management practices, eating disorders, depression, and risky weight loss strategies including illegal drug use and dangerous drug-mixing (see, e.g., Neumark-Sztainer, Paxton, Hannan, Haines, & Story, 2006; Stice, Hayward, Cameron, Killen, & Taylor, 2000; Stice & Shaw, 2003). Idealization of a lean, muscular, and powerful-looking body promotes body dissatisfaction in a fair number of young boys (Smolak, Murnen, & Thompson, 2005), who may be motivated to eat and exercise in unhealthy ways, and to use anabolic steroids and ineffective or even dangerous body building and "nutritional" supplements.

Conceptual Model Informing the Chapter

Obviously, even omnipresent media images and messages do not "cause" eating disorders and poor body image in a direct, "hypodermic," and dose-response fashion. Negative body image is normative in females over age 13–14, and many boys and men are dissatisfied with their levels of fat and muscularity, all the while feeling they weigh too much or too little. Nevertheless, only a relatively small percentage of girls and women develop U-NBI and clinically significant DEB. And among those with significant problems, there are multiple risk factors and causal pathways operating, some of which have little to do with processing of media messages (Smolak, Levine, & Striegel-Moore, 1996; see also Levine & Smolak, 2006).

Accordingly, we conceptualize media as (1) a meta- or macro-context in which other social contexts (e.g., home, school) operate; and (2) a set of features, content, and processes contained within the multiple social contexts in which young people live (Bronfenbrenner, 1979). Consider a girl growing up in a home overseen by a parent who is very concerned about weight, shape, and a slender appearance. The girl is probably going to be exposed to certain types of television and magazines. She is also going to be participating in numerous direct communications, opportunities for observational learning from parents and siblings, and both direct and vicarious behavior-outcome contingencies that support media messages pertaining to (1) the paramount importance of being attractive; (2) the pre-eminence of thinness for attractiveness and the demonstration of control; and (3) the value of technologies and products such as diets and drugs for achieving beauty ideals. Potentially negative effects of ideal-body media messages need to be understood within an ecological framework (see, e.g., Davison & Birch, 2001), because media influences are augmented or buffered by messages from family, friends, teachers, and coaches (Smolak & Levine, 1996; Thompson et al., 1999).

The ultimate effects of this home dynamic on the child are the product of, at the very least, interactions between media, parents, child, and other family members. However, most investigations of media effects on DEB and U-NBI conceptualize the relationship as more or less direct, so contextual factors are statistically controlled. Resulting effects sizes are thus modest (Groesz et al., 2002; Murnen et al., 2007). The effects research summarized in this chapter, then, yields a very conservative estimate of the true media effects on body image and disordered eating, because the collective effect of media (i.e., directly *and* through human agents in various social contexts) is not yet known.

THE IDEAL BODY IN THE MEDIA: CONTENT ANALYTIC RESEARCH

There are at least three reasons to suspect that modern media produce and sustain body dissatisfaction and eating disturbance. First, media are saturated with messages about physical appearance and its significance for gender roles, health, pleasure, happiness, and morality. Second, media in general and appearance-oriented media in particular are immensely popular. Finally, it is hard to comprehend how appearance concerns, body dissatisfaction, and unhealthy eating and weight management could have become so prevalent, influential, and, indeed, normative across age, socioeconomic status, cultures, and subcultures in the absence of the influence of some form of mass communication.

It is hardly a surprise that television, the Internet, film, and other media bombard their enormous audiences with messages about the importance of appearance, the malleability of appearance, and the raw and subtle pleasures of shopping for and using various forms of services and products to improve appearance (Ballentine & Ogle, 2005; Labre & Walsh-Childers, 2003). An ongoing consumer interest in refining appearance is highly profitable.

Unfortunately, media content is rich with unhealthy messages about attractiveness, ideal body sizes and shapes, self-control, desire, food, and weight management (Bordo, 1993; Pope et al., 2000; Spitzer, Henderson, & Zivian, 1999). This is the case even for children's media. For example, Rumble, Cash, and Nashville (2000; cited in Klein & Shiffman, 2006) found that the schematic association of attractiveness and thinness with goodness was present in over 100 female characters appearing in 23 Walt Disney *animated films* (*cel* cartoons) produced over a 60-year period (see also Herbozo, Tantleff-Dunn, Gokee-Larose, & Thompson, 2004). Such associations are also a feature of adult-oriented media. Greenberg, Eastin, Hofschire, Lachlan, and Brownell (2003) analyzed the body sizes of characters in 275 episodes of 56 different *primetime fictional television programs*. About 5% of U.S. women are underweight, but over 30% of female television characters were underweight. The corresponding figures for male characters are 2% and 12%. Thus, from toddler-hood to adulthood, girls and boys have no trouble finding the raw material for maladaptive but entirely normative thin-as-normal and thin-as-ideal schemata (Levine & Harrison, 2004; Smolak & Levine, 1996).

The Female Body Ideal

Content analyses have revealed that the ideal female body showcased on television, in movies, in magazines, and on the Internet can be easily summarized in two phrases: "thin is normative and attractive" and "fat is aberrant and repulsive." Approximately 50% of women in the United States are overweight or obese, but only 13% of female television characters are. Similarly, nearly 60% of men are "fat but" but only 24% of male television characters were overweight or obese (Greenberg et al., 2003). Fatness in both males and females is normative (if not always healthy) in the general population, but it has been "symbolically annihilated" on primetime television, although this erasure is significantly more prominent for females, $X^2(1) = 5.13$, $p < .05$. When overweight characters do appear on television, they are significantly less likely to be portrayed as attractive and to be judged attractive or desirable by other characters (Greenberg et al., 2003).

Mass media also proclaim the glory of thinness and leanness, especially for females, by depicting those attributes as highly desirable *and* by depicting fatness as undesirable, if not intolerable. Fouts and Burggraf (1999, 2000) observed that *thin* female characters in television situation comedies were more likely than heavier female characters to be praised by male characters, and less likely to be insulted by male characters in ways deliberately tied to evocation of "canned" and supportive audience laughter. On the other hand, *fatter* female characters were more likely to be insulted by male characters in ways that garnered audience laughter. Additionally, an analysis of movies and television programs revealed that male characters were three times as likely as female characters to make stigmatizing comments about other characters' fatness, even though males and females were equally likely to be the target of these displays of power (Himes & Thompson, 2007). Mass media forcefully support the culture's stigmatization of fat people, and this prejudice overlaps with stereotypes and prejudices regarding adult females (Harrison, 2000; Puhl & Latner, 2007).

The Male Body Ideal

Although both male and female body ideals are tall and low in body fat, the male ideal has an added feature: exceptional muscularity (Labre, 2005). Since the 1980s magazines have increasingly depicted the male body in a state of objectified undress, such that a significant focus for the camera and viewer is raw, exposed ("chiseled" or "ripped") muscularity (Halliwell, Dittmar, & Orsborn, 2007; Pope et al., 2000). This trend has been accompanied by a surge in the adoration of "bulked up," powerful, and dominant action figures, beginning with toys for younger boys (Pope et al., 2000) and progressing to the principal characters of video games, who "might be regarded as 'virtual action figures' " (Harrison & Bond, 2007, p. 270) for older boys and young men. Professional wrestling's heroes and villains such as Terry "Hulk" Hogan, Dwayne "The Rock" Johnson, and "Stone Cold" Steve Austin are a cultural and economic presence—and, as we have learned from the lives of Arnold Schwarzenegger and Jessie Ventura, a political force, too. Their iconic images are projected *en masse*, on TV, on the sides of vending machines, in films, in magazines, in boxed sets of DVDs containing classic wrestling matches, in lines of action figures, and on billboards and posters.

The Openly Disordered Ideal

The proliferation of hundreds of pro-anorexia (pro-ana) and pro-bulimia (pro-mia) web sites on the Internet has raised alarm about, for example, the effects of "thinspirational" images of emaciation on the body image and eating behavior of impressionable visitors to those sites. Pro-ana sites vary widely in content and tone (Brotsky & Giles, 2007), but many of the best-known ones defiantly and religiously promote AN as a sacred lifestyle rather than a debilitating psychiatric disorder (Norris, Boydell, Pinhas, & Katzman, 2006). Content analyses of pro-ana and pro-mia material on traditional sites and on video-streaming sites such as youtube.com are needed to determine the impact, if any, of potentially harmful media that people already at high risk for an eating disorder—or well entrenched in AN or BN—can choose to access 24 hours a day.

MODELS OF MEDIA EFFECTS ON BODY IMAGE AND DISORDERED EATING

The ingredients for developing a negative body image and DEB are readily available throughout various media. Moreover, this content is synergistic with information and incentives received directly and by observational learning via multiple non-media sources, such as family and peers. We turn now to the two most frequently tested models of media effects on body image, DEB, and eating disorders: Social-cognitive models (those revolving around conscious processing of media information) and social-emotional models (those extending such processing to emotional effects that directly predict eating disturbance).

Social-Cognitive Models

Cultivation

Cultivation analysis (see chapter 3, this volume) has demonstrated that immersion in the media's symbolic worlds is associated with normative beliefs about the world *in vivo*. The slender beauty ideal, framed by other cultivated aspects of the feminine sex role (see chapters 3 & 17, this volume), is not perceived as a mythic fantasy, but rather as ubiquitous and accepted by most people—and therefore all the more desirable because it is cast as normal and achievable (Thompson et al., 1999).

Research on the extent of television viewing and beliefs about human body types and their associations with character supports the process of cultivation. McCreary and Sadava (1999) found a positive correlation between television viewing and Canadian participants' belief that they were overweight, independent of their actual weight, presumably because television exposure encouraged the belief that the excessive thinness portrayed on television is normative. Likewise, a study of elementary school boys and girls in the USA by Harrison (2000) found that, for boys, television exposure was positively correlated with a stereotypical and prejudicial tendency to assume that a fat girl will be lazy, greedy, and have no friends. Harrison's (2003) survey of female college students in the United States supported the cultivation pattern of *mainstreaming*, in that the body-relevant beliefs of women who watched greater amounts of television tended to be more homogeneous and more reflective of television's messages. The more television a woman reported watching, the thinner her ideal waist and hips were. For ideal bust size, however, the mainstreaming pattern emerged: If a woman described herself as smaller-busted, the more television she watched, the more she idealized a larger bust and approved of breast augmentation surgery. Conversely, if a woman described herself as larger-busted, television viewing predicted idealization of a smaller bust and approval of breast reduction surgery.

Thin-ideal Internalization

Social-cognitive models of media influence extend normative beliefs about the *world*, as presented in mass media, to beliefs and attitudes about the *self*. Internalization of the thin body ideal has thus been conceptualized as a necessary link in a chain of influence from mass media → internalization of the thin ideal → body image disturbance → DEB. The most valid and widely used measure of internalization comes from the multi-factorial *Sociocultural Attitudes Toward Appearance Questionnaire* (SATAQ; Thompson, van den Berg, Roehrig, Guarda, & Heinberg, 2004). Two studies of undergraduate women at the University of South Florida (Thompson et al., 2004) indicated that *attention to media as a source of awareness and information* about the desirable thin body was significantly correlated with drive for thinness and body dissatisfaction. However, self-reported levels of *perceived pressure from media* and of *internalization of the slender beauty ideal* were highly correlated with each other and were stronger predictors of precursors of disordered eating. In addition, as hypothesized, scores on the subscales assessing awareness of the media thin ideal, internalization of that ideal, and perceived pressures from media to live up to that ideal were all significantly higher among eating disordered women than among non-disordered controls. Engeln-Maddox (2006) found that the positive correlation between a young woman's expectation that looking like a media ideal will change her life in multiple, positive ways and her degree of body dissatisfaction was fully mediated by her level of thin ideal internalization.

Myers and Crowther (2007) defined "media awareness" as the extent to which young women perceive the content, images, and well-known people in mass media to be important sources of information about being fashionable and attractive. The results of Myers and Crowther's path analysis reinforce the findings of several recent studies that show an important link between internalization of the thin ideal and self-objectification in young women (Forbes, Jobe, & Revak, 2006; Sinclair, 2006). Media awareness was modestly related to internalization of the media ideal, which in turn was positively related to body dissatisfaction through an increase in self-objectification.

There is one population among whom thin-ideal internalization does not appear to be a necessary mediator of media effects on DEB: young children. Harrison (2000) found that, while the extent of television viewing predicted disordered eating among 6–8-year-old girls and boys, it failed to predict the idealization of a thinner body; in fact, television viewing predicted a slight tendency to favor a heavier body at the same time it predicted restrained eating. It is likely that, for young children, television viewing may encourage dieting behavior for reasons other than pursuit of a previously internalized thin body ideal. Research is needed to determine exactly when and how, developmentally, thin-ideal internalization becomes an essential component of the links between media use, self-evaluation, body image, and DEB.

Social Comparison

Many adolescent girls and young women are critical of the restrictive, unrealistic beauty ideals conveyed in ideal-body media. Yet, they are still motivated to seek and use such media for purposes of social comparison, especially if they are convinced that the ideals portrayed represent the social norms adopted and endorsed by their female and male peers (Levine & Harrison, 2004). Surveys of elementary school girls, middle school girls, and college women confirm that females who compare themselves to the models in fashion magazines report greater body dissatisfaction and higher levels of disordered eating. Indeed, some studies suggest the tendency during media exposure to compare one's body and appearance to that of models and celebrities is more important than extent of exposure itself (Botta, 1999; Harrison, 1997).

Far less research has examined whether adolescent boys or young men use media images of models, celebrities, or athletes to define muscularity or good looks, to evaluate their own attractiveness, and to inspire themselves to improve their physique and appearance. Two studies by Smolak and colleagues did find that *internalization of the muscular ideal* was a modest predictor of body dissatisfaction, unhealthy eating, and use of muscle-building techniques for adolescent boys ages 11 through 14 (Smolak, Levine, & Thompson, 2001; Smolak et al., 2005). Nevertheless, in early adolescence at least, SATAQ awareness and internalization subscale scores are much stronger correlates of body esteem and use of weight control techniques for girls than boys. Similarly, studies by Jones (2001) and by Morrison, Kalin, and Morrison (2004) indicated that the tendency to compare oneself to models/celebrities and to same-sex peers on the dimensions of height and weight was positively correlated to body dissatisfaction for boys as well as girls, but the relationships were stronger for girls. However, Jones (2001) found that "body build" comparisons by boys in middle school (ages 11 through 14) to either class of target was a significant predictor of body dissatisfaction, whereas Morrison et al. (2004) did not replicate this relationship for boys in high school (ages 15–17).

Social Learning/Modeling

The process of observational learning (from media "models") outlined in social-cognitive theory (see chapter 6, this volume) is one prominent explanation of how mass media affect beliefs, ideals, attitudes, behaviors, and incentives in regard to food, eating, and desirable weights and shapes (Dittmar, Halliwell, & Ive, 2006; Harrison, 1997; Harrison & Cantor, 1997; Levine & Smolak, 2006, chapter 6). As we have demonstrated, the thin ideal is prevalent in print and electronic media, and thinness is associated with positive attributes and outcomes, whereas fatness is ignored or ridiculed. In the cases of direct advertising, news features about obesity and weight loss, and pro-ana or pro-mia web sites, explicit behavioral instructions for attaining the thin ideal are also provided. This social learning process, even when it is not reinforced by, for example, the comments of people watching TV or reading fashion magazines together, intentionally or incidentally provides media users with multiple incentives to attain the body ideal depicted.

Cognitive-Affective Models

Self-discrepancy Activation

Social-cognitive theory is useful for understanding the acquisition and reinforcement of body ideals, irrational attitudes about thinness and fatness, and unhealthy eating and weight management practices. This paradigm is less adequate for explaining the emotional components underlying the eating disorders. AN, BN, and DEB often operate as seductive but ultimately debilitating methods of coping with noxious emotions, and in particular, agitation, shame, and dejection (Strauman, Vookles, Berenstein, Chaiken, & Higgins, 1991). Food avoidance appears to calm feelings of agitation or anxiety, whereas binge eating and purging can provide immediate and dramatic relief from feelings of dejection and depression.

An *actual-ideal self-discrepancy* occurs when the *perceived* actual self falls significantly short of the ideal self. When an actual-ideal discrepancy occurs on a dimension relevant to self-concept and self-esteem, this disparity tends to evoke disappointment, despair, or dejection (Higgins, 1999; Strauman et al., 1991). Harrison (2001) argued that ideal-body media activate self-ideal discrepancies, thereby increasing feelings of loss or failure that in turn may be ameliorated by binge eating with or without purging. A laboratory experiment by Harrison (2001) showed that, as predicted, adolescent girls and boys with self-ideal discrepancies felt significantly more *dejected* following exposure to a video portraying a teenager being socially *rewarded for being thin*.

According to self-discrepancy theory (Higgins, 1999), in contrast, an *actual-ought discrepancy* occurs when the *perceived* actual\self falls significantly short of the self that the person *believes* others (e.g., parents or peers) feel he or she *ought* to or should be. Harrison (2001) argued that ideal-body media are capable of activating self-ought discrepancies, thereby increasing feelings of agitation and anxiety that in turn may be soothed by food avoidance. As predicted by self-discrepancy theory, and in contrast to the moderating effect of actual-ideal discrepancies, adolescents with actual-ought discrepancies felt more *agitated and anxious* following exposure to a portrayal of a teenager being socially *punished for being fat*. Analysis of additional survey data from the same adolescents showed that self-discrepancies at least partially mediate the positive correlation between media exposure and disordered eating (Harrison, 2001).

RESEARCH SUPPORT FOR EFFECTS

Meta-analyses

The relationships between exposure to mass media, body image, and the DEB spectrum have proven to be complicated and controversial (Harrison & Hefner, 2006; Levine & Harrison, 2004). We can say that a small to modest relationship between media exposure and body image disturbance among females is well-established. A meta-analysis by Groesz et al. (2002) of 25 *experiments* examining media effects on body dissatisfaction in female samples yielded 43 *d* values (i.e., effect sizes representing the standardized difference in body dissatisfaction between control and experimental conditions). Thirty-five (81%) of these *d* values were negative, and the overall *d* value was –0.31 ($z = -7.37$, $p < 0001$), indicating a modest but statistically significant drop in body satisfaction after exposure to thin-ideal images compared to controls. The average effect size was slightly greater for participants who were not yet in college ($d = -.36$), suggesting some degree of heightened sensitivity among adolescents.

An ongoing meta-analysis of cross-sectional and longitudinal *survey* research (Murnen et al., 2007) confirmed that the greater the extent of exposure to television and to magazines, the greater the level of self-reported components of DEB. The predicted positive linear relationships, are statistically significant, but modest. They are also stronger for exposure to fashion and glamour magazines than for exposure to television programming, and stronger for females than for males.

Effects on Thin-Ideal Internalization

Based primarily on cross-sectional survey techniques, most studies support the social cognitive hypothesis that mass media in general, and fashion-glamour magazines in particular, have the potential to encourage widespread and influential internalization of the thin body ideal.

Field et al. (1999) reported that the majority of nearly 550 working class adolescent girls were dissatisfied with their weight and shape. Almost 70% of the sample stated that pictures in magazines influence their conception of the "perfect" body shape, and over 45% indicated that those images motivated them to lose weight. Further, adolescent girls who were more frequent readers of women's magazines were more likely to report being influenced to think about the perfect body, to be dissatisfied with their own body, to want to lose weight, and to diet. In what is likely a demonstration of the widespread reach and power of fashion-glamour magazines for adolescent girls, reading frequency predicted dieting and exercising to lose weight even when weight status, level of schooling (elementary or junior high or high school), and ethnicity were statistically controlled.

A study of Seattle middle school students ages 11 through 14 also revealed that the girls, as compared with the boys, were more invested in appearance-oriented magazines (e.g., *Seventeen*), were more likely to internalize the beauty ideals in them, and had greater body dissatisfaction (Jones, Vigfusdottir, & Lee, 2004). For girls, exposure to appearance-related magazines and to appearance conversations by peers each predicted body dissatisfaction through the mediator of internalization of the media-fueled slender beauty ideal. The path analytic model for girls explained 48% of the variance in body dissatisfaction, whereas the combination of sociocultural variables that predicted boys' body dissatisfaction did not include exposure to appearance-related magazines as a significant predictor and accounted for only 21% of the variance.

The significance of appearance and impression-management concerns in the socialization of young females means that girls are very likely to internalize the thin body ideal, to some degree at least, in late childhood and during the physical and other changes of puberty (Murnen, Smolak, Mills, & Good, 2003; Smolak & Levine, 1996; Smolak & Murnen, 2004; Thompson et al., 1999). Sadly, although this personal investment in the thin ideal is normative and thus socially adaptive in many respects, it is bound to have direct as well as indirect negative effects on self-objectification, attitudes about weight and shape, body image, eating patterns, and weight management efforts (Gordon, 2000; Levine & Smolak, 2006). The parallel process of awareness and internalization of the muscular ideal has a very negative impact on the development of a minority of boys, but such appearance concerns are not an integral aspect of the psychosocial development of males in general (Murnen et al., 2003; Smolak & Levine, 1996). Consequently, messages to boys regarding appearance ideals are not as consistent or clear, which is one reason that internalization of the muscular ideal does not happen as readily. In fact, some adolescent boys may resist thinking and talking about male appearance, media images of bodies, and body image, because these topics are perceived as anti-masculine (Hargreaves & Tiggemann, 2006). Moreover, even when the muscular ideal is internalized, it is not likely to be as influential as internalization of the thin ideal is for girls and women in determining body image, eating behavior, and weight and shape management—unless a male has a very strong, if not obsessive, commitment to defining the self in terms of weight and/or muscularity (Murnen et al., 2003; Pope et al., 2000; Smolak & Murnen, 2004).

Effects on Body Image and DEB

Longitudinal Studies

Although longitudinal research linking media exposure with body image is sparse, early exposure to thin-ideal *television* is correlated with subsequent increases in body-image problems. For Australian girls ages 5 through 8, the number of appearance-focused television programs (but not appearance-focused magazines) viewed predicted a decrease in appearance satisfaction one year later (Dohnt & Tiggemann, 2006). In a sample of White and Black girls ages 7 through 12 living in the United States, overall television exposure predicted the choice of a thinner ideal *adult* body shape, as well as level of disordered eating one year later (Harrison & Hefner, 2006). The findings in both studies were independent of actual body mass (BMI = (weight in kg)/(height in meters^2) or perceived body mass.

Some longitudinal research has replicated the cross-sectional studies in suggesting that effects are more limited for boys than girls. Ricciardelli, McCabe, Lillis, and Thomas (2006) found that the only predictor over time of body dissatisfaction among Australian boys ages 8 through 11 was actual BMI; however, those boys who reported feeling pressure from the media to gain muscle and to control their weight were more likely to report adopting behavioral strategies to actually try to change their bodies. In Harrison and Bond's (2007) longitudinal analysis of boys ages 7 through 10 living in the United States, for White boys, but not Black boys, gaming magazine reading predicted an increase in drive for muscularity one year later, even when BMI and other important variables, such as exposure to other ideal-body magazines, were controlled.

Experimental Studies

Hargreaves and Tiggemann (2004) exposed Australian adolescents ages 13 through 15 to a series of 20 *television* commercials depicting either idealized images or non-appearance-related products and services. Consistent with previous research, girls who viewed images of the thin ideal were more likely than girls in the control condition to compare their own appearance to that of the women in the commercials, and to react to the images with negative feelings (see, e.g., Durkin & Paxton, 2002), and with a reduction in body satisfaction (see Groesz et al., 2002). Boys did respond to repeated presentations of the muscular ideal with appearance comparisons and negative feelings, but their tendency to make self-evaluative social comparison was less than that for girls. This might account for the finding that there was no significant decrease in body satisfaction.

These findings and other experiments conducted by Hargreaves and Tiggemann in

Australia provide compelling evidence for the contention that mass media have negative and cumulative effects on body image in girls and young women. For example, Hargreaves and Tiggemann (2003) demonstrated that those adolescent girls whose body image was most negatively affected by experimental exposure to 20 television commercials featuring the thin ideal tended to have greater levels of body dissatisfaction and drive for thinness 2 years later, even when individual differences in initial level of body dissatisfaction were controlled statistically. It is noteworthy that experiments conducted in Great Britain by Dittmar and Howard (2004) and Halliwell and Dittmar (2004) have shown that it is the thinness of fashion models, not their attractiveness, that accounts for thin-ideal media's immediate negative effects on body image in girls.

Durkin and Paxton (2002) found that images of thin, attractive models from *magazines* functioned like television commercials in producing an immediate drop in body satisfaction in a majority of Australian adolescent girls ages 12–13 and 15–16. However, 32% of the 7th grade girls and 22% of the 10th grade girls in the model-exposure condition reported an *increase* in state body satisfaction. Two studies in the United States by Wilcox and Laird (2000) help explain this potential for a *positive outcome* of the social comparison process. Young women who focused on the slender models in magazines while defocusing attention on themselves were more likely to identify with the models and thus to feel better about their own bodies. Conversely, women who focused on the models and on themselves were more likely to evaluate themselves and to feel worse about their own bodies, probably because this self-conscious division of attention activates actual-ideal and/or actual-ought discrepancies. As compared to self-improvement motives, self-evaluation processes are more likely to reflect and activate "upward" social comparison processes, such as comparing one's body to that of a professional fashion model whose image has been carefully constructed by designers, make-up artists, photographers, and computer technicians. Of course, such a comparison, especially if it occurs automatically and below the threshold of conscious awareness, is likely to generate negative feelings about one's body (Halliwell & Dittmar, 2005).

The importance of the self in directing social comparison, information processing, and emotional responding is also highlighted in Henderson-King and Henderson-King's (1997) finding that only women who were low "self-monitors" tended to feel badly about their bodies immediately after exposure to magazine images of slender beauty. Low self-monitors are typically anxious, introspective, and less able to direct attention away from the self and one's standards. A recent series of studies by noted social comparison researcher Diederik Stapel and colleagues in the Netherlands also focused on undergraduate women who were already dissatisfied with, and presumably self-conscious about, their own bodies (Trampe, Stapel, & Siero, 2007). These women tended to compare their appearance to a wide range of body-shape standards, including other students, fashion models, and celebrities. Further, relative to women who tended to be more satisfied with their own bodies, women who characteristically had high levels of body dissatisfaction were negatively affected by exposure to and comparison with thin, physically attractive people, whether that person was portrayed as a model or not. In fact, women with negative body image felt worse about their bodies after seeing a drawing of a thin *vase* versus a fatter, rounded vase. Women who were more satisfied with their bodies were unlikely to compare themselves to, and consequently feel bad after seeing, models, just as they were unaffected by exposure to either image of a vase. Trampe et al.'s (2007) findings suggest that the tendency of women with higher levels of body dissatisfaction to make broad and unhealthy social comparisons reflects the fact that their body-relevant self-schema (Hargreaves & Tiggemann, 2002), or their self-schema (self-consciousness) in general (Stapel & Tesser, 2001), is activated more readily. Important research remains to be done to understand how aspects of the person, the media, and other contextual variables shape processes of self-relevance, self-activation, attention allocation, social comparison, and self-evaluation.

Social cognitive theory and self-discrepancy theory both incorporate the construct of *schema*. A schema, such as "my appearance" or "my self," is a hypothetical cognitive structure that organizes information, beliefs, assumptions, and feelings so as to direct information processing in a quick and effective although not always adaptive or pleasant manner. Hargreaves and Tiggemann (2002) theorized that girls ages 15 through 18 would be more negatively affected by the thin-beauty ideal in television commercials if these images activate a self-schema emphasizing the core importance of appearance. As predicted, compared to control conditions, appearance-focused commercials did indeed produce greater activation of appearance-related self-schema across all participants. These commercials also generated more overall appearance dissatisfaction for those girls who began the study with a more extensive, emotionally charged, appearance-related self-schema. Regression analyses confirmed that the negative effect on girls' appearance satisfaction of the thin-beauty ideal in commercials was partially mediated by schema activation. In support of a cognitive model that is distinct from social comparison theory, the negative impact of the thin-beauty ideal in television commercials was, unlike previous findings with magazine images, unaffected by the girls' initial level of body dissatisfaction or whether their viewing style was more personal (self-focused) or more detached (image-focused).

The importance of social-cognitive and social-emotional processes in media effects was also evident in Harrison's (2001) study of adolescents' discrepancy-specific emotional reactions, and in a more recent experiment by Harrison, Taylor, and Marske (2006). Following exposure to same-sex thin-ideal slides, college women with body-relevant self-discrepancies ate *less* in the presence of other women, compared to women without body-relevant self-discrepancies or women exposed to no images. Thus, in addition to teaching young people dieting attitudes and behaviors in pursuit of a "to-die-for" body, the visual images and textual/verbal messages contained in thin-ideal media probably remind vulnerable older children and adolescents of their self-discrepancies. This temporarily increases noxious emotions that the person then tries to manage with food avoidance or overindulgence, or both. Repetition of this pattern over days and months could degenerate into a clinically significant eating disorder; it could also increase the probability of overweight and obesity, which are themselves risk factors of U-NBI and DEB in adolescent girls and young women.

Experimental research with boys and men has revealed somewhat different patterns. Recall the study in which Australian adolescents ages 13 through 15 were shown television commercials containing idealized images of muscularity or non-appearance-related products and services (Hargreaves & Tiggemann, 2004). Unlike the girls, boys viewing the idealized images did not experience a drop in body satisfaction compared to boys in the control condition. Research with older males (ages 15–27), however, consistently demonstrates increases in depression and muscle dissatisfaction following exposure to television commercials (see, e.g., Agliata & Tantleff-Dunn, 2004) or magazine advertisements (see, e.g., Humphreys & Paxton, 2004) featuring the muscular male body ideal (see Halliwell et al., 2007, for a review). Arbour and Ginis (2006) found that young men who were already dissatisfied with the amount or the shape of their muscle mass were more susceptible to this negative media effect. Further, general level of body dissatisfaction was not a moderator, and the vulnerability-media interaction was absent when the images were of *hyper*muscular bodybuilders whose massive, "cut" physiques burst the boundaries of realism. The effects of the muscular ideal on males may well be more constrained than the effect of the slender ideal and other appearance cues on females. Specifically, there may be little or no effect unless a fairly specific image of reasonable muscularity is presented to a male who is at an age or developmental stage where he is particularly sensitive to or "schematic" for that aspect of body image.

As predicted by social-cognitive theory, the effects of media on males emerge from a reciprocally determined transaction between the media as source of information and motivation, personal schema and self-discrepancies, expectations, behavioral repertoire, and the context for subsequent initiation or inhibition of behavior. Harrison et al. (2006) showed that college men whose body-relevant self-discrepancies had probably been activated by ideal images of male muscularity behaved very differently than did self-conscious women exposed to the thin ideal: These men ate *more* in the presence of other men than either men without such discrepancies or men who had not been exposed to the ideal-body images. For men the transaction between an appearance self-discrepancy and the self-relevant muscular ideal in the media tends to generate or intensify body image concerns and concomitant negative feelings. These reactions may then motivate a variety of different behaviors, such as over-consumption of food, excessive exercising, anxious checking of one's physique in the mirror, or even abuse of steroids and food supplements (Pope et al., 2000). Also in keeping with social-cognitive theory, Harrison et al.'s (2006) study indicates that subsequent behavior will depend in part on the self-conscious man's expectations as to whether excessive eating, for example, will successfully augment the impression of masculinity.

Pro-DEB Internet Content

Entertainment and commercial media, such as magazines, television, and video games, are usually not designed to make consumers feel miserable about their bodies or to perpetuate disordered eating. In contrast, the proud and defiant intent of many pro-anorexia websites is to celebrate the "lifestyle" of disordered eating. At present, we do not know what effects these sites have on the adolescent girls and young women who avidly seek them out because they already have a full-blown eating disorder. Preliminary evidence from a small study does indicate that pro-ana sites may have a negative effect on young women (Bardone-Cone & Cass, 2006). Much more research is needed to explore the effects of exposure to pro-ana images and text, including material now available and easily accessed at video streaming sites like youtube.com.

RESEARCH-IDENTIFIED MODERATORS

Media Characteristics

What is it about a medium that is responsible for its effects on body image and DEB? Jansen and de Vries (2002) found that repeated *subliminal* presentation of images of the slender beauty ideal did not affect young college women, even if they were sensitive about their weight and committed to dietary restraint. Birkeland et al. (2005) found that images of attractive women decreased the body satisfaction and mood of female undergraduates in the United States, whereas images of appearance-related products, either alone or with the images of the models, did not have any significant effects. Tiggemann and colleagues in Australia (e.g., Tiggemann & Slater, 2004) have shown that music videos, which are saturated with salient (*supraliminal* and "in your face!") visual images and auditory cues pertaining to appearance, gender, sexuality, and objectification, are particularly potent activators of body dissatisfaction. Together, these studies indicate that the negative impact of media images depends on the conscious and, to some extent, cumulative processing of clear, direct, and "attractive" social messages.

This does not mean that more cues, for example, more images in a series, necessarily increase the salience and cumulative impact of media messages. Groesz et al. (2002) found that that the strongest effect (d = .45 across 14 experimental vs. control comparisons) occurred with 9 or fewer stimuli, as compared to 10–19 stimuli (d = .31 across 20 comparisons) or 20 or more stimuli (d = .28 across 9 comparisons). In this regard, Halliwell, Dittmar, and Howe (2005) in Great Britain showed that *ultra-thin* models did not produce more body-focused anxiety than stimuli containing no model, but exposure to average-size but attractive models did offer protection or buffering against the expected negative effect on body dissatisfaction. Recall that Arbour and Ginis's (2006) research with young men showed that the muscular ideal had a stronger negative effect than did exaggerated hyper-muscular images. This analysis suggests an interesting, testable hypothesis: Small but concentrated doses of relatively realistic, non-caricatured ideal-body images produce the most potent negative effect for adolescents and young adults, whereas *children* are more responsive to caricatured models such as action figures and hypermuscular video game characters (Harrison & Bond, 2007; Pope et al., 2000).

Another feature that might be expected to make the slender ideal more salient and thus more influential is the context in which media are consumed. Using a factorial design, Henderson-King, Henderson-King, and Hoffmann (2001) randomly assigned young female undergraduates in the United States to view, in one of three conditions, a long series of either neutral images or slides of idealized slender beauty. In the absence of any males in the viewing room, there was no media effect. In the presence of two *silent* males, women who saw the thin ideals exhibited the expected decrease in body satisfaction. Yet, when the males made brief positive comments about the desirable shape of the female models in 10% of the slides, the overall effect of exposure to the images on body satisfaction was slightly more *positive* than the effect of neutral images. After replicating this counter-intuitive trend, Henderson-King et al. concluded that conscious processing of the males' sexist comments helped the women to activate a stance of critical resistance toward the unhealthy appearance-related media messages. When the thin-ideal media were presented in the context of the silent male gaze, the result was a more automatic priming of social comparison tendencies, appearance self-schema, and/or self-ideal discrepancies, which produce the typical body dissatisfaction.

The studies by Henderson-King et al. (2001) also pointed to one more potentially influential aspect of appearance-related media messages: the interplay between the ideal of slenderness (or muscularity) and cues for *objectification* of the body (Harrison & Frederickson, 2003; Murnen et al., 2003; Smolak & Murnen, 2004). Lavine, Sweeney, and Wagner (1999) found no difference in effects between an experimental condition in which no advertisements were presented and a condition in which women viewed advertisements containing attractive models in non-sexist contexts. Only advertisements portraying attractive models in a sexist and objectified fashion led to an immediate and significant reduction in body satisfaction of males as well as females.

Audience Characteristics

Gender

To reiterate, the effects of ideal-body media, especially for behavioral components of the DEB spectrum, tend to be stronger for females than for males. Harrison (2000) found identical relationships between television exposure and disordered eating among young girls and boys, but as children approach puberty, media exposure remains a consistent predictor of DEB for girls, while losing some potency for boys. On the other hand, media depicting the lean, muscular male body ideal are certainly capable of producing increases in body dissatisfaction among adolescent boys and men, just as media depicting the slender female body ideal produce such dissatisfaction among adolescent girls and women (Groesz et al., 2002).

Race

Research has revealed stronger effects for White, Anglo, or European-American individuals than for individuals from other ethnic backgrounds, in particular African Americans and Latinas (see, e.g., Botta, 2000). Social comparison theory identifies several factors influencing this disparity. In terms of selecting and paying attention to targets, it appears that media effects on Black and Latina girls are largely contingent upon their ability to identify with the models depicted (Frisby, 2004; Schooler, Ward, Merriwether, & Caruthers, 2004). Given that the carefully constructed, prominent, and pervasive media image of a girl or woman who embodies the thin ideal is still very likely to be that of a White or light-hued female with all traces of ethnicity virtually erased (Baker, 2005), individuals from other racial groups have less motivation and fewer opportunities to be affected in a self-relevant way by these images. Nevertheless, survey research points to increasing similarities in effects among Black as well as White girls, especially prior to puberty. In their longitudinal study of Black and White elementary school girls, Harrison and Hefner (2006) found no race differences in the prospective relationship between television viewing and either disordered eating or idealization of a thin adult body. Bodies of color exhibited in mainstream media are becoming increasingly thinner (Baker, 2005), so perhaps the ethnic gap in effects is closing.

Age

As children become youth and adolescents, potential targets of social comparison such as dolls, action figures, and "Power Rangers" are replaced by more adult standards. Lawrie, Sullivan, Davies, and Hill (2006) surveyed a large sample of Australian youth ages 9 through 14. On average, girls and boys strongly agreed that mass media did not promote the "idea you should gain weight." Girls, more than boys, tended to *be unsure* or *agree* that media promoted becoming thinner, although, as they got older, boys as well as girls were increasingly likely to agree that the media have a commitment to the thin ideal. Still, this developmental trend toward certainty about the media ideal was significantly stronger for girls than for boys. Possibly as a reflection of their greater investment in appearance and appearance-oriented mass media (Smolak & Levine, 1996), as they got older, girls but not boys also were more likely to agree that mass media promote a link between the thin ideal and "the idea that you should be more muscular" (p. 357). Overall, as was the case for the Australian boys ages 14 through 16 interviewed by Hargreaves and Tiggemann (2004), the boys in Lawrie et al.'s (2006) study seemed less certain about the direction of media messages for them. This ambiguity or ignorance may lessen boys' risk for negative body image and resulting problems. There is some evidence that girls ages 8 through 11 who for various reasons have become aware of the beauty ideals championed by adult-oriented mass media may be at risk for later problems with body image and eating. Sinton and Birch (2006) studied White girls age 11 in the United States and found that, even when BMI was statistically controlled, recognition or awareness of the thin ideal had weak to moderate correlations with body dissatisfaction and with the importance of appearance to self-evaluation.

Disordered Eating and Negative Body Image

One very robust research finding is that girls and women with a negative body image or an eating disorder are particularly vulnerable to media images of the slender ideal (see, e.g., Groesz et al., 2002). This is probably attributable to the tendency of those girls and women to perceive representations of slender models or celebrities as being more slender than they actually are (King, Touyz, & Charles, 2000), and to actively seek out ideal-body media in a cycle of uses and gratifications that may perpetuate their current condition (Thomsen, McCoy, Williams, & Gustafson, 2002).

Such reciprocal transactions between the nature and context of the medium and the psychology of the perceiver (Smolak & Levine, 1996; see also Levine & Smolak, 2006 and Bandura, Chapter 6, this volume) are the foundations for self-defeating but self-perpetuating cycles of media engagement for certain children and adolescents. Early and more extensive exposure predicts development of harsh prejudice about fat and fat people, appearance concerns, a thinness (or muscularity) schema, and body image disturbance. As emphasized previously, these outcomes increase both attentiveness and vulnerability to thin-ideal media images *and* to the many other forms of unhealthy information and incentives regarding food, appearance, and weight management emanating from family, peers, and influential adults such as coaches (Keery, van den Berg, & Thompson, 2004; Smolak & Levine, 1996; Thompson et al., 1999). Multiple social influences, operating on an older child or on an adolescent who is threatened if not overwhelmed, by ongoing developmental challenges, will probably have multidimensional negative effects on body image, eating, mood, self-concept, and weight-and-shape management (Smolak & Levine, 1996).

Current Body Change Efforts

The transaction between vulnerability and media also underlies the finding that individuals currently engaged in a body-change regimen are particularly susceptible to the influence of ideal-body media, even if this regimen does not display elements of the DEB spectrum. Halliwell et al. (2007) found that young and middle-aged British men felt much worse after viewing only two muscular models than did men who viewed a product, or a slogan, but no model—but only if the men were not exercisers. In fact, if the men were gym users, they tended to feel better about themselves, not worse, following exposure to the muscular models. After nearly 20 years of research on media and body image, much remains to be done in the investigation of vulnerabilities, motives, and other social-cognitive processes that determine when people will make upward social comparisons, when they will make "downward" social comparisons, and what the effects of each will be (Halliwell & Dittmar, 2005; Levine & Harrison, 2004).

The Sociocultural or Ecological Context

During childhood and adolescence, media exposure is part of a constellation of sociocultural factors that promote a thinness schema for girls and the muscularity schema for boys (Harrison & Hefner, 2006; Smolak & Levine, 1996; Thompson et al., 1999). The thinness schema organizes cognitive and emotional components such as the stigmatization of fat, the strong belief that thinness is virtuous, the normalization of dieting as an adult practice, and the knowledge that people are judged by their weight and shape (Levine & Smolak, 2006; Smolak & Levine, 1996). As girls develop through puberty and into late adolescence and early adulthood, shifts in the meaning and importance of peer culture, a growing psychological sophistication, increases in adiposity and size relative to the slender ideal, and a stable concern with "thin vs. fat" as a major criterion in self-evaluation all combine to give new personal and social meaning to "self-consciousness." Note that this process integrates a series of normative developments, although it is certainly affected by non-normative experiences such as sexual trauma, parents' divorce, and physical illness. Thus, developmental tasks and developmental changes during puberty and adolescence coalesce with various ordinary sociocultural influences to highlight actual-ideal and actual-ought self-discrepancies in overlapping realms such as appearance and gender. The salience and accessibility of the self-in-social-context activates and magnifies social comparison processes and other forms of susceptibility to media and peer influences. It is evident that many factors and psychological processes contribute to a state of affairs in which the psychological impact and behavioral consequences of the ubiquitous thin-beauty ideal—as it threatens to become a tyrant in the actual-ideal and/or actual-ought disparity—will likely be greater for vulnerable girls in middle-to-late adolescence than for younger adolescent girls (Durkin & Paxton, 2002; Harrison & Hefner, 2006; Smolak & Levine, 1996; Stapel & Tesser, 2001; Trampe et al., 2007).

Presumed Media Influence on Others

To further complicate matters, the mere presumption of media effects on others may exert its own effect on the individual (see chapter 12, this volume). Park (2005) surveyed over 400 women attending a large university in the United States. As predicted, the number of beauty and fashion magazines read each month was positively related to self-reported determination to be thin. Using path analysis, Park (2005) found that the more issues of beauty and fashion magazines a young woman reads per month, the greater the perceived prevalence of the thin ideal in those magazines. The greater this perceived prevalence, the greater the presumed influence of that ideal on *other women*; and in turn the greater the perceived influence on *self*, which predicted the desire to be thin. Park's (2005) research suggests that more extensive exposure to beauty and fashion magazines fosters strong and influential beliefs that the slender ideal is ubiquitous, that it influences peers, and that this impact on peers influences the person in ways that leave her, too, desiring to be thin(ner).

MITIGATING FACTORS

Media Content

Myers and Crowther (2007) showed that, for young women, endorsement of a feminist perspective reduced the strength of the connection between awareness of the media's thin ideal and internalization of that ideal. The antithesis of a feminist orientation is the current widespread practice in mass media of objectifying women's bodies to sell products and to promote a lifestyle that defines women as consumers of products, while establishing men as consumers of women's bodies (Smolak & Murnen, 2004). Harrison and Fredrickson (2003) examined the effects of exposure to women's *sports* television on adolescent girls' tendency to define themselves in an objectified manner. For White girls (but not Black girls) exposure to "non-lean" sports (e.g., sports such as basketball or soccer whose athletes necessarily have larger, bulky, often more muscular bodies) was associated with a *decrease* in self-objectification compared to no exposure. For White girls, at least, viewing bodies that are larger-than-usual—but clearly healthy, powerful, and functional—had a positive effect. The findings of Harrison and Frederickson's (2003) study are consistent with Halliwell and Dittmar's (2004) research on positive responses to viewing average-size and attractive models.

Media Literacy

"Media literacy" encompasses attitudes and skills that enable one to understand, appreciate, and critically analyze the nature of mass media and one's relationships with them (Levine & Harrison, 2004; Levine & Smolak, 2006). Students in media literacy programs are involved as active, individual learners with the capacity to enrich their own and other people's typically complex understanding and use of mass media in relation to culture. If done well, body-relevant media literacy programs have the potential to redefine the body as a site of public and effective action, not private self-consciousness, shame, and silence (Piran, 2001; see also Levine & Smolak, 2006).

A number of studies have demonstrated that media literacy is a promising development in efforts to help youth develop resistance to ideal-body media messages. Posavac, Posavac, and Weigel (2001) presented American college women who already had a negative body image with one of several versions of a 7-minute media analysis. As predicted, following each intervention, these at-risk women were less likely to engage in social comparison and less likely to become more dissatisfied with their bodies in response to exposure to images of the thin ideal. The most effective inoculation emphasized the clash between the artificial, constructed nature of the slender, flawless, "model look" versus biogenetic realities pertaining to both the diversity of women's actual weights and shapes and to the negative effects of calorie-restrictive dieting in service of the slender ideal. Several recent studies have replicated the finding that exposure to even a brief critical social perspective has desirable immediate outcomes for women with high levels of thin-ideal internalization (Durkin, Paxton, & Wertheim, 2005; Yumamiya, Cash, Melnyk, Posavac, & Posavac, 2005). Lew, Mann, Myers, Taylor, and Bower (2007) showed that one promising direction for development of a healthier, critical perspective in young women who already have a negative body image is learning to make social comparisons on dimensions other than appearance.

Research has indicated that media literacy programs can be effective for children too (Levine & Harrison, 2004; Levine & Smolak, 2006). For example, Wood (2004) compared the effects of a control discussion of peer pressure to a single lesson explaining to girls and boys ages 5 through 11 how technology and fantasy are used to construct unrealistic and unhealthy media images of beauty. Participants in this brief media literacy intervention reported a significant increase in body esteem 2 weeks later. The more intensive, multi-lesson *Free to Be Me* media literacy program for Girl Scouts ages 10 through 12, their parents, and their troop leaders had several positive effects, such as reduced internalization of the thin ideal, that were sustained for 3 months (Neumark-Sztainer, Sherwood, Coller, & Hannan, 2000).

This research, as well as a growing number of controlled outcome studies with Australian girls and boys ages 12 through 14 (Stanford & McCabe, 2005; Wade, Davidson, & O'Dea, 2003; Wilksch, Tiggemann, & Wade, 2006), supports further developments in media literacy as an important element in an ecological approach to prevention (Levine & Smolak, 2006). In the United States, two model prevention programs—ATLAS and ATHENA—for adolescent male and female athletes, respectively, incorporate intensive media literacy training into consciousness-raising and healthy norm development overseen by coaches and captains. Sophisticated research designs and statistical analyses have established that media literacy is one major reason that ATLAS and ATHENA are effective, at 1-year follow-up, in preventing use and abuse of steroids, food supplements, stimulant drugs, and other unhealthy forms of weight and shape management in athletes, dancers, and cheerleaders (Elliot et al., 2004; Elliot & Goldberg, 2008; Goldberg et al., 2000).

Media Activism

If certain media definitely have negative effects, why not replace them with healthier, more positive content? Some media literacy programs (e.g., Neumark-Sztainer et al., 2000) for youth and adolescents include, as a component of prevention, active attempts by the participants and their mentors to challenge unhealthy messages and to create and distribute media with more positive messages (see also Levine & Smolak, 2006).

Transforming mass media is a daunting enterprise, but it is not impossible (Levine & Smolak, 2006). For example, the non-profit organizations Dads and Daughters (www.dadsanddaughters.org) and the National Eating Disorders Association (NEDA; www.nationaleatingdisorders.org) have fused the wide and quick reach of the worldwide web with the spirit of citizen activism to mount many effective protests that have resulted in the termination of advertising campaigns with pernicious messages about beauty, weight, shape, and gender. Based in part on these constructive actions, organizations such as NEDA and the Academy for Eating Disorders (AED; www.aedweb.org) are currently collaborating to offer guidelines for production of more responsible media to the Fashion Designers of America and to journalists who cover fashion and women's health.

Activism also supports positive media developments. Dove's "Campaign for Real Beauty," for instance, features photographs of curvy, underwear-clad women who are not models (www.campaignforrealbeauty.com). The decision by the executives for the Dove brand to showcase women who represent an array that is diverse in size, shape, age, and ethnicity generated a great deal of publicity and more product recognition than a body cream would ordinarily receive (Howard, 2005). As discussed previously, Dittmar and Halliwell's research has indicated that attractive, non-slender (but non-obese) models are as appealing, if not more so, as ultra-thin models, and do not leave women feeling worse about themselves. Thus, it can be lucrative for advertisers to break the mold and feature healthier body ideals. We trust that, as this type of marketing experience and media research accumulates, business communities will jettison the stale defense of "thinness is the only thing our customers want."

CONCLUSION AND ASPIRATIONS

A wide variety of studies, conducted in various countries using a range of accepted quantitative and qualitative methodologies, has demonstrated that mass media function directly and indirectly (through, for example, assumptions about media's influence on peers) to increase the risk of negative body image and the spectrum of disordered eating. This knowledge, coupled with the burgeoning areas of media literacy and media advocacy, is a strong foundation for continuing to develop and evaluate universal prevention programs designed to engage children, adolescents, and adults in the interlocking processes of analyzing and resisting unhealthy media influences, and creating new media to empower participants and to promote healthier social messages.

We hope media effects researchers inside and outside the communication discipline will continue to build on the very solid theoretical and empirical foundation we have outlined by addressing three basic needs. First, we need theoretical models that articulate clearly the transactional relationships between the media content; hypothesized processes such as schema activation, social comparison, affective processes; and the proposed media effects (see, for example, Keery et al., 2004; Myers & Crowther, 2007; and Thompson et al., 2004). Second, these models need to situate the impact of mass media within ecological and developmental contexts (see the work on media and body image by Smolak et al., 2005, and the media practice model of adolescent identity development by Steele & Brown, 1995). For example, a recent study of boys and girls ages 15 through 18 in the United States (Peterson, Paulson, & Williams, 2007) used the multivariate technique of canonical correlations to demonstrate that the self-reported experience of pressures to be thin emanating from peers, mother, and media accounted for over one third of the variance in a set of eating disorder symptoms.

Our final call to action was inspired by the basis of this chapter: collaboration between a communication scholar and an experimental psychologist. Understanding media effects requires analysis of the interplay between media content, the contexts of media use, the perceivers' psychological processes, and the situations in which media effects on body image and DEB are likely to be observed. Therefore, we need to continue to develop valid measures of key theoretical constructs drawn from the many disciplines that have generated investigations of media effects on body image and DEB. The relevant disciplines include, at a minimum, communication, psychology, psychiatry, social work, women's studies, sociology, marketing, men and masculinity, cultural studies, and public health. Refinements in the assessment of media exposure, cultivation of beliefs, and social comparison, for example, should be a top priority in future collaborative efforts to clarify the multiple ways that media messages contribute to poor body image and disturbed eating, both directly and through complex and nuanced processes involving multiple characteristics of the real-world contexts in which young people live, grow, and communicate.

References

Agliata, D., & Tantleff-Dunn, S. (2004). The impact of media exposure on males' body image. *Journal of Social and Clinical Psychology, 23*, 7–22.

American Psychiatric Association. (2000). *Diagnostic and statistical manual of mental disorders* (4th ed., text revision: *DSM-IV-TR*). Washington, DC: Author.

Arbour, K. P., & Ginis, K. A. M. (2006). Effects of exposure to muscular and hypermuscular images on young men's muscularity dissatisfaction and body dissatisfaction. *Body Image, 3*, 153–161.

Baker, C. N. (2005). Images of women's sexuality in advertisements: A content analysis of Black- and White-oriented women's and men's magazines. *Sex Roles, 52*, 13–27.

Ballentine, L. W., & Ogle, J. P. (2005). The making and unmaking of body problems in *Seventeen* magazine, 1992–2003. *Family and Consumer Sciences Research Journal, 33*, 281–307.

Bardone-Cone, A. M., & Cass, K. M. (2006). Investigating the impact of pro-anorexia websites: A pilot study. *European Eating Disorders Review, 14*, 256–262.

Birkeland, R., Thompson, J. K., Herbozo, S., Roehrig, M., Cafri, G., & van den Berg, P. (2005). Media exposure, mood, and body image dissatisfaction: An experimental test of person versus product priming. *Body Image, 2*, 53–61.

Bisaga, K., & Walsh, B. T. (2005). History of the classification of eating disorders. In C. Norring & B. Palmer (Eds.), *EDNOS—Eating Disorders Not Otherwise Specified: Scientific and clinical perspectives on the other eating disorders* (pp. 10–40). London: Routledge.

Bordo, S. (1993). *Unbearable weight: Feminism, Western culture, and the body*. Berkeley: University of California Press.

Botta, R. A. (1999). Television images and adolescent girls' body image disturbance. *Journal of Communication, 49*, 22–41.

Botta, R. A. (2000). The mirror of television: A comparison of Black and White adolescents' body image. *Journal of Communication, 50*, 144–159.

Bronfenbrenner, U. (1979). *The ecology of human development: Experiments by nature and design*. Cambridge MA: Harvard University Press.

Brotsky, S. R., & Giles, D. (2007). Inside the "Pro-ana" community: A covert online participation observation. *Eating Disorders: The Journal of Treatment & Prevention, 15*, 93–109.

Cash, T. F. (2002). The Situational Inventory of Body Image Dysphoria: Psychometric evidence and development of a short form. *International Journal of Eating Disorders, 32*, 362–366.

Cash, T. F., & Pruzinsky, T. (Eds.). (2002). *Body image: A handbook of theory, research, and clinical practice*. New York: Guilford.

Davison, K. K., & Birch, L. L. (2001). Childhood overweight: A contextual model and recommendations for future research. *Obesity Reviews, 2*, 159–171.

Dittmar, H., Halliwell, E., & Ive, S. (2006). Does Barbie make girls want to be thin? The effect of experimental exposure to images of dolls on the body image of 5–8-year-old girls. *Developmental Psychology, 42*, 283–292.

Dittmar, H., & Howard, S. (2004). Thin-ideal internalization and social comparison tendency as moderators of media models' impact on women's body-focused anxiety. *Journal of Social and Clinical Psychology, 23*, 768–791.

Dohnt, H., & Tiggemann, M. (2006). The contribution of peer and media influences to the development of body satisfaction and self-esteem in young girls: A prospective study. *Developmental Psychology, 42*, 929–936.

Durkin, S. J., & Paxton, S. J. (2002). Predictors of vulnerability to reduced body image satisfaction and psychological well-being in response to exposure to idealized female images in adolescent girls. *Journal of Psychosomatic Research, 53*, 995–1005.

Durkin, S. J., Paxton, S. J., & Wertheim, E. H. (2005). How do adolescent girls evaluate body dissatisfaction prevention messages? *Journal of Adolescent Health, 37*, 381–390.

Elliot, D. L., & Goldberg, L. (2008). Athletes Targeting Healthy Exercise and Nutrition Alternativess: Harm reduction/health promotion program for female high school athletes. In C. W. LeCroy & J. E. Mann (Eds.), *Handbook of prevention and intervention programs for adolescent girls* (pp. 205–239). Hoboken, NJ: Wiley.

Elliot, D. L., Goldberg, L., Moe, E. L., DeFrancesco, C. A., Durham, M. B., & Hix-Small, H. (2004). Preventing substance use and disordered eating: Initial outcomes of the ATHENA (Athletes Targeting Health Exercise and Nutrition Alternatives) program. *Archives of Pediatric & Adolescent Medicine, 158*, 1043–1049.

Engeln-Maddox, R. (2006). Buying a beauty standard or dreaming of a new life? Expectations associated with media ideals. *Psychology of Women Quarterly, 30*, 258–266.

Field, A. E., Cheung, L., Wolf, A. M., Herzog, D. B., Gortmaker, S. L., & Colditz, A. (1999).

Exposure to the mass media and weight concerns among girls. *Pediatrics*, *103*, e36. Retrieved August 27, 2007, from http://pediatrics.aapublications.org/cgi/reprint/193.3/e36.

Fouts, G., & Burggraf, K. (1999). Television situation comedies: Female body images and verbal reinforcements. *Sex Roles*, *40*, 473–481.

Fouts, G., & Burggraf, K. (2000). Television situation comedies: Female weight, male negative comments, and audience reactions. *Sex Roles*, *42*, 925–932.

Forbes, G. B., Jobe, R. L., & Revak, J. A. (2006). Relationships between dissatisfaction with specific body characteristics and the Sociocultural Attitudes Toward Appearance Questionnaire-3 and Objectified Body Consciousness Scale. *Body Image*, *3*, 295–300.

Frisby, C. (2004). Does race matter? Effects of idealized images on African American women's perceptions of body esteem. *Journal of Black Studies*, *34*, 323–347.

Goldberg, L., MacKinnon, D. P., Elliot, D. L., Moe, E. L., Clarke, G., & Cheong, J. (2000). The Adolescents Training and Learning to Avoid Steroids Program: Preventing drug use and promoting healthy behaviors. *Archives of Pediatrics & Adolescent Medicine*, *154*, 332–338.

Gordon, R. A. (2000). *Eating disorders: Anatomy of a social epidemic* (2nd ed.). Oxford, UK: Blackwell.

Greenberg, B. S., Eastin, M., Hofschire, L., Lachlan, K., & Brownell, K. D. (2003). Portrayals of overweight and obese individuals on commercial television. *American Journal of Public Health*, *93*, 1342–1348.

Groesz, L. M., Levine, M. P., & Murnen, S. K. (2002). The effect of experimental presentation of thin media images on body dissatisfaction: A meta-analytic review. *International Journal of Eating Disorders*, *31*, 1–16.

Halliwell, E., & Dittmar, H. (2004). Does size matter? The impact of model's body size on women's body-focused anxiety and advertising effectiveness. *Journal of Social and Clinical Psychology*, *23*, 104–122.

Halliwell, E., & Dittmar, H. (2005). The role of self-improvement and self-evaluation motives in social comparisons with idealized female bodies in the media. *Body Image*, *2*, 249–261.

Halliwell, E., Dittmar, H., & Howe, J. (2005). The impact of advertisements featuring ultra-thin or average-size models on women with a history of eating disorders. *Journal of Community & Applied Psychology*, *15*, 406–413.

Halliwell, E., Dittmar, H., & Orsborn, A. (2007). The effects of exposure to muscular male models among men: Exploring the moderating role of gym use and exercise motivation. *Body Image*, *4*, 278–287.

Hargreaves, D., & Tiggemann, M. (2002). The effect of television commercials on mood and body dissatisfaction: The role of appearance-schema activation. *Journal of Social and Clinical Psychology*, *21*, 287–308.

Hargreaves, D., & Tiggemann, M. (2003). Longer-term implications of responsiveness to "thin-ideal" television: support for a cumulative hypothesis of body image disturbance? *European Eating Disorders Review*, *11*, 465–477.

Hargreaves, D., & Tiggemann, M. (2004). Idealized media images and adolescent body image: "Comparing" boys and girls. *Body Image*, *1*, 351–361.

Hargreaves, D., & Tiggemann, M. (2006). "Body image is for girls": A qualitative study of boys' body image. *Journal of Health Pyschology*, *11*, 567–576.

Harrison, K. (1997). Does interpersonal attraction to thin media personalities promote eating disorders? *Journal of Broadcasting and Electronic Media*, *41*, 478–500.

Harrison, K. (2000). Television viewing, fat stereotyping, body shape standards, and eating disorder symptomatology in grade school children. *Communication Research*, *27*(5), 617–640.

Harrison, K. (2001). Ourselves, our bodies: Thin-ideal media, self-discrepancies, and eating disorder symptomatology in adolescents. *Journal of Social and Clinical Psychology*, *20*, 289–323.

Harrison, K. (2003). Television viewers' ideal body proportions: The case of the curvaceously thin woman. *Sex Roles*, *48*, 255–264.

Harrison, K., & Bond, B. J. (2007). Gaming magazines and the drive for muscularity in preadolescent boys: A longitudinal examination. *Body Image*, *4*, 269–277.

Harrison, K., & Cantor, J. (1997). The relationship between media consumption and eating disorders. *Journal of Communication*, *47*, 40–67.

Harrison, K., & Fredrickson, B. L. (2003). Women's sports media, self-objectification, and mental health in Black and White adolescent females. *Journal of Communication*, *53*, 216–232.

Harrison, K., & Hefner, V. (2006). Media exposure, current and future body ideals, and disordered eating among preadolescent girls: A longitudinal panel study. *Journal of Youth and Adolescence*, *3*, 146–156.

Harrison, K., Taylor, L. D., & Marske, A. L. (2006). Women's and men's eating behavior in response to exposure to thin-ideal media images and text. *Communication Research*, *33*, 507–529.

Henderson-King, D., Henderson-King, E., & Hoffmann, L. (2001). Media images and women's self-evaluations: Social context and importance of attractiveness as moderators. *Personality and Social Psychology Bulletin*, *27*, 1407–1416.

Henderson-King, E., & Henderson-King, D. (1997). Media effects on women's body esteem: Social and individual difference factors. *Journal of Applied Social Psychology*, *27*, 399–417.

Herbozo, S., Tantleff-Dunn, S., Gokee-Larose, J., & Thompson, J. K. (2004). Beauty and thinness messages in children's media: A content analysis. *Eating Disorders: The Journal of Treatment and Prevention*, *12*, 21–34.

Higgins, E. T. (1999). When do self-discrepancies have specific relations to emotions? The second-generation question of Tagney, Niedenthal, Covert, and Barlow. *Journal of Personality and Social Psychology*, *77*, 1313–1317.

Himes, S. M., & Thompson, J. K. (2007). Fat stigmatization in television shows and movies: A content analysis. *Obesity*, *15*, 712–718.

Howard, T. (2005, July 8). Ad campaign tells women to celebrate who they are. Retrieved May 19, 2008, from http://www.campaignforrealbeauty.com/press.asp?section=news&id=3073.

Humphreys, P., & Paxton, S. J. (2004). The impact of exposure to idealized male images on adolescent boys' body image. *Body Image*, *1*, 253–266.

Jansen, A., & de Vries, M. (2002). Pre-attentive exposure to the thin female beauty ideal does not affect women's mood, self-esteem, and eating behaviour. *European Eating Disorders Review*, *10*, 208–217.

Jones, D. C. (2001). Social comparison and body image: Attractiveness comparisons to models and peers among adolescent girls and boys. *Sex Roles*, *45*, 645–664.

Jones, D. C., Vigfusdottir, T., & Lee, Y. (2004). Body image and the appearance culture among adolescent girls and boys: An examination of friend conversations, peer criticism, appearance magazines, and the internalization of appearance ideals. *Journal of Adolescent Research*, *19*, 323–339.

Keery, H., van den Berg, P., & Thompson, J. K. (2004). The Tripartite Influence Model of body dissatisfaction and eating disturbance with adolescent girls. *Body Image*, *1*, 237–251.

King, N., Touyz, S., & Charles, M. (2000). The effect of body dissatisfaction on women's perceptions of female celebrities. *International Journal of Eating Disorders*, *27*, 341–347.

Klein, H., & Shiffman, K. S. (2006). Messages about physical attractiveness in animated cartoons. *Body Image*, *3*, 353–363.

Labre, M. P. (2005). Burn fat, build muscle: A content analysis of *Men's Health* and *Men's Fitness*. *International Journal of Men's Health*, *4*, 187–200.

Labre, M. P., & Walsh-Childers, K. (2003). Friendly advice? Beauty messages in Web sites of teen magazines. *Mass Communication & Society*, *6*, 379–396.

Lavine, H., Sweeney, D., & Wagner, S. H. (1999). Depicting women as sex objects in television advertising: Effects on body dissatisfaction. *Personality and Social Psychology Bulletin*, *25*, 1049–1058.

Lawrie, Z., Sullivan, E. A., Davies, P. S. W., & Hill, R. J. (2006). Media influence on the body image of children and adolescents. *Eating Disorders: The Journal of Treatment & Prevention, 14,* 355–364.

Levine, M. P., & Harrison, K. (2004). The role of mass media in the perpetuation and prevention of negative body image and disordered eating. In J. Kevin Thompson (Ed.), *Handbook of eating disorders & obesity* (pp. 695–717). New York: Wiley.

Levine, M. P., & Smolak, L. (2006). *The prevention of eating problems and eating disorders: Theory, research, and practice.* Mahwah, NJ: Erlbaum.

Lew, A-M., Mann, T., Myers, H., Taylor, S. W., & Bower, J. (2007). Thin-ideal media and women's body dissatisfaction: Prevention using downward social comparison on non-appearance dimensions. *Sex Roles, 57,* 543–556.

McCreary, D. R., & Sadava, S. W. (1999). TV viewing and self-perceived health, weight, and physical fitness: Evidence for the cultivation hypothesis. *Journal of Applied Social Psychology, 29,* 2342–2361.

Morrison, T. G., Kalin, R., & Morrison, M. A. (2004). Body-image evaluation and body-image investment among adolescents: A test of sociocultural and social comparison theories. *Adolescence, 39,* 571–592.

Murnen, S. K., Levine, M. P., Groesz, L., & Smith, J. (2007, August). *Do fashion magazines promote body dissatisfaction in girls and women? A meta-analytic review.* Paper presented at the 115th meeting of the American Psychology Association, San Francisco, CA.

Murnen, S. K., Smolak, L., Mills, J. A., & Good, L. (2003). Thin, sexy women and strong, muscular men: Grade-school children's responses to objectified images of women and men. *Sex Roles, 49,* 427–437.

Myers, T. A., & Crowther, J. H. (2007). Sociocultural pressures, thin-ideal internalization, self-objectification, and body dissatisfaction. Could feminist beliefs be a moderating factor? *Body Image, 4,* 296–308.

Neumark-Sztainer, D., Paxton, S. J., Hannan, P., Haines, J., & Story, M. (2006). Does body satisfaction matter? Five-year longitudinal associations between body satisfaction and health in adolescent males and females. *Journal of Adolescent Health, 39,* 244–251.

Neumark-Sztainer D., Sherwood N., Coller, T., & Hannan P. J. (2000). Primary prevention of disordered eating among pre-adolescent girls: Feasibility and short-term impact of community-based intervention. *Journal of the American Dietetic Association, 100,* 1466–1473.

Neumark-Sztainer, D., Wall, M., Guo, J., Story, M., Haines, J., & Eisenberg, M. (2006). Obesity, disordered eating, and eating disorders in a longitudinal study of adolescents: How do dieters fare 5 years later? *Journal of the American Dietetic Association, 106,* 568.

Nielsen, S., Moller-Madsen, S., Isager, T., Jorgensen, J., Pagsberg, K., & Theander, S. (1998). Standardized mortality in eating disorders—a quantitative summary of previously published and new evidence. *Journal of Psychosomatic Research, 44,* 413–434.

Norris, M. L., Boydell, K. M., Pinhas, L., & Katzman, D. K. (2006). Ana and the Internet: A review of pro-anorexia websites. *International Journal of Eating Disorders, 39,* 443–447.

Park, S. Y. (2005). The influence of presumed media influence on women's desire to be thin. *Communication Research, 32,* 594–614.

Peterson, K. A., Paulson, S. E., & Williams, K. K. (2007). Relations of eating disorder symptomatology with perceptions of pressures from mother, peers, and media in adolescent girls and boys. *Sex Roles, 57,* 629–639.

Piran, N. (2001). Re-inhabiting the body from the inside out: Girls transform their school environment. In D. L. Tolman & M. Brydon-Miller (Eds.), *From subjects to subjectivities: A handbook of interpretive and participatory methods* (pp. 218–238). New York: NYU Press.

Pope, H. G., Jr., Phillips, K. A., & Olivardia, R. (2000). *The Adonis Complex: The secret crisis of male body obsession.* New York: The Free Press.

Posavac, H., Posavac, S. S., & Weigel, R. G. (2001). Reducing the impact of media images on women at risk for body image disturbance: Three targeted interventions. *Journal of Social and Clinical Psychology, 20,* 324–340.

Puhl, R. M., & Latner, J. D. (2007). Stigma, obesity, and the health of the nation's children. *Psychological Bulletin, 133,* 557–580.

Ricciardelli, L. A., McCabe, M. P., Lillis, J., & Thomas, K. (2006). A longitudinal investigation of the development of weight and muscle concerns among preadolescent boys. *Journal of Youth and Adolescence, 35,* 177–187.

Rome, E. S., & Ammerman, S. (2003). Medical complications of the eating disorders: An update. *Journal of Adolescent Health, 33,* 418–426.

Schooler, D., Ward, L. M., Merriwether, A., & Caruthers, A. (2004). Who's that girl: Television's role in the body image development of young White and Black women. *Psychology of Women Quarterly, 28,* 38–47.

Sinclair, S. L. (2006). Object lessons: A theoretical and empirical study of objectified body consciousness in women. *Journal of Mental Health Counseling, 28,* 48–68.

Sinton, M. M., & Birch, L. L. (2006). Individual and sociocultural influences on pre-adolescent girls' appearance schemas and body dissatisfaction. *Journal of Youth and Adolescence, 35,* 165–175.

Smolak, L., & Levine, M. P. (1996). Developmental transitions at middle school and college. In L. Smolak, M. P. Levine, & R. H. Striegel-Moore (Eds.), *The developmental psychopathology of eating disorders: Implications for research, prevention, and treatment* (pp. 207–233). Hillsdale, NJ: Erlbaum.

Smolak, L., Levine, M. P., & Striegel-Moore, R. H. (Eds.). (1996). *The developmental psychopathology of eating disorders: Implications for research, prevention, and treatment.* Hillsdale, NJ: Erlbaum.

Smolak, L., Levine, M. P., & Thompson, J. K. (2001). The use of the Sociocultural Attitudes Toward Appearance Questionnaire with middle school boys and girls. *International Journal of Eating Disorders, 29,* 216–223.

Smolak, L., & Murnen, S. K. (2004). A feminist approach to eating disorders. In J. K. Thompson (Ed.), *Handbook of eating disorders and obesity* (pp. 590–605). Hoboken, NJ: Wiley.

Smolak, L., Murnen, S. K., & Thompson, J. K. (2005). Sociocultural influences and muscle building in adolescent boys. *Psychology of Men and Masculinity, 6,* 227–239.

Spitzer, B. L., Henderson, K. A., & Zivian, M. T. (1999). Gender differences in population versus media body sizes: A comparison over four decades. *Sex Roles, 40,* 545–565.

Stanford, J., & McCabe, M. (2005). Sociocultural influences on adolescent boys' body image and body change strategies. *Body Image, 2,* 105–113.

Stapel, D. A., & Tesser, A. (2001). Self-activation increases social comparison. *Journal of Personality and Social Psychology, 81,* 742–750.

Steele, J. R., & Brown, J. D. (1995). Adolescent room culture: Studying media in the context of everyday life. *Journal of Youth and Adolescence, 24,* 551–576.

Stice, E., Cameron, R. P., Killen, J. D., Hayward, C., & Taylor, C. B. (1999). Naturalistic weight-reduction efforts prospectively predict growth in relative weight and onset of obesity among female adolescents. *Journal of Consulting and Clinical Psychology, 67,* 967–974.

Stice, E., Hayward, C., Cameron, R. P., Killen, J. D., & Taylor, C. B. (2000). Body image and eating disturbances predict onset of depression among female adolescents: A longitudinal study. *Journal of Abnormal Psychology, 109,* 438–444.

Stice, E., & Shaw, H. (2003). Prospective relations of body image, eating, and affective disturbances to smoking onset in adolescent girls: How Virginia Slims. *Journal of Consulting and Clinical Psychology, 71,* 129–135.

Strauman, T. J., Vookles, J., Berenstein, V., Chaiken, S., & Higgins, E. T. (1991). Self-discrepancies and vulnerability to body dissatisfaction and disordered eating. *Journal of Personality and Social Psychology, 61,* 946–956.

Thompson, J. K. (Ed.). (2004). *Handbook of eating disorders and obesity.* Hoboken, NJ: Wiley.

Thompson, J. K., Heinberg, L., Altabe, M., & Tantleff-Dunn, S. (1999). *Exacting beauty: Theory, assessment, and treatment of body image disturbance.* Washington, DC: American Psychological Association.

Thompson, J. K., van den Berg, P., Roehrig, M., Guarda, A. S., & Heinberg, L. J. (2004). The Sociocultural Attitudes Toward Appearance Scale-3 (SATAQ-3): Development and validation. *International Journal of Eating Disorders, 35*, 293–304.

Thomsen, S. R., McCoy, K., Williams, M., & Gustafson, R. L. (2002). Motivations for reading beauty and fashion magazines and anorexic risk in college-age women. *Media Psychology, 4*, 113–135.

Tiggemann, M., & Slater, A. (2004). Thin ideals in music television: A source of social comparison and body dissatisfaction. *International Journal of Eating Disorders, 35*, 48–58.

Trampe, D., Stapel, D. A., & Siero, F. W. (2007). On models and vases: Body dissatisfaction and proneness to social comparison effects. *Journal of Personality & Social Psychology, 92*, 106–118.

Wade, T. D., Davidson, S., & O'Dea, J. (2003). A preliminary controlled evaluation of a school-based media literacy and self-esteem program for reducing eating disorder risk factors. *International Journal of Eating Disorders, 33*, 371–383.

Wilcox, K., & Laird, J. D. (2000). The impact of media images of super-slender women on women's self-esteem: Identification, social comparison, and self-perception. *Journal of Research in Personality, 34*, 278–286.

Wilksch, S. M., Tiggemann, M., & Wade, T. D. (2006). Impact of interactive school-based media literacy lessons for reducing internalization of media ideals in young adolescent girls and boys. *International Journal of Eating Disorders, 39*, 385–393.

Wood, K. (2004). Effects of a media intervention program on body image and eating attitudes among children. *University of Wisconsin-La Cross Journal of Undergraduate Research, 7*, 1–6. Retrieved January 12, 2007, from http://www.uwlax.edu/URC/JUR-online/PDF/2004/wood.pdf.

Yumamiya, Y., Cash, T. F., Melnyk, S. E., Posavac, H. D., & Posavac, S. S. (2005). Women's exposure to thin-and-beautiful media images: Body image effects of media-ideal internalization and impact-reduction interventions. *Body Image, 2*, 74–80.

23

INDIVIDUAL DIFFERENCES IN MEDIA EFFECTS

Mary Beth Oliver and K. Maja Krakowiak
Penn State University

The notion that media have powerful, direct effects on individuals is arguably more widely accepted by the general public than by scholars in media effects. Consistent with social scientific conceptualizations of more nuanced media influence, studies in media effects often report small to moderate effect sizes—a situation that has allowed some critics to suggest that the media have no effect or that the effects of media are completely overwhelmed by other social forces. This chapter acknowledges the importance of unexplained variance, and, like some critics, sees it as an issue deserving of attention. However, we take the position that unexplained variance represents the very thing that makes humans interesting, unique, and infinitely worthy of our research attention: individual differences.

The use of the terms "noise" and "error" to refer to individual variations illustrates that individual differences are inherently messy—the list of possible differences that may play important roles in any given media situation is arguably infinite. Indeed, the use of random assignment in most experimental studies is illustrative of the idea that it is virtually impossible to account for the limitless ways that people may vary. This chapter acknowledges the diversity that exists among media audiences, but narrows the focus to those differences that represent enduring dispositions, attitudes, or cognitions. Although these types of individual differences are undoubtedly related to heredity and environment, and are often associated with characteristics such as gender, race, age, class, or experience, the focus of this chapter is on those differences that may vary among individuals who may nevertheless share some demographically based social group. Using this definition, this chapter overviews the variety of ways in which individual differences intersect with media selection, processing, and effects. The topics we consider include enjoyment of and emotional responses to media, the use of media as a means of expressing and inferring individual differences, selective exposure to and perception of media content, individual differences as moderators of media influence, and the ways that media consumption may shape or influence individual differences.

ENJOYMENT AND EMOTIONAL RESPONSE

The diversity that exists in media content is evidence of the importance of individual variations in preferences for, enjoyment of, and responses to specific *types* of media fare.

Research exploring a variety of individual differences suggests that more enduring traits and dispositions play important roles in predicting audience reactions.

Individual Differences as "Needs"

Because many individual difference measures can be conceptualized as "needs" or "affinities," it follows that stimuli that address or fulfill needs should be more frequently sought after and enjoyed. Examples of individual differences that can be conceptualized as "needs" include the need for cognition (Cacioppo & Petty, 1982), the need for affect (Maio & Esses, 2001), and sensation seeking (Zuckerman, 1979), among others. Research that has examined these individual differences and media selection and enjoyment tend to show predictable patterns, with higher levels of need for cognition associated with viewing media content such as news and informational programming (Perse, 1992), higher levels of need for affect associated with greater willingness to view "emotional" than "non-emotional" films (Maio & Esses, 2001), and higher levels of sensation seeking associated with greater viewing and enjoyment of arousing or action-packed media entertainment such as horror films, action adventures, violent programming (including combative sports), or pornography (Aluja-Fabregat & Torrubia-Beltri, 1998; Hoffner & Levine, 2005; McDaniel, 2003; Zuckerman & Litle, 1986).

The number of individuals' needs or desires that may predict media preferences is obviously large, making it somewhat difficult to focus on the particular individual differences that may be consequential. However, Reiss and Wiltz (2004) recently suggested that Reiss's (2000) sensitivity theory of basic desires may be useful in broadly identifying a wide array of motivations predictive of media use and enjoyment. Briefly, sensitivity theory argues for the existence of 16 universal motives, including desires for power, independence, curiosity, vengeance, idealism, and romance, among others. According to this theory, the fulfillment of each of these motives results in the experience of a particular type of joy, such as freedom, wonderment, vindication, fun, and so forth. Although human beings are thought to share basic desires, they differ in how they prioritize them—some individuals rank certain desires as more important than do others. As a result, variations in individuals' desires should be reflected in their media selections and their enjoyment of different types of content. In support of this reasoning, Reiss and Wiltz (2004) found that people who watched more reality television were more strongly motivated by social status, vengeance, social contact, order, and romance, and were less motivated by honor than were individuals who watched fewer reality television shows.

Individual Differences as "Readiness to Respond"

Whereas individual differences conceptualized as "needs" make predictive sense in studies of viewers' enjoyment, other individual differences imply stronger or more intense emotional responses to media portrayals. In this regard, numerous researchers have explored the role of empathy in viewers' reactions to entertainment (Nathanson, 2003; Zillmann, 1991). In general, this research suggests that higher levels of empathy are associated with more intense emotional responses to media portrayals that feature others' misfortunes or suffering. For example, Tamborini, Stiff, and Heidel (1990) reported that higher levels of empathy were positively associated with arousal and coping behaviors (e.g., turning away, covering one's eyes) in response to a frightening film, and were negatively associated with enjoyment. Likewise, Choti, Marston, and Holston

(1987) found that higher levels of empathy predicted greater self-reported sadness and crying in response to sad films, though additional research suggests that such empathic responses are associated with heightened rather than diminished enjoyment (Oliver, 1993).

Just as some individual differences predict more intense emotional responses to media depictions, additional individual differences imply reduced, blunted, or masked responses. For example, Sparks, Pellechia, and Irvine (1999) found that individuals scoring higher on repressive coping styles tended to report lower levels of negative affective responses to a frightening film than their heightened physiological responses would have suggested. Similarly, Oliver, Sargent, and Weaver (1998) reported that agentic (masculine) participants expressed lower levels of disturbance and empathic responding to victims in a violent film than did communal (feminine) participants.

Individual Differences as "Traits"

Although many individual differences imply needs or states of emotional readiness, additional differences can perhaps be best described as enduring dispositions or personality traits. Included here would be individual differences such as shyness, aggressiveness, machiavellianism, deceit, loyalty, optimism, or permissiveness, among hundreds of others, or constellations of traits such as neuroticism, extraversion, and psychoticism (Eysenck, 1990).

Research on the aforementioned types of traits has arguably focused the greatest attention on issues related to media violence, with this research suggesting that violent content appears to be most attractive to individuals harboring dispositions often associated with higher levels of aggression. For example, traits such as psychoticism, machiavellianism, and trait hostility have been shown to positively predict greater interest in and enjoyment of media violence per se and of specific genres such as horror films and violent animation (Aluja-Fabregat, 2000; Bushman, 1995; Krcmar & Kean, 2005; Oliver et al., 1998; Tamborini, Stiff, & Zillmann, 1987; Weaver, 1991). Similar patterns have also been observed for additional types of media content. For example, traits such as rebelliousness, tough-mindedness, machismo, and psychoticism have been associated with greater enjoyment of more violent genres such as hard rock, heavy metal, or rap music (Carpentier, Knobloch, & Zillmann, 2003; Hansen & Hansen, 2000; Robinson, Weaver, & Zillmann, 1996). More recently, Slater (2003) reported that higher levels of aggressiveness among the adolescents in his sample were associated not only with greater viewing of action films, but also with more frequent visits to Internet sites that advocated violent behaviors.

A variety of explanations have been considered to account for the relationship between violence-related traits and preference for violent media content. For example, some researchers have suggested that violent entertainment may be more meaningful to individuals with more aggressive or hostile traits, as such media offerings likely present scenarios, characters, or situations that are familiar and therefore more relevant (Hoffner & Cantor, 1991). In contrast, individuals who harbor antagonistic dispositions may be less vulnerable to feelings of distress or disturbance in response to violent content, thereby allowing them to experience enjoyment from some forms of entertainment (e.g., slasher films, thrillers) that other viewers would find too unsettling. Finally, research on disposition theory and enjoyment of media entertainment might suggest that people with more hostile dispositions may be more likely to see the victims in violent entertainment as more "deserving" of their victimization, thereby increasing the experience of gratification that accrues when "justice is restored," however that justice may be defined by the individual viewer (Oliver & Armstrong, 1995; Raney, 2004; Raney & Bryant, 2002; Zillmann, 1991). Of course, these various explanations are speculative at this point, suggesting that further research is needed to more fully understand the role of personality in predicting preferences for media violence.

Summary

To summarize, enjoyment of media entertainment is highly variable, but numerous studies have demonstrated that many stable and enduring traits and dispositions successfully predict a variety of emotional reactions to media portrayals, gratification included. It is important to keep in mind that this discussion of individual differences does not imply exhaustiveness, nor does it imply mutual exclusivity. Indeed, the consistency of patterns related to viewers' responses likely reflects the fact that many individual differences are related, if not redundant. In addition, there are undoubtedly many additional roles that individual differences may play that await further research. For example, whereas our discussion of individual differences and enjoyment has "treated" these differences as independent variables, it is also plausible that media exposure and enjoyment affect or shape viewer dispositions. We further explore this interpretation of individual differences as dependent variables in the concluding section of this chapter.

EXPRESSING AND INFERRING INDIVIDUAL DIFFERENCES

Given that individual differences serve as predictors of media consumption and enjoyment, it may also be useful to conceptualize media use and preferences as an indicator or expression of our personalities rather than only as outcomes. In addition, with technological advances, the ability of individuals to alter, create, or customize media content allows for further expression of individuals' identities or uniqueness. YouTube video diaries, blogs, customized portals, ring tones, and social networking sites such as Facebook or MySpace are but a few of the examples of media content that individuals can modify to reflect their own personal tastes, dispositions, and interests. Insofar as individual differences serve as useful predictors of media use, enjoyment, and (more recently) media creation and modification, it follows that observations of others' media consumption patterns and preferences may provide (or imply) information about others' dispositions or traits.

Music and Brand Preferences

Musical preferences can convey a great deal of information about an individual's personality, including information about central or core values (e.g., traditional, unconventional, sophisticated, etc.). For some individuals, and particularly adolescents, musical tastes may be so central to self concept that musical selections become a "badge of identity" (North & Hargreaves, 1999). For example, teens and young adults often hang up posters of bands on the walls of their rooms, wear t-shirts featuring musical artists, and increasingly, post lists of their favorite bands, albums, and songs on social networking sites.

Given the importance of music in the expression or display of individual differences, it follows that people may use information about others' musical preferences in forming impressions and making judgments about others' personalities (Rentfrow &

Gosling, 2006; Zillmann & Bhatia, 1989). For example, Zillmann and Bhatia (1989) reported that an individual's association with a specific musical genre (e.g., country music) affected others' level of attraction to that person. Importantly, Rentfrow and Gosling (2006) also recently found that song and genre choices *accurately* reflect certain aspects of individuals' personalities such as agreeableness, emotional stability, and openness. For example, liking of song attributes such as enthusiasm, energy, and amount of singing, and liking of country and hip-hop genres was positively associated with both expressed *and* inferred extraversion.

Of course, expression and judgment of individual differences are not limited to music. For example, Fennis and Pruyn (2007) reported that under certain conditions, people form impressions of individuals based on the brand name that appears on their t-shirts. Specifically, in their study, participants linked the associations they had about a brand (e.g., successful, intelligent, competent) to the person who was wearing the brand name; however, this effect was strongest when the situational context was consistent with the associations the brand evoked (e.g., the Hugo Boss brand appearing in a golf course setting rather than a camping site).

New Media

Changes and developments associated with communication technologies arguably allow for even more elaborate self expression and interpretation by others. Not only are there more venues of media outlets, new media such as the Internet allow for greater selectivity, many new media are mobile and hence become physically associated with users, and many types of technologies employ interactive interfaces that allow individuals the opportunity to become sources rather than only receivers of communication (Sundar, 2007, 2008). For example, many individuals now have elaborate personal pages on networking sites (e.g., Facebook) that detail their hobbies, interests, friends, and aspirations. Likewise, cell phone users can create mobile identities by selecting whom to include in their cell phone networks, and by choosing specific ring tones, wallpapers, and colored covers (Srivastava, 2005). Even signatures included in email communication can convey information about the sender's personality or disposition, as many signatures feature favorite quotes, avatars, or links to websites that the sender finds of interest. Because media customization can be used to express one's individuality, it is not surprising that research suggests that people with a strong need for uniqueness are more prone to customize their cell phones and computers (Marathe, 2007).

Just as people use information about others' musical tastes in forming impressions of others' personalities, recent research suggests that people also form impressions of others on the basis of new technologies. Further, this research also reports that strangers can often accurately infer some aspects of individuals' personalities from online content such as personal websites (Marcus, Machilek, & Schutz, 2006; Vazire & Gosling, 2004), personality profiles on online social-networking websites (Gosling, Gaddis, & Vazire, 2007), and emails (Gill, Oberlander, & Austin, 2006). For example, Gosling et al. (2007) reported that participants who viewed personality profiles on Facebook reached some agreement on the personality dimensions of the page creators, including their levels of extraversion, agreeableness, conscientiousness, emotional stability, and openness to experience. In addition, participants' impressions of the page creator's personality were somewhat accurate in reflecting the actual characteristics of the page creator as measured via the page creator's self reports and the reports from the creator's friends.

Summary

To summarize, research indicates that individuals use traditional media preferences, such as musical genres, to express their individual differences, and that others are able to infer much about individuals' personalities from their media choices. Furthermore, interactive, new media allow users to become sources of communication, thereby enabling them to express their individuality through customization and creation of online content. Those who are exposed to this content through email, personal websites, social networking sites, or via online chatting use these expressions of identity to form fairly accurate impressions of others' personalities. Therefore, media use not only allows individuals to express their individual differences but also informs others of these differences.

SELECTIVE EXPOSURE AND INTERPRETATION

Although preferences for media content and the related use of media as a means of expressing such preferences undoubtedly explain a great deal of media exposure, media selection may also reflect the extent to which the viewer perceives the messages as useful in achieving goals, as informative, or as consistent with or confirming of attitudes or beliefs. This section focuses specifically on individual differences related to attitudes, beliefs, and cognitions, and the role they play in selective exposure and interpretation.

Selection and Avoidance

The idea that individuals select information that is consistent with attitudes and beliefs, and ignore or avoid information that is discrepant is largely understood in terms of theories of cognitive dissonance (Festinger, 1957). In general, this theory argues individuals are motivated to have consistency in their cognitions, and that when inconsistent cognitions exist, people experience cognitive dissonance—an aversive psychological state that motives the alleviation of the dissonance. One implication of this theory is that once a person has established an attitude or belief, that person should be more likely to expose him or herself to congruent information and to avoid incongruent information that would give rise to dissonance.

Many scholars have studied the application of dissonance theory to mass communication. For example, Klapper's (1960) argument that the media serve to reinforce beliefs was largely based on the phenomena of selective exposure to information. More recently, Sunstein (2001) argued that the greater opportunity for selectivity afforded by the Internet will likely result in individuals exposing themselves to only like-minded opinions—a phenomenon he called "The Daily Me."

Consistent with these arguments, a sizable number of studies have found support for the idea that media use patterns often reflect individuals' existing attitudes and beliefs. For example, Sweeney and Gruber (1984) reported that interest in and attention to the Watergate hearings was highest among McGovern supporters, lowest among Nixon supporters, and moderate among undecided citizens. More recently, Iyengar and Hahn (2007) reported similar findings in terms of individuals' selective exposure to news sources encountered on the Internet. Specifically, these authors experimentally assessed how the association of news stories with Fox News, CNN, BBC, or NPR would affect users' interest in reading the stories. As predicted, the political orientation of the users was strongly influential in news selection/avoidance, with Republicans overwhelmingly more likely to select both hard- and soft-news stories associated with Fox, and Democrats more likely to avoid stories from this source. Consistent with Sunstein's (2001) argument, these authors concluded that the Internet provides a unique opportunity for selectivity: "When browsing the web, users can filter or search through masses of text more easily. Thus, as candidates, interest groups, and voters all converge on the Internet, the possibility of selective exposure to political information increases" (p. 19).

Despite studies such as these that show support for the basic processes of selective exposure, the larger body of research employing dissonance models has not gone without criticism. For example, some scholars have argued that individuals may be likely to expose themselves to incongruent information when the information is useful or informative in attaining goals (Freedman & Sears, 1965) or when the information is easily refutable (Frey, 1986). Consequently, though the basic phenomenon of cognitive dissonance and the implications that it has for individual differences in selective exposure are generally supported in the literature, additional research is needed to further examine the individual differences associated with greater and lesser tolerance of dissonance and the manner in which these variations successfully predict selective exposure to and avoidance of media content.

Selective Perception

Although viewers may, at times, selectively choose or avoid congruent and incongruent information, selective exposure is not always necessarily desired, nor is it always an option. Rather, the prevalence of media messages implies that individuals encounter a wide variety of opinions and attitudes, many of which likely conflict with existing beliefs. Whereas inconsistent information may ultimately serve to create dissonance or to *change* viewers' attitudes or beliefs, research on selective perception suggests that individual differences play important roles in viewers' interpretations of media content in ways that may serve to maintain or reinforce existing beliefs (Klapper, 1960).

Perhaps the most frequently studied means by which individuals process incongruent information is via biased assimilation (Lord, Ross, & Lepper, 1979). That is, when individuals hold strong opinions on a given issue, they frequently interpret encountered messages as supportive of or consistent with their position. Such effects have been demonstrated for a variety of different media genres and content types. For example, in terms of entertainment media, Vidmar and Rokeach's (1974) now classic study illustrated the importance of racial attitudes on viewers' responses to *All in the Family*. Although most of the respondents reported viewing and enjoying the program, high-prejudiced individuals tended to interpret the program as sympathetic to the bigoted main character, whereas low-prejudiced individuals tended to interpret the program as sympathetic to the politically liberal main character. Similar evidence of biased assimilation has been demonstrated in terms of viewers' responses to news (Peffley, Shields, & Williams, 1996) and in terms of viewers' responses to politics (Bothwell & Brigham, 1983). For example, Munro et al. (2002) examined viewers' responses to the first presidential debate between Bill Clinton and Bob Dole during the 1996 election, finding that preferences for a given candidate were associated with perceptions that the candidate performed better than his opponent. Importantly, too, these authors also found that participants' affective responses during the debate served as a mediator between pre-debate attitudes and post-debate perceptions, suggesting that biased assimilation may reflect both cognitive and affective/motivational mechanisms.

In contrast to the notion of biased assimilation, research on hostile media perceptions has shown that individuals with strongly held beliefs can sometimes perceive media sources and content as biased *against* their point of view rather than as supportive of it (Vallone, Ross, & Lepper, 1985). For example, research from a hostile-media perspective would suggest that Democrats may be likely to see the media as having a conservative slant, whereas Republicans would be more likely to accuse the media of having a liberal bias. Interestingly, Gunther and Schmitt (2004) found that perceptions of hostility appear to be directed to *media* messages specifically as opposed to messages presented via other channels. These authors interpreted their findings as suggesting a concern among partisan viewers that the media may persuade other "vulnerable" viewers to hold disparate attitudes.

It is important to note that although biased assimilation and hostile-media perceptions appear to suggest conflicting predictions concerning the role of viewers' existing beliefs on perceptions, both perspectives would also imply that responses to media portrayals may ultimately serve to reinforce beliefs. In the case of biased assimilation, beliefs may be reinforced because the portrayal or depiction itself is interpreted to be congruent. In the case of hostile-media perceptions, beliefs may be reinforced because the *source* of incongruent information is perceived as biased and is therefore discounted. Consequently, it appears possible that a given individual may experience both biased assimilation and hostile perceptions simultaneously. For example, a person who is strongly favorable toward a given political candidate may perceive that the candidate provided superior answers in a political debate, while at the same time believe that media coverage of the debate was biased. Although such a scenario seems plausible, research has yet to attend to circumstances under which biased assimilation and hostile perceptions may co-occur, making this direction of research potentially fruitful.

Summary

To summarize, research on viewers' selective exposure and perception highlights the importance that individual differences play in the experience of media content. In general, this body of research shows a tendency for viewers to select and interpret media messages that are consistent with or confirming of their existing attitudes and beliefs. In this regard, research in this area appears to support a limited-effects perspective. Nevertheless, it is important to remember that viewers do not always have control over their media exposure, and that media content is not always sufficiently ambiguous as to allow for multiple interpretations. In addition, whereas individual differences may play a role in reinforcement in some circumstances, in other instances they can serve to allow for or can intensify media influences.

EFFECTS ON VIEWERS

Examinations of individual differences in research on media influence have received much less attention than in studies of viewer selection, response, and interpretation. This general lack of attention likely reflects the idea that individual differences are assumed to be fairly stable. As a consequence, the use of random assignment is the typical procedure employed to account for individual variations representing "noise." However, some models of media effects that explicitly employ individual difference variables as factors in their analyses demonstrate that individual variations can serve as important moderating variables. In addition, we further believe that insofar as media saturation makes media messages an integral part of the day-to-day environments of many people, individual differences in dispositions, temperaments, and traits may reflect this environment and may therefore be important (albeit difficult to test) dependent variables in media effects research.

Individual Differences as Moderators

Effects of media on viewers are obviously not uniform—some individuals may be strongly influenced whereas others are impervious. Studies that have explicitly operationalized the individual differences associated with these variations in influence demonstrate the importance of traits and dispositions as moderating variables. For example, Petty and Wegener's (1998) review of the dual-processing models of persuasion highlighted numerous individual difference variables that play important moderating roles in attitude change, including intelligence, self-esteem, self-monitoring, and need for cognition. These authors pointed out that individual differences can predict not only variations in the types of appeals that are influential, but also the extent to which receivers tend to engage in message scrutiny.

In addition to moderating the direction and nature of media influence, individual characteristics may also heighten or intensify media influences, or may even provide a necessary condition for media influences to occur. For example, network models of media priming argue that semantically related cognitions, feelings, and action tendencies are connected through associative pathways (Berkowitz, 1984; Roskos-Ewoldsen, Roskos-Ewoldsen, & Carpentier, this volume). When a stimulus activates or primes one of the nodes within a cognitive framework, that activation radiates out and primes related thoughts and feelings, thereby increasing the probability that the activated cognitions will be employed in subsequent behaviors and interpretations of new stimuli. As Bushman (1995) pointed out, the importance of individual differences rests on the central role of cognitive networks that allow for the priming of related thoughts—individual differences associated with variations in cognitive networks should predict the extent to which media prime related thoughts and, as a consequence, influence behavior.

Bushman (1995) employed this line of reasoning in a series of studies pertaining to media violence. Specifically, exposure to violent films was shown to increase both aggressive affect and behaviors, but particularly among individuals who scored high on measures of trait aggressiveness. Zillmann and Weaver (2007) recently reported similar patterns of results, showing that exposure to a film featuring violent imagery increased unprovoked aggressive responses, but only among participants scoring high on a trait measure of physical aggression (see also Scharrer, 2005). Likewise, McKenzie-Mohr and Zanna (1990) reported that gender-schematic males (i.e., males scoring high on masculinity and low on femininity) who had viewed pornography were more likely to display sexually suggestive mannerisms in a subsequent interaction with a woman, whereas aschematic males were largely unaffected by the pornography exposure.

Individual Differences as Dependent Variables

It is understandable why individual differences tend to be treated as moderators in experimental research given that some conceptualizations of individual differences focus on biologically driven variations that should remain fairly constant over a person's lifetime. However, social-cognitive conceptualizations of individual differences acknowledge the importance of cultural and social influences on traits and dispositions, allowing for cognitive, emotional, and behavioral elements to strengthen or diminish as a function of environmental changes (Bandura, this volume; Funder, 2001; Mischel & Shoda, 1998). Insofar as media consumption patterns represent an important element in the symbolic environment of many people, these patterns may serve as useful predictors of more enduring and stable effects that could be conceptualized as traits, dispositions, or personality. Although studies of individual differences as dependent variables are understandably rare given that such influence is likely the result of cumulative and long-term exposure, we believe that our speculation concerning this direction of study corresponds with several theoretical frameworks commonly employed in media effects research.

Among theories of media influence that focus on cumulative exposure, cultivation theory has arguably generated the greatest attention, research, and debate (Gerbner, Gross, Morgan, Signorielli, & Shanahan, 2002; Morgan, Shanahan, & Signorielli, this volume). Research from this perspective has tended to operationalize outcomes in terms of social-reality beliefs (rather than more enduring dispositions or traits), meaning that cultivation may not be applicable to studies concerning individual differences. However, research examining cultivation of second-order beliefs or values moves one step closer to assessing individual differences that may represent components of more stable and enduring traits. Indeed, research employing cultivation frameworks to examine the correlations between media exposure and dispositions such as authoritarianism (Shanahan, 1995), materialism (Shrum, Burroughs, & Rindfleisch, 2005), or "mean world" values is consistent with this interpretation. In addition, Shrum's (Shrum, 1995; Shrum & O'Guinn, 1993) research has revealed evidence that media provide heavy viewers with frequent and vivid exemplars that are readily accessible, and that therefore influence individuals' judgments and perceptions. As such, the accessibility of such constructs, and particularly their chronic accessibility (Bargh & Pratto, 1986), may be characterized as representing aspects of a person's knowledge structure, thereby forming the foundation of personality characteristics.

Similarly, the role of media in the development of scripts, mental models, and cognitive associations that are consequential in models such as priming and social learning suggest additional avenues for exploring media influence on individual differences. For example, Anderson and Bushman's (2002) general aggression model (GAM) integrates numerous theories such as script theory, excitation transfer, social learning, and priming to explore the influence of media violence on aggression (see also Anderson & Huesmann, 2003). In brief, GAM conceptualizes aggressive actions as resulting from the combination of situational and person factors, with person factors largely conceptualized as enduring traits or dispositions reflecting scripts, knowledge structures, and schemas that prepare a person to aggress. Within this model, individual differences are thought not only to function as moderators and predictors, but also to reflect experiences, including media consumption. For example, Anderson and Bushman discussed the potential long-term effects of playing violent video games, arguing that cumulative exposure can result in "the creation and automatization of . . . aggression-related knowledge structures [that serve to] change the individual's personality" (p. 42).

Desensitization is a final example of a cumulative-exposure effect that may be useful in explorations of individual differences as dependent variables. A host of studies have demonstrated that exposure to media violence and to violent pornography can result in lower levels of arousal to victims' suffering, to greater levels of callousness, and to a general lack of empathy (Linz, Donnerstein, & Adams, 1989; Linz, Donnerstein, & Penrod, 1988; Thomas, Horton, Lippincott, & Drabman, 1977; Zillmann, 1989; Zillmann & Bryant, 1982; Zillmann & Weaver, 1989). Although studies have typically examined such effects in relatively short durations of time (e.g., hours, days, or weeks), the more enduring cognitive and emotional changes that desensitization may reflect suggest that media portrayals may play a role in the formation of related personality characteristics such as callousness or deviance. Recently, Bartholow and his colleagues have presented similar arguments in their research on video games. Namely, in one set of studies, Bartholow, Sestir, and Davis (2005) reported that heavy playing of violent videogames was associated with higher levels of aggression, but that this relationship was mediated via higher levels of trait hostility and hostile perceptions, and (to a lesser extent) lower levels of empathy. These authors interpreted their results as suggesting that videogame violence leads to changes in long-term personality characteristics (i.e., desensitization), with these long-term changes associated with heightened propensity to aggress. More recently, Bartholow, Bushman, and Sestir (2006) reported that participants who were frequent players of violent video games evidenced brain-related processing of violent images that was indicative of desensitization. These authors concluded that their data provided evidence of ". . . lasting deleterious effects [of violent video games] on brain function and behavior" (p. 538).

The aforementioned examples of how media researchers may usefully employ personality as a dependent variable are far from exhaustive and therefore represent only a sample of potential ways that scholars may usefully examine the cumulative and long-term effects of media on viewers' more enduring and stable dispositions. Although this direction of research will undoubtedly be wrought with a host of methodological challenges, explorations of the role of personality beyond that of predictor or moderator hold promise of demonstrating the important and powerful role of media in affecting viewers in ways that go well beyond the immediate viewing situation.

CONCLUDING COMMENTS

This chapter began with the argument that unexplained variance can be appreciated as representing the opportunity for researchers to explore the importance of individual differences in the media effects process. Whereas research shows that viewers' selection and enjoyment of much media content reflects variations in enduring traits or dispositions, this should not be interpreted as suggesting that individual differences imply only limited or trivial effects. In contrast, it is important to note that the presence of certain traits or dispositions can play a role in predicting the *type* of influence that media may have, but also the *strength* of influence that can be expected. That is, if individual differences are *not* acknowledged, some programs of research run the risk of incorrectly concluding that media have no effects or inconsequentially small effects on viewers.

This cautionary note is not to suggest that individual difference variables become part of every research design. In fact, the measurement of individual differences without theoretical motivation may lead to inflated estimates of the importance of those differences. For example, the ease with which gender is measured in most studies likely creates a scenario in which gender differences are routinely examined—even if not called for by theory—but are reported only if significance is obtained. In contrast, what this reasoning does suggest is that media effects research could certainly benefit from the inclusion of individual differences in a way that is motivated by theory and in a way that extends our understanding of how individual variations serve as important predictors of media use and moderators of media influence. By acknowledging the importance of what the audience brings *to* the viewing situation, media effects research stands to move beyond seeing unexplained variance as only a nuisance, and move toward celebrating diversity in a way that is both methodologically productive and theoretically enriching.

References

Aluja-Fabregat, A. (2000). Personality and curiosity about TV and film violence in adolescents. *Personality and Individual Differences, 29*, 379–392.

Aluja-Fabregat, A., & Torrubia-Beltri, R. (1998). Viewing of mass media violence, perception of violence, personality and academic achievement. *Personality and Individual Differences, 25*, 973–989.

Anderson, C. A., & Bushman, B. J. (2002). Human aggression. *Annual Review of Psychology, 53*, 27–51.

Anderson, C. A., & Huesmann, L. R. (2003). Human aggression: A social-cognitive view. In M. A. Hogg & J. Cooper (Eds.), *Handbook of Social Psychology* (pp. 296–323). London: Sage.

Bargh, J. A., & Pratto, F. (1986). Individual construct accessibility and perceptual selection. *Journal of Experimental Social Psychology, 22*, 293–311.

Bartholow, B. D., Bushman, B. J., & Sestir, M. A. (2006). Chronic violent video game exposure and desensitization to violence: Behavioral and event-related brain potential data. *Journal of Experimental Social Psychology, 42*, 532–539.

Bartholow, B. D., Sestir, M. A., & Davis, E. B. (2005). Correlates and consequences of exposure to video game violence: Hostile personality, empathy, and aggressive behavior. *Personality and Social Psychology Bulletin, 31*, 1573–1586.

Berkowitz, L. (1984). Some effects of thoughts on anti- and prosocial influences of media events: A cognitive-neoassociation analysis. *Psychological Bulletin, 95*, 410–427.

Bothwell, R. K., & Brigham, J. C. (1983). Selective evaluation and recall during the 1980 Reagan-Carter debate. *Journal of Applied Social Psychology, 13*, 427–442.

Bushman, B. J. (1995). Moderating role of trait aggressiveness in the effects of violent media on aggression. *Journal of Personality and Social Psychology, 69*, 950–960.

Cacioppo, J. T., & Petty, R. E. (1982). The need for cognition. *Journal of Personality and Social Psychology, 42*, 116–131.

Carpentier, F. D., Knobloch, S., & Zillmann, D. (2003). Rock, rap, and rebellion: Comparisons of traits predicting selective exposure to defiant music. *Personality and Individual Differences, 35*, 1643–1655.

Choti, S. E., Marston, A. R., & Holston, S. G. (1987). Gender and personality variables in film-induced sadness and crying. *Journal of Social and Clinical Psychology, 5*, 535–544.

Eysenck, H. J. (1990). Biological dimensions of personality. In L. A. Pervin (Ed.), *Handbook of personality and research* (pp. 244–276). New York: Guilford.

Fennis, B. M., & Pruyn, A. T. H. (2007). You are what you wear: Brand personality influences on consumer impression formation. *Journal of Business Research, 60*, 634–639.

Festinger, L. (1957). *A theory of cognitive dissonance*. Evanston, IL: Row, Peterson.

Freedman, J. L., & Sears, D. O. (1965). Selective exposure. In L. Berkowitz (Ed.), *Advances in experimental social psychology* (Vol. 2, pp. 57–97). San Diego, CA: Academic Press.

Frey, D. (1986). Recent research on selective exposure to information. In L. Berkowitz (Ed.), *Advances in experimental social psychology* (Vol. 19, pp. 41–80). San Diego, CA: Academic Press.

Funder, D. C. (2001). Personality. *Annual Review of Psychology, 52*, 197–221.

Gerbner, G., Gross, L., Morgan, M., Signorielli, N., & Shanahan, J. (2002). Growing up with television: Cultivation processes. In J. Bryant & D. Zillmann (Eds.), *Media effects: Advances in theory and research* (2nd ed., pp. 43–67). Mahwah, NJ: Erlbaum.

Gill, A. J., Oberlander, J., & Austin, E. (2006). Rating e-mail personality at zero acquaintance. *Personality and Individual Differences, 40*, 497–507.

Gosling, S. D., Gaddis, S., & Vazire, S. (2007). *Personality impressions based on Facebook profiles*. Paper presented at the International Conference on Weblogs and Social Media, Boulder, CO.

Gunther, A. C., & Schmitt, K. (2004). Mapping boundaries of the hostile media effect. *Journal of Communication, 54*, 55–70.

Hansen, C. H., & Hansen, R. D. (2000). Music and music videos. In D. Zillmann & P. Vorderer (Eds.), *Media entertainment: The psychology of its appeal* (pp. 175–213). Mahwah, NJ: Erlbaum.

Hoffner, C., & Cantor, J. (1991). Perceiving and responding to mass media characters. In J. Bryant & D. Zillmann (Eds.), *Responding to the screen: Reception and reaction processes* (pp. 63–101). Hillsdale, NJ: Erlbaum.

Hoffner, C. A., & Levine, K. J. (2005). Enjoyment of mediated fright and violence: A meta-analysis. *Media Psychology, 7*, 207–237.

Iyengar, S., & Hahn, K. S. (2007). *Red media, blue media: Evidence of ideological polarization in media use*. Paper presented at the annual meeting of the International Communication Association, San Francisco, CA.

Klapper, J. (1960). *The effects of mass communication*. New York: Free Press.

Krcmar, M., & Kean, L. G. (2005). Uses and gratifications of media violence: Personality correlates of viewing and liking violent genres. *Media Psychology, 7*, 399–420.

Linz, D., Donnerstein, E., & Adams, S. M. (1989). Physiological desensitization and judgments about female victims of violence. *Human Communication Research, 15*, 509–522.

Linz, D., Donnerstein, E., & Penrod, S. (1988). Effects of long-term exposure to violent and sexually degrading depictions of women. *Journal of Personality and Social Psychology, 55*, 758–768.

Lord, C. G., Ross, L., & Lepper, M. R. (1979). Biased assimilation and attitude polarization: The effects of prior theories on subsequently considered evidence. *Journal of Personality and Social Psychology, 37*, 2098–2109.

Maio, G. R., & Esses, V. M. (2001). The need for affect: Individual differences in the motivation to approach or avoid emotions. *Journal of Personality, 69*, 583–615.

Marathe, S. S. (2007). *If you build it, they will come—or will they? Need for uniqueness and need for control as psychological predictors of customization*. Paper presented at the annual convention of the International Communication Association, San Francisco.

Marcus, B., Machilek, F., & Schutz, A. (2006). Personality in cyberspace: Personal Web sites as media for personality expressions and impressions. *Journal of Personality and Social Psychology, 90*, 1014–1031.

McDaniel, S. R. (2003). Reconsidering the relationship between sensation seeking and audience preferences for viewing televised sports. *Journal of Sport Management, 17*, 13–36.

McKenzie-Mohr, D., & Zanna, M. P. (1990). Treating women as sexual objects: Look to the (gender schematic) male who has viewed pornography. *Personality and Social Psychology Bulletin, 16*, 296–308.

Mischel, W., & Shoda, Y. (1998). Reconciling processing dynamics and personality dispositions. *Annual Review of Psychology, 49*, 229–258.

Munro, G. D., Ditto, P. H., Lockhart, L. K., Fagerlin, A., Gready, M., & Peterson, E. (2002). Biased assimilation of sociopolitical arguments: Evaluating the 1996 U.S. presidential debate. *Basic and Applied Social Psychology, 24*, 15–26.

Nathanson, A. I. (2003). Rethinking empathy. In J. Bryant, D. Roskos-Ewoldsen, & J. Cantor (Eds.), *Communication and emotion: Essays in honor of Dolf Zillmann* (pp. 107–130). Mahwah, NJ: Erlbaum.

North, A. C., & Hargreaves, D. J. (1999). Music and adolescent identity. *Music Education Research, 1*, 75–92.

Oliver, M. B. (1993). Exploring the paradox of the enjoyment of sad films. *Human Communication Research, 19*, 315–342.

Oliver, M. B., & Armstrong, G. B. (1995). Predictors of viewing and enjoyment of reality-based and fictional crime shows. *Journalism & Mass Communication Quarterly, 72*, 559–570.

Oliver, M. B., Sargent, S. L., & Weaver, J. B. (1998). The impact of sex and gender role self-perception on affective reactions to different types of film. *Sex Roles, 38*, 45–62.

Peffley, M., Shields, T., & Williams, B. (1996). The intersection of race and crime in television news stories: An experimental study. *Political Communication, 13*, 309–327.

Perse, E. M. (1992). Predicting attention to local television news: Need for cognition and motives for viewing. *Communication Reports, 5*, 40–49.

Petty, R. E., & Wegener, D. T. (1998). Attitude change: Multiple roles for persuasion variables. In D. Gilbert, S. T. Fiske, & G. Lindzey (Eds.), *Handbook of social psychology* (4th ed., pp. 323–390). Boston, MA: McGraw-Hill.

Raney, A. A. (2004). Expanding disposition theory: Reconsidering character liking, moral evaluations, and enjoyment. *Communication Theory, 14*, 348–369.

Raney, A. A., & Bryant, J. (2002). Moral judgment and crime drama: An integrated theory of enjoyment. *Journal of Communication, 52*, 402–415.

Reiss, S. (2000). *Who am I? The 16 basic desires that motivate our actions and define our personalities*. New York: Tarcher/Putnam.

Reiss, S., & Wiltz, J. (2004). Why people watch reality TV. *Media Psychology, 6*, 363–378.

Rentfrow, P. J., & Gosling, S. D. (2006). Message in a ballad: The role of music preferences in interpersonal perception. *Psychological Science, 17*, 236–242.

Robinson, T. O., Weaver, J. B., & Zillmann, D. (1996). Exploring the relation between personality and the appreciation of rock music. *Psychological Reports, 78*, 259–269.

Scharrer, E. (2005). Hypermasculinity, aggression, and television violence: An experiment. *Media Psychology, 7*, 353–376.

Shanahan, J. (1995). Television viewing and adolescent authoritarianism. *Journal of Adolescence, 18*, 271–288.

Shrum, L. J. (1995). Assessing the social influence of television: A social cognition perspective on cultivation effects. *Communication Research, 22*, 402–429.

Shrum, L. J., Burroughs, J. E., & Rindfleisch, A. (2005). Television's cultivation of material values. *Journal of Consumer Research, 32*, 473–479.

Shrum, L. J., & O'Guinn, T. C. (1993). Processes and effects in the construction of social-reality: Construct accessibility as an explanatory variable. *Communication Research, 20*, 436–471.

Slater, M. D. (2003). Alienation, aggression, and sensation seeking as predictors of adolescent use of violent film, computer, and website content. *Journal of Communication, 53*, 105–121.

Sparks, G. G., Pellechia, M., & Irvine, C. (1999). The repressive coping style and fright reactions to mass media. *Communication Research, 26*, 176–192.

Srivastava, L. (2005). Mobile phones and the evolution of social behaviour. *Behaviour & information technology, 24*, 111–129.

Sundar, S. S. (2007). The MAIN model: A heuristic approach to understanding technology effects on credibility. In M. J. Metzger & A. J. Flanagin (Eds.), *Digital media, youth, and credibility* (pp. 72–100). Cambridge, MA: The MIT Press.

Sundar, S. S. (2008). Self as source: Agency and customization in interactive media. In E. Konijn, S. Utz, M. Tanis, & S. Barnes (Eds.), *Mediated Interpersonal Communication* (pp. 58–74). New York: Routledge.

Sunstein, C. R. (2001). *Republic.com*. Princeton, NJ: Princeton University Press.

Sweeney, P. D., & Gruber, K. L. (1984). Selective exposure: Voter information preferences and the Watergate affair. *Journal of Personality and Social Psychology, 46*, 1208–1221.

Tamborini, R., Stiff, J., & Heidel, C. (1990). Reacting to graphic horror: A model of empathy and emotional behavior. *Communication Research, 17*, 616–640.

Tamborini, R., Stiff, J., & Zillmann, D. (1987). Preference for graphic horror featuring male versus female victimization: Personality and past film viewing experiences. *Human Communication Research, 13*, 529–552.

Thomas, M. H., Horton, R. W., Lippincott, E. C., & Drabman, R. S. (1977). Desensitization to portrayals of real-life aggression as a function of television violence. *Journal of Personality and Social Psychology, 35*, 450–458.

Vallone, R. P., Ross, L., & Lepper, M. R. (1985). The hostile media phenomenon: Biased perception and perceptions of media bias in coverage of the Beirut massacre. *Journal of Personality and Social Psychology, 49*, 577–585.

Vazire, S., & Gosling, S. D. (2004). e-Perceptions: Personality impressions based on personal websites. *Journal of Personality and Social Psychology, 87*, 123–132.

Vidmar, N., & Rokeach, M. (1974). Archie Bunker's bigotry: A study in selective perception and exposure. *Journal of Communication, 24*, 36–47.

Weaver, J. B. (1991). Exploring the links between personality and media preference. *Personality and Individual Differences, 12*, 1293–1299.

Zillmann, D. (1989). Effects of prolonged consumption of pornography. In D. Zillmann & J. Bryant (Eds.), *Pornography: Research advances and policy considerations* (pp. 127–157). Hillsdale, NJ: Erlbaum.

Zillmann, D. (1991). Empathy: Affect from bearing witness to the emotions of others. In J. Bryant & D. Zillmann (Eds.), *Responding to the screen: Reception and reaction processes* (pp. 135–167). Hillsdale, NJ: Erlbaum.

Zillmann, D., & Bhatia, A. (1989). Effects of associating with musical genres on heterosexual attraction. *Communication Research, 16*, 263–288.

Zillmann, D., & Bryant, J. (1982). Pornography, sexual callousness, and the trivialization of rape. *Journal of Communication, 32*, 10–21.

Zillmann, D., & Weaver, J. B. (1989). Pornography and men's sexual callousness toward women. In D. Zillmann & J. Bryant (Eds.), *Pornography: Research advances and policy considerations* (pp. 95–125). Hillsdale, NJ: Erlbaum.

Zillmann, D., & Weaver, J. B. (2007). Aggressive personality traits in the effects of violent imagery on unprovoked impulsive aggression. *Journal of Research in Personality, 41*, 753–771.

Zuckerman, M. (1979). *Sensation seeking: Beyond the optimal level of arousal*. Hillsdale, NJ: Erlbaum.

Zuckerman, M., & Litle, P. (1986). Personality and curiosity about morbid and sexual events. *Personality and Individual Differences, 7*, 49–56.

24

ENTERTAINMENT AND ENJOYMENT AS MEDIA EFFECTS

Peter Vorderer and Tilo Hartmann
VU University Amsterdam

A BRIEF REVIEW OF MEDIA ENTERTAINMENT RESEARCH

Research on media entertainment clearly has become an established field of study within communication science and media psychology. Although entertainment media had been under-researched for several decades, their significance, content, and consumption were never really questioned. Katz and Foulkes (1962) therefore criticized the lack of systematic research on this topic as early as the 1960s. Beginning in the 1970s, empirical research on entertainment has grown considerably, and it has become a booming field since the late 1990s (cf., Zillmann & Vorderer, 2000). The diversity of entertainment media and their consumption by different users and audiences around the globe create a challenge for theory building and empirical research, and scientific results often seem valid for only a short period of time. Early mediated mass entertainment, such as low-cost novels in the second half of the 19th century or picture-rich newspapers in the early 20th century (Engel, 1997), did not stimulate much scientific concern.

The advent of radio entertainment and movie theatres, however, revealed the importance of entertainment to mass societies' elites (e.g., Carey, 1993). Herzog's (1944) survey studies on the motivation of US-American women to listen to radio soap operas may now be seen as early attempts to systematize what was known about entertainment at this time. Radio soap operas were extremely popular in the 1930s and 1940s. Regularly reaching a wide audience, they were produced in an industrialized manner and implemented advanced business models such as product placement. Katz and Foulkes (1962) were the first to elaborate a motivational framework for entertainment consumption by explaining the preference for such media content through "escapism," i.e., the desire of ordinary people to seek refuge from the negative experiences of everyday life with the world of entertainment media. The substantial contribution of their proposal can hardly be overestimated, as they provided an early psychological perspective on media users' motivation to select specific content repeatedly and discussed underlying experiential processes, such as "identification" with media characters. Nevertheless, their seminal work remained rather isolated and atypical within the Social and Behavioral Sciences for a number of years, partly because the academic community did not consider "entertainment" a serious research topic deserving intellectual scrutiny. This was true particularly for academia in Europe, which held elitist preferences for traditional, i.e., "classic" and "serious" literature and the arts and believed them to be the only appropriate standards of cultural and aesthetic achievement.

The opportunities for empirical research on entertainment did not arise until the 1970s, and occurred for two main reasons. First, political movements of the late 1960s and their accompanying societal change stimulated research explicitly devoted to overcoming elitist and "established" ways of thinking and of evaluating cultural products. These new branches of research sought to reveal the often (or often thought of) ideological quality of mainstream literature and media (cf., Groeben & Vorderer, 1988). Secondly, the field of psychology discovered the relevance of consumption of entertainment for understanding emotion. Comedy, pornography, mediated sports, and other forms of media entertainment trigger affective experiences, which attracted the attention of psychologists, especially that of Percy Tannenbaum (1980) and his mentee, Dolf Zillmann. Zillmann and his early collaborators—most importantly, Jennings Bryant and Joanne Cantor—built upon general foundations from the psychology of emotion and applied experimental methods from psychology to (users of) media entertainment. In doing so, they formed and shaped the beginnings of a systematic, theory-driven inquiry of media entertainment, which still guide and inform contemporary approaches (cf., Bryant, Cantor, & Roskos-Ewoldsen, 2003; Bryant & Miron, 2002; Klimmt & Vorderer, in press; Raney & Bryant, 2002; Vorderer, Klimmt, & Ritterfeld, 2004).

APPROACHING MEDIA ENTERTAINMENT

On the basis of these early approaches this chapter proposes an integrative model of media entertainment and enjoyment. The conceptualization starts from the broad grounds of an ecological perspective, which in turn draws on recent integrative approaches to media entertainment proposed from perspectives such as evolutionary psychology (Miron, 2006; Schwab, 2003), positive psychology (Ryan, Rigby, & Przybylski, 2006; Vorderer, Steen & Chan, 2006), and communication research (Denham, 2004; Frueh, 2002; Vorderer, Klimmt, & Ritterfeld, 2004). Such an ecological perspective regards the user as an organism that exists in a "real" (physical) world but is playfully involved in a "mediated" environment during exposure to media content (Bryant & Miron, 2002). Entertainment, in its broadest sense, is conceptualized as a positive mood-like meta-emotion, which arises from the appreciation of underlying primary emotions (cf., Bartsch, Vorderer, Mangold, & Viehoff, 2008; Frueh, 2002; Wirth & Schramm, 2007). Successful progress towards short- and long-term goals to reach both physiological and psychological life-balance (cf., Damasio, 1999) is seen as a key mechanism of meta-level appreciation.

The User and the Environment

When conceptualizing the media user as a human organism in a specific situational environment (cf., Zillmann & Bryant, 1985a), the term "environment" refers not only to the outer, but also the inner environment ("internal milieu," Damasio, 1999, p. 135). The core of the human organism is the brain, which responds and reaches out to both internal and external environment changes (Damasio, 1999). Therefore, instead of focusing on either the individual or the environment, we should approach psychological processes, like enjoyment, by focusing on underlying brain-environment relationships (cf. Lazarus & Folkman, 1987; Scherer, 2005). The human brain constantly evaluates external and inner environment events ("appraisals;" Roseman & Smith, 2001) that become salient due to certain situational features ("stimulus events," Scherer, 2005, p. 700; "appraisal detectors," Smith & Kirby, 2001). These events become relevant and meaningful (Skaggs & Baron, 2006) because they seem to concern the organism's well-being (Lazarus & Folkman, 1987). Emotions stem from such appraisals of relevant events: "The role of emotions is to provide self-referential value-coding of [internal and external] world events" (Miron, 2006, p. 344). Different layers of the brain are involved in self-referential evaluations of stimuli events, depending on the type of stimulus event (cf. van Reekum & Scherer, 1997; Damasio, 1999). Some events, particularly those on the sensory-motor level (Scherer, 2001), trigger simple and innate appraisal reactions controlled by the "instinctual brain" (cf. van Reekum, 2000; Miron, 2006). However, affective responses are not restricted to simple instincts and stimulus-response sequences. Processes that involve learned response schemes or even plans and action strategies at the conceptual level are thought to provoke more complex appraisal reactions (cf. Scherer, 2001; Miron, 2006).

According to van Reekum (2000, section 1.2),

> one finds a high degree of convergence [in literature] with respect to the appraisal dimensions or criteria postulated by different theories. These include the perception of a change in the environment that captures the subject's attention (novelty and expectancy), the perceived pleasantness or unpleasantness of the stimulus or event (valence), the importance of the stimulus or event to one's goals or concerns (relevance and goal conduciveness or motive consistency), the notion of who or what caused the event (agency or responsibility), the estimated ability to deal with the event and its consequences (perceived control, power or coping potential), and the evaluation of one's own actions in relation to moral standards or social norms (legitimacy), and one's self-ideal.

In general, positive affect results from relationships that are evaluated as both motivationally relevant and congruent, because they conform to a higher goal or are intrinsically pleasurable. If media entertainment is considered to be a positive affective state (cf., "positive meta-emotion," Bartsch, Mangold, Viehoff, & Vorderer, 2006; Bartsch et al., 2008; Wirth & Schramm, 2007), the perception of relevant and beneficial brain-environment-relationships should lie at media entertainment's core.

At the Heart of Appraisals: Life-Balance

Evolutionary theorists argue that "the true object of all the vital mechanisms is [. . .] survival to reproduce" (Schulkin, 2004, p. 22). Therefore, human organisms pursue a basic need for bodily integrity, that is, the assured proper functioning of their inner environment, which is protected and separated from the outer environment by an intact tissue (cf., Damasio, 1999). Thus, the struggle for life-balance, i.e., the constant attempt to avoid severe tissue-damage and maintain the inner environment's functionality, is a key motivation underlying human behavior (Damasio, 1999; cf., "core relational themes," Lazarus, 1991, p. 121). Used here, the term life-balance includes both the balance of physiological resources (cf., "allostasis," Berntson & Cacioppo, 2000) as well as the psychological balance maintained by a higher cognitive subsystem (e.g., "eudaimonic well-being," Schreier, 2006, p. 392; Cabanac, Pouliot, & Everett, 1997, p. 227; Deci & Ryan, 2000). On a physiological level, people must successfully exploit the external environment to balance body temperature and restore energy, thus fueling metabolic processes (cf., "alliesthesia," Cabanac, 1979, p. 7). On a psychological level, for instance, people seek abilities that enable them to maneuver through new or risky situations successfully, which demands proper mental activity (Cabanac, Pouliot & Everett, 1997). Self-determination theory (Deci & Ryan, 2002, 2000) argues that a person's psychological balance depends on the degree to which three innate psychological needs are met: autonomy (acting free of pressure, including urges caused by social norms and values that are not fully internalized), competence (ability to master relevant challenges), and relatedness (social connection to a supportive group). In this view, individuals will be psychologically balanced and maintain a high level of wellbeing to the extent that they feel autonomous, competent, and socially related (cf., Vorderer, Steen, & Chan, 2006).

Pleasure Systems

Throughout the phylogenesis of primates, inner reward-mechanisms developed to indicate the occurrence of a beneficial event (Ohler & Nieding, 2006), or more precisely, beneficial organismic change concurrent with a certain environment (Kahneman, 1999). If activated, such reward mechanisms "tagged" behavior and related situations as pleasurable (Berridge, 2001, 2002). Pleasure "seduce[d] us into good behavior" (Damasio, 1999, p. 78). Throughout the environment of evolutionary adaptedness (EEA; cf., Tooby & Cosmides, 1990), the brain developed higher cognitive functions that moderated the influence of pleasure on behavioral response (Oatley & Mar, 2005). Pleasure became one factor of the hedonic appeal of more complex affective responses that guided behavior (cf., "intrinsic pleasantness" in appraisal checks; Fredrickson, 2001, 2002; Kahneman, 1999; Scherer, 2001, p. 96).

Today's environments differ in many ways from the EEA (Vorderer, Steen, & Chan, 2006), but "pleasure [remains] the oldest and still key function regulating human behavior" (Miron, 2006, p. 344). The human reward system is heavily involved in emotional processes (Bryant & Miron, 2002; Fredrickson, 2001). Therefore, pleasure still guides the struggle for life-balance. Pleasure marks apparent progress towards physiological balance ("physiological pleasure," Cabanac et al., 1997, p. 232; "bottom-up pleasure," Bryant & Miron, 2002) and/or psychological balance (cf., "intellectual pleasure," Cabanac et al., 1997, p. 232; "top-down pleasure," Bryant & Miron, 2002; "intrinsical pleasure," Deci & Ryan, 2000; see also Fredrickson's, 2001, 2002, distinction of "sensory pleasure" and "positive emotions"). Therefore, pleasure may be considered the result of an environmental constellation or stimulus event that is appreciated (van Reekum, 2000). Pleasure and appreciation are closely connected. People often appreciate what they find pleasurable and they enjoy the pleasure if they find something they appreciate. Certainly, then, pleasure—or the appreciation of stimulus events—is key to feeling entertained.

Modern Psychology does not regard pleasure and pain as opposite end points of a bipolar scale. Rather, organisms share both a pleasure-system and a pain-system, which are only partly interconnected (cf., Bryant & Miron, 2002; Damasio, 1999; Ito & Cacioppo, 1999; Lang, 1995). Accordingly, painful events can be pleasurable, but only if the intensity of pleasure trumps that of pain (Davidson, 1992). The orchestra of only partially interconnected subsystems—a pleasure-system, a pain-system, automatic physiological responses and higher-order mental processes—increases an organism's flexibility in the struggle for life-balance. For example, people can go beyond merely striving to stay in healthy environments that provide "pure pleasure" (Miron, 2006). They can also seek and enjoy ambivalent—or even painful—situations that promise mastery and broadening of their resources (Fredrickson, 2001; Lazarus & Folkman, 1987; Rozin, 1999). The same should be true of media entertainment.

The Media "Environment"

Entertainment arises from an interaction between users and their environment (Denham, 2004; Frueh, 2002). Therefore, we should examine the environment in order to understand media entertainment. From a birds-eye perspective, users are situated in their actual environment (e.g., their living-room), which includes media technology. These external and physical features of this setting determine the sensory stimulation of the user. However, users only respond to events that become images in their brain. Physical features of the media affect a user's bodily state, thus creating "inner" stimulus events associated with sensory stimulation (cf., Scherer, 2001). More complex appraisals build on the symbolic meaning a user decodes from a media offering (cf., Bartsch et al., 2006; Scherer, 2001).

Media users can also interpret a media environment in different reception modes: in an involved mode and in a distanced mode (Vorderer, 1993). Users who enter an *involved mode* start to think "within" the depicted mediated world (cf., "transportation," Green, Brock, & Kaufman, 2004; "presence," Hartmann, 2008a; "involvement," Wirth, 2006). Involved users respond to media environments as if they were real; that is, they temporarily seem unaware of their mediated nature (Lee, 2004). Appraisal checks should therefore relate to events within the mediated world. Involvement is likely if the media environment absorbs (Zillmann, 1988) or immerses the user's senses and provides relevant and meaningful insights to the user.

More precisely, an involved state can rest on two different qualities of the media environment (Cupchik, 2002; Zillmann, 2006). Users can be involved as they engage in the *iconic qualities* of the environment. Media representations that match the physical qualities of the imitated real-world-counterparts have high iconicity. For example, some media representations resemble spatial, real world scenarios in such a way that users automatically feel as though they are in the environment (Wirth et al., 2007). Others portray illusions of living entities so vivid that users feel co-present (Hartmann, 2008a). If iconicity is high, the environment and its stimulus events are likely to be considered quite immediate and responsive, which should affect appraisal processes as well. Nevertheless, users can also engage in the symbolic, connotative information they extract from a media offering (Zillmann, 2006). Media content can be of low iconic quality (e.g., a scribbled cartoon figure) but imply a strong symbolic meaning to the user. Symbolic meaning is high if the media environment seems informative regarding general or abstract laws of the real world (Oatley & Mar, 2005). Unlike responses to immediate stimulus events, appraisals of symbolic stimulus events involve higher-order cognitive processing and are probably more open to idiosyncratic interpretations (van Reekum, 2000; Zillmann, 2006).

In contrast to such an involved mode, users can also switch to an *analytical mode* (Vorderer, 1993) and construe the media environment from the "outside," i.e., representing the fictionality or "unrealness" of the depicted events. Appraisals should then relate to formal aspects of the media offering (Tan, 1996) or to the abstract meaning of the exposure situation in general. Alternatively, users can temporarily move their attention away from the media completely and shift their reference frame back to the current real-world environment (Cantor, 2002).

Manipulation of the Environment's Psychological Effectiveness

The exposure situation offers vast freedom for users to effectively regulate their experiences (Schramm & Wirth, 2008; Wirth & Schramm, 2007). As long as the media environment seems more enjoyable than the "real" world, users may be prone to stay in such an involved reception mode. If they need to alter their experience, however, users can quickly adjust the reference frame of their ongoing appraisals. Before the fear that a horror movie induces becomes too disturbing, users may switch to an analytical mode ("this is just a movie") or include particular aspects of the real-world environment (e.g., turning on the lights in the living room, turning off the sound of the movie; cf. "protection cues," Schwab, 2003, p. 305; "re-appraisals," Wirth & Schramm, 2007; "coping strategies," Cantor, 2002, p. 299). By changing their salient environment, and thus the reference frame of appraisal processes, users can return to their actual surroundings, which are often more friendly and healthy. Thus, if a media representation induces overly painful or dissonant states, users may dismantle them before returning to an involved mode. In sum, users' experiences during media exposure do not rest on simple interactions with the media environment. Rather, users encounter a hybrid situation, as they switch from analytical to involved processing (Vorderer, 1993), pay and withdraw attention to and from the media environment, and continue to edit both the sensory stimulation and the meaning of their salient environment to maintain the best experience possible.

Playing With the Environment

The user's capability to edit the environment represented cognitively points to media entertainment as a playful activity (Ohler & Nieding, 2006; Vorderer, 2001). When people start to play, they deal with objects and scenarios in a safe, controlled framework. The framework builds on certain rules (e.g., pretense). What the player perceives has a psychological impact because the game creates a reality on its own that is also strongly attached to the "real" world. Due to the controlled framework, the game can end at any time. Games can be played solely in fantasy (e.g., in daydreaming, Ohler & Nieding, 2006; Singer, 1981), but exposure to media content enables such playful action as well (Vorderer, 2001). If users feel like they are in control of starting or terminating the illusion the actual media offering provides, they can let the simulation unfold in a carefree way. The medium provides tools—objects, characters, scenery, and events—and, altogether, a meaningful world, to mentally play with. Users can also experience activities and accomplishments that they cannot participate in or achieve in their actual lives. Therefore, media environments provide a playground that allows and encourages users to day-dream (Valkenburg & van der Voort, 1994). A mediated playground even trumps real-world games, as it is safer and easier to control, often easier to initiate, and able to offer a variety of experiences impossible in real-world scenarios.

Staying in Control Over the Environment

Some researchers have argued that media users can only play with a media environment if they stay autonomous and in control over the exposure situation (cf., Frueh, 2002). Leisure time, with its lack of demands and necessities, provides a good frame for playful media exposure. Still, the exposure situation and the media offering need to be under control, too. Users are able to control the experiential power of the media environment, as long as they can withdraw cognitively (Cantor, 2002). Users feel in control of the overall exposure situation, as long as they consider the situation to be free of any pressure (Frueh, 2002; Miron, 2006, p. 359). Pressure exists when users feel urged to use a medium, for example, if they follow a compulsive drive to use a medium (cf., LaRose, Lin, & Eastin, 2003), if they need to use the medium to reach an extrinsic goal (Deci & Ryan, 2000), or if they are complying with norms and values that have not been fully incorporated (Koestner & Losier, 2002). Pressure runs counter to pleasure (Deci & Ryan, 2002) and undermines the playful qualities of media exposure. A user who feels compelled to play a video game in the morning, although that violates his intrinsic norms, might still experience pleasure of relief and excitement during the game, but painful dissonance and guilt probably overshadow such positive impressions.

Personal Relevance Versus Play

Other researchers have argued that media users can only playfully engage with media content if the issues portrayed are barely relevant to them (cf., e.g., Frueh, 2002; Schwab, 2003), because only then can protective distancing strategies be applied effectively. Information is deemed irrelevant if it is not of motivational significance (Roseman, 2001). However, irrelevant events do not breed emotional responses. Therefore, enjoyable play needs to deal with issues of personal relevance. Entertaining media offerings are informative (Hartmann, 2008b; Oatley & Mar, 2005; Vorderer et al., 2006). Interesting media environments are opportunities to learn (cf., Silvia, 2006; 2005a, b). Both non-fictional and fictional media offerings can provide relevant insights (Oatley & Mar, 2005; Zillmann, 2006). Fictional media offerings are not completely artificial; they include many authentic features (e.g., humanlike interactions of characters). Compared to non-fictional representations, they often have a greater ability to explicate a deeper truth (Oatley & Mar, 2005) and to inform about general principles on a symbolic level (Zillmann, 2006, p. 216). Perceived content that becomes too relevant, however, increases pressure and undermines enjoyment. For example, a user may feel forced to learn about the plot of a mystery that he or she has not yet solved. Also, protective exit-strategies (to end the media environment experience) could fail if the content relates to problems that exist in the "real" world (cf. Zillmann, 1988). In sum, it seems likely that users' enjoyment of and entertainment from media worlds resemble a tradeoff between complete control, high distance, but little significance on the one hand, and reduced control, the possibility of experiential involvement, but opportunities to learn on the other (cf., Cupchik, 2002; Hartmann, 2008b).

EXPLAINING MEDIA ENTERTAINMENT

Regarding particular media offerings, why do some people enjoy them, while others feel overwhelming frustration and fear or are just unaffected? When is media entertaining?

Researchers have identified various pleasure-related processes thought to be involved in the formation of entertainment. Sensory stimulation and the balance of physiological resources, as well as meaningful events in the salient environment, are believed to lead to primary emotions. Users reappraise the resulting experiences in the light of their mood-regulation and their need for self-realization, often unconsciously. A feeling of entertainment often results from ongoing positive appraisals, i.e., from an appreciation of the primary affective states (Oliver, in press).

Balancing Sensory Stimulation and Physiological Resources

The "right stimulation" and a successful balancing of physiological resources appear to be a crucial mechanism for media enjoyment (cf., theory of affect dependent stimulus arrangement; Zillmann & Bryant, 1985b). A strong physiological imbalance corrupts pleasure or may even be associated with pain. Simple appraisal sequences that breed negative affect are involved in this process (Scherer, 2001). Successful recreation, however, fosters physiological pleasure (Bryant & Miron, 2002; Cabanac, 1971). The stronger the relief is, the greater the pleasure ("alliesthesia," Cabanac, 1979, p. 7). People seek optimal sensory stimulation to maintain well-balanced physiological resources (homeostasis/alleostasis, Berntson & Cacioppo, 2000; Damasio, 1999). This principle applies to diverse physiological resources and systems, including the balancing of blood glucose concentrations, body temperature, and the arousal system. The need for balance also affects the appraisal of external sensory stimulation: External stimuli that help restore balance are pleasurable, but those that promote imbalance can cause injury or pain. Media users therefore choose and arrange the physical features of their exposure situations (e.g., colors, brightness, sound-levels, dynamics) according to the sensory stimulation they desire. Not everyone, for example, appreciates the dazzling colors, surprising sounds, and the pace of cuts typical for music television after a hard working day. Some people will engage in simultaneous activities to enjoy optimal sensory stimulation.

Mood-Management Theory (Zillmann, 1988, 2000b) includes the notion that people employ media to regulate their excitation (cf., "arousal-assumption;" Knobloch-Westerwick, 2006). The theory argues "that levels of excitation that vary within a normal range constitute a necessary, though not sufficient, condition for an individual's feelings of well-being" (Bryant & Miron, 2002, p. 561). Excitatory levels must be balanced and maintained for enjoyment to occur, because it allows users to avoid noxious states. In addition, the successful restoration of balance is thought to promote enjoyment because it breeds pleasurable relief. Indeed, studies have shown that stressed persons who are overly aroused prefer calming and soothing media content (Bryant & Zillmann, 1984; see for overviews Bryant & Miron, 2002; Knobloch-Westerwick, 2006). Likewise, bored and understimulated people prefer exciting media offerings capable of increasing their level of arousal.

The balancing of sensory stimulation and exhausted physiological resources seems to foster pleasure that adds to the overall feeling of being entertained. However, we regard both to be necessary but not sufficient mechanisms of entertainment. Relaxing in a wheel-chair, eating tasty food, or balancing physiological resources in an exposure situation alone does not guarantee entertainment. In addition, and perhaps more importantly, an optimal level of psychological stimulation is necessary to feel entertained.

Primary Emotional Responses to the Salient Environment

If the media environment becomes salient in the mind of the involved user, it replaces the actual environment as the primary reference frame of ongoing appraisals (Wirth & Schramm, 2007; Zillmann, 2006). Processes of character- and group-perception (cf., "parasocial processing," Hartmann, 2008b) may divide the mentally unfolding world into good, neutral, and bad forces ("affective disposition," Raney & Bryant, 2002; Zillmann, 2006). Users may start to feel that they accompany their favorite characters; empathetically, users hold the perspectives of liked characters, which results in a sharing of motivational dispositions, i.e. of goals, hopes, and fears. The events that happen in the mediated world begin to matter and take on meaning. They become emotionally significant ("internal emotions," Oatley, 1994). Some events of the media world may trigger reflexive emotional responses that are rapidly processed (e.g., responses to familiarity and novelty or immediate danger; Cantor, 2002; Miron, 2006). However, most events will probably involve more complex and multi-sequence appraisals (Scherer, 2001). Such events are not only more open to culture-specific or idiosyncratic (and thus also gender- and age-specific) interpretations (van Reekum, 2000), but they might also allow the user to include knowledge of the mediated nature of the event (Wirth & Schramm, 2007).

The Pleasure of Comprehension

"Familiar things tend to be enjoyable, whereas new things tend to be interesting" (Silvia, 2006, p. 25; Reeve, 1989). The identification of novel, unfamiliar stimuli always implies some potential threat (Zajonc, 2001), at least in the form of a cognitive challenge that cannot be met. Familiar aspects, in contrast, are predictable and can be competently processed. The simple pleasure of *comprehension* should apply to the perception of media environments as well. The mere identification of familiar aspects—even if they are disliked on a symbolical level—should evoke mild pleasure and appreciation.

Interest, or *curiosity*, is a related emotion in entertainment media use (cf., Silvia, 2006, 2005a, b). Interest motivates the organism to focus on potentially relevant stimuli that are novel or not fully understood—so-called incongruencies or cognitive challenges (Deci & Ryan, 2002)—but appear to be understandable (Silvia, 2006). Accordingly, if an obscure event is novel, and one's cognitive abilities seem sufficient to cope with the novelty, interest results (Silvia, 2005a). Simple and overly familiar stimuli are not novel and, therefore, barely interesting. Very complex or strong incongruencies, however, are often too challenging cognitively and thus of no interest as well. Interest is strongest if the comprehension skills are just sufficient to master an incongruency (Groeben & Vorderer, 1988).

Heightened arousal accompanies interest. According to Berlyne (1960), comprehension of a once unfamiliar stimulus—or mastery of a cognitive challenge—is pleasurable as it helps to reduce the distress that had been caused by incongruencies. An alternative explanation refers to the growth of the organism (Deci & Ryan, 2000; Reeve, 1989). Interest guides learning processes. Learning helps the human organism gain knowledge about the environment, and thus is key to adaptation throughout ontogenesis. Therefore, the pleasure system rewards comprehension. The excitement caused by incongruent stimuli mingles with reappraisal of the situation once a stimulus is understood, resulting in mild positive affect.

Entertaining media offerings often offer a variety of novel characters, situations, and background scenarios that elicit interest. If novel stimuli constitute cognitive challenges, many media offerings can be regarded as a chain of challenges that impinge on the user. If users have the comprehension skills needed to master the chain of challenges, they are likely to enter a *flow state* (cf., Sherry, 2004) that is characterized by pleasurable absorption in the activity and neglect of time.

Sudden resolution of cognitive incongruencies often causes a rush of euphoria that includes *joy and laughter* (Berlyne, 1969; Zillmann, 2000a). Humor (including funny jokes) develops from a puzzling incongruency that suddenly is resolved. The resolution is often due to a plot or punch-line that allows the audience to comprehend and to solve such incongruency. But in the case of nonsense humor, a resolution might just as well be the realization that there is nothing to resolve (cf. Zillmann, 2000a). Norm-violations and sexual or aggressive content heighten arousal and thus fuel the mild euphoria of a sudden comprehension (cf. Berlyne, 1969), especially for sensation-seekers (Zuckerman, 2006). Humor is omnipresent in many entertaining media offerings, from comedy television shows to action movies, or comedy movies to funny cartoons and books (Zillmann & Bryant, 1991).

Positive Primary Emotions

In general, positive primary emotions result from events that appear to serve a person's motivations or goals, i.e., to broaden and to build his or her resources (Fredrickson, 2001). Media entertainment offerings trigger *happiness* through various means, but the user's perception of "making reasonable progress toward the realization of a goal" is always key (Lazarus, 2001, p. 64). Happiness results from the perception of making reasonable progress toward a goal (Lazarus, 1991; Roseman, 2001). The pleasure of understanding familiar things, the enjoyment of resolving incongruencies, and the humor from comprehension can all be considered specific manifestations of this process. Euphoric happiness can arise from achieving a good outcome in an arousing conflict (Berlyne, 1960; Zillmann, 1983), like in dramatic narratives (Vorderer & Knobloch, 2000), including fictional drama, sports (Zillmann, Bryant, & Sapolsky, 1989) or video games. Happiness can occur as pride, if users attribute the successful outcome to their own efforts (Roseman, 2001; in sports: "basking in reflected glory," Cialdini et al., 1976). Users can even feel malicious happiness, i.e., *schadenfreude*, over others' misfortune if they are unaffiliated with the target individual and the failure seems deserved, like in slapstick comedies (van Dijk, Ouwerkerk, Goslinga & Nieweg, 2005; "disparagement theory of humor," Zillmann, 2000a; Zillmann & Bryant, 1991).

Negative Primary Emotions

In general, negative emotions result from events that imply a serious drawback from goals, violation of rules, or loss of resources. Common negative primary emotions in media entertainment include sadness, anger, fear, fright, shame, and distressful suspense. Those who view tearjerkers and related genres feel *sad*, because they or a closely affiliated person or group perceive a remarkable loss of resources or another strong motivation-incongruent backdrop while, at the same time, the cause of this loss seems to be out of anyone's control (Lazarus, 1991; Roseman & Smith, 2001). Saddening media offerings often deal with the tragic loss of a liked person, either through death or by divorce (cf. Oliver, 1993). *Anger* occurs when people perceive themselves (in case of internally directed anger) or external agents (in case of externally directed anger) to cause the loss (Berkowitz & Harmon-Jones, 2002; Roseman & Smith, 2001). Anger is probably a common emotion in conflicts that include unjust harmful behavior against liked persons or groups (e.g., in sports and other dramas). *Fear and fright reactions* follow from simple appraisals that mark a situation as immediately physically threatening for oneself or an affiliated person or group (see van Reekum, 2000); the horror genre typically stimulates these emotions (Cantor, 2002). Fear-inducing situations that seem to be under control are not immediately endangering and cause positive *thrill* (Balint, 1959; Rozin, 1999), which probably is typical for fast-paced action movies (Zuckerman, 2006). Those who witness others perform norm-incongruent behaviors on shows broadcasted live, such as affect-talks (Bente & Feist, 2000) and talent shows (Nieweg et al., 2006), frequently report shame. Another central primary emotion for many entertaining media offerings is *suspense* (Carroll, 1996; Vorderer & Knobloch, 2000; Vorderer, Wulff & Friedrichsen, 1996). In general, suspense is a state of heightened arousal that results from uncertainty about a motivationally relevant outcome. It is often felt as negative distress (Zillmann, 1996). For suspense to develop, the media offering must tell a narrative, i.e., a causally and chronologically related order of events. It is possible to distinguish between two different structures of suspense-inducing narratives. The narrative either can start with the plot and then question how the plot came to be (here uncertainty exists about what has happened), or anticipate a possible plot, by suggesting a potentially desirable outcome with a certain likelihood (here uncertainty exists about what will happen; cf., affective disposition theory of drama, Zillmann, 1996; Raney & Bryant, 2002).

Reappraising an Emotional Response

In media exposure, the physical environment affects a user's physiology, just like the salient mentally represented environment, the appraisal of which leads to primary emotions. Several researchers, in both Psychology (Mayer & Gaschke, 1988) as well as in Communication Research (Bartsch et al., 2008; Mangold, Unz, & Winterhoff-Spurk, 2001; Oliver, 1993; Wirth & Schramm, 2007), have noted that primary emotions themselves can be subject to reappraisals, which give the occurrence of the affective state a broader context (e.g., the meaning of the exposure situation) and again check for novelty, goal-conduciveness, norm-congruency, controllability, etc. Reappraisals of emotions are thought to result in a more stable mood-like meta-emotion ("background emotion;" Damasio, 1999, p. 51). Feeling entertained by a media offering means meta-level appreciation of the dynamic chain of rather automatic affective states on the primary level.

Why Reappraisals?

Reappraisals connect rather automatic and environment-controlled affective states to higher-order cognitive processes of an elaborate mental system, which links them to more complex planning for the achievement of ideosyncratic short- and long-term goals (cf., Roseman, 2001). It is hard to interrupt the process of automatic primary emotions; "we are about as effective at stopping an emotion as we are at preventing a sneeze" (Damasio, 1999, p. 49). Reappraisals allow the use of phylogenetically more recent and, in adaptive hindsight, superior capabilities to regulate behavior. The organism is able to disengage from behavioral tendencies under environmental control by re-evaluating automatic primary emotions on the basis of more elaborate short- and long-term goals.

Affective responses can be re-evaluated on the basis of a deeper ideosyncratic meaning (Rozin, 1999; Scheele & DuBois, 2006; Skaggs & Baron, 2006) and associated goals (cf., Bartsch et al., 2008) instead of immediate behavioral reactions. Therefore, a recontemplation of spontaneous affect also implies second thoughts on the need and opportunities to cope with a situation (cf., secondary appraisals and coping, Lazarus & Folkman, 1987). Due to reappraisals, users can reconsider the valence of emotions initially felt, leading to the enjoyment of fear (Cantor, 2002) and of pain (Rozin, 1999), or the appreciation of sadness (Oliver, 1993). It is due to reappraisals that entertainment really becomes meaningful.

Reappraisal and Mood-Regulation

Reappraisals can check whether primary emotions promote short-term goals (see "goal-conduciveness," Barsch et al., 2008). In the context of entertainment exposure, mood-regulation seems to be of particular importance. People often turn to the media because they strive for a positive target mood (Zillmann, 1988), but sometimes they might seek a neutral or negative mood as well (Hess, Kacen, & Kim, 2006; Knobloch-Westerwick, 2006; Skaggs & Baron, 2006). Users enjoy their emotional responses to the hybrid environment of the exposure situation, if they imply a move towards their target mood. If the emotional responses run counter to the target mood, however, they deem events unpleasant.

A reappraisal of emotions implies that users also consider whether they need to cope with their emotions, and if so, how to cope with them (Lazarus & Folkman, 1987). If a primary emotion seems to violate a target mood seriously, users are likely to act (cf., Schramm & Wirth, 2008). One effective strategy to dismantle unappreciated negative affect, for example, is to change the reference frame, i.e., the reception mode (Cantor, 2002; Cupchik & Kemp, 2000). By including some of the actual exposure situation, users distance themselves from the media environment. This reduces emotional effects, while responsiveness to the real-world surrounding increases. Choosing the best reference frame might also fuel positive emotions. When the media world triggers less pleasure than users had hoped, they may try to make the best out of it, for example, by appreciating the media environment's aesthetic appeal (Cupchik & Kemp, 2000; Tan, 1996) or by reflecting on the overall positive carefree exposure situation.

Reappraisal and Self-Realization

Human beings need a deeper meaning to their life (Scheele & DuBois, 2006; Schwab, 2003; Skaggs & Baron, 2006). The formation of such a meaning builds on making sense of the evolutionary heritage that so vastly affects one's own behavior. Understanding one's purpose in the world is crucial for successful adaptation throughout life. People therefore strive to develop an identity, i.e., a valid picture of themselves in the world. They also pursue the long-term goal of progress toward their perception of what is ideal. Accordingly, self-determination-theory (Deci & Ryan, 2002, 2000) dwells on Aristotle's notion that psychological growth and integration lie at the heart of human striving. Individuals are thought to strive for growth in the complexity and variety of their abilities and more coherent knowledge about themselves. Events that promise movement towards these long-term goals (cf., Zillmann, 2000b) are often challenging, but also rewarding, as they help people to understand themselves in a better way.

Primary emotions are highly informative events. They reveal how the more archaic bodily instances of behavior control interpret a situation (Schwab, 2008). Being attentive to the unfolding primary emotions should therefore be an effective mechanism that leads to self-realization. In addition, primary emotions can be challenges on their own (Bartsch et al., 2008; Rozin, 1999). Mastering emotional challenges with higher-order cognitive control demonstrates existing skills, and if the emotion is novel, it can reveal enhanced skills as well. Media entertainment products are designed to trigger primary emotions. Therefore, entertainment products can promote self-realization (Bosshart & Macconi, 1989). For example, frequent users of horror movies may be satisfied that they can actualize their skill to stand intense fear (Cantor, 2002). Or, if the fear seems novel, users might feel proud for successfully mastering the emotional challenge. Oliver (1993) links the enjoyment of sad primary emotions during movie exposure to self-realization as well. Sad emotions can inform a user about internalized norms and values (e.g., to feel pity if someone suffers) and thus direct attention to meaningful facets of oneself (cf., Scheele & DuBois, 2006). Primary emotions might also help to actualize and identify one's group-affiliation (Bryant & Miron, 2002).

WHAT IS MEDIA ENTERTAINMENT THEN?

Media offerings, or more precisely situations that include the use of media offerings, are entertaining if they satisfy a user's need to maintain physiological and psychological

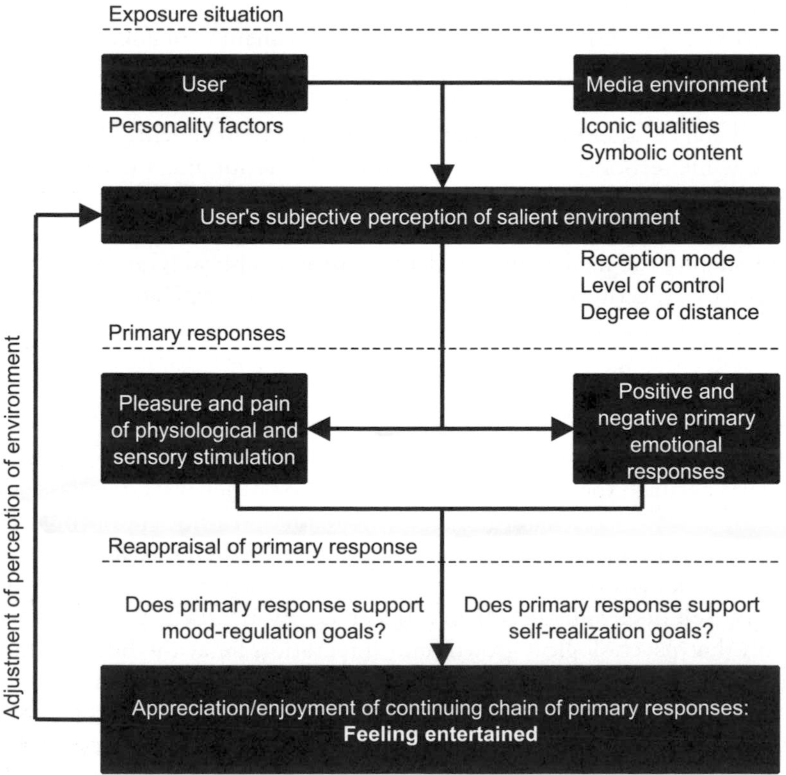

Figure 24.1 Formation of the Feeling to be Entertained by Media

balance. Successful homeostatic regulation causes pleasure, whereas sensory stimulation is unpleasant if it fosters severe imbalance. Comprehension and resolution of cognitive incongruencies are likely to result in positive affect, whereas a lack of cognitive challenges, or incongruencies that are overly complex, create aversion or disinterest. The user's involvement in the media offering triggers both positive and negative primary emotions. Depending on the genre or type of the media offering, certain discrete primary emotions will be characteristic for the exposure situation. Primary emotions are reappraised in light of two motivational stances, mood-regulation and self-realization. The reappraisal fuels a meta-emotion or mood-like background emotion. Enjoyment occurs on a meta-level when the user appreciates his or her primary emotions as motivation-congruent, which includes compliance to intrinsic norms. Users feel entertained over a certain episode (that might resemble the full exposure situation), if they enjoy the ongoing chain of their own primary affective responses. The meta-emotion "entertainment" then rests on the appreciation of both the continuing chain of sensory stimulation and primary emotions stimulated by the present environment and edited by the mood-regulating user throughout a certain episode (see Figure 24.1). Appreciation may depend on how the stimulated affective state corresponds to target-moods and/or the need for self-realization. With varying target-moods and identity processes, entertainment should therefore differ intra-individually (e.g., throughout the day or life-span) as well as inter-individually (e.g., across ages or gender).

References

Balint, M. (1959). *Thrills and regression*. New York: International University Press.

Bartsch, A., Mangold, R., Viehoff, R., & Vorderer P. (2006). Emotional gratifications during media use—an integrative approach. *Communications, 31*, 261–278.

Bartsch, A., Vorderer, P., Mangold, R., & Viehoff, R. (2008). Appraisal of emotions in media use: Towards a process model of meta-emotion and emotion regulation. *Media Psychology, 11*, 7–27.

Bente, G., & Feist, A. (2000). Affect talk and its kin. In D. Zillmann & P. Vorderer (Eds.), *Media entertainment. The psychology of its appeal* (pp. 113–134). Mahwah, NJ: Erlbaum.

Berkowitz, L., & Harmon-Jones, E. (2002). Toward an understanding of the determinants of anger. *Emotion* 4(2), 107–130.

Berlyne, D. E. (1960). *Conflict, arousal, and curiosity*. New York: McGraw-Hill.

Berlyne, D. E. (1969). Laughter, humor, and play. In G. Lindzey & G. Aaronson (Eds.), *The handbook of social psychology: Vol. 3. The individual in a social context* (2nd ed., pp. 795–852). Reading, MA: Addison-Wesley.

Berntson, G. G., & Cacioppo, J. T. (2000). From homeostasis to allodynamic regulation. In J. T. Cacioppo, L. G. Tassinary, & G. G. Berntson (Eds.), *Handbook of psychophysiology* (pp. 459–481). Cambridge, UK: Cambridge University Press.

Berridge, K. C. (2001). Reward learning: Reinforcement, incentives, and expectations. In D. L. Medin (Ed.), *The Psychology of Learning and Motivation* (Vol. 40, pp. 223–278). San Diego: Academic Press.

Berridge, K. C. (2002). Pleasures of the brain. *Brain and Cognition, 52*, 106–128.

Bosshart, L., & Macconi, I. (1989). Media entertainment. *Communication Research Trends, 18*(3), 3–8.

Bryant, J., & Miron, D. (2002). Entertainment as media effect. In J. Bryant & D. Zillmann (Eds.), *Media effects* (2nd ed., pp. 549–582). Mahwah, NJ: Erlbaum.

Bryant, J., & Zillmann, D. (1984). Using television to alleviate boredom and stress. Selective exposure as a function of endorsed excitational states. *Journal of Broadcasting, 28*, 1–20.

Bryant, J., Roskos-Ewoldsen, D. R., & Cantor, J. (Eds.) (2003). *Communication and emotion: Essays in honor of Dolf Zillmann*. Mahwah, NJ: Erlbaum.

Cabanac, M. (1971). Physiological role of pleasure. *Science, 173*, 1103–1107.

Cabanac, M. (1979). Sensory pleasure. *The Quarterly review of biology, 54*, 1–29.

Cabanac, M., Pouliot, C., & Everett, J. (1997). Pleasure as a sign of mental activity. *European Psychologist, 2*(3), 226–234.

Cantor, J. (2002). Fright reactions to mass media. In J. Bryant & D. Zillmann (Eds.), *Media Effects* (2nd ed., pp. 287–306). Mahwah, NJ: Erlbaum.

Carey, J. (1993). *The intellectuals and the masses: Pride and prejudice among the literary intelligentsia, 1880–1939*. New York: St. Martin's Press.

Carroll, N. (1996). The paradox of suspense. In P. Vorderer, H.-J. Wullf, & M. Friedrichsen (Eds.), *Suspense: Conceptualizations, theoretical analyses, and empirical explorations* (pp. 71–91). Mahwah, NJ: Erlbaum.

Cialdini, R. B., Borden, R. J., Thorne, A., Walker, M. R., Freeman, S., & Sloan, L. (1976). Basking in reflected glory: Three (football) field studies. *Journal of Personality and Social Psychology, 34*, 366–375.

Cupchik, G. C. (2002). The evolution of psychical distance as an aesthetic concept. *Culture & Psychology, 8*, 155–187.

Cupchik, G. C., & Kemp, S. (2000). The aesthetics of media fare. In D. Zillmann & P. Vorderer (Eds.), *Media entertainment. The psychology of its appeal* (pp. 249–264). Mahwah, NJ: Erlbaum.

Damasio, A. (1999). *The Feeling of What Happens*. San Diego et al.: Harcourt.

Davidson, R. J. (1992). Anterior cerebral asymmetry and the nature of emotion. *Brain and Cognition, 65*, 245–268.

Deci, E. L., & Ryan, R. M. (2000). The "what" and "why" of goal pursuits: Human needs and the self-determination of behavior. *Psychological Inquiry, 11*, 227–268.

Deci, E. L., & Ryan, R. M. (2002). (Eds.). *Handbook of self-determination research*. Rochester, NY: University of Rochester Press.

Denham, B. E. (2004). Toward an explication of media enjoyment: The synergy of social norms, viewing situations, and program content. *Communication Theory, 4*, 370–387.

Engel, M. (1997). *Tickle the public: 100 years of the popular press*. London: Indigo.

Fredrickson, B. L. (2001). The role of positive emotions in positive psychology: The broaden-and-build theory of positive emotions. *American Psychologist, 56*, 218–226.

Fredrickson, B. L. (2002). Positive emotions. In C. R. Snyder & S. J. Lopez (Eds.), *Handbook of positive psychology* (pp. 120–134). London: Oxford University Press.

Frueh, W. (2002). *Unterhaltung durch das Fernsehen. Eine molare Theorie (A multi-faceted theory of entertainment television)*. Konstanz: UVK.

Green, M. C., Brock, T. C., & Kaufman, G. F. (2004). Understanding media enjoyment: The role of transportation into narrative worlds. *Communication Theory, 56*(1), 163–183.

Groeben, N., & Vorderer, P. (1988). *Leserpsychologie: Lesemotivation—Lektürewirkung*. [Psychology of readers: Reading motivation—reading effects]. Münster: Aschendorff.

Hartmann, T. (2008a). Presence. In Wolfgang Donsbach (Ed.), *The International Encyclopedia of Communication*. Blackwell Reference Online. Retrieved from http://www.communication encyclopedia.com (18 September 2008).

Hartmann, T. (2008b). Parasocial Interactions and New Media Characters. In E. A. Konijn, S. Utz, M. Tanis, & S. Barnes (Eds.). *Mediated Interpersonal Communication* (pp. 177–199). Mahwah, NJ: Erlbaum.

Herzog, H. (1944). What do we really know about daytime serial listeners? In P. F. Lazarsfeld, B. Berelson, & F. N. Stanton (Eds.), *Radio Research, 1942–43* (pp. 3–33). New York: Duell, Sloan and Pearce.

Hess, J. D., Kacen, J. J., & Kim, J. (2006) Mood-management dynamics: The interrelationship between moods and behaviours. *British Journal of Mathematical and Statistical Psychology, 59*, 347–378.

Ito, T. A., & Cacioppo, J. T. (1999). The psychophysiology of utility appraisals. In D. Kahneman, E. Diener, & H. Schwarz (Eds.), *Well-being: The foundations of hedonic psychology* (pp. 470–488). New York: Russell Sage Foundation.

Kahneman, D. (1999). Objective Happiness. In D. Kahneman, E. Diener, & N. Schwarz (Eds.), *Well-being: The foundations of hedonic psychology* (pp. 3–25). New York: Sage.

Katz, E., & Foulkes, D. (1962). On the use of mass media for escape: Clarification of a concept. *Public Opinion Quarterly, 26*, 377–388.

Klimmt, C., & Vorderer, P. (in press). Media Entertainment. In C. Berger, M. Roloff, & D. Roskos-Ewoldsen (Eds.), *Handbook of Communication Science* (2nd ed.). London: Sage.

Knobloch-Westerwick, S. (2006). Mood management: Theory, evidence, and advancements. In J. Bryant & P. Vorderer (Eds.), *Psychology of entertainment* (pp. 239–254). Mahwah, NJ: Erlbaum.

Koestner, R., & Losier, G. F. (2002). Distinguishing three ways of being internally motivated: A closer look at introjection, identification, and intrinsic motivation. In L. Deci & R. M. Ryan (Eds.), *Handbook of self-determination research* (pp. 101–122). Rochester, NY: University of Rochester Press.

Lang, P. (1995). The emotion probe: Studies of motivation and attention. *American Psychologist, 50*, 372–385.

LaRose, R., Lin, C. A., & Eastin, M. S. (2003). Unregulated internet usage: Addiction, habit, or deficient self-regulation? *Media Psychology, 5*, 225–253.

Lazarus, R. S., & Folkman, S. (1987). Transactional theory and research on emotions and coping. *European Journal of Personality, 1*, 141–169.

Lazarus, R. S. (1991). *Emotion and Adaptation*. New York: Oxford University Press.

Lazarus, R. S. (2001). Relational meaning and discrete emotions. In K. R. Scherer, A. Schorr, & T. Johnstone (Eds.), *Appraisal processes in emotion: Theory, methods, research* (pp. 37–67). New York: Oxford University Press.

Lee, K. M. (2004). Presence, explicated. *Communication Theory, 14*, 27–50.

Mangold, R., Unz, D., & Winterhoff-Spurk, P. (2001). Zur Erklärung emotionaler Medienwirkungen: Leistungsfähigkeit, empirische Überprüfung und Fortentwicklung theoretischer Ansätze. In P. Rössler, U. Hasebrink, & M. Jäckel (Eds.), *Theoretische Perspektiven der Rezeptionsforschung* (pp. 163–180). München: Fischer.

Mayer, J. D., & Gaschke, Y. N. (1988). The experience and meta-experience of mood. *Journal of Personality and Social Psychology, 55*, 105–111.

Miron, D. (2006). Emotion and cognition in entertainment. In J. Bryant & P. Vorderer (Eds.), *Psychology of entertainment* (pp. 343–364). Mahwah, NJ: Erlbaum.

Nieweg, M., Van Dijk, W. W., & Ouwerkerk, J. W. (2006). Waarom lachen we om Idols? De rol van zelf-regulatie bij het ervaren van leedvermaak. In R. W. Holland, J. W. Ouwerkerk, R. Ruiter, C. Van Laar, & J. Ham (Eds.), *Jaarboek Sociale Psychologie 2005* (pp. 341–348). Groningen: ASPO.

Oatley, K., & Mar, R. A. (2005). Evolutionary pre-adaptation and the idea of character in fiction. *Journal of Cultural and Evolutionary Psychology, 3(2)*, 181–196.

Oatley, K. (1994). A taxonomy of the emotions of literary response and a theory of identification in fictional narrative. *Poetics, 23*, 53–74.

Ohler, P., & Nieding, G. (2006). Why Play? An Evolutionary Perspective. In P. Vorderer & J. Bryant (Eds.), *Playing Video Games: Motives, Responses, and Consequences* (pp. 101–113). Hillsdale, NJ: Erlbaum.

Oliver, M. B. (1993). Exploring the paradox of the enjoyment of sad films. *Human Communication Research, 19*, 315–342.

Oliver, M. B. (in press). Affect as a predictor of entertainment choice: The utility of looking beyond pleasure. In T. Hartmann (ed.), *Evolving perspectives on media choice*. New York: Routledge.

Raney, A., & Bryant, J. (2002). Moral judgment and crime drama: An integrated theory of enjoyment. *Journal of Communication, 52*(2), 402–415.

Reeve, J. (1989). The interest-enjoyment distinction in intrinsic motivation. *Motivation and emotion, 17*, 353–375.

Roseman, I. J. (2001). A model of appraisal in the emotion system. In K. Scherer, A. Schorr, & T. Johnstone (Eds.), *Appraisal processes in emotion. Theory, methods, research* (pp. 68–91). New York: Oxford University Press.

Roseman, I. J., & Smith, C. A. (2001). Appraisal theory. In K. Scherer, A. Schorr, & T. Johnstone (Eds.). *Appraisal processes in emotion: Theory, methods, research* (pp. 3–19). Oxford: Oxford University Press.

Rozin, P. (1999). Preadaptation and the puzzles and properties of pleasure. In D. Kahneman, E. Diener, & N. Schwarz (Eds.), *Well-Being: The foundations of hedonic psychology* (pp. 109–133). New York: Sage.

Ryan, R. M., Rigby, C. S., & Przybylski, A. (2006). The motivational pull of video games: A self-determination theory approach. *Motivation and Emotion, 30*, 347–363.

Scheele, B., & DuBois, F. (2006). Catharsis as a moral form of entertainment. In J. Bryant & P. Vorderer (Eds.), *Psychology of entertainment* (pp. 405–422). Mahwah, NJ: Erlbaum.

Scherer, K. R. (2001). Appraisal considered as a process of multilevel sequential checking. In K. R. Scherer, A. Schorr, & T. Johnstone (Eds.). *Appraisal processes in emotion: Theory, Methods, Research* (pp. 92–120). New York: Oxford University Press.

Scherer, K. (2005). What are emotions? And how can they be measured? *Social Science Information, 44*, 695–729.

Schramm, H., & Wirth, W. (2008). A case for an integrative view on affect regulation through media usage. *Communications: The European Journal of Communication Research, 33*(1), 27–46.

Schreier, M. (2006). (Subjective) well-being. In J. Bryant, & P. Vorderer (Eds.), *Psychology of entertainment* (pp. 389–404). Mahwah, NJ: Erlbaum.

Schulkin, J. (2004). Introduction. In J. Schulkin (Ed.), *Allostasis, Homeostasis, and the Costs of Adaptation* (pp. 1–17). Cambridge: Cambridge University Press.

Schwab, F. (2003). Unterhaltung. Eine evolutionspsychologische Perspektive. In W. Frueh & H.-J. Stiehler (Eds.), *Theorie der Unterhaltung. Ein interdisziplinärer Diskurs* [A theory of entertainment] (pp. 258–324). Cologne: Von Halem Verlag.

Schwab, F. (2008). Exposure to communication content: Evolutionary theory. In W. Donsbach (Eds.), *The Blackwell International Encyclopedia of Communication*. Oxford: Blackwell.

Sherry, J. L. (2004). Flow and media enjoyment. *Communication Theory, 14*(4), 328–347.

Silvia, P. (2006). *Exploring the psychology of interest*. New York: Oxford University Press.

Silvia, P. J. (2005a). What is interesting? Exploring the appraisal structure of interest. *Emotion, 5*(1), 89–102.

Silvia, P. J. (2005b). Emotional responses to art: From collation and arousal to cognition and emotion. *Review of General Psychology, 9*(4), 342–357.

Singer, J. L. (1981). *Daydreaming and fantasy*. Oxford, UK: Oxford University Press.

Skaggs, B. G., & Baron, C. R. (2006). Searching for meaning in negative events: concept analysis. *Journal of Advanced Nursing, 53*(5), 559–570.

Smith, C. A., & Kirby, L. D. (2001). Toward delivering on the promise of appraisal theory. In K. R. Scherer, A. Schorr, & T. Johnstone (Eds.). *Appraisal processes in emotion: Theory, methods, research* (pp. 121–138). New York: Oxford University Press.

Tan, E. S. (1996). *Emotion and the structure of narrative film: Film as an emotion machine*. Mahwah, NJ: Erlbaum.

Tannenbaum, P. H. (Ed.). (1980). *The entertainment functions of television*. Hillsdale: Erlbaum.

Tooby, J., & Cosmides, L. (1990). The past explains the present: emotional adaptations and the structure of ancestral environments. *Ethology and Sociobiology, 11*, 375–424.

Valkenburg, P. M., & van der Voort, T. H. A. (1994). Influence of TV on daydreaming and creative imagination: A review of research. *Psychological Bulletin, 116*(2), 316–339.

van Dijk, W. W., Ouwerkerk, J. W., Goslinga, S. & Nieweg, M. (2005). Deservingness and Schadenfreude. *Cognition and emotion, 19*(6), 933–939.

van Reekum, C. M., & Scherer, K. R. (1997). Levels of processing for emotion-antecedent appraisal. In G. Matthews (Ed.), *Cognitive science perspectives on personality and emotion*. (pp. 259–300). Amsterdam: Elsevier Science.

van Reekum, C. M. (2000). *Levels of processing in appraisal: Evidence from computer game generated emotions*. Doctoral dissertation, University of Geneva, Switzerland. Retrieved from http://www.unige.ch/cyberdocuments/theses2000/VanReekumC/these.html (September 2007).

Vorderer, P. (1993). Audience involvement and program loyalty. *Poetics, 22*, 89–98.

Vorderer, P. (2001). It's all entertainment—sure. But what exactly is entertainment? *Poetics, 29*, 247–261.

Vorderer, P., Klimmt, C., & Ritterfeld, U. (2004). Enjoyment: At the heart of media entertainment. *Communication Theory, 14*(4), 388–408.

Vorderer, P., & Knobloch, S. (2000). Conflict and suspense in drama. In D. Zillmann & P. Vorderer (Eds.), *Media entertainment. The psychology of its appeal* (pp. 59–73). Mahwah, NJ: Erlbaum.

Vorderer, P., Steen, F. F., & Chan, E. (2006). Motivation. In J. Bryant & P. Vorderer (Eds.), *Psychology of entertainment* (pp. 3–17). Mahwah, NJ: Erlbaum.

Vorderer, P., Wullf, H. J., & Friedrichsen, M. (Eds.). (1996). *Suspense: Conceptualizations, theoretical analyses, and empirical explorations*. Mahwah, NJ: Erlbaum.

Wirth, W., & Schramm, H. (2007). Emotionen, Metaemotionen und Regulationsstrategien bei der Medienrezeption. Ein integratives Modell. In W. Wirth, H.-J. Stiehler, & C. Wünsch (Eds.), *Dynamisch-transaktional denken: Theorie und Empirie der Kommunikationswissenschaft* (pp. 153–184). Köln: Halem Verlag.

Wirth, W. (2006). Involvement. In J. Bryant & P. Vorderer (Eds.), *Psychology of entertainment* (pp. 199–213). Mahwah, NJ: Erlbaum.

Wirth, W., Hartmann, T., Boecking, S., Vorderer, P., Klimmt, C., Schramm, H., Saari, T., Laarni, J., Ravaja, N., Gouveia, F. R., Biocca, F., Gouveia, L. B., Rebeiro, N., Sacau, A., Jäncke, L., Baumgartner T., & Jäncke, P. (2007). A process model of the formation of spatial presence experiences. *Media Psychology, 9*, 493–525.

Zajonc, R. B. (2001). Mere exposure. A gateway to the subliminal. *Current directions in psychological science, 10*, 224–228.

Zillmann, D. (1983). Transfer of excitation in emotional behavior. In J. T. Cacippo & R. E. Petty (Eds.), *Social psychophysiology: A sourcebook* (pp. 215–240). New York: Guilford Press.

Zillmann, D. (1988). Mood management: Using entertainment to full advantage. In L. Donohew, H. E. Sypher & E. T. Higgins (Hrsg.), *Communication, social cognition, and affect* (S. 147–171). Hillsdale, NJ: Erlbaum.

Zillmann, D. (1991). Empathy: Affect from bearing witness to the emotions of others. In J. Bryant & D. Zillmann (Eds.), *Responding to the screen* (pp.135–168). Hillsdale, NJ: Erlbaum.

Zillmann, D. (1996). The psychology of suspense in dramatic exposition. In P. Vorderer, H. J. Wulff, & M. Friedrichsen (Eds.), *Suspense: Conceptualizations, theoretical analyses, and empirical explorations* (pp. 199–231). Mahwah, NJ: Erlbaum.

Zillmann, D. (2000a). Humor and comedy. In D. Zillmann & P. Vorderer (Eds.), *Media entertainment. The psychology of its appeal* (pp. 37–57). Mahwah, NJ: Erlbaum.

Zillmann, D. (2000b). Mood management in the context of selective exposure theory. In M. E. Roloff (Ed.), *Communication Yearbook 23* (pp. 103–123). Thousand Oaks, CA: Sage.

Zillmann, D. (2006). Dramaturgy for Emotions from Fictional Narration. In J. Bryant & P. Vorderer (Eds.), *Psychology of entertainment* (pp. 215–238). Mahwah, NJ: Erlbaum.

Zillmann, D., & Bryant, J. (1985a). Selective-exposure phenomena. In D. Zillmann & J. Bryant (Eds.), *Selective Exposure to Communication* (pp. 1–10). Hillsdale, NJ: Erlbaum.

Zillmann, D., & Bryant, J. (1985b). Affect, mood, and emotion as determinants of selective exposure. In D. Zillmann & J. Bryant (Eds.), *Selective exposure to communication* (pp. 157–190). Hillsdale, NJ: Erlbaum.

Zillmann, D., & Bryant, J. (1991). Responding to comedy: The sense and nonsense in humor. In J. Bryant & D. Zillmann (Eds.), *Responding to the screen: Reception and reaction processes* (pp. 261–279). Hillsdale, NJ: Erlbaum.

Zillmann, D., Bryant, J., & Sapolsky, B. S. (1989). Enjoyment from sports spectatorship. In J. H. Goldstein (Ed.), *Sports, games, and play: Social and psychological viewpoints* (2nd ed., pp. 241–278). Hillsdale, NJ: Erlbaum.

Zillmann, D., & Vorderer, P. (Eds.). (2000). *Media entertainment. The psychology of its appeal.* Mahwah, NJ: Erlbaum.

Zuckerman, M., (2006). Sensation seeking in entertainment. In J. Bryant & P. Vorderer (Eds.), *Psychology of entertainment* (pp. 376–389). Mahwah, NJ: Erlbaum.

25

EFFECTS OF COMPUTER/VIDEO GAMES AND BEYOND

Kwan Min Lee
University of Southern California

Wei Peng
Michigan State University

Namkee Park
University of Oklahoma

In 1958, William A. Higinbotham, an engineer at the Brookhaven National Laboratory, created the world's first computer game, a rudimentary two-player tennis game, to entertain visitors to his lab (Poole, 2000, p. 15). Since then, the computer/video game (from now on computer game) industry has become one of the most aggressively growing business sectors in the United States and in the world. In 2001, U.S. sales of computer games and related hardware increased 43% to $9.4 billion, surpassing movie box-office revenue of $8.3 billion in the same year (Takahashi, 2002). Global sales in the game industry were over $25 billion as early as 2002 and are expected to exceed $46 billion by 2009 (PricewaterhouseCoopers, 2006). In the United States, it is estimated that 67% of American heads of households play computer games (Entertainment Software Association (ESA), 2007). Already in 2000, game playing was regarded as the most entertaining media activity, relegating television watching to the second place (Interactive Digital Software Association (IDSA), 2000). Obviously, games are emerging as one of the most dominant forms of entertainment. This trend will go further, thanks to the increasing penetration of high speed Internet connection and the declining prices of computers, video-game consoles, and mobile entertainment devices.

The growing popularity of computer games and some tragic incidents such as the Columbine High School massacre have sparked various academic studies on social and psychological effects of playing computer games. In the current chapter, we try to provide an extensive review of the computer game literature with a special focus on studies published during the last decade. The current review will cover a wide range of research traditions (from effect studies to uses and gratifications studies) and game genres (from entertainment to serious games). More specifically, we will provide a comprehensive review of the following four research traditions in the game literature—negative effects of violent games; game addiction; positive effects of serious games; uses and gratifications of computer games in general. After the review, we will bring forward some unanswered questions in the current literature and lay out some agenda for future research.

NEGATIVE EFFECTS OF VIOLENT GAMES

As a logical extension of the previous research in media violence, the study of negative effects of violence in computer games has been remarkably accumulated in the last two decades. The debate with respect to the effects of violent games on game users' aggression, however, has been hardly resolved. One stream of research has argued that violent games cause or at least correlate with game users' aggression, especially for kids and adolescents, whereas the other line of research has insisted no significant association between violent games and aggression. This section reviews the two opposing views on the relationship between playing violent games and aggression.

Significant Effects of Computer Game Violence on Aggression

Among various theoretical efforts to explain the ways in which violent computer games affect people's aggression, the general aggression model (GAM: Anderson & Bushman, 2002) is to date the most comprehensive theoretical framework. Integrating several earlier models of human aggression such as social learning theory and social cognitive theory (Bandura, 1973), cognitive neoassociationist model (Berkowitz, 1984), social information processing model (Dodge & Crick, 1990), affective aggression model (Geen, 1990), script theory (Huesmann, 1986), and excitation transfer model (Zillmann, 1983), the GAM claims that aggression is principally geared by the activation and application of aggression-related knowledge structures stored in memory (e.g., scripts or schemas). According to this model, in the case of short-term effects, playing a violent game primes aggressive conditions such as aggressive scripts and perceptual schemata, which in turn increase arousal and create an aggressive affective state (Bushman & Anderson, 2002). In the case of long-term effects, the model explains that hostile knowledge structures can be developed by repeated exposure to violent games, which ultimately create an aggressive personality (Bushman & Anderson, 2002; see Anderson, Gentile, & Buckley, 2007, chapter 5, for a fuller explanation of the model).

Employing the GAM, a vast amount of research has examined violent games' effects on aggression. The research has mainly focused on the negative effects of violent games on aggressive affects, behaviors, thoughts, physical arousal, and pro-social activities. Based on three experiments, one correlational study, and one meta-analysis, Anderson et al. (2004) found that playing violent computer games led to increases in aggressive behavior, aggressive affect, aggressive cognition, physiological arousal, and decreases in pro-social behavior. Similar findings abound. Carnagey and Anderson (2005) discovered that rewarding violent behaviors in computer games increased hostile emotion, aggressive thinking, and aggressive behaviors. In a similar fashion, Gentile, Lynch, Linder, and Walsh (2004) investigated and supported the significant effects of violent games on adolescents' hostility, aggressive behavior, and school performance. Anderson and Murphy (2003) especially examined the impacts of exposure to violent computer games on young women, and found that even brief exposure to a violent game increased aggressive behavior. In addition, they suggested that the effects of violent games on aggression might be greater when game characters played by game users are of the same gender. Bartholow and Anderson (2002) investigated sex differences in the effects of violent games on aggressive behavior and found greater effects for men than for women. A similar result was found in a German context. Krahé and Möller (2004) uncovered significant gender differences in usage and attraction to violent games, which ultimately influenced the acceptance of norms condoning physical aggression.

Some studies have focused on the desensitization effect of violent games. Desensitization, which refers to the attenuation or elimination of cognitive, emotional, and behavioral responses to a stimulus (Rule & Ferguson, 1986), is a strong mechanism that helps reduce psychological and/or physiological reactivity to real violence. In an experiment that measured heart rate (HR) and galvanic skin response (GSR), Carnagey, Anderson, and Bushman (2007) found that participants who played a violent game had lower HR and GSR while viewing filmed real violence compared to participants who played a non-violent game, indicating a physiological desensitization to violence. Funk, Baldacci, Pasold, and Baumgardner (2004) claimed with a more moderate tone that exposure to computer game violence was associated with lower empathy and stronger pro-violence attitudes, yet they could not identify strong relationships between exposure to real-life violence and measures of desensitization. Deselms and Altman (2003) found the desensitization effect only for men with a sample of college students.

There have been a series of attempts to synthesize the existing literature, although they discovered somewhat contrasting findings (e.g., Anderson & Bushman, 2001; Griffiths, 2000; Sherry, 2001). Anderson (2004) updated the effects of playing violent computer games with a meta-analysis based on 46 studies, and argued that more studies of violent games corroborate significant, though not large, effects of computer game violence on aggression. According to the study, the effect sizes of exposure to violent games on aggressive behavior, cognition, affect, pro-social behavior, and physical arousal were, both in experimental and correlational studies, about 0.20 in absolute value, confirming his and others' previous studies.

The Opposing View

The claim of the significant effects of violent games on aggression does not come without criticisms. These criticisms are mainly centered on methodological issues. Some studies (e.g., Freedman, 2002; Olson, 2004) listed the following as the main problems of the existing studies on computer game violence. First, the definitions of aggression are not clear-cut. For instance, in the worst case, the terms, "aggression" and "violence" are used interchangeably, making it almost impossible to distinguish independent and dependent variables from each other. Second, there are few standardized, reliable, and valid measures of aggression and exposure to violent games. Many studies that examined the negative effect of violent games have been conducted in isolation. In other words, studies employed either different types of games or different amount of game exposure time for experiments. Moreover, in many experimental studies participants played the game in a single-player mode in isolation, contrary to reality in which users routinely play games with their friends or other associates (Olson, 2004). As a consequence of the lack of appropriate measures and realistic study settings, a general synthesis of existing studies is hard to achieve. Third, the causal relationship between violent games and aggression in real life is not as straightforward as experimental conditions. It means that (1) it is not easy to take into account all possible mediating variables such as gender, age, personality, and so forth and that (2) a relationship of the opposite direction—aggressive people seek out violent computer games—or a two-way relationship—reinforcing or reciprocal—is also plausible. Fourth, many studies have been conducted with small, non-random, or non-representative samples. Accordingly, the statistical effect size from these studies is relatively too small for physical aggression, and moderate at best for aggressive thinking (Office of the Surgeon General, 2001). Finally, as Anderson (2004) lamented, there is still a paucity of longitudinal studies that could confirm the effect of violent games on a long-term basis. Given that the study of computer games is relatively an emerging field compared to the established research tradition of TV violence, the deficiency of serious longitudinal studies is understandable. Yet, without longitudinal studies, it is hard to not only prove the effect of violent games but also triangulate the existing findings (Williams & Skoric, 2005). In addition to these methodological problems, some argue that, regardless of increase in the number and availability of violent computer games, violence crime has been decreasing in reality (Olson, 2004) and thus the claim that violent games cause aggression is simply misleading.

Not surprisingly, the above arguments are strongly backed up by the game industry such as the Entertainment Software Association (ESA), although these claims are derived originally from academics. Recently, some empirical studies support these claims on the null effect of violent games on aggression. For example, Williams and Skoric (2005) conducted a one-month longitudinal study of a violent "massively multiplayer online role-playing game" (MMORPG) and found no strong effect associated with aggression caused by the game. Baldaro et al. (2004) evaluated the short-term effect of playing a violent computer game on physiological and psychological indicators with a sample of 22 male participants. They discovered that participants who played a violent computer game exhibited higher anxiety and increased systolic blood pressure yet no greater hostility compared to participants who played a non-violent computer game. In addition, a study conducted by Huesmann and Taylor (2006) failed to document a meaningful long-term effect, even though they were able to demonstrate short-term increases in aggression.

Possible Reconciliation

Recognizing the conflicting views on the effects of violent computer games, one study suggests an integrated model with respect to the direction of the relationship between violent games and aggression. Slater, Henry, Swaim, and Anderson (2003) claimed that game users' aggressive tendencies may lead the users to seek out violent games and exposure to violent games, which in turn may reinforce and exacerbate such aggressive tendencies. This so-called "downward spiral model" thus emphasizes a reciprocal relationship between violent games and game users' aggressive tendencies, at the same time focusing on the cumulative characteristic of the association between the two variables. Given that the downward spiral model is based on the assumption that aggressive users seek out violent games in order to satisfy their felt needs, it is theoretically rooted in the uses and gratifications approach (Palmgreen, 1984) and selective exposure theory (Zillmann & Bryant, 1985). Again, however, for the model to be supported as an alternative (or complementary) explanation to the existing literature, more studies are needed.

GAME ADDICTION

Another important negative effect of computer games that has been increasingly discussed in recent years is game addiction. It has been claimed that game addiction may lead to not only social problems such as social isolation or escape from real life but also health problems including seizures or even death. The issue has been fiercely discussed to the extent whether or not the American Medical Association (AMA) has to classify game addiction as a key mental illness. In fact, some medical problems or physical disorders due to game overuse have been reported, including epileptic seizures (e.g., Funatsuka, Fujita, Shirakawa, Oguni, & Osawa, 2001), musculoskeletal disorders, or increased metabolic rate (e.g., Brady & Matthews, 2006). In South Korea, where hundreds of private hospitals and psychiatric clinics are helping game addicts with special treatments, it was also reported that 10 people died in 2005 from game addiction-related causes such as disruptive blood circulation (Faiola, 2006). Moreover, the number of game addicts is far from negligible. In a commercial survey conducted with 1,178 U.S. children and teenagers (ages 8 to 18) in January 2007 by Harris Interactive, it was reported that 8.5% of game users could be classified as addicts (Harris Interactive, 2007). As a response to the increasing trend of game addiction, the AMA, at an annual committee meeting in June 2007, determined that its psychiatric group would examine the issue over the next five years and decide the inclusion of game addiction as an illness. If game addiction is added as a mental illness, it is possible for game addicts to have medications or treatments for healing excessive gaming. Of course, some opposed the AMA's consideration of the inclusion, arguing that game addiction or overuse is simply an individual (bad) habit, rather than a medical problem (Los Angeles Times, 2007). Nevertheless, the fact that game addiction is publicly discussed as a possible medical problem demonstrates that it brings a number of detrimental outcomes whether they are individual or societal problems.

In parallel with the increased interest in game addiction, there have been a few attempts to explain why people are addicted to games. Based on a survey with 1,993 Korean game users, Choi and Kim (2004) suggested a theoretical model for game addiction by integrating the concepts of customer loyalty, flow, personal interaction, and social interaction. According to the model, people are likely to continue to play games when they have optimal experiences while playing games. Optimal experiences, according to the model, can be achieved by effective interaction with the game system and/or pleasant social interaction with other users. Similarly, Wan and Chiou (2006) applied the flow theory and the humanistic needs model as a way to explain psychological motives of game addiction. The results of their study, however, indicated that the flow state was not a key psychological mechanism of game users' addiction. Also, the study discovered that game addicts' compulsive game use was not derived from the pursuit of satisfaction of their need-gratification but from the relief of dissatisfaction.

Game addiction or overuse is particularly associated with MMORPGs (massively multiplayer online role-playing games) since such games are highly social and provide interactive real time applications (AMA, 2007) similar to the factors associated with Internet addiction (Olson, 2004). For instance, MMORPG users spend many more hours devoted to the games compared to other users who play other types of games, and find aspects of the game world more pleasant and satisfying than those of the real world (Ng & Wiemer-Hastings, 2005). The problem of the heavy use of MMORPGs would be that such users are likely to be socially marginalized while experiencing high levels of emotional loneliness and maladaptations to real life social interactions (AMA, 2007). In addition to the increasing use of MMORPGs, the recent launch of Nintendo's Wii and enhanced competition among game console companies are also likely to fuel the addictive nature of games as a way to lock in users to their console.

Meanwhile, a recent study based on a survey of 7,069 game users (Grüsser, Thalemann,

& Griffiths, 2007) investigated the relationship between game addiction and aggression. It found that excessive gaming explained only 1.8% variance of aggression. In addition, with respect to gender difference, Griffiths and Hunt (1998) in a survey with 387 adolescents (12–16 years old) found that males were more likely to be classified as game addicts than females. They also discovered that the earlier children began playing games, the more likely they became addicts.

To sum up, the study of game addiction is still in an early stage despite the heated discussion about its effects on game users' abnormal behaviors and social disorders. As the AMA (2007) properly pointed out, more research is needed to verify game addiction as a mental illness.

POSITIVE EFFECTS OF SERIOUS GAMES

Commercial off-the-shelf (COTS) games are designed to entertain. However, the features of games that afford entertainment can also be utilized for other purposes, such as education. Educational theories inform us that teaching is more effective if students are intrinsically motivated in the learning process, receive continuous feedback, and apply new ideas in a variety of relevant context. This is exactly what game features can offer. Game playing is usually fun and challenging, which motivates students to actively participate. Games also provide a simulated environment where students can apply what they have just learned in different contexts. Therefore, games have great potential to be an effective educational tool. In fact, games with purposes beyond entertainment are called "serious games," including but not limited to games for learning, games for health, and games for policy and social change. Serious games are designed intentionally to achieve these positive effects. In this section, we review the effects of serious games that are used to teach knowledge, attitude, and behavior. Some COTS games are originally designed to entertain, but some unintended positive effects are also found associated with these games. In addition, some COTS games are reapplied by educators for purposes other than entertainment. We will also discuss the positive effects of these COTS games.

Games for Learning

Using the gaming format in teaching was not uncommon even one thousand years ago. The use of digital games in education started in the early 1980s. The early generation of games for learning was limited by the technology capacity and only minimal graphics and interactivity were implemented. In the past decade, due to the technology advancement, many educational games were developed to deliver knowledge of different subject matters, such as economics (Lengwiler, 2004), business and management (Chua, 2005; Hoogeweegen, van Liere, Vervest, van der Meijden, & de Lepper, 2006), language (Kovalik & Kovalik, 2002), mathematics (van Eck & Dempsey, 2002), biology (Clark & Smith, 2004), geography (Mayer, Mautone, & Prothero, 2002), medical education (Mann et al., 2002), and military training (Coleman, 2001). All these games demonstrate that the game-based instruction is effective. However, an early literature review on the effectiveness of using electronic games for education showed that 56% of the studies found no difference between game-based instruction and conventional instruction, 32% found differences favoring simulations/games, 7% favored simulations/games but raised questions about their experimental design, and the remaining 5% found differences favoring conventional instruction (Randel, Morris, & Wetzel, 1992). Poor graphics and low interactivity afforded by early generation games might explain the low rate of effectiveness. A more recent meta-analysis shows that digital games and interactive simulations have advantages over traditional teaching methods for cognitive gain outcomes (Vogel et al., 2006). In addition, games-based instruction seems to be more effective when the subject matter demands active participation and applying the knowledge in specific contexts, such as physics or mathematics (Randel et al., 1992).

Empirical studies have shown that serious games for learning are effective teaching tools. But why can games, as a particular medium, achieve the educational effects? Researchers believe that games embody a number of innate features that facilitate the learning process. First, games are effective because learning takes place within a meaningful context. The game rules in those contexts are usually principles intended to be taught to the players. For instance, for games that teach economics, the game rules follow the economic principles and players need to apply those principles in order to proceed in the games. The game playing experience is thus an experience of applying theoretical principles. This is exactly what situated learning and experiential learning is about. However, if a game is not engaging, the learning effect might not be substantial. The second game feature that promotes effectiveness is the element of fun that motivates players to start to play a game and to continue playing the game even though they need to repeatedly apply the same rules or principles. Players can get frustrated if they get stuck in the game after multiple trials in vain. They can also get bored if they can easily go through the whole game without even trying hard. Most games are thus designed in a way that players will be provided with challenging goals. At the same time, plenty of "just-in-time" information will be available to assist the players. This third game feature matches the learning principle of scaffolding and it is enabled by the interactive feature of games that provides immediate feedback to the players and constantly requires input from the players. Computer games also enable the development of different learning styles, since the speed and the level of difficulty can be adjusted according to the players (Jenkins, 2002).

Besides the games that are intentionally designed to educate, some researchers believe that incidental learning might occur in the process of playing COTS games. Gee (2003) summarized 36 principles in COTS games that actually can teach us about learning and literacy. In fact, there are many examples of COTS games being used in the classroom, including *Civilization, CSI, Age of Empire II, The Sims 2, Age of Mythology*, and *Sim City 4* (Delwiche, 2006; van Eck, 2006). Empirical studies have demonstrated that COTS games are effective in improving strategizing (Jenkins, 2002) and high-level problem solving skills (Greenfield, Brannon, & Lohr, 1994), and enhancing inductive reasoning (Honebein, Carr, & Duffy, 1993). As a number of cognitive skills such as proactive and recursive thinking, systematic organization of information, interpretation of visual information, and general search heuristics are generally required for players to successfully finish games, those cognitive skills naturally will be improved in the process of game playing (Pillay, 2003). In addition, COTS games are particularly effective in improving spatial, mental rotation and visualization skills, and eye-hand coordination (de Lisi & Wolford, 2002).

Games for Health

Computer games have been used for various health-related purposes, particularly for risk prevention, health education, behavioral intervention, and disease self-management. For disease or risk prevention, games have been designed to promote a healthier lifestyle by delivering relevant health information, shifting unhealthy attitudes, and enabling healthy behavior rehearsal. These games are set in a variety of health domains, including promoting healthy nutrition (Peng, in press), safe sexual behavior (Thomas, Cahill, & Santilli, 1997), anti-smoking (Lieberman, 2001), injury prevention (Goodman, Bradley, Paras, Williamson, & Bizzochi, 2006), and early treatments for heart attack (Silverman et al., 2001).

Computer games have been developed to improve self-management skills for coping with certain chronic diseases, such as asthma (Homer et al., 2000; Lieberman, 2001), diabetes (Brown et al., 1997; Lieberman, 2001), and cancer (Cole, Kato, Marin-Bowling, Dahl, & Pollock, 2006). All the games used in the above studies targeted children with aforementioned health problems. Electronic games are believed to be a more advantageous channel to reach children because playing electronic games has become one of the most popular leisure activities of the youth, and thus integrating games into their medical regimen is very likely to be acceptable. In addition, these games provide a fun and engaging environment for behavior rehearsal and repetitive skill practice without taking risk in real life, which is otherwise hard to achieve using traditional approaches. Evaluation studies of these games generally show that players like the games and are willing to use such games to learn more about their health-related issues. However, outcome measures in most of those studies include only attitudinal variables, such as self-efficacy, perceived benefit, and behavior intention. Unfortunately, no actual behavior measures were used in the above studies. It is true that attitudinal variables are mediators for behavior changes that will ultimately lead to positive health outcomes. Yet, without empirical evidence that these games can actually influence health-related behavioral outcomes, it is difficult to convince health providers and policymakers to invest heavily in serious games for health. In fact, Huss et al. (2003) found that an asthma education game did not help kids improve health-related outcomes.

Computer games are also used as a distraction tool to reduce the discomfort caused by medical treatment. COTS games as well as specially designed games can be used for this purpose. Prior research has demonstrated that games are effective in reducing pain and anxiety before surgery (Patel et al., 2006; Rassin, Gutman, & Silner, 2004). Computer games can also serve as effective therapeutic tools (Pope & Bogart, 1996).

The primary reason that games can be an effective channel for health intervention and health education is that they provide a simulated and interactive environment where players can engage in behavioral rehearsal. The simulated environment serves as a safe test-bed for them to practice self-management skills such as taking insulin, checking blood pressure, or checking peak flow. Players can observe detrimental effects of their own mismanagement of a disease without engaging themselves in real danger. For instance, players can observe severe consequences to their game characters if they fail to use an inhaler and learn a lesson. In addition, game players' successes in a simulated environment can increase their self-efficacy for managing their health problems. In addition, the element of fun can motivate players to practice the same skills without getting bored. For many disease self-management processes, the knowledge and skills needed are finite, yet repetitive practice and habit formation are critical. This is exactly what the game format can offer. A well-designed game can be played dozens and even hundreds of times without making players feel bored.

Games for Social Change

Games for education focus on knowledge transfer, and games for health focus on behavioral changes. There are other types of serious games that focus on changing attitudes about political or religious agendas, or simply increasing awareness of social issues. As early as in 1980, a game called *Energy Czar*, an energy crisis simulation game was created. The 2004 presidential election in the Unites States also generated a number of political games. For example, *Howard Dean for Iowa* was created to educate Dean supporters on various grassroots outreach programs. Another noteworthy political game is *PeaceMaker*, in which players can take the role of either the Israeli Prime Minister or the Palestinian President to deal with a variety of events, including diplomatic negotiations, suicide bombers, and interaction with eight other political leaders, so as to reach a peaceful agreement for both sides. By affording perspectives from both sides, this game provides a unique opportunity to inform people of the issues in the region and helps to influence people's attitude towards the other side. *Darfur is dying* is a social issue awareness game to inform people of the crisis in Darfur which made approximately 3 million people leave their home and become refugees. In this game, players take the role of a Darfurian to experience the threats they face every day from the militias. This game has been played by millions of people and is reported to be the most significant source to inform young people of this international crisis. So far, more than dozens of serious games for social change have been made and played. Unfortunately, however, no empirical study has been conducted to evaluate how effective these games are.

USES AND GRATIFICATIONS OF GAMES IN GENERAL

The aforementioned discussions answer the question of what effects (negative and positive) computer games have on the players, yet questions such as what kind of people play games, how frequently people play games, and why people play games remain unanswered. Uses and gratifications is a good approach to investigate these questions. According to the uses and gratifications paradigm (for a general review, see Rubin, 2002), game players are not passive recipients of messages and are not powerless under the influence of games. Rather, players with different demographic and social backgrounds purposely choose a game to satisfy their unique needs or desires. In this section, we summarize computer game studies based on the uses and gratifications research paradigm (especially with regard to differences in gender, age, and personality).

Gender

According to the Entertainment Software Association (2007), 38% of game players are females. Empirical evidence consistently has shown a similar pattern of gender differences. Males tend to play games more often, both at home and in arcades (Phillips, Rolls, Rouse, & Griffiths, 1995). Girls seldom go to arcades, and when they do, more often than not, they are with boys and simply watch how boys play the game (Kiesler, Sproull, & Eccles, 1983). Besides the differences in frequency of game playing, boys also prefer more realistic violent games (Buchman & Funk, 1996). There are a number of explanations for the above gender differences. One possible explanation is that females may feel less comfortable than males with the violent themes that are found in many computer games, and are less comfortable in the arcade atmosphere where such games are played (Kiesler et al., 1983). Another factor might be that these games are generally produced by males and for males. Game contents are dominated by simulations of male activities, such as flying fighter aircraft, driving racing cars, fighting, and doing masculine sports such as football. Even fantasy and strategy games are male-oriented. Female characters appear a lot less frequently. A third explanation is the differences of cognitive abilities of females and males such as the visual and spatial skills. Game playing demands good eye-hand coordination and spatial skills in which males are much better than females.

Age

Computer games were once played only among children and adolescents. The recent data show that games are now being played by more and more adults. Children and adolescents not only play games alone or with friends, but also with parents and family. However, very few studies examine the game playing patterns among different age groups. A relatively outdated study shows that younger subjects were more comfortable with computer games and liked playing those games more. In contrast, older subjects were more afraid of computers, were not aware of the variety of computer games, and did not like playing computer games very much (McClure, 1985). As the Gameboy generation gets older, the major population for computer games has changed also. The average age of game players was 33 as of 2007 (ESA, 2007), indicating that playing games had become one of the major media use activities for the adult population too.

Personality

Personality predicts the frequency of game playing (McClure & Mears, 1984), the enjoyment of games (Holbrook, Chestnut, Oliva, & Greenleaf, 1984), and game addiction (Griffiths & Dancaster, 1995). Frequent game players are more likely to be young males who like competitive activities, science fiction, and challenges (McClure & Mears, 1984). Holbrook et al. (1984) argued that both enjoyment and performance depended on how the personality of the player interacted with the game being played. One particular personality relevant in the gaming context is one's tendency towards visualization as opposed to verbalization. Specifically, visualizers are more likely to enjoy and perform well on visual games while verbalizers are more likely to enjoy and perform well on verbal games. As to the relationship of personality and addiction, Griffiths and Dancaster (1995) demonstrated that Type A personality subjects had a greater increase of arousal than Type B personality subjects while playing games and thus were more likely to become addicted to computer games. A recent study found that people of high physical aggression personality tend to play the game in a more violent way (Peng, Liu, & Mou, 2008).

CONCLUSION AND SUGGESTIONS FOR FUTURE RESEARCH

This chapter reviews the existing literature on the negative and positive effects of computer games. It shows that playing violent entertainment games has negative effects to some extent, though not as strongly as people usually imagine. In general, the previous literature has suggested that violent entertainment games can result in aggressive affects, thoughts, and behaviors. Even non-violent games can have negative impacts on players; MMORPGs can make players be seriously addicted to the games and cause some social, financial, and health problems. Playing games (especially educational games), however, can be beneficial. For instance, computer games can improve motivation, retention, spatial skills, and cognitive skills of players. Computer games can even be used to train soldiers or corporate employees. In addition, computer games can be utilized to help some special groups such as people with health problems. Since kids usually play games with friends and family, computer games might help children to develop social skills as well. Computer games can also be used to promote social causes or increase social awareness as we have seen during presidential elections or international crises. In addition to the studies of games which are based on the media effect research paradigm, game studies based on the uses and gratifications research paradigm were also reviewed. Gender is a very strong predictor for the frequency of game playing. Males and females differ with respect to their preferences of games and their playing patterns. Another important variable is personality. A player's personality influences his or her enjoyment of a game, potential to become addicted to a game, and preference for a particular genre of a game, and how they play the game. Age is also an important factor. Yet, research on this variable is somewhat limited.

As a final remark, we discuss some limitations in the current literature and possible ways to overcome the limitations. First, there is a lack of unique theories on computer games. Current studies mostly borrow theories from the domain of television. However, playing games and watching television are fundamentally different activities in that the former is active and the latter is passive. Therefore, a new set of theories focusing on the interactive nature of game playing is needed. As Sherry (2001) suggested, new theories should be able to explain how and why people are engaged in computer games, and what kind of gratifications players pursue from their game playing. The uses and gratifications approach is a good start to overcome the limitation. New theories on computer games, however, should go beyond the uses and gratifications approach and need to clarify the underlying mechanism of the game engagement and the origin of biological and psychological reasons for diverse individual motivations to play games.

Second, the current literature heavily focuses on the consequences of game playing and as a result fails to explain the nature of game playing as an entertainment experience. We believe that theoretical understanding of the nature of game experience can solve the controversies about the negative effects of game violence and game addiction (see Lee and Peng (2006) for a similar claim). A possible approach to understand the nature of gaming experience is to introduce the concept of presence (see Lee, 2004, for a detailed explication of the concept). As many scholars argue, feelings of presence lie at the heart of media experience (Lombard & Ditton, 1997). Consequently, subjective and objective measures of presence during game playing can give us many insights on the nature of game experience and the underlying mechanisms of how game playing affects game players' attitudes, cognition, and behaviors. A recent study (Lee, Jin, Park, & Kang, 2005) clearly showed the benefits of measuring presence in computer game research.

Finally, the effects of new game interfaces (e.g., Nintendo Wii, Sony PlayStation Eyetoy, DDR (Dance Dance Revolution) Pad), devices (e.g., mobile game devices, PlayStation Portable, Nintendo DS), and technologies (e.g., haptic technologies, 3D graphics) have hardly been examined in the current literature. More than other traditional media experiences, computer gaming experiences are critically affected by technological factors. For example, for the same game, game players might have qualitatively different experiences depending on particular interfaces (e.g., game pad vs. keyboard), devices (e.g., PSP vs. PS2), and technologies (14 inch screen vs. 21 inch screen) that they used while playing the game. Technological factors will also significantly alter possible effects of game playing. For example, violent games played on a small screen with bad audio quality have minimal effects on game players' physiological arousal (Ballard & West, 1996) and aggressive thoughts (Anderson & Dill, 2000) compared with the same game played on a large screen with high fidelity audio. The existing game literature predominantly focuses on the effects of game content factors (e.g., violence, education). With rapid development of game technologies, however, equal attention should be paid to the effects of game technology factors.

References

American Medical Association. (2007). Featured report: Emotional and behavioral effects of computer games and Internet overuse. Retrieved July 22, 2007, from http://www.ama-assn.org/ama/pub/category/17694.html

Anderson, C. A. (2004). An update on the effects of playing violent computer games. *Journal of Adolescence, 27*, 113–122.

Anderson, C. A., & Bushman, B. J. (2001). Effects of violent computer games on aggressive behavior, aggressive cognition, aggressive affect, physiological arousal, and prosocial behavior: A meta-analytical review of the scientific literature. *Psychological Science, 12*, 353–359.

Anderson, C. A., & Bushman, B. J. (2002). Human aggression. *Annual Review of Psychology, 53*, 27–51.

Anderson, C. A., Carnagey, N. L., Flanagan, M., Benjamin, A. J., Eubanks, J., & Valentine, J. C. (2004). Violent computer games: Specific effects of violent content on aggressive thoughts and behavior. *Advances in Experimental Social Psychology, 36*, 199–249.

Anderson, C. A., & Dill, K. E. (2000). Video games and aggressive thoughts, feelings, and behavior in the laboratory and in life. *Journal of Personality and Social Psychology, 78*, 772–790.

Anderson, C. A., Gentile, D. A., & Buckley, K. E. (2007). *Violent computer game effects on children and adolescents: Theory, research, and public policy*. New York: Oxford University Press.

Anderson, C. A., & Murphy, C. R. (2003). Violent computer games and aggressive behavior in young women. *Aggressive Behavior, 29*, 423–429.

Baldaro, B., Tuozzi, G., Codispoti, M., Montebarocci, O., Barbagli, F., Trombini, E., & Rossi, N. (2004). Aggressive and non-violent videogames: Short-term psychological and cardiovascular effects on habitual players. *Stress and Health, 20*, 203–208.

Ballard, M. E., & West, J. R. (1996). Mortal Kombat (tm): The effects of violent videogame play on males' hostility and cardiovascular responding. *Journal of Applied Social Psychology, 26*, 717–730.

Bandura, A. (1973). *Aggression: A social learning theory analysis*. Englewood Cliffs, NJ: Prentice-Hall.

Bartholow, B. D., & Anderson, C. A. (2002). Examining the effects of violent computer games on aggressive behavior: Potential sex differences. *Journal of Experimental Social Psychology, 38*, 283–290.

Berkowitz, L. (1984). Some effects of thoughts on anti- and prosocial influences of media events: A cognitive-neoassociation analysis. *Psychological Bulletin, 95*, 410–427.

Brady, S. S., & Matthews, K. A. (2006). Effects of media violence on health-related outcomes among young men. *Archives of Pediatrics & Adolescent Medicine, 160*, 341–347.

Brown, S. J., Lieberman, D. A., Gemeny, B. A., Fan, Y. C., Wilson, D. M., & Pasta, D. J. (1997). Educational computer game for juvenile diabetes: Results of a controlled trial. *Medical Informatics, 22*, 77–89.

Buchman, D., & Funk, J. B. (1996). Video and computer games in the '90s: Children report time commitment and game preference. *Children Today, 31*, 12–15.

Bushman, B. J., & Anderson, C. A. (2002). Violent computer games and hostile expectations: A test of the General Aggression Model. *Personality and Social Psychology Bulletin, 28*, 1679–1686.

Carnagey, N. L., & Anderson, C. A. (2005). The effects of reward and punishment in violent computer games on aggressive affect, cognition, and behavior. *Psychological Science, 16*, 882–889.

Carnagey, N. L., Anderson, C. A., & Bushman, B. J. (2007). The effect of computer game violence on physiological desensitization to real-life violence. *Journal of Experimental Social Psychology, 43*, 489–496.

Choi, D., & Kim, J. (2004). Why people continue to play online games: In search of critical design factors to increase customer loyalty to online contents. *CyberPsychology & Behavior, 7*, 11–24.

Chua, A. Y. K. (2005). The design and implementation of a simulation game for teaching knowledge management. *Journal of the American Society for Information Science and Technology, 56*, 1207–1216.

Clark, S., & Smith, G. B. (2004). Outbreak!: Teaching clinical and diagnostic microbiology methodologies with an interactive online game. *Journal of College Science Teaching, 34*, 30–33.

Cole, S. W., Kato, P. M., Marin-Bowling, V. M., Dahl, G. V., & Pollock, B. H. (2006). Clinical trial of Re-Mission: A computer game for young people with cancer. *Cyberpsychology & Behavior, 9*, 665–666.

Coleman, D. S. (2001). PC gaming and simulation supports training. *Proceedings of United States Naval Institute, 127*, 73–75.

de Lisi, R., & Wolford, J. L. (2002). Improving children's mental rotation accuracy with computer game playing. *The Journal of Genetic Psychology, 163*, 272–282.

Delwiche, A. (2006). Massively multiplayer online games (MMOs) in the new media classroom. *Educational Technology & Society, 9*, 160–172.

Deselms, J., & Altman, J. (2003). Immediate and prolonged effects of videogame violence. *Journal of Applied Social Psychology, 33*, 1553–1563.

Dodge, K. A., & Crick, N. R. (1990). Social information-processing bases of aggressive behavior in children. *Personality and Social Psychology Bulletin, 16*, 8–22.

Entertainment Software Association. (2007). *Top ten industry facts*. Retrieved August 22, 2007, from http://www.theesa.com/facts/top_10_facts.php

Faiola, A. (2006, May 27). When escape seems just a mouse-click away. *Washington Post*. Retrieved July 22, 2007, from http://www.washingtonpost.com/wp-dyn/content/article/2006/05/26/AR2006052601960_pf.html

Freedman, J. (2002). *Media violence and its effect on aggression: Assessing the scientific evidence*. Toronto, Canada: University of Toronto Press.

Funatsuka, M., Fujita, M., Shirakawa, S., Oguni, H., & Osawa, M. (2001). Study on photo-pattern sensitivity in patients with electronic screen game-induced seizures (ESGS): Effects of spatial resolution, brightness, and pattern movement. *Epilepsia, 42*, 1185–1197.

Funk, J. B., Baldacci, H. B., Pasold, T., & Baumgardner, J. (2004). Violence exposure in real-life, computer games, television, movies, and the Internet: Is there desensitization? *Journal of Adolescence, 27*, 23–29.

Gee, J. P. (2003). *What computer games have to teach us about learning and literacy*. New York: Palgrave Macmillan.

Geen, R. G. (1990). *Human aggression*. Pacific Grove, CA: McGraw Hill.

Gentile, D. A., Lynch, P. J., Linder, J. R., & Walsh, D. A. (2004). The effects of violent computer game habits on adolescent hostility, aggressive behaviors, and school performance. *Journal of Adolescence, 27*, 5–22.

Goodman, D., Bradley, N. L., Paras, B., Williamson, I. J., & Bizzochi, J. (2006). Video gaming promotes concussion knowledge acquisition in youth hockey players. *Journal of Adolescence, 29*, 351–360.

Greenfield, P. M., Brannon, G., & Lohr, D. (1994). Two-dimensional representation of movement through three-dimensional space: The role of computer game expertise. *Journal of Applied Developmental Psychology, 1*, 87–103.

Griffiths, M. D. (2000). Computer game violence and aggression: Comments on "Computer game playing and its relations with aggressive and prosocial behavior" by O. Wiegman and E. G. M. van Schie. *British Journal of Social Psychology, 39*, 147–149 (Part 1).

Griffiths, M. D., & Dancaster, I. (1995). The effect of Type A personality on physiological arousal while playing computer games. *Addictive Behaviors, 20*, 543–548.

Griffiths, M. D., & Hunt, N. (1998). Dependence on computer games by adolescents. *Psychological Reports, 82*, 475–480.

Grüsser, S. M., Thalemann, R., & Griffiths, M. D. (2007). Excessive computer game playing: Evidence for addiction and aggression? *CyberPsychology & Behavior, 10*, 290–292.

Harris Interactive. (2007, April 2). Computer game addiction: Is it real? Retrieved July 22, 2007, from http://www.harrisinteractive.com/news/allnewsbydate.asp?NewsID=1196

Holbrook, M. B., Chestnut, R. W., Oliva, T. A., & Greenleaf, E. A. (1984). Play as a consumption experience: The roles of emotions, performance, and personality in the enjoyment of games. *Journal of Consumer Research, 11*, 728–739.

Homer, C., Susskind, O., Alpert, H. R., Owusu, C., Schneider, L., Rappaport, L. A., et al. (2000). An evaluation of an innovative multimedia educational software program for asthma management: Report of a randomized, controlled trial. *Pediatrics, 106*, 210–215.

Honebein, P. C., Carr, A., & Duffy, T. (1993). The effects of modeling to aid problem solving in computer-based learning environments. In M. R. Simonson & K. Abu-Omar (Eds.), *Annual proceedings of selected research and development presentations at the national convention of the Association for Educational Communications and Technology* (pp. 373–406). Bloomington, IN: Association for Educational Communications and Technology.

Hoogeweegen, M. R., van Liere, D. W., Vervest, P. H. M., van der Meijden, L. H., & de Lepper, I. (2006). Strategizing for mass customization by playing the business networking game. *Decision Support Systems, 42*, 1402–1412.

Huesmann, L. R. (1986). Psychological processes promoting the relation between exposure to media violence and aggressive behavior by the viewer. *Journal of Social Issues, 42*, 125–139.

Huesmann, L. R., & Taylor, L. D. (2006). The role of media violence in violent behavior. *Annual Review of Public Health, 27*, 393–415.

Huss, K., Winkelstein, M., Nanda, J., Naumann, P. L., Sloand, E. D., & Huss, R. W. (2003). Computer game for inner-city children does not improve asthma outcomes. *Journal of Pediatric Health Care, 17*, 72–78.

Interactive Digital Software Association. (2000). *Fast facts about the consumer* [Press release]. No location: Author. Retrieved September 05, 2006, from http://www.idsa.com

Jenkins, H. (2002). Game theory. *Technology Review, 29*, 1–3.

Kiesler, S., Sproull, L., & Eccles, J. S. (1983). Second class citizens. *Psychology Today, 17*, 41–48.

Kovalik, D. L., & Kovalik, L. M. (2002). Language learning simulation: A Piagetian perspective. *Simulation & Gaming, 33*, 345.

Krahé, B., & Möller, I. (2004). Playing violent electronic games, hostile attributional style, and aggression-related norms in German adolescents. *Journal of Adolescence, 27*, 53–69.

Lee, K. M. (2004). Presence, explicated. *Communication Theory, 14*, 27–50.

Lee, K. M., Jin, S., Park, N., & Kang, S. (2005 May). *Effects of narrative on feelings of presence in computer-game playing*. Paper presented at the Annual Conference of the International Communication Association (ICA), New York.

Lee, K. M., & Peng, W. (2006). What do we know about social and psychological effects of computer games? A comprehensive review of the current literature. In P. Vorderer & J. Bryant (Eds.), *Playing computer games: Motives, responses, and consequences* (pp. 327–345). Mahwah, NJ: Erlbaum.

Lengwiler, Y. (2004). A monetary policy simulation game. *Journal of Economic Education, 35*, 175–183.

Lieberman, D. A. (2001). Management of chronic pediatric diseases with interactive health games: Theory and research findings. *Journal of Ambulatory Care Management, 24*, 26–38.

Lombard, M., & Ditton, T. B. (1997). At the heart of it all: The concept of presence. *Journal of*

Computer-Mediated Communication, 13(3). Retrieved September 22, 2006, from http://www.ascusc.org/jcmc/vol3/issue2/lombard.html

Los Angeles Times. (2007, June 25). AMA may identify excessive computer game play as addiction. Retrieved July 20, 2007, from http://www.latimes.com/business/la-fi-games25jun25,1,3023782.story?coll=la-headlines-business&ctrack=1&cset=true

Mann, B. D., Eidelson, B. M., Fukuchi, S. G., Nissman, S. A., Robertson, S., & Jardines, L. (2002). The development of an interactive game-based tool for learning surgical management algorithms via computer. *American Journal of Surgery*, *183*, 305–308.

Mayer, R. E., Mautone, P., & Prothero, W. (2002). Pictorial aids for learning by doing in a multimedia geology simulation game. *Journal of Educational Psychology*, *94*, 171–185.

McClure, R. F. (1985). Age and video game playing. *Perceptual and Motor Skills*, *61*, 285–286.

McClure, R. F., & Mears, F. G. (1984). Video game players: Personality characteristics and demographic variables. *Psychological Reports*, *55*, 271–276.

Ng, B. D., & Wiemer-Hastings, P. (2005). Addiction to the Internet and online gaming. *CyberPsychology & Behavior*, *8*, 110–113.

Office of the Surgeon General (2001). *Youth violence: A report of the Surgeon General*. US Department of Health and Human Services.

Olson, C. K. (2004). Media violence research and youth violence data: Why do they conflict? *Academic Psychiatry*, *28*, 144–150.

Palmgreen, P. (1984). Uses and gratifications: A theoretical perspective. *Communication Yearbook*, 8, 20–55.

Patel, A., Schieble, T., Davidson, M., Tran, M. C. J., Schoenberg, C., Delphin, E., et al. (2006). Distraction with a hand-held computer game reduces pediatric preoperative anxiety. *Pediatric Anesthesia*, *16*, 1019–1027.

Peng, W. (in press). Is a computer game an effective medium for health promotion? Design and evaluation of the RightWay Cafe game to promote a healthy diet for young adults. *Health Communication*.

Peng, W., Liu, M., & Mou, Y. (2008). Do aggressive people play violent computer games in a more aggressive way? Individual difference and idiosyncratic game playing experience. *CyberPsychology & Behavior*, *11*, 157–161.

Phillips, C. A., Rolls, S., Rouse, A., & Griffiths, M. D. (1995). Home video game playing in schoolchildren: A study of incidence and patterns of play. *Journal of Adolescence*, *18*, 687–691.

Pillay, H. (2003). An investigation of cognitive processes engaged in by recreational computer game players: Implications for skills of the future. *Journal of Research on Technology in Education*, *34*, 336–349.

Poole, S. (2000). *Trigger happy: Videogames and the entertainment revolution*. New York: Arcade Publishing.

Pope, A. T., & Bogart, E. H. (1996). Extended attention span training system: Computer game neurotherapy for attention deficit disorder. *Child Study Journal*, *26*, 39–50.

PricewaterhouseCoopers. (2006). Global entertainment and media outlook: 2006–2010. Retrieved May 23, 2007, from http://www.gamasutra.com/php-bin/news_index.php?story=9793

Randel, J. M., Morris, B. A., & Wetzel, C. D. (1992). The effectiveness of games for educational purposes: A review of recent research. *Simulation & Gaming*, *23*, 261–276.

Rassin, M. Gutman, Y. & Silner, D. (2004). Developing a computer game to prepare children for surgery. *AORN Journal*, *80*, 1099–1102.

Rubin, A. M. (2002). The uses-and-gratifications perspective of media effect. In J. Bryant & D. Zillmann (Eds.), *Media effects: Advances in theory and research* (pp. 525–548). Mahwah, NJ: Erlbaum.

Rule, B. K., & Ferguson, T. J. (1986). The effects of media violence on attitude, emotions, and cognitions. *Journal of Social Issues*, *42*, 29–50.

Sherry, J. (2001). The effects of violent computer games on aggression: A meta-analysis. *Human Communication Research*, *27*, 409–431.

Silverman, B. G., Holmes, J., Kimmel, S., Branas, C., Ivins, D., Weaver, R., et al. (2001). Modeling emotion and behavior in animated personas to facilitate human behavior change: The case of the HEART-SENSE game. *Health Care Management Science, 4*, 213–228.

Slater, M. D., Henry, K. L., Swaim, R. C., & Anderson, L. L. (2003). Violent media content and aggressiveness in adolescents: A downward spiral model. *Communication Research, 30*, 713–736.

Takahashi, D. (2002, October 2). Video game industry sees possible slow down. *The Mercury News*. Retrieved February 10, 2007 from http://www.siliconvalley.com/mld/siliconvalley/business/technology/ personal_technology/4201854.htm.

Thomas, R., Cahill, J., & Santilli, L. (1997). Using an interactive computer game to increase skill and self-efficacy regarding safer sex negotiation: Field test results. *Health Education & Behavior, 24*, 71–86.

van Eck, R. (2006). Digital game-based learning: It's not just the digital natives who are restless. *EDUCAUSE Review, 41*, 17–30.

van Eck, R., & Dempsey, J. (2002). The effect of competition and contextualized advisement on the transfer of mathematics skills in a computer-based instructional simulation game. *Etr&D-Educational Technology Research and Development, 50*, 23–41.

Vogel, J. J., Vogel, D. S., Cannon-Bowers, J., Bowers, C. A., Muse, K., & Wright, M. (2006). Computer gaming and interactive simulations for learning: A meta-analysis. *Journal of Educational Computing Research, 34*, 229–243.

Wan, C-S., & Chiou, W-B. (2006). Psychological motives and online games addiction: A test of flow theory and humanistic needs theory for Taiwanese adolescents. *CyberPsychology & Behavior, 9*, 317–324.

Williams, D., & Skoric, M. (2005). Internet fantasy violence: A test of aggression on an online game. *Communication Monographs, 72*, 217–233.

Zillmann, D. (1983). Arousal and aggression. In R. Geen & E. Donnerstein (Eds.), *Aggression: Theoretical and empirical reviews. Vol. 1* (pp. 75–102). New York: Academic Press.

Zillmann, D., & Bryant, J. (1985). *Selective exposure to communication*. Mahwah, NJ: Erlbaum.

26

EFFECTS OF THE INTERNET

Carolyn A. Lin
University of Connecticut

BACKGROUND

Today 70% of American adults are Internet users, according to a national survey conducted during the last month of 2006 (Pew/Internet, 2007a, 2007b). Nonetheless, the term Internet did not become a household word in our culture until America Online (an Internet service provider) and Netscape (a browser service) helped popularize the hypertext-driven World Wide Web (WWW) during the mid-1990s. Prior to these pioneering attempts to commercialize the Internet-use phenomenon in the form in which it is known today, various types of non-hypertext-based Internet networks had existed since the late 1970s and the early 1980s.

Examples of these different forms of precursory Internet services included the Bulletin Board Service (BBS), Usenet (USEr NETwork), and Bitnet (Because It's Time Network), which were primarily used by researchers, universities, or technocrats who enjoyed various text-based newsgroup discussions and email exchanges in a non-centralized network environment. Usenet remains a widely used newsgroup listing and posting service today. The next generation of prototypical Internet services incorporated the technology of graphical user interfaces (GUIs) during the mid-1980s and the mid-1990s. Several commercially launched services, including ViewTron, Prodigy, CompuServ, Genie, and America Online, all achieved some level of commercial success. Only America Online (AOL) remains today as a full-fledged Internet service provider, due to its innovative monthly-fee subscription business model, which proved more successful than the hourly-fee model (adopted by its competitors back then).

Only a decade later, Internet penetration has reached beyond a critical mass in the U.S. It has also become a springboard for developing diversified software applications to change and improve the ways that we use this dynamic medium. These never-ending endeavors to maximize the utilities of Internet technology have led to continuous re-inventions of the way the medium is used and lasting influences on the lives of its users.

INTRODUCTION

To understand the effects of the Internet, it is helpful to examine what people do with the medium when they go online. A glance at the main search categories listed on the homepage of the dominant general search engines—including MSN, Yahoo, and AOL—show the following:

1 News and Weather
2 Entertainment (e.g., TV, movies, music, sports and games)
3 Travel and Tickets
4 Shopping and Products (e.g., automobiles, technology, gadgets and real estate)
5 Directory Information (e.g., residential and email addresses, phone numbers)
6 Careers and Jobs
7 Map and Directions (e.g., city guide)
8 Newsgroups, Chat Rooms, Blogs and Social Networks
9 Dating and Relationships
10 Finance and Investment
11 Advice and Answers (e.g., horoscope)
12 Health and Fitness
13 Lifestyle and Fashion
14 Email and Instant Messenger

Above and beyond these general search categories, the popularity of freelanced blogs (Lenhart & Fox, 2006) and videos posted by individual users on such outlets as YouTube is peaking (Madden, 2007). The hobby sites, including gambling and pornography, continue to attract a large and steady number of users (Griffith & Fox, 2007). The public also utilizes the Internet to search for information about institutions that are for profit and nonprofit, in addition to government Web sites (Horrigan, 2004). Institutions have capitalized the unique capabilities of the Internet to allow their employees to telework and to develop informatics systems to manage organizational tasks (Madden, 2007). Moreover, the Internet, much like the way it was used in its heyday, remains one the most important tools for scientific research and academic learning (Hitlin & Rainie, 2005). The digitization of library information and databases, along with the advent of online distance learning, have helped revolutionize the landscape of how students, teachers, and researchers alike access information and learn.

Table 26.1 broadly summarizes all of the online uses and activities presented above from an individual user's perspective rather than an institutional or organizational perspective.

THE EFFECTS OF ONLINE USE

Compared to other modes of mediated communication channels, the relative advantage of the Internet as a communication medium lies in its technology fluidity. This attribute enables its users to access, distribute, exchange and receive information in multimedia

Table 26.1 Individual Online Use Purposes and Activities

Context	*Activities*	
Social	Friends, Family, & Peers	Relationships & Social Networks
Work	Intranet Communication	Telework & Telecommuting
Play	Entertainment & Recreation	Lifestyle & Hobby
Surveillance	News & Information	Governments & Institutions
Commerce	Transacting Goods & Services	Financial Trades & Transactions
Advice	Questions & Answers	How-To & How Not-To

and multiplatform modalities—of which, some embody greater social presence and information cues—to allow them to multitask in a networked environment (Lin, 2003). For instance, an Internet user can simultaneously chat with a group of friends via instant messenger, reading the email from another friend via Facebook, playing a music video, posting a photo to share, displaying the product information about the new iPod, completing an assignment online, conversing via an Internet phone system, etc.

These fluid and versatile technology attributes of the Internet hence provide its users with better control over the access, creation, distribution and reception of information to and from other online users than any other mediated communication channel. The technical superiority of the Internet, when compared to other modes of communication, is rooted in the constant evolution and reinvention of its applications. As a case in point, one of the most original forms of Internet applications, Listserv, is still being updated on a periodic basis and remains in wide use today. The phenomenon of e-government is another good example where different levels of government have been able to improve its operational efficiencies by allowing citizens to access information and download documents to help facilitate and expedite their services (Jeffres & Lin, 2006).

Owing to the youth of the Internet medium, even with its high penetration ratio (Madden, 2007), empirical work examining the actual long-term social effects of the Internet remains limited. Nonetheless, research on how people use the Internet and the behavioral outcomes of their uses in more narrowly focused topics is available at various levels. To put forth a discussion of the multifaceted effects of the Internet on individuals and society, this chapter will discuss the following slate of topics—developed based on the topical categories of Table 26.1—that reflect individuals' Internet-use activities within the most common settings.

Socializing and Social Networking Context

When people go online to interact with others, their motivations, expectations, behavior, and interaction outcomes could differ from those of other modes of interpersonal communication such as face-to-face interactions. The two fundamental categories of online communication modalities—asynchronous and synchronous—each offer a different set of technical attributes that can enable online users to help reach their communication objectives and outcomes. Asynchronous online communication in a social context allows individual users to send messages directly to each other (e.g., emails) or post messages to a larger group of people (e.g., chatrooms or newsgroups). Synchronous online communication allows individual users to exchange messages in real time (e.g., instant messaging). Both asynchronous and synchronous online communication can involve Internet users who are strangers, acquaintances, friends, relatives, families, and/or co-workers.

CMC allows its users to engage in a communication environment with a reduced number of verbal and nonverbal cues, which is considered a hindrance for developing effective and meaningful interpersonal and relational communication by some (e.g., Burgoon et al., 2002; Cummings, Butler, & Kraut, 2002). Others don't view the lack of a full range of verbal and nonverbal cues as a strong deterrent for fostering meaningful and effective interpersonal communication and relations (Walther, Loh, & Granka, 2005; Walther & Parks, 2002). Walther (1996), for instance, proposed a hyperpersonal communication perspective, which asserted that individuals have the flexibility of constructing and deploying a selective and optimal self-presentation to the receiver. Whether the use of CMC can enable the formation of a meaningful social relationship between individuals depends on how one defines such a relationship. For instance, the expectations and the effects of CMC between individuals could differ drastically between communicators in a weak-tie network (e.g., online support groups) and a close-tie network (e.g., friends) interaction setting.

Re-creating My True Self?

In the context of online communication involving strangers, the nature of these social exchanges is characterized by either a one-on-one or one-to-many communication scenario. The reduced-cues social interaction is appealing to individuals who don't necessarily wish or feel comfortable to socialize in a face-to-face setting (McKenna, Green, & Gleason, 2002). According to McKenna and Bargh (1999, 2000), in face-to-face communication, a number of "gating issues" could prevent an individual from experiencing or achieving a successful communication outcome; these gating issues can include anxiety, oral communication skills, shyness, physical characteristics, etc.

Sheeks and Birchmeier (2007), for instance, found that people who are shy but wish to be social were able to develop a closer and more satisfactory relationship with others online, compared to those who are characterized by high shyness/low sociability, low shyness/high sociability or low shyness/low sociability. Nonetheless, participants' true self-expression was not predictive of the formation of these social relationships. McKenna, Green, and Gleason's (2002) finding suggests that only when online relationships were built on shared interests or sincere disclosure of one's true self, then a healthy and perhaps lasting relationship could potentially flourish.

From the perspective of allowing individuals in society to find a way to become connected in society, the Internet appears to have a positive effect in its facilitator role. But when individuals hide behind the shield provided by the Internet by putting up an idealized self-identity to form relationships with others, this virtual social connection could also help reinforce the psychological rewards associated with the identification with this unreal self-image. This misdirected self-image may lead to negative behavioral outcomes such as Internet infidelity, which has been recognized as a source of marital distress and divorce (Barak & Fisher, 2002; Hertlein & Piercy, 2006).

According to Shouten (1991, p. 413), an individual's identity is the "cognitive and affective understanding of who and what we are." From the perspective of symbolic interaction, an individual's identity is also shaped by the feedback and evaluation provided by others (Blumer, 1969; Solomon, 1983). Schau and Gilly (2003) suggested that when consumers post information about themselves online, the postings are aimed at the discovery of one's self-identity as much as the communication of such identity to others. In the context of online dating, self-identity re-creation can provide individuals with an opportunity to establish an initial relationship with each other. When this online relationship leads to an offline relationship, the issue of how enduring the re-created self-identity may last or may change one's perception about oneself remains largely unknown (Yurchisin, Watchravesringkan, & McCabe, 2005). Nonetheless, the behavior of identity re-creation is popular, even though the positive outcomes of forming a long-term relationship or actual matchmaking offline remain sporadic at best (Frost & Ariely, 2004).

Post and Reach Someone?

In the one-to-many and many-to-many modality of social networking with strangers, the online users typically wish to exchange ideas, knowledge and opinions with others.

The most common modalities of online social networking involve topic-specific news groups or social support groups. The breadth and depth of the news group online is too large for this chapter to explore fully. A list of newsgroup categories that appears on Yahoo (Yahoo! Inc., 2007)—encompassing business and finance, computers and Internet, cultures and community, entertainment and art, family and home, games, government and politics, health and wellness, hobbies and crafts, music, recreation and sports, regional, religion and beliefs, romance and relationships, schools and education, and science—indicates that these news group topics touch upon every aspect of our daily life.

Consistent with the findings regarding establishing individual identity for self-discovery and social acceptance in a one-on-one interaction setting online, the participation in newsgroup interactions was also found to have the benefits of allowing individuals to find group-identification and to increase their self-esteem (Deaux, 1996; Ethier & Deaux, 1994). The ability of individuals to share their ideas, opinions, knowledge, inner thoughts and perhaps an idealized self-image in an uninhibited manner, due to the anonymous nature of these newsgroups, provides these individuals a safe outlet to feel socially connected and to establish themselves as part of a meaningful community in society. Parks and Floyd's (1995) study revealed that people who participated in Internet newsgroups were able to form quality social relationships similar to those offline relationships developed in an in-person setting.

This is especially true with the marginalized population (McKenna & Bargh, 1998), including those with physical limitations such as the hearing-impaired (Bat-Chava, 1994), as participating in these news groups allows these socially disenfranchised individuals to have an outlet for their self identity (true or re-created) to be recognized and accepted, in addition to letting their opinions be heard. These socially isolated individuals may include those who perceive themselves as having stigmatized identities due to their physical appearance (e.g., overweight), physical impediments (e.g., stuttering), physical disabilities (e.g., visually impaired), sexual orientation (e.g., homosexuality), medical conditions (e.g., HIV positive), mental state (e.g., depression), fringe political beliefs, etc.

Can You Feel What I Feel?

Whether individuals feel socially stigmatized or not, seeking social support online is an important aspect of the newsgroup functions. The question of the effects of online support via a weak social-tie network in increasing support-seekers' well-being appears to depend on the social circumstances and the nature of the support issues at stake. Davison, Pennebaker, and Dickerson (2000) conducted a comprehensive comparison of disease categories discussed between face-to-face and online support groups, based on the theory of social comparison (Festinger, 1954). Their findings indicate that, while poorly understood and somewhat overlooked illness conditions were stronger motivators for online-line support seeking, individuals whose illnesses—due to their nature (e.g., AIDs) or the treatment outcomes (e.g., mastectomy)—made them face embarrassment or social stigmatization were also more inclined to seek online support.

Other studies have found that stigmatization was not necessarily the reason for seeking online social support. People may seek online support resources to exert control over their ability to manage their social support needs and outcomes. For instance, a study of diabetic individuals who sought peer support online to help manage their conditions (e.g., dietary control) found such online peer-discussion activity resulted in improved physiological, behavioral, and mental health, and that such activity was as effective as conventional diabetes management (McKay et al., 2002). Another study examining seniors who used SeniorNet and other online support mechanisms tailored for seniors indicated that these seniors reported lower perceived stress in their lives (Wright, 2000).

Online breast-cancer peer-discussion groups were also found to be beneficial to women who had more coping difficulty or received low support from their partners or health-care providers; such online support groups were discovered to be damaging to those women who had strong existing support (Helgeson, Cohen, Schulz, & Yasko, 2000). The authors (Helgeson et al., 2000) suspected that those women who had strong partner or physician support might have utilized the weak social-tie online-support group for advice and intimate discussion that they obtained to reevaluate the support that they had received from their strong social-tie network. These results seem to be consistent with Walther and Boyd's (2002) contention that social support provided by weak social-tie networks online could be more effective than face-to-face social support offered by members of a strong social-tie network, due to the anonymity, access to quality expertise, enhanced expressions of one's emotion, avoidance of embarrassment and lack of obligation to the support providers online. (For a detailed discussion of the Internet and health, see Chapter 21.)

Neither Lonely Nor Isolated?

In the first major field experiment that attempted to study the effects of Internet communication, Kraut et al. (1998) documented how individuals who engaged in communication via the Internet heavily were more socially isolated, lonely, and emotionally depressed. The study was criticized for the lack of a control group, control for external events, or statistical regression that might have confounded with the study's results (Gross, Juvonen, & Gable, 2002; Shapiro, 1999). A follow-up study conducted by Kraut et al. (2002) found that more sociable individuals benefited from socializing on the Internet more than less sociable individuals in a wide range of outcomes, including social involvement, psychological well-being, face-to-face communication, positive affects, and trust in people. Kraut and his colleagues attributed the discrepancies between the earlier and later study in part to the maturation process of computer and Internet use.

Other large-scale survey studies reported that Internet users are not any more socially isolated than non-Internet users. For instance, Dimaggio, Hargittai, Neuman and Robinson (2001) found that people often have expanded social networks as a result of their Internet use. Howard, Raine, and Jones (2001) likewise agreed that the Internet allowed people to extend their social networks by staying in touch with family and friends across distance and time zones. Wellman, Quan Hasse, Witte, and Hampton (2001) contend that heavy Internet users use email to stay connected with people and maintain longer-distance relationships, rather than as a substitute for in-person interpersonal or telephone contact.

Entertainment and Play Context

The Internet, undoubtedly, has become a major source for ready access to entertainment content. This is evidenced by a number of large-scale national studies that have indicated that accessing entertainment-oriented text, graphics, photo images, audio, and audiovisual content—including celebrity news/gossip, fashion, music, sports, hobbies, television programs, and/or films via the Internet—is as common as via the traditional mass media (e.g., Madden & Rainie, 2005; Pew/Internet, 2007a, 2007b). Studies that have examined the social effects of Internet entertainment use purposes have tended to explore individuals' evaluation associated with their use experience and affective outcomes. This body of work is often tied to the media programming, consumer advertising and marketing context.

Uses and Gratifications

The Internet is also regarded as an additional delivery modality and an auxiliary channel for traditional entertainment and media services, in addition to being an alternative outlet for distributing independently produced media content. Individuals who seek entertainment experience from media content online are said to be motivated by a set of cognitive and affective stimulation needs that are similar to those that motivate traditional media use, from the uses and gratifications perspective (Lin, 2001). Applying the uses and gratifications perspective to examine the hedonic "play" aspect (Stephenson, 1988) of Internet media use as a functional alternative to television viewing, Ferguson and Perse (2000) found that people used the Internet primarily to be entertained and to pass time, but not necessarily to become relaxed or gain companionship. Other researchers found relaxation and escape (Parker & Plank, 2000), entertainment, diversion, companionship, surveillance, learning, and interpersonal communication (Lin, 1999) were the reported gratification outcomes for Internet use.

Some have criticized the explanations of psychological outcomes related to Internet use provided by the uses and gratifications perspective as theoretically vague and overly broad (e.g., Knobloch, Carpentier, & Zillmann, 2003; Reagan & Lee, 2007). Theoretical weaknesses notwithstanding, the effects of using the Internet for entertainment or play, as reported by these uses and gratification studies, imply both a positive and negative outcome for the Internet users in terms of receiving cognitive stimulation and affective diversion/escape versus developing potential dependency on the Internet for such psychological gratifications. Applying the uses and gratifications approach as the baseline for exploring dependency on Internet use, Song, LaRose, Eastin, and Lin (2004) identified several dimensions of gratification factors validated in past studies (e.g., Charney & Greenberg, 2002) that are relevant to the triggering of an initial phase of Internet addiction-like use pattern. They maintained that deficient control over compulsive pursuit of these gratification dimensions in a habitual form can transit into uncontrolled impulsive use of the Internet, which can lead to potential pathological Internet use or Internet addiction.

The term "Internet addict" has been adopted by some researchers (e.g., Brenner, 1997; Griffiths, 2000; Young, 1996), which implies a dependency on an activity (or a substance). Withdrawal of this stimulus can generate a mental and physical state that meets the clinical definition of addiction (e.g., withdrawal symptoms), which can carry severe negative psychological and/or physiological consequences. Other researchers have disputed the notion of Internet addiction and regarded excessive use of the Internet as a form of impulsive-control disorder (e.g., LaRose & Eastin, 2002). Terms such as "pathological Internet use" (Davis, 2001; Morahan-Martin & Schumacher, 2000; Young, 1996) and "problematic Internet use" (Caplan, 2002; Shapira et al., 2000) have been utilized to describe this minor form of compulsive behavior. Davis (2001), for instance, considered generalized pathological Internet use—or various forms of maladaptive use of the Internet (e.g., compulsive use of chat rooms or videogames)—as being conceptually different from specific pathological Internet use, which is a form of maladaptive behavior irrespective of the medium (e.g., compulsive use of pornography or gambling online).

LaRose, Lin, and Eastin (2003), in particular, proposed treating such compulsive behavior as a reflection of "deficient self-regulation" of one's impulses—a concept developed based on Bandura's (1991) social cognitive theory—to move the conceptualization of this behavior away from the traditional "disease" or "addiction" model. They further contended that this type of deficient self-regulation fits within the pre-transitional phase, where an individual's compulsive behavior has not yet turned into a problematic dysphoric state which can later lead to the addictive outcome. The concept of deficient self-regulation or low self-control may also be useful in explaining other types of impulsive and compulsive use of the Internet for hedonic gratifications or play purposes—reinforced by the process of operant conditioning—such as pornography (Buzzell, Foss, & Middleton, 2006), online shopping (Kim & LaRose, 2004), and gambling (Johansson & Gotestam, 2004).

Immersed or Addicted?

Similar to the experience of gaining cognitive stimulation and affective release from accessing entertainment or escape oriented content on the Internet, individuals also go online to play videogames to seek similar types of psychological gratifications. The biggest distinction between "interacting" with the entertainment/escape oriented content online and the videogames is that interacting with one's favorite media personalities or celebrities is often limited in a para-social setting, but interacting with other game characters or game players tends to be more "immersed" due to various role-playing opportunities. These role-playing games often involve a number of players who may or may not come from one's close-tie networks. In fact, the most popular multiplayer games (e.g., Diablo or Warcraft) often involve players from around the world.

Multiplayer online role-playing games (MMORPGs) or "heroinware" can perform three social functions, including mass entertainment content, competitive role-playing in a group setting, and social networking. There are several perspectives regarding the effects of these socially and mentally immersive games. One view considers that the most serious and devoted players of videogames display a tendency to displace in-person social interactions with family, friends and others with virtual social interactions. This substitution of online social reality for offline social reality is said to be the culprit for developing Internet addicts. Nonetheless, the overwhelming majority of these players don't seem to exhibit any real negative psychological reactions when they are unable to play the game, compared to about 12% of hard-core anti-social players who strongly prefer virtual over real-world social interactions and may be in danger of evolving into the so-called "Internet addictions" (Ng & Wiemer-Hastings, 2005; Grüsser, Thalemann, & Griffiths, 2007).

Aside from the concern associated with certain players' potentially addictive behavior, there is also a potential problem related to players utilizing these games to enter into a fantasy world—where they assume a different personal identity (e.g., a hero, a villain) to act out various role-playing behaviors (e.g., super-human strength, violence)—that they otherwise would or could not engage in or perform in real life (Young, 1998). However, fascination with role-playing games does not necessarily have to imply addictive behavior. In competitive game playing, players are often driven by their competitive drive instead of potential pathology (e.g., Salguero & Morán, 2002) and the virtual game environment is viewed as a "transitional" space, whereas it allows the players to reflect their true and/or imagined self (Turkle, 1997). Game playing, much like other forms of entertainment uses of the Internet, also has a hedonic aspect.

In fact, the much-discussed potential increase of aggression among players of role-playing violent videogames has not been validated by empirical evidence. For instance, the first longitudinal study (William & Skoric, 2005) demonstrated that there was no relationship between the amount of time spent playing highly violent online videogames and the frequency of exhibiting aggressive behavior in the real world; there were also no differences found between the players and non-players in their level of aggression. Consider a parallel role-playing process that young children often experience. Most children regularly engage in role plays of and dressing up like their idolized heroes or villains (e.g., Superman or Darth Vader), yet few people are concerned about their psychological health.

Charlton and Danforth (2007) made a theoretical distinction between addictive game playing—which comprises such behavioral factors as conflict, behavioral salience, withdrawal, and relapse and reinstatement—and high-engagement styles of game playing, which reflects the game playing behavior of tolerance, euphoria and cognitive salience. Their work was an endeavor to conceptually differentiate the habit of game playing that falls into the clinically defined addictive state from the style of game playing that indicates a strong hedonic stimulation cognitive element.

As empirical work addressing the effects of videogame playing remains in its nascent stage, the American Medical Association (Mundell, 2007) declared that the time to include "Internet/video game addiction" in the next edition of *Diagnostic and Statistical Manual of Mental Disorders* has not yet arrived. With some researchers dismissing the term "Internet addictions" as being misleading, because it is the behavior that people perform on the Internet not the Internet medium itself that is the cause of addiction, the debate regarding the concept of Internet addiction continues.

Surveillance and Information Processing Context

The "true" 24-hour news cycle, which makes news information available to the public around the clock, could not have existed if it were not for the news and media industry's foray into their companion ancillary services online (Bucy, Gantz, & Wang, 2007). This process of disseminating news and information via the Web is different from that of the traditional media delivery methods. Whereas most of the news and information content is virtually free on the Internet, the same is not true with the traditional media. As an economic analysis of such media business models is not the focus of this chapter, the effects of this shifting media economic dynamics can be observed from how individuals access, process, and make use of the news and information that they obtain online in the offline environment.

Media Substitution or Supplementation?

The concept of media substitution, developed based on Lasswell's (1948) work on the potential displacement of radio by television as the dominant entertainment medium, asserts that the audience can change their media-use behavior by replacing the old with the new medium. Early work on media displacement addressed the dynamics of the VCR versus television viewing and movie-going (Childers & Krugman, 1987; Henke & Donahue, 1989; Lin, 1994). In the context of the Internet versus the news and information serviced by the offline media, while a meta-analysis suggested that the Internet news sources have displaced newspapers and network news outlets (Waldfogel, 2002), other studies found more mixed results (Busselle, Reagan, Pinkleton, & Jackson, 1999; Stempel, Hargrove, & Bernt, 2000).

According to Lin (1999), if a new medium is capable of providing its users "superior content, technical benefits and cost efficiency" (p. 24), then the media substitution mechanism could take place. Using these criteria as the baseline, it appears that the Internet news sources are not ready substitutes for offline news sources, as most Internet users still perceive the offline news sources as being more credible than online news sources (Flanagan & Metzer, 2000; Johnson & Kaye, 1998; Kim, Weaver, & Wilnat, 2002). Another study (Lin, Salwen, & Driscoll, 2005) concurs with these findings by reporting that the level of use or loyalty associated with offline news sources including newspapers, radio news, local TV news and cable news was a negative predictor of the displacement for each of these offline news outlets by online news sources.

Additional research also concludes that online media content is more likely to be utilized as a functional supplement to instead of a functional displacement of offline media content (e.g., Lin, 2001). The effects of these substitution or supplementation outcomes have strong implications for how individuals process and learn information. For instance, Eveland and Dunwoody (2002) indicated that a Web page has a very different content layout and structure compared to that of a newspaper page. As a Web page is organized in a nonlinear (or menu-driven) format to permit a nonlinear reading process, a newspaper page is constructed in a linear format to allow a continuous reading sequence.

News and Information Processing

Do individuals have a different way of processing news and information that they access from an offline news source and an online news outlet? The literature that addresses this question remains very limited at this stage of the online-news establishment evolution. According to Tewksbury and Althaus (2000), the focus on breaking news regardless of the social significance of the story nature and the less prominent display of public affairs stories online contributed to less recall of the latter. Tewksbury (2003) contended that the ease of selecting the menu-driven news content of interest online led the users to access stories of specific interest to them and read fewer important public affairs stories, hence bypassing the news flow that is strategically cued by an offline newspaper (e.g., story placement and priming effects).

Graber (2001) suggested that it is important to assess the knowledge structure in news learning and differentiate two types of information from which individuals may benefit when accessing news content. Denotative information, or a simple capturing of factual knowledge through "instinctive" senses, represents a simple absorption of the news content. Connotative information, or a more thoughtful form of information processing, reflects an integration of the different components of the absorbed information. Along the same line of theoretical reasoning, Lin and Salwen (2006) identified information scanning and information skimming as two different information processing approaches for news reading; while the former aims at grasping the news items by poring over the pages to learn the content, the latter focuses on glancing over selective news items via grazing over the pages. Their findings reveal that newspaper readers reported greater skimming activity when reading online news than non-newspaper readers and non-online news readers reported greater scanning activity when reading a newspaper than online news readers.

Eveland, Seo, and Marton (2000) also assessed the different cognitive styles of news information processing and found that the online news is more superior to both print and electronic news offline in structuring their election-related knowledge, in addition to being more conducive in producing accurate recall of such knowledge. Lowrey and Choi (2006) applied the cognitive flexibility theory, which asserts that hypermedia-delivered content—where the material is continuously rearranged from different conceptual views and can help improve information learning (cited in Spiro & Jehng, 1990, p. 171)—to examine how individuals learn from online news stories. Their findings indicate that news stories constructed in the format reflective of the non-linear and cognitive flexibility principles were more enjoyable, not as well understood as a news story, and not more burdensome on the readers' cognitive load.

Bloggers and Amateur Journalists

Cognitive flexibility aside, some Internet users have become active amateur journalists or Web content creators to regularly post their weblogs (blogs) in a textual, image, photographic, audio, and/or video format. The popular "YouTube" site, for example, could also be considered a place for sharing video blogs. Podcasting is another way for Internet content creators to webcast their audio blogs. The topics of blogs are not limited only to journalistic topics and are in fact as broad as newsgroup topics to include such domains as personal journals, opinions, voyeuristic observations, or gossip. The largest number of bloggers (37%) consider their blog content creation as expressing "personal life and experiences," followed by "politics and government" (11%) as a subject related to public-life issues (Lenhart & Fox, 2006).

If publishing a weblog is an example of self expression or a means of establishing one's identity through self dialogues in a public forum, it is useful to review Hermans's (1996, 2001) positioning theory on dialogical self, which asserts a decentralized self where the multiple "I" positions may engage in self dialogues with one another and its parallel socio-cultural worlds.

Likewise, Talamo and Ligorio (2001) identified how individuals construct their virtual identities through dynamic negotiations of dialogical processes with the self. Hevern (2004) considered personal blogs a reflection of constructing a dialogical self and a virtual identity in a threaded process that is composed of selective personal narratives and the reshaping of one's self-identity via multifaceted beliefs and positions.

As the blogging culture remains in its formative stage, little empirical research has been devoted to measure the actual effects of this Internet use behavior on individuals or society as a whole. The preliminary attempts to explicate this social phenomenon tend to focus on gaining a better understanding of the blogged content or the social functions of blogs on journalistic or political discourse. For instance, blogs have been regarded as a new means for individuals to bypass media gatekeepers to participate in public discourse of important political issues and campaigns in a forum that is open to all (Balnaves, Mayrhofer, & Shoesmith, 2004; Deuze, 2003; Williams, et al., 2005). This form of participatory media by amateur journalists challenges as well as supplements the established media as the sole holder of "truths" (Kahn & Kellner, 2004; Matheson, 2004) by breaking stories that were of interest to the public but were either neglected or not uncovered by the press. Some remain ambivalent about the effects of blogging on the journalistic scene, political discourse or social consequences, due to the free-wheeling nature of a blogosphere whose content is neither scrutinized nor accountable to any professional standard (Lawson-Borders & Kirk, 2005).

In essence, the Internet has offered an unprecedented opportunity for average citizens to produce their own freelance and free-form news reporting, documentaries, and commentaries. Gregson (1998) commented that online political chats, discussion boards wsgroups tend to generate sequential monologues instead of true discussion. s are less dismissive, as they consider online political communication to be an er of citizen engagement that can result in political knowledge gain and coordin- . activities that can address their collective concerns (e.g., Davis, 1999; Norris, 1998).

Even though it is too soon to draw any conclusions regarding the effects of weblogs on individuals, media, politics, and society, the blogging activity has added an avenue for public discourse that has proven to be effective in shaking up the political landscape from time to time. The most prominent recent examples include the blogs that recorded then Senator Trent Lott's and Senator George Allen's racist-sounding statements, which ended the former's Majority leadership post (Jensen, 2003) and led to the latter's reelection defeat (Aravosis, 2006). It is safe to say that the phenomenon of blogging is yet another prime example of how the Internet provides individuals with the technological freedom to make their voices heard in the virtual marketplace of ideas.

Civic and Institutional Communication Context

A tandem development alongside politically oriented blogging involves the government and citizens utilizing the Internet as a tool to communicate with each other. Terms such as e-citizen, e-government, or e-democracy are reflective of a desire of as well as a trend towards capitalizing on the versatilities of Internet technology to facilitate greater political participation in democracy and more active citizen engagement with the government. There are optimistic (e.g., Muhlberger, 2005; Tolbert & McNeal, 2003) as well as pessimistic (e.g., Brimber, 2000; Jennings & Zeitner, 2003) views on the promise that e-citizens and their e-government would hold for e-democracy (or e-governance).

It appears that the progress or the utility of e-government remains rudimentary in this phase of its growth curve. In particular, the usability and usefulness of the content on most government Websites are regarded as less than satisfactory, as these websites typically are over-laden with information that requires a very high literacy rate to comprehend and are embedded in information architectures that are difficult to navigate (Hart, Chaparro, & Halcomb, 2006). Parallel to this slow evolution is the still-limited reliable empirical evidence that could shed light on the effects of e-government and how e-government impacts e-democracy. The preliminary research on this topic tends to focus on the content of e-government and the uses of e-government by its citizens.

e-Citizens and e-Government

Despite the strong potential for the Internet to help cultivate a more integrated civic community and civil society that can bridge the gap between the government and its citizenry, Brimber (2000) reported that even political interests did not predict citizen involvement with government via the Web. This finding is not all surprising, as other studies have suggested that local governments have made little progress on e-government (Fletcher, Holden, & Norris, 2003; Moon, 2002). The lack of progress of local e-government is not fully unexpected, as local municipalities don't always possess the resources and expertise to fully develop their websites to meet their constituents' needs.

In light of the lack of clear mission found in the municipal Web sites studied, Musso, Weare, and Hale (2000) identified an entrepreneurial model to foster local economic development and quality of life improvement, in addition to a participatory model to better interest groups' access to the decision-making process and to strengthen social networks for improving public discourse. By expanding on Musso et al.'s (2000) work,

Jeffres and Lin (2006) proposed two parallel local e-government functions—institutional communication (or entrepreneurial model), community communication (or participatory model) and a third function—the mass communication function, reflective of the surveillance, coordination, socialization and entertainment function of the media (Lasswell, 1948; Lemert, 1984; Wright, 1986). Their analysis of the Web sites of the 50 largest U.S. cities revealed that municipal Web sites appear to have captured all three communication functions, with the largest number of links being aimed at providing two mass communication functions—"information surveillance" and "interaction coordination" services.

These two communication functions seem to be similar to the reasons why individuals sought civic engagement—online information seeking and interactive civic messaging—through the use of the Internet, as reported by Shah, Cho, Eveland, and Kwak (2005). In a similar vein, Thomas and Streib (2005) found that the majority of 827 Georgian residents accessed government Web sites for two reasons—getting information and doing business with the government (e.g., filing taxes, buying licenses); a minority of residents accessed these sites to participate in the democratic decision-making processes. In addition, politically partisan ideology was predictive of participation in e-democracy, contrary to Brimber's (2000) earlier finding.

Jensen, Danziger, and Venkatesh (2007) surveyed 1,003 respondents for their use of the Internet as cyber citizens by assessing their democratic engagement in contacting a public official in the local government, obtaining information about public meetings and participating in an online discussion about local politics. Their findings demonstrate that 26.5% of the respondents reported democratic participation and 43% of them did visit a local government Web site for purposes other than democratic engagement. Moreover, respondents' online democratic engagement is also related to contacting online political groups, planning a neighborhood event, and completing a transaction with a local government Web site—or political activities occurring within civil and cyber society—rather than social groups or community-oriented groups.

Instead of investigating the e-citizenry action, Taylor and Kent (2004) examined how Congressional offices engage in Internet-based communication with the public. They found that, while 94% of the 100 Congressional Web sites reviewed primarily function as a tool for providing information to the constituents and the media and 72% of the Congressional staff surveyed confirmed the function as such, "interactive" communication with the public is generally confined to the use of emails. Hence, the dialogic activity via the interactive Internet technology remains under developed and little utilized.

Outreach and External Organizational Communication

The concept of dialogue, as explicated by dialogic theory (Kent & Taylor, 2002; Pearce & Pearce, 2001), has been utilized to explain how organizations communicate with those individuals regarded as their respective internal and external stakeholders. This dialogic process could be particularly effective in producing beneficial results for the participating parties, when the parties are willing to immerse themselves in the co-presence of utterances and cognition to engender a shared willingness for communication and coordination of their action with each other (Riva & Galimberti, 1997).

Welch and Fulla (2005) contended that an organization's willingness to provide feedback opportunity to its constituents (receivers) is the key to facilitating two-way interactive dialogue, a phenomenon emulating McMillan and Huang's (2002) "real-time conversation" construct. Their study of a Web-based community-policing program, which offers updated community crime data to the residents and allows the residents to send email feedback and inquiries, found that this program helps create a shared interlocutory space to change the organizational structure within the police department. Granted responsiveness and structural changes stemming from this type of participatory process will vary depending on an institution's need for accountability and transparency to meet its missions and mandates. The integration of the traditional sender-receiver communication relationship between an institution and its constituency will nevertheless shift over time due to this virtual dialogic process.

These findings suggest that the Internet can be a useful outlet that enables organizations, including government, public, non-profit, or for-profit in their nature, to conduct interactive two-way dialogue with their respective publics about issues of importance to both—such as a national crisis. Hilse and Hoewner (1998) proposed four types of damage that the Internet could add to a crisis situation—reinforcing crisis, absurd crisis (due to the absurd theories and opinions circulated online), affecting crisis (via negative scrutiny) and competence crisis (due to online experts' capability to damage the corporation). Others also echo similar sentiment by pointing out how the Internet can expose the corporation to the public and the inability of the corporate to control the situation (Coombs, 1999; Wheeler, 2001). In light of the fact that a crisis can spread via the Internet quicker than an organization can construct their response, many organizations still choose not to take advantage or take control of the Internet to manage their crisis communication.

For example, Perry, Taylor, and Doerfel's study (2003) reported that 36% of the 50 large organizations experiencing national-level crises (within the 18-month study period) did not utilize the Internet for crisis management. Those organizations (64%) that did employ online crisis management techniques made use of two-way interactive features to communicate with the public (34%), real-time monitoring to provide timely updates (19%), and connecting links to provide others' perspectives (38%), in addition to multimedia presentations (e.g., audio or video recordings). Conway, Ward, Lewis, and Bernhardt's study (2007) also suggests that only 50% of the corporations investigated in their sample integrate the Internet into their crisis communication plan and 48% engage in online monitoring on an irregular basis. The authors surmised that limitations in financial and human resources might be the reason for the lack of proactive management of the Internet's crisis potential.

Telework and Internal Organizational Communication

While organizations can capitalize on the Internet's ubiquity to communicate with their external stakeholders, the Internet can also be "customized" to become an Intranet to serve an organization's internal communication needs. Holtz (2006), for instance, emphasized the importance of using proven effective Web-based Intranet channels for conducting internal corporate dialogue; he recommended the use of: (1) RSS (or really simple syndication) to enable automatic receipt of corporate Web content via the Intranet's "push" technology; (2) (blogs) to open up a dialogue between the CEO and employees to share industry/corporate news or to brainstorm corporate strategies; (3) wiki to create and edit content relevant to research, project management, etc.; (4) podcasting to disseminate internal discussions or updates via the PC or portable digital media players; and (5) social tagging (or folksonomies) to allow easy sharing of content tags between employees to help each other find the important content of interest.

Successful employment of Web-based technology in organizational communication, however, may depend on the nature and structure of the organization. As organizations continue to implement task informating (Zuboff, 1988) to systematically structure, archive and streamline organizational tasks, the outcomes of such technology-driven processes may not always meet the optimistic expectations. For instance, Rice and Schneider (2007) found that converting organizational tasks from a paper-based modality to an information technology-based platform doesn't guarantee an improvement of organizational task cost-efficiency. A related phenomenon that stems from an organization's ability to informate organizational tasks and utilize the Intranet communication network is the practice of telework, which allows workers to telecommute, by substituting work-related travel with the use of information and communication technologies to complete work and transport work products (Sullivan, 2003).

The idea of telework allows the information workers to work at home and only visit the office irregularly. Even though this notion personifies the ideal of how technologies can free individuals from the boundaries of time, distance and physical constraints and still be full-fledged participants of a functioning social (or corporate) system, the practice of teleworking has yet to gain a visible momentum (Pearlson & Saunders, 2001). Based on the limited empirical evidence, it appears that while women favor telework due to their desire to be able to spend more time with their children, men choose telework due to their preference for a non-office physical environment (Bailey & Kurland, 2002).

A main argument that trumpets the virtues of telework is how it affords the workers to balance the demands of their home and work life with more ease (Britton, Halfpenny, Devine, & Mellor, 2004). Nonetheless, the empirical evidence seems to indicate a set of potentially positive and negative outcomes associated with this organizational work modality. For instance, Mann and Holdsworth (2003) found that teleworkers could feel lonely, isolated, irritable, worrisome, and even guilty, and that they experience a higher level of mental stress and physical health symptoms than office workers. Other work has purported that telework has a mostly positive influence on the worker's productivity and personal life, as they have more flexibility in addressing the concerns of both (Hill, Ferris, & Martinson, 2003). As there are no longitudinal studies that can speak to the social consequences of telework, organizations have reported savings in resources associated with employing teleworkers (Harris, 2003; Peters & den Dulk, 2003). According to Atkin and Lau (2007), the success of telework for both the workers and the organizations alike is determined by the commitment from both parties.

This commitment to the organization and workers is fundamental to the organizational e-culture, which is a living ecological organism that grows and/or changes. This concept of living ecological organism is similar to Nardi and O'Day's (1999) concept of information ecology, which emphasizes the importance of proper integration of people, practices, technologies, and values, illustrating the need to treat Web-based communication in an organizational setting as work in progress that needs to adapt to its changing environment. Extending the information ecology concept, Nardi and Whittaker (2002) considered the concept of media ecology as an effective integration of a particular mix of Web-based technologies to accommodate the unique work context and workplace conditions. For instance, Nardi, Whittaker, and Bradner (2000) found that instant messaging allows employees to feel a strong sense of others in their workplace, which helps them establish a more effective communication environment through these instantaneous dialogues.

Such a cognitive response to the preference over a stronger embodiment of social presence of interactive communications between two or multiple parties brings us back to the very beginning of the current discussion, which compares the characteristics of asynchronous and synchronous communication. The theory of social presence emphasizes the "being there" element of social interaction (Short, Williams, & Christie, 1976); a "companion" media richness theory proposes the matching of media modalities capable of communicating more verbal and nonverbal cues with more equivocal tasks (Daft & Lengel, 1984; Trevino, Lengel, & Daft, 1987).

Using these two theories to gauge the perceived physical embodiment of social interaction and the repertoire of communication cues conveyed by the different Internet communication modalities, online videoconferencing and Internet news bulletins may be regarded as the channels that have the strongest and the weakest social presence and media richness, respectively. The theory of technology fluidity, which integrates both the qualitative character and quantitative flow of interactive technology, summarizes the technical attributes of Internet communication to demonstrate the social role of the Internet medium. By revisiting the fluid nature and technical attributes of Internet technology as the baseline that spawns all Internet communication applications and their subsequent social consequences, the current discussion of Internet effects has come to a full circle.

FUTURE RESEARCH IMPLICATIONS

Similar to other forms of subcultures borne out of shared socio-cultural interests or economic necessities, avid users of social communication channels such as instant messaging services or commerce-oriented channels such as eBay, have developed a set of net-etiquettes and net-vernaculars unique to their respective networks. This net-driven culture can also be easily observed via the Internet-use activity of the general public, when one considers how such Internet-originated terminology as "spam" and "Google it" have now become part of our daily lexicon, much like how we use such words as "Kleenex" and "Xerox."

Even though the use of the Internet as an information and communication technology has reached a critical mass in our society, and its social consequences have also started to take root in our culture, communication research on the effects of Internet uses is still limited. Internet effects, in practical terms, refer to the social changes that can be observed and measured at an individual, group, institutional and societal level. As the content of these social changes can be rather diffusive, it is useful to examine them in the contexts of how individuals use the Internet (Liewvrouw & Livingstone, 2002).

It should be noted that the Internet-use activity contexts and categories presented in Table 26.1 only took a snapshot of what the potential for Internet-use applications might be. By the same token, the Internet-use contexts that serve as the basis for the present discussion's explication of Internet effects are also by no means comprehensive nor mutually exclusive. For instance, Internet effects in a family setting or interpersonal trust are implied but not fully explored in the discussion within the socializing and social networking context. Other topics such as deception or rumors that can be easily practiced or spread over the virtual grapevine with little built-in checks and balances also do not receive a detailed discussion in the current chapter.

The difficulty of classifying Internet effects into clear social categories is both a blessing and a curse, as it illustrates the complex phenomenon of this unique medium—capable of being all things to all people—via a fluid platform, one that enables it to interchangeably function as a synchronous and asynchronous interpersonal, group, organizational and mass communication medium. In essence, our traditional conception of the boundaries that demarcate the communication processes into the interpersonal, small group, organizational, and mass communication domain does not fit in well with Internet effects research. What then could help facilitate the expedition of the Internet medium which may be more appropriately conceptualized as an "Intermedia communication" medium (Lin, 2002) or one that possesses the social and technical attributes of all forms of mediated communications?

The answer to this question lies in the conceptual framework that researchers should adopt to investigate Internet effects, which should reflect the multidimensional nature of Internet effects. A good example of approaching Internet effects research through a more socially encompassing perspective is demonstrated in Bargh and McKenna's (2004) review piece, *The Internet and Social Life*, which elucidated the effects of interpersonal interaction in the workplace, personal (close relationships), group membership and social support, as well as community involvement. Other examples of addressing Internet effects in a multifunctional orientation include Lin's (2007) social change typology, which proposed that researchers study the effects of communication and information technologies by examining the functional domains of surveillance, knowledge, communication, entertainment, and commerce, where each functional domain is multidimensional in nature. For instance, the communication domain can encompass social interactions in a one-on-one, group, and institutional setting, which can be a useful framework for examining the potential interrelations between these different interaction scenarios on a continuum.

Provided that it is unlikely for most published journal articles (due to the space limit) to address a wide range of related aspects under a topical focus, efforts could and should be made to cast the chosen topical focus in a more situation- or context-inclusive theoretical and conceptual frame to present the discussion of the literature as well as the empirical findings. The narrow targeting of many of the media and/or Internet effects studies, compounded with the use of a rudimentary experimental setting and student samples, calls into question both the validity as well as reliability of the study results. Bearing these caveats in mind, it is crucial for researchers to conduct their Internet effects research by integrating both micro- and macro-theoretical frameworks as well as collecting empirical data from Internet users in their actual use setting by avoiding the confines of classroom exercises.

More importantly, the pressing issue in Internet effects research predicates on the lack of theories or theoretical development that could help stimulate and hence further advance the intellectual energy and endeavor. The theorizing work that presents such new conceptual thinking for measuring the effects of Internet communication, including the hyperpersonal communication perspective (Walther, 1996), technology fluidity theory (Lin, 2003), and self-regulation deficiency (LaRose et al., 2003), are examples of a good initial effort.

In sum, the reinvention process of how to maximize the social and technical functions of Internet use will march on—independent of the pace of our research progress—accompanied by the continuing emergence of various software programs and wireless mobile devices that will help individuals adapt to these newly invented uses of the Internet medium. In essence, it is necessary for the communication research community to accelerate the pace of producing the best and most up-to-date scientific understanding of the Internet's effects on society. As exemplified by the long list of interdisciplinary references provided by this chapter, Internet effects research is similarly active if not more active in other social science fields.

CONCLUSION

The Internet's effects on society, whether pro-social or anti-social, productive or unproductive, meaningful or meaningless, or negative or positive in relation to individuals' lives as a e-communicators are neither inherently good nor evil. In point of fact, while lonely, isolated, and depressed individuals may rely heavily on social networks online to meet their socializing needs and hence not actively pursue practical social relationships offline, the online social network nevertheless allows them to establish their identity as a virtual social being that can be as real as they perceive it to be.

Due to the youth of the Internet medium in the historical landscape, the debate of a utopian versus a dystopian view of the long-term consequences of incorporating the Internet into our personal and/or work life in forming and managing interpersonal and community relationships will continue (Wellman, 1997). The key to understanding the effects of the Internet on society hence should not focus on how the Internet will change society but how we will shape that change. With its intermedia nature, the Internet medium, for all intents and purposes, is simply a tool for us to produce a set of more or less goal-oriented social and/or institutional outcomes that may or may not be intrinsically effective in meeting the larger ideals of what we perceive to be the most desirable effects on society.

References

Aravosis, J. (2006, August 16). More fall-outs from GOP Senator George Allen's use of racist slur against Indian-American. *Americanblog.com*, Retrieved August 20, 2007, from http:/ www.americablog.com/2006/08/more-fall-out-from-gop-senator-george.html.

Atkin, D. J., & Lau, T. Y. (2007). Information technology and organizational telework. In C. A. Lin & D. J. Atkin (Eds.), *Communication technology and social change: Theory and implications* (pp. 79–100), Mahwah, NJ: Erlbaum.

Bailey, D. E., & Kurland, N. B. (2002). A review and new directions for telework research: Study telework, not teleworkers. *Journal of Organizational Behavior*, *23*(4), 383–400.

Balnaves, M., Mayrhofer, D., & Shoesmith, B. (2004). Media professions and the new humanism. *Journal of Media & Cultural Studies*, *18*, 191–203.

Bandura, A. (1991). Human agency: The rhetoric and the reality. *American Psychologist*, *46*, 157–162.

Barak, A., & Fisher, W.A. (2002). The future of Internet Sexuality. In A. Cooper (Ed.), *Sex and the Internet: A guidebook for clinicians* (pp. 260–280). New York: Brunner-Routledge.

Bargh, J. A., & McKenna, K. Y. A. (2004). The Internet and social life. *Annual Review of Psychology*, *55*, 573–590.

Bat-Chava, Y. (1994). Group identification and the self-esteem of deaf adults. *Personality and Social Psychology Bulletin*, *20*, 494–502.

Blumer, H. (1969). *Symbolic interactionism: Perspective and method*. Englewood Cliffs, NJ: Prentice Hall.

Brenner, V. (1997). Psychology of computer use. XLVII. Parameters of Internet use, abuse and addiction: The first 90 days of the Internet Usage Survey. *Psychological Reports*, *80*, 879–882.

Brimber, B. (2000). The study of information technology and civic engagement. *Political Communication*, *17*(3), 329–333.

Britton, J., Halfpenny, P., Devine, F., & Mellor, R. (2004). The future of regional cities in the information age: The impact of information technology on Manchester's financial and business service sector. *Sociology, 38*(4), 795–814.

Bucy, E. P., Gantz, W., & Wang, Z. (2007). Media technology and the 24-hour news cycle. In C. A. Lin & D. J. Atkin (Eds.), *Communication technology and social change: Theory and implications* (pp. 143–163). Mahwah, NJ: Erlbaum.

Burgoon, J. K., Bonito, J. A., Ramierez, A., Dunbar, N. E., Kam, K., & Fischer, J. (2002). Testing the interactivity principle: Effects of mediation, propinquity, and verbal and nonverbal modalities in interpersonal interaction. *Journal of Communication, 52*, 657–677.

Busselle, R., Reagan, J., Pinkleton, B., & Jackson, K. (1999). Factors affecting Internet use in a saturated access population. *Telematics and Informatics, 16*, 45–58.

Buzzell, T., Foss, D., & Middleton, Z. (2006). Explaining use of online pornography: A test of self-control theory and opportunities for deviance. *Journal of Criminal Justice and Popular Culture, 13*(2), 96–116.

Caplan, S. E. (2002). Problematic Internet use and psychological well-being: Development of a theory-based cognitive-behavioral measurement instrument. *Computers in Human Behavior, 18*, 553–575.

Charlton, J. P., & Danforth, I. D. W. (2007). Distinguishing addiction and high engagement in the context of online game playing. *Computers in Human Behavior, 23*, 1531–1548.

Charney, T., & Greenberg, B. S. (2002). Uses and gratifications of the Internet. In C. A. Lin & D. J. Atkin (Eds.), *Communication technology and society: Audience adoption and uses* (pp. 379–407). Cresskill, NJ: Hampton.

Childers, T., & Krugman, D. (1987). The competitive environment of pay-per-view. *Journal of Broadcasting & Electronic Media, 31*, 335–342.

Conway, T., Ward, M., Lewis, G., & Bernhardt, A. (2007). Internet crisis potential: The importance of a strategic approach to marketing communications. *Journal of Marketing Communications, 13*(3), 213–228.

Coombs, W. T. (1999). *Ongoing crisis communications: Planning, managing and responding*. London: Sage.

Cummings, J., Butler, B., & Kraut, R. (2002). The quality of online social relationships. *Communications of the ACM, 45*, 103–108.

Daft, R. L., & Lengel, R. H. (1984). Information richness: a new approach to managerial behavior and organizational design. *Research in Organizational Behavior, 6*, 191–233.

Davis, R. (1999). *The web of politics: The Internet's impact on the American political system*. New York: Oxford University Press.

Davis, R. A. (2001). A cognitive behavioral model of pathological Internet use. *Computers in Human Behavior, 17*, 187–195.

Davison, K. P., Pennebaker, J. W., & Dickerson, S. S. (2000). Who talks? The social psychology of illness support groups. *American Psychologist, 55*, 205–217.

Deaux, K. (1996). Social identification. In E. T. Higgins & A. W. Kruglanski (Eds.), *Social psychology: Handbook of basic principles* (pp. 777–798). New York: Guilford.

Deuze, M. (2003). The web and its journalisms: Considering the consequences of different types of news media online. *New Media & Society, 5*, 203–230.

Dimaggio, P., Hargittai, E., Neuman, W. R., & Robinson, J. P. (2001). Social implications of the Internet. *Annual Review of Sociology, 27*, 307–336.

Ethier, K. A., & Deaux, K. (1994). Negotiating social identity when contexts change: Maintaining identification and responding to threat. *Journal of Personality and Social Psychology, 67*, 243–251.

Eveland, W. P., & Dunwoody, S. (2002). An investigation of elaboration and selective scanning as method of learning from the web versus print. *Journal of Broadcasting & Electronic Media, 46*, 34–44.

Eveland, W. P., Seo, M., & Marton, K. (2000). Learning from the news in campaign 2000: An experimental comparison of TV news, newspapers, and online news. *Media Psychology, 4*, 355–380.

Ferguson, D. A., & Perse, E. M. (2000). The World Wide Web as a functional alternative to television. *Journal of Broadcasting & Electronic Media, 44*(2), 155–174.

Festinger, L. (1954). A theory of social comparison processes. *Human Relations*, *7*(2), 117–140.

Flanagan, A. J., & Metzer, M. J. (2000). Internet use in the contemporary media environment. *Human Communication Research*, *27*, 153–174.

Fletcher, P. D., Holden, S., & Norris, D. F. (2003). Electronic government at the local level: Progress to date and future issues. *Public Performance and Management Review*, *26*(4), 325–344.

Frost, J., & Ariely, D. (2004). Learning and juggling in online dating. In A. Cheema, S. Hawkins, & J. Srivastava (Eds.), *Proceedings of the Society for Consumer Psychology 2004 Winter conference* (pp. 192). Columbus, OH: Society for Consumer Psychology.

Graber, D. A. (2001). *Processing politics: Learning from television in the Internet age*. Chicago: University of Chicago Press.

Gregson, K. (1998). Conversations & community or sequential monologues: An analysis of politically oriented newsgroups, ASIS 1998 Annual Meeting, Orlando, FL.

Griffiths, M. (2000). Does Internet and computer "addiction" exist? Some case study evidence. *Cyberpsychology & Behavior*, *3*, 211–218.

Griffiths, M., & Fox, S. (2007, September 19). Hobbyists online. *Pew Internet & American Life Project*. Retrieved on September 25, 2007, from http:/www.pewinternet.org/PPF/r/221/report_display.asp.

Gross, E. F., Juvonen, J., & Gable, S. L. (2002). Internet use and well-being in adolescence. *Journal of Social Issues*, *58*(1), 75–90.

Grüsser, S. M., Thalemann, R., & Griffiths, M. D. (2007). Excessive computer game playing: Evidence for addiction and aggression? *Cyberpsychology & Behavior*, *10*(2), 290–292.

Harris, L. (2003). Home-based teleworking and the employment relationship: Managerial challenges and dilemmas. *Personnel Review*, *32*(4), 422–439.

Hart, T. A., Chaparro, B. S., & Halcomb, C. G. (2006, December, 20). Evaluating websites for older adults: Adherence to "senior-friendly" guidelines and end-user performance. *Behavior & Information Technology*, *27*(3), 191–199.

Helgeson, V. S., Cohen, S., Schulz, R., & Yasko, J. (2000). Group support intervention for women with breast cancer: Who benefits from whom? *Health Psychology*, *19*, 107–114.

Henke, L., & Donahue, T. R. (1989). Functional displacement of traditional TV viewing by VCR owners. *Journal of Advertising Research*, *29*, 18–23.

Hermans, H. J. M. (1996). Voicing the self: From information processing to dialogic interchange. *Psychological Bulletin*, *119*, 31–50.

Hermans, H. J. M. (2001). The dialogical self: Toward a theory of personal and cultural positioning. *Culture & Psychology*, *7*, 243–281.

Hertlein, K. M., & Piercy, F. P. (2006). Internet infidelity: A critical review of the literature. *The Family Journal: Counseling and therapy for Couples and Families*, *14*(4), 366–371.

Hevern, V. W. (2004). Threaded identity in cyberspace: Weblogs & positioning in the dialogical self. *Identity: An International Journal of Theory and Research*, *4*(4), 321–335.

Hill, E. J., Ferris, M., & Martinson, V. (2003). Does it matter where you work? A comparison of how three work venues (traditional office, virtual office, and home office) influence aspects of work and personal/family life. *Journal of Vocational Behavior*, *63*(2), 220–241.

Hilse, M., & Hoewner, J. (1998). The communication crisis in the internet and what one can do against it. In M. Crimp (Ed.), *Interactive enterprise communication* (pp. 137–154). Frankfurt: IMK.

Hitlin, P., & Rainie, L. (2005, August). Teens, technology, and school. *Pew Internet & American Life Project*. Retrieved on September 25, 2005, from http:/www.pewinternet.org/pdfs/PIP_Internet_and_schools_05.pdf.

Holtz, S. (2006). The impact of new technologies on internal communication. *Strategic Communication Management*, *10*(1), 22–25.

Horrigan, J. B. (2004, May 24). How Americans get in touch with government. *Pew Internet & American Life Project*. Retrieved on June 12, 2007, from http:/www.pewinternet.org/pdfs/PIP_E-Gov_Report_0504.pdf.

Howard, P. E. N., Raine, L., & Jones, S. (2001). Days and nights on the Internet. *American Behavioral Scientist*, *45*, 383–404.

Jeffres, L. W., & Lin, C. A. (2006). Metro websites as urban communication. *Journal of Computer Mediated Communication, 11*(4). Retrieved January 22, 2007 from http://jcmc.indiana.edu/vol11/issue4/jeffres.html.

Jennings, M. K., & Zeitner, V. (2003). Internet use and civic engagement: A longitudinal analysis. *Public Opinion Quarterly, 67*, 311–334.

Jensen, M. (2003, September/October). Emerging alternatives: A brief history of weblogs. *Columbia Journalism Review, 42*(3), 22–25.

Jensen, M. J., Danziger, J. N., & Venkatesh, A. (2007). Civil society and cyber society: The role of the Internet in communication associations and democratic politics. *The Information Society, 23*, 39–50.

Johansson, A., & Gotestam, K. G. (2004). Problems with computer games without monetary reward: similarity to pathological gambling. *Psychological Reports, 95*(2), 641–650.

Johnson, T. J., & Kaye, B. K. (1998). Cruising is believing? Comparing Internet and traditional sources on media credibility measures. *Journalism & Mass Communication Quarterly, 75*, 325–340.

Kahn, R., & Kellner, D. (2004). New media and Internet activism: From the "Battle of Seattle" to blogging. *New Media & Society, 6*, 87–95.

Kent, M. L., & Taylor, M. (2002). Toward a dialogic theory of public relations. *Public Relations Review, 28*(1), 21–37.

Kim, J., & LaRose, R. (2004). Interactive e-commerce: Promoting consumer efficiency or impulsivity? *Journal of Computer Mediated Communication, 19*(1). Retrieved April 2, 2005, from http:/jcmc.indiana.edu/vol10/issue1/Kim_larose.html.

Kim, S. T., Weaver, D., & Wilnat, L. (2002). Media reporting and perceived credibility of online polls. *Journalism & Mass Communication Quarterly, 77*, 846–864.

Knobloch, S., Carpentier, F. D., & Zillmann, D. (2003). Effects of salience dimensions of information utility on selective exposure to online news. *Journalism & Mass Communication Quarterly, 89*, 91–108.

Kraut, R. E., Patterson, M., Lundmark, V., Kiesler, S., Mukhopadhyay, T., & Scherlis, W. (1998). Internet paradox: A social technology that reduces social involvement and psychological well-being? *American Psychologies, 53*(9), 1017–1032.

Kraut, R., Kiesler, S., Boneva, B., Cummings, V. H., & Crawford, A. (2002). Internet paradox revisited. *Journal of Social Issues, 58*(1), 49–74.

LaRose, R., & Eastin, M. S. (2002). Is online buying out of control? Electronic commerce and consumer self-regulation. *Journal of Broadcasting & Electronic Media, 46*(4), 549–564.

LaRose, R., Lin, C. A., & Eastin, M. S. (2003). Unregulated Internet usage: Addiction, habit or deficient self-regulation? *Media Psychology, 5*, 225–253.

Lasswell, H. D. (1948). The structure and function of communication in society. In L. Bryson (Ed.), *The communication of ideas* (pp. 37–51). New York: Harper.

Lawson-Borders, G., & Kirk, R. (2005). Blogs in campaign communication. *American Behavioral Scientist, 49*(4), 548–559.

Lemert, J. B. (1984). News content and the elimination of mobilizing information: An experiment. *Journalism Quarterly, 61*(2), 243–249.

Lenhart, A., & Fox, S. (2006, July 19). Bloggers: A portrait of Internet's storytellers. *Pew Internet & American Life Project*. Retrieved on August 10, 2007, from http:/www.pewinternet.org/pdfs/PIP%20Bloggers%20Report%20July%2019%202006.pdf.

Liewvrouw, L. A., & Livingstone, S. (Eds.). (2002). *Handbook of new media: social shaping and consequences of ICTs*. London: Sage.

Lin, C. A. (1994). Audience fragmentation in a competitive video marketplace. *Journal of Advertising Research, 34*(6), 1–17.

Lin, C. A. (1999). Predicting online service adoption likelihood among potential subscribers: A motivational approach. *Journal of Advertising Research, 39*(2), 79–89.

Lin, C. A. (2001). Audience attributes, media supplementation and likely online service adoption, *Mass Communication and Society, 4*, 19–38.

Lin, C. A. (2002). Communicating in the information age. In C. A. Lin & D. J. Atkin (Eds.), *Communication technology and society: Audience adoption and uses* (pp. 3–22). Cresskill, NJ: Hampton.

Lin, C. A. (2003). An interactive communication technology adoption model. *Communication Theory, 13*(4), 345–365.

Lin, C. A. (2007). An integrated communication technology and social change typology. In C. A. Lin & D. J. Atkin (Eds.), *Communication technology and social change: Theory and implications* (pp. 283–307), Mahwah, NJ: Erlbaum.

Lin, C. A., & Salwen, M. B. (2006). Utilities of online and offline news use. In X. Li (Ed.), *Internet Newspapers: The making of a mainstream medium* (pp. 209–225). Mahwah, NJ: Erlbaum.

Lin, C. A., Salwen, M. B., & Driscoll, P. D. (2005). Online news as a functional substitute for offline news. In M. B. Salwen, B. Garrison, & P. D. Driscoll (Eds.) *Online news and the public* (pp. 237–255). Mahwah, NJ: Erlbaum.

Lowrey, W., & Choi, J. (2006). The web news story and cognitive flexibility. In X. Li (Ed.), *Internet Newspapers: The making of a mainstream medium* (pp. 99–117). Mahwah, NJ: Erlbaum.

Madden, M. (2006, April). Internet penetration and impact. *Pew Internet & American Life Project*. Retrieved on August 20, 2007 from http:/www.pewinternet.org/pdfs/PIP_Internet_Impact.pdf.

Madden, M. (2007, July 25). Online video. *Pew Internet & American Life Project*. Retrieved on August 25, 2007 from http:/www.pewinternet.org/pdfs/PIP_Online_Video_2007.pdf.

Madden, M., & Rainie, L. (2005, March). Music and video downloading moves beyond P2P. *Pew Internet & American Life Project*. Retrieved on August 25, 2007, from http:/www.pewinternet.org/pdfs/PIP_Filesharing_March05.pdf.

Mann, S., & Holdsworth, L. (2003). The effects of home-based teleworking on work-family conflicts. *Human Resources Development Quarterly, 14*, 35–38.

Matheson, D. (2004). Weblogs and the epistemology of the news: Some trends in online journalism. *New Media & Society, 6*, 443–468.

McKay, H. G., Glasgow, R. E., Feil, E. G., Boles, S. M., & Barrera, M. (2002). Internet-based diabetes management and support: Initial outcomes from the diabetes network project. *Rehabilitation Psychology, 47*, 31–48.

McKenna, K. Y. A., & Bargh, J. A. (1998). Coming out in the age of the Internet: Identity "de-marginalization" through virtual group participation. *Journal of Personality and Social Psychology, 75*, 681–694.

McKenna, K. Y. A., & Bargh, J. A. (1999). Causes and consequences of social interaction on the Internet: A conceptual framework. *Media Psychology, 1*, 249–269.

McKenna, K. Y. A., & Bargh, J. A. (2000). Plan 9 from cyberspace: The implications of the Internet for personality and social psychology. *Personality and Social Psychology Review, 4*, 57–75.

McKenna, K. Y. A., Green, A. S., & Gleason, M. E. J. (2002). Relationship formation on the Internet: What's the big attraction? *Journal of Social Issues, 58*, 9–31.

McMillan, A., & Huang, J. (2002). Measures of perceived interactivity: An exploration of the role and direction of communication, user control, and time in shaping perceptions of interactivity. *Journal of Advertising, 3*, 29–42.

Moon, M. J. (2002). The evolution of e-government among municipalities: Rhetoric or reality? *Public Administration Review, 62*(4), 424–433.

Morahan-Martin, J., & Schumacher, P. (2000). Incidence and correlates of pathological Internet use among college students. *Computers in Human Behavior, 16*, 13–29.

Muhlberger, P. (2005). Human agency and the revitalization of the public sphere. *Political Communication, 22*(2), 163–178.

Mundell, E. J. (2007, June 27). Video games' addictive nature unclear: AMA. *HealthDay Reporter*, Retrieved July 2, 2007, from http:/www.healthday.com/Article.asp?AID=605801.

Musso, J., Weare, C., & Hale, M. (2000). Designing web technologies for local governance reform: Good management or good democracy? *Political Communication, 17*, 1–19.

Nardi, B., & O'Day, V. (1999). *Information ecologies: Using technology with heart*. Cambridge, MA: The MIT Press.

Nardi, B., & Whittaker, S. (2002). The place of face to face communication in distributed work. In P. J. Hinds & S. Kiesler (Eds.), *Distributed work: New research on working across distance using technology* (pp. 83–110). Cambridge, MA: MIT Press.

Nardi, B., Whittaker,S., & Bradner, E. (2000). Interaction and outreaction: Instant messaging in action. *Proceedings of conference on Computer Supported Cooperative Work (CSCW)* (pp. 79–88). Philadelphia: ACM Inc.

Ng, B. D., & Wiemer-Hastings, P. (2005). Addiction to the Internet and online gaming, *Cyberpsychology & Behavior*, 8(20), 110–113.

Norris, P. (1998). Virtual democracy. *Harvard International Journal of Press/Politics*, *3*, 1–4.

Parker, B. J., & Plank, R. E. (2000). A uses and gratifications perspective on the Internet as a new information source. *American Business Review*, *18*, 43–49.

Parks, M. R., & Floyd, K. (1995). Making friends in cyberspace. *Journal of Communication*, *46*, 80–97.

Pearce, K. A., & Pearce, B. W. (2001). The public dialogue consortium's school-web dialogue process: A communication approach to develop citizenship skills and enhance school climate. *Communication Theory*, *11*, 105–123.

Pearlson, K. E., & Saunders, C. S. (2001). There is no place like home: Managing telecommuting paradoxes. *Academy of Management Executive*, *15*(2), 117–129.

Perry, D. C., Taylor, M., & Doerfel, M. L. (2003). Internet-based communication in crisis management. *Management Communication Quarterly*, *17*(2), 206–232.

Peters, P. & den Dulk, L. (2003). Cross-cultural differences in managers' support for home-based telework: A theoretical elaboration. *International Journal of Cross-Cultural Management*, *3*, 329–346.

Pew/Internet. (2007a, January 11). Demographic of Internet users. *Pew Internet & American Life Project*. Retrieved on August 10, 2007, from http:/www.pewinternet.org/trends/User_Demo_1.11.07.htm.

Pew/Internet. (2007b, June 11). Internet activities. *Pew Internet & American Life Project*. Retrieved on September 10, 2007, from http:/www.pewinternet.org/trends/Internet_Activities_8.28.07.htm.

Reagan, J., & Lee, M. J. (2007). Online technology, edutainment, and infotainment. In C. A. Lin & D. J. Atkin (Eds.), *Communication technology and social change: Theory and implications* (pp. 183–200), Mahwah, NJ: Erlbaum.

Rice, E. R., & Schneider, S. (2007). Information technology: analyzing paper and electronic desktop artifacts. In C. A. Lin & D. J. Atkin (Eds.), *Communication technology and social change: Theory and implications* (pp. 101–121), Mahwah, NJ: Erlbaum.

Riva, G., & Galimberti, C. (1997). The psychology of cyberspace: A socio-cognitive framework to computer-mediated communication. *New Ideas in Psychology*, *15*, 141–158.

Salguero, R. A. T., & Morán, R. M. B. (2002). Measuring problem video game playing in adolescents. *Addiction*, *97*, 1601–1606.

Schau, H. J., & Gilly, M. C. (2003). We are what we post? Self-presentation in personal web space. *Journal of Consumer Research*, *30*(3), 385–404.

Shah, D. V., Cho, J., Eveland, W. P., & Kwak, N. (2005). Information and expression in a digital Age. *Communication Research*, *32*(5), 531–564.

Shapira, N. A., Goldsmith, T. D., Keck, P. E., Khosla, U. M., & McElroy, S. L. (2000). Psychiatric features of individuals with problematic internet use. *Journal of Affective Disorders*, *57*, 267–272.

Shapiro, J. S. (1999). Loneliness: Paradox or artifact? *American Psychologies*, *54*(9), 782–783.

Sheeks, M. S., & Birchmeier, Z. P. (2007). Shyness, sociability, and the use of computer-mediated communication in relationship development. *CyberPsychology & Behavior*, *10*, 64–70.

Short, J., Williams, E., & Christie, B. (1976). *The social psychology of telecommunications*. London: Wiley.

Shouten, J. W. (1991). Selves in transition: symbolic consumption in personal rites of passage and identity re-construction. *Journal of Consumer Research*, *17*(March), 412–425.

Solomon, M. R. (1983). The role of products as social stimuli: A symbolic interactionism perspective. *Journal of Consumer Research, 19*(3), 319–329.
Song, I., LaRose, R., Eastin, M. S., & Lin, C. A. (2004). Internet gratifications and Internet addiction: On the uses and abuses of new media. *CyberPsychology & Behavior*, 7, 384–394.
Spiro, R., & Jehng, J. (1990). Cognitive flexibility and hypertext: Theory and technology for the non-linear and multidimensional traversal of complex subject matter. In D. Nix. & R. Spiro (Eds.), *Cognition, education and multimedia: Exploring ideas in high technology* (pp. 163–205). Hillsdale, NJ: Erlbaum.
Stempel, G. H., Hargrove, T., & Bernt, J. P. (2000). Relation of growth of use of the Internet to changes in media use from 1995–1999. *Journalism & Mass Communication Quarterly, 77*, 71–79.
Stephenson, W. (1988). *The play theory of mass communication*. New Brunswick, NJ: Transaction.
Sullivan, C. (2003). What's in a name? Definitions and conceptualisations of teleworking and homeworking. *New Technology, Work & Employment, 18*(3), 158–165.
Talamo, A., & Ligorio, B. (2001). Strategic identities in cyberspace. *Cyberpsychology & Behavior, 4*, 109–122.
Taylor, M., & Kent, M. L. (2004). Congressional web sites and their potential for public dialogue. *Atlantic Journal of Communication, 12*(2), 59–76.
Tewksbury, D. (2003). What do Americans really want to know? Tracking the behavior of news readers on the Internet. *Journal of Communication, 53*(4), 694–710.
Tewksbury, D., & Althaus, S. L. (2000). Differences in knowledge acquisition among readers of the paper and online versions of a national newspaper. *Journalism & Mass Communication Quarterly, 77*, 457–479.
Thomas, J. C., & Streib, G. (2005). E-democracy, E-commerce, and E-research: Examining the electronic ties between citizens and governments. *Administration & Society, 37*(3), 259–279.
Tolbert, C., & McNeal, R. (2003). Unraveling the effects of the Internet on political participation? *Political Research Quarterly, 56*, 175–185.
Trevino, L., Lengel R., & Daft, R. (1987). Media Symbolism, Media Richness, and Media Choice in Organizations. *Communications Research, 14*(5), 553–574.
Turkle, S. (1997). *Life on the screen: Identity and the age of the Internet*. New York: Touchstone.
Waldfogel, J. (2002). *Consumer substitution among media*. Philadelphia: Federal Communications Commission Media Ownership Working Group.
Walther, J. B. (1996). Computer-mediated communication: Impersonal, interpersonal, and hyperpersonal interaction. *Communication Research, 23*, 3–43.
Walther, J. B., & Boyd, S. (2002). Attraction to computer-mediate social support. In C. A. Lin & D. J. Atkin (Eds.), *Communication technology and society: Audience adoption and uses* (pp. 153–188). Cresskill, NJ: Hampton.
Walther, J. B., & Parks, M. R. (2002). Cues filtered out, cues filtered in. Computer-mediated communication and relationship. In M. L. Knapp & J. A. Daly (Eds.), *Handbook of interpersonal communication* (3rd ed., pp. 529–563). Thousand Oaks, CA: Sage.
Walther, J. B., Loh, T., & Granka, L. (2005). Let me count the ways: The interexchange of verbal and nonverbal cues in computer-mediated and face-to-face affinity. *Journal of Language and Social Psychology, 24*(1/1), 36–65.
Welch, E. W., & Fulla, S. (2005). Virtual interactivity between government and citizens: The Chicago police department's citizen ICam application demonstration case. *Political Communication, 22*, 215–236.
Wellman, B. (1997). The road to utopia and dystopia on the information highway. *Contemporary Sociology, 26*(4), 445–449.
Wellman, B., Quan Hasse, A., Witte, J., & Hampton, K. (2001). Does the Internet increase, decrease, or supplement social capital? Social networks, participation, and community commitment. *American Behavioral Scientist, 45*(3), 436–455.
Wheeler, A. (2001). What makes a good corporate reputation. In A. Jolly (Ed.), *Managing corporate reputations* (pp. 7–11), London: Kogan Page.

William, D., & Skoric, M. (2005). Internet fantasy violence: A test of aggression in an online game. *Communication Monographs, 72*, 217–233.

Williams, A. P., Trammell, K. D., Postelnicu, M., Landreville, K., & Martin, J. (2005). Blogging and hyperlinking: Use of the Web to enhance viability during 2004 U.S. campaign. *Journalism Studies*, 6, 177–186.

Wright, C. R. (1986). *Mass communication: A sociological perspective* (3rd ed). New York: Random House.

Wright, K. (2000). Computer-mediated social support, older adults, and coping. *Journal of Communication*, *50*(3), 100–118.

Yahoo! Inc. (2007). Connect with a world of people who share your passions. Retrieved on September 2, 2007, from http:/groups.yahoo.com.

Young, K. S. (1996). Addictive use of the Internet: A case that breaks the stereotype. *Psychological Reports, 79*, 899–902.

Young, K. S. (1998). *Caught in the Net: How to recognize the signs of Internet addiction—and a winning strategy for recovery*. New York: Wiley.

Young, K. S. (1999). Internet addiction: symptoms, evaluation and treatment. In L. Van de Creek & T. Jackson (Eds.), *Innovations in clinical practice: A source book* (pp. 19–31). Sarasota, FL: Professional Resources Press.

Yurchisin, J., Watchravesringkan, K., & McCabe, D. B. (2005). An exploration of identity re-creation in the context of Internet dating. *Social Behavior and Personality*, *33*(8), 735–750.

Zuboff, S. (1988). *In the age of the smart machine: The future of work and power* (3rd ed.). New York: Basic Books.

27

EFFECTS OF MOBILE COMMUNICATION

Scott W. Campbell
University of Michigan

Rich Ling
Telenor Research/University of Michigan

Before reviewing some of the key consequences of mobile communication technology, a brief discussion of how they fit within the media effects paradigm is in order. At the risk of oversimplification, we understand the media effects paradigm as a framework for understanding how mass media content influences attitudes and behavior of audience members. To be fair, it is important to acknowledge that the media effects tradition has grown substantially beyond its roots with a fundamental focus on exposure to media content. In fact, several chapters in this volume highlight how the media effects paradigm has broadened to account for characteristics of audience members, their use of the media, and processes of media production and consumption. For example, McLeod, Kosicki, and McLeod (2002) explained that "understanding political communication effects, because of their dependence on sociopolitical environments, requires examination in broader spatial and temporal contexts than that required by other types of media effects" (p. 216). They argued for expanding the media effects tradition to include consideration of normative expectations, institutional performance, constraints and conventions of the media, and effects on key political actors as well as individual audience members. Like these authors, we also suggest adjustments to the media effects paradigm in order for it to serve as an effective lens for examining the implications of a particular media environment—mobile telephony.

Our argument for broadening the media effects paradigm is grounded in the core assumption that the relationship between communication technologies and their users has fundamentally changed in recent years, from receiving transmitted broadcast messages to interactive engagement in the distribution and production of content. Just as importantly, many of the effects of today's "new media" are not tied to mass communication content, but rather to the processes associated with point-to-point networked interactions. Accordingly, we attempt here to stretch the media effects paradigm beyond the implications of mass communication channels and into the realm of person-to-person mediated interaction. Implied in this is the idea that we move from a situation wherein messages are intended for broadly conceived audiences (advertisements, programs, productions) to a situation where the messages are celebrated for the specific individual with whom we are interacting. With this the question of media effects also changes somewhat. The broadcast version of the question suggests that the collective impact of the message production system as well as the mediation system have some sort of impact on the attitudes and behavior of the individual who is more or less passively receiving the message. With a point-to-point form of mediation, the individual is not passive (e.g., we can shout or coo back at our interlocutor), and the question of "media effect" lies more directly in the effect of the mediation system. In most cases after all, the production of the messages is only another person. Thus, the main difference between co-located and, for example, telephonic interaction is that there is a technical mediation system between the two individuals. In this type of interaction there is not an extensive content production process as with broadcast media. We can ask if the mediation system—be it a PC or a mobile telephone—impacts on the way that the interlocutors interact and in some way reshapes their social contact.

Like television in the 1950s, wireless communication has emerged as one of the defining media of our time, evidenced by the fact that it has become the fastest growing communication technology *ever* (Castells, Fernandez-Ardevol, Qiu, & Sey, 2007). This explosive growth, coupled with publication lag, makes it practically futile for scholarly manuscripts to cite the number of mobile subscriptions worldwide. So we'll simply point out that subscriptions are well into the billions and growing (ITU, 2007). Considering this diffusion rate and, more importantly, the social consequences associated with it, Campbell and Park (2008) argued that we have exited the age of the mass media and entered a new age of personal communication technology.

Marshall McLuhan (1964) is famous for declaring, "The medium is the message." By this, he meant that characteristics of communication technologies shape social order. Following this line of thinking, print media brought about the visual age, while radio, television, and film ushered in the age of mass media. It is worth noting that McLuhan (1967, with Fiore) is also known for the phrase, "The medium is the *massage*," which can serve as a double entendre: (1) that the medium massages the content of a given message and (2) that the prevailing media of his time were characteristic of a "mass" age. We differ from McLuhan's orientation that technologies determine society. However, we do see value in treating them as a lens for understanding how social order is produced and reproduced through systems of communication. In this sense, we agree that much of the 20th century can be characterized as a mass age. That is, up until the latter part of the 20th century, mass communication channels were the predominant media of the time period.[1]

In the 1980s and 1990s we see an important shift from the mass age to an age that Castells (2000) has characterized as "the network society." Castells' basic idea is that advancements in transportation as well as information and communication technologies (ICTs), such as personal computers and the Internet, nourished (but not caused) a fundamental shift in social order—at all levels, from micro to macro—characterized by flexible, decentralized network nodes based on shared interests rather than shared space. In other words, the relationship between communication technologies and their users changed from that of receiving broadcast messages to actively seeking, producing, and distributing content while using the same media for point-to-point networking. Not surprisingly, this change in the relationship between technology and society resulted in a host of new social consequences, including increased alienation and social isolation (see, for example, Kraut et al., 1998; Nie & Erbring, 2000) to new forms of connecting with others and engaging in one's community (see for example, Bimber, 1998; Katz & Aspen, 1997; Rheingold, 1993).

Campbell and Park (2008) argued that the widespread adoption and use of mobile communication technologies mark a new phase in the network society, chiefly characterized by heightened personalization in the relationship between technologies and their users. With these technologies we call to individuals and not to locations. This argument resonates with Castells et al.'s (2007) claim of a "mobile network society," although there is a distinction in that the former emphasizes the centrality of increased personalization which can be seen in mobile as well as non-mobile media (e.g., TIVO), while the latter points to the mobility of wireless technology.[2] Whether mobile communication marks the rise of a new personal communication society, mobile network society, or simply a new wave of communication technology, there are a number of social consequences associated with its explosive and widespread growth. Our aim in this chapter is to examine some key effects of mobile telephony by reviewing how use of the technology is changing the way people live their lives. In doing so, we step outside of the effects of mass media and into the realm of point-to-point networked interaction.

NEW FORMS OF COORDINATION

Mobile communication transforms how people orient to space and time (Ling & Campbell, 2008), which has had profound effects on the way individuals coordinate with one another. Use of the technology to coordinate with others can soften the schedule and afford a great deal of flexibility when making arrangements with others. Ling (2004) pointed out, "As the mobile telephone becomes ubiquitous, it competes with and supplements time-based social coordination . . . Instead of relying on [mechanical time keeping], mobile telephony allows for direct contact that is in many cases more interactive and more flexible than time-based coordination" (p. 59). Ling and Yttri (1999, 2002) characterized this form of mobile phone use as "micro-coordination" and suggested that it entails multiple dimensions, including basic logistics (e.g., redirecting trips that have already started), softening of schedules (e.g., calling someone to let him/her know you are running late), and progressive refinement of an activity, such as filling in details of open-ended plans. These instrumental uses of the mobile phone transform patterns of coordination in many areas of social life, including peer groups, families, and work.

While some may be concerned that mobile communication is supplanting face-to-face communication among peers, evidence from the research suggests otherwise. That is, use of the technology is actually linked to increased face-to-face sociability (Hashimoto et al., 2000; Ishii, 2006). This outcome of mobile phone use can be, at least partially, attributed to the technology's value as a resource for social coordination. To illustrate, a participant in Campbell and Russo's (2003) study of social networks recounted a situation in which mobile communication replaced the traditional practice of holding up giant flagpoles for groups of friends to meet up at an annual jazz festival. The participant explained, "All you had to do was call your friends and say, 'hey, where are you? Let's meet at such-and-such location.' One friend would call another until everyone would meet at some place" (p. 329). This shows how mobile-based point-to-point—or perhaps person-to-person—interaction has real direct impact on our behavior. In short, the media effect of mobile communication is a refined form of social coordination.

Mobile communication has altered coordination patterns among family members as well, especially in households with two-career and otherwise busy parents (Frissen, 2000). The mobile phone allows family members to identify, relay, and manage unscheduled household errands. In addition, parents are better able to keep tabs on and coordinate activities with their children through mobile communication. An interviewee in Ling's (2004) research provided the following examples of messages exchanged with her husband: "Can you drive the youngest one to music lessons?" "Can you get him?" "Can you go to the store and buy milk?" Other parents in the study provided numerous examples along the same lines. Rakow and Navarro (1993) characterized this use of the technology as "remote mothering," and explained that while it offers the benefit of flexibly managing domestic responsibilities, it can also have the negative consequence of reinforcing gender inequities by further tethering women to their domestic roles.

Another area where instrumental use of the mobile phone presents new benefits as well as challenges is in the workplace (Andriessen & Vartiainen, 2006; Julsrud, 2005; Julsrud & Bakke, 2008). Actually, for many individuals the term "workplace" is becoming outdated thanks to the use of computing and telephonic media. For decades, scholars have been studying the practice and effects of telework, which traditionally refers to working from home (Vartiainen, 2006). The use of mobile devices has led to the related, but distinct, form of employment known as mobile work. Like teleworkers, mobile workers spend much of their time away from a fixed location in an office. However, mobile workers are distinct in that they tend to be physically mobile. In fact, there are various types of mobile workers, ranging from on-site workers who move around within a given location to perform their jobs, to nomads who are constantly on the move from one location to another (Lilischkis, 2003). There are numerous benefits of mobile work, including increased flexibility, adaptability, and access to resources. Vartiainen (2006) explained that mobile communication redefines standard work processes, which increases the ability to "transfer information quickly to employees, wherever and whenever. In principle, physical and virtual mobility provide employees with the possibility of being near customers and, at the same time, accessing joint enterprise resources . . . from afar and while moving" (p. 19).

However, the effects of mobile work also have a dark side. Without doubt, it lowers the threshold for communication, thereby making it easier to access resources and fellow workers. However, sometimes that threshold serves a valuable purpose by separating different arenas of social life that are perhaps better off left distinct from one another. Evidence suggests this can be the case when it comes to the boundaries separating work and personal life. In a two-year study of working family members, Chesley (2005) found that mobile communication can cause one's work life to spill over into the home, creating greater stress for both women and men. These effects were more profound for women in the study because for them the spillover was bi-directional. That is, not only were working mothers experiencing work worries at home, but use of the technology also caused issues of home life to bleed into their work environment.

So, the effects of mobile-mediated coordination offer both dividends and costs. On the one hand, individuals have greater flexibility and freedom from the confines of a schedule when making arrangements with others. Paradoxically, this new freedom can lead to feelings of loss of control and psychological distress as individuals struggle to maintain boundaries that have been compromised by mobile communication. Again, here are behavioral and attitudinal impacts that arise in the context of mobile communication technology.

NEW FORMS OF RELATIONAL COMMUNICATION

In addition to coordination, mobile communication has had profound effects on the ways individuals develop and maintain their personal relationships. The mobile phone is a characteristically personal technology. It is carried, even worn, on the body so it travels with the user and can be utilized virtually anytime, anywhere. In addition, subscribers tend to have their own personal account and phone number, which can afford a certain degree of privacy in their use. Text messaging allows for an added layer of privacy because messages can be exchanged "under the radar" of co-present others. Collectively, these affordances of the technology make it highly personal in nature, which helps explain why it has had such a profound effect on patterns of communication in personal community networks. In this section, we will discuss some of the major changes in how users of the technology demonstrate and reinforce social network ties and some of the effects these changes can have on individuals and peer groups.

One of the most obvious effects of mobile communication on sociability is that network ties are able to achieve a state of "perpetual contact" (Katz & Aakhus, 2002). Even when the communication channel is not actively in use, there is the psychological reassurance that communication with a peer is at least possible, and this sense of *possible communication* shapes how people orient to the technology and each other (Campbell, 2008). Ling and Yttri (1999, 2002) have dubbed relational uses of the mobile phone "hyper-coordination." Not surprisingly, hyper-coordination and the heightened sense of connection that comes out of it have led to the strengthening of social network ties. Beyond strengthening these ties, use of the technology has also led to new forms of sociability among close friends and family members.

Of course, use of telephony for relational communication is nothing new. One of the primary functions of the traditional landline telephone is for keeping in touch with friends and family members. This use of the telephone commonly leads to sustained conversations "that are generally spread out in time, long, and sometimes even ritualized, in which taking one's time to converse is a sign of the strength of each person's commitment to the relationship" (Licoppe, 2003, p. 181). Licoppe contrasted this "conversational mode" of landline telephone use with the shorter and more frequent "connected mode" more characteristic of mobile communication. On the surface, these types of mobile messages may appear entirely meaningless, but in actuality they are symbolic gestures of companionship, even intimacy. Johnsen (2003) explained, "The communication has . . . a very important function apart from the instrumental exchange of information. It becomes an information carrier without having content or function except to sustain the idea of a social fellowship" (p. 163). In essence, these types of messages can be regarded as digital gifts (Johnsen, 2003), much like the traditional adolescent practice of passing notes (Ling, 2004). Beyond the symbolic value of these exchanges, they also play a functional role in being connected. Ling and Yttri (2002) explained,

> The receiver is in the thoughts of the sender and when they next meet they will be able to base a certain portion of their further interaction on the exchange of messages. The messages serve to tie the group together through the development of a common history or narrative. (pp. 158–159)

It is clear that network ties are using mobile phones not only to make and maintain connections, but to demarcate peer group boundaries as well. Beyond the use of voice calling and text messaging, relational boundaries are managed through the contact information stored in one's handset. According to Green (2003), having the "right" names in the device helps "to demonstrate one's participation in a peer community" (p. 207). In-group/out-group distinctions can also be reinforced through distinctive uses of voice calling and text messaging. For instance, some teens choose to text message with peers and use the voice calling feature with their parents. This affords the ability to avoid contact with their parents by screening those calls and sending them straight to voicemail. Furthermore, use of text messaging exclusively with peers allows teens to utilize various types of slang and argot unique to their social networks. This practice helps them to demonstrate membership and sharpens the boundaries that distinguish insiders from outsiders (Ling, 2008, 2004; Ling & Yttri, 2002; Taylor & Harper, 2001).

As noted, expressive use of the mobile phone has the effect of strengthening social network ties. In terms of social cohesion, this is both a benefit and a concern. On the one hand, expressive uses of the mobile phone offer a heightened sense connection, belonging, and identity with one's peer group. Family members also benefit by staying in touch with one another while physically separated or living apart, as in the case of migrant workers (Paragas, 2008). On the other hand, there is the concern that social networks can become overly configured through mobile communication. That is, heavy use of the technology may cause one to become "tele-cocooned" in small, insular social groups (Habuchi, 2005; Ito, Okabe, & Anderson, 2008). One possible outcome of this cocooning effect could be that these individuals are connected to their close network of personal ties at the expense of horizontal or weak ties, which might lead to less connection to the "outside" world and limited exposure to alternative voices and perspectives (Campbell & Ling, 2008; Ling, 2008). Research from around the world has shown that mobile communication indeed strengthens the ties among small groups—families and peer groups. The ability to quickly reach one another—either by texting or calling—and to maintain a type of connected presence while physically apart is a hallmark of mobile communication. This means that members are able to develop forms of tacit knowledge with regard to one another's activities and state of mind that were not possible with the landline. Thus, an effect of the media is that it tightens the bonds between individuals within these intimate and friendship groups.

THE SOCIAL EMANCIPATION OF YOUTH

Another area where mobile communication has had an effect on society is in the way that it plays into the emancipation of teens. As noted above, mobile telephony has been widely adopted by young people, indeed teens have been integral in the development of texting as a form of interaction. They have also helped to develop mobile telephone terminals as a type of fashion accessory (Fortunati 2005a; Ling, 2004). The adoption and use of the mobile telephone has reshaped some of the issues associated with adolescents' transition from their families of orientation. It has changed the ways in which teens interact with peers, and thus it has changed the way in which the process of emancipation takes place.

The process of adolescent emancipation is an artifact of modern society. In traditional society there was intergenerational stability. The teen might have learned his/her adult role at the hand of a parent or of another related adult in a master/apprentice relationship. With modern industrial society the dynamics of change are so rapid that the life experience of the child is necessarily different from that of the parent. There are constantly new techniques and new technologies. The social as well as the employment situation of the child is different from that of the parent. The child cannot expect that the knowledge and skills of the parent will be serviceable during their careers. This is not to say that the skills and experience of the parent are without value, only that they need to be modified and adjusted to emergent situations.

This means that the transition from youth to adulthood is a period of separation and preparation. It is a period in which the individual must distance him/herself from parents. In addition he/she must acquire skills and knowledge that was not a part of the previous generation's repertoire. The skills and techniques are often acquired in formal schooling. At the same time there is a large area of social competence that the child needs to develop as they seek out an adult role. There is the mastery of their personal economy, the form of interaction with institutions (educational system, religion, hobbies, etc.). There are the dynamics of dealings with friends, the role of sex and sexuality, their relationship to alcohol, drugs, etc. There is their relationship to work and the expectations within the working world and their need to develop a sense of personal style, identity, and integrity. In short, the experience of adolescence is, in many ways, shaped by the teen and his/her interaction with peers.

These areas of competence are worked out in the interaction with social network ties. It is in this interaction that the mobile telephone has had its impact. The age grading of schools has facilitated the development of peer culture. It is in the peer culture that the individual can develop a sense of the ebb and flow of social interaction. It is there that the adolescent can, for example, establish a sense of identity, be vulnerable among equals, understand social interaction outside the family, and engage in a rich social life with inside humor, nicknames, etc.

The mobile telephone provides a perfect instrument for the cultivation of peer culture, and thus it is a device that affects the emancipation process. As noted in the previous section, the mobile telephone provides the teen with continual access to peers and therefore strengthens the bonds within that group. In addition, the caller ID, voicemail, and texting functions can provide a type of buffering system between the teen and the parent so as to allow the management of that relationship. Thus, in very real and concrete ways, the media of mobile communication affects the way that adolescence is played out.

It is important to note that not all the effects have necessarily been positive. Research has shown, for example, covariance between teen criminality and mobile telephone use. Heavy users of mobile telephony are overrepresented among those who are involved in various forms of deviance (fighting, alcohol and narcotics use, various forms of theft, etc.; Ling 2005b; Pedersen & Samuelsen, 2003).

In these cases, there is not necessarily a linear relationship between deviant activity and mobile phone use. Rather, it is those persons who are extremely heavy users of mobile communication—and in particular voice communication, not text—who are the most likely to also engage in these forms of deviance. In addition, the material shows a broader correlation between sexuality and mobile phone use. In this case the relationship is rather more linear. That is, as the use of mobile communication increases, there is a broadly similar rise in the proclivity to have engaged in sexual activity. The exact mechanism which encourages this correlation is not necessarily well understood. It is likely that the enhanced ability to coordinate trysts facilitates the ability to engage in sexual behavior. Putting this into the broader issue of media effects, it is easy to see that heavy use of this particular medium, i.e., the mobile telephone, seems to have had the effect of facilitating sexuality among all too willing teens.

TEXTING AND SOCIAL INTERACTION

When thinking of text messages, we can also see the influence of the medium on our use of written language. Text mediation via mobile phones has arisen as an important form of interaction. Both the imode based "mobile email" and the GSM-based Short Message System (SMS) allow users to send and receive text messages.

These forms of communication have seen the development of a style of interaction that perhaps encourages the development of an internal slang or argot within the group. The somewhat awkward form of text production (Ling, 2006) and the limited length of messages mean that text messages are often rather limited in scope. This is not to say that the themes touched on in the messages are limited, however. Content analysis (Ling, 2005a) has shown that many messages are concerned with instrumental coordination (a Norwegian database from 2004—in translation—includes messages such as "What are you doing now?" "Are you at home?" and "It will be a little stressful. I have to be home so early. How early will you be in town?"). There are, however, other more expressive themes to be found in the messages ("Happy Birthday" "Enjoy yourselves." Have a nice vacation." and "It took a second to meet you, it took a minute to like you, it took an hour to love you and it will be an eternity to forget you.") Thus, while the majority of the messages are instrumental and "to the point," they can also be used for more emotional ends.

Another dimension of text messages is their role within the peer group. They can easily develop into an internal sociolect. While not as common as often presented in the press, there are different fanciful forms of spelling and creative usage that is developed within teen groups and which becomes a type of badge of membership. In one example from Norway, teens substituted a final "s" in various words with "z." Thus, for example, the word for hug (kos) became "koz" or even "kozzz." This deliberate form of spelling came to be a more generalized marker of teens and in particular teen girls. It was used as a sort of gushing, cuddly form of internal interaction. Interestingly, a rap band lampooned this form of orthography in a song, and consequently it was dropped by the teens. However, within a short time the Norwegian teens had adopted a new form of interaction, namely the integration of various Swedish phrases into their text messages (Ling, 2008).

Thus, the rise of mobile-based texting has had the consequences of enhancing our ability to coordinate interaction, and, more interestingly, it has provided us with a new context in which peers can develop common forms of argot.

THE TRANSFORMATION OF SOCIAL SPACE: FROM PUBLIC TO PRIVATE

The effects of mobile communication addressed so far primarily lie in the private sphere of social life. To be sure, the use of mobile media has important implications for the public sphere as well. It is worth pointing out that the phrase "public sphere" can take on two meanings, one being Habermas' (1989) civic engagement in a civil society, and the other being normative behavior in public settings. Indeed, mobile communication can have effects on social life in both of these areas. First, we address the implications for normative behavior in public locations.

The rapid diffusion of mobile media has transformed the social landscape as individuals make private use of shared space. While mobile phone use in public lowers the threshold of communication for users of the technology, it often does so at the expense of co-present others who are burdened with the unsolicited sounds of rings, chirps, songs, and half-conversations. Because norms for behavior in public settings often conflict with norms for phone conversations (Love & Kewley, 2005; Palen, Salzman, & Youngs, 2001), the boundaries delineating public and private space are increasingly blurred. Although numerous researchers have investigated normative mobile phone use in public (e.g., Campbell, 2004; Campbell & Russo, 2003; Höflich, 2005; Katz, 2006; Ling, 1996, 2002; Murtagh, 2001; Wei & Leung, 1999), we have yet to arrive at a clear "public consensus as to what should be appropriate boundaries or acceptable etiquette for these private behaviors in public space" (Wei & Leung, 1999, p. 13).

The primary effect of mobile phone use in public settings is that co-present others are unwittingly cast into the role of audience member. Believe it or not, some individuals actually enjoy listening to others' mobile conversations because they find it a source of entertainment and curiosity (Fortunati, 2005b; Paragas, 2003). But for the most part, talking on a mobile phone in public settings is an irritation for co-present others (Monk, Carroll, Parker, & Blythe, 2004)

The extent to which it is irritating can depend on the behavior of the mobile phone user, characteristics of the setting, and disposition of the bystander. Users of the technology can mitigate social intrusion during their conversation through behaviors such as turning away from others, diverting their eyes, speaking quietly, and keeping their conversations brief (Campbell, 2004; Ling, 2004; Murtagh, 2001; Paragas, 2003). By taking these measures, mobile phone users effectively carve out "symbolic fences" in an attempt to keep their conversation private from co-present others (Gullestad, 1992; Ling, 1996). However, there are certain places where talking on a mobile phone is socially unacceptable regardless of user behavior. Theaters and classrooms stand out as particularly inappropriate places for talking on a mobile, but some consider restaurants, stores, churches, meetings, trains, public toilets, and buses to be problematic as well (Campbell, 2006; Campbell & Russo, 2003; Caporael & Xie, 2003; Ling, 1996; Wei & Monk, et al., 2004; Leung, 1999). Complicating matters, perceptions of mobile phone use in public can vary across cultural contexts (Campbell, 2007). For example, talking on a mobile while riding on a bus is forbidden—or at least heavily frowned upon—in Japan, while it is common practice in many other societies (Okabe & Ito, 2005). Even within cultures assessments can vary according to individual personality traits, such as extroversion, neuroticism, and psychoticism (Love & Kewley, 2005). Indeed, the transformation of the public sphere into private space is one of the most prominent effects of mobile media. However, the extent to which and how this effect is experienced is deeply situated in social context.

MOBILE COMMUNICATION AND SOCIAL CAPITAL

The cultivation of social capital has been attracting increased attention from social science researchers in recent years. Much of this attention stems from stark warnings about its deterioration in American society in the last few decades, evidenced by declining levels of trust in American government as well as formal and informal social engagement (Putnam, 1995, 2000). In his definition of social capital, Putnam (1995) explained, "By analogy with notions of physical capital and human capital—tools and training that enhance individual productivity—'social capital' refers to features of social organization such as networks, norms, and social trust that facilitate coordination and cooperation for mutual benefit" (p. 67). In other words, social capital is the *relational matter* that constitutes the social fabric of society, and includes both formal involvement in politics, groups, and clubs, as well as informal socializing with friends and family members.

In addition to empirical evidence of its decline (at least in the US), scholarly interest in social capital has also been fueled by the widespread adoption and use of new ICTs, which offer both promise and peril for social capital. Much of the research in this area so far has focused on the links between Internet use and social capital. As noted above, the findings range from increased feelings of alienation (see, for example, Kraut et al., 1998; Nie & Erbring, 2000) to increased social connection, community involvement, and civic engagement (see for example, Bimber, 1998; Katz & Aspen, 1997; Rheingold, 1993). Although most investigations on the effects of ICT have targeted the Internet, the links between mobile communication and social capital are now emerging as a budding area of interest.

Findings in the research show that mobile phone use can be linked to both formal and, especially, informal dimensions of social capital. To point out a few examples: a representative survey of the US indicated that 90% of mobile phone users feel the technology helps foster face-to-face social encounters (University of Michigan, 2006); a pan-European study showed that a vast majority of mobile phone users regard the technology as helpful in coordinating social activities (69%) and for staying in contact with peers and family (70%) (Ling, 2004); and a study of Japanese youth indicated that peers who live in close proximity use the technology to supplement rather than supplant face-to-face interaction (Ishii, 2006).

There is also evidence that mobile phone use is positively related to formal dimensions of social capital, although these links are not as prevalent as those to informal socializing. In a study of several European countries and Israel, Ling, Yttri, Andersen, and DiDuca (2003) found that text messaging is significantly related to membership in formal organizations, such as social clubs, community groups, and political organizations. Similarly, Campbell and Kwak (2007) found that for some users, voice calling is positively related to community engagement and participation in civic affairs, although this relationship depends on the nature of one's social network.

This area of research is still in the nascent stage, therefore conclusions about how mobile communication contributes to or detracts from involvement in formal community groups and civic activities must be tentative. However, it is clear that the technology can play a powerful role in political change in other ways. In conjunction with other ICTs, mobile phones are increasingly used to form "smart mobs," or "sudden epidemics of cooperation," that can lead to rapid social and political change (Rheingold, 2002, p. 175). One notable example is the overthrow of Filipino president Joseph Estrada in January 2001. Enraged over the government's refusal to pursue charges of corruption, Filipino citizens used their mobile phones to help organize a massive demonstration that lasted four days and culminated in the ousting of Estrada by military officials who sided with the protesters (Rheingold, 2002). Other examples of mobile phone use for rapid and large-scale political change have been reported in South Korea, Spain (Castells et al., 2007), and elsewhere (Rheingold, 2002).

Put into the context of media effects, we see here the use of a medium to directly motivate fellow protesters to participate in a mass action. There is no vague link between the broadcast message and the attitudes of the public. Rather, there is a real link between the viral spread of the message from person to person via their mobile phones. The result, in the case of these social protests, was that the recipient of the message both sent the message further and also he/she participated in protest.

To be sure, the emergence of mobile media is having a profound effect on the extent to which and how members of certain societies cooperate to bring about political change. However, it is important to point out that such use of mobile telephony is not happening in a vacuum, but rather as part of a much larger media landscape in which the lines separating interpersonal from mass communication are increasingly blurred. While this blurring effect challenges some of the traditional classification systems of media scholars, it affords users of the technology new opportunities to initiate and shape social change. As Castells (2007) argued, "the rise of insurgent politics cannot be separated from the emergence of a new kind of media space . . . Appropriating the new forms of communication, people have built their own system of mass communication, via SMS, blogs, vlogs, podcasts, wikis, and the like" (pp. 246–247).

CONCLUDING REMARKS: USERS AS CO-CREATORS OF MOBILE MEDIA

In this chapter we have highlighted some of the most salient effects of mobile telephony on individuals and society at large. By framing the discussion from the perspective of the technology's "effects," we have emphasized a directional flow of influence from the technology to society. Indeed, there are important areas of social change that come out of the diffusion and use of mobile telephony, including changes in how people coordinate their daily lives, carry out social relations, make private use of public space, etc. However, we feel it is important to acknowledge that the direction of influence also flows the other way. Just as the technology has "effects" on its users (as well as non-users), so too do these individuals have important effects on the technology. There is a robust body of literature in the field of science and technology studies that establishes how technologies are socially constructed by those who develop, use, and even reject them (see for example, Bjiker, Hughes, & Pinch, 1987). This is especially true with innovations in communication, since a fundamental outcome of communication itself is that people rub off on one another. Human beings are socially contagious in how they think and how they act. As a result, how people think about and use technologies, such as the mobile phone, is a product of social context and social contact.

Mobile media are constructed at all levels of social order, from the individual to the collective. At the individual level, users create symbolic meanings for the technology by customizing the way it looks and operates to suit their personal preferences. Katz and Sugiyama (2005) explained that individual users of the technology achieve the status of co-creators "by manipulating these devices to reflect personal tastes and to represent themselves to the outside world" (p. 79). This type of manipulation is accomplished with stickers, jewelry, ring tones, screen images, and endless other customizations. Mobile telephony is also shaped at the social network level. Attitudes about which phones are "cool," as well as where and how the technology should be used are influenced by the attitudes of our close personal ties (Campbell & Russo, 2003). Adoption itself is frequently a matter of social influence when parents or friends pass their handsets on after getting a new one. Furthermore, cultural differences and regional trends in mobile communication practices show how the technology is socially constructed at macro as well as micro levels of social order (Campbell, 2007; Castells et al., 2007). As noted above, the Japanese have developed their own distinctive norms for mobile phone use, especially on public transportation vehicles (Okabe & Ito, 2005).

Without doubt, studying the effects of mobile communication is an important endeavor as it focuses our attention on the impact of a medium (the mobile communication system) on what might otherwise be direct interpersonal interaction. Adoption and use of the technology brings about important changes in how people relate to each other and go about their daily lives. However, it is important for researchers to be mindful that these effects are not solely attributable to the technology or exposure to it. The effects and uses of mobile media are situated in social context and shaped by social forces. Text messaging is a fantastic example of this. With such limited keypads, character length, and screen sizes, text messaging was never intended to become the phenomenon that it has today. Yet users of the technology, especially younger users, have developed innovative appropriations and language patterns to support the emergent "thumb culture" (Glotz, Bertschi, & Locke, 2005). While the effects of mobile media are clearly profound, so too are the effects of those who shape how the technology is perceived and used.

Notes

1. There have obviously been other forms of point-to-point communication during this period. The traditional landline telephone was actually on the scene before many forms of mass media such as the radio, TV, and even film (Fischer, 1992).
2. Although they advance the phrase "mobile network society," Castells et al. (2007) suggest that in many cases, it is autonomy and not mobility that is the greatest appeal of the technology.

References

Andriessen, J. H., & Vartiainen, M. (2006). *Mobile virtual work: A new paradigm?* Berlin: Springer.

Bimber, B. (1998). The Internet and political transformation: Populism, community, and accelerated pluralism. *Polity, 31*, 133–160.

Bjiker, W. E., Hughes, T. P., & Pinch, T. J. (1987). *The social construction of technological systems: New directions in the sociology and history of technology*. Cambridge, MA: MIT Press.

Campbell, S. W. (2004). *Normative mobile phone use in public settings*. Paper presented at the annual meeting of the National Communication Association, Chicago.

Campbell, S. W. (2006). Perceptions of mobile phones in college classrooms: Ringing, cheating, and classroom policies. *Communication Education, 55*(3), 280–294.

Campbell, S. W. (2007). A cross-cultural comparison of perceptions and uses of mobile telephony. *New Media and Society, 9*(2), 343–363.

Campbell, S. W. (2008). Mobile technology and the body: Apparatgeist, fashion, and function. In J. Katz (Ed.), *Handbook of mobile communication studies* (pp. 153–164). Cambridge, MA: MIT Press.

Campbell, S. W., & Kwak, N. (2007). Mobile communication and social capital in localized, globalized, and scattered networks. Paper presented at the ICA pre-conference, Mobile Communication: Bringing us Together or Tearing us Apart?, San Francisco.

Campbell, S. W., & Ling, R. (2008). Conclusion: Mobile communication in space and time – furthering the theoretical dialogue. In R. Ling & S. Campbell (Eds.), *The mobile communication research series: Reconstruction of space and time through mobile communication practices* (pp. 251–260). New Brunswick, NJ: Transaction Publishers.

Campbell, S. W., & Park, Y. (2008). Social implications of mobile telephony: The rise of personal communication society. *Sociology Compass, 2*(2), 371–387.

Campbell, S. W., & Russo, T. C. (2003). The social construction of mobile telephony: An application of the social influence model to perceptions and uses of mobile phones within personal communication networks. *Communication Monographs, 70*(4), 317–334.

Caporael, L. R., & Xie, B. (2003). Breaking time and place: Mobile technologies and reconstituted identities. In J. Katz (Ed.), *Machines that become us: The social context of communication technology* (pp. 219–232). New Brunswick, NJ: Transaction.

Castells, M. (2000). *The rise of network society* (2nd ed.). Oxford: Blackwell.

Castells, M., Fernandez-Ardevol, M., Qiu, J., & Sey, A. (2007). *Mobile communication and society: A global perspective*. Cambridge, MA: MIT Press.

Chesley, N. (2005). Blurring boundaries? Linking technology use, spillover, individual distress, and family satisfaction. *Journal of Marriage and Family, 67*, 1237–1248.

Fischer, C. S. (1992). *America calling: A social history of the telephone to 1940*. Berkeley: University of California Press.

Fortunati, L. (2005a). Mobile phones and fashion in post-modernity. *Telektronikk, 3/4*, 35–48.

Fortunati, L. (2005b). Mobile telephone and the presentation of self. In R. Ling & P. Pedersen (Eds.), *Mobile communications: Re-negotiation of the social sphere* (pp. 203–218). London: Springer.

Frissen, V. (2000). ICT in the rush hour of life. *The Information Society, 16*, 65–75.

Glotz, P., Bertschi, S., & Locke, C. (Eds.). (2005). *Thumb culture: The meaning of mobile phones for society*. New Brunswick, NJ: Transaction.

Green, N. (2003). Outwardly mobile: Young people and mobile technologies. In J. Katz (Ed.), *Machines that become us: The social context of personal communication technology* (pp. 201–218). New Brunswick, NJ: Transaction.

Gullestad, M. (1984). *Kitchen-table society*. Oslo: Universitetsforlaget.

Gullestad, M. (1992). *The art of social relations: essays on culture, social action and everyday life in modern Norway*. Oslo: Universitetsforlaget.

Habermas, J. (1989). *The structural transformation of the public sphere: An inquiry into a category of bourgeois society* (T. Burger, Trans.). Cambridge, MA: MIT Press. (Original work published 1962).

Habuchi, I. (2005). Accelerating reflexivity. In M. Ito, D. Okabe, & M. Matsuda (Eds.), *Personal, portable, pedestrian: Mobile phones in Japanese life* (pp. 165–182). Cambridge, MA: MIT Press.

Hashimoto, Y., Ishii, K., Nakamura, I., Korenaga, R., Tsuji, D., & Mori, Y. (2000). Keitai denwa wo chyuushin to suru tsusin media riyo ni kansuru chosa kenkyu [A study on mobile phone and other communication media usage]. *Tokyo Daigaku Shyakai Joho Kenkyusyo Chosa Kenkyu Kiyo, 14*, 83–192.

Höflich, J. R. (2005). The mobile phone and the dynamic between public and private communication: Results of an international exploratory study. In P. Glotz, S. Bertschi, & C. Locke (Eds.), *Thumb culture: The meaning of mobile phones for society* (pp. 123–136). New Brunswick, NJ: Transaction.

International Telecommunication Union. (2007, May). *ICT free statistics home page*. Retrieved May 2, 2007, from http://www.itu.int/itu-d/ict/statistics/

Ishii, K. (2006). Implications of mobility: The uses of personal communication media in everyday life. *Journal of Communication, 56*(2), 346–365.

Ito, M., Okabe, D., & Anderson, K. (2008). Portable objects in three global cities: The personalization of urban places. In R. Ling & S. Campbell (Eds.), *The mobile communication research series: Reconstruction of space and time through mobile communication practices* (pp. 67–88). New Brunswick, NJ: Transaction.

Johnsen, T. E. (2003). The social context of the mobile phone use of Norwegian teens. In J. Katz (Ed.), *Machines that become us: The social context of communication technology* (pp. 161–170). New Brunswick, NJ: Transaction.

Julsrud, T. E. (2005). Behavioral changes at the mobile workplace: A symbolic interactionist approach. In R. Ling & P. Pedersen (Eds), *Mobile communications: Re-negotiation of the social sphere* (pp. 93–112). London: Springer-Verlag.

Julsrud, T. E., & Bakke, J. W. (2008). Trust, friendship and expertise: The use of email, mobile dialogues, and SMS to develop and sustain social relations in a distributed work group. In R. Ling & S. Campbell (Eds.), *The mobile communication research series: Reconstruction of space and time through mobile communication practices* (pp. 159–190). New Brunswick, NJ: Transaction Publishers.

Katz, J. E. (2006). *Magic in the air*. New Brunswick, NJ: Transaction.

Katz, J. E., & Aakhus, M. A. (Eds.), (2002). *Perpetual contact: Mobile communication, private talk, public performance*. Cambridge, UK: Cambridge University Press.

Katz, J. E., & Aspen, P. (1997). A nation of strangers? *Communications of the ACM, 40*, 81–86.

Katz, J. E., & Sugiyama, S. (2005). Mobile phones as fashion statements: The co-creation of mobile communication's public meaning. In R. Ling & P. Pedersen (Eds.), *Mobile communications: Re-negotiation of the social sphere* (pp. 63–81). London: Springer.

Kraut, R., Patterson, M., Lundmark, V., Kiesler, S., Mukopadhyay, T., & Scherlis, W. (1998). Internet paradox: A social technology that reduces social involvement and psychological well-being? *American Psychologist, 53*(9), 1017–1031.

Licoppe, C. (2003). Two modes of maintaining interpersonal relations through telephone: From the domestic to the mobile phone. In J. Katz (Ed.), *Machines that become us: The social context of communication technology* (pp. 171–186). New Brunswick, NJ: Transaction.

Lilischkis, S. (2003). *More yo-yos, pendulums and nomads: Trends of mobile and multi-location work in the information society* (Issue report no. 36). Socio-economic trends assessment for the digital revolution.

Ling, R. (1996). *One can talk about common manners!: The use of mobile telephones in inappropriate situations* (Report 32/96). Kjeller, Norway: Telenor Research and Development.

Ling, R. (2002). *The social juxtaposition of mobile telephone conversations in public spaces*. Paper presented at the Conference on Social Consequences of Mobile Telephones, Chunchon, Korea.

Ling, R. (2004). *The mobile connection: The cell phone's impact on society*. San Francisco: Morgan Kaufman.

Ling, R. (2005a). The sociolinguistics of SMS: An analysis of SMS use by a random sample of Norwegians. In R. Ling & P. Pedersen (Eds), *Mobile communications: Re-negotiation of the social sphere* (pp. 335–350). London: Springer-Verlag.

Ling, R. (2005b). Mobile communications vis-à-vis teen emancipation, peer group integration and deviance. In R. Harper, A. Taylor, & L. Palen (Eds.), *The inside text: Social perspectives on SMS in the mobile age* (pp. 175–192). London: Kluwer.

Ling, R. (2006). *The length of text messages and the use of predictive texting: Who uses it and how much do they have to say?* Paper presented at the annual meeting of the Association of Internet Researchers, Brisbane, Australia.

Ling, R. (2008). *New tech, new ties: How mobile communication reshapes social cohesion*. Cambridge, MA: MIT Press.

Ling, R., & Campbell, S. W. (Eds.) (2008). *The mobile communication research series: Reconstruction of space and time through mobile communication practices*. New Brunswick, NJ: Transaction Publishers..

Ling, R., & Yttri, B. (1999). *Nobody sits at home and waits for the telephone to ring: Micro and hyper-coordination through the use of the mobile phone* (Report 30/99). Kjeller, Norway: Telenor Research and Development.

Ling, R., & Yttri, B. (2002). Hyper-coordination via mobile phones in Norway. In J. Katz & M. Aakhus (Eds.), *Perpetual contact: Mobile communication, private talk, public performance* (pp. 139–169). Cambridge, UK: Cambridge University Press.

Love, S., & Kewley, J. (2005). Does personality affect people's attitudes towards mobile phone use in public places? In R. Ling & P. Pedersen (Eds), *Mobile communications: Re-negotiation of the social sphere* (pp. 273–284). London: Springer-Verlag.

McLuhan, M. (1964). *Understanding media: The extensions of man*. New York: New American Library.

McLuhan, M., & Fiore, Q. (1967). *The medium is the massage: An inventory of effects*. New York: Bantam Books.

Monk, A., Carroll, J., Parker, S., & Blythe, M. (2004). Why are mobile phones annoying? *Behavior and information technology*, *23*, 33–41.

Murtagh, G. M. (2001). Seeing the "rules:" Preliminary observations of action, interaction and mobile phone use. In B. Brown, N. Green, & R. Harper (Eds.), *Wireless world: Social and interactional aspects of the mobile age* (pp. 81–91). London: Springer.

Nie, N., & Erbring, L. (2000). *Internet and society: A preliminary report*. The Stanford Institute for the Quantitative Study of Society. Retrieved May 17, 2007, from http://www.stanford.edu/group/siqss/Press_Release/internetStudy.html.

Okabe, D., & Ito, M. (2005). *Keitai* in public transportation. In M. Ito, D. Okabe, & M. Matsuda (Eds.), *Personal, portable, pedestrian: Mobile phones in Japanese life* (pp. 165–182). Cambridge, MA: MIT Press.

Palen, L., Salzman, M., & Youngs, E. (2001). Discovery and integration of mobile communications in everyday life. *Personal and Ubiquitous Computing*, *5*, 109–122.

Paragas, F. (2003). *Being mobile with the mobile: Cellular telephony and renegotiations of public transport as public sphere*. Paper presented at the Front Stage/Back Stage: Mobile Communication and the Renegotiation of the Social Sphere Conference, Grimstad, Norway.

Paragas, F. (2008). Migrant workers and mobile phones: Technological, temporal, and spatial simultaneity. In R. Ling & S. Campbell (Eds.), *The mobile communication research series: Reconstruction of space and time through mobile communication practices* (pp. 39–68). New Brunswick, NJ: Transaction Publishers.

Pedersen, W., & Samuelsen, S. O. (2003). Nye mønstre av seksualatferd blant ungdom. *Tidsskrift for Den norske lœgeforeningen*, *21*, 3006–3009.

Putnam, R. D. (1995). Bowling alone: America's declining social capital. *Journal of Democracy*, *6*, 65–78.

Putnam, R. D. (2000). *Bowling alone: The collapse and revival of American community*. New York: Simon & Schuster.

Rakow, L. F., & Navarro, V. (1993). Remote mothering and the parallel shift: Women meet the cellular telephone. *Critical Studies in Mass Communication*, *10*, 144–157.

Rheingold, H. (1993). *The virtual community: Homesteading on the electronic frontier*. New York: HarperCollins.

Rheingold, H. (2002). *Smart mobs: The next social revolution*. Cambridge, MA: Perseus.

Taylor, A. S., & Harper, R. (2001). *Talking "activity:" Young people and mobile phones*. Paper presented at the CHI 2001 Workshop: Mobile communications: Understanding users, adoption, and design, Seattle, WA. Retrieved February 5, 2002, from http://www.cs.colorado.edu/_/palen/chi_workshop.

University of Michigan. (2006). *On the move: The role of cellular communications in American life*. Ann Arbor.

Vartiainen, M. (2006). Mobile virtual work—concepts, outcomes, and challenges. In J. Andriessen & M. Vartiainen (Eds.), *Mobile virtual work: A new paradigm?* (pp. 13–44). Berlin: Springer.

Wei, R., & Leung, L. (1999). Blurring public and private behaviors in public space: Policy challenges in the use and improper use of the cell phone. *Telematics and Informatics*, *16*, 11–26.

AUTHOR INDEX

SUBJECT INDEX